The Sacred Rights of Conscience

The Sacred Rights of Conscience

SELECTED READINGS ON

RELIGIOUS LIBERTY AND CHURCH-STATE RELATIONS

IN THE AMERICAN FOUNDING

Edited and with an Introduction by

Daniel L. Dreisbach *and* Mark David Hall

LIBERTY FUND

Indianapolis

This book is published by Liberty Fund, Inc., a foundation established to
encourage study of the ideal of a society of free and responsible individuals.

The cuneiform inscription that serves as our logo and as
the design motif for our endpapers is the earliest-known written
appearance of the word "freedom" (*amagi*), or "liberty." It is taken from a
clay document written about 2300 B.C. in the Sumerian
city-state of Lagash.

c 10 9 8 7 6 5 4 3 2
p 10 9 8 7 6 5 4 3 2

Library of Congress Cataloging-in-Publication Data
Sacred rights of conscience : selected readings on religious liberty and church-state relations in the
American founding / edited and with an introduction by Daniel L. Dreisbach and Mark David Hall.
p. cm.
Includes bibliographical references and index.
ISBN 978-0-86597-714-3 (hardcover : alk. paper) —
ISBN 978-0-86597-715-0 (pbk. : alk. paper)
1. Freedom of religion—United States—History—18th century—Sources. 2. Church and state—
United States—History—18th century—Sources. 3. United States—Church history—
18th century—Sources. 4. Freedom of religion—United States—History—19th century—
Sources. 5. Church and state—United States—History—19th century—Sources.
6. United States—Church history—19th century—Sources. I. Dreisbach, Daniel L.
II. Hall, Mark David, 1966–
BR516.S23 2009
323.44′2097309033—dc22   2009005093

Liberty Fund, Inc.
8335 Allison Pointe Trail, Suite 300
Indianapolis, Indiana 46250-1684

I believe there are many good men, of sound integrity, of unblemished morals, and truly lovers of their country in every denomination of christians. On this subject, it matters not with me, whether a man be a stated member of *this* or *that* church, whether he be in communion with that established in *Old* England, or in *New;* provided he be a good man, actuated by evangelical principles and motives, and will stand fast in the liberty wherewith Christ has made him free. I disdain the low singularities of a party. I desire that every man may think and judge for himself in religion, and enjoy all the sacred rights and liberties of conscience in full.

    —SAMUEL SHERWOOD, Scriptural Instructions
    to Civil Rulers, and all Free-born Subjects,
    August 31, 1774

You are, with all convenient despatch, to repair to Canada, and make known to the people of that country, the wishes and intentions of the Congress with respect to them. . . .

    You are further to declare, that we hold sacred the rights of conscience, and may promise to the whole people, solemnly in our name, the free and undisturbed exercise of their religion; and, to the clergy, the full, perfect, and peaceable possession and enjoyment of all their estates; that the government of every thing relating to their religion and clergy, shall be left entirely in the hands of the good people of that province, and such legislature as they shall consititute; Provided, however, that all other denominations of Christians be equally entitled to hold offices, and enjoy civil privileges, and the free exercise of their religion, and be totally exempt from the payment of any tythes or taxes for the support of any religion.

    —Instructions of the Continental Congress to
    commissioners appointed to Canada, March 20, 1776

The importance of religion to civil society and government, is great indeed, as it keeps alive the best sense of moral obligation, a matter of such extensive utility, especially in respect to an oath, which is one of the principal instruments of government. The fear and reverence of God, and the terrors of eternity, are the most powerful restraints upon the minds of men. And hence it is of special importance in a free government, the spirit of which being always friendly to the sacred rights of conscience, it will hold up the gospel as the great rule of faith and practice.

    —PHILLIPS PAYSON, An Election-Sermon,
    May 27, 1778

That some of the natural rights of mankind are unalienable, and subject to no control but that of the Diety. Such are the SACRED RIGHTS OF CONSCIENCE. Which in a state of nature, and of civil society[,] are exactly the same. They can neither be parted with nor controled, by any human authority whatever.

    —SAMUEL STILLMAN, An Election Sermon,
    May 26, 1779

The more I reflect upon the history of mankind, the more I am disposed to think that it is our duty to secure the essential rights of the people, by every precaution; for not an avenue has been left unguarded, through which oppression could possibly enter in any government[,] without some enemy of the public peace and happiness improving the opportunity to break in upon the liberties of the people; and none have been more frequently successful in the attempt, than those who have covered their ambitious designs under the garb of a fiery zeal for religious orthodoxy. What has happened in other countries and in other ages, may very possibly happen again in our own country, and for aught we know, before the present generation quits the stage of life. We ought therefore in a *bill of rights* to secure, in the first place, by the most express stipulation, the sacred rights of conscience.

    —AN OLD WHIG, no. V (Philadelphia)
    Independent Gazetteer, 1787

There are other branches of knowledge, which will be of great advantage to men in power. It is, at least, desireable that they should have a tolerable acquaintance with *natural law*—that they understand the *natural* rights of men, which are the same, under every species of government, and do not owe their origin to the social compact. Such, in a peculiar manner, are the sacred RIGHTS OF CONSCIENCE.

    —CHANDLER ROBBINS, An Election Sermon,
    May 25, 1791

Religion and civil government, are not one and the same thing: tho' both may, and are designed to embrace some of the same objects, yet the former, extends its obligations and designs immensely beyond what the latter can pretend to: and it hath rights and prerogatives, with which the latter may not intermeddle. Still, there are many ways, in which civil government may give countenance, encouragement, and even support to religion, without invading the prerogatives of the Most High; or, touching the inferior, tho sacred rights of conscience: and in doing of which, it may not only shew its friendly regard to christianity, but derive important advantages to itself.

—TIMOTHY STONE, Election Sermon, May 10, 1792

I do therefore issue this my proclamation, recommending to all who shall be piously disposed to unite their hearts and voices in addressing at one and the same time their vows and adorations to the Great Parent and Sovereign of the Universe that they . . . render Him thanks for the many blessings He has bestowed on the people of the United States; . . . and particularly that He has blessed the United States with a political Constitution founded on the will and authority of the whole people and guaranteeing to each individual security, not only of his person and his property, but of those sacred rights of conscience so essential to his present happiness and so dear to his future hopes; that with those expressions of devout thankfulness be joined supplications to the same Almighty Power that He would look down with compassion on our infirmities; that He would pardon our manifold transgressions and awaken and strengthen in all the wholesome purposes of repentance and amendment. . . .

—JAMES MADISON, Proclamation, July 23, 1813

CONTENTS

PART I
Antecedents of the Principles Governing Religious Liberty and Church-State Relations in America

PART II

Creating the Principles Governing Religious Liberty and
Church-State Relations in Colonial America

—

PART III

*Framing the Constitutional Principles Governing Religious Liberty and
Church-State Relations in the American Founding*

PART IV

*Defining and Testing the Constitutional Principles Governing Religious
Liberty and Church-State Relations in the New Nation*

ILLUSTRATIONS

INTRODUCTION

The Pursuit of Religious Liberty in America

RELIGION IS WOVEN TIGHTLY into the fabric of the American experiment. In the traditional telling of the story, early colonists crossed the Atlantic Ocean's treacherous waters to escape religious persecution in the Old World and to search for religious liberty in the New World. (The story's more heroic versions omit less noble motivations that drew immigrants to these shores—ambition, avarice, adventure, etc.) The Pilgrims, followed by the Puritans, were called of God to build a "city set upon a Hill" (Matt. 5:14), to create a new Zion in New England's wilderness. Even before they stepped ashore, as revealed in the Mayflower Compact (1620) and in John Winthrop's "Modell of Christian Charitie" (1630), these pious English settlers committed themselves to establish Bible commonwealths and remake the world in conformity with God's laws. Differing in mission and doctrine, their English cousins to the south in Virginia, more than a decade before, similarly believed that their venture was directed by the hand of Almighty God. These are among the defining themes of the American story, which were perpetuated by the first English settlers and persist to this day in the public mind as integral features of American identity and mythology.

An invocation of divine blessing and acknowledgment of a sacred mission to spread the Gospel are recurring themes in colonial charters and other expressions of the colonists' political enterprise. The Second Charter of Virginia (1609), like the first in 1606, proclaimed that "the principal effect, which we can desire or expect of this action, is the conversion and reduction of the people in those parts unto the true worship of God and Christian Religion."[1] The signatories to the Mayflower Compact affirmed that they had embarked on their voyage "for the glory of God, and advancement of the Christian Faith."[2]

Early colonial laws consciously drew on biblical codes, often providing specific biblical references lest there be any doubt about the source. The New England Puritans, especially, found biblical precedent for republican government and other principles of civil government in God's instructions to the Children of Israel. Their divine mission, they believed, was to establish Bible commonwealths in God's New Israel.

American culture has been characterized by an extraordinary diversity of religious sects that has shaped

---

1. The Second Charter of Virginia (1609), in William Waller Hening, ed., *The Statutes at Large; Being a Collection of all the Laws of Virginia, From the First Session of the Legislature, in the Year 1619* (New-York, 1823), 1:97.

2. The Mayflower Compact (1620), in *Colonial Origins of the American Constitution: A Documentary History*, ed. Donald S. Lutz (Indianapolis: Liberty Fund, 1998), 32.

church-state relationships and fueled the drive for re-ligious liberty. Many Europeans saw the New World as a refuge from religious oppression. The opportunity to worship God as one chooses, without fear of restraint or persecution, drew many settlers to America's shores (and continues to attract immigrants in the twenty-first century). The eighteenth-century historian Daniel Neal said of the New England settlers, religion was "the chief motive of their retreating into these parts [North America]." In their settlements, they hoped "they might be delivered from the hands of their oppressors, and enjoy the free liberty of their consciences."[3] Samuel West sounded this familiar theme in his 1776 Election Day Sermon preached before the Massachusetts Council and House of Representatives: "Our fathers fled from the rage of prelatical tyranny and persecution, and came into this land in order to enjoy liberty of conscience."[4] The promise of religious freedom enticed immigrants to the New World's vast unsettled territories.

The first English settlements were, for the most part, religiously homogenous communities. And while many immigrants were drawn to these shores by the promise of religious toleration, once established in the New World, they often did not welcome into their own communities people whose religious beliefs and practices differed from their own.

As European settlements grew in number and size up and down the Atlantic seaboard, there was a corresponding increase in the religious diversity in colonial America. Religious pluralism was initially fueled by the migration of diverse sects to America. A splintering of familiar Christian denominations, triggered by rearticulations of doctrine and practice and, at times, prompted by religious revivals, further increased sectarian diversity.

3. Daniel Neal, *The History of the Puritans or Protestant Non-Conformists*, second edition corrected, 2 vols. (London, 1754), 1:543.

4. Samuel West, A Sermon Preached Before the Honorable Council, and the Honorable House of Representatives, of the Colony of the Massachusetts-Bay, in New-England. May 29th, 1776 (Boston: John Gill, 1776), 57, reprinted in John Wingate Thornton, ed., *The Pulpit of the American Revolution; or, The Political Sermons of the Period of 1776* (Boston: Gould and Lincoln, 1860), 311.

The first Europeans in the New World encountered native people with various religious beliefs and practices. Spanish and French Catholics, arriving long before the English colonists, established North American settlements and missions to the north, south, and west of the territories that would later become the English colonies. The diverse sects found in the British colonies, at least early in the colonial period, were for the most part variant forms of Protestantism. The first New England settlers, the Pilgrims and the Puritans, were offshoots of the Church of England. These faith communities adopted congregational, presbyterian, or episcopal forms of church government. The Church of England, or Anglicanism, with its episcopal form of governance, became firmly entrenched in Virginia and colonies to the south. African religions were introduced into the colonies by slaves, who began arriving in Virginia even before the Pilgrims set foot on New England's rocky coasts. The Reformed Church in America was established by Dutch and French settlers in New Netherland before the Massachusetts Bay colony was founded. Maryland was established in the 1630s by the Roman Catholic Calvert family, in part, as a haven for their coreligionists. At about the same time, Swedish Lutherans settled territory along the Delaware River, and the first Baptists began arriving in British North America. In 1654, Sephardic Jews, fleeing Portuguese persecution in Brazil, landed in New Amsterdam. The first Quakers arrived in Boston in the mid-1650s where they met with severe persecution, including public executions. They thrived in the face of opposition, growing in influence and numbers throughout the colonies. Around the same time, French Huguenots (Protestants) began immigrating in large numbers. Presbyterianism gained in strength from Connecticut to the Carolinas, accompanying a stream of Scotch-Irish immigration, starting in the late seventeenth century and continuing into subsequent centuries. Before the end of the seventeenth century, German Mennonites (Anabaptists) began to settle in Pennsylvania. Early in the next century, more Mennonites, Dunkers, Amish, Moravians, Brethren,

Schwenkfelders, Lutherans, and the German Reformed arrived in the great German migration. A German Sabbatarian (Seventh-Day Baptist) community was founded in Ephrata, Pennsylvania, in 1732. By the 1760s, Methodist societies began to spring up throughout the colonies. The Methodist Episcopal Church in America was formally organized in 1784. Mother Ann Lee, founder of the Shaker movement in America, arrived from England in 1774 with a small band of followers. Unitarian and Universalist congregations were organized in New England in the following years. This is only a sampling of the denominational diversity in the colonies. The nineteenth century witnessed an even greater expansion in new religious sects, driven by still more immigrant groups, native development in religious belief and practice, and spiritual revivals.

What were the practical consequences of the extraordinary religious diversity in the New World?

First, it was a potential source of rivalry and conflict among the sects competing for adherents and public recognition (and, sometimes, the legal and financial favor of the civil state). There are ample illustrations of such tension turning hostile and even bloody. Many sects suffered persecution and even death in their new homeland. This diversity was also an opportunity for accommodation and cooperation among the numerous sects. Although memory is more frequently drawn to dramatic clashes, the story of religions in America is, indeed, most remarkable for the amity and general respect among the diverse sects that were planted and flourished side by side in the American soil. Thomas Jefferson recounted an example of sectarian cooperation in his own richly diverse community of Charlottesville, Virginia: "In our village of Charlottesville," he reported, "there is a good degree of religion, with a small spice only of fanaticism. We have four sects, but without either church or meeting-house. The court-house is the common temple, one Sunday in the month to each. Here, Episcopalian and Presbyterian, Methodist and Baptist, meet together, join in hymning their Maker, listen with attention and devotion to each others'

preachers, and all mix in society with perfect harmony."[5]

Second, this extraordinary religious diversity necessitated working out the terms of, initially, religious toleration and, eventually, religious liberty. In jurisdictions where rulers and citizens are *all* of one faith, there is little demand for a policy of religious liberty. But where those who wield state power and citizens come from many denominations and where multiple sects compete for followers and public favor, peaceful coexistence requires a workable policy of toleration. Europeans learned this in the wake of the Reformation, which produced fractures in Christendom, and in the bloody wars of religion that followed. And very early in the colonial experience, American colonists began to grapple with these vexing issues, culminating in the bold policies of religious liberty enshrined in Article 16 of the Virginia Declaration of Rights (1776), the Virginia Statute for Establishing Religious Freedom (1786), and the First Amendment to the United States Constitution (1791).

Third, America's extraordinary religious diversity, once manifested, made it difficult to establish and sustain a formal ecclesiastical establishment, such as had existed in Europe. Most of the original colonies had some form of religious establishment, but as sectarian diversity increased and the colonies transitioned from British colonies to independent republics, their ecclesiastical establishments became less and less viable. By the time the national Constitution was crafted in the late 1780s, many influential citizens, despite some Enlightenment influences, continued to believe religion's place (and role) in the polity must be prominent and public, and some continued to support the established church in their respective states, but very few advocated a national ecclesiastical establishment. The religious diversity of the new constitutional republic meant that the establishment of a national church was practically untenable. No de-

5. Letter from Thomas Jefferson to Doctor Thomas Cooper, November 2, 1822, in *The Writings of Thomas Jefferson*, ed. Andrew A. Lipscomb and Albert Ellery Bergh, 20 vols. (Washington, D.C.: Thomas Jefferson Memorial Association, 1905), 15:404.

nomination was sufficiently dominant to claim the legal favor of the national regime, and there was little likelihood that a political consensus would emerge as to which sect or combination of sects should constitute a "Church of the United States." James Madison, an ardent foe of ecclesiastical establishments, thought religious pluralism contributed greatly to religious liberty. Drawing on Voltaire's famous aphorism, Madison argued:

> If there were a majority of one sect, a bill of rights would be a poor protection for liberty. Happily for the states, they enjoy the utmost freedom of religion. This freedom arises from that multiplicity of sects, which pervades America, and which is the best and only security for religious liberty in any society. For where there is such a variety of sects, there cannot be a majority of any one sect to oppress and persecute the rest. . . . [T]he United States abound in such a variety of sects, that it is a strong security against religious persecution, and is sufficient to authorise a conclusion, that no one sect will ever be able to out-number or depress the rest.[6]

Religious pluralism, in short, compelled a rethinking of the prudential and constitutional place of and role for religion, faith-based perspectives, and pious citizens in a society without a religious establishment.

Few Americans of the seventeenth and eighteenth centuries doubted the value and utility of a vibrant religious—specifically Christian—culture. What was disputed was the most effective way to nurture popular religion and extend its influence in society. The prevailing view of the early colonial period was that insofar as religion was indispensable to social order and stability, it was the duty of all citizens to support religion through the auspices of the civil state, which officially and legally endorsed a particular sect or denomination. Establishmentarians feared that the failure to establish a church and to provide it with the civil state's sustaining aid would impair religion's vitality and influence in society.

By the second half of the eighteenth century, the old arrangement of one state, one church was increasingly challenged by an unlikely coalition of religious dissenters, nonconformists, and moderate Enlightenment rationalists who agitated for a termination of legal privileges for one particular sect or combination of sects over all others. As jurisdictions abandoned ecclesiastical establishments toward the end of the eighteenth century and early nineteenth century, matters of one's belief or disbelief, association with and support of a particular minister or religious society were left to the voluntary choice of citizens, and increasingly the civil state could not condition civil rights and prerogatives on a citizen's religious beliefs. Each religious belief system was to be left free to compete in the free and open marketplace of ideas where, as Jefferson confidently predicted, "truth is great and will prevail if left to herself . . . unless by human interposition disarmed of her natural weapons, free argument and debate."[7] Moreover, opponents of state churches often argued that disestablishment and competition among religious sects in the marketplace of ideas, in the words of Madison, resulted "in the greater purity & industry of the pastors & in the greater devotion of their flock."[8] Disestablishment required sects to compete to survive. Churches and their clergy had to be exemplary and industrious, demonstrating to the world the purity and efficacy of

---

6. James Madison, Speech in the Virginia Convention, June 12, 1788, in *The Papers of James Madison*, ed. Robert A. Rutland, Charles F. Hobson et al. (Charlottesville: University Press of Virginia, 1977), 11:130–31. See also Gaillard Hunt, "James Madison and Religious Liberty," *Annual Report of the American Historical Association for the Year 1901*, 2 vols. (Washington, D.C.: Government Printing Office, 1902), 1:170 (Madison was fond of quoting Voltaire's aphorism: "If one religion only were allowed in England, the Government would possibly become arbitrary; if there were two, the people would cut each other's throats; but as there are such a multitude, they all live happy and in peace."); Publius (James Madison), *The Federalist*, Number 51, in *The Papers of James Madison*, ed. Rutland, Hobson et al., 10:478–79 ("In a free government, the security for civil rights must be the same as that for religious rights. It consists in the one case in the multiplicity of interests, and in the other, in the multiplicity of sects.").

7. "A Bill for Establishing Religious Freedom," in *The Papers of Thomas Jefferson*, ed. Julian P. Boyd et al., 31 vols. to date (Princeton, N.J.: Princeton University Press, 1950–), 2:546.

8. Letter from James Madison to Jasper Adams, September 1833, in *Religion and Politics in the Early Republic: Jasper Adams and the Church-State Debate*, ed. Daniel L. Dreisbach (Lexington: University Press of Kentucky, 1996), 118–20.

their faith. Churches were forced to rely on the voluntary support of adherents rather than the benevolence of the civil state. Conversely, there was a growing belief in the founding era that religious establishments (state ecclesiastical monopolies) led to complacency, corruption, and intolerance; whereas, the combination of competition among sects, religious liberty, and disestablishment created an environment in which religions could flourish and beneficently inform public culture. Disestablishmentarians argued with growing confidence that the termination of state aid for one particular church facilitated a vibrant religious culture in which the best and purest religion would dominate. This, they said, was good for the church, good for society, and good for the civil state.

Christianity has made a vital contribution to American political thought and institutions. As evidenced by the documents compiled in this volume, the founders drew on diverse intellectual sources, including Lockean liberalism, classical republicanism, the common law, and the Scottish Enlightenment. Yet these traditions were often viewed through Christian lenses, and the founders were in some cases directly influenced by their understanding of biblical teachings and their religious traditions.[9] Indeed, America's founders were far more likely to cite the Bible in their political writings than they were documents from other intellectual traditions.[10]

Scholars who believe Christianity had an important influence on America's founders sometimes disagree about the precise nature of its impact, but there is broad agreement that most founders believed the following: (1) Human nature is sinful, so political institutions should be designed to prevent the concentration of power and to check the abuse of power vested in human agents. Because men are not angels, Madison counseled in *The Federalist Papers*, "[a]mbition must be made to counteract ambition."[11] Constitutional notions of limited government, rule of law, due process, separation of powers among the three branches of the national government, federalism, and representative government all reflect this awareness of mankind's fallen nature. (2) A legitimate "Civil Body Politick," in the words of the Mayflower Compact, is based on a compact (or covenant) between rulers and the ruled and/or among members of the political community.[12] Modern American constitutions arise in part from a Judeo-Christian concept of covenant. (3) God created transcendent standards of right and wrong that serve as the foundation for natural rights. (4) Christianity—particularly the Protestant Reformed version of Christianity prevalent in America in the founding era—allowed or even required rebellion against tyrannical governments. (To this day, outside America the War for American Independence is often referred to as the "Presbyterian Rebellion.")[13] (5) Men and women are created in the

9. For broad arguments regarding the influence of Christianity, see Ellis Sandoz, *A Government of Laws: Political Theory, Religion and the American Founding* (Baton Rouge: Louisiana State University Press, 1990); Barry Alan Shain, *The Myth of American Individualism: The Protestant Origins of American Political Thought* (Princeton, N.J.: Princeton University Press, 1994); and Michael Novak, *On Two Wings: Humble Faith and Common Sense at the American Founding* (San Francisco: Encounter Books, 2002). For representative works on the impact of religion on individual founders, see Daniel L. Dreisbach, Mark David Hall, and Jeffry H. Morrison, eds., *The Forgotten Founders on Religion and Public Life* (Notre Dame, Ind.: University of Notre Dame Press, forthcoming); Daniel L. Dreisbach, Mark D. Hall, and Jeffry H. Morrison, eds., *The Founders on God and Government* (Lanham, Md.: Rowman and Littlefield Publishers, 2004); Mark David Hall, *The Political and Legal Philosophy of James Wilson, 1742–1798* (Columbia: University of Missouri Press, 1997); Jeffry H. Morrison, *John Witherspoon and the Founding of the American Republic* (Notre Dame, Ind.: University of Notre Dame Press, 2005); and Garrett Ward Sheldon, *The Political Philosophy of James Madison* (Baltimore: Johns Hopkins University Press, 2001).

10. See Donald S. Lutz, "The Relative Influence of European Writers on Late Eighteenth-Century American Political Thought," *American Political Science Review* 78 (1984): 189–97.

11. Publius (James Madison), *The Federalist*, Number 51, in *The Papers of James Madison*, ed. Rutland, Hobson, et al., 10:477.

12. The Mayflower Compact (1620), in *Colonial Origins of the American Constitution*, ed. Lutz, 32.

13. See Sydney E. Ahlstrom, *A Religious History of the American People* (New Haven, Conn.: Yale University Press, 1972), 350 (the Reformed theological tradition was "the religious heritage of three-fourths of the American people in 1776"). See also on this topic Alan Heimert, *Religion and the American Mind: From the Great Awakening to the Revolution* (Cambridge, Mass.: Harvard University Press, 1966), and Mark A. Noll, *America's God: From Jonathan Edwards to Abraham Lincoln* (New York: Oxford University Press, 2002).

image of God and therefore should be treated with dignity. This, of course, did not immediately translate into equal treatment in all respects, but it arguably set the groundwork for principles of due process of law, the abolition of slavery, the equal treatment of women, penal reform, and so forth. (6) Finally, and of particular relevance to this volume, there is a difference between liberty and license. In James Wilson's words, "[w]ithout liberty, law loses its nature and its name, and becomes oppression. Without law, liberty also loses its nature and its name, and becomes licentiousness."[14]

This list could be extended, but the above examples are representative of ways in which Christianity may have influenced American political thought. Of course one might agree that America's founders adhered to these ideas but conclude that they did so for altogether different reasons. And it is almost certainly the case that specific founders believed the same thing for a variety of reasons. Tracing the sources of influence can become complicated, but the documents in this collection suggest that, at a minimum, it is unwise to ignore the influence of Christianity on the American political experiment.

The religious beliefs of the founding fathers, as revealed in the record and their personal testimonies, ranged from orthodox Christianity to skepticism about Christian claims and doctrine. Despite these differences, there was broad agreement that religion and morality (informed by religious values) were "indispensable supports" for social order and political prosperity. Indeed, this was a virtually unchallenged assumption of the age.

The challenge confronted by the founders of the American constitutional regime was how to nurture personal responsibility and social order in a system of self-government. Tyrants and authoritarian rulers could use the whip and rod to compel people to behave as they desired, but this approach was unacceptable for a self-governing people. The founders preferred that a pervasive civic virtue incline citizens to be self-controlled, self-regulating. They concluded that religion—either for genuinely spiritual or merely utilitarian reasons—was indispensable to this project. "[T]o promote true religion is the best and most effectual way of making a virtuous and regular people," the Presbyterian divine John Witherspoon opined.[15] Indeed, religion, and the virtue it fostered, was more important for a free, self-governing people than, perhaps, for any other society. Accordingly, the founders looked to religion to develop the internal moral compass that would prompt citizens to behave in a controlled, disciplined manner and, thereby, promote social discipline and a civil polity in which all citizens enjoyed life, liberty, and the pursuit of happiness.

James H. Hutson has called this "the founding generation's syllogism": "virtue and morality are necessary for free, republican government; religion is necessary for virtue and morality; religion is, therefore, necessary for republican government."[16] Furthermore, many founders believed that *religious liberty* was a desirable precondition for an effective republican government. They knew from history that religion could survive in the face of state persecution; however, they also believed freedom—freedom of religious worship and expression—could facilitate a vibrant religious culture that, in turn, fostered virtue and political prosperity.

The literature of the founding era is replete with expressions and reflections of this vision of the role of religion in a republican system of government. No one made the argument more famously or succinctly than George Washington in this Farewell Address in September 1796:

---

14. Kermit L. Hall and Mark David Hall, eds., *Collected Works of James Wilson* (Indianapolis: Liberty Fund, 2007), 1:435. For Wilson, law and religion were intimately connected. In the lecture following the one from which this quote is taken, he wrote that "religion and law are twin sisters, friends, and mutual assistants. Indeed, these two sciences run into each other. The divine law, as discovered by reason and the moral sense, forms an essential part of both." Ibid., 1:499.

15. John Witherspoon, *Lectures on Moral Philosophy*, ed. Varnum Lansing Collins (Princeton, N.J.: Princeton University Press, 1912), 110.

16. James H. Hutson, *Religion and the Founding of the American Republic* (Washington, D.C.: Library of Congress, 1998), 81.

Of all the dispositions and habits which lead to political prosperity, Religion and morality are indispensable supports. In vain would that man claim the tribute of Patriotism, who should labour to subvert these great Pillars of human happiness, these firmest props of the duties of Men and citizens. The mere Politician, equally with the pious man[,] ought to respect and to cherish them. A volume could not trace all their connections with private and public felicity. Let it simply be asked where is the security for property, for reputation, for life, if the sense of religious obligation *desert* the oaths, which are the instruments of investigation in Courts of Justice? And let us with caution indulge the supposition, that morality can be maintained without religion. Whatever may be conceded to the influence of refined education on minds of peculiar structure, reason and experience both forbid us to expect that National morality can prevail in exclusion of religious principle.

'Tis substantially true, that virtue or morality is a necessary spring of popular government. The rule indeed extends with more or less force to every species of free Government. Who that is a sincere friend to it, can look with indifference upon attempts to shake the foundation of the fabric[.][17]

This theme is ubiquitous in the political literature of the era. For example, John Adams wrote in 1776: "Statesmen, my dear Sir, may plan and speculate for liberty, but it is religion and morality alone, which can establish the principles upon which freedom can securely stand. The only foundation of a free constitution is pure virtue."[18] On October 11, 1782, the Continental Congress issued a Thanksgiving Day Proclamation, authored by the Presbyterian clergyman and signer of the Declaration of Independence,

John Witherspoon, declaring that "the practice of true and undefiled religion . . . is the great foundation of public prosperity and national happiness."[19] Benjamin Rush, another venerated signer of the Declaration of Independence, opined in 1786: "the only foundation for a useful education in a republic is to be laid in RELIGION. Without this [religion], there can be no virtue, and without virtue there can be no liberty, and liberty is the object and life of all republican governments."[20] David Ramsay, physician, delegate to the Continental Congress, and the first major historian of the American Revolution, wrote in 1789: "Remember that there can be no political happiness without liberty; that there can be no liberty without morality, and that there can be no morality without religion."[21] Charles Carroll of Maryland, a Roman Catholic and signer of the Declaration of Independence, similarly remarked: "without morals a republic cannot subsist any length of time; they therefore who are decrying the Christian religion, whose morality is so sublime & pure . . . are undermining the solid foundation of morals, the best security for the duration of free governments."[22] The interdependence of religion, religious liberty, and political prosperity was acknowledged in the Northwest Ordinance (1787), one of the organic laws of the United States of America, which declared that, because "Religion, Morality and knowledge being necessary to good government and the happiness of mankind," "[n]o person" in the territories, "demeaning himself in a peaceable and orderly manner shall ever be mo-

17. George Washington, Farewell Address, September 19, 1796, in *The Writings of George Washington,* ed. John C. Fitzpatrick, 37 vols. (Washington, D.C.: Government Printing Office, 1931–40), 35:229–30. In a March 3, 1797, letter "to the Clergy of Different Denominations Residing in and near the City of Philadelphia," Washington said, "[I do believe] that *Religion* and *Morality* are the essential pillars of Civil society." Ibid., 35:416.

18. Letter from John Adams to Zabdiel Adams, June 21, 1776, in *The Works of John Adams, Second President of the United States,* ed. Charles Francis Adams, 10 vols. (Boston: Little, Brown and Co., 1854), 9:401.

19. Thanksgiving Proclamation of October 11, 1782, in *Journal of the Continental Congress, 1774–1789,* ed. Gaillard Hunt (Washington, D.C.: Government Printing Office, 1914), 23:647. See also Morrison, *John Witherspoon and the Founding of the American Republic,* 21.

20. Benjamin Rush, Thoughts upon the Mode of Education Proper in a Republic (1786), in Charles S. Hyneman and Donald S. Lutz, eds., *American Political Writing during the Founding Era: 1760–1805,* 2 vols. (Indianapolis: Liberty Fund, 1983), 1:681.

21. David Ramsay, *The History of the American Revolution,* 2 vols. (London, 1790), 2:356.

22. Charles Carroll of Carrollton to James McHenry, November 4, 1800, in Bernard C. Steiner, *The Life and Correspondence of James McHenry* (Cleveland: Burrows Bros., 1907), 475.

lested on account of his mode of worship or religious sentiments."[23]

In short, a vibrant religious culture, facilitated by religious liberty, was thought necessary to nurture civic virtue, preserve social order, and promote political prosperity. The free exercise of religion guarantee was written into the First Amendment in order to foster a society in which religion could flourish, free from the restraints or interference of the national government, and to create an environment in which moral leaders could speak boldly, without inhibition or fear of retribution, against immorality and corruption in the public arena. The extolling of morality, facilitated by religious liberty, was not only beneficial to the citizenry at large, but also essential in preserving the "republican virtues" of the American system of self-government.

For this reason, public acknowledgments, exercises, and expressions of religion were not conduct the civil state merely tolerated out of benevolence or as a matter of human rights; rather, the expansive influence of religion (and religious values) in the polity and a vibrant religious culture were deemed essential to the very survival of the civil state. The civil state's respect for religion and religious liberty, in other words, was viewed as an act of self-preservation. The civil state's survival, the founders believed, was dependent on Christian values and morality permeating the community, informing public values, softening the people's prejudices, guiding the consciences of political leaders, and shaping law and public policy.

This was not an argument in favor of an established church or compelled allegiance to a particular creed or bishop; rather, the contention was that the political order must acknowledge and nurture basic religious values in order to prosper. Religious liberty created an environment in which religion and religious values could flourish and thereby foster the values that give citizens a capacity for self-government.

The triumph of religious liberty over mere toleration is arguably America's greatest contribution to, and innovation of, political society. This principle was expressed in Article 16 of the Virginia Declaration of Rights, adopted by the Virginia Convention on June 12, 1776. George Mason, the Declaration's architect and chief draftsman, initially framed Article 16 in the language of religious toleration. Although James Madison was certainly interested in all portions of the Declaration, only the final article "providing for religious toleration, stirred him to action." In "his first important public act,"[24] Madison objected to Mason's use of the word "toleration" because it dangerously implied that religious exercise was a mere privilege that could be granted or revoked at the pleasure of the civil state, and was not assumed to be a natural, indefeasible right. Mason's proposal reflected the most liberal policies of the age and went further than any previous declaration in force in Virginia, but it did not go far enough to satisfy Madison. He wanted to replace "toleration" with the concept of absolute equality in religious belief and exercise. As early as 1774, Madison had come to think of religious toleration, the ultimate objective of most reformers of his day, as an inadequate halfway point on the road to religious liberty. He eventually concluded that religious toleration, whether granted by the civil state or by a religious establishment, was inconsistent with freedom of conscience. Historically speaking, religious *toleration* stands in contrast to religious *liberty*. The former often assumes an established church and is always a revocable grant of the civil state rather than a natural, unalienable right.[25] In Madison's mind, the right of religious exercise was too important to be cast

23. Northwest Ordinance (1787), in *Journals of the Continental Congress, 1774–1789* (Washington, D.C.: Government Printing Office, 1936), 32:340 (July 13, 1787).

24. Editorial Note, *The Papers of James Madison*, ed. William T. Hutchinson and William M. E. Rachal (Chicago: University of Chicago Press, 1962), 1:171.

25. For an extreme expression of this view, see Thomas Paine's 1791 declamation in *Rights of Man:* "Toleration is not the *opposite* of Intolerance, but is the *counterfeit* of it. Both are despotisms. The one assumes to itself the right of withholding Liberty of Conscience, and the other of granting it. The one is the Pope armed with fire and faggot, and the other is the Pope selling or granting indulgences." Paine, *Rights of Man* (1791), in *The Writings of Thomas Paine*, ed. Moncure Daniel Conway, 4 vols. (New York: G. P. Putnam's Sons, 1894), 2:325.

in the form of a mere privilege allowed by the ruling civil polity and enjoyed as a grant of governmental benevolence. Instead, he viewed religious liberty as a fundamental and irrevocable right, possessed equally by all citizens, that must be placed beyond the reach of civil magistrates and subject only to the dictates of a free conscience.

Madison proposed revisions to Mason's draft that punctuated his aversion to the concept of mere toleration and his belief that all men are equally entitled to the free exercise of religious belief. He replaced Mason's tentative statement, "all Men shou'd enjoy the fullest Toleration in the Exercise of Religion," with the phrase, "all men are equally entitled to the full and free exercise of [religion] accord[in]g to the dictates of Conscience." He recognized that religious duties are prior to civil obligations. The logic of Mason's phrasing was that because religion "can be governed only by Reason and Conviction, not by Force or Violence," for practical reasons "all Men shou'd enjoy the fullest Toleration."[26] By contrast, the practical difficulty of governing religious opinion, whether by coercion or persuasion, concerned Madison less; rather, he sought to remove religion—and matters of conscience—from the cognizance of the civil state. Key to Madison's restatement was the word "equally," which the Virginia Convention retained in subsequent drafts. This language meant that the unlearned Separate Baptists of the central Piedmont had religious rights equal to those of the well-heeled Anglican aristocrats of the Tidewater. All citizens enjoyed absolute equality in religious belief.

This great achievement of the American experiment was later enshrined in the Virginia Statute for Establishing Religious Freedom and the First Amendment to the United States Constitution. George Washington also recognized it in an eloquent 1790 address to a Hebrew Congregation in Newport, Rhode Island:

> The Citizens of the United States of America have a right to applaud themselves for having given to mankind examples of an enlarged and liberal policy: a policy worthy of imitation. All possess alike liberty of conscience and immunities of citizenship. It is now no more that toleration is spoken of, as if it was by the indulgence of one class of people, that another enjoyed the exercise of their inherent natural rights. For happily the Government of the United States, which gives to bigotry no sanction, to persecution no assistance requires only that they who live under its protection should demean themselves as good citizens, in giving it on all occasions their effectual support.[27]

There were differences of opinion in the founding era regarding the precise meaning of religious liberty in the American context. Among the issues debated were the extent to which the civil state, consistent with the principles of religious liberty, could identify with religion or cooperate with and aid religious institutions. Some Americans maintained that religious liberty did not preclude official recognition and even promotion of religion in general, while others argued that religious liberty necessitated a separation between the institutions of the church and the civil state. (Interestingly, religious liberty guarantees coexisted with various manifestations of religious establishment in many late eighteenth- and early nineteenth-century state constitutions.) The content, scope, and application of religious liberty were debated in the early republic, and they continue to agitate the public mind today.

Another recurring theme of religion in the American experiment is the consistent desire of Americans to define church-state arrangements at a community or local level. From the first English settlements in

---

26. "Declaration of Rights and Form of Government in Virginia," [May 16–June 29, 1776], in Hutchinson and Rachal, eds., *The Papers of James Madison*, 1:172–75. See generally Daniel L. Dreisbach, "George Mason's Pursuit of Religious Liberty in Revolutionary Virginia," *Virginia Magazine of History and Biography* 108, no. 1 (2000): 5–44.

27. Letter from George Washington to the Hebrew Congregation in Newport, Rhode Island [August 18, 1790], in *The Papers of George Washington*, Presidential Series, ed. Dorothy Twohig et al. (Charlottesville: University Press of Virginia, 1996), 6:285.

North America, the new Americans sought to establish and maintain church-state policies and religious practices for their own communities. They resisted efforts initiated by higher civil authorities in either the Old World or the New to impose church-state arrangements upon them and, for the most part, lived in relative harmony with neighboring communities, some of which were of very different faith traditions.

Although most colonies eventually established churches, under which dissenters bristled, proponents often defended this arrangement as local (or at least regional) control of church-state policies. Establishmentarian laws and policies in some colonies harshly restricted the religious rights and practices of dissenters. Some colonies, and later states, with legally established churches, however, were fairly tolerant of dissenting sects asserting some measure of autonomy in church-state matters within their respective communities. Some jurisdictions had general or multiple religious establishments, which allowed diverse expressions of religious establishment to emerge at a local level. The Massachusetts Constitution of 1780, for example, permitted multiple establishments, although in practice it favored Congregationalism. Diverse denominations, including Baptist, Episcopalian, Quaker, and Unitarian, received support from the public treasury, and in some towns the Baptists, despite reservations about religious establishments, garnered sufficient support to become "the establishment and their ministers received their salaries from the town treasuries."[28] When the former colonies came together to form a union following independence from Great Britain, each state jealously guarded its prerogative to define church-state policies within its own borders and eschewed notions of a national ecclesiastical establishment.

---

28. Leonard W. Levy, *The Establishment Clause: Religion and the First Amendment*, 2d ed. (Chapel Hill: University of North Carolina Press, 1994), 33. See also William G. McLoughlin, *New England Dissent, 1630–1833: The Baptists and the Separation of Church and State*, 2 vols. (Cambridge, Mass.: Harvard University Press, 1971), 1:675. Similar patterns of multiple establishments could be found in Massachusetts at the end of the seventeenth century. Levy, *The Establishment Clause*, 17–18.

This persistent impulse on the part of Americans to define church-state arrangements at the local level was ultimately constitutionalized with the ratification of the First Amendment. This measure explicitly prohibited the establishment of a national church and implicitly affirmed state jurisdiction in matters of church-state relations. This was a manifestation of federalism, a fundamental feature of American constitutionalism.

By the time of the Constitutional Convention of 1787, there was remarkably little popular sentiment for the establishment of a *national* church. There were many reasons for the broad support of a national policy of nonestablishment. The extraordinary religious pluralism left no denomination or sect with the demographic dominance or political clout to assert itself as the established church of the new nation. The rising, though limited, influence of moderate Enlightenment, rationalist thought, especially among a small class of intellectual elites, partly accounts for this. A comparatively few skeptics in the founding generation worried that unchecked religious zeal could perpetuate intolerance and bigotry, such as had spawned the Spanish Inquisition. For a growing number of religious dissenters, religious establishments were a dreaded source of persecution, and they agitated for the termination of legal favors and privileges granted to one particular church. As noted earlier, many pious citizens were coming to the conclusion that Christianity was purer and more vital in the absence of establishments and when it relied on the voluntary support of adherents. There were also some zealous advocates of an established church at the state level who opposed a national ecclesiastical establishment because they feared a national church would displace the existing church-state arrangements in their respective states. Even among the most pious, religiously devout citizens, including many establishmentarians, few advocated for a national church.

The apparent paradox of simultaneously affirming an ecclesiastical establishment at the state level while eschewing a national establishment points to a defining feature of the constitutional principles governing religious liberty and church-state relations. The United States Constitution, as a matter of federalism, denied the national regime the authority to establish a religion or prohibit its free exercise, but left unchanged the prerogative of states to determine their own policies regarding religion. The First Amendment prohibitions were applicable against the national government only. The nonestablishment provision, for example, expressly prohibited Congress from making "law respecting an establishment of religion" and, by implication, proscribed the national government from interfering with existing state religious establishments and church-state arrangements. This meant the Constitution left the states free to establish a religion, disestablish a religion, or implement policies that discriminated for or against a specific sect. And, indeed, various forms and manifestations of religious establishment, from established churches to religious test oaths for public officials and voters, remained the law in some states well into the nineteenth century.

This understanding of the constitutional principles was virtually unchallenged in the founding era and was confirmed by the U.S. Supreme Court. Chief Justice John Marshall, writing for a united Court in *Barron v. Baltimore* (1833), affirmed that "[t]he Constitution was ordained and established by the people of the United States for themselves, for their own government, and not for the Government of the individual States." He then declared that the liberties guaranteed in the Bill of Rights "contain no expression indicating an intention to apply them to the state governments."[29] Specifically addressing religious liberty in the Constitution, the Supreme Court ruled unanimously in *Permoli v. Municipality* (1845) that "[t]he Constitution makes no provision for protecting the citizens of the respective States in their religious liberties; this is left to the state constitutions and laws: nor is there any inhibition imposed by the Constitution of the United States in this respect on

the states."[30] Justice Joseph Story concurred in his authoritative *Commentaries on the Constitution of the United States* (1833). The purpose of the First Amendment, he wrote, was "to exclude from the national government all power to act upon the subject [of religion]." He further opined that "the whole power over the subject of religion is left exclusively to the state governments, to be acted upon according to their own sense of justice, and the state constitutions."[31] It was not until the twentieth century that the Supreme Court overturned this understanding by incorporating the First Amendment guarantees into the due process of law clause of the Fourteenth Amendment (1868), thereby applying these provisions against state governments.

"A page of history," Supreme Court Justice Oliver Wendell Holmes remarked, "is worth a volume of logic."[32] In no area of public life is this adage more true than in the troubled relations between religion and public life. Students of religion and politics, church and state, and American political theology have, thus, consistently turned to the pages of history to inform their interpretations of the prudential and constitutional relationships between religion and civil government. Madison agreed that any discussion of church and state is appropriately and profitably illuminated by history. "[O]n this question," he wrote, "experience will be an admitted umpire."[33] The U.S. Supreme Court has long relied on history, especially the dramatic disestablishment struggle in revolutionary Virginia, to guide its interpretation of the First Amendment religion provisions. In the Supreme Court's first major nonestablishment of religion case in 1947, Justice Hugo L. Black opined that the First Amendment religious clause should be construed "in the light of its history and the evils it was

30. *Permoli v. Municipality*, 44 U.S. (3 Howard) 589, 609 (1845).

31. Joseph Story, *Commentaries on the Constitution of the United States*, 3 vols. (Boston: Hilliard, Gray, and Co., 1833), 3:730–31, sec. 1873.

32. *New York Trust Co. v. Eisner*, 256 U.S. 345, 349 (1921).

33. Letter from James Madison to Jasper Adams, September 1833, in Dreisbach, ed., *Religion and Politics in the Early Republic*, 117.

29. *Barron v. Baltimore*, 32 U.S. (7 Peters) 243, 250 (1833).

designed forever to suppress."[34] Justice Wiley B. Rutledge similarly remarked: "No provision of the Constitution is more closely tied to or given content by its generating history than the religious clause of the First Amendment. It is at once the refined product and the terse summation of that history."[35] In appealing to history, the Supreme Court has often relied on the views of a very small cast of characters.[36] For instance, Justice Tom C. Clark proclaimed in *Abington v. Schempp* (1963) that "the views of Madison and Jefferson, preceded by Roger Williams, came to be incorporated not only in the Federal Constitution but likewise in those of most of our States."[37] Few would dispute that these three men played an important role in the development of church-state relations in America, but their views do not constitute the whole story. One purpose of this volume is to paint a richer and fuller portrait of the development of church-state relations and religious liberty in America, drawing on the writings and experiences of both the famous and the sometimes forgotten individuals who contributed to this aspect of American life.

Church-state relations have been a source of controversy since the first English settlements in the New World and continue to provoke energetic debate and intellectual discourse. Indeed, rarely in American history has the relationship between religion and public life been more widely discussed and intensely debated than it is today. Few topics in public life are more appropriately informed by a thorough understanding of history. Therefore, this collection of primary documents was conceived to introduce modern readers to the history of religious liberty and church-state relations in the American experience. This volume surveys the evolving relationship between public religion and American social, legal, and political culture from the colonial era to the early national period,

and explores the social and political forces that defined the concept of religious liberty and shaped church-state relations in America.

The Sacred Rights of Conscience combines important primary documents with editorial notes providing context and, where appropriate, brief commentary. Documents and topics were selected on the basis of the importance of their contribution to American political and intellectual thought, the saliency of the ideas they illustrate, and relevancy to enduring themes of church-state relations. In general, we favored public papers, such as constitutions, laws, or public addresses, as opposed to private reflections contained in letters or diaries. We do not doubt the utility of the latter for shedding light on a particular founder's views; however, public papers, more than private writings, were accessible to a general audience and available for others to base their actions and opinions upon and to inform public sentiment and policy. The documents we selected also illustrate the rich diversity of perspectives on the role of religion in American society and reveal the roots of modern church-state controversies. We looked for documents that represented diverse political, ideological, theological, and regional viewpoints.

The selected documents are organized topically and, generally, chronologically within each theme. The primary focus is on the evolution of a distinctive American doctrine of religious liberty. The documents trace the development of American church-state relations from the biblical and European sources that influenced church-state thought in colonial America, to the crafting of distinctive American approaches to church-state relations, to the flourishing of denominational pluralism facilitated by the First Amendment's religious liberty and nonestablishment provisions, and to the critical testing of the content and application of the prudential and constitutional principles governing religion's role in an increasingly secular, pluralistic society.

The material has been arranged to emphasize the content and intensity of the continuing public debate in America on the scope of religious liberty and the

---

34. *Everson v. Board of Education,* 330 U.S. 1, 14–15 (1947).

35. *Everson,* 330 U.S. at 33 (Rutledge, J., dissenting).

36. See Mark David Hall, "Jeffersonian Walls and Madisonian Lines: The Supreme Court's Use of History in Religion Clause Cases," *Oregon Law Review* 85 (2006): 563–614.

37. *Abington School District v. Schempp,* 374 U.S. 203, 214 (1963).

relation of religion to public life. A few of the documents are reproduced from unpublished original sources, such as several Virginia petitions in chapter 6 and the letters in chapter 12. The remainder comes from reputable primary sources. The documents have been edited very lightly. Except where noted or for the very occasional correction of obvious typographical errors and addition of punctuation marks in brackets to enhance clarity, we have preserved the original grammar, punctuation, capitalization, italicization, and spelling as found in the primary sources from which the documents have been reproduced, even though they are sometimes idiosyncratic and archaic. A printer's convention of the seventeenth and eighteenth centuries was to use a long letter *s* in place of the short letter *s*. To make the text more accessible to the modern reader, we have replaced the long *s* with the short *s*. (Other printer's conventions found occasionally in these documents include the use of *u* for *v* and *i* for *j*.) Any word or words in the original texts that we could not decipher with certainty have been placed in brackets. The reprinted documents (and excerpts) range in length from a short paragraph to several dozen pages. Footnotes indicated by "Eds." or "Trans." have been added by us. If a footnote was written by an editor of a volume from which we obtained a document, we identify the note as being by this person. Otherwise all notes are in the original texts. Our preference was to reproduce pieces in their entirety, but space limitations forced us to reproduce only selected portions of lengthy texts or works that contained repetitive material or passages unrelated to the general themes of this volume. We have tried to avoid excerpts so brief that it deprives the reader of valuable context.

Each chapter is prefaced by a brief introduction providing context for the selected documents. Short headnotes accompany most documents. The volume also contains a variety of resources and pedagogical aids designed to enhance its value as a supplemental textbook or reference work for students of religion in American history. Recommendations for further reading are located at the end of each chapter. We

have also provided a bibliography of major works on religion in American public life that directs readers to additional primary sources and secondary literature. The appendixes include a chronology of church-state developments in American history and an outline of deliberations in the first federal Congress leading to the language of the First Amendment religious clause.

Collectively, these documents provide a vivid reminder that religion was a dynamic factor in shaping American social, legal, and political culture, and that there has been a struggle since the inception of the American republic to define the prudential and constitutional role of religion in public culture. Many of the selected documents have a striking contemporary quality to them. The style, language, and themes of church-state debate today are much the same as they have been for four centuries. The place of religion in a pluralistic society and the secularization of public life are sources of controversy today, just as they were in revolutionary Virginia, the first Congress, and the early republic.

There is a *very* long list of individuals and institutions who have generously assisted us in preparing this volume. Even if we could remember everyone who has contributed to the project, we could not possibly name them all. We trust those individuals whose contributions we fail to identify by name will accept our thanks anonymously. There are a few individuals and institutions, however, that must escape anonymity.

We are especially grateful for the direction of the late James McClellan, former director of publications at Liberty Fund, who conceived of this project and encouraged us to see it through to completion. We are also grateful for the wise counsel, endless encouragement, generous support, and careful editing of Madelaine Cooke, Laura Goetz, and Patti Ordower. We received immeasurable benefit from volumes published by Liberty Fund edited by Bruce Frohnen, Charles S. Hyneman, Philip B. Kurland, Ralph Lerner, Donald S. Lutz, and Ellis Sandoz. We also thank the scholars who reviewed and commented on various drafts of our table of contents.

relation of religion to public life. A few of the documents are reproduced from unpublished original sources, such as several Virginia petitions in chapter 6 and the letters in chapter 12. The remainder comes from reputable primary sources. The documents have been edited very lightly. Except where noted or for the very occasional correction of obvious typographical errors and addition of punctuation marks in brackets to enhance clarity, we have preserved the original grammar, punctuation, capitalization, italicization, and spelling as found in the primary sources from which the documents have been reproduced, even though they are sometimes idiosyncratic and archaic. A printer's convention of the seventeenth and eighteenth centuries was to use a long letter *s* in place of the short letter *s*. To make the text more accessible to the modern reader, we have replaced the long *s* with the short *s*. (Other printer's conventions found occasionally in these documents include the use of *u* for *v* and *i* for *j*.) Any word or words in the original texts that we could not decipher with certainty have been placed in brackets. The reprinted documents (and excerpts) range in length from a short paragraph to several dozen pages. Footnotes indicated by "Eds." or "Trans." have been added by us. If a footnote was written by an editor of a volume from which we obtained a document, we identify the note as being by this person. Otherwise all notes are in the original texts. Our preference was to reproduce pieces in their entirety, but space limitations forced us to reproduce only selected portions of lengthy texts or works that contained repetitive material or passages unrelated to the general themes of this volume. We have tried to avoid excerpts so brief that it deprives the reader of valuable context.

Each chapter is prefaced by a brief introduction providing context for the selected documents. Short headnotes accompany most documents. The volume also contains a variety of resources and pedagogical aids designed to enhance its value as a supplemental textbook or reference work for students of religion in American history. Recommendations for further reading are located at the end of each chapter. We have also provided a bibliography of major works on religion in American public life that directs readers to additional primary sources and secondary literature. The appendixes include a chronology of church-state developments in American history and an outline of deliberations in the first federal Congress leading to the language of the First Amendment religious clause.

Collectively, these documents provide a vivid reminder that religion was a dynamic factor in shaping American social, legal, and political culture, and that there has been a struggle since the inception of the American republic to define the prudential and constitutional role of religion in public culture. Many of the selected documents have a striking contemporary quality to them. The style, language, and themes of church-state debate today are much the same as they have been for four centuries. The place of religion in a pluralistic society and the secularization of public life are sources of controversy today, just as they were in revolutionary Virginia, the first Congress, and the early republic.

There is a *very* long list of individuals and institutions who have generously assisted us in preparing this volume. Even if we could remember everyone who has contributed to the project, we could not possibly name them all. We trust those individuals whose contributions we fail to identify by name will accept our thanks anonymously. There are a few individuals and institutions, however, that must escape anonymity.

We are especially grateful for the direction of the late James McClellan, former director of publications at Liberty Fund, who conceived of this project and encouraged us to see it through to completion. We are also grateful for the wise counsel, endless encouragement, generous support, and careful editing of Madelaine Cooke, Laura Goetz, and Patti Ordower. We received immeasurable benefit from volumes published by Liberty Fund edited by Bruce Frohnen, Charles S. Hyneman, Philip B. Kurland, Ralph Lerner, Donald S. Lutz, and Ellis Sandoz. We also thank the scholars who reviewed and commented on various drafts of our table of contents.

They include Todd Breyfogle; Thomas E. Buckley, S.J.; James H. Hutson; George M. Marsden; Jeffry H. Morrison; Mark A. Noll; Michael Novak; Paul Otto; Ellis Sandoz; Barry Alan Shain; Garrett Ward Sheldon; James R. Stoner, Jr.; Graham Walker; and John G. West, Jr. As well, we are grateful to Joshua W. D. Smith for providing excellent translations of Latin, Greek, and French passages. We also acknowledge the assistance of archivists, curators, and reference librarians at American University, George Fox University, the Library of Congress, and the Virginia State Library. On a personal note, Daniel Dreisbach thanks his wife, Joyce, and two daughters, Mollie and Moriah, for their endless patience and good humor during the course of this and other projects. Mark Hall is grateful for support provided by George Fox University through the Herbert Hoover Distinguished Professorship, grants from the Faculty Development Committee, and research and secretarial assistance from Karlyn Fleming, Samuel Greene, Janna McKee, and Rachel Sparks. As well, he is indebted to the Earhart Foundation for critical support. Finally, he is grateful for the patience and love of his wife, Miriam, and children, Joshua, Lydia, and Anna.

We hope this volume will prove a useful resource for students of religion in American public life. Given the extensive and continuing influence of history in analyzing the prudential and constitutional place of religion in the American polity, we believe this collection of historical documents will cast light not only on the past but also on the present and the future of the American experiment in liberty under law.

Part I

ANTECEDENTS OF THE

PRINCIPLES GOVERNING RELIGIOUS LIBERTY

AND CHURCH-STATE RELATIONS

IN AMERICA

CHAPTER ONE

Biblical and European Heritages

WHEN COLONIAL AMERICANS thought about the proper relationship between church and state they drew from a variety of biblical and European sources. Because the vast majority of Americans were inheritors of the Protestant doctrine of *sola scriptura,* they turned first to the Bible for guidance when creating or modifying social and political institutions in the New World. In some instances biblical passages speak directly to political issues. For example, Romans 13:1–7 states that Christians are to obey the civil government, whereas Acts 5:27–29 suggests that the obligation is not absolute. In other cases, Scriptures informed basic principles relevant to society and politics (e.g., Genesis 1:26–27, I Peter 2:18–3:6, and Exodus 20:1–17). Of course there were disagreements among the colonists about the meaning or relevance of some passages, but few Americans questioned the normative authority of the Holy Bible.

Well-educated Americans, who were generally in the best positions to shape church-state relations in the New World, were also familiar with great European writers on the subject. Some of these thinkers, such as St. Thomas Aquinas, exercised an indirect influence, whereas others were viewed as important authorities—especially John Calvin in Puritan New England and John Locke in late eighteenth-century America. Even some who were generally vilified, such as Thomas Hobbes, contributed to the general intellectual context that informed American approaches to church-state relations and religious liberty. As well, minority groups, like the Anabaptists, presented important alternatives to dominant understandings of what a Christian commonwealth should look like.

Americans were also greatly influenced by English approaches to church-state relations. They were aware of, and typically bound by, English laws such as the Act of Supremacy and, later, the Act of Toleration. Southern colonies largely followed British practices and provided government support for the Church of England. New England colonies, on the other hand, were dominated by Puritans who had been frustrated by their inability to reform thoroughly the Church of England. Establishments in those colonies differed significantly from their English antecedents—and this occasionally led to conflicts. Finally, as we will see, some colonies took a different path altogether and refused to establish an official state church. In addition to laws, ecclesiastical documents, like the Thirty-nine Articles and the Westminster Confession, had a profound impact on how early Americans viewed church-state relations.

KING JAMES VERSION
OF THE HOLY SCRIPTURES

The following biblical passages are among the most frequently cited in early America concerning political authority and the pious citizen's obligations to, and relationship with, civil authorities. The texts are from the Authorized Version, often referred to as the King James Version, of 1611.

Genesis 1:26–27

26 And God said, Let us make man in our image, after our likeness: and let them have dominion over the fish of the sea, and over the fowl of the air, and over the cattle, and over all the earth, and over every creeping thing that creepeth upon the earth.

27 So God created man in his *own* image, in the image of God created he him; male and female created he them.

Genesis 3:1–24

1 Now the serpent was more subtile than any beast of the field which the LORD God had made. And he said unto the woman, Yea, hath God said, Ye shall not eat of every tree of the garden?

2 And the woman said unto the serpent, We may eat of the fruit of the trees of the garden:

Reprinted from *The Holy Bible* (New York: American Bible Society, 1816).

3 But of the fruit of the tree which *is* in the midst of the garden, God hath said, Ye shall not eat of it, neither shall ye touch it, lest ye die.

4 And the serpent said unto the woman, Ye shall not surely die:

5 For God doth know that in the day ye eat thereof, then your eyes shall be opened, and ye shall be as gods, knowing good and evil.

6 And when the woman saw that the tree *was* good for food, and that it *was* pleasant to the eyes, and a tree to be desired to make *one* wise, she took of the fruit thereof, and did eat, and gave also unto her husband with her; and he did eat.

7 And the eyes of them both were opened, and they knew that they *were* naked; and they sewed fig leaves together, and made themselves aprons.

8 And they heard the voice of the LORD God walking in the garden in the cool of the day: and Adam and his wife hid themselves from the presence of the LORD God amongst the trees of the garden.

9 And the LORD God called unto Adam, and said unto him, Where *art* thou?

10 And he said, I heard thy voice in the garden, and I was afraid, because I *was* naked; and I hid myself.

11 And he said, Who told thee that thou *wast* naked? Hast thou eaten of the tree, whereof I commanded thee that thou shouldest not eat?

12 And the man said, The woman whom thou gavest *to be* with me, she gave me of the tree, and I did eat.

13 And the LORD God said unto the woman, What *is* this *that* thou hast done? And the woman said, The serpent beguiled me, and I did eat.

14 And the LORD God said unto the serpent, Because thou hast done this, thou *art* cursed above all cattle, and above every beast of the field; upon thy belly shalt thou go, and dust shalt thou eat all the days of thy life:

15 And I will put enmity between thee and the woman, and between thy seed and her seed; it shall bruise thy head, and thou shalt bruise his heel.

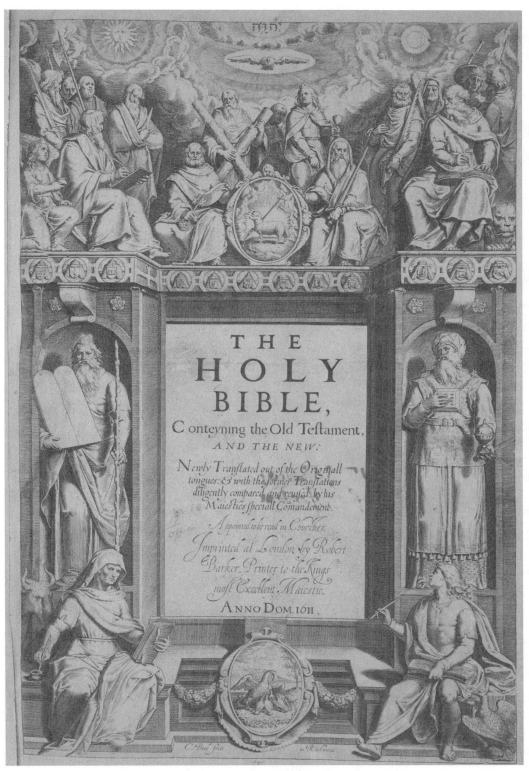

Title page of *The Holy Bible, Conteyning the Old Testament and the New,* London: Robert Baker, 1611. Rare Book and Special Collections Division, Library of Congress.

16 Unto the woman he said, I will greatly multiply thy sorrow and thy conception; in sorrow thou shalt bring forth children; and thy desire *shall be* to thy husband, and he shall rule over thee.

17 And unto Adam he said, Because thou hast hearkened unto the voice of thy wife, and hast eaten of the tree, of which I commanded thee, saying, Thou shalt not eat of it: cursed *is* the ground for thy sake; in sorrow shalt thou eat *of* it all the days of thy life;

18 Thorns also and thistles shall it bring forth to thee; and thou shalt eat the herb of the field:

19 In the sweat of thy face shalt thou eat bread, till thou return unto the ground; for out of it wast thou taken: for dust thou *art,* and unto dust shalt thou return.

20 And Adam called his wife's name Eve; because she was the mother of all living.

21 Unto Adam also and to his wife did the LORD God make coats of skins, and clothed them.

22 And the LORD God said, Behold, the man is become as one of us, to know good and evil: and now, lest he put forth his hand, and take also of the tree of life, and eat, and live for ever:

23 Therefore the LORD God sent him forth from the garden of Eden, to till the ground from whence he was taken.

24 So he drove out the man: and he placed at the east of the garden of Eden cherubim, and a flaming sword which turned every way, to keep the way of the tree of life.

— • —

Exodus 1:15–21

15 And the king of Egypt spake to the Hebrew midwives, of which the name of the one *was* Shiphrah, and the name of the other Puah;

16 And he said, When ye do the office of a midwife to the Hebrew women, and see *them* upon the stools, if it *be* a son, then ye shall kill him; but if it *be* a daughter, then she shall live.

17 But the midwives feared God, and did not as the king of Egypt commanded them, but saved the men children alive.

18 And the king of Egypt called for the midwives, and said unto them, Why have ye done this thing, and have saved the men children alive?

19 And the midwives said unto Pharaoh, Because the Hebrew women *are* not as the Egyptian women; for they *are* lively, and are delivered ere the midwives come in unto them.

20 Therefore God dealt well with the midwives: and the people multiplied, and waxed very mighty.

21 And it came to pass, because the midwives feared God, that he made them houses.

— • —

Exodus 18:13–27

13 And it came to pass on the morrow, that Moses sat to judge the people: and the people stood by Moses from the morning unto the evening.

14 And when Moses' father-in-law saw all that he did to the people, he said, What *is* this thing that thou doest to the people? Why sittest thou thyself alone, and all the people stand by thee from morning unto even?

15 And Moses said unto his father-in-law, Because the people come unto me to inquire of God:

16 When they have a matter, they come unto me; and I judge between one and another, and I do make *them* know the statutes of God, and his laws.

17 And Moses' father-in-law said unto him, The thing that thou doest *is* not good.

18 Thou wilt surely wear away, both thou, and this people that *is* with thee: for this thing *is* too heavy for thee; thou art not able to perform it thyself alone.

19 Hearken now unto my voice, I will give thee counsel, and God shall be with thee: Be thou for the

people to Godward, that thou mayest bring the causes unto God:

20 And thou shalt teach them ordinances and laws, and shalt show them the way wherein they must walk, and the work that they must do.

21 Moreover thou shalt provide out of all the people able men, such as fear God, men of truth, hating covetousness; and place *such* over them, *to be* rulers of thousands, *and* rulers of hundreds, rulers of fifties, and rulers of tens:

22 And let them judge the people at all seasons: and it shall be, *that* every great matter they shall bring unto thee, but every small matter they shall judge: so shall it be easier for thyself, and they shall bear *the burden* with thee.

23 If thou shalt do this thing, and God command thee *so,* then thou shalt be able to endure, and all this people shall also go to their place in peace.

24 So Moses hearkened to the voice of his father-in-law, and did all that he had said.

25 And Moses chose able men out of all Israel, and made them heads over the people, rulers of thousands, rulers of hundreds, rulers of fifties, and rulers of tens.

26 And they judged the people at all seasons: the hard causes they brought unto Moses, but every small matter they judged themselves.

27 And Moses let his father-in-law depart; and he went his way into his own land.

Exodus 20:1–17

1 AND God spake all these words, saying,

2 I *am* the LORD thy God, which have brought thee out of the land of Egypt, out of the house of bondage.

3 Thou shalt have no other gods before me.

4 Thou shalt not make unto thee any graven image, or any likeness *of any thing* that *is* in heaven above, or that *is* in the earth beneath, or that *is* in the water under the earth:

5 Thou shalt not bow down thyself to them, nor serve them: for I the LORD thy God *am* a jealous God, visiting the iniquity of the fathers upon the children unto the third and fourth *generation* of them that hate me;

6 And showing mercy unto thousands of them that love me, and keep my commandments.

7 Thou shalt not take the name of the LORD thy God in vain: for the LORD will not hold him guiltless that taketh his name in vain.

8 Remember the sabbath day, to keep it holy.

9 Six days shalt thou labor, and do all thy work:

10 But the seventh day *is* the sabbath of the LORD thy God: *in it* thou shalt not do any work, thou, nor thy son, nor thy daughter, thy manservant, nor thy maidservant, nor thy cattle, nor thy stranger that *is* within thy gates:

11 For *in* six days the LORD made heaven and earth, the sea, and all that in them *is,* and rested the seventh day: wherefore the LORD blessed the sabbath day, and hallowed it.

12 Honor thy father and thy mother: that thy days may be long upon the land which the LORD thy God giveth thee.

13 Thou shalt not kill.

14 Thou shalt not commit adultery.

15 Thou shalt not steal.

16 Thou shalt not bear false witness against thy neighbor.

17 Thou shalt not covet thy neighbor's house, thou shalt not covet thy neighbor's wife, nor his manservant, nor his maidservant, nor his ox, nor his ass, nor any thing that *is* thy neighbor's.

Leviticus 25:10

10 And ye shall hallow the fiftieth year, and proclaim liberty throughout *all* the land unto all the in-

habitants thereof: it shall be a jubilee unto you; and ye shall return every man unto his possession, and ye shall return every man unto his family.

———

Leviticus 26:1–46*

1 Ye shall make you no idols nor graven image, neither rear you up a standing image, neither shall ye set up any image of stone in your land, to bow down unto it: for I am the LORD your God.

2 Ye shall keep my sabbaths, and reverence my sanctuary: I am the LORD.

3 If ye walk in my statutes, and keep my commandments, and do them;

4 Then I will give you rain in due season, and the land shall yield her increase, and the trees of the field shall yield their fruit.

5 And your threshing shall reach unto the vintage, and the vintage shall reach unto the sowing time: and ye shall eat your bread to the full, and dwell in your land safely.

6 And I will give peace in the land, and ye shall lie down, and none shall make you afraid: and I will rid evil beasts out of the land, neither shall the sword go through your land.

7 And ye shall chase your enemies, and they shall fall before you by the sword.

8 And five of you shall chase an hundred, and an hundred of you shall put ten thousand to flight: and your enemies shall fall before you by the sword.

9 For I will have respect unto you, and make you fruitful, and multiply you, and establish my covenant with you.

10 And ye shall eat old store, and bring forth the old because of the new.

11 And I will set my tabernacle among you: and my soul shall not abhor you.

12 And I will walk among you, and will be your God, and ye shall be my people.

13 I am the LORD your God, which brought you forth out of the land of Egypt, that ye should not be their bondmen; and I have broken the bands of your yoke, and made you go upright.

14 But if ye will not hearken unto me, and will not do all these commandments;

15 And if ye shall despise my statutes, or if your soul abhor my judgments, so that ye will not do all my commandments, but that ye break my covenant:

16 I also will do this unto you; I will even appoint over you terror, consumption, and the burning ague, that shall consume the eyes, and cause sorrow of heart: and ye shall sow your seed in vain, for your enemies shall eat it.

17 And I will set my face against you, and ye shall be slain before your enemies: they that hate you shall reign over you; and ye shall flee when none pursueth you.

18 And if ye will not yet for all this hearken unto me, then I will punish you seven times more for your sins.

19 And I will break the pride of your power; and I will make your heaven as iron, and your earth as brass:

20 And your strength shall be spent in vain: for your land shall not yield her increase, neither shall the trees of the land yield their fruits.

21 And if ye walk contrary unto me, and will not hearken unto me; I will bring seven times more plagues upon you according to your sins.

22 I will also send wild beasts among you, which shall rob you of your children, and destroy your cattle, and make you few in number; and your highways shall be desolate.

23 And if ye will not be reformed by me by these things, but will walk contrary unto me;

24 Then will I also walk contrary unto you, and will punish you yet seven times for your sins.

25 And I will bring a sword upon you, that shall avenge the quarrel of my covenant: and when ye are gathered together within your cities, I will send the

* Cf. Deuteronomy 28.

pestilence among you; and ye shall be delivered into the hand of the enemy.

26 And when I have broken the staff of your bread, ten women shall bake your bread in one oven, and they shall deliver you your bread again by weight: and ye shall eat, and not be satisfied.

27 And if ye will not for all this hearken unto me, but walk contrary unto me;

28 Then I will walk contrary unto you also in fury; and I, even I, will chastise you seven times for your sins.

29 And ye shall eat the flesh of your sons, and the flesh of your daughters shall ye eat.

30 And I will destroy your high places, and cut down your images, and cast your carcases upon the carcases of your idols, and my soul shall abhor you.

31 And I will make your cities waste, and bring your sanctuaries unto desolation, and I will not smell the savour of your sweet odours.

32 And I will bring the land into desolation: and your enemies which dwell therein shall be astonished at it.

33 And I will scatter you among the heathen, and will draw out a sword after you: and your land shall be desolate, and your cities waste.

34 Then shall the land enjoy her sabbaths, as long as it lieth desolate, and ye be in your enemies' land; even then shall the land rest, and enjoy her sabbaths.

35 As long as it lieth desolate it shall rest; because it did not rest in your sabbaths, when ye dwelt upon it.

36 And upon them that are left alive of you I will send a faintness into their hearts in the lands of their enemies; and the sound of a shaken leaf shall chase them; and they shall flee, as fleeing from a sword; and they shall fall when none pursueth.

37 And they shall fall one upon another, as it were before a sword, when none pursueth: and ye shall have no power to stand before your enemies.

38 And ye shall perish among the heathen, and the land of your enemies shall eat you up.

39 And they that are left of you shall pine away in their iniquity in your enemies' lands; and also in the iniquities of their fathers shall they pine away with them.

40 If they shall confess their iniquity, and the iniquity of their fathers, with their trespass which they trespassed against me, and that also they have walked contrary unto me;

41 And that I also have walked contrary unto them, and have brought them into the land of their enemies; if then their uncircumcised hearts be humbled, and they then accept of the punishment of their iniquity:

42 Then will I remember my covenant with Jacob, and also my covenant with Isaac, and also my covenant with Abraham will I remember; and I will remember the land.

43 The land also shall be left of them, and shall enjoy her sabbaths, while she lieth desolate without them: and they shall accept of the punishment of their iniquity: because, even because they despised my judgments, and because their soul abhorred my statutes.

44 And yet for all that, when they be in the land of their enemies, I will not cast them away, neither will I abhor them, to destroy them utterly, and to break my covenant with them: for I am the Lord their God.

45 But I will for their sakes remember the covenant of their ancestors, whom I brought forth out of the land of Egypt in the sight of the heathen, that I might be their God: I am the Lord.

46 These are the statutes and judgments and laws, which the Lord made between him and the children of Israel in mount Sinai by the hand of Moses.

Deuteronomy 13:1–5

1 If there arise among you a prophet, or a dreamer of dreams, and giveth thee a sign or a wonder,

2 And the sign or the wonder come to pass, whereof he spake unto thee, saying, Let us go after other gods, which thou hast not known, and let us serve them;

3 Thou shalt not hearken unto the words of that prophet, or that dreamer of dreams: for the Lord your God proveth you, to know whether ye love the Lord your God with all your heart and with all your soul.

4 Ye shall walk after the Lord your God, and fear him, and keep his commandments, and obey his voice, and ye shall serve him, and cleave unto him.

5 And that prophet, or that dreamer of dreams, shall be put to death; because he hath spoken to turn *you* away from the Lord your God, which brought you out of the land of Egypt, and redeemed you out of the house of bondage, to thrust thee out of the way which the Lord thy God commanded thee to walk in. So shalt thou put the evil away from the midst of thee.

Deuteronomy 17:1–20

1 Thou shalt not sacrifice unto the Lord thy God any bullock, or sheep, wherein is blemish, or any evilfavouredness: for that is an abomination unto the Lord thy God.

2 If there be found among you, within any of thy gates which the Lord thy God giveth thee, man or woman, that hath wrought wickedness in the sight of the Lord thy God, in transgressing his covenant,

3 And hath gone and served other gods, and worshipped them, either the sun, or moon, or any of the host of heaven, which I have not commanded;

4 And it be told thee, and thou hast heard of it, and inquired diligently, and, behold, it be true, and the thing certain, that such abomination is wrought in Israel:

5 Then shalt thou bring forth that man or that woman, which have committed that wicked thing, unto thy gates, even that man or that woman, and shalt stone them with stones, till they die.

6 At the mouth of two witnesses, or three witnesses, shall he that is worthy of death be put to death; but at the mouth of one witness he shall not be put to death.

7 The hands of the witnesses shall be first upon him to put him to death, and afterward the hands of all the people. So thou shalt put the evil away from among you.

8 If there arise a matter too hard for thee in judgment, between blood and blood, between plea and plea, and between stroke and stroke, being matters of controversy within thy gates: then shalt thou arise, and get thee up into the place which the Lord thy God shall choose;

9 And thou shalt come unto the priests the Levites, and unto the judge that shall be in those days, and inquire; and they shall shew thee the sentence of judgment:

10 And thou shalt do according to the sentence, which they of that place which the Lord shall choose shall shew thee; and thou shalt observe to do according to all that they inform thee:

11 According to the sentence of the law which they shall teach thee, and according to the judgment which they shall tell thee, thou shalt do: thou shalt not decline from the sentence which they shall shew thee, to the right hand, nor to the left.

12 And the man that will do presumptuously, and will not hearken unto the priest that standeth to minister there before the Lord thy God, or unto the judge, even that man shall die: and thou shalt put away the evil from Israel.

13 And all the people shall hear, and fear, and do no more presumptuously.

14 When thou art come unto the land which the Lord thy God giveth thee, and shalt possess it, and shalt dwell therein, and shalt say, I will set a king over me, like as all the nations that are about me;

15 Thou shalt in any wise set him king over thee, whom the Lord thy God shall choose: one from among thy brethren shalt thou set king over thee: thou mayest not set a stranger over thee, which is not thy brother.

16 But he shall not multiply horses to himself, nor cause the people to return to Egypt, to the end that he should multiply horses: forasmuch as the Lord hath said unto you, Ye shall henceforth return no more that way.

17 Neither shall he multiply wives to himself, that his heart turn not away: neither shall he greatly multiply to himself silver and gold.

18 And it shall be, when he sitteth upon the throne of his kingdom, that he shall write him a copy of this law in a book out of that which is before the priests the Levites:

19 And it shall be with him, and he shall read therein all the days of his life: that he may learn to fear the Lord his God, to keep all the words of this law and these statutes, to do them:

20 That his heart be not lifted up above his brethren, and that he turn not aside from the commandment, to the right hand, or to the left: to the end that he may prolong his days in his kingdom, he, and his children, in the midst of Israel.

I Samuel 8

1 And it came to pass, when Samuel was old, that he made his sons judges over Israel.

2 Now the name of his firstborn was Joel; and the name of his second, Abiah: *they were* judges in Beersheba.

3 And his sons walked not in his ways, but turned aside after lucre, and took bribes, and perverted judgment.

4 Then all the elders of Israel gathered themselves together, and came to Samuel unto Ramah,

5 And said unto him, Behold, thou art old, and thy sons walk not in thy ways: now make us a king to judge us like all the nations.

6 But the thing displeased Samuel, when they said, Give us a king to judge us. And Samuel prayed unto the Lord.

7 And the Lord said unto Samuel, Hearken unto the voice of the people in all that they say unto thee: for they have not rejected thee, but they have rejected me, that I should not reign over them.

8 According to all the works which they have done since the day that I brought them up out of Egypt even unto this day, wherewith they have forsaken me, and served other gods, so do they also unto thee.

9 Now therefore hearken unto their voice: howbeit yet protest solemnly unto them, and show them the manner of the king that shall reign over them.

10 And Samuel told all the words of the Lord unto the people that asked of him a king.

11 And he said, This will be the manner of the king that shall reign over you: He will take your sons, and appoint *them* for himself, for his chariots, and *to be* his horsemen; and *some* shall run before his chariots.

12 And he will appoint him captains over thousands, and captains over fifties; and *will set them* to ear his ground, and to reap his harvest, and to make his instruments of war, and instruments of his chariots.

13 And he will take your daughters *to be* confectionaries, and *to be* cooks, and *to be* bakers.

14 And he will take your fields, and your vineyards, and your oliveyards, *even* the best *of them,* and give *them* to his servants.

15 And he will take the tenth of your seed, and of your vineyards, and give to his officers, and to his servants.

16 And he will take your menservants, and your maidservants, and your goodliest young men, and your asses, and put *them* to his work.

17 He will take the tenth of your sheep: and ye shall be his servants.

18 And ye shall cry out in that day because of your king which ye shall have chosen you; and the LORD will not hear you in that day.

19 Nevertheless the people refused to obey the voice of Samuel; and they said, Nay; but we will have a king over us;

20 That we also may be like all the nations; and that our king may judge us, and go out before us, and fight our battles.

21 And Samuel heard all the words of the people, and he rehearsed them in the ears of the LORD.

22 And the LORD said to Samuel, Hearken unto their voice, and make them a king. And Samuel said unto the men of Israel, Go ye every man unto his city.

II Chronicles 7:14

14 If my people, which are called by my name, shall humble themselves, and pray, and seek my face, and turn from their wicked ways; then will I hear from heaven, and will forgive their sin, and will heal their land.

Proverbs 14:34

34 Righteousness exalteth a nation: but sin *is* a reproach to any people.

Proverbs 29:2

2 When the righteous are in authority, the people rejoice: but when the wicked beareth rule, the people mourn.

Isaiah 49:22–23

22 Thus saith the Lord GOD, Behold, I will lift up mine hand to the Gentiles, and set up my standard to the people: and they shall bring thy sons in *their* arms, and thy daughters shall be carried upon *their* shoulders.

23 And kings shall be thy nursing fathers, and their queens thy nursing mothers: they shall bow down to thee with *their* face toward the earth, and lick up the dust of thy feet; and thou shalt know that I *am* the LORD: for they shall not be ashamed that wait for me.

Isaiah 60:12

12 For the nation and kingdom that will not serve thee shall perish; yea, *those* nations shall be utterly wasted.

Matthew 5:38–48

38 Ye have heard that it hath been said, An eye for an eye, and a tooth for a tooth:

39 But I say unto you, That ye resist not evil: but whosoever shall smite thee on thy right cheek, turn to him the other also.

40 And if any man will sue thee at the law, and take away thy coat, let him have *thy* cloak also.

41 And whosoever shall compel thee to go a mile, go with him twain.

42 Give to him that asketh thee, and from him that would borrow of thee turn not thou away.

43 Ye have heard that it hath been said, Thou shalt love thy neighbor, and hate thine enemy.

44 But I say unto you, Love your enemies, bless them that curse you, do good to them that hate you, and pray for them which despitefully use you, and persecute you;

45 That ye may be the children of your Father which is in heaven: for he maketh his sun to rise on the evil and on the good, and sendeth rain on the just and on the unjust.

46 For if ye love them which love you, what reward have ye? do not even the publicans the same?

47 And if ye salute your brethren only, what do ye more *than others?* do not even the publicans so?

48 Be ye therefore perfect, even as your Father which is in heaven is perfect.

Matthew 22:15–22*

15 Then went the Pharisees, and took counsel how they might entangle him in *his* talk.

16 And they sent out unto him their disciples with the Herodians, saying, Master, we know that thou art true, and teachest the way of God in truth, neither carest thou for any *man:* for thou regardest not the person of men.

17 Tell us therefore, What thinkest thou? Is it lawful to give tribute unto Caesar, or not?

* Cf. Mark 12:13–17; Luke 20:20–26.

18 But Jesus perceived their wickedness, and said, Why tempt ye me, ye hypocrites?

19 Show me the tribute money. And they brought unto him a penny.

20 And he saith unto them, Whose is this image and superscription?

21 They say unto him, Caesar's. Then saith he unto them, Render therefore unto Caesar the things which are Caesar's; and unto God the things that are God's.

22 When they had heard *these words,* they marveled, and left him, and went their way.

Luke 22:38

38 And they said, Lord, behold, here are two swords. And he said unto them, It is enough.

John 18:36

36 Jesus answered, My kingdom is not of this world: if my kingdom were of this world, then would my servants fight, that I should not be delivered to the Jews: but now is my kingdom not from hence.

Acts 5:27–29

27 And when they had brought them, they set *them* before the council: and the high priest asked them,

28 Saying, Did not we straitly command you that ye should not teach in this name? and, behold, ye have

filled Jerusalem with your doctrine, and intend to bring this man's blood upon us.

29 Then Peter and the *other* apostles answered and said, We ought to obey God rather than men.

———————

Romans 13:1–8

1 LET every soul be subject unto the higher powers. For there is no power but of God: the powers that be are ordained of God.

2 Whosoever therefore resisteth the power, resisteth the ordinance of God: and they that resist shall receive to themselves damnation.

3 For rulers are not a terror to good works, but to the evil. Wilt thou then not be afraid of the power? do that which is good, and thou shalt have praise of the same:

4 For he is the minister of God to thee for good. But if thou do that which is evil, be afraid; for he beareth not the sword in vain: for he is the minister of God, a revenger to *execute* wrath upon him that doeth evil.

5 Wherefore *ye* must needs be subject not only for wrath, but also for conscience' sake.

6 For, for this cause pay ye tribute also: for they are God's ministers, attending continually upon this very thing.

7 Render therefore to all their dues: tribute to whom tribute *is due;* custom to whom custom; fear to whom fear; honor to whom honor.

8 Owe no man any thing, but to love one another: for he that loveth another hath fulfilled the law.

———————

II Corinthians 6:14–18

14 Be ye not unequally yoked together with unbelievers: for what fellowship hath righteousness with unrighteousness? and what communion hath light with darkness?

15 And what concord hath Christ with Belial? or what part hath he that believeth with an infidel?

16 And what agreement hath the temple of God with idols? for ye are the temple of the living God; as God hath said, I will dwell in them, and walk in *them;* and I will be their God, and they shall be my people.

17 Wherefore come out from among them, and be ye separate, saith the Lord, and touch not the unclean *thing;* and I will receive you,

18 And will be a Father unto you, and ye shall be my sons and daughters, saith the Lord Almighty.

———————

I Peter 2:9–3:6*

9 But ye *are* a chosen generation, a royal priesthood, a holy nation, a peculiar people; that ye should show forth the praises of him who hath called you out of darkness into his marvelous light:

10 Which in time past *were* not a people, but *are* now the people of God: which had not obtained mercy, but now have obtained mercy.

11 Dearly beloved, I beseech *you* as strangers and pilgrims, abstain from fleshly lusts, which war against the soul;

12 Having your conversation honest among the Gentiles: that, whereas they speak against you as evildoers, they may by *your* good works, which they shall behold, glorify God in the day of visitation.

13 Submit yourselves to every ordinance of man for the Lord's sake: whether it be to the king, as supreme;

14 Or unto governors, as unto them that are sent by him for the punishment of evildoers, and for the praise of them that do well.

* Cf. Titus 3:1–2; I Timothy 2:1–3.

15 For so is the will of God, that with well doing ye may put to silence the ignorance of foolish men:

16 As free, and not using *your* liberty for a cloak of maliciousness, but as the servants of God.

17 Honor all *men*. Love the brotherhood. Fear God. Honor the king.

18 Servants, *be* subject to *your* masters with all fear; not only to the good and gentle, but also to the froward.

19 For this *is* thankworthy, if a man for conscience toward God endure grief, suffering wrongfully.

20 For what glory *is it*, if, when ye be buffeted for your faults, ye shall take it patiently? but if, when ye do well, and suffer *for it*, ye take it patiently, this *is* acceptable with God.

21 For even hereunto were ye called: because Christ also suffered for us, leaving us an example, that ye should follow his steps:

22 Who did no sin, neither was guile found in his mouth:

23 Who, when he was reviled, reviled not again; when he suffered, he threatened not; but committed *himself* to him that judgeth righteously:

24 Who his own self bare our sins in his own body on the tree, that we, being dead to sins, should live unto righteousness: by whose stripes ye were healed.

25 For ye were as sheep going astray; but are now returned unto the Shepherd and Bishop of your souls.

Chapter 3

1 LIKEWISE, ye wives, *be* in subjection to your own husbands; that, if any obey not the word, they also may without the word be won by the conversation of the wives;

2 While they behold your chaste conversation *coupled* with fear.

3 Whose adorning, let it not be that outward *adorning* of plaiting the hair, and of wearing of gold, or of putting on of apparel;

4 But *let it be* the hidden man of the heart, in that which is not corruptible, *even the ornament* of a meek and quiet spirit, which is in the sight of God of great price.

5 For after this manner in the old time the holy women also, who trusted in God, adorned themselves, being in subjection unto their own husbands:

6 Even as Sarah obeyed Abraham, calling him lord: whose daughters ye are, as long as ye do well, and are not afraid with any amazement.

EUROPEAN INFLUENCES

City of God (410–26)

On the Correction of the Donatists, Letter to Boniface (c. 417)

ST. AUGUSTINE (354–430)

The most important Latin church father, St. Augustine was born in North Africa, baptized as a Christian in 387 after a brilliant career in rhetoric, and made Bishop of Hippo in 395. His more than 113 books include the first western autobiography, *Confessions* (c. 397). After the sack of Rome in 410, Augustine authored the magisterial *City of God*. The "heavenly city" and "earthly city" are often misunderstood to be the institutional church and worldly government respectively, but Augustine's formulation reflects a more sophisticated analysis of the animating loves and ends of human societies—the love of God and of neighbor in charity, and the love of self and the desire to dominate one's fellows.

Contrary to many early church fathers, Augustine contended that Christians could rightly fulfill their duties to serve in civil government and fight in just wars. He argued that "an unjust law is no law at all." Although initially opposed to the use of force in ecclesiastical matters, after 400 he reluctantly acknowledged the use of civil power as a means of correcting and educating schismatics. This position is reflected in the following excerpt from a letter to Boniface, a Roman tribune in Africa. His interpretation of the gospel's phrase "compel them to come in" was used in subsequent centuries to legitimize the use of state power by the church, often in ways that Augustine himself would likely not have supported.

City of God (410–26)

28 Of the Quality of the Two Cities, the Earthly and the Heavenly

Two cities, then, have been created by two loves: that is, the earthly by love of self extending even to contempt of God, and the heavenly by love of God extending to contempt of self.[1] The one, therefore, glories in itself, the other in the Lord; the one seeks glory from men, the other finds its highest glory in God, the Witness of our conscience. The one lifts up its head in its own glory; the other says to its God, "Thou art my glory, and the lifter up of mine head."[2] In the Earthly City, princes are as much mastered by the lust for mastery as the nations which they subdue are by them; in the Heavenly, all serve one another in charity, rulers by their counsel and subjects by their obedience. The one city loves its own strength as displayed in its mighty men; the other says to its God, "I will love Thee, O Lord, my strength."[3]

Thus, in the Earthly City, its wise men, who live according to man, have pursued the goods of the body

or of their own mind, or both. Some of them who were able to know God "glorified Him not as God, neither were thankful; but became vain in their imagination, and their foolish heart was darkened. Professing themselves to be wise" (that is, exalting themselves in their wisdom, under the dominion of pride), "they became fools, and changed the glory of the incorruptible God into an image made like to corruptible man, and to birds, and fourfooted beasts, and creeping things" (for in adoring images of this kind they were either the leaders of the people or their followers); "and they worshipped and served the creature more than the Creator, Who is blessed forever."[4] In the Heavenly City, however, man has no wisdom beyond the piety which rightly worships the true God, and which looks for its reward in the fellowship not only of holy men, but of angels also, "that God may be all in all."[5]

On the Correction of the Donatists, Augustine to Boniface (c. 417)

In short, since they aren't able to show that they are being compelled in a direction that is bad for them, they argue that they should not be forced in a good direction. However, we indicated that Christ used force on Paul; the church imitates her Lord in using force on the people in question, having waited without using force on anyone until the prophetic predictions about the faith of kings and nations were fulfilled.

(24) Furthermore, the saying of the blessed apostle Paul makes complete sense in this context: *Prepared*

Bk. XIV, chap. 28, reprinted from *The City of God against the Pagans*, ed. and trans. R. W. Dyson (Cambridge: Cambridge University Press, 1998), 632–33. © in the selection, translation, and editorial matter Cambridge University Press 1998. Reprinted by permission of Cambridge University Press.

1. Cf. *Enarrat. in Psalm.*, 64,22.
2. Psalm 3,3.
3. Psalm 18,1.

4. Rom. 1,21ff.
5. I Cor. 15,28.

Reprinted from *Augustine Political Writings*, ed. E. M. Atkins and R. J. Dodaro (Cambridge: Cambridge University Press, 2001), 188–89. © in the selection, translation, and editorial matter Cambridge University Press 2001.

to avenge all disobedience, once your earlier obedience is fulfilled [2 Cor 10.6, Latin]. In this spirit too the Lord himself ordered guests first to be invited to his great feast, and subsequently compelled to come. For when his servants replied to him *Lord, your orders have been carried out, and there is still room,* he replied, *Go out into the pathways and hedgerows and force everyone you find to come in* [Lk 14.16–24].

The *earlier obedience* then is fulfilled in those who were, first of all, gently invited. Disobedience was forcibly checked, though, in those who were compelled. After all, what does, *Force them to come in* mean? For in the first place he said *invite,* and then they answered, *Your orders have been carried out, and there is still room.*

Maybe he wanted them to take this as meaning that they should be forced by terrifying miracles? But many divine miracles were performed among those who were first called, in particular among the Jews (it was said of them, *The Jews seek signs* [1 Cor 1.22]). Among the gentiles too in apostolic times such miracles lent credibility to the gospel; if therefore the command was to force people by means such as that, then we should, properly speaking, believe that the first set of guests (as I said) were forced.

Therefore if the church receives power through God's generosity and at the appropriate time, because of the king's religion and faith, and uses this to force anyone to come in who is found on *the pathways and in the hedgerows* (that is, in heresies and in schisms), they should not criticise the fact that they are being compelled, but concentrate on *where* they are being compelled to go. The Lord's banquet is the unity of the body of Christ, not only in the sacrament of the altar, but also *in the bond of peace* [Eph 4.3]. Now we are certainly able to say of *them* very truthfully that they would force no one in a good direction; for anyone they force, they force only in a bad direction.

(25) Admittedly before the laws which are used to force them to come to the holy banquet were despatched to Africa, several of the brethren—and I was one of them—thought otherwise. It seemed that although the madness of the Donatists was raging left,

right and centre, we should not petition the emperors to order this heresy to be entirely suppressed by imposing a penalty on those who wanted to embrace it; rather they ought to decree that anyone who preached Catholic truth by word of mouth, or chose it by their decision, should be protected from the violence of their fury. . . .

On the Government of Princes (1267)

ST. THOMAS AQUINAS (1225–74)

An Italian Dominican theologian, St. Thomas is best known for his magisterial *Summa theologiae.* The following excerpt from *De regimine principum* (On the Government of Princes) reflects his views of church-state relations.

Chapter xv: That the government of a king is like the Divine government, and that such government may be compared to the steering of a ship. Also, a comparison is here made between priestly and royal dominion.

Just as the foundation of a city or kingdom can fittingly be inferred from the example of the creation of the world, so also can the proper government of the former be inferred from the government of the latter. First of all, however, it must be noted that to govern is to guide what is governed in a suitable fashion to its proper end. Thus a ship is said to be governed when it is steered on its right course to port by the industry of the sailors. If, therefore, something is directed towards an end external to itself, as a ship is to harbour, the duty of its governor will be not only to

Reprinted from *St. Thomas Aquinas Political Writings,* ed. and trans. R. W. Dyson; chap. 15, pp. 39–42. © in the selection, translation, and editorial matter Cambridge University Press 2002. Reprinted with the permission of Cambridge University Press.

preserve the thing itself, but also to guide it towards its final end; whereas if there were something with no end outside itself, then the sole task belonging to the ruler would be the preservation of the thing itself in perfect condition.

But nothing of the latter kind [i.e. nothing with no end outside itself] is found in the world [*in rebus*] apart from God, Who is the end of all things; and the care of that which is directed towards an end outside itself is beset with a number of difficulties. For perhaps there is one person whose responsibility it is to preserve the thing itself and another whose task is to lead it towards a higher perfection, as in the case of the ship, from which we have drawn an example of government. For the carpenter has the task of repairing any damage which the ship has sustained, whereas the mariner bears the responsibility for guiding the ship to port. And so it happens also in the case of a man. For the physician has the task of preserving a man's life in a healthy condition; the steward has to supply him with the necessaries of life; the task of the teacher is to see to it that he understands the truth; and that of the moral counsellor is to ensure that he lives according to reason. And if man were not directed towards some good external to himself, the foregoing forms of care would suffice.

But there is a certain extraneous good which awaits man after he has lived this mortal life: namely, the final blessedness to which he looks forward in the enjoyment of God after death. For as the Apostle says (2 Corinthians 5:6): "While we are in the body, we are absent from the Lord." The Christian man, then, for whom that blessedness has been won by the blood of Christ, and for the attainment of which he has received the earnest of the Holy Spirit, has need of another, spiritual, care by which he is guided towards the harbour of eternal salvation. And this is the kind of care shown to the faithful by the ministers of the Church of Christ.

We must make the same judgment in regard to the end of the whole community as we do of one person. If the end of man were some good existing only in himself, therefore, the final end of government would similarly be to acquire and preserve that good for the whole community. Thus if that ultimate end, whether of one man or of a community, were the life and health of the body, the physicians would have the duty of governing. And if the final end were abundant wealth, the steward would be king of the community. And if the good were that the community might achieve knowledge of the truth, the king would have the duty of a teacher. But it seems that the end for which a community is brought together is to live according to virtue; for men come together so that they may live well in a way that would not be possible for each of them living singly. For the good is life according to virtue, and so the end of human association is a virtuous life.

An indication of this lies in the fact that only those who share with one another in the task of living well are deemed to be parts of a community. For if men came together for the sake of life merely, both animals and slaves would have a part in civil society; if for the sake of acquiring wealth, all those engaged in commerce together would belong to one city. But we see that only those are counted as members of a community who are guided in living well under the same laws and by the same government. But because the man who lives according to virtue is also directed towards a further end, which, as we have already said above, consists in the enjoyment of the Divine, the end of the whole community of mankind must therefore be the same as it is for one man. The final end of a multitude united in society, therefore, will not be to live according to virtue, but through virtuous living to attain to the enjoyment of the Divine. Now if it were possible to achieve this end through natural human virtue alone, it would necessarily belong to the king's duty to guide men to this end; for, as we suppose, it is to the king that the supreme ruling power in human affairs is entrusted, and government is of a higher order according to the finality of the end to which it is directed. For we find that it is always the one who has responsibility for the final end who directs those who carry out the tasks leading to the final end. For example, the captain whose responsibility it is to direct the navigation of the ship commands him who constructs the ship to make the kind of ship most suitable for his purposes; and the citizen who makes use of arms gives orders to the blacksmith as to what kind of arms he is to forge. But because the enjoyment of Divinity is an end which a man cannot attain through human virtue alone, but only through Divine virtue, according to the Apostle at Romans 6:23: "The grace of God is eternal life," it is not human but Divine rule that will lead us to this end. And government of this kind belongs only to that King Who is not only man, but also God: that is, to our Lord Jesus Christ, Who by making men sons of God, has led them to the glory of heaven.

This, then, is the government given to Him, which shall not pass away and by reason of which He is called in Holy Scripture not only priest but king. As Jeremiah says (23:5): "A king shall reign and be wise." Hence a royal priesthood is derived from Him; and, what is more, all who believe in Christ, insofar as they are His members, are called kings and priests. The administration of this kingdom, therefore, is entrusted not to earthly kings, but to priests, so that spiritual and earthly things may be kept distinct; and in particular to the Supreme Priest, the successor of Peter, the Vicar of Christ, the Roman Pontiff, to whom all the kings of the Christian people should be subject, as if to the Lord Jesus Christ Himself. For those who are responsible for intermediate ends should be subject to one who is responsible for the ultimate end, and be directed by his command. Since the priesthood of the gentiles and the worship of their gods existed only for the sake of acquiring those temporal goods which are entirely directed to the good of the community and which it is therefore the duty of kings to secure, it was suitable that the priests of the gentiles should be subject to their kings. Again, under the old law, those who embraced the true religion were promised temporal goods not by demons, but by God; and so we read that, under the old law, priests were subject to kings. But under the new law there is a higher priesthood, by which men are conducted towards heavenly goods;

and so, under the law of Christ, kings must be subject to priests.

For this reason it came about by the wondrous dispensation of Divine providence that in the city of Rome, which God foresaw would be the principal seat of the Christian people in time to come, the custom gradually grew up that the rulers of the city should be subject to the priests. For as Valerius Maximus declares:

> Even in matters relating to the dignity of the highest majesty, our city has always affirmed that all things should be placed after religion. For this reason, holders of secular authority have never doubted that they ought to serve sacred authority, thereby showing their belief that the government of human affairs will be properly conducted only by those who are good and constant servants of the Divine power.

Again, because it was to come to pass also that the religion of the Christian priesthood would flourish with particular vigour in Gaul, Divine providence permitted that the gentile priests of the Gauls, who were called Druids, should be the interpreters of the law throughout Gaul, as Caesar relates in the book which he wrote on the Gallic war.

Temporal Authority: To What Extent It Should Be Obeyed (1523)

MARTIN LUTHER (1483–1546)

Luther, the chief architect of the Protestant Reformation in Germany, faced profound opposition from princes allied with the Roman Catholic Church. The following excerpt illustrates his views on the obligation of Christians to obey ungodly rulers and the role

Excerpts reprinted from *Luther's Works*, vol. 45, ed. Walther I. Brandt (Philadelphia: Fortress Press, 1962), 111–15. © 1962 Fortress Press. Used by permission.

Martin Luther, engraving by Charles Edward Wagstaff. © Hulton-Deutsch Collection/CORBIS.

of civil authorities in combating heresy. Although Luther's positions had potentially radical implications, when the German peasants revolted in 1525 he made it clear that religious equality was not the same as political equality (see, for instance, Luther's *Against the Robbing and Murdering Hordes of Peasants* [1525]).

If your prince or temporal ruler commands you to side with the pope, to believe thus and so, or to get rid of certain books, you should say, "It is not fitting that Lucifer should sit at the side of God. Gracious sir, I owe you obedience in body and property; command me within the limits of your authority on earth, and I will obey. But if you command me to believe or to get rid of certain books, I will not obey; for then you are a tyrant and overreach yourself, commanding where you have neither the right nor the authority," etc. Should he seize your property on account of this and punish such disobedience, then blessed are you; thank God that you are worthy to suffer for the sake of the divine word. Let him rage, fool that he is; he will meet his judge. For I tell you, if you fail to withstand him, if you give in to him and let him take away your faith and your books, you have truly denied God.

Let me illustrate. In Meissen, Bavaria, the Mark, and other places, the tyrants have issued an order that all copies of the New Testament are everywhere to be turned in to the officials. This should be the response of their subjects: They should not turn in a single page, not even a letter, on pain of losing their salvation. Whoever does so is delivering Christ up into the hands of Herod, for these tyrants act as murderers of Christ just like Herod. If their homes are ordered searched and books or property taken by force, they should suffer it to be done. Outrage is not to be resisted but endured; yet we should not sanction it, or lift a little finger to conform, or obey. For such tyrants are acting as worldly princes are supposed to act, and worldly princes they surely are. But the world is God's enemy; hence, they too have to do what is antagonistic to God and agreeable to the world, that they may not be bereft of honor, but remain worldly princes. Do not wonder, therefore, that they rage and mock at the gospel; they have to live up to their name and title.

You must know that since the beginning of the world a wise prince is a mighty rare bird, and an upright prince even rarer. They are generally the biggest fools or the worst scoundrels on earth; therefore, one must constantly expect the worst from them and look for little good, especially in divine matters which concern the salvation of souls. They are God's executioners and hangmen; his divine wrath uses them to punish the wicked and to maintain outward peace. Our God is a great lord and ruler; this is why he must also have such noble, highborn, and rich hangmen and constables. He desires that everyone shall copiously accord them riches, honor, and fear in abundance. It pleases his divine will that we call his hang-men gracious lords, fall at their feet, and be subject to them in all humility, so long as they do not ply their trade too far and try to become shepherds instead of hangmen. If a prince should happen to be wise, up-right, or a Christian, that is one of the great miracles, the most precious token of divine grace upon that land. Ordinarily the course of events is in accordance with the passage from Isaiah 3 [:4], "I will make boys their princes, and gaping fools shall rule over them"; and in Hosea 13 [:11], "I will give you a king in my anger, and take him away in my wrath." The world is too wicked, and does not deserve to have many wise and upright princes. Frogs must have their storks.

Again you say, "The temporal power is not forcing men to believe; it is simply seeing to it externally that no one deceives the people by false doctrine; how could heretics otherwise be restrained?" Answer: This the bishops should do; it is a function entrusted to them and not to the princes. Heresy can never be re-strained by force. One will have to tackle the problem in some other way, for heresy must be opposed and dealt with otherwise than with the sword. Here God's word must do the fighting. If it does not succeed, cer-tainly the temporal power will not succeed either, even if it were to drench the world in blood. Heresy is a spiritual matter which you cannot hack to pieces with iron, consume with fire, or drown in water. God's word alone avails here, as Paul says in II Corinthians 10 [:4–5], "Our weapons are not carnal, but mighty in God to destroy every argument and proud obstacle that ex-alts itself against the knowledge of God, and to take every thought captive in the service of Christ."

Moreover, faith and heresy are never so strong as when men oppose them by sheer force, without God's word. For men count it certain that such force is for a wrong cause and is directed against the right, since it proceeds without God's word and knows not how to further its cause except by naked force, as brute beasts do. Even in temporal affairs force can be used only after the wrong has been legally condemned. How much less possible it is to act with force, without justice and God's word, in these lofty spiritual mat-

ters! See, therefore, what fine, clever nobles they are! They would drive out heresy, but set about it in such a way that they only strengthen the opposition, rous-ing suspicion against themselves and justifying the heretics. My friend, if you wish to drive out heresy, you must find some way to tear it first of all from the heart and completely turn men's wills away from it. With force you will not stop it, but only strengthen it. What do you gain by strengthening heresy in the heart, while weakening only its outward expression and forcing the tongue to lie? God's word, however, enlightens the heart, and so all heresies and errors vanish from the heart of their own accord.

The Schleitheim Confession of Faith (1527)

Anabaptists have never been numerous in America, but their understanding of the gospel has often led to tensions between them and the civil state. The Schleitheim Confession was an important and early statement of Anabaptist distinctives. Drafted by Mi-chael Sattler of Germany, the document was ratified by an assembly of Swiss Anabaptists in 1527. Widely circulated, it drew critical responses from Ulrich Zwingli, John Calvin, and others. The fourth, sixth, and seventh articles are reprinted below. The words in brackets were inserted by the text's translator to clarify the text. The words in parentheses are a part of the original text.

Fourth. We are agreed [as follows] on separation: A separation shall be made from the evil and from the

Excerpts reprinted from *Mennonite Quarterly Review* 19 (1945): 249–53, published by the Mennonite Historical Society, Goshen College, Go-shen, Ind. Used by permission of *Mennonite Quarterly Review*.

wickedness which the devil planted in the world; in this manner, simply that we shall not have fellowship with them [the wicked] and not run with them in the multitude of their abominations. This is the way it is: Since all who do not walk in the obedience of faith, and have not united themselves with God so that they wish to do His will, are a great abomination before God, it is not possible for anything to grow or issue from them except abominable things. For truly all creatures are in but two classes, good and bad, believing and unbelieving, darkness and light, the world and those who [have come] out of the world, God's temple and idols, Christ and Belial; and none can have part with the other.

To us then the command of the Lord is clear when He calls upon us to be separate from the evil and thus He will be our God and we shall be His sons and daughters.

He further admonishes us to withdraw from Babylon and the earthly Egypt that we may not be partakers of the pain and suffering which the Lord will bring upon them.

From all this we should learn that everything which is not united with our God and Christ cannot be other than an abomination which we should shun and flee from. By this is meant all popish and antipopish works and church services, meetings and church attendance, drinking houses, civic affairs, the commitments [made in] unbelief and other things of that kind, which are highly regarded by the world and yet are carried on in flat contradiction to the command of God, in accordance with all the unrighteousness which is in the world. From all these things we shall be separated and have no part with them for they are nothing but an abomination, and they are the cause of our being hated before our Christ Jesus, Who has set us free from the slavery of the flesh and fitted us for the service of God through the Spirit Whom He has given us.

Therefore there will also unquestionably fall from us the unchristian, devilish weapons of force—such as sword, armor and the like, and all their use [either] for friends or against one's enemies—by virtue of the word of Christ, Resist not [him that is] evil. . . .

Sixth. We are agreed as follows concerning the sword: The sword is ordained of God outside the perfection of Christ. It punishes and puts to death the wicked, and guards and protects the good. In the Law the sword was ordained for the punishment of the wicked and for their death, and the same [sword] is [now] ordained to be used by the worldly magistrates.

In the perfection of Christ, however, only the ban is used for a warning and for the excommunication of the one who has sinned, without putting the flesh to death,—simply the warning and the command to sin no more.

Now it will be asked by many who do not recognize [this as] the will of Christ for us, whether a Christian may or should employ the sword against the wicked for the defense and protection of the good, or for the sake of love.

Our reply is unanimously as follows: Christ teaches and commands us to learn of Him, for He is meek and lowly in heart and so shall we find rest to our souls. Also Christ says to the heathenish woman who was taken in adultery, not that one should stone her according to the law of His Father (and yet He says, As the Father has commanded me, thus I do), but in mercy and forgiveness and warning, to sin no more. Such [an attitude] we also ought to take completely according to the rule of the ban.

Secondly, it will be asked concerning the sword, whether a Christian shall pass sentence in worldly dispute and strife such as unbelievers have with one another. This is our united answer: Christ did not wish to decide or pass judgment between brother and brother in the case of the inheritance, but refused to do so. Therefore we should do likewise.

Thirdly, it will be asked concerning the sword, Shall one be a magistrate if one should be chosen as such? The answer is as follows: They wished to make Christ king, but He fled and did not view it as the arrangement of His Father. Thus shall we do as He did, and follow Him, and so shall we not walk in darkness. For He Himself says, He who wishes to come after me, let him deny himself and take up his cross and follow me. Also, He Himself forbids the [employment of] the force of the sword saying, The worldly princes lord it over them, etc., but not so shall it be with you. Further, Paul says, Whom God did foreknow He also did predestinate to be conformed to the image of His Son, etc. Also Peter says, Christ has suffered (not ruled) and left us an example, that ye should follow His steps.

Finally it will be observed that it is not appropriate for a Christian to serve as a magistrate because of these points: The government magistracy is according to the flesh, but the Christians' is according to the Spirit; their houses and dwelling remain in this world, but the Christians' are in heaven; their citizenship is in this world, but the Christians' citizenship is in heaven; the weapons of their conflict and war are carnal and against the flesh only, but the Christians' weapons are spiritual, against the fortification of the devil. The worldlings are armed with steel and iron, but the Christians are armed with the armor of God, with truth, righteousness, peace, faith, salvation and the Word of God. In brief, as is the mind of Christ toward us, so shall the mind of the members of the body of Christ be through Him in all things, that there may be no schism in the body through which it would be destroyed. For every kingdom divided against itself will be destroyed. Now since Christ is as it is written of Him, His members must also be the same, that His body may remain complete and united to its own advancement and upbuilding.

Seventh. We are agreed as follows concerning the oath: The oath is a confirmation among those who are quarreling or making promises. In the Law it is commanded to be performed in God's Name, but only in truth, not falsely. Christ, who teaches the perfection of the Law, prohibits all swearing to His [followers], whether true or false,—neither by heaven, nor by the earth, nor by Jerusalem, nor by our head,—and that for the reason which He shortly thereafter gives, For you are not able to make one hair white or black. So you see it is for this reason that all swearing is forbidden: we cannot fulfill that which we promise when we swear, for we cannot change [even] the very least thing on us.

Now there are some who do not give credence to the simple command of God, but object with this question: Well now, did not God swear to Abraham by Himself (since He was God) when He promised him that He would be with him and that He would be his God if he would keep His commandments,—why then should I not also swear when I promise to someone? Answer: Hear what the Scripture says: God, since He wished more abundantly to show unto the heirs the immutability of His counsel, inserted an oath, that by two immutable things (in which it is impossible for God to lie) we might have a strong consolation. Observe the meaning of this Scripture: What God forbids you to do, He has power to do, for everything is possible for Him. God swore an oath to Abraham, says the Scripture, so that He might show that His counsel is immutable. That is, no one can withstand nor thwart His will; therefore He can keep His oath. But we can do nothing, as is said above by Christ, to keep or perform [our oaths]: therefore we shall not swear at all [*nichts schweren*].

Then others further say as follows: It is not forbidden of God to swear in the New Testament, when it is actually commanded in the Old, but it is forbidden only to swear by heaven, earth, Jerusalem and our head. Answer: Hear the Scripture, He who swears by heaven swears by God's throne and by Him who sitteth thereon. Observe: it is forbidden to swear by heaven, which is only the throne of God: how much more is it forbidden [to swear] by God Himself! Ye fools and blind, which is greater, the throne or Him that sitteth thereon?

Further some say, Because evil is now [in the world, and] because man needs God for [the establishment of] the truth, so did the apostles Peter and Paul also swear. Answer: Peter and Paul only testify of that which God promised to Abraham with the oath. They themselves promise nothing, as the example indicates clearly. Testifying and swearing are two different things. For when a person swears he is in the first place promising future things, as Christ was promised to Abraham Whom we a long time afterwards received. But when a person bears testimony he is testifying about the present, whether it is good or evil, as Simeon spoke to Mary about Christ and testified, Behold this (child) is set for the fall and rising of many in Israel, and for a sign which shall be spoken against.

Christ also taught us along the same line when He said, Let your communication be Yea, yea; Nay, nay; for whatsoever is more than these cometh of evil. He says, Your speech or word shall be yea and nay. (However) when one does not wish to understand, he remains closed to the meaning. Christ is simply Yea and Nay, and all those who seek Him simply will understand His Word. Amen.

Institutes of the Christian Religion (1559)

JOHN CALVIN (1509–64)

Calvin was born in France but lived most of his adult life in Geneva, Switzerland, which he helped govern in 1536–38 and 1541–64. In 1536 he published the first edition of his *Institutes of the Christian Religion,* a volume that he revised significantly until its final 1559 edition. The work has proven enormously influential among his followers, who were represented most prominently in America by the Puritans. The following passages were translated from the 1559 edition of the *Institutes.*

Vol. II, bk. IV, chap. XI, sec. 8, and bk. IV, chap. XX, secs. 1, 31–32, reprinted from *Calvin: Institutes of the Christian Religion* (Library of Christian Classics Series), ed. John T. McNeill (Philadelphia: Westminster Press, 1960). Used by permission of Westminster John Knox Press.

Book IV, Chapter XI

Means of Grace: Holy Catholic Church
8. The worldly power of the bishops contradicts the meaning of this office

Even though we have not mentioned everything that could be presented here, and also what we have said has been confined to a few words, I trust we have won such a victory as to leave no reason for anyone to doubt that the spiritual power on which the pope with his whole royal entourage preens himself is an impious tyranny opposed to God's Word and unjust toward his people. Indeed, under the term "spiritual power" I include boldness in formulating new doctrines by which they have turned the wretched people away from the original purity of God's Word, the wicked traditions with which they have ensnared them, and the pretended ecclesiastical jurisdiction which they exercise through suffragans and officials. For if we allow Christ a kingdom among us, it can only result in this whole kind of dominion being at once cast down and falling into ruin.

Moreover, we are not presently concerned to discuss the power of the sword, which they also claim, because it is not exercised over consciences. Yet in this respect it is worth noting that they are always like themselves, that is, far removed from what they wish to be regarded, pastors of the church.

I do not blame the individual faults of men, but the common crime of the whole order, the veritable plague of the order, since it is thought to be mutilated unless it be decked out with opulence and proud titles. If we seek the authority of Christ in this matter, there is no doubt that he wished to bar the ministers of his Word from civil rule and earthly authority when he said, "The rulers of the Gentiles lord it over them, . . . but you do not do so" [Matt. 20:25–26; Luke 22:25–26 p.]. He means not only that the office of pastor is distinct from that of prince but also that the things are so different that they cannot come together in one man.

For that Moses carried both offices at once was, in the first place, through a rare miracle; secondly, it was a temporary arrangement, until things might be better ordered. But when a definite form is prescribed by the Lord, the civil government is left to Moses; he is ordered to resign the priesthood to his brother [Ex. 18:13–26]. And rightly; for it is beyond nature that one man should be sufficient for both burdens.

This has been in all ages carefully observed in the church. And no one of the bishops, so long as any true form of the church endured, thought of usurping the right of the sword. Thus, in the age of Ambrose it was a common proverb that "emperors coveted the priesthood more than priests the empire." In the minds of all has been engraved what Ambrose subsequently says: "To the emperor belong the palaces; to the priest the churches."

Book IV, Chapter XX

Civil Government

1. Differences between spiritual and civil government

Now, since we have established above that man is under a twofold government, and since we have elsewhere discussed at sufficient length the kind that resides in the soul or inner man and pertains to eternal life, this is the place to say something also about the other kind, which pertains only to the establishment of civil justice and outward morality.

For although this topic seems by nature alien to the spiritual doctrine of faith which I have undertaken to discuss, what follows will show that I am right in joining them, in fact, that necessity compels me to do so. This is especially true since, from one side, insane and barbarous men furiously strive to overturn this divinely established order; while, on the other side, the flatterers of princes, immoderately praising their power, do not hesitate to set them against the rule of God himself. Unless both these evils are checked, purity of faith will perish. Besides, it is of no slight importance to us to know how lovingly God has provided in this respect for mankind, that greater zeal for piety may flourish in us to attest our gratefulness.

First, before we enter into the matter itself, we must keep in mind that distinction which we previ-

John Calvin. © Archivo Iconografico, S.A./CORBIS.

ously laid down so that we do not (as commonly happens) unwisely mingle these two, which have a completely different nature. For certain men, when they hear that the gospel promises a freedom that acknowledges no king and no magistrate among men, but looks to Christ alone, think that they cannot benefit by their freedom so long as they see any power set up over them. They therefore think that nothing will be safe unless the whole world is reshaped to a new form, where there are neither courts, nor laws, nor magistrates, nor anything which in their opinion restricts their freedom. But whoever knows how to distinguish between body and soul, between this present fleeting life and that future eternal life, will without difficulty know that Christ's spiritual Kingdom and the civil jurisdiction are things completely distinct. Since, then, it is a Jewish vanity to seek and enclose Christ's Kingdom within the elements of this world, let us rather ponder that what Scripture clearly teaches is a spiritual fruit, which we gather from Christ's grace; and let us remember to keep within its own limits all that freedom which is promised and offered to us in him. For why is it that the same apostle who bids us stand and not submit to the "yoke of bondage" [Gal. 5:1] elsewhere forbids slaves to be anxious about their state [I Cor. 7:21], unless it be that spiritual freedom can perfectly well exist along with civil bondage? These statements of his must also be taken in the same sense: In the Kingdom of God "there is neither Jew nor Greek, neither male nor female, neither slave nor free" [Gal. 3:28, Vg.; order changed]. And again, "there is not Jew nor Greek, uncircumcised and circumcised, barbarian, Scythian, slave, freeman; but Christ is all in all" [Col. 3:11 p.]. By these statements he means that it makes no difference what your condition among men may be or under what nation's laws you live, since the Kingdom of Christ does not at all consist in these things. . . .

31. Constitutional defenders of the people's freedom

But however these deeds of men are judged in themselves, still the Lord accomplished his work through them alike when he broke the bloody scepters of arrogant kings and when he overturned intolerable governments. Let the princes hear and be afraid.

But we must, in the meantime, be very careful not to despise or violate that authority of magistrates, full of venerable majesty, which God has established by the weightiest decrees, even though it may reside with the most unworthy men, who defile it as much as they can with their own wickedness. For, if the correction of unbridled despotism is the Lord's to avenge, let us not at once think that it is entrusted to us, to whom no command has been given except to obey and suffer.

I am speaking all the while of private individuals. For if there are now any magistrates of the people, appointed to restrain the willfulness of kings (as in ancient times the ephors were set against the Spartan kings, or the tribunes of the people against the Roman consuls, or the demarchs against the senate of the Athenians; and perhaps, as things now are, such power as the three estates exercise in every realm when they hold their chief assemblies), I am so far from forbidding them to withstand, in accordance

with their duty, the fierce licentiousness of kings, that, if they wink at kings who violently fall upon and assault the lowly common folk, I declare that their dissimulation involves nefarious perfidy, because they dishonestly betray the freedom of the people, of which they know that they have been appointed protectors by God's ordinance.

32. Obedience to man must not become disobedience to God

But in that obedience which we have shown to be due the authority of rulers, we are always to make this exception, indeed, to observe it as primary, that such obedience is never to lead us away from obedience to him, to whose will the desires of all kings ought to be subject, to whose decrees all their commands ought to yield, to whose majesty their scepters ought to be submitted. And how absurd would it be that in satisfying men you should incur the displeasure of him for whose sake you obey men themselves! The Lord, therefore, is the King of Kings, who, when he has opened his sacred mouth, must alone be heard, before all and above all men; next to him we are subject to those men who are in authority over us, but only in him. If they command anything against him, let it go unesteemed. And here let us not be concerned about all that dignity which the magistrates possess; for no harm is done to it when it is humbled before that singular and truly supreme power of God. On this consideration, Daniel denies that he has committed any offense against the king when he has not obeyed his impious edict [Dan. 6:22–23, Vg.]. For the king had exceeded his limits, and had not only been a wrongdoer against men, but, in lifting up his horns against God, had himself abrogated his power. Conversely, the Israelites are condemned because they were too obedient to the wicked proclamation of the king [Hos. 5:13]. For when Jeroboam molded the golden calves, they, to please him, forsook God's Temple and turned to new superstitions [I Kings 12:30]. With the same readiness, their descendants complied with the decrees of their kings. The prophet sharply reproaches them for embracing the king's edicts [Hos.

5:11]. Far, indeed, is the pretense of modesty from deserving praise, a false modesty with which the court flatterers cloak themselves and deceive the simple, while they deny that it is lawful for them to refuse anything imposed by their kings. As if God had made over his right to mortal men, giving them the rule over mankind! Or as if earthly power were diminished when it is subjected to its Author, in whose presence even the heavenly powers tremble as suppliants! I know with what great and present peril this constancy is menaced, because kings bear defiance with the greatest displeasure, whose "wrath is a messenger of death" [Prov. 16:14], says Solomon. But since this edict has been proclaimed by the heavenly herald, Peter—"We must obey God rather than men" [Acts 5:29]—let us comfort ourselves with the thought that we are rendering that obedience which the Lord requires when we suffer anything rather than turn aside from piety. And that our courage may not grow faint, Paul pricks us with another goad: That we have been redeemed by Christ at so great a price as our redemption cost him, so that we should not enslave ourselves to the wicked desires of men— much less be subject to their impiety [I Cor. 7:23].

GOD BE PRAISED

Act of Supremacy (1534)

Act of Uniformity (1559)

Thirty-nine Articles of the Church of England (1562, 1801)

Beginning in 1527, King Henry VIII (r. 1509–47) requested Pope Clement VII's permission to divorce his wife, Catherine of Aragon. When the Pope refused, Henry sought to remove the English church from Rome's authority. Upon his insistence, Parliament passed the Act of Supremacy in 1534, which declared Henry to be the "supreme head of the Church of England." Papal authority over Britain formally ended when Henry accepted this title in 1535.

The Act of Supremacy was repealed in 1555 during the reign of Henry's Catholic daughter, Mary I (r. 1553–58). However, in 1558 Henry's Protestant daughter Elizabeth ascended to the throne, where she reigned until 1603. She crafted what became known as the Elizabethan Settlement, which created a national church clearly independent of Rome but with doctrines and practices designed to be relatively inoffensive to Catholics. Parliament aided this settlement by reinstituting the Act of Supremacy, although this time it styled the monarch "the Supreme Governor of the Church of England." In the same year it passed the Act of Uniformity which, among other things, made church attendance mandatory and required all churches to use the *Book of Common Prayer*. In 1562, a convocation of the Church of England adopted the Thirty-nine Articles, a basic summary of Anglican beliefs, and all clergymen were required to subscribe to them by a 1571 act of Parliament. The following excerpts from the Act of Uniformity and the Thirty-nine Articles illustrate both the civil state's significant role in governing the church and Elizabeth's attempt to craft a compromise that would alleviate religious tensions in her realm. The text for the Articles is from the authorized London edition of 1571.

After the American Revolution, the American branch of the Church of England reorganized itself as the Protestant Episcopal Church. In 1801, the General Convention of this body approved a revised version of the Thirty-nine Articles. Revisions primarily concerned with the relationship between church and state are reprinted below.

An Act Concerning the King's Highness to be Supreme Head of the Church of England and to have Authority to Reform and Redress all Errors, Heresies and Abuses in the Same (1534)

Albeit the King's Majesty justly and rightfully is and ought to be the supreme head of the Church of England, and so is recognized by the clergy of this realm in their Convocations; yet nevertheless for corroboration and confirmation thereof, and for increase of virtue in Christ's religion within this realm of England, and to repress and extirpate all errors, heresies, and other enormities and abuses heretofore used in the same, Be it enacted by authority of this present Parliament that the King our sovereign lord, his heirs and successors kings of this realm, shall be taken, accepted, and reputed the only supreme head in earth of the Church of England called Anglicana Ecclesia, and shall have and enjoy annexed and united to the imperial crown of this realm as well the title and style thereof, as all honors, dignities, preeminences, jurisdictions, privileges, authorities, immunities, profits, and commodities, to the said dignity of supreme head of the same Church belonging and appertaining. And that our said sovereign lord, his heirs and successors kings of this realm, shall have full power and authority from time to time to visit, repress, redress, reform, order, correct, restrain, and amend all such errors, heresies, abuses, offences, contempts, and enormities, whatsoever they be, which by any manner spiritual authority or jurisdiction ought or may lawfully be reformed, repressed, ordered, redressed, corrected, restrained, or amended, most to the pleasure of Almighty God, the increase of virtue in Christ's religion, and for the conservation of the peace, unity and tranquility of this realm: any usage, custom, foreign laws, foreign authority, prescription, or any other thing or things to the contrary hereof notwithstanding.

Reprinted from *Statutes of the Realm* (London: Record Commission, 1817), 3:492. Spelling and punctuation modernized by the editors of the Liberty Fund edition.

An Acte for the Uniformitie of Common Prayoure and Dyvyne Service in the Churche, and the Administration of the Sacramentes (1559)

WHERE at the deathe of our late sovereigne lorde King Edwarde the Syxte, there remayned one uniforme order of common service and prayour, and of thadministracōn of sacramentes rites and ceremonies in the Churche of Englande, whiche was setfurthe in one booke, entituled The Booke of Common Prayour and administracōn of Sacramentes and other rites and ceremonies in the Churche of Englande, authorized by Acte of Pliament holden in the fifthe and sixthe yeres of our sayd late sovereigne lorde Kyng Edwarde the Syxthe, intituled An Acte for thuniformitee of cōmon prayour and administracōn of the sacramentes; the whiche was repealed and taken away by Acte of Pliament in the first yere of the raigne of our late sovereigne ladye Quene Marie, to the greate decaye of the due honour of God and discomforte to the professoures of the truthe of Christes religion: BE IT therfore enacted by thaucthoritee of this p͂nte Pliamt, that the said estatute of repeale and everye thinge therin conteyned, onely concerning the sayd booke and the service administration of sacramentes rites and ceremonies conteyned or appointed in or by the said booke, shalbee voide and of none effecte from and after the feast of the Nativitye of St John Baptist next coming; and that the sayd booke withe thorder of service and of the administracōn of sacramentes rytes and ceremonies withe thalteracōn and addicōns

Reprinted from *Statutes Revised*, 3rd rev. ed. (London: His Majesty's Stationery Office, 1950), I:311–12.

therin added and appointed by this estatute, shall stande and bee from and after the sayd feaste of the Natyvitee of Sainte John Baptiste in full force and effecte according to the tenoure and effecte of this estatute; annye thing in the aforesaid statute of repeale to the contrarye notwithestanding.

———

Thirty-nine Articles of the Church of England

English Edition, 1571

XXXVI

Of consecration of Bishops and ministers
The booke of Consecration of *Archbyshops, and* Byshops, and orderyng of Priestes and Deacons, *lately set foorth in the time of Edwarde the sixt, and confyrmed at the same tyme by aucthoritie of Parliament,* doth conteyne all thinges necessarie to suche consecration and orderyng: neyther hath it any thing, that of it selfe is superstitious *or* vngodly. And therefore, whosoeuer are consecrate or ordered accordyng *to the rites of that booke, since the seconde yere of the aforenamed king Edwarde, vnto this time or hereafter shal be consecrated or ordered accordyng to the same rites,* we decree all such to be ryghtly, orderly, and lawfully consecrated and ordered.

XXXVII

Of the ciuill Magistrates
The Queenes Maiestie hath the cheefe power in this Realme of Englande, and other her dominions, vnto whom the cheefe gouernment of all estates of this Realme, *whether they be Ecclesiasticall or Ciuile, in all causes doth apparteine, and is not, nor ought to be subiect to any forraigne iurisdiction.*

Where we attribute to the Queenes Maiestie the cheefe gouernment, by whiche titles we vnderstande the mindes of some slanderous folkes to be offended: we geue not to our princes the ministring either of God's word, or of Sacraments, the which thing the iniunctions also lately set forth by Elizabeth our Queene, doth most plainlie testifie: But that only prerogatiue whiche we see to haue ben geuen always to all godly Princes in holy Scriptures by God him selfe, that is, that they should rule all estates and degrees committed to their charge by God, whether they be Ecclesiasticall or Temporall, and restraine with the ciuill sworde the stubberne and euyll doers.

The bishop of Rome hath no iurisdiction in this Realme of Englande.

The lawes of the Realme may punishe Christian men with death, for heynous and greeuous offences.

It is lawfull for Christian men, at the commaundement of the Magistrate, to weare weapons, and serue in the warres.

XXXVIII

Of Christian mens goodes, which are not common
The ryches and goodes of Christians are not common, as touching the ryght, title, and possession of the same, as certayne Anabaptistes do falsely boast. Notwithstandyng euery man ought of suche thinges as he possesseth, liberally to geue almes to the poore, accordyng to his habilitie.

XXXIX

Of a Christian mans othe
As we confesse that vayne and rashe swearing is forbidden Christian men by our Lord Jesus Christe, and James his Apostle: So we iudge that Christian religion doth not prohibite, but that a man may sweare when the Magistrate requireth, in a cause of faith and charitie, so it be done accordyng to the prophetes teaching, in iustice, iudgement, and trueth.

Reprinted from *The Creeds of Christendom*, vol. 3: *The Evangelical Protestant Creeds, with Translations*, ed. Philip Schaff, rev. David S. Schaff, 6th ed. (1931; Grand Rapids, Mich.: Baker Book House, 1983), 3:511–14.

American Revisions, 1801

XXXVI

Of Consecration of Bishops and Ministers
The Book of Consecration of Bishops, and Ordering
of Priests and Deacons, *as set forth by the General Convention of this Church in* 1792, doth contain all things
necessary to such Consecration and Ordering; neither hath it any thing that, of itself, is superstitious
and ungodly. And, therefore, whosoever are consecrated or ordered according to *said Form,* we decree
all such to be rightly, orderly, and lawfully consecrated
and ordered.

XXXVII

Of the Power of *the Civil Magistrates*
*The Power of the Civil Magistrate extendeth to all men,
as well Clergy as Laity, in all things temporal; but hath
no authority in things purely spiritual. And we hold it
to be the duty of all men who are professors of the Gospel,
to pay respectful obedience to the Civil Authority, regularly and legitimately constituted.*

Of the Laws of Ecclesiastical Polity
(1590s)

RICHARD HOOKER (1554–1600)

The great Anglican divine and apologist for the Elizabethan settlement Richard Hooker published the
first four volumes of his magnum opus *Of the Laws of
Ecclesiastical Polity* in 1594. The fifth appeared in 1597;
and books 6, 8, and 7 were published posthumously in

Bk. VIII, chap. 1, secs. 1–4, reprinted by permission of the publishers from
The Folger Library Edition of the *Works of Richard Hooker,* vol. 3, *Of the
Laws of Ecclesiastical Polity,* ed. P. G. Stanwood (Cambridge, Mass.: The
Belknap Press of Harvard University Press, 1981), 316–24; © 1977 by the
President and Fellows of Harvard College.

1648, 1651, and 1662 respectively. Although focused on
ecclesiastical debates, the work also influenced political philosophers, as evidenced by John Locke's numerous references to "the Judicious Hooker" throughout his *Second Treatise.* The selections reprinted below
illustrate Hooker's view of the proper relationship between church and state.

The Eighth Book, Chapter I

*An Admonition concerning Mens Judgments
about the Question of Regall Power*
1. We come now to the last thing, wherof there is
controversie moved, namely the *power* of *Supreme Jurisdiction,* which for distinction sake, we call the
power of *Ecclesiasticall Dominion.*

It was not thought fitt in the *Jewes Commonwealth*
that the exercise of *Supremacie Ecclesiasticall* should be
denied unto him, to whom the exercise of *Chieftie
Civill* did appertaine, and therefore their kings were
invested with both. This power they gave unto *Simon,*
[a]when they consented that he should be their *Prince,*
not only to sett men over the workes and over the
Countrie, and over the weapons and over the fortresses, but also to provide for *the holy things,* and that
he should be obeyed of every man and that all the
writinges in the *Countrie* should be made in his *name,
and that it should not be lawful for any of the people or
Priests to withstand his words or to call any Congregation in the Countrie without him.* And if it be happilie
surmised that thus much was given unto *Simon* as being both *Prince* and *High Priest,* which otherwise (being only their *Civill Governour*) he could not lawfully
have enjoyed, we must note that all this is no more
then the ancient *Kings* of that people had being *Kings
and not Priests.* By this power *David, Asa, Jehosaphat,
Ezekias, Josias* and the rest made those lawes and orders, which the Sacred Historie speaketh of concerning matter of meer religion, the affayres of the *Temple*

a. 1.Maccab. 14:41.42.

and *Service* of God. Finally had it not been by the vertue of this power, how should it possibly have come to pass that the pietie or impietie of the *King* did alwaies accordingly change the publique face of religion, which thing the *Priests* by themselves never did, neither could at any time hinder from being done? Had the *Priests* alone been possessed with all power in *Spirituall* affayres how should any lawe concerning matter of religion have been made, but only by them? In them it had been and not in the *King*, to change the face of religion at any time. The altering of religion, the making of *Ecclesiasticall* lawes with other the like actions belonging unto the power of dominion are still termed the deedes of the *Kinge*, to shewe that in him was placed *Supremacie* of power even in this kinde over all, and that unto their *High Priestes* the same was never committed, saving only at such times as their *Priestes* were also *Kings* or *Princes* over them.

According to the patterne of which example the like power in causes *Ecclesiasticall* is by the lawes of this Realme annexed unto the *Crowne*. And there are which imagine, that kings being meer lay persons, doe by this meanes exceed the lawfull boundes of their calling. Which thinge to the ende that they may perswade, they first make a necessarie separation perpetuall and personall between the *Church* and *Commonwealth*. Secondly they so tie all kinde of power *Ecclesiasticall* unto the *Church* as if it were in every degree their only right, which are by proper spirituall function termed *Church-Governours* and might not to *Christian Princes* any wise appertaine. To lurk under shifting ambiguities and equivocations of wordes in matters of principall weight is childish. A *Church* and a *Commonwealth* we graunt are thinges in nature the one distinguished from the other, a *Commonwealth* is one way, and a *Church* an other way defined. In their opinion the *Church* and the *Commonwealth* are corporations not distinguished only in nature and definition, but in subsistence perpetually severed, so that they that are of the one can neither appointe, nor execute in whole nor in part the dueties which belong unto them, which are of the other, without open

breach of the lawe of *God,* which hath devided them, and doth require that being so devided they should distinctly and severally worke as depending both upon *God* and not hanging one upon the others approbation for that which either hath to doe.

We say that the care of religion being common unto all *Societies* politique, such *Societies* as doe embrace the true religion, have the name of the *Church* given unto every of them for distinction from the rest. So that every body politique hath some religion, but the *Church* that religion, which is only true. Truth of religion is that proper difference, whereby a *Church* is distinguished from other politique societies of men. We heare meane true religion in grosse, and not according to every particuler for they which in some particuler pointes of religion doe swarve from the truth, may neverthelesse most truly, if we compare them to men of an heathenish religion, be saide to hold and professe that religion which is true. For which cause theire being of old so many politique *Societies* established throughout the world only the *Commonwealth* of *Israel* which had the truth of religion, was in that respect the *Church* of *God*. And the *Church* of *Jesus Christ* is every such politique societie of men as doth in religion hold that truth which is proper to *Christianitie*. As a politique *Societie* it doth maintaine religion; as a *Church* that religion which *God* hath revealed by *Jesus Christ*. With us therefore the name of a *Church* importeth only a *Societie* of men first united into some publique forme of regiment and secondly distinguished from other *Societies,* by the exercise of *Christian* religion. With them on the other side the name of the *Church* in this present question importeth not only a multitude of men, so united and so distinguished, but also further the same divided necessarily and perpetuallie from the body of the *Commonwealth.* So that even in such a politique *Societie,* as consisteth of none but *Christians,* yet the *Church* of *Christ* and the *Commonwealth* are two corporations independently each subsisting by it self. We hold that seing there is not any man of the *Church* of *England,* but the same man is also a member of the *Commonwealth,* nor any man a member of the *Com-*

monwealth which is not also of the *Church* of *England,* therefore as in a figure *triangular* the base doth differ from the sides thereof, and yet one and the self same line, is both a base and also a side; a side simplie, a base if it chance to be the bottome and underlie the rest: So albeit properties and actions of one kinde doe cause the name of a Commonwealth, qualities and functions of an other sort the name of a *Church* to be given unto a multitude, yet one and the self same multitude may in such sort be both and is so with us, that no person appertayning to the one can be denied to be also of the other. Contrariwise (unless they against us should hold that the *Church* and the *Commonwealth* are two both distinct and separate societies, of which two the one comprehendeth always persons not belonging to the other) that which they doe, they could not conclude out of the difference between the *Church* and the *Commonwealth;* namely, that *Bishops* may not meddle with the affayres of the commonwealth because they are governours of an other corporation, which is the *Church,* nor *Kings,* with making lawes for the *Church* because they have government not of this corporation, but of an other divided from it, the *Commonwealth,* and the walles of separation between these two must for ever be upheld. They hold the necessitie of personall separation which cleane excludeth the power of one mans dealing in both, we of naturall which doth not hinder, but that one and the same person may in both beare a principall sway.

The causes of common received errour in this pointe seeme to have been especially two: One, that they who embrace true religion living in such Commonwealths as are opposite thereunto and in other publique affayres retayning civill Communion, with such are constrayned for the exercise of their religion to have a severall Communion with those who are of the same religion with them. This was the state of the *Jewish Church* both in *Egypte* and *Babylon,* the state of *Christian Churches* a long time after *Christ.* And in this case because the proper affayres and actions of the *Church,* as it is the *Church,* have no dependencie upon the lawes or upon the Governours of the Civill

state, an opinion hath thereby growne, that even so it should be alwayes. This was it which deceived *Allen* in his writing of his *Apologie. The Apostles* (sayth he) *did governe the Church in Rome when Nero did bare rule, even as at this daye in all the Turkes Dominions the Church hath a spirituall Regiment without dependence and so ought she to have, live she amongst Heathens or with Christians.*

An other occasion of which misconceipte is, that thinges appertayning unto religion are both distinguished from other affayres and have always had in the *Church* speciall persons chosen to be exercised about them. By which distinction of spirituall affayres and persons therein imployed from temporall, the error of personall separation always necessary between the *Church* and the *Commonwealth* hath strengthened it self; for of every politique societie that being true which Aristotle hath, namely, [b] *That the scope thereof is not simplie to live, nor the duetie so much to provide for life as for meanes of living well,* and that even as the soule is the worthier part of man, so humane societies are much more to care for that which tendeth properly unto the soules estate then for such temporall thinges as this life doth stand in need of. Other proof there needes none to shewe that as by all men [c] *the kingdome of God is first to be sought for:* So in all commonwealths things spirituall ought above temporall to be provided for. [d] And of things spirituall the chiefest is *Religion.* For this cause persons and thinges imployed peculiarly about the affayres of religion are by an excellencie termed *Spirituall.* [e] The *Heathen* themselves had their *Spirituall Lawes* causes and offices alwayes severed from their *temporall.* Neither did this make two independent states amongst them. *God* by revealing true religion doth make them that receive it his *Church.* Unto the *Jewes* he so revealed the truth of religion, that he gave them in speciall consideration lawes not only for the administration of things spirituall, but also temporall. The Lord himself appoint-

b. Aristotle Polit. l. 3. c. 6. pag. 102.
c. Mt. 6.
d. Arist. Pol. lib. 3. cap. 16. p. 196.
e. Arist. Pol. 123. l. 10. et 181. l. 28. Liv. Lib. 1º.

ing both the one and the other in that *Commonwealth,* did not thereby distract it into severall independent *Communities,* but instituted severall functions of one and the same *Communitie.* Some reason therefore must be alleaged, why it should be otherwise in the *Church* of *Christ.*

Three kinde of proofes for confirmation of the foresayd separation between the Church and Commonwealth. The first taken from difference of affayres and offices in each.

I shall not need to spend any great store of wordes in answearing that which is brought out of holy *Scripture* to shewe that secular and Ecclesiasticall affayres and offices are distinguished, neither that which hath been borrowed from antiquitie using by phrase of speech to oppose the *Commonwealth* to the *Church* of *Christ;* neither yet the reasons, which are wont to be brought forth as witnesses that the *Church* and *Commonwealth* are always distinct. For whither *a Church* and *a Commonwealth* doe differ is not the question we strive for, but our controversie is concerning the kinde of distinction, whereby they are severed the one from the other; whither, as under *Heathen Kings* the church did deale with her own affayres within her selfe, without depending at all upon any in civill authoritie, and the *Commonwealth* in hers altogether without the privitie of the *Church,* so it ought to continue still even in such *Commonwealths* as have now publiklie embraced the truth of *Christian religion,* whither they ought to be evermore two societies in such sort severall and distinct.

I ask therefore what societie that was, that was in *Rome,* whereunto the *Apostle* did give the name of the *Church* of *Rome* in his time? If they answere as needes they must that the *Church* of *Rome* in those days was that whole societie of men which in *Rome* professed the name of *Christ* and not that religion which the lawes of the *Commonwealth* did then authorize, we say as much and therefore graunte that the *Commonwealth* of *Rome* was one societie and the *Church* of *Rome* an other, in such sort as there was between them no mutuall dependencie. But when whole *Rome* became *Christian,* when they all embraced the Ghos-

pell, and made lawes in the defence thereof, if it be held that the *Church* and the *Commonwealth* of *Rome* did then remayne as before, there is no way how this could be possible save only one, and that is, They must restraine the name of the *Church* in a *Christian Commonwealth* to the *Clergie,* excluding all the residue of beleevers both *Prince* and *People.* For if all that beleeve, be conteyned in the name of the *Church,* how should the *Church* remayne by personall subsistencie divided from the *Commonwealth* when the whole *Commonwealth* doth beleeve? The *Church* and the *Commonwealth* therefore are in this case personally one societie, which societie being termed a *Commonwealth* as it liveth under whatsoever forme of secular lawe and regiment, a *Church* as it hath the *Spirituall* lawe of *Jesus Christ,* forasmuch as these two lawes conteine so many and so different offices, there must of necessitie be appointed in it some to one charge and some to another, yet without deviding the whole and making it two severall impaled societies.

The difference therefore either of [f]affayres or offices Ecclesiasticall from secular is no argument that the *Church* and the *Commonwealth* are always separate and independent the one from the other, which thing even *Allen* himself considering somewhat better doth in this point a little correct his former judgment before mentioned, and confesseth in his defence of English Catholiques that *The power politicall hath her Princes, Lawes, Tribunalls: The Spirituall her Prelates, Canons, Councells, Judgments, and those (when the Princes are Pagans) wholy separate, but in Christian Commonwealths joyned though not confounded.* Howbeit afterwardes his former sting appeareth againe. For in a *Christian Commonwealth* he holdeth that the *Church* ought not to depende at all upon the authoritie of any civill person whatsoever, as in *England* he sayth it doth.

f. 2.Chro. 19:8. 11. Heb. 5:1. 1.Thess. 5:12. T.C. l. 3. p. 151.

The First London Baptist Confession of Faith (1646)

The origins of the Baptists have been much disputed, but most observers agree that "The First London Baptist Confession of Faith" holds an important place in Baptist history. Agreed to by seven London Baptist congregations in 1644, the Confession was revised in the light of Puritan agitation for uniformity in 1645 and was reprinted in 1646. Excerpts from this latter edition concerned with religious liberty and church-state relations are reprinted below.

XLVIII

A civil (Rom. xiii. 1, 2, 3, 4; 1 Pet. ii. 13, 14; 1 Tim. ii. 1, 2, 3) magistracy is an ordinance of God, set up by him for the punishment of evil doers, and for the praise of them that do well; and that in all lawful things, commanded by them, subjection ought to be given by us in the Lord, not only for wrath, but for conscience' sake; and that we are to make supplications and prayers for kings, and all that are in authority, that under them we may live a quiet and peaceable life, in all godliness and honesty.

The supreme magistracy of this kingdom we acknowledge to be the King and Parliament (now established) freely chosen by the kingdom, and that we are to maintain and defend all civil laws and civil officers made by them, which are for the good of the commonwealth: and we acknowledge with thankfulness that God hath made this present king and parliament honourable in throwing down the prelatical hierarchy, because of their tyranny and oppression over us, under which this kingdom long groaned, for

Reprinted from *Confessions of Faith, and Other Public Documents,* ed. Edward Bean Underhill (London: Haddon Brothers for the Hanserd Knollys Society, 1854), 44–48.

which we are ever engaged to bless God, and honour them for the same. And concerning the worship of God, there is but one Lawgiver, which is able to save and destroy, James iv. 12, which is Jesus Christ, who hath given laws and rules sufficient in his word for his worship; and for any to make more, were to charge Christ with want of wisdom or faithfulness, or both, in not making laws enough, or not good enough for his house: surely it is our wisdom, duty, and privilege to observe Christ's laws only, Psa. ii. 6, 9, 10, 12. So it is the magistrate's duty to tender the liberty of men's consciences, Eccl. viii. 8, (which is the tenderest thing unto all conscientious men, and most dear unto them, and without which all other liberties will not be worth the naming, much less enjoying) and to protect all under them from all wrong, injury, oppression, and molestation; so it is our duty not to be wanting in nothing which is for their honour and comfort. And whatsoever is for the well-being of the commonwealth wherein we live, it is our duty to do; and we believe it to be our express duty, especially in matters of religion, to be fully persuaded in our minds of the lawfulness of what we do, as knowing *whatsoever is not of faith is sin:* and as we cannot do anything contrary to our understandings and consciences, so neither can we forbear the doing of that which our understandings and consciences bind us to do; and if the magistrate should require us to do otherwise, we are to yield our persons in a passive way to their power, as the saints of old have done, James v. 4. And thrice happy shall he be, that shall lose his life for witnessing (though but for the least tittle) of the truth of the Lord Jesus Christ, 1 Pet. v., Gal. v.

XLIX

But in case we find not the magistrate to favour us herein, (Acts ii. 40, 41; iv. 19; v. 28, 29, 41; xx. 23; 1 Thess. iii. 3; Phil. i. 28, 29; Dan. iii. 16, 17; vi. 7, 10, 22, 23,) yet we dare not suspend our practice, because we believe we ought to go on in obedience to Christ, in professing the faith which was once delivered to the saints, which faith is declared in the holy scriptures, and this our confession of faith a part of them; and that we are to witness to the truth of the old and new testament unto the death, if necessity require, in the midst of all trials and afflictions, as his saints of old have done, not accounting our goods, lands, wives, children, fathers, mothers, brethren, sisters; yea, and our own lives dear unto us, so we may finish our course with joy, remembering always, that we ought to (1 Tim. vi. 13, 14, 15; Rom. xii. 1, 8; 1 Cor. xiv. 37) obey God rather than men, who will, when we have finished our course and kept the faith, give us (Rev. ii. 20) the crown of righteousness; to (2 Tim. iv. 6, 7, 8; Rom. xiv. 10, 12; 2 Cor. v. 10; Psa. xlix. 7; Psa. l. 22) whom we must give an account of all our actions, and no man being able to discharge us of the same.

L

It is lawful for a Christian to be a magistrate or civil officer; and also it is lawful to take an oath, so it be in truth, and in judgment, and in righteousness, for confirmation of truth and ending of all strife; and that by rash and vain oaths the Lord is provoked, and this land mourns. Acts viii. 38; x. 1, 2, 35, 44; Rom. xvi. 23; Deut. vi. 13; Rom. i. 9; 2 Cor. x. 11; Jer. iv. 2; Heb. vi. 16.

LI

We are to give unto all men whatsoever is their due, as their place, age, and estate require; and that we defraud no man of anything, but to do unto all men as we would they should do unto us. 1 Thess. iv. 6; Rom. xiii. 5, 6, 7; Matt. xxii. 21; Tit. iii.; 1 Pet. ii. 15, 17; v. 5; Eph. v. 21, 23; vi. 1, 9; Tit. iii. 1, 2, 3.

LII

There shall be a (Acts xxiv. 15; 2 Cor. v. 10; Rom. xiv. 12) resurrection of the dead, both of the just and unjust, and every one shall give an account of himself to God, that every one may receive the things done in his body, according to that he hath done, whether it be good or bad.

The Conclusion

Thus we desire to give unto Christ that which is his, and unto all lawful authority that which is their due: and to owe nothing to any man but love, to live quietly and peaceably, as it becometh saints, endeavouring in all things to keep a good conscience, and to do unto every man (of what judgment soever) as we would they should do unto us; that as our practice is, so it may prove us to be a conscionable, quiet, and harmless people (no ways dangerous or troublesome to human society), and to labour and work with our hands that we may not be chargeable to any, but to give to him that needeth, both friends and enemies, accounting it more excellent to give than to receive. Also we confess that we know but in part, and that we are ignorant of many things which we desire and seek to know; and if any shall do us that friendly part to show us from the word of God that we see not, we shall have cause to be thankful to God and them. But if any man shall impose upon us anything that we see not to be commanded by our Lord Jesus Christ, we should in his strength rather embrace all reproaches and tortures of men, to be stripped of all outward comforts, and if it were possible, to die a thousand deaths, rather than to do anything against the least tittle of the truth of God, or against the light of our own consciences. And if any shall call what we have said heresy, then do we with the apostle acknowledge, that after the way they call heresy, worship we the God of our fathers, disclaiming all heresies (rightly so called) because they are against Christ, and to be stedfast and immovable, always abounding in obedience to Christ, as knowing our labour shall not be in vain in the Lord.

PSAL. LXXIV. 21, 22

Arise, O God, plead thine own cause: remember how the
foolish man blasphemeth thee daily.
Oh, let not the oppressed return ashamed, but let the poor
and needy praise thy name.
Come, Lord Jesus! come quickly.

FINIS

Westminster Confession of Faith (1646, 1788)

During the midst of the English Civil War (1642–51), Parliament commissioned an assembly of "divines" to meet at Westminster Abbey to draft plans to reform the Church of England. Among the most influential of the documents produced by the assembly was the Westminster Confession of Faith, which was completed in 1646 and first published in 1647. With a few revisions, the Confession was adopted by the English Parliament as *Articles of Christian Religion* in 1648. Although the standards were nullified in England with the restoration of the monarchy and Anglican episcopacy in 1660, they remained tremendously influential in Scotland and America. Below are excerpts from the 1646 Confession particularly relevant to church-state relations, as well as selected revisions of the Confession made in 1788 by American Presbyterians.

Original, 1646

Chapter XX. Of Christian Liberty, and Liberty of Conscience

I. The liberty which Christ hath purchased for believers under the gospel consists in their freedom from the guilt of sin, the condemning wrath of God, the curse of the moral law; and in their being delivered from this present evil world, bondage to Satan, and dominion of sin, from the evil of afflictions, the sting of death, the victory of the grave, and everlasting damnation; as also in their free access to God, and their yielding obedience unto him, not out of slavish

Chaps. XX, XXII, XXIII, and XXXI reprinted from *The Encyclopedia of American Religions: Religious Creeds,* ed. J. Gordon Melton (Detroit: Gale Research, 1988), 225–27 and 229–30; © 1988 Gale Research. Reprinted by permission of The Gale Group.

fear, but a child-like love and willing mind. All which were common also to believers under the law; but under the New Testament the liberty of Christians is further enlarged in their freedom from the yoke of the ceremonial law, to which the Jewish Church was subjected; and in greater boldness of access to the throne of grace, and in fuller communications of the free Spirit of God, than believers under the law did ordinarily partake of.

II. God alone is Lord of the conscience, and hath left it free from the doctrines and commandments of men which are in any thing contrary to his Word, or beside it in matters of faith or worship. So that to believe such doctrines, or to obey such commands out of conscience, is to betray true liberty of conscience; and the requiring of an implicit faith, and an absolute and blind obedience, is to destroy liberty of conscience, and reason also.

III. They who, upon pretense of Christian liberty, do practice any sin, or cherish any lust, do thereby destroy the end of Christian liberty; which is, that, being delivered out of the hands of our enemies, we might serve the Lord without fear, in holiness and righteousness before him, all the days of our life.

IV. And because the power which God hath ordained, and the liberty which Christ hath purchased, are not intended by God to destroy, but mutually to uphold and preserve one another; they who, upon pretense of Christian liberty, shall oppose any lawful power, or the lawful exercise of it, whether it be civil or ecclesiastical, resist the ordinance of God. And for their publishing of such opinions, or maintaining of such practices, as are contrary to the light of nature, or to the known principles of Christianity, whether concerning faith, worship, or conversation; or to the power of godliness; or such erroneous opinions or practices, as, either in their own nature, or in the manner of publishing or maintaining them, are destructive to the external peace and order which Christ hath established in the Church; they may lawfully be called to account, and proceeded against by the censures of the Church, and by the power of the Civil Magistrate.

Chapter XXII. Of Lawful Oaths and Vows

I. A lawful oath is a part of religious worship, wherein, upon just occasion, the person swearing solemnly calleth God to witness what he asserteth or promiseth; and to judge him according to the truth or falsehood of what he sweareth.

II. The name of God only is that by which men ought to swear, and therein it is to be used with all holy fear and reverence; therefore to swear vainly or rashly by that glorious and dreadful name, or to swear at all by any other thing, is sinful, and to be abhorred. Yet as, in matters of weight and moment, an oath is warranted by the Word of God, under the New Testament, as well as under the Old, so a lawful oath, being imposed by lawful authority, in such matters ought to be taken.

III. Whosoever taketh an oath ought duly to consider the weightiness of so solemn an act, and therein to avouch nothing but what he is fully persuaded is the truth. Neither may any man bind himself by oath to any thing but what is good and just, and what he believeth so to be, and what he is able and resolved to perform. Yet it is a sin to refuse an oath touching any thing that is good and just, being imposed by lawful authority.

IV. An oath is to be taken in the plain and common sense of the words, without equivocation or mental reservation. It can not oblige to sin; but in any thing not sinful, being taken, it binds to performance, although to a man's own hurt: nor is it to be violated, although made to heretics or infidels.

V. A vow is of the like nature with a promissory oath, and ought to be made with the like religious care, and to be performed with the like faithfulness.

VI. It is not to be made to any creature, but to God alone: and that it may be accepted, it is to be made voluntarily, out of faith and conscience of duty, in way of thankfulness for mercy received, or for the obtaining of what we want; whereby we more strictly bind ourselves to necessary duties, or to other things, so far and so long as they may fitly conduce thereunto.

VII. No man may vow to do any thing forbidden in the Word of God, or what would hinder any duty therein commanded, or which is not in his own power, and for the performance whereof he hath no promise or ability from God. In which respect, popish monastical vows of perpetual single life, professed poverty, and regular obedience, are so far from being degrees of higher perfection, that they are superstitious and sinful snares, in which no Christian may entangle himself.

Chapter XXIII. Of the Civil Magistrate

I. God, the Supreme Lord and King of all the world, hath ordained civil magistrates to be under him, over the people, for his own glory and the public good, and to this end hath armed them with the power of the sword, for the defense and encouragement of them that are good, and for the punishment of evil-doers.

II. It is lawful for Christians to accept and execute the office of a magistrate when called thereunto; in the managing whereof, as they ought especially to maintain piety, justice, and peace, according to the wholesome laws of each commonwealth, so, for that end, they may lawfully, now under the New Testament, wage war upon just and necessary occasion.

III. The civil magistrate may not assume to himself the administration of the Word and Sacraments, or the power of the keys of the kingdom of heaven: yet he hath authority, and it is his duty to take order, that unity and peace be preserved in the Church, that the truth of God be kept pure and entire, that all blasphemies and heresies be suppressed, all corruptions and abuses in worship and discipline prevented or reformed, and all the ordinances of God duly settled, administered, and observed. For the better effecting whereof he hath power to call synods, to be present at them, and to provide that whatsoever is transacted in them be according to the mind of God.

IV. It is the duty of people to pray for magistrates, to honor their persons, to pay them tribute and other dues, to obey their lawful commands, and to be sub-

ject to their authority, for conscience's sake. Infidelity or difference in religion doth not make void the magistrate's just and legal authority, nor free the people from their due obedience to him: from which ecclesiastical persons are not exempted; much less hath the Pope any power or jurisdiction over them in their dominions, or over any of their people; and least of all to deprive them of their dominions or lives, if he shall judge them to be heretics, or upon any other pretense whatsoever.

Chapter XXXI. Of Synods and Councils

I. For the better government and further edification of the Church, there ought to be such assemblies as are commonly called synods or councils.

II. As magistrates may lawfully call a synod of ministers and other fit persons to consult and advise with about matters of religion; so, if magistrates be open enemies to the Church, the ministers of Christ, of themselves, by virtue of their office, or they, with other fit persons, upon delegation from their churches, may meet together in such assemblies.

III. It belongeth to synods and councils, ministerially, to determine controversies of faith, and cases of conscience; to set down rules and directions for the better ordering of the public worship of God, and government of his Church; to receive complaints in cases of maladministration, and authoritatively to determine the same: which decrees and determinations, if consonant to the Word of God, are to be received with reverence and submission, not only for their agreement with the Word, but also for the power whereby they are made, as being an ordinance of God, appointed thereunto in his Word.

IV. All synods or councils since the apostles' times, whether general or particular, may err, and many have erred; therefore they are not to be made the rule of faith or practice, but to be used as a help in both.

V. Synods and councils are to handle or conclude nothing but that which is ecclesiastical: and are not to intermeddle with civil affairs which concern the commonwealth, unless by way of humble petition in

cases extraordinary; or by way of advice for satisfaction of conscience, if they be thereunto required by the civil magistrate.

American Revisions, 1788

Chapter XXIII

Of the Civil Magistrate

I. God, the supreme Lord and King of all the world, hath ordained civil magistrates, to be, under him, over the people, for his own glory, and the public good: and, to this end, hath armed them with the power of the sword, for the defense and encouragement of them that are good, and for the punishment of evil doers.

II. It is lawful for Christians to accept and execute the office of a magistrate, when called thereunto: in the managing whereof, as they ought especially to maintain piety, justice, and peace, according to the wholesome laws of each commonwealth; so, for that end, they may lawfully, now under the new testament, wage war, upon just and necessary occasion.

III. Civil magistrates may not assume to themselves the administration of the Word and sacraments; or the power of the keys of the kingdom of heaven; or, in the least, interfere in matters of faith. Yet, as nursing fathers, it is the duty of civil magistrates to protect the church of our common Lord, without giving the preference to any denomination of Christians above the rest, in such a manner that all ecclesiastical persons whatever shall enjoy the full, free, and unquestioned liberty of discharging every part of their sacred functions, without violence or danger. And, as Jesus Christ hath appointed a regular government and discipline in his church, no law of any commonwealth should interfere with, let, or hinder, the due exercise thereof, among the voluntary members of *any* denomination of Christians, according to their own profession and belief. It is the duty

Reprinted from *The Westminster Standards* (Philadelphia: Great Commission Publications, 1985), 25 and 32; © 1985 Free Presbyterian Publications.

of civil magistrates to protect the person and good name of all their people, in such an effectual manner as that no person be suffered, either upon pretense of religion or of infidelity, to offer any indignity, violence, abuse, or injury to any other person whatsoever: and to take order, that all religious and ecclesiastical assemblies be held without molestation or disturbance.

IV. It is the duty of people to pray for magistrates, to honor their persons, to pay them tribute or other dues, to obey their lawful commands, and to be subject to their authority, for conscience' sake. Infidelity, or difference in religion, doth not make void the magistrates' just and legal authority, nor free the people from their due obedience to them: from which ecclesiastical persons are not exempted, much less hath the pope any power and jurisdiction over them in their dominions, or over any of their people; and, least of all, to deprive them of their dominions, or lives, if he shall judge them to be heretics, or upon any other pretense whatsoever.

Chapter XXXI

Of Synods and Councils

I. For the better government, and further edification of the church, there ought to be such assemblies as are commonly called *synods* or *councils:* and it belongeth to the overseers and other rulers of the particular churches, by virtue of their office, and the power which Christ hath given them for edification and not for destruction, to appoint such assemblies; and to convene together in them, as often as they shall judge it expedient for the good of the church.

II. It belongeth to synods and councils, ministerially to determine controversies of faith, and cases of conscience; to set down rules and directions for the better ordering of the public worship of God, and government of his church; to receive complaints in cases of maladministration, and authoritatively to determine the same: which decrees and determinations, if consonant to the Word of God, are to be received with reverence and submission; not only for their

agreement with the Word, but also for the power whereby they are made, as being an ordinance of God appointed thereunto in his Word.

III. All synods or councils, since the apostles' times, whether general or particular, may err; and many have erred. Therefore they are not to be made the rule of faith, or practice; but to be used as a help in both.

IV. Synods and councils are to handle, or conclude nothing, but that which is ecclesiastical: and are not to intermeddle with civil affairs which concern the commonwealth, unless by way of humble petition in cases extraordinary; or, by way of advice, for satisfaction of conscience, if they be thereunto required by the civil magistrate.

Leviathan (1651)

THOMAS HOBBES (1588–1679)

Hobbes wrote *Leviathan* while in self-imposed exile in Paris, where he had fled during the English Civil War. Following the publication of the work in 1651, accusations of atheism and fear of French priests convinced him to return to England, where he submitted himself to the Council of State and, in 1660, to the restored monarchy. Although often considered a classical liberal, Hobbes supported almost limitless state power, including authority over religion and religious institutions.

Reprinted from Thomas Hobbes, *Leviathan,* ed. Richard Tuck (Cambridge: Cambridge University Press, 1991), extracts from chaps. 42 and 43, pp. 343–45, 377–78, 402–4.

Chapter XLII

Of Power Ecclesiasticall

But what (may some object) if a King, or a Senate, or other Soveraign Person forbid us to beleeve in Christ? To this I answer, that such forbidding is of no effect; because Beleef, and Unbeleef never follow mens Commands. Faith is a gift of God, which Man can neither give, nor take away by promise of rewards, or menaces of torture. And if it be further asked, What if wee bee commanded by our lawfull Prince, to say with our tongue, what wee beleeve not; must we obey such command? Profession with the tongue is but an externall thing, and no more then any other gesture whereby we signifie our obedience; and wherein a Christian, holding firmely in his heart the Faith of Christ, hath the same liberty which the Prophet Elisha allowed to Naaman the Syrian. Naaman was converted in his heart to the God of Israel; For hee saith (2 *Kings* 5.17.) *Thy servant will henceforth offer neither burnt offering, nor sacrifice unto other Gods but unto the Lord. In this thing the Lord pardon thy servant, that when my Master goeth into the house of Rimmon to worship there, and he leaneth on my hand, and I bow my selfe, in the house of Rimmon; when I bow my selfe in the house of Rimmon, the Lord pardon thy servant in this thing.* This the Prophet approved, and bid him *Goe in peace.* Here Naaman beleeved in his heart; but by bowing before the Idol Rimmon, he denyed the true God in effect, as much as if he had done it with his lips. But then what shall we answer to our Saviours saying, *Whosoever denyeth me before men, I will deny him before my Father which is in Heaven?* This we may say, that whatsoever a Subject, as Naaman was, is compelled to in obedience to his Soveraign, and doth it not in order to his own mind, but in order to the laws of his country, that action is not his, but his Soveraigns; nor is it he that in this case denyeth Christ before men, but his Governour, and the law of his countrey. If any man shall accuse this doctrine, as repugnant to true, and unfeigned Christianity; I ask him, in case there should be a subject in any Christian Common-wealth, that should be inwardly in his

heart of the Mahometan Religion, whether if his Soveraign command him to bee present at the divine service of the Christian Church, and that on pain of death, he think that Mahometan obliged in conscience to suffer death for that cause, rather than to obey that command of his lawfull Prince. If he say, he ought rather to suffer death, then he authorizeth all private men, to disobey their Princes, in maintenance of their Religion, true, or false: if he say, he ought to bee obedient, then he alloweth to himself, that which hee denyeth to another, contrary to the words of our Saviour, *Whatsoever you would that men should doe unto you, that doe yee unto them;* and contrary to the Law of Nature, (which is the indubitable everlasting Law of God) *Do not to another, that which thou wouldest not he should doe unto thee.*

But what then shall we say of all those Martyrs we read of in the History of the Church, that they have needlessely cast away their lives? For answer hereunto, we are to distinguish the persons that have been for that cause put to death; whereof some have received a Calling to preach, and professe the Kingdome of Christ openly; others have had no such Calling, nor more has been required of them than their owne faith. The former sort, if they have been put to death, for bearing witnesse to this point, that Jesus Christ is risen from the dead, were true Martyrs; For a *Martyr* is, (to give the true definition of the word) a Witnesse of the Resurrection of Jesus the Messiah; which none can be but those that conversed with him on earth, and saw him after he was risen: For a Witnesse must have seen what he testifieth, or else his testimony is not good. And that none but such, can properly be called Martyrs of Christ, is manifest out of the words of St. Peter, *Act.* 1.21, 22. *Wherefore of these men which have companyed with us all the time that the Lord Jesus went in and out amongst us, beginning from the Baptisme of John unto that same day hee was taken up from us, must one be ordained to be a Martyr* (that is a Witnesse) *with us of his Resurrection:* Where we may observe, that he which is to bee a Witnesse of the truth of the Resurrection of Christ, that is to say, of the truth of this fundamentall article of Christian Religion, that Jesus was the Christ, must be some Disciple that conversed with him, and saw him before, and after his Resurrection; and consequently must be one of his originall Disciples: whereas they which were not so, can Witnesse no more, but that their antecessors said it, and are therefore but Witnesses of other mens testimony; and are but second Martyrs, or Martyrs of Christs Witnesses.

He, that to maintain every doctrine which he himself draweth out of the History of our Saviours life, and of the Acts, or Epistles of the Apostles; or which he beleeveth upon the authority of a private man, wil oppose the Laws and Authority of the Civill State, is very far from being a Martyr of Christ, or a Martyr of his Martyrs. 'Tis one Article onely, which to die for, meriteth so honorable a name; and that Article is this, that *Jesus is the Christ;* that is to say, He that hath redeemed us, and shall come again to give us salvation, and eternall life in his glorious Kingdome. To die for every tenet that serveth the ambition, or profit of the Clergy, is not required; nor is it the Death of the Witnesse, but the Testimony it self that makes the Martyr: for the word signifieth nothing else, but the man that beareth Witnesse, whether he be put to death for his testimony, or not. . . .

From this consolidation of the Right Politique, and Ecclesiastique in Christian Soveraigns, it is evident, they have all manner of Power over their Subjects, that can be given to man, for the government of mens externall actions, both in Policy, and Religion; and may make such Laws, as themselves shall judge fittest, for the government of their own Subjects, both as they are the Common-wealth, and as they are the Church: for both State, and Church are the same men.

If they please therefore, they may (as many Christian Kings now doe) commit the government of their Subjects in matters of Religion to the Pope; but then the Pope is in that point Subordinate to them, and exerciseth that Charge in anothers Dominion *Iure Civili,* in the Right of the Civill Soveraign; not *Iure Divino,* in Gods Right; and may therefore be discharged of that Office, when the Sovereign for the good of his Subjects shall think it necessary. They may also if they please, commit the care of Religion to one Supreme Pastor, or to an Assembly of Pastors; and give them what power over the Church, or one over another, they think most convenient; and what titles of honor, as of Bishops, Archbishops, Priests, or Presbyters, they will; and make such Laws for their maintenance, either by Tithes, or otherwise, as they please, so they doe it out of a sincere conscience, of which God onely is the Judge. It is the Civill Soveraign, that is to appoint Judges, and Interpreters of the Canonicall Scriptures; for it is he that maketh them Laws. It is he also that giveth strength to Excommunications; which but for such Laws and Punishments, as may humble obstinate Libertines, and reduce them to union with the Rest of the Church, would bee contemned. In summe, he hath the Supreme Power in all causes, as well Ecclesiasticall, as Civill, as far as concerneth actions, and words, for those onely are known, and may be accused; and of that which cannot be accused, there is no Judg at all, but God, that knoweth the heart. And these Rights are incident to all Soveraigns, whether Monarchs, or Assemblies: for they that are the Representants of a Christian People, are Representants of the Church: for a Church, and a Common-wealth of Christian People, are the same thing. . . .

Chapter XLIII

Of what is NECESSARY *for a Man's Reception into the Kingdome of Heaven*

The most frequent praetext of Sedition, and Civill Warre in Christian Common-wealths hath a long time proceeded from a difficulty, not yet sufficiently resolved, of obeying at once, both God, and Man, then when their Commandements are one contrary to the other. It is manifest enough, that when a man receiveth two contrary Commands, and knows that one of them is Gods, he ought to obey that, and not the other, though it be the command even of his lawfull Soveraign (whether a Monarch, or a soveraign Assembly,) or the command of his Father. The difficulty therefore consisteth in this, that men when they are commanded in the name of God, know not in divers Cases, whether the command be from God, or whether he that commandeth, doe but abuse Gods name for some private ends of his own. For as there were in the Church of the Jews, many false Prophets, that sought reputation with the people, by feigned Dreams, and Visions; so there have been in all times in the Church of Christ, false Teachers, that seek reputation with the people, by phantasticall and false Doctrines; and by such reputation (as is the nature of Ambition,) to govern them for their private benefit.

But this difficulty of obeying both God, and the Civill Soveraign on earth, to those that can distinguish between what is *Necessary,* and what is not *Necessary* for their *Reception* into the *Kingdome of God,* is of no moment. For if the command of the Civill Soveraign bee such, as that it may be obeyed, without the forfeiture of life Eternall; not to obey it is unjust; and the precept of the Apostle takes place; *Servants obey your Masters in all things;* and, *Children obey your Parents in all things;* and the precept of our Saviour, *The Scribes and Pharisees sit in Moses Chaire, All therefore they shall say, that observe, and doe.* But if the command be such, as cannot be obeyed, without being damned to Eternall Death, then it were madnesse to obey it, and the Counsell of our Saviour takes place, (*Mat.* 10.28.) *Fear not those that kill the body, but cannot kill the soule.* All men therefore that would avoid, both the punishments that are to be in this world inflicted, for disobedience to their earthly Soveraign, and those that shall be inflicted in the world to come for disobedience to God, have need be taught to distinguish well between what is, and what is not Necessary to Eternall Salvation.

All that is NECESSARY *to Salvation,* is contained in two Vertues, *Faith in Christ,* and *Obedience to Laws.* The latter of these, if it were perfect, were enough to us. But because wee are all guilty of disobedience to Gods Law, not onely originally in Adam, but also actually by our own transgressions, there is required at our hands now, not onely *Obedience* for the rest of our time, but also a *Remission* of

sins for the time past; which Remission is the reward of our Faith in Christ. That nothing else is Necessarily required to Salvation, is manifest from this, that the Kingdome of Heaven is shut to none but to Sinners; that is to say, to the disobedient, or transgressors of the Law; nor to them, in case they Repent, and Beleeve all the Articles of Christian Faith, Necessary to Salvation.

The Great Case of Liberty of Conscience (1670)

WILLIAM PENN (1644–1718)

In 1662 William Penn was expelled from Oxford for his religious nonconformity, and, after he became a Quaker in 1667, he was jailed on several occasions as a result of his activities on behalf of the Society of Friends. Throughout the 1670s and 1680s he wrote a number of essays arguing for religious liberty. The selections below are from one of his most influential works on this subject.

Chap. I

That imposition, restraint, and persecution for conscience sake, highly invade the divine prerogative, and divest the Almighty of a right, due to none besides himself, and that in five eminent particulars.

THE great case of Liberty of Conscience, so often debated and defended (however dissatisfactorily to such as have so little conscience as to persecute for it)

Chaps. 1–3 reprinted from *The Select Works of William Penn,* 4th ed. (London: William Phillips, 1825; New York: Kraus, 1971), 2:133–39. This essay, along with other essays on religious liberty, can be found in *The Political Writings of William Penn,* ed. Andrew R. Murphy (Indianapolis: Liberty Fund, 2002).

is once more brought to public view, by a late act against dissenters, and bill, or an additional one, that we all hoped the wisdom of our rulers had long since laid aside, as what was fitter to be passed into an act of perpetual oblivion. The kingdoms are alarmed at this procedure, and thousands greatly at a stand, wondering what should be the meaning of such hasty resolutions, that seem as fatal as they were unexpected. Some ask what wrong they have done? others, what peace they have broken? and all, what plots they have formed to prejudice the present government, or occasions given to hatch new jealousies of them and their proceedings? being not conscious to themselves of guilt in any such respect.

For mine own part, I publicly confess myself to be a very hearty dissenter from the established worship of these nations, as believing Protestants to have much degenerated from their first principles, and as owning the poor despised Quakers, in life and doctrine, to have espoused the cause of God, and to be the undoubted followers of Jesus Christ, in his most holy, strait, and narrow way, that leads to the eternal rest. In all which I know no treason, nor any principle that would urge me to a thought injurious to the civil peace. If any be defective in this particular, it is equal both individuals and whole societies should answer for their own defaults; but we are clear.

However, all conclude that union very ominous and unhappy, which makes the first discovery of itself by a "John Baptist's head in a charger." They mean that feast which some are designed to make upon the liberties and properties of free-born Englishmen: since to have the entail of those undoubted hereditary rights cut off, for matters purely relative of another world, is a severe beheading in the law: which must be obvious to all, but such as measure the justice of things, only by that proportion they bear with their own interest. A sort of men that seek themselves, though at the apparent loss of whole societies; like to that barbarous fancy of old, which had rather that Rome should burn than it be without the satisfaction of a bonfire. And sad it is, when men have so far stupified their understandings with the strong doses of their private interest, as to become insensible of the public's. Certainly such an over-fondness for self, or that strong inclination to raise themselves in the ruin of what does not so much oppose them, as that they will believe so, because they would be persecuting, is a malignant enemy to that tranquillity, which all dissenting parties seem to believe would be the consequence of a toleration.

In short we say, there can be but two ends in persecution; the one to satisfy (which none can ever do) the insatiable appetites of a decimating clergy (whose best arguments are fines and imprisonments); and the other as thinking therein they do God good service: but it is so hateful a thing upon any account, that we shall make it appear, by this ensuing discourse, to be a declared enemy to God, religion, and the good of human society.

The whole will be small, since it is but an epitome of no larger a tract than fourteen sheets; yet divides itself into the same particulars, every of which we shall defend against imposition, restraint, and persecution, though not with that scope of reason (nor consequently pleasure to the readers) being by other contingent disappointments limited to a narrow stint.

The terms explained, and the question stated
First, By liberty of conscience, we understand not only a mere liberty of the mind, in believing or disbelieving this or that principle or doctrine; but "the exercise of ourselves in a visible way of worship, upon our believing it to be indispensably required at our hands, that if we neglect it for fear or favour of any mortal man, we sin, and incur divine wrath." Yet we would be so understood to extend and justify the lawfulness of our so meeting to worship God, as not to contrive, or abet any contrivance destructive of the government and laws of the land, tending to matters of an external nature, directly or indirectly; but so far only as it may refer to religious matters, and a life to come, and consequently wholly independent of the secular affairs of this, wherein we are supposed to transgress.

Secondly, By imposition, restraint, and persecution, we do not only mean the strict requiring of us to believe this to be true, or that to be false; and upon refusal to incur the penalties enacted in such cases; but by those terms we mean thus much, "any coercive let or hindrance to us, from meeting together to perform those religious exercises which are according to our faith and persuasion."

The question stated

For proof of the aforesaid terms thus given, we singly state the question thus;

Whether imposition, restraint, and persecution, upon persons for exercising such a liberty of conscience as is before expressed, and so circumstantiated, be not to impeach the honour of God, the meekness of the Christian religion, the authority of Scripture, the privilege of nature, the principles of common reason, the well being of government, and apprehensions of the greatest personages of former and latter ages?

First, Then we say, that imposition, restraint, and persecution, for matters relating to conscience, directly invade the divine prerogative, and divest the Almighty of a due, proper to none besides himself. And this we prove by these five particulars:

First, If we do allow the honour of our creation due to God only, and that no other besides himself has endowed us with those excellent gifts of understanding, reason, judgment, and faith, and consequently that he only is the object as well as the author, both of our faith, worship, and service; then whosoever shall interpose their authority to enact faith and worship in a way that seems not to us congruous with what he has discovered to us to be faith and worship (whose alone property it is to do it) or to restrain us from what we are persuaded is our indispensable duty, they evidently usurp this authority, and invade his incommunicable right of government over conscience: for "The inspiration of the Almighty gives understanding: and faith is the gift of God," says the divine writ.

Secondly, Such magisterial determinations carry an evident claim to that infallibility, which Protes-

tants have been hitherto so jealous of owning, that, to avoid the Papists, they have denied it to all but God himself.

Either they have forsook their old plea; or if not, we desire to know when, and where, they were invested with that divine exellency; and whether imposition, restraint, and persecution, were ever deemed by God the fruits of his spirit. However, that itself was not sufficient; for unless it appear as well to us that they have it, as to them who have it, we cannot believe it upon any convincing evidence, but by tradition only; an anti-protestant way of believing.

Thirdly, It enthrones man as king over conscience, the alone just claim and privilege of his Creator; whose thoughts are not as men's thoughts, but has reserved to himself that empire from all the Caesars on earth: for if men, in reference to souls and bodies, things appertaining to this and the other world, shall be subject to their fellow-creatures, what follows, but that Caesar (however he got it) has all, God's share, and his own too? and being lord of both, both are Caesar's, and not God's.

Fourthly, It defeats God's work of grace, and the invisible operation of his eternal spirit, (which can alone beget faith, and is only to be obeyed, in and about religion and worship) and attributes men's conformity to outward force, and corporal punishments. A faith subject to as many revolutions as the powers that enact it.

Fifthly and lastly, Such persons assume the judgment of the great tribunal unto themselves; for to whomsoever men are imposedly or restrictively subject and accountable in matters of faith, worship and conscience; in them alone must the power of judgment reside: but it is equally true that God shall judge all by Jesus Christ; and that no man is so accountable to his fellow-creatures, as to be imposed upon, restrained, or persecuted for any matter of conscience whatever.

Thus, and in many more particulars, are men accustomed to intrench upon divine property, to gratify particular interests in the world; and (at best) through a misguided apprehension to imagine "they do God good service," that where they cannot give faith, they will use force; which kind of sacrifice is nothing less unreasonable than the other is abominable: God will not give his honour to another; and to him only, that searches the heart and tries the reins, it is our duty to ascribe the gifts of understanding and faith, without which none can please God.

Chap. II

They overturn the Christian Religion; 1. In the nature of it, which is meekness; 2. In the practice of it, which is suffering; 3. In the promotion of it, since all farther discoveries are prohibited; 4. In the rewards of it, which are eternal.

THE next great evil which attends external force in matters of faith and worship, is no less than the overthrow of the whole Christian religion; and this we will briefly evidence in these four particulars: 1. That there can be nothing more remote from the nature; 2. The practice; 3. The promotion; 4. The rewards of it.

First, It is the privilege of the Christian faith above the dark suggestions of ancient and modern superstitious traditions, to carry with it a most self-evidencing verity, whichever was sufficient to proselyte believers, without the weak auxiliaries of external power. The Son of God, and great example of the world, was so far from calling his Father's omnipotency in legions of angels to his defence, that he at once repealed all acts of force, and defined to us the nature of his religion in this one great saying of his, "My kingdom is not of this world." It was spiritual, not carnal; accompanied with weapons as heavenly as its own nature, and designed for the good and salvation of the soul, and not the injury and destruction of the body: no gaols, fines, exiles, &c. but "sound reason, clear truth, and strict life." In short, the Christian religion intreats all, but compels none.

Secondly, That restraint and persecution overturn the practice of it. I need go no farther than the allowed martyrologies of several ages, of which the scriptures claim a share; begin with Abel, go down to Moses, so to the Prophets, and then to the meek ex-

ample of Jesus Christ himself; how patiently devoted was he to undergo the contradictions of men! and so far from persecuting any, that he would not so much as revile his persecutors, but prayed for them: thus lived his apostles, and the true Christians of the first three hundred years. Nor are the famous stories of our first reformers silent in the matter; witness the Christian practices of the Waldenses, Lollards, Hussites, Lutherans, and our noble martyrs; who, as became the true followers of Jesus Christ, enacted and confirmed their religion with their own blood, and not with the blood of their opposers.

Thirdly, Restraint and persecution obstruct the promotion of the Christian religion: for if such as restrain, confess themselves "miserable sinners, and altogether imperfect," it either follows, that they never desire to be better, or that they should encourage such as may be capable of farther informing and reforming them: they condemn the Papists for incoffining the scriptures and their worship in an unknown tongue, and yet are guilty themselves of the same kind of fact.

Fourthly, They prevent many of eternal rewards: for where any are religious for fear, and that of men, it is slavish, and the recompence of such religion is condemnation, not peace: besides, it is man that is served; who having no power but what is temporary, his reward must needs be so too: he that imposes a duty, or restrains from one, must reward; but because no man can reward for such duties, no man can or ought to impose them, or restrain from them. So that we conclude imposition, restraint and persecution, are destructive of the Christian religion, in the nature, practice, promotion and rewards of it, which are eternal.

Chap. III

They oppose the plainest testimonies of divine writ that can be, which condemn all force upon conscience.

WE farther say, that imposition, restraint and persecution are repugnant to the plain testimonies and precepts of the scriptures.

1. "The inspiration of the Almighty gives understanding." Job xxxii. 8.

If no man can believe before he understands, and no man understand before he is inspired of God; then are the impositions of men excluded as unreasonable, and their persecutions for non-obedience as inhuman.

2. "Wo unto them that take counsel, but not of me." Isa. xxx. 1.

3. "Wo unto them that make a man an offender for a word, and lay a snare for him that reproves in the gate, and turn aside the just for a thing of nought." Isa. xxix. 15, 21.

4. "Let the wheat and the tares grow together, until the time of the harvest, or end of the world." Matt. xiii. 27, 28, 29.

5. "And Jesus called them unto him, and said, Ye know that the princes of the Gentiles exercise dominion over them, and they that are great exercise authority upon them; but it shall not be so amongst you." Matt. xx. 25, 26.

6. "And Jesus said unto them, Render unto Caesar the things that are Caesar's, and unto God the things that are God's." Luke xx. 25.

7. "When his disciples saw this, (that there were non-conformists then, as well as now) they said, Wilt thou that we command fire to come down from heaven and consume them, as Elias did? but he turned and rebuked them, and said, Ye know not what spirit ye are of; for the Son of man is not come to destroy men's lives, but to save them." Luke ix. 54, 55, 56.

8. "Howbeit, when the Spirit of truth is come, he shall lead you into all truth." John xvi. 8. 13.

9. "But now the anointing which ye have received of him, abides in you; and you need not that any man teach you, (much less impose upon any, or restrain them from what any are persuaded it leads to) but as the same anointing teaches you of all things, and is truth, and is no lie." 1 John ii. 27.

10. "Dearly beloved, avenge not yourselves; but rather give place unto wrath" (much less should any be wrathful that are called Christians, where no oc-

casion is given.) "Therefore if thine enemy hunger, feed him; and if he thirst, give him drink; recompence no man evil for evil." Rom. xii. 19, 20, 21.

11. "For though we walk in the flesh," (that is, in the body, or visible world) "we do not war after the flesh; for the weapons of our warfare are not carnal." 2 Cor. x. 3. (but fines and imprisonments are; and such use not the apostles' weapons that employ those.) "For a bishop, 1 Tim. iii. 3. (saith Paul) must be of good behaviour, apt to teach, no striker; but be gentle unto all men, patient, in meekness instructing, (not persecuting) those that oppose themselves, if God peradventure will give them repentance to the acknowledging of the truth." 2 Tim. ii. 24, 25.

12. Lastly, We shall subjoin one passage more, and then no more of this particular; "Whatsoever ye would that men should do to you, do ye even so to them." Matt. vii. 12. Luke vi. 31.

Now upon the whole, we seriously ask, Whether any should be imposed upon, or restrained, in matters of faith and worship? Whether such practices become the gospel, or are suitable to Christ's meek precepts and suffering doctrine? And lastly, Whether those, who are herein guilty, do to us as they would be done unto by others?

What if any were once severe to you; many are unconcerned in that, who are yet liable to the lash, as if they were not. But if you once thought the imposition of a directory unreasonable, and a restraint from your way of worship unchristian, can you believe that liberty of conscience is changed, because the parties, in point of power, are? Or that the same reasons do not yet remain in vindication of an indulgence for others, that were once employed by you for yourselves? Surely such conjectures would argue gross weakness.

To conclude: Whether persecutors at any time read the scriptures, we know not; but certain we are, such practise as little of them as may be, who with so much delight reject them, and think it no small accession to the discovery of their loyalty, to lead us and our properties in triumph after them.

A Letter on Toleration (1689)

The Second Treatise (1690)

JOHN LOCKE (1632–1704)

In 1683 Locke was forced to flee England for Holland to avoid political persecution. In 1689 he published *Epistola de Tolerantia*, which was translated and published in English in the same year. The following year he returned to England and published *Two Treatises of Government* and *An Essay Concerning Human Understanding*. The selections below are representative of Locke's arguments on behalf of religious liberty and natural rights.

A Letter on Toleration

Now that the whole jurisdiction of the magistrate reaches only to these civil concernments; and that all civil power, right, and dominion, is bounded and confined to the only care of promoting these things; and that it neither can nor ought in any manner to be extended to the salvation of souls; these following considerations seem unto me abundantly to demonstrate.

First, Because the care of souls is not committed to the civil magistrate, any more than to other men. It is not committed unto him, I say, by God; because it appears not that God has ever given any such authority to one man over another, as to compel any one to his religion. Nor can any such power be vested in the magistrate by the consent of the people; because no man can so far abandon the care of his own salvation, as blindly to leave it to the choice of any other, whether prince or subject, to prescribe to him what faith or worship he shall embrace. For no man can, if

Reprinted from John Locke, *A Letter on Toleration*, in *The Works of John Locke in Nine Volumes*, 12th ed. (London: Rivington, 1824), 5:10–13, 33–35, 46–47. Accessed from http://oll.libertyfund.org/title/764.

he would, conform his faith to the dictates of another. All the life and power of true religion consists in the inward and full persuasion of the mind; and faith is not faith, without believing. Whatever profession we make, to whatever outward worship we conform, if we are not fully satisfied in our own mind that the one is true, and the other well-pleasing unto God, such profession and such practice, far from being any furtherance, are indeed great obstacles to our salvation. For in this manner, instead of expiating other sins by the exercise of religion, I say in offering thus unto God Almighty such a worship as we esteem to be displeasing unto him, we add unto the number of our other sins, those also of hypocrisy, and contempt of his Divine Majesty.

In the second place, The care of souls cannot belong to the civil magistrate, because his power consists only in outward force: but true and saving religion consists in the inward persuasion of the mind, without which nothing can be acceptable to God. And such is the nature of the understanding, that it cannot be compelled to the belief of any thing by outward force. Confiscation of estate, imprisonment, torments, nothing of that nature can have any such efficacy as to make men change the inward judgment that they have framed of things.

It may indeed be alleged, that the magistrate may make use of arguments, and thereby draw the heterodox into the way of truth, and procure their salvation. I grant it; but this is common to him with other men. In teaching, instructing, and redressing the erroneous by reason, he may certainly do what becomes any good man to do. Magistracy does not oblige him to put off either humanity or christianity. But it is one thing to persuade, another to command; one thing to press with arguments, another with penalties. This the civil power alone has a right to do; to the other, good-will is authority enough. Every man has commission to admonish, exhort, convince another of errour, and by reasoning to draw him into truth: but to give laws, receive obedience, and compel with the sword, belongs to none but the magistrate. And upon this ground I affirm, that the magistrate's power extends not to the establishing of any article of faith, or forms of worship, by the force of his laws. For laws are of no force at all without penalties, and penalties in this case are absolutely impertinent; because they are not proper to convince the mind. Neither the profession of any articles of faith, nor the conformity to any outward form of worship, as has been already said, can be available to the salvation of souls, unless the truth of the one, and the acceptableness of the other unto God, be thoroughly believed by those that so profess and practise. But penalties are no ways capable to produce such belief. It is only light and evidence that can work a change in men's opinions; and that light can in no manner proceed from corporal sufferings, or any other outward penalties.

In the third place, The care of the salvation of men's souls cannot belong to the magistrate; because, though the rigour of laws and the force of penalties were capable to convince and change men's minds, yet would not that help at all to the salvation of their souls. For, there being but one truth, one way to heaven; what hope is there that more men would be led into it, if they had no other rule to follow but the religion of the court, and were put under a necessity to quit the light of their own reason, to oppose the dictates of their own consciences, and blindly to resign up themselves to the will of their governors, and to the religion which either ignorance, ambition, or superstition had chanced to establish in the countries where they were born? In the variety and contradiction of opinions in religion, wherein the princes of the world are as much divided as in their secular interests, the narrow way would be much straitened; one country alone would be in the right, and all the rest of the world put under an obligation of following their princes in the ways that lead to destruction: and that which heightens the absurdity, and very ill suits the notion of a deity, men would owe their eternal happiness or misery to the places of their nativity.

These considerations, to omit many others that might have been urged to the same purpose, seem unto me sufficient to conclude, that all the power of civil government relates only to men's civil interests, is confined to the care of the things of this world, and hath nothing to do with the world to come.

Let us now consider what a church is. A church then I take to be a voluntary society of men, joining themselves together of their own accord in order to the public worshipping of God, in such a manner as they judge acceptable to him, and effectual to the salvation of their souls.

I say, it is a free and voluntary society. Nobody is born a member of any church; otherwise the religion of parents would descend unto children, by the same right of inheritance as their temporal estates, and every one would hold his faith by the same tenure he does his lands; than which nothing can be imagined more absurd. Thus therefore that matter stands. No man by nature is bound unto any particular church or sect, but every one joins himself voluntarily to that society in which he believes he has found that profession and worship which is truly acceptable to God. The hope of salvation, as it was the only cause of his entrance into that communion, so it can be the only reason of his stay there. For if afterwards he discover any thing either erroneous in the doctrine, or incongruous in the worship of that society to which he has joined himself, why should it not be as free for him to go out as it was to enter? No member of a religious society can be tried with any other bonds but what proceed from the certain expectation of eternal life. A church then is a society of members voluntarily uniting to this end. . . .

In the next place: As the magistrate has no power to impose by his laws the use of any rites and ceremonies in any church, so neither has he any power to forbid the use of such rites and ceremonies as are already received, approved, and practised by any church: because if he did so, he would destroy the church itself; the end of whose institution is only to worship God with freedom, after its own manner.

You will say, by this rule, if some congregations should have a mind to sacrifice infants, or, as the primitive christians were falsely accused, lustfully pollute themselves in promiscuous uncleanness, or practise any other such heinous enormities, is the magistrate obliged to tolerate them, because they are committed in a religious assembly? I answer, No. These things are not lawful in the ordinary course of life, nor in any private house; and therefore neither are they so in the worship of God, or in any religious meeting. But indeed if any people congregated upon account of religion, should be desirous to sacrifice a calf, I deny that that ought to be prohibited by a law. Meliboeus, whose calf it is, may lawfully kill his calf at home, and burn any part of it that he thinks fit. For no injury is thereby done to any one, no prejudice to another man's goods. And for the same reason he may kill his calf also in a religious meeting. Whether the doing so be well-pleasing to God or no, it is their part to consider that do it.—The part of the magistrate is only to take care that the commonwealth receive no prejudice, and that there be no injury done to any man either in life or estate. And thus what may be spent on a feast may be spent on a sacrifice. But if peradventure such were the state of things that the interest of the commonwealth required all slaughter of beasts should be forborn for some while, in order to the increasing of the stock of cattle, that had been destroyed by some extraordinary murrain; who sees not that the magistrate, in such a case, may forbid all his subjects to kill any calves for any use whatsoever? Only it is to be observed, that in this case the law is not made about a religious, but a political matter: nor is the sacrifice, but the slaughter of calves thereby prohibited.

By this we see what difference there is between the church and the commonwealth. Whatsoever is lawful in the commonwealth, cannot be prohibited by the magistrate in the church. Whatsoever is permitted unto any of his subjects for their ordinary use, neither can nor ought to be forbidden by him to any sect of people for their religious uses. If any man may lawfully take bread or wine, either sitting or kneeling, in his own house, the law ought not to abridge him of the same liberty in his religious worship; though in the church the use of bread and wine be very different, and be there applied to the mysteries of faith, and rites of divine worship. But those things that are prejudicial to the commonwealth of a people in their or-

dinary use, and are therefore forbidden by laws, those things ought not to be permitted to churches in their sacred rites. Only the magistrate ought always to be very careful that he do not misuse his authority, to the oppression of any church under pretence of public good.

It may be said, what if a church be idolatrous, is that also to be tolerated by the magistrate? In answer, I ask, what power can be given to the magistrate for the suppression of an idolatrous church, which may not, in time and place, be made use of to the ruin of an orthodox one? For it must be remembered, that the civil power is the same every where, and the religion of every prince is orthodox to himself. If therefore such a power be granted unto the civil magistrate in spirituals, as that at Geneva, for example; he may extirpate, by violence and blood, the religion which is there reputed idolatrous; by the same rule, another magistrate, in some neighbouring country, may oppress the reformed religion; and in India, the christian. The civil power can either change every thing in religion, according to the prince's pleasure, or it can change nothing. If it be once permitted to introduce any thing into religion by the means of laws and penalties, there can be no bounds put to it; but it will in the same manner be lawful to alter every thing, according to that rule of truth which the magistrate has framed unto himself. No man whatsoever ought therefore to be deprived of his terrestrial enjoyments, upon account of his religion. Not even Americans, subjected unto a christian prince, are to be punished either in body or goods for not embracing our faith and worship. If they are persuaded that they please God in observing the rites of their own country, and that they shall obtain happiness by that means, they are to be left unto God and themselves. . . .

Again: That church can have no right to be tolerated by the magistrate, which is constituted upon such a bottom, that all those who enter into it, do thereby ipso facto deliver themselves up to the protection and service of another prince. For by this means the magistrate would give way to the settling of a foreign jurisdiction in his own country, and suffer his own people to be listed, as it were, for soldiers against his own government. Nor does the frivolous and fallacious distinction between the court and the church afford any remedy to this inconvenience; especially when both the one and the other are equally subject to the absolute authority of the same person; who has not only power to persuade the members of his church to whatsoever he lists, either as purely religious, or as in order thereunto; but can also enjoin it them on pain of eternal fire. It is ridiculous for any one to profess himself to be a mahometan only in religion, but in every thing else a faithful subject to a christian magistrate, whilst at the same time he acknowledges himself bound to yield blind obedience to the mufti of Constantinople; who himself is entirely obedient to the Ottoman emperor, and frames the feigned oracles of that religion according to his pleasure. But this mahometan living amongst christians, would yet more apparently renounce their government, if he acknowledged the same person to be head of his church, who is the supreme magistrate in the state.

Lastly, Those are not at all to be tolerated who deny the being of God. Promises, covenants, and oaths, which are the bonds of human society, can have no hold upon an atheist. The taking away of God, though but even in thought, dissolves all. Besides also, those that by their atheism undermine and destroy all religion, can have no pretence of religion whereupon to challenge the privilege of a toleration. As for other practical opinions, though not absolutely free from all errour, yet if they do not tend to establish domination over others, or civil impunity to the church in which they are taught, there can be no reason why they should not be tolerated. . . .

The Second Treatise

6. But though this be a *State of Liberty,* yet it is *not a State of Licence,* though Man in that State have an uncontroleable Liberty, to dispose of his Person or Possessions, yet he has not Liberty to destroy himself, or so much as any Creature in his Possession, but where some nobler use, than its bare Preservation calls for it. The *State of Nature* has a Law of Nature to govern it, which obliges every one: And Reason, which is that Law, teaches all Mankind, who will but consult it, that being all equal and independent, no one ought to harm another in his Life, Health, Liberty, or Possessions. For Men being all the Workmanship of one Omnipotent, and infinitely wise Maker; All the Servants of one Sovereign Master, sent into the World by his order and about his business, they are his Property, whose Workmanship they are, made to last during his, not one anothers Pleasure. And being furnished with like Faculties, sharing all in one Community of Nature, there cannot be supposed any such *Subordination* among us, that may Authorize us to destroy one another, as if we were made for one anothers uses, as the inferior ranks of Creatures are for ours. Every one as he is *bound to preserve himself,* and not to quit his Station wilfully; so by the like reason when his own Preservation comes not in competition, ought he, as much as he can, *to preserve the rest of Mankind,* and may not unless it be to do Justice on an Offender, take away, or impair the life, or what tends to the Preservation of the Life, the Liberty, Health, Limb or Goods of another.

Reprinted from John Locke, *The Second Treatise,* sec. 6, in *Two Treatises of Government,* ed. Peter Laslett (Cambridge: Cambridge University Press, 1960), 270–71.

Toleration Act (1689)

The Toleration Act of 1689 granted freedom of worship to nonconforming (i.e., non-Anglican) Protestants in Great Britain. Catholics and Unitarians were not included in the act, and social and political disabilities for non-Anglicans remained in place.

A N   A C T for Exempting their Majestyes Protestant Subjects dissenting from the Church of England from the Penalties of certaine Lawes.

F O R A S M U C H as some ease to scrupulous Consciences in the Exercise of Religion may be an effectuall meanes to unite their Majesties Protestant Subjects in Interest and Affection Bee it enacted by the King and Queens most excellent Majestyes by and with the advice and consent of the Lords Spirituall and Temporall and the Commons in this present Parliament assembled and by the authoritie of the same That neither the Statute made in the three and twentieth yeare of the Raigne of the late Queene Elizabeth Entituled An Act to Retaine the Queens Majestyes Subjects in their due Obedience, Nor the Statute made in the twenty ninth yeare of the said Queene Intituled An Act for the more speedy and due Execution of certaine Branches of the Statute made in the three and twentyeth yeare of the Queens Majestyes Raigne viz The aforesaid Act, nor that Branch or Clause of a Statute made in the first year of the Raigne of the said Queene Intituled An Act for [the[1]] Uniformity of Common Prayer and Service in the Church and Administration of the Sacraments whereby all persons haveing noe lawfull or reasonable excuse to be absent are required to resort to their Parish Church or Chappell or some usuall place where

the Common Prayer shall be used upon paine of Punishment by the Censures of the Church and alsoe upon paine that every person soe offending shall forfeite for every such Offence twelve pence Nor the Statute made in the third yeare of the Raigne of the late King James (2) Intituled An Act for the better discovering and repressing Popish Recusants Nor that other Statute made in the same yeare Intituled An Act to Prevent and Avoid Dangers which may grow by Popish Recusants Nor any other Law or Statute of this Realme made against Papists or Popish Recusants Except the Statute made in the five and twentyeth yeare of King Charles the Second Intituled An Act for preventing Dangers which may happen from Popish Recusants And except alsoe the Statute made in the thirtyeth yeare of the said King Charles the Second Intituled An Act for the more effectuall preserveing the Kings Person and Government by disableing Papists from sitting in either House of Parlyament Shall be construed to extend to any person or persons dissenting from the Church of England that shall take the Oaths mentioned in a Statute made this present Parliament Intituled An Act for removeing and preventing all Questions and Disputes concerning the assembling and sitting of this present Parliament And shall make and subscribe the Declaration mentioned in a Statute made in the thirtyeth yeare of the Raigne of King Charles the Second Intituled An Act to prevent Papists from sitting in either House of Parlyament Which Oaths and Declaration the Justices of Peace at the generall Sessions of the Peace to be held for the County or Place where such person shall live are hereby required to tender and administer to such persons as shall offer themselves to take make and subscribe the same and thereof to keepe a Register And likewise none of the persons aforesaid shall give or pay as any Fee or Reward to any Officer or Officers belonging to the Court aforesaid above the summe of six pence nor that more then once for his or their Entry of his takeing the said Oaths and makeing and subscribeing the

Reprinted from *Statutes of the Realm* (London: Record Commission, 1819), 6:74–76.
1. interlined on the Roll.

2. the first *O.*

said Declaration Nor above the further summe of six pence for any Certificate of the same to be made out and signed by the Officer or Officers of the said Court.

AND bee it further enacted by the authoritie aforesaid That all and every person and persons already convicted or prosecuted in order to Conviction of Recusancy by Indictment Information Action of Debt or otherwise grounded upon the aforesaid Statutes or any of them that shall take the said Oaths mentioned in the said Statute made this present Parliament and make and subscribe the Declaration aforesaid in the Court of Exchequer or Assizes or Generall or Quarter Sessions to be held for the County where such person lives and to be thence respectively certified into the Exchequer shall be thenceforth exempted and discharged from all the Penalties Seizures Forfeitures Judgements and Executions incurred by force of any the aforesaid Statutes without any Composition Fee or further Charge whatsoever

AND bee it further enacted by the authoritie aforesaid That all and every person and persons that shall as aforesaid take the said Oathes and make and subscribe the Declaration aforesaid shall not be lyable to any Paines Penalties or Forfeitures mentioned in an Act made in the five and thirtyeth yeare of the Raigne of the late Queene Elizabeth Intituled An Act to retaine the Queenes Majestyes Subjects in their due Obedience Nor in an Act made in the two and twentyeth yeare of the Raigne of the late King Charles the Second Intituled An Act to prevent and suppresse seditious Conventicles Nor shall any of the said persons be prosecuted in any Ecclesiasticall Court for or by reason of their Nonconforming to the Church of England

PROVIDED alwayes and bee it enacted by the authoritie aforesaid That if any Assembly of persons dissenting from the Church of England shall be had in any place for Religious Worship with the doores locked barred or bolted dureing any time of such Meeting together all and every person or persons that shall come to and be at such Meeting shall not receive any benefitt from this Law but be lyable to all the Paines and Penalties of all the aforesaid Laws recited in this Act for such their Meeting notwithstanding his takeing the Oaths and his makeing and subscribing the Declaration aforesaid Provided alwayes That nothing herein contained shall be construed to exempt any of the persons aforesaid from paying of Tythes or other Parochiall Duties or any other Duties to the Church or Minister nor from any Prosecution in any Ecclesiasticall Court or elsewhere for the same

AND bee it further enacted by the Authoritie aforesaid That if any Person dissenting from the Church of England as aforesaid shall hereafter be chosen or otherwise appointed to beare the Office of High Constable or Petty Constable Churchwarden Overseer of the Poore or any other Parochiall or Ward Office and such person shall scruple to take upon him any of the said Offices in reguard of the Oathes or any other Matter or Thing required by the Law to be taken or done in respect of such Office every such Person shall and may execute such Office or Employment by a sufficient Deputie by him to be provided that shall comply with the Laws on this behalfe Provided alwayes the said Deputy be allowed and approved by such person [and³] persons in such manner as such Officer or Officers respectively should by Law have beene allowed and approved

AND bee it further enacted by the authoritie aforesaid That noe person dissenting from the Church of England in Holy Orders or pretended Holy Orders or pretending to Holy Orders nor any Preacher or Teacher of any Congregation of dissenting Protestants that shall make and subscribe the Declaration aforesaid and take the said Oaths at the Generall or Quarter Sessions of the Peace to be held for the County Towne Parts or Division where such person lives which Court is hereby impowred to administer the same and shall alsoe declare his approbation of and subscribe the Articles of Religion mentioned in the Statute made in the thirteenth yeare of the Raigne of the late Queene Elizabeth Except the thirty fourth thirty fifth and thirty sixth and these words of the

3. or O.

twentyeth Article [vizt[4]] (the Church hath power to decree Rights or Ceremonies and Authority in Controversies of Faith and yet) shall be lyable to any of the paines or penalties mentioned in an Act made in the seventeenth yeare of the Raigne of King Charles the Second Intituled An Act for restraining Non Conformists from inhabiting in Corporations Nor the penalties mentioned in the aforesaid Act made in the two and twentyeth yeare of his said late Majesties Raigne for or by reason of such persons preaching at any Meeting for the Exercise of Religion Nor to the penalty of one hundred pounds mentioned in an Act made in the thirteenth and fourteenth of King Charles the Second Intituled An Act for the Uniformity of Publique Prayers and Administration of Sacraments and other Rites and Ceremonies And for establishing the Forme of makeing ordaineing and consecrateing of Bishops Priests and Deacons in the Church of England for officiating in any Congregation for the Exercise of Religion permitted and allowed by this Act [PROVIDED alwayes That the makeing and subscribing the said Declaration and the takeing the said Oaths and makeing the Declaration of Approbation and Subscription to the said Articles in manner as aforesaid by every respective person or persons herein before mentioned at such Generall or Quarter Sessions of the Peace as aforesaid shall be then and there entred of Record in the said Court for which six pence shall be paid to the Clerke of the Peace and noe more[5]] Provided that such person shall not at any time preach in any place but with the doores not locked barred or bolted as aforesaid

AND whereas some dissenting Protestants scruple the baptizeing of Infants Bee it enacted by the authoritie aforesaid That every person in pretended Holy Orders or pretending to Holy Orders or Preacher or Teacher that shall subscribe the aforesaid Articles of Religion Except before excepted and alsoe except part of the seven and twentyeth Article touching Infant Baptisme and shall take the said Oathes

4. interlined on the Roll.
5. annexed to the Original Act in a separate Schedule.

and make and subscribe the Declaration aforesaid in manner aforesaid every such person shall enjoy all the Privileges Benefitts and Advantages which any other dissenting Minister as aforesaid might have or enjoy by vertue of this Act

AND bee it further enacted by the authoritie aforesaid That every Teacher or Preacher in Holy Orders or pretended Holy Orders that is a Minister Preacher or Teacher of a Congregation that shall take the Oathes herein required and make and subscribe the Declaration aforesaid And alsoe subscribe such of the aforesaid Articles of the Church of England as are required by this Act in manner aforesaid shall be thenceforth exempted from serveing upon any Jury or from being chosen or appointed to beare the Office of Churchwarden Overseer of the Poore or any other Parochiall or Ward Office or other Office in any Hundred of any Shire City Towne Parish Division or Wapentake

AND bee it further enacted by the authoritie aforesaid That every Justice of the Peace may at any time hereafter require any person that goes to any Meeting for Exercise of Religion to make and subscribe the Declaration aforesaid and alsoe to take the said Oaths or Declaration of Fidelity herein after mentioned in case such person scruples the takeing of an Oath and upon refusall thereof such Justice of the Peace is hereby required to committ such person to Prison without Baile or Maineprize and to certifie the Name of such person to the next Generall or Quarter Sessions of the Peace to be held for that County City Towne Part or Division where such person then resides and if such person soe committed shall upon a second tender at the Generall or Quarter Sessions refuse to make and subscribe the Declaration aforesaid such persons refuseing shall be then and there recorded and he shall be taken thenceforth to all intents and purposes for a Popish Recusant Convict and suffer accordingly and incurr all the penalties and forfeitures of all the aforesaid Laws

AND whereas there are certaine other persons Dissenters from the Church of England who scruple the takeing of any Oath Bee it enacted by the authoritie aforesaid That every such person shall make and subscribe the aforesaid Declaration and alsoe this Declaration of Fidelity following viz

I A B doe sincerely promise and solemnely declare before God and the World that I will be true and faithfull to King William and Queene Mary And I doe solemnly professe and Declare That I doe from my Heart Abhor Detest and Renounce as Impious and Hereticall that damnable Doctrine and Position That Princes Excommunicated or Deprived by the Pope or any Authority of the See of Rome may be Deposed or Murthered by their Subjects or any other whatsoever And I doe declare that no Forreigne [Prince Person[6]] Prelate State or Potentate hath or ought to have any Power Jurisdiction Superiority Preeminence or Authoritie Ecclesiasticall or Spirituall within this Realme.

[And shall subscribe a Profession of their Christian Beliefe in these Words

I A B professe Faith in God the Father and in Jesus Christ his Eternall Sonne the true God and in the Holy Spirit one God blessed for evermore And doe acknowledge the Holy Scriptures of the Old and New Testament to be given by Divine Inspiration,

Which Declarations and Subscription shall be made and entred of Record at the generall Quarter Sessions of the Peace of the County City or place where every such person shall then reside[7]] And every such person that shall make and subscribe the two Declarations and Profession aforesaid being thereunto required shall be exempted from all the pains and penalties of all and every the aforementioned Statutes made against Popish Recusants or Protestant Nonconformists and alsoe from the penalties of an Act made in the fifth yeare of the Raigne of the late Queene Elizabeth Intituled An Act for the Assurance of the Queenes Royall Power over all Estates and Subjects within her Dominions For or by reason of such persons not takeing or refuseing to take the Oath mentioned in the said Act And alsoe from the

penalties of an Act made in the thirteenth and fourteenth yeares of the Raigne of King Charles the Second Intituled An Act for preventing Michiefes that may arise by certaine persons called Quakers refuseing to take lawfull Oaths And enjoy all other the Benefitts Priviledges and Advantages under the like Limitations Provisoes and Conditions which any other Dissenters shall or ought to enjoy by vertue of this Act

PROVIDED always and bee it enacted by the authoritie aforesaid That in case any person shall refuse to take the said Oaths when tendred to them which every Justice of the Peace is hereby impowred to doe such person shall not be admitted to make and subscribe the two Declarations aforesaid though required thereunto either before any Justice of the Peace or at the Generall or Quarter Sessions before or after any Conviction of Popish Recusancy as aforesaid unlesse such person can within thirty one dayes after such tender of the Declarations to him produce two sufficient Protestant Witnesses to testifie upon Oath that they believe him to be a Protestant Dissenter or a Certificate under the Hands of foure Protestants who are conformable to the Church of England or have taken the Oaths and subscribed the Declaration abovementioned and shall alsoe produce a Certificate under the Hands and Seals of six or more sufficient Men of the Congregation to which he belongs owning him for one of them

PROVIDED alsoe and bee it enacted by the Authoritie aforesaid That untill such Certificate under the Hands of six of his Congregation as aforesaid be produced and two Protestant Witnesses come to attest his being a Protestant Dissenter or a Certificate under the Hands of foure Protestants as aforesaid be produced the Justice of the Peace shall and hereby is required to take a Recognizance with two Sureties in the penall Summe of fifty pounds [to be levyed of his Goods and Chattells Lands and Tenements to the use of the King and Queens Majestyes their Heires and Successors[8]] for his produceing the same and if he

---

6. interlined on the Roll.
7. annexed to the Original Act in a separate Schedule.

8. annexed to the Original Act in a separate Schedule.

cannot give such Security to committ him to prison there to remaine untill he has produced such Certificates or two Witnesses as aforesaid

PROVIDED always and it is the true intent and meaning of this Act That all the Laws made and provided for the frequenting of Divine Service on the Lords Day commonly called Sunday shall be still in force and executed against all persons that offend against the said Laws except such persons come to some Congregation or Assembly of Religious Worship allowed or permitted by this Act

PROVIDED always and bee it further enacted by the authoritie aforesaid That neither this Act nor any Clause Article or Thing herein contained shall extend or be construed to extend to give any ease benefitt or advantage to any Papist or Popish Recusant whatsoever or any person that shall deny in his Preaching or Writeing the Doctrine of the Blessed Trinity as it is declared in the aforesaid Articles of Religion

PROVIDED always, and bee it enacted by the Authoritie aforesaid That if any person or persons at any time or times after the tenth day of June doe and shall willingly and of purpose maliciously or contemptuously come into any Cathedrall or Parish Church Chapell or other Congregation permitted by this Act and disquiet or disturbe the same or misuse any Preacher or Teacher such person or persons upon proofe thereof before any Justice of Peace by two or more sufficient Witnesses shall finde two Sureties to be bound by Recognizance in the penall Summe of fifty pounds and in default of such Sureties shall be committed to prison there to remaine till the next Generall or Quarter Sessions and upon conviction of the said offence at the said Generall or Quarter Sessions shall suffer the paine and penalty of twenty pounds [to the use of the King and Queens Majesties their Heirs and Successors[9]]

PROVIDED always That noe Congregation or Assembly for Religious Worship shall be permitted or allowed by this Act untill the place of such Meeting shall be certified to the Bishop of the Diocesse or to the Arch-Deacon of that Archdeaconry [or to the Justices of the Peace at the Generall or Quarter Sessions of the Peace for the County City or Place[10]] in which such Meeting shall be held and registred in the said Bishops or Archdeacons Court respectively or recorded at the said Generall or Quarter Sessions The Register or Clerke of the Peace whereof respectively is hereby required to register the same and to give Certificate thereof to such person as shall demand the same for which there shall be none greater Fee nor Reward taken then the Summe of six pence.

Cato's Letters: Letter 66, "Arbitrary Government proved incompatible with true Religion, whether Natural or Revealed"

CATO [JOHN TRENCHARD (1662–1723) AND THOMAS GORDON (?–1750)]

Between 1720 and 1723 John Trenchard and Thomas Gordon published 138 political essays, first in the *London Journal* and later in the *British Journal*. Like Cato the Younger (95–146 B.C.), under whose name they wrote, they considered themselves opponents of tyranny and corruption and defenders of liberty and republican principles. Their letters were republished in book form and circulated widely throughout Great Britain and her colonies. Letter 66, reprinted below, was published on February 17, 1721.

---

9. annexed to the Original Act in a separate Schedule.

10. annexed to the Original Act in a separate Schedule.
Reprinted from [John Trenchard and Thomas Gordon], *Cato's Letters: or, Essays on Liberty, Civil and Religious, and Other Important Subjects* (1755; reprint, New York: Da Capo, 1971), 1:292–305.

Sir,

I shall shew, in this Paper, that neither the Christian Religion, nor Natural Religion, nor any Thing else that ought to be called Religion, can subsist under tyrannical Governments, now that Miracles are ceased. I readily confess, that such Governments are fertile in Superstition, in wild Whimsies, delusive Phantoms, and ridiculous Dreams; proper to terrify the human Soul, degrade its Dignity, deface its Beauty, and fetter it with slavish and unmanly Fears, to render it a proper Object of Fraud, Grimace, and Imposition; and to make Mankind the ready Dupes of gloomy Impostors, and the tame Slaves of raging Tyrants. For, Servitude established in the Mind, is best established.

But all these bewildered Imaginations, these dark and dreadful Horrors, which banish Reason, and contract and imbitter the Heart, what have they to do with true Religion, unless to destroy it?—That Religion, which improves and enlarges the Faculties of Men, exalts their Spirits, and makes them brave for God and themselves; that Religion, which gives them great and worthy Conceptions of the Deity; and that Religion which inspires them with generous and beneficent Affections to one another, and with universal Love and Benevolence to the whole Creation? No Man can love God, if he love not his Neighbour; and whoever loves his Neighbour, will neither injure, revile, nor oppress him: Nor can we otherwise shew our Love to God, than by kind, humane, and affectionate Actions to his Creatures: *A new Commandment,* says our blessed Saviour, *I give unto you, that ye love one another.*

Almighty God, the great Author of our Nature, and of all Things, who has the Heavens for his Throne, and the Earth for his Footstool, is raised far above the Reach of our Kindness, our Malice, or our Flattery. He derives infinite Happiness from his own infinite Perfections; nor can any frail Power or Actions of ours lessen or improve it: Religion therefore, from which he can reap no Advantage, was instituted by him for the Sake of Men, as the best Means and the strongest Motive to their own Happiness, and mutual Happiness; and by it Men are taught and animated to be useful, assisting, forgiving, kind and merciful one to another. But to hurt, calumniate, or hate one another, for his Sake, and in Defence of any Religion, is a flat Contradiction to *his* Religion, and an open Defiance of the Author of Religion: And to quarrel about Belief and Opinions, which do not immediately and necessarily produce practical Virtue and social Duties, is equally wicked and absurd. This is to be wicked in behalf of Righteousness, and to be cruel out of Piety. A Religion which begets Selfishness and Partiality only to a few, and its own Followers, and which inspires Hatred and Outrage towards all the rest of the World, can never be the Religion of the merciful and impartial Maker and Judge of the World. Speculations are only so far a Part of Religion, as they produce the moral Duties of Religion, general Peace, and unlimited Charity, publick Spirit, Equity, Forbearance, and good Deeds to all Men: And the Worship of God is no longer the Worship of God, than as it warms our Minds with the Remembrance of his gracious Condescensions, his indulgent Care, Bounty, and Providence, exercised towards us; and as it raises and forms our Affections to an Imitation of such his divine and unrestrained Goodness, and to use one another kindly by his great Example, who uses us all so. So that our worthy, tender, and beneficent Behaviour to one another, is the best Way to acknowledge his to us: It is the most acceptable Way that we can worship him, and the Way which he will best accept our Worship: And whatever Devotion has not this Effect, or a contrary Effect, is the dry or mad Freaks of an Enthusiast, and ought to be called by another and a properer Name.

This is a general Idea of true Religion; these are the certain and only Marks of it: All which, as they are opposite to the Essence and Spirit of an arbitrary Government; so every arbitrary Government is an Enemy to the Spirit of true Religion, and defeats its Ends. In these Governments, in Defiance of Religion, Humanity, and common Sense, Millions must be miserable to exalt and embellish One or a Few, and to make them proud, arrogant, and great: Protection and Security are no more; the Spirit of the People is sunk, their Industry discouraged and lost, or only employed to feed Luxury and Pride; and Multitudes starve, that a few may riot and abound. All Love to Mankind is extinct, and Virtue and publick Spirit are dangerous or unknown; while Vice, Falshood, and servile Sycophancy, become necessary to maintain precarious Safety and an ignominious Life: And, in fine, Men live upon the Spoils of one another, like ravenous Fishes and Beasts of Prey: They become rapacious, brutish, and savage to one another, as their cruel Governors are to them all; and, as a further Imitation of such Masters, their Souls are abject, mean, and villainous. To live upon Prey, and worry human Race, is the Genius and Support of Tyrants, as well as of Wolves and Tygers; and it is the Spirit and Practice of Men to resemble their Governors, and to act like them. Virtue and Vice, in Courts, run like Water in a continual Descent, and quickly overflow the inferior Soil.

*Torva Leaena lupum,** &c.

Now, what can be found here to answer the Spirit and Precepts of the Christian Religion, which is all Love, Charity, Meekness, mutual Assistance, and mutual Indulgence; and must either destroy Tyranny, which destroys all these, or be destroyed by it? A Religion given by God, to inspire Men with every social Virtue, and to furnish them with every Argument for social Happiness, will never find Quarter, much less Protection, from a Government, which subsists by an unrelenting War against every Virtue, and all human Felicity. On the contrary, all its divine Doctrines shall be perverted, all its divine Principles mangled, and both its Principles and its Precepts corrupted, disguised, and wrested, to be made free of the Court: Truth will be made to patronize Imposture, and Meekness to support Tyranny: Obedience to equal Laws, and Submission to just Authority, shall be turned into a servile and crouching Subjection to blind Rage and inhuman Fury; complaisant and respective Behaviour into slavish Flattery, and supple Homage to Power; Meekness and Humility into Dejection, Poorness of Spirit, and bodily Prostrations; Charity, Benevolence, and Humanity, into a fiery and outrageous Zeal to propagate fashionable and gainful Opinions: Christian Courage shall be changed into Cruelty and brutish Violence; impartial Justice into savage Severity; Protection into Oppression and Plundering; the Fear of God into the Fear of Man; and the Worship of the Deity into an idolatrous Adoration of a Tyrant.

Though God Almighty sent his only Son into the World to teach his Will to Men, and to confirm his Mission by Wonders and Miracles; yet, having once fully manifested himself and his Law, he has left it to be propagated and carried on by human Means only, according to the Holy Writings inspired by him; and if the Powers of the World will not submit to those Directions, and will neither pursue them themselves, nor suffer their Subjects to pursue them, nor leave them the Means of doing it; then the Christian Religion must take the Fate of all sublunary Things, and be lost from amongst Men, unless Heaven interpose again miraculously in its Favour. Now the Experience of all Ages will convince us, that all tyrannical Princes will be against the Religion which is against them; and either abolish it, or, which is much worse, pervert it into a deadly and unnatural Engine, to increase and defend that Pride and Power, which Christianity abhors; and to promote those Evils and Miseries, which Christianity forbids, and, were it left to itself, would prevent or relieve. A Religion modelled by usurped Power, to countenance Usurpation and Oppression, is as opposite to the Christian Religion, as Tyranny is to Liberty, and Wickedness to Virtue. When Religion is taught to speak Court-Language, and none are suffered to preach it, but such as speak the same Dialect; when those who are Ministers of the Gospel, must be also the Ministers of Ambition, and either sanctify Falshood and Violence, by the Word of Mercy and Truth, or hold their Tongues; when Preferments and worldly Honours are on the Side of Im-

* This refers to Virgil's *Eclogue II*, line 63, which reads: *"Torva leaena lupum sequitur, lupus ipse capellam . . . ,"* or "The cruel lioness pursues the wolf, the wolf himself pursues the she-goat. . . ."—Trans.

posture, and Galleys, Racks and Dungeons, are the Rewards of Conscience and Piety; the Good and Efficacy of Christianity will be as effectually gone, as if it were formally exchanged for *Mahometanism;* and under those Circumstances, if its Name be retained, it is only retained to do Evil, and might be as innocently banished with the Thing.

The Christian Religion has as rarely gained by Courts, as Courts have improved by the Christian Religion; and arbitrary Courts have seldom meddled with it, but either to persecute it, or debase and corrupt it; nor could the Power and Fury of Tyrants ever hurt or weaken it so much, as their pretended Favours and Countenance have done: By appearing for it, they turn their Power most effectually against it. Their avowed Persecution of Christianity, did only destroy Christians; but afterwards, while they set up for protecting none but the true Christians, that is, those that were as bad as themselves, and having no Religion of their own, adopted blindly the Religion of their Prince; and whilst they were for punishing all who were not true Christians, that is, all that were better than themselves, and would take their Religion from no Man's Word, but only from the Word of God; they listed Christians against Christians, and disfigured, and undermined, and banished Christianity itself, by false Friendship to its Professors: And these Professors thus corrupted, joining a holy Title to an impious Cause, concurred in the Conspiracy, and contended fiercely in the Name of Christ for secular Advantages, which Christ never gave nor took, and for a secular Sovereignty, which he rejected, and his Gospel forbids. Thus one Sort of Tyranny was artfully made to support another, and both by a Union of Interests maintained a War against Religion, under Colour of defending it, and fought the Author of it under his own Banner; that is, as Dr. *Tillotson* finely says, *They lied for the Truth, and killed for God's Sake.*

The many various and contradictory Opinions of weak Enthusiasts, or of designing Men, and all the different and repugnant Interpretations of Scripture, published and contended for by them, could have done but small Prejudice to Religion and Society, if human Authority had not interposed with its Penalties and Rewards annexed to the believing or not believing fortuitous Speculations, useless Notions, dry Ideas, and the inconsistent Reveries of disordered Brains; or the selfish Inventions of usurping Popes, ambitious Synods, and turbulent and aspiring Doctors, or the crafty Schemes of discontented or oppressive Statesmen: For all these have been the important Causes, and the wicked Fuel, of religious Wars and Persecutions.

It is so much the general Interest of Society to perform and to encourage all its Members to perform the practical Duties of Religion, that if a stronger and more prevailing Interest were not thrown by Power into the contrary Scale, there would be no Difference amongst Men about the Nature and Extent of their Duties to Magistrates, to Parents, Children, and to Friends and Neighbours: And if these social Duties (the only Duties which human Society, as such, is concerned to promote) were agreed upon and practised, the Magistrate would have no more to do with their Opinions than with their Shape and Complexion; nor could he know, if he would, by what Method to alter them. No Man's Belief is in his own Power, or can be in the Power of another.

The utmost Length that the Power of the Magistrate can in this Matter extend, beyond that of Exhortation, which is in every Man's Power, can be only to make Hypocrites, Slaves, Fools, or Atheists. When he has forced his Subjects to belye their Consciences, or to act against them, he has in Effect driven them out of all Religion, to bring them into his own; and when they thus see and feel the professed Defender of Religion overturning all its Precepts, exhorting by Bribes, rebuking by Stripes, Confiscations and Dungeons, and making Christianity the Instrument of Fury, Ambition, Rapine, and Tyranny; what can they think, but either that he is no Christian, or that Christianity is not true? If they come to suspect it of Imposture, they grow Infidels; if they grow into a Belief that Religion countenances Bitterness, Outrage, and Severities, nay, commands all these, they become

Bigots; the worst and most mischievous Character of the Two: For, Unbelievers, guided by the Rules of Prudence or Good Nature, may be good Neighbours and inoffensive Men; but Bigotry, standing upon the Ruins of Reason, and being conducted by no Light but that of an inflamed Imagination, and a sour, bitter, and narrow Spirit, there is no Violence nor Barbarity which it is not capable of wishing or acting.

Happiness is the chief End of Man, and the saving of his Soul is his chief Happiness; so that every Man is most concerned for his own Soul, and more than any other can be: And if no Obstruction be thrown in his Way, he will for the most part do all in his Power for his own Salvation, and will certainly do it best; and when he has done all that he can, he has done all that he ought: People cannot be saved by Force; nor can all the Powers in the World together make one true Christian, or convince one Man. Conviction is the Province and Effect of Reason; when that fails, nothing but the Grace of God can supply it: And what has the Power and Penalties of Men to do either with Reason or Grace; which being both the Gifts of God, are not to be conquered by Chains, though they may be weakened, and even banished, by worldly Allurements blended with Christianity, and by the worldly Pride of its Professors?

The Methods of Power are repugnant to the Nature of Conviction, which must either be promoted by Exhortation, Kindness, Example, and Arguments, or can never be promoted at all: Violence does, on the contrary, but provoke Men, and confirm them in Error; nor will they ever be brought to believe, that those who barbarously rob them of their present Happiness, can be charitably concerned for their future.

It is evident in Fact, that most of the different religious Institutions now subsisting in the World, have been founded upon Ambition and Pride; and were advanced, propagated, and established, by Usurpation, Faction, and Oppression: They were begun for the most part by Enthusiasts, or by designing and unpreferred Churchmen; or at least occasioned by the continued Usurpations and Insults of cruel and oppressive ones, and always in Times of Faction and general Discontent. Turbulent and aspiring Men, discarded and discontented Courtiers, or ambitious and designing Statesmen, have taken Advantage from these general Disorders, or from the hot and giddy Spirits of an enthusiastical or oppressed People, and from thence have formed Parties; and setting themselves at the Head, formed National Establishments, with the Concurrence of weak Princes, sometimes in Opposition to them, by the Assistance of factious Clergymen and factious Assemblies, often by Tumults and popular Insurrections; and at last, under Pretence of saving Mens Souls, they seized their Property. A small Acquaintance with Ecclesiastical History, and the History of the *Turks* and *Saracens,* will shew such Causes as these to have given Rise to most of the National Religious Establishments upon Earth: Nor can I see how any future one can arise by other Means, whilst Violence and worldly Interest have any thing to do with them.

Such therefore as is the Government of a Country, such will be made its Religion; and no body, I hope, is now to learn what is, and ever will be, the Religion of most Statesmen; even a Religion of Power, to do as little Good and as much Mischief as they please. Nor have Churchmen, when they ruled States, had ever any other View; but having double Authority, had generally double Insolence, and remarkably less Mercy and Regard to Conscience or Property, than others who had fewer Ties to be merciful and just: And therefore the sorest Tyrants have been they, who united in one Person the Royalty and Priesthood. The Pope's Yoke is more grievous than that of any Christian Prince upon Earth; nor is there a Trace of Property, or Felicity, or of the Religion of *Jesus Christ,* found in the Dominions of this Father of *Christendom;* all is Ignorance, Bigotry, Idolatry, Barbarity, Hunger, Chains, and every Species of Misery. The *Caliphs* of *Egypt,* who founded the *Saracen* Empire there, and maintained it for a great while, were at once Kings and Priests; and there never lived more raging Bigots, or more furious and oppressive Barbarians. The Monarchy of *Persia,* which is also a severe Tyranny, has the Priesthood annexed to it; and

the *Sophy* is at the same time the *Caliph*. The *Turkish* Religion is founded on Imposture, blended with outrageous and avowed Violence; and by their Religion, the Imperial Executioner is, next to their *Alcoran,* the most sacred Thing amongst them: And though he be not himself Chief Priest, yet he creates and uncreates him at Pleasure, and is, without the Name of *Mufti,* the Chief Doctor, or rather Author of their Religion; and we all know what Sort of a Religion it is.

In Fact, as arbitrary Princes want a Religion suited to the Genius of their Power, they model their Religion so as to serve all the Purposes of Tyranny; and debase, corrupt, discourage, or persecute all Religion which is against Tyranny, as all true Religion is: For this Reason, not one of the great absolute Princes in *Europe* embraced the *Reformation,* nor would suffer his People to embrace it, but they were all bitter and professed Enemies to it: Whereas all the great free States, except *Poland,* and most of the small free States, became *Protestants.* Thus the *English, Scotch,* the *Dutch,* the *Bohemians,* and *Sweden* and *Denmark,* (which were then free Kingdoms) the greatest Part of *Swisserland,* with *Geneva,* and all the *Hans-Towns,* which were not awed by the Emperor, threw off the *Popish* Yoke: And not one of the free *Popish* States, out of *Italy,* could be ever brought to receive the *Inquisition;* and the State of *Venice,* the greatest free State there, to shew that they received it against their Will, have taken wise Care to render it ineffectual: And many of the *Popish* free States would never come into Persecution, which they knew would impoverish and dispeople them; and therefore the States of *Arragon, Valencia,* and *Catalonia,* opposed, as much as they were able, the Expulsion of the *Moors,* which was a pure Act of Regal Power, to the Undoing of *Spain;* and therefore a destructive and barbarous Act of Tyranny. As to the *Protestant* Countries, which have since lost their Liberties, there is much miserable Ignorance, and much bitter and implacable Bigotry, but little Religion, and no Charity, amongst them.

We look upon *Montezuma,* and other Tyrants, who worshipped God with human Sacrifice, as so many Monsters, and hug ourselves that we have no such Sons of *Moloch* here in *Europe;* not considering, that every Man put to Death for his Religion, by the *Inquisition* and elsewhere, is a real human Sacrifice, as it is burning and butchering Men for God's Sake.

I think no body will deny, but that in King *James's* Time, we owed the Preservation of our Religion to our Liberties, which both our Clergy and People almost unanimously concurred to defend, with a Resolution and Boldness worthy of *Britons* and Freemen. And as the Cause and Blessings of Liberty are still better understood, its Spirit and Interest daily increase. Most of the Bishops, and many of the inferior Clergy, are professedly in the Principles of Civil and Religious Liberty, notwithstanding the strong and early Prejudices of Education. And I hope soon to see them all as thorough Advocates for publick Liberty, as their Predecessors were, upon Grounds less just, in the Times of *Popery;* and then there will be an End of the pernicious and knavish Distinction of *Whig* and *Tory;* and all the World will unite in paying them that Respect which is due to their holy Office.

I shall conclude with this short Application; That as we love Religion, and the Author of it, we ought to love and preserve our Liberties.

G

I am, &c.

The Spirit of the Laws (1748)

MONTESQUIEU (1689–1755)

Charles-Louis de Secondat, the Baron de Montesquieu, a member of the French nobility and, for a time, Parliament, is best known as author of *The Spirit of the Laws.* One of the most cited writers in eighteenth-century American political discourse,

Reprinted from Charles-Louis de Secondat, Baron de Montesquieu, *The Spirit of the Laws,* bk. 25, chaps. 9–12, trans. Thomas Nugent (New York: Hafner Publishing, 1949), 51–54.

Montesquieu was regarded as an authority on separation of powers and the connection between virtue and republican government. The following excerpts concern his views of religious toleration.

Book XXV: Of Laws in Relation to the Establishment of Religion and its External Polity

9. Of Toleration in point of Religion

We are here politicians, and not divines; but the divines themselves must allow that there is a great difference between tolerating and approving a religion.

When the legislator has believed it a duty to permit the exercise of many religions, it is necessary that he should enforce also a toleration among these religions themselves. It is a principle that every religion which is persecuted becomes itself persecuting; for as soon as by some accidental turn it arises from persecution, it attacks the religion which persecuted it; not as religion, but as tyranny.

It is necessary, then, that the laws require from the several religions, not only that they shall not embroil the state, but that they shall not raise disturbances among themselves. A citizen does not fulfil the laws by not disturbing the government; it is requisite that he should not trouble any citizen whomsoever.

10. The same Subject continued

As there are scarcely any but persecuting religions that have an extraordinary zeal for being established in other places (because a religion that can tolerate others seldom thinks of its own propagation), it must, therefore, be a very good civil law, when the state is already satisfied with the established religion, not to suffer the establishment of another.[a]

a. I do not mean to speak in this chapter of the Christian religion; for, as I have elsewhere observed, the Christian religion is our chief blessing. See the end of the preceding chapter, and the "Defence of the Spirit of Laws," part II.

This is then a fundamental principle of the political laws in regard to religion; that when the state is at liberty to receive or to reject a new religion it ought to be rejected; when it is received it ought to be tolerated.

11. Of changing a Religion

A prince who undertakes to destroy or to change the established religion of his kingdom must greatly expose himself. If his government be despotic, he runs a much greater risk of seeing a revolution arise from such a proceeding, than from any tyranny whatsoever, and a revolution is not an uncommon thing in such states. The reason of this is that a state cannot change its religion, manners, and customs in an instant, and with the same rapidity as the prince publishes the ordinance which establishes a new religion.

Besides, the ancient religion is connected with the constitution of the kingdom and the new one is not; the former agrees with the climate and very often the new one is opposed to it. Moreover, the citizens become disgusted with their laws, and look upon the government already established with contempt; they conceive a jealousy against the two religions, instead of a firm belief in one; in a word, these innovations give to the state, at least for some time, both bad citizens and bad believers.

12. Of penal Laws

Penal laws ought to be avoided in respect to religion: they imprint fear, it is true; but as religion has also penal laws which inspire the same passion, the one is effaced by the other, and between these two different kinds of fear the mind becomes hardened.

The threatenings of religion are so terrible, and its promises so great, that when they actuate the mind, whatever efforts the magistrate may use to oblige us to renounce it, he seems to leave us nothing when he deprives us of the exercise of our religion, and to bereave us of nothing when we are allowed to profess it.

It is not, therefore, by filling the soul with the idea of this great object, by hastening her approach to that critical moment in which it ought to be of the highest importance, that religion can be most successfully attacked: a more certain way is, to tempt her by favors, by the conveniences of life, by hopes of fortune; not by that which revives, but by that which extinguishes the sense of her duty; not by that which shocks her, but by that which throws her into indifference at the time when other passions actuate the mind, and those which religion inspires are hushed into silence. As a general rule in changing a religion the invitations should be much stronger than the penalties.

The temper of the human mind has appeared even in the nature of punishments. If we take a survey of the persecutions in Japan,[b] we shall find that they were more shocked at cruel torments than at long sufferings, which rather weary than affright, which are the more difficult to surmount, from their appearing less difficult.

In a word, history sufficiently informs us that penal laws have never had any other effect than to destroy.

Sir William Blackstone. © Bettmann/CORBIS.

Commentaries on the Laws of England (1769)

WILLIAM BLACKSTONE (1723–80)

Blackstone was a lecturer on English law at the University of Oxford. His magisterial *Commentaries on the Laws of England* (4 vols., 1765–69) provided a thorough synthesis of British common law at the time. The *Commentaries* were enormously influential among American jurists.

b. In the "Collection of Voyages that contributed to the establishment of an East India Company," vol. v.

Reprinted from William Blackstone, *Commentaries on the Laws of England*, bk. 4, chap. 4 (Chicago: University of Chicago Press, 1979), 4:41–65.

The fourth volume of Blackstone's *Commentaries* examined "public wrongs," and the fourth chapter of this volume specifically considered "Offenses against God and Religion." This chapter is reprinted in its entirety.

Chapter the Fourth
Of Offences against God and Religion

I N the present chapter we are to enter upon the detail of the several species of crimes and misdemeanors, with the punishment annexed to each by the laws of England. It was observed, in the beginning of this book[a], that crimes and misdemeanors are a breach

a. See pag. 5.

COMMENTARIES

ON THE

LAWS

OF

ENGLAND.

IN FOUR BOOKS.

BY

Sir WILLIAM BLACKSTONE, Knt.
ONE OF HIS MAJESTY's JUDGES OF THE COURT OF COMMON PLEAS.

RE-PRINTED from the BRITISH COPY, PAGE for PAGE with the LAST EDITION.

AMERICA:

PRINTED for the SUBSCRIBERS,

By ROBERT BELL, at the late UNION LIBRARY, in *Third-street,*

PHILADELPHIA. MDCCLXXI.

Title page of *Commentaries on the Laws of England,* by William Blackstone, 1771.

and violation of the public rights and duties, owing to the whole community, considered as a community, in it's social aggregate capacity. And in the very entrance of these commentaries[b] it was shewn, that human laws can have no concern with any but social and relative duties; being intended only to regulate the conduct of man, considered under various relations, as a member of civil society. All crimes ought therefore to be estimated merely according to the mischiefs which they produce in civil society[c]: and, of consequence, private vices, or the breach of mere absolute duties, which man is bound to perform considered only as an individual, are not, cannot be, the object of any municipal law; any farther than as by their evil example, or other pernicious effects, they may prejudice the community, and thereby become a species of public crimes. Thus the vice of drunkenness, if committed privately and alone, is beyond the knowlege and of course beyond the reach of human tribunals: but if committed publicly, in the face of the world, it's evil example makes it liable to temporal censures. The vice of lying, which consists (abstractedly taken) in a criminal violation of truth, and therefore in any shape is derogatory from sound morality, is not however taken notice of by our law, unless it carries with it some public inconvenience, as spreading false news; or some social injury, as slander and malicious prosecution, for which a private recompence is given. And yet drunkenness and lying are *in foro conscientiae* as thoroughly criminal when they are not, as when they are, attended with public inconvenience. The only difference is, that both public and private vices are subject to the vengeance of eternal justice; and public vices are besides liable to the temporal punishments of human tribunals.

ON the other hand, there are some misdemeanors, which are punished by the municipal law, that are in themselves nothing criminal, but are made so by the positive constitutions of the state for public conve-

nience. Such as poaching, exportation of wool, and the like. These are naturally no offences at all; but their whole criminality consists in their disobedience to the supreme power, which has an undoubted right for the well-being and peace of the community to make some things unlawful, which were in themselves indifferent. Upon the whole therefore, though part of the offences to be enumerated in the following sheets are offences against the revealed law of God, others against the law of nature, and some are offences against neither; yet in a treatise of municipal law we must consider them all as deriving their particular guilt, here punishable, from the law of man.

HAVING premised this caution, I shall next proceed to distribute the several offences, which are either directly or by consequence injurious to civil society, and therefore punishable by the laws of England, under the following general heads: first, those which are more immediately injurious to God and his holy religion; secondly, such as violate and transgress the law of nations; thirdly, such as more especially affect the sovereign executive power of the state, or the king and his government; fourthly, such as more directly infringe the rights of the public or common wealth; and, lastly, such as derogate from those rights and duties, which are owing to particular individuals, and in the preservation and vindication of which the community is deeply interested.

FIRST then, of such crimes and misdemesnors, as more immediately offend Almighty God, by openly transgressing the precepts of religion either natural or revealed; and mediately, by their bad example and consequence, the law of society also; which constitutes that guilt in the action, which human tribunals are to censure.

I. Of this species the first is that of *apostacy*, or a total renunciation of christianity, by embracing either a false religion, or no religion at all. This offence can only take place in such as have once professed the true religion. The perversion of a christian to judaism, paganism, or other false religion, was punished by the emperors Constantius and Julian with confiscation of

b. See Vol. I. pag. 123, 124.
c. Beccar. ch. 8.

goods[d]; to which the emperors Theodosius and Valennian added capital punishment, in case the apostate endeavoured to pervert others to the same iniquity[e]. A punishment too severe for any temporal laws to inflict: and yet the zeal of our ancestors imported it into this country; for we find by Bracton[f], that in his time apostates were to be burnt to death. Doubtless the preservation of christianity, as a national religion, is, abstracted from it's own intrinsic truth, of the utmost consequence to the civil state: which a single instance will sufficiently demonstrate. The belief of a future state of rewards and punishments, the entertaining just ideas of the moral attributes of the supreme being, and a firm persuasion that he superintends and will finally compensate every action in human life (all which are clearly revealed in the doctrines, and forcibly inculcated by the precepts, of our saviour Christ) these are the grand foundation of all judicial oaths; which call God to witness the truth of those facts, which perhaps may be only known to him and the party attesting: all moral evidence therefore, all confidence in human veracity, must be weakened by irreligion, and overthrown by infidelity. Wherefore all affronts to christianity, or endeavours to depreciate it's efficacy, are highly deserving of human punishment. But yet the loss of life is a heavier penalty than the offence, taken in a civil light, deserves: and, taken in a spiritual light, our laws have no jurisdiction over it. This punishment therefore has long ago become obsolete; and the offence of apostacy was for a long time the object only of the ecclesiastical courts, which corrected the offender *pro salute animae* [for the salvation (or health) of the soul]. But about the close of the last century, the civil liberties to which we were then restored being used as a cloke of maliciousness, and the most horrid doctrines subversive of all religion being publicly avowed both in discourse and writings, it was found necessary again for the civil power to interpose, by not admitting those miscreants[g] to the privileges of society, who maintained such principles as destroyed all moral obligation. To this end it was enacted by statute 9 & 10 W. III. c.32. that if any person educated in, or having made profession of, the christian religion, shall by writing, printing, teaching, or advised speaking, deny the christian religion to be true, or the holy scriptures to be of divine authority, he shall upon the first offence be rendered incapable to hold any office or place of trust; and, for the second, be rendered incapable of bringing any action, being guardian, executor, legatee, or purchaser of lands, and shall suffer three years imprisonment without bail. To give room however for repentance; if, within four months after the first conviction, the delinquent will in open court publicly renounce his error, he is discharged for that once from all disabilities.

II. A second offence is that of *heresy;* which consists not in a total denial of christianity, but of some of it's essential doctrines, publicly and obstinately avowed; being defined, "*sententia rerum divinarum humano sensu excogitata, palam docta, et pertinaciter defensa*[h]." And here it must also be acknowledged that particular modes of belief or unbelief, not tending to overturn christianity itself, or to sap the foundations of morality, are by no means the object of coercion by the civil magistrate. What doctrines shall therefore be adjudged heresy, was left by our old constitution to the determination of the ecclesiastical judge; who had herein a most arbitrary latitude allowed him. For the general definition of an heretic given by Lyndewode[i], extends to the smallest deviations from the doctrines of holy church: "*haereticus est qui dubitat de fide catholica, et qui negligit servare ea, quae Romana ecclesia statuit, seu servare decreverat.*"* Or, as the statute 2 Hen. IV. c. 15. expresses it

---

* [a heretic is one who doubts the catholic faith and who neglects preserving those things which the Roman church has established or decreed to preserve.]

g. *Mescroyantz* in our antient law-books is the name of unbelievers.

h. 1 Hal. P. C. 384 [an opinion concerning divine matters which has been invented by human understanding, taught openly, and defended obstinately].

i. *cap. de haereticis.*

d. *Cod.* 1. 7. 1.

e. *Ibid.* 6.

f. *l.* 3. *c.* 9.

in English, "teachers of erroneous opinions, contrary to the faith and blessed determinations of the holy church." Very contrary this to the usage of the first general councils, which defined all heretical doctrines with the utmost precision and exactness. And what ought to have alleviated the punishment, the uncertainty of the crime, seems to have enhanced it in those days of blind zeal and pious cruelty. It is true, that the sanctimonious hypocrisy of the canonists went at first no farther than enjoining penance, excommunication, and ecclesiastical deprivation, for heresy; though afterwards they proceeded boldly to imprisonment by the ordinary, and confiscation of goods *in pios usus* [for pious uses]. But in the mean time they had prevailed upon the weakness of bigotted princes to make the civil power subservient to their purposes, by making heresy not only a temporal, but even a capital offence: the Romish ecclesiastics determining, without appeal, whatever they pleased to be heresy, and shifting off to the secular arm the odium and drudgery of executions; with which they themselves were too tender and delicate to intermeddle. Nay they pretended to intercede and pray, on behalf of the convicted heretic, *ut citra mortis periculum sententia circa eum moderetur*[k]: well knowing at the same time that they were delivering the unhappy victim to certain death. Hence the capital punishments inflicted on the antient Donatists and Manichaeans by the emperors Theodosius and Justinian[l]: hence also the constitution of the emperor Frederic mentioned by Lyndewode[m], adjudging all persons without distinction to be burnt with fire, who were convicted of heresy by the ecclesiastical judge. The same emperor, in another constitution[n], ordained that if any temporal lord, when admonished by the church, should neglect to clear his territories of heretics within a year, it should be lawful for good catholics to seise and occupy the lands, and utterly to exterminate the heret-

ical possessors. And upon this foundation was built that arbitrary power, so long claimed and so fatally exerted by the pope, of disposing even of the kingdoms of refractory princes to more dutiful sons of the church. The immediate event of this constitution was something singular, and may serve to illustrate at once the gratitude of the holy see, and the just punishment of the royal bigot: for upon the authority of this very constitution, the pope afterwards expelled this very emperor Frederic from his kingdom of Sicily, and gave it to Charles of Anjou[o].

Christianity being thus deformed by the daemon of persecution upon the continent, we cannot expect that our own island should be entirely free from the same scourge. And therefore we find among our antient precedents[p] a writ *de haeretico comburendo* [that heretics ought to be burned], which is thought by some to be as antient as the common law itself. However it appears from thence, that the conviction of heresy by the common law was not in any petty ecclesiastical court, but before the archbishop himself in a provincial synod; and that the delinquent was delivered over to the king to do as he should please with him: so that the crown had a control over the spiritual power, and might pardon the convict by issuing no process against him; the writ *de haeretico comburendo* being not a writ of course, but issuing only by the special direction of the king in council[q].

But in the reign of Henry the fourth, when the eyes of the christian world began to open, and the seeds of the protestant religion (though under the opprobrious name of lollardy[r]) took root in this kingdom; the clergy, taking advantage from the king's dubious title to demand an increase of their own power, obtained an act of parliament[s], which sharpened the

k. *Decretal. l.* 5. *t.* 40. *c.* 27 [so that on the near side of the danger of death, the sentence concerning him may be moderated].

l. *Cod. l.* 1. *tit.* 5.

m. *c. de haereticis.*

n. *Cod.* 1. 5. 4.

o. Baldus *in Cod.* 1. 5. 4.

p. F. N. B. 269.

q. 1 Hal. P. C. 395.

r. So called not from *lolium,* or tares, (which was afterwards devised, in order to justify the burning of them from Matth. xiii. 30.) but from one Walter Lolhard, German reformer. Mod. Un. Hist. xxvi. 1, 13 Spelm. *Gloss.* 371.

s. 2 Hen. IV. c. 15.

edge of persecution to it's utmost keenness. For, by that statute, the diocesan alone, without the intervention of a synod, might convict of heretical tenets; and unless the convict abjured his opinions, or if after abjuration he relapsed, the sheriff was bound *ex officio*, if required by the bishop, to commit the unhappy victim to the flames, without waiting for the consent of the crown. By the statute 2 Hen. V. c. 7. lollardy was also made a temporal offence, and indictable in the king's courts; which did not thereby gain an exclusive, but only a concurrent jurisdiction with the bishop's consistory.

AFTERWARDS, when the final reformation of religion began to advance, the power of the ecclesiastics was somewhat moderated: for though what heresy *is,* was not then precisely defined, yet we are told in some points what it *is not:* the statute 25 Hen. VIII. c. 14. declaring, that offences against the see of Rome are not heresy; and the ordinary being thereby restrained from proceeding in any case upon mere suspicion; that is, unless the party be accused by two credible witnesses, or an indictment of heresy be first previously found in the king's courts of common law. And yet the spirit of persecution was not then abated, but only diverted into a lay chanel. For in six years afterwards, by statute 31 Hen. VIII. c. 14. the bloody law of the six articles was made, which established the six most contested points of popery, transubstantiation, communion in one kind, the celibacy of the clergy, monastic vows, the sacrifice of the mass, and auricular confession; which points were "determined and resolved by the most godly study, pain, and travail of his majesty: for which his most humble and obedient subjects, the lords *spiritual* and temporal and the commons, in parliament assembled, did not only render and give unto his highness their most high and hearty thanks," but did also enact and declare all oppugners of the first to be heretics, and to be burnt with fire; and of the five last to be felons, and to suffer death. The same statute established a new and mixed jurisdiction of clergy and laity for the trial and conviction of heretics; the reigning prince being then equally intent on destroying the supremacy of the

bishops of Rome, and establishing all other their corruptions of the christian religion.

I SHALL not perplex this detail with the various repeals and revivals of these sanguinary laws in the two succeeding reigns; but shall proceed directly to the reign of queen Elizabeth; when the reformation was finally established with temper and decency, unsullied with party rancour, or personal caprice and resentment. By statute 1 Eliz. c. 1. all former statutes relating to heresy are repealed, which leaves the jurisdiction of heresy as it stood at common law; *viz.* as to the infliction of common censures, in the ecclesiastical courts; and, in case of burning the heretic, in the provincial synod only[t]. Sir Matthew Hale is indeed of a different opinion, and holds that such power resided in the diocesan also; though he agrees, that in either case the writ *de haeretico comburendo* was not demandable of common right, but grantable or otherwise merely at the king's discretion[u]. But the principal point now gained, was, that by this statute a boundary is for the first time set to what shall be accounted heresy; nothing for the future being to be so determined, but only such tenets, which have been heretofore so declared, 1. By the words of the canonical scriptures; 2. By the first four general councils, or such others as have only used the words of the holy scriptures; or, 3. Which shall hereafter be so declared by the parliament, with the assent of the clergy in convocation. Thus was heresy reduced to a greater certainty than before; though it might not have been the worse to have defined it in terms still more precise and particular: as a man continued still liable to be burnt, for what perhaps he did not understand to be heresy, till the ecclesiastical judge so interpreted the words of the canonical scriptures.

FOR the writ *de haeretico comburendo* remained still in force and we have instances of it's being put in execution upon two anabaptists in the seventeenth of Elizabeth, and two Arians in the ninth of James the first. But it was totally abolished, and heresy again

t. 5 Rep. 23. 12 Rep. 56 92.
u. 1 Hal. P. C. 405.

subjected only to ecclesiastical correction, *pro salute animae,* by virtue of the statute 29 Car. II. c. 9. For in one and the same reign, our lands were delivered from the slavery of military tenures; our bodies from arbitrary imprisonment by the *habeas corpus* act; and our minds from the tyranny of superstitious bigotry, by demolishing this last badge of persecution in the English law.

In what I have now said I would not be understood to derogate from the just rights of the national church, or to favour loose latitude of propagating any crude undigested sentiments in religious matters. Of propagating, I say; for the bare entertaining them, without an endeavour to diffuse them, seem hardly cognizable by any human authority. I only mean to illustrate the excellence of our present establishment, by looking back to former times. Every thing is now as it should be: unless perhaps that heresy ought to be more strictly defined, and no prosecution permitted, even in the ecclesiastical courts, till the tenets in question are by proper authority previously declared to be heretical. Under these restrictions, it seems necessary for the support of the national religion, that the officers of the church should have power to censure heretics, but not to exterminate or destroy them. It has also been thought proper for the civil magistrate again to interpose, with regard to one species of heresy, very prevalent in modern times: for by statute 9 & 10 W. III. c. 32. if any person educated in the christian religion, or professing the same, shall by writing, printing, teaching, or advised speaking, deny any one of the persons in the holy trinity to be God, or maintain that there are more Gods than one, he shall undergo the same penalties and incapacities, which were just now mentioned to be inflicted on apostacy by the same statute. And thus much for the crime of heresy.

III. Another species of offences against religion are those which affect the *established church.* And these are either positive, or negative. Positive, as by reviling it's ordinances: or negative, by non-conformity to it's worship. Of both of these in their order.

1. And, first, of the offence of *reviling the ordinances* of the church. This is a crime of a much grosser nature than the other of mere non-conformity: since it carries with it the utmost indecency, arrogance, and ingratitude: indecency, by setting up private judgment in opposition to public; arrogance, by treating with contempt and rudeness what has at least a better chance to be right, than the singular notions of any particular man; and ingratitude, by denying that indulgence and liberty of conscience to the members of the national church, which the retainers to every petty conventicle enjoy. However it is provided by statutes 1 Edw. VI. c. 1. and 1 Eliz. c. 1. that whoever reviles the sacrament of the lord's supper shall be punished by fine and imprisonment: and by the statute 1 Eliz. c. 2. if any *minister* shall speak any thing in derogation of the book of common prayer, he shall be imprisoned six months, and forfeit a year's value of his benefice; and for the second offence he shall be deprived. And if *any person* whatsoever shall in plays, songs, or other open words, speak any thing in derogation, depraving, or despising of the said book, he shall forfeit for the first offence an hundred marks; for the second four hundred; and for the third shall forfeit all his goods and chattels, and suffer imprisonment for life. These penalties were framed in the infancy of our present establishment; when the disciples of Rome and of Geneva united in inveighing with the utmost bitterness against the English liturgy: and the terror of these laws (for they seldom, if ever, were fully executed) proved a principal means, under providence, of preserving the purity as well as decency of our national worship. Nor can their continuance to this time be thought too severe and intolerant; when we consider, that they are levelled at an offence, to which men cannot now be prompted by any laudable motive; not even by a mistaken zeal for reformation: since from political reasons, sufficiently hinted at in a former volume[v], it would now be extremely unadvisable to make any alterations in the service of the church; unless it could be shewn that some manifest impiety or shocking absurdity would follow from continuing it in it's present form. And therefore the

v. Vol. I. pag. 98.

virulent declamations of peevish or opinionated men on topics so often refuted, and of which the preface to the liturgy is itself a perpetual refutation, can be calculated for no other purpose, than merely to disturb the consciences, and poison the minds of the people.

2. NON-CONFORMITY to the worship of the church is the other, or negative branch of this offence. And for this there is much more to be pleaded than for the former; being a matter of private conscience, to the scruples of which our present laws have shewn a very just and christian indulgence. For undoubtedly all persecution and oppression of weak consciences, on the score of religious persuasions, are highly unjustifiable upon every principle of natural reason, civil liberty, or sound religion. But care must be taken not to carry this indulgence into such extremes, as may endanger the national church: there is always a difference to be made between toleration and establishment.

NON-CONFORMISTS are of two sorts: first, such as absent themselves from the divine worship in the established church, through total irreligion, and attend the service of no other persuasion. These by the statutes of 1 Eliz. c. 2. 23 Eliz. c. 1. and 3 Jac. I. c. 4. forfeit one shilling to the poor every lord's day they so absent themselves, and 20 *l.* to the king if they continue such default for a month together. And if they keep any inmate, thus irreligiously disposed, in their houses, they forfeit 10 *l. per* month.

THE second species of non-conformists are those who offend through a mistaken or perverse zeal. Such were esteemed by our laws, enacted since the time of the reformation, to be papists and protestant dissenters: both of which were supposed to be equally schismatics in departing from the national church; with this difference, that the papists divide from us upon material, though erroneous, reasons; but many of the dissenters upon matters of indifference, or, in other words, upon no reason at all. However the laws against the former are much more severe than against the latter; the principles of the papists being deservedly looked upon to be subversive of the civil government, but not those of the protestant dissenters. As

to the papists, their tenets are undoubtedly calculated for the introduction of all slavery, both civil and religious: but it may with justice be questioned, whether the spirit, the doctrines, and the practice of the sectaries are better calculated to make men good subjects. One thing is obvious to observe, that these have once within the compass of the last century, effected the ruin of our church and monarchy; which the papists have attempted indeed, but have never yet been able to execute. Yet certainly our ancestors were mistaken in their plans of compulsion and intolerance. The sin of schism, as such, is by no means the object of temporal coercion and punishment. If through weakness of intellect, through misdirected piety, through perverseness and acerbity of temper, or (which is often the case) through a prospect of secular advantage in herding with a party, men quarrel with the ecclesiastical establishment, the civil magistrate has nothing to do with it; unless their tenets and practice are such as threaten ruin or disturbance to the state. He is bound indeed to protect the established church, by admitting none but it's genuine members to offices of trust and emolument: for, if every sect was to be indulged in a free communion of civil employments, the idea of a national establishment would at once be destroyed, and the episcopal church would be no longer the church of England. But, this point being once secured, all persecution for diversity of opinions, however ridiculous or absurd they may be, is contrary to every principle of sound policy and civil freedom. The names and subordination of the clergy, the posture of devotion, the materials and colour of the minister's garment, the joining in a known or an unknown form of prayer, and other matters of the same kind, must be left to the option of every man's private judgment.

WITH regard therefore to *protestant dissenters,* although the experience of their turbulent disposition in former times occasioned several disabilities and restrictions (which I shall not undertake to justify) to be laid upon them by abundance of statutes[w], yet at

w. 31 Eliz. c. 1. 17 Car. II. c. 2. 22 Car. II. c. 1.

length the legislature, with a spirit of true magnanimity, extended that indulgence to these sectaries, which they themselves, when in power, had held to be countenancing schism, and denied to the church of England. The penalties are all of them suspended by the statute 1 W. & M. st. 2. c. 18. commonly called the toleration act; which exempts all dissenters (except papists, and such as deny the trinity) from all penal laws relating to religion, provided they take the oaths of allegiance and supremacy, and subscribe the declaration against popery, and repair to some congregation registered in the bishop's court or at the sessions, the doors whereof must be always open: and dissenting teachers are also to subscribe the thirty nine articles, except those relating to church government and infant baptism. Thus are all persons, who will approve themselves no papists or oppugners of the trinity, left at full liberty to act as their conscience shall direct them, in the matter of religious worship. But by statute 5 Geo. I. c. 4. no mayor, or principal magistrate, must appear at any dissenting meeting with the ensigns of his office[x], on pain of disability to hold that or any other office: the legislature judging it a matter of propriety, that a mode of worship, set up in opposition to the national, when allowed to be exercised in peace, should be exercised also with decency, gratitude, and humility.

As to *papists*, what has been said of the protestant dissenters would hold equally strong for a general toleration of them; provided their separation was founded only upon difference of opinion in religion, and their principles did not also extend to a subversion of the civil government. If once they could be brought to renounce the supremacy of the pope, they might quietly enjoy their seven sacraments, their purgatory, and auricular confession; their worship of reliques and images; nay even their transubstantiation. But while they acknowledge a foreign power, superior to the sovereignty of the kingdom, they cannot com-

plain if the laws of that kingdom will not treat them upon the footing of good subjects.

Let us therefore now take a view of the laws in force against the papists; who may be divided into three classes, persons professing popery, popish recusants convict, and popish priests. 1. Persons professing the popish religion, besides the former penalties for not frequenting their parish church, are by several statutes, too numerous to be here recited[y], disabled from taking any lands either by descent or purchase, after eighteen years of age, until they renounce their errors; they must at the age of twenty one register their estates before acquired, and all future conveyances and wills relating to them; they are incapable of presenting to any advowson, or granting to any other person any avoidance of the same, in prejudice of the two universities; they may not keep or teach any school under pain of perpetual imprisonment; they are liable also in some instances to pay double taxes; and, if they willingly say or hear mass, they forfeit the one two hundred, the other one hundred marks, and each shall suffer a year's imprisonment. Thus much for persons, who, from the misfortune of family prejudices or otherwise, have conceived an unhappy attachment to the Romish church from their infancy, and publicly profess it's errors. But if any evil industry is used to rivet these errors upon them, if any person sends another abroad to be educated in the popish religion, or to reside in any religious house abroad for that purpose, or contributes any thing to their maintenance when there; both the sender, the sent, and the contributor, are disabled to sue in law or equity, to be executor or administrator to any person, to take any legacy or deed of gift, and to bear any office in the realm, and shall forfeit all their goods and chattels, and likewise all their real estate for life. And where these errors are also aggravated by apostacy, or perversion, where a person is reconciled to the see of Rome or procures others to be reconciled, the offence amounts to high treason. 2. Popish recusants, convicted in a court of law of not attending the service

x. Sir Humphrey Edwin, a lord mayor of London, had the imprudence soon after the toleration-act to go to a presbyterian meeting-house in his formalities: which is alluded to by dean Swift, in his *tale of a tub*, under the allegory of *Jack* getting on a great horse, and eating custard.

y. See Hawkins's pleas of the crown, and Burn's justice.

of the church of England, are subject to the following disabilities, penalties, and forfeitures, over and above those before-mentioned. They can hold no office or employment; they must not keep arms in their houses, but the same may be seised by the justices of the peace; they may not come within ten miles of London, on pain of 100 *l*; they can bring no action at law, or suit in equity; they are not permitted to travel above five miles from home, unless by licence, upon pain of forfeiting all their goods; and they may not come to court, under pain of 100 *l*. No marriage or burial of such recusant, or baptism of his child, shall be had otherwise than by the ministers of the church of England, under other severe penalties. A married woman, when recusant, shall forfeit two thirds of her dower or jointure, may not be executrix or administratrix to her husband, nor have any part of his goods; and during the coverture may be kept in prison, unless her husband redeems her at the rate of 10 *l*. a month, or the third part of all his lands. And, lastly, as a feme-covert recusant may be imprisoned, so all others must, within three months after conviction, either submit and renounce their errors, or, if required so to do by four justices, must abjure and renounce the realm: and if they do not depart, or if they return without the king's licence, they shall be guilty of felony, and suffer death as felons. There is also an inferior species of recusancy, (refusing to make the declaration against popery enjoined by statute 30 Car. II. st. 2. when tendered by the proper magistrate) which, if the party resides within ten miles of London, makes him an absolute recusant convict; or, if at a greater distance, suspends him from having any seat in parliament, keeping arms in his house, or any horse above the value of five pounds. This is the state, by the laws now in being, of a lay papist. But, 3. The remaining species or degree, *viz.* popish priests, are in a still more dangerous condition. By statute 11 & 12 W. III. c. 4. popish priests or bishops, celebrating mass or exercising any parts of their functions in England, except in the houses of embassadors, are liable to perpetual imprisonment. And by the statute 27 Eliz. c. 2. any popish priest, born in the dominions of the crown of England, who shall come over hither from beyond sea, or shall be in England three days without conforming and taking the oaths, is guilty of high treason: and all persons harbouring him are guilty of felony without the benefit of clergy.

THIS is a short summary of the laws against the papists, under their three several classes, of persons professing the popish religion, popish recusants convict, and popish priests. Of which the president Montesquieu observes[z], that they are so rigorous, though not professedly of the sanguinary kind, that they do all the hurt that can possibly be done in cold blood. But in answer to this it may be observed, (what foreigners who only judge from our statute book are not fully apprized of) that these laws are seldom exerted to their utmost rigor: and indeed, if they were, it would be very difficult to excuse them. For they are rather to be accounted for from their history, and the urgency of the times which produced them, than to be approved (upon a cool review) as a standing system of law. The restless machinations of the jesuits during the reign of Elizabeth, the turbulence and uneasiness of the papists under the new religious establishment, and the boldness of their hopes and wishes for the succession of the queen of Scots, obliged the parliament to counteract so dangerous a spirit by laws of a great, and perhaps necessary, severity. The powder-treason, in the succeeding reign, struck a panic into James I, which operated in different ways: it occasioned the enacting of new laws against the papists; but deterred him from putting them in execution. The intrigues of queen Henrietta in the reign of Charles I, the prospect of a popish successor in that of Charles II, the assassination-plot in the reign of king William, and the avowed claim of a popish pretender to the crown, will account for the extension of these penalties at those several periods of our history. But if a time should ever arrive, and perhaps it is not very distant, when all fears of a pretender shall have vanished, and the power and influence of the pope shall become feeble, ridiculous, and despicable, not

z. Sp. L. b. 19. c. 27.

only in England but in every kingdom of Europe; it probably would not then be amiss to review and soften these rigorous edicts; at least till the *civil* principles of the roman-catholics called again upon the legislature to renew them: for it ought not to be left in the breast of every merciless bigot, to drag down the vengeance of these occasional laws upon inoffensive, though mistaken, subjects; in opposition to the lenient inclinations of the civil magistrate, and to the destruction of every principle of toleration and religious liberty.

IN order the better to secure the established church against perils from non-conformists of all denominations, infidels, turks, jews, heretics, papists, and sectaries, there are however two bulwarks erected; called the *corporation* and *test* acts: by the former of which[a] no person can be legally elected to any office relating to the government of any city or corporation, unless, within a twelvemonth before, he has received the sacrament of the lord's supper according to the rites of the church of England: and he is also enjoined to take the oaths of allegiance and supremacy at the same time that he takes the oath of office: or, in default of either of these requisites, such election shall be void. The other, called the test act[b], directs all officers civil and military to take the oaths and make the declaration against transubstantiation, in the court of king's bench or chancery, the next term, or at the next quarter sessions, or (by subsequent statutes) within six months, after their admission; and also within the same time to receive the sacrament of the lord's supper, according to the usage of the church of England, in some public church immediately after divine service and sermon, and to deliver into court a certificate thereof signed by the minister and church-warden, and also to prove the same by two credible witnesses; upon forfeiture of 500 *l*, and disability to hold the said office. And of much the same nature with these is the statute 7 Jac. I. c. 2. which permits no persons to be naturalized or restored in blood, but

such as undergo a like test: which test having been removed in 1753, in favour of the Jews, was the next session of parliament restored again with some precipitation.

THUS much for offences, which strike at our national religion, or the doctrine and discipline of the church of England in particular. I proceed now to consider some gross impieties and general immoralities, which are taken notice of and punished by our municipal law; frequently in concurrence with the ecclesiastical, to which the censure of many of them does also of right appertain; though with a view somewhat different: the spiritual court punishing all sinful enormities for the sake of reforming the private sinner, *pro salute animae;* while the temporal courts resent the public affront to religion and morality, on which all government must depend for support, and correct more for the sake of example than private amendment.

IV. THE fourth species of offences therefore, more immediately against God and religion, is that of *blasphemy* against the Almighty, by denying his being or providence; or by contumelious reproaches of our Saviour Christ. Whither also may be referred all profane scoffing at the holy scripture, or exposing it to contempt and ridicule. These are offences punishable at common law by fine and imprisonment, or other infamous corporal punishment[c]: for christianity is part of the laws of England[d].

V. SOMEWHAT allied to this, though in an inferior degree, is the offence of profane and common *swearing* and *cursing*. By the last statute against which, 19 Geo. II. c. 21. which repeals all former ones, every labourer, sailor, or soldier shall forfeit 1 *s.* for every profane oath or curse, every other person under the degree of a gentleman 2 *s.* and every gentleman or person of superior rank 5 *s.* to the poor of the parish; and, on a second conviction, double; and, for every subsequent conviction, treble the sum first forfeited; with all charges of conviction: and in default of pay-

a. Stat. 13 Car. II. st. 2. c. 1.
b. Stat. 25 Car. II. c. 2.

c. 1 Hawk. P. C. 7.
d. 1 Ventr. 293. 2 Strange, 834.

ment shall be sent to the house of correction for ten days. Any justice of the peace may convict upon his own hearing, or the testimony of one witness; and any constable or peace officer, upon his own hearing, may secure any offender and carry him before a justice, and there convict him. If the justice omits his duty, he forfeits 5 *l*, and the constable 40 *s*. And the act is to be read in all parish churches, and public chapels, the sunday after every quarter day, on pain of 5 *l*. to be levied by warrant from any justice. Besides this punishment for taking God's name in vain in common discourse, it is enacted by statute 3 Jac. I. c. 21. that if in any stage play, interlude, or shew, the name of the holy trinity, or any of the persons therein, be jestingly or profanely used, the offender shall forfeit 10 *l*, one moiety to the king, and the other to the informer.

VI. A sixth species of offences against God and religion, of which our antient books are full, is a crime of which one knows not well what account to give. I mean the offence of *witchcraft, conjuration, inchantment,* or *sorcery*. To deny the possibility, nay, actual existence, of witchcraft and sorcery, is at once flatly to contradict the revealed word of God, in various passages both of the old and new testament: and the thing itself is a truth to which every nation in the world hath in it's turn borne testimony, by either examples seemingly well attested, or prohibitory laws, which at least suppose the possibility of a commerce with evil spirits. The civil law punishes with death not only the sorcerers themselves, but also those who consult them[e]; imitating in the former the express law of God[f], "thou shalt not suffer a witch to live." And our own laws, both before and since the conquest, have been equally penal; ranking this crime in the same class with heresy, and condemning both to the flames[g]. The president Montesquieu[h] ranks them also both together, but with a very different view: laying it down as an important maxim, that we ought to

be very circumspect in the prosecution of magic and heresy; because the most unexceptionable conduct, the purest morals, and the constant practice of every duty in life, are not a sufficient security against the suspicion of crimes like these. And indeed the ridiculous stories that are generally told, and the many impostures and delusions that have been discovered in all ages, are enough to demolish all faith in such a dubious crime; if the contrary evidence were not also extremely strong. Wherefore it seems to be the most eligible way to conclude, with an ingenious writer of our own[i], that in general there has been such a thing as witchcraft; though one cannot give credit to any particular modern instance of it.

Our forefathers were stronger believers, when they enacted by statute 33 Hen. VIII. c. 8. all witchcraft and sorcery to be felony without benefit of clergy; and again by statute 1 Jac. I. c. 12. that all persons invoking any evil spirit, or consulting, covenanting with, entertaining, employing, feeding, or rewarding any evil spirit; or taking up dead bodies from their graves to be used in any witchcraft, sorcery, charm, or inchantment; or killing or otherwise hurting any person by such infernal arts; should be guilty of felony without benefit of clergy, and suffer death. And, if any person should attempt by sorcery to discover hidden treasure, or to restore stolen goods, or to provoke unlawful love, or to hurt any man or beast, though the same were not effected, he or she should suffer imprisonment and pillory for the first offence, and death for the second. These acts continued in force till lately, to the terror of all antient females in the kingdom: and many poor wretches were sacrificed thereby to the prejudice of their neighbours, and their own illusions; not a few having, by some means or other, confessed the fact at the gallows. But all executions for this dubious crime are now at an end; our legislature having at length followed the wise example of Louis XIV in France, who thought proper by an edict to restrain the tribunals of justice from re-

e. *Cod. l. 9. t.* 18.

f. Exod. xxii. 18.

g. 3 Inst. 44.

h. Sp. L. b. 12. c. 5.

i. Mr Addison, Spect. No 117.

ceiving informations of witchcraft[k]. And accordingly it is with us enacted by statute 9 Geo. II. c. 5. that no prosecution shall for the future be carried on against any person for conjuration, witchcraft, sorcery, or inchantment. But the misdemeanor of persons pretending to use witchcraft, tell fortunes, or discover stolen goods by skill in the occult sciences, is still deservedly punished with a year's imprisonment, and standing four times in the pillory.

VII. A SEVENTH species of offenders in this class are all *religious impostors:* such as falsely pretend an extraordinary commission from heaven; or terrify and abuse the people with false denunciations of judgments. These, as tending to subvert all religion, by bringing it into ridicule and contempt, are punishable by the temporal courts with fine, imprisonment, and infamous corporal punishment[l].

VIII. SIMONY, or the corrupt presentation of any one to an ecclesiastical benefice for gift or reward, is also to be considered as an offence against religion; as well by reason of the sacredness of the charge which is thus profanely bought and sold, as because it is always attended with perjury in the person presented[m]. The statute 31 Eliz. c. 6. (which, so far as it relates to the forfeiture of the right of presentation, was considered in a former book[n]) enacts, that if any patron, for money or any other corrupt consideration or promise, directly or indirectly given, shall present, admit, institute, induct, install, or collate any person to an ecclesiastical benefice or dignity, both the giver and taker shall forfeit two years value of the benefice or dignity; one moiety to the king, and the other to any one who will sue for the same. If persons also corruptly resign or exchange their benefices, both the giver and taker shall in like manner forfeit double the value of the money or other corrupt consideration. And persons who shall corruptly ordain or licence any

minister, or procure him to be ordained or licenced, (which is the true idea of simony) shall incur a like forfeiture of forty pounds; and the minister himself of ten pounds, besides an incapacity to hold any ecclesiastical preferment for seven years afterwards. Corrupt elections and resignations in colleges, hospitals, and other eleemosynary corporations, are also punished by the same statute with forfeiture of the double value, vacating the place or office, and a devolution of the right of election for that turn to the crown.

IX. PROFANATION of the lord's day, or *sabbathbreaking,* is a ninth offence against God and religion, punished by the municipal laws of England. For, besides the notorious indecency and scandal, of permitting any secular business to be publicly transacted on that day, in a country professing christianity, and the corruption of morals which usually follows it's profanation, the keeping one day in seven holy, as a time of relaxation and refreshment as well as for public worship, is of admirable service to a state, considered merely as a civil institution. It humanizes by the help of conversation and society the manners of the lower classes; which would otherwise degenerate into a sordid ferocity and savage selfishness of spirit: it enables the industrious workman to pursue his occupation in the ensuing week with health and chearfulness: it imprints on the minds of the people that sense of their duty to God, so necessary to make them good citizens; but which yet would be worn out and defaced by an unremitted continuance of labour, without any stated times of recalling them to the worship of their maker. And therefore the laws of king Athelstan[o] forbad all merchandizing on the lord's day, under very severe penalties. And by the statute 27 Hen. VI. c. 5. no fair or market shall be held on the principal festivals, good friday, or any sunday (except the four sundays in harvest) on pain of forfeiting the goods exposed to sale. And, since, by the statute 1 Car. I. c. 1. no persons shall assemble, out of their own parishes, for any sport whatsoever upon this day; nor, in

---

k. Voltaire *Siecl. Louis xiv.* Mod. Univ. Hist. xxv. 215. Yet Vouglans, *(de droit criminel,* 353. 459.) still reckons up sorcery and witchcraft among the crimes punishable in France.

l. 1 Hawk. P. C. 7.

m. 3 Inst. 156.

n. See Vol. II. pag. 279.

o. *c.* 24.

their parishes, shall use any bull or bear baiting, interludes, plays, or other *unlawful* exercises, or pastimes; on pain that every offender shall pay 3 *s.* 4 *d.* to the poor. This statute does not prohibit, but rather impliedly allows, any innocent recreation or amusement, within their respective parishes, even on the lord's day, after divine service is over. But by statute 29 Car. II. c. 7. no person is allowed to *work* on the lord's day, or use any boat or barge, or expose any goods to sale; except meat in public houses, milk at certain hours, and works of necessity or charity, on forfeiture of 5 *s.* Nor shall any drover, carrier, or the like, travel upon that day, under pain of twenty shillings.

X. DRUNKENNESS is also punished by statute 4 Jac. I. c. 5. with the forfeiture of 5 *s;* or the sitting six hours in the stocks: by which time the statute presumes the offender will have regained his senses, and not be liable to do mischief to his neighbours. And there are many wholsome statutes, by way of prevention, chiefly passed in the same reign of king James I, which regulate the licencing of ale-houses, and punish persons found tippling therein; or the masters of such houses permitting them.

XI. THE last offence which I shall mention, more immediately against religion and morality, and cognizable by the temporal courts, is that of open and notorious *lewdness:* either by frequenting houses of ill fame, which is an indictable offence[p]; or by some grossly scandalous and public indecency, for which the punishment is by fine and imprisonment[q]. In the year 1650, when the ruling powers found it for their interest to put on the semblance of a very extraordinary strictness and purity of morals, not only incest and wilful adultery were made capital crimes; but also the repeated act of keeping a brothel, or committing fornication, were (upon a second conviction) made felony without benefit of clergy[r]. But at the restoration, when men from an abhorrence of the hypocrisy

of the late times fell into a contrary extreme, of licentiousness, it was not thought proper to renew a law of such unfashionable rigour. And these offences have been ever since left to the feeble coercion of the spiritual court, according to the rules of the canon law; a law which has treated the offence of incontinence, nay even adultery itself, with a great degree of tenderness and lenity; owing perhaps to the celibacy of it's first compilers. The temporal courts therefore take no cognizance of the crime of adultery, otherwise than as a private injury[s].

BUT, before we quit this subject, we must take notice of the temporal punishment for having *bastard children,* considered in a criminal light; for with regard to the maintenance of such illegitimate offspring, which is a civil concern, we have formerly spoken at large[t]. By the statute 18 Eliz. c. 3. two justices may take order for the punishment of the mother and reputed father; but what that punishment shall be, is not therein ascertained: though the contemporary exposition was, that a corporal punishment was intended[u]. By statute 7 Jac. I. c. 4. a specific punishment (*viz.* commitment to the house of correction) is inflicted on the woman only. But in both cases, it seems that the penalty can only be inflicted, if the bastard becomes chargeable to the parish: for otherwise the very maintenance of the child is considered as a degree of punishment. By the last mentioned statute the justices may commit the mother to the house of correction, there to be punished and set on work for one year; and, in case of a second offence, till she find sureties never to offend again.

---

p. Poph. 208.
q. 1 Siderf. 168.
r. Scobell. 121.

s. See Vol. III. pag. 139.
t. See Vol. I. pag. 458.
u. Dalt. just. ch. 11.

The Wealth of Nations (1776)

ADAM SMITH (1723–90)

Adam Smith was a professor of moral philosophy at the University of Glasgow and, later, commissioner of customs at Edinburgh. *The Wealth of Nations* is primarily known for its early and articulate defense of capitalism, but it addresses a number of other subjects as well. The following excerpts concern the relationship between ecclesiastical establishments, toleration, and the flourishing (or lack thereof) of religion.

Book V, Chapter I

Article III

Of the Expence of the Institutions for the Instruction of People of All Ages

The institutions for the instruction of people of all ages are chiefly those for religious instruction. This is a species of instruction of which the object is not so much to render the people good citizens in this world, as to prepare them for another and a better world in a life to come. The teachers of the doctrine which contains this instruction, in the same manner as other teachers, may either depend altogether for their subsistence upon the voluntary contributions of their hearers; or they may derive it from some other fund to which the law of their country may entitle them; such as a landed estate, a tythe or land tax, an established salary or stipend. Their exertion, their zeal and industry, are likely to be much greater in the former situation than in the latter. In this respect the teachers of new religions have always had a considerable advantage in attacking those ancient and established

Reprinted from Adam Smith, *An Inquiry into the Nature and Causes of the Wealth of Nations*, bk. 5, chap. 1, pt. 3, art. 3, repr. from the 6th ed. (London: George Bell and Sons, 1908), 2:309–15.

systems of which the clergy, reposing themselves upon their benefices, had neglected to keep up the fervour of faith and devotion in the great body of the people; and having given themselves up to indolence, were become altogether incapable of making any vigorous exertion in defence even of their own establishment. The clergy of an established and well-endowed religion frequently become men of learning and elegance, who possess all the virtues of gentlemen, or which can recommend them to the esteem of gentlemen; but they are apt gradually to lose the qualities, both good and bad, which gave them authority and influence with the inferior ranks of people, and which had perhaps been the original causes of the success and establishment of their religion. Such a clergy, when attacked by a set of popular and bold, though perhaps stupid and ignorant enthusiasts, feel themselves as perfectly defenceless as the indolent, effeminate, and full-fed nations of the southern parts of Asia, when they were invaded by the active, hardy, and hungry Tartars of the North. Such a clergy, upon such an emergency, have commonly no other resource than to call upon the civil magistrate to persecute, destroy, or drive out their adversaries, as disturbers of the public peace. It was thus that the Roman catholic clergy called upon the civil magistrate to persecute the protestants; and the church of England, to persecute the dissenters; and that in general every religious sect, when it has once enjoyed for a century or two the security of a legal establishment, has found itself incapable of making any vigorous defence against any new sect which chose to attack its doctrine or discipline. Upon such occasions the advantage in point of learning and good writing may sometimes be on the side of the established church. But the arts of popularity, all the arts of gaining proselytes, are constantly on the side of its adversaries. In England those arts have been long neglected by the well-endowed clergy of the established church, and are at present chiefly cultivated by the dissenters and by the methodists. The independent provisions, however, which in many places have been made for dissenting teachers, by means of voluntary subscriptions, of trust rights, and other evasions of the law, seem very much to have abated the zeal and activity of those teachers. They have many of them become very learned, ingenious, and respectable men; but they have in general ceased to be very popular preachers. The methodists, without half the learning of the dissenters, are much more in vogue.

In the church of Rome, the industry and zeal of the inferior clergy are kept more alive by the powerful motive of self-interest, than perhaps in any established protestant church. The parochial clergy derive, many of them, a very considerable part of their subsistence from the voluntary oblations of the people; a source of revenue which confession gives them many opportunities of improving. The mendicant orders derive their whole subsistence from such oblations. It is with them, as with the hussars and light infantry of some armies; no plunder, no pay. The parochial clergy are like those teachers whose reward depends partly upon their salary, and partly upon the fees or honoraries which they get from their pupils; and these must always depend more or less upon their industry and reputation. The mendicant orders are like those teachers whose subsistence depends altogether upon their industry. They are obliged, therefore, to use every art which can animate the devotion of the common people. The establishment of the two great mendicant orders of St. Dominic and St. Francis, it is observed by Machiavel, revived, in the thirteenth and fourteenth centuries, the languishing faith and devotion of the catholic church. In Roman catholic countries the spirit of devotion is supported altogether by the monks and by the poorer parochial clergy. The great dignitaries of the church, with all the accomplishments of gentlemen and men of the world, and sometimes with those of men of learning, are careful enough to maintain the necessary discipline over their inferiors, but seldom give themselves any trouble about the instruction of the people.

"Most of the arts and professions in a state," says by far the most illustrious philosopher and historian of the present age, "are of such a nature, that, while they promote the interests of the society, they are also useful or agreeable to some individuals; and in that case, the constant rule of the magistrate, except, perhaps, on the first introduction of any art, is, to leave the profession to itself, and trust its encouragement to the individuals who reap the benefit of it. The artizans, finding their profits to rise by the favour of their customers, increase, as much as possible, their skill and industry; and as matters are not disturbed by any injudicious tampering, the commodity is always sure to be at all times nearly proportioned to the demand.

"But there are also some callings, which, though useful and even necessary in a state, bring no advantage or pleasure to any individual, and the supreme power is obliged to alter its conduct with regard to the retainers of those professions. It must give them public encouragement in order to their subsistence; and it must provide against that negligence to which they will naturally be subject, either by annexing particular honours to the profession, by establishing a long subordination of ranks and a strict dependance, or by some other expedient. The persons employed in the finances, fleets, and magistracy, are instances of this order of men.

"It may naturally be thought, at first sight, that the ecclesiastics belong to the first class, and that their encouragement, as well as that of lawyers and physicians, may safely be entrusted to the liberality of individuals, who are attached to their doctrines, and who find benefit or consolation from their spiritual ministry and assistance. Their industry and vigilance will, no doubt, be whetted by such an additional motive; and their skill in the profession, as well as their address in governing the minds of the people, must receive daily increase, from their increasing practice, study, and attention.

"But if we consider the matter more closely, we shall find, that this interested diligence of the clergy is what every wise legislator will study to prevent; because, in every religion except the true, it is highly pernicious, and it has even a natural tendency to pervert the true, by infusing into it a strong mixture of superstition, folly, and delusion. Each ghostly practitioner, in order to render himself more precious and sacred in the eyes of his retainers, will inspire them with the most violent abhorrence of all other sects, and continually endeavour, by some novelty, to excite the languid devotion of his audience. No regard will be paid to truth, morals, or decency in the doctrines inculcated. Every tenet will be adopted that best suits the disorderly affections of the human frame. Customers will be drawn to each conventicle by new industry and address in practising on the passions and credulity of the populace. And in the end, the civil magistrate will find, that he has dearly paid for his pretended frugality, in saving a fixed establishment for the priests; and that in reality the most decent and advantageous composition, which he can make with the spiritual guides, is to bribe their indolence, by assigning stated salaries to their profession, and rendering it superfluous for them to be farther active, than merely to prevent their flock from straying in quest of new pastures. And in this manner ecclesiastical establishments, though commonly they arose at first from religious views, prove in the end advantageous to the political interests of society."

But whatever may have been the good or bad effects of the independent provision of the clergy; it has, perhaps, been very seldom bestowed upon them from any view to those effects. Times of violent religious controversy have generally been times of equally violent political faction. Upon such occasions, each political party has either found it, or imagined it, for his interest, to league itself with some one or other of the contending religious sects. But this could be done only by adopting, or at least by favouring, the tenets of that particular sect. The sect which had the good fortune to be leagued with the conquering party, necessarily shared in the victory of its ally, by whose favour and protection it was soon enabled in some degree to silence and subdue all its adversaries. Those adversaries had generally leagued themselves with the enemies of the conquering party, and were therefore the enemies of that party. The clergy of this particular sect having thus become complete masters of the field, and their influence and authority with the great

body of the people being in its highest vigour, they were powerful enough to overawe the chiefs and leaders of their own party, and to oblige the civil magistrate to respect their opinions and inclinations. Their first demand was generally, that he should silence and subdue all their adversaries; and their second, that he should bestow an independent provision on themselves. As they had generally contributed a good deal to the victory, it seemed not unreasonable that they should have some share in the spoil. They were weary, besides, of humouring the people, and of depending upon their caprice for a subsistence. In making this demand therefore they consulted their own ease and comfort, without troubling themselves about the effect which it might have in future times upon the influence and authority of their order. The civil magistrate, who could comply with their demand only by giving them something which he would have chosen much rather to take, or to keep to himself, was seldom very forward to grant it. Necessity, however, always forced him to submit at last, though frequently not till after many delays, evasions, and affected excuses.

But if politics had never called in the aid of religion, had the conquering party never adopted the tenets of one sect more than those of another, when it had gained the victory, it would probably have dealt equally and impartially with all the different sects, and have allowed every man to chuse his own priest and his own religion as he thought proper. There would in this case, no doubt, have been a great multitude of religious sects. Almost every different congregation might probably have made a little sect by itself, or have entertained some peculiar tenets of its own. Each teacher would no doubt have felt himself under the necessity of making the utmost exertion, and of using every art both to preserve and to increase the number of his disciples. But as every other teacher would have felt himself under the same necessity, the success of no one teacher, or sect of teachers, could have been very great. The interested and active zeal of religious teachers can be dangerous and troublesome only where there is, either but one sect tolerated in the society, or where the whole of a large society is divided into two or three great sects; the teachers of each acting by concert, and under a regular discipline and subordination. But that zeal must be altogether innocent where the society is divided into two or three hundred, or perhaps into as many thousand small sects, of which no one could be considerable enough to disturb the public tranquillity. The teachers of each sect, seeing themselves surrounded on all sides with more adversaries than friends, would be obliged to learn that candour and moderation which are so seldom to be found among the teachers of those great sects, whose tenets, being supported by the civil magistrate, are held in veneration by almost all the inhabitants of extensive kingdoms and empires, and who therefore see nothing round them but followers, disciples, and humble admirers. The teachers of each little sect, finding themselves almost alone, would be obliged to respect those of almost every other sect, and the concessions which they would mutually find it both convenient and agreeable to make to one another, might in time probably reduce the doctrine of the greater part of them to that pure and rational religion, free from every mixture of absurdity, imposture, or fanaticism, such as wise men have in all ages of the world wished to see established; but such as positive law has perhaps never yet established, and probably never will establish in any country: because, with regard to religion, positive law always has been, and probably always will be, more or less influenced by popular superstition and enthusiasm. This plan of ecclesiastical government, or more properly of no ecclesiastical government, was what the sect called Independents, a sect no doubt of very wild enthusiasts, proposed to establish in England towards the end of the civil war. If it had been established, though of a very unphilosophical origin, it would probably by this time have been productive of the most philosophical good temper and moderation with regard to every sort of religious principle. It has been established in Pennsylvania, where, though the Quakers happen to be the most numerous, the law in reality favours no one sect more than another, and it is there said to have been productive of this philosophical good temper and moderation.

But though this equality of treatment should not be productive of this good temper and moderation in all, or even in the greater part of the religious sects of a particular country; yet provided those sects were sufficiently numerous, and each of them consequently too small to disturb the public tranquillity, the excessive zeal of each for its particular tenets could not well be productive of any very hurtful effects, but, on the contrary, of several good ones: and if the government was perfectly decided both to let them all alone, and to oblige them all to let alone one another, there is little danger that they would not of their own accord subdivide themselves fast enough, so as soon to become sufficiently numerous.

RECOMMENDATIONS FOR FURTHER READING

Ehler, Sidney Z., and John B. Morrall, eds. and trans. *Church and State through the Centuries: A Collection of Historic Documents with Commentaries.* New York: Biblo and Tannen, 1967.

Jordan, W. K. *The Development of Religious Toleration in England.* 4 vols. Gloucester, Mass.: Peter Smith, 1965.

Pelikan, Jaroslav, and Valerie Hotchkiss. *Creeds and Confessions of Faith in the Christian Tradition.* 4 vols. New Haven: Yale University Press, 2003.

Tierney, Brian. *The Crisis of Church and State, 1050–1300.* Englewood Cliffs, N.J.: Prentice-Hall, 1964.

Wood, James E., Jr., E. Bruce Thompson, and Robert T. Miller. *Church and State in Scripture, History and Constitutional Law.* Waco, Tex.: Baylor University Press, 1958.

Part II

CREATING THE PRINCIPLES

GOVERNING RELIGIOUS LIBERTY AND

CHURCH-STATE RELATIONS

IN COLONIAL AMERICA

CHAPTER TWO

Fundamental Laws, Declarations of Rights, and Public Acts on Ecclesiastical Establishments and Religious Liberty in Colonial America

BRITISH COLONIES IN North America were established by grants or charters from the Crown. Unlike the colonies of other European powers, they possessed a great deal of autonomy. Early in their history, colonists were able to create fundamental laws articulating their basic values and political principles. In addition, every colony had a legislature that passed statutory laws governing the colony. Although the British Parliament or king occasionally interfered with these fundamental or statutory laws, such interventions often provoked significant resistance.

The constitutions for Pennsylvania and Carolina were written in England and were intended to set up basic political institutions for these colonies. The governing council for Virginia appointed a governor for the colony, who issued the Virginia Articles to help maintain order. With the exception of documents concerning New Netherland, the texts in this chapter were created by colonists intending to make a new life in America. Some of these are best considered as fundamental or organic laws (e.g., the Mayflower Compact and Providence Agreement), while others are clearly statutory law.

Most colonial Americans believed that church and state were separate institutions, yet they also thought they should support each other. In at least nine colonies this led to the establishment of a state church; in Pennsylvania, Delaware, Rhode Island, and, perhaps, New Jersey, it did not. Even in colonies without established churches, however, it was common to have religious tests for public office and laws promoting Christian practices and morality. As well, all colonies protected the sacred rights of conscience, although the scope and extent of this was greater in some colonies than in others.

Articles, Laws, and Orders, Virginia (1610–11)

The following excerpts from "Articles, Lawes, and Orders, Divine, Politique, and Martiall for the Colony in Virginea" were issued under martial law by the colony's governor, Sir Thomas Gates, and enlarged by subsequent governors and, most notably, the deputy-governor Sir Thomas Dale.

Articles, Lawes, and Orders, Divine, Politique, and Martiall for the Colony in Virginea: first established by Sir Thomas Gates Knight, Lieutenant Generall, the 24th of May 1610. exemplified and approved by the Right Honourable Sir Thomas West Knight, Lord Lawair, Lord Governor and Captaine Generall the 12th day of June 1610. Againe exemplified and enlarged by Sir Thomas Dale Knight, Marshall, and Deputie Governour, the 22nd of June, 1611.

Whereas his Majestie like himselfe a most zealous Prince hath in his owne Realmes a principall care of true Religion, and reverence to God, and hath alwaies strictly commaunded his Generals and Governours, with all his forces wheresoever, to let their waies be like his ends for the glorie of God.

And forasmuch as no good service can be performed, or warre well managed, where militarie discipline is not observed, and militarie discipline cannot be kept, where the rules or chiefe parts thereof, be not certainely set downe, and generally knowne, I have (with the advise and counsell of Sir Thomas Gates Knight, Lieutenant Generall) adhered unto the lawes divine, and orders politique, and martiall of his Lordship (the same exemplified) an addition of such others, as I have found either the necessitie of the present State of the Colonie to require, or the infancie, and weaknesses of the body thereof, as yet able to digest, and doe now publish them to all persons in the Colonie, that they may as well take knowledge of the Lawes themselves, as of the penaltie and punishment, which without partialitie shall be inflicted upon the breakers of the same.

1 First since we owe our highest and supreme duty, our greatest, and all our allegeance to him, from whom all power and authoritie is derived, and flowes as from the first, and onely fountaine, and being especiall souldiers emprest in this sacred cause, we must alone expect our successe from him, who is only the blesser of all good attempts, the King of kings, the commaunder of commaunders, and Lord of Hostes, I do strictly commaund and charge all Captaines and Officers, of what qualitie or nature soever, whether commanders in the field, or in towne, or townes, forts or fortresses, to have a care that the Almightie God bee duly and daily served, and that they call upon their people to heare Sermons, as that also they diligently frequent Morning and Evening praier themselves by their owne exemplar and daily life, and duties herein, encouraging others thereunto, and that such, who shall often and wilfully absent themselves, be duly punished according to the martiall law in that case provided.

2 That no man speake impiously or maliciously, against the holy and blessed Trinitie, or any of the three persons, that is to say, against God the Father, God the Son, and God the holy Ghost, or against the knowne Articles of the Christian faith, upon paine of death.

3 That no man blaspheme Gods holy name upon paine of death, or use unlawful oathes, taking the name of God in vaine, curse, or banne,[1] upon paine of severe punishment for the first offence so committed, and for the second, to have a bodkin[2] thrust through his tongue, and if he continues the blas-

Reprinted by permission from *Colonial Origins of the American Constitution: A Documentary History*, ed. Donald S. Lutz (Indianapolis: Liberty Fund, 1998), 315–17.

---

1. Calling down evil upon a person.
2. A small dagger or stiletto.

Embarkation of the Pilgrims, by Robert W. Weir, oil on canvas, from The Architect of the Capitol.

pheming of Gods holy name, for the third time so offending, he shall be brought to a martiall court, and there receive censure of death for his offence.

4 No man shall use any traiterous words against his Majesties Person, or royall authority upon paine of death.

5 No man shall speake any word, or do any act, which may tend to the derision, or despight[3] of Gods holy word upon paine of death: Nor shall any man unworthily demeane himself unto any Preacher, or Minister of the same, but generally hold them in all reverent regard, and dutiful intreatie,[4] otherwise he the offender shall openly be whipt three times, and ask publike forgivenesse in the assembly of the congregation three several Saboth Daies.

3. Open defiance.
4. Treatment.

6 Everie man and woman duly twice a day upon the first towling of the Bell shall upon the working daies repaire unto the Church, to hear divine Service upon pain of losing his or her dayes allowance for the first omission, for the second to be whipt, and for the third to be condemned to the Gallies for six Moneths. Likewise no man or woman shall dare to violate or breake the Sabboth by any gaming, publique or private abroad, or at home, but duly sanctifie and observe the same, both himselfe and his familie, by preparing themselves at home with private prayer, that they may be the better fitted for the publique, according to the commandements of God, and the orders of our Church, as also every man and woman shall repaire in the morning to the divine service, and Sermons preached upon the Saboth day, and in the afternoon to divine service, and Catechising, upon paine for the first fault to lose their provision, and allowance for the whole weeke following, for the sec-

ond to lose the said allowance, and also to be whipt, and for the third to suffer death.

7 All Preachers or Ministers within this our Colonie, or Colonies, shall in the Forts, where they are resident, after divine Service, duly preach every Sabbath day in the forenoone, and Catechise in the afternoone, and weekly say the divine service, twice every day, and preach every Wednesday, likewise every Minister where he is resident, within the same Fort, or Fortresse, Townes or Towne, shall chuse unto him, foure of the most religious and better disposed as well to informe of the abuses and neglects of the people in their duties, and service to God, as also to the due reparation, and keeping of the Church handsome, and fitted with all reverent observances thereunto belonging: likewise every Minister shall keepe a faithful and true Record, or Church Booke of all Christnings, Marriages, and deaths of such our people, as shall happen within their Fort, or Fortresses, Townes or Towne at any time, upon the burthen of a neglectfull conscience, and upon paine of losing their Entertainment.[5]

8 He that upon pretended malice, shall murther or take away the life of any man, shall bee punished with death.

9 No man shal commit the horrible, and detestable sins of Sodomie upon pain of death; and he or she that can be lawfully convict of Adultery shall be punished with death. No man shall ravish or force any woman, maid or Indian, or other, upon pain of death, and know that he or shee, that shall commit fornication, and evident proofe made thereof, for their first fault shall be whipt, for the second they shall be whipt, and for their third they shall be whipt three times a weeke for one month, and aske publique forgivenesse in the Assembly of the Congregation.

5. Provisions.

The Mayflower Compact (1620)

In 1620, Separatist Puritans, seeking the freedom to practice their faith, arrived in Provincetown Harbor. William Bradford drew up the following "combination" which, in his words, became "the first foundation of their government in this place." The compact, which was signed by every male settler aboard the Mayflower, is often described as the first constitution written in America. Originally styled "Agreement between the Settlers at New Plymouth" and often referred to as "The Plymouth Combination," the agreement was not referred to as "The Mayflower Compact" until 1793.

Agreement between the Settlers at New Plymouth—1620

IN THE NAME OF GOD, AMEN. We, whose names are underwritten, the Loyal Subjects of our dread Sovereign Lord King *James,* by the Grace of God, of *Great Britain, France,* and *Ireland,* King, *Defender of the Faith,* &c. Having undertaken for the Glory of God, and Advancement of the Christian Faith, and the Honour of our King and Country, a Voyage to plant the first Colony in the northern Parts of *Virginia;* Do by these Presents, solemnly and mutually, in the Presence of God and one another, covenant and combine ourselves together into a civil Body Politick, for our better Ordering and Preservation, and Furtherance of the Ends aforesaid: And by Virtue hereof do enact, constitute, and frame, such just and equal Laws, Ordinances, Acts, Constitutions, and Officers, from time to time, as shall be thought most meet and convenient for the general

Reprinted from *The Federal and State Constitutions, Colonial Charters, and Other Organic Laws of the States, Territories, and Colonies,* ed. Francis Newton Thorpe (Washington, D.C.: U.S. Government Printing Office, 1909), 3:1841.

Mayflower Compact, 1620.

Good of the Colony; unto which we promise all due Submission and Obedience. IN WITNESS whereof we have hereunto subscribed our names at *Cape-Cod* the eleventh of *November,* in the Reign of our Sovereign Lord King *James,* of *England, France,* and *Ireland,* the eighteenth, and of *Scotland,* the fifty-fourth, *Anno Domini,* 1620.

Mr. John Carver,
Mr. William Bradford,
Mr Edward Winslow,
Mr. William Brewster,
   Isaac Allerton,
   Myles Standish,
   John Alden,
   John Turner,
   Francis Eaton,
   James Chilton,

John Craxton,
John Billington,
Joses Fletcher,
John Goodman,
Mr. Samuel Fuller,
Mr. Christopher Martin,
Mr. William Mullins,
Mr. William White,
Mr. Richard Warren,
   John Howland,
Mr. Steven Hopkins,
   Digery Priest,
   Thomas Williams,
   Gilbert Winslow,
   Edmund Margesson,
   Peter Brown,
   Richard Britteridge,

George Soule,
Edward Tilly,
John Tilly,
Francis Cooke,
Thomas Rogers,
Thomas Tinker,
John Ridgdale,
Edward Fuller,
Richard Clark,
Richard Gardiner,
Mr. John Allerton,
Thomas English,
Edward Doten,
Edward Liester.

Providence Agreement (1637)

Banished from Massachusetts Bay, Roger Williams and his followers founded the town of Providence, Rhode Island, in 1636. In 1637 they made the following agreement, which differs from most early American compacts in its lack of theological language and in the jurisdictional limitation on town meetings to "civil things."

We whose names are hereunder, desirous to inhabit in the town of Providence, do promise to subject ourselves in active and passive obedience to all such orders or agreements as shall be made for the public good of the body in an orderly way, by the major consent of present inhabitants, masters of families, incorporated together in a Towne fellowship, and oth-

ers whom they shall admit unto them only in civil things.

[Signed by Richard Scott and twelve others.]

Fundamental Orders of Connecticut (1638–39)

Written and adopted by delegates from the towns of Windsor, Hartford, and Wethersfield, Connecticut, the Fundamental Orders is one of the first constitutions written in America. The following excerpts illustrate both the theological commitments of the citizens and their view of church and state.

FORASMUCH as it hath pleased the Allmighty God by the wise disposition of his divyne providence so to Order and dispose of things that we the Inhabitants and Residents of Windsor, Harteford and Wethersfield are now cohabiting and dwelling in and upon the River of Conectecotte and the Lands thereunto adjoyneing; And well knowing where a people are gathered togather the word of God requires that to mayntayne the peace and union of such a people there should be an orderly and decent Goverment established according to God, to order and dispose of the affayres of the people at all seasons as occation shall require; doe therefore assotiate and conjoyne our selves to be as one Publike State or Commonwelth; and doe, for our selves and our Successors and such as shall be adjoyned to us att any tyme hereafter, enter into Combination and Confederation togather, to mayntayne and presearve the liberty and purity of the

Reprinted from *Colonial Origins of the American Constitution: A Documentary History,* ed. Donald S. Lutz (Indianapolis: Liberty Fund, 1998), 162, which took the complete text from Charles Evans, "Oaths of Allegiance in Colonial New England," *Proceedings of the American Antiquarian Society,* n.s., 31 (April 13–October 19, 1921): 424. Evans's spelling is used.

Reprinted from *The Federal and State Constitutions, Colonial Charters, and Other Organic Laws of the States, Territories, and Colonies,* ed. Francis Newton Thorpe (Washington, D.C.: U.S. Government Printing Office, 1909), 1:519–20, 522–23.

gospell of our Lord Jesus which we now professe, as also the disciplyne of the Churches, which according to the truth of the said gospell is now practised amongst us; As also in our Civell Affaires to be guided and governed according to such Lawes, Rules, Orders and decrees as shall be made, ordered & decreed, as followeth:—

1. It is Ordered, sentenced and decreed, that there shall be yerely two generall Assemblies or Courts, the one the second thursday in Aprill, the other the second thursday in September, following; the first shall be called the Courte of Election, wherein shall be yerely Chosen from tyme to tyme soe many Magestrats and other publike Officers as shall be found requisitte: Whereof one to be chosen Governour for the yeare ensueing and untill another be chosen, and noe other Magestrate to be chosen for more then one yeare; provided allwayes there be six chosen besids the Governour; which being chosen and sworne according to an Oath recorded for that purpose shall have power to administer justice according to the Lawes here established, and for want thereof according to the rule of the word of God; which choise shall be made by all that are admitted freemen and have taken the Oath of Fidellity, and doe cohabitte within this Jurisdiction, (having beene admitted Inhabitants by the maior part of the Towne wherein they live,) or the major parte of such as shall be then present. . . .

11. It is ordered, sentenced and decreed, that when any Generall Courte uppon the occasions of the Commonwelth have agreed uppon any summe or somes of mony to be levyed uppon the severall Townes within this Jurisdiction, that a Committee be chosen to sett out and appoynt what shall be the proportion of every Towne to pay of the said levy, provided the Committees be made up of an equall number out of each Towne.

14th January, 1638, the 11 Orders abovesaid are voted.

The Oath of the Governor, for the [Present]

I N. W. being now chosen to be Governor within this Jurisdiction, for the yeare ensueing, and until a new be chosen, doe sweare by the greate and dreadfull name of the everliveing God, to promote the publicke good and peace of the same, according to the best of my skill; as also will mayntayne all lawfull priviledges of this Commonwealth; as also that all wholsome lawes that are or shall be made by lawfull authority here established, be duly executed; and will further the execution of Justice according to the rule of Gods word; so helpe me God, in the name of the Lord Jesus Christ.

The Oath of a Magestrate, for the [Present]

I, N. W. being chosen a Magestrate within this Jurisdiction for the yeare ensueing, doe sweare by the great and dreadfull name of the everliveing God, to promote the publike good and peace of the same, according to the best of my skill, and that I will mayntayne all the lawfull priviledges thereof according to my understanding, as also assist in the execution of all such wholsome lawes as are made or shall be made by lawfull authority heare established, and will further the execution of Justice for the tyme aforesaid according to the righteous rule of Gods word; so helpe me God, etc.

The Laws and Liberties of Massachusets (1647)

In 1647 the General Court enacted "The Book of the General Laws and Libertyes Concerning the Inhabitants of the Massachusets," an organized code of laws and rights. The code retained many of the rights enumerated in the 1641 "The Massachusetts Body of Liberties," but went well beyond it by adding a number of laws regulating the actions of individuals and

Reprinted from *The Laws and Liberties of Massachusetts* (1929; San Marino, Calif.: The Henry E. Huntington Library, 1998), prefatory pages, 1–2, 4–6, 11–12, 18–20, 24–26, 29, 35–37, 45–47, and 55–56.

groups. The following excerpts primarily concern the General Court's approach to the relationship between church and state and the role of civil government in preserving and promoting morality.

To Our Beloved Brethren and Neighbours the Inhabitants of the Massachusets, the Governour, Assistants and Deputies assembled in the Generall Court of that Jurisdiction wish grace and peace in our Lord Jesus Christ.

So soon as God had set up Politicall Government among his people Israel hee gave them a body of lawes for judgement both in civil and criminal causes. These were breif and fundamental principles, yet withall so full and comprehensive as out of them clear deductions were to be drawne to all particular cases in future times. For a Common-wealth without lawes is like a Ship without rigging and steeradge. Nor is it sufficient to have principles or fundamentalls, but these are to be drawn out into so many of their deductions as the time and condition of that people may have use of. And it is very unsafe & injurious to the body of the people to put them to learn their duty and libertie from generall rules, nor is it enough to have lawes except they be also just. Therefore among other priviledges which the Lord bestowed upon his peculiar people, these he calls them specially to consider of, that God was neerer to them and their lawes were more righteous then other nations. God was sayd to be amongst them or neer to them because of his Ordnances established by himselfe, and their lawes righteous because himselfe was their Law-giver: yet in the comparison are implyed two things, first that other nations had somthing of Gods presence amongst them. Secondly that there was also somwhat of equitie in their lawes, for it pleased the Father (upon the Covenant of Redemption with his Son) to restore so much of his Image to lost man as whereby all nations are disposed to worship God, and to advance righ-

teousnes: which appears in that of the Apostle *Rom. 1. 21. They knew God &c:* and in the *2. 14. They did by nature the things conteined in the law of God.* But the nations corrupting his Ordinances (both of Religion, and Justice) God withdrew his presence from them proportionably whereby they were given up to abominable lusts *Rom. 2. 21.* Wheras if they had walked according to that light & law of nature they might have been preserved from such moral evils and might have injoyed a common blessing in all their natural and civil Ordinances: now, if it might have been so with the nations who were so much strangers to the Covenant of Grace, what advantage have they who have interest in this Covenant, and may injoye the special presence of God in the puritie and native simplicitie of all his Ordinances by which he is so neer to his owne people. This hath been no small priviledge, and advantage to us in New-England that our Churches, and civil State have been planted, and growne up (like two twinnes) together like that of Israel in the wildernes by which wee were put in minde (and had opportunitie put into our hands) not only to gather our Churches, and set up the Ordinances of Christ Jesus in them according to the Apostolick patterne by such light as the Lord graciously afforded us: but also withall to frame our civil Politie, and lawes according to the rules of his most holy word whereby each do help and strengthen other (the Churches the civil Authoritie, and the civil Authoritie the Churches) and so both prosper the better without such aemulation, and contention for priviledges or priority as have proved the misery (if not ruine) of both in some other places.

For this end about nine years since wee used the help of some of the Elders of our Churches to compose a modell of the Judiciall lawes of Moses with such other cases as might be referred to them, with intent to make use of them in composing our lawes, but not to have them published as the lawes of this Jurisdiction: nor were they voted in Court. For that book intitled *The Liberties &c:* published about seven years since (which conteines also many lawes and orders both for civil & criminal causes, and is commonly (though without ground) reported to be our Fundamentalls that wee owne as established by Authoritie of this Court, and that after three years experience & generall approbation: and accordingly we have inserted them into this volume under the severall heads to which they belong yet not as fundamentalls, for divers of them have since been repealed, or altered, and more may justly be (at least) amended heerafter as further experience shall discover defects or inconveniences for *Nihil simul natum et perfectum* [Nothing is at once born and perfected]. The same must we say of this present Volume, we have not published it as a perfect body of laws sufficient to carry on the Government established for future times, nor could it be expected that we should promise such a thing. For if it be no disparagement to the wisedome of that High Court of Parliament in England that in four hundred years they could not so compile their lawes, and regulate proceedings in Courts of justice &c: but that they had still new work to do of the same kinde almost every Parliament: there can be no just cause to blame a poor Colonie (being unfurnished of Lawyers and Statesmen) that in eighteen years hath produced no more, nor better rules for a good, and setled Government then this Book holds forth: nor have you (our Bretheren and Neighbours) any cause, (whether you look back upon our Native Country, or take your observation by other States, & Common wealths in Europe) to complaine of such as you have imployed in this service; for the time which hath been spent in making lawes, and repealing and altering them so often, nor of the charge which the Country hath been put to for those occasions, the Civilian gives you a satisfactorie reason of such continuall alterations additions &c: *Crescit in Orbe dolus.**

These Lawes which were made successively in divers former years, we have reduced under severall heads in an alphabeticall method, that so they might the more readilye be found, & that the divers lawes concerning one matter being placed together the scope and intent of the whole and of every of them might the more easily be apprehended: we must confesse we have not been so exact in placing every law under its most proper title as we might, and would have been: the reason was our hasty indeavour to satisfie your longing expectation, and frequent complaints for want of such a volume to be published in print: wherein (upon every occasion) you might readily see the rule which you ought to walke by. And in this (we hope) you will finde satisfastion, by the help of the references under the severall heads, and the Table which we have added in the end. For such lawes and orders as are not of generall concernment we have not put them into this booke, but they remain still in force, and are to be seen in the booke of the Records of the Court, but all generall laws not heer inserted nor mentioned to be still of force are to be accounted repealed.

You have called us from amongst the rest of our Bretheren and given us power to make these lawes: we must now call upon you to see them executed: remembring that old & true proverb, *The execution of the law is the life of the law.* If one sort of you viz: non-Freemen should object that you had no hand in calling us to this worke, and therefore think yourselvs not bound to obedience &c. Wee answer that a subsequent, or implicit consent is of like force in this case, as an expresse precedent power: for in putting your persons and estates into the protection and way of subsistance held forth and exercised within this Jurisdiction, you doe tacitly submit to this Government and to all the wholesome lawes therof, and so is the common repute in all nations and that upon this *Maxim. Qui sentit commodum sentire debet et onus.**

If any of you meet with some law that seemes not to tend to your particular benefit, you must consider that lawes are made with respect to the whole people, and not to each particular person: and obedience to them must be yeilded with respect to the common welfare, not to thy private advantage, and as thou

---

* "Fraud increases in the world." From Edward Coke's reply to the question, "Why do such great volumes of law increase?" Sir Edward Coke, *The Selected Writings and Speeches of Sir Edward Coke*, ed. Steve Sheppard (Indianapolis: Liberty Fund, 2003) 3:1189.—Trans.

* [He who feels the advantage ought also to feel the burden.]

yeildest obedience to the law for common good, but to thy disadvantage: so another must observe some other law for thy good, though to his own damage; thus must we be content to bear õanothers burden and so fullfill the Law of Christ.

That distinction which is put between the Lawes of God and the lawes of men, becomes a snare to many as it is mis-applied in the ordering of their obedience to civil Authoritie; for when the Authoritie is of God and that in way of an Ordinance *Rom. 13. 1.* and when the administration of it is according to deductions, and rules gathered from the word of God, and the clear light of nature in civil nations, surely there is no humane law that tendeth to commõ good (according to those principles) but the same is mediately a law of God, and that in way of an Ordinance which all are to submit unto and that for conscience sake. *Rom. 13. 5.*

By order of the Generall Court.
INCREASE NOWEL
Secr.

The Book of the General Lauues and Libertyes Concerning &c:

FORASMUCH as the free fruition of such Liberties, Immunities, priviledges as humanitie, civilitie & christianity call for as due to everie man in his place, & proportion, without impeachmēt & infringement hath ever been, & ever will be the tranquillity & stability of Churches & Comon-wealths; & the deniall or deprivall therof the disturbance, if not ruine of both:

It is therfore ordered by this Court, & Authority therof, That no mans life shall be taken away; no mans honour or good name shall be stayned; no mans person shal be arrested, restrained, bannished, dismembred nor any wayes punished; no man shall be deprived of his wife or children; no mans goods or estate shal be taken away from him; nor any wayes indamaged under colour of Law or countenance of Authoritie unles it be by the vertue or equity of some expresse law of the Country warranting the same established by a General Court & sufficiently pub-

lished; or in case of the defect of a law in any particular case by the word of God. And in capital cases, or in cases concerning dismēbring or banishmēt according to that word to be judged by the General Court [1641] . . .

Ana-Baptists

Forasmuch as experience hath plentifully & often proved that since the first arising of the Ana-baptists about a hundred years past they have been the Incendiaries of Common-wealths & the Infectors of persons in main matters of Religiõ, & the Troublers of Churches in most places where they have been, & that they who have held the baptizing of Infants ūlawful, have usually held other errors or heresies together therwith (though as hereticks use to doe they have concealed the same untill they espied a fit advantage and opportunity to vent them by way of question or scruple) and wheras divers of this kinde have since our cõming into New-England appeared amongst ourselvs, some wherof as others before them have denied the Ordinance of Magistracy, and the lawfulnes of making warre, others the lawfulnes of Magistrates, and their Inspection into any breach of the first Table: which opinions if coñived at by us are like to be increased among us & so necessarily bring guilt upõ us, infection, & trouble to the Churches & hazzard to the whole Common-wealth:

It is therfore ordered by this Court & Authoritie therof, that if any person or persons within this Jurisdiction shall either openly condemn or oppose the baptizing of Infants, or goe about secretly to seduce others from the approbation or use therof, or shal purposely depart the Congregation at the administration of that Ordinance; or shal deny the Ordinance of Magistracy, or their lawfull right or authoritie to make war, or to punish the outward breaches of the first Table, and shall appear to the Court wilfully and obstinately to continue therin, after due meanes of conviction, everie such person or persons shall be sentenced to Banishment. [1644]. . . .

Bond-slavery

It is ordered by this Court and authoritie therof, that there shall never be any bond-slavery, villenage or captivitie amongst us; unlesse it be lawfull captives, taken in just warrs, and such strangers as willingly sell themselves, or are solde to us: and such shall have the libertyes and christian usages which the law of God established in Israell concerning such persons doth morally require, provided, this exempts none from servitude who shall be judged thereto by Authoritie. [1641]. . . .

Capital Lawes

IF any man after legal conviction shall HAVE OR WORSHIP any other God, but the LORD GOD: he shall be put to death. *Exod.* 22. 20. *Deut.* 13. 6. & 10. *Deut.* 17. 2. 6.

2 If any man or woman be a WITCH, that is, hath or consulteth with a familiar spirit, they shall be put to death. *Exod.* 22. 18. *Levit.* 20. 27. *Deut.* 18. 10. 11.

3 If any person within this Jurisdiction whether Christian or Pagan shall wittingly and willingly presume to BLASPHEME the holy Name of God, Father, Son or Holy-Ghost, with direct, expresse, presumptuous, or high-handed blasphemy, either by wilfull or obstinate denying the true God, or his Creation, or Government of the world: or shall curse God in like manner, or reproach the holy Religion of God as if it were but a politick device to keep ignorant men in awe; or shal utter any other kinde of Blasphemy of the like nature & degree they shall be put to death. *Levit.* 24. 15. 16.

4 If any person shall commit any wilfull MURTHER, which is Man slaughter, committed upon premeditate malice, hatred, or crueltie not in a mans necessary and just defence, nor by meer casualty against his will, he shall be put to death. *Exod.* 21. 12. 13. *Numb.* 35. 31.

5 If any person slayeth another suddenly in his ANGER, or CRUELTY of passion, he shall be put to death. *Levit.* 24. 17. *Numb.* 35. 20. 21.

6 If any person shall slay another through guile, either by POYSONING, or other such devilish practice, he shall be put to death. *Exod.* 21. 14.

7 If any man or woman shall LYE WITH ANY BEAST, or bruit creature, by carnall copulation; they shall surely be put to death: and the beast shall be slain, & buried, and not eaten. *Lev.* 20. 15. 16.

8 If any man LYETH WITH MAN-KINDE as he lieth with a woman, both of them have committed abomination, they both shal surely be put to death: unles the one partie were forced (or be under fourteen years of age in which case he shall be seveerly punished). *Levit.* 20. 13.

9 If any person commit ADULTERIE with a married, or espoused wife; the Adulterer & Adulteresse shal surely be put to death. *Lev.* 20. 19. & 18. 20. *Deu.* 22. 23. 27

10 If any man STEALETH A MAN, or Mankinde, he shall surely be put to death. *Exodus* 21. 16.

11 If any man rise up by FALSE-WITNES wittingly, and of purpose to take away any mans life: he shal be put to death. *Deut.* 19. 16. 18. 16.

12 If any man shall CONSPIRE, and attempt any Invasion, Insurrection, or publick Rebellion against our Common-Wealth: or shall indeavour to surprize any Town, or Townes, Fort, or Forts therin; or shall treacherously, & perfidiously attempt the Alteration and Subversion of our frame of Politie, or Government fundamentally he shall be put to death. *Numb.* 16. 2 *Sam.* 3. 2 *Sam.* 18. 2 *Sam.* 20.

13 If any child, or children, above sixteen years old, and of sufficient understanding, shall CURSE, or SMITE their natural FATHER, or MOTHER; he or they shall be put to death: unles it can be sufficiently testified that the Parents have been very unchristianly negligent in the education of such children; or so provoked them by extream, and cruel correction; that they have been forced therunto to preserve themselves from death or maiming. *Exod.* 21. 17. *Lev.* 20. 9. *Exod.* 21. 15.

14 If a man have a stubborn or REBELLIOUS SON, of sufficient years & ūderstanding (*viz*) sixteen years of age, which will not obey the voice of his Father, or the voice of his Mother, and that when they have chastened him will not harken unto them: then shal his Father & Mother being his natural parēts, lay

hold on him, & bring him to the Magistrates assembled in Court & testifie unto them, that their Son is stubborn & rebellious & will not obey their voice and chastisement, but lives in sundry notorious crimes, such a son shal be put to death. *Deut.* 21. 20. 21.

15 If any man shal RAVISH any maid or single womã, cõmitting carnal copulation with her by force, against her own will; that is above the age of ten years he shal be punished either with death, or with some other greivous punishmẽt according to circumstances as the Judges, or General court shal determin. [1641]. . . .

Children

Forasmuch as the good education of children is of singular behoof and benefit to any Common-wealth; and wher as many parents & masters are too indulgent and negligent of their duty in that kinde. It is therfore ordered that the Select men of everie town, in the severall precincts and quarters where they dwell, shall have a vigilant eye over their brethern & neighbours, to see, first that none of them shall suffer so much barbarism in any of their families as not to indeavour to teach by themselves or others, their children & apprentices so much learning as may inable them perfectly to read the englishtongue, & knowledge of the Capital lawes: upõ penaltie of twentie shillings for each neglect therin. Also that all masters of families doe once a week (at the least) catechize their children and servants in the grounds & principles of Religion, & if any be unable to doe so much: that then at the least they procure such children or apprentices to learn some short orthodox catechism without book, that they may be able to answer unto the questions that shall be propounded to them out of such catechism by their parents or masters or any of the Select men when they shall call them to a tryall of what they have learned in this kinde. And further that all parents and masters do breed & bring up their children & apprentices in some honest lawful calling, labour or imploymẽt, either in husbandry, or some other trade profitable for themselves, and the Common-wealth if they will not or cannot train them up in learning to fit them for

higher imployments. And if any of the Select men after admonitiõ by them given to such masters of families shal finde them still negligent of their dutie in the particulars aforementioned, wherby children and servants become rude, stubborn & unruly; the said Select men with the help of two Magistrats, or the next County court for that Shire, shall take such children or apprentices from them & place them with some masters for years (boyes till they come to twenty one, and girls eighteen years of age compleat) which will more strictly look unto, and force them to submit unto government according to the rules of this order, if by fair means and former instructions they will not be drawn unto it. [1642]

2 *Wheras sundry Gentlemen of qualitie, and others oft times send over their children into this country unto some freinds heer, hoping at the least therby to prevent their extravagant and riotous courses, who notwithstanding by means of some unadvised and ill-affected persons, which give them credit, in expectation their freinds, either in favour to them, or prevention of blemish to themselves, will discharge what ever is done that way, they are no lesse lavish & profuse heer to the great greif of their freinds, dishonour of God & reproach of the Countrie.*

It is therfore ordered by this Court & authoritie therof; That if any person after publication heerof shall any way give credit to any such youth, or other person under twentie one years of age, without order from such their freinds, heer, or elswhere, under their hands in writing they shall lose their debt whatever it be. And further if such youth or other person incur any penalty by such means and have not wherwith to pay, such person, or persons, as are occasions therof shall pay it as delinquents in the like case should doe. [1647] *See Abilitie.*

3 If any parents shall wilfully, and unreasonably deny any childe timely or convenient marriage, or shall exercise any unnaturall severitie towards them, such children shal have libertie to complain to Authoritie for redresse in such cases. [1641]

4 No Orphan during their minority which was not committed to tuition, or service by their parents in

their life time, shall afterward be absolutely disposed of by any without the consent of some Court wherin two Assistants (at least) shall be present, except in case of marriage, in which the approbation of the major part of the Select men, in that town or any one of the next Assistants shall be sufficient. And the minoritie of women in case of marriage shall be till sixteen years. [1646] *See Age. Cap: Laws. Lib: cōmō: marriage.* . . .

Colledge

Wheras through the good hand of God upon us there is a Colledge founded in Cambridge in the County of Midlesex called Harvard Colledge, *for incouragement wherof this Court hath given the summe of four hundred pounds and also the revenue of the Ferrie betwixt Charlstown and Boston and that the well ordering and mannaging of the said Colledge is of great concernment,*

It is therfore ordered by this Court and Authoritie therof, That the Governour & Deputie Govēr: for the time being and all the Magistrates of this Jurisdiction together with the teaching Elders of the six next adjoyning towns *viz:* Cambridge, Water-town, Charlstown, Boston, Roxburie and Dorchester, & the President of the said Colledge for the time being, shal from time to time have full power & authoritie to make and establish all such orders, statutes and constitutions, as they shall see necessary for the instituting, guiding and furthering of the said Colledge, and several members therof, from time to time, in Pietie, Moralitie & Learning, as also to dispose, order and manage to the use and behoof of the said Colledge and members therof, all gifts, legacyes, bequeaths, revenues, lands and donations as either have been, are, or shall be conferred, bestowed, or any wayes shall fall or come to the sayd Colledge. And wheras it may come to passe that many of the Magistrates and said Elders may be absent and otherwise imployed in other weighty affairs whē the said Colledge may need their present help and counsell. It is therfore ordered that the greater number of Magistrates and Elders which shall be present with the President, shall have the power of the whole. Provided that if any constitution, order or orders by them made shall be found hurtfull unto the said Colledg, or the members therof, or to the weal publick then upō appeal of the partie or parties greived, unto the company of Overseers first mentioned, they shal repeal the said order or orders (if they see cause) at their next meeting or stand accountable therof to the next Generall court. [1636 1640 1642]. . . .

Ecclesiasticall:

1 All the people of God within this Jurisdiction who are not in a Church way and be orthodox in judgement and not scandalous in life shall have full libertie to gather themselves into a Church estate, provided they doe it in a christian way with due observation of the rules of Christ revealed in his word. Provided also that the General Court doth not, nor will heerafter approve of any such companyes of men as shall joyne in any pretended way of Church fellowship unles they shall acquaint the Magistrates and the Elders of the neighbour Churches where they intend to joyn, & have their approbation therin.

2 And it is farther ordered, that no person being a member of any Church which shal be gathered without the approbation of the Magistrates and the said Churches shal be admitted to the Freedom of this Common-wealth.

3 Everie Church hath free liberty to exercise all the Ordinances of God according to the rules of the Scripture.

4 Everie Church hath free libertie of election and ordination of all her Officers from time to time. Provided they be able, pious and orthodox.

5 Everie Church hath also free libertie of admission, recommendation, dismission & expulsion or deposall of their Officers and members upon due cause, with free exercise of the disciplin and censures of Christ according to the rules of his word.

6 No injunction shall be put upon any Church, church Officer or member in point of doctrine, worship or disciplin, whether for substance or circumstance besides the institutions of the Lord.

7 Everie Church of Christ hath freedom to celebrate dayes of Fasting and prayer and of Thanksgiving according to the word of God.

8 The Elders of churches also have libertie to meet monthly, quarterly or otherwise in convenient numbers and places, for conference and consultations about christian and church questions and occasions.

9 All Churches also have libertie to deal with any their members in a church way that are in the hands of justice, so it be not to retard and hinder the course therof.

10 Everie Church hath libertie to deal with any Magistrate, Deputy of court, or other Officer whatsoever that is a member of theirs, in a church way in case of apparent and just offence, given in their places, so it be done with due observance and respect.

11 Wee also allow private meetings for edification in Religion amongst christians of all sorts of people so it be without just offence, both for number, time, place and other circumstances.

12 *For the preventing and removing of errour and offence that may grow and spread in any of the Churches in this Jurisdiction, and for the preserving of truth & peace in the severall Churches within themselves, and for the maintainance and exercise of brotherly cōmunion amongst all the Churches in the country.*

It is allowed and ratified by the authoritie of this Court, as a lawfull libertie of the Churches of Christ, that once in every month of the year (when the season will bear it) it shall be lawfull for the Ministers and Elders of the Churches neer adjoyning, together with any other of the Brethren, with the consent of the Churches, to assemble by course in everie several church one after another, to the intent, that after the preaching of the word, by such a Minister as shal be requested therto, by the Elders of the Church where the Assembly is held, the rest of the day may be spent in publick christian conference, about the discussing and resolving of any such doubts & cases of conscience concerning matter of doctrine, or worship, or government of the Church as shall be propounded by any of the Brethren of that Church; with leave also to any other Brother to propound his objections, or

answers, for further satisfaction according to the word of God. Provided that the whole action be guided and moderated by the Elders of the Church where the Assembly is held, or by such others as they shall appoint. And that nothing be concluded & imposed by way of Authoritie from one, or more Churches, upon another, but only by way of brotherly conference & consultations, that the truth may be searched out to the satisfying of every mans conscience in the sight of God according to his word. And because such an Assemblie and the work therof cannot be duly attended if other Lectures be held the same week, it is therfore agreed with the consent of the Churches, that in what week such an Assembly is held all the Lectures in all the neighbouring Churches for the week dayes shall be forborne, that so the publick service of Christ in this Assembly may be transacted with greater diligence & attention. [1641]

13 *Forasmuch as the open contempt of Gods word and Messengers therof is the desolating sinne of civil States and Churches and that the preaching of the word by those whom God doth send, is the chief ordinary means ordained of God for the converting, edifying and saving the soules of the Elect through the presence and power of the Holy-Ghost, therunto promised: and that the ministry of the word, is set up by God in his Churches, for those holy ends: and according to the respect or contempt of the same and of those whom God hath set apart for his own work & imployment, the weal or woe of all Christian States is much furthered and promoted; it is therfore ordered and decreed,*

That if any christian (so called) within this Jurisdiction shall contemptuously behave himselfe toward the Word preached or the Messengers therof called to dispense the same in any Congregation; when he doth faithfully execute his Service and Office therin, according to the will and word of God, either by interrupting him in his preaching, or by charging him falsely with any errour which he hath not taught in the open face of the Church: or like a son of *Korah* cast upon his true doctrine or himselfe any reproach, to the dishonour of the Lord Jesus who hath sent him and to the disparagement of that his holy Ordinance, and making Gods wayes contemptible and ridiculous: that everie such person or persons (whatsoever censure the Church may passe) shall for the first scandall be convented and reproved openly by the Magistrate at some Lecture, and bound to their good behaviour. And if a second time they break forth into the like contemptuous carriages, they shall either pay five pounds to the publick Treasurie; or stand two hours openly upon a block or stool, four foot high on a lecture day with a paper fixed on his breast, written in Capital letters [AN OPEN AND OBSTINATE CONTEMNER OF GODS HOLY ORDINANCES] that others may fear and be ashamed of breaking out into the like wickednes. [1646]

14 It is ordered and decreed by this Court and Authoritie therof; That wheresoever the ministry of the word is established according to the order of the Gospell throughout this Jurisdiction every person shall duly resort and attend therunto respectively upon the Lords days & upon such publick Fast dayes, & dayes of Thanksgiving as are to be generally kept by the appointmēt of Authoritie: & if any person withī this Jurisdictiō shal without just and necessarie cause withdraw himselfe frō hearing the publick ministry of the word after due meanes of conviction used, he shall forfeit for his absence from everie such publick meeting five shillings. All such offences to be heard and determined by any one Magistrate or more from time to time. [1646]

15 *Forasmuch as the peace and prosperity of Churches and members therof as well as civil Rights & Liberties are carefully to be maintained, it is ordered by this Court & decreed,*

That the civil Authoritie heer established hath power and liberty to see the peace, ordinances and rules of Christ be observed in everie Church according to his word. As also to deal with any church-member in a way of civil justice notwithstanding any church relation, office, or interest; so it be done in a civil and not in an ecclesiastical way. Nor shall any church censure degrade or depose any man from any civil dignity, office or authoritie he shall have in the Common-wealth. [1641]

16 *Forasmuch as there are many Inhabitants in divers towns, who leave their several habitations and therby draw much of the in-come of their estates into other towns wherby the ministry is much neglected, it is therfore ordered by this Court and the authoritie therof;*

That from henceforth all lands, cattle and other estates of any kinde whatsoever, shall be lyable to be rated to all cōmon charges whatsoever, either for the Church, Town or Cōmon-wealth in the same place where the estate is from time to time. And to the end there may be a convenient habitation for the use of the ministry in everie town in this Jurisdiction to remain to posterity. It is decreed by the authoritie of this Court that where the major part of the Inhabitants (according to the order of regulating valid town acts) shall graunt, build, or purchase such habitation it shall be good in law, and the particular sum upon each person assessed by just rate, shal be duly paid according as in other cases of town rates. Provided alwayes that such graunt, deed of purchase and the deed of gift therupon to the use of a present preaching Elder and his next successour and so from time to time to his successors: be entred in the town book and acknowledged before a Magistrate, and recorded in the Shire court. [1647] *See charges publ: sec: 3.* ....

Gaming

UPON *complaint of great disorder by the use of the game called* Shuffle-board, *in houses of common entertainment, wherby much pretious time is spent unfruitfully and much wast of wine and beer occasioned, it is therfore ordered and enacted by the Authoritie of this Court;*

That no person shall henceforth use the said game of Shuffle-board in any such house, nor in any other house used as common for such purpose, upon payn for every Keeper of such house to forfeit for every such offence twenty shillings: and for every person playing at the said game in any such house, to forfeit for everie such offence five shillings: Nor shall any person at any time play or game for any monie, or mony-worth upon penalty of forfeiting treble the value therof: one half to the partie informing, the other half to the Treasurie. And any Magistrate may hear and determin any offence against this Law. [1646 1647]. . . .

Heresie

ALTHOUGH *no humane power be Lord over the Faith & Consciences of men, and therfore may not constrein them to beleive or professe against their Consciences: yet because such as bring in damnable heresies, tending to the subversion of the Christian Faith, and destruction of the soules of men, ought duly to be restreined from such notorious impiety, it is therfore ordered and decreed by this Court;*

That if any Christian within this Jurisdiction shall go about to subvert and destroy the christian Faith and Religion, by broaching or mainteining any damnable heresie; as denying the immortalitie of the Soul, or the resurrection of the body, or any sin to be repented of in the Regenerate, or any evil done by the outward man to be accounted sin: or denying that Christ gave himself a Ransom for our sins, or shal affirm that wee are not justified by his Death and Righteousnes, but by the perfection of our own works; or shall deny the moralitie of the fourth commandement, or shall indeavour to seduce others to any the herisies aforementioned, everie such person continuing obstinate therin after due means of conviction shall be sentenced to Bañishment. [1646]. . . .

Idlenes

IT is ordered by this Court and Authoritie therof, that no person, Housholder or other shall spend his time idlely or unproffitably under pain of such punishment as the Court of Assistants or County Court shall think meet to inflict. And for this end it is ordered that the Constable of everie place shall use speciall care and diligence to take knowledge of offenders in this kinde, especially of common coasters, unproffitable fowlers and tobacco takers, and present the same unto the two next Assistants, who shall have power to hear and determin the cause, or transfer it to the next Court. [1633]

Jesuits

THIS *Court taking into consideration the great wars, combustions and divisions which are this day in Europe: and that the same are observed to be raysed and fomented chiefly by the secret underminings, and solicitations of those of the Jesuiticall Order, men brought up and devoted to the religion and court of Rome; which hath occasioned divers States to expell them their territories; for prevention wherof among ourselves, It is ordered and enacted by Authoritie of this Court,*

That no Jesuit, or spiritual or ecclesiastical person [as they are termed] ordained by the authoritie of the Pope, or Sea of Rome shall henceforth at any time repair to, or come within this Jurisdiction: And if any person shal give just cause of suspicion that he is one of such Societie or Order he shall be brought before some of the Magistrates, and if he cannot free himselfe of such suspicion he shall be committed to prison, or bound over to the next Court of Assistants, to be tryed and proceeded with by Bañishment or otherwise as the Court shall see cause: and if any person so banished shall be taken the second time within this Jurisdiction upon lawfull tryall and conviction he shall be put to death. Provided this Law shall not extend to any such Jesuit, spiritual or ecclesiasticall person as shall be cast upon our shoars, by ship-wrack or other accident, so as he continue no longer then till he may have opportunitie of passage for his departure; nor to any such as shall come in company with any Messenger hither upō publick occasions, or any Merchant or Master of any ship, belonging to any place not in emnitie with the State of *England,* or ourselves, so as they depart again with the same Messenger, Master or Merchant, and behave themselves in-offensively during their aboad heer. [1647]. . . .

[Indians]

4 *Considering that one end in planting these parts was to propagate the true Religion unto the Indians: and that divers of them are become subjects to the English and have ingaged themselves to be willing and ready to understand the Law of God, it is therfore ordered and decreed,*

That such necessary and wholsom Laws, which are in force, and may be made from time to time, to reduce them to civilitie of life shall be once in the year (if the times be safe) made known to them, by such fit persons as the General Court shall nominate, having the help of some able Interpreter with them.

Considering also that interpretation of tongues is appointed of God for propagating the Truth: and may therfore have a blessed successe in the hearts of others in due season, it is therfore farther ordered and decreed,

That two Ministers shall be chosen by the Elders of the Churches everie year at the Court of Election, and so be sent with the consent of their Churches (with whomsoever will freely offer themselves to accompany them in that service) to make known the heavenly counsell of God among the Indians in most familiar manner, by the help of some able Interpreter; as may be most available to bring them unto the knowledge of the truth, and their conversation to the Rules of Jesus Christ. And for that end that somthing be allowed them by the General Court, to give away freely unto those Indians whom they shall perceive most willing & ready to be instructed by them.

And it is farther ordered and decreed by this Court; that no Indian shall at any time *powaw*, or performe outward worship to their false gods: or to the devil in any part of our Jurisdiction; whether they be such as shall dwell heer, or shall come hither: and if any shall transgresse this Law, the *Powawer* shall pay five pounds; the Procurer five pounds; and every other countenancing by his presence or otherwise being of age of discretion twenty shillings. [1646]. . . .

Lying

WHERAS *truth in words as well as in actions is required of all men, especially of Christians who are the professed Servants of the God of Truth; and wheras all lying is contrary to truth, and some sorts of lyes are not only sinfull (as all lyes are) but also pernicious to the Publickweal, and injurious to particular persons; it is therfore ordered by this Court and Authoritie therof,*

That everie person of the age of discretion [which is accounted fourteen years] who shall wittingly and willingly make, or publish any Lye which may be pernicious to the publick weal, or tending to the damage or injurie of any particular person, or with intent to deceive and abuse the people with false news or reports: and the same duly proved in any Court or before any one Magistrate (who hath heerby power graunted to hear, and determin all offences against this Law) such person shall be fined for the first offence ten shillings, or if the partie be unable to pay the same then to be set in the *stocks* so long as the said Court or Magistrate shall appoint, in some open place, not exceeding two hours. For the second offence in that kinde wherof any shall be legally convicted the sum of twenty shillings, or be whipped upon the naked body not exceeding ten stripes. And for the third offence that way fourty shillings, or if the partie be unable to pay, then to be whipped with more stripes, not exceeding fifteen. And if yet any shall offend in like kinde, and be legally convicted therof, such person, male or female, shall be fined ten shillings a time more then formerly: or if the partie so offending be unable to pay, then to be whipped with five, or six more stripes then formerly not exceeding fourty at any time.

The aforesaid fines shall be levied, or stripes inflicted either by the Marshal of that Jurisdiction, or Constable of the Town where the offence is committed according as the Court or Magistrate shall direct. And such fines so levied shall be paid to the Treasurie of that Shire where the Cause is tried.

And if any person shall finde himselfe greived with the sentence of any such Magistrate out of Court, he may appeal to the next Court of the same Shire, giving sufficient securitie to prosecute his appeal and abide the Order of the Court. And if the said Court shall judge his appeal causlesse, he shall be double fined and pay the charges of the Court during his Action, or corrected by whipping as aforesaid not exceeding fourtie stripes; and pay the costs of Court and partie complaining or informing, and of Wittnesses in the Case.

And for all such as being under age of discretion that shall offend in lying contrary to this Order their

Parents or Masters shall give them due correction, and that in the presence of some Officer if any Magistrate shall so appoint. Provided also that no person shall be barred of his just Action of Slaunder, or otherwise by any proceeding upon this Order. [1645]. . . .

Marriage

FOR *preventing all unlawfull marriages, it is ordered by this Court and Authoritie therof,*

That after due publication heerof no persons shall be joyned in marriage before the intention of the parties proceeding therin hath been three times published at some time of publick Lecture or Town-meeting, in both the towns where the parties or either of them doe ordinarily reside; or be set up in writing upon some post of their Meeting-house door in publick view, there to stand so as it may easily be read by the space of fourteen dayes. [1639]

2 *And wheras God hath committed the care and power into the hands of Parents for the disposing their Children in marriage: so that it is against Rule to seek to draw away the affections of young maidens under pretence of purpose of marriage before their Parents have given way and allowance in that respect. And wheras it is a common practice in divers places for young men irregularly and disorderly to watch all advantages for their evil purposes to insinuate into the affections of young maidens, by coming to them in places, and seasons unknown to their Parents, for such ends; wherby much evil hath grown amongst us to the dishonour of God and damage of parties, for prevention wherof for time to come it is farther ordered by Authoritie of this Court,*

That whatsoever person from henceforth shall indeavour directly, or indirectly to draw away the affections of any maid in this Jurisdiction under pretence of marriage, before he hath obtained libertie and allowance from her Parents or Governours (or in absence of such) of the neerest Magistrate; he shall forfeit for the first offence five pounds, for the second offence toward the same partie ten pounds, and be bound to forbear any farther attempt and proceedings in that unlawfull designe without, or against the allowance aforesaid. And for the third offence upon in-

formation, or complaint by such Parents or Governours to any Magistrate, giving *Bond* to prosecute the partie, he shall be committed to prison, and upon hearing and conviction by the next Court shall be adjudged to continue in prison untill the Court of Assistants shall see cause to release him. [1647]

3 *Wheras divers persons both men and woemen living within this Jurisdiction whose Wives, and Husbands are in England, or els-where, by means wherof they live under great temptations heer, and some of them committing lewdnes and filthines heer among us, others make love to woemen, and attempt Marriage, and some have attained it; and some of them live under suspicion of uncleannes, and all to the great dishonour of God, reproach of Religion, Common-wealth and Churches, it is therfore ordered by this Court & Authoritie therof (for the prevention of all such future evils)*

That all such married persons as aforesaid shall repair to their said relations by the first opportunitie of shipping upon the pain, or penaltie of twenty pounds, except they can shew just cause to the contrary to the next County Court, or Court of Assistants to be holden at *Boston,* after they are summoned by the Constable there to appear, who are heerby required so to doe upon pain of twenty shillings for everie such default wittingly made. Provided that this Order doe not extend to such as are come over to make way for their families, or are in a transient way only for traffick, or merchandize for some small time. [1647]. . . .

Profane swearing

IT is ordered, and by this Court decreed, that if any person within this Jurisdiction shall *swear* rashly and vainly either by the holy Name of God, or any other oath, he shall forfeit to the common Treasurie for everie such severall offence ten shillings. And it shall be in the power of any Magistrate by *Warrant* to the Constable to call such person before him, and upon sufficient proof to passe sentence, and levie the said penaltie according to the usuall order of Justice. And if such person be not able, or shall utterly refuse to pay the aforesaid Fine, he shal be committed to the

Stocks there to continue, not exceeding three hours, and not lesse then one hour. [1646]

Protestation contra Remonstrance

It is ordered, decreed, and by this Court declared; that it is, and shall be the libertie of any member, or members of any Court, Council or civil Assemblie in cases of making or executing any Order or Law that properly concerneth Religion, or any cause Capital, or Wars, or subscription to any publick Articles, or Remonstrance in case they cannot in judgement and conscience consent to that way the major Vote or Suffrage goes, to make their *contra-Remonstrance* or *Protestation* in speech or writing, and upon their request, to have their dissent recorded in the *Rolls* of that Court, so it be done christianly and respectively, for the manner, and the dissent only be entred without the reasons therof for avoyding tediousnes. [1641]. . . .

Schools

It being one chief project of that old deluder, Satan, to keep men from the knowledge of the Scriptures, as in former times keeping them in an unknown tongue, so in these later times by perswading from the use of Tongues, that so at least the true sense and meaning of the Originall might be clowded with false glosses of Saint-seeming-deceivers; and that Learning may not be buried in the graves of our fore-fathers in Church and Common-wealth, the Lord assisting our indeavours: it is therefore ordered by this Court and Authoritie therof;

That everie Township in this Jurisdiction, after the Lord hath increased them to the number of fifty Housholders shall then forthwith appoint one within their Town to teach all such children as shall resort to him to write and read, whose wages shall be paid either by the Parents or Masters of such children, or by the Inhabitants in general byway of supply, as the major part of those that order the *prudentials* of the Town shall appoint. Provided that those which send their children be not oppressed by paying much more then they can have them taught for in other Towns.

2 And it is farther ordered, that where any Town shall increase to the number of one hundred Families or Housholders they shal set upon a Grammar-School, the Masters therof being able to instruct youth so far as they may be fitted for the Universitie. And if any Town neglect the performance heerof above one year then everie such town shall pay five pounds *per annum* to the next such School, till they shall perform this Order. [1647]. . . .

Presidents and Forms of things frequently used

To (*IB*) Carpenter, of (*D*). You are required to appear at the next Court, holden at (*B*) on the   day of the   month next ensuing; to answer the complaint of (*N C*) for with-holding a debt of   due upon a *Bond* or *Bill:* or for two heifers &c: sold you by him, or for work, or for a trespasse done him in his corn or hay, by your cattle, or for a slaunder you have done him in his name, or for striking him, or the like, and heerof you are not to fail at your peril. Dated the   day of the   month 1641.

To the Marshal or Constable of (*B*) or to their Deputie. You are required to attach the body and goods of (*WF*) and to take *Bond* of him, to the value of   with sufficient Suertie or Suerties for his appearance at the next Court, holden at (*S*) on the   day of the   month; then, and there to answer to the complaint of (*T M*) for &c: *as before.* And so make a true return thereof under your hand. Dated the   day &c:

By the Court.
R F.

Know all men by these presents, that wee (*AB*) of (*D*) Yeoman, and (*C C*) of the same, Carpenter, doe binde ourselves, our Heirs and Executors to (*R P*) Marshal, or *M O* Constable of *D* aforesaid, in   pounds; upon condition that the said *A B* shall personally appear at the next Court, at *S* to answer *L M* in an Action of   And to abide the order of the Court therin, & not to depart without licence.

To the Marshal or Constable of   You are required to *replevie* three heifers of *T P* now distreined or impounded by *A B*, and to deliver them to the said *T P.* Provided he give *Bond* to the value of   with sufficient Suertie or Suerties to prosecute his *Replevin* at the next Court, holden at (*B*) and so from Court to Court till the Cause be ended, and to pay such costs and damages as the said (*A B*) shall by law recover against him; and so make a true return therof under your hand. Dated &c:

By the Court.
R F.

WHERAS upon serious consideration, wee have concluded a confoederacie with the english Colonies of New-Plimouth, Connecticot and New-Haven, as the bond of nature, reason, Religion and respect to our Nation doth require:

Wee have this Court chosen our trustie and well-beloved friends (*S B*) and (*W H*) for this Colonie, for a full and compleat year, as any occasions and exigents may require and particularly for the next Meeting at (*B*). And do invest them with full power and authoritie to treat, and conclude of all things, according to the true tenour and meaning of the Articles of confoederation of the united Colonies, concluded at *Boston* the ninth day of the third month 1643.

I (*A B*) being by Gods providence an Inhabitant within the Jurisdiction of this Common-wealth, doe freely and sincerely acknowledge my selfe to be subject to the Government therof. And doe heer swear by the great and dreadfull Name of the Ever-living God, that I will be true and faithfull to the same, and will accordingly yeild assistance therunto, with my person and estate, as in equitie I am bound: and will also truly indeavour to maintein and preserve all the Liberties & Priviledges therof, submitting my self unto the wholsom Laws made, & established by the same. And farther, that I will not plot or practice any evil against it, or consent to any that shall so doe: but will timely discover and reveal the same to lawfull Authoritie now heer established, for the speedy preventing therof. So help me God in our Lord Jesus Christ.

I (*A B*) being by Gods providence an Inhabitant within the Jurisdiction of this Common-wealth, and

now to be made free; doe heer freely acknowledge my self to be subject to the Government therof: and therfore do heer swear by the great and dreadfull Name of the Ever-living God, that I will be true and faithfull to the same, & will accordingly yeild assistance & support therunto, with my person and estate, as in equitie I am bound, and will also truly indeavour to maintein & preserve all the Liberties and Priviledges therof, submitting my self unto the wholsom Laws made and established by the same. And farther, that I will not plot or practice any evil against it, or consent to any that shall so doe; but will timely discover & reveal the same to lawfull authoritie now heer established, for the speedy prevention therof.

Moreover, I do solemnly binde my self in the sight of God, that when I shall be called to give my voice touching any such matter of this State, wherin Freemen are to deal; I will give my vote and *suffrage* as I shall in mine own conscience judge best to conduce and tend to the publick weal of the Body, without respect of persons, or favour of any man. So help me God &c:

WHERAS you (*J W*) are chosen to the place of a Governour over this Jurisdiction, for this year, and till a new be chosen & sworn: you do heer swear by the Living God, that you will in all things concerning your place, according to your best power and skill carie and demean your self for the said time of your Government, according to the Laws of God, & for the advancement of his Gospell, the Laws of this land, and the good of the people of this Jurisdiction. You shall doe justice to all men without partialitie, as much as in you lyeth: you shall not exceed the limitations of a Governour in your place. So help you God &c:

Selected Laws of Rhode Island (1647)

Rhode Island was a bastion of religious toleration in colonial America, but that did not prevent the legislature from passing laws based on Christian religious or moral principles, as illustrated by the following statutes.

Acts and Orders

Made and agreed upon at the General Court of Election, held at Portsmouth on Rhode-Island, the 19th, 20th, and 21st of May, 1647, for the Colony and Province of Providence.

Witchcraft

Witchcraft is forbidden by this present Assembly to be used in this colony. The penalty imposed by the authority that we are subjected to is felony of death. 1 Jac. 12.

Touching Whoremongers

First of sodomy, which is forbidden by this present Assembly throughout the whole colony, and by sundry statutes of England. 25 Hen. 8, 6; 5 Eliz. 17. It is a vile affection, whereby men given up thereto leave the natural use of woman and burn in their lusts one toward another, and so men with men work that which is unseemly, as that Doctor of the Gentiles in his letter to the Romans once spake, i. 27. The penalty concluded by that state under whose authority we are is felony of death without remedy. See 5 Eliz. 17.

Buggery

Buggery is forbidden by this present Assembly throughout the whole colony, and also strengthened by the same statutes of England. It is a most filthy lying with a beast as with a woman, and is abomination and confusion, the just reward whereof prepared to our hands is felony of death without remedy. See 5 Eliz. 17.

Adultery and Fornication

Are forbidden by this present Assembly throughout the whole colony, with this memento, that the Most High will judge them. 13 Hen. 4. Adultery is declared to be a vile affection, whereby men do turn aside from the natural use of their own wives and do burn in their lusts toward strange flesh; and we do agree that what penalty the wisdom of the state of England has or shall appoint touching that transgression, the accessaries and effects, shall stand in force throughout the whole colony.

An Act Concerning Religion, Maryland (1649)

Lord Baltimore, the first proprietor of Maryland, intended the colony to be a haven for Roman Catholics. In 1649, under his son's direction, the legislature passed an act intended to protect and promote religious toleration. After the Glorious Revolution the law was repealed and, eventually, the Church of England was established in the colony and Catholics were denied the right to vote, hold office, and worship publicly.

Reprinted from *The Earliest Acts and Laws of the Colony of Rhode Island and Providence Plantations, 1647–1719,* with an editorial note by John D. Cushing (Wilmington, Del.: Michael Glazier, 1977), 5, 21, 25–30.

Reprinted from *Archives of Maryland,* ed. William Hand Browne (Baltimore: Maryland Historical Society, 1882), 244–47. Courtesy of the Maryland State Archives. Accessed online at www.msa.md.gov.

Acts of Assembly of the 21th of Aprill 1649. Confirmed by the Lord Proprietary by an instrument under his hand & seale 26th of August 1650 Phillip Calvert.

Acts and Orders of Assembly assented vnto Enacted and made at a Genãll Sessions of the said Assembly held at St Maries on the one and twentieth day of Aprill Anno Dm̃ 1649 as followeth viz.:

An Act concerning Religion

fforasmuch as in a well governed and Xpian Com̃on Weath matters concerning Religion and the honor of God ought in the first place to bee taken, into serious consideracõn and endeavoured to bee settled. Be it therefore ordered and enacted by the Right Honorable Cecilius Lord Baron of Baltemore absolute Lord and Proprietary of this Province with the advise and consent of this Generall Assembly. That whatsoever ꝑson or ꝑsons within this Province and the Islands thereunto belonging shall from henceforth blaspheme God, that is Curse him, or deny our Saviour Jesus Christ to bee the sonne of God, or shall deny the holy Trinity the ffather sonne and holy Ghost, or the Godhead of any of the said Three ꝑsons of the Trinity or the Vnity of the Godhead, or shall use or utter any reproachfull Speeches, words or language concerning the said Holy Trinity, or any of the said three ꝑsons thereof, shalbe punished with death and confiscatõn or forfeiture of all his or her lands and goods to the Lord Proprietary and his heires, And bee it also Enacted by the Authority and with the advise and assent aforesaid. That whatsoever ꝑson or ꝑsons shall from henceforth use or utter any reproachfull words or Speeches concerning the blessed Virgin Mary the Mother of our Saviour or the holy Apostles or Evangelists or any of them shall in such case for the first offence forfeit to the said Lord Proprietary and his heirs Lords and Proprietaries of this Province the sum̃e of ffive pound Sterling or the value thereof to be Levyed on the goods and chattells of every such

ꝑson soe offending, but in case such Offender or Offenders, shall not then have goods and chattells sufficient for the satisfyeing of such forfeiture, or that the same bee not otherwise speedily satisfyed that then such Offender or Offenders shalbe publiquely whipt and bee ymprisoned during the pleasure of the Lord Proprietary or the Leivet. or chiefe Governor of this Province for the time being. And that every such Offender or Offenders for every second offence shall forfeit tenne pound sterling or the value thereof to bee levyed as aforesaid, or in case such offender or Offenders shall not then haue goods and chattells within this Province sufficient for that purpose then to bee publiquely and severely whipt and imprisoned as before is expressed. And that every ꝑson or ꝑsons before mentioned offending herein the third time, shall for such third Offence forfeit all his lands and Goods and bee for ever banished and expelled out of this Province. And be it also further Enacted by the same authority advise and assent that whatsoever ꝑson or ꝑsons shall from henceforth vppon any occasion of Offence or otherwise in a reproachful manner or Way declare call or denominate any ꝑson or ꝑsons whatsoever inhabiting residing traffiqueing trading or comerceing within this Province or within any the Ports, Harbors, Creeks or Havens to the same belonging an heritick, Scismatick, Idolator, puritan, Independant, Prespiterian popish prest, Jesuite, Jesuited papist, Lutheran, Calvenist, Anabaptist, Brownist, Antinomian, Barrowist, Roundhead, Seꝑatist, or any other name or terme in a reproachfull manner relating to matter of Religion shall for every such Offence forfeit and loose the som̃e of tenne shillings sterling or the value thereof to bee levyed on the goods and chattells of every such Offender and Offenders, the one half thereof to be forfeited and paid unto the person and persons of whom such reproachfull words are or shalbe spoken or vttered, and the other half thereof to the Lord Proprietary and his heires Lords and Proprietaries of this Province, But if such ꝑson or ꝑsons who shall at any time vtter or speake any such reproachfull words or Language shall not have Goods or Chattells sufficient and overt

"An Act Concerning Religion," Maryland General Assembly Upper House Proceedings, April 21, 1649, folios 354–59. Courtesy of the Maryland State Archives.

within this Province to bee taken to satisfie the penalty aforesaid or that the same bee not otherwise speedily satisfyed, that then the p̄son or persons soe offending shalbe publickly whipt, and shall suffer imprisonmt. without baile or maineprise vntill hee shee or they respectively shall satisfy the party soe offended or greived by such reproachfull Language by asking him or her respectively forgivenes publiquely for such his Offence before the Magistrate or cheife Officer or Officers of the Towne or place where such Offence shalbe given. And be it further likewise Enacted by the Authority and consent aforesaid That every person and persons within this Province that shall at any time hereafter p̄phane the Sabbath or Lords day called Sunday by frequent swearing, drunkennes or by any vncivill or disorderly recreacōn, or by working on that day when absolute necessity doth not require it shall for every such first offence forfeit 2s. 6d sterling or the value thereof, and for the second offence 5s sterling or the value thereof, and for the third offence and soe for every time he shall offend in like manner afterwards 10s sterling or the value thereof. And in case such offender and offenders shall not have sufficient goods or chattells within this Province to satisfy any of the said Penalties respectively hereby imposed for prophaning the Sabbath or Lords day called Sunday as aforesaid, That in Every such case the p̄tie soe offending shall for the first and second offence in that kinde be imprisoned till hee or shee shall publickly in open Court before the cheife Commander Judge or Magistrate, of that County Towne or precinct where such offence shalbe committed acknowledg the Scandall and offence he hath in that respect given against God and the good and civill Governemt. of this Province And for the third offence and for every time after shall also bee publickly whipt. And whereas the inforceing of the conscience in matters of Religion hath frequently fallen out to be of dangerous Consequence in those commonwealthes where it hath been practised, And for the more quiett and peaceable governemt. of this Province, and the better to p̄serve mutuall Love and amity amongst the Inhabitants thereof. Be it Therefore also

by the Lo: Proprietary with the advise and consent of this Assembly Ordeyned & enacted (except as in this p̄sent Act is before Declared and sett forth) that noe person or p̄sons whatsoever within this Province, or the Islands, Ports, Harbors, Creekes, or havens thereunto belonging professing to beleive in Jesus Christ, shall from henceforth bee any waies troubled, Molested or discountenanced for or in respect of his or her religion nor in the free exercise thereof within this Province or the Islands thereunto belonging nor any way compelled to the beleife or exercise of any other Religion against his or her consent, soe as they be not vnfaithfull to the Lord Proprietary, or molest or conspire against the civill Governemt. established or to bee established in this Province vnder him or his heires. And that all & every p̄son and p̄sons that shall presume Contrary to this Act and the true intent and meaning thereof directly or indirectly either in person or estate willfully to wrong disturbe trouble or molest any person whatsoever within this Province professing to beleive in Jesus Christ for or in respect of his or her religion or the free exercise thereof within this Province other than is provided for in this Act that such p̄son or p̄sons soe offending, shalbe compelled to pay trebble damages to the party soe wronged or molested, and for every such offence shall also forfeit 20s sterling in money or the value thereof, half thereof for the vse of the Lo: Proprietary, and his heires Lords and Proprietaries of this Province, and the other half for the vse of the party soe wronged or molested as aforesaid, Or if the p̄tie soe offending as aforesaid shall refuse or bee vnable to recompense the party soe wronged, or to satisfy such ffyne or forfeiture, then such Offender shalbe severely punished by publick whipping & imprisonmt. during the pleasure of the Lord Proprietary, or his Leivetenāt or cheife Governor of this Province for the tyme being without baile or maineprise And bee it further alsoe Enacted by the authority and consent aforesaid That the Sheriff or other Officer or Officers from time to time to bee appointed & authorized for that purpose, of the County Towne or precinct where every particular offence in this p̄sent Act conteyned shall happen at any time to bee comitted and wherevppon there is hereby a fforfeiture ffyne or penalty imposed shall from time to time distraine and seise the goods and estate of every such ꝑson soe offending as aforesaid against this ꝑsent Act or any ꝑt thereof, and sell the same or any part thereof for the full satisfaccōn of such forfeiture, ffine, or penalty as aforesaid, Restoring vnto the ꝑtie soe offending the Remainder or overplus of the said goods or estate after such satisfaccōn soe made as aforesaid

The ffreemen haue assented. Tho: Hatton Enacted by the Governor Willm Stone

---

Provisional Regulations for the Colonists of New Netherland (1624)

Dutch West India Company Instructions (1656)

Flushing Remonstrance (1657)

Dutch West India Company Instructions (1663)

Holland was one of the most tolerant countries in Europe in the seventeenth century, and the Dutch West India Company largely followed this policy in New Netherland. However, because Quakers had a reputation as disturbers of the peace, in 1657 Governor Peter Stuyvesant issued an order prohibiting citizens from allowing Quakers into their homes and ships from bringing them to the colony. In response, inhabitants of the town of Flushing, Long Island, sent the following remonstrance. Also included are several instructions from the directors of the Dutch West India Company to Governor Stuyvesant.

Provisional Regulations for the Colonists of New Netherland, 1624

Provisional conditions upon which the respective colonists have been engaged in the service of the West India Company and sent out to New Netherland, to take up their abode on the river of Prince Mauritius, or at such other places as shall be assigned to them by the Commander and his Council.

They shall within their territory practice no other form of divine worship than that of the Reformed religion as at present practiced here in this country and thus by their Christian life and conduct seek to draw the Indians and other blind people to the knowledge of God and His Word, without however persecuting any one on account of his faith, but leaving to every one the freedom of his conscience. But if any one among them or within their jurisdiction should wantonly revile or blaspheme the name of God or of our Saviour Jesus Christ, he shall according to the circumstances be punished by the Commander and his Council.

Reprinted from *Documents Relating to New Netherland, 1624–1626, in The Henry E. Huntington Library,* translated and edited by A. J. F. van Laer (San Marino, Calif.: The Henry E. Huntington Library and Art Gallery, 1924), 2–3; © 1924 by The Henry E. Huntington Library and Art Gallery. Reprinted with the permission of the Henry E. Huntington Library.

Dutch West India Company Instructions, 1656

Letter from the Directors to Stuyvesant: Jews to have some privileges; Indian raid on New Amsterdam; Hartford Treaty; Emigration.

The 13th of March 1656

Honorable, Prudent, Pious, Dear, Faithful, ...

The permission given to the *Jews,* to go to *New-Netherland* and enjoy there the same privileges, as they have here, has been granted only as far as civil and political rights are concerned, without giving the said *Jews* a claim to the privilege of exercising their religion in a synagogue or at a gathering; as long therefore, as you receive no request for granting them this liberty of religious exercise, your considerations and anxiety about this matter, are premature and when later something shall be said about it, you can do no better, than to refer them to us and await the necessary order. . . .

Letter from the Directors to Stuyvesant: Trade between Virginia and New Netherland prohibited; Jews; Lutherans; Public Record.

The 14th of June 1656

Honorable, Vigorous, Pious, Dear, Faithful, ...

We have seen and heard with displeasure, that against our orders of the 15th of February 1655, issued at the request of the *Jewish* or *Portuguese* nation, you have forbidden them to trade to *Fort Orange* and the South river, also the purchase of real estate, which is granted to them without difficulty here in this country, and we wish it had not been done and that you had obeyed our orders, which you must always execute punctually and with more respect: *Jews* or *Portuguese* people however shall not be employed in any public service, (to which they are neither admitted in

this city), nor allowed to have open retail shops, but they may quietly and peacefully carry on their business as before said and exercise in all quietness their religion within their houses, for which end they must without doubt endeavor to build their houses close together in a convenient place on one or the other side of *New Amsterdam,*—at their own choice—as they have done here.

We would also have been better pleased, if you had not published the placat against the Lutherans, a copy of which you sent us, and committed them to prison, for it has always been our intention, to treat them quietly and leniently. Hereafter you will therefore not publish such or similar placats without our knowledge, but you must pass it over quietly and let them have free religious exercises in their houses. . . .

———————

Flushing Remonstrance, 1657

Remonstrance of the Inhabitants of Flushing, L. I., against the Law against Quakers and subsequent Proceedings by the Government against them and others favoring Quakers

Right Honnorable.

You have beene pleased to send vp vnto vs a certaine Prohibition or Command that wee shoulde not receive or entertaine any of those people called *Quakers* because they are supposed to bee by some seducers of the people for our parte wee cannot condem them in this case neither can wee stretch out our hands against them to punish bannish or persecute them for out of Christ God is a Consuming fire and it is a feareful to fall into the handes of the liveing God wee desire therefore in this case not to iudge least wee be

Reprinted from *Documents Relating to the Colonial History of the State of New York,* vol. 3 (Albany: Weed, Parsons and Co., 1883), 340–41, 350–51.

Reprinted from *Documents Relating to the Colonial History of the State of New York,* vol. 3 (Albany: Weed, Parsons and Co., 1883), 402–3.

iudged neither to Condem least wee bee Condemed but rather let every man stand and fall to his own. Maister wee are bounde by the Law to doe good vnto all men especially to those of the Household of faith and though for the present wee seeme to bee vnsensible of the law and the Lawgiver: yet when death and the Law assault vs: if we haue our advocate to seeke who shall pleade for vs in this case of Conscience betwixt god and our owne soules the powers of this world can neither attack vs neither excuse vs for if god iustifye who can Condem and if god Condem there is none can justifye and for those Jealowsies and suspitions which some haue of them that they are destructiue vnto Magistracy and Ministery that cannot bee: for the Magistrate hath the Sword in his hand and the Minister hath the Sword in his hand as witnesse those two great examples which all Maiestrates and Ministers are to follow M[oses] and Christ whom god raised vp Maintained and defended against all the Enemies both of flesh and spirit and therefore that which is of god will stand and that which is of man will [come] to noething: and as the Lord hath taught Moses, or the Civill power to giue an outward libertie in the State by the law written in his heart designed [for] the good of all and can truely iudge who is good and who is evill who is true and who is false and can pass definitiue sentence of life or [death] against that man which rises vp against the fundamental law of the States Generall soe [he] hath made his Ministers a savor of life vnto [life ?] and a savor of death vnto death.

The law of loue peace and libertie in the states extending to *Jewes Turkes* and *Egiptians* as they are Considered the sonnes of Adam which is the glory of the outward State of *Holland,* soe loue peace and libertie extending to all in Christ Jesus Condems hatred warre and bondage and becawse our Saviour saith it is Impossible but that offences will come but woe bee vnto him by whom they Commeth our desire is not to offend one of his little ones in what soever forme name or title hee appeares in whether presbiterian independant Baptist or Quaker but shall bee glad to see any thing of god in any of them: desireing to doe vnto all men as wee desire all men shoulde doe vnto vs which is the true law both of Church and State for our Saviour saith this is the Law and the Prophets Therefore if any of these said persons come in loue vnto vs wee cannot in Conscience lay violent hands vpon them but giue them free Egresse and Regresse into our Towne and howses as god shall perswade our Consciences and in this wee are true subiects both of Church and State for wee are bounde by the law of god and man to doe good vnto all men and evill to noe man and this is according to the Pattent and Charter of our Towne giuen vnto vs in the name of the States Generall which wee are not willing to infringe and violate but shall houlde to our pattent and shall remaine your Humble Subiects the inhabitants of *Vlishing* written this 27th of December in the yeare 1657 by mee

TOBIAS FEAKE.
The Marke of WILLIAM NOBLE.
WILLIAM THORNE, seignior.
The mark of WM. THORNE Junior.
EDWARD TARNE?
JOHN STORER.
NATHANIEL HEFFERD.
BENIAMIN HUBBARD.
The marke of WILLIAM PIDGION.
The marke of GEORGE CLERE.
ELIAS DOUGHTIE.
ANTONIE FEILD.
RICHARD STOCTON.
EDWARD GRIFFINE.
NATHANIELL TUE.
EDWARD HEART CLERICUS
NICOLAS BLACKFORD.
The marke of MICAH TUE.
The marke of PHILIPP UD.
EDWARD FFARINGTON.
ROBERT FFIELD, senior.
ROBERT FIELD junior.
NICK COLAS PARSELL.
MICHAEL MILNER.
HENRY TOWNSEND.
GEORGE WRIGHT.

JOHN FOARD.
HENRY SAMTELL.
EDWARD HEART.
JOHN MASTINE.
JOHN TOWNESEND.

Dutch West India Company Instructions, 1663

Your last letter informed us that you had banished from the Province and sent hither by ship a certain Quaker, *John Bowne* by name: although we heartily desire, that these and other sectarians remained away from there, yet as they do not, we doubt very much, whether we can proceed against them rigorously without diminishing the population and stopping immigration, which must be favored at a so tender stage of the country's existence. You may therefore shut your eyes, at least not force people's consciences, but allow every one to have his own belief, as long as he behaves quietly and legally, gives no offence to his neighbors and does not oppose the government. As the government of this city has always practised this maxim of moderation and consequently has often had a considerable influx of people, we do not doubt, that your Province too would be benefitted by it.

Reprinted from *Documents Relating to the Colonial History of the State of New York*, vol. 3 (Albany: Weed, Parsons and Co., 1883), 526.

An Act made at a General Court, Held at Boston, the 20th of October, 1658

A Declaration of the General Court of the Massachusetts Holden at Boston in New-England, October 18, 1659. Concerning the Execution of Two Quakers.

MASSACHUSETTS GENERAL COURT

In 1659 three Quakers, William Robinson, Marmaduke Stevenson, and Mary Dyer, were imprisoned and then banished from Boston upon pain of death. They returned one month later and were sentenced to death. The two men were hanged, but Mary Dyer was granted a last-minute reprieve. Banished once again, she returned shortly thereafter and was hanged on June 1, 1660.

An Act Made at a General Court, Held at Boston, the 20th of October, 1658

4. *Whereas there is a Cursed sect of hereticks, lately risen up in the world, which are commonly called Quakers, who take upon them to be immediately sent of God, and infallibly assisted by the Spirit, to speake and write blasphemous opinions despising government, and the order of God in Church & commonwealth, speaking evil of dignities, reproaching and reviling Magistrates and Ministers, seeking to turn the people from the faith, and gaine proselites to their pernicious wayes. The Court considering the premisses, and to prevent the like mischeife, as by their meanes is wrought in our native land;*

Reprinted from *The Laws and Liberties of Massachusetts, 1641–1691*, comp. John D. Cushing (Wilmington, Del.: Scholarly Resources, 1976), 1:35–36.

Doth hereby Order, And by the Authority of this Court be it Ordered & Enacted, That no *Master* or *Commander of any Ship, Barke, Pinnace, Catch* or other *Vessel,* shall henceforth bring into any harbour, Creek or Cove, within this Jurisdiction, any known *Quaker* or *Quakers,* or any other blasphemous hereticks as aforesayd, upon the penaltie of the forfeiture of *one hundred pounds,* to be forthwith payd to the Treasurer of the Country, except it appeareth that such Master, wanted true notice or information that they were such, and in that case he may cleare himself by his Oath, when sufficient proofe to the contrary is wanting. And for default of paiment of the sayd fine of *one hundred pounds,* or good security for the same, such Master shall be committed to prison, by warrant from any Magistrate, there to continue till the sayd fine be satisfyed to the Treasurer as aforesayd. And the *Master* or *Commander* of any such ship or vessel, that shall bring them being legally convicted, shall give in sufficient security to the Governour or any one or more of the Magistrates to carry them backe to the place, whence he brought them, and on his refusall so to doe, the Governour, or the said Magistrate or Magistrates, shall committ such Master or Commander to prison, there to continue till he shall give in sufficient security to the Content of the Governour or sayd Magistrates. And if any person or persons within this Iurisdiction, shall henceforth entertain & conceale any such *Quaker* or *Quakers* or other *Blasphemous hereticks* (knowing them to be such) every such person shall forfeit to the Countrey, *Fourty shillings* for every houres entertainement and concealment of any *Quaker* or *Quakers,* &c: as aforesayd, and shall be Committed to prison as aforesayd, till the fines be fully satisfyed and payd.

5. And every person or persons, that shall *incourage or defend* any of their pernicious wayes by speaking, writing, or meeting on the Lords day, or at any other time, shall after due meanes of conviction, incurr the penalty ensuing, *viz:* every person so meeting, shall pay to the use of the Country, for every time ten shillings & every one speaking in such meeting, shall forfeit five pounds.

6. If any person shall knowingly import into any harbour of this Jurisdiction, any *Quakers Books* or *Writings,* cōcerning their damnable opinions, he shall forfeit for every such book or writing *Five Pounds,* and whosoever shall disperse or conceale any such book or writing, and it be found with him or her, or in his or her house, & shall not immediately deliver the same to the next Magistrate, shall forfeit and pay *Five Pounds* for dispersing or Concealing every such Book or writing.

7. And every person or persons whatsoever, that shall revile the office or person of Magistrates or Ministers, as is usuall with the Quakers, such Person or Persons shall be *Severely Whipt,* or pay the Summ of *Five Pounds.*

8. And every person that shall publish and maintaine, any Heterodox or erroneous Doctrine, shall be liable to be questioned and Censured by the County Court where he liveth, according to the merit of his offence.

9. *Whereas there is a pernicious Sect commonly called Quakers lately arisen, who by word and writing, have published and maintained many dangerous and horrid tenents, and do take upon them to change & alter, the received laudable customes of our nation in giving Civil respect to equals, or reverence to Superiours, whose actions tend to undermine the Authority of Civil Government, as also to destroy the Order of the churches, by denying all established formes of worship, and by withdrawing from the orderly church assemblies, allowed & approved, by all Orthodox professors of the trueth; and instead thereof & opposition thereunto, frequenting private meetings of their own, Insinuating themselves into the minds of the Simpler, or such as are less affected to the Order & Government of the Church and Commonwealth, whereby divers of our Inhabitants have been infected and seduced, notwithstanding all former Lawes made, (upon experience of their arrogant bold obtrusions, to disseminate their principles amongst us) prohibiting their Comming into this Jurisdiction, they have not been deterred from their impetuous attempts, to undermine our peace, and hasten our ruine.*

For prevention thereof this Court doth Order and Enact, That every person or persons of the Cursed sect of the *Quakers,* who is not an Inhabitant of, but found within this Iurisdiction, shall be apprehended (without warrant, where no Magistrate is at hand) by any Constable Commissiioner or Select Man, and conveyed from Constable to Constable untill they come before the next Magistrate who shall Committ the sayd person or persons to close Prison, there to remaine without Baile, untill the next Court of Assistants where they shall have a Legall tryall, by a speciall jury, and being convicted to be of the sect of the *Quakers,* shall be sentenced to banishment upon paine of Death.

And that every Inhabitant of this Jurisdiction being convicted to be of the aforesayd sect, either by taking up, publishing and defending, the horrid opinions of the *Quakers,* or by stirring up *mutinie, Sedition* or *Rebellion,* against the Government, or by taking up their absurd & destructive practises, *viz* denying Civil respect and reverence to equals and Superiours, withdrawing from our church assemblies, & instead thereof frequenting private meetings of their own, in opposition to church Order, or by adhering to, or approving of any known Quakers, that are opposite to the Orthodox received opinions & practises of the godly, & endeavoring to disaffect others to Civil Government, and church order, and Condemning the practise & proceedings of this Court against the Quakers, manifesting thereby cōplyance with those, whose design is to overthrow the Order established in Church and Common wealth, every such person upon examination and legall conviction before the Court of Assistants in manner as aforesayd shall be committed to close prison, for one Month, and then unless they choose voluntarily to depart the Jurisdiction, shall give bond for their good abbearance and appearance at the next Court of Assistants, where Continuing obstinate, and refusing to retract & reform the aforesaid opinions & practises shall be sentenced to Banishment, upon paine of Death, and in case of the aforesaid voluntary departure not to remaine; or againe to returne into this Iurisdiction without the allowance of the major part of the Councell first had and published, on penalty of being Ban-

ished upon paine of Death, and any one Magistrate, upon information given him, of any such person, shall cause them to be apprehended, and if upon examination of the case he shall according to his best discretion, find just ground for such complaint, he shall commit such person to prison, untill he comes to his tryall as is above expressed.

A Declaration of the General Court of the *Massachusets* Holden at *Boston* in *New-England,* October 18, 1659. Concerning the Execution of Two Quakers.

Although the justice of our proceedings against William Robinson, Marmaduke Stevenson, *and* Mary Dyer, *supported by the Authority of this Court, the Lawes of the country; and the Law of God, may rather perswade us to expect incouragement and commendation from all prudent and pious men, then convince us of any necessity to Apologize for the same, yet forasmuch as men of weaker parts, out of pitty and commiseration (a commendable and Christian virtue yet easily abused, and susceptible of sinister and dangerous impressions) for want of full information, may be less satisfied, and men of perverser principles, may take occasion hereby to calumniate us, and render us as bloody persecutors, to satisfie the one, and stop the mouths of the other, we thought it requisite to declare.*

That about three Years since, divers persons, professing themselves *Quakers,* (of whose pernicious Opinions and Practises we had received intelligence from good hands, from *Barbadoes* to *England,* arrived at *Boston*) whose persons were onely secured, to be sent away by the first opportunity, without censure or punishment, although their professed tenents, tur-

Reprinted from *The Laws and Liberties of Massachusetts, 1641–1691,* comp. John D. Cushing (Wilmington, Del.: Scholarly Resources, 1976), 1:67.

bulent and contemptuous behaviour to Authority would have justified a severer animadversion, yet the prudence of this Court, was exercised, onely in making provision to secure the Peace and Order here established, against their attempts, whose design (we were well assured of by our own experience, as well as by the example of their predecessours in *Munster*) was to undermine and ruine the same,

And accordingly a Law was made and published, prohibiting all Masters of Ships, to bring any *Quakers* into this Jurisdiction, and themselves from comming in, on penalty of the House of Correction, till they could be sent away: Notwithstanding which, by a back Door, they found entrance, and the penalty inflicted on themselves, proving insufficient to restrain their impudent and insolent obtrusions, was increased by the loss of the ears of those that offended the second time, which also being too weak a defence against their impetuous frantick fury, necessitated us to endeavour our security, and upon serious consideration, after the former experiments, by their incessant assaults, a Law was made, that such persons should be banished, on pain of Death, according to the example of *England* in their provision against *Jesuites*, which sentence being regularly pronounced at the last Court of Assistants against the parties above named, and they either returning, or continuing presumptuously in this Jurisdiction, after the time limited, were apprehended, & owning themselves to be the persons banished, were sentenced (by the Court) to death, according the Law aforesaid, which hath been executed upon two of them: *Mary Dyer* upon the petition of her Son, and the mercy and clemency of this Court, had liberty to depart within two dayes, which she hath accepted of.

The consideration of our gradual proceeding, will vindicate us from the clamorous accusations of severity; our own just and necessary defence, calling upon us (other means fayling) to offer the poynt, which these persons have violently, and wilfully rushed upon, and thereby become *felons de se* [felons of themselves], which might it have been prevented, and the Soveraign Law *Salus populi* [welfare of peo-

ple] been preserved, our former proceedings, as well as the sparing of *Mary Dyer*, upon an inconsiderable intercession, will manifestly evince, we desire their lives absent, rather then their death present.

Printed by their order in

Reprinted in *London,* 1659

NEW-ENGLAND.

Edward Rawson, Secretary

FINIS

An Act for the Suppressing the Quakers, Virginia (1659)

Concerns about members of the Society of Friends (Quakers) were not limited to New England, as illustrated by the following Virginia statute.

ACT VI
An Act for the suppressing the Quakers

WHEREAS there is an vnreasonable and turbulent sort of people, comonly called Quakers, who contrary to the law do dayly gather together vnto them vnlaw'll Assemblies and congregations of people teaching and publishing, lies, miracles, false visions, prophecies and doctrines, which have influence vpon the comunities of men both ecclesiasticall and civil endeavouring and attemping thereby to destroy religion, lawes, comunities and all bonds of civil societie, leaveing it arbitrarie to everie vaine and vitious person whether men shall be safe, lawes established, offenders punished, and Governours rule, hereby disturbing the publique peace and just interest, to prevent and

Reprinted from *Colony Laws of Virginia, 1619–1660*, ed. John D. Cushing (Wilmington, Del.: Michael Glazier, 1978), 2:532–33.

restraine which mischiefe, *It is enacted,* That no master or comander of any shipp or other vessell do bring into this collonie any person or persons called Quakers, vnder the penalty of one hundred pounds sterling to be leavied vpon him and his estate by order from the Governour and Council or the comissioners in the severall counties where such shipps shall arrive, That all such Quakers as have beene questioned or shall hereafter arrive shall be apprehended wheresoever they shall be found and they be imprisoned without baile or mainprize till they do abjure this country or putt in security with all speed to depart the collonie and not to returne again: And if any should dare to presume to returne hither after such departure to be proceeded against as contemners of the lawes and magistracy and punished accordingly, and caused again to depart the country, And if they should the third time be so audacious and impudent as to returne hither to be proceeded against as ffelons. That noe person shall entertain any of the Quakers that have heretofore been questioned by the Governour and Council, or which shall hereafter be questioned, nor permit in or near his house any Assemblies of Quakers in the like penalty of one hundred pound sterling, That comissioners and officers are hereby required and authorized as they will answer the contrary at their perill to take notice of this act to see it fully effected and executed, And that no person do presume on their peril to dispose or publish their bookes, pamphlets or libells bearing the title of their tenents and opinions.

Charter of Rhode Island and Providence Plantations (1663)

Roger Williams founded Rhode Island's first permanent settlement in 1636, and the colony received a patent from Parliament in 1643. After the Stuart Restoration, the colony sought and received the following royal charter. The religious liberty protected by the charter and other organic laws of the colony made it a haven for religious minorities throughout the colonial era.

CHARLES THE SECOND, by the grace of *God,* King of England, Scotland, France and Ireland, Defender of the Faith, &c., to all to whome these presents shall come, greeting: *Whereas wee* have been informed, by the humble petition of our trustie and well beloved subject, John Clarke, on the behalf of Benjamine Arnold, William Brenton, William Codington, Nicholas Easton, William Boulston, John Porter, John Smith, Samuell Gorton, John Weeks, Roger Williams, Thomas Olnie, Gregorie Dexter, John Cogeshall, Joseph Clarke, Randall Holden, John Greene, John Roome, Samuell Wildbore, William Ffield, James Barker, Richard Tew, Thomas Harris, and William Dyre, and the rest of the purchasers and ffree inhabitants of our island, called *Rhode-Island,* and the rest of the colonie of Providence Plantations, in the Narragansett Bay, in New-England, in America, that they, pursueing, with peaceable and loyall mindes, their sober, serious and religious intentions, of godlie edifieing themselves, and one another, in the holie Christian ffaith and worshipp as they were perswaded; together with the gaineing over and conver-

Reprinted from *The Federal and State Constitutions, Colonial Charters, and Other Organic Laws of the States, Territories, and Colonies Now or Heretofore Forming the United States of America,* compiled and edited by Francis Newton Thorpe (Washington, D.C.: GPO, 1909), 6:3211–13.

sione of the poore ignorant Indian natives, in those partes of America, to the sincere professione and obedienc of the same ffaith and worship, did, not onlie by the consent and good encouragement of our royall progenitors, transport themselves out of this kingdome of England into America, but alsoe, since their arrivall there, after their first settlement amongst other our subjects in those parts, ffor the avoideing of discorde, and those manie evills which were likely to ensue upon some of those oure subjects not beinge able to beare, in these remote parties, theire different apprehensiones in religious concernements, and in pursueance of the afforesayd ends, did once againe leave theire desireable stationes and habitationes, and with excessive labour and travell, hazard and charge, did transplant themselves into the middest of the Indian natives, who, as wee are infformed, are the most potent princes and people of all that country; where, by the good Providence of God, from whome the Plantationes have taken their name, upon theire labour and industrie, they have not onlie byn preserved to admiration, but have increased and prospered, and are seized and possessed, by purchase and consent of the said natives, to their ffull content, of such lands, islands, rivers, harbours and roades, as are verie convenient, both for plantationes and alsoe for buildinge of shipps, suplye of pypestaves, and other merchandize; and which lyes verie commodious, in manie respects, for commerce, and to accommodate oure southern plantationes, and may much advance the trade of this oure realme, and greatlie enlarge the territories thereof; they haveinge, by neare neighbourhoode to and friendlie societie with the greate bodie of the Narragansett Indians, given them encouragement, of theire owne accorde, to subject themselves, theire people and landes, unto us; whereby, as is hoped, there may, in due tyme, by the blessing of God upon theire endeavours, bee layd a sure ffoundation of happinesse to all America:

And whereas, in theire humble addresse, they have ffreely declared, that it is much on their hearts (if they may be permitted), to hold forth a livlie experiment, that a most flourishing civill state may stand and best bee maintained, and that among our English subjects, with a full libertie in religious concernements; and that true pietye rightly grounded upon gospell principles, will give the best and greatest security to sovereignetye, and will lay in the hearts of men the strongest obligations to true loyaltye: *Now know yee,* that wee beinge willinge to encourage the hopefull undertakeinge of oure sayd loyall and loveinge subjects, and to secure them in the free exercise and enjoyment of all theire civill and religious rights, appertaining to them, as our loveing subjects; and to preserve unto them that libertye, in the true Christian ffaith and worshipp of God, which they have sought with soe much travaill, and with peaceable myndes, and loyall subjectione to our royall progenitors and ourselves, to enjoye; and because some of the people and inhabitants of the same colonie cannot, in theire private opinions, conforms to the publique exercise of religion, according to the litturgy, formes and ceremonyes of the Church of England, or take or subscribe the oaths and articles made and established in that behalfe; and for that the same, by reason of the remote distances of those places, will (as wee hope) bee noe breach of the unitie and unifformitie established in this nation: Have therefore thought ffit, and doe hereby publish, graunt, ordeyne and declare, That our royall will and pleasure is, that noe person within the sayd colonye, at any tyme hereafter, shall bee any wise molested, punished, disquieted, or called in question, for any differences in opinione in matters of religion, and doe not actually disturb the civill peace of our sayd colony; but that all and everye person and persons may, from tyme to tyme, and at all tymes hereafter, freelye and fullye have and enjoye his and theire owne judgments and consciences, in matters of religious concernments, throughout the tract of lande hereafter mentioned; they behaving themselves peaceablie and quietlie, and not useing this libertie to lycentiousnesse and profanenesse, nor to the civill injurye or outward disturbeance of others; any lawe, statute, or clause, therein contayned, or to bee contayned, usage or custome of this realme, to the contrary hereof, in any wise, notwithstanding. And

that they may bee in the better capacity to defend themselves, in theire just rights and libertyes against all the enemies of the Christian ffaith, and others, in all respects, wee have further thought fit, and at the humble petition of the persons aforesayd are gratiously pleased to declare, That they shall have and enjoye the benefitt of our late act of indempnity and ffree pardon, as the rest of our subjects in other our dominions and territoryes have; and to create and make them a bodye politique or corporate, with the powers and priviledges hereinafter mentioned.

Frame of Government of Pennsylvania (1682)

Laws Agreed Upon in England, &c. (1682)

WILLIAM PENN (1644–1718)

The son of Admiral Penn, William converted to Quakerism in his twenties and soon became an avid advocate of religious toleration. To settle a debt owed to his father, Charles II gave William the colony of Pennsylvania in 1681. The following excerpts are from the constitution and laws that Penn wrote to govern the colony.

Frame of Government of Pennsylvania, 1682

The frame of the government of the province of Pensilvania, *in* America: *together with certain* laws *agreed*

Preface reprinted from *The Federal and State Constitutions, Colonial Charters, and Other Organic Laws of the States, Territories, and Colonies Now or Heretofore Forming the United States of America,* comp. and ed. Francis Newton Thorpe (Washington, D.C.: GPO, 1909), 5:3052–54.

upon in England, *by the Governor and divers freemen of the aforesaid province. To be further explained and confirmed there, by the first provincial Council, that shall be held, if they see meet.*

The Preface

When the great and wise *God* had made the world, of all his creatures, it pleased him to chuse man his Deputy to rule it: and to fit him for so great a charge and trust, he did not only qualify him with skill and power, but with integrity to use them justly. This native goodness was equally his honour and his happiness; and whilst he stood here, all went well; there was no need of coercive or compulsive means; the precept of divine love and truth, in his bosom, was the guide and keeper of his innocency. But lust prevailing against duty, made a lamentable breach upon it; and the law, that before had no power over him, took place upon him, and his disobedient posterity, that such as would not live comfortable to the holy law within, should fall under the reproof and correction of the just law without, in a judicial administration.

This the Apostle teaches in divers of his epistles: "The law (says he) was added because of transgression:" In another place, "Knowing that the law was not made for the righteous man; but for the disobedient and ungodly, for sinners, for unholy and prophane, for murderers, for whoremongers, for them that defile themselves with mankind, and for man-stealers, for lyers, for perjured persons," &c., but this is not all, he opens and carries the matter of government a little further: "Let every soul be subject to the higher powers; for there is no power but of *God.* The powers that be are ordained of *God:* whosoever therefore resisteth the power, resisteth the ordinance of *God.* For rulers are not a terror to good works, but to evil: wilt thou then not be afraid of the power? do that which is good, and thou shalt have praise of the same." "He is the minister of God to thee for good." "Wherefore ye must needs be subject, not only for wrath, but for conscience sake."

This settles the divine right of government beyond exception, and that for two ends: first, to terrify evil doers: secondly, to cherish those that do well; which gives government a life beyond corruption, and makes it as durable in the world, as good men shall be. So that government seems to me a part of religion itself, a thing sacred in its institution and end. For, if it does not directly remove the cause, it crushes the effects of evil, and is as such, (though a lower, yet) an emanation of the same Divine Power, that is both author and object of pure religion; the difference lying here, that the one is more free and mental, the other more corporal and compulsive in its operations: but that is only to evil doers; government itself being otherwise as capable of kindness, goodness and charity, as a more private society. They weakly err, that think there is no other use of government, than correction, which is the coarsest part of it: daily experience tells us, that the care and regulation of many other affairs, more soft, and daily necessary, make up much of the greatest part of government; and which must have followed the peopling of the world, had Adam never fell, and will continue among men, on earth, under the highest attainments they may arrive at, by the coming of the blessed *Second Adam,* the *Lord* from heaven. Thus much of government in general, as to its rise and end.

For particular *frames* and *models,* it will become me to say little; and comparatively I will say nothing. My reasons are:

First. That the age is too nice and difficult for it; there being nothing the wits of men are more busy and divided upon. It is true, they seem to agree to the end, to wit, happiness; but, in the means, they differ, as to divine, so to this human felicity; and the cause is much the same, not always want of light and knowledge, but want of using them rightly. Men side with their passions against their reason, and their sinister interests have so strong a bias upon their minds, that they lean to them against the good of the things they know.

Secondly. I do not find a model in the world, that time, place, and some singular emergences have not

Engraving of William Penn by J. Hill after Benjamin West. © Bettmann/corbis

necessarily altered; nor is it easy to frame a civil government, that shall serve all places alike.

Thirdly. I know what is said by the several admirers of *monarchy, aristocracy* and *democracy,* which are the rule of one, a few, and many, and are the three common ideas of government, when men discourse on the subject. But I chuse to solve the controversy with this small distinction, and it belongs to all three: *Any government is free to the people under it* (whatever be the frame) *where the laws rule, and the people are a party to those laws,* and more than this is tyranny, oligarchy, or confusion.

But, lastly, when all is said, there is hardly one frame of government in the world so ill designed by its first founders, that, in good hands, would not do well enough; and story tells us, the best, in ill ones, can do nothing that is great or good; witness the *Jewish* and *Roman* states. Governments, like clocks, go from the motion men give them; and as governments are made and moved by men, so by them they are ruined too. Wherefore governments rather depend upon men, than men upon governments. Let men be good, and the government cannot be bad; if it be ill, they will cure it. But, if men be bad, let the government be never so good, they will endeavor to warp and spoil it to their turn.

I know some say, let us have good laws, and no matter for the men that execute them: but let them consider, that though good laws do well, good men do better: for good laws may want good men, and be abolished or evaded [invaded in Franklin's print] by ill men; but good men will never want good laws, nor suffer ill ones. It is true, good laws have some awe upon ill ministers, but that is where they have not power to escape or abolish them, and the people are generally wise and good: but a loose and depraved people (which is the question) love laws and an administration like themselves. That, therefore, which makes a good constitution, must keep it, *viz:* men of wisdom and virtue, qualities, that because they descend not with worldly inheritances, must be carefully propagated by a virtuous education of youth; for which after ages will owe more to the care and prudence of founders, and the successive magistracy, than to their parents, for their private patrimonies.

These considerations of the weight of government, and the nice and various opinions about it, made it uneasy to me to think of publishing the ensuing frame and conditional laws, forseeing both the censures, they will meet with, from men of differing humours and engagements, and the occasion they may give of discourse beyond my design.

But, next to the power of necessity, (which is a solicitor, that will take no denial) this induced me to a compliance, that we have (with reverence to God, and good conscience to men) to the best of our skill, contrived and composed the *frame* and *laws* of this government, to the great end of all government, viz: *To support power in reverence with the people, and to secure the people from the abuse of power;* that they may be free by their just obedience, and the magistrates honourable, for their just administration: for liberty without obedience is confusion, and obedience without liberty is slavery. To carry this evenness is partly owing to the constitution, and partly to the magistracy:

where either of these fail, government will be subject to convulsions; but where both are wanting, it must be totally subverted; then where both meet, the government is like to endure. Which I humbly pray and hope *God* will please to make the lot of this of *Pensilvania*. Amen.

WILLIAM PENN

Laws Agreed Upon in England, &c., 1682

XXXIV. That all Treasurers, Judges, Masters of the Rolls, Sheriffs, Justices of the Peace, and other officers and persons whatsoever, relating to courts, or trials of causes, or any other service in the government; and all Members elected to serve in provincial Council and General Assembly, and all that have right to elect such Members, shall be such as possess faith in Jesus Christ, and that are not convicted of ill fame, or unsober and dishonest conversation, and that are of one and twenty years of age, at least; and that all such so qualified, shall be capable of the said several employments and privileges, as aforesaid.

XXXV. That all persons living in this province, who confess and acknowledge the one Almighty and eternal God, to be the Creator, Upholder and Ruler of the world; and that hold themselves obliged in conscience to live peaceably and justly in civil society, shall, in no ways, be molested or prejudiced for their religious persuasion, or practice, in matters of faith and worship, nor shall they be compelled, at any time, to frequent or maintain any religious worship, place or ministry whatever.

Articles XXXIV–XXXVII reprinted from *The Federal and State Constitutions, Colonial Charters, and Other Organic Laws of the States, Territories, and Colonies Now or Heretofore Forming the United States of America,* comp. and ed. Francis Newton Thorpe (Washington, D.C.: GPO, 1909), 5:3062–63.

XXXVI. That, according to the good example of the primitive Christians, and the case of the creation, every first day of the week, called the Lord's day, people shall abstain from their common daily labour, that they may the better dispose themselves to worship God according to their understandings.

XXXVII. That as a careless and corrupt administration of justice draws the wrath of God upon magistrates, so the wildness and looseness of the people provoke the indignation of God against a country: therefore, that all such offences against God, as swearing, cursing, lying, prophane talking, drunkenness, drinking of healths, obscene words, incest, sodomy, rapes, whoredom, fornication, and other uncleanness (not to be repeated) all treasons, misprisions, murders, duels, felony, seditions, maims, forcible entries, and other violences, to the persons and estates of the inhabitants within this province; all prizes, stage-plays, cards, dice, May-games, gamesters, masques, revels, bull-baitings, cock-fightings, bear-baitings, and the like, which excite the people to rudeness, cruelty, looseness, and irreligion, shall be respectively discouraged, and severely punished, according to the appointment of the Governor and freemen in provincial Council and General Assembly; as also all proceedings contrary to these laws, that are not here made expressly penal.

The Fundamental Constitutions of Carolina (1669)

The eight proprietors of Carolina adopted the Fundamental Constitutions of Carolina in 1669. Reportedly drafted by John Locke, the document guarantees religious freedom within limits, as illustrated by the following excerpts.

Ninety-five. No man shall be permitted to be a freeman of Carolina, or to have any estate or habitation within it, that doth not acknowledge a God; and that God is publicly and solemnly to be worshipped.

Ninety-six. [As the country comes to be sufficiently planted and distributed into fit divisions, it shall belong to the parliament to take care for the building of churches, and the public maintenance of divines, to be employed in the exercise of religion, according to the Church of England; which being the only true and orthodox, and the national religion of all the King's dominions, is so also of Carolina; and, therefore, it alone shall be allowed to receive public maintenance, by grant of parliament.][a]

Ninety-seven. But since the natives of that place, who will be concerned in our plantation, are utterly strangers to Christianity, whose idolatry, ignorance, or mistake gives us no right to expel or use them ill; and those who remove from other parts to plant there will unavoidably be of different opinions concerning matters of religion, the liberty whereof they will expect to have allowed them, and it will not be reasonable for us, on this account, to keep them out, that civil peace may be maintained amidst diversity of opinions, and our agreement and compact with all men may be duly and faithfully observed; the violation whereof, upon what pretence soever, cannot be without great offence to Almighty God, and great scandal to the true religion which we profess; and also that Jews, heathens, and other dissenters from the purity of Christian religion may not be scared and kept at a distance from it, but, by having an opportunity of acquainting themselves with the truth and

Articles 95–110 reprinted from *The Federal and State Constitutions, Colonial Charters, and Other Organic Laws of the States, Territories, and Colonies Now or Heretofore Forming the United States of America,* comp. and ed. Francis Newton Thorpe (Washington, D.C.: GPO, 1909), 5:2783–85.

a. This article was not drawn up by Mr. Locke, but inserted by some of the chief of the proprietors, against his judgment; as Mr. Locke himself informed one of his friends, to whom he presented a copy of these constitutions.

reasonableness of its doctrines, and the peaceableness and inoffensiveness of its professors, may, by good usage and persuasion, and all those convincing methods of gentleness and meekness, suitable to the rules and design of the gospel, be won over to embrace and unfeignedly receive the truth; therefore, any seven or more persons agreeing in any religion, shall constitute a church or profession, to which they shall give some name, to distinguish it from others.

Ninety-eight. The terms of admittance and communion with any church or profession shall be written in a book, and therein be subscribed by all the members of the said church or profession; which book shall be kept by the public register of the precinct wherein they reside.

Ninety-nine. The time of every one's subscription and admittance shall be dated in the said book or religious record.

One hundred. In the terms of communion of every church or profession, these following shall be three; without which no agreement or assembly of men, upon pretence of religion, shall be accounted a church or profession within these rules:

1st. "That there is a God."

II. "That God is publicly to be worshipped."

III. "That it is lawful and the duty of every man, being thereunto called by those that govern, to bear witness to truth; and that every church or profession shall, in their terms of communion, set down the external way whereby they witness a truth as in the presence of God, whether it be by laying hands on or kissing the bible, as in the Church of England, or by holding up the hand, or any other sensible way."

One hundred and one. No person above seventeen years of age shall have any benefit or protection of the law, or be capable of any place of profit or honor, who is not a member of some church or profession, having his name recorded in some one, and but one religious record at once.

One hundred and two. No person of any other church or profession shall disturb or molest any religious assembly.

One hundred and three. No person whatsoever shall speak anything in their religious assembly irreverently or seditiously of the government or governors, or of state matters.

One hundred and four. Any person subscribing the terms of communion, in the record of the said church or profession, before the precinct register, and any five members of the said church or profession, shall be thereby made a member of the said church or profession.

One hundred and five. Any person striking out his own name out of any religious record, or his name being struck out by any officer thereunto authorized by each church or profession respectively, shall cease to be a member of that church or profession.

One hundred and six. No man shall use any reproachful, reviling, or abusive language against any religion of any church or profession; that being the certain way of disturbing the peace, and of hindering the conversion of any to the truth, by engaging them in quarrels and animosities, to the hatred of the professors and that profession which otherwise they might be brought to assent to.

One hundred and seven. Since charity obliges us to wish well to the souls of all men, and religion ought to alter nothing in any man's civil estate or right, it shall be lawful for slaves, as well as others, to enter themselves, and be of what church or profession any of them shall think best, and, therefore, be as fully members as any freeman. But yet no slave shall hereby be exempted from that civil dominion his master hath over him, but be in all things in the same state and condition he was in before.

One hundred and eight. Assemblies, upon what pretence soever of religion, not observing and performing the above said rules, shall not be esteemed as churches, but unlawful meetings, and be punished as other riots.

One hundred and nine. No person whatsover shall disturb, molest, or persecute another for his speculative opinions in religion, or his way of worship.

One hundred and ten. Every freeman of Carolina shall have absolute power and authority over his negro slaves, of what opinion or religion soever.

RECOMMENDATIONS FOR FURTHER READING

Botein, Stephen. "Religious Dimensions of the Early American State." In *Beyond Confederation: Origins of the Constitution and American National Identity,* edited by Richard Beeman, Stephen Botein, and Edward C. Carter II, 315–30. Chapel Hill: University of North Carolina Press, 1987.

Cobb, Sanford H. *The Rise of Religious Liberty in America: A History.* New York: Macmillan, 1902.

Curry, Thomas J. *The First Freedoms: Church and State in America to the Passage of the First Amendment.* New York: Oxford University Press, 1986.

Greene, Evarts B. *Religion and the State: The Making and Testing of an American Tradition.* New York: New York University Press, 1941.

CHAPTER THREE

Letters, Tracts, and Sermons on Religious Liberty and Duty in Colonial America

ORGANIC AND STATUTORY LAWS, such as those presented in the last chapter, may exist without significant theoretical justification. From the very beginning, however, leading Americans provided sophisticated arguments to support or attempt to change the laws under which they lived. Well into the late 1700s, the most common and influential arguments were based on Christian scripture and theology. In many cases these arguments were made by clergy—who were often the most educated and respected persons in their communities. Nonclergy were just as likely to rely upon biblical arguments, as illustrated by John Winthrop's famous speech aboard the *Arbella*. This speech, along with John Cotton's discourse, Charles Chauncy's sermon, and the Cambridge Platform, represent arguments commonly used by colonial Americans to defend state support and protection of religion.

A commitment to scripture did not guarantee a uniformity of belief regarding church-state relations and the proper extent of religious liberty. For instance, the Reverends Roger Williams, Samuel Davies, and Isaac Backus presented powerful scriptural critiques of existing establishment practices. Al-

though they were not averse to making legal arguments or drawing from other sources to support their positions, in each case they argued for religious liberty on biblical and theological grounds.

As the eighteenth century progressed, extrabiblical authorities and ideas began to play a more prominent role in American political discourse. Among the most important of these sources were the writings of John Locke. Scholars debate whether or not Locke was a Christian and the extent to which his writings are compatible with orthodox Christianity. Regardless of how these questions are answered, virtually all Americans who borrowed Locke's ideas or appealed to him as an authority believed his works to be compatible with, or required by, the Christian faith. Excerpts from works by Elisha Williams and Samuel Adams illustrate how Locke and his ideas could be used by Christian political and religious leaders in eighteenth-century America. Although the extent of his influence in the era remains a subject of debate, few deny that his works had a significant impact on American views on the interaction between church and state and on the nature and extent of religious liberty.

A Modell of Christian Charitie (1630)

Little Speech on Liberty (1645)

JOHN WINTHROP (1588–1649)

John Winthrop was governor or deputy governor of Massachusetts Bay Company almost every year from his arrival in 1630 to his death in 1649. "A Modell of Christian Charitie" was written and preached aboard the *Arbella,* the ship that carried Winthrop to America. The sermon illustrates the Puritan vision of "a Citty upon a Hill" that would serve as an example to the nations.

In 1645, when he was serving as deputy governor, Winthrop was impeached by the colony's lower house for exceeding his constitutional powers. Upon his acquittal, he delivered a "little speech" to his accusers on the nature of liberty.

A Modell of Christian Charitie

Written
On Boarde the Arrabella,
On the Attlantick Ocean.
By the Honorable JOHN WINTHROP *Esquire.*
In His passage, (with the great Company of Religious people, of which Christian Tribes he was the Brave Leader and famous Governor;) from the Island of Great Brittaine, to New-England in the North America.

Anno 1630.

Reprinted from *Winthrop Papers,* ed. Stewart Mitchell (Boston: Massachusetts Historical Society, 1931), 2:282–95. Used by permission of the Massachusetts Historical Society.

Christian Charitie

A Modell Hereof

God Almightie in his most holy and wise providence hath soe disposed of the Condicion of mankinde, as in all times some must be rich some poore, some highe and eminent in power and dignitie; others meane and in subieccion.

The Reason Hereof

1. REAS: *First,* to hold conformity with the rest of his workes, being delighted to shewe forthe the glory of his wisdome in the variety and difference of the Creatures and the glory of his power, in ordering all these differences for the preservacion and good of the whole, and the glory of his greatnes that as it is the glory of princes to haue many officers, soe this great King will haue many Stewards counting himselfe more honoured in dispenceing his guifts to man by man, then if hee did it by his owne immediate hand.

2. REAS: *Secondly,* That he might haue the more occasion to manifest the worke of his Spirit: first, vpon the wicked in moderateing and restraineing them: soe that the riche and mighty should not eate vpp the poore, nor the poore, and dispised rise vpp against theire superiours, and shake off theire yoake; 2ly in the regenerate in exerciseing his graces in them, as in the greate ones, theire loue mercy, gentlenes, temperance etc., in the poore and inferiour sorte, theire faithe patience, obedience etc:

3. REAS: Thirdly, That every man might haue need of other, and from hence they might be all knitt more nearly together in the Bond of brotherly affeccion: from hence it appeares plainely that noe man is made more honourable then another or more wealthy etc., out of any perticuler and singuler respect to himselfe but for the glory of his Creator and the Common good of the Creature, Man; Therefore God still reserues the propperty of these guifts to himselfe as Ezek: 16. 17. he there calls wealthe his gold and his silver etc. Prov: 3. 9. he claimes theire seruice as his due honour the Lord with thy riches etc. All men being thus (by divine providence) rancked into two

sortes, riche and poore; vnder the first, are comprehended all such as are able to liue comfortably by
theire owne meanes duely improued; and all others
are poore according to the former distribution. There
are two rules whereby wee are to walke one towards
another: JUSTICE and MERCY. These are allwayes
distinguished in theire Act and in theire obiect, yet
may they both concurre in the same Subiect in eache
respect; as sometimes there may be an occasion of
shewing mercy to a rich man, in some sudden danger
of distresse, and allsoe doeing of meere Justice to a
poor man in regard of some perticuler contract etc.
There is likewise a double Lawe by which wee are regulated in our conversacion one towardes another: in
both the former respects, the lawe of nature and the
lawe of grace, or the morrall lawe or the lawe of the
gospell, to omitt the rule of Justice as not propperly
belonging to this purpose otherwise then it may fall
into consideracion in some perticuler Cases: By the
first of these lawes man as he was enabled soe withall
[is] commaunded to loue his neighbour as himselfe
vpon this ground stands all the precepts of the morrall
lawe, which concernes our dealings with men. To apply this to the works of mercy this lawe requires two
things first that every man afford his help to another
in every want or distresse Secondly, That hee performe this out of the same affeccion, which makes
him carefull of his owne good according to that of our
Saviour Math: [7.12] Whatsoever ye would that men
should doe to you. This was practised by Abraham
and Lott in entertaineing the Angells and the old
man of Gibea.

The Lawe of Grace or the Gospell hath some dif-
ferance from the former as in these respectes first the
lawe of nature was giuen to man in the estate of innocency; this of the gospell in the estate of regener-
acy: 2ly, the former propounds one man to another,
as the same fleshe and Image of god, this as a brother
in Christ allsoe, and in the Communion of the same
spirit and soe teacheth vs to put a difference betweene
Christians and others. Doe good to all especially to
the household of faith; vpon this ground the Israelites
were to putt a difference betweene the brethren of
such as were strangers though not of the Canaanites.
3ly. The Lawe of nature could giue noe rules for deale-
ing with enemies for all are to be considered as freinds
in the estate of innocency, but the Gospell com-
maunds loue to an enemy. proofe. If thine Enemie
hunger feede him; Loue your Enemies doe good to
them that hate you Math: 5. 44.

This Lawe of the Gospell propoundes likewise a
difference of seasons and occasions there is a time
when a christian must sell all and giue to the poore as
they did in the Apostles times. There is a tyme allsoe
when a christian (though they giue not all yet) must
giue beyond theire abillity, as they of Macedonia.
Cor: 2. 6. likewise community of perills calls for extraordinary liberallity and soe doth Community in
some speciall seruice for the Churche. Lastly, when
there is noe other meanes whereby our Christian
brother may be releiued in this distresse, wee must
help him beyond our ability, rather then tempt God,
in putting him vpon help by miraculous or extraordinary meanes.

This duty of mercy is exercised in the kindes,
Giueing, lending, and forgiueing.

QUEST. What rule shall a man observe in giueing
in respect of the measure?

ANS. If the time and occasion be ordinary he is to
giue out of his aboundance—let him lay aside, as god
hath blessed him. If the time and occasion be extraordinary he must be ruled by them; takeing this withall,
that then a man cannot likely doe too much especially,
if he may leaue himselfe and his family vnder probable meanes of comfortable subsistance.

OBIECTION. A man must lay vpp for posterity,
the fathers lay vpp for posterity and children and he
is worse then an Infidell that prouideth not for his
owne.

ANS: For the first, it is plaine, that it being spoken by way of Comparison it must be meant of the
ordinary and vsuall course of fathers and cannot extend to times and occasions extraordinary; for the
other place the Apostle speakes against such as
walked inordinately, and it is without question, that
he is worse then an Infidell whoe throughe his owne

Sloathe and voluptuousnes shall neglect to prouide for his family.

OBIECTION. The wise mans Eies are in his head (saith Salomon) and foreseeth the plague, therefore wee must forecast and lay vpp against euill times when hee or his may stand in need of all he can gather.

ANS: This very Argument Salomon vseth to perswade to liberallity. Eccle: [11.1.] cast thy bread vpon the waters etc.: for thou knowest not what euill may come vpon the land Luke 16. make you freinds of the riches of Iniquity; you will aske how this shall be? very well. for first he that giues to the poore lends to the lord, and he will repay him euen in this life an hundred fold to him or his. The righteous is euer mercifull and lendeth and his seed enioyeth the blessing; and besides wee know what advantage it will be to vs in the day of account, when many such Witnesses shall stand forthe for vs to witnesse the improuement of our Tallent. And I would knowe of those whoe pleade soe much for layeing vp for time to come, whether they hold that to be Gospell Math: 16. 19. Lay not vpp for yourselues Treasures vpon Earth etc. if they acknowledge it what extent will they allowe it; if onely to those primitiue times lett them consider the reason wherevpon our Saviour groundes it, the first is that they are subiect to the moathe, the rust the Theife. Secondly, They will steale away the hearte, where the treasure is there will the heart be allsoe. The reasons are of like force at all times therefore the exhortacion must be generall and perpetuall which [applies] allwayes in respect of the loue and affeccion to riches and in regard of the things themselues when any speciall seruice for the churche or perticuler distresse of our brother doe call for the vse of them; otherwise it is not onely lawfull but necessary to lay vpp as Joseph did to haue ready vppon such occasions, as the Lord (whose stewards wee are of them) shall call for them from vs: Christ giues vs an Instance of the first, when hee sent his disciples for the Asse, and bids them answer the owner thus, the Lord hath need of him; soe when the Tabernacle was to be builte his [servant] sends to his people to call for their silver and gold etc.; and yeildes them noe other reason but that it was for

his worke, when Elisha comes to the widowe of Sareptah and findes her prepareing to make ready her pittance for herselfe and family, he bids her first prouide for him, he challengeth first gods parte which shee must first giue before shee must serue her owne family, all these teach vs that the lord lookes that when hee is pleased to call for his right in any thing wee haue, our owne Interest wee haue must stand aside, till his turne be serued, for the other wee need looke noe further then to that of John 1. he whoe hath this worlds goodes and seeth his brother to neede, and shutts vpp his Compassion from him, how dwelleth the loue of god in him, which comes punctually to this Conclusion: if thy brother be in want and thou canst help him, thou needst not make doubt, what thou shouldst doe, if thou louest god thou must help him.

QUEST: What rule must wee obserue in lending?

ANS: Thou must obserue whether thy brother hath present or probable, or possible meanes of repayeing thee, if ther be none of these, thou must giue him according to his necessity, rather then lend him as hee requires; if he hath present meanes of repayeing thee, thou art to looke at him, not as an Act of mercy, but by way of Commerce, wherein thou arte to walke by the rule of Justice, but, if his meanes of repayeing thee be onely probable or possible then is hee an obiect of thy mercy thou must lend him, though there be danger of looseing it Deut: 15. 7. If any of thy brethren be poore etc. thou shalt lend him sufficient that men might not shift off this duty by the apparant hazzard, he tells them that though the Yeare of Jubile were at hand (when he must remitt it, if hee were not able to repay it before) yet he must lend him and that chearefully: it may not greiue thee to giue him (saith hee) and because some might obiect, why soe I should soone impoverishe my selfe and my family, he adds with all thy Worke etc. for our Saviour Math: 5. 42. From him that would borrow of thee turne not away.

QUEST: What rule must wee obserue in forgiueing?

ANS: Whether thou didst lend by way of Commerce or in mercy, if he haue noething to pay thee

[thou] must forgiue him (except in cause where thou hast a surety or a lawfull pleadge) Deut. 15. 2. Every seaventh yeare the Creditor was to quitt that which hee lent to his brother if hee were poore as appeares ver: 8[4]: saue when there shall be noe poore with thee. In all these and like Cases Christ was a generall rule Math: 7. 22. Whatsoever ye would that men should doe to you doe yee the same to them allsoe.

QUEST: What rule must wee obserue and walke by in cause of Community of perill?

ANS: The same as before, but with more enlargement towardes others and lesse respect towards our selues, and our owne right hence it was that in the primitiue Churche they sold all had all things in Common, neither did any man say that that which he possessed was his owne likewise in theire returne out of the Captiuity, because the worke was greate for the restoreing of the church and the danger of enemies was Common to all Nehemiah exhortes the Jewes to liberallity and readines in remitting theire debtes to theire brethren, and disposeth liberally of his owne to such as wanted and stands not vpon his owne due, which hee might haue demaunded of them, thus did some of our forefathers in times of persecucion here in England, and soe did many of the faithfull in other Churches whereof wee keepe an honourable remembrance of them, and it is to be obserued that both in Scriptures and latter stories of the Churches that such as haue beene most bountifull to the poore Saintes especially in these extraordinary times and occasions god hath left them highly Commended to posterity, as Zacheus, Cornelius, Dorcas, Bishop Hooper, the Cuttler of Brussells and divers others obserue againe that the scripture giues noe causion to restraine any from being over liberall this way; but all men to the liberall and cherefull practise hereof by the sweetest promises as to instance one for many, Isaiah 58. 6: Is not this the fast that I haue chosen to loose the bonds of wickednes, to take off the heavy burdens to lett the oppressed goe free and to breake every Yoake, to deale thy bread to the hungry and to bring the poore that wander into thy house, when thou seest the naked to cover them etc. then shall thy light breake forthe as the morneing, and thy healthe shall growe speedily, thy righteousnes shall goe before thee, and the glory of the lord shall embrace thee, then thou shalt call and the lord shall Answer thee etc. 2. 10: If thou power out thy soule to the hungry, then shall thy light spring out in darknes, and the lord shall guide thee continually, and satisfie thy Soule in draught, and make fatt thy bones, thou shalt be like a watered Garden, and they shall be of thee that shall build the old wast places etc. on the contrary most heavy cursses are layd vpon such as are straightened towards the Lord and his people Judg: 5. [23] Cursse ye Meroshe because the[y] came not to help the Lord etc. Pro: [21. 13] Hee whoe shutteth his eares from hearing the cry of the poore, he shall cry and shall not be heard: Math: 25. [41] Goe ye curssed into everlasting fire etc. [42.] I was hungry and ye fedd mee not. Cor: 2. 9. 16. [6.] He that soweth spareingly shall reape spareingly.

Haueing allready sett forth the practise of mercy according to the rule of gods lawe, it will be vsefull to lay open the groundes of it allsoe being the other parte of the Commaundement and that is the affeccion from which this exercise of mercy must arise, the Apostle tells vs that this loue is the fullfilling of the lawe, not that it is enough to loue our brother and soe noe further but in regard of the excellency of his partes giueing any motion to the other as the Soule to the body and the power it hath to sett all the faculties on worke in the outward exercise of this duty as when wee bid one make the clocke strike he doth not lay hand on the hammer which is the immediate instrument of the sound but sets on worke the first mouer or maine wheele, knoweing that will certainely produce the sound which hee intends; soe the way to drawe men to the workes of mercy is not by force of Argument from the goodnes or necessity of the worke, for though this course may enforce a rationall minde to some present Act of mercy as is frequent in experience, yet it cannot worke such a habit in a Soule as shall make it prompt vpon all occasions to produce the same effect but by frameing these affeccions of loue in the hearte which will as natiuely bring forthe the other, as any cause doth produce the effect.

The diffinition which the Scripture giues vs of loue is this Loue is the bond of perfection. First, it is a bond, or ligament. 2ly, it makes the worke perfect. There is noe body but consistes of partes and that which knitts these partes together giues the body its perfeccion, because it makes eache parte soe contiguous to other as thereby they doe mutually participate with eache other, both in strengthe and infirmity in pleasure and paine, to instance in the most perfect of all bodies, Christ and his church make one body: the severall partes of this body considered aparte before they were vnited were as disproportionate and as much disordering as soe many contrary quallities or elements but when christ comes and by his spirit and loue knitts all these partes to himselfe and each to other, it is become the most perfect and best proportioned body in the world Eph: 4. 16. "Christ by whome all the body being knitt together by every ioynt for the furniture thereof according to the effectuall power which is in the measure of every perfeccion of partes a glorious body without spott or wrinckle the ligaments hereof being Christ or his loue for Christ is loue["] 1 John: 4. 8. Soe this definition is right Loue is the bond of perfeccion.

From hence wee may frame these Conclusions.

1 first all true Christians are of one body in Christ 1. Cor. 12. 12. 13. 17. [27.] Ye are the body of Christ and members of [your?] parte.

2ly. The ligamentes of this body which knitt together are loue.

3ly. Noe body can be perfect which wants its propper ligamentes.

4ly. All the partes of this body being thus vnited are made soe contiguous in a speciall relacion as they must needes partake of each others strength and infirmity, ioy, and sorrowe, weale and woe. 1 Cor: 12. 26. If one member suffers all suffer with it, if one be in honour, all reioyce with it.

5ly. This sensiblenes and Sympathy of each others Condicions will necessarily infuse into each parte a natiue desire and endeavour, to strengthen defend preserue and comfort the other.

To insist a little on this Conclusion being the product of all the former the truthe hereof will appeare both by precept and patterne i. John. 3. 10. yee ought to lay downe your liues for the brethren Gal: 6. 2. beare ye one anothers burthens and soe fulfill the lawe of Christ.

For patterns wee haue that first of our Saviour whoe out of his good will in obedience to his father, becomeing a parte of this body, and being knitt with it in the bond of loue, found such a natiue sensiblenes of our infirmities and sorrowes as hee willingly yeilded himselfe to deathe to ease the infirmities of the rest of his body and soe heale theire sorrowes: from the like Sympathy of partes did the Apostles and many thousands of the Saintes lay downe theire liues for Christ againe, the like wee may see in the members of this body among themselues. 1. Rom. 9. Paule could haue beene contented to haue beene seperated from Christ that the Jewes might not be cutt off from the body: It is very obseruable which hee professeth of his affectionate part[ak]eing with every member: whoe is weake (saith hee) and I am not weake? whoe is offended and I burne not; and againe. 2 Cor: 7. 13. therefore wee are comforted because yee were comforted. of Epaphroditus he speaketh Phil: 2. 30. that he regarded not his owne life to [do] him seruice soe Phebe. and others are called the seruantes of the Churche, now it is apparant that they serued not for wages or by Constrainte but out of loue, the like wee shall finde in the histories of the churche in all ages the sweete Sympathie of affeccions which was in the members of this body one towardes another, theire chearfullnes in serueing and suffering together how liberall they were without repineing harbourers without grudgeing and helpfull without reproacheing and all from hence they had feruent loue amongst them which onely make[s] the practise of mercy constant and easie.

The next consideracion is how this loue comes to be wrought; Adam in his first estate was a perfect modell of mankinde in all theire generacions, and in him this loue was perfected in regard of the habit, but Adam Rent in himselfe from his Creator, rent all his posterity allsoe one from another, whence it comes that every man is borne with this principle in him, to loue and seeke himselfe onely and thus a man continueth till Christ comes and takes possession of the soule, and infuseth another principle loue to God and our brother. And this latter haueing continuall supply from Christ, as the head and roote by which hee is vnited get the predominency in the soule, soe by little and little expells the former 1 John 4. 7. loue cometh of god and every one that loueth is borne of god, soe that this loue is the fruite of the new birthe, and none can haue it but the new Creature, now when this quallity is thus formed in the soules of men it workes like the Spirit vpon the drie bones Ezek. 37. [7] bone came to bone, it gathers together the scattered bones or perfect old man Adam and knitts them into one body againe in Christ whereby a man is become againe a liueing soule.

The third Consideracion is concerning the exercise of this loue, which is twofold, inward or outward, the outward hath beene handled in the former preface of this discourse, for vnfolding the other wee must take in our way that maxime of philosophy, Simile simili gaudet or like will to like; for as it is things which are carued with disafeccion to eache other, the ground of it is from a dissimilitude or [blank] ariseing from the contrary or different nature of the things themselues, soe the ground of loue is an apprehension of some resemblance in the things loued to that which affectes it, this is the cause why the Lord loues the Creature, soe farre as it hath any of his Image in it, he loues his elect because they are like himselfe, he beholds them in his beloued sonne: soe a mother loues her childe, because shee throughly conceiues a resemblance of herselfe in it. Thus it is betweene the members of Christ, each discernes by the worke of the spirit his owne Image and resemblance in another, and therefore cannot but loue him as he loues himselfe: Now when the soule which is of a sociable nature findes any thing like to it selfe, it is like Adam when Eue was brought to him, shee must haue it one with her-

selfe this is fleshe of my fleshe (saith shee) and bone of my bone shee conceiues a greate delighte in it, therefore shee desires nearenes and familiarity with it: shee hath a greate propensity to doe it good and receiues such content in it, as feareing the miscarriage of her beloued shee bestowes it in the inmost closett of her heart, shee will not endure that it shall want any good which shee can giue it, if by occasion shee be withdrawne from the Company of it, shee is still lookeing towards the place where shee left her beloued, if shee heare it groane shee is with it presently, if shee finde it sadd and disconsolate shee sighes and mournes with it, shee hath noe such ioy, as to see her beloued merry and thriueing, if shee see it wronged, shee cannot beare it without passion, shee setts noe boundes of her affeccions, nor hath any thought of reward, shee findes recompence enoughe in the exercise of her loue towardes it, wee may see this Acted to life in Jonathan and David. Jonathan a valiant man endued with the spirit of Christ, soe soone as hee Discovers the same spirit in David had presently his hearte knitt to him by this linement of loue, soe that it is said he loued him as his owne soule, he takes soe great pleasure in him that hee stripps himselfe to adorne his beloued, his fathers kingdome was not soe precious to him as his beloued David, David shall haue it with all his hearte, himselfe desires noe more but that hee may be neare to him to reioyce in his good hee chooseth to converse with him in the wildernesse even to the hazzard of his owne life, rather then with the greate Courtiers in his fathers Pallace; when hee sees danger towards him, hee spares neither care paines, nor perill to divert it, when Iniury was offered his beloued David, hee could not beare it, though from his owne father, and when they must parte for a Season onely, they thought theire heartes would haue broake for sorrowe, had not theire affeccions found vent by aboundance of Teares: other instances might be brought to shewe the nature of this affeccion as of Ruthe and Naomi and many others, but this truthe is cleared enough. If any shall obiect that it is not possible that loue should be bred or vpheld without hope of requitall, it is graunted but that is not our cause, for this loue is allwayes vnder reward it never giues, but it allwayes receiues with advantage: first, in regard that among the members of the same body, loue and affection are reciprocall in a most equall and sweete kinde of Commerce. 2ly [3ly], in regard of the pleasure and content that the exercise of loue carries with it as wee may see in the naturall body the mouth is at all the paines to receiue, and mince the foode which serues for the nourishment of all the other partes of the body, yet it hath noe cause to complaine; for first, the other partes send backe by secret passages a due proporcion of the same nourishment in a better forme for the strengthening and comforteing the mouthe. 2ly the labour of the mouthe is accompanied with such pleasure and content as farre exceedes the paines it takes: soe is it in all the labour of loue, among christians, the partie loueing, reapes loue againe as was shewed before, which the soule covetts more then all the wealthe in the world. 2ly [4ly]. noething yeildes more pleasure and content to the soule then when it findes that which it may loue fervently, for to loue and liue beloued is the soules paradice, both heare and in heaven: In the State of Wedlock there be many comfortes to beare out the troubles of that Condicion; but let such as haue tryed the most, say if there be any sweetnes in that Condicion comparable to the exercise of mutuall loue.

From the former Consideracions ariseth these Conclusions.

1 First, This loue among Christians is a reall thing not Imaginarie.

2ly. This loue is as absolutely necessary to the being of the body of Christ, as the sinewes and other ligaments of a naturall body are to the being of that body.

3ly. This loue is a divine spirituall nature free, actiue strong Couragious permanent vnder valueing all things beneathe its propper obiect, and of all the graces this makes vs nearer to resemble the virtues of our heavenly father.

4ly, It restes in the loue and wellfare of its beloued, for the full and certaine knowledge of these truthes concerning the nature vse, [and] excellency of this grace, that which the holy ghost hath left recorded 1. Cor. 13. may giue full satisfaccion which is needfull for every true member of this louely body of the Lord Jesus, to worke vpon theire heartes, by prayer meditacion continuall exercise at least of the speciall [power] of this grace till Christ be formed in them and they in him all in eache other knitt together by this bond of loue.

It rests now to make some application of this discourse by the present designe which gaue the occasion of writeing of it. Herein are 4 things to be propounded: first the persons, 2ly, the worke, 3ly, the end, 4ly the meanes.

1. For the persons, wee are a Company professing our selues fellow members of Christ, In which respect only though wee were absent from eache other many miles, and had our imploymentes as farre distant, yet wee ought to account our selues knitt together by this bond of loue, and liue in the excercise of it, if wee would haue comforte of our being in Christ, this was notorious in the practise of the Christians in former times, as is testified of the Waldenses from the mouth of one of the adversaries Aeneas Syluius, mutuo [solent amare] penè antequam norint,* they vse to loue any of theire owne religion even before they were acquainted with them.

2ly. for the worke wee haue in hand, it is by a mutuall consent through a speciall overruleing providence, and a more then an ordinary approbation of the Churches of Christ to seeke out a place of Cohabitation and Consorteshipp vnder a due forme of Government both ciuill and ecclesiasticall. In such cases as this the care of the publique must oversway all private respects, by which not onely conscience, but meare Ciuill pollicy doth binde vs; for it is a true rule that perticuler estates cannott subsist in the ruine of the publique.

3ly. The end is to improue our liues to doe more seruice to the Lord the comforte and encrease of the body of christe whereof wee are members that our

---

* This is a shortened form of the original: *noscunt et amant mutuo paene antequam noverint,* or "They are accustomed to love mutually almost before they have met."—Trans.

selues and posterity may be the better preserued from the Common corrupcions of this euill world to serue the Lord and worke out our Salvacion vnder the power and purity of his holy Ordinances.

4ly for the meanes whereby this must bee effected, they are 2fold, a Conformity with the worke and end wee aime at, these wee see are extraordinary, therefore wee must not content our selues with vsuall ordinary meanes whatsoever wee did or ought to haue done when wee liued in England, the same must wee doe and more allsoe where wee goe: That which the most in theire Churches maineteine as a truthe in profession onely, wee must bring into familiar and constant practise, as in this duty of loue wee must loue brotherly without dissimulation, wee must loue one another with a pure hearte feruently wee must beare one anothers burthens, wee must not looke onely on our owne things, but allsoe on the things of our brethren, neither must wee think that the lord will beare with such faileings at our hands as hee dothe from those among whome wee haue liued, and that for 3 Reasons.

1. In regard of the more neare bond of mariage, betweene him and vs, wherein he hath taken vs to be his after a most strickt and peculiar manner which will make him the more Jealous of our loue and obedience soe he tells the people of Israell, you onely haue I knowne of all the families of the Earthe therefore will I punishe you for your Transgressions.

2ly, because the lord will be sanctified in them that come neare him. Wee know that there were many that corrupted the seruice of the Lord some setting vpp Alters before his owne, others offering both strange fire and strange Sacrifices allsoe; yet there came noe fire from heaven, or other sudden Judgement vpon them as did vpon Nadab and Abihu whoe yet wee may thinke did not sinne presumptuously.

3ly When God giues a speciall Commission he lookes to haue it stricktly obserued in every Article, when hee gaue Saule a Commission to destroy Amaleck hee indented with him vpon certaine Articles and because hee failed in one of the least, and that vpon a faire pretence, it lost him the kingdome,

which should haue beene his reward, if hee had obserued his Commission: Thus stands the cause betweene God and vs, wee are entered into Covenant with him for this worke, wee haue taken out a Commission, the Lord hath giuen vs leaue to drawe our owne Articles wee haue professed to enterprise these Accions vpon these and these ends, wee haue herevpon besought him of favour and blessing: Now if the Lord shall please to heare vs, and bring vs in peace to the place wee desire, then hath hee ratified this Covenant and sealed our Commission, [and] will expect a strickt performance of the Articles contained in it, but if wee shall neglect the observacion of these Articles which are the ends wee haue propounded, and dissembling with our God, shall fall to embrace this present world and prosecute our carnall intencions, seekeing great things for our selues and our posterity, the Lord will surely breake out in wrathe against vs be revenged of such a periured people and make vs knowe the price of the breache of such a Covenant.

Now the onely way to avoyde this shipwracke and to provide for our posterity is to followe the Counsell of Micah, to doe Justly, to loue mercy, to walke humbly with our God, for this end, wee must be knitt together in this worke as one man, wee must entertaine each other in brotherly Affeccion, wee must be willing to abridge our selues of our superfluities, for the supply of others necessities, wee must vphold a familiar Commerce together in all meekenes, gentlenes, patience and liberallity, wee must delight in eache other, make others Condicions our owne reioyce together, mourne together, labour, and suffer together, allwayes haueing before our eyes our Commission and Community in the worke, our Community as members of the same body, soe shall wee keepe the vnitie of the spirit in the bond of peace, the Lord will be our God and delight to dwell among vs, as his owne people and will commaund a blessing vpon vs in all our wayes, soe that wee shall see much more of his wisdome power goodnes and truthe then formerly wee haue beene acquainted with, wee shall finde that the God of Israell is among vs, when tenn of vs shall be able to resist a thousand of our enemies, when hee shall make vs a prayse and glory, that men shall say of succeeding plantacions: the lord make it like that of New England: for wee must Consider that wee shall be as a Citty vpon a Hill, the eies of all people are vppon vs; soe that if wee shall deale falsely with our god in this worke wee haue vndertaken and soe cause him to withdrawe his present help from vs, wee shall be made a story and a by-word through the world, wee shall open the mouthes of enemies to speake euill of the wayes of god and all professours for Gods sake; wee shall shame the faces of many of gods worthy seruants, and cause theire prayers to be turned into Cursses vpon vs till wee be consumed out of the good land whether wee are goeing: And to shutt vpp this discourse with that exhortacion of Moses that faithfull seruant of the Lord in his last farewell to Israell Deut. 30. Beloued there is now sett before vs life, and good, deathe and euill in that wee are Commaunded this day to loue the Lord our God, and to loue one another to walke in his wayes and to keepe his Commaundements and his Ordinance, and his lawes, and the Articles of our Covenant with him that wee may liue and be multiplyed, and that the Lord our God may blesse vs in the land whether wee goe to possesse it: But if our heartes shall turne away soe that wee will not obey, but shall be seduced and worshipp [serue *cancelled*] other Gods our pleasures, and proffitts, and serue them; it is propounded vnto vs this day, wee shall surely perishe out of the good Land whether wee passe over this vast Sea to possesse it;

> Therefore lett vs choose life,
> that wee, and our Seede,
> may liue; by obeyeing his
> voyce, and cleaueing to him,
> for hee is our life, and
> our prosperity.

Little Speech on Liberty

I suppose something may be expected from me, upon this charge that is befallen me, which moves me to speak now to you; yet I intend not to intermeddle in the proceedings of the court, or with any of the persons concerned therein. Only I bless God, that I see an issue of this troublesome business. I also acknowledge the justice of the court, and, for mine own part, I am well satisfied, I was publicly charged, and I am publicly and legally acquitted, which is all I did expect or desire. And though this be sufficient for my justification before men, yet not so before the God, who hath seen so much amiss in my dispensations (and even in this affair) as calls me to be humble. For to be publicly and criminally charged in this court, is matter of humiliation, (and I desire to make a right use of it,) notwithstanding I be thus acquitted. If her father had spit in her face, (saith the Lord concerning Miriam,) should she not have been ashamed seven days? Shame had lien upon her, whatever the occasion had been. I am unwilling to stay you from your urgent affairs, yet give me leave (upon this special occasion) to speak a little more to this assembly. It may be of some good use, to inform and rectify the judgments of some of the people, and may prevent such distempers as have arisen amongst us. The great questions that have troubled the country, are about the authority of the magistrates and the liberty of the people. It is yourselves who have called us to this office, and being called by you, we have our authority from God, in way of an ordinance, such as hath the image of God eminently stamped upon it, the contempt and violation whereof hath been vindicated with examples of divine vengeance. I entreat you to consider, that when you choose magistrates, you take them from among yourselves, men subject to like passions as you are. Therefore when you see infirmities in us, you should reflect upon your own, and that would make you bear the more with us, and not be

Reprinted from *Winthrop's Journal: "History of New England," 1630–1649*, ed. James Kendall Hosmer (New York: Charles Scribner's Sons, 1908), 2:237–39.

severe censurers of the failings of your magistrates, when you have continual experience of the like infirmities in yourselves and others. We account him a good servant, who breaks not his covenant. The covenant between you and us is the oath you have taken of us, which is to this purpose, that we shall govern you and judge your causes by the rules of God's laws and our own, according to our best skill. When you agree with a workman to build you a ship or house, etc., he undertakes as well for his skill as for his faithfulness, for it is his profession, and you pay him for both. But when you call one to be a magistrate, he doth not profess nor undertake to have sufficient skill for that office, nor can you furnish him with gifts, etc., therefore you must run the hazard of his skill and ability. But if he fail in faithfulness, which by his oath he is bound unto, that he must answer for. If it fall out that the case be clear to common apprehension, and the rule clear also, if he transgress here, the error is not in the skill, but in the evil of the will: it must be required of him. But if the case be doubtful, or the rule doubtful, to men of such understanding and parts as your magistrates are, if your magistrates should err here, yourselves must bear it.

For the other point concerning liberty, I observe a great mistake in the country about that. There is a twofold liberty, natural (I mean as our nature is now corrupt) and civil or federal. The first is common to man with beasts and other creatures. By this, man, as he stands in relation to man simply, hath liberty to do what he lists; it is a liberty to evil as well as to good. This liberty is incompatible and inconsistent with authority, and cannot endure the least restraint of the most just authority. The exercise and maintaining of this liberty makes men grow more evil, and in time to be worse than brute beasts: omnes sumus licentia deteriores. This is that great enemy of truth and peace, that wild beast, which all the ordinances of God are bent against, to restrain and subdue it. The other kind of liberty I call civil or federal, it may also be termed moral, in reference to the covenant between God and man, in the moral law, and the politic covenants and constitutions, amongst men them-

selves. This liberty is the proper end and object of authority, and cannot subsist without it; and it is a liberty to that only which is good, just, and honest. This liberty you are to stand for, with the hazard (not only of your goods, but) of your lives, if need be. Whatsoever crosseth this, is not authority, but a distemper thereof. This liberty is maintained and exercised in a way of subjection to authority; it is of the same kind of liberty wherewith Christ hath made us free. The woman's own choice makes such a man her husband; yet being so chosen, he is her lord, and she is to be subject to him, yet in a way of liberty, not of bondage; and a true wife accounts her subjection her honor and freedom, and would not think her condition safe and free, but in her subjection to her husband's authority. Such is the liberty of the church under the authority of Christ, her king and husband; his yoke is so easy and sweet to her as a bride's ornaments; and if through frowardness or wantonness, etc., she shake it off, at any time, she is at no rest in her spirit, until she take it up again; and whether her lord smiles upon her, and embraceth her in his arms, or whether he frowns, or rebukes, or smites her, she apprehends the sweetness of his love in all, and is refreshed, supported, and instructed by every such dispensation of his authority over her. On the other side, ye know who they are that complain of this yoke and say, let us break their bands, etc., we will not have this man to rule over us. Even so, brethren, it will be between you and your magistrates. If you stand for your natural corrupt liberties, and will do what is good in your own eyes, you will not endure the least weight of authority, but will murmur, and oppose, and be always striving to shake off that yoke; but if you will be satisfied to enjoy such civil and lawful liberties, such as Christ allows you, then will you quietly and cheerfully submit unto that authority which is set over you, in all the administrations of it, for your good. Wherein, if we fail at any time, we hope we shall be willing (by God's assistance) to hearken to good advice from any of you, or in any other way of God; so shall your liberties be preserved, in upholding the honor and power of authority amongst you.

A Discourse about
Civil Government (1637–39)

JOHN COTTON (1585–1652)

Born in England, John Cotton came to America in 1633 where he served as a minister in Boston. Cotton wrote more than fifty books and engaged in a number of polemical controversies—notably with Roger Williams. The following essay, sometimes attributed to John Davenport, was written between 1637 and 1639 during the founding of New Haven colony. In it he responds to a critic of limiting the right to vote and hold political office to church members. The essay was not published until 1663.

A Discourse about Civil Government
in a New Plantation:

Where all, or the most considerable part of free Planters profess their desire and purpose of enjoying, & securing to themselves and their Posterity, the pure and peaceable enjoyment of the Ordinances of Christ in Church-fellowship with his People, and have liberty to cast themselves into that Mould or Form of a Common-wealth, which shall appear to be best for them. Tending to prove the Expediency and Necessity in that case of intrusting free Burgesses which are members of Churches gathered amongst them according to Christ, with the power of Chusing from among themselves Magistrates, and men to whom the Managing of all Publick Civil Affairs of Importance is to be committed. And to vindicate the same from an Imputation of an Under-Power upon the

The current text was transcribed from microfilm of the original 1663 pamphlet. We made minor formatting changes, including moving printed marginal notes into footnotes (except marginal notes outlining the argument, which are placed in the text), and we fixed the three errata noted on the last pages of the original pamphlet. Otherwise the text follows the original.—Eds.

Churches of Christ, which hath been cast upon it through a Mistake of the true Date of the Question.

Reverend Sir,

The *Sparrow* being now gone, and one dayes respite from publick Labours on the Lords-day falling to me in courte, I have sought out your Writing, and have reviewed it, and finde (as I formerly expressed to your self) that the Question is misstated by you; and that the Arguments which you produce to prove that which is not denied, are (in reference to this Question) spent in vain, as arrows are when they fall wide of the Marks they should hit, though they strike in a White which the Archer is not called to shoot at.

The terms wherein you state the Question, are these:

Whether the Right and Power of Chusing Civil Magistrates belongs unto The Church of Christ?

To omit all critical Inquiries, in your thus stating the Question, I utterly dislike two things.

1. That you speak of *Civil Magistrates indefinitely, and without limitation;* under which notion, all Magistrates in the world are included, *Turks,* and *Indians,* and *idolaters,* as well as *Christians.* Now no man, I think, holdeth or imagineth, that a Church of Christ hath power and right to Chuse all Civil Magistrates throughout the World: For,

1. In some Countreys there is no Church of Christ, all the inhabitants being Heathen men and Idolaters; and amongst those who are called *Christians,* the number of the Churches of Christ will be found to be so small, and the Members of them so few and mean, that it is impossible that the Right and Power of Choosing Civil Magistrates in all places, should belong to the Churches of Christ.

2. Nor have the Churches countenance of State in all Countreys, but are under Restraint and Persecution in some; as the *Jews* in *Egypt* under *Pharaoh,* and in the Captivity of *Babylon,* and the *Christian Churches* 300 years after Christ persecuted by *Roman Emperours* and in these dayes those Reformed Churches *sub cruce* [under the cross] in *Antwerp,* and other Popish Countreys.

3. In some Countreys the Churches are indeed under the Protection of Magistrates, as Forreigners, permitted quietly to sit down under their Wings: but neither are the Members capable of Magistracy there, nor have they power of Voting in the Choice of Magistrates: Such was that Church of Strangers gathered in *London* by *Johannes Alase,* with allowance of State under the Broad Seal of *England* in *Edw. 6.* Such are the *Dutch* and *French Churches* in *England,* and other Churches in the *Netherlands* at this day.

4. In some Countreys sundry Nations are so mingled, that they have severally an equal Right unto several parts of the Countrey, and therefore though they live in the same general Countrey, yet they are governed by different Laws, and have several Magistrates chosen. Chosen by themselves severally, neither of them being capable of Magistracy in the others parts, nor having Right and Power of Chusing Civil Magistrates there. Thus were the *Israelites* joined with the *Canaanites,* that were left in *Canaan* unsubdued: and thus are the *English* planted in these parts of *America,* where sundry Nations of *Indians* dwell near them, and are Proprietaries of the places which they inhabit. Now he that should affirm, that the Churches of Christ, as such, have Right and Power of choosing Civil Magistrates in such places, seemeth to me more to need Physick then Arguments, to recover him from his Errour.

2. The second thing that I dislike in your stating the Questions, is, in that you make the *Churches of Christ to be the subject of this Right and Power of choosing Civil Magistrates.* For 1. The Church so considered is a Spiritual Political Body, consisting of divers Members Male and Female, Bond and Free; sundry of which are not capable of Magistracy, nor of Voting in the choice of Magistrates, inasmuch as none have that Right and Power but free Burgesses, among whom Women and Servants are not reckoned, though they may be, and are Church members. 2. The Members of the Churches of Christ are considerable under a twofold respect answerable to the twofold man, which is in all the Members of the Church whilst they are in this world, *the inward & the outward*

man.[1] Whereunto the onely wise God hath fitted and appointed two sorts of Administrations, *Ecclesiastical* and *Civil.* Hence they are capable of a twofold Relation, and of Action and Power suitable to them both; *viz. Civil* and *Spiritual,* and accordingly must be exercised about both in their seasons, without confounding those two different states, or destroying either of them, whilest what they transact in civil Affairs, is done by virtue of their civil Relation, their Church state onely fitting them to do it according to God.

Now that the state of the Question may appear, I think it seasonable and necessary to premise a few Distinctions, to prevent all mistakes, if it may be.

Distinction 1

First then, let us distinguish between the two Administrations or Polities, *Ecclesiastical* and *Civil,* which men commonly call *the Church,* and *Commonwealth.* I incline rather to them who speaking of a *Christian Communion,* make the Communion to be the Genus, and the State Ecclesiastical and Civil to be the *Species* of it. For in a Christian Communion there are these different Administrations or Polities or States, Ecclesiastical & Civil: Ecclesiastical Administrations, are a *Divine Order appointed to Believers for holy communion of holy things:* Civil Administrations, are *An Humane Order appointed by God to men for Civil Fellowship of humane things.* Thus Junius defineth them; and maketh 1. Order *The Genus of them both.* 2. God *the Efficient and Author of them both.* 3. Gods Glory *the late End of them both.* 4. Man *the common Subject of both.* And so they agree very well in the *General Nature, Efficient, End* and *Subject;* yet with difference in all. For,

1. Though both agree in this, that there is Order in their Administrations, yet with this difference, that the Guides in the Church have not a Despotical, but

1. 2 Cor. 4.16.

Oeconomical Power only,[2] being *not Lords over Christ's heritage, but stewards and ministers of Christ and of the Church;* the Dominion and Law-giving Power being referred to *Christ* alone, as *he only Head of the Church.* But in the other State he hath given Lordly Power, Authority and Dominion unto men.[3]

2. Though both agree in this, that *Man is the common Subject of them both,* yet with this difference, Man by Nature being a Reasonable and Sociable Creature, capable of Civil Order, is or may be the Subject of Civil Power and State: But Man by Grace called out of the world to fellowship with Jesus Christ, and with his People, is the only Subject of Church-power; yet so, as the Outward man of Church-members is subject to the Civil Power in common with other men, whilest their Inward man is the subject of Spiritual Order and Administrations.

3. Though they both agree in this, that *God is the Efficient and Author of themselves, and that by Christ,* yet not *eadem ratione.* For, God as the Creator and Governour of the world, is the Author of Civil Order and Administrations: But God as in Covenant with his People is Christ, is the Author of Church-Administrations. So likewise Christ, as the Essential Word and Wisdom of God creating and governing the World is the Efficient and Fountain of Civil Order & Administrations:[4] But as Mediator of the New Covenant, & Head of the Church,[5] he establisheth Ecclesiastical Order.

4. Though they both agree in this, that they have *the same last End,* viz. *The Glory of God,* yet they differ in their next Ends; for the next End of Civil Order and Administrations, is *The Preservation of Humane Societies in outward Honour, Justice and Peace;* But the next Ends of Church Order and Administrations, are *The Conversion, Edification, and Salvation of Souls, Pardon of Sin, Power against Sin, Peace with God,* &c.

5. Hence ariseth another Difference about the *Objects* of these different States: for though both agree in this, that they have the *common Welfare* for their aime and scope; yet the things about which the Civil Power is primarily conversant, are *Bodies,* τά Βίωτικά, 2 Cor. 6.4. or τά πρός τόν Βίον, *the things of this life,* as *Goods, Lands, Honour, the Liberties and Peace of the outward man.* The things whereabout the Church Power is exercised, are τά πρός τὸν Θεὸν,[6] *The things of God, as the Souls and Consciences of men, the Doctrine and Worship of God, the Communion of the Saints.* Hence also 1. They have different Laws: 2. Different Officers. 3. Different Power, where by to reduce men to Order, according to their different Objects and Ends. Now that a just harmony may be kept between these two different Orders and Administrations, two Extremes must be avoided: 1. That they be not confounded, either by giving the Spiritual Power, which is proper to the Church, into the hand of the Civil Magistrate, as *Erasius* would have done in the matter of Excommunication. If any Magistrate should presume to thrust himself by his Authority or otherwise, into a Work which properly belongs to a Church-Officer, let him remember what befell *Saul* and *Uzzaih* for so doing: or 2. By giving Civil Power to Church-Officers, who are called to attend only to Spiritual matters and *the things of God,* and therefore may not be distracted from them by Secular intanglements. I say, Church-Officers, not Church-members; for they (not being limited as the Officers are by God) are capable of two different imployments, suting with two different Men in them, in different respects, as hath been said: and as they may lawfully be imployed about things of this life; so they are of all men fittest, being sanctified and dedicated to God to carry on all worldly and civil business to Gods ends, as we shall declare in due time. But concerning Church-Officers I am able with Gods help to prove, that the devolving of Civil Power upon Pastors of Churches, (upon how specious pretences soever it began) gave that Rise to the *Man of Sin,* which at last set his feet on the necks

2. John 1.23; Matth 3.11; I Cor. 3.5.21; 2 Cor. 1.1.24 & 4.5 & 5.20; I Pet. 5.1; Matth. 28.18.

3. Luke 22.25; John 19.10; I Pet. 2.13.

4. Job 1.1,3,10; Col. 1.17; Heb. 1.2,3; Prov. 8:15.

5. Eph. 5.22,23 & 4.8,11.

6. Heb. 5.1.

of the Princes of the Earth, yea, of the Emperours of the World. It was your mistake, when you too confidently affirmed, That *the limiting of the Right and Power of choosing Civil Officers unto free Burgesses that are Members of Churches, brought that Tyranny into the Romish Church, which all the Churches of Christ complain of.* It would well have become you to have better digested your own thoughts, before such words had passed through your lips; for you will never be able to produce any good Author that will confirm what you say. The truth is quite contrary; for that I may instance in *Rome* it self: Had Churches been rightly managed, when the most considerable part in that City embraced the Christian Faith, in the ceasing of the *Ten Persecutions,* that only such as had been fit for that estate, had been admitted into Church fellowship, and they alone had had power, out of themselves to have chosen Magistrates, such Magistrates would not have been chosen, as would have given their Power to the Pope; nor would those Churches have suffered their Pastors to become Worldly Princes and Rulers, as the Pope and his Cardinals are; nor would they have given up the Power of the Church from the Church into the Officers hands, but would have called upon them to *fulfill their Ministry which they had received of the Lord:* and if need were, would by the power of Christ have compelled them so to do: And then where had the Pope Supremacy been, which is made up of the Spoils of the Ecclesiastical and Civil State? but had by the course which now we plead for, been prevented.

2. The second Extreme to be avoided, is, That these two different Orders and States, *Ecclesiastical* and *Civil,* be not set in opposition as contraries, that one should destroy the other, but as coordinate States, in the same place reaching forth help mutually each to other, for the welfare of both, according to God: So that both Officers and Members of Churches be subject, in respect of the outward man, to the Civil Power of those who bear Rule in the Civil State according to God, and teach others so to do: And that the Civil Magistrates and Officers, in regard of the inward man, subject themselves Spiritually to the

power of Christ in Church-Ordinances, and by their Civil Power preserve the same in outward Peace and Purity; and this will best be attained, when the Pastor may say to the Magistrate, as *Gregory Nazianzum* wrote to the Magistrates of *Nazianzum, Scio te ovem mei gregis esse sacri gregis sacram ovem:* I know thou art a Sheep of my flock, a holy Sheep of a holy Flock. Again, *Cum Christo imperas, cum Christo etiam administras, ab eo est tibi gladius, hoc donarium à te purum ei qui dedit conservetur;* that is, Thou rulest with Christ, and administrate to Christ; thou hast the Sword from him: let this gift which thou hast received from him, be kept pure for him. And when the Civil Magistrate in his Church-State, answereth *Ambrose* his description of a good Emperour: *Ipse Imperator bonus intra Ecclesiam, non Supra Ecclesum est.* A good Magistrate is within the Church, not above it. Lastly, when according to *Junius* his description of the Power of the Christian Magistrate in Church-matters, he accounts it his duty to embrace in Fellowship with the whole Church, *ut verum Christi & Ecclesia membrum,* the Laws given by God in the Church, and the means sanctified by him to nourish the inward man, and to protect and defend the same: [*Tanquam Magistratus à Deo Ordinatus*]* for, faith be, *As he is a Christian,* he is *Sancta ovis de sancto Christi grege,* (*i.e.* A holy Sheep of Christ's holy flock). But as a Magistrate he is [*Custos Ordinis vindexq; publici;*] that is, *A preserver of publick order.* Such were (besides the good Kings of *Judah*) Constantine, Theodosius, *& c.* in some measure, though very defective. So much shall serve to have been spoken concerning the first Distinction.

Distinction 2

The Second *Distinction* to be premised for clearing the true State of the Question, is, [*Inter Remp. constitutam & constituendam*] Between a Commonwealth already settled, and a Common-wealth yet to be settled, and wherein men are free to chuse what

---

* These and the following two sets of brackets are in the original text. All others are inserted by the editors.—Eds.

Form they shall judge best. For I conceive, when *Paul* exhorted the *Romans* to *be subject to the higher Powers*, who at that time were Heathen men, and Persecutors, he considered that Civil State as settled, and suted his Advice accordingly. But if he had been to Direct them about laying the Foundation of a Christian Common-wealth, he would not have advised them to chuse such Governours as were out of the Church, but would have seriously forewarned them of the danger whereunto the Church would have been exposed thereby and that unavoidably. And that this may not be thought a slight and uncertain conjecture, let us consider what advice he gave in like cases: Ye know, that writing to persons already Married he exhorteth *the believing wife to live with the unbelieving husband;*[7] yet the same Apostle directeth the same Church in case they were free to make their own choice, to avoid such matches: *Be not unequally yoked* (saith he) *with Infidels; for what fellowship hath righteousness with unrighteousness? And what part hath the believer with the infidel?*[8] In like manner, when *Peter* exhorted Christian *Servants to be subject to their Masters with all fear, not only to the good and gentle, but also to the froward,*[9] he did accommodate his instruction to their present condition. But had he been to direct them in another state being free, to chose what might be best for themselves, he would have expressed himself otherwise, as may appear by this. The same Spirit that inspired *Peter* thus to advise in the case, guided *Paul* further in a different case: *Art thou called being a Servant,* (saith he) *care not for it but if thou maist be free, use it rather.*[10] And that if he had written to a company of Believers in a New Plantation, where the Foundations of the Church and Civil State, and the communion of both, was to be laid for many Generations to come, he would have advised them to take the same course which we plead for, may appear by his reproving the Church in *Corinth*, for carrying *their difference before Heathen Magistrates to be judged by*

them, though he press them to be *Subject to their power.*[11] Had the unbelieving Magistrates cited them to appear before their judgement-seats, he taught them both by Precept and by his Example to submit. But when they were at liberty to compose civil Differences among themselves, and yet they would voluntarily, and of their own accord, chuse to bring their cases before those that were without the Church, this he blameth in them; and that so farre as he demandeth why *they do not rather suffer wrong* then take such a course plainly intimating, that men that profess the fear of God if they be free to make choice of their Civil Judges, (as in this New Plantation we are) they should rather chose such as are Members of the Church for that purpose, then others that are not in that estate. The same Rule holdeth by proportion in all things of like nature: for *Parum par est ratio.**

Distinction 3

The third Distinction to be premised for clearing the truth in this Point, is *between free Burgesses and free Inhabitants in a Civil State.* Concerning whom, there must be had a different consideration. This difference of People living under the same Civil Jurisdiction, is held and observed in all Countreys, as well Heathen as others, as may at large be proved, if it were needful, out of the Histories of all Nations and Times; and the Experience of our Times, as well in our own Native Countrey, as in other places, confirmeth it. In all which, many are Inhabitants that are not Citizens, that are never likely to be numbered among ἀρχονίες, or Rulers: Answerably it is in the case now in question. So that when we urge, that Magistrates be chosen out of free Burgesses, and by them, and that those free Burgesses be chosen out of such as are Members of these Churches, we do not thereby go about to exclude those that are not in Church-Order, from any Civil Right or Liberty that is due unto them as Inhabitants and Planters, as if none should have Lots

7. 1 Cor. 7.13.
8. 2 Cor. 6.14,15.
9. 1 Pet. 2.18.
10. 1 Cor. 7.21.

11. 1 Cor. 5.1.
* [the ratio of equals is equal]

in due proportion with other men, nor the benefit of Justice under the Government where they live, but only Church-members; (for this were indeed to have the Common-wealth swallowed up of the Church) but seeing there ever will be difference between the World and the Church in the same place, and that both men of the world are allowed of God the use and enjoyment of the help of Civil Government, for their quiet and comfortable subsistence in the world: and Church-members (though called out of the world into fellowship with Christ, yet) living in the world, and having many worldly necessities and businesses in common with men of the world that live among them, stand in need of the civil Power to right them against civil injuries, and to protect them in their right, and outward orderly use of their Spirituals, against those that are apt to be injurious to them in the one, or in the other respect; which being without, are not under the Churches Power; and yet living within the Verge of the same Civil Jurisdiction, are under the Civil Power of the Magistrates. Hence it is, that we plead for this Order to be set in Civil Affairs, that such a course may be taken as may best secure to our selves and our posterities the faithful managing of Civil Government for the *common welfare* of all as well in the Church as without; which will then most certainly be effected, when the publick Trust and Power of these matters is committed to such men as are most approved according to God; and these are Church-members,[12] as shall afterward, God assisting, be proved.

Distinction 4

The fourth *Distinction* to be premised for clearing the truth, and to prevent mistakes in this Question, shall be *between the Actions of Church-members.* For some actions are done *by them all, joynily as a Spiritual Body,* in reference to Spiritual ends; and some actions are done only *by some of the Body,* in reference to Civil

12. By *Church Members* in all this Discourse, is meant such as are in full Communion.

ends. Actions of the first sort, are said to be done *by the Church of Christ, as a Church of Christ;* such are *Admission of members, and Excommunication of them according to Christ's order,* and other actions of that kinde; but these fall not under our Question, which is wholly about *the transaction of Civil Affairs:* so that your whole Dispute wanteth a good ground, and your labour about it might well have been spared. Actions of the second sort, are of a larger extent, and reach to businesses of a *Civil Nature,* such as that Civil Judgement whereof *Paul* speaketh, *1 Cor. 6* ἐν τοῖς βίωτι- κοῖς, in *matters that concern this life, as the Lives, Goods,* (and which is dearer to them then both) *the Reputations of men, and their outward Liberty and Peace.* Concerning which, Members fitly chosen out of the Church, and made free Burgesses, are fitter to judge and determine according to God, than other men, and that for weighty Reasons; some whereof are rendered by *Paul* in the Chapter, whereunto others may be added, when we shall argue that Point, the Lord helping us.

Distinction 5

The fifth *Distinction* to be premised for the clearing of the truth in this Point, is *between Places, where all, or the most considerable part of the first and free Planters, profess their desire and purpose of entering into Church-fellowship according to Christ, and of enjoying in that State all the Ordinances in purity and peace, and of securing the same unto their posterity, so farre as men are able;* and *those Places where all or the most considerable part of the first and free Planters are otherwise minded, and profess the contrary.* Our Question is of the first sort, not of the second. As for those of the second sort, if the *major,* or more considerable part among them, will be like Heathen men, without such Church fellowship, as is according to Christ in all things, a Heathen man or meet civil worldly Politician, will be good enough to be their Magistrate; or if this desire to let up Idolatry and Superstition, an Idolatrous and superstitious Governor in the civil State will best sute their ends; and so they may be said to their just reproof and shame, *Like Priest, like People;* and *Like Prince, like People.* Thus sometimes the Lord hath spoken against a licentious people concerning their prophets, *He that will prophecy of wine and strong drink, he shall be the prophet to this people.*[13] He that sometimes giveth such *Guides in the Church* to a people in *his indignation,* doth also sometimes give *Magistrates & Rulers* to a people *in the Civil State* in *his wrath,* when men are *forsaken of him,* and *given up more to affect* outward fancy and *vanity,* then *Gods Order:* as when the *people of Israel sought a King,* without respect to the *right Tribe* from whence by Gods order they ought to expect one, *He gave them a King in his anger, and took him away in his wrath.*[14] In such case, what shall the people of God do that live in such a place? Surely if God give them liberty and ability, they should attend to the voice of God, which hath said in a like case to his people, *Arise and depart, this is not your rest;*[15] and follow *the steps of Christs flock* to any place, *where he causeth his flock to feed, and lye down* under a comfortable shadow *as noon;*[16] As in *Jeroboam's* time, the *Levites left their suburbs, and came to Judah and Jerusalem, and after them of all the Tribes of Israel, such as set their hearts to seek the Lord God of Israel, and strengthened the Kingdome of Judah,* where Gods Ordinances both concerning Civil Government and Religious Worship were better observed. But if Divine Providence doth necessitate their stay and abode in such places, they are to *pray for those in Authority,*[17] that they may become such, as *under whom they may live a quiet and peaceable life, in all godliness and honesty;* and to be *subject to their Power,* even in those things wherein they may not obey their commands, nor seek their help, 1 Cor. 6.1, 2 till God shall give them liberty from the Yoke, either by removing them to those places where fitter Magistrates bear Rule in Civil matters, or by giving them opportunity of Chusing more sutable ones from among themselves.

13. Micah 2.11.
14. Hosea 13.11.
15. Micah 2.10.
16. Cantic 1.6,20.
17. 1 Tim. 2.12.

So much shall serve to have been spoken to the *Distinctions,* which having thus premised, we now proceed to declare the true state of the Question: which is as followeth.

The true state of the Question

Q. Whether a new Plantation, where all or the most considerable part of free Planters profess their purpose and desire of securing in themselves and to their posterity, the pure and peaceable enjoyment of Christ's Ordinances; Whether, I say, such Planters are bound in laying the Foundations of Church and Civil State, to take order, that all the free Burgesses be such as are in fellowship of the Church or Churches which are, or may be gathered according to Christ; and that those free Burgesses have the only power of chusing from among themselves Civil Magistrates, and men to be intrusted with transacting all publick Affairs of Importance, according to the rules and directions of Scripture?

I hold the Affirmative part of the Question upon this ground, that this course will most conduce to the good of both States; and by consequence to the *common welfare of all,* whereunto all men are bound principally to attend in laying the *Foundation of a Common-wealth;* lest Posterity rue the first Miscarriages, when it will be too late to redress them. They that are skillful in Architecture observe, *that the breaking or yielding of a stone on the groundwork of a Building but the breadth of the back of a knife, will make a cleft of more than half a foot in the Fabrick aloft: So important* (saith mine Author) *are fundamental Errours.* The Lord awakens us to look to it in time, and send us his Light and Truth to lead us into the safest wayes in these beginnings.

The Question being thus stated, I now proceed with Gods help to prove the Affirmative part: and thus I argue, to prove that *the Form of Government which is described in the true stating of the Question is the best, and by consequence, that men that are free to chouse (as in new Plantations they are) ought to establish it in a Christian Common-wealth.*

Argument 1.

Theocratie, *or to make the Lord God our Governour,*[18] *is the best Form of Government in a Christian Common-wealth, and which men that are free to chuse (as in new Plantations they are) ought to establish. The Form of Government described in the true stating of the Question is* Theocratic, *or that wherein we make the Lord God our Governour. Therefore that Form of Government which is described in the true stating of the Question, is the best Form of Government in a Christian Common-wealth, and which men that are free to chuse (as in new Plantations they are) ought to establish.* The Proposition is clear of itself. The Assumption I prove thus:

That Form of Government where 1. The people have the power of chusing their Governors are in Covenant with God.[19] *2. Wherein the men chosen by them are godly men, and fitted with a spirit of Government.*[20] *3. In which the Laws they rule by are the Laws of God:*[21] *4. Wherein Laws are executed, inheritances allotted, and civil differences are composed, according to God's appointment:*[22] *5. In which men of God are consulted with in all hard cases, and in matters of Religion,*[23] is the Form which was received and established among the people of *Israel* whilst the Lord God was their Governour, as the places of Scripture alledged shew; and is the very same with that which we plead for, as will appear to him that shall examine the true stating of the Questions. The Conclusion follows necessarily.

Argument 2.

*That Form of Government which giveth unto Christ his due preeminence, is the best Form of Government in a Christian Common-wealth, and which men that are free to chuse (as in new Plantations they are) ought to estab-*lish. *The Form of Government described in the true stating of the Question, is that which giveth unto Christ his due preheminence. Therefore the Form of Government which is described in the true stating of the Question, is the best Form of Government in a Christian Common-wealth, and which men that are free to chuse (as in New Plantations they are) ought to establish.*

The Proposition is proved out of two places of Scripture, Col. 1:15. to 19. *with* Eph. 1.21, 22. From which Texts it doth appear, that it is a preheminence due to Christ, that all things, and all Governments in the world, should serve to Christs ends, for the welfare of the Church whereof he is the Head. For 1. In relation to God, he hath this by Right of Primogenture, as he is *the first-born, and so Heir of all things, higher then the Kings of the earth.* 2. In relation to the World, it is said, *All things were made by him, and for him, and do consist in him,* and therefore it is a preheminence due to him, that they all serve him. 3. In relation to the Church, it is said, *He hath made all things subject under his feet, and hath given him over all things to be Head of the Church, that in all things he might have the preheminence.* And indeed that he upholdeth the Creatures, and the Order that is in them, it is for his Churches sake; when that is once compleat, the world shall soon be at an end. And if you read the stories of the great Monarchies that have been and judge of them by Scripture-light, you will finde they stood or fell, according to God purposed to make use of them about some service to be done about his Church. So that the only considerable part for which the world standeth this day, is the Church: and therefore it is a Preheminence due to Christ, that his Headship over the Church should be exalted and acknowledged, and served by all. In which respect also the Title of *The first-born* is given to the Members of the Church, and they are called *The first-fruits of his Creatures,* to show both their preheminence above others, and that they are fittest to serve to Gods ends.

The Assumption (*That the Form of Government described in the true stating of the Question, doth give unto Christ his due preheminence*) will easily be granted by those that shall consider what Civil Magistrates and

18. Deut. 33.29; Isai. 33:22; Judg. 8.23.
19. Exod. 19.5; Deut. 1.13,14.
20. Exod. 18.21; Deut. 1.13.
21. Numb. 11.24,25; Isa. 33.22.
22. Num 35.29 & 6.27 & 2.3; I Cor. 6.1,2.
23. Deut. 7.8 to 11 & 19.16,17; 2 Cor. 10.4 to 11.

Rulers in the Common wealth those are, who are fittest to serve to Christ's ends for the good and welfare of his Church; which will be evident from two places of Scripture: First, in *Psa. 2.10, 11, 12* you have a description of those that are fitted to order Civil Affairs in the Magistracy to Christ's ends; they are such as are not only wise and learned in matters of Religion but also do reduce their knowledge into practice: they *Worship the Lord in fear;* and not only so, but *Kiss the Son,* which was a solemn & outward *Profession of love;*[24] and *of Subjection,*[25] and *of Religious Worship,*[26] and so fitly serveth to express their joining themselves to the Church of Christ. Secondly, in *Isa. 49.23* it is promised to the Church, that *Kings and Queens shall be their nursing-fathers and nursing-mothers,* and therefore it is added, *They shall worship with their faces to the earth, and lick up the dust of thy feet;* which is a proverbial expression of their voluntary humbling of themselves to Christ in his Ordinances, taken from the manner of the *Persians,* in declaring their Subjection to their Emperour,[27] which the Apostle calls *a voluntary submission to the Gospel,*[28] which is the spirit of the Members of the churches of Christ. And for this Reason it is that the Lord, when he moulded a Communion among his own People, wherein all Civil Administrations should serve to holy ends, he described the men to whom that Trust should be committed, by certain Properties, which also qualified them for fellowship in Church-Ordinances, as *Men of ability and power over their own affections;*[29] secondly, *fearing God, Truly Religious, Men of Courage, hating Covetousness, men of Wisdom, men of understanding,* and *men known or approved of among the people of God, & chosen by the Lord from among their Brethren,* & not a stranger, which is no Brother: the most of which concurre to describe Church members

in a Church rightly gathered and ordered, who are also in respect of their union with Christ and fellowship together, called *Brethren* frequently in the New Testament, wherein the equity of that Rule is established to us.

Objection

Christ will have his due Preheminence, though the Civil Rulers oppose him, and persecute the Churches, as in Rome; *Therefore it is not necessary that this course be taken in Civil Affairs to establish Christs Preheminence.*

Answer

The Question is of a Christian Commonwealth that should willingly subject themselves to Christ, not of a Heathen State that shall perforce be subdued unto Christ. It is concerning what Gods people being free should chuse, not what his enemies are compelled unto.

Argument 3

That Form of Government wherein the best provision is made for the good both of the Church and of the Civil State, is the best Form of Government in a Christian Communion, and which men that are free to chuse (as in new Plantations they are) ought to establish. The Form of Government described in the true stating of the Question, is that wherein the best provision is made for the good both of the Church and Civil State. Therefore the Form of Government described in the true stating of the Question, is the best Form of Government in a Christian Communion, and which men that are free to chuse (as in new Plantations they are) ought to establish. The Proposition (if need be) may be confirmed from the end of all Civil Government & Administrations which is *the publick and common Good,* whether Natural, as in *the preservation of Life and Safety;* or Moral, as *Justice and Honesty in Humane Societies;* or Civil, as *Peace, Liberty of Commerce;* or Spiritual as *to protect the Church in Spiritual, though outward, Order and Administrations in peace & purity.* And this last is principally to be attended unto, and therefore such as are

24. I Pet. 5.14.
25. Gen. 41.40; I Sam. 10.1.
26. Hos. 13.2.
27. *Val. Max.* lib. 7 chap. 3.
28. 2 Cor. 9.13.
29. Exod. 18.21; Deut. 1.13.

intrusted with this care, are called *The Ministers of God,* to note the principal end whereunto they serve, viz. The things wherein God is most directly and immediately honoured, which is in promoting man's Spiritual good, so farre as they are enabled by their Civil Power.

The Assumption (*That the Form of Government in the common-wealth which we plead for, is that wherein the best provision is made for the good both of the Church and of the Civil State*) may appear by the blessing of God which usually is upon the Communion, where the securing of the Spiritual good of men, in the peace and purity of Gods Ordinances, is principally attended unto by all sorts as may be proved by the state of things in the Communion of *Israel,* whilst the service of the Lord was with due care attended to *all the dayes of Joshua, and all the dayes of the Elders that over-lived Joshua, which had known all the works of the Lord which he had done, for Israel.*[30] Many more places of Scripture might be alledged; but I will only note *Psal. 72.* wherein all sorts of good are assured to the Common-wealth, wherein *the fear of God,* that is, Matters of Religion are so regarded, as the preservation thereof to after ages is duely provided for: which how can it be done, if the course described in the true stating of the Question be neglected by those that are free to cast the Common-wealth into what Mould they please?

This *Junius,*[31] a Learned and Godly man, and much exercised in State Affairs, as appears by the Story of Life, saw clearly; and therefore speaking of the Consent and Harmony of the Church and Civil State, in the concurrence of their several Administrations to the welfare of a Christian Common-wealth, he expresseth it by the *conjunction of the Soul and Body in a Man;* and concludeth, that *Nothing will be of so much avail to the welfare of civil Administrations, as will the best Administrations of the Church giving attendance to the holy and just Communion of Saints,* (ut ad parentem officiorum omnium) *as to the Parent of all Duties:* and, that *Nothing will so secure and strengthen Church-Administrations, as that security* (quam praebitura est justa pia Magistratus atque fidelis Πολιτεία) *which the just Administrations of a godly and faithful Magistrate will afford.* Now *Pii & Fideles, Men that are godly and faithfull,* are such as are described in our stating of the Question. And having thus said, he breaks out into an affectionate Admiration of the Happiness of a Communion so ordered: *Ecquid obsecro futurum est, si optima Ecclesia, cum Republicâ optima coalescat? O beatum populum, in quo uno ore, & uno animo, utraq; administratio, ad sanctam communionem cum civili Societate continendam, & augendam conspiraverit! Non minuit illam hac administratio, sed altera[?] alteram stantem, confirmat, labantem, statuminat, collapsam erigit.* Which I thus English: *What I pray may be expected in future times, if the best Church, and the best Common-wealth grow up together? Oh blessed people, among whom each Administration shall conspire with one mouth, and one minde, to conjoyn and advance the Communion of Saints with the Civil Society! One of these Administrations will not detract from the other, but each will confirm the other if it stand, and stay it if it be falling, and raise it up if it be faln down.* And a little after he thus concludeth, *Magistratum cui credita est civilis administratio non in Ecclesia solum, sed etiam ex Ecclesia esse affirmamus; We affirm, that the Magistrate to whom the Civil Administration is committed, is or ought to be not onely in the church, but also taken out of the Church.* Thus *Junius* thought, and taught, and published to the world. And indeed what is more equal, then that he who by Office is to be a *Minister of God,* should be chosen by and out of those who are by open Profession in the Church-estate, the Servants of the Lord and have more helps to know his Minde, and deep engagements to seek his Ends, and observe his Will, then other men? But if any be otherwise minded, let them shew some other course, wherein the publick good may be promoted according to God, with assurance of a blessing by virtue of the Promises.

30. Josh. 24.31.
31. *Junius Eccles.* lib. 3. chap. 5.

Argument 4

The fourth Argument shall be taken out of *1 Cor. 6. ver. 1, to 8*. Whence I thus argue: *That Form of Government wherein the power of Civil Administrations is denied unto unbelievers, and committed to the Saints, is the best Form of Government in a Christian Common-wealth, and which men that are free to chuse (as in new Plantations they are) ought to establish. The Form of Government described in the true stating of the Question, is that wherein the power of Civil Administrations is denied to unbelievers, and committed to the Saints. Therefore the Form of Government described in the true stating of the Question, is the best Form of Government in a Christian Communion, and which men that are free to chuse (as in new Plantations they are) ought to estab-lish.* The Proposition is evident from the Scripture al-ledged. For, the thing which *Paul* blameth in them, is not, that living under unbelieving Magistrates, they submitted to their Civil Judicature when they were cited to appear before their Judgement-seats; but this he reproveth, that when they were free to chuse other Judges, (as in voluntary references they were) they would out of choice be judged under the unjust and not under Saints. His Arguments against this are many and weighty. 1. From the danger of thus exalt-ing unbelievers, and abasing the Saints, in these words, *Dare any of you having a matter against another, be judged under the unjust, and not under the Saints?* 2. From the quality of unbelieving Judges, whom he calleth *unjust*, because they are destitute of the righ-teousness that is by Faith, and which is the Fountain of all true Moral Justice; and because they were ill-affected to Christians, and to the Church of Christ, and part to vex them injuriously, if they had any busi-ness before them; and because though some men out of Christ may be found civilly honest, and morally just, as were also some Heathen men, yet you can have no assurance of their justice, seeing this is the genius and nature of all men out of Christ to be unrighteous. 3. From the property of Church-members, whom he calls *Saints*, that is, men consecrated to God and to his ends in all things; for so they are in their Church-

estate, and by virtue of their Covenant are bound so to be: when as others are (or at least are not mani-fested to be otherwise according to Gods order) worldly-minded, or self-seekers, *minding their own things, and not the things of Jesus Christ.* The 4th Ar-gument is *a majors,* for he saith, *The Saints shall judge the world,* and blames their ignorance that question it: *Know ye not that the Saints shall judge the world?* And thence inferreth, that they should much more have judgement ἐν τοίς Βιωτιχοίς *in matters that con-cern this life,* such are Humane Contracts, mens Goods, and Lives, and outward Liberties. The 5th Argument is from the Wisdom wherewith the Church of God is furnished for all Civil businesses: *Is there not a wise man among you?* as if he should say, It cannot be that more wisdome should be for trans-acting of business according to God, in men that are out of the Church, then in those that are in the Church? howsoever much worldly wisdom is some-times given to men of the world, yet not sufficient to reach Gods ends that is the Priviledge of Saints, they onely are *wise as Serpents,* the other men may be as *subtle as Foxes.* And seeing it is by Christ that *Kings reign, and Princes decree justice,*[32] how can it be sup-posed that Christ, who is the Head of the Church, will furnish others with a Spirit of Wisdome and Government in Civil Matters, and deny it to the Church, Members of his own Body, whom he alone sanctifieth to his end?

The Assumption (*That the Form of Government in the Common-wealth which we plead for, is that wherein the power of civil Administrations is denied to unbeliev-ers, and committed to the Saints*) is evident of itself. For whom doth the Apostle call *Saints* there, but Mem-bers of the Church? when he had said before, they *were sanctified in Christ Jesus, Saints by calling.*[33] Hence it is that he speaks of men esteemed in the Church; v. 4 and of men that can judge between *Brethren, v. 5* which is a Title given to Church-members ordinarily in the New Testament.

32. Prov. 8.15.
33. I Cor. 3.2.

Objection

If it be objected, *He speaketh there of Church-members, in opposition to Infidels which persecuted the truth, not in opposition to men that may fear God, and be accounted Believers, though they be not in Church-fellowship.*

Answer

I Answer, The fear of God, and Faith of those men, may be justly doubted, whose settled abode is in a place where Churches are gather'd and order'd according to Christ, and yet are not after a convenient time joined to them: For if in those times and places where the Name of Christ was a Reproach, men were no sooner converted, then they were *added to the Church*, and their being added to the Church, was made an evidence of their conversion; what may we think of those men who living in times and places where the Ordinances of the Gospel may be enjoyed in purity, with peace in Church-fellowship, do yet live without the Church? 2. Though there be sundry degrees of distance from the church, to be found among men that are out of Church fellowship, as the Heathen are further off than moral Christians, yet the same Spirit of unrighteousness and enmity against Christ, worketh and bears rule in an unconverted Christian, as doth in an unbaptized Heathen: He is unsanctified as the other is, and so unsutable to Gods ends in civil Administrations; and therefore it will not be safe, nor according to the Rule, that where a Church is gathered according to Christ, the Members should be neglected, and such men intrusted with managing the Publick Affairs, as are not in fellowship with them.

Argument 5

The fifth Argument may be taken from the Nature and Power of Church-Order, which when it is managed according to Christ's appointment, affordeth best security to a Christian State, for the faithful discharge of any Trust that shall be committed to those that are under it. Whence I thus argue: *That the Form of Government wherein the power of chusing from among themselves, men to be intrusted with managing all publick Affairs of Importance, is committed to them who are furnished with the best helps for securing to a Christian State the faithfull discharge of such a Trust, is the best Form of Government in a Christian Common-wealth, and which men that are free to chuse (as in new Plantations they are) ought to establish. The Form of Government described in the true stating of the Question is such. Therefore the Form of Government described in the true stating of the Question, is the best Form of Government in a Christian Common-wealth, and which men that are free to chuse (as in new Plantations they are) ought to establish.* The Proposition is undeniable.

The Assumption (*That the Form of Government which we plead for, is that wherein the power of chusing men to be instructed with managing of all publick Affairs of Importance, is committed to them who are furnished with the best helps for securing to a Christian State the faithful discharge of such a Trust*) may be confirmed, by showing what these Helps are; *viz.* 1. That the Members of the Church are *Saints by calling*, i.e. men *separated from the world, and the pollutions thereof*, out of which *they are called, and dedicated to God*, as the *firstborn*, and the *first-fruits* were; and they are qualified, by *the spirit of wisdome and understanding, the spirit of counsel and strength, the spirit of knowledge and the fear of the Lord*, in some measure through fellowship with Christ, to serve God and men *in holiness and righteousness all the dayes of their lives*.[34] 2. That these *Saints by calling* being in Church-Order according to Christ's appointment, are in Covenant with God, and one with another; whereby they are most strictly bound to do faithfully, whatsoever they do to God or men. 3. That by virtue of this Order, they are bound to mutual helpfulness, in Watching over one another, Instructing, Admonishing, and Exhorting one another to prevent sin, or to recover such as are faln, or to encourage one another, and strengthen them in well-doing.

---

34. I Cor. 1.2; John 15.19; Heb. 12.23; James 1.18; Isai. 11.1,2; Luke 1.75; Psal. 50.5; Deut. 26.17,18.

Thus are they bound in a threefold Cable unto all Faithfulness *in all things to God and Man.* The like assurance cannot be had in any other way, if this course be neglected.

Argument 6

The sixth Argument, with which I will conclude, (that I may not weary you with Reading, as I have wearied myself with Writing) shall be taken from *The Danger of devolving this Power upon those that are not in Church-Order.* From whence the Apostle would have men to be affrighted: *Dare any of you having business against another, be judged under the unjust, and not under the Saints?*[35] The Danger therefore that is to be feared in reference to the *Church,* is, The disturbance of the Churches Peace, when Power shall be put into their hands, who being of worldly spirits, hate the Saints and their Communion; and being of the *seed of the Serpent, are at enmity against the seed of the Woman;* and being Satans instruments, who is the *God of this World,* are resisting and fighting against Christ his Kingdome and Government in the Church.[36] 2. Adde hereunto, The Danger of corrupting Church Order, either by compelling them to receive into fellowship unsutable ones, or by imposing upon them Ordinances of men, and worldly Rudiments; or by establishing Idolatrous Worship;[37] or by strengthening Hereticks in subverting the common Faith, as those *Arrian Emperours,* and Idolatrous Kings and States have done, of which we reade so many instances.

Secondly, the Danger to be feared in reference to the Civil State is, 1. The raising of Factions to the disturbance of Publick Peace, whil'st some Magistrates out of the Church, watch their seasons to strengthen themselves against those that are in the Church, till they have wrought them out of Office and Power in the Civil State: and in the mean time, what other can be expected from such unequal mix-

ture in State, but that they should be as *the toes of the feet of Nebuchadnezzar's image,* which *were part of iron, and part of clay,* they should be partly broken, and partly strong, and not comfortably joyn one with another, as iron cannot be mixed with clay.[38] The second Danger to the Civil State, will be, A perverting of *Justice* by Magistrates of worldly spirits, through Bribery, respect of persons, unacquaintance with the Law of God, and injuriousness to the servants of God. But I must break off, lest I grow too tedious. How easily might I adde the Consent of all Nations to this Truth in some proportion, who generally practice accordingly? In our Native Countrey, none are intrusted with managing of Publick Affairs, but *Members of the Church of England,* (as they call them). In *Holland,* when the *Arminian* Party had many Burgomasters on their side, *Grave Maurice* came into divers of their Cities with Troops of Souldiers, by Order from the *States Generall,* and put those *Arminian* Magistrates out of Office, and caused them to chuse only such as were of the *Dutch Churches.* And in *Rotendam* (and I think it is so in other Towns) the *Vreniseap* (who are all of them of the *Dutch Church,* and free Burgers) do out of their own company chuse the Burgomaster, and other Magistrates and Officers. In all Popish Countreys and Plantations, they observe it strictly, to intrust none with managing of Publick Civil Affairs, but such as are *Catholics* (as they speak) and of the *Roman Church.* Yea, in *Turkey* itself, they are careful that none but a man devoted to *Mahomet* bear publick Office. Yea, these very *Indians* that Worship the Devil, will not be under the Government of any *Sagamores,* but such as joyn with them in Observance of their Pawawes *and Idolatries:* That it seems to be a Principle imprinted in the mindes and hearts of all men in the equity of it, *That such a form of Government as best serveth to Establish their Religion, should by the consent of all be Established in the Civil State.*

Other things I might adde, but I hope enough hath been said for Defence and Confirmation of what I

35. I Cor. 6.1.

36. John 15.18; Gen. 3.15; Zech. 3.1; Revel. 12.7.

37. Col. 2.22,23.

38. Dan. 2.42,43.

have affirmed touching this matter. If you remain unsatisfied, I shall desire that you will placidly, and lovingly, and impartially weigh the Grounds of my judgement, and communicate yours if any remain against it, in writing. For though much writing be wearisome unto me, yet I finde it the safer way for me. Now the God of Peace and Truth lead us into all wayes of Peace and Truth, to the Praise of his Grace through *the Lord Jesus Christ,* who is *the Way, the Truth, and the Life. To whom be in all things the Preheminence, and Glory, and Praise.* Amen.

FINIS.

<hr>

Mr. Cottons Letter Lately Printed, Examined and Answered (1644)

The Bloudy Tenent, of Persecution, for Cause of Conscience, discussed, in A Conference betweene Truth and Peace (1644)

Letter from Roger Williams to the Town of Providence (1654)

ROGER WILLIAMS (c. 1603–83)

Williams, a minister in the Church of England, immigrated to America in 1631 in support of the Puritan cause. Banished from Massachusetts Bay in 1635 because of his separatist views, he helped found the colony of Rhode Island, which soon became known as a haven of religious toleration.

Shortly after Williams was exiled, John Cotton wrote a letter to move him "to a more serious sight of your sin, and of the justice of God's hand against it." The epistle was published as a pamphlet in 1643, and Williams's reply, "Mr. Cottons Letter Lately Printed, Examined and Answered," came out the following

year. Williams's essay expresses his views of church-state relations and is most famous for his use of the metaphor of a "hedge or wall of Separation between the Garden of the Church and the Wildernes of the world." Both pamphlets were published in London and were virtually unknown in America until Williams's works were republished in the nineteenth century. The final chapter of the pamphlet is reprinted here.

In 1644 Williams published "The Bloudy Tenent, of Persecution, for Cause of Conscience," written in part to respond to pamphlets by John Cotton and a group of Massachusetts clergy who defended their colony's vision of church-state relations. Selections from this famous defense of religious liberty are reprinted below. Shortly after its publication, Cotton responded with an essay, "The bloudy tenent, washed, and made white in the bloud of the Lambe" (1647), to which Williams rejoined with "The Bloody Tenent yet more Bloody, by Mr. Cotton's Endeavor to wash it in the Blood of the Lamb, etc." (1652).

The final document is a letter written by Williams to the town of Providence in 1654, in response to citizens who objected to the town's requirement of military service.

<hr>

Mr. Cottons Letter Lately Printed, Examined and Answered (1644)

Chap. XXVIII

The close of his Letter is an Answer to a passage of mine, which he repeateth in an Objection thus:

But this you feare is to condemn the witnesses of Jesus (the Separate Churches in *London,* and elswhere) and our jealous God will visit us for such arrearages: yea the curse of the Angel to *Meros* will fall upon us, *because we come not forth to help Jehovah*

Chap. XXVIII reprinted from *The Complete Writings of Roger Williams* (New York: Russell and Russell, 1963), I:106–12.

against the mighty: we pray not for them, we come not at them (but at Parishes frequently) yea we reproach and censure them.

To which he answereth, that neither Christ nor his Apostles after him, nor Prophets before him ever delivered that way. That they feare not the Angels curse, because it is not to help *Iehovah* but Sathan, to withdraw people from the Parishes where they have found more presence of Christ, and evidence of his Spirit then in separated Churches: That they pray not for them because they cannot pray in faith for a blessing upon their Separation: and that it is little comfort to heare of separate Churches, as being the inventions of men, and blames them that being desirous of Reformation, they stumble not only at the inventions of men, but for their sakes at the Ordinances of the Lord, because they separate not only from the Parishes, but from the Church at *Plymouth,* and of that wherof Mr. *Lathrop* was Pastor, who (as he saith) not only refuse all the inventions of men, but choose to serve the Lord in his own Ordinances. Only, lastly he professeth his inward sorrow that my self helpe erring, though zealous soules against the mighty Ordinances of the Lord, which whosoever stumble at shall be broken, because whosoever will not kisse the Sonne (that is, will not heare and embrace the words of his mouth) shall perish in their way.

Ans. However Mr. *Cotton* beleeves and writes of this point, yet hath he not duly considered these following particulars:

First the faithfull labours of many Witnesses of *Iesus Christ,* extant to the world, abundantly proving, that the Church of the Jews under the Old Testament in the type, and the *Church* of the Christians under the New Testament in the Antitype, were both separate from the world; and that when they have opened a gap in the hedge or wall of Separation between the Garden of the Church and the Wildernes of the world, God hath ever broke down the wall it selfe, removed the Candlestick, *&c.* and made his Garden a Wildernesse, as at this day. And that therfore if he will ever please to restore his Garden and Paradice again, it must of necessitie be walled in peculiarly

Roger Williams, drypoint etching, 1936, by Arthur W. Heintzelman, commemorating the tercentenary of the founding of Rhode Island. Courtesy of Roger Williams University.

unto himselfe from the world, and that all that shall be saved out of the world are to be transplanted out of the Wildernes of world, and added unto his Church or Garden.

Secondly, that all the grounds and principles leading to oppose Bishops, Ceremonies, Common Prayer, prostitution of the Ordinances of Christ to the ungodly and to the true practise of Christs own Ordinances, doe necessarily (as before I intimated, and Mr. *Cann* hath fully proved) conclude a separation of holy from unholy, penitent from impenitent, godly from ungodly, *&c.* and that to frame any other building upon such grounds and foundations, is no other then to raise the form of a square house upon the Keele of a Ship, which will never prove a soul saving true Arke or Church of Christ Jesus, according to the Patterne.

Thirdly the multitudes of holy and faithfull men and women, who since Q. *Maries* dayes have witnessed this truth by writing, disputing, and in suffring losse of *goods* and *friends*, in *imprisonments, banishments, death,* &c. I confesse the Nonconformists have suffred also: but they that have suffred for this cause, have farre exceeded, in not only witnessing to those grounds of the Non-conformists but to those Truths also, the unavoidable conclusions of the Nonconformists principles.

Fourthly, what is that which Mr. *Cotton* and so many hundreths fearing God in New *England* walk in, but a way of separation? Of what matter doe they professe to constitute their Churches, but of true godly persons? In what form doe they cast this matter, but by a *voluntary uniting,* or *adding* of such godly persons, whom they carefully examine, and cause to make a *publike confession* of *sinne,* and *profession* of their *knowledge,* and *grace* in Christ? Nay, when other English have attempted to set up a Congregation after the Parishionall way, have they not been supprest? Yea have they not professedly and lately answered many worthy persons, whom they account godly Ministers and people, that they could not permit them to live in the same Common-wealth together with them, if they set up any other Church and Worship then what themselvs practise? Let their own soules, and the soules of others seriously ponder in the feare of God, what should be the Reason why themselves so practising, should persecute others for not leaving open a gap of Liberty to escape *persecution* and the Crosse of Christ, by frequenting the Parishes in Old *England,* which Parishes themselves *persecute* in New England, and will not permit them to breath in the common aire amongst them.

Fifthly, in the Parishes (which Mr. *Cotton* holds but inventions of men) however they would have liberty to frequent the Worship of the Word, yet they separate from the Sacraments: and yet according to Mr. *Cottons* own principles (as before) there is as true Communion in the Ministration of the word in a Church estate, as in the seales: What mystery should be in this, but that here also the Crosse or Gibbet of Christ may be avoyded in a great measure, if persons come to Church, &c.

Lastly, however he saith, *he hath not found such presence of Christ, and evidence of his Spirit in such Churches, as in the Parishes:* What should be the reason of their great rejoycings and boastings of their own Separations in New England, insomuch that some of the most eminent amongst them have affirmed, That even the Apostles Churches were not so pure? Surely if the same New English Churches were in Old England, they could not meet without Persecution, which therfore in Old England they avoid, by frequenting the way of Church-worship (which in New England they Persecute) the Parishes.

Upon these considerations how can Mr. *Cotton* be offended that I should help (as he calls them) any zealous soules, not against the mighty Ordinances of the Lord Jesus, but to seek after the Lord Jesus without halting? Yea why should Mr. *Cotton,* or any desirous to practice Reformation, kindle a fire of Persecution against such zealous soules, especially considering that themselves, had they so inveighed against Bishops, Common Prayer, &c. in Edward the 6. his dayes had been accounted as great Hereticks, in those Reforming times, as any now can be in these: yet would it have been then, and since hath it been great oppression and Tyranny to persecute their consciences, and still will it be for them to persecute the consciences of others in Old or New England.

How can I better end then Mr. *Cotton* doth, by warning, that all that will not kisse the Son (that is, heare and embrace the words of his mouth) shall perish in their way, *Psal.* 2. 12. And I desire Mr. *Cotton* and every soule to whom these lines may come, seriously to consider, in this Contraversie, if the Lord Jesus were himselfe in person in Old or New England, what Church, what Ministry, what Worship, what Government he would set up, and what persecution he would practice toward them that would not receive Him?

FINIS.

The Bloudy Tenent, of Persecution, for Cause of Conscience (1644)

To the Right Honorable, both Houses of the High Court of Parliament

Right Honourable and Renowned Patriots:

Next to the saving of your own *soules* (in the lamentable *shipwrack* of *Mankind*) your taske (as *Christians*) is to save the *Soules*, but as *Magistrates*, the *Bodies* and *Goods* of others.

Many excellent *Discourses* have been presented to your *Fathers* hands and Yours in former and present *Parliaments:* I shall be humbly bold to say, that (in what concernes your duties as *Magistrates*, towards others) a more necessary and seasonable *debate* was never yet presented.

Two things your *Honours* here may please to view (in this Controversie of *Persecution* for cause of *Conscience*) beyond what's extant.

First the whole *Body* of this *Controversie* form'd & pitch'd in true *Battalia* [fighter exercises of soldiers].

Secondly (although in respect of my selfe it be *impar congressus* [unequal contest], yet in the power of that *God* who is *Maximus in Minimis* [greatest in the least], Your Honours shall see the Controversie is discussed with men as able as most, eminent for *abilitie* and *pietie*, Mr. *Cotton*, and the *New English Ministers*.

When the *Prophets* in Scripture have given their *Coats of Armes* and *Escutchions* to *Great Men*, Your *Honours* know the *Babylonian Monarch* hath the *Lyon*, the *Persian* the *Beare*, the *Grecian* the *Leopard*, the *Romane* a *compound* of the former 3. most strange and dreadfull, *Dan.* 7.

Their oppressing, plundring, ravishing, murthering, not only of the *bodies*, but the *soules* of Men are large explaining *commentaries* of such similitudes.

Excerpts reprinted from *The Complete Writings of Roger Williams* (New York: Russell and Russell, 1963), 1:5–9, 29–39.

Your *Honours* have been famous to the end of the World, for your unparallel'd *wisdome, courage, justice, mercie*, in the vindicating your Civill *Lawes, Liberties,* &c. Yet let it not be grievous to your *Honours* thoughts to ponder a little, why all the *Prayers* and *Teares* and *Fastings* in this Nation have not pierc'd the *Heavens*, and quench'd these *Flames*, which yet who knowes how far they'll spread, and when they'll out!

Your *Honours* have broke the jawes of the *Oppressour*, and taken the prey out of their Teeth (*Job.* 29). For which Act I believe it hath pleased the most High *God* to set a *Guard* (not only of Trained Men, but) of mighty *Angels*, to secure your sitting and the Citie.

I feare we are not *pardoned*, though *reprieved:* O that there may be a lengthning of *Londons* tranquilitie, of the *Parliaments* safetie, by *mercy* to the *poore!* Dan. 4.

Right Honorable, *Soule yokes, Soule oppression, plundrings, ravishings,* &c. are of a *crimson* and *deepest dye*, and I believe the chiefe of *Englands* sins, unstopping the Viols of *Englands* present sorrowes.

This glasse presents your *Honours* with *Arguments* from *Religion, Reason, Experience*, all proving that the greatest yoakes yet lying upon *English necks*, (the *peoples* and Your *own*) are of a *spirituall* and *soule* nature.

All former *Parliaments* have changed these yoakes according to their *consciences*, (*Popish* or *Protestant*) 'Tis now your *Honours* turne at *helme*, and (as your *task*, so I hope your *resolution*, not to change (for that is but to turne the wheele, which another *Parliament*, and the very next may turne againe:) but to ease the Subjects and Your selves from a *yoake* (as was once spoke in a case not unlike *Act.* 15.) which neither You nor your Fathers were ever able to beare.

Most *Noble Senatours*, Your *Fathers* (whose *seats* You fill) are mouldred, and mouldring their *braines*, their *tongues*, &c. to *ashes* in the pit of *rottenesse:* They and You must shortly (together with two *worlds* of men) appeare at the great *Barre:* It shall then be no griefe of heart that you have now attended to the *cries* of *Soules, thousands oppressed, millions ravished* by the *Acts* and *Statutes* concerning *Soules*, not yet *repealed.*

THE
BLOVDY TENENT,
of PERSECUTION, for cause of
CONSCIENCE, difcuffed, in
A Conference betweene
TRVTH and PEACE.

VVHO,
In all tender Affection, prefent to the High
Court of Parliament, (as the Refult of
their Difcourfe) thefe, (amongft other
Paffages) of higheft confideration.

Printed in the Year 1644.

Roger Williams, Title page of *The Bloudy Tenent of Persecution, for cause of Conscience*,
1644. Rare Book and Special Collections Division, Library of Congress.

Of *Bodies impoverished, imprisoned,* &c. for their *soules* beliefe, yea slaughtered on heapes for *Religions* controversies in the *Warres* of present and former Ages.

"Notwithstanding the success of later times, (wherein sundry opinions have been hatched about the subject of *Religion*) a man may clearly discerne with his eye, and as it were touch with his finger that according to the verity of holy Scriptures, &c. mens *consciences* ought in no sort to be violated, urged or constrained. And whensoever men have attempted any thing by this violent course, whether openly or by secret meanes, the issue hath beene pernicious, and the cause of great and *wonderfull innovations* in the principallest and mightiest *Kingdomes* and *Countries*, &c."

It cannot be denied to be a pious and prudentiall *act* for Your *Honours* (according to your conscience) to call for the advice of faithfull *Councellours* in the high debates concerning Your owne, and the soules of others.

Yet let it not be imputed as a *crime* for any *suppliant* to the *God* of *Heaven* for You, if in the humble sense of what their soules beleeve, they powre forth (amongst others) these three *requests* at the *Throne* of *Grace*.

First, That neither Your *Honours,* nor those excellent and worthy persons, whose advice you seek, limit the holy *One* of *Israel* to their *apprehensions, debates, conclusions,* rejecting or neglecting the humble and faithfull suggestions of any, though as base as spittle and clay, with which sometimes *Christ Jesus* opens the *eyes* of them that are borne blinde.

Secondly, That the present and future *generations* of the Sons of Men may never have cause to say that such a *Parliament* (as *England* never enjoyed the like) should modell the *worship* of the *living, eternall* and *invisible God* after the *Bias* of any earthly *interest,* though of the highest concernment under the Sunne: And yet, faith that learned Sir *Francis Bacon* (how ever otherwise perswaded, yet thus he confesseth:) "Such as hold *pressure* of *Conscience,* are guided therein by some private *interests* of their owne."

Thirdly, What ever way of *worshipping God* Your owne *Consciences* are perswaded to walke in, yet (from any bloody *act* of violence to the consciences of others) it may bee never told at *Rome* nor *Oxford,* that the *Parliament* of *England* hath committed a greater *rape,* then if they had forced or ravished the bodies of all the women in the *World.*

And that *Englands Parliament* (so famous throughout all Europe and the World) should at last turne *Papists, Prelatists, Presbyterians, Independents, Socinians, Familists, Antinomians,* &c. by confirming all these sorts of Consciences, by Civill force and violence to their Consciences. . . .

Scriptures And Reasons written long since by a *Witnesse* of Iesus Christ, close *Prisoner* in *Newgate,* against *Persecution* in cause of *Conscience;* and sent some while since to Mr. *Cotton,* by a Friend who thus wrote:

In the multitude *of* Councellours *there is safety: It is therefore humbly desired to be instructed in this point: viz.*

Whether Persecution *for cause of* Conscience *be not against the Doctrine of* Iesus Christ *the* King of Kings. *The Scriptures and Reasons are these.*

Because *Christ* commandeth that the *Tares* and *Wheat* (which some understand are those that walke in the *Truth,* and those that walke in *Lies*) should be *let alone* in the *World,* and not *plucked* up untill the *Harvest,* which is the end of the *World, Matth.* 13. 30. 38. &c.

The same commandeth *Matth.* 15. 14. that they that are *Blinde* (as some interpret, led on in false *Religion,* and are offended with him for teaching true *Religion*) should be *let alone,* referring their punishment unto their falling into the *Ditch.*

Againe, *Luke* 9. 54, 55. hee reproved his *Disciples* who would have had *Fire* come downe from Heaven and devoure those *Samaritanes* who would not receive Him, in these words: Ye know not of what *Spirit* ye are, the son of Man is not come to destroy *Mens lives,* but to save them.

Paul the Apostle of our Lord teacheth, 2 *Tim.* 24. 2. That the servant of the Lord must not *strive,* but must be *gentle* toward *all Men,* suffering the Evill Men, instructing them with *meeknesse* that are contrary minded, proving if *God* at any time will give them *repentance,* that they may acknowledge the Truth, and come to *amendment* out of that snare of the *devill,* &c.

According to these blessed *Commandements,* the holy *Prophets* foretold, that when the *Law of Moses* (concerning *Worship*) should cease, and *Christs Kingdome* be established, *Esa.* 2. 4. *Mic.* 4. 3, 4. They shall breake their *Swords* into *Mathookes,* and their *Speares* into *Sithes.* And *Esa.* 11. 9. Then shall none hurt or destroy in all the *Mountaine* of my Holinesse, &c. And when he came, the same he *taught* and *practised,* as before: so did his D*isciples* after him, for the *Weapons* of his *Warfare* are not *carnall* (saith the Apostle) 2 *Cor.* 10.4.

But he chargeth straitly that his Disciples should be so far from persecuting those that would not bee of their Religion, that when they were *persecuted* they should *pray* (*Matth.* 5.) when they were *cursed* they should *blesse,* &c.

And the Reason seemes to bee, because they who now are *Tares,* may hereafter become *Wheat;* they who are now *blinde,* may hereafter *see;* they that now *resist* him, may hereafter *receive* him; they that are now in the *devils snare,* in *adversenesse* to the *Truth,* may hereafter come to *repentance;* they that are now *blasphemers* and *persecutors* (as *Paul* was) may in time become *faithfull* as he; they that are now *idolators* as the *Corinths* once were (1 *Cor.* 6. 9.) may hereafter become *true worshippers* as they; they that are now *no people* of *God,* nor under *mercy* (as the Saints sometimes were, 1 *Pet.* 2. 20.) may hereafter become the people of *God,* and obtaine *mercy,* as they.

Some come not till the 11. houre, *Matth.* 20. 6. if those that come not till the *last houre* should be *destroyed,* because they come not at the *first,* then should they never come but be prevented.

All which *premises* are in all humility referred to your godly wise *consideration.*

Because this *persecution* for cause of *conscience* is against the *profession* and *practice* of *famous Princes.*

First, you may please to consider the speech of *King James,* in his *Majesties Speech* at *Parliament,* 1609. He saith, it is a sure *Rule* in *divinity,* that God never loves to plant his *Church* by *violence* and *bloodshed.*

And in his *Highnesse Apologie,* pag. 4. speaking of such *Papists* that tooke the Oath, thus:

"I gave good proofe that I intended no *persecution* against them for *conscience* cause, but onely desired to bee secured for *civill obedience,* which for *conscience* cause they are bound to performe."

And pag. 60. speaking of *Blackwell* (the *Archpriest*) his *Majesty* saith, "It was never my intention to lay any thing to the said *Arch-Priests* charge (as I have never done to any) for *cause of conscience.*" And in his *Highnesse Exposition* on *Revel.* 20. printed 1588. and after [in] 1603. his *Majesty* writeth thus: "Sixthly, the compassing of the *Saints* and the *besieging* of the *beloved City,* declareth unto us a certaine *note* of a *false Church,* to be *Persecution,* for they come to seeke the *faithfull,* the *faithfull* are them that are sought: the *wicked* are the *besiegers,* the *faithfull* are the *besieged.*"

Secondly, the saying of *Stephen* King of *Poland:* "I am *King* of *Men,* not of *Consciences,* a Commander of *Bodies,* not of *Soules.*"

Thirdly, the *King* of *Bohemia* hath thus written:

"And notwithstanding the success of the later times (wherein sundry *opinions* have beene hatched about the subject of *Religion*) may make one clearly discerne with his *eye,* and as it were to touch with his *Finger,* that according to the veritie of *Holy Scriptures,* and a *Maxime* heretofore told and maintained, by the ancient Doctors of the *Church;* That *mens consciences* ought in no sort to bee *violated, urged,* or *constrained;* and whensoever men have attempted any thing by this *violent course,* whether openly or by secret meanes, the issue hath beene *pernicious,* and the cause of great and wonderfull *Innovations* in the principallest and mightiest *Kingdomes* and *Countries* of all Christen-dome."

And further his *Majesty* saith: "So that once more we doe professe before *God* and the *whole World,* that from this time forward wee are firmly resolved not to *persecute* or *molest,* or suffer to be *persecuted* or *mo-lested,* any person whosoever for *matter of Religion,* no not they that professe *themselves* to be of the *Romish Church,* neither to trouble or disturbe them in the ex-ercise of their *Religion,* so they live conformable to the *Lawes* of the *States,* &c."

And for the practice of this, where is *persecution* for cause of *conscience* except in *England* and where *Pop-ery* reignes, [?] and there neither in all places, as ap-peareth by *France, Poland,* and other places.

Nay, it is not practised amongst the *Heathen* that acknowledge not the *true God,* as the *Turke, Persian,* and others.

Thirdly, because *persecution* for cause of conscience is condemned by the ancient and later *Writers,* yea and *Papists* themselves.

Hilarie against *Auxentius* saith thus: The *Christian Church* doth not *persecute,* but is *persecuted.* And la-mentable it is to see the great folly of these times, and to sigh at the foolish opinion of this world, in that men thinke by humane aide to helpe *God,* and with worldly pompe and power to undertake to defend the *Christian Church.* I aske you *Bishops,* what helpe used the *Apostles* in the publishing of the *Gospel?* with the aid of what power did they preach *Christ,* and con-verted the *Heathen* from their *idolatry* to *God?* When they were in *prisons,* and lay in *chaines,* did they praise and give thankes to God for any *dignities, graces,* and *favours* received from the *Court?* Or do you thinke that *Paul* went about with *Regall Mandates,* or *Kingly authority,* to gather and establish the *Church* of *Christ?* sought he *protection* from *Nero, Vespasian?*

The *Apostles* wrought with their *hands* for their owne *maintenance,* travailing by *land* and *water* from *Towne* to *Citie,* to preach *Christ:* yea the more they were *forbidden,* the more they *taught* and preached *Christ.* But now alas, *humane helpe* must *assist* and *pro-tect* the *Faith,* and give the same countenance to and

by vaine and *worldly honours.* Doe men seek to defend the *Church of Christ?* as if hee by his power were un-able to performe it.

The same against the *Arrians.*

The *Church* now, which formerly by induring *mis-ery* and *imprisonment* was knowne to be a *true Church,* doth now terrifie others by *imprisonment, banishment,* and *misery,* and boasteth that she is highly esteemed of the *world,* when as the true *Church* [she] cannot but be hated of the same.

Tertull. ad Scapulam: It agreeth both with *humane reason,* and *naturall equity,* that every man *worship* God uncompelled, and beleeve what he will; for it neither hurteth nor profiteth any one another mans *Religion* and *Beleefe:* Neither beseemeth it any *Reli-gion* to compell another to be of their *Religion,* which willingly and freely should be imbraced, and not by constraint: for as much as the *offerings* were required of those that freely and with good will offered, and not from the *contrary.*

Jerom. in proaem. lib. 4. in Jeremiam. Heresie must be cut off with the *Sword* of the *Spirit:* let us strike through with the *Arrowes* of the *Spirit* all *Sonnes* and *Disciples* of mis-led *Heretickes,* that is, with *Testimo-nies* of holy *Scriptures.* The slaughter of *Heretickes* is by the word of God.

Brentius upon 1 *Cor.* 3. No man hath power to make or give Lawes to *Christians,* whereby to binde their *consciences;* for willingly, freely, and uncompelled, with a ready desire and cheerfull minde, must those that come, run unto *Christ.*

Luther in his Booke of the *Civill Magistrate* saith; The *Lawes* of the *Civill Magistrates* government ex-tends no further then over the *body* or *goods,* and to that which is *externall:* for over the *soule God* will not suffer any man to *rule:* only he *himselfe* will rule there. Wherefore whosoever doth undertake to give *Lawes* unto the *Soules* and *Consciences* of Men, he usurpeth that *government* himselfe which appertain-eth unto God, &c.

Therefore upon 1 *Kings* 5. In the building of the *Temple* there was no *sound* of *Iron* heard, to signifie that *Christ* will have in his *Church* a *free* and a *willing*

People, not compelled and constrained by *Lawes* and *Statutes.*

Againe he saith upon *Luk.* 22. It is not the true *Catholike Church,* which is defended by the *Secular Arme* or humane Power, but the *false* and *feigned Church,* which although it carries the *Name* of a *Church* yet it denies the power thereof.

And upon *Psal.* 17. he saith: For the true *Church* of *Christ* knoweth not *Brachium saeculare,* which the *Bishops* now adayes, chiefly use.

Againe, in *Postil. Dom.* 1. *post Epiphan.* he saith: Let not *Christians* be *commanded,* but *exhorted:* for, He that willingly will not doe that, whereunto he is friendly exhorted, he is no *Christian:* wherefore they that doe compell those that are not willing, shew thereby that they are not *Christian Preachers,* but *Worldly Beadles.*

Againe, upon 1 *Pet.* 3. [ii: 17] he saith: If the *Civill Magistrate* shall command me to believe thus and thus: I should answer him after this manner: *Lord,* or *Sir,* Looke you to your *Civill* or *Worldly Government,* Your Power extends not so farre as to command any thing in *Gods Kingdome:* Therefore herein I may not heare you. For if you cannot beare it, that any should usurpe *Authoritie* where you have to Command, how doe you thinke that *God* should suffer you to thrust him from his Seat, and to seat your selfe therein?

Lastly, the Papists, the *Inventors of Persecution,* in a wicked Booke of theirs set forth in *K. James* his *Reigne,* thus:

Moreover, the *Meanes* which *Almighty God* appointed his Officers to use in the Conversion of *Kingdomes* and *Nations,* and People, was *Humilitie, Patience, Charitie;* saying, Behold I send you as *Sheepe* in the midst of *Wolves,* Mat. 10. 16. He did not say, Behold I send you as *Wolves* among *Sheepe,* to kill, imprison, spoile and devoure those unto whom they were sent.

Againe *vers.* 7. he saith: They to whom I send you, will deliver you up into *Councells,* and in their *Synagogues* they will scourge you; and to *Presidents* and to *Kings* shall you be led for my sake. He doth not say:

You whom I send, shall deliver the people (whom you ought to convert) unto *Councells,* and put them in Prisons, and lead them to *Presidents,* and *Tribunall Seates,* and make their *Religion Felony* and *Treason.*

Againe he saith, *vers.* 32. When ye enter into an House, salute it, saying, Peace be unto this House: he doth not say, You shall send *Pursevants* to ransack or spoile his House.

Againe he said, *John* 10. The good *Pastour* giveth his life for his Sheep, the *Thiefe* commeth not but to steale, kill and destroy. He doth not say, The *Thiefe* giveth his life for his Sheep, and the Good *Pastour* commeth not but to steale, kill and destroy.

So that we holding our peace, our *Adversaries* themselves speake for us, or rather for the Truth.

To Answer Some Maine Objections

And first, that it is no *prejudice* to the *Common wealth,* if *Libertie* of *Conscience* were suffred to such as doe feare *God* indeed, as is or will be manifest in such mens lives and conversations.

Abraham abode among the *Canaanites* a long time, yet contrary to them in *Religion,* Gen. 13. 7. & 16. 13. Againe he sojourned in *Gerar,* and K. *Abimelech* gave him leave to abide in his Land, *Gen.* 20. 21. 23. 24. [xx, xxi: 33. 34.]

Isaack also dwelt in the same Land, yet contrary in *Religion,* Gen. 26.

Jacob lived 20 yeares in one House with his Unkle *Laban,* yet differed in *Religion,* Gen. 31.

The people of *Israel* were about 430 yeares in that infamous land of *Egypt,* and afterwards 70 yeares in *Babylon,* all which time they differed in *Religion* from the States, *Exod.* 12. & 2 *Chron.* 36.

Come to the time of *Christ,* where *Israel* was under the *Romanes,* where lived divers Sects of *Religion,* as *Herodians, Scribes* and *Pharises, Saduces* and *Libertines, Thudaeans* and *Samaritanes,* beside the Common Religion of the *Jewes, Christ* and his *Apostles.* All which differed from the Common *Religion* of the State, which was like the Worship of *Diana,* which almost the whole world then worshipped, *Acts* 19. 20. [27.]

All these lived under the Government of *Caesar*, being nothing hurtfull unto the *Common-wealth*, giving unto C*aesar* that which was his. And for their *Religion* and Consciences towards God, he left them to themselves, as having no Dominion over their *Soules* and C*onsciences*. And when the Enemies of the Truth raised up any *Tumults*, the wisedome of the *Magistrate* most wisely appeased them, *Acts* 18 14. & 19. 35.

———————

Letter to the Town of Providence

[Providence, January, 1654–5.]
That ever I should speak or write a tittle, that tends to such an infinite liberty of conscience, is a mistake, and which I have ever disclaimed and abhorred. To prevent such mistakes, I shall at present only propose this case: There goes many a ship to sea, with many hundred souls in one ship, whose weal and woe is common, and is a true picture of a commonwealth, or a human combination or society. It hath fallen out sometimes, that both papists and protestants, Jews and Turks, may be embarked in one ship; upon which supposal I affirm, that all the liberty of conscience, that ever I pleaded for, turns upon these two hinges—that none of the papists, protestants, Jews, or Turks, be forced to come to the ship's prayers or worship, nor compelled from their own particular prayers or worship, if they practice any. I further add, that I never denied, that notwithstanding this liberty, the commander of this ship ought to command the ship's course, yea, and also command that justice, peace and sobriety, be kept and practiced, both among the seamen and all the passengers. If any of the seamen refuse to perform their services, or passengers to pay their freight; if any refuse to help, in person or purse, towards the common charges or defence; if any refuse to obey the common laws and orders of the ship, con-

cerning their common peace or preservation; if any shall mutiny and rise up against their commanders and officers; if any should preach or write that there ought to be no commanders or officers, because all are equal in Christ, therefore no masters nor officers, no laws nor orders, nor corrections nor punishments;—I say, I never denied, but in such cases, whatever is pretended, the commander or commanders may judge, resist, compel and punish such transgressors, according to their deserts and merits. This if seriously and honestly minded, may, if it so please the Father of lights, let in some light to such as willingly shut not their eyes.

I remain studious of your common peace and liberty.

ROGER WILLIAMS

═══════════════

The Simple Cobbler of Aggawam in America (1646)

NATHANIEL WARD (1578–1652)

The Reverend Ward was a Cambridge-educated lawyer, clergyman, and pamphleteer. He was a leading Puritan minister in England before immigrating to Massachusetts in 1634 to escape persecution of the Puritans. He served briefly as a minister in Ipswich (then known by the Indian name Aggawam) in northeastern Massachusetts. He is credited with crafting "The Body of Liberties," which was adopted by the General Court of the Massachusetts Bay Company in 1641. Drawing on English common law and the Bible, this influential document was New England's first legal code. *The Simple Cobbler of Aggawam in America,* written under the pseudonym Theodore de la Guard, a purported humble cobbler, is a witty and pungent satire exposing the follies and

Reprinted from *The Complete Writings of Roger Williams* (New York: Russell and Russell, 1963), 1:278–79.

Reprinted from Theodore de la Guard [Nathaniel Ward], *The Simple Cobbler of Aggawam in America* (Boston: Daniel Henchman, 1713), 1–29.

iniquities of Englishmen on both sides of the Atlantic. Ward's curmudgeonly cobbler unapologetically affirms a faith in the omnipotent "Truth of God" and an intolerance of "adversaries of his Truth," denouncing notions of religious toleration.

To The Reader

Gentlemen,
I Pray make a little room for a Cobler, his work was done in time, but a Ship setting Sail one day too soon makes it appear some Weeks too late; Seeing he is so reasonable as to demand no other pay for his labour and leather, but leave to pay us well for our faults, let it be well accepted, as Counsel in our occasions to come, and as Testimony to what is past,

By a Friend

Sutor Ultra Crepidem

EITHER I am in Apoplexy, or that man is in a Lethargy, who doth not now sensibly feel God shaking the Heavens over his head, and the Earth under his feet: The Heavens so, as the Sun begins to turn into darkness, the Moon into blood, the Stars to fall down to the ground; So that little Light of Comfort or Counsel is left to the Sons of Men: The Earth so, as the foundations are failing, the righteous scarce know where to find rest, the inhabitants stagger like drunken men: it is in a manner dissolved both in Religions and Relations: And no marvel; for, they have defiled it by transgressing the Laws, changing the Ordinances, and breaking the Everlasting Covenant. The Truths of God are the Pillars of the World, whereon States and Churches may stand quiet if they will; if they will not, He can easily shake them off into delusions, and distractions enough.

Satan is now in his passions, he feels his passion approaching; he loves to fish in royled waters.

Though that Dragon cannot sting the vitals of the Elect mortally, yet that Beelzebub can fly-blow their Intellectuals miserably: The finer Religion grows, the finer he spins his Cobwebs, he will hold pace with Christ so long as his wits will serve him. He sees himself beaten out of gross Idolatries, Heresies, Ceremonies, where the Light breaks forth with power; he will therefore bestir him to prevaricate Evangelical Truths, and Ordinances, that if they will needs be walking, yet they shall *laborare varicibus,* and not keep their path, he will put them out of time and place; Assassinating for his Engineers, men of Paracelsian parts; well complexioned for honesty; for such are fittest to Mountebank his Chimistry into sick Churches and weak Judgments.

Nor shall he need to stretch his strength overmuch in this work: Too many men having not laid their foundations sure, nor ballasted their Spirits deep with humility and fear, are prest enough of themselves to evaporate their own apprehensions. Those that are acquainted with Story know, it hath ever been so in new Editions of Churches: Such as are least able, are most busy to pudder in the rubbish, and to raise dust in the eyes of more steady Repayrers. Civil Commotions make room for uncivil practises: Religious mutations, for irreligious opinions: Change of Air, discovers currupt bodies; Reformation of Religion, unsound minds. He that hath any well-faced phansy in his Crown, and doth not vent it now, fears the pride of his own heart will dub him dunce for ever. Such a one will trouble the whole *Israel* of God with his most untimely births, though he makes the bones of his vanity stick up, to the view and grief of all that are godly wise. The devil desires no better sport than to see light heads handle their heels, and fetch their carreers in a time, when the Roof of Liberty stands open.

The next perplexed Question, with pious and ponderous men, will be: What should be done for the healing of these comfortless exulcerations. I am the unablest adviser of a thousand, the unworthiest of ten thousand; yet I hope I may presume to assert what follows without just offence.

First, such as have given or taken any unfriendly reports of us *New-English,* should doe well to recollect themselves. We have been reputed a Colluvies of wild Opinionists, swarmed into a remote wilderness to find elbow-room for our Phanatick Doctrines and Practises: I trust our diligence past, and constant sedulity against such persons and courses, will plead better things for us. I dare take upon me, to be the Herauld of *New-England* so far, as to proclaim to the World, in the name of our Colony, that all Familists, Antinomians, Anabaptists, and other Enthusiasts shall have free Liberty to keep away from us, and such as will come to be gone as fast as they can, the sooner the better.

Secondly, I dare aver, that God doth no where in his word tolerate Christian States, to give Tolerations to such adversaries of his Truth, if they have power in their hands to suppress them.

Here is lately brought us an Extract of a *Magna Charta,* so called, compiled between the Sub-planters of a *West-Indian* Island; whereof the first Article of constipulation, firmly provides free stable-room and litter for all kind of Consciences, be they never so dirty or jadish; making it actionable, yea, treasonable, to disturb any man in his Religion, or to discommend it, whatever it be. We are very sorry to see such professed Prophaneness in *English* Professors, as industriously to lay their Religious foundations on the ruine of true Religion; which strictly binds every Conscience *to contend earnestly for the Truth: to preserve unity of Spirit, Faith and Ordinances, to be all like minded, of one accord; every man to take his Brother into his Christian care, to stand fast with one spirit, with one mind, striving together for the faith of the Gospel;* and by no means to permit Heresies or Erronious Opinions: But God abhorring such loathsome beverages, hath in his righteous judgment blasted that enterprize, which might otherwise have prospered well, for ought I know; I presume their case is generally known ere this.

If the Devil might have his free option, I believe he would ask nothing else, but liberty to enfrancize all false Religions, and to embondage the true; nor should he need: It is much to be feared, that lax Tolerations upon State-pretences and planting necessities, will be the next subtle Stratagem he will spread to distate the Truth of God, and supplant the Peace of the Churches. Tolerations in things tolerable, exquisitely drawn out by the lines of the Scripture, and pensil of the Spirit, are the sacred favours of Truth, the due latitudes of Love, the fair Compartiments of Christian fraternity: but irregular dispensations, dealt forth by the facilities of men, are the frontiers of error, the redoubts of Schisme, the perillous irritaments of carnal and spiritual enmity.

My heart hath naturally detested four things: The standing of the Apocrypha in the Bible; Forainers dwelling in my Country, to crowd out Native Subjects into the corners of the Earth; Alchymized Coines; Tolerations of divers Religions, or of one Religion in segregant shapes: He that willingly assents to the last, if he examines his heart by day light, his Conscience will tell him, he is either an Atheist, or an Heretick, or an Hypocrite, or at best a captive to some Lust: Poly-piety is the greatest impiety in the World. True Religion is *Ignis probationis,* which doth *congregare homogenea & segregare heterogenea.*

Not to tolerate things meerly indifferent to weak Consciences, argues a Conscience too strong: pressed uniformity in these, causes much disunity: To tolerate more than indifferents, is not to deal indifferently with God: He that doth it, takes his Scepter out of his hand, and bids him stand by. Who hath to do to institute Religion but God. The power of all Religion and Ordinances, lies in their Purity: their Purity in their Simplicity: then are mixtures pernicious. I lived in a City, where a Papist Preached in one Church, a Lutheran in another, a Calvinist in a third; a Lutheran one part of the day, a Calvinist the other, in the same Pulpit: the Religion of that Place was but motly and meagre, their affections Leopard-like.

If the whole Creature should conspire to do the Creator a mischief, or offer him an insolency, it would be in nothing more, than in erecting untruths against his Truth, or by sophisticating his Truths with humane medleyes: the removing of some one iota in Scripture, may draw out all the life, and traverse all the Truth of the whole Bible: but to authorise an untruth, by a Toleration of State, is to build a Sconce against the walls of Heaven, to batter God out of his Chair: To tell a practical lye, is a great Sin, but yet transient; but to set up a Theorical untruth, is to warrant every lye that lyes from its root to the top of every branch it hath, which are not a few.

I would willingly hope that no Member of the Parliament hath skilfully ingratiated himself into the hearts of the House, that he might watch a time to Midwife out some ungracious Toleration for his own turn, and for the sake of that, some other, I would also hope that a word of general caution should not be particularly misapplied. I am the freer to suggest it, because I know not one man of that mind, my aim is general, and I desire may be so accepted. Yet good Gentlemen, look well about you, and remember how *Tiberius* play'd the Fox with the Senate of *Rome,* and how *Fabius Maximus* cropt his ears for his cunning.

That State is wise, that will improve all pains and patience rather to compose, than tolerate differences in Religion. There is no divine Truth, but hath much Coelestial fire in it from the Spirit of Truth: nor no irreligious untruth, without its proportion of Antifire from the spirit of Error to contradict it: the zeal of the one, the virulency of the other, must necessarily kindle Combustions. Fiery diseases seated in the Spirit, imbroil the whole frame of the body: others more external and cool, are less dangerous. They which divide in Religion, divide in God; they who divide in him, divide beyond *Genus Generalissimum,* where there is no reconciliation, without atonement; that is, without uniting in him, who is One, and in his Truth, which is also one.

Wise are those men who will be perswaded rather to live within the pale of Truth, where they may be quiet, than in the purlieves, where they are sure to be hunted ever and anon, do Authority what it can. Every singular Opinion, hath a singular opinion of it self, and he that holds it a singular opinion of himself, and a simple opinion of all contra-sentients: he that confutes them, must confute all three at once, or else he does nothing; which will not be done without more stir than the Peace of the State or Church can indure.

And prudent are those Christians, that will rather give what may be given, than hazard all by yielding nothing. To sell all Peace of Country, to buy some Peace of Conscience unseasonably, is more avarice than thrift, imprudence than patience: they deal not equally, that set any Truth of God at such a rate; but they deal wisely that will stay till the Market is fallen.

My Prognosticks deceive me not a little, if once within three seven years, Peace prove not such a Penny-worth at most Marts in Christendom, that he that would not lay down his Money, his Lust, his Opinion, his Will, I had almost said the best flower of his Crown for it, while he might have had it; will tell his own heart, he plaid the very ill husband.

Concerning Tolerations, I may further assert.

That Persecution of true Religion, and Toleration of false, are the *Jannes* and *Jambres* to the Kingdom of Christ, whereof the last is far the worst. *Augustines* Tongue had not owed his Mouth one Penny-rent though he had never spake word more in it, but this, *Nullum malum pejus libertate errandi.*

Frederick Duke of *Saxon,* spake not one foot beyond the mark when he said. He had rather the Earth should swallow him up quick, than he should give a toleration to any Opinion against any Truth of God.

He that is willing to tolerate any Religion, or discrepant way of Religion, besides his own, unless it be in matters meerly indifferent, either doubts of his own, or is not sincere in it.

He that is willing to tolerate any unsound Opinion, that his own may also be tolerated, though never so sound, will for a need hang Gods Bible at the Devils girdle.

Every Toleration of false Religions, or Opinions hath as many Errors and Sins in it, as all the false

Religions and Opinions it tolerates, and one found one more.

That State that will give Liberty of Conscience in matters of Religion, must give Liberty of Conscience and Conversation in their Moral Laws, or else the Fiddle will be out of Tune, and some of the strings crack.

He that will rather make an irreligious quarel with other Religions than try the Truth of his own by valuable Arguments, and peaceable Sufferings; either his Religion, or himself is irreligious.

Experience will teach Churches and Christians, that it is far better to live in a State united, though a little Corrupt, than in a State, whereof some Part is incorrupt, and all the rest divided.

I am not altogether ignorant of the eight Rules given by Orthodox Divines about giving Tolerations, yet with their favour I dare affirm,

That there is no Rule given by God for any State to give an affirmative Toleration to any false Religion, or Opinion whatsoever; they must connive in some Cases, but may not concede in any.

That the State of *England* (so far as my Intelligence serves) might in time have prevented with ease, and may yet without any great difficulty deny both Toleration, and irregular connivences *salva Republica.*

That if the State of *England* shall either willingly Tolerate, or weakly connive at such Courses, the Church of that Kingdom will sooner become the Devils dancing-School, than Gods Temple: The Civil State a Bear-garden, than an Exchange: The whole Realm a Pais base than an *England.* And what pity it is, that that Country which hath been the Staple of Truth to all Christendom, should now become the Aviary of Errors to the whole World, let every fearing heart judge.

I take Liberty of Conscience to be nothing but a freedom from Sin, and Error. *Conscientia in tantum libera, inquantum ab errore liberata.* And Liberty of Error nothing but a Prison for Conscience. Then small will be the kindness of a State to build such Prisons for their Subjects.

The Scripture saith, there is nothing makes free but Truth, and Truth saith, there is no Truth but one: If the States of the World would make it their sumoperous Care to preserve this One Truth in its purity and Authority, it would ease you of all other Political cares. I am sure Satan makes it his grand, if not only task, to adulterate Truth; Falshood is his sole Scepter, whereby he first ruffled, and ever since ruined the World.

If Truth be but One, methinks all the Opinionists in *England* should not be all in that One Truth, some of them I doubt are out. He that can extract an unity out of such a disparity, or contract such a disparity into an unity; had need be a better Artist, than ever was *Drebell.*

If two Centers (as we may suppose) be in one Circle, and lines drawn from both to all the points of the Compass, they will certainly cross one another, and probably cut through the Centers themselves.

There is talk of an universal Toleration, I would talk as loud as I could against it, did I know what more apt and reasonable Sacrifice *England* could offer to God for his late performing all his heavenly Truths than an universal Toleration of all hellish Errors, or how they shall make an universal Reformation, but by making Christs Academy the Devils University, where any man may commence Heretick *per saltum;* where he that is *filius Diabolicus,* or *simpliciter pessimus,* may have his grace to go to Hell *cum Publico Privilegio;* and carry as many after him, as he can.

Religio docenda est, non coercenda is a pretty piece of *album Latinum* for some kind of throats that are willingly sore, but *Haeresis dedocenda est non permittenda,* will be found a far better *Diamoron* for the Gargarismes this Age wants, if timely and throughly applyed.

If there be room in *England* for

Familists			*Manes*
Libertines			*Lemures*
Erastians			*Dryades*
Antitrinitarians			*Homadryades*
Anabaptists			*Potamides*
Antiscripturists			*Naiades*
Arminians			*Hinnides*
Manifestarians	the room		*Pierides*
Millinarians	for		*Nereides*
Antinomians			*Pales*
Socinians			*Anonides*
Arrians			*Parcades*
Perfectists			*Castalides*
*Brownists***			*Monides*
Religious *Mortalians*		Good	*Charites*
Men but *Seekers*		Spirits,	*Heliconides*
pernicious *Enthusiasts,*		but very	*Pegasides,*
Heriticks *&c.*		Devils.	*&c.*

In a word room for Hell above ground.

It is said, Though a man have light enough himself to see the Truth, yet if he hath not enough to enlighten others, he is bound to tolerate them, I will engage my self, that all the Devils in *Britanie* shall sell themselves to their shirts, to purchase a Lease of this Position for three of their Lives, under the Seal of the Parliament.

It is said, That Men ought to have Liberty of their Conscience, and that it is Persecution to debar them of it: I can rather stand amazed than reply to this: it is an astonishment to think that the braines of men should be parboyl'd in such impious ignorance; Let all the wits under the Heavens lay their heads together and find an Assertion worse than this (one excepted) I will Petition to be chosen the universal Ideot of the World.

It is said, That Civil Magistrates ought not to meddle with Ecclesiastical matters.

I would answer to this so well as I could, did I not know that some Papers lately brought out of *New-*

* By Brownists, I mean not Independents, but dew-clawd Seperatists: far be it from me to wrong godly Independents. I truely acknowledge that I judge my self neither able nor worthy to honour some of them as they deserve.

England, are going to the Press, wherein the Opinions of the Elders there in a late Synod, concerning this point are manifested, which I suppose will give clearer satisfaction than I can.

The true English of all this their false Latin, is nothing but a general Toleration of all Opinions; which motion if it be like to take, it were very requisite, that the City would repair *Pauls* with all the speed they can, for an English *Pantheon*, and bestow it upon the Sectaries, freely to assemble in, then there may be some hope that *London* will be quiet in time.

But why dwell I so intolerable long about Tolerations, I hope my fears are but Panick, against which I have a double cordial. First, that the Parliament will not though they could: Secondly, that they cannot though they would grant such Tolerations. God who hath so honoured them with eminent Wisdom in all other things, will not suffer them to cast both his, and their Honour in the dust of perpetual Infamy, do what they can; nor shall those who have spent so great a part of their substance in redeeming their Civil Liberties from Usurpation, lose all that remains in enthralling their spiritual Liberty by Toleration.

It is said Opinionists are many, and strong, that *de sunt Vires,* that it is *turbata respublica,* I am very sorry for it, but more sorry, if despondency of mind shall cause the least tergiversation in Gods Worthies, who have receiv'd such pledges of his presence in their late Counsels, and Conflicts. It is not thousands of Opinionists that can pinion his Everlasting armes. I can hardly believe there is a greater unbeliever than my Self, yet I can verily believe that the God of Truth will in a short time scatter them all like smoke before the wind. I confess, I am troubled to see Men so overtroubled about them; I am rather glad to hear the Devil is breaking up house in *England,* and removing some whither else, give him leave to sell all his rags, and odd-ends by the out-cry; and let his petty Chapmen make their Market while they may, upon my poor Credit it will not last long. He that hath done so much for *England* will go on to perfect his own Praise, and his Peoples Peace: Let good men stand still, and behold his further Salvation. He that sitteth in the Heavens laughs at them, the most High hath them in Derision, and their folly shall certainly be manifested to all men.

Yet I dare not but add, and in the Name of God will add, that if any Publick members of Church or State, have been either open fautors, or private abetters of any blasphemous, contagious Opinions; It will be their wisdom to proportion their repentance to their Sin, before God makes them Publick Monuments of Ignominy, and Apostasy.

Thirdly, That all Christian States, ought to disavow and decry all such Errors, by some peremptory Statutary Act, and that in time, that Subjects knowing fully the mind of the State, might not delude themselves with vain hopes of unsufferable Liberties. It is less to say, *Statuatur veritas, ruat Regnum,* than *Fiat justitia, ruat Coelum;* but there is no such danger in either of them. Fear nothing Gentlemen, *Rubiconem transistis, jacta est alea,* ye have turned the Devil out of doors; fling all his old parrel after him out at the windows, lest he makes another errand for it again. *Quae relinquuntur in morbis post indicationem, recidivas facere consuevere.* Christ would have his Church without spot or wrinckle; They that help make it so, shall lose neither honour nor labour: If ye be wise, suffer no more thorns in his sides or your own. When God kindles such fires as these, he doth not usually quench them, till the very scum on the Pot sides be boyled clean away, *Ezek.* 24. 10, 11. Ye were better to do it your selves, than leave it to him: the Arm of the Lord is mighty, his hand very heavy; who can dwell with his devouring fire, and long lasting burnings?

Fourthly, to make speedy provision against Obstinates and Disseminaries: were under favour, two things will be found requisite. First, variety of Penalties, I mean certain, not indefinite: I am a Crabbat against Arbitrary Government. Experience hath taught us here, that political, domestical, and personal respects, will not admit one and the same remedy for all, without sad inconveniences. Secondly, just severity: Persecution hath ever spread Truth, Prosecution scattered Error: Ten of the most Christian Emperors, found that way best; Schollars know whom I mean: Five of the ancient Fathers perswaded to it, of whom *Augustine* was one, who for a time argued hard for indulgency: but upon conference with other Prudent Bishops, altered his judgment, as appears in three of his Epistles, to *Marcellinus, Donatus,* and *Boniface.* I would be understood, not only an Allower, but an humble Petitioner, that ignorant and tender conscienced Anabaptists may have due time and means of conviction.

Fifthly, That every Prophet, to whom God hath given the Tongue of the Learned, should teach, and every Angel who hath a Pen and Inkhorn by his side write against these grieving extravagancies: writing of many Books, I grant is irksome, reading endless. A reasonable man would think Divines had declaimed sufficiently upon these Themes. I have ever thought the Rule given, *Titus* 3. 10. which cuts the work short and sharp to be more properly prevalent, than wearisome waiting upon unweariable Spirits. It is a most toylsome task to run the wild-goose chase after a well-breath'd Opinionist: they delight in vitilitigation: it is an itch that loves a life to be scrubd: they desire not satisfaction, but satisdiction, whereof themselves must be judges: yet in new eruptions of Error with new objections, silence is sinful.

As for my self, I am none of the disputers of this world: all I can do, is to guess when men speak true or false Divinity: If I can but find the Parental root, or formal reason of a Truth, I am quiet; if I cannot, I shore up my slender judgement as long as I can, with two or three the handsomest Props I can get: I shall therefore leave Arguments to acuter heads, and only speak a word of Love, with all Christian respect to our dear Brethren in *England,* which are against Baptizing of Infants: I intreat them to consider these few things seriously and meekly. First, what a high pitch of boldness it is for man to cut a principal Ordinance out of the Kingdom of God; If it be but to make a dislocation, which so far disgoods the Ordinance, I fear it altogether unhallows it, to transplace or transtime a stated Institution of Christ, without his direction, I think, is to destroy it. Secondly, what a Cruelty it is to devest Children of that only external Priviledge which their heavenly Father hath bequeathed them, to interest them visibly in Himself, His Son, His Spirit, His Covenant of Grace, and the tender bosome of their careful Mother the Church. Thirdly, what an Inhumanity it is, to deprive Parents of that comfort they may take from the Baptism of their Infants dying in their Childhood. Fourthly, How unseasonable and unkindly it is, to interturbe the State and Church with these Amalekitish on-sets, when they are in their extream pangs of travail with their lives. Fifthly, to take a through view of those who have preambled this by path. Being sometimes in the Crowds of foraign Wederdopers, that is, Anabaptists, and prying into their inward frames with the best eyes I had; I could not but observe these disguised guises in the generality of them. First, a flat formality of Spirit without salt or savour in the spiritualties of Christ, as if their Religion began and ended in their Opinion. Secondly, a shallow slighting of such as discent from them, appearing too often in their faces, speeches and carriages. Thirdly, a feeble, yet peremptory obstinacy; seldome are any of them reclaimed. Fourthly, a shameful sliding into other such tarpauling tenets, to keep themselves dry from the showers of Justice, as a rational mind would never entertain, if it were not Error-blasted from Heaven and Hell. I should as shrewdly suspect that Opinion, that will cordially corrive with two or three sottish errors, as that faith that can professedly live with two or three sordid sins. I dare not fear our godly Brethren in *England* to be yet coming to this pass; how soon they may, themselves know not, the times are slippery: They will undoubtedly find God as jealous of his Ordinances, as themselves are zealous of their Opinions.

Sixthly, that Authority ought to see their Subjects Children Baptized, though their Parents judgments be against it, if there be no other Evangelical bar in the way.

Seventhly, that prudent men, especially Young, should do well not to ingage themselves in conference with Errorists, without a good calling and great caution; their breath is contagious, their leprey spread-

ing: receive not him that is weak saith the Apostle to doubtful disputations; much less may they run themselves into dangerous Sophistications. He usually hears best in their Meetings, that stops his ears closest; he opens his Mouth to best purpose, that keeps it shut, and he doth best of all, that declines their company as wisely as he may.

Brethren, have an extraordinary care also of the late Theosophers, that teach men to climb to Heaven upon a ladder of lying figments. Rather than the Devil will lose his game, he will out-shoot Christ in his own bow; he will out-law the Law, quite out of the Word and World: over-Gospel the Gospel, and quidanye Christ, with Sugar and Rats-bane. He was Professor not long since at *Schlestat* in *Alsatia,* where he learned, that no Poyson is so deadly as the Poyson of Grace.

The wisest way, when all is said, is with all humility and fear, to take Christ as himself hath revealed himself in his Gospel, and not as the Devil presents him to prestigiated fansies. I have ever hated the way of the Rosie-Crucians, who reject things as Gods Wisdom hath tempered them, and will have nothing but their Spirits. If I were to give Physick to Spryts, I would do so too: but when I want Physick for my body, I would not have my Soul tartared: nor my Animal Spirits purged any way, but by my Natural, and those by my bodily humours, and those by such Ordinaries, as have the nearest vicinage to them, and not by Metaphysical Limbeckings. I cannot think that *materia prima* or *secunda,* should be good for me, that am at least, *Materia millessima sexcentefima quadragesimaquinta.*

Here I hold my self bound to set up a Beacon, to give warning of a new-sprung Sect of Phrantasticks, which would perswade themselves and others, that they have discovered the Norst-west passage to Heaven. These wits of the game, cry up and down in Corners such bold ignotions of a new Gospel, new Christ, new Faith, and new gay-nothings, as trouble unsetled heads, querulous hearts, and not a little grieve the Spirit of God. I desire all good men may be saved from their Lunatick Creed, by Infidelity; and rather believe these torrid overtures will prove in time nothing but horrid raptures down to the lowest hell, from which he that would be delivered, let him avoid these blasphemers, a late fry of croaking Frogs, not to be indured in a Religious State, no, if it were possible, not an hour.

As some are playing young Spaniel, questing at every bird that rises; so others, held very good men, are at a dead stand, not knowing what to do or say; and are therefore called Seekers, looking for new Nuntio's from Christ, to assoil these benighted questions, and to give new Orders for new Churches. I crave leave with all respect to tell them, that if they look into *Act.* 20. 20, 25. *Gal.* 1. 8, 9. 1 *Tim.* 6. 13, 16. and find them not there; they may happily seek as the young Prophets did for *Elijah's* corps, where it never was, nor ever will be found.

I cannot imagine why the Holy Ghost should give *Timothy* the solemnest charge, was ever given Mortal man, to observe the Rules he had given, till the coming of Christ, if new things must be expected.

Wo to them, who ever they be, that so trouble the ways of God that they who have found the way to Heaven cannot find the way to Church: And wo be to them, that so gaze at the glorious light, they say, will break forth in the thousand years to come, that they make little of the gracious Truth that hath been revealed these sixteen hundred years past. And wo be to them that so under-value the first Master Builders, I mean the Apostles of Christ, that unless he sends wiser than they, He must be accounted less faithful in his house than *Moses* was.

I have cause enough to be as Charitable to others as any man living; yet I cannot but fear, that those men never Moored their Anchors well in the firm soil of Heaven; that are weather-waft up and down with every eddy-wind of every new doctrine. The good Spirit of God doth not usually tie up the Helm, and suffer Passengers to Heaven to ride a drift, hither and thither, as every wave and current carries them: that is a fitter course for such as the Apostle calls wandring Stars and Meteors, without any certain motion, hurried about with tempests, bred of the Exhalations of

their own Pride and Self-wittedness: whose damnation sleepeth not, and to whom the mist of darkness is reserved for ever, that they may suffer irreparable shipwrack upon the Sands and Rocks of their own Errors, being of old ordained to condemnation.

Eightly, let all considerate men beware of ungrounded Opinions in Religion: Since I knew what to fear, my heart hath dreaded three things: a blazing Star appearing in the Air: a State Comet, I mean a favourite rising in a Kingdom; a new Opinion spreading in Religion: these are Exorbitances: which is a formidable word; a *vacuum* and an exorbitancy, are mundicidious evils. Concerning Novelties of Opinions; I shall express my thoughts in these brief passages. First, that Truth is the best boone God ever gave the World: there is nothing in the World, World, any further than Truth makes it so, it is better than any creat' *Ens* or *Bonem,* which are but Truths twins. Secondly, the least Truth of Gods Kingdom, doth in its place uphold the whole Kingdom of his Truths; Take away the least *vericulum* out of the World, and it unworlds all, potentially, and may unravel the whole texture actually, if it be not conserved by an Arm of Superiordinary Power. Thirdly, the least Evangelical Truth is more worth than all the Civil Truths in the World, that are meerly so. Fourthly, that Truth is the Parent of all liberty whether Political or Personal; so much untruth, so much thraldom, *Joh.* 8. 32.

Hence it is, that God is so jealous of his Truths, that he hath taken order in his due justice: First, that no practical Sin is so Sinful as some error in judgment; no man so accursed with indelible infamy and dedolent impenitency as Authors of Heresie. Secondly, that the least Error, if grown sturdy and pressed, shall set open the Spittle-door of all the squint-ey'd, wry-necked, and brasen-faced Errors that are or ever were of that litter; if they be not enough to serve its turn, it will beget more, though it hath not one crust of reason to maintain them. Thirdly, that that State which will permit Errors in Religion, shall admit Errors in Policy unavoidably. Fourthly, that that Policy which will suffer irreligious

Errors, shall suffer the loss of so much Liberty in one kind or other, I will not exempt *Venice, Rhaguse,* the *Cantons,* the *Netherlands,* or any.

An easie head may soon demonstrate, that the Prementioned Planters, by Tolerating all Religions, had immazed themselves in the most intolerable confusions and inextricable thraldoms the World ever heard of. I am perswaded the Devil himself was never willing with their proceedings, for fear it would break his wind and wits to attend such a Province. I speak it seriously, according to my meaning. How all Religions should enjoy their liberty Justice its due regularity, Civil cohabitation moral honesty, in one and the same Jurisdiction, is beyond the Artique of my comprehension. If the whole conclave of Hell can so compromise, exadverse, and diametrical contradictions, as to compolitize such a multimonstrous maufrey of heteroclytes and quicquidlibets quietly; I trust I may say with all humble reverence, they can do more than the Senate of Heaven. My *modus loquendi* pardoned: I intirely wish much welfare and more wisdom to that Plantation.

It is greatly to be lamented, to observe the wanton fearlessness of this Age, especially of Younger Professors, to greet new Opinions and Opinionists: as if former truths were grown Superannuate, and Sapless, if not altogether antiquate. *Non senescet veritas.* No man ever saw a gray hair on the head or beard of any Truth wrinckle, or morphew on its face: The bed of Truth is green all the year long. He that cannot solace himself with any saving truth, as affectionately as at the first acquaintance with it, hath not only a fastidious, but an adulterous Heart.

If all be true we hear, Never was any People under the Sun, so sick of new Opinions as *English-men,* nor of new fashions as *English-women:* If God help not the one, and the Devil leave not helping the other, a blind man may easily foresee what will become of both. I have spoken what I intend for the present to men; I shall speak a word to the Women anon: in the mean time I intreat them to prepare Patience.

Ninthly, that godly humble Christians ought not to wonder impatiently at the wonderful works of God

in these times: it is full Season for him to work Soveraign work, to vindicate his Soveraignty, that men may fear before him. States are unstated, Rulers grown Over-rulers, Subjects worse than men, Churches decayed. Tofts, Professors, empty casks filled with unholy humours; I speak not of all, but too many; I condemn not the generation of the just, God hath his remnant, whom he will carefully preserve. If it be time for men to take up Defensive Arms against such as are called Gods, upon the point of *Salus populi,* it is high time for him that is God indeed, to draw his Sword against Worms and no Men, upon the point of *Majestas imperij:* The piercing of his Sword shall discover the thoughts of many hearts.

Lastly, I dare aver, that it ill becomes Christians any thing well-shod with the preparation of the Gospel, to meditate flight from their dear Country upon these disturbances. Stand your grounds ye *Eleazars* and *Shammahs,* stir not a foot so long as you have half a foot of ground to stand upon: after one or two such Worthies, a great Victory may be regained, and flying *Israel* may return to a rich spoils. *English-men,* be advised to love *England,* with your hearts and to preserve it by your Prayers. I am bold to say that since the pure Primitive Time, the Gospel never thrived so well in any soil on Earth, as in the *British,* nor is the like goodness of Nature, or Cornucopian plenty elsewhere to be found: if ye lose that Country and find a better before you come to Heaven, my Cosmography failes me. I am far from discouraging any, whom necessity of Conscience or Condition thrusts out by head and shoulders: if God calls any into a Wilderness, He will be no Wilderness to them, *Jer.* 2. 31. witness his large beneficence to us here beyond expectation.

Ye say, why come not we over to help the Lord against the Mighty, in these Sacred Battailes?

I answer, many here are diligently observing the counsel of the same Prophet, 22. 10. *Weep not for him that is dead, neither bemoan him; but weep for him that is gone away and shall return no more to see his Native Country.* Divers make it an Article of our *American* Creed, which a celebrate Divine of *England* hath observed upon *Heb.* 11. 9. That no man ought to forsake his own Country, but upon extraordinary cause, and when that cause ceaseth, he is bound in Conscience to return if he can: We are looking to him who hath our hopes and seasons in his only wise hand.

In the mean time we desire to bow our knees before the Throne of Grace day and night, that the Lord would be pleased in his tender mercy to still the sad unquietness and per-peracute contentions, or that most comfortable and renowned Island, that at length He may have Praise in his Churches, and his Churches Peace in Him, through Jesus Christ. . . .

The Cambridge Platform (1648)

THE CAMBRIDGE SYNOD

Between 1646 and 1648, representatives from Massachusetts churches met in Cambridge to determine the proper relationship among Puritan churches in the colony. The resultant Cambridge Platform, sometimes called "A Platform of Church Discipline," is an important statement of Congregational ecclesiology. The following excerpts illustrate the Congregationalists' view of the proper relationship between individuals and churches, churches and churches, and church and state. Richard Mather, John Cotton, and Ralph Partridge played important roles in drafting the document.

The Cambridge Platform did not resolve ecclesiological debates among the New England Puritans. In 1708, Connecticut Congregationalists adopted the Saybrook Platform, a document that favored the more centralized form of church government preferred by Presbyterians.

Chaps. 13–17 reprinted from *Creeds and Confessions of Faith in the Christian Tradition,* ed. Jaroslav Pelikan and Valerie Hotchkiss (New Haven and London: Yale University Press, 2003), 3:81–91.

Chapter 13. Of Church Members, Their Removal from One Church to Another, and of Letters of Recommendation and Dismission

1. Church members may not remove or depart from the church, and so from one another, as they please, nor without just and weighty cause, but ought to live and dwell together, forasmuch as they are commanded not to forsake the assembling of themselves together. Such departure tends to the dissolution and ruin of the body, as the pulling of stones and pieces of timber from the building, and of members from the natural body, tend to the destruction of the whole.

2. It is therefore the duty of church members, in such times and places when counsel may be had, to consult with the church whereof they are members about their removal, that accordingly they have their approbation, may be encouraged, or otherwise desist. They who are joined with consent should not depart without consent, except forced thereunto.

3. If a member's departure be manifestly unsafe and sinful, the church may not consent thereunto; for in so doing they should not act in faith and should partake with him in his sin. If the case be doubtful and the person not to be persuaded, it seemeth best to leave the matter unto God, and not forcibly to detain him.

4. Just reasons for a member's removal of himself from the church are: (1) If a man cannot continue without partaking in sin; (2) In case of personal persecution, so Paul departed from the disciples at Damascus; also in case of general persecution, when all are scattered; (3) In case of real, and not only pretended, want of competent subsistence, a door being opened for a better supply in another place, together with the means of spiritual edification. In these or like cases, a member may lawfully remove, and the church cannot lawfully detain him.

5. To separate from a church either out of contempt of their holy fellowship or out of covetousness or for greater enlargements with just grief to the church, or out of schism or want of love, and out of a spirit of contention in respect of some unkindness or some evil only conceived or, indeed, in the church which

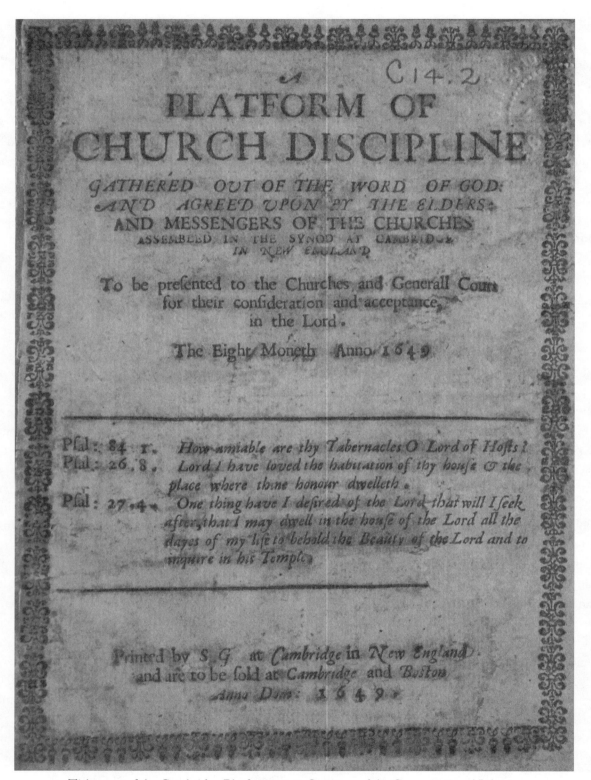

Title page of the Cambridge Platform, 1648. Courtesy of the Congregational Library, Boston, Massachusetts.

might and should be tolerated and healed with a spirit of meekness, and of which evil the church is not yet convinced (though perhaps himself be) nor admonished—for these or the like reasons to withdraw from public communion, in word or seals or censures, is unlawful and sinful.

6. Such members as have orderly removed their habitation ought to join themselves unto the church in order where they do inhabit if it may be. Otherwise they can neither perform the duties nor receive the privileges of members. Such an example, tolerated in some, is apt to corrupt others, which if many should follow, would threaten the dissolution and confusion of churches, contrary to the Scripture.

7. Order requires that a member thus removing have letters testimonial and of dismission from the church whereof he yet is unto the church whereunto he desireth to be joined, lest the church should be deluded, that the church may receive him in faith and not be corrupted by receiving deceivers and false brethren. Until the person dismissed be received into another church, he ceaseth not by his letters of dismission to be a member of the church whereof he was. The church cannot make a member no member but by excommunication.

8. If a member be called to remove only for a time, where a church is, letters of recommendation are requisite and sufficient for communion with that church in the ordinances and in their watch; as Phoebe, a servant of the church at Cenchrea, had letters written for her to the church of Rome, that she might be received as becometh saints.

9. Such letters of recommendation and dismission were written for Apollos, for Marcus to the Colossians, for Phoebe to the Romans, for sundry others to other churches; and the apostle telleth us that some persons, not sufficiently known otherwise, have special need of such letters, though he for his part had no need thereof. The use of them is to be a benefit and help to the party for whom they are written, and for the furthering of his receiving amongst the saints in the place whereto he goeth, and the due satisfaction of them in their receiving of him.

Chapter 14. Of Excommunication and Other Censures

1. The censures of the church are appointed by Christ for the preventing, removing, and healing of offenses in the church; for the reclaiming and gaining of offending brethren; for the deterring others from the like offenses; for purging out the leaven which may infect the whole lump; for vindicating the honor of Christ and of his church, and the holy profession of the gospel; and for preventing the wrath of God that may justly fall upon the church if they should suffer his covenant and the seals thereof to be profaned by notorious and obstinate offenders.

2. If an offense be private (one brother offending another), the offender is to go and acknowledge his repentance for it unto his offended brother, who is then to forgive him. But if the offender neglect or refuse to do it, the brother offended is to go and convince and admonish him of it, between themselves privately. If thereupon the offender be brought to repent of his offense, the admonisher hath won his brother. But if the offender hear not his brother, the brother offended is to take with him one or two more, that in the mouth of two or three witnesses every word may be established (whether the word of admonition if the offender receive it, or the word of complaint if he refuse it). For if he refuse it, the offended brother is by the mouth of the elders to tell the church. And if he hear the church and declare the same by penitent confession, he is recovered and gained. And if the church discern him to be willing to hear, yet not fully convinced of his offense, as in the case of heresy, they are to dispense to him a public admonition, which, declaring the offender to lie under the public offense of the church, doth thereby withhold or suspend him from the holy fellowship of the Lord's supper, till his offense be removed by penitent confession. If he still continue obstinate, they are to cast him out by excommunication.

3. But if the offense be more public at first, and of a more heinous and criminal nature, to wit, such as are condemned by the light of nature, then the

church, without such gradual proceeding, is to cast out the offender from their holy communion, for the further mortifying of his sin and the healing of his soul, in the day of the Lord Jesus.

4. In dealing with an offender, great care is to be taken that we be neither overstrict or rigorous nor too indulgent or remiss; our proceeding herein ought to be with a spirit of meekness, considering ourselves, lest we also be tempted, and that the best of us have need of much forgiveness from the Lord. Yet the winning and healing of the offender's soul being the end of these endeavors, we must not daub with untempered mortar, nor heal the wounds of our brethren slightly: on some have compassion, others save with fear.

5. While the offender remains excommunicate, the church is to refrain from all member-like communion with him in spiritual things, and also from all familiar communion with him in civil things farther than the necessity of natural or domestic or civil relations do require, and are therefore to forbear to eat and drink with him, that he may be ashamed.

6. Excommunication being a spiritual punishment, it doth not prejudice the excommunicate in, nor deprive him of, his civil rights, and therefore toucheth not princes or other magistrates in point of their civil dignity or authority. And, the excommunicate being but as a publican and a heathen, heathens being lawfully permitted to come to hear the word in church assemblies, we acknowledge therefore the like liberty of hearing the word may be permitted to persons excommunicate that is permitted unto heathen. And because we are not without hope of his recovery, we are not to account him as an enemy but to admonish him as a brother.

7. If the Lord sanctify the censure to the offender, so as by the grace of Christ he doth testify his repentance, with humble confession of his sin and judging of himself, giving glory unto God, the church is then to forgive him and to comfort him and to restore him to the wonted brotherly communion which formerly he enjoyed with them.

8. The suffering of profane or scandalous livers to continue in fellowship and partake in the sacraments is doubtless a great sin in those that have power in their hands to redress it and do it not. Nevertheless, inasmuch as Christ and his apostles in their times, and the prophets and other godly in theirs, did lawfully partake of the Lord's commanded ordinances in the Jewish church, and neither taught nor practiced separation from the same though unworthy ones were permitted therein; and inasmuch as the faithful in the church of Corinth, wherein were many unworthy persons and practices, are never commanded to absent themselves from the sacraments because of the same—therefore the godly in like cases are not presently to separate.

9. As separation from such a church wherein profane and scandalous livers are tolerated is not presently necessary, so for the members thereof, otherwise worthy, hereupon to abstain from communicating with such a church in the participation of the sacraments is unlawful. For as it were unreasonable for an innocent person to be punished for the faults of others wherein he hath no hand and whereunto he gave no consent, so it is more unreasonable that a godly man should neglect duty and punish himself in not coming for his portion in the blessing of the seals as he ought, because others are suffered to come that ought not. Especially, considering that himself doth neither consent to their sin nor to their approaching to the ordinance in their sin nor to the neglect of others who should put them away and do not, but on the contrary doth heartily mourn for these things, modestly and seasonably stir up others to do their duty. If the church cannot be reformed, they may use their liberty, as is specified in chapter 13, section 4. But this all the godly are bound unto, even everyone to do his endeavor, according to his power and place, that the unworthy may be duly proceeded against by the church to whom this matter doth appertain.

Chapter 15. Of the Communion of Churches One with Another

1. Although churches be distinct and therefore may not be confounded one with another, and equal and

Two views of the New York City skyline displaying an increase in church steeples and in ecclesiastical diversity during a forty-year period. *Above,* a view of Fort George with the City of New York, engraving by I. Carwithan, c. 1730. Geography & Map Division (LC-USZ62-19360), Library of Congress. *Below,* prospect of the City of New York from *New York Pocket Almanac, 1771.* Courtesy American Antiquarian Society.

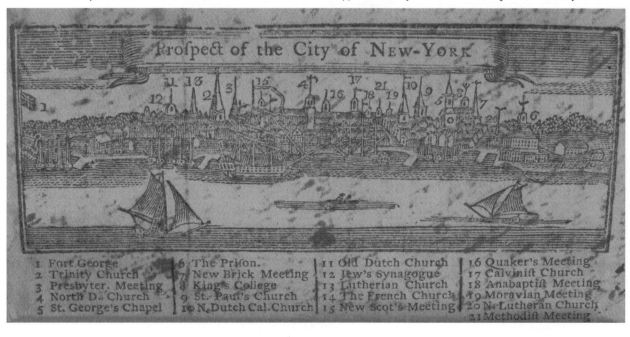

Profpect of the City of NEW-YORK

1 Fort George
2 Trinity Church
3 Presbyter. Meeting
4 North D. Church
5 St. George's Chapel

6 The Prifon.
7 New Brick Meeting
8 King's College
9 St. Paul's Church
10 N. Dutch Cal. Church

11 Old Dutch Church
12 Jew's Synagogue
13 Lutherian Church
14 The French Church
15 New Scot's Meeting

16 Quaker's Meeting
17 Calvinift Church
18 Anabaptift Meeting
19 Moravian Meeting
20 N. Lutheran Church
21 Methodift Meeting

therefore have not dominion one over another, yet all the churches ought to preserve church communion one with another, because they are all united unto Christ, not only as a mystical but as a political head; whence is derived a communion suitable thereunto.

2. The communion of churches is exercised sundry ways:

(1) By way of mutual care in taking thought for one another's welfare;

(2) By way of consultation one with another when we have occasion to require the judgment and counsel of other churches, touching any person or cause wherewith they may be better acquainted than ourselves. As the church of Antioch consulted with the apostles and elders of the church at Jerusalem about the question of circumcision of the Gentiles and about the false teachers that broached that doctrine. In which case, when any church wanteth light or peace amongst themselves, it is a way of communion of churches (according to the word) to meet together by their elders and other messengers in a synod, to consider and argue the points in doubt or difference, and having found out the way of truth and peace, to commend the same by their letters and messengers to the churches, whom the same may concern. But if a church be rent with divisions amongst themselves, or lie under any open scandal, and yet refuse to consult with other churches for healing or removing of the same, it is a matter of just offense both to the Lord Jesus and to other churches, as betraying too much want of mercy and faithfulness, not to seek to bind up the breaches and wounds of the church and brethren. And therefore the state of such a church calleth aloud upon other churches to exercise a fuller act of brotherly communion, to wit, by way of admonition.

(3) A third way, then, of communion of churches is by way of admonition, to wit, in case any public offense be found in a church, which they either discern not or are slow in proceeding to use the means for the removing and healing of. Paul had no authority over Peter; yet when he saw Peter not walking with a right foot, he publicly rebuked him before the church. Though churches have no more authority over one another than one apostle had over another, yet as one apostle might admonish another, so may one church admonish another, and yet without usurpation. In which case, if the church that lieth under offense do not hearken to the church which doth admonish her, the church is to acquaint other neighbor churches with that offense which the offending church still lieth under, together with their neglect of the brotherly admonition given unto them. Whereupon those other churches are to join in seconding the admonition formerly given. And if still the offending church continue in obstinacy and impenitency, they may forbear communion with them, and are to proceed to make use of the help of a synod or council of neighbor churches walking orderly (if a greater cannot conveniently be had) for their conviction. If they hear not the synod, the synod having declared them to be obstinate, particular churches, approving and accepting of the judgment of the synod, are to declare the sentence of noncommunion respectively concerning them. And thereupon, out of a religious care to keep their own communion pure, they may justly withdraw themselves from participation with them at the Lord's table, and from such other acts of holy communion as the communion of churches doth otherwise allow and require. Nevertheless, if any members of such a church as lieth under public offense do not consent to the offense of the church, but do in due sort bear witness against it, they are still to be received to wonted communion; for it is not equal that the innocent should suffer with the offensive. Yea furthermore, if such innocent members, after due waiting in the use of all good means for the healing of the offense of their own church, shall at last (with the allowance of the counsel of neighbor churches) withdraw from the fellowship of their own church and offer themselves to the fellowship of another, we judge it lawful for the other church to receive them (being otherwise fit) as if they had been orderly dismissed to them from their own church.

(4) A fourth way of communion of churches is by way of participation: the members of one church oc-

casionally coming unto another, we willingly admit them to partake with us at the Lord's table, it being the seal of our communion not only with Christ, nor only with the members of our own church, but also with all the churches of the saints. In which regard we refuse not to baptize their children presented to us if either their own minister be absent or such a fruit of holy fellowship be desired with us. In like case such churches as are furnished with more ministers than one do willingly afford one of their own ministers to supply the place of an absent or sick minister of another church for a needful season.

(5) A fifth way of church communion is by way of recommendation when a member of one church hath occasion to reside in another church: if but for a season, we commend him to their watchful fellowship by letters of recommendation; but if he be called to settle his abode there, we commit him, according to his desire, to the fellowship of their covenant by letters of dismission.

(6) A sixth way of church communion is, in case of need, to minister relief and succor one unto another, either of able members to furnish them with officers, or of outward support to the necessities of poorer churches, as did the churches of the Gentiles contribute liberally to the poor saints at Jerusalem.

3. When a company of believers purpose to gather into church fellowship, it is requisite for their safer proceeding and the maintaining of the communion of churches that they signify their intent unto the neighbor churches walking according unto the order of the gospel, and desire their presence and help and right hand of fellowship, which they ought readily to give unto them when there is no just cause of excepting against their proceedings.

4. Besides these several ways of communion, there is also a way of propagation of churches. When a church shall grow too numerous, it is a way and fit season to propagate one church out of another, by sending forth such of their members as are willing to remove and to procure some officers to them as may enter with them into church estate amongst themselves. As bees, when the hive is too full, issue forth by swarms and are gathered into other hives, so the churches of Christ may do the same upon like necessity, and therein hold forth to them the right hand of fellowship, both in their gathering into a church and in the ordination of their officers.

Chapter 16. Of Synods

1. Synods orderly assembled, and rightly proceeding according to the pattern, Acts 15, we acknowledge as the ordinance of Christ, and, though not absolutely necessary to the being, yet many times, through the iniquity of men and perverseness of times, necessary to the well-being of churches, for the establishment of truth and peace therein.

2. Synods, being spiritual and ecclesiastical assemblies, are therefore made up of spiritual and ecclesiastical causes. The next efficient cause of them, under Christ, is the power of the churches, sending forth their elders [and] other messengers, who, being met together in the name of Christ, are the matter of a synod. And they, in arguing, debating, and determining matters of religion according to the word and publishing the same to the churches whom it concerneth, do put forth the proper and formal acts of a synod, to the conviction of errors and heresies, and the establishment of truth and peace in the churches, which is the end of a synod.

3. Magistrates have power to call a synod, by calling to the churches to send forth their elders and other messengers to counsel and assist them in matters of religion. But yet the constituting of a synod is a church act, and may be transacted by the churches even when civil magistrates may be enemies to churches and to church assemblies.

4. It belongeth unto synods and councils: to debate and determine controversies of faith and cases of conscience; to clear from the word holy directions for the holy worship of God and good government of the church; to bear witness against maladministration and corruption in doctrine or manners in any particular church, and to give direction for the reformation thereof; not to exercise church censures in

way of discipline, nor any other act of church authority or jurisdiction, which that presidential synod did forbear.

5. The synod's directions and determinations, so far as consonant to the word of God, are to be received with reverence and submission, not only for their agreement therewith (which is the principal ground thereof, and without which they bind not at all), but also secondarily, for the power whereby they are made, as being an ordinance of God appointed thereunto in his word.

6. Because it is difficult, if not impossible, for many churches to come all together in one place in all their members universally, therefore they may assemble by their delegates or messengers, as the church of Antioch went not all to Jerusalem, but some select men for that purpose. Because none are or should be more fit to know the state of the churches, nor to advise of ways for the good thereof, than elders, therefore it is fit that in the choice of the messengers for such assemblies they have special respect unto such. Yet inasmuch as not only Paul and Barnabas but certain others also were sent to Jerusalem from Antioch, Acts 15, and when they were come to Jerusalem, not only the apostles and elders but other brethren also do assemble and meet about the matter, therefore synods are to consist both of elders and other church members, endowed with gifts and sent by the churches, not excluding the presence of any brethren in the churches.

Chapter 17. Of the Civil Magistrate's Power in Matters Ecclesiastical

1. It is lawful, profitable, and necessary for Christians to gather themselves into church estate and therein to exercise all the ordinances of Christ according unto the word, although the consent of the magistrate could not be had thereunto, because the apostles and Christians in their time did frequently thus practice, when the magistrates, being all of them Jewish or pagan and mostly persecuting enemies, would give no countenance or consent to such matters.

2. Church government stands in no opposition to civil government of commonwealths, nor any entrencheth upon the authority of civil magistrates in their jurisdictions, nor any whit weakeneth their hands in governing; but rather strengtheneth them and furthereth the people in yielding more hearty and conscionable obedience unto them, whatever some ill-affected persons to the ways of Christ have suggested, to alienate the affections of kings and princes from the ordinances of Christ. As if the kingdom of Christ in his church could not rise and stand without the falling and weakening of their government, which is also of Christ. Whereas the contrary is most true, that they may both stand together and flourish, the one being helpful unto the other in their distinct and due administrations.

3. The power and authority of magistrates is not for the restraining of churches or any other good works, but for helping in and furthering thereof. And therefore the consent and countenance of magistrates, when it may be had, is not to be slighted or lightly esteemed; but on the contrary, it is part of that honor due to Christian magistrates to desire and crave their consent and approbation therein, which being obtained, the churches may then proceed in their way with much more encouragement and comfort.

4. It is not in the power of magistrates to compel their subjects to become church members and to partake at the Lord's table. For the priests are reproved that brought unworthy ones into the sanctuary; then as it was unlawful for the priests, so it is unlawful to be done by civil magistrates. Those whom the church is to cast out if they were in, the magistrate ought not to thrust into the church nor to hold them therein.

5. As it is unlawful for church officers to meddle with the sword of the magistrate, so it is unlawful for the magistrate to meddle with the work proper to church officers. The acts of Moses and David, who were not only princes but prophets, were extraordinary, therefore not imitable. Against such usurpation the Lord witnessed by smiting Uzziah with leprosy for presuming to offer incense.

6. It is the duty of the magistrate to take care of matters of religion, and to improve his civil authority for the observing of the duties commanded in the first, as well as for observing of the duties commanded in the second table. They are called "gods." The end of the magistrate's office is not only the quiet and peaceable life of the subject in matters of righteousness and honesty, but also in matters of godliness, yea of all godliness. Moses, Joshua, David, Solomon, Asa, Jehoshaphat, Hezekiah, Josiah are much commended by the Holy Ghost for the putting forth their authority in matters of religion. On the contrary, such kings as have been failing this way are frequently taxed and reproved by the Lord. And not only the kings of Judah, but also Job, Nehemiah, the king of Nineveh, Darius, Artaxerxes, Nebuchadnezzar, whom none looked at as types of Christ (though were it so, there were no place for any just objection) are commended in the book of God for exercising their authority this way.

7. The object of the power of the magistrate are not things merely inward, and so not subject to his cognizance and view, as unbelief, hardness of heart, erroneous opinions not vented, but only such things as are acted by the outward man. Neither is their power to be exercised in commanding such acts of the outward man, and punishing the neglect thereof, as are but mere inventions and devices of men, but about such acts as are commanded and forbidden in the word, yes, such as the word doth clearly determine, though not always clearly to the judgment of the magistrate or others, yet clearly in itself. In these he of right ought to put forth his authority, though ofttimes actually he doth it not.

8. Idolatry, blasphemy, heresy, venting corrupt and pernicious opinions that destroy the foundation, open contempt of the word preached, profanation of the Lord's day, disturbing the peaceable administration and exercise of the worship and holy things of God, and the like are to be restrained and punished by civil authority.

9. If any church, one or more, shall grow schismatical, rending itself from the communion of other churches, or shall walk incorrigibly or obstinately in any corrupt way of their own, contrary to the rule of the word, in such case the magistrate is to put forth his coercive power as the matter shall require. The tribes on this side Jordan intended to make war against the other tribes for building the altar of witness, whom they suspected to have turned away therein from following of the Lord.

The Essential Rights and Liberties of Protestants (1744)

ELISHA WILLIAMS (1694–1755)

Williams was, among other things, a Congregationalist pastor, Yale rector, member of the Connecticut Assembly, and judge on the Connecticut Superior Court. In 1742 Connecticut passed a statute aimed at restraining the itinerant revivalists of the First Great Awakening. In this pamphlet, Williams argues for an extensive, but not unlimited, liberty of conscience in religious matters.

Sir,

I now give you my thoughts on the questions you lately sent me. As you set me the task, you must take the performance as it is without any apology for its defects. I have wrote with the usual freedom of a friend, aiming at nothing but truth, and to express my self so as to be understood. In order to answer your main enquiry concerning the extent of the civil magistrate's power respecting religion; I suppose it needful to look back to the end, and therefore to the original of it: By which means I suppose a just notion may

Excerpts reprinted from *Political Sermons of the American Founding Era, 1730–1805*, ed. Ellis Sandoz, 2nd ed. (Indianapolis: Liberty Fund, 1998), 1:55–63. © 1998, Liberty Fund, Inc. Reprinted by permission.

A feafonable PLEA

FOR

The Liberty of Confcience,

AND

The Right of private Judgment,

In Matters of RELIGION,

Without any Controul from *human Authority.*

Being a LETTER,

From a Gentleman in the *Maffachufetts-Bay* to his Friend in *Connecticut.*

WHEREIN

Some Thoughts on the Origin, End, and Extent of the *Civil Power*, with brief Confiderations on feveral late Laws in *Connecticut*, are humbly offered.

By a Lover of TRUTH *and* LIBERTY.

Matth. xxii. 21.---- *Render unto* Cæfar *the Things which are* Cæfar's; *and unto* GOD, *the Things that are* GOD's.

" If our Purfes be *Cæfar's*, our Confciences are GOD's : ---
" and if *Cæfar's* Commands interfere with GOD's, we
" muft *obey* GOD *rather than Men*.--- HENRY on the Place.

BOSTON : Printed and Sold by S. KNEELAND and T. GREEN in Queenftreet. 1744.

Elisha Williams, *The Essential Rights and Liberties of Protestants*, 1744.

be formed of what is properly their business or the object of their power; and so without any insuperable difficulty we may thence learn what is out of that compass.

That the sacred scriptures are the alone rule of faith and practice to a Christian, all Protestants are agreed in; and must therefore inviolably maintain, that every Christian has *a right of judging for himself* what he is to believe and practice in religion according to that rule: Which I think on a full examination you will find perfectly inconsistent with any power in the civil magistrate to make any penal laws in matters of religion. Tho' Protestants are agreed in the profession of that principle, yet too many in practice have departed from it. The evils that have been introduced thereby into the Christian church are more than can be reckoned up. Because of the great importance of it to the Christian and to his standing fast in that liberty wherewith CHRIST has made him free, you will not fault me if I am the longer upon it. The more firmly this is established in our minds; the more firm shall we be against all attempts upon our Christian liberty, and better practice that Christian charity towards such as are of different sentiments from us in religion that is so much recommended and inculcated in those sacred oracles, and which a just understanding of our Christian rights has a natural tendency to influence us to. And tho' your sentiments about some of those points you demand my thoughts upon may have been different from mine; yet I perswade my self, you will not think mine to be far from the truth when you shall have throughly weighed what follows. But if I am mistaken in the grounds I proceed upon or in any conclusion drawn from true premises, I shall be thankful to have the same pointed out: Truth being what I seek, to which all must bow first or last.

To proceed then as I have just hinted, I shall first, briefly consider *the Origin and End of Civil Government.*

First, as to the origin—Reason teaches us that all men are naturally equal in respect of jurisdiction or dominion one over another. Altho' true it is that children are not born in this full state of equality, yet they are born to it. Their parents have a sort of rule & jurisdiction over them when they come into the world, and for some time after: But it is but a temporary one; which arises from that duty incumbent on them to take care of their offspring during the imperfect state of childhood, to preserve, nourish and educate them (as the workmanship of their own almighty Maker, to whom they are to be accountable for them), and govern the actions of their yet ignorant nonage, 'till reason shall take its place and ease them of that trouble. For GOD having given man an understanding to direct his actions, has given him therewith a freedom of will and liberty of acting, as properly belonging thereto, within the bounds of that law he is under: And whilst he is in a state wherein he has no understanding of his own to direct his will, he is not to have any will of his own to follow: He that understands for him must will for him too. But when he comes to such a state of reason as made the father free, the same must make the son free too: For the freedom of man and liberty of acting according to his own will (without being subject to the will of another) is grounded on his having reason, which is able to instruct him in that law he is to govern himself by, and make him know how far he is left to the freedom of his own will. So that we are born free as we are born rational. Not that we have actually the exercise of either as soon as born; age that brings one, brings the other too. This natural freedom is not a liberty for every one to do what he pleases without any regard to any law; for a rational creature cannot but be made under a law from its Maker: But it consists in a freedom from any *superiour power on earth,* and not being under the will or legislative authority of man, and having only the law of nature (or in other words, of its Maker) for his rule.

And as reason tells us, all are born thus naturally equal, i.e. with an equal right to their persons; so also with an equal right to their preservation; and therefore to such things as nature affords for their subsistence. For which purpose GOD was pleased to make a grant of the earth in common to the children of men, first to Adam and afterwards to Noah and his sons: as the Psalmist says, Psal. 115. 16. And altho' no one has originally a private dominion exclusive of the rest of mankind in the earth or its products, as they are consider'd in this their natural state; yet since GOD has given these things for the use of men and given them reason also to make use thereof to the best advantage of life; there must of necessity be a means to appropriate them some way or other, before they can be of any use to any particular person. And every man having a property in his own person, the *labour of his body and the work of his hands* are properly his own, to which no one has right but himself; it will therefore follow that when he removes any thing out of the state that nature has provided and left it in, he has mixed his labour with it and joined something to it that is his own, and thereby makes it his property. He having removed it out of the common state nature placed it in, it hath by this labour something annexed to it that excludes the common right of others; because this labour being the unquestionable property of the labourer, no man but he can have a right to what that is once joined to, at least where there is enough and as good left in common for others. Thus every man having a natural right to (or being the proprietor of) his own person and his own actions and labour and to what he can honestly acquire by his labour, which we call property; it certainly follows, that no man can have a right to the person or property of another: And if every man has a right to his person and property; he has also a right to defend them, and a right to all the *necessary means of defence,* and so has a right of punishing all insults upon his person and property.

But because in *such a state of nature,* every man must be judge of the breach of the law of nature and executioner too (even in his own case) and the greater part being no strict observers of equity and justice; the enjoyment of property in this state is not very safe. Three things are wanting in this state (as the celebrated Lock observes) to render them safe; *viz.* an established known law received and allowed by common consent to be the standard of right and wrong, the common measure to decide all controversies be-

tween them: For tho' the law of nature be intelligible to all rational creatures; yet men being biassed by their interest as well as ignorant for want of the study of it, are not apt to allow of it as a law binding to them in the application of it to their particular cases. There wants also a *known and indifferent judge* with authority to determine all differences according to the established law: for men are too apt to be partial to themselves, and too much wanting in a just concern for the interest of others. There often wants also in a state of nature, *a power to back and support the sentence when right, and give it due execution.* Now to remedy these inconveniencies, reason teaches men to join in society, to unite together into a commonwealth under some form or other, to make a body of laws agreable to the law of nature, and institute one common power to see them observed. It is they who thus unite together, *viz.* the people, who make and alone have right to make the laws that are to take place among them; or which comes to the same thing, appoint those who shall make them, and who shall see them executed. For every man has an equal right to the preservation of his person and property; and so an equal right to establish a law, or to nominate the makers and executors of the laws which are the guardians both of person and property.

Hence then the fountain and original of all civil power is from the people, and is certainly instituted for their sakes; or in other words, which was the second thing proposed, *The great end of civil government, is the preservation of their persons, their liberties and estates, or their property.* Most certain it is, that it must be for their own sakes, the rendering their condition better than it was in what is called a state of nature (a state without such establish'd laws as before mentioned, or without any common power) that men would willingly put themselves out of that state. It is nothing but their own good can be any rational inducement to it: and to suppose they either should or would do it on any other, is to suppose rational creatures ought to change their state with a design to make it worse. And that good which in such a state they find a need of, is no other than a *greater security of enjoyment of what belonged to them.* That and that only can then be the true reason of their uniting together in some form or other they judge best for the obtaining that greater security. That greater security therefore of life, liberty, money, lands, houses, family, and the like, which may be all comprehended under that of person and property, is the sole end of all civil government. I mean not that all civil governments (as so called) are thus constituted: (tho' the British and some few other nations are through a merciful Providence so happy as to have such). There are too too many arbitrary governments in the world, where the people don't make their own laws. These are not properly speaking governments but tyrannies; and are absolutely against the law of GOD and nature. But I am considering things as they be in their own nature, what reason teaches concerning them: and herein have given a short sketch of what the celebrated Mr. Lock in his *Treatise of Government* has largely demonstrated; and in which it is justly to be presumed all are agreed who understand the natural rights of mankind.

Thus having seen what the end of civil government is; I suppose we see a fair foundation laid for the determination of the next thing I proposed to consider: Which is, *What liberty or power belonging to man as he is a reasonable creature does every man give up to the civil government whereof he is a member.* Some part of their natural liberty they do certainly give up to the government, for the benefit of society and mutual defence (for in a political society every one even an infant has the whole force of the community to protect him), and something therefore is certainly given up to the whole for this purpose. Now the way to know what branches of natural liberty are given up, and what remain to us after our admission into civil society, is to consider the ends for which men enter into a state of government. For so much liberty and no more is departed from, as is necessary to secure those ends; the rest is certainly our own still. And here I suppose with the before-mentioned noble assertor of the liberties of humane nature; *all that is given up* may be reduced to two heads.

1st. The power that every one has in a state of nature *to do whatever he judgeth fit,* for the preservation of his person and property and that of others also, within the permission of the law of nature, he gives up to be regulated by laws made by the society, so far forth as the preservation of himself (his person and property) and the rest of that society shall require.

And, 2. The power of punishing he wholly gives up, and engages his natural force (which he might before employ in the execution of the law of nature by his own single authority as he thought fit) to assist the executive power of the society as the law thereof shall require. For (he adds) being now in a new state wherein he is to enjoy many conveniencies, from the labour assistance and society of others in the same community, as well as protection from its whole strength; he is to part also with as much of his natural liberty and providing for himself, as the good and safety of the society shall require; which is not only necessary but just, since the other members of the society do the like. Now if the giving up these powers be sufficient to answer those ends for which men enter into a state of government, *viz.* the better security of their persons and properties; then no more is parted with; and therefore all the rest is ours still. This I rest on as certain, *that no more natural liberty or power is given up than is necessary for the preservation of person and property.*

I design not to mention many particulars which according to this rule I suppose are not parted with by entering into a state of government: what is reducible to one or two general heads is sufficient to our present purpose. Tho' as I pass I cannot forbear taking notice of *one point of liberty* which all members of a free state and particularly Englishmen think belonging to them, and are fond of; and that is the right that every one has *to speak his sentiments openly concerning such matters as affect the good of the whole.* Every member of a community ought to be concerned for the whole, as well as for his particular part: His life and all, as to this world is as it were embarked in the same bottom, and is perpetually interested in the good or ill success thereof: Whenever therefore he sees a rock on which

there is a probability the vessel may split, or if he sees a sand that may swallow it up, or if he foresees a storm that is like to arise; his own interest is too deeply concerned not to give notice of the danger: And the right he has to his own life and property gives him a right to speak his sentiments. If the pilot or captain don't think fit to take any notice of it, yet it seems to be certain they have no right to stop the mouth of him who thinks he espys danger to the whole ships crew, or to punish the well-meaning informer. A man would scarce deserve the character of a *good member of society* who should receive to be silent on all occasions, and never mind, speak or guard against the follies or ignorance of mistakes of those at the helm. And government rather incourages than takes away a liberty, the use of which is so needful and often very beneficial to the whole, as experience has abundantly shown.

But not to detain you here,

I. The members of a civil state or society do retain their natural liberty *in all such cases* as have no relation to the ends of such a society. In a state of nature men had a right to read Milton or Lock for their instruction or amusement: and why they do not retain this liberty under a government that is instituted for the preservation of their persons and properties, is inconceivable. From whence can such a society derive any right to hinder them from doing that which does not affect the ends of that society? Should a government therefore restrain the free use of the scriptures, prohibit men the reading of them, and make it penal to examine and search them; it would be a manifest usurpation upon the common rights of mankind, as much a violation of natural liberty as the attack of a highwayman upon the road can be upon our civil rights. And indeed with respect to the sacred writings, men might not only read them if the government did prohibit the same, but they would be bound by a higher authority to read them, notwithstanding any humane prohibition. The pretence of any authority to restrain men from reading the same, is wicked as well as vain. But whether in some cases that have no relation to the ends of government and

wherein therefore men retain their natural liberty; if the civil authority should attempt by a law to restrain men, people might not be oblig'd to submit therein, is not here at all the question: tho' I suppose that in such case wherein they ought to submit, the obligation thereto would arise from some other consideration, and not from the supposed law; there being no binding force in a law where a rightful authority to make the same is wanting.

II. The members of a civil state *do retain their natural liberty or right of judging for themselves in matters of religion.* Every man has an equal right to follow the dictates of his own conscience in the affairs of religion. Every one is under an indispensable obligation to search the scripture for himself (which contains the whole of it) and to make the best use of it he can for his own information in the will of GOD, the nature and duties of Christianity. And as every Christian is so bound; so he has an unalienable right to judge of the sense and meaning of it, and to follow his judgment wherever it leads him; even an equal right with any rulers be they civil or ecclesiastical. This I say, I take to be an original right of the humane nature, and so far from being given up by the individuals of a community that it cannot be given up by them if they should be so weak as to offer it. Man by his constitution as he is a reasonable being capable of the knowledge of his Maker; is a moral & accountable being: and therefore as every one is accountable for himself, he must reason, judge and determine for himself. That faith and practice which depends on the judgment and choice of any other person, and not on the person's own understanding judgment and choice, may pass for religion in the synagogue of Satan, whose tenet is that ignorance is the mother of devotion; but with no understanding Protestant will it pass for any religion at all. No action is a religious action without understanding and choice in the agent. Whence it follows, the rights of conscience are sacred and equal in all, and strictly speaking unalienable. This *right of judging every one for himself in matters of religion* results from the nature of man, and is so inseperably connected therewith, that a man can no more part with it than he can with his power of thinking: and it is equally reasonable for him to attempt to strip himself of the power of reasoning, as to attempt the vesting of another with this right. And whoever invades this right of another, be he pope or Caesar, may with equal reason assume the other's power of thinking, and so level him with the brutal creation. A man may alienate some branches of his property and give up his right in them to others; but he cannot transfer the rights of conscience, unless he could destroy his rational and moral powers, or substitute some other to be judged for him at the tribunal of GOD.

But what may further clear this point and at the same time shew the extent of this right of private judgment in matters of religion, is this truth, That the sacred scriptures are the alone rule of faith and practice to every individual Christian. Were it needful I might easily show, the sacred scriptures have all the characters necessary to constitute a just and proper rule of faith and practice, and that they alone have them. It is sufficient for all such as acknowledge the divine authority of the scriptures, briefly to observe, that GOD the author has therein declared he has given and designed them to be our only rule of faith and practice. Thus says the apostle Paul, 2 Tim. 3. 15, 16; That *they are given by Inspiration from* GOD, *and are profitable for Doctrine, for Reproof, for Correction, for Instruction in Righteousness; that the Man of* GOD *may be perfect, thoroughly furnished unto every good Work.* So the apostle John in his gospel, Chap. 20. ver. 31. says; *These Things are written that ye might believe that* JESUS *is the* CHRIST, *the Son of* GOD, *and that believing ye might have Life through his Name.* And in his first epistle, Chap. 5. ver. 13. *These Things have I written, that ye may know that ye have eternal Life, and that ye may believe on the Name of the Son of* GOD. These passages show that what was written was to be the standing rule of faith and practice, compleat and most sufficient for such an end, designed by infinite wisdom in the giving them, containing every thing needful to be known and done by Christians, or such as believe on the name of the Son of GOD. Now in-

asmuch as the scriptures are the only rule of faith and practice to a Christian; hence every one has an unalienable right to read, enquire into, and impartially judge of the sense and meaning of it for himself. For if he is to be governed and determined therein by the opinions and determinations of any others, the scriptures cease to be a rule to him, and those opinions or determinations of others are substituted in the room thereof. But you will say, *The Priest's Lips should keep Knowledge, and they should seek the Law at his Mouth,* Mal. 2. 7. Yes; that is, it is their duty to explain the scriptures, and the people's duty at the same time to search the scriptures to see whether those things they say are so. Acts 17. 11. The officers CHRIST has commissioned in his church, as pastors or bishops, are to teach his laws, to explain as they are able the mind & will of CHRIST laid down in the scriptures; but they have no warrant to make any laws for them, nor are their sentiments the rule to any Christian, who are *all commanded to prove all Things, to try the Spirits whether they be of* GOD. 1 Thes. 5. 21. 1 Joh. 4. 1. *I speak as to wise Men,* says Paul, *judge ye what I say,* 1 Cor. 10. 15. These and many other texts I might have alledg'd, entirely answer the objection, and establish the point before us. . . .

Civil Magistrates Must Be Just, Ruling in the Fear of God (1747)

CHARLES CHAUNCY (1705–87)

One of the most important forms of political literature in seventeenth- and eighteenth-century America was the political sermon. Ministers might preach such sermons on election days, to commemorate special occasions, or to address contemporary issues. The

Excerpts reprinted from *Political Sermons of the American Founding Era, 1730–1805,* ed. Ellis Sandoz, 2nd ed., 2 vols. (Indianapolis: Liberty Fund, 1998), 1:141–77. © 1998, Liberty Fund, Inc. Reprinted by permission.

Civil Magiftrates *muft be juft, ruling in the Fear of God.*

S E R M O N

A

Preached before His EXCELLENCY

William Shirley, Efq;

The Honourable

His Majefty's COUNCIL,

AND

Houfe of Reprefentatives,

Of the Province of the

Maffachufetts-Bay in N.England;

May 27. 1747.

Being the ANNIVERSARY for the ELECTION of His Majefty's Council for faid Province.

By *Charles Chauncy,* D. D.

One of the Paftors of the firft Church in BOSTON.

Deut. XVI. 20. *That which is altogether juft fhalt thou follow---.*

N. B. The feveral Paragraphs which, for want of Time, were omitted in Preaching, are inferted in their proper Places, and, for Diftinction's fake, comprehended in Crotchets.

B O S T O N:

Printed by Order of the Honourable Houfe of REPRESENTATIVES. 1747.

Charles Chauncy, *Civil Magistrates Must Be Just, Ruling in the Fear of God,* 1747.

full texts of some of the most important of these sermons are found in *Political Sermons of the American Founding Era, 1730–1805*, edited by Ellis Sandoz.

Charles Chauncy, longtime pastor of the First Church in Boston, preached the following election-day sermon before the legislature and governor on May 27, 1747. The sermon was later published with additions by the author. The following text contains the sermon as it was originally delivered.

━━━━━━━━━━━━━━━━━━━

The God of Israel said, the Rock of Israel spake to me; he that ruleth over Men must be just, ruling in the Fear of God.

II Sam. xxiii. 3.

If we may judge by the manner in which these words are introduced, there are none in all the bible, applicable to civil rulers, in their publick capacity, of more solemn importance.

The last words of good men are commonly tho't worthy of particular notice; especially, if they are great as well as good, of an elevated station as well as character in life. This is a consideration that adds weight to my text. For it is enrolled among the last words of one of the best and greatest men that ever lived. Such was David, "the man after God's own heart," who was raised up from low life to the regal dignity, and stiled, on that account, "the anointed of the God of Jacob."

And was my text nothing more than his own private sentiments, formed with due care, upon long observation and experience, it might well deserve the particular attention of all in civil power; especially, as he was a man of extraordinary knowledge, penetration and wisdom, as well as piety; and, at the same time, singularly qualified to make a judgment in an affair of this nature, as he was called into publick service from a youth, and had for many years reigned king in Israel.

But it is not only David that here speaks. The words are rather God's than his. For they are thus prefaced, *The God of Israel said, the rock of Israel spake to me.* "That God who had selected the Jews to be his people, and was their God so as he was not the God of other nations; the rock on whom their political state was built, and on whom it depended for support and protection": This God spake unto David, either by Samuel, or Nathan, or some other inspired prophet, or himself immediately from heaven, saying, as in the words I have read to you, *He that ruleth over men must be just, ruling in the fear of God.* It is certainly some momentous truth, highly worthy of the most serious consideration of civil rulers, that is here delivered, or it would not have been ushered in with so much solemnity.

Some read the words, (agreable eno' to the original, as criticks observe) *there shall be a ruler over men that shall be just, ruling in the fear of God;* and refer them to Christ, as agreeing with other prophecies, which describe him as a "king that shall reign in righteousness," and be of "quick understanding in the fear of the Lord": But if they be allowed to look forward to him that has since "come forth out of Zion," they were also designed for the instruction and benefit of Solomon, David's son and appointed successor to the throne of Israel. And by analogy they are applicable to civil rulers, in their various stations, in all ages of the world.

In this view I shall now consider them, under the two following heads obviously contained in them.

I. There is a certain order among mankind, according to which some are entrusted with power to rule over others.

II. Those who rule over others must be just, ruling in the fear of God.

The whole will then be applied to the occasions of the day.

I. I am to say, in the first place, there is a certain order among men, according to which some are entrusted with power to rule over others. This is evidently supposed in the text; and 'tis supposed, not as a bare fact, but a fact that has taken place conformably to the will of God, and the reason of things.

This, to be sure, is the truth of the case, in it self considered. Order and rule in society, or, what means the same thing, civil government, is not a contrivance of arbitrary and tyrannical men, but a regular state of things, naturally resulting from the make of man, and his circumstances in the world. Had man abode in innocency, his nature as a sociable creature, and his condition as a dependent one, would probably have led to some sort of civil superiority: As, among the inhabitants of the upper world, there seems to be a difference of order, as well as species; which the scripture intimates, by speaking of them in the various stile of *thrones, dominions, principalities, powers, archangels and angels*. But however it would have been, had man continued in obedience to his maker, government is rendered a matter of necessity by the introduction of sin into the world. Was there no civil rule among men, but every one might do that which was right in his own eyes, without restraint from humane laws, there would not be safety any where on the earth. No man would be secure in the enjoyment, either of his liberty, or property, or life: But every man's hand would be against his fellow; and mankind must live in perpetual danger, from that oppression, rapine and violence, which would make this world rather a hell, than a fit place to dwell happily in.

The present circumstances of the human race are therefore such, by means of sin, that 'tis necessary they should, for their mutual defence and safety, combine together in distinct societies, lodging as much power in the hands of a few, as may be sufficient to restrain the irregularities of the rest, and keep them within the bounds of a just decorum. Such a superiority in some, and inferiority in others, is perfectly adjusted to the present state of mankind. Their circumstances require it. They could not live, either comfortably or safely without it.

And from hence, strictly and properly speaking, does that civil order there is among men take rise. Nor will it from hence follow, that government is a mere humane constitution. For as it originates in the reason of things, 'tis, at the same time, essentially founded on the will of God. For the voice of reason is the voice of God: And he as truly speaks to men by the reason of things, their mutual relations to and dependencies on each other, as if he uttered his voice from the excellent glory. And in this way, primarily, he declares his will respecting a civil subordination among men. The sutableness of order and superiority, both to the nature of man, and his circumstances in the world, together with its necessary connection, in the nature of things, with his safety and happiness, is such an indication of the divine pleasure, that there should be government, as cannot be gainsay'd nor resisted.

Only it must be remembered here, a distinction ought always to be made between government in its general notion, and particular form and manner of administration. As to the latter, it cannot be affirmed, that this or that particular form of government is made necessary by the will of God and reason of things. The mode of civil rule may in consistency with the public good, admit of variety: And it has, in fact, been various in different nations: Nor has it always continued the same, in the same nation. And one model of government may be best for this community, and another for that; nay, that model which may be best for the same community at one time, may not be so at another. So that it seems left to the wisdom of particular communities to determine what form of government shall take place among them; and, so long as the general ends of society are provided for and secured, the determination may be various, according to the various circumstances, policies, tempers and interests of different communities.

And the same may be said of the manner of vesting particular persons with civil power, whether supreme or subordinate. This is not so fix'd by the divine will, as that all nations are obliged to one and the same way of devolving the administration of rule. The supreme authority in Israel, 'tis true, from which, of course, all subordinate power in that state was derived, was settled by God himself on David, and entail'd on his family to descend in a lineal succession. But it does not appear, that this was ever intended to be a rule obligatory on all nations of the earth: Nor have they kept to it; but have varied in their manner of designing persons for, and introducing them into, the several places of civil trust. And this seems to be a matter alterable in its nature, and proper to be variously determined according to the different circumstances of particular nations.

But 'tis quite otherwise in respect of government itself, in its general notion. This is not a matter of meer humane prudence, but of moral necessity. It does not lie with men to determine at pleasure, whether it shall or shall not take place; but, considering their present weak, exposed and dependent condition, 'tis unalterably right and just there should be rule and superiority in some, and subjection and inferiority in others: And this therefore is invariably the will of God; his will manifested by the moral fitness and reason of things.

And the will of God, as discovered in the revelations of scripture, touching government among men, perfectly coincides with his will primarily made known, upon the same head, by the constitution of things: Or rather, 'tis more clearly and fully opened. For kings, and princes, and nobles, and *all the judges of the earth,* are here represented* as *reigning and ruling by God:* Yea, they are stiled, *the ministers of God*†; and *the powers that be* are declared to be *ordained of God*‡: And, upon this consideration, *subjection to them* is demanded, *for conscience sake* §; and *whosoever resisteth,* is looked upon as *resisting the ordinance of God.*¶ From all which it is apparent, there is no more room to dispute the divinity of civil rule upon the foot of revelation, than of reason.

And thus we have seen, not only that some among men have rule over others, but that it is reasonable in itself, and agreable to the will of God, it should be so.

And 'tis easy to collect from the whole, the true design of that power some are entrusted with over others. It is not merely that they might be distinguished from, and set above vulgar people; much less that they might live in greater pomp, and be revered

* Prov. 8. 15, 16.
† Rom. 13. 4.
‡ Verse 1.
§ Verse 5.
¶ Verse 2.

as gods on earth; much less still that they might be in circumstances to oppress their fellow-creatures, and trample them under their feet: But it is for the general good of mankind; to keep confusion and disorder out of the world; to guard men's lives; to secure their rights; to defend their properties and liberties; to make their way to justice easy, and yet effectual, for their protection when innocent, and their relief when injuriously treated; and, in a word, to maintain peace and good order, and, in general, to promote the public welfare, in all instances, so far as they are able. But this leads me to the next head of discourse, which is what I have principally in view; *viz.*

II. Those who rule over others must be *just, ruling in the fear of God.* Here I shall distinctly say,

1. They must be just. They ought to be so in their private capacity; maintaining a care to exhibit in their conduct towards all they are concerned with, a fair transcript of that fundamental law of the religion of Jesus, as well as eternal rule of natural justice, "all things whatsoever ye would that men should do to you, do ye even so to them." But private justice, tho' necessary in all, yet is not the virtue here especially intended. The injunction respects those who rule over men; and 'tis as magistrates, not private members of society, that they are required to be just.

And this duty includes in it more than a negation of unrighteousness. 'Tis not enough that rulers are not unjust; that they don't betray the trusts reposed in them; that they don't defraud the public; that they don't oppress the subject, whether in a barefac'd manner, or in a more covert way; by downright violence, or under the cloak of law: 'Tis not enough, I say, that rulers don't, in these and such like ways, pervert judgment and justice; but, besides all this, they must be positively righteous. Being possess'd of an inward, steady, uniform principle of justice, setting them, in a good measure, above the influence of private interest, or party views, they must do that which is equal and right, in their various stations, from the king in supreme, to the lowest in authority under him.

It would carry me too far beyond the hour assigned me, should I make a distribution of rulers into their several ranks, and mention the more special acts of justice respectively required of them. I shall therefore content my self with speaking of them chiefly in the collective sense; pointing out, under a few general heads, some of the more important articles wherein they should approve themselves just. And they are such as these.

1. They must be just in the *use of their power;* confining it within the limits prescribed in the constitution they are under. Whatever power any are vested with, 'tis delegated to them according to some civil constitution. And this, so long as it remains the constitution, they are bound in justice to conform themselves to: To be sure, they ought not to act in violation of any of its main and essential rights. Especially, is this an important point of justice, where the constitution is branched into several parts, and the power originally lodged in it, is divided, in certain measures, to each part, in order to preserve a ballance in the whole. Rulers, in this case, in either branch of the government, are bounded by the constitution, and obliged to keep within the proper limits assigned them; never clashing in the exercise of their power, never encroaching upon the rights of each other, in any shape, or under any pretence whatever. They have severally and equally a right to that power which is granted to them in the constitution, and to wrest it out of each other's hands, or to obstruct one another in the regular legal exercise of it, is evidently unjust. As in the British constitution, which devolves the power of the state, in certain proportions, on *King, Lords* and *Commons,* they have neither of them a right to invade the province of the other, but are required, by the rule of righteousness, to keep severally within their own boundaries, acting in union among themselves, and consistency with the constitution. If the prerogatives of the King are sacred, so also are the rights of Lords and Commons: And if it would be unjust in Lords or Commons, to touch, in any instance, the prerogative of the crown; so would it be in the crown, to invade the rights, which are legally settled in Lords and Commons: In either of these cases, the law of righteousness is violated: Nor does the manner in which it is done make any essential difference; for, if one part of the government is really kept from exerting it self, according to the true meaning of the constitution, whether it be done openly, or by secret craft; by compulsion or corruption, the designed ballance is no longer preserved; and which way soever the scale turns, whether on the side of sovereignty, or popularity, 'tis forced down by a false weight, which, by degrees, will overturn the government, at least, according to this particular model.

And the case is just the same in all dependent governments, as in those whose power originates in themselves: Especially, where the derived constitution, like that of Great-Britain, is divided into several ruling parts, and distributes the granted powers and priviledges severally among these ruling parts, to each their limited portion. The constitution is here evidently the grand rule to all cloathed with power, or claiming priviledge, in either branch of the government. And 'tis indeed a fundamental point of justice, that they keep respectively within the bounds marked out to them in the constitution. Rulers in one branch of the state should not assume the power delegated to those in another: Nay, so far should they be from this, that they should not, in any degree, lessen their just weight in the government; much less may they contrive, by an undue application to their hopes or fears, or by working on their ambition, or covetousness, or any other corrupt principle; much less, I say, may they contrive to influence them to give up their power, or, what is as bad, to use it unfaithfully, beside the intention for which it was committed to them. These are certainly methods of injustice; and, if put in practice, will, by a natural causality, weaken, and, by degrees, destroy those checks which rulers are mutually designed to have one upon another; the effect whereof must be tyranny, or anarchy, either of which will be of fatal consequence.

2. Another general instance wherein rulers should be just, relates to the *laws by which they govern.*

To be sure, if they would be just, they must make no laws but what bear this character. They should not, when upon the business of framing and passing acts, suffer themselves to be swayed by any wrong biass, either from self-will, or self-interest; the smiles or frowns of men greater than themselves; or the humour of the populace: But should bring the proposed laws to a fair and impartial examination, not only in their reference to the temper, genius and circumstances of the community, but to that justice also which is founded in the nature of things, and the will of the supreme legislator: And if they should appear to be inconsistent with this eternal rule of equity, they ought not to countenance them, but should do what they can to prevent their establishment. And the rather, because should they enact that into a statute, which is unrighteous; especially, if it be plainly and grosly so, they would be chargeable with "framing mischief by a law": The guilt whereof would be the more aggravated, as power, in this case, would be on the side of oppression; and, what is as bad, as unrighteousness, by this means, would take a dreadful spread thro' the community. For as the laws are the rule for the executive powers in the government, if these are unjust, all that is done consequent upon a regard to them, must be unjust too. That would be the state of things which Solomon describes, when he says, "I saw under the sun the place of judgment, that wickedness was there; and the place of righteousness, that iniquity was there": Than which, there cannot be given a more terrible representation of the unhappy effect of a disregard to justice in the making of laws.

But rulers, in order to their answering the character of just, must not satisfy themselves with making none but righteous laws; but must provide also, so far as may be, a sufficiency of such to restrain the sons of wickedness, men of avaricious minds, and no consciences, from that rapine and violence, those frauds and oppressions, in their various kinds and degrees, which their lusts would prompt them to perpetrate, to the damage of society, and in violation of all that is right and just.

Besides which, they should be particular in their care to guard the important and extensive article of commerce; calculating laws so as that they may have a tendency to oblige every member of the community, to use the methods of fairness and honesty in their dealings with one another: In order whereto, one of the main things necessary is, to fix the precise weight and measure, according to which these and those commodities shall be bought and sold; hereby rendring the practice of honesty easy and familiar, while, at the same time, it is made a matter of difficulty, as well as hazard, for this member of the community to defraud that, by palming on him a less quantity than he bargain'd, for, and expected to receive.

And if justice in rulers should shew itself by reducing the things that are bought and sold to weight and measure, much more ought it to be seen in ascertaining the medium of trade, as nearly as may be, to some determinate value. For this, whether it be money, or something substituted to pass in lieu of it, is that for which all things are exchanged in commerce. And if this, which is of such universal use in the affair of traffick, be a thing variable and uncertain, of one value this week, and another the next, 'tis difficult to conceive, how justice should take place between man and man, in their dealings with one another. If the measure we call a foot might gradually, in the space of a few months or years, lengthen into a yard, or shorten into an inch; every one sees, it would, if used as a measure in trade, tend to spread unrighteousness in a community, rather than justice. So, if the weight we call a pound might gradually, in the like space, increase or diminish one half; 'tis past dispute, it would be an occasion of general iniquity, rather than a means to promote honesty. And the case is really the same (however insensible we may be of it) with respect to the passing medium in a government. If what we call a shilling, may, in a gradual way, in the course of a few months or years, rise in value so as to be equal to two or three, or sink in proportion; 'tis impossible, in the nature of things, but a wide door should be opened for oppression and injustice. An upright man, in this case, would find it extreamly difficult to do himself justice, or others he might be concerned with in business. And for those of dishonest minds, and no principles of honour or religion, if men of craft and foresight, they would have it very much in their power to enrich themselves by being unjust to their neighbour.

I am sensible, the case may be so circumstanced in a government, especially if it be a dependent one, as that it may be extreamly difficult, if not impossible, while they have no money, to keep that which passes, in the room of it, from varying in it's real worth. But it is not very difficult; to be sure, it is not impossible, to pitch upon some certain standard, to which the current medium may be so related, as that it's true value, at different times, may be nearly ascertained: And if this was established as the rule in all public payments, as well as private contracts and bargains, it would be no other than what is right. It would certainly tend, not only to do every one justice, but to put it very much out of the power of men of no probity "to go beyond and defraud their brother": Whereas, while the medium is connected with no established certain standard, but continually varies in it's real worth, it must be, in the natural course of things, an occasion of great injustice.

There is yet another thing, belonging to this head, wherein rulers should approve themselves just; and that is, the *execution of the laws*.

To go on,

3. Another instance wherein rulers should be just, respects the debts that may be due from the public. A government may be in debt, as well as private men. Their circumstances may be such, as to render it adviseable for them to borrow money, either of other governments, or within themselves: Or, they may have occasion to make purchases, or to enter into contracts, upon special emergencies, which may bring them in debt. In which cases, the rule of justice is the same to magistrates, as to men in a private life. They must pay that which they owe, according to the true meaning of their engagements, without fraud or delay.

In fine, they may be in debt to their own officers, whether in higher or lower station, the proper business of whose office calls off their attention from other affairs. And as their time, and care, and tho't,

are employed in the service of the public, a public maintenance is their just due. "Who goeth a warfare any time at his own charge? Who planteth a vineyard, and eateth not of the fruit thereof? Or, who feedeth a flock, and eateth not of the milk of the flock? Say I these things as a man? Or saith not the law the same also?"[*] For it is written, "For this cause pay you tribute; for they are God's ministers, attending continually upon this very thing.[†] Render unto Caesar the things that are Caesar's."[‡]

Nor is it sufficient that they be supported according to the condition of men in low life. This may be tho't enough, if not too much, by those who imagine, that the more strait-handed they are upon the head of allowances, the more serviceable they shall be to the public. But there is such a thing in the state, as a "withholding more than is meet." And it really tends to the damage of a government. Too scant an allowance may unhappily prove a temptation to officers, to be hard upon those dependent on them; and what they may injuriously squeeze out of them, by one artful contrivance or another, may turn out more to the hurt of the community, than if twice that sum had been paid out of the public treasury, and this evil, by means hereof, had been prevented. Besides, 'tis no ways fitting, that men cloathed with honour and power should be brought down to a level with vulgar people, in the support that is granted them. Their outward circumstances should be elevated in proportion to their civil character, that they may be better able to support the visible dignity of their station, and command that respect which is due to men of their figure. He that is *governour should eat the bread of a governour;* and subordinate officers should be maintained, according to the rank they bear in the state: Nor ought their honourable maintenance to be tho't a matter of *meer* bounty; 'tis rather a debt, which can't be withheld without injustice.

* I Cor. 5. 7, 8.
† Rom. 13. 6.
‡ Matth. 22. 21.

4. Another general instance wherein rulers should be just, concerns the liberties and priviledges of the subject. In all governments there is a reserve of certain rights in favour of the people: In some, they are few in kind, and small in degree: In others, they are both great and numerous; rendring the people signally happy whose lot it is to be favoured with the undisturbed enjoyment of them. And it would be no wonder, if they should keep a jealous eye over them, and think no cost too much to be expended, for the defence and security of them: Especially, if they were the purchase of wise and pious ancestors, who submitted to difficulties, endured hardships, spent their estates, and ventured their lives, that they might transmit them as an inheritance to their posterity.

And shall such valuable, dear-bought rights be neglected, or invaded by the rulers of a people? 'Tis a principal part of that justice which is eternally expected of them, as they would not grosly pervert one of the main ends of their office, to preserve and perpetuate to every member of the community, so far as may be, the full enjoyment of their liberties and priviledges, whether of a civil or religious nature.

Here I may say distinctly,

As rulers would be just, they must take all proper care to preserve entire the civil rights of a people. And the ways in which they should express this care are such as these.

They should do it by appearing in defence of their liberties, if called in question, and making use of all wise and sutable methods to prevent the loss of them: Nor can they be too active, diligent or laborious in their endeavours upon this head: Provided always, the priviledges in danger are worth contending for, and such as the people have a just right and legal claim to. Otherwise, there may be hazard of losing real liberties, in the strife for those that are imaginary; or valuable ones, for such as are of trifling consideration.

They should also express this care, by seasonably and faithfully placing a proper guard against the designs of those, who would rule in a dispotic manner, to the subversion of the rights naturally or legally vested in the people. And here 'tis a great mistake to suppose, there can be danger only from those in the highest station. There may, 'tis true, be danger from this quarter: And it has sometimes proved so in fact: An unhappy instance whereof was seen in the arbitrary reign of King James the second, in person at home, and by his representative here; as a check to which, those entrusted with the guardianship of the nation's rights were spirited to take such measures, as issued in that revolution, and *establishment of the succession*, on which his present majesty's claim to the British throne is dependent. May the succession be continued in his royal house forever! And may the same spirit, which settled it there, prevail in the rulers of the English nation, so long as the sun and moon shall endure!

But, as I said, a people's liberties may be in danger from others, besides those in the highest rank of government. The men who strike in with the popular cry of liberty and priviledge, working themselves, by an artful application to the fears and jealousies of the people, into their good opinion of them as lovers of their country, if not the only stanch friends to it's interests, may, all the while, be only aiming at power to carry every thing according to their own sovereign pleasure: And they are, in this case, most dangerous enemies to the community; and may, by degrees, if not narrowly watched, arrive to such an height, as to be able to serve their own ends, by touching even the people in their most valuable rights. And these commonly are the men, thro' whose influence, either as primary managers, or tools to others, they suffer most in their real liberties.

In fine, they should express this care in a constant readiness to bear due testimony against even the smaller encroachments upon the liberty of the subject, whether by private men's invading one another's rights, or by the tyranny of inferiour officers, who may treat those under their power, as tho' they had no natural rights, not to say a just claim to the invaluable priviledges of *Englishmen*.

The ancient Romans have set an illustrious example in this kind. Such was the provision they made

to secure the people's priviledges, that it was dangerous for any man, tho' in office, to act towards the
meanest freeman of Rome in violation of the meanest
of them. Hence the magistrates who ordered Paul
and Silas to be *beaten uncondemned, feared when they
heard they were Romans.* And Lysias, the chief captain, was filled with the like fear for commanding,
that Paul should be examined with scourging; when
he understood, that he was born a freeman of Rome.
And it would have a good tendency to secure to the
people the enjoyment of their liberties, if these
smaller instances of illegal power were carefully and
severely chastised.

But justice in rulers should be seen likewise in their
care of the religious rights and liberties of a people.
Not that they are to exert their authority in *settling
articles of faith,* or *imposing modes of worship,* so as that
all must frame their belief, and order their practice,
according to their decisions, or lie exposed to penalties of one kind or another. This would be to put
men under restraint, as to the exercise of their religious rights: Nor are penal laws at all adjusted in their
nature, to enlighten men's minds, or convince their
judgment. This can be done only by good reason:
And this therefore is the only proper way of applying
to reasonable creatures.

Justice in rulers should therefore put them upon
leaving every member of the community, without respect of persons, freely to choose his own religion,
and profess and practice it according to that external
form, which he apprehends will be most acceptable
to his maker: Provided, his religion is such as may
consist with the public safety: Otherwise, it would be
neither wisdom nor justice in the government to tolerate it.

Nor is this all; but they should guard every man
from all insult and abuse on account of his religious
sentiments, and from all molestation and disturbance, while he endeavours the propagation of them,
so far as he keeps within the bounds of decency, and
approves himself a peaceable member of society.

Besides which, it would be no more than reasonable, if, as christian magistrates, they distinguished
those in their regards, who professed the religion of
JESUS, and in that way, which, to them, was most
agreable to scripture rule. They should be guardians
to such christian societies, by defending their constitution; by countenancing their manner of worship; by
maintaining the liberties granted to them in the
gospel-charter, in all their regular exercises, whether
in church assemblies for the performance of the services of piety, or the choice of officers, or the administration of discipline; or in councils, greater or less,
for the help and preservation of each other: And, in
fine, by owning those who minister to them in sacred
things, and providing for their support, according to
that rule in scripture, as well as common equity,
"They that preach the gospel should live of the gospel": Or if they are generally and wrongfully kept out
of a great part of that support, which has been engaged, and is justly due to them, by taking their case
into consideration, and doing what may be effectual
for their relief.

This last instance of the care of rulers, I the rather
mention, because it falls in so exactly with the circumstances of the pastors of the churches in this
province. There is not, I believe, an order of men, in
the land, more universally, or to a greater degree, injured and oppressed in regard of their just dues.
While others have it, in some measure, in their power
to right themselves, by rising in their demands, in
proportion to the sinking of the current medium,
they are confined to a nominal quantum, which every
day varies in its real worth, and has been gradually
doing so, 'till it is come to that pass, that many of
them don't receive more than one half, or two thirds
of the original value they contracted for. And to this
it is owing, that they are diverted from their studies,
discouraged in their work, and too frequently treated
with contempt. And what is an aggravation of their
difficulty, their only desiring that justice may be done
them, often makes an uneasiness among their people:
And if they urge it; to be sure, if they demand it, 'tis
great odds but there ensues thereupon contention and
strife, and, at last, such a general alienation of affection, as puts an entire end to their usefulness.

Suffer me, my fathers in the government, as I have this opportunity of speaking in your presence, to beseech the exercise of your authority, on the behalf, (may I not say) of so valuable and useful a part of the community: And the rather, because some special provision for their relief seems to be a matter of justice, and not meer favour; as it is by means of the public bills, tho' contrary to the design of the government, that they are injured. And might not this be made, without any great expence either of time or pains, and so as to be effectual too, to put it out of the power of people to turn off their ministers with any thing short of the true value of what they agreed with them for, when they settled among them? This is all they desire: And as it is nothing more than common equity, would it not be hard, if they should be still left to groan under their oppressions, and to have no helper?

The great and general court, it must be acknowledged, more than twenty years since, "upon serious consideration of the great distresses, that many of the ministers within this province laboured under, with respect to their support, resolved, that it was the indispensable duty of the several towns and parishes, to make additions to the maintenance of their respective ministers; and therein to have regard to the *growing difference in the value of the bills of credit,* from what they had sometimes been." And thereupon "earnestly recommended the speedy and chearful practice of this duty to the several congregations within this province." And that the recommendation might be universally known and comply'd with, "Ordered, that their resolve should be publickly read on the next Lord's day after the receipt thereof, and at the anniversary meeting of the several towns in the month of March next" following.*

---

* The resolve refer'd to above, and in part quoted, it's tho't proper to insert at large; and is in these words.

At a great and general court or assembly for his majesty's province of the Massachusetts-Bay in New-England, begun and held at Boston, upon Wednesday May 26, 1725.

The following resolve pass'd both houses, and was consented to by his honour the lieutenant governor. *Viz.*

Upon serious consideration of the great distresses that many of the ministers

And it is with thankfulness that we take notice of this instance of the care of our civil fathers; tho' we are sorry, we must, at the same time, say, it was generally treated with neglect by our congregations, as being void of power.

It will not be pretended, but that the distresses of the ministers, and from the same cause too, the sinking of the medium, are vastly greater now, than they were twenty years ago: And if it was then reasonable, in the great and general court, to recommend it to the several congregations, throughout the province, as their indispensable duty, to make additions to the maintenance of their ministers, and therein to have regard to the lower value of the bills of credit, from what they formerly were; it is certainly now high time to oblige them to this: Especially, as the grievances of the ministers have often, since that day, upon these occasions, been opened to their civil fathers, whose interposition has been humbly and earnestly intreated. But I would not be too pressing: Neither have I said thus much on my own account, who am not, thro' the goodness of God, in suffering circumstances myself, but in very pity to many of my poor brethren who are; because there may be danger lest guilt should lie on the government, if they take no notice of the sighing of so considerable a body of men; and be-

---

of the gospel within this province labour under, with respect to their support or maintenance, their salaries being generally paid in the public bills of credit of this province, altho' many of the ministers contracted with their people in the time when silver money passed in payment; and the necessaries of life, such as cloathing, provisions, together with labour and other things, now demand so much more of the bills of credit than heretofore;

Resolved, that it is the indispensable duty of the several towns precincts and parishes of this province, to make such additions to the salaries or maintenance of their respective ministers, as may honourably support and encourage them in their work; and therein to have regard as well to the time of the contract between the minister and people, and the specie therein mentioned, as to the great and growing difference in the value of the bills of credit, from what they have sometimes been. And this court do therefore most earnestly recommend the speedy and chearful practice of this duty, to the several congregations and religious assemblies within this province: And that this resolve be publickly read on the next Lord's day after the receipt hereof, in the afternoon before the congregation be dismiss'd; and at the anniversary meeting of the several towns or precincts in the province in the month of March next.

By order of the great and general court or assembly,

Josiah Willard, Secr.

cause, I verily believe, the offerings of the Lord are too often despised, by reason of that poverty those are unrighteously reduced to, by whom they are presented.

But to return,

5. Another instance of justice in rulers relates to the defence of the state, and it's preservation in peace and safety.

6thly, and finally, rulers should be just to promote the general welfare and prosperity of a people, by discouraging, on the one hand, idleness, prodigality, prophaneness, uncleanness, drunkenness, and the like immoralities, which tend, in the natural course of things, to their impoverishment and ruin: And by encouraging, on the other hand, industry, frugality, temperance, chastity, and the like moral virtues, the general practice whereof are naturally connected with the flourishing of a people in every thing that tends to make them great and happy. As also, by rendring the support of government as easy as is consistent with it's honour and safety; by calculating laws to set forward those manufactures which may be of public benefit; by freeing trade, as much as possible, from all unnecessary burdens; and, above all, by a wise and sutable provision for the instruction of children and youth: In order whereunto effectual care should be taken for the encouragement and support, not only of private schools, but of the public means of education. Colleges ought to be the special care of the government, as it is from hence, principally, that it has it's dependence for initiating the youth in those arts and sciences, which may furnish them, as they grow up in the world, to be blessings both in church and state. It would certainly be unrighteous, not to protect these societies in the full and quiet enjoyment of such rights as have been freely and generously granted to them: And if they should not have within themselves a sufficiency for the support of their officers, it would be a wrong to the community, not to do what was further wanting towards their comfortable and honourable support.

And having thus, in a general and imperfect manner, gone over the more important instances, wherein rulers should be just, it might now be proper to enlarge on the obligations they are under to be so: But the time will allow me only to suggest as follows.

Application

It now remains to apply what has been said to rulers and people.

And 'tis fit I should first turn the discourse into an address to your Excellency, as it has pleased God and the king to advance you to the first seat of government, among those who bear rule in this province.

The administration, sir, is devolved on you in the darkest day, it may be, New-England ever saw; when there was never more occasion for distinguishing talents in a governour, to direct the public counsels, and minister to the relief and comfort of a poor people, groaning under the calamities of war and debt, and, what is worse than both, an unhappy medium, that fills the land with oppression and distress. We would hope, it was because the Lord loved this people, that he has set you over us; and that he intends to honour you as the instrument in delivering us from the perplexing difficulties wherewith our affairs are embarrass'd.

We have had experience of your Excellency's superior wisdom, knowledge, steadiness, resolution, and unwearied application in serving the province: And would herefrom encourage our selves to depend on you for every thing, that may reasonably be expected of a chief ruler, furnished with capacities fitted to promote the public happiness.

We rejoice to see so many posts in the government, at the disposal of your Excellency, either alone, or in conjunction with your council, filled with men of capacity, justice and religion: And as the public good is so much dependent on the nomination and appointment of well qualified persons to sustain the various offices in the province, we promise our selves your eye will be upon the faithful of the land, and that, while you contemn every vile person, you will honour them that fear the Lord. And should any attempt by indirect means to obtain places of trust which others better deserve, we assure ourselves your Excellency will resent such an affront, and testify a just displeasure against the persons who shall dare to offer it.

The opinion we have of your Excellency's integrity and justice, forbids the least suspicion of a design in you to invade the civil charter-rights of this people. And tho' you differ in your sentiments from us, as to the model of our church-state, and the external manner of our worship; yet we can securely rely on the generosity of your principles to protect us in the full enjoyment of those ecclesiastical rights we have been so long in possession of: And the rather, because your Excellency knows, that our progenitors enterprized the settlement of this country principally on a religious account; leaving their native land, and transporting themselves and their families, at a vast expence, and at the peril of their lives, into this distant, and then desolate wilderness, that they might themselves freely enjoy, and transmit to us their posterity, *that manner of worship and discipline,* which we look upon, as they did, most agreable to the purity of God's word.

Your Excellency knows too well the worth of learning, and the advantage of a liberal education, not to be strongly dispos'd to cherish the college, which has, from the days of our fathers, been so much the glory of New-England: And we doubt not, you will be always tender of its rights, and exert your self, as there may be occasion, for its defence and welfare.

And as your Excellency is our common father, we repair to you as the friend and patron of all that is dear and valuable to us; depending that you will employ your time, your thought, your authority, your influence and best endeavours, to ease our burdens, to lead us out of the labyrinths we have run into, and to make us a happy and prosperous people.

We can wish nothing better for your Excellency than the divine presence enabling you to act, in your whole administration, under the influence of a steady principle of justice, and an habitual awe and reverence of that God, for whom ultimately you derived your authority, and to whom you are accountable for the use of it. This will recommend you to the love, and

entitle you to the praise of an obliged happy people; this will yield you undisturbed ease of mind under the cares and burdens of government; this will brighten to you the shades of death, embalm your memory after you are dead, and, what is infinitely more desireable, give you boldness when great and small shall stand before the Son of man, and procure for you that blessed euge, from the mouth of your divine Saviour and Master, "Well done, good and faithful servant: Enter thou into the joy of thy Lord."

Permit me, in the next place, with a becoming respect, to apply myself to the honourable his majesty's council, and the honourable house of representatives; whose desire has ordered me into this desk.

Through the goodness of God, we see the return of this anniversary for the exercise of one of those charter-rights, granted to our fathers, and continued to us, on the wise and faithful management whereof, the public happiness is very much dependent.

His majesty's council, this afternoon to be elected, is an happy medium between the king and the people, and wisely designed to preserve a due ballance between the prerogatives of the one, and the privileges of the other. And as they constitute one branch of the legislature, they have a share in framing and passing all acts and orders. To them it appertains to assist the chief ruler with their advice upon all emergent occasions, especially in the court's recess. And without their consent, none of the civil posts in the government can be filled; in consequence whereof, no judges can be appointed, no courts erected, no causes tried, no sentences executed, but by persons who have had their approbation: All which, by shewing the weight of this order of men in the state, bespeaks the importance of this day's business, and, at the same time, demands a proportionable care and faithfulness in the discharge of it.

It is not, gentlemen, a trifling concern you have before you; an affair wherein you may act with carelessness or inattention; with a party or partial spirit; out of affection to friends, or complaisance to superiors; much less upon the corrupt design of making instruments to be imployed and managed to serve your own private schemes. It is not for yourselves only that you are empowered and called to vote in the elections of this day, but for your God, your king and your country: And you will be unjust to them all, if you give your voice as moved by any considerations, but those which are taken from the real characters of men, qualifying them to sit at the council-board.

You all know, from the oracles of God, how men must be furnished, in order to their being fit to be chosen into places of such important trust; that they must be wise and understanding, and known to be so among their tribes; that they must be *able men, and men of truth, men that fear God, and hate covetousness.* And 'tis to be hoped, we have a sufficiency of such, in the land, to constitute his majesty's council. It would be lamentable indeed, if we had not. 'Tis your business, gentlemen, to seek them out. And with you will the fault principally lie, if we have not the best men in the country for councillors; men of capacity and knowledge, who are well acquainted with the nature of government in general, and the constitution, laws, priviledges and interests of this people in particular: Men of known piety towards God, and fidelity to their king and country: Men of a generous spirit, who are above acting under the influence of narrow and selfish principles: Men of unquestionable integrity, inflexible justice, and undaunted resolution, who will dare not to give their consent to unrighteous acts, or mistaken nominations; who will disdain, on the one hand, meanly to withdraw, when speaking their minds with freedom and openness may expose them to those who set them up, and may have it in their power to pull them down, or, on the other, to accommodate their conduct, in a servile manner, to their sentiments and designs; in fine, who will steadily act up to their character, support the honour of their station, and approve themselves invariably faithful in their endeavours to advance the public weal.

These are the men, 'tis in your power, my honourable fathers, to choose into the council; and these are the men for whom, in the name of God, and this whole people, I would earnestly beg every vote this day: And suffer me to say, these are the men you will all send in your votes for, if you are yourselves men of integrity and justice, and exercise your elective-power, not as having concerted the matter beforehand, in some party-juncto, but under the influence of a becoming awe of that omnipresent righteous God, whose eye will be upon you, to observe how you vote, and for whom you vote, and to whom you must finally render an account, before the general assembly of angels and men, for this day's transaction.

We bow our knees to the alwise sovereign Being, who presides over the affairs of the children of men, in humble and fervent supplications, that he would govern your views, direct your tho'ts, and lead you into a choice that he shall own and succeed, to promote the best interests of this people.

And when the elections of this day are over, and the several branches of the legislature shall proceed upon the affairs of the public, we promise ourselves you will act as those, who have upon their minds a just sense of the vast importance of the trust that is reposed in you.

To you is committed the defence of the province, the guardianship of it's liberties and priviledges, the protection of it's trade, and the care of it's most valuable interests: And never was there a time, wherein it's circumstances more urgently called upon you to exert yourselves, in seeking it's welfare.

Religion is not in such a flourishing state, at this day, but that it needs the countenance of your example, and the interposition of your authority, to keep it from insult and contempt. We thankfully acknowledge the pious care, the legislature has lately taken to restrain the horrid practice of cursing and swearing, which so generally prevailed, especially in this, and our other sea-port towns, to the dishonour of God, and our reproach as wearing the name of christians. And if laws still more severe are necessary, to guard the day and worship of God from prophanation, we can leave it with your wisdom to enact such, as may tend to serve so good a design. And tho' we would be far from desiring, that our rulers should espouse a party in religion; yet we cannot but hope, they will never do any thing to encourage those, who may have arrived at such an height in spiritual pride, as to say, in their practice, to their brethren as good as themselves, "stand by thy self, come not near me; for I am holier than thou": Concerning whom the blessed God declares, "These are a smoke in my nose, a fire that burneth all the day." And as for those, be their character, persuasion, or party, what it will, who, under the notion of appearing zealous for God, his truths or ways, shall insult their betters, vilify their neighbours, and spirit people to strife and faction, we earnestly wish the civil arm may be stretched forth to chastise them: And if they suffer, 'twill be for disturbing the peace of society; the evil whereof is rather aggravated than lessened, by pretences to advance the glory of God and the interest of religion.

We are thankful for the good and wholesome laws which have been made, from time to time, for the suppression of vice, in it's various kinds; and, in particular, for the restraint that has been laid upon those, who may be inclined to excessive drinking. Alas! that such multitudes, notwithstanding, are overtaken with this fault. Hard drinking is indeed become common all over the land. And 'tis astonishing to think what quantities of strong drink are consumed among us! Unless some, well capable of forming a judgment, are very much mistaken, more a great deal is needlessly and viciously consumed than would suffice to answer the whole charge, both of church and state. A reproach this, to any people! And if something further is not done by the government, to prevent the use that is made of strong drink, it will, in a little time, prove the destruction of the country, in the natural course of things; if God should not positively testify his displeasure against such horrid intemperance. It may deserve your consideration, my fathers, whether one occasion of this scandalous consumption of strong drink, has not been the needless multiplication of taverns, as well as more private licensed houses, that are too commonly used for tipling, and serve to little purpose, but to tempt people, in low life sinfully to waste their time, and spend their substance.

But there is nothing more needs your awaken'd attention, my honoured fathers in the government, than the unhappy state of this people by means of the current medium. Whatever wise and good ends might be proposed at first, and from time to time, in the *emission of bills of credit*, they have proved, in the event, a cruel engine of oppression. It may be, there was scarce ever a province under more melancholly circumstances, by reason of injustice, which is become almost unavoidable. Sad is the case of your men of nominal salaries: And much to be pitied also are those widows and orphans, who depend on the loan of their money for a subsistance: While yet, these last, of all persons in the community, should be most carefully guarded against every thing that looks like oppression. This sin, when widows and fatherless children are the persons wronged by it, is heinously aggravated in the sight of a righteous God; as may easily be collected from that emphatical prohibition, so often repeated in all parts of the bible, "Thou shalt not oppress the widow, nor the fatherless." But the oppression reigning in the land, is not confined to this order or that condition of persons, but touches all without exception. None escape its pernicious influence, neither high nor low, rich nor poor. Like an over-bearing flood, it makes its way thro' the province; and all are sufferers by it, in a less or greater degree, and feel and own themselves to be so.

And will you, our honoured rulers, by any positive acts, or faulty neglects, suffer your selves to be instrumental in the continuance of such a state of things? God forbid! We don't think you would designedly do any thing to countenance oppression, or neglect any thing that might have a tendency to remove it out of the land.

Neither can we think, that any former assemblies have knowingly acted, in the *emission of public bills*, upon dishonest principles: Tho' it may be feared, whether the righteous God, in holy displeasure at the sins both of rulers and people, may not have witheld counsel from our wise men, and scattered darkness in their paths: And if, in consequence hereof, there has been disunion in the sentiments of our civil fathers, concerning the public medium, and unsteadiness in their conduct, 'tis no matter of wonder: Nor, upon this supposition, is it hard to be accounted for, that injustice, by means of the paper currency, should have taken such a general and dreadful spread, thro' the land.

But, by what means soever we became involved in these perplexities, 'tis certainly high time to make a pause, and consider what may be done that will be effectual towards the recovering and maintaining justice and honesty, that we may be called the *city of righteousness, the faithful city.*

It would be culpable vanity in me, to attempt to prescribe to our honourable legislature; yet may I, without going beyond my line, after the example of the great apostle of the gentiles, reason with you of public righteousness, and its connection with a judgment to come.

You are, my fathers, accountable to that God whose throne is in the heavens, in common with other men. And his eyes behold your conduct in your public capacity, and he sees and observes it, not merely as a spectator, but an almighty righteous judge, one who enters all upon record in order to a reckoning another day. And a day is coming, it lingers not, when you shall all stand upon a level, with the meanest subjects, before the tremendous bar of the righteous judge of all the earth, and be called upon to render an account, not only of your private life, but of your whole management as entrusted with the concerns of this people.

Under the realising apprehension of this, suffer me, in the name of God, (tho' the most unworthy of his servants) to advise you to review the public conduct, respecting the passing bills, and to do whatever may lay in your power to prevent their being the occasion of that injustice, which, if continued much longer, will destroy the small remains of common honesty that are still left in the land, and make us an abhorrence to the people that delight in righteousness.

Let me beseech you, sirs, for the sake of this poor people, and for the sake of your own souls, when you shall stand before the dreadful bar of the eternal judgment, to lay aside all party designs and private considerations, and to deliberate upon this great affair, with a single view to the public good, and under the uniform influence of a steady principle of righteousness; for, as the wise man observes, "transgressors shall be taken in their own naughtiness," while "the righteousness of the upright shall deliver them, and their integrity shall guide them"; and again, "as for the upright, the Lord directeth their way."

If there needs any excuse for my wonted plainness of speech, I can only say; my conscience beareth me witness, that what I have said has proceeded, not from want of a decent respect for those who are my civil fathers, but from faithfulness to God, whose I am, and whom I desire to serve, as well as from an ardent love to my dear country, which I am grieved to behold in tears, by reason of "the oppressions that are done under the sun."

Custom might now demand an address to my fathers and brethren in the ministry; but as a sermon will be preached to the clergy tomorrow, by one who is every way my superior, and from whom I expect myself to receive instruction, I shall no otherwise apply to them than as they may be concerned in the exhortation to the people, which, agreably to the preceeding discourse, speaketh in the words of the inspired Solomon, "Fear God, and honour the king."

Be, first of all, concerned to become truly religious; men of piety towards God, faith in our Lord Jesus Christ, and the subjects of that regenerating change, which shall renew your whole inner man, and form you to a resemblance of the blessed Jesus, in the moral temper of his mind.

And let your religion now discover itself in all proper ways; particularly, in doing your duty to those, whom it hath pleased God to entrust with power to rule over you.

Be exhorted to "make supplications, prayers and intercessions, with giving of thanks, for the king in supreme, and for all in authority" under him, that by means of their wise, and gentle, and just administrations in government, we may "lead quiet and peaceable lives in all godliness and honesty."

And as subjection to civil rulers is so peremptorily demanded of you, by the laws of our holy religion, that you can't be good christians without it, let me caution you, on the one hand, not to "despise dominion," nor "speak evil of dignities": And, on the other, let me "put you in mind to be subject to principalities and powers, and to obey magistrates; submitting to every ordinance of man for the Lord's sake: Whether it be to the king, as supreme; or unto governours, as unto them that are sent by him, for the punishment of evil doers, and for the praise of them that do well: For so is the will of God."

And as rulers are the ministers of God, his authoris'd deputies, for the people's good, and continually, so far as they answer the ends of their institution, attend on this very thing: "For this cause pay you tribute also": And do it, not grudgingly, but with a chearful mind, in obedience to that glorious sovereign Being, who has said, "render unto Caesar the things that are Caesar's."

In fine, let me call upon you to "render unto all their dues." Abhor the little arts of fraud and deceit that are become so common, in this day of growing dishonesty. Make use of conscience in your dealings with your neighbour; and be fair and equitable, wherein you may have to do with him in a way of commerce. In conformity to the righteous God, love righteousness, and discover that you do so, by constantly living in the practice of it: Always bearing it in mind, that he, "whose eyes behold, and whose eyelids try the children of men," will hereafter descend from heaven, "to give to every man according as his work shall be." Behold! He cometh with clouds, and we shall, every one of us, see him. We are hastening to another world; and it will not be long, before we shall all be together again, in a much more numerous assembly, and upon a far greater occasion, even that of being tried for our future existence, at the dreadful tribunal of the impartial judge of the quick and dead. The good Lord so impress the thought upon the hearts of us all, whether rulers, or ministers, or peo-

ple, as that it may have an abiding influence on us, engaging us to be faithful and just in our respective places: And now may we hope, of the mercy of God, thro' the merits of our saviour Jesus Christ, to be acquitted at the bar of judgment, pronounced blessed, and bid to inherit the kingdom prepared from the foundation of the world.

AMEN

State of Religion among the Protestant Dissenters in Virginia (1751)

SAMUEL DAVIES (1723–61)

In 1747 Davies was sent as a Presbyterian evangelist to Hanover, Virginia. He met with stiff opposition from proponents of the state's established church—the Church of England. The following selections from his 1751 pamphlet illustrate some of the concerns of Presbyterian dissenters, as well as their rights and liabilities under Virginia and English law. Davies is often credited for helping to demonstrate that the Act of Toleration applied in Virginia. He died shortly after replacing Jonathan Edwards as president of the College of New Jersey (Princeton) in 1759.

I have Reason to hope Sir, there are and have been a *few Names* in various Parts of the Colony, who are sincerely seeking the Lord, and groping after Religion, in the Communion of the Church of *England;* which I charitably presume from my finding there were a few of this happy Character in & about *Han-*

Excerpts reprinted from *State of Religion among the Protestant Dissenters in Virginia; in a Letter to the Rev. Mr. Joseph Bellamy, of Bethlem, in New-England: from the Reverend Mr. Samuel Davies, V.D.M. in Hanover County, Virginia* (Boston: S. Kneeland, 1751), 5–8, 29–44.

over before the late Revival of Religion. Such were awakened, as they have told me, either by their own serious Reflections, suggested and enforced by divine Energy; or on reading some Authors of the last Century, particularly *Bolton, Baxter, Flavel, Bunyan,* &c. Some of them were wont to attend on publick Worship in the established Church without much murmuring at the Entertainments there; tho' they were sensible these were vastly inferior to what past Ages were favoured with, and often wondered if there were such Doctrines taught any where in the World at present, as they found in the Writings of these good Men. Others of them, tho' they had no Objections against the Ceremonies of the Church of *England,* except a few who were shocked at the impracticable Obligations imposed upon the Sponsors in Baptism, were utterly dissatisfied with the usual Doctrines taught from the Pulpit. Tho' these were generally true, and would have been useful, in their Connection with the Scheme of evangelical Doctrines; yet so many necessary Truths were neglected, as rendered those that were inculcated of very little Service. The whole System of what is distinguished by the Name of *experimental Religion,* was past over in Silence. The *Depravity of humane Nature,* the *Necessity of Regeneration, and it's Pre-requisites, Nature and Effects,* the *various Exercises of pious Souls according to their several Cases,* &c. these were omitted; and without these, you know Sir, the finest Declamations on moral Duties or speculative Truths, will be but wretched Entertainment to hungry Souls. Such a maim'd System is not the compleat Religion of J E S U S, that glories in the amiable *Symmetry,* mutual *Dependency* and *Subserviency* of all its Doctrines, as its peculiar Characteristic. Had the *whole Counsel of God* been declared, had all the Doctrines of the Gospel been solemnly and faithfully preached in the established Church; I am perswaded there would have been but few Dissenters in these Parts of *Virginia;* for, as I observed, their first Objections were not against the peculiar *Rites* & *Ceremonies* of that Church, much less against her excellent *Articles;* but against the general Strain of the *Doctrines* delivered from the Pulpit, in which

these Articles were opposed, or (which was the more common Case) *not mentioned at all:* so that at first they were not properly *Dissenters from* the original Constitution of the Church of *England,* but the most strict *Adherents to* it, and only dissented from those that had forsaken it, tho' they still usurped the Denomination. But tho' such Impartiality in preaching the Gospel might have prevented the Advancement of the Interest of the Dissenters *as a Party,* it would have tended to promote the infinitely more valuable Interests of the blessed Redeemer: and had this been the Case, our Zeal and Industry to convert them to *Presbyterianism,* would have been almost superfluous, and quite disproportioned.—And here Sir, it may be proper to observe, That when in this Narrative I speak of the Increase of Dissenters in these Parts with an Air of Satisfaction, I do not boast of them as meer *Captures* from the Church of *England,* but as hopefully *sincere Proselytes to living Religion,* or at least as lying open to Conviction, and in the Way of more profitable Means. I cannot indeed but conscienciously dissent from some of the Peculiarities of that Church; and it tends a little to heighten our Satisfaction, when such as agree with us in *Essentials,* and appear truly pious, do also agree with us in *Circumstantials;* for as Agreement is the Foundation and Measure of social Love, *this* must be co-extended with *that:* Yet as I am fully perswaded *the Kingdom of God is not Meat & Drink, but Righteousness and Peace and Joy in the Holy Ghost;* and that Persons of superiour Piety and Judgment have used these Rites and Ceremonies with Approbation; I think the Alteration of Men's Principles and Practice with Respect to these Things *only,* without being born again of God, is a wretched Conversion; and it would inspire me with much greater Joy to see a *pious Church-man,* than a *graceless Presbyterian.* I cheerfully embrace the Sentiments of that illustrious Divine Mr. *Howe,** "*That without the Effusion of the Spirit from high,*" to fashion the Hearts of Men into a Conformity to the blessed God, and to prepare them for a happy Immortality,

* See *Howe's* Works, Vol. II. p. 474.

"*it matters little, and signifies to me scarce one Straw, what Party of us is uppermost:* The most Righteous, (*as they may be vogu'd*) *will be but as Bryars & scratching Thorns; and it is better to suffer by such than to be of them.*" The chief Reason Sir, why I call upon you to congratulate the Increase of the Dissenters here, and rejoyce in it my self, is, because I have Ground to hope that the Number of the Heirs of Heaven is augmented in some *Proportion,* tho' alas! not to an Equality; and to triumph on inferior Accounts, would argue the narrow Genius of a *Bigot.*——

'Tis likely, Sir, you may desire some Account of the State of Religion in other Counties where Dissenters are settled; and therefore, as I have undertaken this History, and as I know not any other Way in which you may receive as full Information, I shall endeavour to gratify you.

There is an immense Quantity of Land unsettled to the Westward of *Hanover,* between this and *Missisippii*-River; to which People from most of the Northern Colonies, particularly from *Pennsylvania* and *New-Jersey,* are yearly removing in vast Multitudes. The three Frontier Counties of this Colony, *Frederick, Augusta,* and *Lunenburg,* which are prodigiously large, are chiefly inhabited by such; especially *Augusta,* in which there are very few others. There is also a considerable Number of them in *Amelia* County and *Albemarle.* They are generally *Irish* People, and were educated in the *Presbyterian* Religion, and have seen no Reason to change their Religion with their Residence. As their Encouragement tends to the great Advantage of the Colony, and there are but few *Virginians* among them, especially in *Augusta* and *Frederick,* to be proselyted; the Council, (who, I verily believe, are possess'd with a noble Spirit of Patriotism to promote the temporal Welfare of their Country) have given them, or the Ministers that have officiated among them, but little Molestation. There are two Congregations of them, one in *Albemarle,* and one in *Augusta* County, belonging to the Synod of *Philadelphia,* that have Ministers settled among them: but those that have put themselves under the Care of *New-Castle* Presbytery belonging to the

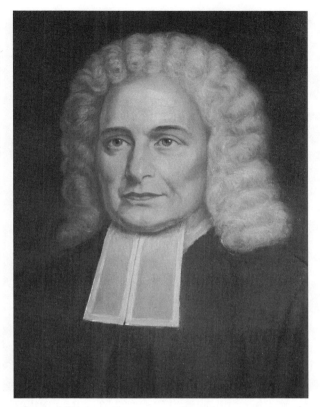

Samuel Davies, oil on canvas. Used by permission of the Union Theological Seminary and Presbyterian School of Christian Education.

Synod of *New-York,* (which are vastly more numerous) notwithstanding their zealous and repeated Endeavours, are still destitute of Ministers, by Reason of the Scarcity of Ministers and Multitude of Vacancies in said Presbytery. They are sufficiently numerous to form 5 distinct Congregations, three at least in *Augusta,* one in *Frederica,* and one at least in *Lunenburg* and *Amelia.* The only Method our Presbytery has been capable to take to supply them, is, to send some of its Members or Candidates to officiate transiently among them, as long and as frequently as the Circumstances of their own Congregations or of other Vacancies would permit; but notwithstanding all the Supplies they could obtain this Way, some of them, particularly *Lunenburg,* have been above a Year together without one Sermon. I hope that one of them may obtain a settled Minister soon, as I am told, there is a pious popular Youth,* sent by *New-Brunswick* Presbytery among them, whose Heart seems disposed to settle somewhere in *Virginia:* But truly, Sir, I have no Prospect how the rest shall be furnished with stated Ministers; for I can now count up at least 6 or 7 vacant Congregations in *Pennsylvania,* and 2 or 3 in *Maryland,* besides the 5 mentioned in the Frontier Counties of *Virginia,* and a Part of my Congregation, which I would willingly declare vacant, had they Opportunity of obtaining another Minister:† And there are but 12 Members in *New-Castle* Presbytery, each of whom has a stated Charge; and two or three Candidates, who are pre-engaged to vacant Congregations in *Pennsylvania:* From whence you may easily calculate the Disproportion of our Ministers to the Vacancies. Our Number indeed has been increased of late Years by the Licensure of sundry pious Youth, who make up the most of the Number mentioned; and I have the pleasing Prospect of the Licensure of 3 or 4 more within a few Years: But our Vacancies increase almost as fast as our Ministers, by the Settlement of new Places, or by the breaking out of religious Concern in Places where there were little or no Appearances of it before; upon which they generally apply to our Presbytery: And the Lord removes from us all Occasion to boast of our Number, by advancing some of our most useful Members, in the Bloom of Life, and in the midst of their Successes, from their painful Labours below, to join the Church triumphant in eternal Rest. Mr. *Robinson* and Mr. *Dean,* led the Way; and I have lately had the melancholy Account, that the great Mr. *Samuel Blair,* the brightest Light in these Parts of *Zion,* is just on the Wing to follow.—*My Father! my Father! the Chariots of Israel, and the Horsemen thereof!* The very Tho't strikes a Terror to the Friends of *Zion.* On these Ac-

counts, Sir, I am afraid the most of these Vacancies in *Virginia,* cannot be settled with Ministers from *New-Castle* Presbytery this considerable Time; which is the more affecting, as they have been destitute these 8 or 10 Years, i.e. since their first Settlement. You may easily conjecture I mention this as an Inducement to faithful Ministers from *New-England* and elsewhere, where they may be spared, to *come into our Macedonia to help us.*

Tho' these Congregations have been hitherto destitute of the stated Ministrations of the Gospel; yet the Itenerations of my Brethren among them, have been attended with very considerable Success. Mr. *Robinson,* as I intimated before, took a Tour thro' these Frontier Counties, and into *North-Carolina,* about seven Years ago. He underwent great Hardships in *Carolina,* without much Success, by Reason of the Fewness of the Inhabitants at that Time; who were generally such uncultivated Savages, that there was little Prospect of doing them much Service without continuing a long Time among them to teach them the first Rudiments of Christianity; and so scattered, that but very few of them could convene in one Place to hear. The Case is indeed happily altered there since that Time, as the Inhabitants are vastly more numerous, and some Persons that had a religious Education are settled among them. A new Congregation, I think upon *Pee-dee River,* sent a Petition to me last Year to be presented to *New-Castle* Presbytery for a Minister, subscribed by more than a Hundred Persons, chiefly Heads of Families; and one of my Correspondents there informs me, that they are very sufficient to maintain a Minister. Our Presbytery appointed Mr. *James Finley* to visit them; but by Indisposition he was prevented; so that they have lain wholly destitute hitherto, and are like to do so, unless they can obtain some foreign Assistance, besides what our Presbytery can afford them. Besides this, I hear of sundry other Places in *North-Carolina,* that are ripening very fast for the Gospel: And Oh! that the Lord would THRUST *forth Labourers into that Part of his Harvest;* for I am afraid but few will go thither, 'till they are *thrust* and constrained by an ir-

---

* The Rev. Mr. *John Todd.*

† There are perhaps 20 or 30 Places where there is a Number of Families, thirsting after the Word, besides these mentioned; which require transient Supplies; but as they are not yet sufficient to form distinct Congregations, and maintain Ministers of their own, I have not numbred them among the vacant Congregations.

resistible Zeal, and a providential Concurrence of Circumstances.—

But I find I must suppress the rest, lest I tire you, and lose the Historian in the Poet.

Mr. *Robinson* continued, I think, 15 Sabbaths in *Lunenburg* and *Amelia,* and left sundry spiritual Children there behind him. A considerable Number of *Virginians,* who knew nothing of real Religion before, were awakened by his Ministry; and their Conduct since gives Ground for a charitable Judgment concerning them. Sundry also that had removed thither from the Northward, and had a religious Education, and a System of orthodox Principles, were convinced of their unregenerate Condition, and that they had had but a *Form of Godliness without the Power,* who now appear solid Christians.—At their repeated Solicitations, I spent about a Fortnight preaching among them the Beginning of this Month [*June*]; and tho' they seem sensibly languishing for the Want of the Means of Grace, yet sundry give agreable Evidences of real Religion; and there is a Prospect of doing much Service, were they furnished with a faithful Minister. I met with most Encouragement in a Part of *Amelia* County, where very few had heard any of my Brethren. The Assemblies were large even on Week Days, and sometimes there appeared much Solemnity and Affection among them. There appears the greatest Probability, that if they had faithful Preaching frequently, many of them would be turned to the Lord; and it was really afflictive to me, that the Necessity of my own Congregation constrained me to leave them so soon, and refuse sundry Invitations they gave me to preach in other Places in the County. I believe another Congregation would soon be gathered there, had they frequent Preaching.

In *Augusta,* there is a great Number of solid and warm Christians; some of whom were such when they came thither, & others have experienced a happy Change since. There was a pretty general Awakening there some Years ago under the Ministry of Mr. *Dean* (now at Rest) and Mr. *Byram;* the Effects of which in sundry Instances are still apparent; and the Itinerations of most of my Brethren before & since, have

been bless'd with Success. I believe three Ministers might live very comfortably among them.

I have no general Acquaintance in *Frederic* County, tho' I have pass'd thro' it, and preached frequently in some Parts of it: but I am credibly informed by such of my Brethren as have been often there, that there has been a considerable Awakening there some Years ago, which has had a blessed Issue in many, and that the Congregation is in promising Circumstances, and has been endeavouring, tho' unsuccessfully, to obtain a Minister, for sundry Years.

You will no doubt, be glad to have some certain Information of the State of Religion in *Maryland;* and therefore, tho' I now live at a great Distance from the Places there where it flourishes, yet as I preached at most of them formerly, when the religious Commotion was at its Height, and as I have heard of no remarkable Alterations in them since, I shall give the following concise Account; which you may depend upon as true.

There has been a considerable *Revival* (shall I call it?) or *first Plantation* of Religion in *Baltimore* County, which lies along *Susquehannah* River, bordering on *Pennsylvania,* where, I'm informed, Mr. *Whittlesey* (with whom I find, you are acquainted) is like to settle.—Of this Mr. *S. Blair,* if I remember rightly, gives an Account in, *The Christian History;* and therefore I shall say no more of it.

In *Kent* County and *Queen Ann's,* which lie between *Cheasapeak* Bay and *Delaware,* a Number of careless Sinners have been awakened and hopefully brought to Christ. The Work was begun and chiefly carried on by the Instrumentality of that favoured Man Mr. *Robinson;* whose Success, whenever I reflect upon it, astonishes me. Oh! he did much in a little Time; and who would not chuse so expeditious a Pilgrimage thro' this World? There is in these Places a considerable Congregation; and they have made repeated Essays to obtain a settled Minister, but are not like to succeed 'till our Number is increased.

There was a great Stir about Religion in a Place called *Buckingham,* on the Sea-shore, about four Years ago, when I was there; but it was not then come to Maturity. It has spread since, and issued in a hopeful Conversion in sundry Instances; and I am informed they are now sufficient to constitute a Congregation, and are waiting for a Minister.

But the most glorious Display of divine Grace in *Maryland* has been in and about *Somerset* County, which lies at some Distance from *Cheasapeak* Bay on the Eastern Shore. It began, I think, in the Year 1745, by the Ministry of Mr. *Robinson;* and was afterwards carried on by sundry Ministers that preach'd transiently there. I was there about two Months, when the Work was at its Height; and I never saw such a deep and spreading Concern among People in my Life as then appeared among them: The Assemblies were numerous, tho' it was in the Extremity of a cold Winter, and unwearied in attending the Word; and frequently there were very few among them that did not give some plain Indications of Distress or Joy. Oh! these were the happiest Days that ever my Eyes saw, or are, as I fear, like to see. Since that, the Harvest seems over there; tho' considerable Gleanings, I hear, are still gathered; and many of the late Converts give the utmost Reason to presume their final Perseverance. There had been a Congregation of Presbyterians there for many Years; but they were reduced almost to nothing before the late Revival; when many of the Church-People were brought under deep Impressions, and cordially joined with them; so that now they form at least one large Congregation; and after many fruitless Attempts, they have lately been so happy as to obtain the Reverend Mr. *Hugh Henry* for their Minister, a Youth of a good Genius and undoubted Piety, who will I trust, be an extensive Blessing to that Part of the Colony.

I might, Sir, have been more particular on most of Things in this Narrative; but as a *general* View may perhaps be sufficient to you and the Public, and is most convenient to me in my present Hurry, I have declined it.—The indigested Order and other Inaccuries you will easily discern, are proper Objects for your Candour and Generosity; and I have no other Apology to make, but that the unavoidable Hurry of the Bearer on a Business of the greatest Importance

to the Interest of Religion in *Virginia,* in which we doubt not of your hearty Concurrence, will not suffer me to transcribe this first Draft.

I shall prize it, dear Sir, as an inestimable Blessing, if you and others of the Lord's Servants and People in distant Parts, favour us with the Concurrence of your Prayers to promote the declining Work of Religion among us; which is the only Way I can expect the Assistance of most of them.

The Constancy of your Correspondence, Sir, affords me peculiar Satisfaction in my present solitary Situation: And if any of the sacred Character, in any Parts of the Church where this Narrative may come, should condescend to favour me with their Correspondence, I should most gratefully acknowledge it, and make them the best Returns in my Power. Our Acquaintance with the State of the Church in various Parts, qualifies us to adapt our Prayers to it; and therefore such mutual Intelligences may be of special Service to us in our Intercessions.

May your divine Master bless you, dear Sir, and succeed your Ministrations! And may the Spirit be richly poured forth from on high on that favoured Land where you reside.

I am,

Reverend Sir,

Your very affectionate Brother

and Servant,

in the Kingdom and Patience

of Jesus Christ

Samuel Davies

Hanover,
June 28. 1751.

Appendix

I at first intended, Sir, to have said Nothing of a particular Restraint impos'd upon us at present by the civil Government; lest I should seem fond of raising the Cry of *Persecution,* which is very indecent in the Followers of the uncomplaining Lamb of God, especially when there is in Truth so little Occasion for it; or to fling injurious Reflections on His Majesty's Council for this Colony, for whom I have the profoundest Veneration on Account both of their honourable Character and their Accomplishments for it; and under whose indulgent Administration we enjoy so many civil and sacred Liberties.

But as I know not, Sir, but this Narrative may come into the Hands of some who may have some Influence to secure our Priviledges, or procure their Enlargement, if it may be judged that we lie under any illegal Restraints; and as the Matter is not only public in this Colony, but has been lately laid before the Government in *England* by the President & Council, for Advice; I shall venture to give you the following short, simple Narrative of it; without any tedious Argumentations upon it; and without injurious Aspersions, which are far from my Heart.

The General Court, as I informed you, have licensed seven Meeting-Houses for me to officiate in; and I should not desire to have their Number and my Fatigues encreased, were not the Circumstances of the Dissenters in *Virginia* extraordinary & peculiar. There are a few of them in sundry Counties besides these in which the licensed Houses are, who are too weak to maintain a Minister of their own; and were they never so able, they could not obtain one in the present Scarcity of Ministers. These have given me repeated and importunate Invitations to come and preach among them; but I judged it imprudent to comply till the Places were legally licensed. Upon this some of them, with a View to obtain my Labours transiently among them, at least on Week Days, and the Visits of my Brethren in their Itinerations, have petitioned the Courts of their respective Counties for Licenses for Places convenient to them; but they have either been denied, or the License granted by the County Court has been nullified by the Council; which has discouraged others that they have made no Application. This is a Disadvantage to the People, not only as they are thereby deprived of the Preaching of the Word, but as they are exposed to the intolerable Hardship of carrying their Children so great a Way to be baptized.

The Council has superseded a License granted by a County Court on the Presumption, "*That it does not belong to a County Court to proceed in such Affairs;* and, *That a dissenting Minister has no legal Right to more Meeting-Houses than one.*" And these two Points have been submitted to the Determination of those to whose Province it belongs in *England;* but no Answer is yet arriv'd.

The taking the Authority from County Courts of administring the legal Qualifications to Ministers and licensing Meeting-Houses, would be no great Disadvantage to us in *Hanover,* because we might easily apply to the Commander in Chief, or the General Court; and therefore 'tis of small Importance with me how it be determined; tho' it would occasion a considerable Difficulty to those that live 2 or 300 Miles distant from *Williamsburg.*

But the restraining a dissenting Minister to but *one* Meeting-House would be a prodigious Grievance to the People in their present Circumstances.—This, Sir, is not a proper Place to debate the Legality of it, nor does it belong to my Province to determine it; yet I may inoffensively suggest the following Remarks upon it, as Matters of Speculation to the Curious, and of Determination to those in Authority.

His Majesty's private Instructions with Respect to Dissenters, to the Governour or Commander in Chief, (so far as I can recollect them from a transient View, which the Hon. Col. Lee, our late President favoured me with) run thus *verbatim,* "You are to tolerate all Dissenters (except Papists) who lead quiet and inoffensive Lives"—But how can such Dissenters be tolerated, who by Reason of Weakness and the Scarcity of Ministers, cannot obtain a Minister of their own, unless they may legally share in the Labours of a Minister with other Places, which cannot be without a Plurality of Meeting-Houses under the Care of one Minister?

The Act of Toleration (which has been received by our Legislature*) does not determine the Number of

---

* This Act was received *An. quart. Reginae Annae,* in these Words, "If any Person being of the Age of twenty-one Years, or upwards, shall willfully absent him or herself from Divine Service at his or her Parish Church or Chapel, the Space of one Month, (EXCEPTING AS IS EXCEPTED IN AN ACT OF PARLIAMENT PASSED IN THE FIRST YEAR

Meeting-Houses, but only gives a general Toleration to legally qualified Ministers to officiate in Places legally licensed: And may it not be reasonably presumed from hence, That the *Number* is left to be determined according to the peculiar Circumstances of particular Congregations?

Farther; The said Act expresly says,—"That all the Laws made and provided for the frequenting of divine Service on the Lord's-Day, commonly called *Sunday,* shall be still in Force, and executed against all Persons that offend against the said Laws, except such Persons come to some Congregation or Assembly of religious Worship, allowed or permitted by this Act." But how can Persons come to such Congregation or Assembly, unless a Place within their Reach be licensed for that Purpose? If this Liberty be denied them, are they not obliged, according to *the Act of Toleration* it self, to attend constantly on Worship in the established Church? And if so, where is their Toleration?

Finally; It is a very common Thing in this Colony, and allowed expresly by Law, that where the Parish is of great Extent, and cannot be divided into sundry, each of them capable to maintain a Minister, to erect 2, 3 or 4 Churches or Chappels of Ease, for the Conveniency of the Parish, where the Minister officiates alternately, or in Proportion to the Number of People: And since the Reason for a Plurality of Meeting-Houses among us, is the same; why is it not equally legal?—Sundry under Things might be suggested; but I forbear.

I am, *ut anté*

<hr/>

OF K. WILLIAM AND Q. MARY, entitled, *An Act for exempting their Majesty's Protestant Subjects dissenting from the Church of* England, *from the Penalty of certain Laws*)—Every such Person—being lawfully convicted, by Confession, or otherwise,—shall forfeit and pay, for every such Offence, the Sum of Five Shillings, or fifty Pounds of Tobacco."

The Rights of the Colonists, A List of Violations of Rights and a Letter of Correspondence (1772)

SAMUEL ADAMS (1722–1803)

John Adams's cousin Samuel was for years the most dominant politician in Massachusetts. One of the first and most articulate advocates of American independence, Adams penned the following letter for Boston's Committee of Correspondence in 1772.

Adopted by the Town of Boston, November 20, 1772

The Committee appointed by the Town the second Instant "to State the Rights of the Colonists and of this Province in particular, as Men, as Christians, and as Subjects; to communicate and publish the same to the several Towns in this Province and to the World as the sense of this Town with the Infringements and Violations thereof that have been, or from Time to Time may be made. Also requesting of each Town a free Communication of their Sentiments Reported—

First, a State of the *Rights* of the Colonists and of this Province in particular—

Secondly, A List of the *Infringements,* and Violations of those Rights.—

Thirdly, A Letter of Correspondence with the other Towns.—

1st. Natural Rights of the Colonists as Men.—

Among the Natural Rights of the Colonists are these First. a Right to *Life;* Secondly to *Liberty;*

Excerpts reprinted from *The Writings of Samuel Adams,* ed. Harry Alonzo Cushing (New York: Octagon, 1968), 2:350–56. "The Rights of the Colonists, A List of Violations of Rights and a Letter of Correspondence" first appeared in the *Boston Record Commissioners' Report,* vol. xviii, pp. 94–108.

thirdly to *Property;* together with the Right to support and defend them in the best manner they can— Those are evident Branches of, rather than deductions from the Duty of Self Preservation, commonly called the first Law of Nature—

All Men have a Right to remain in a State of Nature as long as they please: And in case of intollerable Oppression, Civil or Religious, to leave the Society they belong to, and enter into another.—

When Men enter into Society, it is by voluntary consent; and they have a right to demand and insist upon the performance of such conditions, And previous limitations as form an equitable *original compact.*—

Every natural Right not expressly given up or from the nature of a Social Compact necessarily ceded remains.—

All positive and civil laws, should conform as far as possible, to the Law of natural reason and equity.—

As neither reason requires, nor religeon permits the contrary, every Man living in or out of a state of civil society, has a right peaceably and quietly to worship God according to the dictates of his conscience.—

"Just and true liberty, equal and impartial liberty" in matters spiritual and temporal, is a thing that all Men are clearly entitled to, by the eternal and immutable laws Of God and nature, as well as by the law of Nations, & all well grounded municipal laws, which must have their foundation in the former.—

In regard to Religeon, mutual tolleration in the different professions thereof, is what all good and candid minds in all ages have ever practiced; and both by precept and example inculcated on mankind: And it is now generally agreed among christians that this spirit of toleration in the fullest extent consistent with the being of civil society "is the chief characteristical mark of the true church"* & In so much that Mr. Lock has asserted, and proved beyond the possibility of contradiction on any solid ground, that such tol-

eration ought to be extended to all whose doctrines are not subversive of society. The only Sects which he thinks ought to be, and which by all wise laws are excluded from such toleration, are those who teach Doctrines subversive of the Civil Government under which they live. The Roman Catholicks or Papists are excluded by reason of such Doctrines as these "that Princes excommunicated may be deposed, and those they call *Hereticks* may be destroyed without mercy; besides their recognizing the Pope in so absolute a manner, in subversion of Government, by introducing as far as possible into the states, under whose protection they enjoy life, liberty and property, that solecism in politicks, Imperium in imperio* leading directly to the worst anarchy and confusion, civil discord, war and blood shed—

The natural liberty of Men by entring into society is abridg'd or restrained so far only as is necessary for the Great end of Society the best good of the whole—

In the state of nature, every man is under God, Judge and sole Judge, of his own rights and the injuries done him: By entering into society, he agrees to an Arbiter or indifferent Judge between him and his neighbours; but he no more renounces his original right, than by taking a cause out of the ordinary course of law, and leaving the decision to Referees or indifferent Arbitrations. In the last case he must pay the Referees for time and trouble; he should be also willing to pay his Just quota for the support of government, the law and constitution; the end of which is to furnish indifferent and impartial Judges in all cases that may happen, whether civil ecclesiastical, marine or military.—

"The natural liberty of man is to be free from any superior power on earth, and not to be under the will or legislative authority of man; but only to have the law of nature for his rule."—

In the state of nature men may as the *Patriarchs* did, employ hired servants for the defence of their lives, liberty and property: and they should pay them

---

* See Locks Letters on Toleration.

* A Government within a Government—

reasonable wages. Government was instituted for the purposes of common defence; and those who hold the reins of government have an equitable natural right to an honourable support from the same principle "that the labourer is worthy of his hire" but then the same community which they serve, ought to be assessors of their pay: Governors have no right to seek what they please; by this, instead of being content with the station assigned them, that of honourable servants of the society, they would soon become Absolute masters, Despots, and Tyrants. Hence as a private man has a right to say, what wages he will give in his private affairs, so has a Community to determine what they will give and grant of their Substance, for the Administration of publick affairs. And in both cases more are ready generally to offer their Service at the proposed and stipulated price, than are able and willing to perform their duty.—

In short it is the greatest absurdity to suppose it in the power of one or any number of men at the entering into society, to renounce their essential natural rights, or the means of preserving those rights when the great end of civil government from the very nature of its institution is for the support, protection and defence of those very rights: the principal of which as is before observed, are life, liberty and property. If men through fear, fraud or mistake, should *in terms* renounce and give up any essential natural right, the eternal law of reason and the great end of society, would absolutely vacate such renunciation; the right to freedom being *the gift* of God Almighty, it is not in the power of Man to alienate this gift, and voluntarily become a slave—

2d. *The Rights of the Colonists as Christians*—

These may be best understood by reading—and carefully studying the institutes of the great Lawgiver and head of the Christian Church: which are to be found closely written and promulgated in the *New Testament*—

By the Act of the British Parliament commonly called the Toleration Act, every subject in England Except Papists &c was restored to, and re-established in, his natural right to worship God according to the dictates of his own conscience. And by the Charter of this Province it is granted ordained and established (that it is declared as an original right) that there shall be liberty of conscience allowed in the worship of God, to all christians except Papists, inhabiting or which shall inhabit or be resident within said Province or Territory.* Magna Charta itself is in substance but a constrained Declaration, or proclamation, and promulgation in the name of King, Lord, and Commons of the sense the latter had of their original inherent, indefeazible natural Rights,† as also those of free Citizens equally perdurable with the other. That great author that great jurist, and even that Court writer Mr. Justice Blackstone holds that this recognition was justly obtained of King John sword in hand: and peradventure it must be one day sword in hand again rescued and preserved from total destruction and oblivion.—

An Appeal to the Public for Religious Liberty (1773)

ISAAC BACKUS (1724–1806)

A Baptist minister from Massachusetts, Backus was a fervent advocate of religious liberty and disestablishment. The following excerpts are from one of his most influential pamphlets on religious liberty.

Introduction

Inasmuch as there appears to us a real need of such an appeal, we would previously offer a few thoughts

* See 1. Wm. and Mary. St. 2. C. 18—and Massachusetts Charter.
† Lord Cokes Im. Blackstone, Commentaries—Vol. 1st. Page 122.
Excerpts reprinted from *Political Sermons of the American Founding Era, 1730–1805*, ed. Ellis Sandoz, 2nd ed., 2 vols. (Indianapolis: Liberty Fund, 1998), 1:331–59. © 1998, Liberty Fund, Inc. Reprinted by permission.

AN
APPEAL
TO THE
PUBLIC
FOR
RELIGIOUS LIBERTY,

Againſt the Oppreſſions of the preſent Day.
By Isaac Backus.

Brethren, ye have been called unto Liberty ; only uſe
not Liberty for an occaſion to the Fleſh, but by love
ſerve one another.   GAL. V. 13.

BOSTON :

Printed by JOHN BOYLE in Marlborough-Street.
MDCCLXXIII.

Isaac Backus, *An Appeal to the Public for Religious Liberty*, 1773.

concerning the general nature of liberty and government, and then shew wherein it appears to us, that our religious rights are encroached upon in this land.

It is supposed by multitudes, that in submitting to government we give up some part of our liberty, because they imagine that there is something in their nature incompatible with each other. But the word of truth plainly shews, that man first lost his freedom by breaking over the rules of government; and that those who now speak great swelling words about liberty, while they despise government, are themselves servants of corruption. What a dangerous error, yea, what a root of all evil then must it be, for men to imagine that there is any thing in the nature of true government that interferes with true and full liberty! A grand cause of this evil is, ignorance of what we are, and where we are; for did we view things in their true light, it would appear to be as absurd and dangerous, for us to aspire after any thing beyond our capacity, or out of the rule of our duty, as it would for the frog to swell till he bursts himself in trying to get as big as the ox, or for a beast or fowl to dive into the fishes element till they drown themselves. *Godliness with contentment is great gain:* But they that *will* take a contrary course *fall into temptation, and a snare, and into many foolish and hurtful lusts, which drown men in destruction and perdition.* 1 Tim. 6. 6, 9.

The true liberty of man is, to know, obey and enjoy his Creator, and to do all the good unto, and enjoy all the happiness with and in his fellow-creatures that he is capable of; in order to which the law of love was written in his heart, which carries in it's nature union and benevolence to being in general, and to each being in particular, according to it's nature and excellency, and to it's relation and connexion to and with the supreme Being, and ourselves. Each rational soul, as he is a part of the whole system of rational beings, so it was and is, both his duty and his liberty to regard the good of the whole in all his actions. To love ourselves, and truly to seek our own welfare, is both our liberty and our indispensible duty; but the conceit that man could advance either his honor or happiness, by disobedience instead of obedience, was first injected by the father of lies, and all such conceits ever since are as false as he is.

Before man imagined that submission to government, and acting strictly by rule was confinement, and that breaking over those bounds would enlarge his knowledge and happiness, how clear were his ideas! (even so as to give proper names to every creature) and how great was his honor and pleasure! But no sooner did he transgress, than instead of enjoying the boldness of innocency, and the liberties of paradise, he sneaks away to hide himself; and instead of clear and just ideas, he adopted that master of all absurdities (which his children follow to this day) of thinking to hide from omniciency, and of trying to deceive him who knows every thing! Instead of good and happiness, he felt evil, guilt and misery; and in the room of concord was wrangling, both against his Creator and his fellow-creature, even so that she who was before loved as his own flesh, he now accuses to the great Judge. By which it appears, that the notion of man's gaining any dignity or liberty by refusing an intire submission to government, was so delusive, that instead of it's advancing him to be as gods, it sunk him down into a way of acting like the beasts and like the devil! the beasts are actuated by their senses and inclinations, and the devil pursues his designs by deceit and violence. With malicious reflections upon God, and flattering pretences to man, he drew him down to gratify his eyes and his taste with forbidden fruit: and he had no sooner revolted from the authority of heaven, than the beauty and order of his family was broken; he turns accuser against the wife of his bosom, his first son murders the next, and then lies to his Maker to conceal it; and that lying murderer's posterity were the first who broke over the order of marriage which God had instituted; and things proceeded from bad to worse, till all flesh had corrupted his way, and the earth was filled with violence, so that they could no longer be borne with, but by a just vengeance were all swept away, only one family.

Yet all this did not remove the dreadful distemper from man's nature, for the great Ruler of the universe directly after the flood, gave this as one reason why he would not bring such another while the earth remains, namely, *For the imagination of man's heart is evil from his youth,** so that if he was to drown them as often as they deserved it, one deluge must follow another continually. Observe well where the distemper lies; evil imaginations have usurped the place of reason and a well informed judgment, and hold them in such bondage, that instead of being governed by those noble faculties, they are put to the horrid drugery of seeking out inventions, for the gratification of *fleshly lusts, which war against the soul;* and to guard against having these worst of all enemies detected and subdued; enemies which are so far from being God's creatures, that strictly speaking, they have no being at all in themselves, only are the privation of his creatures well-being; therefore sin, with it's offspring death, will, as to those who are saved, be *swallowed up in victory.* Sin is an enemy both to God and man, which was begotten by satan, and was conceived and brought forth by man; for lust when it is conceived bringeth forth sin, and sin when it is finished bringeth forth death.†

Now how often have we been told, that he is not a freeman but a slave, whose person and goods are not at his own but anothers disposal? And to have foreigners come and riot at our expence and in the fruit of our labours, has often been represented to be worse than death. And should the higher powers appear to deal with temporal oppressors according to their deserts, it would seem strange indeed, if those who have suffered intolerably by them, should employ all their art and power to conceal them, and so to prevent their being brought to justice! But how is our world filled with such madness concerning spiritual tyrants! How far have pride and infidelity, covetousness and luxury, yea deceit and cruelty, those foreigners which came from hell, carried their influence, and spread their baneful mischiefs in our world! Yet who is willing to own that he has been deceived and enslaved by them? Who is willing honestly to bring them forth to justice!

All acknowledge that these enemies are among us, and many complain aloud of the mischiefs that they do; yet even those who lift their heads so high as to laugh at the atonement of Jesus, and the powerful influences of the Spirit, and slight public & private devotion, are at the same time very unwilling to own that they harbour pride, infidelity, or any other of those dreadful tyrants. And nothing but the divine law refered to above, brought home with convincing light and power, can make them truly sensible of the soul-slavery that they are in: and 'tis only the power of the gospel that can set them free from sin, so as to become the servants of righteousness: can deliver them from these enemies, so as to *serve God in holiness* all their days. And those who do not thus know the truth, and have not been made free thereby,* yet have never been able in any country to subsist long without some sort of government; neither could any of them ever make out to establish any proper government without calling in the help of the Deity. However absurd their notions have been, yet they have found human sight and power to be so short and weak, and able to do so little toward watching over the conduct, and guarding the rights of individuals, that they have been forced to appeal to heaven by oaths, and to invoke assistance from thence to avenge the cause of the injured upon the guilty. Hence it is so far from being necessary for any man to give up any part of his real liberty in order to submit to government, that all nations have found it necessary to submit to some government in order to enjoy any liberty and security at all.

We are not insensible that the general notion of liberty, is for each one to act or conduct as he pleases; but that government obliges us to act toward others by law and rule, which in the imagination of many, interferes with such liberty; though when we come to the light of truth, what can possibly prevent it's being the highest pleasure, for every rational person, to love God with all his heart, and his neighbour as himself, but corruption and delusion? which, as was before

* Gen. 4. 19. and 6. 13, 15. and 8. 21.
† Eccl. 7. 29. 1 Pet. 2. 11. Jam. 1. 14, 15.

* Rom. 6. 18. Luke 1. 74, 75. John 8. 32.

noted, are foreigners and not originally belonging to man. Therefore the divine argument to prove, that those who promise liberty while they despise government are servants of corruption is this; *For of whom a man is overcome, of the same is he brought in bondage.* 2 Pet. 2. 18, 19. He is so far from being *free* to act the man, that he is a bond slave to the worst of tyrants. And not a little of this tyranny is carried on by such an abuse of language, as to call it liberty, for men to yield themselves up, to be so foolish, disobedient and deceived, as to *serve divers lusts and pleasures.* Tit. 3. 3.

Having offered these few thoughts upon the general nature of government and liberty, it is needful to observe, that God has appointed two kinds of government in the world, which are distinct in their nature, and ought never to be confounded together; one of which is called civil, the other ecclesiastical government. And tho' we shall not attempt a full explanation of them, yet some essential points of difference between them are necessary to be mentioned, in order truly to open our grievances.

Section I

Some essential points of difference between civil and ecclesiastical government.

1. The forming of the constitution, and appointment of the particular orders and offices of civil government is left to human discretion, and our submission thereto is required under the name of their being, the ordinances of men for the Lord's sake. 1 Pet. 2. 13, 14. Whereas in ecclesiastical affairs we are most solemnly warned not to be *subject to ordinances, after the doctrines and commandments of men.* Col. 2. 20, 22. And it is evident that he who is the only worthy object of worship, has always claimed it as his sole prerogative, to determine by express laws, what his worship shall be, who shall minister in it, and how they shall be supported. How express were his appointments concerning these things by Moses? And so wise and good a ruler as Solomon, was not intrusted with any legislative power upon either of these articles, but had

the exact dimensions of the temple, the pattern and weight of every vessel, with the treasuries of the dedicate things, and the courses of the priests and Levites, all given to him in *writing by the Spirit,* through the hand of his father David. 1 Chron. 28. 11–19. And so strict were God's faithful servants about these matters, that Daniel who in a high office in the Persian court, behaved so well that his most envious and crafty foes, could find no occasion against him, nor fault in him concerning the kingdom, till they fell upon the device of moving the king to make a decree about worship, that should interfere with Daniel's obedience to his God; yet when that was done, he would not pay so much regard to it as to shut his windows. Dan. 6. 4–11. And when the Son of God, who is the great Law-giver and King of his church, came and blotted out the handwriting of the typical ordinances, and established a better covenant, or constitution of his church, upon better promises, we are assured that he was *faithful in all his house, and counted worthy of more glory than Moses.* What vacancy has he then left for faliable men to supply, by making new laws to regulate and support his worship? especially if we consider,

2. That as the putting any men into civil office is of men, of the people of the world; so officers have truly no more authority than the people give them: And how came the people of the world by any ecclesiastical power? They arm the magistrate with the sword, that he may be a minister of God *to them for good,* and might execute wrath upon evil doers; and for this cause they pay them tribute: upon which the apostle proceeds to name those divine commandments which are comprehended in love to our neighbour, and which work *no ill to him.* Surely the inspired writer had not forgotten the first and great command of love to God; but as this chapter treats the most fully of the nature and end of civil government of any one in the new-testament, does it not clearly shew that the crimes which fall within the magistrates jurisdiction to punish, are only such as work ill to our neighbour? Rom. 13. 1–10. While church government respects our behaviour toward God as well as man.

3. All acts of executive power in the civil state, are to be performed in the name of the king or state they belong to; while all our religious acts are to be done in the *name of the Lord Jesus;* and so are to be performed *heartily as to the Lord, and not unto men.* And it is but lip service, and vain worship, if our *fear toward him is taught by the precepts of men.* Col. 3. 17, 23. Isa. 29. 13. Mat. 15. 9. It is often pleaded, that magistrates ought to do their duty in religious as well as civil affairs. That is readily granted; but what is their duty therein? Surely it is to *bow to the name of Jesus,* and to serve him with holy reverence; and if they do the contrary they may expect to *perish from the way.* Phil. 2. 10. Psa. 2. 10–12. But where is the officer that will dare to come in the name of the Lord to demand, and forcibly to take, a tax which was imposed by the civil state! And can any man in the light of truth, maintain his character as a minister of Christ, if he is not contented with all that Christ's name and influence will procure for him, but will have recourse to the *kings of the earth,* to force money from the people to support him under the name of an embassador of the God of heaven! Does not such conduct look more like the way of those who made *merchandize of slaves and souls of men,* than it does like the servants who were content to be as their master, who said, *He that heareth you heareth me; and he that despiseth you despiseth me?* Rev. 18. 9, 13. Luke 10. 3–16.

4. In all civil governments some are appointed to judge for others, and have power to compel others to submit to their judgment: but our Lord has most plainly forbidden us, either to assume or submit to any such thing in religion. Mat. 23. 1–9. Luke 22. 25–27. He declares, that the cause of his coming into the world, was to bear *witness unto the truth;* and says he, *Every one that is of the truth heareth my voice.* This is the nature of his kingdom, which he says, *is not of this world:* and gives that as the reason why his servants should not fight, or defend him with the sword. John. 18. 36, 37. And it appears to us that the true difference and exact limits between ecclesiastical and civil government is this, That the church is armed with light and truth, to pull down the strong holds of iniquity,

and to gain souls to Christ, and into his church, to be governed by his rules therein; and again to exclude such from their communion, who will not be so governed; while the state is armed with the sword to guard the peace, and the civil rights of all persons and societies, and to punish those who violate the same. And where these two kinds of government, and the weapons which belong to them, are well distinguished, and improved according to the true nature and end of their institution, the effects are happy, and they do not at all interfere with each other: but where they have been confounded together, no tongue nor pen can fully describe the mischiefs that have ensued; of which the Holy Ghost gave early and plain warnings. He gave notice to the church, that the main of those antichristian confusions and abominations, would be drawn by philosophy and deceit, from the *hand-writing of ordinances* that Christ has blotted out. And to avoid the same, directs the saints to walk in Christ Jesus *as they received him,* rooted and built up in him, and stablished in the faith *as they have been taught;* viewing that they are *complete in him, which is the head over all principality and power.* Therefore he charges them not to be beguiled into a voluntary humility, by such fleshly minds as do not hold this head, but would subject them to ordinances after the doctrines and commandments of men. Col. 2.

Now 'tis well known that this glorious head made no use of secular force in the first sitting up of the gospel church, when it might seem to be pecularly needful if ever; and it is also very evident, that ever since men came into the way of using force in such affairs, their main arguments to support it have been drawn from the old Jewish constitution and ordinances. And what work has it made about the head as well as members of the church?

First they moved Constantine, a secular prince, to draw his sword against heretics; but as all earthly states are changeable, the same sword that Constantine drew against heretics, Julian turned against the orthodox. However, as the high priest's sentence in the Jewish state, decided matters both for prince and people, the same deceitful pilosophy that had gone so far, never left plotting till they had set up an ecclesiastical head over kingdoms as well as churches, who with Peter's keys was to open and shut, bind and loose, both in spiritual and temporal affairs. But after many generations had groaned under this hellish tyranny, a time came when England renounced that head, and set up the king as their head in ecclesiastical as well as civil concernments; and though the free use of the scriptures which was then introduced, by a divine blessing, produced a great reformation, yet still the high places were not taken away, & the lord bishops made such work in them, as drove our fathers from thence into America. The first colony that came to this part of it carried the reformation so far, as not to make use of the civil force to save the people to support religious ministers (for which they have had many a lash from the tongues & pens of those who were fond of that way) but the second colony, who had not taken up the cross so as to separate from the national church before they came away, now determined to pick out all that they thought was of universal and moral equity in Moses's laws, and so to frame a christian common-wealth here.* And as the Jews were ordered not to set up any rulers over them who were not their brethren; so this colony resolved to have no rulers nor voters for rulers, but brethren in their churches. And as the Jews were required to inflict corporal punishments, even unto death, upon non-conformers to their worship, this commonwealth did the like to such as refused to conform to their way; and they strove very hard to have the church govern the world, till they lost their charter; since which, they have yielded to have the world govern the church, as we shall proceed to shew.

Section II

. . . In civil states the power of the whole collective body is vested in a few hands, that they may with better advantage defend themselves against injuries from abroad, and correct abuses at home, for which end a

* Massachusetts history, vol. 3. p. 161.

few have a right to judge for the whole society; but in religion each one has an equal right to judge for himself; for we must all appear before the judgment seat of Christ, that every one may receive the things *done in his body,* according to that he hath done (not what any earthly representative hath done for him) 2 Cor. 5. 10. And we freely confess that we can find no more warrant from divine truth, for any people on earth to constitute any men their representatives, to make laws to impose religious taxes, than they have to appoint Peter or the Virgin Mary to represent them before the throne above. We are therefore brought to a stop about paying so much regard to such laws, as to give in annual certificates to the other denomination, as we have formerly done.

1. Because the very nature of such a practice implies an acknowledgment, that the civil power has a right to set one religious sect up above another, else why need we give certificates to them any more than they to us? It is a tacit allowance that they have a right to make laws about such things, which we believe in our consciences they have not. For,

2. By the foregoing address to our legislature, and their committees report thereon, it is evident, that they claim a right to tax us from civil obligation, as being the representatives of the people. But how came a civil community by any ecclesiastical power? how came the kingdoms of this world to have a right to govern in Christ's kingdom which is *not of this world!*

3. That constitution not only emboldens people to *judge the liberty of other mens consciences,* and has carried them so far as to tell our general assembly, that they conceived it to be a *duty they owed to God* and their country, not to be dispensed with, to lay before them the springs of their neighbours actions;* but it also requires something of the same nature from us. Their laws require us annually to certify to them, what our belief is concerning the conscience of every

* How are men deluded to think they do God service, when they violate his word! 1 Cor. 4. 5. Would not the same principle carry them to kill Christ's disciples under the same pretence? John 16. 2.

person that assembles with us, as the condition of their being exempted from taxes to other's worship. And only because our brethren in Bellingham, left that clause about the conscience out of their certificates last year, a number of their society who live at Mendon were taxed, and lately suffered the spoiling of their goods to uphold pedobaptist worship.

4. The scheme we oppose evidently tends to destroy the purity and life of religion; for the inspired apostle assures us, that the church is *espoused as a chaste virgin to Christ*, and is obliged to be *subject to him in every thing*, as a true wife is to her husband. Now the most chaste domestic obedience, does not at all interfere with any lawful subjection to civil authority; but for a woman to admit the highest ruler in a nation into her husband's place, would be adultery or whoredom; and how often are mens inventions about worship so called in the sacred oracles?* And does it not greatly concern us all, earnestly to search out and put away such evils, as we would desire to escape the awful judgments that such wickedness has brought on other nations! Especially if we consider that not only the purity, but also the very life and being of religion among us is concerned therein; for 'tis evident that Christ has given as plain laws to determine what the duty of people is to his ministers, as he has the duty of ministers to his people; and most certainly he is as able to enforce the one as the other. The common plea of our opponents is, that people will not do their duty if rulers do not enforce it; but does not the whole book of God clearly shew, that ministers as often fail of doing their duty as the people do? And where is the care of rulers to punish minis-

ters for their unfaithfulness? They often talk about equality in these affairs, but where does it appear! As Christ is the head of all principality and power; so the *not holding the head, from which all the body by joints and bands having nourishment ministred, and knit together, increaseth with the increase of God*, but bringing in an earthly power between Christ and his people, has been the grand source of anti-christian abominations, and of settling men down in *a form of godliness*, while they *deny the power thereof*. Has not this earthly scheme prevailed so far in our land, as to cause many ministers, instead of *taking heed to the ministry received from the Lord*; and instead of *watching for souls as those who must give an account*,* rather to act as if they were not accountable to any higher power, than that of the men who support them? and on the other hand, how do many people behave as if they were more afraid of the collector's warrant, and of an earthly prison, than of Him who sends his ministers to preach his gospel, and says, *He that receiveth whomsoever I send, receiveth me;* but declares, That it shall be more tolerable in the day of judgment for Sodom, than for those who receive them not?† Yea, as if they were more afraid of an earthly power than of our great King and Judge, who can this night require the soul of him that layeth up *treasure for himself, and is not rich towards God;* and will sentence all either to heaven or hell, according as they have treated Him well or ill, in his ministers and members.‡

5. The custom which they want us to countenance, is very hurtful to civil society: for by the law of Christ *every man*, is not only allowed, but also required, to judge for himself, concerning the circumstantials as well as the essentials, of religion, and to act according to the *full persuasion of his own mind;* and he contracts guilt to his soul if he does the contrary. Rom. 14. 5, 23.

---

* Psalm 106. 39. We delight not in hard names, but every vice ought to be called by it's proper name; and the custom in this adulterous age of calling those, natural children, which God calls children of whoredom, has doubtless had a pernicious effect upon many to embolden them to go on in their filthy ways. God charged his ancient church with playing the harlot, because she said, *I will go after my lovers, that gave me my bread and my water;—For she did not know that I gave her corn*, &c. Hosea 2. 5, 8. By which it appears, that to fix our dependence upon any other beside the divine Being, and to pursue any method beside his directions, to obtain the necessaries and comforts of life, is whoredom; and does not the chief sin of the mother of harlots lie in her fixing this dependence upon the kings of the earth? Rev. 18. 3–13.

* Col. 4. 17. Heb. 13. 17.
† Joh. 13. 20. Luk. 10. 10–12.
‡ Luk. 12. 20, 21. Mat. 25. 31, &c.

RECOMMENDATIONS FOR FURTHER READING

Bonomi, Patricia U. *Under the Cope of Heaven: Religion, Society, and Politics in Colonial America.* New York: Oxford University Press, 1986.

Hall, Timothy L. *Separating Church and State: Roger Williams and Religious Liberty.* Urbana: University of Illinois Press, 1998.

McLoughlin, William G. *New England Dissent, 1630–1833: The Baptists and the Separation of Church and State.* 2 vols. Cambridge: Harvard University Press, 1971.

Sandoz, Ellis, ed. *Political Sermons of the American Founding Era: 1730–1805.* 2nd ed., 2 vols. Indianapolis, Ind.: Liberty Fund, 1998.

Shain, Barry Alan. *The Myth of American Individualism: The Protestant Origins of American Political Thought.* Princeton: Princeton University Press, 1994.

Stout, Harry S. *The New England Soul: Preaching and Religious Culture in Colonial New England.* New York: Oxford University Press, 1986.

Part III

FRAMING THE CONSTITUTIONAL
PRINCIPLES GOVERNING RELIGIOUS LIBERTY
AND CHURCH-STATE RELATIONS IN
THE AMERICAN FOUNDING

CHAPTER FOUR

The Continental and Confederation Congresses and Church-State Relations

FROM THEIR INCEPTION, Great Britain's colonies in North America were largely self-governing with respect to internal affairs. Parliament's attempts in the 1760s and 1770s to assert control over the colonies and, particularly, to raise tax revenues without their consent, led to a series of increasingly violent clashes between American patriots and British officials. After the Boston Tea Party of 1773, Parliament passed a series of repressive measures that became known in America as the Coercive, or Intolerable, Acts. In response, colonial leaders formed the First Continental Congress, which met from September 5, 1774, to October 26, 1774. The Second Continental Congress, which convened on May 10, 1775, remained in place until the new national government under the United States Constitution took power in 1789.

Although it was a continuation of the same body, after the states ratified the Articles of Confederation in 1781 the Second Continental Congress became known as "the Congress of the Confederation," or "the Confederation Congress."

The powers of the Continental and Confederation congresses were extremely limited. At least until the late 1780s, most Americans assumed that the state or local governments would exercise most civil authority. Congress did have the power, however, to pass laws on a few national and international issues. It could also request states to take certain actions. The following documents illustrate how members of these congresses approached church-state issues within the context of a limited national government.

Letter of John Adams to Abigail Adams (September 16, 1774)

The First Continental Congress convened on September 5, 1774. On September 6 delegates voted to invite the Reverend Jacob Duché to open their proceedings with prayer on the following day. John Adams (1735–1826), a leading advocate of independence and future vice president and president of the United States, sent this account of the prayer to his wife. Psalm 35, the psalm to which Adams refers, begins "Plead my cause, O LORD, with them that strive with me: fight against them that fight against me."

Phyladelphia Septr. 16. 1774

Having a Leisure Moment, while the Congress is assembling, I gladly embrace it to write you a Line.

When the Congress first met, Mr. Cushing made a Motion, that it should be opened with Prayer. It was opposed by Mr. Jay of N. York and Mr. Rutledge of South Carolina, because we were so divided in religious Sentiments, some Episcopalians, some Quakers, some anabaptists, some Presbyterians and some Congregationalists, so that We could not join in the same Act of Worship. Mr. S. Adams arose and said he was no Bigot, and could hear a Prayer from a Gentleman of Piety and Virtue, who was at the same Time a Friend to his Country. He was a Stranger in Phyladelphia, but had heard that Mr. Duché (Dushay they pronounce it) deserved that Character, and therefore he moved that Mr. Duché, an episcopal Clergyman, might be desired, to read Prayers to the Congress, tomorrow Morning. The Motion was seconded and passed in the Affirmative. Mr. Randolph

our President, waited on Mr. Duché, and received for Answer that if his Health would permit, he certainly would. Accordingly next Morning he appeared with his Clerk and in his Pontificallibus, and read several Prayers, in the established Form; and then read the Collect for the seventh day of September, which was the Thirty fifth Psalm. You must remember this was the next Morning after we heard the horrible Rumour, of the Cannonade of Boston. I never saw a greater Effect upon an Audience. It seemed as if Heaven had ordained that Psalm to be read on that Morning.

After this Mr. Duche, unexpected to every Body struck out into an extemporary Prayer, which filled the Bosom of every Man present. I must confess I never heard a better Prayer or one, so well pronounced. Episcopalian as he is, Dr. Cooper himself never prayed with such fervour, such Ardor, such Earnestness and Pathos, and in Language so elegant and sublime—for America, for the Congress, for The Province of Massachusetts Bay, and especially the Town of Boston. It has had an excellent Effect upon every Body here.

I must beg you to read that Psalm. If there was any Faith in the sortes Virgilianae, or sortes Homericae, or especially the Sortes biblicae, it would be thought providential.

It will amuse your Friends to read this Letter and the 35th. Psalm to them. Read it to your Father and Mr. Wibirt. I wonder what our Braintree Churchmen would think of this? Mr. Duché is one of the most ingenious Men, and best Characters, and greatest orators in the Episcopal order, upon this Continent—Yet a Zealous Friend of Liberty and his Country.

I long to see my dear Family. God bless, preserve and prosper it. Adieu.

John Adams

Reprinted from *Letters of Delegates to Congress, 1774 to 1789*, ed. Paul H. Smith (Washington, D.C.: Library of Congress, 1976), 74–75.

Congressional Resolution Calling for a Day of Public Humiliation, Fasting, and Prayer (June 1775)

The Continental Congress first issued a call for "public humiliation, prayer, and fasting" in June 1775. It was authored by Presbyterian clergyman and Princeton president John Witherspoon. On July 20, the day set for the fast, "Congress attended *en masse* Reverend Duché's Episcopalian church in the morning and Dr. Francis Allison's First Presbyterian Church in the afternoon."*

As the great Governor of the World, by his supreme and universal Providence, not only conducts the course of nature with unerring wisdom and rectitude, but frequently influences the minds of men to serve the wise and gracious purposes of his providential government; and it being, at all times, our indispensible duty devoutly to acknowledge his superintending providence, especially in times of impending danger and public calamity, to reverence and adore his immutable justice as well as to implore his merciful interposition for our deliverance:

This Congress, therefore, considering the present critical, alarming and calamitous state of these colonies, do earnestly recommend that Thursday, the 20th day of July next, be observed, by the inhabitants of all the English colonies on this continent, as a day of public humiliation, fasting and prayer; that we may, with united hearts and voices, unfeignedly confess and deplore our many sins; and offer up our joint supplications to the all-wise, omnipotent, and merciful Disposer of all events; humbly beseeching him to forgive our iniquities, to remove our present calamities, to avert those desolating judgments, with which we are threatened, and to bless our rightful sovereign, King George the third, and [to] inspire him with wisdom to discern and pursue the true interest of all his subjects, that a speedy end may be put to the civil discord between Great Britain and the American colonies, without farther effusion of blood: And that the British nation may be influenced to regard the things that belong to her peace, before they are hid from her eyes: That these colonies may be ever under the care and protection of a kind Providence, and be prospered in all their interests; That the divine blessing may descend and rest upon all our civil rulers, and upon the representatives of the people, in their several assemblies and conventions, that they may be directed to wise and effectual measures for preserving the union, and securing the just rights and priviledges of the colonies; That virtue and true religion may revive and flourish throughout our land; And that all America may soon behold a gracious interposition of Heaven, for the redress of her many grievances, the restoration of her invaded rights, a reconcilation with the parent state, on terms constitutional and honorable to both; And that her civil and religious priviledges may be secured to the latest posterity.

And it is recommended to Christians, of all denominations, to assemble for public worship, and to abstain from servile labour and recreations on said day.

*Derek Davis, *Religion and the Continental Congress, 1774–1789* (New York: Oxford University Press, 2000), 86.
Reprinted from *Journals of the Continental Congress: 1774–1789,* ed. Worthington Chauncey Ford (Washington, D.C.: GPO, 1904), 1:87–88.

Rules and Orders for the Continental Army (June 1775)

The Continental Congress attempted to promote religion and virtuous behavior in the Continental Army, as illustrated by the first three of sixty-nine rules passed by Congress in June 1775.

Resolved, That the following Rules and Orders be attended to, and observed by such forces as are or may hereafter be raised for the purposes aforesaid.

Article I. That every officer who shall be retained, and every soldier who shall serve in the Continental Army, shall, at the time of his acceptance of his commission or inlistment, subscribe these rules and regulations. And that the officers and soldiers, already of that army, shall also, as soon as may be, subscribe the same; from the time of which subscription every officer and soldier, shall be bound by those regulations. But if any of the officers or soldiers, now of the said army, do not subscribe these rules and regulations, then they may be retained in the said army, subject to the rules and regulations under which they entered into the service, or be discharged from the service, at the option of the Commander in chief.

Art. II. It is earnestly recommended to all officers and soldiers, diligently to attend Divine Service; and all officers and soldiers who shall behave indecently or irreverently at any place of Divine Worship, shall, if commissioned officers, be brought before a court-martial, there to be publicly and severely reprimanded by the President; if non-commissioned officers or soldiers, every person so offending, shall, for his first offence, forfeit One Sixth of a Dollar, to be deducted out of his next pay; for the second offence, he shall not only forfeit a like sum, but be confined for twenty-four hours, and for every like offence, shall suffer and pay in like manner; which money so forfeited, shall be applied to the use of the sick soldiers of the troop or company to which the offender belongs.

Art. III. Whatsoever non-commissioned officer or soldier shall use any profane oath or execration, shall incur the penalties expressed in the second article; and if a commissioned officer be thus guilty of profane cursing or swearing, he shall forfeit and pay for each and every such offence, the sum of Four Shillings, lawful money. . . .

Congressional Chaplains (1775–88)

Members of the Continental Congress regularly invited clergy to open their sessions with prayer and occasionally attended religious services as a body. On July 9, 1776, Congress appointed Jacob Duché chaplain to Congress. Upon his resignation in October of that year, Congress voted to pay him one hundred fifty dollars in acknowledgment of his services. Duché donated the money to "widows and children" of fallen Pennsylvania officers. In late 1777 Duché changed his mind about the wisdom of independence and fled to England.

Congress replaced Duché with Episcopalian minister William White and Presbyterian minister George Duffield. They served until 1784, at which point Congress made the position subject to annual appointment. In 1788 Congress voted to pay chaplains regularly. The following excerpts from the *Journals of the Continental Congress* illustrate Congress's approach to chaplains.

July 15, 1775

On motion, *Resolved*, That the Congress will, on Thursday next, attend divine service together, both morning and after noon.

Resolved, That Mr. [Thomas] Lynch, and Mr. [John] Dickinson, wait on Mr. [Jacob] Duché, and request him to preach for the Congress on next Thursday morning, and to wait upon Doctr. [Francis] Allison, and request him to preach at his Church for the Congress, on the after noon of the said day.

July 9, 1776

Resolved, That the Rev. Mr. J. Duché be appointed chaplain to Congress, and that he be desired to attend every morning at 9 o'Clock.

October 17, 1776

Mr. Duché having, by letter, informed the president, that the state of his health, and his parochial duties, were such, as obliged him to decline the honour of continuing chaplain to the Congress,

Resolved, That Mr. president be desired to return the thanks of this house to the Rev. Mr. Duché, for the devout and acceptable manner in which he discharged his duty during the time he officiated as chaplain to it; and that 150 dollars be presented to him, as an acknowledgment from the house for his services.

October 30, 1776

Mr. Duché having, by a letter to the president, acknowledged his obligations for the kind manner in which Congress have expressed their approbation of his services, requests, as he accepted their appoint-

Excerpts reprinted from *Journals of the Continental Congress: 1774–1789*, ed. Worthington Chauncey Ford (Washington, D.C.: GPO, 1904), 2:185; 5:530; 6:886–87, 911; 34:71.

ment from motives perfectly disinterested, that ~~Mr. Hancock will please to put~~ the 150 dollars voted to him, may be applied to the relief of the widows and children of such of the Pensylvania officers, as have fallen in battle in the service of their country:

Resolved, That the money be deposited with the council of safety of Pensylvania, to be applied agreeable to the request and desire of Mr. Duché.

February 29, 1788

A motion being made by Mr. [Paine] Wingate seconded by Mr. [Dyre] Kearny

That two chaplains be appointed for Congress whose salaries shall not exceed three hundred dollars each per Annum to commence from the day of their appointment,

On the question to agree to this the yeas and nays being required by Mr. [Dyre] Kearny

New hampshire		
Mr. Gillman	ay	⎫ ay
Mr. Wingate	ay	⎭
Massachusetts		
Mr. Dane	ay	⎫
Mr. Otis	ay	⎬ ay
Mr. Thatcher	no	⎭
Connecticut		
Mr. Mitchel	no	⎫
Mr. Cook	ay	⎬ ay
Mr. Wadsworth	ay	⎭
New York		
Mr. Hamilton	ay	⎫ ay
Mr. Gansevort	ay	⎭
New Jersey		
Mr. Clarke	ay	⎫ ay
Mr. Dayton	ay	⎭
Pensylvania		
Irvine	ay	⎫
Mr. Armstrong	no	⎬ no
Mr. Reid	no	⎭
Delaware		
Mr. Kearny	ay	⎫ ay
Mr. Mitchel	ay	⎭
Maryland		
Mr. Howard	no	⎫ d
Mr. Contee	ay	⎭
Virginia		
Mr. Madison	ay	⎫
Mr. Griffin	ay	⎬ ay
Mr. Brown	ay	⎭
N[orth] Carolina		
Mr. White	ay	
S[outh] Carolina		
Mr. Huger	no	⎫
Mr. Parker	ay	⎬ no
Mr. Tucker	no	⎭

So it was resolved in the affirmative.

The Declaration of Independence
(July 4, 1776)

On July 2, 1776, the Continental Congress approved Richard Henry Lee's resolution "That these United Colonies are, and of right ought to be, free and independent States, that they are absolved from all allegiance to the British Crown, and that all political connection between them and the State of Great Britain is, and ought to be, totally dissolved." Congress had earlier appointed a committee consisting of John Adams, Roger Sherman, Benjamin Franklin, Robert R. Livingston, and Thomas Jefferson to write a declaration of independence. Jefferson wrote the first draft, which was amended by Adams and Franklin. Congress then debated, amended, and passed the Declaration on July 4, 1776.

IN CONGRESS, JULY 4, 1776
The Unanimous Declaration of the Thirteen
United States of America

WHEN, in the course of human events, it becomes necessary for one people to dissolve the political bands which have connected them with another, and to assume, among the powers of the earth, the separate and equal station to which the laws of nature and of nature's God entitle them, a decent respect to the opinions of mankind requires that they should declare the causes which impel them to the separation.

We hold these truths to be self-evident: that all men are created equal; that they are endowed, by their Creator, with certain unalienable rights; that among these are life, liberty, and the pursuit of happiness.

Reprinted from *The Public Statutes at Large of the United States of America,* ed. Richard Peters (Boston: Charles C. Little and James Brown, 1845), 1:1–3.

That to secure these rights, governments are instituted among men, deriving their just powers from the consent of the governed; that whenever any form of government becomes destructive of these ends, it is the right of the people to alter or to abolish it, and to institute a new government, laying its foundation on such principles, and organizing its powers in such form, as to them shall seem most likely to effect their safety and happiness. Prudence, indeed, will dictate, that governments long established, should not be changed for light and transient causes; and accordingly all experience hath shown, that mankind are more disposed to suffer, while evils are sufferable, than to right themselves by abolishing the forms to which they are accustomed. But when a long train of abuses and usurpations, pursuing invariably the same object, evinces a design to reduce them under absolute despotism, it is their right, it is their duty, to throw off such government, and to provide new guards for their future security. Such has been the patient sufferance of these colonies; and such is now the necessity which constrains them to alter their former systems of government. The history of the present King of Great Britain is a history of repeated injuries and usurpations, all having in direct object the establishment of an absolute tyranny over these states. To prove this, let facts be submitted to a candid world.

He has refused his assent to laws the most wholesome and necessary for the public good.

He has forbidden his governors to pass laws of immediate and pressing importance, unless suspended in their operation till his assent should be obtained; and when so suspended, he has utterly neglected to attend to them.

He has refused to pass other laws for the accommodation of large districts of people, unless those people would relinquish the right of representation in the legislature; a right inestimable to them, and formidable to tyrants only. He has called together legislative bodies at places unusual, uncomfortable, and distant from the depository of their public records, for the sole purpose of fatiguing them into compliance with his measures.

He has dissolved representative houses repeatedly, for opposing, with manly firmness, his invasions on the rights of the people.

He has refused for a long time, after such dissolutions, to cause others to be elected; whereby the legislative powers, incapable of annihilation, have returned to the people at large for their exercise; the state remaining, in the mean time, exposed to all the dangers of invasion from without, and convulsions within.

He has endeavored to prevent the population of these States; for that purpose obstructing the laws for naturalization of foreigners; refusing to pass others to encourage their migrations hither, and raising the conditions of new appropriations of lands.

He has obstructed the administration of justice, by refusing his assent to laws for establishing judiciary powers.

He has made judges dependent on his will alone, for the tenure of their offices, and the amount and payment of their salaries.

He has erected a multitude of new offices, and sent hither swarms of officers, to harass our people, and eat out their substance.

He has kept among us, in times of peace, standing armies, without the consent of our legislatures.

He has affected to render the military independent of, and superior to the civil power.

He has combined with others to subject us to a jurisdiction foreign to our constitution, and unacknowledged by our laws; giving his assent to their acts of pretended legislation:

For quartering large bodies of armed troops among us;

For protecting them, by a mock trial, from punishment for any murders which they should commit on the inhabitants of these States;

For cutting off our trade with all parts of the world;

For imposing taxes on us without our consent;

For depriving us, in many cases, of the benefits of trial by jury;

For transporting us beyond seas to be tried for pretended offences;

For abolishing the free system of English laws in a neighbouring province, establishing therein an arbitrary government, and enlarging its boundaries, so as to render it at once an example and fit instrument for introducing the same absolute rule into these colonies;

For taking away our charters, abolishing our most valuable laws, and altering fundamentally the forms of our governments;

For suspending our own legislatures, and declaring themselves invested with power to legislate for us in all cases whatsoever.

He has abdicated government here, by declaring us out of his protection, and waging war against us.

He has plundered our seas, ravaged our coasts, burnt our towns, and destroyed the lives of our people.

He is at this time transporting large armies of foreign mercenaries to complete the works of death, desolation, and tyranny, already begun with circumstances of cruelty and perfidy, scarcely paralleled in the most barbarous ages, and totally unworthy the head of a civilized nation.

He has constrained our fellow-citizens, taken captive on the high seas, to bear arms against their country, to become the executioners of their friends and brethren, or to fall themselves by their hands.

He has excited domestic insurrections amongst us, and has endeavoured to bring on the inhabitants of our frontiers the merciless Indian savages, whose known rule of warfare is an undistinguished destruction of all ages, sexes, and conditions.

In every stage of these oppressions we have petitioned for redress in the most humble terms. Our repeated petitions have been answered only by repeated injury. A prince, whose character is thus marked by every act which may define a tyrant, is unfit to be the ruler of a free people.

Nor have we been wanting in attentions to our British brethren. We have warned them, from time to time, of attempts by their legislature to extend an unwarrantable jurisdiction over us. We have reminded them of the circumstances of our emigration and settlement here. We have appealed to their native justice and magnanimity, and we have conjured them by the ties of our common kindred to disavow these usurpations, which would inevitably interrupt our connexions and correspondence. They too have been deaf to the voice of justice and of consanguinity. We must, therefore, acquiesce in the necessity which denounces our separation, and hold them, as we hold the rest of mankind, enemies in war, in peace friends.

We, therefore, the representatives of the UNITED STATES OF AMERICA, in General Congress assembled, appealing to the Supreme Judge of the world for the rectitude of our intentions, do, in the name, and by authority of the good people of these colonies, solemnly publish and declare, That these United Colonies are, and of right ought to be, FREE and INDEPENDENT STATES; that they are absolved from all allegiance to the British crown, and that all political connexion between them and the state of Great Britain is, and ought to be, totally dissolved; and that, as FREE and INDEPENDENT STATES, they have full power to levy war, conclude peace, contract alliances, establish commerce, and to do all other acts and things which INDEPENDENT STATES may of right do. And for the support of this Declaration, with a firm reliance on the protection of DIVINE PROVIDENCE, we mutually pledge to each other our lives, our fortunes, and our sacred honour.

JOHN HANCOCK.

New Hampshire.—Josiah Bartlett, William Whipple, Matthew Thornton.

Massachusetts Bay.—Samuel Adams, John Adams, Robert Treat Paine, Elbridge Gerry.

Rhode Island, &c.—Stephen Hopkins, William Ellery.

Connecticut.—Roger Sherman, Samuel Huntington, William Williams, Oliver Wolcott.

New York.—William Floyd, Philip Livingston, Francis Lewis, Lewis Morris.

New Jersey.—Richard Stockton, John Witherspoon, Francis Hopkinson, John Hart, Abraham Clark.

Pennsylvania.—Robert Morris, Benjamin Rush, Benjamin Franklin, John Morton, George Clymer, James Smith, George Taylor, James Wilson, George Ross.

Delaware.—Caesar Rodney, George Read, Thomas McKean.

Maryland.—Samuel Chase, William Paca, Thomas Stone, Charles Carroll of Carrollton.

Virginia.—George Wythe, Richard Henry Lee, Thomas Jefferson, Benjamin Harrison, Thomas Nelson, Jun., Francis Lightfoot Lee, Carter Braxton.

North Carolina.—William Hooper, Joseph Hewes, John Penn.

South Carolina.—Edward Rutledge, Thomas Hayward, Jun., Thomas Lynch, Jun., Arthur Middleton.

Georgia.—Button Gwinnett, Lyman Hall, George Walton.

Congressional Resolution Calling for a Day of Thanksgiving (November 1, 1777)

Shortly after the surrender of General Burgoyne in New York, Congress appointed a committee consisting of Samuel Adams, Richard Henry Lee, and Daniel Roberdeau to write a recommendation to the states for a day of thanksgiving. The following resolution was approved by Congress on November 1, 1777.

The committee appointed to prepare a recommendation to these states, to set apart a day of thanksgiving, brought in a report; which was agreed to as follows:

Reprinted from *Journals of the Continental Congress: 1774–1789*, ed. Worthington Chauncey Ford (Washington, D.C.: GPO, 1904), 9:854–55.

STATE OF NEW-HAMPSHIRE.

THE COUNCIL and ASSEMBLY of said State, have ordered,-- that the following Proclamation of the Hon'ble Continental CONGRESS, for a General THANKSGIVING throughout the United-States, be printed, and sent to the several religious Societies in this State, to be observed, agreeable to the Directions therein.

M. WEARE, (PRESIDENT of THE COUNCIL.

E. THOMPSON, Secretary.

A PROCLAMATION
For a General THANKSGIVING,
Throughout the United-States of AMERICA.

In *CONGRESS, November* 1, 1777.

FORASMUCH as it is the indispensible Duty of all Men, to adore the superintending Providence of *Almighty GOD*, to acknowledge with Gratitude their Obligation to *Him* for Benefits received, and to implore such further Blessings as they stand in Need of ; and it having pleased Him, in his abundant Mercy, not only to continue to us the innumerable Bounties of his common Providence ; but also to smile upon us, in the Prosecution of a *just and necessary WAR*, for the Defence and Establishment of our unalienable Rights and Liberties ; particularly, in that he hath been pleased in so great a Measure to prosper the Means used for the Support of our Troops, and to crown our Arms with most signal Success :

IT is therefore recommended to the Legislative or executive Powers of these several *UNITED STATES*, to set apart *THURSDAY*, the eighteenth Day of December next, for solemn *THANKSGIVING* and *PRAISE* : That at one Time and with one Voice the good People may express the grateful Feelings of their Hearts, and consecrate themselves to the Service of their Divine Benefactor ; and that together with their sincere Acknowledgments and Offerings they may join the penitent Confession of their manifold Sins whereby they had forfeited every Favour, and their humble and earnest Supplication that *GOD*, thro' the Merits of *Jesus Christ*, would mercifully forgive and blot them out of Remembrance ; that it may please him graciously to afford his Blessing on the Government of these states respectively, and prosper the public Council of the whole ; to inspire our Commanders both by Land and Sea, and all under them, with that Wisdom & Fortitude which may render them fit Instruments, under the Providence of *Almighty GOD*, to secure for these *United-States*, the greatest of all human Blessings, *Independence* and *Peace* ; that it may please him to prosper the Trade and Manufactures of the People, and the Labour of the Husbandman, that our Land may yet yield its Increase ; to take schools and Seminaries of Education, so necessary for cultivating the Principles of true Liberty, Virtue, and Piety, under his nurturing Hand ; and to prosper the Means of Religion for the Promotion and Enlargement of that Kingdom which consisteth in *Righteousness, Peace, and Joy in the Holy Ghost.*

And is it further recommended, that servile Labour and Recreation, altho' at other Times innocent, may be unbecoming the Purpose of this Appointment, be omitted on so solemn an Occasion.

Extract from the Minutes,

Attest,   CHA. THOMPSON, Secretary.

GOD save the UNITED-STATES of AMERICA.

EXETER; Printed by ZECHARIAH FOWLE, 1777.

Congressional Thanksgiving Day Proclamation, November 1, 1777.
Rare Book and Special Collections Division, Library of Congress.

Forasmuch as it is the indispensable duty of all men to adore the superintending providence of Almighty God; to acknowledge with gratitude their obligation to him for benefits received, and to implore such farther blessings as they stand in need of; and it having pleased him in his abundant mercy not only to continue to us the innumerable bounties of his common providence, but also to smile upon us in the prosecution of a just and necessary war, for the defence and establishment of our unalienable rights and liberties; particularly in that he hath been pleased in so great a measure to prosper the means used for the support of our troops and to crown our arms with most signal success: It is therefore recommended to the legislative or executive powers of these United States, to set apart Thursday, the eighteenth day of December next, for solemn thanksgiving and praise; that with one heart and one voice the good people may express the grateful feelings of their hearts, and consecrate themselves to the service of their divine benefactor; and that together with their sincere acknowledgments and offerings, they may join the penitent confession of their manifold sins, whereby they had forfeited every favour, and their humble and earnest supplication that it may please God, through the merits of Jesus Christ, mercifully to forgive and blot them out of remembrance; that it may please him graciously to afford his blessing on the governments of these states respectively, and prosper the public council of the whole; to inspire our commanders both by land and sea, and all under them, with that wisdom and fortitude which may render them fit instruments, under the providence of Almighty God, to secure for these United States the greatest of all human blessings, independence and peace; that it may please him to prosper the trade and manufactures of the people and the labour of the husbandman, that our land may yet yield its increase; to take schools and seminaries of education, so necessary for cultivating the principles of true liberty, virtue and piety, under his nurturing hand, and to prosper the means of religion for the promotion and enlargement of that kingdom which

consisteth "in righteousness, peace and joy in the Holy Ghost."

And it is further recommended, that servile labour, and such recreation as, though at other times innocent, may be unbecoming the purpose of this appointment, be omitted on so solemn an occasion.

The Articles of Confederation and Perpetual Union (November 1777)

The Articles of Confederation were passed by the Continental Congress in 1777 and went into effect after ratification by the thirteenth state in 1781. Articles referencing God or religion are reprinted below.

To all to whom these presents shall come,
    We, the undersigned, Delegates of the States affixed to our names, send greeting:

Whereas the Delegates of the United States of America in Congress assembled, did on the fifteenth day of November, in the year of our Lord one thousand seven hundred and seventy-seven, and in the second year of the Independence of America, agree to certain Articles of Confederation and Perpetual Union between the states of New Hampshire, Massachusetts Bay, Rhode Island and Providence Plantations, Connecticut, New York, New Jersey, Pennsylvania, Delaware, Maryland, Virginia, North Carolina, South Carolina, and Georgia, in the words following, viz.

ARTICLES OF CONFEDERATION AND PERPETUAL UNION,

between the States of New Hampshire, Massachu-

Excerpts reprinted from *The Public Statutes at Large of the United States of America*, ed. Richard Peters (Boston: Charles C. Little and James Brown, 1845), 1:4, 8–9.

setts Bay, Rhode Island and Providence Plantations, Connecticut, New York, New Jersey, Pennsylvania, Delaware, Maryland, Virginia, North Carolina, South Carolina, and Georgia.

ARTICLE 1. The style of this confederacy shall be, "THE UNITED STATES OF AMERICA"

ART. 2. Each State retains its sovereignty, freedom, and independence, and every power, jurisdiction, and right, which is not by this confederation, expressly delegated to the United States, in Congress assembled.

ART. 3. The said States hereby severally enter into a firm league of friendship with each other, for their common defence, the security of their liberties, and their mutual and general welfare, binding themselves to assist each other against all force offered to, or attacks made upon them, or any of them, on account of religion, sovereignty, trade, or any other pretence whatever. . . .

ART. 13. Every State shall abide by the determinations of the United States, in Congress assembled, on all questions which by this confederation are submitted to them. And the articles of this confederation shall be inviolably observed by every State, and the Union shall be perpetual; nor shall any alteration at any time hereafter be made in any of them, unless such alteration be agreed to in a Congress of the United States, and be afterwards confirmed by the legislatures of every State.

And whereas it hath pleased the great Governor of the world to incline the hearts of the legislatures we respectively represent in Congress, to approve of, and to authorize us to ratify the said articles of confederation and perpetual union, Know ye, that we, the undersigned delegates, by virtue of the power and authority to us given for that purpose, do, by these presents, in the name and in behalf of our respective constituents, fully and entirely ratify and confirm each and every of the said articles of confederation and perpetual union, and all and singular the matters and things therein contained. And we do further solemnly plight and engage the faith of our respective constituents, that they shall abide by the determi-

nations of the United States, in Congress assembled, on all questions which by the said confederation are submitted to them; and that the articles thereof shall be inviolably observed by the States we respectively represent, and that the Union shall be perpetual. In witness whereof, we have hereunto set our hands, in Congress.

Done at Philadelphia, in the State of Pennsylvania, the 9th day of July, in the year of our Lord 1778, and in the third year of the Independence of America.

Congressional Resolution Recommending the Promotion of Morals (October 1778)

The Continental Congress did not have the power to promote directly religion and morality in the nation at large. However, it had the power to recommend that the states do so, and it utilized this power from time to time as indicated below.

On motion, That Congress come to the following resolutions:

"Whereas true religion and good morals are the only solid foundations of public liberty and happiness:

"*Resolved,* That it be, and it is hereby earnestly recommended to the several states, to take the most effectual measures for the encouragement thereof, and for the suppressing of theatrical entertainments, horse racing, gaming, and such other diversions as are productive of idleness, dissipation, and a general depravity of principles and manners.

Reprinted from *Journals of the Continental Congress: 1774–1789*, ed. Worthington Chauncey Ford (Washington, D.C.: GPO, 1904), 12:1001.

"*Resolved*, That all officers in the army of the United States, be, and hereby are strictly enjoined to see that the good and wholesome rules provided for the discountenancing of prophaneness and vice, and the preservation of morals among the soldiers, are duly and punctually observed."

Congressional Resolution Calling for a Day of Fasting, Humiliation, and Prayer (March 20, 1779)

On March 4, 1779, Congress appointed Gouverneur Morris, William Henry Drayton, and William Paca to a committee to "prepare a recommendation to the several states to set apart a day of fasting humiliation and prayer." The following draft, written in Morris's hand, with additions in John Jay's hand (in brackets), was approved by Congress on March 20, 1779.

The committee appointed to prepare a recommendation to several states to set apart a day of fasting, humiliation, and prayer brought in a draft that was taken into consideration and agreed to as follows.

Whereas, in just punishment of our manifold transgressions, it hath pleased the Supreme Disposer of all events to visit these United States with a ~~destructive~~ calamitous war, through which His divine Providence hath, hitherto, in a wonderful manner, conducted us, so that we might acknowledge that the race is not to the swift, nor the battle to the strong: and whereas, ~~there is but too much Reason to fear that~~ notwithstanding the chastisements received and

Reprinted from *Journals of the Continental Congress: 1774–1789*, ed. Worthington Chauncey Ford (Washington, D.C.: GPO, 1904), 13:343–44.

benefits bestowed, too few have been sufficiently awakened to a sense of their guilt, or warmed ~~our Bosoms~~ with gratitude, or taught to amend their lives and turn from their sins, that so He might turn from His wrath. And whereas, from a consciousness of what we have merited at His hands, and an ~~just~~ apprehension that the malevolence of our disappointed enemies, like the incredulity of Pharaoh, may be used as the scourge of Omnipotence to vindicate his slighted Majesty, there is reason to fear that he may permit much of our land to become the prey of the spoiler, ~~and the Blood of the innocent be poured out that~~ our borders to be ravaged, and our habitations destroyed:

Resolved, That it be recommended to the several states to appoint the first Thursday in May next, to be a day of fasting, ~~Thanksgiving~~ humiliation and prayer to Almighty God, that he will be pleased to avert those impending calamities which we have but too well deserved: that he will grant us his grace to repent of our sins, and amend our lives, according to his holy word: that he will continue that wonderful protection which hath led us through the paths of danger and distress: that he will be a husband to the widow and a father to the fatherless children, who weep over the barbarities of a savage enemy: that he will grant us patience in suffering, and fortitude in adversity: that he will inspire us with humility and moderation, and gratitude in prosperous circumstances: that he will give wisdom to our councils, firmness to our resolutions, and victory to our arms. ~~That he will have Mercy on our Foes, and graciously forgive them, and turn their Hearts from Enmity to Love.~~

That he will bless the labours of the husbandman, and pour forth abundance, so that we may enjoy the fruits of the earth in due season.

[That he will cause union, harmony, and mutual confidence to prevail throughout these states: that he will bestow on our great ally all those blessings which may enable him to be gloriously instrumental in protecting the rights of mankind, and promoting the

PROCLAMATION.

WHEREAS, in juſt Puniſhment of our manifold Tranſgreſſions, it hath pleaſed the Supreme Diſpoſer of all Events to viſit theſe United States with a calamitous War, through which his Divine Providence hath hitherto in a wonderful Manner conducted us, ſo that we might acknowledge that the Race is not to the Swift, nor the Battle to the Strong: AND WHEREAS, notwithſtanding the Chaſtiſements received and Benefits beſtowed, too few have been ſufficiently awakened to a Senſe of their Guilt, or warmed with Gratitude, or taught to amend their Lives and turn from their Sins, that ſo he might turn from his Wrath: AND WHEREAS, from a Conſciouſneſs of what we have merited at his Hands, and an Apprehenſion that the Malevolence of our diſappointed Enemies, like the Incredulity of Pharaoh, may be uſed as the Scourge of Omnipotence to vindicate his ſlighted Majeſty, there is Reaſon to fear that he may permit much of our Land to become the Prey of the Spoiler, our Borders to be ravaged, and our Habitations deſtroyed:

RESOLVED,

THAT it be recommended to the ſeveral States to appoint the Firſt *Thurſday* in *May* next to be a Day of Faſting, Humiliation, and Prayer to Almighty God, that he will be pleaſed to avert thoſe impending Calamities which we have but too well deſerved: That he will grant us his Grace to repent of our Sins, and amend our Lives according to his Holy Word: That he will continue that wonderful Protection which hath led us through the Paths of Danger and Diſtreſs: That he will be a Huſband to the Widow, and a Father to the fatherleſs Children, who weep over the Barbarities of a Savage Enemy: That he will grant us Patience in Suffering, and Fortitude in Adverſity: That he will inſpire us with Humility, Moderation, and Gratitude in proſperous Circumſtances: That he will give Wiſdom to our Councils, Firmneſs to our Reſolutions, and Victory to our Arms: That he will bleſs the Labours of the Huſbandman, and pour forth Abundance, ſo that we may enjoy the Fruits of the Earth in due Seaſon: That he will cauſe Union, Harmony, and mutual Confidence to prevail throughout theſe States: That he will beſtow on our great Ally all thoſe Bleſſings which may enable him to be gloriouſly inſtrumental in protecting the Rights of Mankind, and promoting the Happineſs of his Subjects: That he will bountifully continue his paternal Care to the Commander in Chief, and the Officers and Soldiers of the United States: That he will grant the Bleſſings of Peace to all contending Nations, Freedom to thoſe who are in Bondage, and Comfort to the Afflicted: That he will diffuſe Uſeful Knowledge, extend the Influence of True Religion, and give us that Peace of Mind which the World cannot give: That he will be our Shield in the Day of Battle, our Comforter in the Hour of Death, and our kind Parent and merciful Judge through Time and through Eternity.

Done in CONGRESS, *this Twentieth Day of March, in the Year of Our Lord One Thouſand Seven Hundred and Seventy-Nine, and in the Third Year of our Independence.*

JOHN JAY, Preſident.

Atteſt. CHARLES THOMSON, Secretary.

PHILADELPHIA: PRINTED BY HALL AND SELLERS.

Congressional Fast Day Proclamation, March 20, 1779.
Rare Book and Special Collections Division, Library of Congress.

happiness of his subjects ~~and advancing the Peace and Liberty of Nations. That he will give to both Parties to this Alliance, Grace to perform with Honor and Fidelity their National Engagements~~]. That he will bountifully continue his paternal care to the commander in chief, and the officers and soldiers of the United States: that he will grant the blessings of peace to all contending nations, freedom to those who are in bondage, and comfort to the afflicted: that he will diffuse useful knowledge, extend the influence of true religion, and give us that peace of mind, which the world cannot give: that he will be our shield in the day of battle, our comforter in the hour of death, and our kind parent and merciful judge through time and through eternity.

Done in Congress, this 20th day of March, in the year of our Lord one thousand seven hundred and seventy-nine, and in the third year of our independence.

JOHN JAY, *President*

Attest,   CHARLES THOMSON, *Secretary*

Congressional Resolution Calling for a Day of Thanksgiving and Prayer (October 1780)

A congressional committee composed of Samuel Adams, William Houston, and Frederick Muhlenberg drafted, and Congress approved, the following recommendation shortly after Benedict Arnold's intended treachery was discovered and General Cornwallis abandoned his invasion of North Carolina.

Congress took into consideration the resolution reported for setting apart a day of thanksgiving and prayer, and agreed to the following draught:

Whereas it hath pleased Almighty God, the Father of all mercies, amidst the vicissitudes and calamities of war, to bestow blessings on the people of these states, which call for their devout and thankful acknowledgments, more especially in the late remarkable interposition of his watchful providence, in rescuing the person of our Commander in Chief and the army from imminent dangers, at the moment when treason was ripened for execution; in prospering the labours of the husbandmen, and causing the earth to yield its increase in plentiful harvests; and, above all, in continuing to us the enjoyment of the gospel of peace;

It is therefore recommended to the several states to set apart Thursday, the seventh day [of December next, to be observed as a day of public thanksgiving and prayer; that all the people may assemble on that day to celebrate the praises of our Divine Benefactor; to confess our unworthiness of the least of his favours, and to offer our fervent supplications to the God of all grace; that it may please him to pardon our heinous transgressions and incline our hearts for the future to keep all his laws ~~that it may please him still to afford us the blessing of health~~; to comfort and relieve our brethren who are any wise afflicted or distressed; to smile upon our husbandry and trade ~~and establish the work of our hands~~; to direct our publick councils, and lead our forces, by land and sea, to victory; to take our illustrious ally under his special protection, and favor our joint councils and exertions for the establishment of speedy and permanent peace; to cherish all schools and seminaries of education, ~~build up his churches in their most holy faith~~ and to cause the knowledge of Christianity to spread over all the earth.

Done in Congress, the 18th day of October, 1780, and in the fifth year of the independence of the United States of America.]

Reprinted from *Journals of the Continental Congress: 1774–1789*, ed. Worthington Chauncey Ford (Washington, D.C.: GPO, 1904), 18:950–51. The prayer is in the writing of James Duane except the portion in brackets, which is in the writing of Samuel Adams.

Texts Concerning the National Seal (August 1776 and June 1782)

Following America's declaration of independence, Congress decided that the nation needed an official seal. A committee consisting of Benjamin Franklin, John Adams, and Thomas Jefferson began the process of creating a seal, a process that was completed six years and two committees later. The final version drew from the three committees (especially the work of William Barton [1754–1817] for the third committee) and was assembled by Charles Thomson (1729–1824), secretary to Congress (1774–89) and first American translator of the Bible from Greek to English (1808). He translated the Old Testament from the Greek Septuagint rather than the Hebrew text. The following documents reflect some of the religious imagery that the creators of the seal considered, rejected, and adopted.

Benjamin Franklin's Draft (August 1776)

Moses in the Dress of a High Priest[a] standing on the Shore, and extending his Hand over the Sea, thereby causing the same to overwhelm Pharoah who is sitting in an open Chariot, a Crown on his Head & a[b] Sword in his Hand. Rays from a Pillar of Fire in the Clouds[c] reaching to Moses, expressing to express that he acts by the Command of the Deity

Motto, *Rebellion to Tyrants is Obedience to God.*

Franklin's draft reprinted from Richard S. Patterson and Richardson Dougall, *The Eagle and the Shield: A History of the Great Seal of the United States* (Washington, D.C.: GPO, 1976), 14.

a. The words "in the Dress of a High Priest" are inserted with a caret and deleted.

b. The article "a" is inserted with a caret.

c. The words "in the Clouds" are inserted with a caret.

Thomas Jefferson's Draft (August 1776)

Pharaoh sitting in an open chariot, a crown on his head & a sword in his hand passing thro' the divided waters of the Red sea in pursuit of the Israelites: rays from a pillar of fire in the cloud, expressive of the divine presence, reachi & command, reaching to Moses who stands on the shore &, extending his hand over the sea, causes it to overwhelm Pharaoh. Motto. Rebellion to tyrants is obed^{ce} to god.

Charles Thomson's Report to Congress (June 1782)

On the report of the secretary of the United States in Congress assembled, to whom were referred the several reports on the device for a great seal, to take order:

The device for an armorial atchievement and reverse of the great seal for the United States in Congress assembled, is as follows:

ARMS. Paleways of thirteen pieces, argent and gules; a chief, azure; the escutcheon on the breast of the American bald eagle displayed proper, holding in his dexter talon an olive branch, and in his sinister a bundle of thirteen arrows, all proper, and in his beak a scroll, inscribed with this motto, *"E pluribus Unum."**

For the CREST. Over the head of the eagle, which appears above the escutcheon, a glory, or, breaking through a cloud, proper, and surrounding thirteen stars, forming a constellation, argent, on an azure field.

Jefferson's draft reprinted from ibid., 16.

Thomson's report reprinted from *Journals of the Continental Congress: 1774–1989*, ed. Worthington Chauncey Ford (Washington, D.C.: GPO, 1904), 22:338–40.

* [out of many, one]

THE

HOLY BIBLE,

Containing the OLD and NEW

TESTAMENTS:

Newly translated out of the

ORIGINAL TONGUES;

And with the former

TRANSLATIONS

Diligently compared and revised.

PHILADELPHIA:

PRINTED AND SOLD BY R. AITKEN, AT POPE'S
HEAD, THREE DOORS ABOVE THE COFFEE
HOUSE, IN MARKET STREET.
M.DCC.LXXXII.

Title page of *The Holy Bible, Containing Old and New Testaments:*
Newly Translated out of the Original Tongues, Philadelphia: R. Aitken, 1782.
Rare Book and Special Collections Division, Library of Congress.

REVERSE. A pyramid unfinished. In the zenith, an eye in a triangle, surrounded with a glory proper. Over the eye these words, *"Annuit Coeptis."** On the base of the pyramid the numerical letters MDCCLXXVI. And underneath the following motto, *"Novus Ordo Seclorum."* †

Remarks and explanation:

The escutcheon is composed of the Chief and pale, the two most honorable ordinaries. The pieces, paly, represent the several States all joined in one solid compact entire, supporting a Chief which unites the whole and represents Congress. The motto alludes to this Union. The pales in the Arms are kept closely united by the Chief and the Chief depends on that union, and the strength resulting from it for its support, to denote the Confederacy of the United States of America, and the preservation of their Union through Congress. The colours of the pales are those used in the flag of the United States of America. White signifies purity and innocence. Red hardiness and valour and Blue the colour of the Chief signifies vigilance perseverance and justice. The Olive Branch and arrows denote the power of peace and war which is exclusively vested in Congress. The Constellation denotes a new State taking its place and rank among other sovereign powers. The escutcheon is borne on the breast of an American Eagle without any other supporters, to denote that the United States of America ought to rely on their own virtue.

Reverse: The Pyramid signifies strength and duration. The eye over it and the motto allude to the many signal interpositions of providence in favour of the American cause. The date underneath is that of the Declaration of Independence, and the words under it signify the beginning of the new American Era, which commences from that date.[1]

Aitken's Bible (January 21, 1781, and September 12, 1782)

Before the War of Independence, English Bibles were imported into America from Great Britain. The war curtailed this trade, leading to a severe shortage of Bibles. In 1777, a group of pastors petitioned Congress to address this problem. A congressional committee recommended the importation of twenty thousand Bibles, but provided no funds to do so. In 1781, Robert Aitken (1734–1802), a Presbyterian elder and congressional printer, asked Congress to authorize him to publish the first American edition of the Holy Scriptures in the English language. Congress provided the following endorsement, but no subsidy. The Pennsylvania legislature, however, offered Aitken a one-hundred-fifty-pound, interest-free loan to complete his work, and ten thousand copies of his Bible were printed with the congressional endorsement.

Aitken's Petition (January 21, 1781)

To the Honourable The Congress of the United States of America
The Memorial of Robert Aitken of the City of Philadelphia, Printer
Humbly Sheweth
That in every well regulated Government in Christendom The Sacred Books of the Old and New Testament, commonly called the Holy Bible, are printed and published under the Authority of the Sovereign

---

* "He favors (or has favored) our undertaking." This may have been derived from Virgil's *Aeneid,* Book IX, line 625: *Iuppiter omnipotens, audacibus adnue coeptis,* or "Almighty Jupiter, favor my bold undertaking."—Trans.

† [New Order of the Ages (or Centuries)]

1. This report, in the writing of Charles Thomson, is in the *Papers of the Continental Congress,* No. 23, folio 113. It was adapted from a report by William Barton which was, in its turn, an "improvement on the Secretary's device," as the indorsement states. It is on folio 131. The Secretary's device is on folio 179, the drawing accompanying it being on folio 180. The first device offered by Barton is on folio 137. His second was approved by the committee, reported to Congress May 9, 1782, and referred to the Secretary of Congress to take order June 13, as the indorsement shows. It is on folio 181, the drawing accompanying it, and the indorsement, being on folio 117.

Papers of Continental Congress, item no. 41, I, folio 63.

South-Carolina.	Mr. Rutledge	no	
	Mr. Ramfay	no	
	Mr. Izard	no	no
	Mr. Gervais	no	
	Mr. Middleton	no	
Georgia,	Mr. Jones	ay	ay
	Mr. Few	ay	

So it paffed in the negative.

The queftion being taken on the refpective quotas of the feveral ftates was agreed to, and the report of the grand committee confirmed.

T H U R S D A Y, September 12, 1782.

Whereas James Innes, efquire, who was on the 9th day of July laft elected to the office of judge advocate, has not fignified his acceptance, and it being intimated to Congrefs that he declines to accept the office :

Refolved, That Wednefday next be affigned for electing a judge advocate.

The committee, confifting of Mr. Duane, Mr. M'Kean and Mr. Witherfpoon, to whom was referred a memorial of Robert Aitkin, printer, dated January 21ft, 1781, refpecting an edition of the holy fcriptures, report,

"That Mr. Aitkin has at a great expence now finifhed an American edition of the holy fcriptures in Englifh ; that the committee have from time to time attended to his progrefs in the work ; that they alfo recommended it to the two chaplains of Congrefs to examine and give their opinion of the execution, who have accordingly reported thereon.

The recommendation and report being as follows :

"Philadelphia, September 1ft, 1782.

Reverend gentlemen,

Our knowledge of your piety and public fpirit leads us without apology to recommend to your particular attention the edition of the holy fcriptures publifhing by Mr. Aitkin. He undertook this expenfive work at a time, when from the circumftances of the war an Englifh edition of the bible could not be imported, nor any opinion formed how long the obftruction might continue. On this account particularly he deferves applaufe and encouragement. We therefore wifh you, reverend gentlemen, to examine the execution of the work, and if approved to

give

Congressional Resolution, September 12, 1782, Endorsing Robert Aitken's Bible, Philadelphia: David C. Claypoole, 1782, from the *Journals of Congress*.
Rare Book and Special Collections Division, Library of Congress.

give it the fanction of your judgment and the weight of your recommendation. We are, with very great refpect, your moft obedient humble fervants,

    (Signed.)   JAMES DUANE, chairman, in behalf of a committee of Congrefs on Mr. Aitkin's memorial.

Reverend doctor White and reverend
  Mr. Duffield, chaplains of the United States in Congrefs affembled."

Report.

" Gentlemen,

Agreeably to your defire we have paid attention to Mr. Robert Aitkin's impreffion of the holy fcriptures of the old and new teftament. Having felected and examined a variety of paffages throughout the work, we are of opinion that it is executed with great accuracy as to the fenfe, and with as few grammatical and typographical errors as could be expected in an undertaking of fuch magnitude. Being ourfelves witneffes of the demand for this invaluable book, we rejoice in the prefent profpect of a fupply, hoping that it will prove as advantageous as it is honourable to the gentleman, who has exerted himfelf to furnifh it at the evident rifque of private fortune. We are, gentlemen, your very refpectful and humble fervants,

    (Signed.)   William White,
                    George Duffield.

Honourable James Duane, efquire,
  chairman, and the other honourable gentlemen of the committee of Congrefs on Mr. Aitkin's memorial.
  Philadelphia, September 10, 1782."
  Whereupon,

Refolved, That the United States in Congrefs affembled highly approve the pious and laudable undertaking of Mr. Aitkin, as fubfervient to the intereft of religion as well as an inftance of the progrefs of arts in this country, and being fatisfied from the above report, of his care and accuracy in the execution of the work, they recommend this edition of the bible to the inhabitants of the United States, and hereby authorife him to publifh this recommendation in the manner he fhall think proper.

                        FRIDAY,

Powers, in order to prevent the fatal confusion that would arise, and the alarming Injuries the Christian Faith might suffer from the spurious and erroneous Editions of Divine Revelation. That your Memorialist has no doubt but this work is an Object worthy the attention of the Congress of the United States of America, who will not neglect spiritual security, while they are virtuously contending for temporal blessings. Under this persuasion your Memorialist begs leave to inform your Honours that he both begun and made considerable progress in a neat Edition of the Holy Scriptures for the use of schools, But being cautious of suffering his copy of the Bible to Issue forth without the sanction of Congress, Humbly prays that your Honours would take this important matter into serious consideration & would be pleased to appoint one Member or Members of your Honourable Body to inspect his work so that the same may be published under the Authority of Congress. And further, your Memorialist prays, that he may be Commissioned or otherwise appointed & Authorized to print and vend Editions of, the Sacred Scriptures, in such manner and form as may best suit the wants and demands of the good people of these States, provided the same be in all things perfectly consonant to the Scriptures as heretofore Established and received amongst us.

And as in Duty bound your Memorialist shall ever pray.

Robt Aitken

Congressional Endorsement of Aitken's Bible (September 12, 1782)

The committee, consisting of Mr. [James] Duane, Mr. [Thomas] McKean and Mr. [John] Wither-

Reprinted from *Journals of the Continental Congress: 1774–1789*, ed. Worthington Chauncey Ford (Washington, D.C.: GPO, 1904), 23:572–74.

spoon, to whom was referred a ~~petition~~ memorial of Robert Aitken, printer, dated 21 January, 1781, respecting an edition of the holy scriptures, report,

That Mr. Aitken has at a great expence now finished an American edition of the holy scriptures in English; that the committee have, from time to time, ~~conferred with him~~ attended to his progress in the work: that they also recommended it to the two chaplains of Congress to examine and give their opinion of the execution, who have accordingly reported thereon:

The recommendation and report being as follows:

PHILADELPHIA, *1 September, 1782*
Rev. Gentlemen, Our knowledge of your piety and public spirit leads us without apology to recommend to your particular attention the edition of the holy scriptures publishing by Mr. Aitken. He undertook this expensive work at a time, when from the circumstances of the war, an English edition of the Bible could not be imported, nor any opinion formed how long the obstruction might continue. On this account particularly he deserves applause and encouragement. We therefore wish you, reverend gentlemen, to examine the execution of the work, and if approved, to give it the sanction of your judgment and the weight of your recommendation. We are with very great respect, your most obedient humble servants,

(Signed)   JAMES DUANE, *Chairman,*
In behalf of a committee of Congress on Mr. Aitken's memorial.
Rev. Dr. White and Rev. Mr. Duffield, chaplains of the United States in Congress assembled.

REPORT

Gentlemen, Agreeably to your desire, we have paid attention to Mr. Robert Aitken's impression of the holy scriptures, of the old and new testament. Having selected and examined a variety of passages throughout the work, we are of opinion, that it is executed with great accuracy as to the sense, and with as few grammatical and typographical errors as could be expected in an undertaking of such magnitude. Being ourselves witnesses of the demand for this invaluable book, we rejoice in the present prospect of a supply, hoping that it will prove as advantageous as it is honorable to the gentleman, who has exerted himself to furnish it at the evident risk of private fortune. We are, gentlemen, your very respectful and humble servants,

(Signed)   WILLIAM WHITE,
GEORGE DUFFIELD.

PHILADELPHIA, September 10, 1782.
Hon. James Duane, esq. chairman, and the other hon. gentlemen of the committee of Congress on Mr. Aitken's memorial.

Whereupon, Resolved, That the United States in Congress assembled, highly approve the pious and laudable undertaking of Mr. Aitken, as subservient to the interest of religion as well as an instance of the progress of arts in this country, and being satisfied from the above report, of his care and accuracy in the execution of the work, they recommend this edition of the Bible to the inhabitants of the United States, and hereby authorise him to publish this recommendation in the manner he shall think proper.

Congressional Resolution Calling for a Day of Thanksgiving (October 18, 1783)

On September 3, 1783, representatives from the United States and Great Britain signed the Treaty of Paris, which marked the end of the War of American Independence and the beginning of British recognition of American independence. The next month, Congress issued the following "proclamation for a day of thanksgiving." The proclamation was drafted by a committee consisting of James Duane, Samuel Huntington, and Samuel Holten.

By the United States in Congress assembled

A PROCLAMATION

Whereas it hath pleased the Supreme Ruler of all human events, to dispose the hearts of the late belligerent powers to put a period to the effusion of human blood, by proclaiming a cessation of all hostilities by sea and land, and these United States are not only happily rescued from the dangers ~~distresses~~ and calamities ~~which they have so long and so magnanimously sustained~~ to which they have been so long exposed, but their freedom, sovereignty and independence ultimately acknowledged ~~by the king of Great Britain~~. And whereas in the progress of a contest on which the most essential rights of human nature depended, the interposition of Divine Providence in our favour hath been most abundantly and most graciously manifested, and the citizens of these United States have every ~~possible~~ reason for praise and gratitude to the God of their salvation. Impressed, therefore, with an exalted sense of ~~the magnitude of~~ the blessings by which we are surrounded, and of our entire dependence on that Almighty Being, from whose goodness and bounty they are derived, the United States in Congress assembled do recommend it to the several States, to set apart the second Thursday in December next, as a day of public thanksgiving, that all the people may then assemble to celebrate with ~~one voice~~ grateful hearts and united voices, the praises of their Supreme and all bountiful Benefactor, for his numberless favors and mercies. That he hath been pleased to conduct us in safety through all the perils and vicissitudes of the war; that he hath given us unanimity and resolution to adhere to our just rights; that he hath raised up a powerful ally to assist us in supporting them, and hath so far crowned our united efforts with success, that in the course of the present year, hostilities have ceased, and we are left in

Reprinted from *Journals of the Continental Congress: 1774–1789*, ed. Worthington Chauncey Ford (Washington, D.C.: GPO, 1904), 25:699–701.

the undisputed possession of our liberties and independence, and of the fruits of our own land, and in the free participation of the treasures of the sea; that he hath prospered the labour of our husbandmen with plentiful harvests; and above all, that he hath been pleased to continue to us the light of the blessed gospel, and secured to us in the fullest extent the rights of conscience in faith and worship. And while our hearts overflow with gratitude, and our lips set forth the praises of our great Creator, that we also offer up fervent supplications, that it may please him to pardon all our offences, to give wisdom and unanimity to our public councils, to cement all our citizens in the bonds of affection, and to inspire them with an earnest regard for the national honor and interest, to enable them to improve the days of prosperity by every good work, and to be lovers of peace and tranquillity; that he may be pleased to bless us in our husbandry, our commerce and navigation; to smile upon our seminaries and means of education, to cause pure religion and virtue to flourish, to give peace to all nations, and to fill the world with his glory.

Done by the United States in Congress assembled, witness his Excellency ELIAS BOUDINOT, our President, this 18th day of October, in the year of our Lord one thousand seven hundred and eighty-three, and of the sovereignty and independence of the United States of America the eighth.

An Ordinance for the Government of the Territory of the United States, North-West of the River Ohio [Northwest Ordinance] (July 1787)

Congress passed the following ordinance to create a government for American territories between the Ohio and Mississippi rivers. It also provided for the formation of new states within this region. The ordinance contains several passages related to religion, which are excerpted below.

And for extending the fundamental principles of civil and religious liberty, which form the basis whereon these republics, their laws and constitutions are erected; to fix and establish those principles as the basis of all laws, constitutions and governments, which forever hereafter shall be formed in the said territory; to provide also for the establishment of States and permanent government therein, and for their admission to a share in the federal Councils on an equal footing with the original States, at as early periods as may be consistent with the general interest,

It is hereby Ordained and declared by the authority aforesaid, That the following Articles shall be considered as Articles of compact between the Original States and the people and States in the said territory, and forever remain unalterable, unless by common consent, *to wit,*

Article the First. No person demeaning himself in a peaceable and orderly manner shall ever be molested on account of his mode of worship or religious sentiments in the said territory. . . .

Excerpts reprinted from *Journals of the Continental Congress: 1774–1789,* ed. Worthington Chauncey Ford (Washington, D.C.: GPO, 1904), 32:339–41.

An ORDINANCE for the GOVERNMENT of the TERRITORY of the UNITED STATES, North-West of the RIVER OHIO.

BE IT ORDAINED by the United States in Congress assembled, That the said territory, for the purposes of temporary government, be one district, subject, however, to be divided into two districts, as future circumstances may, in the opinion of Congress, make it expedient.

Be it ordained by the authority aforesaid, That the estates both of resident and non-resident proprietors in the said territory, dying intestate, shall descend to, and be distributed among their children, and the descendants of a deceased child in equal parts; the descendants of a deceased child or grand-child, to take the share of their deceased parent in equal parts among them: And where there shall be no children or descendants, then in equal parts to the next of kin, in equal degree; and among collaterals, the children of a deceased brother or sister of the intestate, shall have in equal parts among them their deceased parents share; and there shall in no case be a distinction between kindred of the whole and half blood; saving in all cases to the widow of the intestate, her third part of the real estate for life, and one third part of the personal estate; and this law relative to descents and dower, shall remain in full force until altered by the legislature of the district. ———— And until the governor and judges shall adopt laws as herein after mentioned, estates in the said territory may be devised or bequeathed by wills in writing, signed and sealed by him or her, in whom the estate may be, (being of full age) and attested by three witnesses; —and real estates may be conveyed by lease and release, or bargain and sale, signed, sealed, and delivered by the person being of full age, in whom the estate may be, and attested by two witnesses, provided such wills be duly proved, and such conveyances be acknowledged, or the execution thereof duly proved, and be recorded within one year after proper magistrates, courts, and registers shall be appointed for that purpose; and personal property may be transferred by delivery, saving, however, to the French and Canadian inhabitants, and other settlers of the Kaskaskies, Saint Vincent's, and the neighbouring villages, who have heretofore professed themselves citizens of Virginia, their laws and customs now in force among them, relative to the descent and conveyance of property.

Be it ordained by the authority aforesaid, That there shall be appointed from time to time, by Congress, a governor, whose commission shall continue in force for the term of three years, unless sooner revoked by Congress; he shall reside in the district, and have a freehold estate therein, in one thousand acres of land, while in the exercise of his office.

There shall be appointed from time to time, by Congress, a secretary, whose commission shall continue in force for four years, unless sooner revoked, he shall reside in the district, and have a freehold estate therein, in five hundred acres of land, while in the exercise of his office; it shall be his duty to keep and preserve the acts and laws passed by the legislature, and the public records of the district, and the proceedings of the governor in his executive department; and transmit authentic copies of such acts and proceedings, every six months, to the secretary of Congress: There shall also be appointed a court to consist of three judges, any two of whom to form a court, who shall have a common law jurisdiction, and reside in the district, and have each therein a freehold estate in five hundred acres of land, while in the exercise of their offices; and their commissions shall continue in force during good behaviour.

The governor and judges, or a majority of them, shall adopt and publish in the district, such laws of the original states, criminal and civil, as may be necessary, and best suited to the circumstances of the district, and report them to Congress, from time to time, which laws shall be in force in the district until the organization of the general assembly therein, unless disapproved of by Congress; but afterwards the legislature shall have authority to alter them as they shall think fit.

The governor for the time being, shall be commander in chief of the militia, appoint and commission all officers in the same, below the rank of general officers; all general officers shall be appointed and commissioned by Congress.

Previous to the organization of the general assembly, the governor shall appoint such magistrates and other civil officers, in each county or township, as he shall find necessary for the preservation of the peace and good order in the same: After the general assembly shall be organized, the powers and duties of magistrates and other civil officers shall be regulated and defined by the said assembly; but all magistrates and other civil officers, not herein otherwise directed, shall, during the continuance of this temporary government, be appointed by the governor.

For the prevention of crimes and injuries, the laws to be adopted or made shall have force in all parts of the district, and for the execution of process, criminal and civil, the governor shall make proper divisions thereof—and he shall proceed from time to time, as circumstances may require, to lay out the parts of the district in which the Indian titles shall have been extinguished, into counties and townships, subject, however, to such alterations as may thereafter be made by the legislature.

So soon as there shall be five thousand free male inhabitants, of full age, in the district, upon giving proof thereof to the governor, they shall receive authority, with time and place, to elect representatives from their counties or townships, to represent them in the general assembly; provided that for every five hundred free male inhabitants there shall be one representative, and so on progressively with the number of free male inhabitants, shall the right of representation increase, until the number of representatives shall amount to twenty-five, after which the number and proportion of representatives shall be regulated by the legislature: provided that no person be eligible or qualified to act as a representative, unless he shall have been a citizen of one of the United States three years and be a resident in the district, or unless he shall have resided in the district three years, and in either case shall likewise hold in his own right, in fee simple, two hundred acres of land within the same:—Provided also, that a freehold in fifty acres of land in the district, having been a citizen of one of the states, and being resident in the district; or the like freehold and two years residence in the district shall be necessary to qualify a man as an elector of a representative.

The representatives thus elected, shall serve for the term of two years, and in case of the death of a representative, or removal from office, the governor shall issue a writ to the county or township for which he was a member, to elect another in his stead, to serve for the residue of the term.

The general assembly, or legislature, shall consist of the governor, legislative council, and a house of representatives. The legislative council shall consist of five members, to continue in office five years, unless sooner removed by Congress, any three of whom to be a quorum, and the members of the council shall be nominated and appointed in the following manner, to wit: As soon as representatives shall be elected, the governor shall appoint a time and place for them to meet together, and, when met, they shall nominate ten persons, residents in the district, and each possessed of a freehold in five hundred acres of land, and return their names to Congress; five of whom Congress shall appoint and commission to serve as aforesaid; and whenever a vacancy shall happen in the council, by death or removal from office, the house of representatives shall nominate two persons, qualified as aforesaid, for each vacancy, and return their names to Congress; one of whom Congress shall appoint and commission for the residue of the term; and every five years, four months at least before the expiration of the time of service of the members of council, the said house shall nominate ten persons, qualified as aforesaid, and return their names to Congress, five of whom Congress shall appoint and commission to serve as members of the council five years, unless sooner removed. And the governor, legislative council, and house of re-

Northwest Ordinance, July 1787. Rare Book and Special Collections Division, Library of Congress.

Article the Third. Religion, Morality <u>and knowledge being necessary to good government and the happiness of mankind,</u> Schools and the means of education shall forever be encouraged. The utmost good faith shall always be observed towards the Indians, their lands and property shall never be taken from them without their consent; and in their property, rights and liberty, they never shall be invaded or disturbed, unless in just and lawful wars authorised by Congress; but laws founded in justice and humanity shall from time to time be made, for preventing wrongs being done to them, and for preserving peace and friendship with them.

RECOMMENDATIONS FOR FURTHER READING

Davis, Derek H. *Religion and the Continental Congress, 1774–1789: Contributions to Original Intent.* New York: Oxford University Press, 2000.

Humphrey, Edward Frank. *Nationalism and Religion in America, 1774–1789.* Boston: Chipman Law Publishing Co., 1924.

Withington, Ann Fairfax. *Toward a More Perfect Union: Virtue and the Formation of American Republics.* New York: Oxford University Press, 1991.

CHAPTER FIVE

State Constitutions, Laws, and Papers on Church and State in Revolutionary America

ON MAY 10, 1776, the Continental Congress approved a resolution recommending "to the respective assemblies and conventions of the United Colonies, where no government sufficient to the exigencies of their affairs have been hitherto established, to adopt such government as shall, in the opinion of the representatives of the people, best conduce to the happiness and safety of their constituents in particular, and America in general."[1] Most of the newly independent states followed this advice, writing new constitutions and, over the next decade, significantly revising their statutory laws to reflect the republican principles of the Revolution. The exact content of these principles, and the way in which they should be reflected by constitutional or statutory law, was the subject of much debate. This was particularly true with respect to religious liberty and religious establishments.

Church-state contests in the Revolutionary Era are sometimes described as a struggle between intolerant Christians, represented by John Adams and the Massachusetts Constitution of 1780 and Patrick Henry and "A Bill Establishing a Provision for Teachers of the Christian Religion" on the one side, and Enlightenment Deists, represented by Thomas Jefferson and his "A Bill for Establishing Religious Freedom" and James Madison and his "Memorial and Remonstrance" on the other. Telling the tale in this way, however, obscures more than it illuminates. Notably, it suggests that advocates of state support for religion were far more intolerant than they tended to be, and that opponents of establishment were hostile toward religion, in general, or any state support of religion, more specifically.

Virtually all Americans in the Revolutionary Era agreed with George Washington's view that of "all the dispositions and habits which lead to political prosperity, Religion and morality are indispensable supports."[2] Moreover, most believed that morality depended on religion—and by religion they almost uniformly meant Christianity. The central question with respect to issues such as whether a civil state should have an established faith, or how that faith should be supported, was how best to promote a vibrant religious culture that would influence public life. By the last quarter of the eighteenth century, proponents of establishment argued increasingly that clergy from different denominations should be supported by the civil state, and that law-abiding religious dissenters should be tolerated. On the other hand, opponents of establishments tended to reject them on religious grounds, and even those who may

---

1. Chauncy Ford, ed., *Journals of the Continental Congress* (Washington, D.C.: Government Printing Office, 1906), 4:342.

2. George Washington, "Farewell Address," 1796 (see p. 468, below).

have been more influenced by Enlightenment rationalism framed their arguments in religious language. Moreover, many opponents of formal establishments did not oppose all government aid to or support of religion.

The following excerpts from constitutions, laws, and state papers reflect different approaches to religious liberty and the proper relationship between church and state. Virginia is overrepresented in this and the following chapter because Virginia's debates over disestablishment have greatly influenced subsequent historians and jurists.

Virginia Declaration of Rights, Articles XV and XVI (1776)

George Mason (1725–92), an important leader of the American Revolution and, later, opponent of the U.S. Constitution, was the chief architect of Virginia's 1776 Declaration of Rights. This document exercised enormous influence on later bills of rights. The draft and final versions of articles most concerned with religion and morality are reprinted below. One significant change was the removal of the word "toleration" from Mason's draft of what became Article XVI, which was done at the insistence of James Madison, who believed it dangerously implied that religious liberty was a grant from the civil state that could be revoked at will rather than a natural right.

Mason's Draft (May 1776)

That no free Government, or the Blessings of Liberty, can be preserved to any People, but by a firm adherence to Justice, Moderation, Temperance, Frugality, and Virtue and by frequent Recurrence to fundamental Principles.

That as Religion, or the Duty which we owe to our divine and omnipotent Creator, and the Manner of discharging it, can be governed only by Reason and Conviction, not by Force or Violence; and therefore that all Men shou'd enjoy the fullest Toleration in the Exercise of Religion, according to the Dictates of Conscience, unpunished and unrestrained by the Magistrate, unless, under Colour of Religion, any Man disturb the Peace, the Happiness, or Safety of Society, or of Individuals. And that it is the mutual

Mason's draft reprinted from *The Papers of George Mason, 1727–1792*, ed. Robert A. Rutland and published in three volumes for the Omohundro Institute of Early American History and Culture (Chapel Hill: University of North Carolina Press, 1971), 1:278. © 1971 by the University of North Carolina Press. Used by permission of the publisher.

Duty of all, to practice Christian Forbearance, Love and Charity towards Each other.

Final Version (June 12, 1776)

SEC. 15. That no free government, or the blessings of liberty, can be preserved to any people, but by a firm adherence to justice, moderation, temperance, frugality, and virtue, and by frequent recurrence to fundamental principles.

SEC. 16. That religion, or the duty which we owe to our Creator, and the manner of discharging it, can be directed only by reason and conviction, not by force or violence; and therefore all men are equally entitled to the free exercise of religion, according to the dictates of conscience; and that it is the mutual duty of all to practise Christian forbearance, love, and charity towards each other.

Final version reprinted from *The Federal and State Constitutions, Colonial Charters, and Other Organic Laws of the States, Territories, and Colonies*, comp. and ed. Francis Newton Thorpe (Washington, D.C.: GPO, 1909), 7:3814.

Pennsylvania Constitutions, 1776 and 1790

Pennsylvania never had an established church, and it often provided greater protection for religious liberty than other colonies. As well, its constitution of 1776 was the most democratic of all the Revolutionary Era constitutions. Even in Pennsylvania, however, religious liberty was not absolute. The following excerpts from the Pennsylvania constitutions of 1776 and 1790 illustrate the state's approach to religious liberty.

Pennsylvania Constitution of 1776

A Declaration of the Rights of the Inhabitants of the Commonwealth, or State of Pennsylvania

I. That all men are born equally free and independent, and have certain natural, inherent and inalienable rights, amongst which are, the enjoying and defending life and liberty, acquiring, possessing and protecting property, and pursuing and obtaining happiness and safety.

II. That all men have a natural and unalienable right to worship Almighty God according to the dictates of their own consciences and understanding: And that no man ought or of right can be compelled to attend any religious worship, or erect or support any place of worship, or maintain any ministry, contrary to, or against, his own free will and consent: Nor can any man, who acknowledges the being of a God, be justly deprived or abridged of any civil right as a citizen, on account of his religious sentiments or peculiar mode of religious worship: And that no authority can or ought to be vested in, or assumed by any power whatever, that shall in any case interfere with, or in any manner controul, the right of conscience in the free exercise of religious worship. . . .

VIII. That every member of society hath a right to be protected in the enjoyment of life, liberty and property, and therefore is bound to contribute his proportion towards the expence of that protection, and yield his personal service when necessary, or an equivalent thereto: But no part of a man's property can be justly taken from him, or applied to public uses, without his own consent, or that of his legal representatives: Nor can any man who is conscientiously scrupulous of bearing arms, be justly compelled thereto, if he will pay such equivalent, nor are the people bound by any laws, but such as they have in like manner assented to, for their common good. . . .

Excerpts reprinted from *The Federal and State Constitutions, Colonial Charters, and Other Organic Laws of the States, Territories, and Colonies,* comp. and ed. Francis Newton Thorpe (Washington, D.C.: GPO, 1909), 5:3082–85, 3091.

Plan or Frame of Government for the Commonwealth or State of Pennsylvania

SECT. 10. A quorum of the house of representatives shall consist of two-thirds of the whole number of members elected; and having met and chosen their speaker, shall each of them before they proceed to business take and subscribe, as well the oath or affirmation of fidelity and allegiance hereinafter directed, as the following oath or affirmation, viz:

I——— do swear (or affirm) that as a member of this assembly, I will not propose or assent to any bill, vote, or resolution, which shall appear to me injurious to the people; nor do or consent to any act or thing whatever, that shall have a tendency to lessen or abridge their rights and privileges, as declared in the constitution of this state; but will in all things conduct myself as a faithful honest representative and guardian of the people, according to the best of my judgment and abilities.

And each member, before he takes his seat, shall make and subscribe the following declaration, viz:

I do believe in one God, the creator and governor of the universe, the rewarder of the good and the punisher of the wicked. And I do acknowledge the Scriptures of the Old and New Testament to be given by Divine inspiration.

And no further or other religious test shall ever hereafter be required of any civil officer or magistrate in this State. . . .

SECT. 45. Laws for the encouragement of virtue, and prevention of vice and immorality, shall be made and constantly kept in force, and provision shall be made for their due execution: And all religious societies or bodies of men heretofore united or incorporated for the advancement of religion or learning, or for other pious and charitable purposes, shall be encouraged and protected in the enjoyment of the privileges, immunities and estates which they were accustomed to enjoy, or could of right have enjoyed, under the laws and former constitution of this state.

Pennsylvania Constitution of 1790

Article VII

SECTION 1. The legislature shall, as soon as conveniently may be, provide, by law, for the establishment of schools throughout the State, in such manner that the poor may be taught gratis.

SEC. 2. The arts and sciences shall be promoted in one or more seminaries of learning.

SEC. 3. The rights, privileges, immunities, and estates of religious societies and corporate bodies shall remain as if the constitution of this State had not been altered or amended.

Article VIII

Members of the general assembly, and all officers, executive and judicial, shall be bound, by oath or affirmation, to support the constitution of this commonwealth, and to perform the duties of their respective offices with fidelity.

Article IX

That the general, great, and essential principles of liberty and free government may be recognized and unalterably established, we declare—

SECTION 1. That all men are born equally free and independent, and have certain inherent and indefeasible rights, among which are those of enjoying and defending life and liberty, of acquiring, possessing, and protecting property and reputation, and of pursuing their own happiness.

SEC. 2. That all power is inherent in the people, and all free governments are founded on their authority and instituted for their peace, safety, and happiness. For the advancement of those ends, they have at all times an unalienable and indefeasible right to alter, reform, or abolish their government, in such manner as they may think proper.

SEC. 3. That all men have a natural and indefeasible right to worship Almighty God according to the dictates of their own consciences; that no man can of right be compelled to attend, erect, or support any place of worship, or to maintain any ministry, against his consent; that no human authority can, in any case whatever, control or interfere with the rights of conscience; and that no preference shall ever be given, by law, to any religious establishments or modes of worship.

SEC. 4. That no person, who acknowledges the being of a God and a future state of rewards and punishments, shall, on account of his religious sentiments, be disqualified to hold any office or place of trust or profit under this commonwealth.

South Carolina Constitution of 1778

South Carolina's constitution of 1778 set forth a system for the support of Protestant Christianity.

Article XXI

And whereas the ministers of the gospel are by their profession dedicated to the service of God and the cure of souls, and ought not to be diverted from the great duties of their function, therefore no minister of the gospel or public preacher of any religious persuasion, while he continues in the exercise of his pastoral function, and for two years after, shall be el-

Excerpts reprinted from *The Federal and State Constitutions, Colonial Charters, and Other Organic Laws of the States, Territories, and Colonies,* comp. and ed. Francis Newton Thorpe (Washington, D.C.: GPO, 1909), 5:3099–3100.

Articles XXI and XXXVIII reprinted from *The Federal and State Constitutions, Colonial Charters, and Other Organic Laws of the States, Territories, and Colonies,* comp. and ed. Francis Newton Thorpe (Washington, D.C.: GPO, 1909), 6:3253, 3255–57.

igible either as governor, lieutenant-governor, a member of the senate, house of representatives, or privy council in this State. . . .

Article XXXVIII

That all persons and religious societies who acknowledge that there is one God, and a future state of rewards and punishments, and that God is publicly to be worshipped, shall be freely tolerated. The Christian Protestant religion shall be deemed, and is hereby constituted and declared to be, the established religion of this State. That all denominations of Christian Protestants in this State, demeaning themselves peaceably and faithfully, shall enjoy equal religious and civil privileges. To accomplish this desirable purpose without injury to the religious property of those societies of Christians which are by law already incorporated for the purpose of religious worship, and to put it fully into the power of every other society of Christian Protestants, either already formed or hereafter to be formed, to obtain the like incorporation, it is hereby constituted, appointed, and declared that the respective societies of the Church of England that are already formed in this State for the purpose of religious worship shall still continue incorporate and hold the religious property now in their possession. And that whenever fifteen or more male persons, not under twenty-one years of age, professing the Christian Protestant religion, and agreeing to unite themselves in a society for the purposes of religious worship, they shall, (on complying with the terms hereinafter mentioned,) be, and be constituted a church, and be esteemed and regarded in law as of the established religion of the State, and on a petition to the legislature shall be entitled to be incorporated and to enjoy equal privileges. That every society of Christians so formed shall give themselves a name or denomination by which they shall be called and known in law, and all that associate with them for the purposes of worship shall be esteemed as belonging to the society so called. But that previous to the establishment and incorporation of the respective societies of every denomination as aforesaid, and in order to entitle them thereto, each society so petitioning shall have agreed to and subscribed in a book the following five articles, without which no agreement or union of men upon pretence of religion shall entitle them to be incorporated and esteemed as a church of the established religion of this State:

1st. That there is one eternal God, and a future state of rewards and punishments.

2d. That God is publicly to be worshipped.

3d. That the Christian religion is the true religion.

4th. That the holy scriptures of the Old and New Testaments are of divine inspiration, and are the rule of faith and practice.

5th. That it is lawful and the duty of every man being thereunto called by those that govern, to bear witness to the truth.

And that every inhabitant of this State, when called to make an appeal to God as a witness to truth, shall be permitted to do it in that way which is most agreeable to the dictates of his own conscience. And that the people of this State may forever enjoy the right of electing their own pastors or clergy, and at the same time that the State may have sufficient security for the due discharge of the pastoral office, by those who shall be admitted to be clergymen, no person shall officiate as minister of any established church who shall not have been chosen by a majority of the society to which he shall minister, or by persons appointed by the said majority, to choose and procure a minister for them; nor until the minister so chosen and appointed shall have made and subscribed to the following declaration, over and above the aforesaid five articles, viz: "That he is determined by God's grace out of the holy scriptures, to instruct the people committed to his charge, and to teach nothing as required of necessity to eternal salvation but that which he shall be persuaded may be concluded and proved from the scripture; that he will use both public and private admonitions, as well to the sick as to the whole within his cure, as need shall require and occasion shall be given, and that he will be diligent in prayers, and in reading of the same; that he will be diligent to frame and fashion his own self and his family according to the doctrine of Christ, and to make both himself and them, as much as in him lieth, wholesome examples and patterns to the flock of Christ; that he will maintain and set forwards, as much as he can, quietness, peace, and love among all people, and especially among those that are or shall be committed to his charge. No person shall disturb or molest any religious assembly; nor shall use any reproachful, reviling, or abusive language against any church, that being the certain way of disturbing the peace, and of hindering the conversion of any to the truth, by engaging them in quarrels and animosities, to the hatred of the professors, and that profession which otherwise they might be brought to assent to. No person whatsoever shall speak anything in their religious assembly irreverently or seditiously of the government of this State. No person shall, by law, be obliged to pay towards the maintenance and support of a religious worship that he does not freely join in, or has not voluntarily engaged to support. But the churches, chapels, parsonages, glebes, and all other property now belonging to any societies of the Church of England, or any other religious societies, shall remain and be secured to them forever. The poor shall be supported, and elections managed in the accustomed manner, until laws shall be provided to adjust those matters in the most equitable way.

Massachusetts Constitution (1780)

The Massachusetts Constitution of 1780 was drafted in large part by John Adams (1735–1826), debated by the state constitutional convention of 1779–80, and ratified by voters in the state in 1780. The constitution remains in effect today, although articles involving religion have been annulled or significantly amended.

Preamble

The end of the institution, maintenance, and administration of government, is to secure the existence of the body politic, to protect it, and to furnish the individuals who compose it with the power of enjoying in safety and tranquillity their natural rights, and the blessings of life: and whenever these great objects are not obtained, the people have a right to alter the government, and to take measures necessary for their safety, prosperity, and happiness.

The body politic is formed by a voluntary association of individuals: it is a social compact, by which the whole people covenants with each citizen, and each citizen with the whole people, that all shall be governed by certain laws for the common good. It is the duty of the people, therefore, in framing a constitution of government, to provide for an equitable mode of making laws, as well as for an impartial interpretation and a faithful execution of them; that every man may, at all times, find his security in them.

We, therefore, the people of Massachusetts, acknowledging, with grateful hearts, the goodness of the great Legislator of the universe, in affording us, in the course of His providence, an opportunity, deliberately and peaceably, without fraud, violence, or surprise, of entering into an original, explicit, and solemn compact with each other; and of forming a new constitution of civil government, for ourselves and posterity; and devoutly imploring His direction in so interesting a design, do agree upon, ordain, and establish, the following *Declaration of Rights, and Frame of Government,* as the CONSTITUTION OF THE COMMONWEALTH OF MASSACHUSETTS.

Preamble and Declaration of Rights, Articles I–X reprinted from *The Federal and State Constitutions, Colonial Charters, and Other Organic Laws of the States, Territories, and Colonies,* comp. and ed. Francis Newton Thorpe (Washington, D.C.: GPO, 1909), 3:1888–91.

Part the First

A Declaration of the Rights of the Inhabitants of the Commonwealth of Massachusetts

Article I. All men are born free and equal, and have certain natural, essential, and unalienable rights; among which may be reckoned the right of enjoying and defending their lives and liberties; that of acquiring, possessing, and protecting property; in fine, that of seeking and obtaining their safety and happiness.

II. It is the right as well as the duty of all men in society, publicly, and at stated seasons, to worship the SUPREME BEING, the great Creator and Preserver of the universe. And no subject shall be hurt, molested, or restrained, in his person, liberty, or estate, for worshipping GOD in the manner and season most agreeable to the dictates of his own conscience; or for his religious profession of sentiments; provided he doth not disturb the public peace, or obstruct others in their religious worship.

III. As the happiness of a people, and the good order and preservation of civil government, essentially depend upon piety, religion, and morality; and as these cannot be generally diffused through a community but by the institution of the public worship of GOD, and of public instructions in piety, religion, and morality: Therefore, to promote their happiness, and to secure the good order and preservation of their government, the people of this commonwealth have a right to invest their legislature with power to authorize and require, and the legislature shall, from time to time, authorize and require, the several towns, parishes, precincts, and other bodies politic, or religious societies, to make suitable provision, at their own expense, for the institution of the public worship of GOD, and for the support and maintenance of public Protestant teachers of piety, religion, and morality, in all cases where such provision shall not be made voluntarily.

And the people of this commonwealth have also a right to, and do, invest their legislature with authority to enjoin upon all the subjects an attendance upon the instructions of the public teachers aforesaid, at stated times and seasons, if there be any on whose instructions they can conscientiously and conveniently attend.

Provided, notwithstanding, that the several towns, parishes, precincts, and other bodies politic, or religious societies, shall, at all times, have the exclusive right of electing their public teachers, and of contracting with them for their support and maintenance.

And all moneys paid by the subject to the support of public worship, and of the public teachers aforesaid, shall, if he require it, be uniformly applied to the support of the public teacher or teachers of his own religious sect or denomination, provided there be any on whose instructions he attends; otherwise it may be paid towards the support of the teacher or teachers of the parish or precinct in which the said moneys are raised.

And every denomination of Christians, demeaning themselves peaceably, and as good subjects of the commonwealth, shall be equally under the protection of the law: and no subordination of any one sect or denomination to another shall ever be established by law.

IV. The people of this commonwealth have the sole and exclusive right of governing themselves, as a free, sovereign, and independent state; and do, and forever hereafter shall, exercise and enjoy every power, jurisdiction, and right, which is not, or may not hereafter be, by them expressly delegated to the United States of America, in Congress assembled.

V. All power residing originally in the people, and being derived from them, the several magistrates and officers of government, vested with authority, whether legislative, executive, or judicial, are their substitutes and agents, and are at all times accountable to them.

VI. No man, nor corporation, or association of men, have any other title to obtain advantages, or particular and exclusive privileges, distinct from those of the community, than what arises from the consideration of services rendered to the public; and this title being in nature neither hereditary, nor transmissible to children, or descendants, or relations by blood, the idea of a man born a magistrate, lawgiver, or judge, is absurd and unnatural.

VII. Government is instituted for the common good; for the protection, safety, prosperity, and happiness of the people; and not for the profit, honor, or private interest of any one man, family, or class of men: Therefore the people alone have an incontestible unalienable, and indefeasible right to institute government; and to reform, alter, or totally change the same, when their protection, safety, prosperity, and happiness require it.

VIII. In order to prevent those who are vested with authority from becoming oppressors, the people have a right, at such periods and in such manner as they shall establish by their frame of government, to cause their public officers to return to private life; and to fill up vacant places by certain and regular elections and appointments.

IX. All elections ought to be free; and all the inhabitants of this commonwealth, having such qualifications as they shall establish by their frame of government, have an equal right to elect officers, and to be elected, for public employments.

X. Each individual of the society has a right to be protected by it in the enjoyment of his life, liberty, and property, according to standing laws. He is obliged, consequently, to contribute his share to the expense of this protection; to give his personal service, or an equivalent, when necessary: but no part of the property of any individual can, with justice, be taken from him, or applied to public uses, without his own consent, or that of the representative body of the people. In fine, the people of this commonwealth are not controllable by any other laws than those to which their constitutional representative body have given their consent. And whenever the public exigencies require that the property of any individual should be appropriated to public uses, he shall receive a reasonable compensation therefor.

A Bill Concerning Religion, Virginia (1779)

Borrowing from article 38 of South Carolina's constitution of 1778, "A Bill Concerning Religion" would have redefined toleration and establishment in Virginia. The Virginia Legislature debated the bill, tabled it, and never considered it again.

FOR the encouragement of Religion and virtue, and for removing all restraints on the mind in its inquiries after truth, *Be it enacted by the General Assembly,* that all persons and Religious Societies who acknowledge that there is one *God,* and a future State of rewards and punishments, and that *God* ought to be publickly worshiped, shall be freely tolerated.

The Christian Religion shall in all times coming be deemed, and held to be the established Religion of this Commonwealth; and all Denominations of Christians demeaning themselves peaceably and faithfully, shall enjoy equal privileges, civil and Religious.

To accomplish this desirable purpose without injury to the property of those Societies of Christians already incorporated by Law for the purpose of Religious Worship, and to put it fully into the power of every other Society of Christians, either already formed or to be hereafter formed to obtain the like incorporation, *Be it farther enacted,* that the respective Societies of the *Church of England* already formed in this Commonwealth, shall be continued Corporate, and hold the Religious property now in their possession for ever.

Reprinted from Thomas E. Buckley, *Church and State in Revolutionary Virginia, 1776–1787* (Charlottesville: University Press of Virginia, 1977), 185–88. © 1977 The University of Virginia Press. Used by permission of the publisher.

Whenever　　　free male Persons not under twenty one Years of Age professing the Christian Religion, shall agree to unite themselves in a Society for the purposes of Religious Worship, they shall be constituted a Church, and esteemed and regarded in Law as of the established Religion of this Commonwealth, and on their petition to the General Assembly shall be entitled to be incorporated and shall enjoy equal Privileges with any other Society of Christians, and all that associate with them for the purpose of Religious Worship, shall be esteemed as belonging to the Society so called.

Every Society so formed shall give themselves a name or denomination by which they shall be called and known in Law. *And it is farther enacted,* that previous to the establishment and incorporation of the respective Societies of every denomination as aforesaid, and in order to entitle them thereto, each Society so Petitioning shall agree to and subscribe in a Book the following five Articles, without which no agreement or Union of Men upon pretence of Religious Worship shall entitle them to be incorporated and esteemed as a Church of the Established Religion of this Commonwealth.

First, That there is one Eternal God and a future State of Rewards and Punishments.

Secondly, That God is publickly to be Worshiped.

Thirdly, That the Christian Religion is the true Religion.

Fourthly, That the Holy Scriptures of the old and new Testament are of divine inspiration, and are the only rule of Faith.

Fifthly, That it is the duty of every Man, when thereunto called by those who Govern, to bear Witness to truth.

And that the People may forever enjoy the right of electing their own Teachers, Pastors, or Clergy; and at the same time that the State may have Security for the due discharge of the Pastoral Office by those who shall be admitted to be Clergymen, Teachers, or Pastors, no Person shall officiate as Minister of any established Church who shall not have been chosen by a Majority of the Society to which he shall be Min-

ister, or by the Persons appointed by the said Majority to chose and procure a Minister for them, nor until the Minister so chosen shall have made and subscribed the following declaration, over and above the aforesaid five Articles, to be made in some Court of Record in this Commonwealth, viz.:

"That he is determined by *God's* Grace out of the Holy Scriptures to instruct the people committed to his charge, and to teach nothing (as required of necessity to eternal Salvation) but that which he shall be persuaded may be concluded and proved from the Scriptures; that he will use both publick and private admonitions, with prudence and discretion, as need shall require, and occasion shall be given; that he will be diligent in prayers and in reading the Holy Scriptures, and in such Studies as lead to the knowledge of the same; that he will be diligent to frame and fashion himself and his Family according to the doctrines of Christ, and to make both himself and them, as much as in him lieth, wholesome examples and patterns to the flock of Christ; and that he will maintain and set forward, as much as he can, peace and love among all people, and especially among those that are or shall be committed to his charge."

No Person whatsoever shall speak any thing in their Religious Assemblies disrespectfully or Seditiously of the Government of this State.

And that permanent encouragement may be given for providing a sufficient number of ministers and teachers to be procured and continued to every part of this Commonwealth, *Be it farther enacted,* that the sum of　　　pounds of Tobacco, or such rate in Money, as shall be Yearly settled for each County by the Court thereof, according to the Current Price, shall be paid annually for every Tithable by the Person enlisting the same, for and towards the Support of Religious Teachers and places of Worship in manner following: Within　　　Months after the passing of this Act every freeholder, Housekeeper, & person possessing Tithables, shall enroll his or her name with the Clerk of the County of which he or she shall be an Inhabitant, at the same time expressing to the Support of what Society or denomination of Christians he or she would chose to contribute; which enrollment shall be binding upon each such Person, untill he or she shall in like manner cause his or her name to be enrolled in any other Society.

The Clerk of each County Court shall Annually before the day of , deliver to the Trustees of each Religious Society, a list of the several names enrolled in his office as Members of such Society, with the number of Tithables belonging to each, according to the List taken and returned that Year. Whereupon such Trustees respectively shall meet and determine how the Assessment aforesaid upon such Tithables shall be laid out for the support of their teachers or places of Worship, according to the true intent of this Act; and having entered such disposition in a Book to be kept for that purpose, shall deliver a Copy thereof to the Sheriff, together with the List of Tithables so received from the Clerk, and such Sheriff shall on or before the day of , then next following, Collect, Levy, or Distrain for the amount of such Assessment, which he shall account for and pay to the several Persons to whom he shall have been directed to pay it by the Trustees of each respective Society, deducting Insolvents and Six *per Centum* for Collection.

If any Person shall fail to enlist his Tithables, the Sheriff shall nevertheless Collect or distrain for the Assessment aforesaid in like manner as if he or she had done so, and pay the same to that Religious Society of which he or she shall be enrolled as a Member. And should any Person liable to this Assessment fail to procure himself to be enrolled according to this Act, or to make his Election at the time of paying his Assessment to the Sheriff, the Sheriff shall nevertheless Levy in like manner the Assessment for his or her Tithables, and lay an Account upon Oath of all Tobacco or Monies so Collected before his Court in the Month of Annually; or if no Court be then held, at the next Court which shall be here thereafter, who shall apportion the same between the several Religious Societies in the Parish in which such Person or Persons shall reside, according to the amount of the Assessment for each to be paid to the Order

of such Trustees for the purposes of this Act. And every Sheriff shall Annually before the day of , enter into Bond, with sufficient Security to be approved by the County Court, for the faithful Collection and disbursement of all Tobacco or monies received in consequence of this Act; and the Trustees of any Religious Society, or any Creditor to whom Money may by them be Ordered to be paid, on motion in the County Court, having given him ten days previous notice thereof, may have Judgment against any delinquent Sheriff and his Securities, his or their Executors or Administrators, for what shall appear to be due from him to such Society or Creditor, or may bring suit on the Bond given by the Sheriff; and the Bond shall not be discharged by any Judgment had thereon, but shall remain as a Security against him, and may be put in Suit as often as any breach shall happen, until the whole Penalty shall have been Levied.

And if any Society or Church so established, shall refuse to appoint some Person to receive their Quota of the Assessment from the Sheriff, the Money shall remain in his hands for one Year; and if then no person properly appointed shall apply for such Money, the same shall by the County Court be equally apportioned between the several Religious Societies in the parish in which such person or persons shall reside, in proportion to the amount of the Assessment for each Society.

The Clerks of the respective County Courts shall be entitled to the same fees for making out and delivering the lists of Tithables required by this Act as they are entitled to for the like services in other cases.

And be it farther enacted, that so much of an Act of Assembly passed in the Year 1748, intituled "An Act for the Support of the Clergy, and for the regular Collecting and paying the Parish Levies," as respects the Levying, Collecting, and payment of the Salaries of the Clergy of the *Church of England* which has been suspended by several Acts of the General Assembly; and also so much of an Act intituled "*ministers to be inducted*," as required Ordination by a *Bishop* in *England,* be and the same are hereby Repealed.

A Bill for Establishing Religious Freedom, Virginia (1779 and 1786)

Drafted by Thomas Jefferson (1743–1826) in 1777, "A Bill for Establishing Religious Freedom" was first introduced in the Virginia Legislature in 1779. The bill was reintroduced by James Madison in October 1785 and eventually signed into law on January 16, 1786. It is commonly referred to as "The Virginia Statute for Religious Freedom." Italicized words in Jefferson's original draft below were removed by the General Assembly. The Act as adopted begins: "Whereas, Almighty God. . . ."

SECTION I. WELL *aware that the opinions and belief of men depend not on their own will, but follow involuntarily the evidence proposed to their minds; that* Almighty God hath created the mind free, *and manifested his supreme will that free it shall remain by making it altogether insusceptible of restraint;* that all attempts to influence it by temporal punishments, or burthens, or by civil incapacitations, tend only to beget habits of hypocrisy and meanness, and are a departure from the plan of the holy author of our religion, who being lord both of body and mind, yet chose not to propagate it by coercions on either, as was in his Almighty power to do, *but to extend it by its influence on reason alone;* that the impious presumption of legislators and rulers, civil as well as ecclesiastical, who, being themselves but fallible and uninspired men, have assumed dominion over the faith of others, setting up their own opinions and modes of thinking as the only true and infallible, and as such endeavoring to impose them on others, hath

Reprinted from *Report of the Committee of Revisors Appointed by the General Assembly of Virginia in 1776* (Richmond: Dixon and Holt, 1784), 58–59.

established and maintained false religions over the greatest part of the world and through all time: That to compel a man to furnish contributions of money for the propagation of opinions which he disbelieves *and abhors,* is sinful and tyrannical; that even the forcing him to support this or that teacher of his own religious persuasion, is depriving him of the comfortable liberty of giving his contributions to the particular pastor whose morals he would make his pattern, and whose powers he feels most persuasive to righteousness; and is withdrawing from the ministry those temporary rewards, which proceeding from an approbation of their personal conduct, are an additional incitement to earnest and unremitting labours for the instruction of mankind; that our civil rights have no dependance on our religious opinions, any more than our opinions in physics or geometry; that therefore the proscribing any citizen as unworthy the public confidence by laying upon him an incapacity of being called to offices of trust and emolument, unless he profess or renounce this or that religious opinion, is depriving him injuriously of those privileges and advantages to which, in common with his fellow citizens, he has a natural right; that it tends also* to currupt the principles of that *very* religion it is meant to encourage, by bribing, with a monopoly of worldly honours and emoluments, those who will externally profess and conform to it; that though indeed these are criminal who do not withstand such temptation, yet neither are those innocent who lay the bait in their way; *that the opinions of men are not the object of civil government, nor under its jurisdiction;* that to suffer the civil magistrate to intrude his powers into the field of opinion and to restrain the profession or propagation of principles on supposition of their ill tendency is a dangerous falacy, which at once destroys all religious liberty, because he being of course judge of that tendency will make his opinions the rule of judgment, and approve or condemn the sentiments of others only as they shall square with or differ from his own; that it is time enough for the

* The act replaced "also" with "only."—Eds.

rightful purposes of civil government for its officers to interfere when principles break out into overt acts against peace and good order; and finally, that truth is great and will prevail if left to herself; that she is the proper and sufficient antagonist to error, and has nothing to fear from the conflict unless by human interposition disarmed of her natural weapons, free argument and debate; errors ceasing to be dangerous when it is permitted freely to contradict them.

SECT. II. *WE the General Assembly of Virginia do enact** that no man shall be compelled to frequent or support any religious worship, place, or ministry whatsoever, nor shall be enforced, restrained, molested, or burthened in his body or goods, nor shall otherwise suffer, on account of his religious opinions or belief; but that all men shall be free to profess, and by argument to maintain, their opinions in matters of religion, and that the same shall in no wise diminish, enlarge, or affect their civil capacities.

SECT. III. AND though we well know that this Assembly, elected by the people for the ordinary purposes of legislation only, have no power to restrain the acts of succeeding Assemblies, constituted with powers equal to our own, and that therefore to declare this act irrevocable would be of no effect in law; yet we are free to declare, and do declare, that the rights hereby asserted are of the natural rights of mankind, and that if any act shall be hereafter passed to repeal the present or to narrow its operation, such act will be an infringement of natural right.

A Bill for Punishing Disturbers of Religious Worship and Sabbath Breakers, Virginia (1786)

Framed by Thomas Jefferson and introduced in the Virginia Legislature by James Madison in October 1785, the following statute was enacted in November 1786.

SECTION I. BE it enacted by the General Assembly, that no officer, for any civil cause, shall arrest any minister of the gospel, licensed according to the rules of his sect, and who shall have taken the oath of fidelity to the commonwealth, while such minister shall be publicly preaching or performing religious worship in any church, chapel, or meeting-house, on pain of imprisonment and amercement, at the discretion of a jury, and of making satisfaction to the party so arrested.

SECT. II. AND if any person shall of purpose, maliciously, or contemptuously, disquiet or disturb any congregation assembled in any church, chapel, or meeting-house, or misuse any such minister being there, he may be put under restraint during religious worship, by any Justice present, which Justice, if present, or if none be present, then any Justice before whom proof of the offence shall be made, may cause the offender to find two sureties to be bound by recognizance in a sufficient penalty for his good behavior, and in default thereof shall commit him to prison, there to remain till the next court to be held for the same county; and upon conviction of the said offence before the said court, he shall be further punished by imprisonment and amercement at the discretion of a jury.

---

* The act replaced this language with "Be it enacted by the General Assembly."—Eds.

Reprinted from *Report of the Committee of Revisors Appointed by the General Assembly of Virginia in 1776* (Richmond: Dixon and Holt, 1784), 59.

Sect. III. If any person on Sunday shall himself be found labouring at his own or any other trade or calling, or shall employ his apprentices, servants or slaves in labour, or other business, except it be in the ordinary houshold offices of daily necessity, or other work of necessity or charity, he shall forfeit the sum of ten shillings for every such offence, deeming every apprentice, servant, or slave so employed, and every day he shall be so employed as constituting a distinct offence.

A Bill for Appointing Days of Public Fasting and Thanksgiving, Virginia (1779)

Framed by Thomas Jefferson and introduced in the Virginia Legislature by James Madison in October 1785, the following bill was assigned to the Committee of the Whole in 1786 and was never enacted.

Be it enacted by the General Assembly, that the power of appointing days of public fasting and humiliation, or thanksgiving, throughout this commonwealth, may in the recess of the General Assembly, be exercised by the Governor, or Chief Magistrate, with the advice of the Council; and such appointment shall be notified to the public, by a proclamation, in which the occasion of the fasting or thanksgiving shall be particularly set forth. Every minister of the gospel shall on each day so to be appointed, attend and perform divine service and preach a sermon, or discourse, suited to the occasion, in his church, on pain of forfeiting fifty pounds for every failure, not having a reasonable excuse.

Reprinted from *The Papers of Thomas Jefferson*, ed. Julian P. Boyd, vol. 2, *1777 to 18 June 1779* (Princeton: Princeton University Press, 1950), 556. Reprinted by permission of Princeton University Press.

A Bill Establishing a Provision for Teachers of the Christian Religion, Virginia (1784)

Drafted by a committee chaired by Patrick Henry in 1784, this bill would have provided a general assessment to support ministers from every denomination. On Christmas Eve of 1784, the Virginia Legislature postponed final action on the bill until the legislature's fall 1785 session. After sustained opposition led by James Madison, no final action was taken on the measure.

Whereas the general diffusion of Christian knowledge hath a natural tendency to correct the morals of men, restrain their vices, and preserve the peace of society, which cannot be effected without a competent provision for learned teachers, who may be thereby enabled to devote their time and attention to the duty of instructing such citizens, as from their circumstances and want of education, cannot otherwise attain such knowledge; and it is judged that such provision may be made by the Legislature, without counteracting the liberal principle heretofore adopted and intended to be preserved by abolishing all distinctions of preeminence amongst the different societies or communities of Christians;

Be it therefore enacted by the General Assembly, That for the support of Christian teachers,   per centum on the amount, or   in the pound on the amount, or   in the pound on the sum payable for tax on the property within this Commonwealth, is hereby assessed, and shall be paid by every person chargeable with the said tax at the time the same shall

Reprinted from Thomas E. Buckley, *Church and State in Revolutionary Virginia, 1776–1787* (Charlottesville: University Press of Virginia, 1977), 188–89. © 1977 The University of Virginia Press. Used by permission of the publisher.

become due; and the Sheriffs of the several Counties shall have power to levy and collect the same in the same manner and under the like restrictions and limitations, as are or may be prescribed by the laws for raising the revenues of this State.

And be it enacted, That for every sum so paid, the Sheriff or Collector shall give a receipt, expressing therein to what society of Christians the person from whom he may receive the same shall direct the money to be paid, keeping a distinct account thereof in his books. The Sheriff of every Country, shall, on or before the _____ day of _____ in every year, return to the Court upon oath, two alphabetical lists of the payments to him made, distinguishing in columns opposite to the names of the persons who shall have paid the same, the society to which the money so paid was by them appropriated; and one column for the names where no appropriation shall be made. One of which lists, after being recorded in a book to be kept for that purpose, shall be filed by the Clerk in his office; and the other shall by the Sheriff be fixed up in the Court-house, there to remain for the inspection of all concerned. And the Sheriff, after deducting a five per centum for the collection, shall forthwith pay to such persons or persons as shall be appointed to receive the same by the Vestry, Elders, or Directors, however denominated of each such society, the sum so stated to be due to that society; or in default thereof, upon the motion of such person or persons to the next or any succeeding Court, execution shall be awarded for the same against the Sheriff and his security, his and their executors or administrators; provided that ten days previous notice be given of such motion. And upon every such execution, the Officer serving the same shall proceed to immediate sale of the estate taken, and shall not accept of security for payment at the end of three months, nor to have the goods forthcoming at the day of sale, for his better direction wherein, the Clerk shall endorse upon every such execution that no security of any kind shall be taken.

And be it further enacted, That the money to be raised by virtue of this act, shall be by the Vestries, Elders, or Directors of each religious society, appropriated to a provision for a Minister or Teacher of the Gospel of their denomination, or the providing places of divine worship, and to none other use whatsoever; except in the denominations of Quakers and Menonists, who may receive what is collected from their members, and place it in their general fund, to be disposed of in a manner which they shall think best calculated to promote their particular mode of worship.

And be it enacted, That all sums which at the time of payment to the Sheriff or Collector may not be appropriated by the person paying the same, shall be accounted for with the Court in manner as by this Act is directed; and after deducting for his collection, the Sheriff shall pay the amount thereof (upon account certified by the Court to the Auditors of Public Accounts, and by them to the Treasurer) into the Public Treasury, to be disposed of under the direction of the General Assembly, for the encouragement of seminaries of learning within the Counties whence such sums shall arise, and to no other use or purpose whatsoever.

Resolutions and Address by the Maryland House of Delegates (January 8, 1785)

In 1785, the Maryland Assembly submitted to the people a general assessment bill that would provide support to clergy from multiple denominations. The House of Delegates approved the following resolutions and address in support of the measure. It was published on January 18, 1785, in the *Maryland Journal and Baltimore Advertiser.* After much debate, the voters of Maryland rejected the measure.

By the House of Delegates, January 8, 1785.

RESOLVED, That it is the opinion of this house, that the happiness of the people, and the good order and preservation of civil government, depend upon morality, religion, and piety; and that these cannot be generally diffused through a community, but by the *public* worship of Almighty God.

RESOLVED, That it is the opinion of this house, that it is highly necessary, and the indispensable duty of the legislature of this state, to discourage vice and immorality, to enact a law for the support and encouragement of the christian religion, as the best means of manifesting our gratitude to God for his past mercies and deliverances, and procuring his blessing and favour upon all our future endeavours, for the honor, prosperity, and happiness of this country.

RESOLVED, That it is the opinion of this house, that agreeably to the constitution and form of government, it is proper for the general assembly to lay a general and equal tax on all the citizens of this state, of all denominations of christians (as far as their present circumstances will permit) for the support of the ministers of the gospel of all societies of christians within this state, without any preference or discrimination.

By order,   W. Harwood, Clk.

An Address of the House of Delegates of Maryland to their Constituents

THE Resolves hereunto prefixed are the foundation of a *bill* highly interesting both to your temporal and everlasting concerns, which we have ordered to be published for your consideration; and we wish to draw your most serious attention, not only to its *form* and *substance*, but to its *principles* and probable operation.

The house of delegates, your immediate representatives in general assembly, have not entered hastily upon this great business. They have long beheld a growing indifference to religion and things sacred, very alarming to the interests of morality, peace and good order in society. They found themselves called

The text was transcribed from *Maryland Journal* 12, no. 5 (January 8, 1785): 2.

upon, in their legislative capacity, not only by the mournful voice of *Religion* herself, but by the voice of the constitution, and numerous petitions from our constituents; all which were still further enforced, in the most powerful manner, by an *address* of the governor and council (in the month of May, seventeen hundred and eighty-three) in the following pathetic words: "It is far from our intentions to embarrass your deliberations with a variety of objects; but we cannot pass over matters of so high concernment as *religion* and *learning*. The sufferings of the *ministers* of the gospel of *all denominations* during the war, have been very considerable; and the perseverance and firmness of those who discharged their sacred functions, under many discouraging circumstances, claim our acknowledgments and thanks. The Bill of Rights and Form of Government recognize the principle of *public support for the ministers* of the gospel, and ascertain the mode. Anxiously solicitous for the blessings of government, and the welfare and happiness of our citizens, and thoroughly convinced of the powerful influence of religion, when diffused by its respectable teachers, we beg leave most seriously and warmly to recommend, among the first objects of your attention, *on the return of peace*, the making such provision, as the constitution, in this case, authorizes and approves."

Being called upon, in this solemn manner, to consider the high concernments of *religion* and *learning*, as one of the first objects of legislative attention, upon the happy *return of peace*; some suitable provision hath been accordingly made for the latter of these (namely *learning*) by the foundation of two *colleges*, (viz. one upon each shore) connected together, as one *university*, upon such liberal principles as (it is hoped) will merit a continuance of the public approbation, and be productive of the most lasting advantages to our posterity.

The bill (herewith published) is intended to make the best provision in the power of the legislature, for the former of these great concernments, namely the support and advancement of *religion* among all denominations of *christians*, without preference or distinction, as is set forth in the *resolutions* prefixed, which contain principles so universally received, that it cannot be supposed they will meet with a dissenting voice among mankind, if considered by themselves, without any other view than as conducive to the general happiness of society.

That *religion* hath the most powerful influence upon *manners*, and hath been more or less interwoven with the very frame and texture of every *civil* government upon earth, needs but little proof.

The *savages* of the wilderness around us can bear testimony to this truth; and the ancient *Romans*, the wisest and the greatest of the nations, unenlightened by immediate *revelation*, owed more of their grandeur to their *religious institutions*, than either to their strength or stratagem. *Religion* pervaded their whole system of laws; its precepts regulated their conduct in *peace* and war; and if at any time, in the dire extremity of affairs, *the safety of the commonwealth*, their *supreme law*, required the least deviation from the *laws* of religion, yet still they paid a strict regard to its external sanctions and appearances, and threw a veil over the statues of their gods, to persuade the people, that the gods did either not see, or (for that time) would connive or dispense with the great and necessary, although otherwise sacrilegious action!

If we come to *revelation*, the government of the *Jews* under the Old Testament was wholly a *theocracy* or *government of religion*, instituted by God himself as their *supreme lawgiver;* and their empire was great and flourishing, or miserable and depressed, as they obeyed or forsook his holy laws. And as to the *New Testament*, where shall we find a system of religion which conduces so effectually to the good order, peace and happiness of society, as the *religion of Christ*? Whatsoever things are honest, pure, lovely, and of *good report*, are enforced by it, under the sacred sanction of everlasting rewards and punishments.

If we come to our situation in America, and recall to memory the many arduous contests of the late war, while we were laying the foundations of our present liberty and happiness; religion, both in belief and practice, was considered as our principal support and stay. How frequent were our appeals to Heaven for the justice of our cause? How many our days of fasting and prayer, to implore the Divine protection on the success of our arms? And how many our days of thanksgiving for mercies received? By all which, religion was, at least, acknowledged in our *national* councils, as having the most powerful influence on the minds of men, in order to lead them to a sense of duty, and the faithful discharge of it as good citizens.

The right and duty of the legislative or supreme power to interpose in matters of religion, so far as concerns the general peace and welfare of the community, and "to make suitable provision, at the public expence, for the institution of the public worship of God," are fully acknowledged and recognised under the American revolution.

By the constitution of this state, no man can hold any office of profit or trust, without professing and declaring "his belief in the christian religion." Government can have no confidence in that man who is under no religious tie, and who believes neither Heaven nor Hell, or, in other words, a future state of rewards and punishments. What the celebrated commentator on the law of England delivers on this subject, deserves the most serious attention.

"The preservation of *christianity*, as a *national religion*, is (abstracted from its own intrinsic truth) of the utmost consequence to the civil state, which a single instance will sufficiently demonstrate. The belief of a future state of rewards and punishments, the entertaining just ideas of the moral attributes of the Supreme Being, and a firm persuasion that he superintends, and will finally compensate, every action of human life, (all which are clearly revealed in the doctrines, and forcibly inculcated by the precepts, of our Saviour Christ) are the grand foundation of all *judicial oaths*, which call God to witness the truth of those facts, which perhaps may be only known to him and the party attesting; all moral evidence, therefore, all confidence in human veracity, must be weakened by irreligion, and overthrown by infidelity."

Upon the whole, since *religion* has such an intimate connexion with *government*, and is so conducive to the happiness of mankind in this world, as well as their best preparation for the happiness of the world to come, we cannot but consider it as the indispensable duty of every wise and virtuous legislature, to make the most early and permanent provision for the administration and support of both.

We have now stated the *principles* of the bill, and our motives for bringing it before you at this time. The subject is of the utmost magnitude, and it is your duty to weigh it with the greatest deliberation and temper. It requires no depth of learning, nor any other exertion than that of a common understanding, love to your country, and christian forbearance, one with another.

In considering it therefore you will remember, that in *religion,* as well as *government,* the *labourer* is *worthy of his hire;* that the ministers of the gospel among us, for the future, must chiefly be our own natives; that their profession will deprive them, for the most part, of any other means of getting a livelihood, or providing for their families; that they ought to be endued with considerable learning and knowledge to be respectable and useful in their sacred calling; and that without a competent support in prospect, few men will put themselves to the expence of a liberal education for the ministry; and the discharge of its sacred functions will be left chiefly to those, whose ignorance would render them improper even to be entrusted with any of our worldly affairs.

Objections will probably be made to the proposed mode of supporting the ministers. It may be called a *poll-tax,* and yielding *partial* favours, to raise one denomination of christians above others, contrary to the Declaration of Rights. But let such objections be well weighed before they lead you to any injurious suspicions of the integrity of your representatives. Let it be considered, whether they come from the friends or enemies to the general principles of the bill—those who wish for any legal support to the ministers of religion, or those who profess themselves opposed to it.

Consider the whole frame and spirit of the bill. It declares the most perfect *equality;* and if your representatives were so weak or wicked as to design any thing contrary to the constitution, they are at least wise enough to know that the act would be *null* and *void* in itself.

A *poll-tax,* such as was levied under the old constitution (where the expence of *government* was *not* supported in proportion to property and the benefits to be derived, but by the head) is justly declared *grievous* and *oppressive* by the Bill of Rights.

The instruction to be given to all men, from the word of God, is equally important, to the *rich* and *poor;* and the souls of both are alike precious in the *Maker's* sight. Yet still the *rich* man will pay in proportion to the number of his family and the taxables dependent upon him, which is just and reasonable. Nevertheless the sum to be paid by every individual, when thus borne equally by *all,* will be small indeed compared to the burden which now falls upon a *few;* while many of the *rich* and *sordid,* as well as many of lower degree, whose profligate lives are a reproach to society, escape wholly *free.*

Whether the tax shall be raised upon property in general, or in any other mode, will be maturely considered by your representatives, when they shall have further opportunity of consulting you thereon. Let what is best upon the whole be done. Your representatives *will* not, they *cannot,* do any thing injurious to your interest, which is inseparable from their own.

The great and almost only point is—"Whether or not it be necessary, and the desire of a majority of the good people of this state, that some suitable provision should be made by *law,* for the support of the christian religion according to the Bill of Rights, and the *resolutions* of your representatives hereunto prefixed?"

Upon this great question, your INSTRUCTIONS are desired; and while you give them, we beseech you to exercise all possible temper and discretion; considering yourselves as in the presence of your *Almighty Creator;* and that the judgment which you are to pronounce may be finally decisive upon the future *religion, glory, honour* and *happiness* of your country and posterity, to the latest generations!

THO. COCKEY DEYE,
Speaker of the House of Delegates

State Constitutional Provisions and Proclamations Related to Religion

B. F. MORRIS (1810–67)

B. F. Morris compiled a vast array of primary source documents on church-state relations in early America which were published in *Christian Life and Character of the Civil Institutions of the United States* (1864). The following excerpt from that work surveys a wide range of state constitutions and proclamations.

The Constitution of Pennsylvania,

Adopted in 1776, declares that the Legislature shall consist of "persons most noted for wisdom and virtue," and that every member should subscribe the following declaration:—

I do believe in one God, the Creator and Governor of the universe, the Rewarder of the good, and the Punisher of the wicked; and I acknowledge the Scriptures of the Old and New Testaments to be given by inspiration.

The Constitution of North Carolina,

Bearing date 1776, declares

That no person who should deny the being of a God, or the truth of the Protestant religion, or the divine authority of either the Old or New Testaments, or who should hold religious principles incompatible with the freedom and safety of the State, should be capable of holding any office or place of trust in the civil government of this State.

Reprinted from B. F. Morris, *Christian Life and Character of the Civil Institutions of the United States, Developed in the Official and Historical Annals of the Republic* (Philadelphia: George W. Childs, 1864), 233–44.

Delaware,

In her first Constitution, formed during the Revolution, made the following declaration:—

That every citizen who should be chosen a member of either house of the Legislature, or appointed to any other office, should be required to subscribe to the following declaration:—"I do profess faith in God the Father, and in the Lord Jesus Christ his only Son, and in the Holy Ghost, one God and blessed for evermore; and I do acknowledge the Holy Scriptures of the Old and New Testaments to be given by divine inspiration."

Maryland

Formed a State Constitution in 1776, and the Declaration of Rights (Art. XIX.) says,—

That as it is the duty of every man to worship God in such manner as he thinks most acceptable to him, all persons professing the Christian religion are equally entitled to protection in their religious liberty. And (in Art. XXXV.) "That no other qualification ought to be required on admission to any office of trust or profit than such oath of support and fidelity to this State, and such oath of office, as shall be directed by this Constitution or the Legislature of this State, *and a declaration of belief in the Christian religion.*"

The Constitution also authorized the Legislature "to lay a general tax for the support of the Christian religion."

New Jersey,

In her Constitution formed in 1776, declares

That there shall be no establishment of any one religious sect in this province in preference to another, and that no Protestant inhabitant of this colony shall be denied the enjoyment of any civil right on account of his religious principles; but

That all persons professing a belief in the faith of any Protestant sect, and who should demean himself peaceably under the government, should be capable of being elected unto any office of profit or trust, or of being a member of either branch of the Legislature.

The following instructions from the Legislature of New Jersey to its delegates in Congress in 1777 will exhibit the high Christian sentiments of the men who directed the civil and military concerns of the Revolution. Among the delegates were John Witherspoon and Elias Boudinot. The Legislature instructs as follows:

> 1. We hope you will habitually bear in mind that the success of the great cause in which the United States are engaged depends upon the favor and blessing of Almighty God; and therefore you will neglect nothing which is competent to the Assembly of the States for promoting *piety* and *good morals* among the people at large. But especially we desire that you may give attention to this circumstance in the government of the army, taking care that such of the articles of war as forbid profaneness, riot, and debauchery be observed and enforced with all due strictness and severity. This, we apprehend, is absolutely necessary for the encouragement and maintenance of good discipline, and will be the means of recruiting the army with men of credit and principle,—an object ardently to be wished, but not to be expected if the warmest friends of their country should be deterred from sending their sons and connections into the service, lest they should be tainted with impious and immoral notions and contract vicious habits.

New Hampshire

Formed a State Constitution in 1776, and in it declares

> That morality and piety, rightly grounded on evangelical principles, would give the best and greatest security to government, and would lay in the hearts of men the strongest obligation to due subjection; and that the knowledge of these was most likely to be propagated by the institution of the public worship of the Deity and instruction in morality and religion.

The Constitution of the same State in 1792 empowered the Legislature to adopt measures "for the support and maintenance of public Protestant teachers of piety, religion, and morality."

The province of New Hampshire, in a convention composed of one hundred and forty-four deputies appointed by the various towns in the province aforesaid, after resolving "that we heartily approve of the proceedings of the late grand Continental Congress," passed the following:—

> Lastly, we earnestly entreat you, at this time of tribulation and distress, when your enemies are urging you to despair, when every scene around is full of gloom and horror, that, in imitation of your pious forefathers, you implore the divine Being, who alone is able to deliver you from your present unhappy and distressing situation, to espouse your righteous cause, secure your liberties, and fix them on a firm and lasting basis.

The Constitution of Georgia,

Adopted in 1777, declares that "all the members of the Legislature shall be of the Protestant religion."

The Constitution of Vermont

Declares that

> Every sect or denomination of Christians ought to observe the Sabbath or Lord's Day, and keep up some sort of religious worship, which to them shall seem most agreeable to the revealed will of God.

Connecticut,

In Part 7, sec. 1 of her Constitution, declared that,—

> It being the duty of all men to worship the Supreme Being, the great Creator and Preserver of the Universe, and their right to render that worship in the mode most consistent with the dictates of their consciences, no person shall, by law, be compelled to join or support, nor be classed with or associated to, any congregation,

church, or religious association. But every person now belonging to such congregation, church, or religious association shall remain a member thereof, until he shall have separated himself therefrom, in the manner hereinafter provided. And each and every society or denomination of Christians in this State shall have and enjoy the same and equal powers, rights, and privileges, and shall have power and authority to support and maintain the ministers or teachers of their respective denominations, and to build and repair houses for public worship, by a tax on the members of any such society only, to be laid by a major vote of the legal voters assembled at any society meeting, warned and held according to law, or in any other manner.

The Charter of Rhode Island,

Granted by Charles II., in 1682–83, and which continued to be the Constitution of that Commonwealth till 1843, says,—

The object of the colonists is to pursue, with peace and loyal minds, their sober, serious, and religious intentions of godly edifying themselves and one another in the holy Christian faith and worship, together with the gaining over and conversion of the poor ignorant Indian natives to the sincere profession and obedience of the same faith and worship.

The Constitution of New York,

Though less full and explicit on the subject than those of other States, yet contains an organic act recognizing the Christian religion. The Constitution of 1777 has the following articles, the same as those inserted in the Constitution formed in 1821:—

And *Whereas* we are required, by the benevolent principles of rational liberty, not only to expel civil tyranny, but also to guard against that spiritual oppression and intolerance wherewith the bigotry and ambition of weak and wicked priests and princes have scourged mankind: this Convention doth further, in the name

and by the authority of the good people of this State, ORDAIN, DETERMINE, and DECLARE that the free exercise and enjoyment of religious profession and worship, without discrimination or preference, shall forever hereafter be allowed within this State to all mankind: *Provided,* That the liberty of conscience hereby granted shall not be so construed as to excuse acts of licentiousness or justify practices inconsistent with the peace or safety of this State.

And *Whereas* the ministers of the gospel are, by their profession, dedicated to the service of God and the cure of souls, and ought not to be diverted from the great duties of their functions: therefore, no minister of the gospel, or priest of any denomination whatsoever, shall, at any time hereafter, under any pretence or description whatever, be eligible to or capable of holding any civil or military office or place within this State.

An examination of the present Constitutions of the various States, now existing, will show that the Christian religion and its institutions are recognized as the religion of the Government and the nation.

The recognitions of Christianity in the State Constitutions are of three kinds. 1. These instruments are usually dated in the *year of our Lord.* 2. Nearly all of them refer to the observance of Sunday by the Chief Executive Magistrate, in the same way in which such observance is referred to in the Constitution of the United States. 3. All the State Constitutions, or legislation under them, guard with vigilance the religious observance of the Christian Sabbath, and punish, with greater or less severity, all unlawful violation of the day. 4. Definite constitutional provisions not only recognizing the Christian religion, but affording it countenance, encouragement, and protection.

"In perusing the thirty-four Constitutions of the United States, we find all of them recognizing Christianity as the well-known and well-established religion of the communities whose legal, civil, and political foundations they are. The terms of this recognition are more or less distinct in the Constitutions of the different States; but they exist in all of them. The reason why any degree of indistinctness exists in any of them, unquestionably, is that at their forma-tion it never came into the minds of the framers to suppose that the existence of Christianity as the re-ligion of their communities could ever admit of a question. Nearly all these Constitutions recognize the customary observance of Sunday; and a suitable observance of this day includes a performance of all the peculiar duties of the Christian faith. The Con-stitution of Vermont declares that 'every sect or de-nomination of Christians ought to observe the Sab-bath or Lord's Day, and keep up some sort of religious worship, which to them shall seem most agreeable to the revealed will of God.' The Constitutions of Mas-sachusetts and Maryland are among those which do not prescribe the observance of Sunday: yet the for-mer declares it to be 'the right, as well as the duty, of all men in society, publicly and at stated seasons to worship the Supreme Being, the great Creator and Preserver of the universe;' and the latter requires every person appointed to any office of profit or trust to 'subscribe a declaration of his belief in the Chris-tian religion.' Two of them concur in the sentiment that 'morality and piety, rightly grounded on evan-gelical principles, will be the best and greatest security to government; and that the knowledge of these is most likely to be propagated through a society by the institution of the public worship of the Deity, and of public instruction in morality and religion.' Only a small part of what the Constitutions of the States contain in regard to the Christian religion is here cited. At the same time, they all grant the free exercise and enjoyment of religious profession and worship, with some slight discriminations, to all mankind. The principle obtained by the foregoing inductive ex-amination of our State Constitutions is this:—THE PEOPLE OF THE UNITED STATES HAVE RE-TAINED THE CHRISTIAN RELIGION AS THE FOUNDATION OF THEIR CIVIL, LEGAL, AND POLITICAL INSTITUTIONS; WHILE THEY HAVE REFUSED TO CONTINUE A LEGAL PREFERENCE TO ANY ONE OF ITS FORMS OVER ANY OTHER."

In 1838, the Legislature of New York, in a report from the Committee on Petitions, "praying a repeal of the laws for the observance of the Sabbath," by a vote nearly unanimous rejected the petition, and de-clared that,—

In all countries, some kind of religion or other has existed in all ages. No people on the face of the globe are without a prevailing national religion. Magistrates have sought in many countries to strengthen civil gov-ernment by an alliance with some particular religion and an intolerant exclusion of all others. But those who have wielded this formidable power have rendered it a rival instead of an auxiliary to the public welfare,—a fetter instead of a protection to the rights of conscience. With us it is wisely ordered that no one religion shall be es-tablished by law, but that all persons shall be left free in their choice and in their mode of worship. Still, *this is a Christian nation.* Ninety-nine hundredths, if not a larger proportion, of our whole population, believe in the general doctrines of the Christian religion. Our Government depends for its being on the virtue of the people,—on that virtue that has its foundation in the morality of the Christian religion; and that religion is the common and prevailing faith of the people. There are, it is true, exceptions to this belief; but general laws are not made for excepted cases. There are to be found, here and there, the world over, individuals who enter-tain opinions hostile to the common sense of mankind on subjects of honesty, humanity, and decency; but it would be a kind of republicanism with which we are not acquainted in this country, which would require the great mass of mankind to yield to and be governed by this few.

It is quite unnecessary to enter into a detailed review of all the evidences that Christianity is the common creed of this nation. We know it, and we feel it, as we know and feel any other unquestioned and admitted truth; the evidence is all around us, and before us, and with us. We know, too, that the exceptions to this gen-eral belief are rare,—so very rare that they are sufficient only, like other exceptions, to prove a general rule.

The following papers reflect the Christian tone of the civil government and people of New York during the era of the Revolution:—

Die Saturnii, 9 ho. A.M., July 8, 1775

The Continental Congress having recommended it to the inhabitants of the Colonies to keep the twentieth day of *July* instant, 1775, as a day of fasting and prayer, this Congress does strictly enjoin all persons in this colony religiously to observe the said recommendation. And we, being taught by that holy religion, declared by the merciful *Jesus* and sealed by his blood, that we ought to acknowledge the hand of *God* in all public calamities, and being thoroughly convinced that the Great Disposer of events regardeth the hearts of his creatures, do most earnestly recommend it to all men to conform themselves to the pure dictates of Christianity, and by deep repentance, and sincere amendment of their lives, implore of our heavenly Father that favor and protection which he alone can give.

Committee-Chamber, New York, May, 1776

Whereas the honorable Continental Congress have appointed and earnestly recommend "that the 17th inst. (being to-morrow) be observed by the United Colonies as a day of humiliation, fasting, and prayer, that we may with united hearts confess and bewail our manifold sins and transgressions against *God,* and, by a sincere repentance and amendment of life, as a people, appease his righteous displeasure against us, humbly imploring his assistance to frustrate the cruel purposes of our unnatural enemies, and, by inclining their hearts to justice and peace, prevent the further effusion of human blood; but if, continuing deaf to the voice of reason and humanity, and inflexibly bent on desolation and war, they constrain us to repel their hostile invasions by open resistance, that it may please the Lord of hosts, the God of armies, to animate our officers and soldiers with invincible fortitude, to guard and protect them in the day of battle, and to crown the Continental armies, by sea and land, with victory and success; that he may bless all our representatives in General Congress, Provincial Congress, Conventions, and Committees; preserve and strengthen their union, give wisdom and stability to their councils, and direct the most efficient measures for establishing the rights of *America* on the most honorable and permanent basis; that he would be graciously pleased to bless all the people in these colonies with health and plenty, and grant that a spirit of incorruptible patriotism and of pure and undefiled religion may universally prevail, and that this continent may be speedily restored to the blessings of peace and liberty, and enabled to transmit them inviolate to the latest posterity."

It is therefore expected that all the inhabitants of this city and county do, on the morrow, abstain from all and every kind of servile labor, business, and employment, and attend upon divine service in public, which will be performed in all churches in this city; that no persons (but such as are in the Continental service, whose business may require it) will be permitted to cross the ferries, ride or walk out of town, or about the streets, for amusement or diversion; and that all parents and masters will be careful to restrain their children from playing and straggling about this city on the ensuing day, which ought to be, and we trust will be, regarded as the most solemn day this devoted continent has ever yet beheld.

A true copy from the minutes. Published by order of the Committee,

JOSEPH WINTER, *Secretary*

The following extracts from a proclamation issued by the Great and General Court of Massachusetts Bay in January, 1776, exhibit the high Christian character of the government of that Commonwealth:—

As the happiness of the people is the sole end of government, so the consent of the people is the only foundation of it, in reason, morality, and the natural fitness of things. And therefore every act of government, every exercise of sovereignty, against or without the consent of the people, is injustice, usurpation, and tyranny.

It is a maxim of every government that there must exist somewhere a supreme, sovereign, absolute, and uncontrollable power; but this power resides always in the body of the people, and it never was or can be delegated to one man or a few,—the great Creator having never given to men a right to invest authority over them unlimited either in duration or degree.

When kings, ministers, governors, or legislators, therefore, instead of exercising the powers intrusted to them according to the principles, forms, and propositions stated by the constitution and established by the original compact, prostitute those powers to the purposes of oppression,—to subvert instead of supporting a free constitution,—to destroy instead of preserving the lives, liberties, and properties of the people,—they are no longer to be deemed magistrates vested with a sacred character, but become public enemies, and ought to be resisted.

The present generation may be congratulated on the acquisition of a form of government more immediately, in all its branches, under the influence and control of the people, and therefore more free and happy than was enjoyed by their ancestors. But, as a government so popular can be supported only by universal knowledge and virtue in the body of the people, it is the duty of all ranks to promote the means of education for the rising generation, as well as true religion, purity of manners, and integrity of life, among all orders and degrees.

That piety and virtue, which alone can secure the freedom of any people, may be encouraged, and vice and immorality suppressed, the Great and General Court have thought fit to issue this proclamation, commanding and enjoining it upon the good people of this colony that they lead sober, religious, and peaceable lives, avoiding all blasphemies, contempt of the Holy Scriptures and of the Lord's Day, and all other crimes and misdeameanors, all debauchery, profaneness, corruption, revelry, all riotous and tumultuous proceedings, and all immoralities whatsoever; and that they decently and reverently attend the public worship of God, at all times acknowledging with gratitude his merciful interposition in their behalf, devoutly confiding in him as the God of armies, by whose favor and protection alone they may hope for success in their present conflict.

And all judges, justices, sheriffs, grand jurors, tithing-men, and all other civil officers within this colony, are hereby strictly enjoined and commanded that they contribute all in their power, by their example, towards a general reformation of manners, and that they bring to condign punishment every person who shall commit any of the crimes or misdemeanors aforesaid, or that shall be guilty of any immoralities whatsoever; and that they use their utmost endeavors to have the

resolves of the Congress and the good and wholesome laws of this colony duly carried into execution.

And as ministers of the gospel within this colony have, during the late relaxation of the powers of civil government, exerted themselves for our safety, it is hereby recommended to them still to continue their virtuous labors for the good of the people, inculcating by their public ministry and private example the necessity of religion, morality, and good order.

Ordered, That the foregoing proclamation be read at the opening of every superior court of judicature, &c. and inferior court of common pleas and court of general sessions for the peace within this colony, by their respective clerks, and at the annual town meetings, in March, in each town. And it is hereby recommended to the several ministers of the gospel throughout this colony to read the same in their respective assemblies, on the Lord's Day next after receiving, immediately after divine service.

By order of the General Court.

In Council, January 19, 1776. In the House of Representatives, January 23, 1776.

GOD SAVE THE PEOPLE!

In January, 1777, the Legislature of the State of Massachusetts Bay addressed to the people, through civil officers and Christian ministers, a paper on the great conflict then in progress, which, after presenting the condition of the country, closes in these words:—

We, therefore, for the sake of religion, for the enjoyment whereof your ancestors fled to this country, for the sake of your laws and future felicity, entreat you to act vigorously and firmly in this critical condition of your country. And we doubt not but that your humble exertions, under the smiles of Heaven, will insure that success and freedom due to the wise man and patriot.

Above all, we earnestly exhort you to contribute all within your power to the encouragement of those virtues for which the Supreme Being has declared that he will bestow his blessing upon a nation, and to the discouragement of those vices for which he overturns kingdoms in his wrath; and that at all proper times and seasons you seek to him, by prayer and supplication, for deliverance from the calamities of war, duly considering that, without his powerful aid and gracious interposition, all your endeavors must prove abortive and vain.

The Christian views of the people and government of the colony of Massachusetts are further disclosed by the following proclamations:—

Provincial Congress, Concord, Mass.,

Saturday, April 15, 1775, A.D.

Whereas it hath pleased the righteous Sovereign of the universe, in just indignation against the sins of a people long blessed with inestimable privileges, civil and religious, to suffer the plots of wicked men on both sides of the Atlantic, who for many years have incessantly labored to sap the foundation of our public liberties, so far to succeed that we see the New England colonies reduced to the ungracious alternative of a tame submission to a state of absolute vassalage to the will of a despotic minister, or of preparing themselves to defend at the hazard of their lives the inalienable rights of themselves and posterity against the avowed hostilities of their parent state, who openly threaten to wrest them from their hands by fire and sword.

In circumstances dark as these, it becomes us, as men and Christians, to reflect that, whilst every prudent measure should be taken to ward off the impending judgment, or to prepare to act in a proper manner under them when they come, at the same time, all confidence must be withheld from the means we use, and repose only on *that God* who rules in the armies of heaven, and without whose blessing the best human counsels are but foolishness, and all created power vanity.

It is the happiness of the church, that when the powers of earth and hell are combined against it, and those who should be nursing fathers become its persecutors, then the Throne of Grace is of the easiest access, and its appeal thither is graciously invited by that Father of Mercies who has assured it that "when his children ask bread, he will not give them a stone." Therefore, in compliance with the laudable practice of the people of God in all ages, with humble regard to the steps of Divine Providence towards this oppressed, threatened, and endangered people, and especially in obedience to the command of Heaven, that binds us to call on him in the day of trouble:

Resolved, That it be, and hereby is, recommended to the good people of this colony, of all denominations, that *Thursday,* the eleventh day of *May* next, be set apart as a day of public humiliation, fasting, and prayer; that a total abstinence from servile labor and recreation be observed, and all their religious assemblies solemnly convened, to humble themselves before *God,* under the heavy judgments felt and feared; to confess the sins they have commited; to implore the forgiveness of all our transgressions; a spirit of repentance and reformation; and a blessing on the husbandry, manufactures, and other lawful employments of this people; and especially that the union of the *American colonies* in defence of their rights (for which hitherto we desire to thank *Almighty God*) may be preserved and confirmed; that the Provincial, and especially the Continental, Congresses, may be directed to such measures as *God* will countenance; that the people of *Great Britain* and their rulers may have their eyes opened to discern the things that make for the peace of the nation and all its connections; and that *America* may soon behold a gracious interposition of Heaven for the redress of her many grievances, the restoration of all her invaded liberties, and their security to the latest generations.

Ordered, That the foregoing be copied, authenticated, and sent to all the religious assemblies in this colony.

Watertown, Nov. 20

A Proclamation for a Public Thanksgiving

Although, in consequence of the unnatural, cruel, and barbarous measures adopted and pursued by the British administration, great and distressing calamities are brought upon our distressed country, and in this colony in particular we feel the dreadful effects of a *civil war,* by which America is stained with the blood of her valiant sons, who have bravely fallen in the laudable defence of our rights and privileges; our capital, once the seat of justice, opulence, and virtue, is unjustly wrested from its proper owners, who are obliged to flee from the iron hand of tyranny, or held in the unrelenting arms of oppression; our seaports greatly distressed, and towns burnt by the foes who have acted the part of barbarous incendiaries; and although the wise and holy Governor of the world has, in his righteous providence, sent droughts into this colony; and wasting sickness into many of our towns; yet we have the greatest reasons to adore and praise the Supreme Disposer of all events, who deals infinitely better with us than we deserve, and amidst all his judgments hath remembered mercy, by causing the voice of health again to be heard amongst us; instead of famine, affording to an ungrateful people a competency of the necessaries and comforts of life; in remarkably protecting and preserving our troops when in apparent danger, while our *enemies,* with all their boasted skill and strength, have met with *loss, disappointment,* and *defeat;* and, in the course of his good providence, the Father of all Mercies hath bestowed upon us many other favors which call for our grateful acknowledgments:

Therefore, We have thought fit, with the advice of the Council and House of Representatives, to appoint Thursday, the 23d of November instant, to be observed throughout this colony as a day of public *thanksgiving;* hereby calling upon ministers and people to meet for religious worship on the said day, and *devoutly* to offer up their unfeigned praise to Almighty God, the source and benevolent bestower of all good, for his affording the necessary means of subsistence, though our commerce has been prevented and the supplies from the fishery denied us; that the lives of our officers and soldiers have been so remarkably preserved, while our enemies have fallen before them; that the vigorous efforts which have been made to excite the savage vengeance of the wilderness and to rouse the Indians in arms, that an unavoidable destruction might come upon our fron-

tier, have been almost miraculously defeated; that our unnatural enemies, instead of ravaging the country with uncontrolled sway, are confined within such narrow limits, to their own mortification and distress, environed by an *American* army, *brave* and *determined;* and that our rights and privileges, both civil and religious, are so far preserved to us, notwithstanding all efforts to deprive us of them.

And to offer up humble and fervent prayers to Almighty God for the whole British empire, especially for the United American Colonies; that he would bless our civil rulers, and lead them into wise and prudent measures at this dark and difficult day; that he would endow our General Court with all that wisdom which is profitable to direct; that he would graciously smile upon our endeavors to restore peace, preserve our rights and privileges and hand them down to posterity; that he would grant wisdom to the American Congress equal to their important station; that he would direct the generals and the American armies, wherever employed, and give them success and victory; that he would preserve and strengthen the hands of the *United Colonies;* that he would pour his Spirit upon all orders of men through the land, and bring us to a hearty repentance and reformation, and purify and sanctify all his churches, and make ours Emanuel's land; that he would spread the knowledge of the Redeemer throughout the whole earth, and fill the world with his glory. And all servile labor is forbidden on this day.

Given under our hands, at the Council-Chamber at Watertown, the fourth day of November, in the year of our Lord one thousand seven hundred and seventy-five.

By their Honors' command

JAMES OTIS   PERCY MORTON, *Dep. Secy.*

GOD SAVE THE PEOPLE!

RECOMMENDATIONS FOR FURTHER READING

Buckley, Thomas E., S.J. *Church and State in Revolutionary Virginia, 1776–1787.* Charlottesville: University Press of Virginia, 1977.

Curry, Thomas J. *The First Freedoms: Church and State in America to the Passage of the First Amendment.* New York: Oxford University Press, 1986.

Miller, William Lee. *The First Liberty: America's Foundation in Religious Freedom.* Washington, D.C.: Georgetown University Press, 2003.

Wilson, John K. "Religion under the State Constitutions, 1776–1800." *Journal of Church and State* 32 (1990): 753–73.

Witte, John, Jr. "'A Most Mild and Equitable Establishment of Religion': John Adams and the Massachusetts Experiment." In *Religion and the New Republic: Faith in the Founding of America,* edited by James H. Hutson, 1–40. Lanham, Md.: Rowman and Littlefield, 2000.

CHAPTER SIX

Petitions, Essays, and Sermons on Church and State in Revolutionary America

REVISIONS OF STATE CONSTITUTIONS and laws prompted widespread discussion about political institutions, rights, and duties. With respect to religious liberty and church-state relations, Americans argued most fervently about whether or not states should have an established faith and how religious minorities should be treated. Through petitions, essays, and sermons Americans made their views known to their fellow citizens and state legislatures.

As suggested in the last chapter, one notable feature of the following documents is the extent to which virtually every author professed (with apparent sincerity, in most cases) that religion—particularly Christianity—is a good thing. It is rare to find arguments for disestablishment on the grounds that religion is dangerous, although Madison does suggest

in *Federalist* nos. 10 and 51 that religion can be a cause of faction. Americans, of course, differed on whether or how civil governments should encourage religion, a debate which is reflected in the following texts. As well, in spite of the widespread support for religious toleration, the extent to which full civil rights should extend to religious minorities, such as Catholics and Jews, remained a subject of controversy.

This chapter includes documents by authors from a variety of denominations and states. As in the last chapter, Virginia is overrepresented because of the influence debates over disestablishment there have had among subsequent historians and jurists. The last three documents arguably fall outside the Revolutionary Era, but they are included here because their themes and concerns are similar to those of other documents in this chapter.

Petition of the German Congregation of Culpeper, Virginia (October 1776)

The following petition to the "President and Delegates of the Convention of the Commonwealth of Virginia" illustrates some of the disabilities under which Virginia dissenters lived.

To The Hon'ble the President and Delegates of the Convention of the Commonwealth of Virginia—

The Petition of the German Congregation of the County of Culpeper. Sheweth:

That our Fathers who liv'd under an Arbitrary Prince in Germany, and the Germans being particularly invited by the Hon'ble William Penn. Senr. Esqr. Proprietor of the Province of Pennsilvania to settle his Province; which, with the faith they had in the Provincial Charters, given and granted from the British Crown, and that the Germans there, enjoyed freedom in the Exercise of Religion as well as other ways, and that they only supported their own Church and Poor. Our Fathers Ventured their Lives and Fortunes to come into a Land of Liberty (I. E.) from a Europian Egypt to an American Canaan, to enjoy those sweets of freedom, which God created for all men. They journeyed from Germany to London & and there agreed with a Captain, to land them and their Families in Pensylvania; but he prov'd false, and landed them against their Will and agreement in Virginia, and sold them for Servants.—

On our arrival, the loss of their Estates, and the snare the Captain had draw'd them in, was not equal with the loss they were at, in not understanding the English Tongue, which rendered it impossible to join in the worship of God; till they were free, and the Lord directed a Zoar for them, where they could exercise themselves in the Christian Religion as they were taught by their Parents in Europe.

Soon after they were gethered to the Plase where we now live, they Concluded to erect a Church and School-House. But 1st they being just free were to Poor, 2d the Laws of the Country was against them, & 3ly the Arbitrary Power of Bishops. However, with sincere Prayer to God, that he would be Merciful to them, they petitioned the Governour & House of Burgesses, acquainted them with their Distress, and ask'd redress of their Grievance; which was so far granted that they had license to collect Money, build a Church, call a Minister, Worship God in a Congregation, & practice the Christian Religion as they were taught by their Parents in Europe.

Full of Love and Gratitude for this advance, and trusting that the Lord would further give his Grace to this Religious design; they send Three of the Congregation to Europe, who acquainted their Brethren there, with the Mercy they received from God, through the Act of Assembly and ask'd them for Assistance. The Reverend Doctor Tiegenhaken, Chaplain to the Royal House of England assisted them as much as was in his Power; sent Letters in favour of them, to our Bretheren in Germany, which caus'd that they rais'd a tolerable sum of German money, of the free Gifts of the Germans and other People, with which they build a Church, School-House, and purchased some land and Negroes as an Estate to the Church. But that Estate is not near sufficient to support the Church Expense and Minister.

And thro' our poverty we are oblig'd to pay Parochial Charges, as well as support our own Church, which still leaves many of us distress'd and as we are fellow-citizens in common, and still cannot understand the English Tongue and as we are now with our fellow citizens are oblig'd to bleed to Freedom, and Contribute our proportional part of the Expense of the War, and are not breaking from the establish'd Church, as do the common Discenders, we humbly pray, that we may hereafter be exempted from further

Reprinted from *Virginia Magazine of History and Biography* 18 (Richmond: House of the Society, 1910; repr. New York: Kraus Reprint Corporation, 1968), 268–70.

payment of Parochial Charges, other then sufficient to support our own Church and Poor. And that our Ministers who are hitherto received from the German Lutheran North American Ministerii, under whose Direction we at present are; may have full right and privilege and administration of their office with their Bretheren in Pennsylvania, or the establish'd Church Ministers in Virginia, so far as may extend to the Members of their own Church only; and your Petitioners as in Duty bound shall ever pray &c.

Petitions to the Virginia Legislature (1776–77)

When the Virginia Legislature began debating the fate of the Church of England, which had been Virginia's established church since its earliest days, it was inundated with hundreds of petitions. This debate took place following the adoption of Article XVI of the Virginia Declaration of Rights with its affirmation that "all men are equally entitled to the free exercise of religion." The following four petitions were presented to the Virginia Legislature in late 1776 and early 1777.

Petition of Sundry Inhabitants of Prince Edward County, Virginia (October 11, 1776)

Oct. 11th.

To the Honourable the President and House of Delegates of the Commonwealth of Virginia, to meet at Williamsburg the first Tuesday in October 1776.

Reprinted from *Virginia Magazine of History and Biography* 18 (Richmond: House of the Society, 1910; repr. New York: Kraus Reprint Corporation, 1968), 40.

The Petition of Sundry of the Inhabitants of Prince Edward County, respectfully sheweth,

That we heartily approve, and chearfully submit ourselves to the form of Government adopted at your last session; hoping that our united American States will long continue free and Independent. The last Article of the Bill of Rights we also esteem as the rising Sun of religious Liberty, to *relieve* us from a long night of ecclesiastic Bondage: and we do most earnestly request and expect that you would go on to complete what is so nobly begun; raise religious as well as civil Liberty to the Zenith of Glory, and make Virginia an Asylum for free enquiry, knowledge, and the virtuous of every Denomination. Justice to ourselves and *Posterity,* as well as a regard to the honour of the Common Wealth, makes it our indispensable Duty, in particular to intreat, That without Delay, you would pull down all Church Establishments; abolish every Tax upon Conscience and private judgment; and leave each Individual to rise or sink according to his Merit, and the general Laws of the Land. The whole amounts of what we desire is, That our Honourable Legislature would blot out every vestige of British Tyranny and Bondage, and define accurately between civil and ecclesiastic authority; then leave our Lord Jesus Christ the Honour of being the sole Lawgiver and Governor in his Church; and every one in the Things of Religion to stand or fall to Him; he being in this respect the only rightful Master.

Memorial of the Presbytery of Hanover, Virginia (October 24, 1776)

To the Honourable the General Assembly of Virginia:

The Memorial of the Presbytery of Hanover humbly represents, That your memorialists are governed by the same sentiments which have inspired the united States of America, and are determined that nothing in our power and influence shall be wanting to give success to their common Cause. We would also represent, that, Dissenters from the Church of England in this Country, have ever been desirous to conduct themselves as peaceable members of the civil Government; for which reason, they have hitherto submitted to several ecclesiastic burthens and restrictions that are inconsistent with equal liberty. But now when the many and grievous oppressions of our mother Country have laid this Continent under the necessity of casting off the yoke of tyranny, and of forming independent Governments upon equitable and liberal foundations, we flatter ourselves, that we shall be freed from all the incumbrances which a spirit of Domination, prejudice, or bigotry hath interwoven with most other political systems. This we are the more strongly encouraged to expect by the *Declaration of Rights* so universally applauded for that dignity, firmness, and precision with which it delineates and asserts the privileges of society, and the prerogatives of human nature; and which we embrace as the *Magna Charta* of our Commonwealth, that can never be violated without endangering the grand superstructure it was designed to sustain. Therefore we rely upon this *Declaration,* as well as the justice of our honourable Legislature, to secure us the *free exercise of Religion, according to the dictates of our Consciences;* and we should fall short in our duty to ourselves, and the many and numerous congregations under our Care, were we upon this occasion to neglect laying

The text was transcribed from microfilm of the original Memorial and follows the original. Library of Virginia, Religious Petitions, Part 1, 1774–1785. Miscellaneous Reel 425A, October 24, 1776.

before you a State of the religious Grievances under which we have hitherto laboured, that they no longer may be continued in our present form of Government.

It is well known that in the frontier Counties, which are justly supposed to contain a fifth part of the inhabitants of Virginia, the dissenters have borne the heavy burthens of purchasing Glebes, building Churches, and supporting the established Clergy, when there are very few Episcopalians either to assist in bearing the expences, or to reap the advantage; and that throughout the other parts of the Country there are also many thousands of zealous friends and defenders of our State, who, besides the invidious and disadvantageous restrictions to which they have been subjected, annually pay large taxes to support an Establishment, from which their consciences and principles oblige them to dissent: all which are confessedly so many violations of their natural Rights; and in their consequences a restraint upon freedom of inquiry and private judgment.

In this enlightened age, and in a land where all of every denomination are united in the most strenuous efforts to be free; we hope and expect, that our Representatives will cheerfully concur in removing every species of religious as well as civil bondage. Certain it is that every argument for civil liberty gains additional strength when applied to liberty in the concerns of Religion; and there is no argument in favour of establishing the Christian Religion, but what may be pleaded with equal propriety for establishing the tenets of Mahommed by those who believe the Alcoran; or, if this be not true, if it is at least impossible for the Magistrate to adjudge the right of preference among the various Sects that profess the Christian Faith without erecting a Chair of Infallibility which would lead us back to the Church of Rome.

We beg leave further to represent that Religious Establishments are highly injurious to the temporal interests of any Community. Without insisting upon the ambition and the arbitrary practices of those who are favored by Government, or the intriguing seditious Spirit which is commonly excited by this, as well as every other kind of oppression, such Establishments greatly retard population, and consequently the progress of Arts, Sciences, and Manufactories; witness the rapid growth and improvements of the Northern Provinces compared with this. No one can deny that the more early settlement and the many superior advantages of our Country, would have invited multitudes of Artificers, mechanics, and the useful members of Society to fix their habitation among us, who have either remained in the place of their nativity, or preferred worse civil Governments, and a more barren soil, when they might enjoy the rights of conscience more fully than they had a prospect of doing it in this. From which we infer, that Virginia might now have been the Capitol of America, and a match for the British Arms without depending upon others for the necessaries of War, had it not been prevented by her religious establishment.

Neither can it be made appear that the Gospel needs any such civil aid. We rather conceive that when our Blessed Saviour declares his kingdom is not of the world, he renounces all dependence upon State power; and as his *weapons are spiritual,* and were only designed to have influence upon the judgment & heart of man, we are persuaded that if mankind were left in the quiet possession of their unalienable religious privileges, Christianity, as in the days of the Apostles, would continue to prevail and flourish in the greatest purity, by its own native excellence, and under the all-disposing providence of God.

We would also humbly represent, that the only proper objects of civil Government are the happiness and protection of men in the present state of existence; the security of the life, liberty, and property of the Citizens; and to restrain the vicious and encourage the virtuous by wholesome laws equally extending to every individual. But that the *duty which we owe our Creator and the manner of discharging it can only be directed by reason and conviction;* and is no where cognizable but at the Tribunal of the Universal Judge.

Therefore we ask no Ecclesiastical Establishments for ourselves, neither can we approve of them when granted to others; this indeed would be giving *exclu-*

sive or separate emoluments and privileges to one set (or sect) of men without any special *public services* to the common reproach and injury of every other denomination. And for the reasons recited, we are induced earnestly to entreat that all laws now in force in the Common Wealth, which countenance religious domination may be speedily repealed; that all of every religious sect may be protected in the full exercise of their several modes of worship; and exempted from all taxes for the support of any Church whatsoever further than what may be agreeable to their own private choice or voluntary obligation. This being done, all partial and invidious distinctions will be abolished, to the great honor and interest of the State, and every one be left to stand or fall according to merit, which can never be the case so long as any one denomination is established in preference to others.

That the great Sovereign of the Universe may inspire you with unanimity, wisdom, and resolution; and bring you to a just determination on all the important concerns before you, is the fervent prayer of your Memorialists.

Signed by Order of the Presbytery
John Todd, Moderator
Caleb Wallace, P. Clk.

———————

Memorial from Clergy of the Established Church, Virginia (November 8, 1776)

To the Honorable the Speaker and Gentlemen of the House of Delegates—

The Memorial of a considerable number of the Clergy of the established Church in Virginia . . . .

Reprinted from *Virginia Magazine of History and Biography* 18 (Richmond: House of the Society, 1910; repr. New York: Kraus Reprint Corporation, 1968), 146–48.

. . . . setting forth that your Memorialists, having understood that various Petitions have been presented to the Honorable the Assembly, praying the abolition of the established Church in this State, wish to represent that when they undertook the charge of Parishes in Virginia, they depended on the publick Faith for the receiving of that Recompence for their services, during Life or good Behaviour, which the Laws of the Land promised, a Tenure which to them appears of the same sacred nature as that by which every man in the State holds, & has secured to him, his private Property; and that such of them, as are not yet provided for, entered into Holy Orders—expecting to receive the several Emoluments which such religious Establishment offered; that from the nature of their Education they are precluded from gaining a tolerable subsistence in any other way of Life: & that therefore they think it would be inconsistent with justice, either to deprive the present Incumbents of Parishes of any Rights or Profits they hold or enjoy; or to cut off from such as are now in orders & unbeneficed, those Expectations which originated from the Laws of the Land & which have been the means of disqualifying them for any other Profession or way of Life—

Also, That though your Memorialists are far from favouring Encroachments on the religious Rights of any Sect or Denomination of men, yet they conceive that a religious Establishment in a State is conducive to its Peace and Happiness. They think the opinions of mankind have a very considerable influence over their Practice; and that it therefore cannot be improper for the legislative Body of a State to consider how such opinions as are most consonant to Reason & of the best Efficacy in human affairs, may be propagated and supported. That for their Part are of opinion that the Doctrines of Christianity have a greater Tendency to produce Virtue amongst men than any human Laws or Institutions; & that these can be best taught & preserved in their Purity in an established Church, which gives Encouragements to men to study & acquire a competent knowledge of the Scriptures: and they think that if these great Pur-

poses can be answered by a religious Establishment, the Hardships which such a Regulation might impose on Individuals, or even Bodies of men, ought not to be considered.

Also, That whilst your Memorialists are fully persuaded of the good Effects of religious Establishment in general, they are more particularly convinced of the Excellency of the religious Establishment which has hitherto subsisted in this State:

That they ground their convictions on the Experience of 150 years, during which Period order & internal Tranquillity, true Piety & Virtue have more prevailed than in most other Parts of the world; & on the mild & tolerating spirit of the Church established, which with all christian charity & Benevolence has regarded Dissenters of every Denomination, & has shewn no Disposition to restrain them in the Exercise of their Religion: That it appears to your Memorialists that the mildness of the church Establishment has heretofore been acknowledged by those very Dissenters, who now aim at its Ruin, many of whom emigrate from other countries to settle in this, from Motives, we may reasonably suppose, of Interest & Happiness[.]

Also, That your Memorialists apprehend many bad consequences from abolishing the church Establishment. They cannot suppose, should all Denominations of Christians be placed upon a Level, that this Equality will continue, or that no attempt will be made by any Sect for the superiority, & they foresee that much confusion, probably civil commotions, will attend the contest. They also dread the ascendency of that Religion which permits its Professors to threaten Destruction to the Commonwealth, in order to serve their own private Ends.

Lastly, That though the justice & Expediency of continuing the church Establishment is a matter of which your Memorialists themselves have no Doubt, yet they wish that the final Determination of your honorable House be deferred, till the general sentiments of the good People of this Commonwealth can be collected, as your Memorialists have the best Reasons to believe that a majority of them desire to see the Church Establishment continued: as the sentiments of the People have been attended to in other Instances, they submit it to your consideration, whether some Regard should not be paid in their sentiments in a matter, which so nearly concerns them, as that of Religion.

Memorial of the Presbytery of Hanover, Virginia (June 3, 1777)

To the Honourable the General Assembly of Virginia.

The memorial of the Presbytery of Hanover, humbly represents,—That your memorialists and the religious denomination with which we are connected, are most sincerely attached to the common interests of the American States, and are determined that our most fervent prayers and strenuous endeavours shall ever be united with our fellow subjects to repel the assaults of tyranny and to maintain our common rights. In our former memorial we have expressed our hearty approbation of the Declaration of Rights, which has been made and adopted as the basis of the laws and government of this State; and now we take the opportunity of testifying that nothing has inspired us with greater confidence in our Legislature, than the late act of Assembly declaring that equal liberty, as well religious as civil, shall be universally extended to the good people of this country; and that all the oppressive acts of parliament respecting religion which have been formerly enacted in the mother country, shall henceforth be of no validity or force in this commonwealth. As also exempting dissenters from all levies, taxes, and impositions, whatsoever, towards supporting the church of England as it now

Reprinted from *American Presbyterians* 63, no. 4 (winter 1985), 362–65. Virginia General Assembly, Legislative Petitions (Record Group 78). Miscellaneous Petition, dated June 3, 1777. State government records collection, The Library of Virginia. Used by permission of The Library of Virginia.

is or hereafter may be established. We would, therefore have given our honourable Legislature no further trouble on this subject, but we are sorry to find that there yet remains a variety of opinions touching the propriety of a general assessment, or whether every religious society shall be left to voluntary contributions for the maintenance of the ministers of the gospel who are of different persuasions. As this matter is deferred by our Legislature to the discussion and final determination of a future Assembly, when the opinions of the country, in general, shall be better known; we think it our indispensable duty again to repeat a part of the prayer of our former memorial, "That dissenters of every denomination may be exempted from all taxes for the support of any church whatsoever, further than what may be agreeable to the private choice or voluntary obligation of every individual; while the civil magistrates no otherwise interfere, than to protect them all in the full and free exercise of their several modes of worship." We then represented as the principal reason upon which this request is founded, that the only proper objects of civil governments are, the happiness and protection of men in the present state of existence, the security of the life, liberty, and property of the citizens, and to restrain the vicious and encourage the virtuous by wholesome laws equally extending to every individual: and that the duty which we owe our Creator, and the manner of discharging it, can only be directed by reason and conviction, and is no where cognizable but at the tribunal of the universal Judge.

To illustrate and confirm these assertions, we beg leave to observe, that to judge for ourselves, and to engage in the exercise of religion agreeable to the dictates of our own consciences is an unalienable right, which upon the principles that the gospel was first propagated, and the reformation from Popery carried on, can never be transferred to another. Neither does the church of Christ stand in need of a *general assessment* for its support; and most certain we are that it would be no advantage, but an injury to the society to which we belong: and as every good Christian believes that Christ has ordained a complete system of laws for the government of his kingdom, so we are persuaded that, by his providence, he will support it to its final consummation. In the fixed belief of this principle, that the kingdom of Christ, and the concerns of religion, are beyond the limits of civil control, we should act a dishonest, inconsistent part, were we to receive any emoluments from human establishments for the support of the gospel.

These things being considered, we hope we shall be excused for remonstrating against a general assessment for any religious purpose. As the maxims have long been approved, that every servant is to obey his master; and that, the hireling is accountable for his conduct to him from whom he receives his wages; in like manner, if the Legislature has any rightful authority over the ministers of the gospel in the exercise of their sacred office, and it is their duty to levy a maintenance for them as such; then it will follow that they may revive the old establishment in its former extent; or ordain a new one for any sect they think proper; they are invested with a power not only to determine, but it is incumbent on them to declare, who shall preach, what they shall preach; to whom, when, at what places they shall preach; or to impose any regulations and restrictions upon religious societies that they may judge expedient. These consequences are so plain as not to be denied; and they are so entirely subversive of religious liberty, that if they should take place in Virginia, we should be reduced to the melancholy necessity of saying with the Apostles in like cases "Judge ye whether it is best to obey God or man;" and also of acting as they acted.

Therefore, as it is contrary to our principles and interest; and, as we think, subversive of religious liberty, we do again most earnestly entreat that our Legislature would never extend any assessment for religious purposes to us, or to the congregations under our care. And your memorialists, as in duty bound, shall ever pray for, and demean themselves as peaceable subjects, of, civil government.

Signed by order of the Presbytery.
RICHARD SANKEY, *Moderator.*
[Timber Ridge, 25 April 1777]

Worcestriensis, Number IV (September 4, 1776)

The pseudonymous author Worcestriensis, "from Worcester," published a series of essays during the War of American Independence in the Boston newspaper *Massachusetts Spy*. In the following essay the author argues for both religious toleration and state support of religion.

To the Hon. LEGISLATURE of the STATE of MASSACHUSETTS-BAY

The subject of this disquisition (begun in my last) which is humbly offered to your consideration, is the promotion and establishment of religion in the State. In the course of the reasoning, it was suggested that a toleration of all religious principles (in other words, of all professions, modes & forms of worship) which do not sap the foundation of good government, is consistent with equity and the soundest policy. To establish this, as well as the general doctrine is my present design.

We live in [an] age of the world, in which the knowledge of the arts and sciences, calm and dispassionate enquiries and sound reasoning have been carried to surprising lengths, much to the honor of mankind. The rights of men and things, as well in an intellectual as a civil view, have by able writers, friends of human nature, been ascertained with great degrees of precision. Therefore it now becomes us in all our words and action to do nothing ungenerous, nothing unworthy the dignity of our *rational nature*.

In a well regulated state, it will be the business of the Legislature to prevent sectaries of different de-

Reprinted from *American Political Writing during the Founding Era, 1760–1805*, ed. Charles S. Hyneman and Donald S. Lutz (Indianapolis: Liberty Fund, 1983), 1:449–54. © Liberty Fund, 1983. Reprinted by permission.

nominations from molesting and disturbing each other; to ordain that no part of the community shall be permitted to perplex and harrass the other for any supposed heresy, but that each individual shall be allowed to have and enjoy, profess and maintain his own system of religion, provided it does not issue in *overt acts* of treason against the state undermining the peace and good order of society.

To allow one part of a society to lord it over the faith and consciences of the other, in religious matters is the ready way to set the whole community together by the ears. It is laying a foundation for persecution in the abstract; for (as the judicious MONTESQUIEU observes) "it is a principle that every religion which is persecuted, becomes itself persecuting; for as soon as by some accidental turn it arises from persecution, it attacks the religion that persecuted it; not as a religion but as a tyranny."

It is necessary then that the laws require from the several religions, not only that they shall not embroil the State, but that they shall not raise disturbances among themselves. A citizen does not fulfill the laws by not disturbing the government; it is requisite that he should not trouble any citizen whomever.

Compulsion, instead of making men religious, generally has a contrary tendency, it works not conviction, but most naturally leads them into hypocrisy. If they are honest enquirers after truth; if their articles of belief differ from the creed of their *civil* superiors, compulsion will bring them into a sad *dilemma*. If they are conformists to what they do not believe, great uneasiness of mind must continuously perplex them. If they stand out and persist in nonconformity, they subject themselves to pains and penalties. There is further this ill consequence resulting from the establishment of religious dominion, viz. That an endeavor to suppress nonconformists, will increase, rather than diminish their number: For, however strange it may appear, yet indubitable facts prove that mankind [is] naturally compassionate [toward] those who are subjected to pains and hardships for the sake of their religion, and very frequently join with them

and espouse their cause, raise sedition and faction, and endanger the public peace.

Whoever will read the history of Germany (not to mention the mother of harlots) will find this exemplified, in a manner and degree sufficient to shock any one who is not destitute of every spark of humanity. Calvinists and remonstrants made the religious divisions of the people: sometimes one party then the other was superior in their bloody disputes.

The fire first began among and between the congregations of different persuasions (calvinistic and arminian) the women and children came to blows and women pulled each others caps and hair as they passed and repassed the streets after (what they called divine) service was over in the several congregations, and the children gave each other bloody noses. This brought on civil dissention and altercation, until at length, rivers of blood in quarrels about things entirely immaterial and useless, relative either to this world or the other were shed; the nearest kindred embrued their hands in each others blood, subjects withdrew their allegiance and tumbled their rulers from their seats.

This is a true representation of facts, and is sufficient to deter any legislature from enacting laws requiring conformity to any particular mode or profession of religion, under pains of persecution in case of refusal.

This is not suggested because a *persecuting spirit* has of late years been conspicuous among the inhabitants of this state. On the contrary, a candid, catholic, and benevolent disposition has increased and prevailed. The principle reason why this is exhibited is, that as the GOOD PEOPLE of this and its sister states had just cause to alter and amend their civil constitution, so also, it is probable, the legislature of this State will take into consideration the eclesiastical discipline and government, and make such alterations and amendments in the constitution of the churches, as by them, in their wisdom shall be thought proper. We would therefore guard against everything that might be construed to have the least colour of a persecuting tendency, that so the law, relative to religion, may be the most candid, catholic and rational, that the nature of human society will admit of.

Perhaps some sticklers for establishments, requiring conformity to the prevailing religion, may now enquire whether, upon the principles above laid down, any legal establishment at all can take place? and if any, what? In answer to such querists, I would say that if by an establishment they intend the enacting and ordaining laws obliging dissenters from any certain religion to conform thereto, and, in case of nonconformity, subjecting them to pains, penalties and disabilities, in this sense there can and ought to be none. The establishment contended for in this disquisition, is of a different kind, and must result from a different legal Procedure.

It must proceed only from the benign frames of the legislature from an encouragement of the GENERAL PRINCIPLES of religion and morality, recommending free inquiry and examination of the doctrines said to be divine; using all possible and lawful means to enable its subjects to discover the truth, and to entertain good and rational sentiments, and taking mild and parental measures to bring about the design; these are the most probable means to bring about that establishment of religion which is recommended, and a settlement on an immoveable BASIS. It is lawful for the directors of a state to give preference to that profession of religion which they take to be true, and they have right to inflict penalties on those who notoriously violate the laws of natural religion, and thereby disturb the public peace. The openly profane come within their penal jurisdiction. There is no stronger cement of society than a sacred regard to OATHS; nothing binds stronger to the observation of the laws, therefore the public safety, and the *honor* of the SUPREME BEING require that public *profaneness,* should bring down the public vengeance upon those who dare hurl profanities at the throne of OMNIPOTENCE, and thereby *lessen* the reverence of the people for oaths, and solemn appeals to almighty

God, and so shaking the foundation of good order and security in society. The same may be said of all Profaneness, and also of debauchery, which strike a fatal blow at the root of good regulation, and the well-being of the state.

And now with regard to the positive interposition of civil magistracy in behalf of religion, I would say, that what has been above suggested with respect to *toleration,* will not disprove the right of the legislature to exert themselves in favor of one religious profession rather than another, they have a right of private judgment as well as others, and are BOUND to do their *utmost* to propagate *that* which they esteem to be true. This they are to do by providing *able* and *learned* TEACHERS, to instruct the people in the knowledge of what they deem the truth, maintaining them by the public money, though at the same time they have no right in the least degree to endeavor the depression of professions of any religious denomination. Nor let it be said (in order to a perfect toleration) that all religious denominations have an equal right to public countenance, for this would be an evident infringement on the right of private judgment in the members of the legislature.

If the greatest part of the people, coincide with the public authority of the State in giving the prefference to any one religious system and creed, the dissenting few, though they cannot conscientiously conform to the prevailing religion, yet ought to acquiesce and rest satisfied that their religious Liberty is not *diminished.*

This suggestion starts a question, which has caused much debate among persons of different religious sentiments, viz. Whether a minor part of a parish or other corporation, are, or can be consistently obliged to contribute to the maintenance and support of a minister to them disagreeable, who is approved by the majority.

This is answered by a very able writer in the following manner, viz. "that this will stand upon the same footing with their contributing towards the expence of a war, which they think not necessary or prudent. If no such power were admitted, covetousness would drive many into dissenting parties in order to save their money.

So that none can reasonably blame a government for requiring such a *general Contribution,* and in this case it seems fit it should be yielded to, as the determination of those to whose guardianship the minority have committed themselves and their possessions.

We hope and trust that you, Hon. directors of this State, will exert yourselves in the cultivation and promotion of pure and RATIONAL RELIGION among your constituents. If there were no arguments to be drawn from the consideration of a *future* world, yet those drawn from the great influence of religion upon the LAWS and the *observance* of them, must, and ought to prevail."

I would add, that our Legislature of the last year have declared that "a Government so popular can be supported only by universal Knowledge and VIRTUE, in the body of the people."

In addition to this, I shall produce the opinion of the above cited *Montesquieu* (a great *authority!*) and so conclude this number.

"Religion may support a state, when the laws themselves are incapable of doing it.

"Thus when a kingdom is frequently agitated by civil wars, religion may do much by obliging one part of the state to remain always quiet.

"A prince who loves and fears religion, is a lion, who stoops to the hand that strokes or to the voice that appeases him. He who fears and hates religion, is like the savage beast, that growls and bites the chain which prevents his flying on the passenger. He who has no religion at all, is that terrible animal; who perceives his liberty only when he tears in pieces, and when he devours."

WORCESTRIENSIS

A Declaration of the Rights, of the Inhabitants of the State of Massachusetts-Bay, in New-England (1779)

ISAAC BACKUS (1724–1806)

In 1779, Noah Alden, an elder in a Baptist church, was elected a delegate to the Massachusetts constitutional convention. He wrote to New England Baptist leader Isaac Backus asking his opinion as to "what are the rights of the people" and how a "Bill of Rights ought to be drawn." In response, Backus wrote the following bill of rights.

1 All men are born equally free and independant, and have certain natural, inherent and unalienable rights, among which are the enjoying and defending life and liberty, acquiring, possessing, and protecting property, and pursuing and obtaining happiness and safety.

2 As God is the only worthy object of all religious worship, and nothing can be true religion but a voluntary obedience unto his revealed will, of which each rational soul has an equal right to judge for itself, every person has an unalienable right to act in all religious affairs according to the full persuasion of his own mind, where others are not injured thereby. And civil rulers are so far from having any right to empower any person or persons, to judge for others in such affairs, and to enforce their judgments with the sword, that their power ought to be exerted to protect all persons and societies, within their jurisdiction

Reprinted by permission of the publishers from *Isaac Backus on Church, State, and Calvinism: Pamphlets, 1754–1789,* ed. William G. McLoughlin (Cambridge, Mass.: The Belknap Press of Harvard University Press), 487–89. © 1968 by the President and Fellows of Harvard College.

from being injured or interrupted in the free enjoyment of this right, under any pretense whatsoever.

3 The people of this State have the sole, exclusive, and inherent right of governing and regulating the internal police of the same.

4 As all civil rulers derive their authority from the people, so they are accountable to them for the use they make of it.

5 The great end of government being for the good of the governed, and not the honor or profit of any particular persons or families therein, the community hath an unalienable right to reform, alter, or new form their constitution of government as that community shall judge to be most conducive to the public weal.

6 It being essential to civil freedom that every elector of officers should give his vote with an unbiased mind, whoever shall make use of any sort of bribery, or party influence, either to get into office, or to keep himself in place thereby seeks to rob the freemen of their birthright and ought to be looked upon as an enemy to liberty, and not to be trusted with any public office. Elections ought to be free and frequent.

7 Every member of civil society hath a right to be protected in the enjoyment of life, liberty and property, and therefore is bound to contribute his proportion towards the expenses of that protection, and to yield his personal services, when necessary, or an equivolent thereto: but no part of any man's property can justly be taken from him, or applied to public uses, without his own consent, or that of his legal representatives: and no man ought to be compelled to bear arms, who conscientiously scruples the lawfulness of it, if he will pay such equivolent; nor are the people bound by any laws, but such as they have in like manner assented to, for their common good.

8 In all prosecutions for criminal offences, a man hath a right to be heard by himself and his council, to demand the cause and nature of his accusation, to be confronted with the witnesses, to call for evidence in his favor, and a speady public trial, by an impartial jury of the country, without whose consent he cannot be found guilty. Nor can he be compelled to give evi-

Isaac Backus, oil on canvas. Used by permission of Andover Newton Theological School.

dence against himself; nor can any man be justly deprived of his liberty, except by the laws of the land, or the judgment of his peers.

9 The people have a right to hold themselves, their houses, papers and possessions free from search or seizure; therefore warrants without oaths or affirmations first made, affording a sufficient foundation for them, and whereby an officer or messenger may be required to search suspected places, or seize any person or persons, his or their property, not particularly described, are contrary to that right, and ought not to be granted.

10 In all controversies respecting property, and in suits between man and man, the parties have a right to trial by jury, which ought to be held sacred.

11 The people have a right to freedom of speech, and of writing and publishing their sentiments; therefore the freedom of the press ought not to be restrained.

12 The people have a right to bear arms for the defense of themselves and the state; and as standing armies, in time of peace, are dangerous to liberty, they ought not to be kept up; and the military should be kept under strict subordination to, and governed by, the civil power.

13 A frequent recurrence to the first principles of government, and a firm adherence to justice, moderation, temperance, industery, and frugality, are absolutely necessary to preserve the great blessings of government and liberty; and the people have a right to assemble together, to consult about these great concerns, to instruct their representatives, and to apply to the legislature for a redress of grievances, by address, petition or remonstrance.

Bill of Rights
1779

Sermon Delivered at a Public Thanksgiving after Peace (1782)

JOHN WITHERSPOON (1722–94)

Presbyterian clergyman, Princeton president, and longtime member of the Continental Congress, John Witherspoon preached the following thanksgiving sermon in 1782. In it he reflects on God's providential aid during the War of American Independence and on the role of civil government in promoting religion and morality.

PSAL. iii. 8
Salvation belongeth unto the Lord

MY BRETHREN,

We are met together in obedience to public authority, to keep a day of solemn thanksgiving to God, for the goodness of his providence to the United States of America, in the course of a war, which has now lasted seven years, with a powerful and formidable nation. We are particularly called upon to give thanks for the signal successes with which it hath pleased him to bless our arms and those of our allies, in the course of the last year, and the campaign which is now drawing to a close. I need say nothing of the importance of the great contest in which we have been so long engaged, or the interesting alternative which depends upon the issue, as these seem to have been felt in the fullest manner by all ranks in this country, from the beginning. The language even of the common people will convince every man of reflection that they are universally sensible how much is at stake. My proper business, therefore, is to engage every pious hearer to adore the providence of God in general, to offer with sincerity and gratitude the sacrifice of praise for his many mercies, and to make a wise and just improvement of the present promising situation of public affairs.

Many who now hear me are witnesses, that it has never been my practice, for reasons which appear to me to be good, to intermix politics with the ordinary service of the sanctuary, on the weekly returns of the Christian Sabbath, further than fervent supplications to the throne of grace, for divine direction to the public counsels, and assistance to those who are employed in the public service. But on days of this kind it becomes part of a minister's duty to direct the attention of the hearers to events of a public nature. This you know I did with great concern, and at considerable length, six years ago on a public fast day. I would therefore willingly, in this more advanced period, take a view of what is past, and endeavour to direct you in what remains, of your duty to God, to your country, and to yourselves.

Reprinted from *The Works of John Witherspoon* (Edinburgh: Ogle and Aikman et al., 1804–5), 5:237–70.

For this purpose I have chosen the words of the Psalmist David now read, which are part of a psalm generally thought to have been composed by the royal author before the war with Absalom, his unnatural son, was wholly finished; but when he had such presages of success as made him speak the language of faith and confidence. "I laid me down and slept: I awaked, for the Lord sustained me. I will not be afraid of ten thousands of people that have set themselves against me round about. Arise, O Lord, save me, O my God; for thou hast smitten all mine enemies upon the cheek-bone; thou hast broken the teeth of the ungodly. Salvation belongeth unto the Lord; thy blessing is upon thy people. Selah."

In discoursing upon this subject I propose, through the assistance of divine grace,

I. To explain and state the proper meaning of this expression or sentiment of the inspired Psalmist, "Salvation belongeth unto the Lord."

II. To lay before you a succinct view of what the United States of America owe to divine Providence in the course of the present war.

III. To make a practical improvement of the subject for your instruction and direction.

First, then, I am to explain and state the proper meaning of this expression or sentiment of the inspired Psalmist, "Salvation belongeth unto the Lord." This I mean to do by adhering strictly to what appears to be the mind of the Spirit of God in the passage before us, as well as in a manner agreeable to the analogy of faith. As religion is the same in substance in every age, the reflections of pious persons on the course of Providence, arise from the same examples, and lead to the same end. The words may justly be supposed to contain the Psalmist's thankful acknowledgment of the past mercies of God, as well as the foundation of his future security. They carry in them a general confession of the influence of divine Providence upon every event, and in particular with respect to salvation, or deliverance from impending danger. In this view when he says, "Salvation belong-

John Witherspoon, by Charles Willson Peale, 1783–84. Used by permission of Independence National Historical Park.

eth unto the Lord," it seems to imply the three following things.

1. That "salvation belongeth unto the Lord," as distinguished from human or created help, and therefore all confidence in man stands opposed to the sentiment expressed by the holy Psalmist in the text. It is not opposed to the use or application of, but to an excessive or undue reliance on human means, or second causes of any kind. It implies, that success in any attempt is to be ultimately attributed to God. That it is he who by his providence provides outward means, who raises up friends to his people, or causes "their enemies to be at peace with them." That it is he who in cases of difficulty and danger directs their hands to war and their fingers to fight, and finally crowns their endeavours with success. Whether therefore the outward advantages are great or small, whether the expectation or the probability of success has been strong

or weak, he who confesses that salvation belongeth unto God, will finally give the glory to him. Confidence before, and boasting after the event, are alike contrary to this disposition. If any person desires to have his faith in this truth confirmed or improved, let him read the history of mankind in a cool and considerate manner, and with a serious frame of spirit. He will then perceive that every page will add to his conviction. He will find that the most important events have seemed to turn upon circumstances the most trivial, and the most out of the reach of human direction. A blast of wind, a shower of rain, a random shot, a private quarrel, the neglect of a servant, a motion without intention, or a word spoken by accident and misunderstood, has been the cause of a victory or defeat which has decided the fate of empires. Whoever, with these facts in his view, believes the constant influence and over-ruling power of divine providence, will know what the Psalmist means when he says, "Salvation belongeth unto the Lord."

2. In this sentiment the Psalmist seems to have had in view the *omnipotence* of Providence; that nothing is impossible with God; that there is no state so dangerous, no enemy so formidable, but he is able to work deliverance. He has not only the direction and government of means and second causes, but is himself superior to all means. The word *salvation,* when it is applied in Scripture to temporal danger, generally signifies a great and distinguished deliverance. Thus it is used by Moses, Exodus xiv. 13. "Stand still and see the salvation of God"; and in the same manner, 1 Sam. xiv. 45. "Shall Jonathan die, who hath wrought this great salvation in Israel?" When, therefore, a person or people are threatened with evils of the most dreadful kind; when they are engaged in a conflict very unequal; when they are driven to extremity, and have no resource left as means of defence; then, if the cause in which they are engaged is righteous and just, they may cry to God for relief. The sentiment expressed by the Psalmist ought to bear them up against despair, and they may say as the angel to the father of the faithful, "Is there any thing too hard for the Lord?" There are many instances in Scripture of sig-

nal deliverance granted to the servants of God, some of them even wholly miraculous, which teach us to set our hope in his mercy, and not to suffer his mighty works to slip out of our minds. This is the exercise of faith in an unchangeable God—"the same yesterday, to-day, and for ever."

3. This sentiment has respect to the mercy and goodness of God, or his readiness to hear the cry of the oppressed, and send deliverance to his people. This circumstance is necessary to be taken in, to make him the proper object of faith and trust; and it must be combined with the other, to give us a complete view of the influence of Providence. Power and wisdom alone give an imperfect display of the divine character. It would give little support under the pressure of affliction, to have a general or theoretical persuasion that all things are possible with God; but if we believe his readiness to interpose, and see our title clear to implore his help, we have that hope which is justly called "the anchor of the soul, sure and stedfast." In this sense salvation belongeth unto God; it is his prerogative, it is his glory. The promise so often repeated in the same or similar terms, is addressed both to nations and particular persons. "He shall call upon me, and I will answer him. I will be with him in trouble, to deliver him, and to honour him. The righteous cry, and the Lord heareth, and delivereth him out of all his troubles. Many are the afflictions of the righteous; but the Lord delivereth him out of them all."

Having briefly stated these known and general truths, I proceed to the *second* and principal thing proposed, which was to lay before you a succinct view of what the United States of America owe to divine providence, in the course of the present war. On considering this part of the subject, a difficulty presents itself as to the manner of handling it. I am desirous of doing it some measure of justice, and at the same time of avoiding excessive prolixity, or a tedious enumeration of particular facts. To unite these two purposes as much as possible, I will divide what I have to say into distinct branches; and after a few words of illustration on each of them, leave it to every hearer to add such further examples as may have fallen within his own observation. The branches I would separately consider are the following: 1. Signal successes, or particular and providential favours to us in the course of the war. 2. Preservation from difficulties and evils which seemed to be in our situation unavoidable, and, at the same time, next to insurmountable. 3. Confounding the counsels of our enemies, and making them hasten on the change which they desired to prevent.

1. Signal successes, or providential favours to us in the course of the war. Here I must mention what happened at the beginning of the contest, and prevented us from being crushed in the very out-set, although it is now in a manner wholly forgotten. Let us remember our true situation, after we had made the most public and peremptory declarations of our determination to defend our liberties. There was a willing spirit, but unarmed hands. Our enemies have all along charged us with a deliberate concerted purpose of breaking with them, and setting up an independent empire. The falsehood of this accusation might be made to appear from many circumstances; as there being no pre contract among the states themselves, nor any attempt to engage allies or assistance in Europe, and several others. But though there were no other argument at all, it is sufficiently proved by the total want of arms and ammunition to supply us even during the first stages of resistance. The nakedness of the country in this respect is well known; and our enemies endeavoured to avail themselves of it, by taking every measure to prevent their being brought to us. This difficulty was got over by many providential supplies, without the care or foresight of those who were at the head of affairs, and particularly by many unexpected captures from our enemies themselves.

How contrary to human appearance and human conjectures have many circumstances turned out! It was universally supposed at first, that we should be able to do nothing at all at sea, because of the great naval power of the enemy, yet the success of our private vessels has been one of the most powerful means

of distressing them, and supporting us. I cannot help in particular taking notice, that the eastern states, which were the first objects of their vengeance, were actually in their possession, and seemed to be devoted to pillage and destruction; yet in a short time they were delivered, and have in the course of the war acquired a greater accession of wealth and power, than it is probable they could have done in the same period of security and peace.

It falls to be taken notice of under this branch of the subject, that our most signal successes have generally been when we had the weakest hopes or the greatest fears. What could be more discouraging than our situation at the close of the year 1776; when, after General Howe's arrival with so powerful and well appointed an armament, our army, enlisted but for a few months, was almost entirely dispersed? Yet then did the surprise of the Hessians at Trenton, and the subsequent victory at Princeton, raise the drooping spirits of the country, and give a new turn to our affairs. These advantages redounded greatly to the honour of the commander in chief who planned, and the handful of troops with him who executed the measures, as is confessed by all; yet were they of still greater moment to the cause of America in general, than they were brilliant as military exploits. This place and neighbourhood having been the scene of these actions, cannot but make them and their consequences fresh in the memory of every one who now hears me.

The great victory over General Burgoyne and his army, (weakened at Bennington, and taken prisoners at Saratoga) which opened the eyes of Europe in general, and in some degree even of Britain, happened at a time when many were discouraged. It happened when after the losses of Brandy-Wine and Germantown, the British were in possession of Philadelphia, and the Congress of the United States were obliged to fly to a distant part of the country. It happened not long after our disgraceful flight from Ticonderoga, and the scandalous loss of that post, which was every where said and thought to be the key of the continent, and the possession of it essential to our security. We must not omit to observe, that this victory over a numerous army of British regulars, was obtained by an army composed in a great measure of militia suddenly collected, and freemen of the country who turned out as volunteers.

In the same manner our late astonishing success in the south began when our affairs in that part of the continent wore a most discouraging aspect. The year 1781, which began with mutiny in the northern army, and weakness in the southern, produced more instances of gallantry and military prowess than all the former, and was closed with a victory more glorious to us, and more humiliating to the enemy, than any thing that had before happened during the course of the war.

It was surely a great favour of Providence to raise up for us so great and illustrious an ally in Europe. This prince has assisted us, as you all know, in a very powerful and effectual manner, and has granted that assistance upon a footing so generous as well as just, that our enemies will not yet believe, but there must be some secret and partial stipulations in favour of himself and his subjects, although no such thing exists.

Let me add to all these, the providing for us a person who was so eminently qualified for the arduous task of commander in chief of the armies of the United States. I must make some apology here. None who know me, I think, will charge me with a disposition to adulation or gross flattery of living characters. I am of opinion, and have often expressed it, that the time for fixing a man's character is after death has set his seal upon it, and favour, fear and friendship are at an end. For this reason I do not mean to give a general or full character of the person here in view. But in speaking of the kindness of Providence to the United States, it would be a culpable neglect not to mention that several of his characteristic qualities seem so perfectly suited to our wants, that we must consider his appointment to the service, and the continued health with which he has been blessed, as a favour from the God of heaven. Consider his coolness and prudence, his fortitude and perseverance, his happy talent of engaging the affections of all ranks, so that he is equally acceptable to the citizen and to the soldier—to the state in which he was born, and to every other on the continent. To be a brave man, or skilful commander, is common to him with many others; but this country stood in need of a comprehensive and penetrating mind, which understood the effect of particular measures in bringing the general cause to an issue. When we contrast his character and conduct with those of the various leaders that have been opposed to him; when we consider their attempts to blast each other's reputation, and the short duration of their command, we must say that Providence has fitted him for the charge, and called him to the service.

This head can hardly be better closed, than with the extraordinary interposition of divine Providence for the discovery of the black treachery of Arnold, who intended to put one of the most important fortresses, and the general himself, into the enemies hands. This design was ripe for execution, and the time of execution was at hand. As there was no suspicion of the traitor, no measures were, or could be taken for preventing it. The meeting of the spy with two friends of America, which was entirely casual, the unaccountable embarrassment of that artful person, when with a little address he might easily have extricated himself, and indeed the whole circumstances of that affair, clearly point out the finger of God.

I might have added many more instances of the favour of Providence in particular events, but what have been mentioned, I think, are fully sufficient for the purpose for which they are adduced, and will lead the hearers to the recollection of others of a similar kind.

The second part of my observations must be on the difficulties and dangers which seemed to be in our situation unavoidable, and, at the same time, next to insurmountable. The first of this kind which I shall mention is dissension, or the opposition of one colony to another. On this our enemies reckoned very much, from the beginning. Even before the war broke out, reasoners seemed to build their hopes of the colonies not breaking off from the mother country for ages, upon the impossibility of their uniting their strength, and forming one compact body, either for offence or resistance. To say the truth, the danger was great and real. It was on this account foreseen and dreaded, and all true patriots were anxious to guard against it. Great thanks, doubtless, are due to many citizens in every state, for their virtuous efforts to promote the general union. These efforts have not been without effect; but I am of opinion, that union has been hitherto preserved and promoted to a degree that no man ventured to predict, and very few had the courage to hope for. I confess myself, from the beginning, to have apprehended more danger from this than from any other quarter, and must now declare that my fears have been wholly disappointed, and my hopes have been greatly exceeded. In the public councils no mark of dissension, in matters of importance, has ever appeared; and I take upon me further to say, that every year has obliterated colonial distinctions, and worn away local prejudices, so that mutual affection is at present more cordial, and the views and works of the whole more uniform, than ever they were at any preceding period.

Having mentioned the union and harmony of the United States, it will be very proper to add, that the harmony that has prevailed in the allied army is another signal mercy, for which we ought to be thankful to God. It is exceedingly common for dissension to take place between troops of different nations, when acting together. In the English history we meet with few examples of conjunct expeditions, with sea and land forces, in which the harmony has been complete. Our enemies did not fail to make use of every topic, which they apprehended would be inflammatory and popular, to produce jealousies between us and our allies. Yet it has been wholly in vain. Not only have the officers and soldiers of the American and French armies acted together with perfect cordiality, but the troops of our allies have met with a hearty welcome wherever they have been, from the people of the country; and, indeed, just such a reception as shews they were esteemed to be of the utmost importance and utility to the American cause.

Another difficulty we had to encounter was the want of money and resources for carrying on the war.

To remedy this evil an expedient was fallen upon which I do not look upon myself as obliged either to justify or approve. It was, however, embraced by the plurality as necessary, and, upon the whole, less hazardous than any other which in our situation was practicable. The difficulty of raising, clothing, paying and supporting an army, with a depreciated currency, which its own nature, the arts of interested persons, and the unwearied attempts of our enemies were pushing on to annihilation, may be easily perceived. Yet the war has not only been supported, but we have seen the fall and ruin of the money itself, without the least injury to the public cause. Without injury, did I say? it was to the unspeakable benefit of the public cause. Many private persons, indeed, have suffered such injury as not only merits pity, but calls for redress, and I hope the time will come, when all the redress shall be given that the nature of the thing and the state of the country will admit. In the mean time, when we reflect upon what is past, we have a proof of the general attachment of the country to the cause of liberty, the strongest perhaps that can well be conceived, and we see a circumstance from which we feared the greatest evil, adding its force to many others, in blinding our enemies, misleading their measures, and disappointing their expectations.

Another difficulty we had before us was the being obliged to encounter the whole force of the British nation, with an army composed of raw soldiers, unacquainted with military discipline. The difficulty was increased by our own conduct, viz. filling our army with soldiers enlisted for short periods. The views of those who preferred this method were certainly very honourable, though the wisdom of it is at least very disputable. They hoped it would make every man in America a soldier in a short time. This effect, indeed, it has in a good degree produced, by the frequent calls of the militia wherever the enemy appeared. They also apprehended danger from a standing army, unconnected with civil life, who, after they had conquered their enemies, might give cause of jealousy to their friends. The history of other countries in general, and in particular that of the civil wars in England against Charles the First, seemed to give plausibility to this reason, though from several circumstances there was less cause of fear in America, than would have been in one of the European states. However, the measure was resolved upon by the plurality at first, and we felt the inconvenience of it very severely; but it pleased God to preserve us from utter destruction, to set bounds to the progress of our enemies, and to give time to the states to make better and more effectual provision for their final overthrow.

The only other danger I shall mention was that of anarchy and confusion, when government under the old form was at an end, and every state was obliged to establish civil constitutions for preserving internal order, at the very same time that they had to resist the efforts of a powerful enemy from without. This danger appeared so considerable, that some of the king of Great Britain's governors ran off early, as they themselves professed, in order to augment it. They hoped that universal disorder would prevail in every colony, and not only defeat the measures of the friends of liberty, but be so insupportable to the people in general, as to oblige them to return to their subjection, for their own sakes, and to be rid of a still greater evil. This danger, through the divine blessing, we happily, and indeed entirely escaped. The governors by their flight ripened every measure, and hastened on the change by rendering it visibly necessary. Provincial conventions were held, city and county committees were every where chosen, and such was the zeal for liberty, that the judgment of these committees was as perfectly submitted to, and their orders more cheerfully and completely executed, than those of any regular magistrates, either under the old government or since the change. At the same time every state prepared and settled their civil constitutions, which have now all taken place, and, except in very few instances, without the least discord or dissatisfaction. Happily for us in this state, our constitution has now subsisted near seven years, and we have not so much as heard the voice of discontent. I speak on this head of what is known to every hearer, and indeed

to the whole world; and yet I am persuaded, that to those who reflect upon it, it will appear next to miraculous. Although so much was to be done in which every man was interested, although the colonies were so various and extensive, and the Parliament of Great Britain was threatening, and its army executing vengeance against us, yet the whole was completed in little more than a year, with as much quietness and composure as a private person would move his family and furniture from one house, and settle them in another.

The third branch of my observations shall consist of a few instances in which the counsels of our enemies have been confounded, and their measures have been such as to hasten on the change which they desired to prevent. As to the first of these, nothing can be more remarkable than the ignorance and error in which they have continued from the first rise of the controversy to the present time, as to the state of things, and the dispositions of men in America. Even those at the head of affairs in Great Britain, have not only constantly given out, but in my opinion have sincerely believed, that the great body of the people were upon their side, and were only misled into rebellion by a few factious leaders. At the same time, the very same persons, without being sensible of the absurdity, have affirmed that this country was groaning under the oppression of its rulers, and longed to be delivered from it. Now these things could not both be true. If the first had been true, these leaders must have been popular and acceptable in a high degree, and have had the most extensive influence. If the last had been true, they must have been inwardly and universally detested. But how many circumstances might have convinced them of the falsehood of both these assertions? The vast extent of the states, and the concurrence of all ranks and classes of men, which was so early, so uniform, and so notorious, plainly prove that no such thing could have happened, without a strong and rooted inclination in the people themselves, and such as no address or management of interested persons could have produced. Besides, those who know how fluctuating a body the Congress is, and what continual changes take place in it, as to men, must perceive the absurdity of their making or succeeding in any such attempt. The truth is, the American Congress owes its existence and its influence to the people at large. I might easily shew, that there has hardly any great or important step been taken, but the public opinion has gone before the resolutions of that body; and I wish I could not say, that they have been sometimes very slow in hearing and obeying it.

As to the other assertion, it was still more manifestly false, and they had greater opportunities of perceiving it to be so. If Congress, or those in public trust in any state, had tyrannized over the people, or wantonly oppressed them, the usurpation would, in the nature of things, have come to a speedy period. But what if I should say, that this pretence of our enemies, in an equivocal sense, is indeed true; and yet this truth doth but the more clearly demonstrate their error and delusion. It is true that Congress has, in many instances, been obliged to have recourse to measures in themselves hard and oppressive, and confessed to be so, which yet have been patiently submitted to, because of the important purpose that was to be served by them. Of this kind was the emission of paper money, the passing of tender laws, compelling all into the militia, draughting the militia to fill the regular army, pressing provisions and carriages, and many others of the like nature. Two things are remarkable in this whole matter: one, that every imposition for the public service fell heaviest upon those who were the friends of America; the lukewarm or contrary minded always finding some way of shifting the load from their own shoulders; the other, that from the freedom of the press in this country, there never were wanting the boldest and most inflammatory publications, both against men and measures. Yet neither the one nor the other, nor both united, had any perceptible influence in weakening the attachment of the people. If this account is just, and I am confident it is known to be so by almost all who now hear me, what less than judicial blindness could have made our enemies so obstinate in the contrary sentiments? Such, however, we know has been the case, and as the

whole of their proceedings have been grounded on mistakes, it is no wonder that they have been both injudicious and unsuccessful.

This matter may be explained in the following manner. They supposed that they had only a few discontented particulars to apprehend and punish, and an army to conquer in no respects comparable to their own; but in addition to this they had the lost affections of a whole people to recover. The first, which was almost of no consequence at all, they bent their whole force to effect, in council and in the field. The other they supposed was already done, or not worth the doing; and therefore every measure they took had a quite different intention, and a quite opposite effect. In all this they were fortified and confirmed by the sentiments, discourse, and conduct of the disaffected in America. These unhappy people, from the joint influence of prejudice, resentment and interest, were unwearied in their endeavours to mislead their friends. Their prejudice deserves to be mentioned first. This was great indeed. They had generally such an exalted idea of the power of Britain, that they really considered it as madness to resist. I could mention many sentiments uttered by them, which could hardly fail of making the hearers to smile at their gross ignorance, and more than childish timidity. Resentment also joined its force. They were sometimes roughly handled by the multitude at the beginning of the controversy. This led them to wish for revenge, and as they could not inflict it themselves, to call for it from their friends in England. To these two circumstances we may add, that the road to favour was plainly that of flattery; and therefore their opinions and intelligence were generally such as they supposed would be most acceptable to those who had it in their power to provide for them, or promote them. Such was the effect of these circumstances united, that time will constrain every body to confess, that the partizans and friends of the English in America, have done more essential injury to their cause, than the greatest and boldest of their enemies.

The above distinction between overcoming the armed force of the states, and regaining the people's hearts, is the true key to explain the proceedings, and account for the events of the war. Every measure taken by Great Britain, from the beginning, instead of having the least tendency to gain the affections of the people of this country, had, and one would think must have been seen to have the most powerful influence in producing the contrary effect. Without mentioning every separate particular, I will only consider a little the cruelty and severity with which the war has been carried on; because I am firmly of opinion, that the spirit and temper of our enemies in this contest, has been the principal cause of the disappointment of their attempts. In this the cabinet and counsellors in Great Britain, and the officers and soldiers of their armies in America, have nothing to reproach each other with. If the barbarity of the army has ever equalled, certainly it has never exceeded the cruelty of several of the acts of parliament. I will not enumerate these acts which are so well known, and which some years ago were so often mentioned in every publication; but shall only tell you with what view I desire you to recollect them. Every one of these acts, on their being known in America, served to increase the union of the states, to fill the hearts of the citizens with resentment, and to add vigour to the soldier's arm.

After the example of their employers at home, the commanders of the British armies, their officers and soldiers, and indeed all their adherents, seemed to have been animated with a spirit of implacable rancour, mingled with contempt, towards the Americans. This is to be understood of the general run or greatest number of every class, always admitting that there were particular exceptions, whose honour and principle controuled or overcame the national prejudice. Neither perhaps is it in any of them to be ascribed so much to the national character, as to the nature and subject of the quarrel. It has been long observed, that civil wars are carried on with much greater fury, and attended with acts of greater barbarity, than wars between independent nations. The fact, however, of their barbarity is certain; and no less so is the powerful influence which this conduct has

had in defeating their expectations, either of reconciliation or submission.

The barbarous treatment of the American prisoners through the whole war, but especially at the beginning, when their enemies were confident of success, is a melancholy subject indeed, and will be a stain upon the British name to future ages. No part of America can be ignorant of this, having witnesses in every state, in the few that returned alive out of their hands. But we in this state, through which they passed to their homes, can never forget the appearance of the emaciated spectres who escaped, or were exchanged from British dungeons or prison-ships. Neither was it possible for the people in general not to be struck with the contrast when exchanges took place, and they saw companies of British prisoners going home hale and hearty, bearing every mark of their having been supplied with comfortable provisions, and treated with humanity in every other respect. I am not to enlarge upon these known and fertile subjects. The only reason of their being introduced, is to shew the effect which spectacles of this kind must have had upon the public mind, and their influence in rendering the return of the people of this country to submission to the parent state altogether impossible.

The inhuman treatment of the American prisoners by the British, was not more remarkable than their insolence and rapacity towards the people of the country wherever their power extended. The abuse and contempt poured upon the inhabitants in discourse, and the indiscriminate plunder of their property, could not but in the most powerful manner alienate their affections. Many who hear me at present have had so full conviction of this truth in their own experience, that it is unnecessary to offer any proof of it. It is of importance however to observe, that this impolitic oppression was the true and proper cause of the general concourse of the inhabitants of this State to the American standard, in the beginning of the year 1777, and their vigorous exertions ever since against the incursions of the enemy from New York. I confess I was not so much surprised at such conduct when they possessed this part of the country, because they were then flushed with victory, and had scarcely an idea that they would fail of final success. But when we consider that their conduct has been the same, or even worse, in the southern States, we can hardly help wondering at their infatuation. Surely there was time enough before the year 1780, to have convinced them that insolence and cruelty were not the means of bringing back a revolted people; and yet by all accounts their treatment of the inhabitants in Georgia, South and North Carolina, in that year, was even more barbarous than had been experienced by the people here three years before.

I shall only further mention, that it seems plainly to have been not by accident, but in consequence of general orders or a prevailing disposition, that they treated, wherever they went, places of public worship (except those of the Episcopal denomination) with all possible contempt and insult. They were in general used, not only for hospitals, but storehouses, barracks, riding schools and prisons, and in many places they were torn to pieces wantonly, and without any purpose to be served by it, but wreaking their vengeance on the former possessors. What influence must this have had upon the minds of the people! What impression must have been made upon the few who remained, and were witnesses to these acts of profanation, when in those places where they had been accustomed to hear nothing but the word and the worship of God, their ears were stunned with the horrid sound of cursing and blasphemy! This was done very early in Boston, and repeated in every part of the continent with increasing rage.

I have chosen on this part of the subject to insist only on what was general, and therefore must be supposed to have had an extensive influence. It would have been easy to have collected many particular acts of barbarity, but as these might be accounted for from the degeneracy and savage disposition of the persons who were severally guilty of them, they would not have been so conclusive for the purpose for which they were adduced. I shall therefore omit every thing of this kind, except one of the earliest instances of

their barbarity, because it happened in one of the streets of this place, viz. massacring in cold blood a minister of the gospel, who was not, nor ever had been in arms, and received his death wound while on his knees begging mercy.

Upon the whole, nothing appears to me more manifest, than that the separation of this country from Britain has been of God; for every step the British took to prevent, served to accelerate it, which has generally been the case when men have undertaken to go in opposition to the course of Providence, and to make war with the nature of things.

I proceed to make some practical improvement of the subject, for your instruction and direction. And,

In the first place, it is our duty to give praise to God for the present happy and promising state of public affairs. This is what we are called to, and making profession of, by our meeting together at the present time. Let it then be more than a form. Let the disposition of your hearts be correspondent to the expressions of your lips. While we who are here alive before God this day, recollect with tenderness and sympathy with surviving relations, the many valuable lives that have been lost in the course of the war, let us give thanks to God who hath spared us as monuments of his mercy, who hath given us the satisfaction of seeing our complete deliverance approaching, and those liberties, civil and religious, for which we have been contending, established upon a lasting foundation. It will be remembered by many, that I have early and constantly expressed my disapprobation of self-confidence, and vain-glorious boasting. To many American soldiers I have said, Seldom boast of what you have done, but never of what you only mean to do. This was not occasioned by any doubt or hesitation I ever had as to the probable issue of the war, from the apparent state of things, and the course of human events, but by a deep conviction of the sinfulness of this practice, either in a nation or person. Now, therefore, that we have come so far in opposition to a formidable enemy, it is certainly our duty to say, that "salvation belongeth unto the Lord." This indeed is not only the duty of every person with respect to what is past, but is the way to support and animate us in what remains of the warfare, and dispose us to make a suitable improvement of the settlement which we hope is not very distant.

2. We ought to testify our gratitude to God for the many signal interpositions of his providence in our behalf, by living in his fear, and by a conversation such as becometh the gospel. This is not only a tribute we owe to him for every mercy, and therefore for those of a public nature, but it is the only way by which public prosperity can become a real mercy to us. Eternity is of yet greater moment than any earthly blessing. Their state is little to be envied, who are free as citizens, but slaves as sinners. All temporal comforts derive their value from their being the fruits of divine goodness, the evidence of covenant love, and the earnest of everlasting mercy. It is therefore our indispensable duty to endeavour to obtain the sanctified improvement of every blessing, whether public or personal. There is the greater necessity of insisting on this at present, that though a time of national suffering or jeopardy has some advantages for alarming the consciences of the secure, it hath also some disadvantages, and frequently occasions such distraction of mind as is little favourable to the practice of piety. We know by sad experience, that the regular administration of divine ordinances, the observation of the Sabbath, and the good order of the country in general, have been much disturbed by the war. The public service seemed many times to justify what would otherwise have been highly improper. This contributed to introduce a licentiousness of practice, and to protect those from restraint or reproof, who I am afraid in many cases rather yielded to inclination than submitted to necessity. Now, therefore, when by the blessing of God our distresses are removed, we ought to return to punctuality as to public order, as well as conscientious strictness in every part of our practice.

3. In the third place, it is our duty to testify our gratitude to God, by usefulness in our several stations; or in other words, by a concern for the glory of God, the public interest of religion, and the good of others.

This is the duty of every person, even of the lowest station, at all times. Even the meanest and most unconnected hath still some small bounds within which his influence and example may be useful. But it is especially the duty of those who are distinguished from others by their talents, by their station, or by office and authority. I shall at present consider it chiefly as the duty of two sorts of persons, ministers and magistrates, those who have the direction of religious societies, and those who are vested with civil authority. As to the first of these, they are under the strongest obligations to holiness and usefulness in their own lives, and diligence in doing good to others. The world expects it from them, and demands it of them. Many of this class of men have been peculiarly the objects of the hatred and detestation of the enemy, in the course of this war. Such, therefore, as have been spared to see the return of peace and security, are bound by the strongest ties to improve their time and talents in their Master's service. But what I have peculiarly in view is, strictness in religious discipline, or the inspection of the morals of their several societies. By our excellent constitution they are well secured in their religious liberty. The return which is expected from them to the community is, that by the influence of their religious government, their people may be the more regular citizens, and the more useful members of society. I hope none here will deny, that the manners of the people in general are of the utmost moment to the stability of any civil society. When the body of a people are altogether corrupt in their manners, the government is ripe for dissolution. Good laws may hold the rotten bark some longer together, but in a little time all laws must give way to the tide of popular opinion, and be laid prostrate under universal practice. Hence it clearly follows, that the teachers and rulers of every religious denomination are bound mutually to each other, and to the whole society, to watch over the manners of their several members.

(2.) Those who are vested with civil authority ought also, with much care, to promote religion and good morals among all under their government. If we give credit to the holy Scriptures, he that ruleth must be just, ruling in the fear of God. It is a truth of no little importance to us in our present situation, not only that the manners of a people are of consequence to the stability of every civil society, but that they are of much more consequence to free states, than to those of a different kind. In many of these last, a principle of honour, and the subordination of ranks, with the vigour of despotic authority, supply the place of virtue, by restraining irregularities and producing public order. But in free states, where the body of the people have the supreme power properly in their own hands, and must be ultimately resorted to on all great matters, if there be a general corruption of manners, there can be nothing but confusion. So true is this, that civil liberty cannot be long preserved without virtue. A monarchy may subsist for ages, and be better or worse under a good or bad prince; but a republic once equally poised, must either preserve its virtue or lose its liberty, and by some tumultuous revolution, either return to its first principles, or assume a more unhappy form.

From this results a double duty, that of the people themselves, who have the appointment of rulers, and that of their representatives, who are intrusted with the exercise of this delegated authority. Those who wish well to the State, ought to chuse to places of trust, men of inward principle, justified by exemplary conversation. Is it reasonable to expect wisdom from the ignorant, fidelity from the profligate, assiduity and application to public business from men of a dissipated life? Is it reasonable to commit the management of public revenue, to one who hath wasted his own patrimony? Those, therefore, who pay no regard to religion and sobriety in the persons whom they send to the legislature of any state, are guilty of the greatest absurdity, and will soon pay dear for their folly. Let a man's zeal, profession, or even principles as to political measures, be what they will, if he is without personal integrity and private virtue as a man, he is not to be trusted. I think we have had some instances of men who have roared for liberty in taverns, and were most noisy in public meetings, who yet have turned traitors in a little time. Suffer me on this subject to make another remark. I have not yet heard of any Christian State in which there were not laws against immorality. But with what judgment will they be made, or with what vigour will they be executed, by those who are profane and immoral in their own practice? Let me suppose a magistrate on the bench of justice administering an oath to a witness, or passing sentence of death on a criminal, and putting him in mind of a judgment to come: With what propriety, dignity, or force, can any of these be done by one who is known to be a blasphemer or an infidel, by whom in his convivial hours every thing that is serious and sacred is treated with scorn?

But if the people in general ought to have regard to the moral character of those whom they invest with authority, either in the legislative, executive, or judicial branches, such as are so promoted may perceive what is, and will be expected from them. They are under the strongest obligations to do their utmost to promote religion, sobriety, industry, and every social virtue, among those who are committed to their care. If you ask me, what are the means which civil rulers are bound to use for attaining these ends, further than the impartial support and faithful guardianship of the rights of conscience? I answer that example itself is none of the least. Those who are in high station and authority, are exposed to continual observation, and therefore their example is both better seen, and hath greater influence than that of persons of inferior rank. I hope it will be no offence in speaking to a Christian assembly, if I say that reverence for the name of God, a punctual attendance on the public and private duties of religion, as well as sobriety and purity of conversation, are especially incumbent on those who are honoured with places of power and trust.

But I cannot content myself with this. It is certainly the official duty of magistrates to be "a terror to evil doers, and a praise to them that do well." That society will suffer greatly, in which there is no care taken to restrain open vice by exemplary punishment. It is often to be remarked, in some of the corrupt governments of Europe, that whatever strictness may be used, or even impartiality in rendering justice between man and man, yet there is a total and absolute relaxation as to what is chiefly and immediately a contempt of God. Perhaps a small trespass of a poor man on property, shall be pursued by a vindictive party, or punished by a tyrannical judge with the utmost severity, when all the laws against swearing, Sabbath breaking, lewdness, drunkenness and riot, shall be a dead letter, and more trampled upon by the judges themselves, than by the people who are to be judged. Those magistrates who would have their authority both respected and useful, should begin at the source, and reform or restrain that impiety towards God, which is the true and proper cause of every disorder among men. O the short-sightedness of human wisdom, to hope to prevent the effect, and yet nourish the cause! Whence come dishonesty and petty thefts? I say, from idleness, Sabbath-breaking, and uninstructed families. Whence come deceits of greater magnitude, and debts unpaid? from sloth, luxury, and extravagance. Whence come violence, hatred, and strife? from drunkenness, rioting, lewdness, and blasphemy. It is common to say of a dissolute liver, that he does harm to none but himself; than which I think there is not a greater falsehood that ever obtained credit in a deceived world. Drunkards, swearers, profane and lascivious jesters, and the whole tribe of those who do harm to none but themselves, are the pests of society, the corrupters of the youth, and, in my opinion, for the risk of infection, thieves and robbers are less dangerous companions.

Upon the whole, my brethren, after we have contended in arms for liberty from foreign domination, let us guard against using our liberty as a cloke for licentiousness, and thus poisoning the blessing after we have attained it. Let us endeavour to bring into, and keep in credit and reputation, every thing that may serve to give vigour to an equal republican constitution. Let us cherish a love of piety, order, industry, frugality. Let us check every disposition to luxury, effeminacy, and the pleasures of a dissipated life. Let us in public measures put honour upon modesty and self-denial, which is the index of real merit. And in

our families let us do the best by religious instruction, to sow the seeds which may bear fruit in the next generation. We are one of the body of confederated States. For many reasons I shall avoid making any comparisons at present, but may venture to predict, that whatsoever State among us shall continue to make piety and virtue the standard of public honour, will enjoy the greatest inward peace, the greatest national happiness, and in every outward conflict will discover the greatest constitutional strength.

Notes on the State of Virginia, Query XVII and Query XVIII (1782)

THOMAS JEFFERSON (1743–1826)

In 1781, Thomas Jefferson, who was serving as governor of Virginia, received a series of questions from François de Barbé-Marbois, secretary of the French legation in Philadelphia. He answered Marbois in 1782, printed two hundred private copies of his *Notes* in 1784, and cooperated with their publication in Paris and London in 1787 and America in 1788.

Query XVII

The different religions received into that state?

The first settlers in this country were emigrants from England, of the English church, just at a point of time when it was flushed with complete victory over the religious of all other persuasions. Possessed, as they became, of the powers of making, administering and executing the laws, they shewed equal intolerance in this country with their Presbyterian

Reprinted from *The Works of Thomas Jefferson,* ed. Paul Leicester Ford (New York and London: G. P. Putnam's Sons, 1904–5), 4:74–84.

brethren, who had emigrated to the northern government. The poor Quakers were flying from persecution in England. They cast their eyes on these new countries as asylums of civil and religious freedom; but they found them free only for the reigning sect. Several acts of the Virginia assembly of 1659, 1662, and 1693, had made it penal in parents to refuse to have their children baptized; had prohibited the unlawful assembling of Quakers; had made it penal for any master of a vessel to bring a Quaker into the state; had ordered those already here, and such as should come thereafter, to be imprisoned till they should abjure the country; provided a milder punishment for their first and second return, but death for their third; had inhibited all persons from suffering their meetings in or near their houses, entertaining them individually, or disposing of books which supported their tenets. If no capital execution took place here, as did in New-England, it was not owing to the moderation of the church, or spirit of the legislature, as may be inferred from the law itself; but to historical circumstances which have not been handed down to us. The Anglicans retained full possession of the country about a century. Other opinions began then to creep in, and the great care of the government to support their own church, having begotten an equal degree of indolence in its clergy, two thirds of the people had become dissenters at the commencement of the present revolution. The laws indeed were still oppressive on them, but the spirit of the one party had subsided into moderation, and of the other had risen to a degree of determination which commanded respect.

The present state of our laws on the subject of religion is this. The convention of May 1776, in their declaration of rights, declared it to be a truth, and a natural right, that the exercise of religion should be free; but when they proceeded to form on that declaration the ordinance of government, instead of taking up every principle declared in the bill of rights, and guarding it by legislative sanction, they passed over that which asserted our religious rights, leaving them as they found them. The same convention, however, when they met as a member of the general assembly in October 1776, repealed all *acts of parliament* which had rendered criminal the maintaining any opinions in matters of religion, the forbearing to repair to church, and the exercising any mode of worship; and suspended the laws giving salaries to the clergy, which suspension was made perpetual in October 1779. Statutory oppressions in religion being thus wiped away, we remain at present under those only imposed by the common law, or by our own acts of assembly. At the common law, *heresy* was a capital offence, punishable by burning. Its definition was left to the ecclesiastical judges, before whom the conviction was, till the statute of the I El. c. I. circumscribed it, by declaring that nothing should be deemed heresy but what had been so determined by authority of the canonical scriptures, or by one of the four first general councils, or by some other council having for the grounds of their declaration the express and plain words of the scriptures. Heresy, thus circumscribed, being an offence at the common law, our act of assembly of October 1777, c. 17 gives cognizance of it to the general court, by declaring that the jurisdiction of that court shall be general in all matters at the common law. The execution is by the writ *De haeretico comburendo.** By our own act of assembly of 1705, c. 30, if a person brought up in the christian religion denies the being of a God, or the trinity, or asserts there are more Gods than one, or denies the christian religion to be true, or the scriptures to be of divine authority, he is punishable on the first offence by incapacity to hold any office or employment ecclesiastical, civil, or military; on the second by disability to sue, to take any gift or legacy, to be guardian, executor or administrator, and by three years imprisonment, without bail. A father's right to the custody of his own children being founded in law on his right of guardianship, this being taken away, they may of course be severed from him and put, by the authority of a court, into more orthodox hands. This is a summary view of that religious slavery under which a people have

* [concerning heretics, who must be burned]

been willing to remain who have lavished their lives and fortunes for the establishment of their civil freedom. The error seems not sufficiently eradicated, that the operations of the mind, as well as the acts of the body, are subject to the coercion of the laws.[1] But our rulers can have authority over such natural rights, only as we have submitted to them. The rights of conscience we never submitted, we could not submit. We are answerable for them to our God. The legitimate powers of government extend to such acts only as are injurious to others. But it does me no injury for my neighbor to say there are twenty gods, or no god. It neither picks my pocket nor breaks my leg. If it be said his testimony in a court of justice cannot be relied on, reject it then, and be the stigma on him. Constraint may make him worse by making him a hypocrite, but it will never make him a truer man. It may fix him obstinately in his errors, but will not cure them. Reason and free inquiry are the only effectual agents against error. Give a loose to them, they will support the true religion by bringing every false one to their tribunal, to the test of their investigation. They are the natural enemies of error, and of error only. Had not the Roman government permitted free inquiry, christianity could never have been introduced. Had not free inquiry been indulged, at the aera of the reformation, the corruptions of christianity could not have been purged away. If it be restrained now, the present corruptions will be protected, and new ones encouraged. Was the government to prescribe to us our medicine and diet, our bodies would be in such keeping as our souls are now. Thus in France the emetic was once forbidden as a medicine, and the potatoe as an article of food. Government is just as infallible, too, when it fixes systems in physics. Galileo was sent to the inquisition for affirming that the earth was a sphere; the government had declared it to be as flat as a trencher, and Galileo was obliged to abjure his error. This error however at length prevailed, the earth became a globe, and Descartes declared it was whirled round its axis by a vortex. The

government in which he lived was wise enough to see that this was no question of civil jurisdiction, or we should all have been involved by authority in vortices. In fact the vortices have been exploded, and the Newtonian principles of gravitation is now more firmly established, on the basis of reason, than it would be were the government to step in and to make it an article of necessary faith. Reason and experiment have been indulged, and error has fled before them. It is error alone which needs the support of government. Truth can stand by itself. Subject opinion to coercion: whom will you make your inquisitors? Fallible men; men governed by bad passions, by private as well as public reasons. And why subject it to coercion? To produce uniformity. But is uniformity of opinion desireable? No more than of face and stature. Introduce the bed of Procrustes then, and as there is danger that the large men may beat the small, make us all of a size, by lopping the former and stretching the latter. Difference of opinion is advantageous in religion. The several sects perform the office of a Censor morum over each other. Is uniformity attainable? Millions of innocent men, women and children, since the introduction of Christianity, have been burnt, tortured, fined, imprisoned: yet we have not advanced one inch towards uniformity. What has been the effect of coercion? To make one half the world fools, and the other half hypocrites. To support roguery and error all over the earth. Let us reflect that it is inhabited by a thousand millions of people. That these profess probably a thousand different systems of religion. That ours is but one of that thousand. That if there be but one right, and ours that one, we should wish to see the 999 wandering sects gathered into the fold of truth. But against such a majority we cannot effect this by force. Reason and persuasion are the only practicable instruments. To make way for these, free inquiry must be indulged; and how can we wish others to indulge it while we refuse it ourselves. But every state, says an inquisitor, has established some religion. "No two, say I, have established the same." Is this a proof of the infallibility of establishments? Our sister states of Pennsylvania and New York, however,

1. Furneaux passim.—*T. J.*

have long subsisted without any establishment at all. The experiment was new and doubtful when they made it. It has answered beyond conception. They flourish infinitely. Religion is well supported; of various kinds indeed, but all good enough; all sufficient to preserve peace and order: or if a sect arises whose tenets would subvert morals, good sense has fair play, and reasons and laughs it out of doors, without suffering the state to be troubled with it. They do not hang more malefactors than we do. They are not more disturbed with religious dissentions. On the contrary, their harmony is unparalleled, and can be ascribed to nothing but their unbounded tolerance, because there is no other circumstance in which they differ from every nation on earth. They have made the happy discovery, that the way to silence religious disputes, is to take no notice of them. Let us too give this experiment fair play, and get rid, while we may, of those tyrannical laws. It is true we are as yet secured against them by the spirit of the times. I doubt whether the people of this country would suffer an execution for heresy, or a three years imprisonment for not comprehending the mysteries of the trinity. But is the spirit of the people an infallible, a permanent reliance? Is it government? Is this the kind of protection we receive in return for the rights we give up? Besides, the spirit of the times may alter, will alter. Our rulers will become corrupt, our people careless. A single zealot may commence persecuter, and better men be his victims. It can never be too often repeated, that the time for fixing every essential right on a legal basis is while our rulers are honest, and ourselves united. From the conclusion of this war we shall be going down hill. It will not then be necessary to resort every moment to the people for support. They will be forgotten therefore, and their rights disregarded. They will forget themselves, but in the sole faculty of making money, and will never think of uniting to effect a due respect for their rights. The shackles, therefore, which shall not be knocked off at the conclusion of this war, will remain on us long, will be made heavier and heavier, till our rights shall revive or expire in a convulsion.

Query XVIII

The particular customs and manners that may happen to be received in that State?

It is difficult to determine on the standard by which the manners of a nation may be tried, whether *catholic* or *particular*. It is more difficult for a native to bring to that standard the manners of his own nation, familiarized to him by habit. There must doubtless be an unhappy influence on the manners of our people produced by the existence of slavery among us. The whole commerce between master and slave is a perpetual exercise of the most boisterous passions, the most unremitting despotism on the one part, and degrading submissions on the other. Our children see this, and learn to imitate it; for man is an imitative animal. This quality is the germ of all education in him. From his cradle to his grave he is learning to do what he sees others do. If a parent could find no motive either in his philanthropy or his self-love, for restraining the intemperance of passion towards his slave, it should always be a sufficient one that his child is present. But generally it is not sufficient. The parent storms, the child looks on, catches the lineaments of wrath, puts on the same airs in the circle of smaller slaves, gives a loose to the worst of passions, and thus nursed, educated, and daily exercised in tyranny, cannot but be stamped by it with odious peculiarities. The man must be a prodigy who can retain his manners and morals undepraved by such circumstances. And with what execrations should the statesman be loaded, who permitting one half the citizens thus to trample on the rights of the other, transforms those into despots, and these into enemies, destroys the morals of the one part, and the amor patriae of the other. For if a slave can have a country in this world, it must be any other in preference to that in which he is born to live and labour for another: in which he must lock up the faculties of his nature, contribute as far as depends on his individual endeavours to the evanishment of the human race, or entail his own miserable condition on the endless generations proceeding from him. With the morals of the people, their industry also is destroyed. For in a warm climate, no man will labour for himself who can make another labour for him. This is so true, that of the proprietors of slaves a very small proportion indeed are ever seen to labour. And can the liberties of a nation be thought secure when we have removed their only firm basis, a conviction in the minds of the people that these liberties are of the gift of God? That they are not to be violated but with his wrath? Indeed I tremble for my country when I reflect that God is just: that his justice cannot sleep forever: that considering numbers, nature and natural means only, a revolution of the wheel of fortune, an exchange of situation, is among possible events: that it may become probable by supernatural interference! The Almighty has no attribute which can take side with us in such a contest.—But it is impossible to be temperate and to pursue this subject through the various considerations of policy, of morals, of history natural and civil. We must be contented to hope they will force their way into every one's mind. I think a change already perceptible, since the origin of the present revolution. The spirit of the master is abating, that of the slave rising from the dust, his condition mollifying, the way I hope preparing, under the auspices of heaven, for a total emancipation, and that this is disposed, in the order of events, to be with the consent of the masters, rather than by their extirpation.

Petition for Equality by the Philadelphia Synagogue to Council of Censors of Pennsylvania (1783)

The Pennsylvania Constitution of 1776 required that before representatives took office they had to "swear (or affirm)" that they believed the "New Testament to be given by Divine inspiration." It also provided for a Council of Censors, which was to meet every seven years to determine whether the constitution needed to be amended. When the Council met in 1783, leaders of the Philadelphia synagogue sent to it the following petition. The Council considered the petition on December 23, 1783, tabled it, and took no further action. However, when the state rewrote its constitution in 1789–90, the disability was removed (see relevant texts in chapter 5).

To the honourable the COUNCIL OF CENSORS, assembled agreeable to the Constitution of the State of Pennsylvania.

The Memorial of Rabbi Ger. Seixas of the Synagogue of the Jews at Philadelphia, Simon Nathan their Parnass or President, Asher Myers, Bernard Gratz and Haym Salomon the Mahamad, or Associates of their council, in behalf of themselves and their bretheren Jews, residing in Pennsylvania,

Most respectfully sheweth,

THAT by the tenth section of the Frame of Government of this Commonwealth, it is ordered that each member of the general assembly of representatives of the freemen of Pennsylvania, before he takes his seat, shall make and subscribe a declaration, which ends in these words, "I do acknowledge the Scriptures of the old and new Testament to be given by divine inspiration," to which is added an assurance, that "no further or other religious test shall ever hereafter be required of any civil officer or magistrate in this state."

Your memorialists beg leave to observe, that this clause seems to limit the civil rights of your citizens to one very special article of the creed; whereas by the second paragraph of the declaration of the rights of the inhabitants, it is asserted without any other limitation than the professing the existence of God, in plain words, "that no man who acknowledge the being of a God can be justly deprived or abridged of any civil rights as a citizen, on account of his religious sen-

Reprinted from *A Documentary History of the Jews in the United States, 1654–1875*, ed. Morris U. Schappes, 3rd ed. (New York: Schocken Books, 1971), 64–66.

timents." But certainly this religious test deprives the Jews of the most eminent rights of freemen, solemnly ascertained to all men who are not professed Atheists.

May it please your Honors,

Although the Jews in Pennsylvania are but few in number, yet liberty of the people in one country, and the declaration of the government thereof, that these liberties are the rights of the people, may prove a powerful attractive to men, who live under restraints in another country. Holland and England have made valuable acquisitions of men who, for their religious sentiments, were distressed in their own countries.— And if Jews in Europe or elsewhere, should incline to transport themselves to America, and would, for reason of some certain advantage of the soil, climate, or the trade of Pennsylvania, rather become inhabitants thereof, than of any other state; yet the disability of Jews to take seat among the representatives of the people, as worded by the said religious test, might determine their free choice to go to New-York, or to any other of the United States of America, where there is no such like restraint laid upon the nation and religion of the Jews, as in Pennsylvania.—Your memorialists cannot say that the Jews are particularly fond of being representatives of the people in assembly or civil officers and magistrates in the state; but with great submission they apprehend that a clause in the constitution, which disables them to be elected by their fellow citizens to represent them in assembly, as [is?] a stigma upon their nation and their religion, and it is inconsonant with the second paragraph of the said bill of rights; otherwise Jews are as fond of liberty as other religious societies can be, and it must create in them a displeasure, when they perceive that for their professed dissent to a doctrine, which is inconsistent with their religious sentiments, they should be excluded from the most important and honourable part of the rights of a free citizen.

Your memorialists beg farther leave to represent, that in the religious books of the Jews, which are or may be in every man's hands, there are no such doctrines or principles established, as are inconsistent with the safety and happiness of the people of Penn-

sylvania, and that the conduct and behaviour of the Jews in this and the neighbouring states, has always tallied with the great design of the revolution; that the Jews of Charlestown, New-York, New-Port and other posts, occupied by the British troops, have distinguishedly suffered for their attachment to the revolution principles; and their brethren at St. Eustatius, for the same cause, experienced the most severe resentments of the British commanders. The Jews of Pennsylvania in proportion to the number of their members, can count with any religious society whatsoever, the whigs among either of them; they have served some of them in the continental army; some went out in the militia to fight the common enemy; all of them have chearfully contributed to the support of the militia, and of the government of this state; they have no inconsiderable property in lands and tenements, but particularly in the way of trade, some more, some less, for which they pay taxes; they have, upon every plan formed for public utility, been forward to contribute as much as their circumstances would admit of; and as a nation or a religious society, they stand unimpeached of any matter whatsoever, against the safety and happiness of the people.

And your memorialists humbly pray, that if your honours, from any other consideration than the subject of this address, should think proper to call a convention for revising the constitution, you would be pleased to recommend this to the notice of that convention.

Circular to the States (1783)

GEORGE WASHINGTON (1732–99)

George Washington was appointed by Congress to be commander-in-chief of the Continental Army in 1775, a position he held until the end of the war in 1783. Upon resigning his commission, he sent a circular letter to the state governors. The following excerpts illustrate Washington's view of the relationship between religion and the republic.

Head Quarters, Newburgh, June 8, 1783

Sir: The great object for which I had the honor to hold an appointment in the Service of my Country, being accomplished, I am now preparing to resign it into the hands of Congress, and to return to that domestic retirement, which, it is well known, I left with the greatest reluctance, a Retirement, for which I have never ceased to sigh through a long and painful absence, and in which (remote from the noise and trouble of the World) I meditate to pass the remainder of life in a state of undisturbed repose; But before I carry this resolution into effect, I think it a duty incumbent on me, to make this my last official communication, to congratulate you on the glorious events which Heaven has been pleased to produce in our favor, to offer my sentiments respecting some important subjects, which appear to me, to be intimately connected with the tranquility of the United States, to take my leave of your Excellency as a public Character, and to give my final blessing to that Country, in whose service I have spent the prime of my life, for whose sake I have consumed so many anxious days and watchfull nights, and whose happiness being extremely dear to me, will always constitute no inconsiderable part of my own.

Impressed with the liveliest sensibility on this pleasing occasion, I will claim the indulgence of dilating the more copiously on the subjects of our mutual felicitation. When we consider the magnitude of the prize we contended for, the doubtful nature of the contest, and the favorable manner in which it has terminated, we shall find the greatest possible reason for gratitude and rejoicing; this is a theme that will afford infinite delight to every benevolent and liberal mind, whether the event in contemplation, be considered as the source of present enjoyment or the parent of future happiness; and we shall have equal occasion to felicitate ourselves on the lot which Providence has assigned us, whether we view it in a natural, a political or moral point of light.

The Citizens of America, placed in the most enviable condition, as the sole Lords and Proprietors of a vast Tract of Continent, comprehending all the various soils and climates of the World, and abounding with all the necessaries and conveniencies of life, are now by the late satisfactory pacification, acknowledged to be possessed of absolute freedom and Independency; They are, from this period, to be considered as the Actors on a most conspicuous Theatre, which seems to be peculiarly designated by Providence for the display of human greatness and felicity; Here, they are not only surrounded with every thing which can contribute to the completion of private and domestic enjoyment, but Heaven has crowned all its other blessings, by giving a fairer oppertunity for political happiness, than any other Nation has ever been favored with. Nothing can illustrate these observations more forcibly, than a recollection of the happy conjuncture of times and circumstances, under which our Republic assumed its rank among the Nations; The foundation of our Empire was not laid in the gloomy age of Ignorance and Superstition, but at an Epocha when the rights of mankind were better understood and more clearly defined, than at any former period, the researches of the human mind, after social happiness, have been carried to a great extent, the

Reprinted from *The Writings of George Washington, from the Original Manuscript Sources, 1745–1799*, ed. John C. Fitzpatrick (Washington, D.C.: GPO, 1938), 26:483–87, 496.

Treasures of knowledge, acquired by the labours of Philosophers, Sages and Legislatures, through a long succession of years, are laid open for our use, and their collected wisdom may be happily applied in the Establishment of our forms of Government; the free cultivation of Letters, the unbounded extension of Commerce, the progressive refinement of Manners, the growing liberality of sentiment, and above all, the pure and benign light of Revelation, have had a meliorating influence on mankind and increased the blessings of Society. At this auspicious period, the United States came into existence as a Nation, and if their Citizens should not be completely free and happy, the fault will be intirely their own.

Such is our situation, and such are our prospects: but notwithstanding the cup of blessing is thus reached out to us, notwithstanding happiness is ours, if we have a disposition to seize the occasion and make it our own; yet, it appears to me there is an option still left to the United States of America, that it is in their choice, and depends upon their conduct, whether they will be respectable and prosperous, or contemptable and miserable as a Nation; This is the time of their political probation, this is the moment when the eyes of the whole World are turned upon them, this is the moment to establish or ruin their national Character forever, this is the favorable moment to give such a tone to our Federal Government, as will enable it to answer the ends of its institution, or this may be the ill-fated moment for relaxing the powers of the Union, annihilating the cement of the Confederation, and exposing us to become the sport of European politics, which may play one State against another to prevent their growing importance, and to serve their own interested purposes. For, according to the system of Policy the States shall adopt at this moment, they will stand or fall, and by their confirmation or lapse, it is yet to be decided, whether the Revolution must ultimately be considered as a blessing or a curse: a blessing or a curse, not to the present age alone, for with our fate will the destiny of unborn Millions be involved.

With this conviction of the importance of the present Crisis, silence in me would be a crime; I will therefore speak to your Excellency, the language of freedom and of sincerity, without disguise; I am aware, however, that those who differ from me in political sentiment, may perhaps remark, I am stepping out of the proper line of my duty, and they may possibly ascribe to arrogance or ostentation, what I know is alone the result of the purest intention, but the rectitude of my own heart, which disdains such unworthy motives, the part I have hitherto acted in life, the determination I have formed, of not taking any share in public business hereafter, the ardent desire I feel, and shall continue to manifest, of quietly enjoying in private life, after all the toils of War, the benefits of a wise and liberal Government, will, I flatter myself, sooner or later convince my Countrymen, that I could have no sinister views in delivering with so little reserve, the opinions contained in this Address.

There are four things, which I humbly conceive, are essential to the well being, I may even venture to say, to the existence of the United States as an Independent Power:

1st. An indissoluble Union of the States under one Federal Head.

2dly. A Sacred regard to Public Justice.

3dly. The adoption of a proper Peace Establishment, and

4thly. The prevalence of that pacific and friendly Disposition, among the People of the United States, which will induce them to forget their local prejudices and policies, to make those mutual concessions which are requisite to the general prosperity, and in some instances, to sacrifice their individual advantages to the interest of the Community.

These are the Pillars on which the glorious Fabrick of our Independency and National Character must be supported; Liberty is the Basis, and whoever would dare to sap the foundation, or overturn the Structure, under whatever specious pretexts he may attempt it, will merit the bitterest execration, and the severest punishment which can be inflicted by his injured Country. . . .

It remains then to be my final and only request, that your Excellency will communicate these sentiments to your Legislature at their next meeting, and that they may be considered as the Legacy of One, who has ardently wished, on all occasions, to be useful to his Country, and who, even in the shade of Retirement, will not fail to implore the divine benediction upon it.

I now make it my earnest prayer, that God would have you, and the State over which you preside, in his holy protection, that he would incline the hearts of the Citizens to cultivate a spirit of subordination and obedience to Government, to entertain a brotherly affection and love for one another, for their fellow Citizens of the United States at large, and particularly for their brethren who have served in the Field, and finally, that he would most graciously be pleased to dispose us all, to do Justice, to love mercy, and to demean ourselves with that Charity, humility and pacific temper of mind, which were the Characteristicks of the Divine Author of our blessed Religion, and without an humble imitation of whose example in these things, we can never hope to be a happy Nation.

Memorials of the Presbytery of Hanover, Virginia (1784–85)

The following three memorials were sent by the Presbytery of Hanover to the General Assembly of the Commonwealth of Virginia. Of particular concern to the Presbytery were proposals to incorporate the Episcopal Church, disposal of the assets already possessed by the Episcopal Church, and, in the final memorial, the fate of Patrick Henry's "Bill Establishing a Provision for Teachers of the Christian Religion."

Memorial of the Presbytery of Hanover, Virginia

Adopted May 20, 1784,
Received by General Assembly, May 26, 1784

To the Honourable the Speaker & House of Delegates
of Virginia.
Gentlemen,

The united Clergy of the Presbyterian Church of Virginia, assembled in Presbytery, request your attention to the following representation. In the late arduous struggle for every thing dear to us, a desire of perfect liberty, and political equality animated every class of Citizens. An entire and everlasting freedom from every species of ecclesiastical domination, a full and permanent security of the unalienable rights of Conscience & private judgment, and an equal share of the protection & favour of Government to all Denominations of Christians, were particular objects of our expectation and irrefragable claim. The happy revolution effected by the virtuous exertions of our

The text was transcribed from microfilm of the original Memorial and follows the original. Library of Virginia, Religious Petitions, Part 1, 1774–1785. Miscellaneous Reel 425a, May 26, 1784.

Countrymen of various opinions in religion, was a favourable opportunity for obtaining these desirable objects without faction, Contention or Complaint. All ranks of men almost felt the claims of justice when the Rod of oppression had scourged them into sensibility, & the powerful band of Common danger had cordially united them together against civil encroachments. The members therefore of every religious Society had a right to expect, and most of them did expect, that former invidious & exclusive distinctions, preferences, and emoluments conferred by the State on any one sect above others would have been wholly removed. They justly supposed that any partiality of this kind, any particular & illicit connexion or commerce between the State & one description of Christians more than another on account of peculiar *opinions* in religion, or in anything else, would be unworthy of the representatives of a people perfectly free and an infringement of that religious liberty, which enhances the value of other privileges in a state of Society.

We, therefore, and the numerous body of Citizens in our Communion, as well as in many others, are justly dissatisfied & uneasy that our expectations from the Legislature have not been answered in these important respects. We regret that the prejudices of Education, the influence of partial custom, and habits of thinking confirmed by these, have too much confounded the distinction between matters purely religious, and the objects of human Legislation, and have occasioned Jealousy & dissatisfaction by injurious inequalities, respecting things which are connected with religious opinion, towards different sects of Christians. That this uneasiness may not appear to be entertained without ground, we would wish to state the following unquestionable facts for the Consideration of the House of Delegates.

The security of our religious Rights upon equal and impartial ground instead of being made a fundamental part of our Constitution as it ought to have been, is left to the precarious fate of Common Law. A matter of general & essential concern to the people, is committed to the hazard of the prevailing opinion of

a majority of the Assembly at its different Sessions. In consequence of this the Episcopal Church was virtually regarded as the Constitutional Church, the Church of the State at the Revolution, and was left by the framers of our present Government in that station of unjust pre-eminence which she had formerly acquired under the smiles of royal favour. And even when the late oppressive Establishment of that Church was at length acknowledged an unreasonable hardship by the Assembly in 1776, a Superiority & distinction in name was still retained and it was expressly styled the established Church as before; which title was continued as late as the year 1778, and never formally disclaimed: our common danger at that time not permitting that opposition to the injustice of such distinction which is required and deserved.

But "a seat on the right hand of temporal glory as the "established mother Church" was not the only inequality then countenanced," and still subsisting, of which we now have reason to regret & Complain: substantial advantages were also confirmed and secured to her by a partial & inequitable decree of Government. We hoped the time past would have sufficed for the enjoyment of these emoluments which that church long possessed without controul by the abridgement of the equal privileges of others, and the aid of their property wrested from them by the hand of Usurpation, but we were deceived. An estate computed to be worth several hundred thousand pounds in Churches, Glebes, &c., derived from the pockets of all religious Societies, was exclusively and unjustly appropriated to the benefit of one, without compensation or restitution to the rest, who in many places were in large majority of the Inhabitants.

Nor is this the whole of the injustice we have felt in matters connected with religious opinion. The Episcopal Church is actually incorporated & known in law as a body, so that it can receive and possess property for ecclesiastical purposes without trouble or risk in securing it, while other Christian communities are obliged to trust to the precarious fidelity of Trustees chosen for the purpose. The Episcopal Clergy are considered as having a right ex officio to celebrate marriages throughout the State, while unnecessary hardships & restrictions are imposed upon other Clergymen in the law relating to that subject passed in 1780, which confines their exercise of that function to those Counties where they receive a special licence from the Court by recommendation, for recording which they are charged with certain fees by the Clerk and which exposes them to a heavy fine for delay in returning certificates of marriages to the office.

The Vestries of the different parishes, a remnant of hierarchical domination, have a right by law to levy money from the people of all denominations for certain purposes; and yet these Vestrymen are exclusively required by law to be members of the Episcopal Church, and to subscribe a conformity to its doctrines & disciplines as professed & practised in England. Such preferences, distinctions, and advantages granted by the Legislature exclusively to one sect of Christians, are regarded by a great number of your constituents as glaringly unjust and dangerous. Their continuance so long in a Republic without animadversion or correction by the assembly, affords just ground for alarm & complaint to a people who feel themselves by the favour of providence happily free, who are conscious of having deserved as well from the State as those who are most favoured; who have an undoubted right to think themselves as orthodox in opinion upon every subject as others, & whose privileges are as dear to them. Such partiality to any system of religious opinion whatever is inconsistent with the intention & proper object of well directed Government, and obliges men of reflexion to consider the Legislature which indulges it, as a party in religious differences instead of the common Guardian and equal Protector of every class of Citizens in their religious as well as civil rights. We have hitherto restrained our complaints from reaching our Representatives, that we might not be thought to take advantage from times of confusion, or critical situations of Government in an unsettled state of Convulsion and wars, to obtain what is our clear and uncontestable rights. But as the happy restoration of peace affords leisure for reflection, we wish to state our sense of the objects of this memorial to your honourable house upon the present occasion, that it may serve to remind you of what might be unnoticed in a multitude of business and remain as a remonstrance against future encroachments from any quarter. That uncommon liberality of Sentiments, which seems daily to gain ground in this enlightened period, encourages us to hope from your wisdom & integrity, Gentlemen, a redress of every grievance & remedy of every abuse. Our invaluable privileges have been purchased by the common blood and treasure of our Countrymen of different names and opinions, and therefore ought to be secured in full and perfect equality to them all. We are willing to allow a full share of Credit to our fellow citizens, however distinguished in name from us, for their spirited exertions in our arduous struggle for Liberty, we would not wish to charge any of them, either minister or people, with open disaffection to the common cause of America, or with crafty dissimulation or indecision, till the issue of the war was certain, so as to oppose their obtaining equal privileges in Religion; but we will resolutely engage against any monopoly of the honours and rewards of Government by any one sect of Christians more than the rest, for we shun not a Comparison with any of our brethren for our efforts in the cause of our Country, and assisting to establish her liberties, and therefore esteem it unreasonable that any of them should reap Superior advantages for, at most, but equal merit. We expect from the representatives of a free people, that all partiality and prejudice on any account whatever will be laid aside and that the happiness of the Citizens at large will be secured upon the broad basis of perfect political equality. This will engage confidence in Government, and unsuspicious affection towards our fellow Citizens. We hope that the Legislature will adopt some measures to remove present inequality and resist any attempt either at their present session or hereafter to continue those which we now complain of. Thus by preserving a proper regard to every religious denomination as the common protectors of piety and Virtue, you will remove every real ground of Contention, and allay every jealous Commotion on the score of Religion. The Citizens of Virginia will feel themselves free, unsuspicious, and happy in this respect. Strangers will be encouraged to share our freedom & felicity, and when civil and religious liberty go hand in hand, our late prosperity will bless the wisdom and Virtue of their fathers. We have the Satisfaction to assure you that we are steady well-wishers to the State, and your h'ble Servants.

The Presbytery of Hanover

Memorial of the Presbytery of Hanover, Virginia

Adopted October 28, 1784,
Received by General Assembly, November 12, 1784

To the Honourable Speaker and House of Delegates of
   Virginia.
Gentlemen,

   The united clergy of the Presbyterian church of Virginia assembled in Presbytery, beg leave again to address your honourable house, upon a few important subjects, in which we find ourselves interested as citizens of this State.

   The freedom we possess is so rich a blessing, and the purchase of it has been so high, that we would ever wish to cherish a spirit of vigilant attention to it, in every circumstance of possible danger. We are anxious to retain a full share of all the privileges which our happy revolution affords, and cannot but feel alarmed at the continued existence of any infringe-

Reprinted from *American Presbyterians* 63, no. 4 (winter 1985), 367–70. Virginia General Assembly, Legislative Petitions (Record Group 78). Miscellaneous Petition, dated November 12, 1784. State government records collection, The Library of Virginia. Used by permission of The Library of Virginia.

ment upon them, or even any indirect attempt tending to this. Impressed with this idea as men, whose rights are sacred and dear to them, ought to be, we are obliged to express our sensibility upon the present occasion, and we naturally direct our appeal to you, gentlemen, as the public guardians of your country's happiness and liberty, who are influenced we hope by that wisdom and justice which your high station requires. Conscious of the rectitude of our intentions and the strength of our claims, we wish to speak our sentiments freely upon these occasions, but at the same time with all that respectful regard, which becomes us, when addressing the representatives of a great and virtuous people. It is with pain that we find ourselves obliged to renew our complaints upon the subjects stated in our memorial last spring. We deeply regret that such obvious grievances should exist unredressed in a Republic, whose end ought to be the happiness of all the citizens. We presumed that immediate redress would have succeeded a clear and just representation of them; as we expect, that it is always the desire of our representatives to remove real grounds of uneasiness, and allay jealous commotions amongst the people. But as the objects of the memorial, though very important in their nature, and more so in their probable consequences, have not yet been obtained, we request that the house of delegates would be pleased to recollect what we had the honour to state to them in that paper at their last sessions; to resume the subject in their present deliberation; and to give it that weight which its importance deserves. The uneasiness which we feel from the continuance of the grievances just referred to, is increased under the prospect of an addition to them by certain exceptionable measures said to be proposed to the Legislature.—We have understood that a comprehensive incorporating act, has been and is at present in agitation, whereby ministers of the gospel as such, of certain descriptions, shall have legal advantages which are not proposed to be extended to the people at large of any denomination. A proposition has been made by some gentlemen in the house of delegates we are told, to extend the grace to us, amongst others, in our professional capacity. If this be so, we are bound to acknowledge with gratitude our obligations to such gentlemen for their inclination to favour us with the sanction of public authority in the discharge of our duty. But as the scheme of incorporating clergymen, *independent of the religious communities to which they belong,* is inconsistent with our ideas of propriety, we request the liberty of declining any such solitary honour should it be again proposed. To form clergymen into a distinct order in the community, and especially where it would be possible for them to have the principal direction of a considerable public estate by such incorporation, has a tendency to render them independent, at length, of the churches whose ministers they are; and this has been too often found by experience to produce ignorance, immorality, and neglect of the duties of their station.

Besides, if clergymen were to be erected by the State into a distinct political body, detached from the rest of the citizens, with the express design of "enabling them to direct spiritual matters," which we all possess without such formality, it would naturally tend to introduce that antiquated and absurd system, in which government is owned, in effect, to be the fountain head of spiritual influences to the church. It would establish an immediate, a peculiar, and for that very reason, in our opinion, illicit connexion between government, and such as were thus distinguished. The Legislature in that case would be the head of a religious party, and its dependent members would be entitled to all decent reciprocity, to a becoming paternal and fostering care. This we suppose, would be giving a preference, and creating a distinction between citizens equally good, on account of something entirely foreign from civil merit, which would be a source of endless jealousies, and inadmissible in a republic or any other well-directed government.—The principle too, which this system aims to establish, is both false and dangerous to religion, and we take this opportunity to remonstrate and protest against it. The real ministers of true religion, derive their authority to act in the duties of their profession from a higher source than any Legislature on earth, however

respectable. Their office relates to the care of the soul, and preparing it for a future state of existence, and their administrations are, or ought to be, of a spiritual nature suited to this momentous concern. And it is plain from the very nature of the case, that they should neither expect, nor receive from government any permission or direction in this respect. We hope therefore that the House of Delegates shares so large a portion of that philosophic and liberal discernment, which prevails in America at present, as to see this matter in its proper light—and that they will understand too well the nature of their duty, as the equal and common guardians of the chartered rights of all the citizens, to permit a connexion of this kind we have just now mentioned, to subsist between them and the spiritual instructors of any religious denomination in the State.—The interference of government in religion, cannot be indifferent to us, and as it will probably come under consideration at the present session of the Assembly, we request the attention of the honourable House, to our sentiments upon this head.

We conceive that human legislation, ought to have human affairs[1] alone for its concern. Legislators in free States possess delegated authority, for the good of the community at large in its political or civil capacity.

The existence, preservation and happiness of society should be their only object; and to this their public cares should be confined. Whatever is not materially connected with this, lies not within their province as statesmen. The thoughts, the intentions, the faith, and the consciences of men, with their modes of worship, lie beyond their reach, and are ever to be referred to a higher and more penetrating tribunal. These internal and spiritual matters cannot be measured by human rules, nor be amenable to human laws. It is the duty of every man, for himself, to take care of his immortal interests in a future state, where we are to account for our conduct as individuals; and

---

1. The second copy of this Memorial has added above the line here the words "as they relate to this world."

it is by no means the business of a Legislature to attend to this, for THERE governments and states as collective bodies shall no more be known.

Religion, therefore, as a spiritual system, and its ministers in a professional capacity, ought not to be under the direction of the State.

Neither is it necessary to their existence that they should be publicly supported by a legal provision for the purpose, as tried experience hath often shown; although it is absolutely necessary to the existence and welfare of every political combination of men in society, to have the support of religion and its solemn institutions, as affecting the conduct of rational beings more than human laws can possibly do. On this account it is wise policy in legislators to seek its alliance and solicit its aid in a civil view, because of its happy influence upon the morality of its citizens, and its tendency to preserve the veneration of an oath, or an appeal to heaven, which is the cement of the social union. It is upon this principle alone, in our opinion, that a legislative body has a right to interfere in religion at all, and of consequence we suppose that this interference ought only to extend to the preserving of the public worship of the Deity, and the supporting of institutions for inculcating the great fundamental principles of all religion, without which society could not easily exist. Should it be thought necessary at present for the Assembly to exert this right of supporting religion in general by an assessment on all the people, we would wish it to be done on the most *liberal plan.* A general assessment of the kind we have heard proposed is an object of such consequence that it excites much anxious speculation amongst your constituents.

We therefore earnestly pray that nothing may be done in the case, inconsistent with the proper objects of human legislation or the Declaration of Rights as published at the Revolution. We hope that the assessment will not be proposed under the idea of supporting religion as a spiritual system, relating to the care of the soul and preparing it for its future destiny. We hope that no attempt will be made to point out articles of faith, that are not essential to the preser-

vation of society; or to settle modes of worship; or to interfere in the internal government of religious communities; *or to render the ministers of religion independent of the will of the people whom they serve.* We expect from our representatives, that careful attention to the political equality of all the citizens, which a Republic ought ever to cherish; and that no scheme of an assessment will be encouraged which will violate the happy privilege we now enjoy of thinking for ourselves in all cases where conscience is concerned.

We request the candid indulgence of the honourable house to the present address; and their most favourable construction of the motives which induce us to obtrude ourselves into public notice. We are urged by a sense of duty. We feel ourselves impressed with the importance of the present crisis. We have expressed ourselves in the plain language of freemen, upon the interesting subjects which called for animadversion; and we hope to stand excused with you, gentlemen, for the manner in which it is executed, as well as for the part we take in the public interests of the community. In the present important moment, we conceived it criminal to be silent; and have therefore attempted to discharge a duty which we owe to our religion as Christians; to ourselves as freemen; and to our posterity, who ought to receive from us a precious birthright of perfect freedom and political equality.

That you may enjoy the direction of Heaven in your present deliberations, and possess in a high degree the spirit of your exalted station, is the prayer of your sincere well wishers,[2]

THE PRESBYTERY OF HANOVER

—————

2. In the second copy of the Memorial the words "humble servants" are substituted for "well wishers."

Memorial of the Presbytery of Hanover, Virginia

Adopted August 13, 1785,
Received by General Assembly, November 2, 1785

To the Honourable the General Assembly of the
Commonwealth of Virginia.

The Ministers and Lay Representatives of the Presbyterian Church in Virginia, assembled in Convention, beg leave to address you.

As citizens of the State, not so by accident but choice, and having willingly conformed to the system of civil policy adopted for our government, and defended it with the foremost at the risk of every thing dear to us, we feel ourselves deeply interested in all the measures of the Legislature.

When the late happy Revolution secured to us an exemption from British control, we hoped that the gloom of injustice and usurpation would have been forever dispelled by the cheering rays of liberty and independence. This inspired our hearts with resolution in the most distressful scenes of adversity and nerved our arm in the day of battle. But our hopes have since been overcast with apprehension when we found how slowly and unwillingly, ancient distinctions among the citizens on account of religious opinions were removed by the Legislature. For although the glaring partiality of obliging all denominations to support the one which had been the favourite of government, was pretty early withdrawn, yet an evident predilection in favour of that church, still subsisted in the acts of the Assembly. Peculiar distinctions and the honour of an important name, were still continued;

Reprinted from *American Presbyterians* 63, no. 4 (winter 1985), 370–73. Virginia General Assembly, Legislative Petitions (Record Group 78). Miscellaneous Petition, dated November 2, 1785. State government records collection, The Library of Virginia. Used by permission of The Library of Virginia.

Note from James Smylie: Two copies of the Fourth Memorial are cataloged in the Virginia State Library, and two emendations have been made after comparing the two documents.

and these are considered as equally partial and injurious with the ancient emoluments. Our apprehensions on account of the continuance of these, which could have no other effect than to produce jealous animosities, and unnecessary contentions among different parties, were increased when we found that they were tenaciously adhered to by government notwithstanding the remonstrances of several Christian societies. To increase the evil a manifest disposition has been shown by the State, to consider itself as possessed of supremacy in *spirituals*, as well as *temporals;* and our fears have been realized in certain proceedings of the General Assembly at their last sessions. The engrossed bill for establishing a provision for the teachers of the Christian religion and the act for incorporating the Protestant Episcopal Church, so far as it secures to that church, the churches, glebes, &c. procured at the expense of the whole community, are not only evidences of this, but of an impolitic partiality which we are sorry to have observed so long.

We therefore in the name of the Presbyterian Church in Virginia, beg leave to exercise our privilege as freemen in remonstrating against the former absolutely, and against the latter under the restrictions above expressed.

We oppose the Bill,

Because it is a departure from the proper line of legislation;

Because it is unnecessary, and inadequate to its professed end—impolitic, in many respects—and a direct violation of the Declaration of Rights.

The end of civil government is security to the temporal liberty and property of mankind, and to protect them in the free exercise of religion. Legislators are invested with powers from their constituents, for this purpose only; and their duty extends no farther. Religion is altogether personal, and the right of exercising it unalienable; and it is not, cannot, and ought not to be, resigned to the will of the society at large; and much less to the Legislature, which derives its authority wholly from the consent of the people, and is limited by the original intention of civil associations.

We never resigned to the control of government, our right of determining for ourselves, in this important article; and acting agreeably to the convictions of reason and conscience, in discharging our duty to our Creator. And therefore, it would be an unwarrantable stretch of prerogative, in the Legislature, to make laws concerning it, except for protection. And it would be a fatal symptom of abject slavery in us, were we to submit to the usurpation.

The Bill is also an unnecessary, and inadequate expedient for the end proposed. We are fully persuaded of the happy influence of Christianity upon the morals of men; but we have never known it, in the history of its progress, so effectual for this purpose, as when left to its native excellence and evidence to recommend it, under the all directing providence of God, and free from the intrusive hand of the civil magistrate. Its Divine Author did not think it necessary to render it dependent on earthly governments. And experience has shown, that this dependence, where it has been effected, has been an injury rather than an aid. It has introduced corruption among the teachers and professors of it, wherever it has been tried, for hundreds of years, and has been destructive of genuine morality, in proportion to the zeal of the powers of this world, in arming it with the sanction of legal terrors, or inviting to its profession by honours and rewards.

It is urged, indeed, by the abettors of this bill, that it would be the means of cherishing religion and morality among the citizens. But it appears from fact, that these can be promoted only by the internal conviction of the mind, and its voluntary choice, which such establishments cannot effect.

We farther remonstrate against the bill as an impolitic measure:

It disgusts so large a proportion of citizens, that it would weaken the influence of government in other respects, and diffuse a spirit of opposition to the rightful exercise of constitutional authority, if enacted into a law:

It partially supposes the Quakers and Menomists to be more faithful in conducting the religious interests of their societies, than the other sects—which we apprehend to be contrary to fact:

It unjustly subjects men who may be good citizens, but who have not embraced our common faith, to the hardship of supporting a system, they have not as yet believed the truth of; and deprives them of their property, for what they do not suppose to be of importance to them:

It establishes a precedent for farther encroachments, by making the Legislature judges of religious truth. If the Assembly have a right to determine the preference between Christianity, and the other systems of religion that prevail in the world, they may also, at a convenient time, give a preference to some favoured sect among Christians:

It discourages the population of our country by alarming those who may have been oppressed by religious establishments in other countries, with fears of the same in this: and by exciting our own citizens to emigrate to other lands of greater freedom:

It revives the principle which our ancestors contested to blood, of attempting to reduce all religions to one standard by the force of civil authority:

And it naturally opens a door for contention among citizens of different creeds, and different opinions respecting the extent of the powers of government.

The bill is also a direct violation of the Declaration of Rights, which ought to be the standard of all laws. The sixteenth article is clearly infringed upon by it, and any explication which may have been given of it by the friends of this measure in the Legislature, so as to justify a departure from its literal construction, might also be used to deprive us of other fundamental principles of our government.

For these reasons, and others that might be produced, we conceive it our duty to remonstrate and protest against the said bill; and earnestly urge that it may not be enacted into a law.

We also wish to engage your attention a little farther, while we request a revision of the act for incorporating the Protestant Episcopal Church: and state our reasons for this request. We do not desire to oppose the incorporation of that church for the better management of its *temporalities;* neither do we wish to lessen the attachment of any of the members of the Legislature, in a private capacity, to the interests of that church. We rather wish to cultivate a spirit of forbearance and charity towards the members of it, as the servants of one common Master who differ in some particulars from each other. But we cannot consent that they shall receive particular notice or favour from government as a Christian Society; nor peculiar distinctions or emoluments.

We find by the act, that the convenience of the Episcopal Church hath been consulted by it, in the management of their interests as a religious society, at the expense of other denominations. Under the former establishment, there were perhaps few men who did not, at length, perceive the hardships and injustice of a compulsory law, obliging the citizens of this State by birthright free, to contribute to the support of a religion, from which their reason and conscience obliged them to dissent. Who then would not have supposed that the same sense of justice, which induced the Legislature to dissolve the grievous establishment, would also have induced them to leave to common use, the property in churches, glebes, &c., which had been acquired by common purchase.

To do otherwise was, as we conceive, to suppose that long prescription could sanction injustice; and that to persist in error, is to alter the essential difference between right and wrong. As Christians also, the subjects of Jesus Christ, who are wholly opposed to the exercise of spiritual powers by civil rulers, we conceive ourselves obliged to remonstrate against that part of the incorporating act, which authorises and directs the regulation of spiritual concerns. This is such an invasion of Divine prerogative, that it is highly exceptionable on that account, as well as on account of the danger to which it exposes our religious liberties. Jesus Christ hath given sufficient authority to his church, for every lawful purpose: and it is forsaking his authority and direction, for that of fallible men, to expect or to grant the sanction of civil law to authorise the regulation of any Christian so-

ciety. It is also dangerous to our liberties, because it creates an invidious distinction on account of religious opinions, and exalts to a superior pitch of grandeur, as the church of the State, a society which ought to be contented with receiving the same protection from government, which the other societies enjoy, without aspiring to superior notice or regard. The Legislature assumes to itself by that law, the authoritative direction of this church is spirituals; and can be considered in no other light than its head, peculiarly interested in its welfare; a matter which cannot be indifferent to us—though this authority has only as yet been extended to those who have requested it or acquiesced in it. This church is now considered as the only regular church in the view of the law: and it is thereby raised to a state of unjust pre-eminence over others. And how far it may increase in dignity and influence in the State, by these means, at a future day, and especially when aided by the emoluments which it possesses, and the advantages of funding a very large sum of money without account, time alone can discover. But we esteem it our duty to oppose the act thus early, before the matter be entangled in precedents more intricate and dangerous. Upon the whole, therefore, we hope that the exceptionable parts of this act will be repealed by your honourable House; and that all preferences, distinctions, and advantages, contrary to the fourth article of the Declaration of Rights will be forever abolished.

We regret that full equality in all things, and ample protection and security to religious liberty were not incontestibly fixed in the constitution of the government. But we earnestly request that the defect may be remedied, as far as it is possible for the Legislature to do it, by the adopting the bill in the revised laws for establishing religious freedom. (Chap. 82 of the Report.)

That Heaven may illuminate your minds with all that wisdom which is necessary for the important purposes of your deliberation, is our earnest wish. And we beg leave to assure you, that however warmly we may engage in preserving our religion free from the shackles of human authority, and opposing claims of spiritual domination in civil powers, we are zealously disposed to support the government of our country, and to maintain a due submission to the lawful exercise of its authority.

Signed by order of the Convention.

JOHN TODD, *Chairman*
Attest, DANIEL MCCALLA, *Clerk*

Petitions For and Against Religious Assessment from Westmoreland County, Virginia (November 1784)

Two groups of citizens from Westmoreland County, Virginia, sent the following petitions to the Virginia General Assembly urging legislators to, respectively, pass or defeat "A Bill Establishing a Provision for Teachers of the Christian Religion" (see chapter 5).

Petition in Favor of the Bill (November 2, 1784)

Petition of Sundry Inhabitants of the County of Westmoreland

To The Honourable Assembly of Virginia

Your Petitioners having considered the Bill for Establishing a Provision for the Teachers of the Christian Religion are of Opinion that Religion is absolutely requisite for the well ordering of Society and the aid of Government: and that it's Pastors should be comfortably provided for: It being highly unreasonable to suppose that any set of men could devote their time of Fortune to the Attainment of Education

The text was transcribed from microfilm of the original Petition and follows the original except for a few changes to punctuation and capitalization to conform to modern usage. Library of Virginia, Reel 2001, Box 253, Folder 21, image 82.

unless they should Expect to be enabled to preserve a decent and respectable rank in life.

Therefore do we pray that the Bill for that purpose referred to our consideration may be enacted. We further pray that your honourable Assembly will take into consideration the Distinguished part of our Fellow Creatures, who, upon the Destruction of the Old Vestries are left destitute and that some mode may be adopted whereby they may be supported at the General Expense and not left alone to solicit the Cold hand of Charity.

Petition Against the Bill (November 2, 1784)

To the Honourable the Speaker; and Gentlemen of the House of Delegates

The petition of the Inhabitants of the County of Westmoreland humbly showeth that whereas it pleased your Honourable House to publish a Bill Obliging the Inhabitants of their State to pay the Teachers of the Christian Religion and have required their Opinions Concerning it:

Your Petitioners do therefore most earnestly declare against it, believing it to be contrary to the spirit of the Gospel and the Bill of Rights and that Legislature should not assume the power of establishing Modes of Religion, directing the manner of divine Worship, or the Method of supporting it's Teachers.

Certain it is that the Holy Author of our Religion not only supported and maintained his Gospel in the world for several hundred years without the aid of Civil Power, but against all the powers of the Earth. The excellent purity of it's precepts and the unblamable behavior of it's Ministers (with the divine Bless-

The text was transcribed from microfilm of the original Memorial and follows the original except for a few changes to punctuation and capitalization to conform to modern usage. Library of Virginia, Reel 2001, Box 253, Folder 21, images 85 and 86.

ing) made it's way thro all opposition. Nor was it the better for the Church when Constantine first established Christianity by human Law's. True: there was rest from persecution. But how soon over Run with Error, Superstition, and Immorality; how unlike were Ministers then, to what they were before, both in orthodoxy of principle and purity of Life.

But it is said Religion is taking it's Flight, and that Deism with it's banefull Influence is spreading itself over the state. If so, it must be owing to other Causes, not the want of religious Establishment. Let your Laws punish the Vices and Immoralities of the Times, and let there not be wanting such men placed in Power, who by their Example shall recommend Religion and by their Faithfullness shall scourge the growing Vices of the Age. Let ministers manifest to the world "that they are inwardly moved by the Holy Ghost to take upon them that Office," that they seek the good of Mankind and not worldly Interest. Let their doctrines be scriptural and their Lives upright. Then shall Religion (if departed) speedily return, and Deism be put to open shame, and it's dreaded Consequences removed—

But what good purpose would such Assessment answer? Would it introduce any more usefull and faithful Men into the Ministry? Surely not; those whom divine Grace hath called to that work will esteem it their highest Honor to perform the Ministerial Function. On the Contrary, it likely would Call in many Hirelings whose chief motive would be temporal Interest.

That religious Establishment and Government are linked together, and that the latter cannot exist without the former, is Contrary to Experience. Witness the state of Pennsylvania, wherein no such Establishment hath taken place; their Government stands firm; and which of the neighbouring States has better members, of brighter morals, and more upright Character? That matters of Religion are not the object of Civil Government, nor under it's jurisdiction, that to compel a man to furnish Contributions of money for the propagation of Opinions which he disbelieves and Abhors is sinfull and Tyranical, that even

the forcing him to support this or that Teacher of his own Religious persuasion is depriving him of the Comfortable liberty of giving his Contributions to the particular Pastor whose Morals he would make his Pattern.

As Christ the head of the Church has left plain Directions concerning Religion, and the manner of supporting its Teachers which should be by free Contributions, should Legislature step into the Field of Religion and Assume the Liberty of exercising this power over Religious Societies they would Bind a heavy Yoke on them which would be grievous to bear. Let religious Societies Manage the affairs of Religion and Government exercise it's Concern about the Civil Right and Temporal privileges of Man. That, as the Constitution of this State declares all ministers of the Gospel Incapable of being elected members of either House of Assembly, so it is hoped the Assembly will never undertake to direct matters Concerning the Ministry, or the support of it.

Our Bill of Rights which says "That all Men by Nature are equally free, so No Man or sett of men are instilled to exclusive or separate Emoluments or privileges from the Community, but in Consideration of Publick Services." Those who are not of the Christian Religion are by the Assesment Bill denied the privileges which by Nature they are said to be intitled to and from the declaration of Rights, they might reasonably expect.

Finally as such Tax is against the Spirit of the Gospel, since Christ supported and maintained it for several hundred years, not only without such aid, but against all the Powers of the Earth; If it is not the Object of Civil Government, if it would not introduce any more usefull and faithfull men into the Ministry; as it would not Revive decayed Religion nor stop the growth of Deism, and if Against the Bill of Rights, your humble Petitioners trust that the wisdom and uprightness of Your Honourable House will leave them entirely free in Matters of Religion, and the manner of supporting its Teachers. That so peace and Harmony may Abound, which otherwise would be much disturbed; and they shall ever pray & etc.

A Memorial and Remonstrance Against Religious Assessments (1785)

JAMES MADISON (1751–1836)

In the 1780s, as a member of the Virginia Legislature, James Madison engaged in a long-running battle with Patrick Henry and his allies over the propriety of government support for ministers. In response to "A Bill Establishing a Provision for Teachers of the Christian Religion" (see chapter 5), Madison wrote the following memorial, which was printed, circulated, and signed by opponents of the bill throughout Virginia.

[ca. 20 June 1785]
To the Honorable the General Assembly
of the Commonwealth of Virginia
A Memorial and Remonstrance

We the subscribers, citizens of the said Commonwealth, having taken into serious consideration, a Bill printed by order of the last Session of General Assembly, entitled "A Bill establishing a provision for Teachers of the Christian Religion," and conceiving that the same if finally armed with the sanctions of a law, will be a dangerous abuse of power, are bound as faithful members of a free State to remonstrate against it, and to declare the reasons by which we are determined. We remonstrate against the said Bill,

1. Because we hold it for a fundamental and undeniable truth, "that Religion or the duty which we owe to our Creator and the manner of discharging it, can be directed only by reason and conviction, not by force or violence." The Religion then of every man must be left to the conviction and conscience of every man; and it is the right of every man to exercise it as

Reprinted from *The Papers of James Madison*, ed. Robert A. Rutland et al. (Chicago and London: University of Chicago Press, 1973), 8:298–304.

these may dictate. This right is in its nature an unalienable right. It is unalienable, because the opinions of men, depending only on the evidence contemplated by their own minds cannot follow the dictates of other men: It is unalienable also, because what is here a right towards men, is a duty towards the Creator. It is the duty of every man to render to the Creator such homage and such only as he believes to be acceptable to him. This duty is precedent, both in order of time and in degree of obligation, to the claims of Civil Society. Before any man can be considered as a member of Civil Society, he must be considered as a subject of the Governour of the Universe: And if a member of Civil Society, who enters into any subordinate Association, must always do it with a reservation of his duty to the General Authority; much more must every man who becomes a member of any particular Civil Society, do it with a saving of his allegiance to the Universal Sovereign. We maintain therefore that in matters of Religion, no mans right is abridged by the institution of Civil Society and that Religion is wholly exempt from its cognizance. True it is, that no other rule exists, by which any question which may divide a Society, can be ultimately determined, but the will of the majority; but it is also true that the majority may trespass on the rights of the minority.

2. Because if Religion be exempt from the authority of the Society at large, still less can it be subject to that of the Legislative Body. The latter are but the creatures and vicegerents of the former. Their jurisdiction is both derivative and limited: it is limited with regard to the co-ordinate departments, more necessarily is it limited with regard to the constituents. The preservation of a free Government requires not merely, that the metes and bounds which separate each department of power be invariably maintained; but more especially that neither of them be suffered to overleap the great Barrier which defends the rights of the people. The Rulers who are guilty of such an encroachment, exceed the commission from which they derive their authority, and are Tyrants. The People who submit to it are governed by laws made nei-

To the Honorable the General Assembly of the Commonwealth of Virginia: A Memorial and Remonstrance, holograph, James Madison, June 1785. The Papers of James Madison, Manuscript Division, Library of Congress.

ther by themselves nor by an authority derived from them, and are slaves.

3. Because it is proper to take alarm at the first experiment on our liberties. We hold this prudent jealousy to be the first duty of Citizens, and one of the noblest characteristics of the late Revolution. The free men of America did not wait till usurped power had strengthened itself by exercise, and entangled the question in precedents. They saw all the consequences in the principle, and they avoided the consequences by denying the principle. We revere this lesson too much soon to forget it. Who does not see that the same authority which can establish Christianity, in exclusion of all other Religions, may establish with the same ease any particular sect of Christians, in exclusion of all other Sects? that the same authority which can force a citizen to contribute three pence only of his property for the support of any one establishment, may force him to conform to any other establishment in all cases whatsoever?

4. Because the Bill violates that equality which ought to be the basis of every law, and which is more indispensible, in proportion as the validity or expediency of any law is more liable to be impeached. If "all men are by nature equally free and independent," all men are to be considered as entering into Society on equal conditions; as relinquishing no more, and therefore retaining no less, one than another, of their natural rights. Above all are they to be considered as retaining an "*equal* title to the free exercise of Religion according to the dictates of Conscience." Whilst we assert for ourselves a freedom to embrace, to profess and to observe the Religion which we believe to be of divine origin, we cannot deny an equal freedom to those whose minds have not yet yielded to the evidence which has convinced us. If this freedom be abused, it is an offence against God, not against man: To God, therefore, not to man, must an account of it be rendered. As the Bill violates equality by subjecting some to peculiar burdens, so it violates the same principle, by granting to others peculiar exemptions. Are the Quakers and Menonists the only sects who think a compulsive support of their Religions unnecessary

and unwarrantable? Can their piety alone be entrusted with the care of public worship? Ought their Religions to be endowed above all others with extraordinary privileges by which proselytes may be enticed from all others? We think too favorably of the justice and good sense of these denominations to believe that they either covet pre-eminences over their fellow citizens or that they will be seduced by them from the common opposition to the measure.

5. Because the Bill implies either that the Civil Magistrate is a competent Judge of Religious Truth; or that he may employ Religion as an engine of Civil policy. The first is an arrogant pretension falsified by the contradictory opinions of Rulers in all ages, and throughout the world: the second an unhallowed perversion of the means of salvation.

6. Because the establishment proposed by the Bill is not requisite for the support of the Christian Religion. To say that it is, is a contradiction to the Christian Religion itself, for every page of it disavows a dependence on the powers of this world: it is a contradiction to fact; for it is known that this Religion both existed and flourished, not only without the support of human laws, but in spite of every opposition from them, and not only during the period of miraculous aid, but long after it had been left to its own evidence and the ordinary care of Providence. Nay, it is a contradiction in terms; for a Religion not invented by human policy, must have pre-existed and been supported, before it was established by human policy. It is moreover to weaken in those who profess this Religion a pious confidence in its innate excellence and the patronage of its Author; and to foster in those who still reject it, a suspicion that its friends are too conscious of its fallacies to trust it to its own merits.

7. Because experience witnesseth that ecclesiastical establishments, instead of maintaining the purity and efficacy of Religion, have had a contrary operation. During almost fifteen centuries has the legal establishment of Christianity been on trial. What have been its fruits? More or less in all places, pride and indolence in the Clergy, ignorance and servility in the

laity, in both, superstition, bigotry and persecution. Enquire of the Teachers of Christianity for the ages in which it appeared in its greatest lustre; those of every sect, point to the ages prior to its incorporation with Civil policy. Propose a restoration of this primitive State in which its Teachers depended on the voluntary rewards of their flocks, many of them predict its downfall. On which Side ought their testimony to have greatest weight, when for or when against their interest?

8. Because the establishment in question is not necessary for the support of Civil Government. If it be urged as necessary for the support of Civil Government only as it is a means of supporting Religion, and it be not necessary for the latter purpose, it cannot be necessary for the former. If Religion be not within the cognizance of Civil Government how can its legal establishment be necessary to Civil Government? What influence in fact have ecclesiastical establishments had on Civil Society? In some instances they have been seen to erect a spiritual tyranny on the ruins of the Civil authority; in many instances they have been seen upholding the thrones of political tyranny: in no instance have they been seen the guardians of the liberties of the people. Rulers who wished to subvert the public liberty, may have found an established Clergy convenient auxiliaries. A just Government instituted to secure & perpetuate it needs them not. Such a Government will be best supported by protecting every Citizen in the enjoyment of his Religion with the same equal hand which protects his person and his property; by neither invading the equal rights of any Sect, nor suffering any Sect to invade those of another.

9. Because the proposed establishment is a departure from that generous policy, which, offering an Asylum to the persecuted and oppressed of every Nation and Religion, promised a lustre to our country, and an accession to the number of its citizens. What a melancholy mark is the Bill of sudden degeneracy? Instead of holding forth an Asylum to the persecuted, it is itself a signal of persecution. It degrades from the equal rank of Citizens all those whose opinions in Re-

ligion do not bend to those of the Legislative authority. Distant as it may be in its present form from the Inquisition, it differs from it only in degree. The one is the first step, the other the last in the career of intolerance. The magnanimous sufferer under this cruel scourge in foreign Regions, must view the Bill as a Beacon on our Coast, warning him to seek some other haven, where liberty and philanthrophy in their due extent, may offer a more certain repose from his Troubles.

10. Because it will have a like tendency to banish our Citizens. The allurements presented by other situations are every day thinning their number. To superadd a fresh motive to emigration by revoking the liberty which they now enjoy, would be the same species of folly which has dishonoured and depopulated flourishing kingdoms.

11. Because it will destroy that moderation and harmony which the forbearance of our laws to intermeddle with Religion has produced among its several sects. Torrents of blood have been spilt in the old world, by vain attempts of the secular arm, to extinguish Religious discord, by proscribing all difference in Religious opinion. Time has at length revealed the true remedy. Every relaxation of narrow and rigorous policy, wherever it has been tried, has been found to assuage the disease. The American Theatre has exhibited proofs that equal and compleat liberty, if it does not wholly eradicate it, sufficiently destroys its malignant influence on the health and prosperity of the State. If with the salutary effects of this system under our own eyes, we begin to contract the bounds of Religious freedom, we know no name that will too severely reproach our folly. At least let warning be taken at the first fruits of the threatened innovation. The very appearance of the Bill has transformed "that Christian forbearance, love and charity," which of late mutually prevailed, into animosities and jealousies, which may not soon be appeased. What mischiefs may not be dreaded, should this enemy to the public quiet be armed with the force of a law?

12. Because the policy of the Bill is adverse to the diffusion of the light of Christianity. The first wish

of those who enjoy this precious gift ought to be that it may be imparted to the whole race of mankind. Compare the number of those who have as yet received it with the number still remaining under the dominion of false Religions; and how small is the former! Does the policy of the Bill tend to lessen the disproportion? No; it at once discourages those who are strangers to the light of revelation from coming into the Region of it; and countenances by example the nations who continue in darkness, in shutting out those who might convey it to them. Instead of Levelling as far as possible, every obstacle to the victorious progress of Truth, the Bill with an ignoble and unchristian timidity would circumscribe it with a wall of defence against the encroachments of error.

13. Because attempts to enforce by legal sanctions, acts obnoxious to so great a proportion of Citizens, tend to enervate the laws in general, and to slacken the bands of Society. If it be difficult to execute any law which is not generally deemed necessary or salutary, what must be the case, where it is deemed invalid and dangerous? And what may be the effect of so striking an example of impotency in the Government, on its general authority?

14. Because a measure of such singular magnitude and delicacy ought not to be imposed, without the clearest evidence that it is called for by a majority of citizens, and no satisfactory method is yet proposed by which the voice of the majority in this case may be determined, or its influence secured. "The people of the respective counties are indeed requested to signify their opinion respecting the adoption of the Bill to the next Session of Assembly." But the representation must be made equal, before the voice either of the Representatives or of the Counties will be that of the people. Our hope is that neither of the former will, after due consideration, espouse the dangerous principle of the Bill. Should the event disappoint us, it will still leave us in full confidence, that a fair appeal to the latter will reverse the sentence against our liberties.

15. Because finally, "the equal right of every citizen to the free exercise of his Religion according to the dictates of conscience" is held by the same tenure with all our other rights. If we recur to its origin, it is equally the gift of nature; if we weigh its importance, it cannot be less dear to us; if we consult the "Declaration of those rights which pertain to the good people of Virginia, as the basis and foundation of Government," it is enumerated with equal solemnity, or rather studied emphasis. Either then, we must say, that the Will of the Legislature is the only measure of their authority; and that in the plenitude of this authority, they may sweep away all our fundamental rights; or, that they are bound to leave this particular right untouched and sacred: Either we must say, that they may controul the freedom of the press, may abolish the Trial by Jury, may swallow up the Executive and Judiciary Powers of the State; nay that they may despoil us of our very right of suffrage, and erect themselves into an independent and hereditary Assembly or, we must say, that they have no authority to enact into law the Bill under consideration. We the Subscribers say, that the General Assembly of this Commonwealth have no such authority: And that no effort may be omitted on our part against so dangerous an usurpation, we oppose to it, this remonstrance; earnestly praying, as we are in duty bound, that the Supreme Lawgiver of the Universe, by illuminating those to whom it is addressed, may on the one hand, turn their Councils from every act which would affront his holy prerogative, or violate the trust committed to them: and on the other, guide them into every measure which may be worthy of his blessing, may redound to their own praise, and may establish more firmly the liberties, the prosperity and the happiness of the Commonwealth.

The Federalist Papers, Number 10 (1787)

The Federalist Papers, Number 51 (1788)

PUBLIUS [JAMES MADISON]

The Federalist Papers were written by James Madison, Alexander Hamilton, and John Jay in 1787 and 1788 to promote New York's ratification of the federal constitution. Although none of the papers focus on religion per se, the following excerpts from two of Madison's most famous essays contain his view that religion can be a dangerous source of faction. They also set forth his remedy for the problem of factions—religious or otherwise.

The Federalist Papers, Number 10

The latent causes of faction are thus sown in the nature of man; and we see them everywhere brought into different degrees of activity, according to the different circumstances of civil society. A zeal for different opinions concerning religion, concerning government, and many other points, as well of speculation as of practice; an attachment to different leaders ambitiously contending for pre-eminence and power; or to persons of other descriptions whose fortunes have been interesting to the human passions, have, in turn, divided mankind into parties, inflamed them with mutual animosity, and rendered them much more disposed to vex and oppress each other than to co-operate for their common good. So strong is this propensity of mankind to fall into mutual animosi-

ties, that where no substantial occasion presents itself, the most frivolous and fanciful distinctions have been sufficient to kindle their unfriendly passions and excite their most violent conflicts. But the most common and durable source of factions has been the various and unequal distribution of property. Those who hold and those who are without property have ever formed distinct interests in society. Those who are creditors, and those who are debtors, fall under a like discrimination. A landed interest, a manufacturing interest, a mercantile interest, a moneyed interest, with many lesser interests, grow up of necessity in civilized nations, and divide them into different classes, actuated by different sentiments and views. The regulation of these various and interfering interests forms the principal task of modern legislation, and involves the spirit of party and faction in the necessary and ordinary operations of the government. . . .

The other point of difference is, the greater number of citizens and extent of territory which may be brought within the compass of republican than of democratic government; and it is this circumstance principally which renders factious combinations less to be dreaded in the former than in the latter. The smaller the society, the fewer probably will be the distinct parties and interests composing it; the fewer the distinct parties and interests, the more frequently will a majority be found of the same party; and the smaller the number of individuals composing a majority, and the smaller the compass within which they are placed, the more easily will they concert and execute their plans of oppression. Extend the sphere, and you take in a greater variety of parties and interests; you make it less probable that a majority of the whole will have a common motive to invade the rights of other citizens; or if such a common motive exists, it will be more difficult for all who feel it to discover their own strength, and to act in unison with each other. Besides other impediments, it may be remarked that, where there is a consciousness of unjust or dishonorable purposes, communication is always checked by distrust in proportion to the number whose concurrence is necessary.

Hence, it clearly appears, that the same advantage which a republic has over a democracy, in controlling the effects of faction, is enjoyed by a large over a small republic,—is enjoyed by the Union over the States composing it. Does the advantage consist in the substitution of representatives whose enlightened views and virtuous sentiments render them superior to local prejudices and schemes of injustice? It will not be denied that the representation of the Union will be most likely to possess these requisite endowments. Does it consist in the greater security afforded by a greater variety of parties, against the event of any one party being able to outnumber and oppress the rest? In an equal degree does the increased variety of parties comprised within the Union, increase this security. Does it, in fine, consist in the greater obstacles opposed to the concert and accomplishment of the secret wishes of an unjust and interested majority? Here, again, the extent of the Union gives it the most palpable advantage.

The influence of factious leaders may kindle a flame within their particular States, but will be unable to spread a general conflagration through the other States. A religious sect may degenerate into a political faction in a part of the Confederacy; but the variety of sects dispersed over the entire face of it must secure the national councils against any danger from that source. A rage for paper money, for an abolition of debts, for an equal division of property, or for any other improper or wicked project, will be less apt to pervade the whole body of the Union than a particular member of it; in the same proportion as such a malady is more likely to taint a particular county or district, than an entire State.

In the extent and proper structure of the Union, therefore, we behold a republican remedy for the diseases most incident to republican government. And according to the degree of pleasure and pride we feel in being republicans, ought to be our zeal in cherishing the spirit and supporting the character of Federalists.

PUBLIUS

The Federalist Papers, Number 51

It is of great importance in a republic not only to guard the society against the oppression of its rulers, but to guard one part of the society against the injustice of the other part. Different interests necessarily exist in different classes of citizens. If a majority be united by a common interest, the rights of the minority will be insecure. There are but two methods of providing against this evil: the one by creating a will in the community independent of the majority—that is, of the society itself; the other, by comprehending in the society so many separate descriptions of citizens as will render an unjust combination of a majority of the whole very improbable, if not impracticable. The first method prevails in all governments possessing an hereditary or self-appointed authority. This, at best, is but a precarious security; because a power independent of the society may as well espouse the unjust views of the major, as the rightful interests of the minor party, and may possibly be turned against both parties. The second method will be exemplified in the federal republic of the United States. Whilst all authority in it will be derived from and dependent on the society, the society itself will be broken into so many parts, interests, and classes of citizens, that the rights of individuals, or of the minority, will be in little danger from interested combinations of the majority. In a free government the security for civil rights must be the same as that for religious rights. It consists in the one case in the multiplicity of interests, and in the other in the multiplicity of sects. The degree of security in both cases will depend on the number of interests and sects; and this may be presumed to depend on the extent of country and number of people comprehended under the same government. This view of the subject must particularly recommend a proper federal system to all the sincere and considerate friends of republican government, since it shows that

Reprinted from Alexander Hamilton, John Jay, and James Madison, *The Federalist*, ed. George W. Carey and James McClellan (Indianapolis: Liberty Fund, 2001), 356–58. © Liberty Fund, Inc., 2001. Reprinted by permission.

in exact proportion as the territory of the Union may be formed into more circumscribed Confederacies, or States oppressive combinations of a majority will be facilitated: the best security, under the republican forms, for the rights of every class of citizens, will be diminished: and consequently the stability and independence of some member of the government, the only other security, must be proportionately increased. Justice is the end of government. It is the end of civil society. It ever has been and ever will be pursued until it be obtained, or until liberty be lost in the pursuit. In a society under the forms of which the stronger faction can readily unite and oppress the weaker, anarchy may as truly be said to reign as in a state of nature, where the weaker individual is not secured against the violence of the stronger; and as, in the latter state, even the stronger individuals are prompted, by the uncertainty of their condition, to submit to a government which may protect the weak as well as themselves; so, in the former state, will the more powerful factions or parties be gradually induced, by a like motive, to wish for a government which will protect all parties, the weaker as well as the more powerful. It can be little doubted that if the State of Rhode Island was separated from the Confederacy and left to itself, the insecurity of rights under the popular form of government within such narrow limits would be displayed by such reiterated oppressions of factious majorities that some power altogether independent of the people would soon be called for by the voice of the very factions whose misrule had proved the necessity of it. In the extended republic of the United States, and among the great variety of interests, parties, and sects which it embraces, a coalition of a majority of the whole society could seldom take place on any other principles than those of justice and the general good; whilst there being thus less danger to a minor from the will of a major party, there must be less pretext, also, to provide for the security of the former, by introducing into the government a will not dependent on the latter, or, in other words, a will independent of the society itself. It is no less certain than it is important, notwith-

standing the contrary opinions which have been entertained, that the larger the society, provided it lie within a practical sphere, the more duly capable it will be of self-government. And happily for the REPUBLICAN CAUSE, the practicable sphere may be carried to a very great extent, by a judicious modification and mixture of the FEDERAL PRINCIPLE.

PUBLIUS

An Essay on the Influence of Religion in Civil Society (1788)

THOMAS REESE (1742–94)

Thomas Reese, a native of Pennsylvania and graduate of Princeton, was an influential Presbyterian minister in South Carolina. This essay, written in the context of the disestablishment of the Anglican Church in South Carolina, argues that the civil magistrate may, "without invasion of the rights of conscience, take measures for the instruction of subjects in the important doctrines and precepts of Christianity."

That our laws do not operate with sufficient force, is a truth too glaring to escape observation. It is seen, felt, and lamented by every sincere lover of his country. Different causes, no doubt, co-operate to produce this effect. To investigate all these, does not fall in with my present design; though it might be of singular service to the state. For as in the human, so in the body politic, the cause of a disease being once discovered, the remedy is more easily prescribed, and the deleterious effect more successfully counteracted. It is more to my purpose to observe, that the general ne-

Reprinted from Thomas Reese, *An Essay on the Influence of Religion in Civil Society* (Charleston: Markland & McIver, 1788), 3–8, 19–22, 42–46, 60–86.

glect of religion which prevails among us, is one great, if not the chief cause, why our laws are so feeble in their operation. Immorality is the natural consequence of impiety. An irreligious, will always be an immoral, people; and among such, good and wholesome laws can never be executed with punctuality.

Some of our laws may be erroneous or defective, and not framed with a sufficient regard to the spirit of the people; and this hath been assigned by superficial thinkers as the only reason why they are not carried into execution. This, I think, is a great mistake. Our laws though they may partake of that imperfection which is the common mark of all human productions, are in general salutary, and calculated to promote our political happiness. Here lies the grand defect; a defect which is not to be attributed solely or even principally to the badness of our laws, but to some other causes. Whatever these may be, the effect is sufficiently alarming, and threatens a speedy dissolution of our government. Let our laws be ever so good, if they are not properly executed, our government can be of no long duration.

A transient view of those states and kingdoms, which have made the most striking figure in the history of the world, and which have been most renowned for the felicity of their government, will convince us, that religion was by them always considered as a matter of great importance to civil society.

The greatest politicians and most celebrated legislators of antiquity depended much on this to give sanction to their laws, and make them operate with vigour and facility.

If we carefully consider the nature of religion and of civil government, we will be led to conclude, that in this they did not act at random; but from the most profound knowledge of human nature, and the dictates of the soundest policy. The manners of the people, though so little attended to by our legislators, are confessed by all to be of the utmost consequence in a commonwealth. The most profligate politician can expatiate on the necessity of good morals; but we hear little of religion from our most respectable statesmen. When the discussion is of politics, she is generally

kicked out of doors, as having nothing to do either with morality or civil policy. The inseparable connection between this daughter of heaven and her genuine offspring morality, is forgotten, and her influence on civil society almost wholly overlooked.

For the better arrangement of our thoughts on this extensive subject, we shall—

I. Consider religion under its more general notion, as comprehending the belief of a deity, a providence, and future state of rewards and punishments.

II. We shall consider the christian religion in particular; and, as we pass along, endeavour to show the influence of both on civil society.

That religion is of great importance to society is universally acknowledged. Assuming this for granted, let us proceed to enquire how it operates to produce those effects which are confessed to be of such singular service. It is a common observation, that we are so formed as to be greatly influenced by whatever works upon our hopes or our fears. Now it is by taking hold on these that religion produces those salutary effects of which we now speak; thus restraining men from vice by the dread of punishment, and alluring them to virtue by the hope of reward. These are the two principles, or if you please, passions, in human nature, which first prompted men to enter into the social union; fear of violence from each other, and hope of security by association. And it is only by working on these passions, that the union of men in the social state can be rendered permanent, and laws operate with that energy which is necessary to obtain their end.

They who firmly believe that there is a God who governs the world, who sees all their actions, and who will certainly reward virtue and punish vice, must undoubtedly be influenced by this belief; and restrained, at least in some measure, from evil, and excited to good.

It must be confessed indeed, that there are too many who profess to believe the doctrines of religion, who seem to be very little influenced by them. Hurried away by the violence of their passions, they frequently transgress the bounds which religion prescribes, and prefer the gratification of present appetite to the enjoyment of future good. But we must not hence conclude, that religion is in no degree a curb to the licentiousness of men. They who in some instances act thus contrary to their principles, would go much further, were they void of those principles, and the reins laid on the neck of appetite. It will not follow, that because religion does not restrain from immorality totally and universally, therefore it is no restraint at all. By the same way of reasoning, we might prove, that civil laws lay no restraint upon men, because they do not entirely restrain all men, at all times and in all instances.

In order that we may be more fully convinced of the utility, and even necessity of religion, to the well being, we might venture to say, to the very existence of civil society, it will be necessary a little to enquire into the essential defects of the best constituted government possible.

If we consider the end of civil society, and the evils it was designed to remedy, we will be convinced from its very nature, that it cannot reach that end, nor guard against those evils, without the aid of religion. Let it suffice to observe, that *security* of *life*, *liberty* and *property*, is the precise and specific end of the social compact. Other advantages it brings with it, and answers many other valuable purposes. But the evils for which it was designed as a remedy, are injustice, violence, rapine, mutual slaughter and bloodshed. The manner in which men aim at the cure of these evils, is by laws enacted with common consent, enforced by a sanction, and committed to the magistrate to be strictly and impartially carried into execution.

That civil government may fully and completely obtain its end, it is necessary that its laws should have such a sanction, and operate in such a manner, as to prevent or punish all crimes whatsoever, which may be injurious to the community, or tend to its dissolution. It will, I suppose, be readily granted on all hands, that there never were, nor ever will be, laws so sanctioned as to operate in this manner. Hence appears the insufficiency of civil society to answer its end.

The two great sanctions of all laws have been generally reckoned *reward* and *punishment*, and indeed without these two sanctions, every one must see, that government cannot, in any tolerable degree, answer its end, or laws operate in such a manner as is necessary to secure its very existence. But civil society, without the support of religion, is altogether destitute of one of these sanctions; and can apply the other but in a very partial manner, and under great restrictions.

I. Civil society wholly wants the *sanction* of *reward*.

In an age and place so highly enlightened in the nature and principles of sound policy, I shall not enter into a formal proof, that reward is not, and cannot be the sanction of civil society, considered in itself. It will be sufficient just to observe, "that no state whatever can possess a fund large enough to reward all its subjects for obedience to the laws, unless it be first drawn from them by a tax, to be paid back as a reward." Government can indeed, and it hath been the custom in all governments, to reward particular subjects for eminent services; but every one must see, that this is something very different from the idea of reward considered as the sanction of civil laws. A reward barely for obedience to the good and wholesome laws of his country, is what no wise subject expects, and no society can* bestow. Without entering any further into this subject, we shall take it for granted that civil society, in itself, totally wants one of those sanctions which are necessary to enforce its laws. That this is a

---

* It may perhaps be said that protection is the reward conferred on every individual for his observance of the laws. And here I imagine, if any where, it is that so many have fallen into a mistake in this matter. To this it may be briefly replied, that protection is a debt due from *all* to *every individual*, for that portion of his natural liberty which he hath given up in the original compact. If protection, in strict propriety of speech, be reward, then with drawing it must be punishment, which it is not invariably, but only accidentally. The consequence of withdrawing protection is, or at least always ought to be, banishment. But banishment is not always a punishment. It becomes so only by accident. It is so intentionally, but not always consequentially. Punishment is not of the essence of banishment; for it would be easy to put a case where banishment must be considered, not as a punishment, but a very great blessing. This shows that protection considered as reward, is not the sanction of human laws in the same sense that punishment is, to which it ought to be properly opposed, if indeed it be the sanction of reward.

very great and essential defect, will, we hope, be allowed by every competent judge. How, and in what degree religion supplies this defect, will be seen hereafter. At present let us a little enquire,

II. Into the effects of punishment considered as a sanction. This is the proper and only sanction of civil laws. But how imperfectly it can be enforced by society will appear from the following considerations.

I. Civil government cannot punish secret crimes.

That these abound in every society, is matter of universal experience; that they are injurious to it, is too plain to admit of the least doubt; that they are even multiplied by it, a little attention to human nature, will evince. When men are restrained from open transgression, by the terror of laws and the dread of punishment, it is natural for them to fly to the covert of secrecy, that they may evade the laws, and escape with impunity. They know that civil judicatures take cognizance only of those crimes which are apparent: and if they can only conceal their guilt from the eyes of men, they are sure to escape that punishment which is the sanction of human laws. This will deter them from open violence, but at the same time, spur them on to secret craft and stratagem. This will lead them to study and improve all the latent arts of mischief and malice: and the very security which society affords, by throwing men off their guard, gives designing villains an opportunity of practising these with greater success. I crave the readers particular attention to this circumstance, as it is of the first importance to the point in hand, and in the clearest manner shows the necessity of religion in civil government. . . .

It is well known that three different opinions have been advanced on this head: some founding it on the *moral sense,* others on the *essential difference* of things, and others on the *will* of *God.* Strictly speaking, perhaps this last only, can properly oblige *men.* But in order to maintain this, it is not necessary to exclude the other two from all influence on morality. Where is the absurdity of allowing all three a share in leading men to the practice of virtue? Without determining any thing positively concerning this matter, we have

endeavored to prove, that religion cannot be considered as unnecessary, even on the principles of those who are most strongly attached to the *moral sense* and the *essential difference.* These two have indeed, of late, been the hobby-horses of their respective patrons. They make the principal figure in the writings of most of our modern moralists, not to say divines. The *will* of God, or what comes nearly to the same thing, *religion,* which is indeed the only proper and stable foundation of morality, is either wholly excluded, or brought in only by the bye, as a matter of little or no consequence. These fine-spun systems, however much they may display the ingenuity of their authors, have but very little tendency to promote virtue, and reform the manners of the people; and therefore can be of little service to society. It is not easy to see how the *moral sense,* or the *essential difference,* or both taken together, when considered as wholly distinct from religion, if indeed they can be so considered, can properly establish the sanction of future reward and punishment. This we have shewn is of the greatest moment to civil government; and hence arises the singular utility of religion.

The abstract beauty of virtue may operate upon profound reasoners,—that pleasure which arises from those actions which the moral sense approves, may have its weight with men of elegant minds and delicate sentiments; but neither of them will have much effect upon the great body of mankind. They will be always found to operate but very faintly upon the *many,* who have, generally, "quick senses, strong passions and gross intellects." This single observation shows of how little consequence they are, when compared with religion, which is calculated to operate upon the bulk of the common people in every society.

Upon the whole, tho' we should grant that other things co-operate with religion in supplying the defects of civil society, we need not fear to conclude, that this is the most proper, and at the same time, the most powerful remedy.

Before we conclude this part, it will be necessary to add a few words concerning the use of oaths, which *may* be considered as a distinct argument, to prove the influence of religion on civil society. Solemn oaths, as far as I can learn, have obtained in all civilized nations. It is well known, what amazing force and influence they had upon the Romans in the virtuous period of their republic. In the greatest extremity, and most pressing dangers, these were their *dernier* resort. We have instances enough of this in their history. Let one suffice in this place: After the battle of Cannae, the people were struck with such a panic terror, that they talked of removing to Sicily. But Scipio had the address to obtain an oath from them, that they would not leave Rome. The dread of violating this oath overwhelmed all other apprehensions. "Rome," says the excellent Montesquieu, "was a ship held by two anchors, religion and morality, in the midst of a furious tempest."

If Mr. Locke, and the American politicians, argue right, all legitimate government is originally founded on compact. This compact is usually ratified by solemn oaths. The chief magistrate, who is invested with the supreme executive power, is bound by oath, faithfully and impartially to execute the laws, and govern agreeably to them. In like manner, every citizen is bound to aid and support him, as far as he acts conformably to his solemn engagement. Among us, it is well known, that all civil officers from the governor down to the constable, are obliged by oath, to the discharge of their respective trusts. The policy, and even necessity of all this, is very obvious; for altho' our civil officers are amenable for their conduct, and liable to be punished upon conviction, this can be no security against clandestine fraud. Here the religion of an oath is necessary, to restrain them from those secret *mal-practices,* which, however injurious to the public, cannot be legally detected. The security of life and property depends, in a great measure, upon oaths. The innocent cannot be absolved, nor the guilty punished without them. In the most important judicial proceedings, the verdict ultimately rests upon their validity. Take away the use of these religious affirmations, and our courts of judicature must cease, or be almost entirely useless. In a word civil government can by no means be carried on without them. If oaths

be thus necessary to the administration of government, religion must be so; for where there is no religion, there can be no oath. Take away the belief of a deity, a providence and future state, and there is an end of all oaths at once. In every oath a deity is invoked, as a witness and avenger, if we deviate from the truth. The atheist, therefore, cannot be bound by it. He who believes there is no providence or future state, can be in no dread of punishment, either in this or a coming world, if he can only elude human judicatures. The greatest free thinker, or most abandoned profligate in our country, would place very little dependence on the oath of one who believes there is neither God nor devil, heaven nor hell. Civil laws do indeed hold out a severe punishment to deter men from perjury; but as it is one of those crimes, of which a person can seldom be legally convicted, such laws strike but little terror, and are of very little service. The perjured villain may repeat his crime an hundred times without any danger from human laws. If therefore, the laws of religion have no hold upon him, his oath is perfectly insignificant, especially, where he is under temptation to depart from the truth. We may therefore venture to affirm, that the obligation of oaths is properly founded on religion; and that whatever weight we allow them above a simple affirmation, arises from a supposition, that the *deponent* believes there is a God, the *rewarder* of truth and the *avenger* of perjury, to whom he makes a solemn appeal. This single consideration, were there no other arguments, is sufficient to evince the utility, and even the necessity of religion to civil society. For if government cannot be carried on without the use of oaths, and the validity of these depend upon religion, the consequence is unavoidable, that civil society cannot subsist without religion. We proceed to the second head of argument.

In order to show the influence of the christian religion on civil society, it will be necessary to consider—the doctrines it teaches—the worship it enjoins—and the precepts it inculcates. The two first, shall be treated briefly; the last requires a more ample discussion. . . .

1. That benevolent disposition which Christianity requires, has a direct tendency to promote the peace and happiness of men in a state of society.

Christianity is beyond comparison the purest and most extensive system of benevolence which hath ever been published to the world. It every where breathes the spirit of love, and inculcates the laws of kindness and humanity. That good will towards men which it requires is universal, and embraces the whole human race. It is not confined to the narrow circle of friends and relations, but extends even to enemies. The precept of our Savior which requires us to love, do good to, and pray for our enemies, is peculiar to Christianity; at least we do not find it so expressly taught, and particularly enforced, by any other religion. The Jews entertained an implacable hatred against all those who were not of their own nation and religion. Their malevolence to all but their own brethren, was so remarkable, that the heathens have taken notice of it. "Their fidelity," says Tacitus, "is inviolable, and their pity ready towards each other; but to all others they bear a mortal hatred." The apostle Paul, a more impartial judge, gives them the same character. "They please not God, and are contrary to all men." They even thought themselves at liberty to indulge their malice against private enemies of their own nation. Though the precepts of their law, rightly understood, were far from allowing such a malevolent disposition, it is certain that by their corrupt interpretations, they drew this inference from them. And it must be confessed, that the god-like duty of loving our enemies, was not so clearly revealed, and so expressly inculcated, under the Jewish, as under the Christian dispensation. Here we have it enforced by the noblest of all considerations, namely, the resemblance it gives us to the deity, who indiscriminately showers down the common blessings of his providence, both on his friends and enemies. The bloody and vindictive spirit of the Mahometan religion is well known. Grotius has emphatically characterized it in a few words. "Mahometis religio in armis nata, nihil spirat nisi arma, armis propagatur." "The religion of Mahomet originated in arms, breathes nothing but arms, is propagated by arms." The civil institutions of the Greeks, particularly those of Sparta, were principally directed to war. Conquest, rapine, blood-shed, triumph, were their chief aim. To rob and plunder their neighbors was so far from being reckoned infamous among them, that they gloried in it. And it is worthy of observation, that these institutions were admired by their philosophers, and approved by their oracles. Aristotle is not ashamed to affirm, "That war with barbarians is natural." The Romans were little better than the robbers and butchers of the world. Their fame, wealth, power, and grandeur, arose principally from the conquest and spoils of those whom they made or found their enemies. They were so infamous for their unjust wars and public robberies, that Cicero himself scruples not to declare, "that if every one had his own, they must return to their old cottages." In a word, the many instances of flagrant injustice and cruelty publicly approved both by the Greeks and Romans, show, that they had scarce any idea of that universal benevolence, that humane, gentle and peaceable disposition, which the precepts of our religion so strongly recommend and enforce.* War was their trade, and their religion restrained them from nothing which they imagined might extend their empire and increase their power. Some of the heathen moralists have told us that faith is to be kept with an enemy; and that injuries should be forgiven, on the repentance and acknowledgement of the offender; but I do not recollect that one of them before the Christian aera, requires men to love those who are in a state of actual enmity with them. To do good to such, to pray for them, and

---

* It must be confessed, that Christian nations have, in many instances, shown too little regard to the spirit of their religion, in the wars they have commenced and carried on. They have often been cruel and unjust, contrary to that humane and peaceable disposition enjoined by the gospel. It cannot, however, be denied, that Christianity hath had a considerable influence on men, and laid them under great restraints in this respect. The history of Europe evidently shows how much it tends to check the ferocity and soften the rugged manners of those nations who embrace it. If I mistake not, it produced a remarkable change on the Roman empire. We do not find the same cruel and sanguinary disposition prevailing after it became Christian. War is divested of half its horrors by the mild and gentle spirit of Christianity.

promote their happiness, is a pitch of philanthropy, to which Christianity alone teaches us to aspire. How much such a disposition tends to the peace and happiness of men in the social state, is obvious at first view. Love is the great cement of society, and a principal bond of union among its members. As malice, hatred, envy, and all the inimical passions, naturally tend to disunite men, and destroy that concord, which is the greatest strength and security of government; so mutual love sweetly and powerfully attracts and binds them to each other. He who loves his neighbor as himself, and sincerely desires his happiness, needs no other motive to excite him to the most exact and careful performance of all the social duties. A heart overflowing with benevolence to our fellowmen will be a more powerful restraint from injury, and a stronger excitement to beneficence, than all the terror of civil laws. This noble and generous principle will operate uniformly and efficaciously; and by an internal, secret impulse, direct and spur us on to a careful observance of all the laws of kindness and humanity. Prompted by an ardent wish to promote the happiness of all around us, we will perform every kind office with a pleasure and facility unknown to a narrow and selfish mind. We will often forget or overlook our own interest to oblige a friend, to vindicate the innocent, relieve the distressed and succour the miserable. He who is conformed to the temper, governed by the precepts, and influenced by the example of the benevolent Jesus, will, like the good Samaritan, pour balm even into the wounds of an enemy; will feed him when hungry, cloath him when naked, return him good for evil, and blessing for cursing. In a word, that unbounded benevolence which Christianity requires, necessarily leads to the performance of all the duties of charity, hospitality, gratitude, mercy and compassion, which we have shown human laws cannot enforce, and which are nevertheless necessary to the peace and happiness of civil government.

Let it be further observed here, that Christianity not only enjoins meekness and benevolence, but expressly condemns a contrary disposition. A malicious and vindictive temper is directly opposite to the precepts of the gospel. Hear the apostle Paul on this subject, "Dearly beloved, avenge not yourselves, but rather give place unto wrath; for it is written, vengeance is mine; I will repay, saith the Lord. Therefore, if thine enemy hunger, feed him; if he thirst, give him drink; for, in so doing, thou shalt heap coals of fire upon his head." This is perfectly consistent with the precepts and example of his meek and heavenly master, who teaches us to expect forgiveness only, on condition that we forgive others. "But if you do not forgive neither will your father, who is in heaven, forgive your trespasses." The same precept and example is illustrated and enforced, with incomparable strength and beauty, in the parable of the debtors and creditors, Mat. 18. from the 23d verse to the close. . . .

III. That temperance and moderation which the precepts of Christianity require, are of great importance to civil society, and evidently tend to promote public good.

It is a trite observation, that society, by cultivating the arts of life, greatly increases our wants; and consequently inflames our appetites in proportion. The wants of nature are few, and easily supplied; but those created by society, which may be called artificial, are without bounds or number. In the social state, therefore, where mens wants are so numerous, and the desire of satisfying them so highly excited, temperance and moderation must be peculiarly necessary. It is too plain to need any proof, that by far the greater part of those evils which disturb society, flow from the inordinate appetites and ungoverned passions of men. An immoderate desire of those things which have, at least, the appearance of *natural good*, and which are generally thought necessary to our happiness in polished life, is the source of numberless civil crimes. A too eager and violent pursuit of wealth, honor, power and sensual gratification, prompts men to rapine, violence, cruelty, oppression, and every species of injustice. Hence flows a long train of evils, which bring a consumption on the body politic, destroy public happiness, and overturn kingdoms and empires. The principal design, therefore, of civil laws, is to check the fury of exorbitant appetite, restrain the unruly passions, and keep them within the bounds which reason and common good require. How imperfectly they answer this design, and how much they need the aid of religion for this purpose, the experience of all ages is a sufficient proof. All the restraint which civil government can lay upon the passions, is by prohibiting and punishing some of their most dangerous effects: but religion, by enjoining a due government of all our appetites, teaches us to eradicate from our minds the very cause of those effects. *That* only lops off some of the most noxious branches; *this* strikes at the root: *that* only counteracts or diverts the streams; *this* dries up the fountain.

Temperance is a very comprehensive virtue; and, as enjoined by Christianity, not only requires a certain moderation in *eating* and *drinking;* but in all those affections, pursuits and enjoyments, which are liable to become faulty by excess. He who professes to govern his life by the precepts of the gospel, must be temperate in all things. His moderation must be conspicuous to all, and visible in the whole of his deportment. Thus exhorts the inspired Apostle: "Let your moderation be known to all men." But though our religion so strictly prohibits all kinds of intemperance, it allows us a free use of the gifts of Providence, and deprives us of no pleasure or enjoyment, which is not injurious to ourselves, or prejudicial to others. The Stoic Philosophers, who have said so many excellent things on temperance, and whose morality, in the opinion of Jerome, came nearest to the Christian, absurdly taught that the passions ought to be wholly eradicated. According to them, all the tender emotions of love and pity, all the sweet sensibilities, and melting affections of nature, must be extinguished, as unworthy of a philosopher. Thus, before men can become wise and virtuous, they must divest themselves of all the tender feelings of humanity, and be transformed into statues. How much more excellent and reasonable the precepts of Christianity! They require us not to eradicate, but to govern and regulate our passions, in such a manner, as is most worthy of the dignity, and most conducive to the perfection and felicity of rational creatures. They point

out the objects on which we ought to fix them, the degree in which they should be indulged, and show their due balance and subordination. Were it possible for men to bring themselves to that total insensibility, which was the pride and boast of the Stoic, it would deprive them of a great part of that happiness which they derive from a reciprocal exchange of kind affections and mutual offices of love, which constitutes one of the principal bonds, as well as chief felicities of social life. How well soever the doctrines of the Stoics in general were calculated to form the good citizen, the *dogma* we are now speaking of, not to mention other parodoxes which they held, was far from being favorable to society. Had the *retortion* of nature permitted their much desired *apathy,* they would have made very awkward members of the community. Reason is too weak to rouse men to that vigor and activity, which are necessary for the discharge of the social duties. The impulse of the passions is therefore requisite, and they are implanted in us for this purpose. The vessel which is stripped of its sails, though the rudder be ever so good, is not likely to reach the port. What sails are to a ship, passions are to the man. Let them be under the conduct of reason; give them the due tone; keep them within the bounds of moderation which Christianity prescribes, and they will invariably tend to social happiness. Thus tempered and restrained, they are a principal source of social enjoyment, give the necessary spring and energy to civil life, and impel us only to such actions and pursuits, as serve at once to promote both private and public good. Hence we see how far the morality of the gospel surpasses that of the *Porch,* the most celebrated, and indeed the most perfect, to be found among the heathen sages. It is more conformable to the constitution of our nature, better adapted to our present condition, and hath a greater tendency to promote the ends of civil government.

I suppose it will be readily acknowledged, that drunkenness, gluttony and lawless lust, not to mention many other evil consequences which flow from them, enervate the body, debase the mind, and tend to unfit us for the discharge of those duties which we owe to society. As far, therefore, as the precepts of Christianity restrain men from these vices, so far they must be useful to government. We have no laws, at least none which operate, for the punishment of drunkenness, though it is detrimental to the state, by introducing diseases, destroying the health and vigor of its inhabitants, and reducing thousands of families to want and misery. As to those against uncleanness, they are so seldom carried into execution, that we might almost as well be without them. If, therefore, men are under no restraint from religion, they are left at full liberty to abandon themselves to those vicious courses. A regard to credit and reputation, or a dread of infamy, cannot restrain men from such practices, where they are so common as not to be disgraceful; and where the number of transgressors exempts them from censure or reproach. How far this is the case in many parts of our state, I leave others to say; and only remark, that the abominable mixture of colors in our capital, as well as in some other places, and the scenes of lewdness, riot and debauchery, common in town and country, are too plain a proof of our dissolute manners, and a melancholy presage of approaching ruin. I am sensible we have no small number amongst us, and those too of high rank and considerable political influence, who make light of these crimes; but it is not the less true, that they are attended with effects highly dangerous to government, and open a wide door to a group of political evils, which menace destruction to our country. Whatever men of loose morals may think of these things, to those who consider their pernicious tendency, they are sufficiently alarming, and clearly indicate the necessity of a reformation. All that *can*, ought to be done by civil laws for this purpose; but I am persuaded that nothing but a sense of religion, and a regard to the precepts of Christianity, will prove effectual.

But, not to dwell any longer on these instances of intemperance, which are a reproach to reason, and transform men into brutes; we proceed to observe, that the moderation which Christianity enjoins in the pursuit of wealth greatly tends to the advantage of society. Avarice is insatiable, and productive of infinite

mischief in government. The most numerous and flagrant acts of injustice, and the most atrocious crimes, even murder itself, may be often traced to an immoderate desire of riches, as their source. Experience confirms the assertion of the Apostle, "The love of money is the root of all evil." As an immoderate love of wealth, therefore, is one principal source of those crimes which plainly tend to the subversion of society, it is of great moment that it should be curbed; and whatever hath a tendency to keep it in proper bounds, must be subservient to public good. Christianity gives us such a striking picture of the empty and unsatisfying, as well as dangerous, nature of riches, as cannot fail to have a mighty influence on the minds of all those who have a cordial belief of its truth. He who has a full conviction that "a man's life consisteth not in the abundance of the things which he possesseth," and pays a due regard to those divine precepts, which forbid us to set our hearts on earthly possessions, will be moderate in his pursuit of riches. Sensible of their uncertain and ensnaring nature, he will be under little temptation to use fraud or violence in order to acquire them. Contented with food and raiment, he is not anxious to amass great wealth; and if God should please to prosper his moderate care and diligence and bless him with abundance, he has a heart open to distress, and is ready to pity and relieve the miserable. Sensible that he is only a steward of the good things God hath given him, and that he must be accountable for the use he makes of his estate, he is careful not to consume it in luxury, nor make it the fuel of lust. He keeps the golden mean between the miser and the prodigal; not hoarding up uselessly, nor spending profusely, but contributing according to his ability in promoting such designs as are useful to the public; feeding the hungry, clothing the naked, or instructing the ignorant. Such is the temper of the man formed upon the precepts of the gospel: and how admirably it is adapted to promote the peace and happiness of society, is too plain to need illustration. If this Christian moderation were more prevalent among us, how many acts of extortion, oppression, fraud and rapine; how much strife and contention, envy and emulation, would it prevent? It would be a much stronger security against these and a thousand other irregularities, than the dread of human laws, though framed with the highest wisdom, and executed with the greatest punctuality.

But further; Christianity is not more favorable to government by moderating our love of riches, than by enjoining an honest care and diligence as the means of acquiring a comfortable subsistence. Idleness, sloth and negligence, in our several occupations, are as expressly condemned by our religion, as a too eager and violent pursuit of the world. Thus we are guarded against two extremes equally pernicious to society. Extreme poverty and want stimulate men to theft, robbery and many other dishonest practices, highly injurious to the community. Those who are extremely poor, and those who are extremely rich, are generally the most vicious: and though their vices may be of different kinds, they are equally opposite to public good. The *mean* in life is most desirable: and this is generally the result of that moderate care and diligence which the precepts of Christianity require. They who are placed between the extremes of want and abundance, are generally the best members of society, most happy themselves, and contribute most to the happiness of others. Over-grown estates are seldom acquired or enjoyed, in a manner wholly consistent with Christianity. They are often a curse and incumbrance to their owners, and a source of many evils in society, by introducing luxury, sensuality and effeminacy, with a long train of vices, which have always been the destruction of governments; and are peculiarly repugnant to the spirit, and hostile to the liberty and happiness of a republic. But as it is a thing possible, that men may both acquire and possess ample fortunes, consistently with the Christian character, and the happiness of the community; and as such have it in their power to be most extensively useful, both to the public and individuals, Christianity is of singular service in restraining them from the abuse, and fixing the true use of riches.

This naturally leads us to take notice of the influence which Christianity has, in moderating our pursuit of those things which are reckoned *comfortable, elegant* and *ornamental* in civil life.

It is not easy, precisely to ascertain, how far Christianity permits us to indulge to the enjoyment of those things which are not necessary to the support of nature; or to what degree we may innocently gratify an elegant taste, in magnificent buildings, sumptuous tables, splendor of dress, equipage, &c. This subject has been greatly embroiled by *monks* and *mystics,* who have cried out an *abuse,* whenever the gifts of Providence were used further than is necessary for the bare sustenance of life. It is needless to show the absurdity of this notion, and how little ground Christianity affords for such a supposition. The *bare necessary* is reckoned sufficiently beggarly among us: and we have much more reason to guard against excess and intemperance, than a rigid austerity and superstitious abstinence. Though our bountiful Creator "hath given us richly all things to enjoy," and Christianity permits us to use the comforts, conveniencies, and even the elegancies of life, it requires a certain temperance and moderation in the enjoyment of these things. To suppose otherwise would be unreasonable, and contrary to the spirit and general strain of its precepts. To use the gifts of Providence to our own injury, in person or fortune, or to the injury of others to whom we stand related, or are obliged to assist, is prohibited by Christianity. This, as I take it, is a pretty accurate definition of *luxury,* which is undoubtedly vicious, and as contrary to the precepts of our religion, as it is pernicious to civil society. When a man indulges himself in sumptuous fare, so as to enervate his body and debauch his mind; when he gratifies his taste for elegance, grandeur and magnificence, in building, furniture, dress, equipage, &c. to such a degree, as to embarrass his estate, plunge himself in debt, and bring his family to beggary, he certainly passes the bounds of moderation. Imprudence is too soft a name for such a conduct. It is highly criminal. For by acting in this manner, he not only injures himself; but is chargeable with great injustice to others. Had he kept within the bounds which religion, and even reason, prescribes, he might have lived comfortably, though perhaps not splendidly, and bestowed liberally to those, who reduced by unavoidable misfortunes, had a right to share in his bounty. The man who regulates his mode of living by a strict and conscientious regard to the precepts of the gospel, will always endeavor to manage his affairs with such economy, that his expences may not exceed his income. Though he may have a taste for the *grand* and *elegant* in life, he will not always gratify it, even when in his power; but often sacrifice the *pleasures of imagination* to the more sublime and God-like pleasure of relieving the real wants of the poor and needy. Although his estate may permit, and rank require him, to live in a magnificent and splendid manner, he will study moderation and simplicity, as far as possible without incurring the imputation of meanness. A regard to religion, the love of his country, and a desire to promote public good, will lead him to this; lest by the influence of his example, luxury should be encouraged, and others carried into a train of expences which they cannot honestly support. In a word, the real Christian, though he may possess an affluent fortune, to which you may add, if you please, a noble and refined taste, is careful to keep both in due subordination to the honor of God and the good of men; and neither uses the one, nor indulges the other, to the detriment of civil society. All who consider the fatal effects and dangerous tendency of luxury, will acknowledge, that Christianity in this view is of great importance to the state. In all rich and flourishing republics, *sumptuary laws* have been generally thought necessary; but they seldom fully answer the end designed by them. A strict regard to that moderation which Christianity requires, would have much greater influence, and lay a more effectual curb on luxury, than the most rigorous sumptuary laws. How much we need the influence of religion in this particular, is too plain to admit of a doubt. If luxury be an "abuse of the gifts of Providence," there is certainly a great deal of it among us. Our progress in this vice since the close of the war, has been so amazingly rapid, that I could not believe it, were I not convinced by my own senses. The nature of our government, the losses we have sustained, and

the debts we have contracted, in the course of a bloody and desolating war, call for the severest oeconomy and the most exact frugality; and yet such is the profusion, prodigality and extravagance, which generally prevail among our citizens, that a sagacious politician would be almost tempted to pronounce us in the last stage of political corruption. As a free and independent state, we are but in infancy; and yet we have many flagrant marks of a republic in rapid decline. "We have luxury and avarice," no uncommon conjunction; "public poverty, and private opulence."* Profaneness, riot, dissipation and debauchery have, in many places, arrived to a height which is really astonishing. If, in the course of a few years, we are so far gone in these vices, who can look forward, only one century, without trembling for posterity? The unsettled condition of our government, and the warm political contentions which take place amongst us, are the natural consequence of our present situation; and neither very surprising, nor much to be dreaded; but our rapid progress in luxury, which will naturally increase with our wealth and commerce, is an alarming circumstance, and a sure harbinger of impending ruin. We already begin to feel the fatal effects of our prodigality and extravagance. It is known to all, what great numbers of our citizens are involved in debt. Not a few of them are so irrecoverably sunk, that they have relinquished all hopes of payment. This is generally reckoned no small evil; and is, at this moment, the source of infinite discontent and uneasiness in the state. Whence arises this evil so much complained of? We may, I think, pronounce without hesitation, that *an immoderate desire of high and expensive living* is the principal and most general cause. Our citizens seem to be seized with a general emulation to surpass each other in every article of expence. Those who possess

---

* "Nos habemus luxuriam atque avaritiam; publice egestatem, privatim opulentiam." Rome had existed 600 years before the patriot could say this: In the early ages of the commonwealth, it was quite otherwise: "Patriae enim rem unusquisque, non suam augere properebat; pauperque in divite, quam dives in paupere imperio, versari malebat." Valerius Max. Such is the disposition which ought to prevail among *us* in this early stage of our republic: but how far it is otherwise, no one can be ignorant, who is capable of the smallest observation.

affluent fortunes lead the way, and set the example. Others, whose estates are not sufficient to bear them out, madly adopt the same expensive system, and in order to support it, contract debts which they have no rational prospect of discharging. All they seem to wish, is to obtain credit, to figure away, and make a brilliant appearance at the expence of others. It is too plain, many of them enter into engagements without the most distant prospect of complying with them. They make no efforts for this purpose; but plunge deeper and deeper into the vortex of extravagance. If they can only indulge their fondness for pleasure, show and vanity, and shine upon the property of the honest and industrious, they care not what becomes either of their creditors or their country. Rich and sumptuous fare, expensive diversions, costly entertainments, the pomp, parade and splendor of dress and equipage: these are the things which have involved thousands; and among other mischiefs, have obliged our legislature to stop the course of justice; or, at least, to clog it in such a manner, that an honest creditor may starve, before he can recover his just due. Indeed there are a number of these desperate debtors, who seem determined to hazard every extreme rather than discharge their just debts: for they are sensible, if they do this, they must retrench from their luxury, and many of them be reduced to beggary. At a certain period of the Roman republic, it was common for a bold tribune, who aimed at popularity, to propose a total abolition of all debts: and if the ruinous scheme of credit be continued as in times past, I shall not be at all surprized, if such a motion should be made in our assembly. Something which appears to me nearly tantamount, hath already been done.—A *paper currency*, on the footing some plead for, would produce nearly the same effect.

The weight of our taxes is also a matter of great complaint; and none complain more heavily, than those who live most prodigally. You may hear a man *cursing* our assembly, and exclaiming against the tax, when the very *silver* on the *trappings of his horse* would pay his proportion of it. He can find money to eat and drink, and dress like a gentleman; he has guineas upon guineas to stake at a horse race or a gaming table: but not a farthing to pay his tax. Is it at all strange, that men of this cast cannot pay their public or private debts? If they would only retrench from their superfluities, and be frugal and industrious; if they would live within the limits of their income, and observe those bounds of moderation which common prudence, reason and religion require, most of them would find little difficulty in paying their taxes. Their extravagant taste for high and expensive living, is the principal reason, why they *cannot*, or rather *will not*, discharge their public dues. Every one who considers the heavy debts we have incurred by the war, must be sensible that a weighty tax is necessary.* Honor, justice and our own real interest equally require, that this debt should be discharged: and he who refuses to sacrifice a few of the luxuries, or elegancies of life, for this purpose, in my judgment, discovers very little of a republican spirit, as well as very little regard to honor and justice. A few years of oeconomy, industry and frugality, would extricate us from all the difficulties which arise from our debts, and make our public faith as respectable as it is now contemptible. But is not my design to insist on all the evils which our extravagance hath already brought upon us. Every one who will only reason a little on the subject, and trace effects to their causes, must be convinced, they are numerous. The destructive tendency of luxury is a beaten topic: we shall not therefore repeat what hath been said by many excellent writers on this subject. The history of the world points to this, as the rock on which the state-vessel hath most commonly split. It

---

* Those who complain of the weight of our taxes, readily acknowledge the justice of discharging the debts contracted by the war; but at the same time alledge, that very little of our money is applied this way—that our civil list, which, say they, is enormous, swallows up the greater part; and, in general, that those who have the management of our finances, lavish out the public money without any regard to that severe oeconomy which our present situation requires. I do not take upon me to say, this is the case; but if it be, it is a still further proof, that the political grievances we labor under, are the consequence of extravagance, prodigality and luxury. If the salaries of our civil officers be too high, the evil may be easily traced to luxury as the original cause. If our assembly deal out the public money unnecessarily, and in such a manner as proves detrimental to the state, what is this but public profusion and extravagance?

stands conspicuous; and if we run upon it with our eyes open, we deserve to perish. The majestic ruins of mighty kingdoms and empires present themselves to our view, as an awful, but friendly warning of our danger from this quarter. Rome, once so famous for her contempt of wealth, her virtue and her valour; Rome, so renowned for the excellence of her civil institutions, and the wisdom of her policy, at last fell a sacrifice to luxury. The spoils of Greece and the riches of the East, proved her ruin, and overturned that mighty fabric which it had been the work of ages to rear. A general dissolution of manners took place—virtue fled—vice broke in like an irresistible torrent;

—— *Saevior armis*
Luxuria incubuit victumque ulciscitur orbem.*   J U V.

The judicious reader must be sensible, how easy it would be to enlarge here, by selecting many other precepts besides those already treated, and showing their influence on civil society.

That strict regard to chastity and conjugal fidelity which Christianity enjoins—the prohibition of Poligamy, which is allowed by other religions, and which is as contrary to the intention of nature, as it is unfavorable to public happiness—all those precepts which point out and enforce the several duties required of us in the different stations and relations of civil and domestic life, particularly as *magistrates* and *subjects, rulers* and *ruled:* All these so evidently tend to promote our happiness in the social state, that it may be thought tedious and unnecessary to insist upon them.

Upon the whole, what hath been said is, we trust, sufficient to demonstrate how admirably the Christian religion is adapted to co-operate with good and wholesome civil laws, and how much it tends to promote the peace and happiness of men in a state of society. Let us, for a moment, admit the supposition, that the doctrines of Christianity were firmly be-

lieved, cordially embraced, and its precepts diligently practised, by all our citizens; and it may easily be conceived what a happy effect it would have. What love, what peace and harmony, what firm union, perfect order and ready obedience to every wholesome institution and wise regulation, would then take place amongst us! To what an exalted pitch of true greatness, glory, grandeur and felicity might we arrive! The bare thought is sufficient to transport every lover of his country. It is not indeed to be expected, that such a sacred regard to religion should ever become universal among any people; but from the effect which would follow on this supposition, we may see, that it must ever be productive of good to society, as far as it prevails. The more strongly men are influenced by its motives, and the more perfactly they are conformed to its precepts, the better members of civil society they will be: and the greater the number of such in any state, other things being equal, the higher it will rise in the scale of political glory and happiness. "Righteousness exalteth a nation, but sin is a reproach to any people." As vice degrades a nation, renders them contemptible, and at last terminates in public misery and ruin: so virtue, which is the necessary result of piety, exalts, ennobles, and leads them to true substantial glory and felicity.

'Tis fix'd! by Fate irrevocably fix'd!
Virtue and *vice* are empire's *life* and *death.*
                                        Y O U N G.

Conclusion

If religion be of that importance to the state which we have been endeavoring to prove, it certainly merits the public attention; and those who are engaged in the arduous and important task of government, ought to avail themselves of its force, to give vigour to the operation, and facilitate the execution of wise and wholesome laws. The most intelligent of my readers will perhaps blame me for taking so much pains to

---

* "Luxury, more cruel than arms, lies upon [Rome] and avenges a conquered world." From Juvenal, *Sixth Satire*, line 293.—Trans.

prove what very few either doubt or deny. To this I can only say, that how well soever the truths insisted upon are known and believed, it is clear they have been too much over-looked: and if what hath been offered may serve, in any measure, to draw the public attention to this important object, I shall not regret the labor I have bestowed. All our politicians will readily grant, that the morality of the people is a matter of no small moment, especially in republics; but many of them seem to forget the inseparable connection between religion and morality. They appear not sufficiently sensible, how impossible it is to preserve purity of morals among the people at large, even in the lax political sense of that expression, without a sense of religion. A complete morality, independent of all religion, is merely visionary, and never, in fact existed. It is the dream of theory spinners, and the unmeaning language of pidling profligate politicians. The necessity of morality to the commonwealth being once granted, the necessity of religion will unavoidably follow; and certainly that which is necessary, not only to the *well-being*, but to the very *existence* of civil society, must be worthy the attention of civil rulers. Without entering into any dispute concerning the power of civil magistrates *circa sacra* [concerning sacred things], we lay it down as certain, that they may do much for the support and encouragement of religion, without the least encroachment on the prerogative of him who is the supreme head of the church. They may, and ought to do much, by their pious example, which in persons of high rank and authority has an amazing weight and influence. They may without any invasion of the rights of conscience, take measures for the instruction of subjects in the important doctrines and precepts of Christianity, which so evidently tend to the safety of the body politic. If measures of this nature were ever necessary in any government, they are so in South-Carolina. The greater part of our citizens are ignorant of religion to a degree which is equally astonishing and deplorable. Whole settlements may be found, where but very few can so much as read the scriptures. There are some hundreds, one might venture to say, some thousands of young persons growing up among us, almost as ignorant of the God who made them, as the Hottentots of Africa. Instructed in no one duty which they owe, either to God or man, is it reasonable to suppose, they will ever make good citizens or useful members of the community? Brought up, as many of them are, in the most abject poverty and the most criminal idleness, and taught no kind of employment by which they can procure an honest subsistence, must we not expect they will prove pests of society? Restrained by no obligations of virtue or religion, stimulated by want, and sharpened by keen necessity, they are expert only in stealing; and in time, will, no doubt, make dextrous horse-thieves. Do we not find in fact, that those settlements, where idleness, ignorance and irreligion most prevail, are at once the seminaries and asylums of public offenders? Here the laws are not executed at all, or with the greatest difficulty; and in some of them the people are scarcely one degree above downright barbarism. Is there any other method to bring them out of this state, and make them honest and worthy citizens, but by diffusing knowledge among them, and instructing their children in the principles of religion and morality? And is not this an object worthy of the public attention? Aside compassion to the souls of men, which should strongly operate with those who profess themselves Christians, our own peace and happiness, as a political body, evidently require it. If parents either cannot, or will not provide for, and educate their children, in a proper manner, it would certainly be just and expedient, to take them out of their hands, and have them brought up in such a way, as might afford some rational prospect of their being useful to society. This would be, at once, an act of charity and compassion to the children, and highly beneficial to the state.

One principal reason why ignorance is so prevalent among our citizens, is the want of public teachers, properly qualified to instruct them in the doctrines and precepts of Christianity. If our country were properly supplied with able, pious and faithful ministers, it would doubtless be one of the most promising means to diffuse religious knowledge, stem the torrent of vice, and promote the practice of piety and virtue. Without attempting to prove, I make no scruple boldly to affirm, that the preaching of the gospel in its genuine purity and simplicity, is the most powerful mean to reform the manners of men. If so, is it reasonable to expect, that a reformation will take place, while this mean is neglected? Can we rationally hope, that a sense of religion will be kept alive in the hearts of men, when there are none amongst them, whose stated business it is to explain its doctrines and inculcate its precepts? It is the appointment of the great Author of our religion, that there should be such an order of men. And when they conduct themselves with that gravity and dignity which become their office; when they are zealous, active and diligent in preaching, instructing, reproving, and, by their holy and exemplary lives, give weight and influence to their doctrines, we are authorized to expect the most salutary effects from their ministrations. Had we a sufficient number of such clergymen fixed in the different parts of our state, it would be a singular blessing, and greatly facilitate the execution of our laws. Were this the case, we might expect, that our citizens would be more generally enlightened in the nature and end of government, and the several duties they owe to society, more sensible of the necessity of order in the body politic, and of submission to all these civil ordinances which are subservient to the common good. Virtue would be more countenanced and promoted, vice more discouraged, and a stronger curb laid on the licentious and profane.

But how are such clergymen to be obtained? how supported? "Hoc opus, hic labor." We do not take upon us to dictate. We point out the influence of religion on civil society, the need we have of that influence, and give one reason why we are so deficient in the knowledge and practice of Christianity.

It may, however, be observed, that the most probable means of furnishing our country with useful pastors, is to promote learning, and educate pious and promising youth among ourselves. The encouragement of literature on this, and many other accounts,

should be considered as a very capital object of public attention in South Carolina. It is neither for our honor, nor our interest, to have our learned departments filled up with foreigners. How far this is the case, none can be ignorant. To say nothing of the inundation of Physicians from Great-Britain, Ireland and the northern states, we have not so much as one learned clergyman amongst us, who is a native of South Carolina. Of the few ministers who are settled in our state, the greater number are illiterate. Some of these are no doubt useful: but if their learning equalled their piety and zeal, they would certainly be much more so; and religion would be more solid and rational, than it is at present in many places. The most able and judicious of these illiterate preachers, are sensible of the disadvantages they labour under, and lament their want of a liberal education; but at the same time, urge the difficulty of obtaining it, and the deplorable ignorance which prevails, as their excuse for assuming the character of public instructors. And in truth, considering the state of learning among us, and the scarcity of religious teachers, this argument appears to me to have no small weight. If such preachers were capable of nothing further than to inculcate the doctrine of a future state, and press upon men the necessity of moral and social duties, even this would be of no small utility to the state. It requires but little knowledge to instruct many of our citizens, and they who can only read the scriptures in their own language, may do much good in many parts of our country, by teaching the grossly ignorant, and reforming the notoriously vicious. After all, it must be confessed, that they would be much more useful, were their knowledge more enlarged, and their education more liberal: and if a method could be fallen upon to make learning cheap and convenient, this would be more generally the case. This is the point at which we ought to aim, and the most spirited efforts should be made for this purpose. While learning continues so expensive, as it is at present amongst us, we cannot expect it to become general. The more opulent only will be able to give their sons a liberal education; and there is little probability, that any considerable number of these will devote themselves to the service of the church.*

It is the opinion of many, that the best way to supply ourselves with clergymen, is to encourage their emigration from Great-Britain and Ireland. In our provincial state this plan was not altogether ineligible; but, in our present circumstances, I think there are strong political objections against it. An important revolution hath taken place. We are now an independent people, and have rejected the government of Great-Britain, as equally odious and intolerable. Those men, whom it is proposed to bring in amongst us, are the subjects of king George III; and in justice to them, it is to be supposed, loyal subjects. Their education has a deep tincture of the government under which they have lived. They have been brought up with that predilection for monarchy, and that superstitious reverence for royalty, and the high-sounding title of *king,* which is usual in regal governments. Can we reasonably expect that men of this description will generally have the same strong attachment to our country, the same high respect to our republican forms of government, as those who are educated among us, and imbibe the principles and spirit of freedom and independence with the milk of their mothers? Have we any ground to hope, that they will show the same zeal for the support and prosperity of our free constitutions, as the natives of America, whose fathers have suffered so much for their establishment?

Some of these gentlemen, who have ventured to cross the water since the establishment of peace, and are now in quest of settlements amongst us, make no scruple to declare their hatred and contempt of our

government; and express their great regret that the revolution ever took place. "Better," say they, "we had still continued our connection with England; we would have now been a much more happy people." That they should hold such language, is not all surprising. It is the natural result of their education, and the prejudices which hang about them in favor of a kingly government: and how plainly it tends to embroil our government, and facilitate our return to a servile dependence on Great-Britain, is sufficiently obvious. Others, who have more prudence, and better know how to accommodate themselves to their interest, are silent on the matter. Few, if any of them, discover that cordial approbation of our government, or interest themselves in our welfare with that ardor which we find in true republicans. Indeed, it would be unseasonable to expect it. Suppose 40 or 50 of these foreign clergymen settled in different parts of our state; suppose them to be as respectable as men of their function ought to be, and to have that influence on the minds of their people, which is necessary to render them useful, it is easy, I think, to see what might be the consequence to the state. How weak soever this objection may appear to some, it shows at least, that in a political view, it is most eligible to have a clergy well affected to our government: and the most probable method of obtaining such, is to promote learning in our own country.

As to the method of supporting our clergy, it seems to be the most general opinion, especially among those formerly called Dissenters, that it should be by the free contributions of the people. And indeed no other mode appears more eligible, where people are generally sensible of the utility of religion, and disposed to contribute according to their abilities for its support. It ought however to be considered, that in many parts of our state, the people are so totally sunk in vice and ignorance, that they have scarcely any idea of the necessity and importance of religion; and consequently will not exert themselves, either to obtain or support public teachers. And yet, these are the people who most need instruction. What is to be done in this case? Can nothing, consistent with justice and

---

* As our form of government tends to an aristocracy, if learning were properly diffused, it might, I think, serve to counteract this tendency in some measure. In a republic, offices of high trust and preferment ought to be rotatory, and diffused as much as possible. If learning be confined to a few of the most wealthy, it will naturally tend to keep these offices in a few hands; the consequence of which will be, that the rich and learned *few* will rule and oppress the poor and ignorant *many.* Every proud politic *aristocrat* knows, that if he can keep a people in poverty and ignorance; he can *ride* them at pleasure, and will therefore strenuously oppose every attempt of the legislature to put learning upon such a footing, that it may be acquired by those of lower rank.

the rights of conscience, be attempted by civil authority to oblige persons of this description to contribute to the support of religion? If religion be of that utility to government, which we have been endeavoring to show, it will certainly follow, that every citizen reaps advantage from it in a political view; and therefore ought to contribute for its support. Nor is there any more injustice in obliging him to this by law, than in obliging him to pay a public tax for the support of government: because religion is absolutely necessary to government; and were it not for this, he would be deprived of those benefits which he enjoys from the social union. We may therefore venture to affirm, that every member of civil society ought, and may be justly obliged by law, to pay something for the support of religion. Nor will there be any just cause of complaint on the score of conscience, provided every one be left at liberty to pay to whatever denomination of the clergy he pleases. We do not take upon us to affirm that such a law ought to be made: some difficulties would probably arise in the execution of it. We only show, that such a law would have nothing in it unjust, were it thought expedient. If properly executed, it would, I think, have at least one good effect; it would excite people to make some efforts to obtain fixed clergymen among themselves. It is easy to foresee, that avarice on the one hand, and contempt of religion on the other, will rake up many objections against this plan: but as we only just throw out the hint, and are far from being sanguine on the matter, we shall not, at present, take any notice of these. There is, however, one objection which, with me, has no small weight, and which, no doubt, will operate strongly with all those who wish well to religion. If the law proposed could be so framed and executed, as to afford support and encouragement only to the pious, sober and diligent of all denominations, it would certainly be of singular service to the state; but the great danger is, that those of the opposite character would probably be supported and encouraged. Could matters be so managed, as to guard against this, I should not hesitate a moment to pronounce such a law highly expedient and salutary. This

may perhaps be difficult, and could I think it absolutely impracticable, I would be one of the last men in South-Carolina to propose, or consent to, a law of this nature. It would be an intolerable hardship indeed, to be obliged to give our money for the maintenance of idle, ignorant or vicious ecclesiastics. But however true this may be, if those who so violently oppose every other mode of supporting religion but by voluntary contribution, would properly consider the situation of our country, and what vast numbers there are amongst us, who neither do nor will assist in maintaining the teachers of religion, unless they be compelled by law; if, I say, they would consider these, and many other things, which might be urged, they would not wholly reprobate every attempt to encourage religion at the public expence. We have the best religion in the world. There is no other so well adapted to the genius of a free and independent people, so favorable to liberty and the natural rights of men: nor is there any other which so commodiously falls in with that form of government which we have pitched upon, the supreme end and sole object of which is the common good.* Tyranny and oppression of every kind are condemned by the precepts, and utterly repugnant to the spirit of Christianity. It must be corrupted, abused and perverted, before it can be brought to speak the language of despotism, and give countenance to arbitrary power. There is not a despotic government on the face of the earth, where it prevails in any considerable degree of purity. We ought not, therefore, to spare a little cost and pains to support and encourage a religion so friendly to equal government and laws; and which so directly tends to promote the great designs of the American revolution. A sufficient number of useful pastors might be supported with but very little expence to the

---

* Montesquieu, with his usual penetration, has observed, that the Catholic religion is most agreeable to monarchy, and the protestant to a republic. Indeed the Popish system contains many things which must be unfavorable to any form of civil government whatever. Such are indulgencies, bodily penance, dispensing with oaths, celibacy of the clergy, monastic institutions; to say nothing of the enormous power claimed by the Pope in things meerly civil, and the superiority which he arrogates over all Christian rulers.

public. I am none of those who wish to heap wealth upon ecclesiastics, and make them wholly independent of the people. This would be highly impolitic, and the ready way to destroy their usefulness, by making them proud, luxurious, indolent and negligent of their duty. But they certainly ought to have what is sufficient to keep them above that contempt, which, unhappily among us, is too often connected with a certain degree of honest poverty. It requires little less than the resolution of a martyr to undertake the sacred employment, where a man has no reasonable prospect of a maintenance for himself and his family. When the road to wealth and honor lies open to gentlemen of a liberal education, in so many other ways, we cannot reasonably expect, that many of them will prefer an employment, from which they can look for little else in this world, but poverty and contempt. This is very much the case at present, especially amongst those formerly called Dissenters, many of whom seem to expect, that men will sacrifice every earthly consideration to the desire of saving souls. It would be well, if they could find a sufficient number of this temper; but as Christianity requires no such sacrifice, and gives those who preach the gospel a right to live by the gospel, few, I believe, will think it their duty to relinquish this right, and engage in a work at once so arduous and painful, without some hope of a comfortable subsistence. If, therefore, we would enjoy those advantages which flow from religion, we must give proper encouragement to its ministers; and support them in such a manner, that the prospect of extreme indigence, may not deter them from entering into the sacred office. And if our citizens had a proper sense of the importance of religion, even in a political view, they would think it no great hardship to contribute their part for this purpose.

What others think of it, I know not; but to me it appears clearer than the sun, that we never can be a great, happy or respectable people, while religion is generally despised and neglected among us. A general corruption of morals, will always be the consequence of a general contempt of religion. The more irreligious a people are, the more vicious; and the more vicious, generally speaking, the more miserable. However slowly vice may operate, in the end it brings sure and inevitable perdition on the body politic. I hear some of my countrymen bewailing our political factions and civil dissensions; others lamenting the precarious state of our trade, the scarcity of money and the weight of our taxes; but, I confess, none of all these appears to me half so alarming as our rapid progress in vice. Faction, tumult and intestine commotions, may be compared to certain acute and violent diseases, which, though for a short time, they cruelly ravage the human frame; yet, where the constitution is good, a crisis is frequently made, the disorder thrown off, and the body restored to its pristine health and vigor: but vice, like a deadly poison, sometimes slow, but always sure in its operation, infects every member of the political body, corrupts the whole mass, and issues in certain destruction. Many, who wish well to their country, are greatly alarmed with the dread of an aristocracy, and seem to think, that nothing is so much to be feared, as the undue influence of a few wealthy and aspiring gentlemen in the lower parts of our state, who, they imagine, are combining to seize our liberties, and engross all the power into their own hands. I will not affirm that we are in no danger from this quarter. Our government naturally tends to an aristocracy; and we cannot be too careful to guard against the encroachments of power, and watch over those privileges which we have so dearly purchased. But trust me, my dear countrymen, it is not a matter of much moment to a people sunk in vice, what their form of government is. None can make them happy. There is a certain point of moral corruption, to which if we once arrive, we can no longer exist as a republic. A revolution must then of consequence take place, and some other kind of government better suited to our circumstances, and the spirit of the people, be adopted. There is a degree of vice which utterly debases human nature, and renders men incapable either to think, or judge, or act for themselves. When they come to this, they are prepared for slavery, and it is necessary, perhaps best for them, to have a master. The history of the most noted republics shows how vain must be all the efforts of a few virtuous men, to support our constitution and preserve our liberty, when once that virtue, which is the basis of freedom, and the very soul of a democracy, is no more. When Caesar passed the Rubicon, he saw that Rome must have a master; and why not Caesar as well as another? The virtuous and gallant spirit of Brutus could not brook this master. He thought that by sacrificing the tyrant, he could abolish the tyranny, and restore the republic; but he found himself mistaken. The sacrifice was not acceptable to the people. The Roman spirit was departed; and instead of resuming their liberty, they ungratefully rose up against their deliverers. A second triumvirate was formed, worse than the first; and the lords of the world servilely surrendered their liberties into the hands of a boy. We are surprized at this; but it was perhaps the best thing they could do, as circumstances then stood.

There is, therefore, no other way to preserve our liberty, but by preserving our virtue.

> Whatever secondary props may rise
> From POLITICS, to build the public peace,
> The basis is the MANNERS of the LAND.
> When rotten these, the politicians wiles
> But struggle with destruction; as a child
> With giants huge; or giants with a Jove,
>
> YOUNG

Suffer me then, my dear countrymen, to address you with all seriousness on this subject. After having displayed so much virtue and valor, in the course of a most arduous and trying struggle; and at last, through the signal interposition of Heaven, brought our affairs to such a happy issue, what a reproach will it be to us, if by suffering ourselves to be effeminated with luxury, and plunged in vice, we tarnish all that glory which we have acquired, and lose the fruits of so much blood and treasure! Would you preserve those liberties, which have been bought with the blood of thousands of your brave countrymen? Be virtuous. Would you rise to that summit of glory and felicity which was the end of your separation from Great-Britain? Promote religion; and endeavor to stem that torrent of vice which threatens to break in upon us, and blast all those sanguine hopes, which animated us to do and suffer so much in the cause of freedom. Let the rich and the great use their influence to encourage purity of morals, and inspire their fellow-citizens with those sentiments of religion and virtue, which are so absolutely necessary to our political welfare. How happy would it be for us, if such would consider how much it is in their power, to suppress vice, and promote the cause of virtue! Were I permitted to address them with freedom, it would be in the following strain.

GENTLEMEN,

You owe an immense debt to your country. Providence hath placed you in an exalted station. Your wealth and rank make you respectable; your gentle and commanding manners, give an irresistible force and charm to your example. In *you*, virtue and religion appear in their most lovely and alluring forms. As you, of all men, have it most in your power to spread the infection of vice, and corrupt the manners of the multitude: so none can more effectually recommend piety and virtue, or more successfully restrain the licentious and the profligate. Only set the example—we are ready to follow you. You are no strangers to the influence of a court on the morals of a kingdom. What courts are in monarchies, you are in a republic: you give the tone and tincture to our manners; and if you be dissolute in your morals and profligate in your lives, the infection will in time spread through all inferior ranks, and corrupt the whole mass of the people.

Do you profess yourselves lovers of your country? Do you desire its prosperity? Do you wish to see the laws respected and good order preserved? And are you convinced that purity of morals, and consequently religion, is necessary for this purpose? Lead the way then; show us a pattern we may dare to imitate; and use that influence and authority which Heaven has put into your hands, so that you may be a "Terror to evil-doers, and a praise to those that do well." This is the only road to true honor and renown; this is the most effectual way to advance the glory of your country, to make your names respectable while you live, and your memory dear to posterity.

But I wish not to confine this address to those only of high rank and figure: permit me therefore, my dear countrymen, to call upon you all, of whatever rank, character, or station, to lend your aid; and by your example and influence do your utmost, for the suppression of vice and the encouragement of virtue. There is none of you in a station so low, or circumstances so obscure, as to put it wholly out of your power to contribute, in some degree, for this purpose. The longer I consider the subject, the more fully I am convinced of the fatal effects of vice, and the absolute necessity of piety and purity of morals, in order to make us a great and a happy people: and there is no other way in which you can more effectually promote the prosperity of your country, than by the practice of these. Do you love your country? Do you wish to discharge the debt you owe to society? Do you desire to be happy here, and enjoy eternal felicity hereafter? Show your respect for that religion you profess; and endeavor to conform your lives to the precepts of Christianity. "True religion always enlarges the heart, and strengthens the social tie." If you be good Christians, you can never fail of being good citizens.

The God of Heaven hath favored us, in common with the other States of America, with many singular blessings. He has given us many advantages which no other people on the face of the earth have ever enjoyed; and if we improve these advantages in a proper manner, we may soon be the wonder and envy of the world. But if we forget the kind hand which covered us in the hour of danger, and conducted us through a sea of troubles to the calm haven of peace and security; if we abuse the gifts of Providence, turn our liberty to licentiousness, and provoke the vengeance of Heaven by our daring impiety, and shocking immoralities; what can we expect, but that a righteous God will give us up to the fatal consequences of our own vices, and inflict upon us that punishment which we justly deserve? Hath he so visibly and remarkably interposed in our behalf; wrought so many signal deliverances for us, and poured out so many blessings upon us; and shall we, by our ingratitude and abuse of his distinguishing mercies, provoke him to withdraw them from us, and hold us up to the world as a monument of what an impious and ungrateful people may expect from his hand? Forbid it my countrymen! Forbid it gratitude!—Forbid it Heaven!

The Rights of Conscience Inalienable (1791)

JOHN LELAND (1754–1841)

John Leland was a Baptist minister and an active opponent of state establishments in Virginia, Massachusetts, and Connecticut. A native New Englander, Leland spent nearly fifteen years as an itinerant preacher in central Virginia where he was instrumental in allying evangelical dissenters with Jefferson and Madison in the struggle for religious liberty. He wrote the following pamphlet in 1791.

There are four principles contended for, as the foundation of civil government, viz., birth, property, grace, and compact. The first of these is practised upon in all hereditary monarchies, where it is believed that the son of a monarch is entitled to dominion upon the decease of his father, whether he be a wise man or a fool. The second principle is built upon in all aristocratical governments, where the rich landholders have the sole rule of all their tenants, and make laws at pleasure which are binding upon all. The third principle is adopted by those kingdoms and states that require a religious test to qualify an officer of state, proscribing all non-conformists from civil

Reprinted from *The Writings of John Leland*, ed. L. F. Greene (New York: Arno Press, 1969), 179–92.

and religious liberty. This was the error of Constantine's government, who first established the Christian religion by law, and then proscribed the Pagans, and banished the Arian heretics. This error also filled the heads of the Anabaptists, in Germany, who were re-sprinklers. They supposed that none had a right to rule but gracious men. The same error prevails in the See of Rome, where his holiness exalts himself above all who are called gods, (i.e., kings and rulers,) and where no Protestant heretic is allowed the liberty of a citizen. This principle is also pleaded for in the Ottoman empire, where it is death to call in question the divinity of Mahomet, or the authenticity of the Alcoran.

The same evil has entwined itself into the British form of government, where, in the state establishment of the church of England, no man is eligible to any office, civil or military, without he subscribes to the thirty-nine articles and book of common prayer; and even then, upon receiving a commission for the army, the law obliges him to receive the sacrament of the Lord's supper, and no non-conformist is allowed the liberty of his conscience without he subscribes to all the thirty-nine articles but about four. And when that is done, his purse-strings are drawn by others to pay preachers in whom he puts no confidence, and whom he never hears.

This was the case in several of the southern states, until the revolution, in which the church of England was established.

The fourth principle, (compact,) is adopted in the American states, as the basis of civil government. This foundation appears to be a just one, by the following investigation.

Suppose a man to remove to a desolate island, and take a peaceable possession of it, without injuring any, so that he should be the honest inheritor of the isle. So long as he is alone, he is the absolute monarch of the place, and his own will is his law, which law is as often altered or repealed as his will changes. In process of time, from this man's loins ten sons are grown to manhood, and possess property. So long as they are all good men, each one can be as absolute, free, and

sovereign as his father: but one of the ten turns vagrant, by robbing the rest. This villain is equal to, if not an over-match for any one of the nine: not one of them durst engage him in single combat. Reason and safety both dictate to the nine the necessity of a confederation, to unite their strength together to repel or destroy the plundering knave. Upon entering into confederation, some compact or agreement would be stipulated by which each would be bound to do his equal part in fatigue and expense. It would be necessary for these nine to meet at stated times to consult means of safety and happiness. A shady tree, or small cabin, would answer their purpose, and, in case of disagreement, four must give up to five.

In this state of things, their government would be perfectly democratic, every citizen being a legislator.

In a course of years, from these nine there arises nine thousand: their government can be no longer democratic—prudence would forbid it. Each tribe, or district, must then choose their representative, who, for the term that he is chosen, has the whole political power of his constituents. These representatives, meeting in assembly, would have power to make laws binding on their constituents, and while their time was spent in making laws for the community, each one of the community must advance a little of his money as a compensation therefor. Should these representatives differ in judgment, the minor must be subject to the major, as in the case above.

From this simple parable, the following things are demonstrated: First, that the law was not made for a righteous man, but for the disobedient. Second, that righteous men have to part with a little of their liberty and property to preserve the rest. Third, that all power is vested in, and consequently derived from the people. Fourth, that the law should rule over rulers, and not rulers over the law. Fifth, that government is founded on compact. Sixth, that every law made by legislators, inconsistent with the compact, modernly called a constitution, is usurping in the legislators, and not binding on the people. Seventh, that whenever government is found inadequate to preserve the liberty and property of the people, they have an indubitable right to alter it so as to answer those purposes. Eighth, that legislators, in their legislative capacity, cannot alter the constitution, for they are hired servants of the people to act within the limits of the constitution.

From these general observations, I shall pass on to examine a question which has been the strife and contention of ages. The question is, *"Are the rights of conscience alienable, or inalienable?"*

The word *conscience,* signifies *common science,* a court of judicature which the Almighty has erected in every human breast: a *censor morum* [judge of conduct] over all his conduct. Conscience will ever judge right, when it is rightly informed, and speak the truth when it understands it. But to advert to the question, "Does a man, upon entering into social compact, surrender his conscience to that society, to be controlled by the laws thereof; or can he, in justice, assist in making laws to bind his children's consciences before they are born?" I judge not, for the following reasons:

First. Every man must give an account of himself to God, and therefore every man ought to be at liberty to serve God in a way that he can best reconcile to his conscience. If government can answer for individuals at the day of judgment, let men be controlled by it in religious matters; otherwise, let men be free.

Second. It would be sinful for a man to surrender that to man, which is to be kept sacred for God. A man's mind should be always open to conviction, and an honest man will receive that doctrine which appears the best demonstrated: and what is more common than for the best of men to change their minds? Such are the prejudices of the mind, and such the force of tradition, that a man who never alters his mind, is either very weak or very stubborn. How painful then must it be to an honest heart, to be bound to observe the principles of his former belief, after he is convinced of their imbecility? And this ever has, and ever will be the case, while the rights of conscience are considered alienable.

Third. But supposing it was right for a man to bind his *own* conscience, yet surely it is very iniquitous to bind the consciences of his children—to make fetters

John Leland, from *The Baptist Encyclopaedia,*
ed. William Cathcart, 1881.

for them before they are born, is very cruel. And yet such has been the conduct of men in almost all ages, that their children have been bound to believe and worship as their fathers did, or suffer shame, loss, and sometimes life, and at best to be called dissenters, because they dissent from that which they never joined voluntarily. Such conduct in parents, is worse than that of the father of Hannibal who imposed an oath upon his son, while a child, never to be at peace with the Romans.

Fourth. Finally, religion is a matter between God and individuals: the religious opinions of men not being the objects of civil government, nor in any way under its control.

It has often been observed by the friends of religion established by human laws, that no state can long continue without it; that religion will perish, and nothing but infidelity and atheism prevail.

Are these things facts? Did not the Christian religion prevail during the first three centuries, in a more glorious manner than ever it has since, not only without the aid of law, but in opposition to all the laws of haughty monarchs? And did not religion receive a deadly wound by being fostered in the arms of civil power and regulated by law? These things are so.

From that day to this, we have but a few instances of religious liberty to judge by; for, in almost all states, civil rulers, by the investigation of covetous priests, have undertaken to steady the ark of religion by human laws; but yet we have a few of them without leaving our own land.

The state of Rhode Island has stood above one hundred and sixty years without any religious establishment. The state of New York never had any. New Jersey claims the same. Pennsylvania has also stood from its first settlement until now upon a liberal foundation; and if agriculture, the mechanical arts and commerce, have not flourished in these states, equal to any of the others, I judge wrong.

It may further be observed, that all the states now in union, saving two or three in New England, have no legal force used about religion, in directing its course, or supporting its preachers. And, moreover, the federal government is forbidden by the constitution, to make any laws, establishing any kind of religion. If religion cannot stand, therefore, without the aid of law, it is likely to fall soon, in our nation, except in Connecticut and Massachusetts.

To say that "religion cannot stand without a state establishment," is not only contrary to fact, (as has been proved already,) but is a contradiction in phrase. Religion must have stood a time before any law could have been made about it; and if it did stand almost three hundred years without law, it can still stand without it.

The evils of such an establishment, are many.

First. Uninspired, fallible men make their own opinions tests of orthodoxy, and use their own systems, as Pocrustes used his iron bedstead, to stretch and measure the consciences of all others by. Where no toleration is granted to non-conformists, either ignorance and superstition prevail, or persecution rages; and if toleration is granted to restricted nonconformists, the minds of men are biased to embrace that religion which is favored and pampered by law, and thereby hypocrisy is nourished; while those who cannot stretch their consciences to believe anything and everything in the established creed, are treated with contempt and opprobrious names; and by such means, some are pampered to death by largesses, and others confined from doing what good they otherwise could, by penury. The first lie under a temptation to flatter the ruling party, to continue that form of government which brings them in the sure bread of idleness; the last to despise that government, and those rulers, that oppress them. The first have their eyes shut to all further light, that would alter the religious machine; the last are always seeking new light, and often fall into enthusiasm. Such are the natural evils of the establishment of religion by human laws.

Second. Such establishments not only wean and alienate the affections of one from another, on account of the different usage they receive in their religious sentiments, but are also very impolitic, especially in new countries; for what encouragement can strangers have to migrate with their arts and wealth into a state, where they cannot enjoy their religious sentiments without exposing themselves to the law? when, at the same time, their religious opinions do not lead them to be mutinous. And further, how often have kingdoms and states been greatly weakened by religious tests! In the time of the persecution in France, not less than twenty thousand people fled for the enjoyment of religious liberty.

Third. These establishments metamorphose the church into a creature, and religion into a principle of state, which has a natural tendency to make men conclude that *Bible religion* is nothing but a *trick of state;* hence it is that the greatest part of the well-informed in literature are overrun with deism and infidelity; nor is it likely that it will ever be much better, while preaching is made a trade of emolument. And if there is no difference between *Bible religion* and *state religion,* I shall soon fall into infidelity.

Fourth. There are no two kingdoms and states that establish the same creed and formalities of faith, which alone proves their debility. In one kingdom a man is condemned for not believing a doctrine that he would be condemned for believing in another kingdom. Both of these establishments cannot be right, but both of them can be, and surely are, wrong.

First. The nature of such establishments, further, is to keep from civil office the best of men. Good men cannot believe what they cannot believe, and they will not subscribe to what they disbelieve, and take an oath to maintain what they conclude is error; and, as the best of men differ in judgment, there may be some of them in any state: their talents and virtue entitle them to fill the most important posts, yet, because they differ from the established creed of the state, they cannot—will not fill those posts; whereas villains make no scruple to take any oath.

If these, and many more evils, attend such establishments, what were, and still are, the causes that ever there should be a state establishment of religion in any empire, kingdom, or state?

The causes are many—some of which follow:

First. The love of importance is a general evil. It is natural to men to dictate for others: they choose to command the bushel and use the whip-row: to have the halter around the necks of others, to hang them at pleasure.

Second. An over-fondness for a particular system or sect. This gave rise to the first human establishment of religion, by Constantine the Great. Being converted to the Christian system, he established it in the Roman empire, compelled the Pagans to submit, and banished the Christian heretics; built fine chapels at public expense, and forced large stipends for the preachers. All this was done out of love to the Christian religion; but his love operated inadvertently, for he did the Christian church more harm than all the persecuting emperors ever did. It is said, that in his day a voice was heard from heaven, saying: "Now is poison spued into the churches." If this voice was not heard, it, nevertheless, was a truth; for, from that day to this, the Christian religion has been made a stirrup to mount the steed of popularity, wealth and ambition.

Third. To produce uniformity in religion. Rulers often fear that if they leave every man to think, speak, and worship as he pleases, that the whole cause will be wrecked in diversity; to prevent which, they establish some standard of orthodoxy, to effect uniformity. But, is uniformity attainable? Millions of men, women and children, have been tortured to death, to produce uniformity, and yet the world has not advanced one inch towards it. And as long as men live in different parts of the world, have different habits, education and interests, they will be different in judgment, humanly speaking.

Is uniformity of sentiments, in matter of religion, essential to the happiness of civil government? Not at all. Government has no more to do with the religious opinions of men, than it has with the principles of mathematics. Let every man speak freely without fear, maintain the principles that he believes, worship according to his own faith, either one God, three Gods, no God, or twenty Gods; and let government protect him in so doing, i.e., see that he meets with no personal abuse, or loss of property, for his religious opinions. Instead of discouraging him with proscriptions, fines, confiscations or death, let him be encouraged, as a free man, to bring forth his arguments and maintain his points with all boldness; then, if his doctrine is false, it will be confuted, and if it is true, (though ever so novel,) let others credit it.

When every man has this liberty, what can he wish for more? A liberal man asks for nothing more of government.

The duty of magistrates is, not to judge of the divinity or tendency of doctrines; but when those principles break out into overt acts of violence, then to use the civil sword and punish the vagrant for what he has done, and not for the religious phrenzy that he acted from.

It is not supposable that any established creed contains the whole truth, and nothing but the truth; but supposing it did, which established church in the world has got it? All bigots contend for it, each society cries out, "the temple of the Lord are we." Let one society be supposed to be in possession of the whole, let that society be established by law; the creed of faith that they adopt, be consecrated so sacred to government, that the man that disbelieves it must die; let this creed finally prevail over the whole world. I ask, what honor truth gets by all this? None at all. It is famed of a Prussian, called John the Cicero, that by one oration he reconciled two contending princes, actually in war; but, says the historian, "it was his six thousand horse that had the most persuasive oratory." So when one creed or church prevails over another, being armed with a coat of mail, law and sword, truth gets no honor by the victory. Whereas if all stand upon one footing, being equally protected by law, as citizens, (not as saints,) and one prevails over another by cool investigation and fair argument, then truth gains honor; and men more firmly believe it, than if it was made an essential article of salvation by law.

Truth disdains the aid of law for its defence—it will stand upon its own merit. The heathen worshipped a goddess, called truth, stark naked, and all human decorations of truth, serve only to destroy her virgin beauty. It is error, and error alone, that needs human support; and whenever men fly to the law or sword to protect their system of religion, and force it upon others, it is evident that they have something in their system that will not bear the light, and stand upon the basis of truth.

Fourth. The common objection, "that the ignorant part of the community are not capacitated to judge for themselves," supports the Popish hierarchy, and all Protestant, as well as Turkish and Pagan establishments in idea.

But is this idea just? Has God chosen many of the wise and learned? Has he not hid the mystery of gospel truth from them, and revealed it unto babes? Does the world by wisdom know God? Did many of the rulers believe in Christ when he was upon earth? Were not the learned clergy (the scribes) his most inveterate enemies? Do not great men differ as much as little men in judgment? Have not almost all lawless

errors crept into the world through the means of wise men (so called)? Is not a simple man, who makes nature and reason his study, a competent judge of things? Is the Bible written (like Caligula's laws) so intricate and high, that none but the letter learned (according to common phrase) can read it? Is not the vision written so plain that he that runs may read it? Do not those who understand the original languages, that the Bible was written in, differ as much in judgment as others? Are the identical copies of Matthew, Mark, Luke and John, together with the epistles in every university, and in the hands of every master of arts? If not, have not the learned to trust to a human transcription, as much as the unlearned have to a translation? If these questions, and others of the like nature, can be confuted; then I will confess that it is wisdom for a conclave of bishops, or a convocation of clergy to frame a system out of the Bible, and persuade the legislature to legalize it. No; it would be attended with so much expense, pride, domination, cruelty and bloodshed, that let me rather fall into infidelity; for no religion at all, is better than that which is worse than none.

Fifth. The groundwork of these establishments of religion is, *clerical influence.* Rulers, being persuaded by the clergy that an establishment of religion by human laws, would promote the knowledge of the gospel, quell religious disputes, prevent heresy, produce uniformity, and finally be advantageous to the state; establish such creeds as are framed by the clergy; and this they often do more readily, when they are flattered by the clergy; that if they thus defend the truth, they will become nursing fathers to the church, and merit something considerable for themselves.

What stimulates the clergy to recommend this mode of reasoning is:

First. Ignorance, not being able to confute error by fair argument.

Second. Indolence, not being willing to spend any time to confute the heretical.

Third. But chiefly covetousness, to get money, for it may be observed that in all these establishments, settled salaries for the clergy, recoverable by law, are sure to be interwoven; and was not this the case, I am well convinced that there would not be many, if any religious establishments in the Christian world.

Having made the foregoing remarks, I shall next make some observations on the religion of Connecticut.

If the citizens of this state, have anything in existence that looks like a religious establishment, they ought to be very cautious; for being but a small part of the world, they can never expect to extend their religion over the whole of it, without it is so well founded that it cannot be confuted.

If one-third part of the face of the globe is allowed to be seas, the earthly parts would compose four thousand five hundred and fifty such states as Connecticut. The American empire would afford above two-hundred of them. And as there is no religion in this empire, of the same stamp as the Connecticut standing order, upon the Say-Brook platform, they may expect one hundred and ninety-nine against one at home, and four thousand five hundred and forty-nine against one abroad.

Connecticut and New-Haven were separate governments till the reign of Charles II. when they were incorporated together by a charter; which charter is still considered, by some, as the basis of government.

At present, there are in the state about one hundred and sixty-eight Presbyterial, Congregational and Consociated preachers; thirty-five Baptist, twenty Episcopalians, ten separate Congregationals, and a few other denominations. The first are the standing order of Connecticut; to whom all others have to pay obeisance. Societies of the standing order are formed by law; none have a right to vote therein but men of age, who possess property to the amount of £40, or are in full communion in the church. Their choice of ministers is by major vote; and what the society agree to give him annually, is levied upon all within the limits of the society-bounds; except they bring a certificate to the clerk of the society, that they attend worship elsewhere, and contribute to the satisfaction of the society where they attend. The money being levied on the people, is distrainable by law; and perpet-

ually binding on the society till the minister is dismissed by a council, or by death, from his charge.

It is not my intention to give a detail of all the tumults, oppression, fines and imprisonments, that have heretofore been occasioned by this law religion. These things are partly dead and buried, and if they did not rise of themselves, let them sleep peaceably in the dust forever. Let it suffice on this head, to say, that it is not possible, in the nature of things, to establish religion by human laws, without perverting the design of civil law and oppressing the people.

The certificate that a dissenter produces to the society clerk, must be signed by some officer of the dissenting church, and such church must be Christian; for heathens, deists, and Jews, are not indulged in the certificate law; all of them, as well as Turks, must therefore be taxed for the standing order, although they never go among them, or know where the meeting-house is.

This certificate law is founded on this principle, "that it is the duty of all persons to support the gospel and the worship of God." Is this principle founded in justice? Is it the duty of a deist to support that which he believes to be a cheat and imposition? Is it the duty of a Jew to support the religion of Jesus Christ, when he really believes that he was an impostor? Must the Papists be forced to pay men for preaching down the supremacy of the pope, who they are sure is the head of the church? Must a Turk maintain a religion, opposed to the Alkoran, which he holds as the sacred oracle of heaven? These things want better confirmation. If we suppose that it is the duty of all these to support the Protestant Christian religion, as being the best religion in the world; yet how comes it to pass, that human legislatures have a right to force them so to do? I now call for an instance, where Jesus Christ, the author of his religion, or the apostles, who were divinely inspired, ever gave orders to, or intimated, that the civil powers on earth, ought to force people to observe the rules and doctrine of the gospel.

Mahomet called in the use of the law and sword, to convert people to his religion; but Jesus did not—does not.

It is the duty of men to love God with all their hearts, and their neighbors as themselves; but have legislatures authority to punish men if they do not; so there are many things that Jesus and the apostles taught, that men ought to obey, which yet the civil law has no concern in.

That it is the duty of men, who are taught in the word, to communicate to him that teaches, is beyond controversy; but that it is the province of the civil law to force them to do so, is denied.

The charter of Charles II., is supposed to be the basis of government in Connecticut; and I request any gentleman to point out a single clause in that charter, which authorizes the legislature to make any religious laws, establish any religion, or force people to build meeting-houses or pay preachers. If there is no such constitutional clause, it follows, that the laws are usurpatory in the legislatures, and not binding on the people. I shall here add, that if the legislature of Connecticut, have a right to establish the religion which they prefer to all religions, and force men to support it, then every legislature or legislator has the same authority; and if this be true, the separation of the Christians from the Pagans, the departure of the Protestant from the Papists, and the dissent of the Presbyterians from the church of England, were all schisms of a criminal nature; and all the persecution that they have met with, is just the effect of their stubbornness.

The certificate law supposes, first, that the legislature have power to establish a religion; this is false. Second, that they have authority to grant indulgence to non-conformists; this is also false, for a religious liberty is a right and not a favor. Third, that the legitimate power of government extends to force people to part with their money for religious purposes; this cannot be proved from the New Testament.

The certificate law has lately passed a new modification. Justices of the peace must now examine them; this gives ministers of state a power over religious concerns that the New Testament does not. To examine the law, part by part, would be needless, for the whole of it is wrong.

From what is said, this question arises, "are not contracts with ministers, i.e., between ministers and people, as obligatory as any contracts whatever?" The simple answer is, yes. Ministers should share the same protection of the law that other men do, and no more. To proscribe them from seats of legislation, etc., is cruel. To indulge them with an exemption from taxes and bearing arms is a tempting emolument. The law should be silent about them; protect them as citizens, not as sacred officers, for the civil law knows no sacred religious officers.

In Rhode Island, if a congregation of people agree to give a preacher a certain sum of money for preaching, the bond is not recoverable by law.*

This law was formed upon a good principle, but, unhappily for the makers of that law, they were incoherent in the superstructure.

The principle of the law, is, that the gospel is not to be supported by law; that civil rulers have nothing to do with religion, in their civil capacities; what business had they then to make that law? The evil seemed to arise from blending religious *right* and religious *opinions* together. Religious *right* should be protected to *all* men, religious *opinion* to none; i.e. government should confirm the first unto all; the last unto none: each individual having a *right* to differ from all others in *opinion* if he is so persuaded. If a number of people in Rhode Island, or elswhere, are of opinion that ministers of the gospel ought to be supported by law, and choose to be bound by a bond to pay him, government has no just authority to declare that bond illegal; for, in so doing, they interfere with private contracts, and deny the people the liberty of conscience. If these people bind nobody but themselves, who is injured by their religious opinions? But if they bind an individual besides themselves, the bond is fraudulent, and ought to be declared illegal. And here lies the

---

* Some men, who are best informed in the laws of Rhode Island, say, if ever there was such an act in that state, there is nothing like it in existence at this day; and perhaps it is only cast upon them as a stigma, because they have ever been friends to religious liberty. However, as the principle is supposable, I have treated it as a real fact: and this I have done the more willingly, because nine-tenths of the people believe it is a fact.

mischief of Connecticut religion. My lord, major vote, binds all the minor part, unless they submit to idolatry; i.e., pay an acknowledgement to a power that Jesus Christ never ordained in his church; I mean produce a certificate. Yea further, Jews, Turks, heathens and deists, if such there are in Connecticut, are bound, and have no redress; and further, this bond is not annually given, but for life, except the minister is dismissed by a number of others, who are in the same predicament with himself.

Although it is no abridgement of religious liberty for congregations to pay their preachers by legal force, in the manner prescribed above, yet it is anti Christian; such a church cannot be a church of Christ, because they are not governed by Christ's laws, but by the laws of state; and such ministers do not appear like ambassadors of Christ, but like ministers of state.

The next question is this, "Suppose a congregation of people have agreed to give a minister a certain sum of money annually, for life or during good behaviour, and in a course of time, some or all of them change their opinions, and verily believe that the preacher is in a capital error; and really from conscience, dissent from him, are they still bound to comply with their engagements to the preacher?" This question is supposable, and I believe there have been a few instances of the kind.

If men have bound themselves, honor and honesty call upon them to comply; but God and conscience call upon them to come out from among them, and let such blind guides alone.* Honor and honesty are amiable virtues; but God and conscience call to perfidiousness. This shows the impropriety of such contracts, which always may, and sometimes do lead into such labyrinths. It is time enough to pay a man after his labor is over. People are not required to communicate to the *teacher* before they are *taught*. A man, called of God to preach, feels a necessity to preach, and a woe if he does not. And if he is sent by Christ,

---

* The phrase of *blind guides*, is not intended to cast contempt upon any order of religious preachers, for, let a preacher be orthodox or heterodox, virtuous or vicious, he is always a *blind guide* to those who differ from him in opinion.

he looks to him and his laws for support; and if men comply with their duty, he finds relief; if not, he must go to his field, as the priests of old did. A man cannot give a more glaring proof of his covetousness and irreligion, than to say, "If you will give me so much, then I will preach, but if not, be assured I will not preach to you."

So that in answering the question, instead of determining which of the evils to choose, either to disobey God and conscience, or break honor and honesty, I would recommend an escape of both evils, by entering into no such contracts; for the natural evils of imprudence that men are fallen into, neither God nor man can prevent.

A minister must have a hard heart to wish men to be forced to pay him, when through conscience, enthusiasm, or private pique, they dissent from his ministry. The spirit of the Gospel disdains such measures.

The question before us, is not applicable to many cases in Connecticut: the dissenting churches make no contracts for a longer term than a year, and most of them make none at all. Societies of the *standing order*, rarely bind themselves, in contract with preachers, without binding others beside themselves; and when that is the case the bond is fraudulent; and if those who are bound involuntarily can get clear, it is no breach of honor or honesty.

A few additional remarks shall close my piece.

First. The Church of Rome was at first constituted according to the gospel; and at that time her faith was spoken of through the whole world. Being espoused to Christ, as a chaste virgin, she kept her bed pure for her husband almost three hundred years; but afterwards she played the whore with the kings and princes of this world, who, with their gold and wealth, came in unto her, and she became a strumpet. And, as she was the first Christian church that ever forsook the laws of Christ for her conduct, and received the laws of his rivals, i.e., was established by human law, and governed by the legalized edicts of councils, and received large sums of money to support her preachers and her worship, by the force of civil power, she is called the *mother of harlots;* and all Protestant churches, who are regulated by law, and force people to support their preachers, build meeting-houses, and otherwise maintain their worship, are *daughters* of this holy *mother*.

Second. I am not a citizen of Connecticut—the religious laws of the state do not oppress me, and I expect never will personally; but a love to religious liberty in general, induces me thus to speak. Were I a resident in the state, I could not give or receive a certificate to be exempted from ministerial taxes; for, in so doing, I should confess that the legislature had authority to pamper one religious order in the state, and make all others pay obeisance to that sheaf. It is high time to know whether all are to be free alike, and whether ministers of state are to be lords over God's heritage.

And here I shall ask the citizens of Connecticut, whether, in the months of April and September, when they choose their deputies for the assembly, they mean to surrender to them the rights of conscience, and authorize them to make laws binding on their consciences? If not, then all such acts are contrary to the intention of constituent power, as well as unconstitutional and anti-Christian.

Third. It is likely that one part of the people in Connecticut believe, in conscience, that gospel preachers should be supported by the force of law; and the other part believe that it is not in the province of civil law to interfere, or any ways meddle with religious matters. How are both parties to be protected by law in their conscientious belief?

Very easily. Let all those whose consciences dictate that they ought to be taxed by law to maintain their preacher, bring in their names to the society clerk, by a certain day, and then assess them all, according to their estates, to raise the sum stipulated in the contract, and all others go free. Both parties, by this method, would enjoy the full liberty of conscience, without oppressing one another—the laws use no force in matters of conscience—the evil of Rhode Island law be escaped—and no person could find fault with it, in a political point of view, but those who fear the consciences of too many would lie dormant, and,

therefore, wish to force them to pay. Here let it be noted, that there are many in the world who believe, in conscience, that a minister is not entitled to any acknowledgement for his services, without he is so poor that he cannot live without it; and thereby convert a gospel debt to alms. Though this opinion is not founded either on reason or scripture, yet it is a better opinion than that which would force them to pay a preacher by human law.

Fourth. How mortifying must it be to foreigners, and how far from conciliatory is it to citizens of the American states, that when they come into Connecticut to reside, they must either conform to the religion of Connecticut, or produce a certificate? Does this look like religious liberty, or human friendship? Suppose that man, whose name need not be mentioned, but which fills every American heart with pleasure and awe, should remove to Connecticut for his health, or any other cause, what a scandal would it be to the state, to tax him to support a Presbyterian minister, unless he produced a certificate, informing them that he was an Episcopalian.

Fifth. The federal constitution certainly had the advantage of any of the state constitutions, in being made by the wisest men in the whole nation, and after an experiment of a number of years trial upon republican principles; and that constitution forbids Congress ever to establish any kind of religion, or require any religious test to qualify any officer in any department of federal government. Let a man be Pagan, Turk, Jew or Christian, he is eligible to any post in that government. So that if the principles of religious liberty, contended for in the foregoing pages, are supposed to be fraught with Deism, fourteen states in the Union are now fraught with the same. But the separate states have not surrendered that supposed right of establishing religion to Congress. Each state retains all its power, saving what is given to the general government, by the federal constitution. The assembly of Connecticut, therefore, still undertake to guide the helm of religion; and if Congress were disposed, yet they could not prevent it, by any power vested in them by the states. Therefore, if any of the people of

Connecticut feel oppressed by the certificate law, or any other of the like nature, their proper mode of procedure will be to remonstrate against the oppression, and petition the assembly for a redress of the grievance.

Sixth. Divines generally inform us that there is a time to come, (called the Latter Day Glory,) when the knowledge of the Lord shall cover the earth, as the waters do the sea, and that this day will appear upon the destruction of antichrist. If so, I am well convinced that Jesus will first remove all the hinderances of religious establishments, and cause all men to be free in matters of religion. When this is effected, he will say to the kings and great men of the earth: "Now, see what I can do: ye have been afraid to leave the church and gospel in my hands alone, without steadying the ark by human law, but now I have taken the power and kingdom for myself, and will work for my own glory." Here let me add that, in the southern states, where there has been the greatest freedom from religious oppression, where liberty of conscience is entirely enjoyed, there has been the greatest revival of religion; which is another proof that true religion can, and will prevail best, where it is left entirely to Christ.

RECOMMENDATIONS FOR FURTHER READING

Albanese, Catherine L. *Sons of the Fathers: The Civil Religion of the American Revolution.* Philadelphia: Temple University Press, 1976.

Brauer, Jerald C., ed. *Religion and the American Revolution.* Philadelphia: Fortress Press, 1976.

Dreisbach, Daniel L., Mark D. Hall, and Jeffry H. Morrison, eds. *The Founders on God and Government.* Lanham, Md.: Rowman and Littlefield, 2004.

Noll, Mark A. *Christians in the American Revolution.* Grand Rapids: Christian University Press, 1977.

CHAPTER SEVEN

References to God and the Christian Religion in the U.S. Constitution

A STRIKING FEATURE of the United States Constitution of 1787 is its lack of explicit acknowledgments of God and the Christian religion. The Constitution, in this respect, departed from the pattern of most public documents of the day, including state constitutions, which were replete with references to and claims of Christian devotion and supplications to a Supreme Being. The omission is remarkable because, despite any revolutionary ardor of the time, there was little sentiment that the new republican order broke with the prevailing Christian traditions of the American people.

Although slight references to the Deity and Christian custom can be found in the national Constitution (see, for example, the Article I, section 7, clause 2 mention of "Sunday" and the Article VII reference to "the Year of our Lord"), unlike the Declaration of Independence (1776) and most public documents of the era, there is no clear affirmation of the existence of a superintendent, transcendent being and no acknowledgment that society and civil government are dependent on and governed by God. Delegates to the Constitutional Convention noted this omission. Also, some critics in state ratifying conventions as well as in the general public decried the omission as a defect in the proposed Constitution.

The complaint was less about what the Constitution said than about its silence—its failure to identify the Christian foundations upon which, it was believed, all political institutions should rest. During the ratification debates and well into the nineteenth century, persistent and often vocal critics protested the document's failure to acknowledge God appropriately. Some warned that God would withhold favor from a nation that failed to acknowledge Him; and, indeed, calamities in the early republic, such as the War of 1812, were often blamed on this constitutional omission. For many years, some religious societies even instructed their members to refrain from voting in national elections until the U.S. Constitution was amended to acknowledge God as the ruler of all nations and author of supreme law. This dissatisfaction, which has been expressed throughout American history, has sustained several national campaigns to amend the Constitution to recognize God and the republic's Christian character and heritage.

Commentators, then and now, have offered numerous explanations for the Constitution's lack of explicit theistic or Christian references. Some have argued, for example, that the constitutional framers deliberately laid the foundations for a strictly secular polity. Others have speculated that a mention of God was not thought necessary in a purely political and legal document. Another explanation is that the framers minimized religious references in the Constitution in order to avoid potentially divisive sectarian conflicts in the already difficult and contentious proceedings. Still others have argued that the Constitution omitted more explicit references to God and religion because the framers thought that, as a matter of federalism, religion's interaction with the civil state was a matter of state (not national) jurisdiction. (And, indeed, most states in the founding era retained features of religious establishment, and state constitutions were replete with acknowledgments of the Deity and the Christian religion.)

This debate in the early republic raises fundamental questions about the place and role of religion—specifically Christianity—in the American constitutional tradition.

Call for Prayer in the Constitutional Convention (June 28, 1787)

BENJAMIN FRANKLIN (1706–90)

By late June, the Constitutional Convention of 1787 was mired in dissension. In a memorable speech, the venerable Benjamin Franklin recommended that "prayers imploring the assistance of Heaven, and its blessings on our deliberations, be held in this Assembly every morning." Franklin's solemn proposal and the subsequent discussion in the Convention chambers are reprinted from James Madison's convention notes.

Benjamin Franklin, by Joseph Wright.
© The Corcoran Gallery of Art/CORBIS.

[Dr. Franklin.][1]

Mr. President

The small progress we have made after 4 or five weeks close attendance & continual reasonings with each other—our different sentiments on almost every question, several of the last producing as many noes as ays, is methinks a melancholy proof of the imperfection of the Human Understanding. We indeed seem to feel[2] our own want of political wisdom, since we have been running about in search of it. We have gone back to ancient history for models of Government, and examined the different forms of those Re-

publics which having been formed with the seeds of their own dissolution now no longer exist. And we have viewed Modern States all round Europe, but find none of their Constitutions suitable to our circumstances.

In this situation of this Assembly, groping as it were in the dark to find political truth, and scarce able to distinguish it when presented to us, how has it happened, Sir, that we have not hitherto once thought of humbly applying to the Father of lights to illuminate our understandings? In the beginning of the Contest with G. Britain, when we were sensible of danger we had daily prayer in this room for the divine protection.—Our prayers, Sir, were heard, and they were graciously answered. All of us who were engaged in the struggle must have observed frequent instances of a Superintending providence in our favor. To that kind providence we owe this happy opportunity of

---

Reprinted from *The Records of the Federal Convention of 1787*, ed. Max Farrand, rev. ed. (New Haven and London: Yale University Press, 1987), 1:450–52.

1. Madison originally made an abstract of Franklin's speech in about 200 words. This was later stricken out—and this note made: "see opposite page & insert the speech of Doctr F in this place." On the opposite page under the heading "June 28, in convention" is the speech which is here given—but without Franklin's name.

Among the Franklin Papers in the Library of Congress is a copy of this speech differing hardly at all from the text except in more frequent use of capitals.

2. "feel" is underscored in Franklin MS.

consulting in peace on the means of establishing our future national felicity. And have we now forgotten that powerful friend? or do we imagine that we no longer need his assistance? I have lived, Sir, a long time, and the longer I live, the more convincing proofs I see of this truth—*that God*[3] *governs in the affairs of men.* And if a sparrow cannot fall to the ground without his notice, is it probable that an empire can rise without his aid? We have been assured, Sir, in the sacred writings, that "except the Lord build the House they labour in vain that build it." I firmly believe this; and I also believe that without his concurring aid we shall succeed in this political building no better than the Builders of Babel: We shall be divided by our little partial local interests; our projects will be confounded, and we ourselves shall become a reproach and bye word down to future ages. And what is worse, mankind may hereafter from this unfortunate instance, despair of establishing Governments by Human Wisdom and leave it to chance, war and conquest.

I therefore beg leave to move—that henceforth prayers imploring the assistance of Heaven, and its blessings on our deliberations, be held in this Assembly every morning before we proceed to business, and that one or more of the Clergy of this City be requested to officiate in that service ———

Mr. Sharman seconded the motion.

Mr. Hamilton & several others expressed their apprehensions that however proper such a resolution might have been at the beginning of the convention, it might at this late day, 1. bring on it some disagreeable animadversions. & 2. lead the public to believe that the embarrassments and dissentions within the convention, had suggested this measure. It was answered by Docr. F. Mr. Sherman & others, that the past omission of a duty could not justify a further omission—that the rejection of such a proposition would expose the Convention to more unpleasant animadversions than the adoption of it: and that the alarm out of doors that might be excited for the state

of things within would at least be as likely to do good as ill.

Mr. Williamson, observed that the true cause of the omission could not be mistaken. The Convention had no funds.

Mr. Randolph proposed in order to give a favorable aspect to ye. measure, that a sermon be preached at the request of the convention on 4th of July, the anniversary of Independence,—& thenceforward prayers be used in ye Convention every morning. Dr. Frankn. 2ded. this motion After several unsuccessful attempts for silently postponing the matter by adjourng. the adjournment was at length carried, without any vote on the motion.[4]

4. In the Franklin MS. the following note is added:—"The Convention, except three or four persons, thought Prayers unnecessary."

U.S. Constitution (1788)

The United States Constitution, some commentators have argued, contains words and phrases with religious connotations or that reflect Christian customs. Among them are the Article I, section 7, omission of "Sunday" in the number of days in which a president must decide to sign or veto a bill, and the Article VII reference to "the Year of our Lord." Insofar as an "oath is an appeal to God, . . . and always expresses or supposes an imprecation of his judgment upon us, if we prevaricate,"[1] the Constitution's four oath provisions (Article I, section 3, clause 6; Article II, section 1, clause 8; Article VI, clause 3; and Amendment 4) also acknowledge sacred obligations (see chapter 10 for the texts of these clauses).

---

3. "God" twice underscored in Franklin MS.

1. John Witherspoon, *Lectures on Moral Philosophy*, ed. Varnum Lansing Collins (Princeton: Princeton University Press, 1912), 130.

Preamble

We, the people of the United States, in order to form a more perfect Union, establish justice, insure domestic tranquillity, provide for the common defence, promote the general welfare, and secure the blessings of liberty to ourselves and our posterity, do ordain and establish this Constitution for the United States of America.

Article I, Section 7, Clause 2

Every bill which shall have passed the House of Representatives and the Senate, shall, before it become a law, be presented to the President of the United States; if he approve he shall sign it, but if not he shall return it, with his objections, to that House in which it shall have originated, who shall enter the objections at large on their journal, and proceed to reconsider it. If after such reconsideration two thirds of that House shall agree to pass the bill, it shall be sent, together with the objections, to the other House, by which it shall likewise be reconsidered, and if approved by two thirds of that House, it shall become a law. But in all such cases the votes of both Houses shall be determined by yeas and nays, and the names of the persons voting for and against the bill shall be entered on the journal of each House respectively. If any bill shall not be returned by the president within ten Days, (Sundays excepted,) after it shall have been presented to him, the same shall be a law, in like manner as if he had signed it, unless the Congress by their adjournment prevent its return, in which case it shall not be a law.

Article VII

The ratification of the conventions of nine States, shall be sufficient for the establishment of this Constitution between the States so ratifying the same.

Done in Convention by the unanimous consent of the States present, the seventeenth day of September,

Reprinted from *The Public Statutes at Large of the United States of America*, ed. Richard Peters (Boston: Little and Brown, 1845), 1:10, 12, 19–20.

in the year of our lord one thousand seven hundred and eighty-seven, and of the independence of the United States of America the twelfth. In witness whereof we have hereunto subscribed our names. . . .

The Federalist Papers, Number 37 (1788)

PUBLIUS [JAMES MADISON]

In *The Federalist Papers,* Number 37, James Madison, reviewing the "difficulties encountered by the [constitutional] convention," said it is impossible for a citizen of "pious reflection" not to see the work of God in the convention's achievement.

In reviewing the defects of the existing confederation, and showing that they cannot be supplied by a government of less energy than that before the public, several of the most important principles of the latter fell of course under consideration. But as the ultimate object of these papers is, to determine clearly and fully the merits of this constitution, and the expediency of adopting it, our plan cannot be completed without taking a more critical and thorough survey of the work of the convention; without examining it on all its sides; comparing it in all its parts, and calculating its probable effects. . . .

Would it be wonderful if, under the pressure of all these difficulties, the convention should have been forced into some deviations from that artificial structure and regular symmetry, which an abstract view of the subject might lead an ingenious theorist to bestow

Reprinted from Alexander Hamilton, John Jay, and James Madison, *The Federalist,* ed. George W. Carey and James McClellan (Indianapolis: Liberty Fund, 2001), 179, 184–85. © Liberty Fund, Inc., 2001. Reprinted by permission.

on a constitution planned in his closet, or in his imagination? The real wonder is, that so many difficulties should have been surmounted; and surmounted with an unanimity almost as unprecedented, as it must have been unexpected. It is impossible for any man of candour to reflect on this circumstance, without partaking of the astonishment. It is impossible, for the man of pious reflection, not to perceive in it a finger of that Almighty Hand, which has been so frequently and signally extended to our relief in the critical stages of the revolution.

We had occasion in a former paper, to take notice of the repeated trials which have been unsuccessfully made in the United Netherlands, for reforming the baneful and notorious vices of their constitution. The history of almost all the great councils and consultations, held among mankind for reconciling their discordant opinions, assuaging their mutual jealousies, and adjusting their respective interests, is a history of factions, contentions, and disappointments; and may be classed among the most dark and degrading pictures, which display the infirmities and depravities of the human character. If, in a few scattered instances, a brighter aspect is presented, they serve only as exceptions to admonish us of the general truth; and by their lustre to darken the gloom of the adverse prospect to which they are contrasted. In revolving the causes from which these exceptions result, and applying them to the particular instance before us, we are necessarily led to two important conclusions. The first is, that the convention must have enjoyed in a very singular degree, an exemption from the pestilential influence of party animosities; the diseases most incident to deliberative bodies, and most apt to contaminate their proceedings. The second conclusion is, that all the deputations composing the convention, were either satisfactorily accommodated by the final act; or were induced to accede to it, by a deep conviction of the necessity of sacrificing private opinions and partial interests to the public good; and by a despair of seeing this necessity diminished by delays or by new experiments.

PUBLIUS

Letter from William Williams to the Landholder, *The American Mercury* (February 11, 1788)

William Williams of Lebanon, Connecticut (1731–1811), a prominent Connecticut politician and a signer of the Declaration of Independence, expressed consternation in a letter to "A Landholder" that the proposed national Constitution did not explicitly acknowledge God, and he recommended affixing the following preamble to the Constitution to correct this alleged defect. (The complete text of Williams's letter is reprinted in chapter 8.)

When the clause in the 6th Article, which provides that "no religious test should ever be required as a qualification to any office or trust, etc." came under consideration, I observed I should have chose that sentence, and anything relating to a religious test, had been totally omitted rather than stand as it did; but still more wished something of the kind should have been inserted, but with a reverse sense so far as to require an explicit acknowledgment of the being of a God, His perfections, and His providence, and to have been prefixed to, and stand as, the first introductory words of the Constitution in the following or similar terms, viz.: *We the people of the United States, in a firm belief of the being and perfections of the one living and true God, the creator and supreme Governor of the world, in His universal providence and the authority of His laws: that He will require of all moral agents an account of their conduct, that all rightful powers among men are ordained of, and mediately derived*

Excerpt reprinted from *The Documentary History of the Ratification of the Constitution*, vol. 3: *Ratification of the Constitution by the States: Delaware, New Jersey, Georgia, Connecticut*, ed. Merrill Jensen (Madison: State Historical Society of Wisconsin, 1978), 589. Reprinted with permission of the Wisconsin Historical Society.

from God, therefore in a dependence on His blessing and acknowledgment of His efficient protection in establishing our Independence, whereby it is become necessary to agree upon and settle a Constitution of federal government for ourselves, and in order to form a more perfect union, etc., as it is expressed in the present introduction, do ordain, etc. . . . .

Essay by Elihu, *The American Mercury* (February 18, 1788)

This essay by Elihu, originally published in the Hartford, Connecticut, *American Mercury,* responded to William Williams's recommendation for a revised preamble to the U.S. Constitution acknowledging God and the nation's dependence on Him. (A "Letter by David," reprinted in chapter 8, was written in response to this essay.)

Reprinted from *The Documentary History of the Ratification of the Constitution,* vol. 3: *Ratification of the Constitution by the States: Delaware, New Jersey, Georgia, Connecticut,* ed. Merrill Jensen (Madison: State Historical Society of Wisconsin, 1978), 590–92. Reprinted with permission of the Wisconsin Historical Society.

Elihu, American Mercury, 18 February

I was afraid, and durst not shew mine opinion. I said days should speak and multitude of years should teach wisdom. Great men are not always wise, neither doth age understand judgment. I will answer. I also will shew mine opinion. The Spirit within me constraineth me. I will speak that I may be refreshed. Let me not accept any man's person, neither let me give flattering titles unto man. etc. Job, chap. XXXII.

It was an objection against the Constitution, urged in the late Convention, that the being of a God was not explicitly acknowledged in it. It has been reported that an honorable gentleman, who gave his vote in favor of the Constitution, has since expressed his discontent by an expression no less remarkable than this, "that they (speaking of the framers of the Constitution) had not allowed God a seat there"!!

Another honorable gentleman who gave his vote in like manner, has published a *specimen of an introductory acknowledgment of a God* such as should have been *in his opinion* prefixed to the Constitution, viz.: *We the people of the United States, in a firm belief of the being and perfections of the one living and true God, the creator and supreme Governor of the world, in His universal providence and the authority of His laws: that He will require of all moral agents an account of their conduct, that all rightful powers among men are ordained of, and mediately derived from God, therefore in a dependence on His blessing and acknowledgment of His efficient protection in establishing our Independence, whereby it is become necessary to agree upon and settle a Constitution of federal government for ourselves*—This introduction is likewise to serve as a religious test, for he says *"instead of none, no other religious test should ever be required, etc."*

In treating of a *being* who is above comprehension there may be a certain degree of propriety in using language that is so; if any reader's brain is too weak to obtain a distinct idea of a writer's meaning, I am sensible it may be retorted that a writer is not obliged to furnish his readers with comprehension. Neither is there any law to oblige him to write comprehensible matter, which is a great comfort to me; as I shall not stop to think, but proceed to give mine opinion! Should any body of men, whose characters were unknown to me, form a plan of government, and prologue it with a long pharisaical harangue about God and religion, I should suspect a design to cheat and circumvent us, and their cant, and semblance of superior sanctity would be the ground of my suspicion. If they have a plan founded on good sense, wisdom, and experience, what occasion have they to make use of God, His providence, or religion, like old cunning monks to gain our assent to what is in itself rational and just? "There must be (tis objected) some proof, some evidence that we the people acknowledge the being of a God." Is this a thing that wants proof? Is this a thing that wants constitutional establishment in the United States? It is almost the only thing that all universally are agreed in; everybody believes there is a God; not a man of common sense in the United States denies or disbelieves it. *The fool hath said in his heart there is no God,* but was there ever a wise man said such a thing? No, not in any age or in any country. Besides, if it was not so, if there were unbelievers, as it is a matter of faith, it might as well be admitted; for we are not to bind the consciences of men by laws or constitutions. The mind is free; it may be convinced by reasoning, but cannot be compelled by laws *or constitutions,* no, nor by fire, faggot, or the halter. Such an acknowledgment is moreover useless *as a religious test*—it is calculated to exclude from office *fools* only, who believe there is no God; and the people of America are now become so enlightened that no fool hereafter (it is hoped) will ever be promoted to any office or high station.

An honorable gentleman objects that God has no seat allowed him. Is this only to find fault with the Constitution because he had no hand in making it? Or is he serious? Would he have given God a seat there? For what purpose? To get a name for sanctity that he might have it in his power to impose on the people? The time has been when nations could be kept in awe with stories of gods sitting with legislators and dictating laws; with this lure, cunning politicians have established their own power on the credulity of the people, shackling their uninformed minds with incredible tales. But the light of philosophy has arisen in these latter days, miracles have ceased, oracles are silenced, monkish darkness is dissipated, and even witches at last hide their heads. Mankind are no longer to be deluded with fable. Making the glory of God subservient to the temporal interest of men is a wornout trick, and a pretense to superior sanctity and special grace will not much longer promote weakness over the head of wisdom.

A low mind may imagine that God, like a foolish old man, will think himself slighted and dishonored if he is not complimented with a seat or a prologue of recognition in the Constitution, but those great philosophers who formed the Constitution had a higher idea of the perfection of that INFINITE MIND which governs all worlds than to suppose they could add to his honor or glory, or that He would be pleased with such low familiarity or vulgar flattery.

The most shining part, the most brilliant circumstance in honor of the framers of the Constitution is their avoiding all appearance of craft, declining to dazzle even the superstitious by a hint about grace or ghostly knowledge. They come to us in the plain language of common sense and propose to our understanding a system of government as the invention of mere human wisdom; no deity comes down to dictate it, not even a God appears in a dream to propose any part of it.

A knowledge of human nature, the aid of philosophy, and the experience of ages are seen in the very face of it; whilst it stands forth like a magnificent STATUE of gold. Yet, there are not wanting FANATICS who would crown it with the periwig of an old monk and wrap it up in a black cloak—whilst *political quackery* is contending to secure it with fetters and decorate it with a leather apron!!

═══════════════════════════════

Letter from Benjamin Rush to Elias Boudinot(?) (July 9, 1788)

In this letter, probably written to the former president of the Continental Congress Elias Boudinot (1740–1821), Dr. Benjamin Rush (1745–1813), a signer of the Declaration of Independence, described a Fourth of July, 1788, procession in Philadelphia and opined on

Excerpts reprinted from *Letters of Benjamin Rush,* ed. L. H. Butterfield (Princeton: Princeton University Press, 1951), 1:470, 474–75. Used by permission of the Adams Manuscript Trust, the Massachusetts Historical Society.

the hand of Divine Providence in crafting the U.S. Constitution.

———————————

My dear Friend,   Philadelphia, 9th July, 1788

Herewith you will receive an account of our late procession in honor of the establishment of the Federal Government. It was drawn up by Judge Hopkinson, a gentleman to whose patriotism, ingenuity, and taste our city is much indebted for the entertainment.

To this account I cannot help adding a few facts and remarks that occurred during the day and which were of too minute or speculative a nature to be introduced in the general account published by order of the committee of arrangement.

The procession gave universal pleasure. Never upon any occasion during the late war did I see such deep-seated joy in every countenance. Foreigners speak of it in the highest terms, and many of them who have seen the splendid processions of coronations in Europe declare that they all yield in the effect of pleasure to our hasty exhibition instituted in honor of our Federal Government. . . .

The Clergy formed a very agreeable part of the procession. They manifested by their attendance their sense of the connection between religion and good government. They amounted to seventeen in number. Four and five of them marched arm in arm with each other to exemplify the Union. Pains were taken to connect ministers of the most dissimilar religious principles together, thereby to show the influence of a free government in promoting Christian charity. The Rabbi of the Jews locked in the arms of two ministers of the gospel was a most delightful sight. There could not have been a more happy emblem contrived of that section of the new Constitution which opens all its power and offices alike not only to every sect of Christians but to worthy men of *every* religion. . . .

I must not forget to mention that the weather proved uncommonly favorable to the entertainment.

The sun was not to be seen till near two o'clock, at which time the procession was over. A pleasant and cooling breeze blew all day from the south, and in the evening the sky was illuminated by a beautiful aurora borealis. Under this head another fact is equally worthy of notice. Notwithstanding the haste in which the machines were made and the manner in which they were drawn through the streets, and notwithstanding the great number of women and children that were assembled on fences, scaffolds, and roofs of the houses to see the procession, *no one* accident happened to anybody. These circumstances gave occasion for hundreds to remark that "Heaven was on the federal side of the question."

It would be ungrateful not to observe that there have been less equivocal signs, in the course of the formation and establishment of this government, of heaven having favored the federal side of the question. The union of twelve states in the *form,* and of ten states in the *adoption,* of the Constitution in less than ten months, under the influence of local prejudices, opposite interests, popular arts, and even the threats of bold and desperate men, is a solitary event in the history of mankind. I do not believe that the Constitution was the offspring of inspiration, but I am as perfectly satisfied that the Union of the States, in its *form* and *adoption,* is as much the work of a Divine Providence as any of the miracles recorded in the Old and New Testament were the effects of a divine power.

'Tis done! We have become a nation. America has ceased to be the only power in the world that has derived no benefit from her declaration of independence. We are more than repaid for the distresses of the war and the disappointments of the peace. The torpid resources of our country already discover signs of life and motion. We are no longer the scoff of our enemies. The reign of violence is over. Justice has descended from heaven to dwell in our land, and ample restitution has at last been made to human nature by our new Constitution for all the injuries she has sustained in the old world from arbitrary government, false religions, and unlawful commerce. . . .

Letter from Benjamin Rush to John Adams (June 15, 1789)

In this June 1789 letter to Vice President John Adams, the venerable Dr. Benjamin Rush of Philadelphia (1745–1813), a signer of the Declaration of Independence, reported the wish of many pious citizens that "the name of the Supreme Being had been introduced somewhere in the new Constitution."

Philadelphia, June 15th, 1789

Dear Sir,

... Many pious people wish the name of the Supreme Being had been introduced somewhere in the new Constitution. Perhaps an acknowledgement may be made of his goodness or of his providence in the proposed amendments. In all enterprises and parties I believe the *praying* are better allies than the *fighting* part of communities.

I am, dear sir, with great regard, your affectionate and steady friend,

Benjn Rush

Excerpt reprinted from *Letters of Benjamin Rush*, ed. L. H. Butterfield (Princeton: Princeton University Press, 1951), 1:516–17. Used by permission of the Adams Manuscript Trust, the Massachusetts Historical Society.

Address of the Presbytery of the Eastward to George Washington (October 28, 1789)

Letter from George Washington to the Presbyterian Ministers of Massachusetts and New Hampshire (November 2, 1789)

In October 1789, a delegation of Presbyterian ministers and ruling elders from Massachusetts and New Hampshire wrote the new president, George Washington. The Presbyterians lamented the absence of "some Explicit acknowledgement of the *only true God and Jesus Christ, whom he hath sent* inserted somewhere in the *Magna Charta* of our country." In his reply, Washington dispelled the notion that the U.S. Constitution's lack of a religious designation or a reference to the deity indicated hostility or indifference toward religion, thereby deftly diffusing a criticism that had nearly derailed the Constitution's ratification.

Address of the Presbytery of the Eastward to George Washington

[28 Oct. 1789]

We the Ministers and ruling Elders delegated to represent the Churches in Massachusetts and New Hampshire which compose the first Presbytery of the eastward, now holding a stated session in this Town, beg leave to approach your presence with genuine feelings of the deepest veneration and highest esteem.

Reprinted from *The Papers of George Washington*, ed. W. W. Abbot and Dorothy Twohig; Presidential Series, vol. 4: *September 1789–January 1790*, ed. Dorothy Twohig (Charlottesville and London: University of Virginia Press, 1993), 275–77. © 1993 The University of Virginia Press. Used by permission of the publisher.

George Washington, by Gilbert Stuart.
© Francis G. Mayer/CORBIS.

We ask the honor of a place among the multitudes of good citizens who are ambitious of expressing the heartfelt satisfaction, with which they bid you welcome to these eastern parts of your government.

In unison with rejoicing millions, we felicitate our country, and ourselves on your unanimous election to the highest office a nation can bestow—and on your acceptance of the trust with every evidence, which a citizen can give of being actuated thereto by the purest principles of patriotism, of piety and of self-denial.

Great was the joy of our hearts to see the late tedious and destructive war terminated in a safe and honorable peace—to see the liberty and independence of our country happily secured—to see wise constitutions of civil government peaceably established in the several States—and especially to see a confederation of them all finally agreed on by the general voice. But amid all our joy, we ever contemplated with regret the want of efficiency in the federal government—we ardently wished for a form of national union which should draw the cord of amity more closely around the several States—which should concentrate their separate interests—and reduce the freemen of *America* to *one* great Body—ruled by *One* head, and animated by one Soul.

And now we devoutly offer our humble tribute of praise and thanksgiving to the all-gracious *Father* of *lights* who has inspired our public Councils with a wisdom and firmness, which have effected that desireable purpose, in so great a measure by the National-Constitution, and who has fixed the eyes of all America on you as the worthiest of its Citizens to be entrusted with the execution of it.

Whatever any may have supposed wanting in the original plan, we are happy to find so wisely providing in its amendments; and it is with peculiar satisfaction we behold how easily the entire confidence of the People, in the Man who sits at the helm of Government, has eradicated every remaining objection to its form.

Among these we never considered the want of *a religious test,* that grand engine of persecution in every tyrant's hand: But we should not have been alone in rejoicing to have seen some Explicit acknowledgement of the *only true God and Jesus Christ, whom he hath sent* inserted some where in the *Magna Charta* of our country.

We are happy to find, however, that this defect has been amply remedied, in the face of all the world, by the piety and devotion, in which your first public act of office was performed—by the religious observance of the Sabbath, and of the public worship of *God,* of which you have set so eminent an example—and by the warm strains of christian and devout affections, which run through your late proclamation, for a general thanksgiving.

The catholic spirit breathed in all your public acts supports us in the pleasing assurance that no religious establishments—no exclusive privileges tending to elevate one denomination of Christians to the depression of the rest, shall ever be ratified by the signature of the *President* during your administration.

On the contrary we bless God that your whole deportment bids all denominations confidently to expect to find in you the watchful guardian of their equal liberties—the steady Patron of genuine christianity—and the bright Exemplar of those peculiar virtues, in which its distinguishing doctrines have their proper effect.

Under the nurturing hand of a Ruler of such virtues, and one so deservedly revered by all ranks, we joyfully indulge the hope that virtue and religion will revive and flourish—that infidelity and the vices ever attendant in its train, will be banished [from] every polite circle; and that rational piety will soon become fashionable there; and from thence be diffused among all other ranks in the community.

Captivated with the delightful prospect of a national reformation rising out of the influence of your authority and example; we find the fullest encouragement to cherish the hope of it, from the signal deeds of pious and patriotic heroism, which marked the steps of the Father of his country, from the memorable hour of his appearance in Congress, to declare the disinterested views, with which he accepted the command of her armies, to that hour, not less memorable, when, having gloriously acquitted himself in that important trust, and completely accomplished the design of it, he appeared in the same great Assembly again; and resigned his commission into the hands that gave it.

But glorious as your course has been as a Soldier in arms, defending your country, and the rights of mankind; we exult in the presage that it will be far outshone by the superior lustre of a more glorious career now before you, as the Chief Magistrate of your nation—protecting, by just and merciful laws—and by a wise, firm, and temperate execution of them, enhancing the value of those inestimable rights and privileges, which you have so worthily asserted to it by your sword.

Permit us then, great Sir, to assure you that whilst it ever shall be our care, in our several places, to inculcate those principles, drawn from the pure fountains of light and truth, in the sacred scriptures, which can best recommend your virtues to their imitation, and which, if generally obeyed, would contribute essentially to render your people happy, and your government prosperous; Our unceasing prayers to the *great Sovereign of all* nations, shall be that your important life, and all your singular talents may be the special care of an indulgent Providence for many years to come; that your administration may be continued to your country, under the peculiar smiles of Heaven, long enough to advance the interests of learning to the zenith—to carry the arts and sciences to their destined perfection—to chace ignorance, bigotry, and immorality off the stage—to restore true virtue, and the religion of *Jesus* to their deserved throne in our land: and to found the liberties of America, both religious and civil, on a basis which no era of futurity shall ever see removed: and, finally, that, when you have thus done—free grace may confer on you, as the reward of all your great labours, the unfading laurels of an everlasting crown.

Letter from George Washington to the Presbyterian Ministers of Massachusetts and New Hampshire

[Portsmouth, N.H., 2 November 1789]

Gentlemen,

The affectionate welcome, which you are pleased to give me to the eastern parts of the union, would leave me without excuse, did I fail to acknowledge the sensibility, which it awakens, and to express the most sincere return that a grateful sense of your goodness can suggest.

Reprinted from *The Papers of George Washington*, ed. W. W. Abbot and Dorothy Twohig; Presidential Series, vol. 4: *September 1789–January 1790*, ed. Dorothy Twohig (Charlottesville and London: University Press of Virginia, 1993), 274. © 1993 The University of Virginia Press. Used by permission of the publisher.

To be approved by the praise-worthy is a wish as natural to becoming ambition, as its consequence is flattering to our self-love—I am, indeed, much indebted to the favorable sentiments which you entertain towards me, and it will be my study to deserve them.

The tribute of thanksgiving which you offer to "the gracious Father of lights" for his inspiration of our public-councils with wisdom and firmness to complete the national constitution, is worthy of men, who, devoted to the pious purposes of religion, desire their accomplishment by such means as advance the temporal happiness of their fellow-men—and, here, I am persuaded, you will permit me to observe that the path of true piety is so plain as to require but little political direction. To this consideration we ought to ascribe the absence of any regulation, respecting religion, from the Magna-Charta of our country.

To the guidance of the ministers of the gospel this important object is, perhaps, more properly committed—It will be your care to instruct the ignorant, and to reclaim the devious—and, in the progress of morality and science, to which our government will give every furtherance, we may confidently expect the advancement of true religion, and the completion of our happiness.

I pray the munificent Rewarder of virtue that your agency in this good work may receive its compensation here and hereafter.

G: Washington

A Discourse, in Two Parts (1812)

President Dwight's Decisions of Questions Discussed by the Senior Class in Yale College, in 1813 and 1814 (1833)

TIMOTHY DWIGHT, JR. (1752–1817)

Timothy Dwight, grandson of Jonathan Edwards, president of Yale College, and Congregationalist minister, represented the view that the U.S. Constitution's failure to acknowledge God was a defect and exposed the nation to divine punishment.

A Discourse, in Two Parts

We formed our Constitution without any acknowledgment of God; without any recognition of his mercies to us, as a people, of his government, or even of his existence. The [Constitutional] Convention, by which it was formed, never asked, even once, his direction, or his blessing upon their labors. Thus we commenced our national existence under the present system, without God. I wish I could say, that a disposition to render him the reverence, *due to his* great *Name,* and the gratitude, demanded by his innumerable mercies, had been more public, visible, uniform, and fervent. . . .

Excerpts reprinted from *A Discourse, in Two Parts* (Utica, N.Y.: Ira Merrill, 1812), 38.

President Dwight's Decisions of Questions Discussed by the Senior Class in Yale College, in 1813 and 1814

It is highly discreditable to us that we do not acknowledge God in our Constitution. Now it is remarkable that the grossest nations and individuals, in their public acts, and in their declarations, manifestoes, proclamations, &c. always recognize the superintendency of a supreme being. Even Napoleon does it. We, however, have neglected to do it. God says: "They who despise me shall be lightly esteemed"; and we have rendered ourselves liable, as a nation, to his displeasure. The corruption which is now rapidly extending in this country, gives reason for apprehension that we are soon to suffer the punishment to which we have exposed ourselves.

Excerpts reprinted from *President Dwight's Decisions of Questions Discussed by the Senior Class in Yale College, in 1813 and 1814* (New York: J. Leavitt; Boston: Crocker & Brewster, 1833), 111–12.

A Scriptural View of the Character, Causes, and Ends of the Present War (1815)

ALEXANDER M'LEOD (1773–1833)

Scottish-born Presbyterian minister and theologian Alexander M'Leod lamented the U.S. Constitution's failure to acknowledge God in *A Scriptural View of the Character, Causes, and Ends of the Present War.* This essay, which is excerpted below, meditated on the causes for the War of 1812.

The public immoralities of the constitution of our federal government, may, although more numerous in detail, be classed under two heads, viz. *Disrespect for God—and violation of human liberty.* By the terms of the national compact, God is not at all acknowledged, and holding men in slavery is authorized. Both these are evils.

1. *God is not acknowledged by the constitution.* In a federative government, erected over several distinct and independent states, retaining each the power of local legislation, it is not to be expected that specific provision should be made for the interests of religion in particular congregations. The general government is erected for the general good of the United States, and especially for the management of their foreign concerns: but no association of men for moral purposes can be justified in an entire neglect of the Sovereign of the world. Statesmen in this country had undoubtedly in their eye the abuse of religion for mere political purposes, which in the nations of the old world, had corrupted the sanctuary, and laid the foundation for the persecution of godly men. The principal writers, upon government, friendly to the cause of civil liberty in the kingdoms of Europe, had generally advocated principles, which, in their application, have led, upon the part of civilians, to a disrespect for religion itself; and these principles had no small influence upon the founders of this republic. This was the case in a remarkable degree with the continental politicians; nor are Sydney and Locke to be entirely exempted from the charge. In the overthrow of those particular establishments, favourable to the church of England, which existed here before the revolution, it was natural, considering the state of religious information in the community, to go to an opposite extreme. But no consideration will justify the framers of the federal constitution, and the administration of the government, in withholding a recognition of *the Lord and his Anointed* from the grand charter of the nation. On our daily bread, we ask a blessing. At our ordinary meals, we acknowledge the Lord of the world. We begin our last testament for disposing of worldly estates, in the name

Reprinted from *A Scriptural View of the Character, Causes, and Ends of the Present War* (New York: Eastburn, Kirk; Whiting and Watson; and Smith and Forman, 1815), 54–56.

of God: and shall we be guiltless, with the bible in our hands, to disclaim the christian religion as a body politic?* . . .

* If it be true, as has been asserted, by men who had the opportunity of knowing the fact, that Benjamin Franklin proposed, in the [constitutional] convention, the introduction into the constitution, of an article professing submission to the Lord, and that he was overruled, the sin and the reproach on the part of his opponents is the greater. It is certainly true, that an administration, often said to be more friendly to christianity, than that which has recently existed, has disclaimed that religion in the following words: viz. *"The government of the United States is not, in any sense, founded on the christian religion. It has in itself, no character of enmity against the laws or religion of Mussulmen."*
Tripoli Treaty, Art. 11. U.S. Laws, Vol. IV.
This treaty, ratified in the year 1797, was thereby made the supreme law of the land. *Const. Art. 6. Sect.* 2. In a discourse published in 1803, the author has vindicated *Christ's power over the nations.*

Prince Messiah's Claims to Dominion over All Governments (1832)

JAMES R. WILLSON (1780 – 1853)

James R. Willson, a Reformed Presbyterian clergyman and theologian, denounced the U.S. Constitution for its inattention to God and Christian principles. His criticisms of the Constitution in *Prince Messiah's Claims to Dominion over All Governments*, excerpted below, provoked great debate and even public burnings of the tract when it was published.

Prince Messiah's Claims to Dominion over All Governments: and the Disregard of His Authority by the United States, in the Federal Constitution

I. *In the theory of the government.*

1. Atheists, Deists, Jews, Pagans, and profane men, of the most abandoned manners, are as eligible to office by the United States constitution, as men fearing God and hating covetousness. Its words are:—"No religious test shall ever be required as a qualification to any office or public trust under the United States." U.S. Con. art. VI. sec. III. God's law is:—"Elect able men, such as fear God, men of truth, hating covetousness."* "He that ruleth over men must be just, ruling in the fear of God."† This command of Jehovah prescribes, at least, *Three Religious Tests,* in these words.

1. "Fearers of God"—those who worship him. How shall we know that any man fears God, unless he makes a profession of his faith in Christ?

2. *"Men of truth"*—such as are sound in the faith, not mere professors of religion—for the Pagan professes to fear God; but one who receives the true gospel of God.

3. "Hating covetousness"—"just men" in their dealings—men who perform the duties enjoined in the second table of the law—not profane swearers, Sabbath breakers, card players, and libertines. This is common sense too. What can be more absurd than to set over a nation as rulers, men who hate God, men of lies, and lovers of covetousness? But the constitution says expressly, that what God commands, shall not be done. This is surely a very great and direct moral evil in the constitution. The constitution, in effect, says to Prince Messiah, your command is, that your friends shall be entrusted with power; but it shall not be done. Your enemies are as competent to bear rule, as your friends.

2. There is no recognition of the law of God, in the instrument which gives the nation its national organization.—The law of God is not named, and there is not any allusion to such a law, so far as the writer

Reprinted from *Prince Messiah's Claims to Dominion over All Governments, and the Disregard of His Authority by the United States, in the Federal Constitution* (Albany: Packard, Hoffman and White, 1832), 21–26.
* Exodus 18:21.—Eds.
† II Samuel 23:3.—Eds.

has perceived, except in two instances. The one is in these words:—"I do solemnly swear (or affirm) that I will faithfully execute the office of President of the United States." Art. II. sec. I. specification VIII. Here there is an allusion to the third commandment; or at least to the declaration, "An oath for confirmation is an end of all strife."* It is pleasant to a lover of the Lord's law, to find even this remote allusion. But was it intended to honor the law of the Lord, as recorded in the Holy Scriptures? However agreeable to the benevolent heart to think so, we are constrained to think not. The affirmation will pass for the oath. Many infidels swear oaths in courts, without intending to admit the truth of the Scriptures, or to honor Messiah. Infidels were known at the time when the constitution was framed, to swear oaths of office, and to swear as witnesses. Heathens are known to have sworn very solemnly by Jove, Hercules, &c. The mere swearing is not at all distinctive of Paganism, Mahometanism, or of Christianity.

The other instance occurs, Art. I. sec. VII. specification II. "If any bill shall not be returned by the President within ten days (Sundays excepted) after it shall have been presented," &c. This implies that governmental business may be omitted on the Sabbath. The constitution would not compel the President to spend the Sabbath in examining bills. He may, if he chooses, have that day for devotion. As a matter of fact, such was the influence of Christianity in the nation, that congressional, judiciary, and executive proceedings were suspended on the Lord's day. The constitution did not enjoin its violation by the executive. But its binding force is not affirmed even by fair implication. The suspension of the legislative business, the closing of the federal courts, and the President's not issuing proclamations, on the first day of the week, with the hiring of a chaplain by Congress, do not altogether amount to a recognition of the law of God, much less of the Christian religion. Thousands of professed deists, men who regard the

whole Bible as a fabrication of priestcraft, do close their shops and offices on the Sabbath, hire preachers, and go to church on that holy day, without at all intending to pledge themselves to Christianity. The mention of Sunday in this connection, is a mere accommodation to popular sentiment.

It is, indeed, astonishing, that in a Christian commonwealth, where the great majority of the citizens were attached to some Protestant church, a constitution of government could have been framed, with only two very remote and indirect *allusions merely* to the law and Bible of God. The fact demonstrates, how very careful the framers were to avoid every word, that might be construed into a declaration of respect to the statutes of Jehovah.

That the national functionaries have so understood it all along, appears from the reports made by Col. Johnston,† both in the Senate and in the House of Representatives; and from the fact that Congress made the doctrine of the reports, national principles; for they, on the reasons assigned, refused to stop the mail. The essence of both these reports is, that the law of God does not bind the government of the United States, and that to admit the obligation of the statutes of Jehovah, would be (*horresco referens*) a monstrous evil. Truly, Messiah is a merciful Prince.

3. The "King of Kings and Lord of Lords" is not acknowledged, by the remotest allusion, to the claims of his holy government. Hence the nation says:—"We will not have this man to reign over us."‡ A fundamental theory, or maxim on which the convention proceeded, rendered such an acknowledgment impossible. The maxim is this—"all men, whatever may be their religious, or irreligious tenets, have an equal right to participate in the civil privileges of the commonwealth." There were infidels in the convention—at present, it is sufficient to mention Dr. Franklin and Mr. Madison. Had there been any act of homage to

---

* Hebrews 6:16.—Eds.

† Col. Richard M. Johnston.—Eds.

‡ Luke 19:14.—Eds.

Messiah, Lord of all, it would have excluded every infidel, Jew and Pagan, from all those offices, to which an oath to the constitution was annexed.

To have honored Christ, would have introduced a religious test. The utter exclusion of any moral qualifications or test, rendered it impossible to acknowledge either Messiah the King, or the Christian religion, without self-contradiction.—As the right to reign and the duty of obedience are correlates, it is certainly true, since Messiah is the Prince of the kings of the earth, that the national constitution is sinful in refusing this allegiance.

However infidels may rage, and imagine a vain thing,* they that love the Saviour of sinners, and wish to honor the Son of God who died to save them, will mourn over the dishonor which has been done to their Lord and King, by this nation.

4. *The constitution positively declares that nothing shall be done by the government for the advancement of the Christian religion.* "Congress shall make no law respecting an establishment of religion." Amendments, Art. i. The words are not Congress shall not *establish* any religion; but "no law *respecting* the establishment of religion." Whatever has any *respect* to religion, or *tends* to give it stability, is prohibited by this article. Any act of homage to Almighty God, is religion. Any law that would encourage or countenance an act of homage to Jehovah, would tend to the establishment of religion.—Here, then, is an institution which some men say is an ordinance of God, but which does solemnly disclaim the doctrine of being ordained by him; and which formally proclaims that it will not do any thing to promote the glory of his holy name. What should we say of the ambassador of a nation, who would publicly announce his intention to do no act for promoting the honor of those whom he represents? We have the promise of our God, that in New Testament times it shall be otherwise: "Kings shall be thy nursing fathers, and their Queens thy nursing mothers; they shall bow down to thee, with their face toward the earth, and lick up the dust of thy

feet."† On the theory of the U.S. Constitution, this cannot take place.

Why treat thus all religion? Why disfranchise, by a solemn act, the church of the living God? Is the benevolent, pure, holy, heaven-born religion of Emmanuel, hostile to the happiness of the republic? Shall commerce, agriculture, the arts, literature—all the other lawful pursuits, be countenanced, fostered, protected, and established, on as permanent a basis, as possible, and the true religion be put under the ban of the empire? But, they say, let religion alone. Do they, however, adopt the *laisez nous faire* [leave us be], in relation to manufactures and trade? No. We cherish all, but respecting the advancement of religion, congress shall never do any thing. When the child is born, were the father and mother to say, *laisez l'infant faire*—leave the babe to itself—would that be to act as a nursing father and mother? Surely no. There must be a far different kind of constitution among the nations, when the promise is fulfilled, that "Kings shall be nursing fathers."—God Almighty says, in the text quoted above, that civil rulers *shall* nurse the church—the Constitution says they *shall not.* Which is right? "Ah! sinful nation, laden with iniquity."‡ God spares the world for the sake of his redeemed, that his moral subjects on earth may be, by the gospel of his son, reclaimed from sin and rebellion—that on the earth, through his own holy religion, he may expatiate the glories of redemption. The constitution says religion shall be discountenanced by the Congress of the United States.

5. *There is no acknowledgment of Almighty God, nor any, even the most remote, token of national subjection to Jehovah, the Creator.* It is believed, that there never existed, previous to this constitution, any national deed like this, since the creation of the world. A nation having no God! In vain shall we search the annals of pagan Greece and Rome, of modern Asia, Africa, pagan America, and the isles of the sea—they have all worshipped some God. The United States have

---

* Psalm 2:1; Acts 4:25.—Eds.

† Isaiah 49:23.—Eds.
‡ Isaiah 1:4.—Eds.

none.—But here let us pause over this astounding fact. Was it a mere omission? Did the convention that framed the constitution *forget* to name the living God? Was this an omission in some moment of national phrenzy, when the nation forgot God? That, indeed, were a great sin. God says, "the nations that *forget* God, shall be turned into hell."* It was not, however, a thoughtless act, an undesigned omission. It was a deliberate deed, whereby God was rejected; and in the true atheistical spirit of the whole instrument, and of course, done with intent to declare national independence of the Lord of hosts. We have seen that the convention was convened to correct what was thought to be improper in the old articles of confederation. These articles were ratified 1778, July 9th. The enacting clause has these words:—"And whereas, it hath pleased the great Governor of the world, to incline the hearts of the legislatures, we respectively represent in Congress, to approve of the said articles of confederation—know ye, that we entirely ratify," &c. Here the formal reason of the ratification is, that the great Governor of the world inclined the hearts of the state legislatures to adopt the instrument. This did acknowledge Jehovah. Deists could unite, and Deists did unite in this deed; for there was no recognition of Messiah. Among the Deists, who subscribed these articles, we find Thomas McKean and Doct. Franklin. It was a radical defect in that deed, that the Lord Jesus was not recognized as Sovereign of the United States. It was a perilous period of our history, and perhaps even Deists had some faint knowledge of the nation's need of the divine aid.

When, on the 17th of December, 1787, nine years, three months and eight days after the ratification of the old Articles, the present U.S. Constitution was adopted; there is no allusion to "the *Great Governor of the Universe.*" Can any man believe, that the name of the Lord God was thus expunged, without agreement by learned men, who examined every thing? No. But we have evidence that God was formally and solemnly rejected. "Franklin," it is said, by men who had an opportunity of knowing, "proposed in the convention, the introduction, into the Constitution, of an article professing submission to the Lord, and he was overruled."† Doct. Franklin was notoriously a Deist, and those who overruled his motion, must have been worse than Deists—even Atheists. Can any man doubt that they were "without God," or Atheists? Who, of them all, gave any decisive evidence of their being Christians, except William Few? I do not speak certainly. But a biography of the members of that convention, as to their *fearing God,* would not, it is believed, add much to the moral honor of our country.

When the country was plainly in peril, and the arm of Jehovah perceived to be necessary for our defence, then the God of creation was acknowledged. But when he had conducted our armies to victory, and set our country free from the oppression of foreign despotism—then with a blackness of ingratitude, and an atheistical impiety, his name was erased from the fundamental law of the empire. There was still another aggravation of this national sin. After, as is affirmed, I think, on good authority, the convention had been some days in session, and was rent by the most violent passions, with little, perhaps no prospect of success in forming a constitution, it was proposed by Franklin, and resolved to open the sessions by prayer to God. The business, from the adoption of that measure, proceeded with some degree of harmony. After such a demonstration of the presence and mercy of the Lord, was it not enough, (as Doct. Mason,‡ of New-York, said in another case,) *"to make the Devil blush,"* that they proceeded deliberately to blot his name from the constitution?

Of the convention, in this and not a few other transactions, it may be said, in scripture style, "They did not that which was right in the sight of the Lord." . . .

---

* Psalm 9:17.—Eds.

† Sermons on the late war, by the Rev. Dr. M'Leod, of New-York, pp. 56, 57. See the Manuscript Minutes of the Convention.

‡ Dr. John Mitchell Mason.—Eds.

A Brief Exposition of the Constitution of the United States (1833)

JAMES A. BAYARD, JR. (1799–1880)

James Bayard, Jr., of Delaware, a U.S. senator and attorney, offered explanations for the U.S. Constitution's failure to recognize the existence and providence of God in his much-respected commentary on the Constitution.

To add the sanction of religious obligation, to this supremacy of the general government, the senators and representatives of the Union, and the members of the several State legislatures, and all executive and judicial officers, both of the United States and of the several States, are bound by oath or affirmation, to support this Constitution. The Constitution of the Union is thus incorporated into, and made an essential part of the Constitution of each State; so that every department of the State government is to submit to it, and acknowledge its authority; and a State legislature, or executive, acting in opposition to it, violates the will of its constituents, as directly as if it disregarded its own particular Constitution.

"But no religious test shall ever be required as a qualification to any office or public trust under the United States." The people of the United States were so fully aware of the evils which arise from the union of Church and State, and so thoroughly convinced of its corrupting influence, upon both religion and government, that they introduced this prohibition into the fundamental law.

It has been made an objection to the Constitution, by some, that it makes no mention of religion, contains no recognition of the existence and providence of God; as though his authority were slighted or disregarded. But such is not the reason of the omission. The convention, which framed the Constitution, comprised some of the wisest and best men in the nation; men who were firmly persuaded, not only of the divine origin of the Christian religion, but also, of its importance to the temporal and eternal welfare of men. The people, too, of this country, were generally impressed with religious feelings; and felt, and acknowledged, the superintendence of God, who had protected them through the perils of war, and blessed their exertions to obtain civil and religious freedom. But there were reasons why the introduction of religion into the Constitution, would have been unseasonable, if not improper.

In the first place, it was intended exclusively for *civil* purposes, and religion could not be regularly mentioned, because it made no part of the agreement between the parties. They were about to surrender a portion of their civil rights, for the security of the remainder; but each retained his religious freedom, entire and untouched, as a matter between himself and his God, with which government could not interfere. But even if this reason had not existed, it would have been difficult, if not impossible, to use any expression on this subject, which would have given general satisfaction. The difference between the various sects of Christians is such, that while all have much in common, there are many points of variance; so that in an instrument, where all are entitled to equal consideration, it would be difficult to use terms in which all could cordially join. Besides, the whole Constitution was a compromise, and it was foreseen that it would meet with great opposition, before it would be finally adopted. It was therefore important to restrict its provisions to things absolutely necessary, so as to give as little room as possible to cavil. Moreover, it was impossible to introduce into it, even an expression of gratitude to the Almighty, for the formation of the present government; for when the Constitution was framed, and submitted to the people, it was entirely uncertain whether it would ever be ratified, and the government might, therefore, never be established.

Excerpt reprinted from *A Brief Exposition of the Constitution of the United States*, 2nd ed. (Philadelphia: Hogan & Thompson, 1845), 141–43.

The prohibition of any religious test for office was wise, because its admission would lead to hypocrisy and corruption. The purity of religion is best preserved by keeping it separate from government; and the surest means of giving to it, its proper influence in society, is by the dissemination of correct principles, through the medium of education. The experience of this country has proved, that religion may flourish in all its vigour and purity, without the aid of a national establishment; and the religious feeling of the community is the best guarantee for the religious administration of government.

RECOMMENDATIONS FOR FURTHER READING

Dreisbach, Daniel L. "In Search of a Christian Commonwealth: An Examination of Selected Nineteenth-Century Commentaries on References to God and the Christian Religion in the United States Constitution." *Baylor Law Review* 48 (1996): 927–1000.

Kramnick, Isaac, and R. Laurence Moore. *The Godless Constitution: The Case Against Religious Correctness.* New York: W. W. Norton, 1996.

CHAPTER EIGHT

The Religious Test Ban of the U.S. Constitution

THE FIRST AMENDMENT is not the only constitutional provision that substantively addresses religious concerns. Article VI, clause 3, of the original Constitution, drafted by the Philadelphia Convention of 1787 and ratified by the states in 1788, includes a clause that provides: "no religious Test shall ever be required as a Qualification to any Office or public Trust under the United States." This provision followed language in Article VI instructing all national and state officeholders to take an oath or affirmation to support the Constitution.

The genesis of the ban on religious tests was a proposal purportedly offered by South Carolina delegate Charles Pinckney at the Constitutional Convention in May 1787, which stated that "[t]he Legislature of the United States shall pass no Law on the subject of Religion."[1] This measure in the so-called Pinckney Plan was not acted upon immediately. Pinckney opined that "the prevention of Religious Tests, as qualifications to Offices of Trust or Emolument . . . [, is] a provision the world will expect from you, in the establishment of a System founded on Republi-

can Principles, and in an age so liberal and enlightened as the present."[2]

Three months later, on August 20, Pinckney once again broached the subject. This time he moved to add the following clause: "No religious test or qualification shall ever be annexed to any oath of office under the authority of the United States." The proposal was referred to a committee without further recorded deliberation or action. Ten days later, on August 30, during debate on qualifications for federal office and employment, the religious test ban was once again placed on the table at Pinckney's insistence. In deference to Quakers and some other sects, the convention discussed adding the words "or affirmation" after the word "oath" in an oath clause. Pinckney then moved to join the test ban with the proposed "oath or affirmation" clause; the motion was the subject of a brief debate. James Madison reported that Roger Sherman of Connecticut "thought [the ban] unnecessary, the prevailing liberality being a sufficient security [against] such tests." Gouverneur Morris of Pennsylvania and General Charles Cotesworth Pinckney of South Carolina (the other Pinckney's second cousin) both voiced support for the motion in unreported speeches. Pinckney's motion was agreed to *nemine contradicente* [with no one oppos-

---

1. Max Farrand, ed., *The Records of the Federal Convention of 1787*, rev. ed., 4 vols. (New Haven, Conn.: Yale University Press, 1937), 3:599; Jonathan Elliot, ed., *The Debates in the Several State Conventions on the Adoption of the Federal Constitution*, 2nd ed., 5 vols. (Philadelphia: J. B. Lippincott, 1859), 5:131 (May 29, 1787); ibid., 1:148.

2. Farrand, ed., *Records of the Federal Convention*, 3:122.

ing]. The convention then gave its approval to "the whole Article." According to Madison's notes, North Carolina alone opposed it, and Maryland was divided. The *Convention Journal,* however, perhaps taking Sherman's comments into account, reported that the Connecticut delegation was also divided on the proposal. The article, as approved, was forwarded to the Committee on Style, which crafted the final language incorporated into Article VI of the Constitution.

The provision generated energetic debate among the general public and in the state ratifying conventions. A recurring theme was that moral restraint fostered by the Christian religion was essential to social order and civic virtue. The ban on religious tests, opponents said, suggested an inattentiveness to the vital requirement of a society to ordain moral rulers committed to protecting and assisting public morals, as well as religion. Once it is conceded that not all religions are conducive to good government and social stability, then there are plausible grounds for excluding adherents of some religions from public office, opponents argued. Proponents of a federal religious test ban framed the debate in terms of religious liberty. Oliver Ellsworth, a Connecticut Federalist and delegate at the Constitutional Convention, offered a succinct defense of the test ban: "my countrymen, the sole purpose and effect of it is to exclude persecution, and to secure to you the important right of religious liberty."

For centuries, religious test oaths have been a favored instrument for preserving ecclesiastical establishments. Accordingly, modern commentators often describe the test ban as the cornerstone of the secular state and a constitutional expression of church-state separation. Interestingly, however, religious liberty and nonestablishment provisions coexisted with religious test oaths in many state constitutions of the founding era, indicating that the founding generation did not consider these concepts incompatible. Moreover, the inclusion of religious tests in many state constitutions of the era suggests that they conformed to popular wishes. An alternative interpretation is that the federal test ban was not driven by a general denunciation of religious tests as a matter of principle. Indeed, there were delegates at the Constitutional Convention who endorsed the Article VI test ban and had previously participated in crafting religious tests for their state constitutions. Their support for the federal test ban was, perhaps, rooted in the principle of federalism which denied the national government all jurisdiction in religious matters, including the authority to administer religious tests. There was a consensus that religion was a matter best left to the individual citizen and to their respective state governments. Some founders arguably supported a federal test ban because they valued religious tests required under state laws, and they feared a federal test might displace existing state test oaths and religious establishments. Even among the most ardent proponents of Article VI, few denied the advantage of placing citizens with strong religious values in public office. The issues warmly debated were federalism and the efficacy of a national religious test for attaining this objective.

Letter from Benjamin Franklin to Richard Price (October 9, 1780)

Both Benjamin Franklin (1706–90) and his correspondent Richard Price (1723–91), a Welsh-born nonconformist minister and moral philosopher, opposed religious test oaths. This letter was written in the wake of public debates concerning such measures in the Massachusetts Constitution of 1780.

Dear Sir,   Passy, Oct. 9. 1780

Besides the Pleasure of their Company, I had the great Satisfaction of hearing by your two valuable Friends, & learning from your Letter, that you enjoy a good State of Health. May God continue it as well for the Good of Mankind as for your Comfort. I thank you much for the second Edition of your excellent Pamphlet. I forwarded that you sent to Mr. Dana, he being in Holland.—I wish also to see the Piece you have written as Mr Jones tells me, on Toleration.—I do not expect that your new Parliament will be either wiser or honester than the last. All Projects to procure an Honest one, by Place Bills, &c appear to me vain and Impracticable. The true Cure I imagine is to be found only in rendring all Places unprofitable, and the King too poor to give Bribes & Pensions. Till this is done, which can only be by a Revolution, and I think you have not Virtue enough left to procure one, your Nation will always be plundered; & obliged to pay by Taxes the Plunderers for Plundering & Ruining. Liberty & Virtue therefore join in the Call, COME OUT OF HER, MY PEOPLE! I am fully of your Opinion respecting Religious

Tests; but tho' the People of Massachusetts have not in their new Constitution kept quite clear of them; yet if we consider what that People were 100 Years ago, we must allow they have gone great Lengths in Liberality of Sentiment, on religious Subjects; and we may hope for greater Degrees of Perfection when their Constitution some years hence shall be revised. If Christian Preachers had continued to teach as Christ & his Apostles did, without Salaries, and as the Quakers now do, I imagine Tests would never have existed: For I think they were invented not so much to secure Religion itself, as the Emoluments of it.—When a Religion is good, I conceive that it will support itself; and when it cannot support itself, and God does not take care to support, so that its Professors are oblig'd to call for the help of the Civil Power, 'tis a Sign, I apprehend, of its being a bad one. But I shall be out of my Depth if I wade any deeper in Theology, & I will not trouble you with Politicks, nor with News which are almost as uncertain: But conclude with a heartfelt Wish, to embrace you once more, & enjoy your sweet Society in Peace, among our honest, worthy, ingenious Friends at the London.

Adieu

On Test Laws, Oaths of Allegiance and Abjuration, and Partial Exclusions from Office (March 1787)

NOAH WEBSTER (1758–1843)

Noah Webster, who went on to great fame as an educator and lexicographer, denounced test laws in this brief essay written prior to the Constitutional Con-

Reprinted from *The Papers of Benjamin Franklin*, vol. 33: *July 1 through November 15, 1780*, ed. Barbara B. Oberg (New Haven and London: Yale University Press, 1997), 389–90. Used by permission of Yale University's Sterling Memorial Library.

Excerpt reprinted from Noah Webster, Jun., *A Collection of Essays and Fugitiv Writings: On Moral, Historical, Political and Literary Subjects* (Boston: I. Thomas and E. T. Andrews, 1790), 151–53.

vention of 1787. Webster was a close observer of the Convention and became a dedicated supporter of the proposed national Constitution.

━━━━━━━━━━━━━━━━━

Philadelphia, March, 1787

On Test Laws, Oaths *of* Allegiance *and* Abjuration, *and* Partial Exclusions *from* Office

To change the current of opinion, is a most difficult task, and the attempt is often ridiculed. For this reason, I expect the following remarks will be passed over with a slight reading, and all attention to them cease with a hum.

The revisal of the test law has at length passed by a respectable majority of the Representativs of this State. This is a prelude to wiser measures; people are just awaking from delusion. The time will come (and may the day be near!) when all test laws, oaths of allegiance, abjuration, and partial exclusions from civil offices, will be proscribed from this land of freedom.

Americans! what was the origin of these discriminations? What is their use?

They originated in savage ignorance, and they are the instruments of slavery. Emperors and generals, who wished to attach their subjects to their persons and government; who wished to exercise despotic sway over them, or prosecute villanous wars, (for mankind have always been butchering each other) found the solemnity of oaths had an excellent effect on poor superstitious soldiers and vassals; oracles, demons, eclipses; all the terrifying phenomena of nature, have at times had remarkable effects in securing the obedience of men to tyrants. Oaths of fealty, and farcical ceremonies of homage, were very necessary to rivet the chains of feudal vassals; for the whole system of European tenures was erected on jurisdiction, and is supported solely by ignorance, superstition, artifice, or military force. Oaths of allegiance may possibly be still necessary in Europe, where there are so many contending powers contiguous to each other: But what is their use in America? To secure fidelity to the State, it will be answered. But where is the danger of defection? Will the inhabitants join the British in Nova Scotia or Canada? Will they rebel? Will they join the savages, and overthrow the State? No; all these are visionary dangers. My countrymen, if a State has any thing to fear from its inhabitants, the constitution or the laws must be wrong. Danger cannot possibly arise from any other cause.

Permit me to offer a few ideas to your minds; and let them be the subject of more than one hour's reflection.

An oath creates no new obligation. A witness, who swears to tell the whole truth, is under no new obligation to tell the whole truth. An oath reminds him of his duty; he swears to do as he ought to do; that is, he adds an express promise to an implied one. A moral obligation is not capable of addition or diminution.

When a man steps his foot into a State, he becomes subject to its general laws. When he joins it as a member, he is subject to all its laws. The act of entering into society, binds him to submit to its laws, and to promote its interest. Every man, who livs under a government, is under allegiance to that government. Ten thousand oaths do not increase the obligation upon him to be a faithful subject.

But, it will be asked, how shall we distinguish between the friends and enemies of the government? I answer, by annihilating all distinctions. A good constitution, and good laws, make good subjects. I challenge the history of mankind to produce an instance of bad subjects under a good government. The test law in Pensylvania has produced more disorder, by making enemies in this State, than have cursed all the union besides. During the war, every thing gave way to force; but the feelings and principles of war ought to be forgotten in peace.

Abjuration! a badge of folly, borrowed from the dark ages of bigotry. If the government of Pennsylvania is better than that of Great Britain, the subjects will prefer it, and abjuration is perfectly nugatory. If not, the subject will have his partialities in spite of any solemn renunciation of a foreign power.

But what right has even the Legislature to deprive any class of citizens of the benefits and emoluments of civil government? If any men have forfeited their lives or estates, they are no longer subjects; they ought to be banished or hung. If not, no law ought to exclude them from civil emoluments. If any have committed public crimes, they are punishable; if any have been guilty, and have not been detected, the oath, as it now stands, obliges them to confess their guilt. To take the oath, is an implicit acknowledgement of innocence; to refuse it, is an implicit confession that the person has aided and abetted the enemy. This is rank despotism. The inquisition can do no more than force confession from the accused.

I pray God to enlighten the minds of the Americans. I wish they would shake off every badge of tyranny. Americans!—The best way to make men honest, is to let them enjoy equal rights and privileges; never suspect a set of men will be rogues, and make laws proclaiming that suspicion. Leave force to govern the wretched vassals of European nabobs, and reconcile subjects to your own constitutions by their excellent nature and beneficial effects. No man will commence enemy to a government which givs him as many privileges as his neighbors enjoy.

Records of the Constitutional Convention of 1787

The records of the Constitutional Convention of 1787 reveal the evolution of the texts of both the Article VI, clause 3, oath clause and the religious test ban.

Records of the Constitutional Convention of 1787, excerpts. Reprinted from *The Records of the Federal Convention of 1787*, ed. Max Farrand, rev. ed. (New Haven and London: Yale University Press, 1966), vols. 1 and 2.

The following excerpts, drawing on the Convention Journal and notes taken by delegates James Madison, William Paterson, and Robert Yates, are recorded in Max Farrand's *The Records of the Federal Convention of 1787* (hereafter *Records*).

━━━━━━━━━━━━━━━━━━━━━━

Records, 1:22; Madison, May 29
[Resolution proposed by Mr. Randolph in Convention]

14. Resd. that the Legislative Executive & Judiciary powers within the several States ought to be bound by oath to support the articles of Union

Records, 1:28; Paterson, May 29
Governor Randolph's Propositions

5. That the leg. ex. and judy. Officers should be bound by Oath to observe the Union.

Records, 1:122; Madison, June 5

propos. 14. "*requiring oath from the State officers to support national Govt.*" was postponed after a short uninteresting conversation; ⟨the votes, Con. N. Jersey. Md. Virg: S.C. Geo. ay
   N.Y. Pa. Del. N.C. . . . . no
   Massachusetts. . . . divided⟩[1]

Records, 1:194; Journal, June 11

It was then moved and seconded to agree to the 14 resolution submitted by Mr Randolph namely

"Resolved that the legislative, executive, and judiciary powers within the several States ought to be bound by oath to support the articles of union"

It was then moved by Mr Martin seconded by

---

1. Vote taken from Journal.

to strike out the words "within the several States"

and on the question to strike out.

it passed in the negative [Ayes—4; noes—7.] It was then moved and seconded to agree to the 14th resolution as submitted by Mr. Randolph

And on the question to agree to the same.

it passed in the affirmative [Ayes—6; noes—5.]

Records, 1:203–4; Madison, June 11

⟨Resolution 14.⟩ requiring oaths from the ⟨members of the State Govts.⟩ to observe the Natl. Constitution ⟨& laws, being⟩ considered.

Mr. Sharman opposed it as unnecessarily intruding into the State jurisdictions.

Mr. Randolph considered ⟨it⟩ as necessary to prevent that competition between the National Constitution & laws & those of the particular States, which had already been felt. The officers of the States are already under oath to the States. To preserve a due impartiality they ought to be equally bound to the Natl. Govt. The Natl. authority needs every support we can give it. The Executive & Judiciary of the States, notwithstanding their nominal independence on the State Legislatures are in fact, so dependent on them, that unless they be brought under some tie ⟨to⟩ the Natl. system, they will always lean too much to the State systems, whenever a contest arises between the two.

Mr. Gerry did not like the clause. He thought there was as much reason for requiring an oath of fidelity to the States, from Natl. officers, as vice. versa.

Mr. Luther Martin moved to strike out the ⟨words⟩ requiring such an oath from the State Officers ⟨viz "within the several States."⟩ observing that if the new oath should be contrary to that already taken ⟨by them⟩ it would be improper; if coincident the oaths already taken will be sufficient.

On the question for striking out as proposed by Mr. L. Martin

Massts. no. Cont. ay. N.Y. no. N.J. ay. Pa. no. Del. ay. Md. ay. Va. no. N.C. no. S.C. no. Geo. no. [Ayes—4; noes—7.]

Question on whole ⟨Resolution as proposed by Mr. Randolph;⟩

Massts. ay. Cont. no. N.Y. no. N.J. no. Pa. ay. Del. no. Md. no. Va. ay. N.C. ay. S.C. ay. Geo. ay. [Ayes—6; noes—5.]

Records, 1:207; Yates, June 11

Mr. Williamson. This resolve will be unnecessary, as the union will become the law of the land.

Governor Randolph. He supposes it to be absolutely necessary. Not a state government, but its officers will infringe on the rights of the national government. If the state judges are not sworn to the observance of the new government, will they not judicially determine in favor of their state laws? We are erecting a supreme national government; ought it not to be supported, and can we give it too many sinews?

Mr. Gerry rather supposes that the national legislators ought to be sworn to preserve the state constitutions, as they will run the greatest risk to be annihilated—and therefore moved it.

For Mr. Gerry's amendment, 7 ayes, 4 noes.

Main question then put on the clause or resolve—6 ayes, 5 noes. New-York in the negative.

Records, 1:227; Journal, June 13
[State of the resolutions submitted to the consideration of the House by Mr. Randolph, as agreed to in a Committee of the whole House.]

Resolved that the Legislative, Executive, and judiciary powers within the several States ought to be bound by oath to support the articles of union

Records, 1:237; Madison, June 13
[Report of the Committee of Whole on Mr. Randolph's propositions.]

18. Resd. that the Legislative, Executive, & Judiciary powers within the several States ought to be bound by oath to support the articles of Union

Records, 2:84; Journal, July 23

It was moved and seconded to add after the word "States" in the 18 resolution, the words "and of the national government"

    which passed in the affirmative

On the question to agree to the 18th resolution as amended namely

    "That the legislative, Executive, and Judiciary Powers within the several States, and of the national Government, ought to be bound by oath to support the articles of union"

Records, 2:87–88; Madison, July 23

    Resoln. 18. "requiring the Legis: Execut: & Judy. of the States to be bound by oath to support the articles of Union". taken into consideration.

    Mr. Williamson suggests that a reciprocal oath should be required from the National officers, to support the Governments of the States.

    Mr. Gerry moved to insert as an amendmt. that the oath of the Officers of the National Government also should extend to the support of the Natl. Govt. which was agreed to nem. con.

    Mr. Wilson said he was never fond of oaths, considering them as a left handed security only. A good Govt. did not need them. and a bad one could not or ought not to be supported. He was afraid they might too much trammel the Members of the Existing Govt in case future alterations should be necessary; and prove an obstacle to Resol: 17. just agd. to.

    Mr. Ghorum did not know that oaths would be of much use; but could see no inconsistency between them and the 17. Resol: or any regular amendt. of the Constitution. The oath could only require fidelity to the existing Constitution. A constitutional alteration of the Constitution, could never be regarded as a breach of the Constitution, or of any oath to support it.

    Mr Gerry thought with Mr. Ghorum there could be no shadow of inconsistency in the case. Nor could he see any other harm that could result from the Res-

olution. On the other side he thought one good effect would be produced by it. Hitherto the officers of ⟨the two⟩ Governments had considered them as distinct from, not as parts of the General System, & had in all cases of interference given a preference to the State Govts. The proposed oaths will cure that error.—

    The Resoln. (18). was agreed to nem. con.—

Records, 2:334–35; Journal, August 20

It was moved and seconded to refer the following propositions to the Committee of five. . . .

    No religious test or qualification shall ever be annexed to any oath of office under the authority of the United States:

Records, 2:340–41; Madison, August 20

Mr. Pinkney submitted sundry propositions—. . . 8. forbidding religious tests. . . .—these were referred to the Committee of detail for consideration & report.

Records, 2:461; Journal, August 30

It was moved or seconded to add the words "or affirmation" after the word "oath" 20 article

    which passed in the affirmative.

On the question to agree to the 20 article as amended it passed in the affirmative [Ayes—8; noes—1; divided—2.]

It was moved and seconded to add the following clause to the 20 Article.

    "But no religious test shall ever be required as a qualification to any office or public trust under the authority of the United States"

    which passed unan: in the affirmative

Records, 2:468; Madison, August 30

    Art: XX. taken up.—"or affirmation" was added after "oath."

    Mr. Pinkney. moved to add to the art:—"but no religious test shall ever be required as a qualification to any office or public trust under the authority of the U. States"

Mr. Sherman thought it unnecessary, the prevailing liberality being a sufficient security agst. such tests.

Mr. Govr. Morris & Genl. Pinkney approved the motion,

The motion was agreed to nem: con: ⟨and then the whole Article, N-C. only no—& Md. divided.⟩[2]

Records, 2:579; Proceedings of Convention Referred to the Committee of Style and Arrangement, September 10

XX.

The Members of the Legislatures, and the executive and judicial officers of the United States, and of the several States, shall be bound by oath or affirmation to support this Constitution.

But no religious test shall ever be required as a qualification to any office or public trust under the authority of the United States.

Records, 2:603; Report of Committee of Style, September 12

VI.

The senators and representatives beforementioned, and the members of the several state legislatures, and all executive and judicial officers, both of the United States and of the several States, shall be bound by oath or affirmation, to support this constitution; but no religious test shall ever be required as a qualification to any office or public trust under the United States.

U.S. Constitution, Article VI, Clause 3 (1788)

One of the most innovative and distinctively American features of the U.S. Constitution was the ban on religious tests for national officeholders. It also proved to be one of the most controversial in the ratification debates, raising fundamental questions about religion's role in civic life. The eighteenth-century mind viewed oath-taking as a profoundly religious act; therefore, Article VI, clause 3, invited questions about the relationship between the religious test ban and the immediately preceding oath clause. Critics asked whether there was a conflict between the oath clause and the test ban. Related questions concerned whether the Constitution redefined oath-taking as a strictly secular obligation, or whether the oath requirement should be viewed as a sacred obligation and the test ban as a prohibition on only sect-specific oaths that discriminated among religious denominations.

The Senators and Representatives before mentioned, and the members of the several State legislatures, and all executive and judicial officers, both of the United States and of the several States, shall be bound, by oath or affirmation, to support this Constitution; but no religious test shall ever be required as a qualification to any office or public trust under the United States.

---

2. The Journal records Connecticut's vote also as divided. *Records,* 2:460; 2:468 n. 26.

Reprinted from *The Public Statutes at Large of the United States of America,* ed. Richard Peters (Boston: Little and Brown, 1845), 1:19.

Letter from Jonas Phillips to the President and Members of the Constitutional Convention (September 7, 1787)

This letter by Jonas Phillips (1736–1803), a Philadelphia merchant who identified himself as "one of the people called Jews," is the only known communication addressed to the president and members of the national Constitutional Convention by an individual petitioner on the subject of religious liberty. Phillips decried the oath clause in the Pennsylvania Constitution, requiring a belief in the Divine inspiration of the New Testament, which excluded Jews from public office, and he petitioned the Convention to avoid such language in the fruits of their labors.

Sires

With leave and submission I address myself To those in whome there is wisdom understanding and knowledge. they are the honourable personages appointed and Made overseers of a part of the terrestrial globe of the Earth, Namely the 13 united states of america in Convention Assembled, the Lord preserve them amen—

I the subscriber being one of the people called Jews of the City of Philadelphia, a people scattered and despersed among all nations do behold with Concern that among the laws in the Constitution of Pennsylvania their is a Clause Sect. 10 to viz—I do believe in one God the Creature and governour of the universe the Rewarder of the good and the punisher of the wicked—and I do acknowledge the scriptures of the old and New testement to be given by a devine in-

Reprinted from *The Records of the Federal Convention of 1787*, ed. Max Farrand, rev. ed. (New Haven and London: Yale University Press, 1987), 3:78–79.

spiration—to swear and believe that the new testement was given by devine inspiration is absolutely against the Religious principle of a Jew. and is against his Conscience to take any such oath—By the above law a Jew is deprived of holding any publick office or place of Government which is a Contridectory to the bill of Right Sect 2. viz

That all men have a natural and unalienable Right To worship almighty God according to the dectates of their own Conscience and understanding, and that no man aught or of Right can be Compelled to attend any Relegious Worship or Erect or support any place of worship or Maintain any minister contrary to or against his own free will and Consent nor Can any man who acknowledges the being of a God be Justly deprived or abridged of any Civil Right as a Citizen on account of his Religious sentiments or peculiar mode of Religious Worship, and that no authority Can or aught to be vested in or assumed by any power what ever that shall in any Case interfere or in any manner Controul the Right of Conscience in the free Exercise of Religious Worship—

It is well known among all the Citizens of the 13 united States that the Jews have been true and faithful whigs, and during the late Contest with England they have been foremost in aiding and assisting the States with their lifes and fortunes, they have supported the Cause, have bravely faught and bleed for liberty which they Can not Enjoy—

Therefore if the honourable Convention shall in ther Wisdom think fit and alter the said oath and leave out the words to viz—and I do acknoweledge the scripture of the new testement to be given by devine inspiration then the Israeletes will think them self happy to live under a government where all Relegious societys are on an Eaquel footing—I solecet this favour for my self my Childreen and posterity and for the benefit of all the Isrealetes through the 13 united States of america

My prayers is unto the Lord. May the people of this States Rise up as a great and young lion, May they prevail against their Enemies, May the degrees of honour of his Excellencey the president of the Convention George Washington, be Extollet and Raise up. May Every one speak of his glorious Exploits. May God prolong his days among us in this land of Liberty—May he lead the armies against his Enemys as he has done hereuntofore—May God Extend peace unto the united States—May they get up to the highest Prosperetys—May God Extend peace to them and their seed after them so long as the Sun and moon Endureth—and may the almighty God of our father Abraham Isaac and Jacob endue this Noble Assembly with wisdom Judgement and unamity in their Councells, and may they have the Satisfaction to see that their present toil and labour for the wellfair of the united States may be approved of, Through all the world and perticular by the united States of america is the ardent prayer of Sires

Your Most devoted obed Servant

Jonas Phillips

Philadelphia 24th Ellul 5547 or Sepr 7th 1787

Letter from James Madison to Edmund Pendleton (October 28, 1787)

In this letter to Edmund Pendleton (1721–1803), one of Virginia's elder statesmen who later served as president of the Virginia ratifying convention, Madison contemplated the commonalities between oaths, in general, and religious tests.

New York Octr. 28. 1787

. . . Is not a religious test as far as it is necessary, or would operate, involved in the oath itself? If the person swearing believes in the supreme Being who is

Excerpt reprinted from *The Papers of James Madison,* ed. Robert A. Rutland et al. (Chicago and London: University of Chicago Press, 1977), 10:223.

invoked, and in the penal consequences of offending him, either in this or a future world or both, he will be under the same restraint from perjury as if he had previously subscribed a test requiring this belief. If the person in question be an unbeliever in these points and would notwithstanding take the oath, a previous test could have no effect. He would subscribe it as he would take the oath, without any principle that could be affected by either. . . .

Js. MADISON JR.

An Examination of the Constitution for the United States of America (1788)

AN AMERICAN CITIZEN [TENCH COXE]

Tench Coxe (1755–1824) of Pennsylvania, a member of the Confederation Congress and prolific Federalist pamphleteer, wrote widely circulated essays in support of the national Constitution proposed in 1787. In this passage, he celebrated Article VI's removal of restrictions on national officeholders.

Number IV

The security for national safety and happiness, resulting from other parts of the foederal Government.

. . . No *religions* test is ever to be required of any officer or servant of the United States. The people may employ *any wise and good citizen* in the execution of the various duties of the government. In Italy, Spain, and Portugal, *no protestant* can hold a public trust. In England *every Presbyterian, and other person not of their established church,* is incapable of holding an of-

Reprinted from *An Examination of the Constitution for the United States of America* (Philadelphia: Zachariah Poulson, 1788), 15–16.

fice. No such *impious* deprivation of the rights of men can take place under the new foederal constitution. The convention has the honour of proposing *the first public act,* by which any nation has ever *divested itself* of a power, every exercise of which is *a trespass on the Majesty of Heaven.*

No qualification *in monied or landed property* is required by the proposed plan; nor does it admit any preference from the preposterous distinctions of *birth and rank.* The office of the President, a Senator, and a Representative, and every other place of *power or profit,* are therefore open *to the whole body of the people.* Any wise, informed and upright man, be his property what it may, *can exercise the trusts and powers of the state,* provided he possesses the moral, religious and political virtues which are necessary to secure the confidence of his fellow citizens. . . .

A Landholder [Oliver Ellsworth], No. 7, *Connecticut Courant* (December 17, 1787)

Letter from William Williams to the Landholder, *The American Mercury* (February 11, 1788)

In a sharp exchange over ratification of the proposed national Constitution, "A Landholder" [Oliver Ellsworth (1745–1807)], a Connecticut delegate to the Constitutional Convention of 1787, and William Williams (1731–1811), a leading Connecticut politician, debated the propriety of religious tests for officeholders. Ellsworth defended Article VI on the grounds that it was designed "to exclude persecution and to secure . . . the important right of religious liberty." Williams opined that "divine and human wisdom, with universal experience, have approved and established them [oaths] as useful and a security to

mankind." Ellsworth's essay, the seventh in his "Landholder" series written in support of ratification, was first published in the *Connecticut Courant,* December 17, 1787. Williams's response was printed in *The American Mercury,* February 11, 1788.

A Landholder [Oliver Ellsworth], No. 7, *Connecticut Courant* (December 17, 1787)

To the Landholders and Farmers.

I have often admired the spirit of candor, liberality, and justice with which the Convention began and completed the important object of their mission. "In all our deliberations on this subject," say they, "we kept steadily in our view, that which appears to us the greatest interest of every true American, the consolidation of our union, in which is involved our prosperity, felicity, safety, perhaps our national existence. This important consideration, seriously and deeply impressed on our minds, led each state in the Convention to be less rigid on points of inferior magnitude, than might otherwise have been expected; and thus the Constitution which we now present is the result of a spirit of amity, and of that mutual deference and concession, which the peculiarity of our political situation rendered indispensable."[1]

Let us, my fellow citizens, take up this Constitution with the same spirit of candor and liberality; consider it in all its parts; consider the important advantages which may be derived from it and the fatal consequences which will probably follow from rejecting it. If any objections are made against it, let us

Reprinted from *The Documentary History of the Ratification of the Constitution,* vol. 3: *Ratification of the Constitution by the States: Delaware, New Jersey, Georgia, Connecticut,* ed. Merrill Jensen (Madison: State Historical Society of Wisconsin, 1978), 497–501. © State Historical Society of Wisconsin 1978. Reprinted with permission of the Wisconsin Historical Society.

1. See President of the Convention to the President of the Congress, 17 September 1787.

obtain full information on the subject and then weigh these objections in the balance of cool impartial reason. Let us see, if they be not wholly groundless. But, if upon the whole, they appear to have some weight, let us consider well whether they be so important that we ought on account of them to reject the whole Constitution. Perfection is not the lot of human institutions; that which has the most excellencies and fewest faults is the best that we can expect.

Some very worthy persons, who have not had great advantages for information, have objected against that clause in the Constitution which provides that "no religious Test shall ever be required as a qualification to any office or public trust under the United States." They have been afraid that this clause is unfavorable to religion. But, my countrymen, the sole purpose and effect of it is to exclude persecution and to secure to you the important right of religious liberty. We are almost the only people in the world who have the full enjoyment of this important right of human nature. In our country, every man has a right to worship God in that way which is most agreeable to his own conscience. If he be a good and peaceable citizen, he is liable to no penalties or incapacities on account of his religious sentiments; or, in other words, he is not subject to persecution.

But in other parts of the world, it has been, and still is, far different. Systems of religious error have been adopted in times of ignorance. It has been the interest of tyrannical kings, popes, and prelates to maintain these errors. When the clouds of ignorance began to vanish, and the people grew more enlightened, there was no other way to keep them in error but to prohibit their altering their religious opinions by severe persecuting laws. In this way, persecution became general throughout Europe. It was the universal opinion that one religion must be established by law, and that all who differed in their religious opinions must suffer the vengeance of persecution. In pursuance of this opinion, when popery was abolished in England, and the Church of England was established in its stead, severe penalties were inflicted upon all who dissented from the Established Church.

In the time of the civil wars, in the reign of Charles I, the Presbyterians got the upper hand and inflicted legal penalties upon all who differed from them in their sentiments respecting religious doctrines and discipline. When Charles II was restored, the Church of England was likewise restored, and the Presbyterians and other dissenters were laid under legal penalties and incapacities. It was in this reign that a religious test was established as a qualification for office; that is, a law was made requiring all officers civil and military (among other things) to receive the Sacrament of the Lord's Supper, according to the usage of the Church of England, written [within] six months after their admission to office, under the penalty of £500 and disability to hold the office. And by another statute of the same reign, no person was capable of being elected to any office relating to the government of any city or corporation unless, within a twelvemonth before, he had received the Sacrament according to the rites of the Church of England. The pretense for making these severe laws, by which all but churchmen were made incapable of any office civil or military, was to exclude the Papists; but the real design was to exclude the Protestant dissenters. From this account of test laws, there arises an unfavorable presumption against them. But if we consider the nature of them and the effects which they are calculated to produce, we shall find that they are useless, tyrannical, and peculiarly unfit for the people of this country.

A religious test is an act to be done, or profession to be made, relating to religion (such as partaking of the Sacrament according to certain rites and forms, or declaring one's belief of certain doctrines), for the purpose of determining whether his religious opinions are such that he is admissible to a public office. A test in favor of any one denomination of Christians would be to the last degree absurd in the United States. If it were in favor of either Congregationalists, Presbyterians, Episcopalians, Baptists, or Quakers, it would incapacitate more than three-fourths of the American citizens for any public office; and thus degrade them from the rank of freemen. There needs no argument to prove that the majority of our citizens would never submit to this indignity.

If any test act were to be made, perhaps the least exceptionable would be one requiring all persons appointed to office to declare, at the time of their admission, their belief in the being of a God and in the divine authority of the Scriptures. In favor of such a test, it may be said that one who believed these great truths will not be so likely to violate his obligations to his country, as one who disbelieves them; we may have greater confidence in his integrity. But I answer: his making a declaration of such a belief is no security at all. For suppose him to be an unprincipled man, who believes neither the Word nor the being of a God, and to be governed merely by selfish motives, how easy is it for him to dissemble? How easy is it for him to make a public declaration of his belief in the creed which the law prescribes; and excuse himself by calling it a mere formality? This is the case with the test laws and creeds in England. The most abandoned characters partake of the Sacrament in order to qualify themselves for public employments. The clergy are obliged by law to administer the ordinance unto them; and thus to prostitute the most sacred office of religion, for it is a civil right in the party to receive the Sacrament. In that country, subscribing to the Thirty-Nine Articles is a test for admission into holy orders. And it is a fact that many of the clergy do this; when, at the same time, they totally disbelieve several of the doctrines contained in them. In short, test laws are utterly ineffectual; they are no security at all, because men of loose principles will, by an external compliance, evade them. If they exclude any persons, it will be honest men, men of principle, who will rather suffer an injury than act contrary to the dictates of their consciences. If we mean to have those appointed to public offices who are sincere friends to religion, we the people who appoint them must take care to choose such characters and not rely upon such cobweb-barriers as test laws are.

But to come to the true principle by which this question ought to be determined: The business of civil government is to protect the citizen in his rights, to defend the community from hostile powers, and to promote the general welfare. Civil government has no business to meddle with the private opinions of the people. If I demean myself as a good citizen, I am accountable not to man, but to God, for the religious opinions which I embrace and the manner in which I worship the Supreme Being. If such had been the universal sentiments of mankind, and they had acted accordingly, persecution, the bane of truth and nurse of error with her bloody axe and flaming hand, would never have turned so great a part of the world into a field of blood.

But while I assert the right of religious liberty, I would not deny that the civil power has a right, in some cases, to interfere in matters of religion. It has a right to prohibit and punish gross immoralities and impieties because the open practice of these is of evil example and public detriment.

For this reason, I heartily approve of our laws against drunkenness, profane swearing, blasphemy, and professed atheism. But in this state, we have never thought it expedient to adopt a test law; and yet I sincerely believe we have as great a proportion of religion and morality as they have in England, where every person who holds a public office must be either a saint by law or a hypocrite by practice. A test law is the parent of hypocrisy, and the offspring of error and the spirit of persecution. Legislatures have no right to set up an inquisition and examine into the private opinions of men. Test laws are useless and ineffectual, unjust and tyrannical; therefore, the Convention have done wisely in excluding this engine of persecution and providing that no religious test shall ever be required.

Letter from William Williams to the Landholder, *The American Mercury* (February 11, 1788)

Since the Federal Constitution has had so calm, dispassionate, and rational a discussion, and so happy an issue, in the late worthy Convention of this state, I did not expect any members of that honorable body to be challenged in a newspaper, and especially by name and by anonymous writers, on account of their opinion, or decently expressing their sentiments relative to the great subject then under consideration or any part of it. Nor do I yet see the propriety or happy issue of such a proceeding. However, as a gentleman in your paper feels uneasy that every sentiment contained in his publications (tho in general they are well written) is not received with perfect acquiescence and submission, I will endeavor to satisfy him, or the candid reader, by the same channel that I am not so reprehensible as he supposes, in the matter referred to.

When the clause in the 6th Article, which provides that "no religious test should ever be required as a qualification to any office or trust, etc." came under consideration, I observed I should have chose that sentence, and anything relating to a religious test, had been totally omitted rather than stand as it did; but still more wished something of the kind should have been inserted, but with a reverse sense so far as to require an explicit acknowledgment of the being of a God, His perfections, and His providence, and to have been prefixed to, and stand as, the first introductory words of the Constitution in the following or similar terms, viz.: *We the people of the United States, in a firm belief of the being and perfections of the one living and true God, the creator and supreme Governor of the world, in His universal providence and the au-*

Reprinted from *The Documentary History of the Ratification of the Constitution*, vol. 3: *Ratification of the Constitution by the States: Delaware, New Jersey, Georgia, Connecticut*, ed. Merrill Jensen (Madison: State Historical Society of Wisconsin, 1978), 588–90. © State Historical Society of Wisconsin 1978. Reprinted with permission of the Wisconsin Historical Society.

thority of His laws: that He will require of all moral agents an account of their conduct, that all rightful powers among men are ordained of, and mediately derived from God, therefore in a dependence on His blessing and acknowledgment of His efficient protection in establishing our Independence, whereby it is become necessary to agree upon and settle a Constitution of federal government for ourselves, and in order to form a more perfect union, etc., as it is expressed in the present introduction, do ordain, etc. And instead of none, that no other religious test should ever be required, etc. And that supposing, but not granting, this would *be no security at all,* that it would make hypocrites etc.; yet this would not be a sufficient reason against it, as it would be a public declaration against, and disapprobation of, men who did not, even with sincerity, make such a profession, and they must be left to the Searcher of Hearts; that it would, however, be the voice of the great body of the people and an acknowledgment proper and highly becoming them to express on this great and only occasion, and, according to the course of Providence, one means of obtaining blessings from the Most High. But that since it was not, and so difficult and dubious to get it inserted, I would not wish to make it a capital objection; that I had no more idea of a religious test which should restrain offices to any particular sect, class, or denomination of men or Christians, in the long list of diversity, than to regulate their bestowments by the stature or dress of the candidate. Nor did I believe one sensible catholic man in the state wished for such a limitation; and that therefore the newspaper observations and reasonings (I named no author) against a test, in favor of any one denomination of Christians, and the sacrilegious injunctions of the test laws of England, etc., combated objections which did not exist and *was building up a man of straw and knocking him down again.* These are the same and only ideas and sentiments I endeavored to communicate on that subject, tho perhaps not precisely in the same terms, as I had not written, nor preconceived them, except the proposed test; and whether there is any reason in them or not, I submit to the public.

I freely confess such a test and acknowledgment would have given me great additional satisfaction; and I conceive the arguments against it, on the score of hypocrisy, would apply with equal force against requiring an oath from any officer of the united or individual states, and, with little abatement, to any oath in any case whatever. But divine and human wisdom, with universal experience, have approved and established them as useful and a security to mankind.

I thought it was my duty to make the observations in this behalf, which I did, and to bear my testimony for God. And that it was also my duty to say *the Constitution*, with this and some other faults of another kind, was yet too wise and too necessary to be rejected.

P.S. I could not have suspected the Landholder (if I know him) to be the author of the piece referred to; but if he or any other is pleased to reply, without the signature of his proper name, he will receive no further answer or notice from me.

The Federalist Papers, Number 52 (1788)

The Federalist Papers, Number 57 (1788)

PUBLIUS [JAMES MADISON]

In *The Federalist Papers,* numbers 52 and 57, James Madison observed the practical consequence of the Article VI religious test ban.

The Federalist Papers, Number 52

The first view to be taken of this part of the government, relates to the qualifications of the electors, and the elected.

Those of the former are to be the same with those of the electors of the most numerous branch of the state legislatures. The definition of the right of suffrage is very justly regarded as a fundamental article of republican government. It was incumbent on the convention, therefore, to define and establish this right in the constitution. . . .

The qualifications of the elected, being less carefully and properly defined by the state constitutions, and being at the same time more susceptible of uniformity, have been very properly considered and regulated by the convention. A representative of the United States must be of the age of twenty-five years; must have been seven years a citizen of the United States; must, at the time of his election, be an inhabitant of the state he is to represent, and during the time of his service, must be in no office under the United States. Under these reasonable limitations, the door of this part of the federal government is open to merit of every description, whether native or adoptive, whether young or old, and without regard to poverty or wealth, or to any particular profession of religious faith. . . .

Reprinted from Alexander Hamilton, John Jay, and James Madison, *The Federalist,* ed. George W. Carey and James McClellan (Indianapolis: Liberty Fund, 2001), 272, 273. © Liberty Fund, Inc., 2001. Reprinted by permission.

The Federalist Papers, Number 57

Who are to be the electors of the federal representatives? Not the rich, more than the poor; not the learned, more than the ignorant; not the haughty heirs of distinguished names, more than the humble sons of obscure and unpropitious fortune. The electors are to be the great body of the people of the United States. They are to be the same who exercise the right in every state of electing the correspondent branch of the legislature of the state.

Who are to be the objects of popular choice? Every citizen whose merit may recommend him to the esteem and confidence of his country. No qualification of wealth, of birth, of religious faith, or of civil profession, is permitted to fetter the judgment, or disappoint the inclination of the people. . . .

Reprinted from Alexander Hamilton, John Jay, and James Madison, *The Federalist,* ed. George W. Carey and James McClellan (Indianapolis: Liberty Fund, 2001), 295–96. © Liberty Fund, Inc., 2001. Reprinted by permission.

Letter from James Madison to Edmund Randolph (April 10, 1788)

This passage was written in response to Edmund Randolph's query, in a letter dated February 29, 1788, whether the Article VI exception implied "that the congress by the general words had power over religion." Randolph (1753–1813), a delegate to the national Constitutional Convention and then governor of Virginia, conveyed Madison's explanation to the Virginia ratifying convention in a speech on June 10, 1788 (see p. 391).

As to the religious test, I should conceive that it can imply at most nothing more than that without that exception, a power would have been given to impose an oath involving a religious test as a qualification for office. The constitution of necessary offices being given to the Congress, the proper qualifications seem to be evidently involved. I think too there are several other satisfactory points of view in which the exception might be placed. . . .

Excerpt reprinted from James Madison, *The Papers of James Madison,* ed. Robert A. Rutland and Charles F. Hobson, Presidential Series, vol. 11: *7 March 1788–1 March 1789* (Charlottesville: University Press of Virginia, 1977), 19. © 1977 The University of Virginia Press. Used by permission of the publisher.

Luther Martin, *The Genuine Information* (1788)

Essay by Samuel, (Boston) *Independent Chronicle and Universal Advertiser* (January 10, 1788)

A Friend to the Rights of the People, (New Hampshire) *Freeman's Oracle* (February 8, 1788)

Letter by David, *Massachusetts Gazette* (March 7, 1788)

Aristocrotis, *The Government of Nature Delineated; or An Exact Picture of the New Federal Constitution* (1788)

The most vociferous critics of the Article VI prohibition on religious tests were the Anti-Federalists who thought that, especially compared to their respective state constitutions, this provision was, at best, inattentive to the vital contribution of religion to the polity and, at worst, hostile to religion. They sought to raise doubts about the propriety of Article VI in order to derail ratification of the proposed national Constitution. The following writings illustrate the Anti-Federalist critique of the proposed test ban.

The observations of Luther Martin (1748–1826), Maryland's attorney general and a delegate to the Constitutional Convention, were contained in his report on the proposed Constitution to the Maryland Legislature. Concerned about the powers granted to the central government, Martin vigorously opposed the Constitution's ratification. ("Letter by David" was written in response to Elihu's essay, which is reprinted in chapter 7.)

Luther Martin, *The Genuine Information* (1788)

The part of the system, which provides that *no religious test* shall ever be required as a qualification to any office or public trust under the United States, was adopted by a great majority of the convention, and without much debate,—however, there were some members *so unfashionable* as to think that a *belief of the existence of a Deity,* and of a *state of future rewards and punishments* would be some security for the good conduct of our rulers, and that in a Christian country it would be at *least decent* to hold out some distinction between the professors of Christianity and downright infidelity or paganism. . . .

Reprinted from Luther Martin, *The Genuine Information, Delivered to the Legislature of the State of Maryland* (Philadelphia: Eleazer Oswald, 1788), 80.

Essay by Samuel

But some have supposed, they have a *salvo* for all difficulties, that may arise in said Constitution, by the 5th Art. entitled *amendments provided.* But all amendments, are effectually guarded against in the

Excerpt reprinted from *The Complete Anti-Federalist,* ed. Herbert J. Storing (Chicago and London: University of Chicago Press, 1981), 4:195–96.

next Art. paragraph 3. For there we find, all the members of Congress, and all the members of the several State Legislatures, and all the Executive and Judicial officers, both of the United States, and of the several States, are to be bound by oath or affirmation to support this Constitution. How then can we have any amendments, as speciously pretended in said 5th Article? When all those from whom only it can originate, are to be bound by oath, to support this as it is. Besides, it is not likely, that the President, or Congress, would be so impolitic, as to oppress so large a proportion of the States at once, as two thirds; therefore, there is no probability, and scarcely possibility, that ever a motion of two thirds should arise. Moreover, could we obtain a Convention, and by them amendments proposed; they might lie dormant forever, if the Congress did not see cause to appoint how the amendments should be ratified; which is not to be expected, if the amendments should be to diminish their power; so that all the parade about amendments, comes to nothing. But to return to the oath; there is something very singular in the manner of the oath; that all Continental and State officers, should be bound by oath, to preserve, protect, defend and support this Constitution. And not rather be under oath, to preserve, protect, defend and support the United States, or the people thereof, in their rights and privileges; it may from this no doubt be expected that Proclamations will conclude GOD SAVE THE CONSTITUTION!

In the same paragraph, in which the above oath is instituted, all religion is expressly rejected, from the Constitution. Was there ever any State or kingdom, that could subsist, without adopting some system of religion? Not so much as to own the being, and government of a Deity; or any acknowledgment of him! or having any revelation from him! Should we adopt such a rejection of religion as this, the words of Samuel to Saul, will literally apply to us,—*Because thou hast rejected the word of the Lord, he hath also rejected thee from being king.*[*] We may justly expect, that God

* I Samuel 15:23.—Eds.

will reject us, from that self government, we have obtained thro' his divine interposition: Or being able to keep up government and order among us; for he has commanded the rulers of the earth, to kiss the son, lest he be angry, and they perish from the way.

If civil rulers won't acknowledge God, he won't acknowledge them; and they must perish from the way. And there can be no rational doubt, that the prevailing neglect of acknowledging God in the time of the revolution, and since, is the cause of our having such convulsions as have been among us; we are perishing from the way. . . .

A Friend to the Rights of the People, *Anti-Foederalist, No. I*

Upon the discarding of all religious tests, Art. 6, clause 3—But no religious test shall ever be required as a qualification to any office, or public trust under the United States, according to this we may have a Papist, a Mohomatan, a Deist, yea an Atheist at the helm of Government: all nations are tenacious of their religion, and all have an acknowledgment of it in their civil establishment; but the new plan requires none at all; none in Congress, none in any member of the legislative bodies; none in any single officer of the United States; all swept off at one stroke totally contrary to our state plans.—But will this be good policy to discard all religion? It may be said the meaning is not to discard it, but only to shew that there is no need of it in public officers; they may be as faithful without as with—this is a mistake—when a man has no regard to God and his laws nor any belief of a future state; he will have less regard to the laws of men, or to the most solemn oaths or affirmations; it is acknowledged by all that civil governments can't well

be supported without the assistance of religion; I think therefore that so much deference ought to be paid to it, as to acknowledge it in our civil establishment; and that no man is fit to be a ruler of protestants, without he can honestly profess to be of the protestant religion. . . .

Letter by David

Mr. Allen,

A Connecticut writer, whose very curious production, under the signature of Elihu, was *honoured* with a place in your Gazette of the 26th of February, in treating of religious acknowledgements and professions, appears to consider all who retain any symptoms of religion, as rogues or fools. It is not my intention to become a polemick divine, nor to enter into a dispute with those, whose argument, if it proves any thing, proves that their own hearts are not under the influence of religion. I mean only to consider the matter in a political view, in order, if we can, to determine whether the state ought or ought not to interfere at all in religious concernments.

It is agreed on all hands, that the business of government is to secure the subjects in the enjoyment of their lives, liberty and property, and that it must be furnished with all the powers necessary to attain so desirable an object. It is clearly impossible to secure the subject unless the invasions of lawless men can be restrained. There have been but three ways hitherto invented by which the turbulent passions of mankind are controlled; 1st. By punishing offenders, 2d. By rewarding virtuous actions, and 3d. By prepossessing the people in favour of virtue by affording publick protection to religion. The first method is least eligible of them all unless when it is absolutely necessary; and the more frequent it becomes, the less ef-

Excerpt reprinted from *The Complete Anti-Federalist,* ed. Herbert J. Storing (Chicago and London: University of Chicago Press, 1981), 4:242.

Reprinted from *The Complete Anti-Federalist,* ed. Herbert J. Storing (Chicago and London: University of Chicago Press, 1981), 4:246–48.

ficacious it is. The second is in its own nature very confined, and can take place only in a few of the most exalted instances, so that it can produce no effect upon the body of mankind. The third method then, by forming the opinion of the people at large in favour of virtue and religion, is in theory the most probable, and if we find in practice it has been most successful, we shall hardly hesitate to say, that religion is a proper subject for publick protection and encouragement.

If we examine the history of mankind, under whatever dispensation of religion they lived, we find, that while their circumstances were improving, they attended much to their religious system. They frequently acknowledged the superintendence of the Gods, and sought their protection. They are careful to train up their children in the religion of their ancestors, and it has been generally if not always a fundamental article that moral offences would be punished by the Deity, even if they escaped the laws of human society, unless satisfaction was made to the sovereign of the universe for the violation of good order. Every nation, I believe, has committed the care of religion to the government, and almost every government has adopted some institution for instructing the subjects both old and young in principles, which had a direct tendency to secure the practice of good morals and consequently the peace of society. In Europe it has been carried to an absurd extreme. It gave rise to an elective monarchy, which claimed jurisdiction over the different states and princes, and pervaded all parts of their dominions. As it was an empire, founded in opinion, and in principles which took fast hold of the human mind, kings could not always defend themselves by force from its encroachments on their prerogatives. After the reformation, which Luther boldly begun, the reformed countries deprived the pope of his supremacy, and transferred it to themselves. Still however they took care to provide means for the instruction of the subjects, because that religion had always been found to attach the professors of it to what they conceived to be good order and the constitution they lived under. No good reason has been given why the government should not pro-vide for their instruction in such principles as tend to secure internal peace, any more than for instructing the people in the arts of defence. The power indeed, like any other power, may be abused; but it by no means follows that government should not be possessed of it under certain limitations.

The practice of our own country has been uniformly in favour of a limited power of this kind in the government. We have from the beginning had laws in favour of a learned and able clergy, and have provided means for their education and support. We have had and still have laws for a due observance of the Sabbath; and our annual fasts and thanksgivings are not only uniform proofs of the exercise of such a power; but are instances of the propriety of our conduct in making frequent and publick acknowledgments of our dependence upon the Deity. Never did any people possess a more ardent love of liberty than the people of this state; yet that very love of liberty has induced them to adopt a religious test, which requires all publick officers to be of some Christian, protestant persuasion, and to abjure all foreign authority. Thus religion secures our independence as a nation, and attaches the citizens to our own government.

I know it is a common objection against religious tests, that they bind only those who are good men, and do not exclude bad ones. The same remark is true of oaths; yet every government requires them, and an oath is, as much as a test, a religious declaration. Nothing can be urged in favour of one which does not apply to the other. It is true, indeed, that bad men will agree to either. Still however, those, whose avowed principles are unfriendly to the system of the country, will be excluded: And there are two descriptions of men that ought to be excluded. These are Papists and Atheists. The latter should be excluded because they have no principles of virtue, and the former because they acknowledge a foreign head, who can relieve them from the obligation of an oath. There is therefore no publick dependence upon either, and men publickly and avowedly of either description should be excluded.

We have now seen what have been the principles generally adopted by mankind, and to what degree they have been adopted in our own state. Before we decide in favour of our practice, let us see what has been the success of those who have made no publick provision for religion. Unluckily we have only to consult our next neighbours. In consequence of this publick inattention they derive the vast benefit of being able to do whatever they please without any compunction. Taught from their infancy to ridicule our formality as the effect of hypocrisy, they have no principles of restraint but laws of their own making; and from such laws may Heaven defend us. If this is the success that attends leaving religion to shift wholly for itself, we shall be at no loss to determine, that it is not more difficult to build an elegant house without tools to work with, than it is to establish a durable government without the publick protection of religion. What the system is which is most proper for our circumstances will not take long to determine. It must be that which has adopted the purest moral principles, and which is interwoven in the laws and constitution of our country, and upon which are founded the habits of our people. Upon this foundation we have established a government of influence and opinion, and therefore secured by the affections of the people; and when this foundation is removed, a government of mere force must arise.

David

Aristocrotis, *The Government of Nature Delineated; or An Exact Picture of the New Federal Constitution*

Carlisle 1788

There are many other rights claimed by the people besides these mentioned; but as they are of little consequence, I shall leave the discussion of them to the new congress themselves, who no doubt will be quick sighted enough to discern them, and prudent enough to provide for their removal. But before I conclude, I must take notice of an incumbrance upon government, which have been more general in its operation than any yet mentioned; viz. religion. There has been but few nations in the world, where the people possessed the privilege of electing their rulers; of prefixing a bill of rights to their constitutions, enjoyed a free press, or trial by jury; but there was never a nation in the world whose government was not circumscribed by religion. It intermingled itself so much with the Jewish system, that it is difficult to distinguish between some of the functions of the magistrates and those of the priests. In some stages of their commonwealth, the high priest was also the supreme civil magistrate. Religion had also a decisive influence in the Grecian and Roman systems of jurisprudence; their augurs could in many cases put a negative on the decrees of their senates; and countermand the orders of their consuls and dictators.—In our own times, the most absolute rulers in the world, find their power abridged by religion. The grand signior possesses an authority very similar to the principle of nature which I have stated; yet his power is limitted by religion;—for wherever it interposes, the will of the sovereign must submit to its decrees: "When the koran hath prescribed any religious rite; hath enjoined any moral duty; or hath confirmed by its sanction any political maxim. The command of the sultan cannot overturn that which an higher authority hath established."

Excerpts reprinted from *The Complete Anti-Federalist*, ed. Herbert J. Storing (Chicago and London: University of Chicago Press, 1981), 3:205–8.

Even the Venetian government, which of all other seems to be formed on the best model, (though much inferior to our new plan) is nevertheless embarrassed with religion; but what need I mention particulars, since every government in the world, as I observed before, has, in a lesser or greater degree felt this inconvenience. Indeed it seems to have formed an essential part of them; such a part as could not be expunged without annihilating the whole systems; and though this might have been done, yet the shallow brains of those antiquated legislators, could not devise a possibility of avoiding the same radical evil in any new system they could frame; so that this direful incumbrance has hitherto proved too powerful for the united efforts of all the legislators and philosophers that ever appeared in the world to conquer. But what is the world to the federal convention! but as the drop of a bucket, or the small dust in the balance! What the world could not accomplish from the commencement of time till now, they easily performed in a few moments, by declaring, that "no religious test shall ever be required as a qualification to any office, or public trust; under the united states." This is laying the ax to the root of the tree; whereas other nations only lopped off a few noxious branches. This is purifying the fountain; the streams must of course be pure. By this provision the convention hath prudently removed the distemper from the head, and secured it from contamination.—The certain method to preserve the members from catching the infection. Religion, is certainly attended with dangerous consequences to government: it hath been the cause of millions being slaughtered, whose lives and services might have been of use to their masters; but in a peculiar manner the christian religion, which has these several centuries past prevailed over a great part of Europe, and is professed by a great many of the vulgar in this country, is of all others the most unfavourable to a government founded upon nature; because it pretends to be of a supernatural divine origin, and therefore sets itself above nature. Its precepts are likewise so rigid and severe, as to render it impossible for any

gentleman of fashion or good breeding to comply with them in any sense, without a manifest violation of decorum, and an abandonment of every genteel amusement and fashionable accomplishment; but another capital objection against this singular system of religion is, that it prohibits slavery, which is so essential to government, that it cannot exist, with any degree of energy, without it, for all the subjects of a good government ought to be slaves in a political sense; or as they were anciently termed, vassals; that is, their persons and property must be entirely at the will and disposal of their masters; which is ingeniously provided for in the new constitution, under the articles of taxation and discipline of the militia.

The congress must certainly extirpate from their dominions such a religion as this that is an enemy to so many good things. By this means the clergy may be annihilated,* who have always been an ambitious, aspiring and restless set of men, ever grasping at honours and distinctions, which is the unalienable prerogative of those of illustrious descent: they also by their address and cunning, gain an ascendency, and assume an authority over the people, which is only proper for the rulers to possess; but perhaps it may be urged that some sort of religion is necessary to awe

---

* When first I perused this construction, I expected the clergy, to a man, would have opposed it; but in this I am happily deceived; they are the most strenuous advocates it has got; this appeared to me unaccountable, that an order of men, ever jealous of their own power and interest, should favour a constitution which would eventually destroy both; but I presume they have secret assurance that one or two denominations of clergy, are to have fixed stipends established under the new constitution. This, they expect will relieve them from their state of dependance they are now in. It is natural for them to wish something surer for a living, than the good will of the people, their hearers. It is very well to amuse them with such alluring stories as these, while their services is needed. Working on their avarice and ambition is the sure way to engage them; and when the constitution is once established, and they have no more useful, but rather hurtful, sound policy will dictate evasions plausible enough to disengage gentlemen from the accomplishment of their promise; and the most noisy and dangerous of them, may have their mouths stopped, by bestowing sinecures on them in the civil, military, or naval department: such as the collector of taxes, excise, or impost duties: this will suit them better than their present employments; for preaching is a great restraint upon gentlemen of modern morality.

the minds of the vulgar, and keep them in subjection to government. I grant, weak, feeble governments, such as our present systems, may stand in need of the visionary terrors of religion for their support; but such an energetic government as the new constitution, disdains such contemptible auxiliaries as the belief of a Deity, the immortality of the soul, or the resurrection of the body, a day of judgment, or a future state of rewards and punishments. Such bug-bears as these are too distant and illusory to claim the notice of the new congress. The present state of punishments, which will be within their immediate reach to inflict, will answer the end infinitely better. But if some religion must be had, the religion of nature will certainly be preferred by a government founded upon the law of nature.—One great argument in favour of this religion is, that most of the members of the grand convention are great admirers of it; and they certainly are the best models to form our religious, as well as our civil belief on. This religion also admits of proper degrees and distinctions amongst mankind; but the other does not; for it commands to call no man upon earth master or lord. From these remarks, I think it evident, that the grand convention hath dexterously provided for the removal of every thing that hath ever opperated as a restraint upon government in any place or age of the world. But perhaps some weak heads may think that the constitution itself will be a check upon the new congress; but this I deny, for the convention has so happily worded themselves, that every part of this constitution, either bears double meaning, or no meaning at all; and if any concessions are made to the people in one place, it is effectually cancelled in another; so that in fact this constitution is much better and gives more scope to the rulers than they durst safely take if there was no constitution at all; for then the people might contend that the power was inherent in them, and that they had made some implied reserves in the original grant; but now they cannot, for every thing is expressly given away to government in this plan. Perhaps some people may think that power, which the house of representatives pos-

sesses, of impeaching the officers of government will be a restraint upon them; but this entirely vanishes, when it is considered that the senate hath the principal say in appointing these officers, and that they are the sole judges of all impeachments. Now it would be absurd to suppose that they would remove their own servants for performing their secret orders perhaps. For the interest of rulers and the ruled will then be two distinct things. The mode of electing the president is another excellent regulation, most wisely calculated to render him the obsequious machine of congress. He is to be chosen by electors appointed in such manner as the state legislators shall direct: but then the highest in votes cannot be president, without he has the majority of all the electors; and if none have this majority, then the congress is to chuse president out of the five highest on the return. By this means the congress will always have the making of the president after the first election; so that if the reigning president pleases his masters, he need be under no apprehensions of being turned out for any severities used to the people, for though the congress may not have influence enough to procure him the majority of the votes of the electoral college, yet they will always be able to prevent any other from having such a majority, and to have him returned among the five highest, so that they may have the appointing of him themselves.

Debate in Connecticut Ratifying
Convention (January 9, 1788)

Debate in Massachusetts Ratifying
Convention (January 19, 23, 30,
and February 4, 1788)

Debate in Virginia Ratifying
Convention (June 6, 10, and 12, 1788)

Debate in North Carolina Ratifying
Convention (July 30, 1788)

The propriety of the Article VI prohibition on religious tests provoked spirited debate in several state ratifying conventions. Selected excerpts from these debates, as reported in Jonathan Elliot's *The Debates in the Several State Conventions on the Adoption of the Federal Constitution,* are reproduced below.

Debate in Connecticut Ratifying
Convention (January 9, 1788)

January 9, 1788

Hon. OLIVER WOLCOTT. . . . I do not see the necessity of such a *test* as some gentlemen wish for. The Constitution enjoins an oath upon all the officers of the United States. This is a direct appeal to that God who is the avenger of perjury. Such an appeal to him is a full acknowledgment of his being and providence. An acknowledgment of these great truths is all that the gentleman contends for. For myself, I should be content either with or without that clause in the Constitution which excludes test laws. Knowledge and

Excerpt reprinted from Jonathan Elliot, *The Debates in the Several State Conventions on the Adoption of the Federal Constitution,* 2nd ed. (New York: Burt Franklin, n.d.; Ayer Reprint, 1987), 2:201–2.

liberty are so prevalent in this country, that I do not believe that the United States would ever be disposed to establish one religious sect, and lay all others under legal disabilities. But as we know not what may take place hereafter, and any such test would be exceedingly injurious to the rights of free citizens, I cannot think it altogether superfluous to have added a clause, which secures us from the possibility of such oppression. I shall only add, that I give my assent to this Constitution, and am happy to see the states in a fair way to adopt a Constitution which will protect their rights and promote their welfare. . . .

Debate in Massachusetts Ratifying
Convention (January 19, 23, 30,
and February 4, 1788)

SATURDAY, *January* 19, 1788, A.M.—The Hon. Mr. SINGLETARY thought we were giving up all our privileges, as there was no provision that men in power should have any *religion;* and though he hoped to see Christians, yet, by the Constitution, a Papist, or an Infidel, was as eligible as they. It had been said that men had not degenerated; he did not think men were better now than when men after God's own heart did wickedly. He thought, in this instance, we were giving great power to we know not whom.

Gen. BROOKS, (of Medford.)—If good men are appointed, government will be administered well. But what will prevent bad men from mischief, is the question. If there should be such in the Senate, we ought to be cautious of giving power; but when that power is given, with proper checks, the danger is at an end. When men are answerable, and within the

Excerpts reprinted from Jonathan Elliot, *The Debates in the Several State Conventions on the Adoption of the Federal Constitution,* 2nd ed. (New York: Burt Franklin, n.d.; Ayer Reprint, 1987), 2:44–45, 88–90, 116–20, 148–49.

reach of responsibility, they cannot forget that their political existence depends upon their good behavior. The Senate can frame no law but by consent of the Representatives, and is answerable to that house for its conduct. If that conduct excites suspicion, they are to be impeached, punished, (or prevented from holding any office, which is great punishment.) If these checks are not sufficient, it is impossible to devise such as will be so. . . .

January 23, 1788

Mr. PARSONS, (of Newburyport.) . . .

It has been objected that the Constitution provides no religious test by oath, and we may have in power unprincipled men, atheists and pagans. No man can wish more ardently than I do that all our public offices may be filled by men who fear God and hate wickedness; but it must remain with the electors to give the government this security. An oath will not do it. Will an unprincipled man be entangled by an oath? Will an atheist or a pagan dread the vengeance of the Christian's God, a being, in his opinion, the creature of fancy and credulity? It is a solecism in expression. No man is so illiberal as to wish the confining places of honor or profit to any one sect of Christians; but what security is it to government, that every public officer shall swear that he is a Christian? For what will then be called Christianity? One man will declare that the Christian religion is only an illumination of natural religion, and that he is a Christian; another Christian will assert that all men must be happy hereafter in spite of themselves; a third Christian reverses the image, and declares that, let a man do all he can, he will certainly be punished in another world; and a fourth will tell us that, if a man use any force for the common defence, he violates every principle of Christianity. Sir, the only evidence we can have of the sincerity of a man's religion is a good life; and I trust that such evidence will be required of every candidate by every elector. That man who acts an honest part to his neighbor, will, most probably, conduct honorably towards the public. . . .

January 30, 1788

Dr. JARVIS. . . .

In the conversation on Thursday, on the sixth article which provides that "no religious test shall ever be required as a qualification to any office," &c., several gentlemen urged that it was a departure from the principles of our forefathers, who came here for the preservation of their religion; and that it would admit deists, atheists, &c., into the general government; and, people being apt to imitate the examples of the court, these principles would be disseminated, and, of course, a corruption of morals ensue. Gentlemen on the other side applauded the liberality of the clause, and represented, in striking colors, the impropriety, and almost impiety, of the requisition of a test, as practised in Great Britain and elsewhere. In this conversation, the following is the substance of the observations of the

Rev. Mr. SHUTE. Mr. President, to object to the latter part of the paragraph under consideration, which excludes a religious test, is, I am sensible, very popular; for the most of men, somehow, are rigidly tenacious of their own sentiments in religion, and disposed to impose them upon others as the *standard* of truth. If, in my sentiments upon the point in view, I should differ from some in this honorable body, I only wish from them the exercise of that candor, with which true religion is adapted to inspire the honest and well-disposed mind.

To establish a religious test as a qualification for offices in the proposed federal Constitution, it appears to me, sir, would be attended with injurious consequences to some individuals, and with no advantage to the *whole*.

By the injurious consequences to individuals, I mean, that some, who, in every other respect, are qualified to fill some important post in government, will be excluded by their not being able to stand the religious test; which I take to be a privation of part of their civil rights.

Nor is there to me any conceivable advantage, sir, that would result to the whole from such a test. Un-

principled and dishonest men will not hesitate to subscribe to *any thing* that may open the way for their
advancement, and put them into a situation the better
to execute their base and iniquitous designs. Honest
men alone, therefore, however well qualified to serve
the public, would be excluded by it, and their country
be deprived of the benefit of their abilities.

In this great and extensive empire, there is, and will
be, a great variety of sentiments in religion among its
inhabitants. Upon the plan of a religious test, the
question, I think, must be, Who shall be excluded
from national trusts? Whatever answer bigotry may
suggest, the dictates of candor and equity, I conceive,
will be, *None.*

Far from limiting my charity and confidence to
men of my own denomination in religion, I suppose,
and I believe, sir, that there are worthy characters
among men of every denomination—among the
Quakers, the Baptists, the Church of England, the
Papists; and even among those who have no other
guide, in the way to virtue and heaven, than the dictates of natural religion.

I must therefore think, sir, that the proposed plan
of government, in this particular, is wisely constructed; that, as all have an equal claim to the blessings of the government under which they live, and
which they support, so none should be excluded from
them for being of any particular denomination in religion.

The presumption is, that the eyes of the people will
be upon the faithful in the land; and, from a regard
to their own safety, they will choose for their rulers
men of known abilities, of known probity, of good
moral characters. The apostle Peter tells us that God
is no respecter of persons, but, in every nation, he that
feareth him, and worketh righteousness, is *acceptable*
to him. And I know of no reason why men of such a
character, in a community of whatever denomination
in religion, *caeteris paribus* [with other things being
equal], with other suitable qualifications, should not
be *acceptable* to the people, and why they may not be
employed by them with safety and advantage in the
important offices of government. The exclusion of a

religious test in the proposed Constitution, therefore,
clearly appears to me, sir, to be in favor of its adoption.

Col. JONES (of Bristol) thought, that the rulers
ought to believe in God or Christ, and that, however
a test may be prostituted in England, yet he thought,
if our public men were to be of those who had a good
standing in the church, it would be happy for the
United States, and that a person could not be a good
man without being a good Christian.

The conversation on the Constitution, by paragraphs, being ended,

Mr. PARSONS moved, *that this Convention do assent to, and ratify, this Constitution.*

Mr. NEAL rose, and said, that, as the Constitution
at large was now under consideration, he would just
remark, that the article which respected the Africans
was the one which lay on his mind; and, unless his
objections to that were removed, it must, how much
soever he liked the other parts of the Constitution,
be a sufficient reason for him to give his negative
to it.

Col. JONES said, that one of his principal objections was, the omission of a religious test.

Rev. Mr. PAYSON. Mr. President, after what has
been observed, relating to a religious test, by gentlemen of acknowledged abilities, I did not expect that
it would again be mentioned, as an objection to the
proposed Constitution, that such a test was not required as a qualification for office. Such were the abilities and integrity of the gentlemen who constructed
the Constitution, as not to admit of the presumption,
that they would have betrayed so much vanity as to
attempt to erect bulwarks and barriers to the throne
of God. Relying on the candor of this Convention, I
shall take the liberty to express my sentiments on the
nature of a religious test, and shall endeavor to do it
in such propositions as will meet the approbation of
every mind.

The great object of religion being God supreme,
and the seat of religion in man being the heart or conscience, *i.e.,* the reason God has given us, employed
on our moral actions, in their most important consequences, as related to the tribunal of God, hence I

infer that God alone is the God of the conscience, and, consequently, attempts to erect human tribunals for the consciences of men are impious encroachments upon the prerogatives of God. Upon these principles, had there been a religious test as a qualification for office, it would, in my opinion, have been a great blemish upon the instrument. . . .

February 4, 1788

Major LUSK concurred in the idea already thrown out in the debate, that, although the insertion of the amendments in the Constitution was devoutly wished, yet he did not see any reason to suppose they ever would be adopted. Turning from the subject of amendments, the major entered largely into the consideration of the 9th section, and, in the most pathetic and feeling manner, described the miseries of the poor natives of Africa, who are kidnapped and sold for slaves. With the brightest colors he painted their happiness and ease on their native shores, and contrasted them with their wretched, miserable, and unhappy condition, in a state of slavery. From this subject he passed to the article dispensing with the qualification of a religious test, and concluded by saying, that he shuddered at the idea that Roman Catholics, Papists, and Pagans might be introduced into office, and that Popery and the Inquisition may be established in America.

Rev. Mr. BACKUS. Mr. President, I have said very little in this honorable Convention; but I now beg leave to offer a few thoughts upon some points in the Constitution proposed to us, and I shall begin with the exclusion of any religious test. Many appear to be much concerned about it; but nothing is more evident, both in reason and the Holy Scriptures, than that religion is ever a matter between God and individuals; and, therefore, no man or men can impose any religious test, without invading the essential prerogatives of our Lord Jesus Christ. Ministers first assumed this power under the Christian name; and then Constantine approved of the practice, when he adopted the profession of Christianity, as an engine

of state policy. And let the history of all nations be searched from that day to this, and it will appear that the imposing of religious tests hath been the greatest engine of tyranny in the world. And I rejoice to see so many gentlemen, who are now giving in their rights of conscience in this great and important matter. Some serious minds discover a concern lest, if all religious tests should be excluded, the Congress would hereafter establish Popery, or some other tyrannical way of worship. But it is most certain that no such way of worship can be established without any religious test. . . .

Debate in Virginia Ratifying Convention (June 6, 10, and 12, 1788)

June 6, 1788

Mr. MADISON then arose— . . .

I confess to you, sir, were uniformity of religion to be introduced by this system, it would, in my opinion, be ineligible; but I have no reason to conclude that uniformity of government will produce that of religion. This subject is, for the honor of America, perfectly free and unshackled. The government has no jurisdiction over it: the least reflection will convince us there is no danger to be feared on this ground. . . .

Tuesday, *June* 10, 1788

Gov. RANDOLPH.

Freedom of religion is said to be in danger. I will candidly say, I once thought that it was, and felt great

Excerpts reprinted from Jonathan Elliot, *The Debates in the Several State Conventions on the Adoption of the Federal Constitution,* 2nd ed. (New York: Burt Franklin, n.d.; Ayer Reprint, 1987), 3:93, 204–5, 313–18, 328, 330.

repugnance to the Constitution for that reason. I am willing to acknowledge my apprehensions removed; and I will inform you by what process of reasoning I did remove them. The Constitution provides that "the senators and representatives before mentioned, and the members of the several state legislatures, and all executive and judicial officers, both of the United States and of the several states, shall be bound, by oath or affirmation, to support this Constitution; but no religious test shall ever be required as a qualification to any office or public trust under the United States." It has been said that, if the exclusion of the religious test were an exception from the general power of Congress, the power over religion would remain. I inform those who are of this opinion, that no power is given expressly to Congress over religion. The senators and representatives, members of the state legislatures, and executive and judicial officers, are bound, by oath or affirmation, to support this Constitution. This only binds them to support it in the exercise of the powers constitutionally given it. The exclusion of religious tests is an exception from this general provision, with respect to oaths or affirmations. Although officers, &c., are to swear that they will support this Constitution, yet they are not bound to support one mode of worship, or to adhere to one particular sect. It puts all sects on the same footing. A man of abilities and character, of any sect whatever, may be admitted to any office or public trust under the United States. I am a friend to a variety of sects, because they keep one another in order. How many different sects are we composed of throughout the United States! How many different sects will be in Congress! We cannot enumerate the sects that may be in Congress! And there are now so many in the United States, that they will prevent the establishment of any one sect, in prejudice to the rest, and will forever oppose all attempts to infringe religious liberty. If such an attempt be made, will not the alarm be sounded throughout America? If Congress should be as wicked as we are foretold they will be, they would not run the risk of exciting the resentment of all, or most, of the religious sects in America. . . .

June 12, 1788

Mr. HENRY.

We are told that all powers not given are reserved. I am sorry to bring forth hackneyed observations. But, sir, important truths lose nothing of their validity or weight, by frequency of repetition. The English history is frequently recurred to by gentlemen. Let us advert to the conduct of the people of that country. The people of England lived without a declaration of rights till the war in the time of Charles I. That king made usurpations upon the rights of the people. Those rights were, in a great measure, before that time undefined. Power and privilege then depended on implication and logical discussion. Though the declaration of rights was obtained from that king, his usurpations cost him his life. The limits between the liberty of the people, and the prerogative of the king, were still not clearly defined.

The rights of the people continued to be violated till the Stuart family was banished, in the year 1688. The people of England magnanimously defended their rights, banished the tyrant, and prescribed to William, Prince of Orange, by the bill of rights, on what terms he should reign; and this bill of rights put an end to all construction and implication. Before this, sir, the situation of the public liberty of England was dreadful. For upwards of a century, the nation was involved in every kind of calamity, till the bill of rights put an end to all, by defining the rights of the people, and limiting the king's prerogative. Give me leave to add (if I can add any thing to so splendid an example) the conduct of the American people. They, sir, thought a bill of rights necessary. It is alleged that several states, in the formation of their government, omitted a bill of rights. To this I answer, that they had the substance of a bill of rights contained in their constitutions, which is the same thing. I believe that Connecticut has preserved it, by her Constitution, her royal charter, which clearly defines and secures the great rights of mankind—secures to us the great, important rights of humanity; and I care not in what form it is done.

Of what advantage is it to the American Congress to take away this great and general security? I ask, Of what advantage is it to the public, or to Congress, to drag an unhappy debtor, not for the sake of justice, but to gratify the malice of the plaintiff, with his witnesses, to the federal court, from a great distance? What was the principle that actuated the Convention in proposing to put such dangerous powers in the hands of any one? Why is the trial by jury taken away? All the learned arguments that have been used on this occasion do not prove that it is secured. Even the advocates for the plan do not all concur in the certainty of its security. Wherefore is religious liberty not secured? One honorable gentleman, who favors adoption, said that he had had his fears on the subject. If I can well recollect, he informed us that he was perfectly satisfied, by the powers of reasoning, (with which he is so happily endowed,) that those fears were not well grounded. There is many a religious man who knows nothing of argumentative reasoning; there are many of our most worthy citizens who cannot go through all the labyrinths of syllogistic, argumentative deductions, when they think that the rights of conscience are invaded. This sacred right ought not to depend on constructive, logical reasoning.

When we see men of such talents and learning compelled to use their utmost abilities to convince themselves that there is no danger, is it not sufficient to make us tremble? Is it not sufficient to fill the minds of the ignorant part of men with fear? If gentlemen believe that the apprehensions of men will be quieted, they are mistaken, since our best-informed men are in doubt with respect to the security of our rights. Those who are not so well informed will spurn at the government. When our common citizens, who are not possessed with such extensive knowledge and abilities, are called upon to change their bill of rights (which, in plain, unequivocal terms, secures their most valuable rights and privileges) for construction and implication, will they implicitly acquiesce? Our declaration of rights tells us that "all men are by nature free and independent," &c. [Here Mr. Henry read the declaration of rights.] Will they exchange these rights for logical reasons? If you had a thousand acres of land dependent on this, would you be satisfied with logical construction? Would you depend upon a title of so disputable a nature? The present opinions of individuals will be buried in entire oblivion when those rights will be thought of. That sacred and lovely thing, religion, ought not to rest on the ingenuity of logical deduction. Holy religion, sir, will be prostituted to the lowest purposes of human policy. What has been more productive of mischief among mankind than religious disputes? Then here, sir, is a foundation for such disputes, when it requires learning and logical deduction to perceive that religious liberty is secure. . . .

Mr. MADISON. . . .

The honorable member has introduced the subject of religion. Religion is not guarded; there is no bill of rights declaring that religion should be secure. Is a bill of rights a security for religion? Would the bill of rights, in this state, exempt the people from paying for the support of one particular sect, if such sect were exclusively established by law? If there were a majority of one sect, a bill of rights would be a poor protection for liberty. Happily for the states, they enjoy the utmost freedom of religion. This freedom arises from that multiplicity of sects which pervades America, and which is the best and only security for religious liberty in any society; for where there is such a variety of sects, there cannot be a majority of any one sect to oppress and persecute the rest. Fortunately for this commonwealth, a majority of the people are decidedly against any exclusive establishment. I believe it to be so in the other states. There is not a shadow of right in the general government to intermeddle with religion. Its least interference with it would be a most flagrant usurpation. I can appeal to my uniform conduct on this subject, that I have warmly supported religious freedom. It is better that this security should be depended upon from the general legislature, than from one particular state. A particular state might concur in one religious project. But the United States abound in such a variety of sects, that it is a strong security against religious persecution; and it is sufficient to authorize a conclusion, that no one sect will ever be able to outnumber or depress the rest. . . .

Debate in North Carolina Ratifying Convention (July 30, 1788)

Wednesday, *July* 30, 1788

The last clause of the 6th article read.

Mr. HENRY ABBOT, after a short exordium, which was not distinctly heard, proceeded thus: Some are afraid, Mr. Chairman, that, should the Constitution be received, they would be deprived of the privilege of worshipping God according to their consciences, which would be taking from them a benefit they enjoy under the present constitution. They wish to know if their religious and civil liberties be secured under this system, or whether the general government may not make laws infringing their religious liberties. The worthy member from Edenton mentioned sundry political reasons why treaties should be the supreme law of the land. It is feared, by some people, that, by the power of making treaties, they might make a treaty engaging with foreign powers to adopt the Roman Catholic religion in the United States, which would prevent the people from worshipping God according to their own consciences. The worthy member from Halifax has in some measure satisfied my mind on this subject. But others may be dissatisfied. Many wish to know what *religion* shall be established. I believe a majority of the community are Presbyterians. I am, for my part, against any exclusive establishment; but if there were any, I would prefer

Excerpts reprinted from Jonathan Elliot, *The Debates in the Several State Conventions on the Adoption of the Federal Constitution,* 2nd ed. (New York: Burt Franklin, n.d.; Ayer Reprint, 1987), 4:191–200, 206, 208–9, 212–13.

the Episcopal. The exclusion of religious tests is by many thought dangerous and impolitic. They suppose that if there be no religious test required, pagans, deists, and Mahometans might obtain offices among us, and that the senators and representatives might all be pagans. Every person employed by the general and state governments is to take an oath to support the former. Some are desirous to know how and by whom they are to swear, since no religious tests are required—whether they are to swear by Jupiter, Juno, Minerva, Proserpine, or Pluto. We ought to be suspicious of our liberties. We have felt the effects of oppressive measures, and know the happy consequences of being jealous of our rights. I would be glad some gentleman would endeavor to obviate these objections, in order to satisfy the religious part of the society. Could I be convinced that the objections were well founded, I would then declare my opinion against the Constitution. [Mr. Abbot added several other observations, but spoke too low to be heard.]

Mr. IREDELL. Mr. Chairman, nothing is more desirable than to remove the scruples of any gentleman on this interesting subject. Those concerning religion are entitled to particular respect. I did not expect any objection to this particular regulation, which, in my opinion, is calculated to prevent evils of the most pernicious consequences to society. Every person in the least conversant in the history of mankind, knows what dreadful mischiefs have been committed by religious persecutions. Under the color of religious tests, the utmost cruelties have been exercised. Those in power have generally considered all wisdom centred in themselves; that they alone had a right to dictate to the rest of mankind; and that all opposition to their tenets was profane and impious. The consequence of this intolerant spirit had been, that each church has in turn set itself up against every other; and persecutions and wars of the most implacable and bloody nature have taken place in every part of the world. America has set an example to mankind to think more modestly and reasonably—that a man may be of different religious sentiments from our own, without being a bad member of society. The principles of toleration, to the honor of this age, are doing away those errors and prejudices which have so long prevailed, even in the most intolerant countries. In the Roman Catholic countries, principles of moderation are adopted which would have been spurned at a century or two ago. I should be sorry to find, when examples of toleration are set even by arbitrary governments, that this country, so impressed with the highest sense of liberty, should adopt principles on this subject that were narrow and illiberal.

I consider the clause under consideration as one of the strongest proofs that could be adduced, that it was the intention of those who formed this system to establish a general religious liberty in America. Were we to judge from the examples of religious tests in other countries, we should be persuaded that they do not answer the purpose for which they are intended. What is the consequence of such in England? In that country no man can be a member in the House of Commons, or hold any office under the crown, without taking the sacrament according to the rites of the Church. This, in the first instance, must degrade and profane a rite which never ought to be taken but from a sincere principle of devotion. To a man of base principles, it is made a mere instrument of civil policy. The intention was, to exclude all persons from offices but the members of the Church of England. Yet it is notorious that dissenters qualify themselves for offices in this manner, though they never conform to the Church on any other occasion; and men of no religion at all have no scruple to make use of this qualification. It never was known that a man who had no principles of religion hesitated to perform any rite when it was convenient for his private interest. No test can bind such a one. I am therefore clearly of opinion that such a discrimination would neither be effectual for its own purposes, nor, if it could, ought it by any means to be made. Upon the principles I have stated, I confess the restriction on the power of Congress, in this particular, has my hearty approbation. They certainly have no authority to interfere in the establishment of any religion whatsoever; and I am astonished that any gentleman should conceive

they have. Is there any power given to Congress in matters of religion? Can they pass a single act to impair our religious liberties? If they could, it would be a just cause of alarm. If they could, sir, no man would have more horror against it than myself. Happily, no sect here is superior to another. As long as this is the case, we shall be free from those persecutions and distractions with which other countries have been torn. If any future Congress should pass an act concerning the religion of the country, it would be an act which they are not authorized to pass, by the Constitution, and which the people would not obey. Every one would ask, "Who authorized the government to pass such an act? It is not warranted by the Constitution, and is barefaced usurpation." The power to make treaties can never be supposed to include a right to establish a foreign religion among ourselves, though it might authorize a toleration of others.

But it is objected that the people of America may, perhaps, choose representatives who have no religion at all, and that pagans and Mahometans may be admitted into offices. But how is it possible to exclude any set of men, without taking away that principle of religious freedom which we ourselves so warmly contend for? This is the foundation on which persecution has been raised in every part of the world. The people in power were always right, and every body else wrong. If you admit the least difference, the door to persecution is opened. Nor would it answer the purpose, for the worst part of the excluded sects would comply with the test, and the best men only be kept out of our counsels. But it is never to be supposed that the people of America will trust their dearest rights to persons who have no religion at all, or a religion materially different from their own. It would be happy for mankind if religion was permitted to take its own course, and maintain itself by the excellence of its own doctrines. The divine Author of our religion never wished for its support by worldly authority. Has he not said that the gates of hell shall not prevail against it? It made much greater progress for itself, than when supported by the greatest authority upon earth.

It has been asked by that respectable gentleman (Mr. Abbot) what is the meaning of that part, where it is said that the United States shall *guaranty* to every state in the Union a republican form of government, and why a *guaranty* of religious freedom was not included. The meaning of the guaranty provided was this: There being thirteen governments confederated upon a republican principle, it was essential to the existence and harmony of the confederacy that each should be a republican government, and that no state should have a right to establish an aristocracy or monarchy. That clause was therefore inserted to prevent any state from establishing any government but a republican one. Every one must be convinced of the mischief that would ensue, if any state had a right to change its government to a monarchy. If a monarchy was established in any one state, it would endeavor to subvert the freedom of the others, and would, probably, by degrees succeed in it. This must strike the mind of every person here, who recollects the history of Greece, when she had confederated governments. The king of Macedon, by his arts and intrigues, got himself admitted a member of the Amphictyonic council, which was the superintending government of the Grecian republics; and in a short time he became master of them all. It is, then, necessary that the members of a confederacy should have similar governments. But consistently with this restriction, the states may make what change in their own governments they think proper. Had Congress undertaken to guaranty religious freedom, or any particular species of it, they would then have had a pretence to interfere in a subject they have nothing to do with. Each state, so far as the clause in question does not interfere, must be left to the operation of its own principles.

There is a degree of jealousy which it is impossible to satisfy. Jealousy in a free government ought to be respected; but it may be carried to too great an extent. It is impracticable to guard against all possible danger of people's choosing their officers indiscreetly. If they have a right to choose, they may make a bad choice.

I met, by accident, with a pamphlet, this morning, in which the author states, as a very serious danger, that the pope of Rome might be elected President. I confess this never struck me before; and if the author had read all the qualifications of a President, perhaps his fears might have been quieted. No man but a native, or who has resided fourteen years in America, can be chosen President. I know not all the qualifications for pope, but I believe he must be taken from the college of cardinals; and probably there are many previous steps necessary before he arrives at this dignity. A native of America must have very singular good fortune, who, after residing fourteen years in his own country, should go to Europe, enter into Romish orders, obtain the promotion of cardinal, afterwards that of pope, and at length be so much in the confidence of his own country as to be elected President. It would be still more extraordinary if he should give up his popedom for our presidency. Sir, it is impossible to treat such idle fears with any degree of gravity. Why is it not objected, that there is no provision in the Constitution against electing one of the kings of Europe President? It would be a clause equally rational and judicious.

I hope that I have in some degree satisfied the doubts of the gentleman. This article is calculated to secure universal religious liberty, by putting all sects on a level—the only way to prevent persecution. I thought nobody would have objected to this clause, which deserves, in my opinion, the highest approbation. This country has already had the honor of setting an example of civil freedom, and I trust it will likewise have the honor of teaching the rest of the world the way to religious freedom also. God grant both may be perpetuated to the end of time!

Mr. Abbot, after expressing his obligations for the explanation which had been given, observed that no answer had been given to the question he put concerning the form of an *oath*.

Mr. Iredell. Mr. Chairman, I beg pardon for having omitted to take notice of that part which the worthy gentleman has mentioned. It was by no means from design, but from its having escaped my memory, as I have not the conveniency of taking notes. I shall now satisfy him in that particular in the best manner in my power.

According to the modern definition of an oath, it is considered a "solemn appeal to the Supreme Being, for the truth of what is said, by a person who believes in the existence of a Supreme Being and in a future state of rewards and punishments, according to that form which will bind his conscience most." It was long held that no oath could be administered but upon the New Testament, except to a Jew, who was allowed to swear upon the Old. According to this notion, none but Jews and Christians could take an oath; and heathens were altogether excluded. At length, by the operation of principles of toleration, these narrow notions were done away. Men at length considered that there were many virtuous men in the world who had not had an opportunity of being instructed either in the Old or New Testament, who yet very sincerely believed in a Supreme Being, and in a future state of rewards and punishments. It is well known that many nations entertain this belief who do not believe either in the Jewish or Christian religion. Indeed, there are few people so grossly ignorant or barbarous as to have no religion at all. And if none but Christians or Jews could be examined upon oath, many innocent persons might suffer for want of the testimony of others. In regard to the form of an oath, that ought to be governed by the religion of the person taking it. I remember to have read an instance which happened in England, I believe in the time of Charles II. A man who was a material witness in a cause, refused to swear upon the book, and was admitted to swear with his uplifted hand. The jury had a difficulty in crediting him; but the chief justice told them, he had, in his opinion, taken as strong an oath as any of the other witnesses, though, had he been to swear himself, he should have kissed the book. A very remarkable instance also happened in England, about forty years ago, of a person who was admitted to take an oath according to the rites of his own country, though he was a heathen. He was an East Indian, who had a great suit in chancery, and his answer upon oath to a bill filed against him was absolutely necessary. Not believing either in the Old or New Testament, he could not be sworn in the accustomed manner, but was sworn according to the form of the Gentoo religion, which he professed, by touching the foot of a priest. It appeared that, according to the tenets of this religion, its members believed in a Supreme Being, and in a future state of rewards and punishments. It was accordingly held by the judges, upon great consideration, that the oath ought to be received; they considering that it was probable those of that religion were equally bound in conscience by an oath according to their form of swearing, as they themselves were by one of theirs; and that it would be a reproach to the justice of the country, if a man, merely because he was of a different religion from their own, should be denied redress of an injury he had sustained. Ever since this great case, it has been universally considered that, in administering an oath, it is only necessary to inquire if the person who is to take it, believes in a Supreme Being, and in a future state of rewards and punishments. If he does, the oath is to be administered according to that form which it is supposed will bind his conscience most. It is, however, necessary that such a belief should be entertained, because otherwise there would be nothing to bind his conscience that could be relied on; since there are many cases where the terror of punishment in this world for perjury could not be dreaded. I have endeavored to satisfy the committee. We may, I think, very safely leave religion to itself; and as to the form of the oath, I think this may well be trusted to the general government, to be applied on the principles I have mentioned.

Gov. JOHNSTON expressed great astonishment that the people were alarmed on the subject of religion. This, he said, must have arisen from the great pains which had been taken to prejudice men's minds against the Constitution. He begged leave to add the following few observations to what had been so ably said by the gentleman last up.

I read the Constitution over and over, but could not see one cause of apprehension or jealousy on this subject. When I heard there were apprehensions that the pope of Rome could be the President of the United States, I was greatly astonished. It might as well be said that the king of England or France, or the Grand Turk, could be chosen to that office. It would have been as good an argument. It appears to me that it would have been dangerous, if Congress could intermeddle with the subject of religion. True religion is derived from a much higher source than human laws. When any attempt is made, by any government, to restrain men's consciences, no good consequence can possibly follow. It is apprehended that Jews, Mahometans, pagans, &c., may be elected to high offices under the government of the United States. Those who are Mahometans, or any others who are not professors of the Christian religion, can never be elected to the office of President, or other high office, but in one of two cases. First, if the people of America lay aside the Christian religion altogether, it may happen. Should this unfortunately take place, the people will choose such men as think as they do themselves. Another case is, if any persons of such descriptions should, notwithstanding their religion, acquire the confidence and esteem of the people of America by their good conduct and practice of virtue, they may be chosen. I leave it to gentlemen's candor to judge what probability there is of the people's choosing men of different sentiments from themselves.

But great apprehensions have been raised as to the influence of the Eastern States. When you attend to circumstances, this will have no weight. I know but two or three states where there is the least chance of establishing any particular religion. The people of Massachusetts and Connecticut are mostly Presbyterians. In every other state, the people are divided into a great number of sects. In Rhode Island, the tenets of the Baptists, I believe, prevail. In New York, they are divided very much: the most numerous are the Episcopalians and the Baptists. In New Jersey, they are as much divided as we are. In Pennsylvania, if any sect prevails more than others, it is that of the Quakers. In Maryland, the Episcopalians are most numerous, though there are other sects. In Virginia,

there are many sects; you all know what their religious sentiments are. So in all the Southern States they differ; as also in New Hampshire. I hope, therefore, that gentlemen will see there is no cause of fear that any one religion shall be exclusively established.

Mr. CALDWELL thought that some danger might arise. He imagined it might be objected to in a political as well as in a religious view. In the first place, he said, there was an invitation for Jews and pagans of every kind to come among us. At some future period, said he, this might endanger the character of the United States. Moreover, even those who do not regard religion, acknowledge that the Christian religion is best calculated, of all religions, to make good members of society, on account of its morality. I think, then, added he, that, in a political view, those gentlemen who formed this Constitution should not have given this invitation to Jews and heathens. All those who have any religion are against the emigration of those people from the eastern hemisphere.

Mr. SPENCER was an advocate for securing every unalienable right, and that of worshipping God according to the dictates of conscience in particular. He therefore thought that no one particular religion should be established. Religious tests, said he, have been the foundation of persecutions in all countries. Persons who are conscientious will not take the oath required by religious tests, and will therefore be excluded from offices, though equally capable of discharging them as any member of the society. It is feared, continued he, that persons of bad principles, deists, atheists, &c., may come into this country; and there is nothing to restrain them from being eligible to offices. He asked if it was reasonable to suppose that the people would choose men without regarding their characters. Mr. Spencer then continued thus: Gentlemen urge that the want of a test admits the most vicious characters to offices. I desire to know what test could bind them. If they were of such principles, it would not keep them from enjoying those offices. On the other hand, it would exclude from offices conscientious and truly religious people, though equally capable as others. Conscientious persons would not take such an oath, and would be therefore excluded. This would be a great cause of objection to a religious test. But in this case, as there is not a religious test required, it leaves religion on the solid foundation of its own inherent validity, without any connection with temporal authority; and no kind of oppression can take place. I confess it strikes me so. I am sorry to differ from the worthy gentleman. I cannot object to this part of the Constitution. I wish every other part was as good and proper.

Gov. JOHNSTON approved of the worthy member's candor. He admitted a possibility of Jews, pagans, &c., emigrating to the United States; yet, he said, they could not be in proportion to the emigration of Christians who should come from other countries; that, in all probability, the children even of such people would be Christians; and that this, with the rapid population of the United States, their zeal for religion, and love of liberty, would, he trusted, add to the progress of the Christian religion among us. . . .

Mr. SPAIGHT.

No sect is preferred to another. Every man has a right to worship the Supreme Being in the manner he thinks proper. No test is required. All men of equal capacity and integrity, are equally eligible to offices. Temporal violence might make mankind wicked, but never religious. A test would enable the prevailing sect to persecute the rest. I do not suppose an infidel, or any such person, will ever be chosen to any office, unless the people themselves be of the same opinion. He says that Congress may establish ecclesiastical courts. I do not know what part of the Constitution warrants that assertion. It is impossible. No such power is given them. The gentleman advises such amendments as would satisfy him, and proposes a mode of amending before ratifying. If we do not adopt first, we are no more a part of the Union than any foreign power. It will be also throwing away the influence of our state to propose amendments as the condition of our ratification. If we adopt first, our representatives will have a proportionable weight in bringing about amendments, which will not be the case if we do not adopt. It is adopted by ten states already. The question, then, is, not whether the Constitution be good, but whether we will or will not confederate with the other states. The gentleman supposes that the liberty of the press is not secured. The Constitution does not take it away. It says nothing of it, and can do nothing to injure it. But it is secured by the constitution of every state in the Union in the most ample manner.

Mr. WILSON wished that the Constitution had excluded Popish priests from offices. As there was no test required, and nothing to govern them but honor, he said that when their interest clashed with their honor, the latter would fly before the former. . . .

Mr. LANCASTER.

As to a religious test, had the article which excludes it provided none but what had been in the states heretofore, I would not have objected to it. It would secure religion. Religious liberty ought to be provided for. I acquiesce with the gentleman, who spoke, on this point, my sentiments better than I could have done myself. For my part, in reviewing the qualifications necessary for a President, I did not suppose that the pope could occupy the President's chair. But let us remember that we form a government for millions not yet in existence. I have not the art of divination. In the course of four or five hundred years, I do not know how it will work. This is most certain, that Papists may occupy that chair, and Mahometans may take it. I see nothing against it. There is a disqualification, I believe, in every state in the Union—it ought to be so in this system. It is said that all power not given is retained. I find they thought proper to insert negative clauses in the Constitution, restraining the general government from the exercise of certain powers. These were unnecessary if the doctrine be true, that every thing not given is retained. From the insertion of these we may conclude the doctrine to be fallacious. Mr. Lancaster then observed, that he would disapprove of the Constitution as it then stood. His own feelings, and his duty to his constituents, induced him to do so. Some people, he said, thought a delegate might act independently of the people. He thought otherwise, and that every delegate was bound by their instructions, and if he did any thing repugnant to their wishes, he betrayed his trust. He thought himself bound by the voice of the people, whatever other gentlemen might think. He would cheerfully agree to adopt, if he thought it would be of general utility; but as he thought it would have a contrary effect, and as he believed a great majority of the people were against it, he would oppose its adoption. . . .

Proposed Amendment, South Carolina Ratifying Convention (May 23, 1788)

A proposed amendment offered by the South Carolina convention addressed questions about the interplay between the Article VI oath clause and the religious test ban. Interestingly, in the *New Haven Gazette,* Connecticut Federalist Roger Sherman insisted that the South Carolina amendment was unnecessary because "it may be considered as a clerical omission and be inserted without calling a convention, as it now stands the effect will be the same."*

RESOLVED that the third section of the Sixth Article ought to be amended by inserting the word "*other*" between the words "*no*" and "*religious.*"

* "A Citizen of New Haven [Roger Sherman]," *New Haven Gazette,* December 18, 1788, in *The Documentary History of the First Federal Elections, 1788–1790,* ed. Gordon DenBoer (Madison: University of Wisconsin Press, 1984), 2:16.
Reprinted from *Creating the Bill of Rights: The Documentary Record from the First Federal Congress,* ed. Helen E. Veit, Kenneth R. Bowling, and Charlene Bangs Bickford (Baltimore and London: Johns Hopkins University Press, 1991), 15, 16.

Commentaries on the Constitution of the United States, §§ 1837–43 (1833)

JOSEPH STORY (1779–1845)

The eminent nineteenth-century jurist, Joseph Story, associate justice of the U.S. Supreme Court and Harvard University's Dane Professor of Law, commented on the Article VI oath clause and religious test ban in his influential 1833 *Commentaries on the Constitution of the United States.*

Chapter XLIII

Oaths of Office—Religious Test— Ratification of Constitution

§ 1837. The next clause is, "The senators and representatives before mentioned, and the members of the several state legislatures and all executive and judicial officers, both of the United States and of the several states, shall be bound by oath or affirmation to support the constitution.[1] But no religious test shall ever be required as a qualification to any office or public trust under the United States."

§ 1838. That all those, who are entrusted with the execution of the powers of the national government, should be bound by some solemn obligation to the due execution of the trusts reposed in them, and to support the constitution, would seem to be a proposition too clear to render any reasoning necessary in

Reprinted from Joseph Story, *Commentaries on the Constitution of the United States* (Boston: Hilliard, Gray; Cambridge, Mass.: Brown, Shattuck, 1833), 3:702–9.

1. This clause, requiring an oath of the state and national functionaries to support the constitution, was at first carried by a vote of six states against five; but it was afterwards unanimously approved. Journ. of Convention, p. 114, 197. On the final vote, it was adopted by a vote of eight states against one, two being divided. Id. 313. The clause respecting a religious test was unanimously adopted. Id. 313.

support of it. It results from the plain right of society to require some guaranty from every officer, that he will be conscientious in the discharge of his duty. Oaths have a solemn obligation upon the minds of all reflecting men, and especially upon those, who feel a deep sense of accountability to a Supreme being. If, in the ordinary administration of justice in cases of private rights, or personal claims, oaths are required of those, who try, as well as of those, who give testimony, to guard against malice, falsehood, and evasion, surely like guards ought to be interposed in the administration of high public trusts, and especially in such, as may concern the welfare and safety of the whole community. But there are known denominations of men, who are conscientiously scrupulous of taking oaths (among which is that pure and distinguished sect of Christians, commonly called Friends, or Quakers,) and therefore, to prevent any unjustifiable exclusion from office, the constitution has permitted a solemn affirmation to be made instead of an oath, and as its equivalent.

§ 1839. But it may not appear to all persons quite so clear, why the officers of the state governments should be equally bound to take a like oath, or affirmation; and it has been even suggested, that there is no more reason to require that, than to require, that all of the United States officers should take an oath or affirmation to support the state constitutions. A moment's reflection will show sufficient reasons for the requisition of it in the one case, and the omission of it in the other. The members and officers of the national government have no agency in carrying into effect the state constitutions. The members and officers of the state governments have an essential agency in giving effect to the national constitution. The election of the president and the senate will depend, in all cases, upon the legislatures of the several states; and, in many cases, the election of the house of representatives may be affected by their agency. The judges of the state courts will frequently be called upon to decide upon the constitution, and laws, and treaties of the United States; and upon rights and claims growing out of them. Decisions ought to be,

Joseph Story, engraving.
© Stapleton Collection/CORBIS.

as far as possible, uniform; and uniformity of obligation will greatly tend to such a result. The executive authority of the several states may be often called upon to exert powers, or allow rights, given by the constitution, as in filling vacancies in the senate, during the recess of the legislature; in issuing writs of election to fill vacancies in the house of representatives; in officering the militia, and giving effect to laws for calling them; and in the surrender of fugitives from justice. These, and many other functions, devolving on the state authorities, render it highly important, that they should be under a solemn obligation to obey the constitution. In common sense, there can be no well-founded objection to it. There may be serious evils growing out of an opposite course.[2] One of the objections, taken to the articles of confederation, by an enlightened state, (New-Jersey,) was, that

2. The Federalist, No. 44; 1 Tuck. Black. Comm. App. 370, 371; Rawle on Constitution, ch. 19, p. 191, 192.

no oath was required of members of congress, previous to their admission to their seats in congress. The laws and usages of all civilized nations, (said that state,) evince the propriety of an oath on such occasions; and the more solemn and important the deposit, the more strong and explicit ought the obligation to be.[3]

§ 1840. As soon as the constitution went into operation, congress passed an act,[4] prescribing the time and manner of taking the oath, or affirmation, thus required, as well by officers of the several states, as of the United States. On that occasion, some scruple seems to have been entertained, by a few members, of the constitutional authority of congress to pass such an act.[5] But it was approved without much opposition. At this day, the point would be generally deemed beyond the reach of any reasonable doubt.[6]

§ 1841. The remaining part of the clause declares, that "no religious test shall ever be required, as a qualification to any office or public trust, under the United States." This clause is not introduced merely for the purpose of satisfying the scruples of many respectable persons, who feel an invincible repugnance to any religious test, or affirmation. It had a higher object; to cut off for ever every pretence of any alliance between church and state in the national government. The framers of the constitution were fully sensible of the dangers from this source, marked out in the history of other ages and countries; and not wholly unknown to our own. They knew, that bigotry was unceasingly vigilant in its stratagems, to secure to itself an exclusive ascendancy over the human mind; and that intolerance was ever ready to arm itself with all the terrors of the civil power to exterminate those, who doubted its dogmas, or resisted its infallibility. The Catholic and the Protestant had alternately waged the most ferocious and unrelenting warfare on each other; and Protestantism itself, at the very moment, that it was proclaiming the right of pri-

vate judgment, prescribed boundaries to that right, beyond which if any one dared to pass, he must seal his rashness with the blood of martyrdom.[7] The history of the parent country, too, could not fail to instruct them in the uses, and the abuses of religious tests. They there found the pains and penalties of non-conformity written in no equivocal language, and enforced with a stern and vindictive jealousy. One hardly knows, how to repress the sentiments of strong indignation, in reading the cool vindication of the laws of England on this subject, (now, happily, for the most part abolished by recent enactments,) by Mr. Justice Blackstone, a man, in many respects distinguished for habitual moderation, and a deep sense of justice. "The second species," says he "of nonconformists, are those, who offend through a mistaken or perverse zeal. Such were esteemed by our laws, enacted since the time of the reformation, to be papists, and protestant dissenters; both of which were supposed to be equally schismatics in not communicating with the national church; with this difference, that the papists divided from it upon material, though erroneous, reasons; but many of the dissenters, upon matters of indifference, or, in other words, upon no reason at all. Yet certainly our ancestors were mistaken in their plans of compulsion and intolerance. The sin of schism, as such, is by no means the object of temporal coercion and punishment. If, through weakness of intellect, through misdirected piety, through perverseness and acerbity of temper, or, (which is often the case,) through a prospect of secular advantage in herding with a party, men quarrel with the ecclesiastical establishment, the civil magistrate has nothing to do with it; unless their tenets and practice are such, as threaten ruin or disturbance to the state. He is bound, indeed, to protect the established church; and, if this can be better effected, by admitting none but its genuine members to offices of trust and emolument, he is certainly at liberty so to do; the disposal of offices being matter of favour and discretion. But, this point being once secured, all

3. 2 Pitk. Hist. 22; 1 Secret Journ. of Congress, June 25, 1778, p. 374.
4. Act of 1st June, 1789, ch. 1.
5. Lloyd's Debates, 218 to 225; 4 Elliot's Debates, 139 to 141.
6. See also *M'Culloh* v. *Maryland,* 4 Wheat. R. 415, 416.

7. See 4 Black. Comm. 44, 53, and ante, Vol. I, § 53.

persecution for diversity of opinions, however ridiculous or absurd they may be, is contrary to every principle of sound policy and civil freedom. The names and subordination of the clergy, the posture of devotion, the materials and colour of the minister's garment, the joining in a known, or an unknown form of prayer, and other matters of the same kind, must be left to the option of every man's private judgment."[8]

§ 1842. And again: "As to papists, what has been said of the protestant dissenters would hold equally strong for a general toleration of them; provided their separation was founded only upon difference of opinion in religion, and their principles did not also extend to a subversion of the civil government. If once they could be brought to renounce the supremacy of the pope, they might quietly enjoy their seven sacraments, their purgatory, and auricular confession; their worship of reliques and images; nay even their transubstantiation. But while they acknowledge a foreign power, superior to the sovereignty of the kingdom, they cannot complain, if the laws of that kingdom will not treat them upon the footing of good subjects."[9]

§ 1843. Of the English laws respecting papists, Montesquieu observes, that they are so rigorous, though not professedly of the sanguinary kind, that they do all the hurt, that can possibly be done in cold blood. To this just rebuke, (after citing it, and admitting its truth,) Mr. Justice Blackstone has no better reply to make, than that these laws are seldom exerted to their utmost rigour; and, indeed, if they were, it would be very difficult to excuse them.[10] The meanest apologist of the worst enormities of a Roman emperor could not have shadowed out a defence more servile, or more unworthy of the dignity and spirit of a freeman. With one quotation more from the same authority, exemplifying the nature and objects of the

English test laws, this subject may be dismissed. "In order the better to secure the established church against perils from non-conformists of all denominations, infidels, Turks, Jews, heretics, papists, and sectaries, there are, however, two bulwarks erected, called the corporation and test-acts. By the former of which, no person can be legally elected to any office relating to the government of any city or corporation, unless, within a twelvemonth before, he has received the sacrament of the Lord's supper according to the rights of the church of England; and he is also enjoined to take the oaths of allegiance and supremacy, at the same time, that he takes the oath of office; or, in default of either of these requisites, such election shall be void. The other, called the test-act, directs all officers, civil and military, to take the oaths, and make the declaration against transubstantiation, in any of the king's courts at Westminster, or at the quarter sessions, within six calendar months after their admission; and also within the same time to receive the sacrament of the Lord's supper, according to the usage of the church of England, in some public church immediately after divine service and sermon; and to deliver into court a certificate thereof signed by the minister and church-warden, and also to prove the same by two credible witnesses, upon forfeiture of 500*l*, and disability to hold the said office. And of much the same nature with these is the statute 7 Jac. I. c. 2., which permits no persons to be naturalized, or restored in blood, but such as undergo a like test; which test, having been removed in 1753, in favour of the Jews, was the next session of parliament restored again with some precipitation."[11] It is easy to foresee, that without some prohibition of religious tests, a successful sect, in our country, might, by once possessing power, pass test-laws, which would secure to themselves a monopoly of all the offices of trust and profit, under the national government.[12]

8. 4 Black. Comm. 52, 53.
9. 4 Black. Comm. 54, 55.
10. 4 Black. Comm. 57.

11. See also 2 Kent's Comm. Lect. 24, (2 edit.) p. 35, 36; Rawle on the Constitution, ch. 10, p. 121; 1 Tuck. Black. Comm. App. 296; 2 Tuck. Black. Comm. App. Note (G.), p. 3.
12. See ante, Vol. II, § 621.

RECOMMENDATIONS FOR FURTHER READING

Bradley, Gerard V. "The No Religious Test Clause and the Constitution of Religious Liberty: A Machine That Has Gone of Itself." *Case Western Reserve Law Review* 37 (1987): 674–747.

Dreisbach, Daniel L. "The Constitution's Forgotten Religion Clause: Reflections on the Article VI Religious Test Ban." *Journal of Church and State* 38 (1996): 261–95.

CHAPTER NINE

The First Amendment to the U.S. Constitution

THE MOST INFLUENTIAL constitutional pronouncement on religious liberty and church-state relations is the First Amendment to the U.S. Constitution. Drafted by the first federal Congress in 1789, ratified by the states and added to the Constitution in 1791, the Amendment states: "Congress shall make no law respecting an establishment of religion, or prohibiting the free exercise thereof." The interpretation and application of these sixteen words have been the source of much debate and litigation in American history.

Many Americans in 1787 thought the proposed national constitution insufficiently safeguarded religious liberty. Accordingly, a number of state ratifying conventions proposed amendments to the new Constitution—namely an enumeration of rights that included religious liberty. When the first Congress convened in New York City in the summer of 1789, Representative James Madison led the efforts to frame a bill of rights. Although Madison is often called the "Father of the Bill of Rights," the legislative history of the amendment reveals that some of his proposals concerning religion were rejected altogether, and others were amended by his fellow members of the U.S. House of Representatives and the Senate. The texts of the congressional debates are included in this chapter, and a summary of them is contained in the second appendix (pp. 637–39).

Although diverse interpretations can be drawn from the recorded congressional debates and text of the amendment, broad agreement exists for several modest conclusions. Some commentators argue that the First Amendment was designed to achieve more in terms of religious liberty or church-state separation, but the following principles provide a starting point for any analysis of the religion provisions that are consistent with the history of the framing of these clauses.

First, the First Amendment proscribed the creation of a national church, departing from the English model of an ecclesiastical establishment. The framers sought to protect all religious sects and denominations from the discrimination that would result if Congress conferred upon one religious sect or combination of sects legal preference or special favors that were denied others. It did not require civil government to hold all religion in utter indifference or to strip public life of all religious discourse, values, or symbols.

Second, the First Amendment implicitly affirmed state jurisdiction in religious matters. Congress, in other words, was not only prohibited from establishing a national church, but also it was denied authority to interfere with existing state religious establishments. The U.S. Supreme Court confirmed that the Bill of Rights, in general, and the religion clauses of the First Amendment, more specifically, were not binding on the states in *Barron v. Baltimore,* 32 U.S. (7 Peters) 243 (1833), and *Permoli v. New Orleans,* 44 U.S. (3 Howard) 589 (1845), respectively. (However, in the mid-twentieth century, the Supreme Court incorporated the First Amendment's religion provisions into the Fourteenth Amendment's due process of law clause, thereby making these provisions applicable to the states.)

Third, the First Amendment protected individual citizens from actions by the national regime that inhibited the free exercise of religion. The precise definition and scope of this liberty is far from clear; however, the absolutist tenor of the language suggests a far-reaching limitation on the national government's power to interfere with voluntary religious practices. At the very least, the free-exercise provision was meant to prevent Congress from prohibiting or compelling any form of religious worship. A plausible reading of the amendment, consistent with the understandings of religious liberty in 1789, is that it affirmed a right to worship God according to the dictates of one's conscience, free from coercion, punishment, interference, or discrimination by the national government. Moreover, it ensured freedom to profess and support one's religious belief without diminishing one's civil rights and capacities.

Although the legislative history reveals much about the original understanding and purposes of the First Amendment's religion provisions, many questions about the interpretation of this text remain unanswered. For example, to what extent is the national government authorized to assist or encourage religion generally; or does the free-exercise provision relieve a believer of an obligation to comply with a valid, facially neutral law of general applicability on the ground that the law inhibits the adherent's religious exercise; or what was the intended relationship between the amendment's nonestablishment and free-exercise clauses? These are questions that continue to vex modern church-state relations.

Objections to This Constitution of Government (c. September 16, 1787)

GEORGE MASON (1725–92)

George Mason was a member of the Federal Convention, but he disagreed with the final draft of the Constitution and refused to sign the document. Shortly after the convention concluded, he penned a set of objections and circulated them among friends. They were published without his approval in Philadelphia on October 4, 1787, and were soon reprinted throughout the states. The opening paragraph of his objections is reprinted below.

[*ca.* 16 September 1787]

Objections to This Constitution of Government

There is no Declaration of Rights, and the laws of the general government being paramount to the laws and constitution of the several States, the Declarations of Rights in the separate States are no security. Nor are the people secured even in the enjoyment of the benefit of the common law. . . .

George Mason, by Louis Mathieu Didier Guillaume, 1858. Used by permission of the Virginia Historical Society, Richmond, Virginia.

Proposed Amendments (October 1, 1787)

RICHARD HENRY LEE (1732–94)

On September 18, 1787, George Mason sent a letter and a copy of his objections to his friend, Richard Henry Lee, who was serving in the Confederation Congress. Lee proposed a set of amendments to the Constitution, which were rejected by Congress before the body sent the document to the states for ratification. On October 1, Lee sent Mason a report of

Excerpt reprinted from *The Papers of George Mason, 1727–1792,* ed. Robert A. Rutland (Chapel Hill: University of North Carolina Press, 1970), 3:991. © 1970 by the University of North Carolina Press. Used by permission of the publisher.

Excerpts reprinted from *The Papers of George Mason, 1727–1792,* ed. Robert A. Rutland (Chapel Hill: University of North Carolina Press, 1970), 3:997–98. © 1970 by the University of North Carolina Press. Used by permission of the publisher.

Congress's actions, a suggestion for the Virginia legislature, and a copy of his proposed amendments. The following excerpts focus on his concerns regarding a bill of rights.

Suppose when the Assembly recommended a Convention to consider this new Constitution they were to use some words like these—It is earnestly recommended to the good people of Virginia to send their most wise & honest Men to this Convention that it may undergo the most intense consideration before a plan shall be without amendments adopted that admits of abuses being practised by which the best interests of this Country may be injured and Civil Liberty greatly endanger'd. This might perhaps give a decided Tone to the business.

Please to send my Son Ludwell a Copy of the Amendments proposed by me to the new Constitution sent herewith.

[enclosure]   [1 October 1787]
It having been found from Universal experience that the most express declarations and reservations are necessary to protect the just rights and liberty of Mankind from the silent powerful and ever active conspiracy of those who govern—And it appearing to be the sense of the good people of America by the various Bills or Declarations of Rights whereon the Governments of the greater number of the States are founded; that such precautions are proper to restrain and regulate the exercise of the great powers necessarily given to Rulers—In conformity with these principles, and from respect for the public sentiment on this subject it is submitted

That the new Constitution proposed for the Government of the U. States be bottomed upon a declaration, or Bill of Rights, clearly and precisely stating the principles upon which this Social Compact is founded to wit, That the right of Conscience in matters of Religion shall not be violated—That the free-

dom of the Press shall be secured—That the trial by Jury in Criminal and Civil cases, and the modes prescribed by the Common Law for safety of Life in criminal prosecutions shall be held sacred— . . .

Objections to the Constitution (February 28, 1788)

JOHN LELAND (1754–1841)

John Leland, a native of Massachusetts, was licensed to preach by the Baptists in 1775 and moved to Virginia in the fall of 1776. An important advocate of religious liberty, he wrote a series of objections to the proposed Constitution. Fellow Baptist Joseph Spencer sent a copy of these objections to James Madison so that he could refute them. Objections related to the absence of a bill of rights and protections for religious liberty are excerpted below.

According, to your request, I here send you my objections to the *Foederal Constitution*, which are as follows,

1st. There is no Bill Rights, whenever Number of men enter into a State of Socity, a Number of individual Rights must be given up to Socity, but there should always be a memorial of those not surrendred, otherwise every natural & domestic Right becomes alianable, which raises Tyranny at once, & this is as necessary in one Form of Goverment as in another—
. . .

Excerpts reprinted from *The Documentary History of the Ratification of the Constitution*, vol. 8: *Ratification of the Constitution by the States: Virginia*, ed. John P. Kaminski and Gaspare J. Saladino (Madison: State Historical Society of Wisconsin, 1988), 425, 426. © State Historical Society of Wisconsin 1988. Reprinted with permission of the publisher.

10ly. What is dearest of all—*Religious Liberty*, is not Sufficiently Secured, No religious test is required as a Qualification to fill any office under the United States, but if a Majority of Congress with the presedent favour one Systom more then another, they may oblige all others to pay to the Support of their System as Much as they please, & if Oppression dose not ensue, it will be owing to the Mildness of Administration & not to any Constitutional defense, & if the Manners of People are so far Corrupted, that they cannot live by republican principles, it is Very Dangerous leaving religious Liberty at their Marcy— . . .

A Farmer, No. 1 (February 15, 1788) and No. 7 (April 11, 1788)

JOHN FRANCIS MERCER (1759–1821)

"A Farmer" was likely John Francis Mercer, a delegate to the Federal Convention who refused to sign the Constitution and who returned to Maryland to lead the Anti-Federalist forces there. He penned a series of seven essays for the *Maryland Gazette* responding to Federalist author Alexander Contee Hanson, who wrote under the pseudonym of Aristides. Excerpts from his first and seventh essays concerning a bill of rights and religious liberty are reprinted below.

I
15 February 1788

When men, to whom the guardianship of public liberty has been committed, discover a neglect if not

Excerpts reprinted from *The Complete Anti-Federalist*, ed. Herbert J. Storing (Chicago and London: University of Chicago Press, 1981), 5:9–10, 60–63.

contempt for a bill of rights—when they answer reasons by alledging a fact,—which fact too, is no fact at all—it becomes a duty to bear testimony against such conduct, for silence and acquiescence in political language are synonimous terms.

If men were as anxious about reality as appearance, we should have fewer professions of disinterested patriotism—true patriotism like true piety, is incompatible with an ostentatious personal display.

In a world more cautious than correct, the intrusion of private names in a public cause, is generally considered as a sacrifice of prudence to vanity, and not unfrequently censured as impertinent—in either view it is unreasonable to require it—It is more, it is inadmissible—it would be betraying one of those inestimable rights of an individual, over which society should have no controul—the freedom of the press— and the only recompence for the treason, would be a boundless increase of private malice.

That men who profess an attachment to the liberty of the press, should also require names, is one of those instances of human weakness and inconsistency, that deserves rather pity than resentment. Political as well as religious freedom has ever been and forever will be destroyed by that invariable tendency of enthusiasts and bigots to mark out as objects of public resentment and persecution, those who presume to dispute their opinions or question their infallibility—and whilst there are men, enthusiasm and bigotry will prevail— it is the natural predominance of the passions over reason—The citizens of America are not yet so agitated by the phrenzy of innovation as to forget—that the object of public inquiry is, or ought to be, *truth*— that to convert *truth* into *falsehood, right* into *wrong*, is equally beyond the reach of the *good*, the *bad*, the *great* and the *humble*—A great name may indeed *impose falsehood* for *truth*—*wrong* for *right*—and whenever such voluntarily offer themselves, there may be ground for suspicion—But the people may listen with safety to those, who assert no other claim to their attention, than the *reason* and *merit* of their remarks.

To assert that bills of rights have always originated from, or been considered as grants of the King or

Prince, and that the liberties which they secure are the gracious concessions of the sovereign, betrays an equal ignorance of history and of law, or what in effect amounts to the same thing a violent and precipitate zeal.

I believe no writer in the most venal age, has ever openly asserted this doctrine, but the prostituted, rotten Sir Robert Filmer, and Aristides—And the man who at this day would contend in England that their bill of rights is the grant of the King, would find the general contempt his only security—In saying this, I sincerely regret that the name of Aristides should be joined with that of Sir Robert Filmer, and I freely acknowledge that no contemptible degree of talents, and integrity render him who uses it, much more worthy of the very respectable association he has selected for himself—But the errors of such men alone are dangerous—the man who has too much activity of mind, or restlessness to be quiet, qualities to engage public and private esteem, talents to form and support an opinion, fortitude to avow it, and too much pride to be convinced, will at all times have weight in a free country, (especially where indolence is the general characteristic) though that weight he will always find impaired in proportion as he indulges levity, caprice and passion. . . .

A Farmer

VII
11 April 1788

Human misery is wound up to its highest pitch in this last stage of corruption, to which the social union can arrive:—At length the poor, wretched beings, who, let whatever be the change, and in every preceding gradation of government, have invariably fallen from bad to worse—turn their weary eyes, from a world which presents so frightful a prospect—to the world of hope,—the kingdom that is to come hereafter—the only solace and comfort of those who are miserable here;—there all the fond images of equality, which men are fated ever to retain, are once more revived—Scenes of never-ending bliss are painted in the most delightful colours—the imagination grows warm with the prospect—mad with the hopes of celestial happiness, the souls of all men seem anxious to take their flight, to their Omnipotent Author—the Sovereign Legislator of nature—who, peerless and above all, dispences equal law to willing minds:—The people flock in crouds to hear preachers—who, exalted by the presence of numerous and passionate audiences, are elevated into flights of native eloquence, surpassing the strains of the most studied oratory:—The people mind nothing but preaching; the things of this miserable world, are despised when put in competition with the joys of Paradise—agriculture is neglected—famine ensues—government is at length roused for want of plunder and a supply of luxuries—the sword of coercion is drawn—but it increases the phrenzy—One martyr makes fifty converts—such was the first rise of the Christian religion, as it is exactly and pathetically described by the historic pen of Ammianus Marcellinus:—The empire torn by intestine convulsions becomes an easy prey to any bold invader.

Thus it is that barbarity—cruelty and blood which stain the history of religion, spring from the corruption of civil government, and from that never-dying hope and fondness for a state of equality, which constitutes an essential part of the soul of man:—A chaos of darkness obscures the downfal of empire, intermixed with gleams of light, which serve only to disclose scenes of desolation and horror—From the last confusion springs order:—The bold spirits who pull down the ancient fabric—erect a new one, founded on the natural liberties of mankind, and *where civil government is preserved free, there can be no religious tyranny*—the sparks of bigotry and enthusiasm may and will crackle, but can never light into a blaze.—

The truth of these remarks appear from the histories of those two great revolutions of European government, which seem to have convulsed this earth to the centre of its orb, and of which we have compleat record—The Roman and the Gothic, or as it is more commonly called the feudal constitution:—In the infancy of the Roman republic, when enterprizing and free, their conquests were rapid, because beneficial to the conquered (who were admitted to a participation of their liberty) their religion, although devoid, was not only unstained by persecution, but censurably liberal—they received without discrimination the Gods of the countries they subdued, into the list of their deities, until Olympus was covered with an army of demigods as numerous as the legions of Popish Saints; and we find the Grecian divinities adored with more sincere piety at Rome, than at Athens.—Rome was then in the zenith of her glory—in the days of her wretched decline—in the miserable reigns of Caracalla, Eliagabalus and Commodus.— Ammianus and others, inform us that the Christians were butchered like sheep, for reviving the old exploded doctrine of a future state, in which Emperors and Senators were to be placed on a level with the poorest and most abject of mankind:—And in the succeeding despotisms when christianity became the established religion, it grew immediately as corrupt in its infancy, as ever it has proved at any period since— the most subtle disquisitions of a metaphysical nature became the universal rage—the more incomprehensible—the more obstinately were they maintained, and in fine, the canonized Austin or Ambrose, (I forget which) closed his laborious enquiries, with this holy position—*that he believed, because it was impossible.* At length the great question, whether the three persons of the divinity, were three or one, became publickly agitated, and threw all mankind into a flame—Councils after councils, composed of all the wisdom of the divines, were assembled, and at length the doctrine that three were one prevailed, and such would have been the determination had it been proposed that three were sixteen—because misery is the foundation, upon which error erects her tyranny over the vulgar mind.—After this determination the arm of the Magistrate was called in, and those poor misled Arians who were still so wicked as to imagine that three must be three, were not only declared guilty of a most abominable and damnable heresy, but were thenceforth exterminated by fire and sword.

In the first age of the *Gothic* government, those free and hardy adventurers, deserted their Idols and embraced the doctrines of Christianity with ardent sincerity:—The King and a large majority of a nation, would be converted and baptized with as much celerity as the ceremony could be performed—but still liberty in the temporal, secured freedom in the spiritual administration: Christians and Pagan citizens lived together in the utmost harmony—Those bold and hardy conquerors would never listen to Bishops who advised persecution, and held in sovereign contempt all those metaphysical distinctions with which a pure religion has been disgraced, in order to cloak villainous designs and support artful usurpations of civil powers in feeble and turbulent governments. The Gothic institutions were however much sooner corrupted from internal vices than the Roman, and the undeniable reason was, that in the former, government by representation was admitted almost coeval with their first inundations;—whereas with the Romans, the democratic branch of power, exercised by the people personally, rendered them invincible both in war and peace—the virtue of this internal institution could only be subdued by the greatness of its external acquisition—extensive empire ruined this mighty fabric—a superstructure, which overshadowed the then known world, was too mighty for the foundation confined within the walls of a city—the wealth imported by the Scipios from Spain and Afric, and by Flaminius, Lucullus, Sylla and Pompey, from the East, enabled the *few* to corrupt the *many*—a case that can never exist but where the legislative power resides exclusively in the citizens of the town—The Roman republic then became diseased at the heart, but as it was ages in forming, so it required ages of corruption to destroy a robust constitution where every atom was a nerve: It was not so with the Gothic constitution, mortal disease soon made its appearance there—Civil liberty was early destroyed by the insolence and oppressions of the great—The temporal power availed itself of that spiritual influence which nature has given religion over the hearts of men—A religion, the divinity of which is demonstrable by reason alone, unassisted by revelation became the corrupt instrument of usurpation.—Those who were the authors of the disorders which disgraced civil government, cut the reins of ecclesiastical persecution: And an universal and tyrannic confusion was mingled with absurdities that excite both ridicule and horror. We see a Duke of Gandia (who was betrayed and assassinated by that monster of perfidy Caesar Borgia, the bastard of the infamous Pope Alexander the VIth) in the last moments of his existence, begging the cut throat son, that he would intercede with his father, the Pope, in favour of his poor soul, that it might not be kept long in purgatory, but dispatched as soon as possible to Heaven, to dispute the infallibility of those vice-gerents of God, who generally patterned after the devil, was considered as an heresy more damnable than blaspheming the most high. Religious tyranny continued in this state, during those convulsions which broke the aristocracies of Europe, and settled their governments into mixed monarchies: A ray of light then beamed—but only for a moment—the turbulent state and quick corruption of mixed monarchy, opened a new scene of religious horror—Pardons for all crimes committed and to be committed, were regulated by ecclesiastical law, with a mercantile exactitude, and a Christian knew what he must pay for murdering another better than he now does the price of a pair of boots: At length some bold spirits began to doubt whether wheat flour, made into paste, could be actually human flesh, or whether the wine made in the last vintage could be the real blood of Christ, who had been crucified upwards of 1400 years—Such was the origin of the Protestant reformation—at the bare mention of such heretical and dangerous doctrine, striking (as they said) at the root of all religion, the sword of power leaped from its scabbard, the smoke that arose from the flames, to which the most virtuous of mankind, were without mercy committed, darkened all Europe for ages; tribunals, armed with frightful tortures, were every where erected, to make men confess opinions, and then they were solemnly burned for confessing, whilst priest and people sang hymns around them; and the fires of persecution are scarcely yet extinguished. *Civil and religious liberty are inseparably*

interwoven—whilst government is pure and equal—religion will be uncontaminated:—The moment government becomes disordered, bigotry and fanaticism take root and grow—they are soon converted to serve the purpose of usurpation, and finally, religious persecution reciprocally supports and is supported by the tyranny of the temporal powers.

A Farmer

Letter from Thomas Jefferson to James Madison (December 20, 1787)

Thomas Jefferson, while American minister to France, sent James Madison a letter detailing what he did and did not like about the proposed Constitution. His concerns regarding the lack of a bill of rights are reprinted below.

I will now add what I do not like. First the omission of a bill of rights providing clearly and without the aid of sophisms for freedom of religion, freedom of the press, protection against standing armies, restriction against monopolies, the eternal and unremitting force of the habeas corpus laws, and trials by jury in all matters of fact triable by the laws of the land and not by the law of Nations. To say, as Mr. Wilson does that a bill of rights was not necessary because all is reserved in the case of the general government which is not given, while in the particular ones all is given which is not reserved might do for the Audience to whom it was addressed, but is surely gratis dictum [statement for no reward], opposed by strong infer-

Excerpt reprinted from *The Papers of Thomas Jefferson*, ed. Julian P. Boyd (Princeton: Princeton University Press, 1955), 12:440. © 1955 Princeton University Press.

ences from the body of the instrument, as well as from the omission of the clause of our present confederation which had declared that in express terms. It was a hard conclusion to say because there has been no uniformity among the states as to the cases triable by jury, because some have been so incautious as to abandon this mode of trial, therefore the more prudent states shall be reduced to the same level of calamity. It would have been much more just and wise to have concluded the other way that as most of the states had judiciously preserved this palladium, those who had wandered should be brought back to it, and to have established general right instead of general wrong. Let me add that a bill of rights is what the people are entitled to against every government on earth, general or particular, and what no just government should refuse, or rest on inference. . . .

Letter from James Madison to Thomas Jefferson (October 17, 1788)

The following excerpt from a letter Madison wrote to Jefferson in the midst of the first elections under the newly ratified Constitution illustrates his thinking about the virtues and vices of adding a bill of rights to the Constitution.

The little pamphlet herewith inclosed will give you a collective view of the alterations which have been proposed for the new Constitution. Various and numerous as they appear they certainly omit many of the true grounds of opposition. The articles relating to

Excerpt reprinted from James Madison, *The Papers of James Madison*, ed. Robert A. Rutland and Charles F. Hobson, vol. 11: *7 March 1788–1 March 1789* (Charlottesville: University Press of Virginia, 1977), 297–300. © 1977 The University of Virginia Press. Used by permission of the publisher.

Treaties—to paper money, and to contracts, created more enemies than all the errors in the System positive & negative put together. It is true nevertheless that not a few, particularly in Virginia have contended for the proposed alterations from the most honorable & patriotic motives; and that among the advocates for the Constitution, there are some who wish for further guards to public liberty & individual rights. As far as these may consist of a constitutional declaration of the most essential rights, it is probable they will be added; though there are many who think such addition unnecessary, and not a few who think it misplaced in such a Constitution. There is scarce any point on which the party in opposition is so much divided as to its importance and its propriety. My own opinion has always been in favor of a bill of rights; provided it be so framed as not to imply powers not meant to be included in the enumeration. At the same time I have never thought the omission a material defect, nor been anxious to supply it even by *subsequent* amendment, for any other reason than that it is anxiously desired by others. I have favored it because I supposed it might be of use, and if properly executed could not be of disservice. I have not viewed it in an important light 1. because I conceive that in a certain degree, though not in the extent argued by Mr. Wilson, the rights in question are reserved by the manner in which the federal powers are granted. 2. because there is great reason to fear that a positive declaration of some of the most essential rights could not be obtained in the requisite latitude. I am sure that the rights of Conscience in particular, if submitted to public definition would be narrowed much more than they are likely ever to be by an assumed power. One of the objections in New England was that the Constitution by prohibiting religious tests opened a door for Jews Turks & infidels. 3. because the limited powers of the federal Government and the jealousy of the subordinate Governments, afford a security which has not existed in the case of the State Governments, and exists in no other. 4. because experience proves the inefficacy of a bill of rights on those occasions when its controul is most needed. Repeated violations of these parchment barriers have been committed by overbearing majorities in every State. In Virginia I have seen the bill of rights violated in every instance where it has been opposed to a popular current. Notwithstanding the explicit provision contained in that instrument for the rights of Conscience it is well known that a religious establishment wd. have taken place in that State, if the legislative majority had found as they expected, a majority of the people in favor of the measure; and I am persuaded that if a majority of the people were now of one sect, the measure would still take place and on narrower ground than was then proposed, notwithstanding the additional obstacle which the law has since created. Wherever the real power in a Government lies, there is the danger of oppression. In our Governments the real power lies in the majority of the Community, and the invasion of private rights is *chiefly* to be apprehended, not from acts of Government contrary to the sense of its constituents, but from acts in which the Government is the mere instrument of the major number of the constituents. This is a truth of great importance, but not yet sufficiently attended to: and is probably more strongly impressed on my mind by facts, and reflections suggested by them, than on yours which has contemplated abuses of power issuing from a very different quarter. Wherever there is an interest and power to do wrong, wrong will generally be done, and not less readily by a powerful & interested party than by a powerful and interested prince. The difference, so far as it relates to the superiority of republics over monarchies, lies in the less degree of probability that interest may prompt abuses of power in the former than in the latter; and in the security in the former agst. oppression of more than the smaller part of the society, whereas in the former it may be extended in a manner to the whole. The difference so far as it relates to the point in question— the efficacy of a bill of rights in controuling abuses of power—lies in this, that in a monarchy the latent force of the nation is superior to that of the sovereign, and a solemn charter of popular rights must have a great effect, as a standard for trying the validity of public acts, and a signal for rousing & uniting the superior force of the community; whereas in a popular Government, the political and physical power may be considered as vested in the same hands, that is in a majority of the people, and consequently the tyrannical will of the sovereign is not [to] be controuled by the dread of an appeal to any other force within the community. What use then it may be asked can a bill of rights serve in popular Governments? I answer the two following which though less essential than in other Governments, sufficiently recommend the precaution. 1. The political truths declared in that solemn manner acquire by degrees the character of fundamental maxims of free Government, and as they become incorporated with the national sentiment, counteract the impulses of interest and passion. 2. Altho' it be generally true as above stated that the danger of oppression lies in the interested majorities of the people rather than in usurped acts of the Government, yet there may be occasions on which the evil may spring from the latter sources; and on such, a bill of rights will be a good ground for an appeal to the sense of the community. Perhaps too there may be a certain degree of danger, that a succession of artful and ambitious rulers, may by gradual & well-timed advances, finally erect an independent Government on the subversion of liberty. Should this danger exist at all, it is prudent to guard agst. it, especially when the precaution can do no injury. At the same time I must own that I see no tendency in our governments to danger on that side. It has been remarked that there is a tendency in all Governments to an augmentation of power at the expence of liberty. But the remark as usually understood does not appear to me well founded. Power when it has attained a certain degree of energy and independence goes on generally to further degrees. But when below that degree, the direct tendency is to further degrees of relaxation, until the abuses of liberty beget a sudden transition to an undue degree of power. With this explanation the remark may be true; and in the latter sense only is it in my opinion applicable to the Governments in America. It is a melancholy reflection that liberty should be equally exposed to danger whether the Government have too much or too little power, and that the line which divides these extremes should be so inaccurately defined by experience.

Supposing a bill of rights to be proper the articles which ought to compose it, admit of much discussion. I am inclined to think that *absolute* restrictions in cases that are doubtful, or where emergencies may overrule them, ought to be avoided. The restrictions however strongly marked on paper will never be regarded when opposed to the decided sense of the public; and after repeated violations in extraordinary cases, they will lose even their ordinary efficacy. Should a Rebellion or insurrection alarm the people as well as the Government, and a suspension of the Hab. Corp. be dictated by the alarm, no written prohibitions on earth would prevent the measure. Should an army in time of peace be gradually established in our neighbourhood by Britn: or Spain, declarations on paper would have as little effect in preventing a standing force for the public safety. The best security agst. these evils is to remove the pretext for them. With regard to monopolies they are justly classed among the greatest nusances in Government. But is it clear that as encouragements to literary works and ingenious discoveries, they are not too valuable to be wholly renounced? Would it not suffice to reserve in all cases a right to the Public to abolish the privilege at a price to be specified in the grant of it? Is there not also infinitely less danger of this abuse in our Governments, than in most others? Monopolies are sacrifices of the many to the few. Where the power is in the few it is natural for them to sacrifice the many to their own partialities and corruptions. Where the power, as with us, is in the many not in the few, the danger can not be very great that the few will be thus favored. It is much more to be dreaded that the few will be unnecessarily sacrificed to the many. . . .

Selected Amendments Proposed by the State Ratifying Conventions

Amendments to the U.S. Constitution were formally proposed by ratifying conventions in seven states, and by minorities in conventions in three states. Those most relevant to religious liberty are reprinted below.

Amendment Proposed by the Pennsylvania Minority (December 12, 1787)

1. The right of conscience shall be held inviolable; and neither the legislative, executive nor judicial powers of the United States shall have authority to alter, abrogate or infringe any part of the constitution of the several States, which provide for the preservation of liberty in matters of religion.

Reprinted from John Bach McMaster and Frederick D. Stone, *Pennsylvania and the Federal Constitution, 1787–1788* (1888; reprint, New York: Da Capo Press, 1970), 461.

Amendment Proposed by the Massachusetts Minority (February 6, 1788)

[T]hat the said Constitution be never construed to authorize Congress to infringe the just liberty of the press, or the rights of conscience; or to prevent the people of the United States, who are peaceable citi-

Reprinted from *The Complete Bill of Rights: The Drafts, Debates, Sources, and Origins,* ed. Neil H. Cogan (New York and Oxford: Oxford University Press, 1997), 12. © 1997 Oxford University Press. Used by permission of Oxford University Press, Inc.

zens, from keeping their own arms; or to raise standing armies, unless when necessary for the defence of the United States, or of some one or more of them; or to prevent the people from petitioning, in a peaceable and orderly manner, the federal legislature, for a redress of grievances; or to subject the people to unreasonable searches and seizures of their persons, papers or possessions.

Amendment Proposed by the Maryland Minority (April 26, 1788)

12. That there be no national religion established by law, but that all persons be equally entitled to protection in their religious liberty.

Reprinted from *The Complete Bill of Rights: The Drafts, Debates, Sources, and Origins*, ed. Neil H. Cogan (New York and Oxford: Oxford University Press, 1997), 11. © 1997 Oxford University Press. Used by permission of Oxford University Press, Inc.

Amendment Proposed by the New Hampshire Ratifying Convention (June 21, 1788)

Eleventh
    Congress shall make no Laws touching Religion, or to infringe the rights of Conscience.

Amendments Proposed by the Virginia Ratifying Convention (June 27, 1788)

That there be a Declaration or Bill of Rights asserting and securing from encroachment the essential and unalienable Rights of the People in some such manner as the following:

First, That there are certain natural rights of which men, when they form a social compact cannot deprive or divest their posterity, among which are the enjoyment of life and liberty, with the means of acquiring, possessing and protecting property, and pursuing and obtaining happiness and safety. . . .

. . . NINETEENTH, That any person religiously scrupulous of bearing arms ought to be exempted upon payment of an equivalent to employ another to bear arms in his stead.

TWENTIETH, That religion or the duty which we owe to our Creator, and the manner of discharging it can be directed only by reason and conviction, not by force or violence, and therefore all men have an equal, natural and unalienable right to the free exercise of religion according to the dictates of conscience, and that no particular religious sect or society ought to be favored or established by Law in preference to others.

Reprinted from *Creating the Bill of Rights: The Documentary Record from the First Federal Congress*, ed. Helen E. Veit, Kenneth R. Bowling, and Charlene Bangs Bickford (Baltimore and London: Johns Hopkins University Press, 1991), 17.

Reprinted from *Creating the Bill of Rights: The Documentary Record from the First Federal Congress*, ed. Helen E. Veit, Kenneth R. Bowling, and Charlene Bangs Bickford (Baltimore and London: Johns Hopkins University Press, 1991), 17, 19.

Amendments Proposed by the New York Ratifying Convention (July 26, 1788)

That all power is originally vested in and consequently derived from the People, and that Government is instituted by them for their common Interest Protection and Security.

That the enjoyment of Life, Liberty and the pursuit of Happiness are essential rights which every Government ought to respect and preserve.

That the Powers of Government may be reassumed by the People, whensoever it shall become necessary to their Happiness; that every Power, Jurisdiction and Right, which is not by the said Constitution clearly delegated to the Congress of the United States, or the departments of the Government thereof, remains to the People of the several States, or to their respective State Governments to whom they may have granted the same; And that those Clauses in the said Constitution, which declare, that Congress shall not have or exercise certain Powers, do not imply that Congress is entitled to any Powers not given by the said Constitution; but such Clauses are to be construed either as exceptions to certain specified Powers, or as inserted merely for greater Caution.

That the People have an equal, natural and unalienable right, freely and peaceably to Exercise their Religion according to the dictates of Conscience, and that no Religious Sect or Society ought to be favoured or established by Law in preference of others.

Amendments Proposed by the North Carolina Ratifying Convention (August 1, 1788)

19th. That any person religiously scrupulous of bearing arms ought to be exempted upon payment of an equivalent to employ another to bear arms in his stead.

10. [20th.] That religion, or the duty which we owe to our Creator, and the manner of discharging it, can be directed only by reason and conviction, not by force or violence, and therefore all men have an equal, natural and unalienable right, to the free exercise of religion according to the dictates of conscience, and that no particular religious sect or society ought to be favoured or established by law in preference to others.

Reprinted from *The Complete Bill of Rights: The Drafts, Debates, Sources, and Origins,* ed. Neil H. Cogan (New York and Oxford: Oxford University Press, 1997), 12. © 1997 Oxford University Press. Used by permission of Oxford University Press, Inc.

Amendments Proposed by the Rhode Island Ratifying Convention (May 29, 1790)

4th. That religion, or the duty which we owe to our Creator, and the manner of discharging it, can be directed only by reason and conviction, and not by force or violence, and therefore all men, have an equal, natural and unalienable right to the free exercise of religion according to the dictates of conscience, and that no particular religious sect or society ought to be favoured, or established by law in preference to others.

Reprinted from *Creating the Bill of Rights: The Documentary Record from the First Federal Congress,* ed. Helen E. Veit, Kenneth R. Bowling, and Charlene Bangs Bickford (Baltimore and London: Johns Hopkins University Press, 1991), 21–22.

Reprinted from *The Complete Bill of Rights: The Drafts, Debates, Sources, and Origins,* ed. Neil H. Cogan (New York and Oxford: Oxford University Press, 1997), 12–13. © 1997 Oxford University Press. Used by permission of Oxford University Press, Inc.

Speech in the First Congress Introducing Amendments to the U.S. Constitution (June 8, 1789)

JAMES MADISON (1751–1836)

Although he did not initially support adding a bill of rights to the U.S. Constitution, James Madison promised voters he would advocate for one if elected to the U.S. House of Representatives. One of his first acts as a congressman was to introduce and defend a bill of rights.

MR. MADISON. I am sorry to be accessary to the loss of a single moment of time by the house. If I had been indulged in my motion, and we had gone into a committee of the whole, I think we might have rose, and resumed the consideration of other business before this time; that is, so far as it depended on what I proposed to bring forward. As that mode seems not to give satisfaction, I will withdraw the motion, and move you, sir, that a select committee be appointed to consider and report such amendments as are proper for Congress to propose to the legislatures of the several States, conformably to the 5th article of the constitution. I will state my reasons why I think it proper to propose amendments; and state the amendments themselves, so far as I think they ought to be proposed. If I thought I could fulfil the duty which I owe to myself and my constituents, to let the subject pass over in silence, I most certainly should not trespass upon the indulgence of this house. But I cannot do this; and am therefore compelled to beg a

Reprinted from James Madison, *The Papers of James Madison*, ed. Robert A. Rutland and Charles F. Hobson, vol. 12: *2 March 1789–20 January 1790*, with a supplement *24 October 1775–24 January 1789* (Charlottesville: University Press of Virginia, 1979), 197–209. © 1979 The University of Virginia Press. Used by permission of the publisher.

patient hearing to what I have to lay before you. And I do most sincerely believe that if congress will devote but one day to this subject, so far as to satisfy the public that we do not disregard their wishes, it will have a salutary influence on the public councils, and prepare the way for a favorable reception of our future measures. It appears to me that this house is bound by every motive of prudence, not to let the first session pass over without proposing to the state legislatures some things to be incorporated into the constitution, as will render it as acceptable to the whole people of the United States, as it has been found acceptable to a majority of them. I wish, among other reasons why something should be done, that those who have been friendly to the adoption of this constitution, may have the opportunity of proving to those who were opposed to it, that they were as sincerely devoted to liberty and a republican government, as those who charged them with wishing the adoption of this constitution in order to lay the foundation of an aristocracy or despotism. It will be a desirable thing to extinguish from the bosom of every member of the community any apprehensions, that there are those among his countrymen who wish to deprive them of the liberty for which they valiantly fought and honorably bled. And if there are amendments desired, of such a nature as will not injure the constitution, and they can be ingrafted so as to give satisfaction to the doubting part of our fellow citizens; the friends of the federal government will evince that spirit of deference and concession for which they have hitherto been distinguished.

It cannot be a secret to the gentlemen in this house, that, notwithstanding the ratification of this system of government by eleven of the thirteen United States, in some cases unanimously, in others by large majorities; yet still there is a great number of our constituents who are dissatisfied with it; among whom are many respectable for their talents, their patriotism, and respectable for the jealousy they have for their liberty, which, though mistaken in its object, is laudable in its motive. There is a great body of the people falling under this description, who at present feel much inclined to join their support to the cause of federalism, if they were satisfied in this one point: We ought not to disregard their inclination, but, on principles of amity and moderation, conform to their wishes, and expressly declare the great rights of mankind secured under this constitution. The acquiescence which our fellow citizens shew under the government, calls upon us for a like return of moderation. But perhaps there is a stronger motive than this for our going into a consideration of the subject; it is to provide those securities for liberty which are required by a part of the community. I allude in a particular manner to those two states who have not thought fit to throw themselves into the bosom of the confederacy: it is a desirable thing, on our part as well as theirs, that a re-union should take place as soon as possible. I have no doubt, if we proceed to take those steps which would be prudent and requisite at this juncture, that in a short time we should see that disposition prevailing in those states that are not come in, that we have seen prevailing [in] those states which are.

But I will candidly acknowledge, that, over and above all these considerations, I do conceive that the constitution may be amended; that is to say, if all power is subject to abuse, that then it is possible the abuse of the powers of the general government may be guarded against in a more secure manner than is now done, while no one advantage, arising from the exercise of that power, shall be damaged or endangered by it. We have in this way something to gain, and, if we proceed with caution, nothing to lose; and in this case it is necessary to proceed with caution; for while we feel all these inducements to go into a revisal of the constitution, we must feel for the constitution itself, and make that revisal a moderate one. I should be unwilling to see a door opened for a reconsideration of the whole structure of the government, for a re-consideration of the principles and the substance of the powers given; because I doubt, if such a door was opened, if we should be very likely to stop at that point which would be safe to the government itself: But I do wish to see a door opened to

consider, so far as to incorporate those provisions for the security of rights, against which I believe no serious objection has been made by any class of our constituents, such as would be likely to meet with the concurrence of two-thirds of both houses, and the approbation of three-fourths of the state legislatures. I will not propose a single alteration which I do not wish to see take place, as intrinsically proper in itself, or proper because it is wished for by a respectable number of my fellow citizens; and therefore I shall not propose a single alteration but is likely to meet the concurrence required by the constitution.

There have been objections of various kinds made against the constitution: Some were levelled against its structure, because the president was without a council; because the senate, which is a legislative body, had judicial powers in trials on impeachments; and because the powers of that body were compounded in other respects, in a manner that did not correspond with a particular theory; because it grants more power than is supposed to be necessary for every good purpose; and controuls the ordinary powers of the state governments. I know some respectable characters who opposed this government on these grounds; but I believe that the great mass of the people who opposed it, disliked it because it did not contain effectual provision against encroachments on particular rights, and those safeguards which they have been long accustomed to have interposed between them and the magistrate who exercised the sovereign power: nor ought we to consider them safe, while a great number of our fellow citizens think these securities necessary.

It has been a fortunate thing that the objection to the government has been made on the ground I stated; because it will be practicable on that ground to obviate the objection, so far as to satisfy the public mind that their liberties will be perpetual, and this without endangering any part of the constitution, which is considered as essential to the existence of the government by those who promoted its adoption.

The amendments which have occurred to me, proper to be recommended by congress to the state legislatures, are these:

First. That there be prefixed to the constitution a declaration—That all power is originally vested in, and consequently derived from the people.

That government is instituted, and ought to be exercised for the benefit of the people; which consists in the enjoyment of life and liberty, with the right of acquiring and using property, and generally of pursuing and obtaining happiness and safety.

That the people have an indubitable, unalienable, and indefeasible right to reform or change their government, whenever it be found adverse or inadequate to the purposes of its institution.

Secondly. That in article 1st. section 2, clause 3, these words be struck out, to wit, "The number of representatives shall not exceed one for every thirty thousand, but each state shall have at least one representative, and until such enumeration shall be made." And that in place thereof be inserted these words, to wit, "After the first actual enumeration, there shall be one representative for every thirty thousand, until the number amount to   after which the proportion shall be so regulated by congress, that the number shall never be less than   nor more than   but each state shall after the first enumeration, have at least two representatives; and prior thereto."

Thirdly. That in article 1st, section 6, clause 1, there be added to the end of the first sentence, these words, to wit, "But no law varying the compensation last ascertained shall operate before the next ensuing election of representatives."

Fourthly. That in article 1st, section 9, between clauses 3 and 4, be inserted these clauses, to wit, The civil rights of none shall be abridged on account of religious belief or worship, nor shall any national religion be established, nor shall the full and equal rights of conscience be in any manner, or on any pretext infringed.

The people shall not be deprived or abridged of their right to speak, to write, or to publish their sentiments; and the freedom of the press, as one of the great bulwarks of liberty, shall be inviolable.

The people shall not be restrained from peaceably assembling and consulting for their common good; nor from applying to the legislature by petitions, or remonstrances for redress of their grievances.

The right of the people to keep and bear arms shall not be infringed; a well armed, and well regulated militia being the best security of a free country: but no person religiously scrupulous of bearing arms, shall be compelled to render military service in person.

No soldier shall in time of peace be quartered in any house without the consent of the owner; nor at any time, but in a manner warranted by law.

No person shall be subject, except in cases of impeachment, to more than one punishment, or one trial for the same offence; nor shall be compelled to be a witness against himself; nor be deprived of life, liberty, or property without due process of law; nor be obliged to relinquish his property, where it may be necessary for public use, without a just compensation.

Excessive bail shall not be required, nor excessive fines imposed, nor cruel and unusual punishments inflicted.

The rights of the people to be secured in their persons, their houses, their papers, and their other property from all unreasonable searches and seizures, shall not be violated by warrants issued without probable cause, supported by oath or affirmation, or not particularly describing the places to be searched, or the persons or things to be seized.

In all criminal prosecutions, the accused shall enjoy the right to a speedy and public trial, to be informed of the cause and nature of the accusation, to be confronted with his accusers, and the witnesses against him; to have a compulsory process for obtaining witnesses in his favor; and to have the assistance of counsel for his defence.

The exceptions here or elsewhere in the constitution, made in favor of particular rights, shall not be so construed as to diminish the just importance of other rights retained by the people; or as to enlarge the powers delegated by the constitution; but either as actual limitations of such powers, or as inserted merely for greater caution.

Fifthly. That in article 1st, section 10, between clauses 1 and 2, be inserted this clause, to wit:

No state shall violate the equal rights of conscience, or the freedom of the press, or the trial by jury in criminal cases.

Sixthly. That article 3d, section 2, be annexed to the end of clause 2d, these words to wit: but no appeal to such court shall be allowed where the value in controversy shall not amount to _____ dollars: nor shall any fact triable by jury, according to the course of common law, be otherwise re-examinable than may consist with the principles of common law.

Seventhly. That in article 3d, section 2, the third clause be struck out, and in its place be inserted the clauses following, to wit:

The trial of all crimes (except in cases of impeachments, and cases arising in the land or naval forces, or the militia when on actual service in time of war or public danger) shall be by an impartial jury of freeholders of the vicinage, with the requisite of unanimity for conviction, of the right of challenge, and other accustomed requisites; and in all crimes punishable with loss of life or member, presentment or indictment by a grand jury, shall be an essential preliminary, provided that in cases of crimes committed within any county which may be in possession of an enemy, or in which a general insurrection may prevail, the trial may by law be authorised in some other county of the same state, as near as may be to the seat of the offence.

In cases of crimes committed not within any county, the trial may by law be in such county as the laws shall have prescribed. In suits at common law, between man and man, the trial by jury, as one of the best securities to the rights of the people, ought to remain inviolate.

Eighthly. That immediately after article 6th, be inserted, as article 7th, the clauses following, to wit:

The powers delegated by this constitution, are appropriated to the departments to which they are respectively distributed: so that the legislative department shall never exercise the powers vested in the executive or judicial; nor the executive exercise the powers vested in the legislative or judicial; nor the judicial exercise the powers vested in the legislative or executive departments.

The powers not delegated by this constitution, nor prohibited by it to the states, are reserved to the States respectively.

Ninthly. That article 7th, be numbered as article 8th.

The first of these amendments, relates to what may be called a bill of rights; I will own that I never considered this provision so essential to the federal constitution, as to make it improper to ratify it, until such an amendment was added; at the same time, I always conceived, that in a certain form and to a certain extent, such a provision was neither improper nor altogether useless. I am aware, that a great number of the most respectable friends to the government and champions for republican liberty, have thought such a provision, not only unnecessary, but even improper, nay, I believe some have gone so far as to think it even dangerous. Some policy has been made use of perhaps by gentlemen on both sides of the question: I acknowledge the ingenuity of those arguments which were drawn against the constitution, by a comparison with the policy of Great-Britain, in establishing a declaration of rights; but there is too great a difference in the case to warrant the comparison: therefore the arguments drawn from that source, were in a great measure inapplicable. In the declaration of rights which that country has established, the truth is, they have gone no farther, than to raise a barrier against the power of the crown; the power of the legislature is left altogether indefinite. Altho' I know whenever the great rights, the trial by jury, freedom of the press, or liberty of conscience, came in question in that body, the invasion of them is resisted by able advocates, yet their Magna Charta does not contain any one provision for the security of those rights, respecting which, the people of America are most alarmed. The freedom of the press and rights of conscience, those choicest privileges of the people, are unguarded in the British constitution.

But altho' the case may be widely different, and it may not be thought necessary to provide limits for the legislative power in that country, yet a different opinion prevails in the United States. The people of many states, have thought it necessary to raise barriers against power in all forms and departments of government, and I am inclined to believe, if once bills of rights are established in all the states as well as the federal constitution, we shall find that altho' some of them are rather unimportant, yet, upon the whole, they will have a salutary tendency.

It may be said, in some instances they do no more than state the perfect equality of mankind; this to be sure is an absolute truth, yet it is not absolutely necessary to be inserted at the head of a constitution.

In some instances they assert those rights which are exercised by the people in forming and establishing a plan of government. In other instances, they specify those rights which are retained when particular powers are given up to be exercised by the legislature. In other instances, they specify positive rights, which may seem to result from the nature of the compact. Trial by jury cannot be considered as a natural right, but a right resulting from the social compact which regulates the action of the community, but is as essential to secure the liberty of the people as any one of the pre-existent rights of nature. In other instances they lay down dogmatic maxims with respect to the construction of the government; declaring, that the legislative, executive, and judicial branches shall be kept separate and distinct: Perhaps the best way of securing this in practice is to provide such checks, as will prevent the encroachment of the one upon the other.

But whatever may be [the] form which the several states have adopted in making declarations in favor of particular rights, the great object in view is to limit and qualify the powers of government, by excepting out of the grant of power those cases in which the government ought not to act, or to act only in a particular mode. They point these exceptions sometimes against the abuse of the executive power, sometimes against the legislative, and, in some cases, against the community itself; or, in other words, against the majority in favor of the minority.

In our government it is, perhaps, less necessary to guard against the abuse in the executive department than any other; because it is not the stronger branch of the system, but the weaker: It therefore must be levelled against the legislative, for it is the most powerful, and most likely to be abused, because it is under the least controul; hence, so far as a declaration of rights can tend to prevent the exercise of undue power, it cannot be doubted but such declaration is proper. But I confess that I do conceive, that in a government modified like this of the United States, the great danger lies rather in the abuse of the community than in the legislative body. The prescriptions in favor of liberty, ought to be levelled against that quarter where the greatest danger lies, namely, that which possesses the highest prerogative of power: But this [is] not found in either the executive or legislative departments of government, but in the body of the people, operating by the majority against the minority.

It may be thought all paper barriers against the power of the community, are too weak to be worthy of attention. I am sensible they are not so strong as to satisfy gentlemen of every description who have seen and examined thoroughly the texture of such a defence; yet, as they have a tendency to impress some degree of respect for them, to establish the public opinion in their favor, and rouse the attention of the whole community, it may be one mean to controul the majority from those acts to which they might be otherwise inclined.

It has been said by way of objection to a bill of rights, by many respectable gentlemen out of doors, and I find opposition on the same principles likely to be made by gentlemen on this floor, that they are unnecessary articles of a republican government, upon the presumption that the people have those rights in their own hands, and that is the proper place for them to rest. It would be a sufficient answer to say that this objection lies against such provisions under the state governments as well as under the general government; and there are, I believe, but few gentlemen who are inclined to push their theory so far as to say that a declaration of rights in those cases is either ineffectual or improper. It has been said that in the federal government they are unnecessary, because the powers are enumerated, and it follows that all that are not granted by the constitution are retained: that the constitution is a bill of powers, the great residuum being the rights of the people; and therefore a bill of rights cannot be so necessary as if the residuum was thrown into the hands of the government. I admit that these arguments are not entirely without foundation; but they are not conclusive to the extent which has been supposed. It is true the powers of the general government are circumscribed; they are directed to particular objects; but even if government keeps within those limits, it has certain discretionary powers with respect to the means, which may admit of abuse to a certain extent, in the same manner as the powers of the state governments under their constitutions may to an indefinite extent; because in the constitution of the United States there is a clause granting to Congress the power to make all laws which shall be necessary and proper for carrying into execution all the powers vested in the government of the United States, or in any department or officer thereof; this enables them to fulfil every purpose for which the government was established. Now, may not laws be considered necessary and proper by Congress, for it is them who are to judge of the necessity and propriety to accomplish those special purposes which they may have in contemplation, which laws in themselves are neither necessary or proper; as well as improper laws could be enacted by the state legislatures, for fulfilling the more extended objects of those governments. I will state an instance which I think in point, and proves that this might be the case. The general government has a right to pass all laws which shall be necessary to collect its revenue; the means for enforcing the collection are within the direction of the legislature: may not general warrants be considered necessary for this purpose, as well as for some purposes which it was supposed at the framing of their constitutions the state governments had in view. If there was reason for restraining the state governments from exercising this power, there is like reason for restraining the federal government.

It may be said, because it has been said, that a bill of rights is not necessary, because the establishment of this government has not repealed those declarations of rights which are added to the several state constitutions: that those rights of the people, which had been established by the most solemn act, could not be annihilated by a subsequent act of that people, who meant, and declared at the head of the instrument, that they ordained and established a new system, for the express purpose of securing to themselves and posterity the liberties they had gained by an arduous conflict.

I admit the force of this observation, but I do not look upon it to be conclusive. In the first place, it is too uncertain ground to leave this provision upon, if a provision is at all necessary to secure rights so important as many of those I have mentioned are conceived to be, by the public in general, as well as those in particular who opposed the adoption of this constitution. Beside some states have no bills of rights, there are others provided with very defective ones, and there are others whose bills of rights are not only defective, but absolutely improper; instead of securing some in the full extent which republican principles would require, they limit them too much to agree with the common ideas of liberty.

It has been objected also against a bill of rights, that, by enumerating particular exceptions to the grant of power, it would disparage those rights which were not placed in that enumeration, and it might follow by implication, that those rights which were not singled out, were intended to be assigned into the hands of the general government, and were consequently insecure. This is one of the most plausible arguments I have ever heard urged against the admission of a bill of rights into this system; but, I conceive, that may be guarded against. I have attempted it, as gentlemen may see by turning to the last clause of the 4th resolution.

It has been said, that it is unnecessary to load the constitution with this provision, because it was not found effectual in the constitution of the particular states. It is true, there are a few particular states in which some of the most valuable articles have not, at one time or other, been violated; but does it not follow but they may have, to a certain degree, a salutary effect against the abuse of power. If they are incorporated into the constitution, independent tribunals of justice will consider themselves in a peculiar manner the guardians of those rights; they will be an impenetrable bulwark against every assumption of power in the legislative or executive; they will be naturally led to resist every encroachment upon rights expressly stipulated for in the constitution by the declaration of rights. Beside this security, there is a great probability that such a declaration in the federal system would be inforced; because the state legislatures will jealously and closely watch the operations of this government, and be able to resist with more effect every assumption of power than any other power on earth can do; and the greatest opponents to a federal government admit the state legislatures to be sure guardians of the people's liberty. I conclude from this view of the subject, that it will be proper in itself, and highly politic, for the tranquility of the public mind, and the stability of the government, that we should offer something, in the form I have proposed, to be incorporated in the system of government, as a declaration of the rights of the people.

In the next place I wish to see that part of the constitution revised which declares, that the number of representatives shall not exceed the proportion of one for every thirty thousand persons, and allows one representative to every state which rates below that proportion. If we attend to the discussion of this subject, which has taken place in the state conventions, and even in the opinion of the friends to the constitution, an alteration here is proper. It is the sense of the people of America, that the number of representatives ought to be encreased, but particularly that it should not be left in the discretion of the government to diminish them, below that proportion which certainly is in the power of the legislature as the constitution now stands; and they may, as the population of the country encreases, increase the house of representatives to a very unwieldy degree. I confess I always thought this part of the constitution defective, though not dangerous; and that it ought to be particularly attended to whenever congress should go into the consideration of amendments.

There are several lesser cases enumerated in my proposition, in which I wish also to see some alteration take place. That article which leaves it in the power of the legislature to ascertain its own emolument is one to which I allude. I do not believe this is a power which, in the ordinary course of government, is likely to be abused, perhaps of all the powers granted, it is least likely to abuse; but there is a seeming impropriety in leaving any set of men without controul to put their hand into the public coffers, to take out money to put in their pockets; there is a seeming indecorum in such power, which leads me to propose a change. We have a guide to this alteration in several of the amendments which the different conventions have proposed. I have gone therefore so far as to fix it, that no law, varying the compensation, shall operate until there is a change in the legislature; in which case it cannot be for the particular benefit of those who are concerned in determining the value of the service.

I wish also, in revising the constitution, we may throw into that section, which interdicts the abuse of certain powers in the state legislatures, some other provisions of equal if not greater importance than those already made. The words, "No state shall pass any bill of attainder, ex post facto law, &c." were wise and proper restrictions in the constitution. I think there is more danger of those powers being abused by the state governments than by the government of the United States. The same may be said of other powers which they possess, if not controuled by the general principle, that laws are unconstitutional which infringe the rights of the community. I should therefore wish to extend this interdiction, and add, as I have stated in the 5th resolution, that no state shall violate the equal right of conscience, freedom of the press, or trial by jury in criminal cases; because it is proper that every government should be disarmed of powers which trench upon those particular rights. I know in some of the state constitutions the power of the government is controuled by such a declaration, but others are not. I cannot see any reason against obtaining even a double security on those points; and nothing can give a more sincere proof of the attachment of those who opposed this constitution to these great and important rights, than to see them join in obtaining the security I have now proposed; because it must be admitted, on all hands, that the state governments are as liable to attack these invaluable privileges as the general government is, and therefore ought to be as cautiously guarded against.

I think it will be proper, with respect to the judiciary powers, to satisfy the public mind on those points which I have mentioned. Great inconvenience has been apprehended to suitors from the distance they would be dragged to obtain justice in the supreme court of the United States, upon an appeal on an action for a small debt. To remedy this, declare, that no appeal shall be made unless the matter in controversy amounts to a particular sum: This, with the regulations respecting jury trials in criminal cases, and suits at common law, it is to be hoped will quiet and reconcile the minds of the people to that part of the constitution.

I find, from looking into the amendments proposed by the state conventions, that several are particularly anxious that it should be declared in the constitution, that the powers not therein delegated, should be reserved to the several states. Perhaps words which may define this more precisely, than the whole of the instrument now does, may be considered as superfluous. I admit they may be deemed unnecessary; but there can be no harm in making such a declaration, if gentlemen will allow that the fact is as stated. I am sure I understand it so, and do therefore propose it.

These are the points on which I wish to see a revision of the constitution take place. How far they will accord with the sense of this body, I cannot take upon me absolutely to determine; but I believe every gentleman will readily admit that nothing is in contemplation, so far as I have mentioned, that can endanger the beauty of the government in any one important feature, even in the eyes of its most sanguine admirers. I have proposed nothing that does not appear to me as proper in itself, or eligible as patronised by a respectable number of our fellow citizens; and if we can make the constitution better in the opinion of those who are opposed to it, without weakening its frame, or abridging its usefulness, in the judgment of those who are attached to it, we act the part of wise and liberal men to make such alterations as shall produce that effect.

Having done what I conceived was my duty, in bringing before this house the subject of amendments, and also stated such as I wish for and approve, and offered the reasons which occurred to me in their support; I shall content myself for the present with moving, that a committee be appointed to consider of and report such amendments as ought to be proposed by congress to the legislatures of the states, to become, if ratified by three-fourths thereof, part of the constitution of the United States. By agreeing to this motion, the subject may be going on in the committee, while other important business is proceeding to a conclusion in the house. I should advocate greater dispatch in the business of amendments, if I was not convinced of the absolute necessity there is of pursuing the organization of the government; because I think we should obtain the confidence of our fellow citizens, in proportion as we fortify the rights of the people against the encroachments of the government.

Debates in the First Congress on the Religion Clauses (1789)

James Madison is often called the "Father of the Bill of Rights," and he undoubtedly played an important role in its creation. However, some of his proposals were rejected, and others were amended by members of the House and Senate. Unfortunately, records of debates about the religion clauses are quite limited, but the excerpts below give some indication of the religion clauses' path through Congress.

Religion Clauses from Madison's June 8, 1789, Speech

Fourthly. That in article 1st, section 9, between clauses 3 and 4, be inserted these clauses, to wit, The civil rights of none shall be abridged on account of religious belief or worship, nor shall any national religion be established, nor shall the full and equal rights of conscience be in any manner, or on any pretext infringed. . . .

The right of the people to keep and bear arms shall not be infringed; a well armed, and well regulated militia being the best security of a free country: but no person religiously scrupulous of bearing arms, shall be compelled to render military service in person. . . .

Fifthly. That in article 1st, section 10, between clauses 1 and 2, be inserted this clause, to wit:

No state shall violate the equal rights of conscience, or the freedom of the press, or the trial by jury in criminal cases.

Draft Proposals from House Committee of Eleven (July 21–28, 1789)*

The people have certain natural rights which are retained by them when they enter into Society, Such are the rights of Conscience in matters of religion; of acquiring property and of pursuing happiness & Safety; of Speaking, writing and publishing their Sentiments with Decency and Freedom; of peaceably assembling to consult their common good, and of applying to Government by petition or remonstrance for redress of grievances. Of these rights therefore they Shall not be deprived by the Government of the united States. . . .

The militia shall be under the government of the laws of the respective States, when not in the actual Service of the united States, but such rules as may be prescribed by Congress for their uniform organization & discipline shall be observed in officering and training them, but military Service shall not be required of persons religiously scrupulous of bearing arms. . . .

Reprinted from James Madison, *The Papers of James Madison*, ed. Robert A. Rutland and Charles F. Hobson, vol. 12: *2 March 1789–20 January 1790*, with a supplement *24 October 1775–24 January 1789* (Charlottesville: University Press of Virginia, 1979), 201, 202. © 1979 The University of Virginia Press. Used by permission of the publisher.

Reprinted from Scott D. Gerber, "Roger Sherman and the Bill of Rights," *Polity* 28, no. 4 (summer 1996): 532, 533. © Northeastern Political Science Association. Used by permission of Scott D. Gerber.

* These proposals, recorded in the handwriting of Roger Sherman, are sometimes referred to as "Sherman's Proposals." The evidence suggests, however, that Sherman was simply the committee's scribe. For further discussion, see Scott D. Gerber, "Roger Sherman and the Bill of Rights," *Polity* 28, no. 4 (summer 1996): 521–40.—Eds.

Religion Clauses from House Committee Report (July 28, 1789)

[4] Art. 1, Sec. 9—Between Par. 2 and 3 insert, "No religion shall be established by law, nor shall the equal rights of conscience be infringed." . . .

[6] "A well regulated militia, composed of the body of the people, being the best security of a free State, the right of the people to keep and bear arms shall not be infringed, but no person religiously scrupulous shall be compelled to bear arms." . . .

[12] Art. 1, Sec. 10, between the 1st and 2d Par. insert, "No State shall infringe the equal rights of conscience, nor the freedom of speech, or of the press, nor of the right of trial by jury in criminal cases."

Reprinted from *Creating the Bill of Rights: The Documentary Record from the First Federal Congress*, ed. Helen E. Veit, Kenneth R. Bowling, and Charlene Bangs Bickford (Baltimore and London: Johns Hopkins University Press, 1991), 30, 31.

House Debate over Religion Clauses (1789)

Amendments to the Constitution

Saturday, August 15

The House again went into a Committee of the whole on the proposed amendments to the constitution, Mr. BOUDINOT in the chair.

The fourth proposition being under consideration, as follows:

Article 1. Section 9. Between paragraphs two and three insert "no religion shall be established by law, nor shall the equal rights of conscience be infringed."

Mr. SYLVESTER had some doubts of the propriety of the mode of expression used in this paragraph.

Reprinted from *The Debates and Proceedings in the Congress of the United States*, vol. 1: *March 3, 1789–March 3, 1791* (Washington, D.C.: Gales and Seaton, 1834), 757–59, 778–80, 783–84, 795–96.

He apprehended that it was liable to a construction different from what had been made by the committee. He feared it might be thought to have a tendency to abolish religion altogether.

Mr. VINING suggested the propriety of transposing the two members of the sentence.

Mr. GERRY said it would read better if it was, that no religious doctrine shall be established by law.

Mr. SHERMAN thought the amendment altogether unnecessary, inasmuch as Congress had no authority whatever delegated to them by the constitution to make religious establishments; he would, therefore, move to have it struck out.

Mr. CARROLL.—As the rights of conscience are, in their nature, of peculiar delicacy, and will little bear the gentlest touch of governmental hand; and as many sects have concurred in opinion that they are not well secured under the present constitution, he said he was much in favor of adopting the words. He thought it would tend more towards conciliating the minds of the people to the Government than almost any other amendment he had heard proposed. He would not contend with gentlemen about the phraseology, his object was to secure the substance in such a manner as to satisfy the wishes of the honest part of the community.

Mr. MADISON said, he apprehended the meaning of the words to be, that Congress should not establish a religion, and enforce the legal observation of it by law, nor compel men to worship God in any manner contrary to their conscience. Whether the words are necessary or not, he did not mean to say, but they had been required by some of the State Conventions, who seemed to entertain an opinion that under the clause of the constitution, which gave power to Congress to make all laws necessary and proper to carry into execution the constitution, and the laws made under it, enabled them to make laws of such a nature as might infringe the rights of conscience, and establish a national religion; to prevent these effects he presumed the amendment was intended, and he thought it as well expressed as the nature of the language would admit.

Mr. HUNTINGTON said that he feared, with the gentleman first up on this subject, that the words might be taken in such latitude as to be extremely hurtful to the cause of religion. He understood the amendment to mean what had been expressed by the gentleman from Virginia; but others might find it convenient to put another construction upon it. The ministers of their congregations to the Eastward were maintained by the contributions of those who belonged to their society; the expense of building meeting-houses was contributed in the same manner. These things were regulated by by-laws. If an action was brought before a Federal Court on any of these cases, the person who had neglected to perform his engagements could not be compelled to do it; for a support of ministers, or building of places of worship might be construed into a religious establishment.

By the charter of Rhode Island, no religion could be established by law; he could give a history of the effects of such a regulation; indeed the people were now enjoying the blessed fruits of it. He hoped, therefore, the amendment would be made in such a way as to secure the rights of conscience, and a free exercise of the rights of religion, but not to patronize those who professed no religion at all.

Mr. MADISON thought, if the word national was inserted before religion, it would satisfy the minds of honorable gentlemen. He believed that the people feared one sect might obtain a pre-eminence, or two combine together, and establish a religion to which they would compel others to conform. He thought if the word national was introduced, it would point the amendment directly to the object it was intended to prevent.

Mr. LIVERMORE was not satisfied with that amendment; but he did not wish them to dwell long on the subject. He thought it would be better if it was altered, and made to read in this manner, that Congress shall make no laws touching religion, or infringing the rights of conscience.

Mr. GERRY did not like the term national, proposed by the gentleman from Virginia, and he hoped it would not be adopted by the House. It brought to his mind some observations that had taken place in the conventions at the time they were considering the present constitution. It had been insisted upon by those who were called antifederalists, that this form of Government consolidated the Union; the honorable gentleman's motion shows that he considers it in the same light. Those who were called antifederalists at that time complained that they had injustice done them by the title, because they were in favor of a Federal Government, and the others were in favor of a national one; the federalists were for ratifying the constitution as it stood, and the others not until amendments were made. Their names then ought not to have been distinguished by federalists and antifederalists, but rats and antirats.

Mr. MADISON withdrew his motion, but observed that the words "no national religion shall be established by law," did not imply that the Government was a national one; the question was then taken on Mr. Livermore's motion, and passed in the affirmative, thirty-one for, and twenty against it. . . .

Monday, August 17

The House again resolved itself into a committee, Mr. BOUDINOT in the chair, on the proposed amendments to the constitution. The third clause of the fourth proposition in the report was taken into consideration, being as follows: "A well regulated militia, composed of the body of the people, being the best security of a free state, the right of the people to keep and bear arms shall not be infringed; but no person religiously scrupulous shall be compelled to bear arms."

Mr. GERRY.—This declaration of rights, I take it, is intended to secure the people against the maladministration of the Government; if we could suppose that, in all cases, the rights of the people would be attended to, the occasion for guards of this kind would be removed. Now, I am apprehensive, sir, that this clause would give an opportunity to the people in power to destroy the constitution itself. They can declare who are those religiously scrupulous, and prevent them from bearing arms.

What, sir, is the use of a militia? It is to prevent the establishment of a standing army, the bane of liberty. Now, it must be evident, that, under this provision, together with their other powers, Congress could take such measures with respect to a militia, as to make a standing army necessary. Whenever Governments mean to invade the rights and liberties of the people, they always attempt to destroy the militia, in order to raise an army upon their ruins. This was actually done by Great Britain at the commencement of the late revolution. They used every means in their power to prevent the establishment of an effective militia to the eastward. The Assembly of Massachusetts, seeing the rapid progress that administration were making to divest them of their inherent privileges, endeavored to counteract them by the organization of the militia; but they were always defeated by the influence of the Crown.

Mr. SENEY wished to know what question there was before the committee, in order to ascertain the point upon which the gentleman was speaking.

Mr. GERRY replied that he meant to make a motion, as he disapproved of the words as they stood. He then proceeded. No attempts that they made were successful, until they engaged in the struggle which emancipated them at once from their thraldom. Now, if we give a discretionary power to exclude those from militia duty who have religious scruples, we may as well make no provision on this head. For this reason, he wished the words to be altered so as to be confined to persons belonging to a religious sect scrupulous of bearing arms.

Mr. JACKSON did not expect that all the people of the United States would turn Quakers or Moravians; consequently, one part would have to defend the other in case of invasion. Now this, in his opinion, was unjust, unless the constitution secured an equivalent: for this reason he moved to amend the clause, by inserting at the end of it, "upon paying an equivalent, to be established by law."

Mr. SMITH, of South Carolina, inquired what were the words used by the conventions respecting this amendment. If the gentleman would conform to what was proposed by Virginia and Carolina, he would second him. He thought they were to be excused provided they found a substitute.

Mr. JACKSON was willing to accommodate. He thought the expression was, "No one, religiously scrupulous of bearing arms, shall be compelled to render military service, in person, upon paying an equivalent."

Mr. SHERMAN conceived it difficult to modify the clause and make it better. It is well known that those who are religiously scrupulous of bearing arms, are equally scrupulous of getting substitutes or paying an equivalent. Many of them would rather die than do either one or the other; but he did not see an absolute necessity for a clause of this kind. We do not live under an arbitrary Government, said he, and the States, respectively, will have the government of the militia, unless when called into actual service; besides, it would not do to alter it so as to exclude the whole of any sect, because there are men amongst the Quakers who will turn out, notwithstanding the religious principles of the society, and defend the cause of their country. Certainly it will be improper to prevent the exercise of such favorable dispositions, at least whilst it is the practice of nations to determine their contests by the slaughter of their citizens and subjects.

Mr. VINING hoped the clause would be suffered to remain as it stood, because he saw no use in it if it was amended so as to compel a man to find a substitute, which, with respect to the Government, was the same as if the person himself turned out to fight.

Mr. STONE inquired what the words "religiously scrupulous" had reference to: was it of bearing arms? If it was, it ought so to be expressed.

Mr. BENSON moved to have the words "but no person religiously scrupulous shall be compelled to bear arms," struck out. He would always leave it to the benevolence of the Legislature, for, modify it as you please, it will be impossible to express it in such a manner as to clear it from ambiguity. No man can claim this indulgence of right. It may be a religious persuasion, but it is no natural right, and therefore ought to be left to the discretion of the Government.

If this stands part of the constitution, it will be a question before the Judiciary on every regulation you make with respect to the organization of the militia, whether it comports with this declaration or not. It is extremely injudicious to intermix matters of doubt with fundamentals.

I have no reason to believe but the Legislature will always possess humanity enough to indulge this class of citizens in a matter they are so desirous of; but they ought to be left to their discretion.

The motion for striking out the whole clause being seconded, was put, and decided in the negative—22 members voting for it, and 24 against it. . . .

The committee then proceeded to the fifth proposition:

Article 1. section 10. between the first and second paragraph, insert "no State shall infringe the equal rights of conscience, nor the freedom of speech or of the press, nor of the right of trial by jury in criminal cases."

Mr. TUCKER.—This is offered, I presume, as an amendment to the constitution of the United States, but it goes only to the alteration of the constitutions of particular States. It will be much better, I apprehend, to leave the State Governments to themselves, and not to interfere with them more than we already do; and that is thought by many to be rather too much. I therefore move, sir, to strike out these words.

Mr. MADISON conceived this to be the most valuable amendment in the whole list. If there was any reason to restrain the Government of the United States from infringing upon these essential rights, it was equally necessary that they should be secured against the State Governments. He thought that if they provided against the one, it was as necessary to provide against the other, and was satisfied that it would be equally grateful to the people.

Mr. LIVERMORE had no great objection to the sentiment, but he thought it not well expressed. He wished to make it an affirmative proposition; "the equal rights of conscience, the freedom of speech or of the press, and the right of trial by jury in criminal cases, shall not be infringed by any State."

This transposition being agreed to, and Mr. TUCKER's motion being rejected, the clause was adopted. . . .

Thursday, August 20

The House resumed the consideration of the report of the Committee of the whole on the subject of amendment to the constitution.

Mr. AMES's proposition was taken up. Five or six other members introduced propositions on the same point, and the whole were, by mutual consent, laid on the table. After which, the House proceeded to the third amendment, and agreed to the same.

On motion of Mr. AMES, the fourth amendment was altered so as to read "Congress shall make no law establishing religion, or to prevent the free exercise thereof, or to infringe the rights of conscience." This being adopted,

The first proposition was agreed to.

Mr. SCOTT objected to the clause in the sixth amendment, "No person religiously scrupulous shall be compelled to bear arms." He observed that if this becomes part of the constitution, such persons can neither be called upon for their services, nor can an equivalent be demanded; it is also attended with still further difficulties, for a militia can never be depended upon. This would lead to the violation of another article in the constitution, which secures to the people the right of keeping arms, and in this case recourse must be had to a standing army. I conceive it, said he, to be a legislative right altogether. There are many sects I know, who are religiously scrupulous in this respect; I do not mean to deprive them of any indulgence the law affords; my design is to guard against those who are of no religion. It has been urged that religion is on the decline; if so, the argument is more strong in my favor, for when the time comes that religion shall be discarded, the generality of persons will have recourse to these pretexts to get excused from bearing arms.

Mr. BOUDINOT thought the provision in the clause, or something similar to it, was necessary. Can any dependence, said he, be placed in men who are conscientious in this respect? or what justice can there be in compelling them to bear arms, when, according to their religious principles, they would rather die than use them? He adverted to several instances of oppression on this point, that occurred during the war. In forming a militia, an effectual defence ought to be calculated, and no characters of this religious description ought to be compelled to take up arms. I hope that in establishing this Government, we may show the world that proper care is taken that the Government may not interfere with the religious sentiments of any person. Now, by striking out the clause, people may be led to believe that there is an intention in the General Government to compel all its citizens to bear arms.

Some further desultory conversation arose, and it was agreed to insert the words "in person" to the end of the clause; after which, it was adopted, as was the fourth, fifth, sixth, seventh, and eighth clauses of the fourth proposition; then the fifth, sixth, and seventh propositions were agreed to, and the House adjourned.

Religion Clauses from House Resolution and Articles of Amendment (August 24, 1789)

Article the Third

Congress shall make no law establishing religion or prohibiting the free exercise thereof, nor shall the rights of Conscience be infringed.

Reprinted from *Creating the Bill of Rights: The Documentary Record from the First Federal Congress,* ed. Helen E. Veit, Kenneth R. Bowling, and Charlene Bangs Bickford (Baltimore and London: Johns Hopkins University Press, 1991), 38, 41.

Article the Fourth

The Freedom of Speech, and of the Press, and the right of the People peaceably to assemble, and consult for their common good, and to apply to the Government for a redress of grievances, shall not be infringed.

Article the Fifth

A well regulated militia, composed of the body of the People, being the best security of a free State, the right of the People to keep and bear arms, shall not be infringed, but no one religiously scrupulous of bearing arms, shall be compelled to render military service in person.

Article the Fourteenth

No State shall infringe the right of trial by Jury in criminal cases, nor the rights of conscience, nor the freedom of speech, or of the press. . . .

Monday, August 24*

Mr. Benson, from the committee appointed, reported, according to order, an arrangement of the articles of amendment to the Constitution of the United States as agreed to by the House on Friday last; also, a resolution proper to be prefixed to the same; which resolution he delivered in at the Clerk's table, where the same was twice read, and agreed to by the House, as followeth:

"*Resolved by the Senate and House of Representatives of the United States of America in Congress assembled, two-thirds of both Houses deeming it necessary,* That the following articles be proposed to the Legislatures of the several States, as amendments to the Constitution of the United States, all or any of which articles, when ratified by three-fourths of the said Legisla-

* Reprinted from *Journal of the House of Representatives* (Washington, D.C.: Gales and Seaton, 1826), 1:89.

tures, to be valid, to all intents and purposes, as part of the said Constitution."

Ordered, That the Clerk of this House do carry to the Senate a fair engrossed copy of the said proposed articles of amendment, and desire their concurrence. . . .

Senate Debate over Religion Clauses

September 3, 1789

On motion, To amend Article third, and to strike out these words, "Religion or prohibiting the free Exercise thereof," and insert, "One Religious Sect or Society in preference to others,"
> It passed in the Negative.

On motion, For reconsideration,
> It passed in the Affirmative.

On motion, That Article the third be striken out,
> It passed in the Negative.

On motion, To adopt the following, in lieu of the third Article,

"Congress shall not make any law, infringing the rights of conscience, or establishing any Religious Sect or Society,"
> It passed in the Negative.

On motion, To amend the third Article, to read thus—

"Congress shall make no law establishing any particular denomination of religion in preference to another, or prohibiting the free exercise thereof, nor shall the rights of conscience be infringed"—
> It passed in the Negative.

On the question upon the third Article as it came from the House of Representatives—

It passed in the Negative.

On motion, To adopt the third Article proposed in the Resolve of the House of Representatives, amended by striking out these words—

"Nor shall the rights of conscience be infringed"—
> It passed in the Affirmative. . . .

September 9, 1789

On motion, To amend Article the third, to read as follows:

"Congress shall make no law establishing articles of faith or a mode of worship, or prohibiting the free exercise of religion, or abridging the freedom of speech, or the press, or the right of the people peaceably to assemble, and petition to the Government for the redress of grievances"—
> It passed in the Affirmative.

On motion, To strike out the fourth Article,
> It passed in the Affirmative.

On motion, To amend Article the fifth, by inserting these words, "For the common defence," next to the words "Bear arms"—
> It passed in the Negative.

Amendment Concerning Religion as Agreed to by the Senate (September 14, 1789)

Article the Third

Congress shall make no law establishing articles of faith, or a mode of worship, or prohibiting the free

Reprinted from *Senate Legislative Journal: Documentary History of the First Federal Congress of the United States of America, March 4, 1789–March 3, 1791,* ed. Linda Grant De Pauw (Baltimore and London: Johns Hopkins University Press, 1977), 151, 166.

Reprinted from *Creating the Bill of Rights: The Documentary Record from the First Federal Congress,* ed. Helen E. Veit, Kenneth R. Bowling, and Charlene Bangs Bickford (Baltimore and London: Johns Hopkins University Press, 1991), 48.

exercise of religion, or abridging the freedom of speech, or of the press, or the right of the people peaceably to assemble, and to petition to the government for a redress of grievances.

Article the Fourth

A well regulated militia, being necessary to the security of a free State, the right of the people to keep and bear arms, shall not be infringed.

Amendment Concerning Religion as Agreed to by the Conference Committee

*Consisting of Representatives James Madison (Va.), Roger Sherman (Conn.), and John Vining (Del.), and Senators Oliver Ellsworth (Conn.), Charles Carroll (Md.), and William Paterson (N.J.).**

ART. 3. Congress shall make no law respecting an establishment of religion, or prohibiting a free exercise thereof, or abridging the freedom of speech, or of the press, or the right of the people peaceably to assemble, and to petition the Government for a redress of grievances.

Reprinted from *The Debates and Proceedings in the Congress of the United States*, vol. 1: *March 3, 1789–March 3, 1791* (Washington, D.C.: Gales and Seaton, 1834), 948.

* This version was accepted by the House on September 24, 1791, and the Senate on September 25, and was sent to the States for ratification.—Eds.

U.S. Constitution, Amendment 1 (1791)

Twelve amendments were approved by Congress and sent to the states for ratification. However, the first of these proposals was never ratified, and the second was not ratified until 1992, when it became the Twenty-seventh Amendment. The third proposal was ratified by the requisite number of states on December 15, 1791, thus becoming the First Amendment.

ART. I. Congress shall make no law respecting an establishment of religion, or prohibiting the free exercise thereof; or abridging the freedom of speech, or of the press; or the right of the people peaceably to assemble, and to petition the government for a redress of grievances.

Reprinted from *The Public Statutes at Large of the United States of America*, ed. Richard Peters (Boston: Little and Brown, 1845), 1:21.

Commentaries on the Constitution of the United States, §§ 1863–73 (1833)

JOSEPH STORY (1779–1845)

Associate justice of the U.S. Supreme Court and Harvard University's professor of law, Joseph Story was a preeminent nineteenth-century jurist. The following excerpts illustrate his views on the religion clauses of the First Amendment.

---

§ 1863. Let us now enter upon the consideration of the amendments, which, it will be found, principally regard subjects properly belonging to a bill of rights.

§ 1864. The first is, "Congress shall make no law

respecting an establishment of religion, or prohibiting the free exercise thereof; or abridging the freedom of speech, or of the press; or the right of the people peaceably to assemble, and to petition government for a redress of grievances."

§ 1865. And first, the prohibition of any establishment of religion, and the freedom of religious opinion and worship.

How far any government has a right to interfere in matters touching religion, has been a subject much discussed by writers upon public and political law. The right and the duty of the interference of government, in matters of religion, have been maintained by many distinguished authors, as well those, who were the warmest advocates of free governments, as those, who were attached to governments of a more arbitrary character.[1] Indeed, the right of a society or government to interfere in matters of religion will hardly be contested by any persons, who believe that piety, religion, and morality are intimately connected with the well being of the state, and indispensable to the administration of civil justice. The promulgation of the great doctrines of religion, the being, and attributes, and providence of one Almighty God; the responsibility to him for all our actions, founded upon moral freedom and accountability; a future state of rewards and punishments; the cultivation of all the personal, social, and benevolent virtues;—these never can be a matter of indifference in any well ordered community.[2] It is, indeed, difficult to conceive, how any civilized society can well exist without them. And at all events, it is impossible for those, who believe in the truth of Christianity, as a divine revelation, to

doubt, that it is the especial duty of government to foster, and encourage it among all the citizens and subjects. This is a point wholly distinct from that of the right of private judgment in matters of religion, and of the freedom of public worship according to the dictates of one's conscience.

§ 1866. The real difficulty lies in ascertaining the limits, to which government may rightfully go in fostering and encouraging religion. Three cases may easily be supposed. One, where a government affords aid to a particular religion, leaving all persons free to adopt any other; another, where it creates an ecclesiastical establishment for the propagation of the doctrines of a particular sect of that religion, leaving a like freedom to all others; and a third, where it creates such an establishment, and excludes all persons, not belonging to it, either wholly, or in part, from any participation in the public honours, trusts, emoluments, privileges, and immunities of the state. For instance, a government may simply declare, that the Christian religion shall be the religion of the state, and shall be aided, and encouraged in all the varieties of sects belonging to it; or it may declare, that the Catholic or Protestant religion shall be the religion of the state, leaving every man to the free enjoyment of his own religious opinions; or it may establish the doctrines of a particular sect, as of Episcopalians, as the religion of the state, with a like freedom; or it may establish the doctrines of a particular sect, as exclusively the religion of the state, tolerating others to a limited extent, or excluding all, not belonging to it, from all public honours, trusts, emoluments, privileges, and immunities.

§ 1867. Now, there will probably be found few persons in this, or any other Christian country, who would deliberately contend, that it was unreasonable, or unjust to foster and encourage the Christian religion generally, as a matter of sound policy, as well as of revealed truth. In fact, every American colony, from its foundation down to the revolution, with the exception of Rhode Island, (if, indeed, that state be an exception,) did openly, by the whole course of its laws and institutions, support and sustain, in some

Reprinted from Joseph Story, *Commentaries on the Constitution of the United States* (Boston: Hilliard, Gray; Cambridge, Mass.: Brown, Shattuck, 1833), 3:722–31.

1. See Grotius, B. 2, ch. 20, § 44 to 51; Vattell, B. 1, ch. 12, § 125, 126; Hooker's Ecclesiastical Polity, B. 5, § 1 to 10; Bynkershoeck, 2 P. J. Lib. 2, ch. 18; Woodeson's Elem. Lect. 3, p. 49; Burlemaqui, Pt. 3, ch. 3, p. 171, and Montesq. B. 24, ch. 1 to ch. 8, ch. 14 to ch. 16, B. 25, ch. 1, 2, 9, 10, 11, 12.

2. See Burlemaqui, Pt. 3, ch. 3, p. 171, &c.; 4 Black. Comm. 43.

form, the Christian religion; and almost invariably gave a peculiar sanction to some of its fundamental doctrines. And this has continued to be the case in some of the states down to the present period, without the slightest suspicion, that it was against the principles of public law, or republican liberty.[3] Indeed, in a republic, there would seem to be a peculiar propriety in viewing the Christian religion, as the great basis, on which it must rest for its support and permanence, if it be, what it has ever been deemed by its truest friends to be, the religion of liberty. Montesquieu has remarked, that the Christian religion is a stranger to mere despotic power. The mildness so frequently recommended in the gospel is incompatible with the despotic rage, with which a prince punishes his subjects, and exercises himself in cruelty.[4] He has gone even further, and affirmed, that the Protestant religion is far more congenial with the spirit of political freedom, than the Catholic. "When," says he, "the Christian religion, two centuries ago, became unhappily divided into Catholic and Protestant, the people of the north embraced the Protestant, and those of the south still adhered to the Catholic. The reason is plain. The people of the north have, and will ever have, a spirit of liberty and independence, which the people of the south have not. And, therefore, a religion, which has no visible head, is more agreeable to the independency of climate, than that, which has one."[5] Without stopping to inquire, whether this remark be well founded, it is certainly true, that the parent country has acted upon it with a severe and vigilant zeal; and in most of the colonies the same rigid jealousy has been maintained almost down to our own times. Massachusetts, while she has promulgated in her BILL OF RIGHTS the importance and necessity of the public support of religion, and the worship of God, has authorized the legislature to require it only for Protestantism. The language of that bill of rights is remarkable for its pointed affirmation

of the duty of government to support Christianity, and the reasons for it. "As," says the third article, "the happiness of a people, and the good order and preservation of civil government, essentially depend upon piety, religion, and morality; and as these cannot be generally diffused through the community, but by the institution of the public worship of God, and of public instructions in piety, religion, and morality; therefore, to promote their happiness and to secure the good order and preservation of their government, the people of this Commonwealth have a right to invest their legislature with power to authorize, and require, and the legislature shall from time to time authorize and require, the several towns, parishes, &c. &c. to make suitable provision at their own expense for the institution of the public worship of God, and for the support and maintenance of public *protestant* teachers of piety, religion, and morality, in all cases where such provision shall not be made voluntarily." Afterwards there follow provisions, prohibiting any superiority of one sect over another, and securing to all citizens the free exercise of religion.

§ 1868. Probably at the time of the adoption of the constitution, and of the amendment to it, now under consideration, the general, if not the universal, sentiment in America was, that Christianity ought to receive encouragement from the state, so far as was not incompatible with the private rights of conscience, and the freedom of religious worship. An attempt to level all religions, and to make it a matter of state policy to hold all in utter indifference, would have created universal disapprobation, if not universal indignation.[6]

§ 1869. It yet remains a problem to be solved in human affairs, whether any free government can be permanent, where the public worship of God, and the support of religion, constitute no part of the policy or duty of the state in any assignable shape. The future experience of Christendom, and chiefly of the American states, must settle this problem, as yet new in the

---

3. 2 Kent's Comm. Lect. 34, p. 35 to 37; Rawle on Const. ch. 10, p. 121, 122.

4. Montesq. Spirit of Laws, B. 24, ch. 3.

5. Montesq. Spirit of Laws, B. 24, ch. 5.

6. See 2 Lloyd's Deb. 195, 196.

history of the world, abundant, as it has been, in experiments in the theory of government.

§ 1870. But the duty of supporting religion, and especially the Christian religion, is very different from the right to force the consciences of other men, or to punish them for worshipping God in the manner, which, they believe, their accountability to him requires. It has been truly said, that "religion, or the duty we owe to our Creator, and the manner of discharging it, can be dictated only by reason and conviction, not by force or violence."[7] Mr. Locke himself, who did not doubt the right of government to interfere in matters of religion, and especially to encourage Christianity, at the same time has expressed his opinion of the right of private judgment, and liberty of conscience, in a manner becoming his character, as a sincere friend of civil and religious liberty. "No man, or society of men," says he, "have any authority to impose their opinions or interpretations on any other, the meanest Christian; since, in matters of religion, every man must know, and believe, and give an account for himself."[8] The rights of conscience are, indeed, beyond the just reach of any human power. They are given by God, and cannot be encroached upon by human authority, without a criminal disobedience of the precepts of natural, as well as of revealed religion.

§ 1871. The real object of the amendment was, not to countenance, much less to advance Mahometanism, or Judaism, or infidelity, by prostrating Christianity; but to exclude all rivalry among Christian sects, and to prevent any national ecclesiastical establishment, which should give to an hierarchy the exclusive patronage of the national government. It thus cut off the means of religious persecution, (the vice and pest of former ages,) and of the subversion of the rights of conscience in matters of religion, which had been trampled upon almost from the days of the Apostles to the present age.[9] The history of the parent country had afforded the most solemn warnings and melancholy instructions on this head;[10] and even New-England, the land of the persecuted puritans, as well as other colonies, where the Church of England had maintained its superiority, would furnish out a chapter, as full of the darkest bigotry and intolerance, as any, which could be found to disgrace the pages of foreign annals.[11] Apostacy, heresy, and nonconformity had been standard crimes for public appeals, to kindle the flames of persecution, and apologize for the most atrocious triumphs over innocence and virtue.[12]

§ 1872. Mr. Justice Blackstone, after having spoken with a manly freedom of the abuses in the Romish church respecting heresy; and, that Christianity had been deformed by the demon of persecution upon the continent, and that the island of Great Britain had not been *entirely* free from the scourge,[13] defends the final enactments against nonconformity in England, in the following set phrases, to which, without any material change, might be justly applied his own sarcastic remarks upon the conduct of the Roman ecclesiastics in punishing heresy.[14] "For nonconformity to the worship of the church," (says he,) "there is much more to be pleaded than for the former, (that

---

7. Virginia Bill of Rights, 1 Tuck. Black. Comm. App. 296; 2 Tuck. Black. Comm. App. note G. p. 10, 11.

8. Lord King's Life of Locke, p. 373.

9. 2 Lloyd's Deb. 195.

10. 4 Black. Comm. 41 to 59.

11. Ante, Vol. I. § 53, 72, 74.

12. See 4 Black. Comm. 43 to 59.

13. "*Entirely*"! Should he not have said, *never* free from the scourge, as more conformable to historical truth?

14. 4 Black. Comm. 45, 46.—His words are: "It is true, that the sanctimonious hypocrisy of the Canonists went, at first, no further, than enjoining penance, excommunication, and ecclesiastical deprivation for heresy, though afterwards they proceeded to imprisonment by the ordinary, and confiscation of goods *in pios usus*. But in the mean time they had prevailed upon the weakness of bigotted princes to make the civil power subservient to their purposes, by making heresy not only a temporal, but even a capital offence; the Romish Ecclesiastics determining, without appeal, whatever they pleased, to be heresy, and shifting off to the secular arm the odium and the drudgery of executions, with which they themselves were too tender and delicate to intermeddle. Nay, they pretended to intercede, and pray in behalf of the convicted heretic, *ut citra mortis periculum sententia circum eum moderatur*, well knowing, at the same time, that they were delivering the unhappy victim to certain death." 4 Black. Comm. 45, 46. Yet the learned author, in the same breath, could calmly vindicate the outrageous oppressions of the Church of England upon Catholics and Dissenters with the unsuspecting satisfaction of a bigot.

is, reviling the ordinances of the church,) being a matter of private conscience, to the scruples of which our *present* laws have shown a very just, and Christian indulgence. For undoubtedly all persecution and oppression of weak consciences, on the score of religious persuasions, are highly unjustifiable upon every principle of natural reason, civil liberty, or sound religion. But care must be taken not to carry this indulgence into such extremes, as may endanger the national church. There is always a difference to be made between toleration and establishment."[15] Let it be remembered, that at the very moment, when the learned commentator was penning these cold remarks, the laws of England merely tolerated protestant dissenters in their public worship upon certain conditions, at once irritating and degrading; that the test and corporation acts excluded them from public and corporate offices, both of trust and profit; that the learned commentator avows, that the object of the test and corporation acts was to exclude them from office, in common with Turks, Jews, heretics, papists, and other sectaries;[16] that to deny the Trinity, however conscientiously disbelieved, was a public offence, punishable by fine and imprisonment; and that, in the rear of all these disabilities and grievances, came the long list of acts against papists, by which they were reduced to a state of political and religious slavery, and cut off from some of the dearest privileges of mankind.[17]

§ 1873. It was under a solemn consciousness of the dangers from ecclesiastical ambition, the bigotry of spiritual pride, and the intolerance of sects, thus exemplified in our domestic, as well as in foreign annals, that it was deemed advisable to exclude from the national government all power to act upon the subject.[18] The situation, too, of the different states equally proclaimed the policy, as well as the necessity of such an exclusion. In some of the states, episcopalians constituted the predominant sect; in others, presbyterians; in others, congregationalists; in others, quakers; and in others again, there was a close numerical rivalry among contending sects. It was impossible, that there should not arise perpetual strife and perpetual jealousy on the subject of ecclesiastical ascendancy, if the national government were left free to create a religious establishment. The only security was in extirpating the power. But this alone would have been an imperfect security, if it had not been followed up by a declaration of the right of the free exercise of religion, and a prohibition (as we have seen) of all religious tests. Thus, the whole power over the subject of religion is left exclusively to the state governments, to be acted upon according to their own sense of justice, and the state constitutions; and the Catholic and the Protestant, the Calvinist and the Arminian, the Jew and the Infidel, may sit down at the common table of the national councils, without any inquisition into their faith, or mode of worship.[19]

---

15. 4 Black. Comm. 51, 52.

16. 1 Black. Comm. 58.

17. 1 Black. Comm. 51 to 59.—Mr. Tucker, in his Commentaries on Blackstone, has treated the whole subject in a manner of most marked contrast to that of Mr. J. Blackstone. His ardour is as strong, as the coolness of his adversary is humiliating, on the subject of religious liberty. 2 Tuck. Black. Comm. App. Note G. p. 3, &c. See also 4 Jefferson's Corresp. 103, 104; Jefferson's Notes on Virginia, 264 to 270; 1 Tuck. Black. Comm. App. 296.

18. 2 Lloyd's Debates, 195, 196, 197.—"The sectarian spirit," said the late Dr. Currie, "is uniformly selfish, proud, and unfeeling." (Edinburgh Review, April, 1832, p. 125.)

19. See 2 Kent's Comm. Lect. 24, (2d edition, p. 35 to 37); Rawle on Const. ch. 10, p. 121, 122; 2 Lloyd's Deb. 195. See also Vol. II. § 621.

RECOMMENDATIONS FOR FURTHER READING

Adams, Arlin M., and Charles J. Emmerich. *A Nation Dedicated to Religious Liberty: The Constitutional Heritage of the Religion Clauses.* Philadelphia: University of Pennsylvania Press, 1990.

Bradley, Gerard V. *Church-State Relationships in America.* Westport, Conn.: Greenwood Press, 1987.

Cord, Robert L. *Separation of Church and State: Historical Fact and Current Fiction.* New York: Lambeth Press, 1982.

Glenn, Gary D. "Forgotten Purposes of the First Amendment Religion Clauses." *Review of Politics* 49 (1987): 340–67.

Levy, Leonard W. *The Establishment Clause: Religion and the First Amendment.* 2d ed. Chapel Hill: University of North Carolina Press, 1994.

Malbin, Michael J. *Religion and Politics: The Intentions of the Authors of the First Amendment.* Washington, D.C.: American Enterprise Institute, 1978.

McClellan, James. "The Making and the Unmaking of the Establishment Clause." In *A Blueprint for Judicial Reform,* edited by Patrick B. McGuigan and Randall R. Rader, 295–325. Washington, D.C.: Free Congress Research and Education Foundation, 1981.

McConnell, Michael W. "The Origins and Historical Understanding of Free Exercise of Religion." *Harvard Law Review* 103 (1990): 1409–1517.

Part IV

DEFINING AND TESTING

THE CONSTITUTIONAL PRINCIPLES

GOVERNING RELIGIOUS LIBERTY

AND CHURCH-STATE RELATIONS

IN THE NEW NATION

CHAPTER TEN

Religion and the Public Policy and Culture of the New Nation

SCHOLARS AND JURISTS often debate the founders' views of religious liberty and church-state relations. These arguments sometimes focus narrowly on congressional and ratification debates about the First Amendment. While these are important, significant insights into the founders' views concerning the proper scope of religious liberty and role of religion in public life may be gained by considering more broadly the actions and rhetoric of the first congresses and presidents.

Some scholars and jurists argue that the first Congress's actions concerning religion are particularly important as this Congress wrote and proposed to the states the First Amendment. If the same Congress that authored the nonestablishment of religion provision also arranged for paid legislative chaplains, the argument goes, clearly the nonestablishment provision was not intended to prohibit such chaplains. Opponents of paid legislative chaplains, however, respond that the intent of the authors of the First Amendment is not controlling in the contemporary context or that the first Congress was simply inconsistent. Still other scholars contend that, instead of attempting to find guidance on specific issues, it is more profitable to attempt to discern broad principles that underlie the founders' views of religious liberty and church-state relations.

Congressional and presidential actions and rhetoric in the early republic are also meaningful because the men holding national offices were directly or indirectly accountable to American voters, so their public acts may be taken as a measure of public opinion. The following texts suggest that religion played an important role in America's political culture. Even a president such as Thomas Jefferson, who thought the First and Tenth amendments prevented him from issuing calls for national prayer and fasting, made significant use of religious rhetoric in his presidential addresses.

OATHS OF OFFICE (1788–91)

Historically, oaths have been seen as essential for ensuring the loyalty and fidelity of citizens and elected officials. In the Christian West, oaths usually invoke God as the witness of the oath taker's veracity. The U.S. Constitution requires federal and state officers to swear to protect the Constitution, and the first statute passed by Congress concerned oath taking.

Although oaths traditionally invoke God, the only oath spelled out in the Constitution does not. Moreover, the presidential oath of office and congressional legislation concerning oaths are written so as to accommodate Quakers and others who refuse to take oaths but do not object to "affirming" promises. Although not required by the Constitution, George Washington took his oath of office with his right hand on the Bible and, according to tradition, ended it with an appeal to God. Most presidents have followed his precedent, and only one (Franklin Pierce) has opted to "affirm" rather than "swear" the oath.

U.S. Constitution (1788)

Article I, Section 3

The Senate shall have the sole power to try all impeachments. When sitting for that purpose, they shall be on oath or affirmation. When the President of the United States is tried, the Chief Justice shall preside; and no person shall be convicted without the concurrence of two thirds of the members present.

Reprinted from *The Public Statutes at Large of the United States of America*, ed. Richard Peters (Boston: Charles C. Little and James Brown, 1845), 1:11, 16, 19.

Article II, Section 1

Before he enter on the execution of his office, he shall take the following oath or affirmation:

"I do solemnly swear, (or affirm,) that I will faithfully execute the office of President of the United States, and will, to the best of my ability, preserve, protect, and defend the Constitution of the United States."

Article VI, Section 3

The Senators and Representatives before mentioned, and the members of the several State legislatures, and all executive and judicial officers, both of the United States and of the several States, shall be bound, by oath or affirmation, to support this Constitution; but no religious test shall ever be required as a qualification to any office or public trust under the United States.

An Act to Regulate the Time and Manner of Administering Certain Oaths (June 1, 1789)

SEC. 1. *Be it enacted by the Senate and* [*House of*] *Representatives of the United States of America in Congress assembled,* That the oath or affirmation required by the sixth article of the Constitution of the United States, shall be administered in the form following, to wit: "I, A. B. do solemnly swear or affirm (as the case may be) that I will support the Constitution of the United States." The said oath or affirmation shall be administered within three days after the passing of this act, by any one member of the Senate, to the President of the Senate, and by him to all the mem-

Reprinted from *The Public Statutes at Large of the United States of America*, ed. Richard Peters (Boston: Charles C. Little and James Brown, 1845), 1:23–24.

bers and to the secretary; and by the Speaker of the House of Representatives, to all the members who have not taken a similar oath, by virtue of a particular resolution of the said House, and to the clerk: and in case of the absence of any member from the service of either House, at the time prescribed for taking the said oath or affirmation, the same shall be administered to such member, when he shall appear to take his seat.

SEC. 2. *And be it further enacted,* That at the first session of Congress after every general election of Representatives, the oath or affirmation aforesaid, shall be administered by any one member of the House of Representatives to the Speaker; and by him to all the members present, and to the clerk, previous to entering on any other business; and to the members who shall afterwards appear, previous to taking their seats. The President of the Senate for the time being, shall also administer the said oath or affirmation to each Senator who shall hereafter be elected, previous to his taking his seat: and in any future case of a President of the Senate, who shall not have taken the said oath or affirmation, the same shall be administered to him by any one of the members of the Senate.

SEC. 3. *And be it further enacted,* That the members of the several State legislatures, at the next sessions of the said legislatures, respectively, and all executive and judicial officers of the several States, who have been heretofore chosen or appointed, or who shall be chosen or appointed before the first day of August next, and who shall then be in office, shall, within one month thereafter, take the same oath or affirmation, except where they shall have taken it before; which may be administered by any person authorized by the law of the State, in which such office shall be holden, to administer oaths. And the members of the several State legislatures, and all executive and judicial officers of the several States, who shall be chosen or appointed after the said first day of August, shall, before they proceed to execute the duties of their respective offices, take the foregoing oath or affirmation, which shall be administered by the person or persons, who

by the law of the State shall be authorized to administer the oath of office; and the person or persons so administering the oath hereby required to be taken, shall cause a record or certificate thereof to be made, in the same manner, as, by the law of the State, he or they shall be directed to record or certify the oath of office.

SEC. 4. *And be it further enacted,* That all officers appointed, or hereafter to be appointed under the authority of the United States, shall, before they act in their respective offices, take the same oath or affirmation, which shall be administered by the person or persons who shall be authorized by law to administer to such officers their respective oaths of office; and such officers shall incur the same penalties in case of failure, as shall be imposed by law in case of failure in taking their respective oaths of office.

SEC. 5. *And be it further enacted,* That the secretary of the Senate, and the clerk of the House of Representatives for the time being, shall, at the time of taking the oath or affirmation aforesaid, each take an oath or affirmation in the words following, to wit: "I, A. B. secretary of the Senate, or clerk of the House of Representatives (as the case may be) of the United States of America, do solemnly swear or affirm, that I will truly and faithfully discharge the duties of my said office, to the best of my knowledge and abilities."

APPROVED, June 1, 1789.

B. F. Morris, Christian Life and Character of the Civil Institutions of the United States (1864)

THE first session of Congress after the adoption of the Federal Constitution opened with distinct leg-

Reprinted from B. F. Morris, *Christian Life and Character of the Civil Institutions of the United States, Developed in the Official and Historical Annals of the Republic* (Philadelphia: George W. Childs, 1864), 270–73.

islative recognitions of the Christian religion. Washington was inaugurated and took the oath of office on the 30th of April, 1789. Congress, the day before the inauguration, passed the following:—

> *Resolved,* That, after the oath shall be administered to the President, the Vice-President, and members of the Senate, the Speaker and members of the House of Representatives, will accompany him to St. Paul's Chapel, to hear divine service performed by the chaplains.

Chancellor Livingston administered the oath of office, and Mr. Otis held up the Bible on its crimson cushion. The President, as he bowed to kiss its sacred page, at the same time laying his hand on the open Bible, said, audibly, "I swear," and added, with fervency, that his whole soul might be absorbed in the supplication, "So help me God." Then the Chancellor said, "It is done!" and, turning to the multitude, waved his hand, and, with a loud voice, exclaimed, "Long live George Washington!" This solemn scene concluded, he proceeded with the whole assembly, on foot, to St. Paul's Church, where prayers suited to the occasion were read by Dr. Provost, Bishop of the Protestant Episcopal Church in New York, who had been appointed one of the chaplains of Congress.

Previous to his inauguration, on the morning of the same day, a general prayer-meeting of the various denominations of Christians in New York was held for the special object of praying for God's blessing to rest on the President and the new Government. The notice of the prayer-meeting is among the old files of the "New York Daily Advertiser," dated Thursday, April 23, 1789, and is as follows:—

> As we believe in an overruling Providence and feel our constant dependence upon God for every blessing, so it is undoubtedly our duty to acknowledge him in all our ways and commit our concerns to his protection and mercy. The ancient civilized heathen, from the mere dictates of reason, were uniformly excited to this; and we find from their writings that they engaged in no important business, especially what related to the welfare

of a nation, without a solemn appeal to Heaven. How much more becoming and necessary is such a conduct in Christians, who believe not only in the light of nature, but are blessed with a divine revelation which has taught them more of God and of their obligations to worship him than by their reason they ever could have investigated!

It has been the wish of many pious persons in our land that at the framing of our new Constitution a solemn and particular appeal to Heaven had been made; and they have no doubt but Congress will soon call upon the whole nation to set apart a day for fasting and prayer for the express purpose of invoking the blessing of Heaven on our new Government. But this, in consequence of the distance of some of the States, cannot immediately take place: in the meanwhile, the inhabitants of this city are favored with the opportunity of being present on the very day on which the Constitution will be fully organized, and have it thus in their power to accommodate their devotions exactly to the important season.

In this view, it gave universal satisfaction to hear it announced last Sunday from the pulpits of our churches that, on the morning of the day on which our illustrious President will be invested with his office, the bells will ring at nine o'clock, when the people may go up and in a solemn manner commit the new Government, with its important train of consequences, to the holy protection and blessings of the Most High. An early hour is prudently fixed for this peculiar act of devotion, and it is designed wholly for prayer: it will not detain the citizens very long, or interfere with any of the other public business of the day.

It is supposed Congress will adopt religious solemnities by fervent prayer with their chaplains, in the Federal Hall, when the President takes his oath of office; but the people feel a common interest in this great transaction, and whether they approve of the Constitution as it now stands, or wish that alterations may be made, it is equally their concern and duty to leave the cause with God and refer the issue to his gracious providence. In doing this, the inauguration of our President and the commencement of our national character will be introduced with the auspices of religion, and our enlightened rulers and people will bear a consistent part in a business which involves the weal or woe of themselves and posterity.

I have heard that the notification respecting this hour of prayer was made in almost all the churches of the city, and that some of those who omitted the publication intend, notwithstanding, to join in that duty; and, indeed, considering the singular circumstances of the day, which in many respects exceed any thing recorded in ancient or modern history, it cannot be supposed that the serious and pious of any denomination will hesitate in going up to their respective churches and uniting at the throne of grace with proper prayers and supplications on this occasion. *"I was glad when they said unto me, Let us go into the house of the Lord."*—(DAVID.)

The people came out from the churches where Mason, Livingston, Provost, Rodgers, and other clergymen had given passionately earnest and eloquent expression to that reverent and profound desire for God's blessing upon the President and Government which filled all hearts, so universal was a religious sense of the importance of the occasion.

"The scene," said one, "was solemn and awful beyond description. It would seem extraordinary that the administration of an oath—a ceremony so very common and familiar—should to so great a degree excite public curiosity; but the circumstances of the President's election, the importance of his past services, the concourse of the spectators, the devout fervency with which he repeated the oath, and the reverential manner in which he bowed down and kissed the sacred volume,—all these conspired to render it one of the most august and interesting spectacles ever exhibited. It seemed, from the number of witnesses, to be a solemn appeal to heaven and earth at once. In regard to this great and good man I may be an enthusiast, but I confess I was under an awful and religious persuasion that the gracious Ruler of the universe was looking down at that moment with peculiar complacency on an act which to a part of his creatures was so very important."

After divine service had been performed, Washington and the officers of the new Government and the members of Congress returned to the Federal Hall, where his inaugural was delivered.

———

Fourth Amendment to the U.S. Constitution (1791)

The right of the people to be secure in their persons, houses, papers, and effects, against unreasonable searches and seizures, shall not be violated; and no warrants shall issue, but upon probable cause, supported by oath or affirmation, and particularly describing the place to be searched, and the persons or things to be seized.

Reprinted from *The Public Statutes at Large of the United States of America,* ed. Richard Peters (Boston: Charles C. Little and James Brown, 1845), 1:21.

RELIGION AND THE PRESIDENCY

Inaugural Addresses, 1789–1813

Presidents almost always use religious rhetoric or images in their inaugural addresses. A notable exception to this rule is George Washington's second address, which at 135 words is the shortest to date. This was in contrast with Washington's first inaugural address, which devotes considerable attention to religious themes. Excerpts from the following addresses illustrate how America's earliest presidents incorporated religion into their inaugural addresses. Selections from Thomas Jefferson's second address can be found in chapter 12 of this volume.

George Washington (1789)

The First Inaugural Address

[April 30, 1789]
Fellow Citizens of the Senate and the House of Representatives.

Among the vicissitudes incident to life, no event could have filled me with greater anxieties than that of which the notification was transmitted by your order, and received on the fourteenth day of the present month. On the one hand, I was summoned by my Country, whose voice I can never hear but with veneration and love, from a retreat which I had chosen with the fondest predilection, and, in my flattering

Reprinted from *The Writings of George Washington, from the Original Manuscript Sources, 1745–1799*, ed. John C. Fitzpatrick (Washington, D.C.: GPO, 1939), 30:291–96.

hopes, with an immutable decision, as the asylum of my declining years: a retreat which was rendered every day more necessary as well as more dear to me, by the addition of habit to inclination, and of frequent interruptions in my health to the gradual waste committed on it by time. On the other hand, the magnitude and difficulty of the trust to which the voice of my Country called me, being sufficient to awaken in the wisest and most experienced of her citizens, a distrustful scrutiny into his qualifications, could not but overwhelm with dispondence, one, who, inheriting inferior endowments from nature and unpractised in the duties of civil administration, ought to be peculiarly conscious of his own deficencies. In this conflict of emotions, all I dare aver, is, that it has been my faithful study to collect my duty from a just appreciation of every circumstance, by which it might be affected. All I dare hope, is, that, if in executing this task I have been too much swayed by a grateful remembrance of former instances, or by an affectionate sensibility to this transcendent proof, of the confidence of my fellow-citizens; and have thence too little consulted my incapacity as well as disinclination for the weighty and untried cares before me; my *error* will be palliated by the motives which misled me, and its consequences be judged by my Country, with some share of the partiality in which they originated.

Such being the impressions under which I have, in obedience to the public summons, repaired to the present station; it would be peculiarly improper to omit in this first official Act, my fervent supplications to that Almighty Being who rules over the Universe, who presides in the Councils of Nations, and whose providential aids can supply every human defect, that his benediction may consecrate to the liberties and happiness of the People of the United States, a Government instituted by themselves for these essential purposes: and may enable every instrument employed in its administration to execute with success, the functions allotted to his charge. In tendering this homage to the Great Author of every public and private good, I assure myself that it expresses your sentiments not less than my own; nor those of my fellow-citizens at large, less than either. No People can be bound to acknowledge and adore the invisible hand, which conducts the Affairs of men more than the People of the United States. Every step, by which they have advanced to the character of an independent nation, seems to have been distinguished by some token of providential agency. And in the important revolution just accomplished in the system of their United Government, the tranquil deliberations and voluntary consent of so many distinct communities, from which the event has resulted, cannot be compared with the means by which most Governments have been established, without some return of pious gratitude along with an humble anticipation of the future blessings which the past seem to presage. These reflections, arising out of the present crisis, have forced themselves too strongly on my mind to be suppressed. You will join with me I trust in thinking, that there are none under the influence of which, the proceedings of a new and free Government can more auspiciously commence.

By the article establishing the Executive Department, it is made the duty of the President "to recommend to your consideration, such measures as he shall judge necessary and expedient." The circumstances under which I now meet you, will acquit me from entering into that subject, farther than to refer to the Great Constitutional Charter under which you are assembled; and which, in defining your powers, designates the objects to which your attention is to be given. It will be more consistent with those circumstances, and far more congenial with the feelings which actuate me, to substitute, in place of a recommendation of particular measures, the tribute that is due to the talents, the rectitude, and the patriotism which adorn the characters selected to devise and adopt them. In these honorable qualifications, I behold the surest pledges, that as on one side, no local prejudices, or attachments; no seperate views, nor party animosities, will misdirect the comprehensive and equal eye which ought to watch over this great assemblage of communities and interests: so, on another, that the foundations of our National policy will be laid in the pure and immutable principles of private morality; and the pre-eminence of a free Government, be exemplified by all the attributes which can win the affections of its Citizens, and command the respect of the world.

I dwell on this prospect with every satisfaction which an ardent love for my Country can inspire: since there is no truth more thoroughly established, than that there exists in the oeconomy and course of nature, an indissoluble union between virtue and happiness, between duty and advantage, between the genuine maxims of an honest and magnanimous policy, and the solid rewards of public prosperity and felicity: Since we ought to be no less persuaded that the propitious smiles of Heaven, can never be expected on a nation that disregards the eternal rules of order and right, which Heaven itself has ordained: And since the preservation of the sacred fire of liberty, and the destiny of the Republican model of Government, are justly considered as *deeply*, perhaps as *finally* staked, on the experiment entrusted to the hands of the American people.

Besides the ordinary objects submitted to your care, it will remain with your judgment to decide, how far an exercise of the occasional power delegated by the Fifth article of the Constitution is rendered expedient at the present juncture by the nature of objections which have been urged against the System, or by the degree of inquietude which has given birth to them. Instead of undertaking particular recommendations on this subject, in which I could be guided by no lights derived from official opportunities, I shall again give way to my entire confidence in your discernment and pursuit of the public good: For I assure myself that whilst you carefully avoid every alteration which might endanger the benefits of an United and effective Government, or which ought to await the future lessons of experience; a reverence for the characteristic rights of freemen, and a regard for the public harmony, will sufficiently influence your deliberations on the question how far the former can be more impregnably fortified, or the latter be safely and advantageously promoted.

To the preceeding observations I have one to add, which will be most properly addressed to the House of Representatives. It concerns myself, and will therefore be as brief as possible. When I was first honoured with a call into the Service of my Country, then on the eve of an arduous struggle for its liberties, the light in which I contemplated my duty required that I should renounce every pecuniary compensation. From this resolution I have in no instance departed. And being still under the impressions which produced it, I must decline as inapplicable to myself, any share in the personal emoluments, which may be indispensably included in a permanent provision for the Executive Department; and must accordingly pray that the pecuniary estimates for the Station in which I am placed, may, during my continuance in it, be limited to such actual expenditures as the public good may be thought to require.

Having thus imparted to you my sentiments, as they have been awakened by the occasion which brings us together, I shall take my present leave; but not without resorting once more to the benign parent of the human race, in humble supplication that since he has been pleased to favour the American people, with opportunities for deliberating in perfect tranquility, and dispositions for deciding with unparellelled unanimity on a form of Government, for the security of their Union, and the advancement of their happiness; so his divine blessing may be equally *conspicuous* in the enlarged views, the temperate consultations, and the wise measures on which the success of this Government must depend.

John Adams (March 4, 1797)

On this subject it might become me better to be silent or to speak with diffidence; but as something may be expected, the occasion, I hope, will be admitted as an apology if I venture to say that if a preference, upon principle, of a free republican government, formed upon long and serious reflection, after a diligent and impartial inquiry after truth; if an attachment to the Constitution of the United States, and a conscientious determination to support it until it shall be altered by the judgments and wishes of the people, expressed in the mode prescribed in it; if a respectful attention to the constitutions of the individual States and a constant caution and delicacy toward the State governments; if an equal and impartial regard to the rights, interest, honor, and happiness of all the States in the Union, without preference or regard to a northern or southern, an eastern or western, position, their various political opinions on unessential points or their personal attachments; if a love of virtuous men of all parties and denominations; if a love of science and letters and a wish to patronize every rational effort to encourage schools, colleges, universities, academies, and every institution for propagating knowledge, virtue, and religion among all classes of the people, not only for their benign influence on the happiness of life in all its stages and classes, and of society in all its forms, but as the only means of preserving our Constitution from its natural enemies, the spirit of sophistry, the spirit of party, the spirit of intrigue, the profligacy of corruption, and the pestilence of foreign influence, which is the angel of destruction to elective governments; if a love of equal laws, of justice, and humanity in the interior administration; if an inclination to improve agriculture, commerce, and manufacturers for necessity, convenience, and defense; if a spirit of equity and humanity toward the aboriginal nations of America, and a dis-

Reprinted from *Inaugural Addresses of the Presidents of the United States, from George Washington 1789 to George Bush 1989*, Bicentennial Edition (Washington, D.C.: GPO, 1989), 11–12.

position to meliorate their condition by inclining them to be more friendly to us, and our citizens to be more friendly to them; if an inflexible determination to maintain peace and inviolable faith with all nations, and that system of neutrality and impartiality among the belligerent powers of Europe which has been adopted by this Government and so solemnly sanctioned by both Houses of Congress and applauded by the legislatures of the States and the public opinion, until it shall be otherwise ordained by Congress; if a personal esteem for the French nation, formed in a residence of seven years chiefly among them, and a sincere desire to preserve the friendship which has been so much for the honor and interest of both nations; if, while the conscious honor and integrity of the people of America and the internal sentiment of their own power and energies must be preserved, an earnest endeavor to investigate every just cause and remove every colorable pretense of complaint; if an intention to pursue by amicable negotiation a reparation for the injuries that have been committed on the commerce of our fellow-citizens by whatever nation, and if success can not be obtained, to lay the facts before the Legislature, that they may consider what further measures the honor and interest of the Government and its constituents demand; if a resolution to do justice as far as may depend upon me, at all times and to all nations, and maintain peace, friendship, and benevolence with all the world; if an unshaken confidence in the honor, spirit, and resources of the American people, on which I have so often hazarded my all and never been deceived; if elevated ideas of the high destinies of this country and of my own duties toward it, founded on a knowledge of the moral principles and intellectual improvements of the people deeply engraven on my mind in early life, and not obscured but exalted by experience and age; and, with humble reverence, I feel it to be my duty to add, if a veneration for the religion of a people who profess and call themselves Christians, and a fixed resolution to consider a decent respect for Christianity among the best recommendations for the public service, can enable me in any degree to comply with your wishes, it shall be my strenuous endeavor that this sagacious injunction of the two Houses shall not be without effect.

With this great example before me, with the sense and spirit, the faith and honor, the duty and interest, of the same American people pledged to support the Constitution of the United States, I entertain no doubt of its continuance in all its energy, and my mind is prepared without hesitation to lay myself under the most solemn obligations to support it to the utmost of my power.

And may that Being who is supreme over all, the Patron of Order, the Fountain of Justice, and the Protector in all ages of the world of virtuous liberty, continue His blessing upon this nation and its Government and give it all possible success and duration consistent with the ends of His providence.

Thomas Jefferson (1801)

First Inaugural Address in the Washington, D.C.

Wednesday, March 4, 1801

Friends and Fellow-Citizens:

Called upon to undertake the duties of the first executive office of our country, I avail myself of the presence of that portion of my fellow-citizens which is here assembled to express my grateful thanks for the favor with which they have been pleased to look toward me, to declare a sincere consciousness that the task is above my talents, and that I approach it with those anxious and awful presentiments which the greatness of the charge and the weakness of my powers so justly inspire. A rising nation, spread over a wide and fruitful land, traversing all the seas with the

Reprinted from *Inaugural Addresses of the Presidents of the United States, from George Washington 1789 to George Bush 1989*, Bicentennial Edition (Washington, D.C.: GPO, 1989), 13–17.

rich productions of their industry, engaged in commerce with nations who feel power and forget right, advancing rapidly to destinies beyond the reach of mortal eye—when I contemplate these transcendent objects, and see the honor, the happiness, and the hopes of this beloved country committed to the issue, and the auspices of this day, I shrink from the contemplation, and humble myself before the magnitude of the undertaking. Utterly, indeed, should I despair did not the presence of many whom I here see remind me that in the other high authorities provided by our Constitution I shall find resources of wisdom, of virtue, and of zeal on which to rely under all difficulties. To you, then, gentlemen, who are charged with the sovereign functions of legislation, and to those associated with you, I look with encouragement for that guidance and support which may enable us to steer with safety the vessel in which we are all embarked amidst the conflicting elements of a troubled world.

During the contest of opinion through which we have passed the animation of discussions and of exertions has sometimes worn an aspect which might impose on strangers unused to think freely and to speak and to write what they think; but this being now decided by the voice of the nation, announced according to the rules of the Constitution, all will, of course, arrange themselves under the will of the law, and unite in common efforts for the common good. All, too, will bear in mind this sacred principle, that though the will of the majority is in all cases to prevail, that will to be rightful must be reasonable; that the minority possess their equal rights, which equal law must protect, and to violate would be oppression. Let us, then, fellow-citizens, unite with one heart and one mind. Let us restore to social intercourse that harmony and affection without which liberty and even life itself are but dreary things. And let us reflect that, having banished from our land that religious intolerance under which mankind so long bled and suffered, we have yet gained little if we countenance a political intolerance as despotic, as wicked, and capable of as bitter and bloody persecutions. During the throes and convulsions of the ancient world, during

the agonizing spasms of infuriated man, seeking through blood and slaughter his long-lost liberty, it was not wonderful that the agitation of the billows should reach even this distant and peaceful shore; that this should be more felt and feared by some and less by others, and should divide opinions as to measures of safety. But every difference of opinion is not a difference of principle. We have called by different names brethren of the same principle. We are all Republicans, we are all Federalists. If there be any among us who would wish to dissolve this Union or to change its republican form, let them stand undisturbed as monuments of the safety with which error of opinion may be tolerated where reason is left free to combat it. I know, indeed, that some honest men fear that a republican government can not be strong, that this Government is not strong enough; but would the honest patriot, in the full tide of successful experiment, abandon a government which has so far kept us free and firm on the theoretic and visionary fear that this Government, the world's best hope, may by possibility want energy to preserve itself? I trust not. I believe this, on the contrary, the strongest Government on earth. I believe it the only one where every man, at the call of the law, would fly to the standard of the law, and would meet invasions of the public order as his own personal concern. Sometimes it is said that man can not be trusted with the government of himself. Can he, then, be trusted with the government of others? Or have we found angels in the forms of kings to govern him? Let history answer this question.

Let us, then, with courage and confidence pursue our own Federal and Republican principles, our attachment to union and representative government. Kindly separated by nature and a wide ocean from the exterminating havoc of one quarter of the globe; too high-minded to endure the degradations of the others; possessing a chosen country, with room enough for our descendants to the thousandth and thousandth generation; entertaining a due sense of our equal right to the use of our own faculties, to the acquisitions of our own industry, to honor and confidence from our fellow-citizens, resulting not from birth, but from our actions and their sense of them; enlightened by a benign religion, professed, indeed, and practiced in various forms, yet all of them inculcating honesty, truth, temperance, gratitude, and the love of man; acknowledging and adoring an overruling Providence, which by all its dispensations proves that it delights in the happiness of man here and his greater happiness hereafter—with all these blessings, what more is necessary to make us a happy and a prosperous people? Still one thing more, fellow-citizens—a wise and frugal Government, which shall restrain men from injuring one another, shall leave them otherwise free to regulate their own pursuits of industry and improvement, and shall not take from the mouth of labor the bread it has earned. This is the sum of good government, and this is necessary to close the circle of our felicities.

About to enter, fellow-citizens, on the exercise of duties which comprehend everything dear and valuable to you, it is proper you should understand what I deem the essential principles of our Government, and consequently those which ought to shape its Administration. I will compress them within the narrowest compass they will bear, stating the general principle, but not all its limitations. Equal and exact justice to all men, of whatever state or persuasion, religious or political; peace, commerce, and honest friendship with all nations, entangling alliances with none; the support of the State governments in all their rights, as the most competent administrations for our domestic concerns and the surest bulwarks against antirepublican tendencies; the preservation of the General Government in its whole constitutional vigor, as the sheet anchor of our peace at home and safety abroad; a jealous care of the right of election by the people—a mild and safe corrective of abuses which are lopped by the sword of revolution where peaceable remedies are unprovided; absolute acquiescence in the decisions of the majority, the vital principle of republics, from which is no appeal but to force, the vital principle and immediate parent of despotism; a well disciplined militia, our best reliance in

peace and for the first moments of war, till regulars may relieve them; the supremacy of the civil over the military authority; economy in the public expense, that labor may be lightly burthened; the honest payment of our debts and sacred preservation of the public faith; encouragement of agriculture, and of commerce as its handmaid; the diffusion of information and arraignment of all abuses at the bar of the public reason; freedom of religion; freedom of the press, and freedom of person under the protection of the habeas corpus, and trial by juries impartially selected. These principles form the bright constellation which has gone before us and guided our steps through an age of revolution and reformation. The wisdom of our sages and blood of our heroes have been devoted to their attainment. They should be the creed of our political faith, the text of civic instruction, the touchstone by which to try the services of those we trust; and should we wander from them in moments of error or of alarm, let us hasten to retrace our steps and to regain the road which alone leads to peace, liberty, and safety.

I repair, then, fellow-citizens, to the post you have assigned me. With experience enough in subordinate offices to have seen the difficulties of this the greatest of all, I have learnt to expect that it will rarely fall to the lot of imperfect man to retire from this station with the reputation and the favor which bring him into it. Without pretensions to that high confidence you reposed in our first and greatest revolutionary character, whose preeminent services had entitled him to the first place in his country's love and destined for him the fairest page in the volume of faithful history, I ask so much confidence only as may give firmness and effect to the legal administration of your affairs. I shall often go wrong through defect of judgment. When right, I shall often be thought wrong by those whose positions will not command a view of the whole ground. I ask your indulgence for my own errors, which will never be intentional, and your support against the errors of others, who may condemn what they would not if seen in all its parts. The approbation implied by your suffrage is a great consolation to me for the past, and my future solicitude will be to retain the good opinion of those who have bestowed it in advance, to conciliate that of others by doing them all the good in my power, and to be instrumental to the happiness and freedom of all.

Relying, then, on the patronage of your good will, I advance with obedience to the work, ready to retire from it whenever you become sensible how much better choice it is in your power to make. And may that Infinite Power which rules the destinies of the universe lead our councils to what is best, and give them a favorable issue for your peace and prosperity.

———

James Madison

First Inaugural Address

March 4, 1809

To cherish peace and friendly intercourse with all nations having correspondent dispositions; to maintain sincere neutrality towards belligerent nations; to prefer in all cases, amicable discussion and reasonable accommodation of differences, to a decision of them by an appeal to Arms; to exclude foreign intrigues and foreign partialities, so degrading to all Countries, and so baneful to free ones; to foster a spirit of independence too just to invade the rights of others, too proud to surrender our own, too liberal to indulge unworthy prejudices ourselves, and too elevated not to look down upon them in others; to hold the Union of the States as the basis of their peace and happiness; to support the Constitution, which is the cement of the Union, as well in its limitations as in its authorities; to respect the rights and authorities reserved to the States and to the people, as equally incorporated with,

Reprinted from James Madison, *The Papers of James Madison*, ed. Robert A. Rutland et al., Presidential Series, vol. 1: *1 March–30 September 1809* (Charlottesville: University Press of Virginia, 1984), 16–18, 509. © 1984 The University of Virginia Press. Used by permission of the publisher.

and essential to the success of, the general system; to avoid the slightest interference with the rights of conscience, or the functions of religion so wisely exempted from civil jurisdiction; to preserve in their full energy, the other salutary provisions in behalf of private and personal rights, and of the freedom of the press; to observe oeconomy in public expenditures; to liberate the public resources by an honorable discharge of the public debts; to keep within the requisite limits a standing military force, always remembering, that an Armed and trained militia is the firmest bulwark of Republics; that without standing Armies their liberty can never be in danger; nor with large ones, safe; to promote by authorized means, improvements friendly to agriculture, to manufactures and to external as well as internal commerce; to favor, in like manner, the advancement of science and the diffusion of information as the best aliment to true liberty; to carry on the benevolent plans which have been so meritoriously applied to the conversion of our aboriginal neighbours from the degradation and wretchedness of savage life, to a participation of the improvements of which the human mind and manners are susceptible in a civilized state: As far as sentiments and intentions such as these can aid the fulfilment of my duty, they will be a resource which cannot fail me.

It is my good fortune, moreover, to have the path in which I am to tread, lighted by examples of illustrious services, successfully rendered in the most trying difficulties, by those who have marched before me. Of those of my immediate predecessor, it might least become me here to speak. I may however, be pardoned for not suppressing the sympathy with which my heart is full, in the rich reward he enjoys in the benedictions of a beloved Country, gratefully bestowed for exalted talents, zealously devoted, thro' a long career, to the advancement of its highest interest and happiness.

But the source to which I look for the aids which alone can supply my deficiences, is in the well tried intelligence and virtue of my fellow Citizens, and in the Councils of those representing them, in the other

Departments associated in the care of the national interests. In these my confidence will, under every difficulty be best placed; next to that which we have all been encouraged to feel in the guardianship and guidance of that Almighty Being whose power regulates the destiny of nations, whose blessings have been so conspicuously dispensed to this rising Republic, and to whom we are bound to address our devout gratitude for the past, as well as our fervent supplications and best hopes for the future.

James Madison

Second Inaugural Address

March 4, 1813

About to add the solemnity of an oath to the obligations imposed by a second call to the station in which my country heretofore placed me, I find in the presence of this respectable assembly an opportunity of publicly repeating my profound sense of so distinguished a confidence and of the responsibility united with it. The impressions on me are strengthened by such an evidence that my faithful endeavors to discharge my arduous duties have been favorably estimated, and by a consideration of the momentous period at which the trust has been renewed. From the weight and magnitude now belonging to it I should be compelled to shrink if I had less reliance on the support of an enlightened and generous people, and felt less deeply a conviction that the war with a powerful nation, which forms so prominent a feature in our situation, is stamped with that justice which invites the smiles of Heaven on the means of conducting it to a successful termination. . . .

Presidential Proclamations (1789–1815)

Colonial and state governments and the Continental and Confederation congresses often issued calls for prayer and fasting or thanksgiving. The first Congress asked President Washington to issue a thanksgiving proclamation, a request with which he complied. Many presidents have followed this practice, but Thomas Jefferson believed such calls to be a violation of the First and Tenth amendments and so refused to issue them. Although James Madison acceded to Congress's request for calls for "public humiliation and prayer" and thanksgiving during and after the War of 1812, he later noted in a private document after leaving public office that he thought such appeals to be unconstitutional (see James Madison, "Detached Memoranda," in chapter 14).

George Washington (October 3, 1789)

Thanksgiving Proclamation

City of New York, October 3, 1789

Whereas it is the duty of all Nations to acknowledge the providence of Almighty God, to obey his will, to be grateful for his benefits, and humbly to implore his protection and favor, and Whereas both Houses of Congress have by their joint Committee requested me "to recommend to the People of the United States a day of public thanks-giving and prayer to be observed by acknowledging with grateful hearts the many signal favors of Almighty God, especially by affording them an opportunity peaceably to establish a form of government for their safety and happiness."

Reprinted from *The Writings of George Washington, from the Original Manuscript Sources, 1745–1799,* ed. John C. Fitzpatrick (Washington, D.C.: GPO, 1939), 30:427–28.

Now therefore I do recommend and assign Thursday the 26th. day of November next to be devoted by the People of these States to the service of that great and glorious Being, who is the beneficent Author of all the good that was, that is, or that will be. That we may then all unite in rendering unto him our sincere and humble thanks, for his kind care and protection of the People of this country previous to their becoming a Nation, for the signal and manifold mercies, and the favorable interpositions of his providence, which we experienced in the course and conclusion of the late war, for the great degree of tranquillity, union, and plenty, which we have since enjoyed, for the peaceable and rational manner in which we have been enabled to establish constitutions of government for our safety and happiness, and particularly the national One now lately instituted, for the civil and religious liberty with which we are blessed, and the means we have of acquiring and diffusing useful knowledge and in general for all the great and various favors which he hath been pleased to confer upon us.

And also that we may then unite in most humbly offering our prayers and supplications to the great Lord and Ruler of Nations and beseech him to pardon our national and other transgressions, to enable us all, whether in public or private stations, to perform our several and relative duties properly and punctually, to render our national government a blessing to all the People, by constantly being a government of wise, just and constitutional laws, discreetly and faithfully executed and obeyed, to protect and guide all Sovereigns and Nations (especially such as have shown kindness unto us) and to bless them with good government, peace, and concord. To promote the knowledge and practice of true religion and virtue, and the encrease of science among them and Us, and generally to grant unto all Mankind such a degree of temporal prosperity as he alone knows to be best.

George Washington (January 1, 1795)

When we review the calamities which afflict so many other nations, the present condition of the United States affords much matter of consolation and satisfaction. Our exemption hitherto from foreign war, an increasing prospect of the continuance of that exemption, the great degree of internal tranquillity we have enjoyed, the recent confirmation of that tranquillity by the suppression of an insurrection which so wantonly threatened it, the happy course of our public affairs in general, the unexampled prosperity of all classes of our citizens, are circumstances which peculiarly mark our situation with indications of the Divine beneficence toward us. In such a state of things it is in an especial manner our duty as a people, with devout reverence and affectionate gratitude, to acknowledge our many and great obligations to Almighty God and to implore Him to continue and confirm the blessings we experience.

Deeply penetrated with this sentiment, I, George Washington, President of the United States, do recommend to all religious societies and denominations, and to all persons whomsoever, within the United States to set apart and observe Thursday, the 19th day of February next, as a day of public thanksgiving and prayer, and on that day to meet together and render their sincere and hearty thanks to the Great Ruler of Nations for the manifold and signal mercies which distinguish our lot as a nation, particularly for the possession of constitutions of government which unite and by their union establish liberty with order; for the preservation of our peace, foreign and domestic; for the seasonable control which has been given to a spirit of disorder in the suppression of the late insurrection, and generally, for the prosperous course of our affairs, public and private; and at the same time humbly and fervently to beseech the kind Author of these blessings graciously to prolong them

Reprinted from U.S. House and Senate, *A Compilation of the Messages and Papers of the Presidents* (New York: Bureau of National Literature, 1897), 1:171–72.

to us; to imprint on our hearts a deep and solemn sense of our obligations to Him for them; to teach us rightly to estimate their immense value; to preserve us from the arrogance of prosperity, and from hazarding the advantages we enjoy by delusive pursuits; to dispose us to merit the continuance of His favors by not abusing them; by our gratitude for them, and by a correspondent conduct as citizens and men; to render this country more and more a safe and propitious asylum for the unfortunate of other countries; to extend among us true and useful knowledge; to diffuse and establish habits of sobriety, order, morality, and piety, and finally, to impart all the blessings we possess, or ask for ourselves, to the whole family of mankind.

In testimony whereof I have caused the seal of the United States of America to be affixed to these presents, and signed the same with my hand.

[SEAL]   Done at the city of Philadelphia, the 1st day of January, 1795, and of the Independence of the United States of America the nineteenth.

Go. Washington

By the President:
E DM: R ANDOLPH

John Adams, by Thomas Spear after Gilbert Stuart.
© Bettmann/CORBIS.

John Adams

Proclamation for a National Fast

23 March, 1798

As the safety and prosperity of nations ultimately and essentially depend on the protection and blessing of Almighty God; and the national acknowledgment

of this truth is not only an indispensable duty, which the people owe to him, but a duty whose natural influence is favorable to the promotion of that morality and piety, without which social happiness cannot exist, nor the blessings of a free government be enjoyed; and as this duty, at all times incumbent, is so especially in seasons of difficulty and of danger, when existing or threatening calamities, the just judgments of God against prevalent iniquity, are a loud call to repentance and reformation; and as the United States of America are at present placed in a hazardous and afflictive situation, by the unfriendly disposition, conduct, and demands of a foreign power, evinced by repeated refusals to receive our messengers of reconciliation and peace, by depredations on our commerce, and the infliction of injuries on very many of our fellow-citizens, while engaged in their lawful business on the seas;—under these considerations, it has appeared to me that the duty of imploring the

Reprinted from Charles Francis Adams, ed., *The Works of John Adams, Second President of the United States* (Boston: Little, Brown, 1854), 9:169–70.

mercy and benediction of Heaven on our country, demands at this time a special attention from its inhabitants.

I have therefore thought fit to recommend, and I do hereby recommend, that Wednesday, the 9th day of May next, be observed throughout the United States, as a day of solemn humiliation, fasting and prayer; that the citizens of these States, abstaining on that day from their customary worldly occupations, offer their devout addresses to the Father of mercies, agreeably to those forms or methods which they have severally adopted as the most suitable and becoming; that all religious congregations do, with the deepest humility, acknowledge before God the manifold sins and transgressions with which we are justly chargeable as individuals and as a nation; beseeching him at the same time, of his infinite grace, through the Redeemer of the world, freely to remit all our offences, and to incline us, by his Holy Spirit, to that sincere repentance and reformation which may afford us reason to hope for his inestimable favor and heavenly benediction; that it be made the subject of particular and earnest supplication, that our country may be protected from all the dangers which threaten it, that our civil and religious privileges may be preserved inviolate, and perpetuated to the latest generations, that our public councils and magistrates may be especially enlightened and directed at this critical period, that the American people may be united in those bonds of amity and mutual confidence, and inspired with that vigor and fortitude by which they have in times past been so highly distinguished, and by which they have obtained such invaluable advantages, that the health of the inhabitants of our land may be preserved, and their agriculture, commerce, fisheries, arts, and manufactures, be blessed and prospered, that the principles of genuine piety and sound morality may influence the minds and govern the lives of every description of our citizens, and that the blessings of peace, freedom, and pure religion, may be speedily extended to all the nations of the earth.

And finally I recommend, that on the said day, the duties of humiliation and prayer be accompanied by fervent thanksgiving to the bestower of every good gift, not only for having hitherto protected and preserved the people of these United States in the independent enjoyment of their religious and civil freedom, but also for having prospered them in a wonderful progress of population, and for conferring on them many and great favors conducive to the happiness and prosperity of a nation.

Given, &c.

JOHN ADAMS

John Adams

Proclamation for a National Fast

6 MARCH, 1799

As no truth is more clearly taught in the volume of inspiration, nor any more fully demonstrated by the experience of all ages, than that a deep sense and a due acknowledgment of the governing providence of a Supreme Being, and of the accountableness of men to Him as the searcher of hearts and righteous distributor of rewards and punishments, are conducive equally to the happiness and rectitude of individuals, and to the well-being of communities; as it is, also, most reasonable in itself, that men who are made capable of social acts and relations, who owe their improvements to the social state, and who derive their enjoyments from it, should, as a society, make their acknowledgments of dependence and obligation to Him, who hath endowed them with these capacities, and elevated them in the scale of existence by these distinctions; as it is, likewise, a plain dictate of duty, and a strong sentiment of nature, that in circumstances of great urgency and seasons of imminent

Reprinted from Charles Francis Adams, ed., *The Works of John Adams, Second President of the United States* (Boston: Little, Brown, 1854), 9:172–74.

danger, earnest and particular supplications should be made to Him who is able to defend or to destroy; as, moreover, the most precious interests of the people of the United States are still held in jeopardy by the hostile designs and insidious acts of a foreign nation, as well as by the dissemination among them of those principles, subversive of the foundations of all religious, moral, and social obligations, that have produced incalculable mischief and misery in other countries; and as, in fine, the observance of special seasons for public religious solemnities, is happily calculated to avert the evils which we ought to deprecate, and to excite to the performance of the duties which we ought to discharge, by calling and fixing the attention of the people at large to the momentous truths already recited, by affording opportunity to teach and inculcate them, by animating devotion, and giving to it the character of a national act:

For these reasons I have thought proper to recommend, and I do hereby recommend accordingly, that Thursday, the twenty-fifth day of April next, be observed, throughout the United States of America, as a day of solemn humiliation, fasting, and prayer; that the citizens, on that day, abstain as far as may be from their secular occupations, devote the time to the sacred duties of religion, in public and in private; that they call to mind our numerous offences against the most high God, confess them before him with the sincerest penitence, implore his pardoning mercy, through the Great Mediator and Redeemer, for our past transgressions, and that, through the grace of his Holy Spirit, we may be disposed and enabled to yield a more suitable obedience to his righteous requisitions in time to come; that he would interpose to arrest the progress of that impiety and licentiousness in principle and practice, so offensive to himself and so ruinous to mankind; that he would make us deeply sensible, that "righteousness exalteth a nation, but that sin is the reproach of any people"; that he would turn us from our transgressions, and turn his displeasure from us; that he would withhold us from unreasonable discontent, from disunion, faction, sedition, and insurrection; that he would preserve our country from the desolating sword; that he would save our cities and towns from a repetition of those awful pestilential visitations under which they have lately suffered so severely, and that the health of our inhabitants, generally, may be precious in his sight; that he would favor us with fruitful seasons, and so bless the labors of the husbandman as that there may be food in abundance for man and beast; that he would prosper our commerce, manufactures, and fisheries, and give success to the people in all their lawful industry and enterprise; that he would smile on our colleges, academies, schools, and seminaries of learning, and make them nurseries of sound science, morals, and religion; that he would bless all magistrates from the highest to the lowest, give them the true spirit of their station, make them a terror to evil-doers, and a praise to them that do well; that he would preside over the councils of the nation at this critical period, enlighten them to a just discernment of the public interest, and save them from mistake, division, and discord; that he would make succeed our preparations for defence, and bless our armaments by land and by sea; that he would put an end to the effusion of human blood and the accumulation of human misery among the contending nations of the earth, by disposing them to justice, to equity, to benevolence, and to peace; and that he would extend the blessings of knowledge, of true liberty, and of pure and undefiled religion, throughout the world.

And I do, also, recommend that, with these acts of humiliation, penitence, and prayer, fervent thanksgiving to the author of all good be united, for the countless favors which he is still continuing to the people of the United States, and which render their condition as a nation eminently happy, when compared with the lot of others.

Given, &c.

JOHN ADAMS

James Madison

Presidential Proclamation

[9 July 1812]

WHEREAS the Congress of the United States, by a joint Resolution of the two Houses, have signified a request, that a day may be recommended, to be observed by the People of the United States, with religious solemnity, as a day of public Humiliation and Prayer: and whereas such a recommendation will enable the several religious denominations and societies so disposed, to offer, at one and the same time, their common vows and adorations to Almighty God, on the solemn occasion produced by the war, in which he has been pleased to permit the injustice of a foreign power to involve these United States; I do therefore recommend the *third Thursday in August next,* as a convenient day, to be so set apart, for the devout purposes of rendering to the Sovereign of the Universe, and the Benefactor of mankind, the public homage due to his holy attributes; of acknowleging the transgressions which might justly provoke the manifestations of His divine displeasure; of seeking His merciful forgiveness, and His assistance in the great duties of repentance & amendment; and, especially, of offering fervent supplications, that in the present season of calamity and war, he would take the American People under His peculiar care and protection; that He would guide their public councils, animate their patriotism, and bestow His blessing on their arms; that He would inspire all nations with a love of justice & of concord, and with a reverence for the unerring precept of our holy religion, to do to others as they would require that others should do to them; and, finally, that turning the hearts of our enemies from the violence and injustice which sway their councils against us, He would hasten a restoration of

Reprinted from James Madison, *The Papers of James Madison,* ed. Robert A. Rutland et al., Presidential Series, vol. 4: *5 November 1811–9 July 1812,* with a supplement, *5 March 1809–19 October 1811,* ed. J. C. A. Stagg et al. (Charlottesville: University Press of Virginia, 1999), 581–82. © 1999 The University of Virginia Press. Used by permission of the publisher.

the blesings of Peace. Given at Washington the ninth day of July, in the year of our Lord one thousand eight hundred and twelve.

JAMES MADISON
By the President,
JAMES MONROE,
Secretary of State

———

James Madison (July 23, 1813)

A Proclamation

Whereas the Congress of the United States, by a joint resolution of the two Houses, have signified a request that a day may be recommended to be observed by the people of the United States with religious solemnity as a day of public humiliation and prayer; and

Whereas in times of public calamity such as that of the war brought on the United States by the injustice of a foreign government it is especially becoming that the hearts of all should be touched with the same and the eyes of all be turned to that Almighty Power in whose hand are the welfare and the destiny of nations:

I do therefore issue this my proclamation, recommending to all who shall be piously disposed to unite their hearts and voices in addressing at one and the same time their vows and adorations to the Great Parent and Sovereign of the Universe that they assemble on the second Thursday of September next in their respective religious congregations to render Him thanks for the many blessings He has bestowed on the people of the United States; that He has blessed them with a land capable of yielding all the necessaries and requisites of human life, with ample means for convenient exchanges with foreign coun-

Reprinted from *A Compilation of the Messages and Papers of the Presidents* (New York: Bureau of National Literature, 1897), 2:517–18.

tries; that He has blessed the labors employed in its cultivation and improvement; that He is now blessing the exertions to extend and establish the arts and manufactures which will secure within ourselves supplies too important to remain dependent on the precarious policy or the peaceable dispositions of other nations, and particularly that He has blessed the United States with a political Constitution founded on the will and authority of the whole people and guaranteeing to each individual security, not only of his person and his property, but of those sacred rights of conscience so essential to his present happiness and so dear to his future hopes; that with those expressions of devout thankfulness be joined supplications to the same Almighty Power that He would look down with compassion on our infirmities; that He would pardon our manifold transgressions and awaken and strengthen in all the wholesome purposes of repentance and amendment; that in this season of trial and calamity He would preside in a particular manner over our public councils and inspire all citizens with a love of their country and with those fraternal affections and that mutual confidence which have so happy a tendency to make us safe at home and respected abroad; and that as He was graciously pleased heretofore to smile on our struggles against the attempts of the Government of the Empire of which these States then made a part to wrest from them the rights and privileges to which they were entitled in common with every other part and to raise them to the station of an independent and sovereign people, so He would now be pleased in like manner to bestow His blessing on our arms in resisting the hostile and persevering efforts of the same power to degrade us on the ocean, the common inheritance of all, from rights and immunities belonging and essential to the American people as a coequal member of the great community of independent nations; and that, inspiring our enemies with moderation, with justice, and with that spirit of reasonable accommodation which our country has continued to manifest, we may be enabled to beat our swords into plowshares and to enjoy in peace every man the fruits of his honest industry and the rewards of his lawful enterprise.

If the public homage of a people can ever be worthy the favorable regard of the Holy and Omniscient Being to whom it is addressed, it must be that in which those who join in it are guided only by their free choice, by the impulse of their hearts and the dictates of their consciences; and such a spectacle must be interesting to all Christian nations as proving that religion, that gift of Heaven for the good of man, freed from all coercive edicts, from that unhallowed connection with the powers of this world which corrupts religion into an instrument or an usurper of the policy of the state, and making no appeal but to reason, to the heart, and to the conscience, can spread its benign influence everywhere and can attract to the divine altar those freewill offerings of humble supplication, thanksgiving, and praise which alone can be acceptable to Him whom no hypocrisy can deceive and no forced sacrifices propitiate.

Upon these principles and with these views the good people of the United States are invited, in conformity with the resolution aforesaid, to dedicate the day above named to the religious solemnities therein recommended.

Given at Washington, this 23d day of July, A.D. 1813.

[SEAL]   JAMES MADISON

James Madison (November 16, 1814)

A Proclamation

The two Houses of the National Legislature having by a joint resolution expressed their desire that in the present time of public calamity and war a day may be recommended to be observed by the people of the

Reprinted from *A Compilation of the Messages and Papers of the Presidents* (New York: Bureau of National Literature, 1897), 2:543.

United States as a day of public humiliation and fasting and of prayer to Almighty God for the safety and welfare of these States, His blessing on their arms, and a speedy restoration of peace, I have deemed it proper by this proclamation to recommend that Thursday, the 12th of January next, be set apart as a day on which all may have an opportunity of voluntarily offering at the same time in their respective religious assemblies their humble adoration to the Great Sovereign of the Universe, of confessing their sins and transgressions, and of strengthening their vows of repentance and amendment. They will be invited by the same solemn occasion to call to mind the distinguished favors conferred on the American people in the general health which has been enjoyed, in the abundant fruits of the season, in the progress of the arts instrumental to their comfort, their prosperity, and their security, and in the victories which have so powerfully contributed to the defense and protection of our country, a devout thankfulness for all which ought to be mingled with their supplications to the Beneficent Parent of the Human Race that He would be graciously pleased to pardon all their offenses against Him; to support and animate them in the discharge of their respective duties; to continue to them the precious advantages flowing from political institutions so auspicious to their safety against dangers from abroad, to their tranquillity at home, and to their liberties, civil and religious; and that He would in a special manner preside over the nation in its public councils and constituted authorities, giving wisdom to its measures and success to its arms in maintaining its rights and in overcoming all hostile designs and attempts against it; and, finally, that by inspiring the enemy with dispositions favorable to a just and reasonable peace its blessings may be speedily and happily restored.

Given at the city of Washington, the 16th day of November, 1814, and of the Independence of the United States the thirty-eighth.

[SEAL]   JAMES MADISON

James Madison (March 4, 1815)

A Proclamation

The Senate and House of Representatives of the United States have by a joint resolution signified their desire that a day may be recommended to be observed by the people of the United States with religious solemnity as a day of thanksgiving and of devout acknowledgments to Almighty God for His great goodness manifested in restoring to them the blessing of peace.

No people ought to feel greater obligations to celebrate the goodness of the Great Disposer of Events and of the Destiny of Nations than the people of the United States. His kind providence originally conducted them to one of the best portions of the dwelling place allotted for the great family of the human race. He protected and cherished them under all the difficulties and trials to which they were exposed in their early days. Under His fostering care their habits, their sentiments, and their pursuits prepared them for a transition in due time to a state of independence and self-government. In the arduous struggle by which it was attained they were distinguished by multiplied tokens of His benign interposition. During the interval which succeeded He reared them into the strength and endowed them with the resources which have enabled them to assert their national rights and to enhance their national character in another arduous conflict, which is now so happily terminated by a peace and reconciliation with those who have been our enemies. And to the same Divine Author of Every Good and Perfect Gift we are indebted for all those privileges and advantages, religious as well as civil, which are so richly enjoyed in this favored land.

It is for blessings such as these, and more especially for the restoration of the blessing of peace, that I now recommend that the second Thursday in April next be set apart as a day on which the people of every re-

Reprinted from *A Compilation of the Messages and Papers of the Presidents* (New York: Bureau of National Literature, 1897), 2:545–46.

ligious denomination may in their solemn assemblies unite their hearts and their voices in a freewill offering to their Heavenly Benefactor of their homage of thanksgiving and of their songs of praise.

Given at the city of Washington on the 4th day of March, A.D. 1815, and of the Independence [SEAL] of the United States the thirty-ninth.

JAMES MADISON

George Washington's Letters and Farewell Address

Americans often call George Washington "the father of our country"—and with good reason. After leading the Continental Army during the War of American Independence and lending his prestige to the Constitutional Convention of 1787, he served two terms as the nation's first president. Historians and political scientists routinely rank him as one of America's greatest presidents. Washington's views on religious liberty and the role of religion in public life are reflected well by the following documents composed when he was president. Although Alexander Hamilton wrote an early draft of the Farewell Address, he did so with Washington's views in mind, and the president took an active role in revising it. Relevant excerpts from both the draft and the final version are included below.

Letter from George Washington to the United Baptist Churches of Virginia

Gentlemen, [New York, May 1789]

I request that you will accept my best acknowledgments for your congratulation on my appointment to the first office in the nation. The kind manner in which you mention my past conduct equally claims the expression of my gratitude.

After we had, by the smiles of Heaven on our exertions, obtained the object for which we contended, I retired at the conclusion of the war, with an idea that my country could have no farther occasion for my services, and with the intention of never entering again into public life: But when the exigence of my country seemed to require me once more to engage in public affairs, an honest conviction of duty superseded my former resolution, and became my apology for deviating from the happy plan which I had adopted.

If I could have entertained the slightest apprehension that the Constitution framed in the Convention, where I had the honor to preside, might possibly endanger the religious rights of any ecclesiastical Society, certainly I would never have placed my signature to it; and if I could now conceive that the general Government might ever be so administered as to render the liberty of conscience insecure, I beg you will be persuaded that no one would be more zealous than myself to establish effectual barriers against the horrors of spiritual tyranny, and every species of religious persecution—For you, doubtless, remember that I have often expressed my sentiment, that every man, conducting himself as a good citizen, and being accountable to God alone for his religious opinions, ought to be protected in worshipping the Deity according to the dictates of his own conscience.

Reprinted from George Washington, *The Papers of George Washington*, ed. W. W. Abbot and Dorothy Twohig, Presidential Series, vol. 2: *April–June 1789*, ed. Dorothy Twohig (Charlottesville and London: University of Virginia Press, 1987), 423–24. © 1987 The University of Virginia Press. Used by permission of the publisher.

To the Hebrew Congregation in New Port, Rhode Island.

Gentlemen,

While I receive with much satisfaction your address replete with expressions of affection and esteem; I rejoice in the opportunity of assuring you that I shall always retain a grateful remembrance of the cordial welcome I experienced in my visit to New Port from all classes of citizens.

The reflection on the days of difficulty and danger which are past is rendered the more sweet from a consciousness that they are succeeded by days of uncommon prosperity and security. If we have wisdom to make the best use of the advantages with which we are now favored, we cannot fail, under the just administration of a good government to become a great and a happy people.

The citizens of the United States of America have a right to applaud themselves for having given to mankind examples of an enlarged and liberal policy, a policy worthy of imitation. All possess alike liberty of conscience and immunities of citizenship. It is now no more than

George Washington to the Hebrew Congregation in Newport, Rhode Island, August 18, 1790. Manuscript Division, The Papers of George Washington, Library of Congress.

that toleration is spoken of, as if it was by the indulgence of one class of people, that another enjoyed the exercise of their inherent natural rights. For happily the government of the United States, which gives to bigotry no sanction, to persecution no assistance, requires only that they who live under its protection should demean themselves as good citizens, in giving it on all occasions their effectual support.

It would be inconsistent with the frankness of my character not to avow that I am pleased with your favorable opinion of my administration, and fervent wishes for my felicity.

May the children of the Stock of Abraham, who dwell in this land, continue to merit and enjoy the good will of the other inhabitants, while every one shall sit in safety under his own vine and fig-tree, and there shall be none to make him afraid.

May the Father of all mercies scatter light and not darkness in our paths, and make us all in our several vocations useful here, and in his own due time and way everlastingly happy.

G Washington.

While I recollect with satisfaction that the religious Society of which you are Members, have been, throughout America, uniformly, and almost unanimously, the firm friends to civil liberty, and the persevering Promoters of our glorious revolution; I cannot hesitate to believe that they will be the faithful Supporters of a free, yet efficient general Government. Under this pleasing expectation I rejoice to assure them that they may rely on my best wishes and endeavors to advance their prosperity.

In the meantime be assured, Gentlemen, that I entertain a proper sense of your fervent supplications to God for my temporal and eternal happiness.

G. Washington

Letter from George Washington to the Hebrew Congregation in Newport, Rhode Island

Gentlemen.   [Newport, R.I., 18 August 1790]

While I receive, with much satisfaction, your Address replete with expressions of affection and esteem; I rejoice in the opportunity of assuring you, that I shall always retain a grateful remembrance of the cordial welcome I experienced in my visit to Newport, from all classes of Citizens.

The reflection on the days of difficulty and danger which are past is rendered the more sweet, from a consciousness that they are succeeded by days of uncommon prosperity and security. If we have wisdom to make the best use of the advantages with which we are now favored, we cannot fail, under the just ad-

ministration of a good Government, to become a great and a happy people.

The Citizens of the United States of America have a right to applaud themselves for having given to mankind examples of an enlarged and liberal policy: a policy worthy of imitation. All possess alike liberty of conscience and immunities of citizenship. It is now no more that toleration is spoken of, as if it was by the indulgence of one class of people, that another enjoyed the exercise of their inherent natural rights. For happily the Government of the United States, which gives to bigotry no sanction, to persecution no assistance requires only that they who live under its protection should demean themselves as good citizens, in giving it on all occasions their effectual support.

It would be inconsistent with the frankness of my character not to avow that I am pleased with your favorable opinion of my Administration, and fervent wishes for my felicity. May the Children of the Stock of Abraham, who dwell in this land, continue to merit and enjoy the good will of the other Inhabitants; while every one shall sit in safety under his own vine and figtree, and there shall be none to make him afraid. May the father of all mercies scatter light and not darkness in our paths, and make us all in our several vocations useful here, and in his own due time and way everlastingly happy.

Go: Washington

Alexander Hamilton's Draft of Washington's Farewell Address (July 1796)

∧my fellow Citizens

If benefits have resulted to you _∧_ from these services, let it always be remembered to your praise and as an instructive example in our annals that the constancy of your support amidst appearances ~~sometimes~~ _frequently_ _sometimes_ dubious ~~discouraging~~ vicissitudes of fortune _∧often discouraging_ and ~~not infrequently want of success~~ in situations in which not infrequently want of success has seconded the ~~suggesti~~ criticisms of malevolence was the essential prop ~~and guarantee~~ of ~~of~~ the efforts and _∧the guarantee of the_ measures by which they were atchieved. ~~I will not be restrained by personal considerations of personal delicacy from paying you the tribute of declaring~~ Profoundly penetrated with this idea, I shall carry it with me to my retirement and to my grave as a lively incitement to unceasing vows (the only returns I can henceforth make) that Heaven may continue to You the choicest tokens of the beneficence merited by national piety and morality—that your union and brotherly affection may be perpetual—that the free constitution, which is the work of your own hands may be sacredly maintained—that its administration in every department may be stamped with wisdom and virtue—that in fine the happiness of the People of these States under the auspices of liberty may be made complete by so careful a preservation & so prudent a use of this blessing as will acquire them the glorious satisfaction of recommending it to the affection the praise—and the adoption of every nation which is yet a stranger to it. . . .

This being the point in your political fortress against which the batteries of internal and external enemies will be most constantly and actively however covertly and insidiously levelled, it is of the utmost importance that you should appreciate in its full force the immense value of your political Union to your national and individual happiness—that you should cherish towards it an affectionate and immoveable attachment and that you should watch for its preservation with jealous _∧ and eagle eyed_ _∧_ solicitude.

For this you have every motive of sympathy and interest. Children for the most part of a common country, that country ~~ought~~ claims and ought to concentrate your affections. The name of American must always ~~exalt your character &~~ gratify _∧ and exalt_ the just pride of patriotism more than any denomination which can be derived from local discrimination. ~~Religion morality~~ _You have_ with slight shades of difference the same religion manners habits & political _∧ laws institutions &_ principles. You have in a common cause fought and triumphed to gether. The independence and liberty you enjoy are the work of ~~your united~~ _∧ joint councils_ efforts—dangers sufferings & successes. By your Union you atchieved them, by your union you will most effectually maintain them. . . .

To all those dispositions which promote ~~the~~ political happiness, Religion and Morality are essential _prosperity_ props. In vain does ~~he~~ _∧ that man_ claim the praise of patriotism who labours to subvert or undermine these great pillars of human happiness these ~~sure foundations~~ firmest foundations of ~~all~~ the duties of men and citizens. The mere politician equally with the pious man ought to respect and cherish them. A volume could not trace all their connections with private and public happiness. Let it simply be asked where is the security for ~~reputation~~ property for reputation for life if the sense of moral and religious obligation deserts the oaths which are administered in ~~the~~ Courts of Justice? Nor _the instruments of Investigation_ ought we to flatter ourselves that morality can be separated from religion. Concede as much as may be asked to the effect of refined education in minds of peculiar structure—can we believe—can we in _a_

Excerpts reprinted from _The Papers of Alexander Hamilton_, ed. Harold C. Syrett (New York and London: Columbia University Press, 1974), 20:268–70, 280–82, 287–88. © 1974 Columbia University Press. Used by permission of the publisher.

Draft of George Washington's Farewell Address, July 1796, by Alexander Hamilton.
Manuscript Division, Library of Congress.

prudence suppose that national morality can be maintained in exclusion of religious principles? Does it not require the aid of a generally received and divinely authoritative Religion?

^a main & necessary
Tis essentially true that virtue or morality is ^ ~~an~~
spring
~~indispensable prop~~ of popular or republican Governments. The rule indeed extends with more or less force to all free Governments. Who that is a prudent & sincere friend to them can look with indifference on the ravages which are making in the foundation of the Fabric? Religion? The uncommon means which of late have been directed to this fatal end seem to make it in a particular of manner the duty of the Re-
a
tiring Chief of ~~his~~ nation to warn his country against tasting of the poisonous draught.

Cultivate also industry and frugality. They are auxiliaries of good morals and ~~sour~~ great sources of private and national prosperity. Is there not room for regret that our propensity to expence exceeds the maturity of our Country for expense? Is there not more luxury among us, in various classes, than ~~the~~ suits the actual period of our national progress?
^the apology for
Whatever may be ^ ~~said of~~ luxury in a Country mature ~~in wealth and~~ in all the arts which are its ministers and the means of national opulence—can it promote the advantage of a young agricultural Country little advanced in manufactures and not much advanced in wealth? . . .

Cherish good faith and Justice towards, and peace and harmony with all nations. Religion and morality
enjoins
~~demand~~ this conduct And It cannot be, but that true
demands ~~dictates~~
policy equally ^~~demands~~ it. It will be worthy of a free enlightened and at ~~not~~ no distant period a great na-
^to mankind
tion to give ^the magnanimous and too novel example ~~to mankind~~ of a people ~~and go~~ invariably governed
an exalted justice & benevolence.   a
by those exalted views. Who can ~~say~~ doubt that in~~the~~ long course of time and events the fruits of such a conduct would richly repay any temporary advantages which might be lost by a steady adherence to

the plan? Can it be that Providence has not connected
permanent felicity
the ^ ~~happiness~~ of a nation with its virtue? The ex-
recommended by   which
periment is ~~worthy of~~ every sentiment ~~that~~ ennobles human nature. Alas! is it rendered impossible by its vices? . . .
incidents
Though in reviewing the ~~events~~ of my administration I am unconscious of intentional error—I am yet too sensible of my own deficiencies not to think it probable that I have committed many errors. I deprecate the evils to which they may tend—and fervently implore the Almighty to avert or mitigate them. I shall carry with me nevertheless the hope that my motives will continue to be viewed by my Country with indulgence & that after forty five years of my life devoted with an upright zeal to the public service the faults of inadequate abilities will be consigned to oblivion as myself must soon be to the mansions of rest.

Neither Ambition nor interest has been the impelling cause of my actions. I never designedly misused any power confided to me. The fortune with which I came into office is not bettered otherwise than by that ~~value~~ improvement in the value of property which the natural progress and peculiar prosperity of our country have produced. I retire
without cause for a blush—
with ~~an~~ a pure heart ~~with no sentiment alien to your true interests~~ with no alien sentiment to the ardor of those vows for the happiness of his Country which is so natural to a Citizen who sees in it ~~with undefiled hand and with ardent~~ vows for ~~the happiness of a~~
which is   himself   his
~~Country~~, ^ the native soil of ~~myself~~ and ^ progenitors for four generations.

George Washington's Farewell Address (September 19, 1796)

If benefits have resulted to our country from these services, let it always be remembered to your praise, and as an instructive example in our annals, that, under circumstances in which the Passions agitated in every direction were liable to mislead, amidst appearances sometimes dubious, viscissitudes of fortune often discouraging, in situations in which not unfrequently want of Success has countenanced the spirit of criticism, the constancy of your support was the essential prop of the efforts, and a guarantee of the plans by which they were effected. Profoundly penetrated with this idea, I shall carry it with me to my grave, as a strong incitement to unceasing vows that Heaven may continue to you the choicest tokens of its beneficence; that your Union and brotherly affection may be perpetual; that the free constitution, which is the work of your hands, may be sacredly maintained; that its Administration in every department may be stamped with wisdom and Virtue; that, in fine, the happiness of the people of these States, under the auspices of liberty, may be made complete, by so careful a preservation and so prudent a use of this blessing as will acquire to them the glory of recommending it to the applause, the affection, and adoption of every nation which is yet a stranger to it. . . .

For this you have every inducement of sympathy and interest. Citizens by birth or choice, of a common country, that country has a right to concentrate your affections. The name of AMERICAN, which belongs to you, in your national capacity, must always exalt the just pride of Patriotism, more than any appellation derived from local discriminations. With slight shades of difference, you have the same Religeon, Manners, Habits and political Principles. You have

in a common cause fought and triumphed together. The independence and liberty you possess are the work of joint councils, and joint efforts; of common dangers, sufferings and successes. . . .

Of all the dispositions and habits which lead to political prosperity, Religion and morality are indispensable supports. In vain would that man claim the tribute of Patriotism, who should labour to subvert these great Pillars of human happiness, these firmest props of the duties of Men and citizens. The mere Politician, equally with the pious man ought to respect and to cherish them. A volume could not trace all their connections with private and public felicity. Let it simply be asked where is the security for property, for reputation, for life, if the sense of religious obligation *desert* the oaths, which are the instruments of investigation in Courts of Justice? And let us with caution indulge the supposition, that morality can be maintained without religion. Whatever may be conceded to the influence of refined education on minds of peculiar structure, reason and experience both forbid us to expect that National morality can prevail in exclusion of religious principle.

'Tis substantially true, that virtue or morality is a necessary spring of popular government. The rule indeed extends with more or less force to every species of free Government. Who that is a sincere friend to it, can look with indifference upon attempts to shake the foundation of the fabric.

Promote then as an object of primary importance, Institutions for the general diffusion of knowledge. In proportion as the structure of a government gives force to public opinion, it is essential that public opinion should be enlightened. . . .

Observe good faith and justice towds. all Nations. Cultivate peace and harmony with all. Religion and morality enjoin this conduct; and can it be that good policy does not equally enjoin it? It will be worthy of a free, enlightened, and, at no distant period, a great Nation, to give to mankind the magnanimous and too novel example of a People always guided by an exalted justice and benevolence. Who can doubt that in the course of time and things the fruits of such a

Excerpts reprinted from *The Writings of George Washington, from the Original Manuscript Sources, 1745–1799*, ed. John C. Fitzpatrick (Washington, D.C.: GPO, 1940), 35:217–20, 229–31, 237–38.

Final manuscript of George Washington's Farewell Address, 1796. From *Washington's Farewell Address*, edited by Victor Hugo Paltsits (New York: New York Public Library, 1935), 105.

plan would richly repay any temporary advantages wch. might be lost by a steady adherence to it? Can it be, that Providence has not connected the permanent felicity of a Nation with its virtue? The experiment, at least, is recommended by every sentiment which ennobles human Nature. Alas! is it rendered impossible by its vices? . . .

Though in reviewing the incidents of my Administration, I am unconscious of intentional error, I am nevertheless too sensible of my defects not to think it probable that I may have committed many errors. Whatever they may be I fervently beseech the Almighty to avert or mitigate the evils to which they may tend. I shall also carry with me the hope that my Country will never cease to view them with indulgence; and that after forty five years of my life dedicated to its Service, with an upright zeal, the faults of incompetent abilities will be consigned to oblivion, as myself must soon be to the Mansions of rest.

Relying on its kindness in this as in other things, and actuated by that fervent love towards it, which is so natural to a Man, who views in it the native soil of himself and his progenitors for several Generations; I anticipate with pleasing expectation that retreat, in which I promise myself to realize, without alloy, the sweet enjoyment of partaking, in the midst of my fellow Citizens, the benign influence of good Laws under a free Government, the ever favourite object of my heart, and the happy reward, as I trust, of our mutual cares, labours and dangers.

Letter from George Washington to the Clergy of Different Denominations Residing in and near the City of Philadelphia

[March 3, 1797]

Gentlemen: Not to acknowledge with gratitude and sensibility the affectionate addresses and benevolent wishes of my fellow Citizens on my retiring from public life, would prove that I have been unworthy of the Confidence which they have been pleased to repose in me.

And, among those public testimonies of attachment and approbation, none can be more grateful than that of so respectable a body as yours.

Believing, as I do, that *Religion* and *Morality* are the essential pillars of Civil society, I view, with unspeakable pleasure, that harmony and brotherly love which characterizes the Clergy of different denominations, as well in this, as in other parts of the United States; exhibiting to the world a new and interesting spectacle, at once the pride of our Country and the surest basis of universal Harmony.

That your labours for the good of Mankind may be crowned with success; that your temporal enjoyments may be commensurate with your merits; and that the future reward of good and faithful Servants may be your's, I shall not cease to supplicate the Divine Author of life and felicity.

Reprinted from *The Writings of George Washington, from the Original Manuscript Sources, 1745–1799,* ed. John C. Fitzpatrick (Washington, D.C.: GPO, 1940), 35:416–17.

Letter from John Adams to the Officers of the First Brigade of the Third Division of the Militia of Massachusetts (October 11, 1798)

11 October, 1798

GENTLEMEN,

I have received from Major-General Hull and Brigadier-General Walker your unanimous address from Lexington, animated with a martial spirit, and expressed with a military dignity becoming your character and the memorable plains on which it was adopted.

While our country remains untainted with the principles and manners which are now producing desolation in so many parts of the world; while she continues sincere, and incapable of insidious and impious policy, we shall have the strongest reason to rejoice in the local destination assigned us by Providence. But should the people of America once become capable of that deep simulation towards one another, and towards foreign nations, which assumes the language of justice and moderation while it is practising iniquity and extravagance, and displays in the most captivating manner the charming pictures of candor, frankness, and sincerity, while it is rioting in rapine and insolence, this country will be the most miserable habitation in the world; because we have no government armed with power capable of contending with human passions unbridled by morality and religion. Avarice, ambition, revenge, or gallantry, would break the strongest cords of our Constitution as a whale goes through a net. Our Constitution was made only for a moral and religious people. It is wholly inadequate to the government of any other.

An address from the officers commanding two thousand eight hundred men, consisting of such sub-stantial citizens as are able and willing at their own expense completely to arm and clothe themselves in handsome uniforms, does honor to that division of the militia which has done so much honor to its country.

Oaths in this country are as yet universally considered as sacred obligations. That which you have taken and so solemnly repeated on that venerable spot, is an ample pledge of your sincerity and devotion to your country and its government.

JOHN ADAMS

CONGRESSIONAL CHAPLAINS AND ACTIONS OF CONGRESS (1789)

The first Congress's most important act concerning religion was to pass what became the First Amendment (see chapter 9). Before it did so, however, it agreed to appoint and pay congressional chaplains. Congress also reauthorized the Northwest Ordinance, originally passed by the Confederation Congress in 1787, which contains several provisions relevant to religious liberty and church-state relations.

Reprinted from Charles Francis Adams, ed., *The Works of John Adams, Second President of the United States* (Boston: Little, Brown, 1854), 9: 228–29.

Congressional Chaplains, 1789

Wednesday, April 15, 1789

The committee appointed the 7th of April, to prepare a system of rules to govern the two Houses in cases of conference, to take into consideration the manner of electing chaplains, and to confer thereon with a committee of the House of Representatives, reported:

That they had conferred with a committee of the House of Representatives, for that purpose appointed.

Whereupon,

Resolved, That, in every case of an amendment to a bill agreed to in one House and dissented to in the other, if either House shall request a conference, and appoint a committee for that purpose, and the other House shall also appoint a committee to confer, such committees shall, at a convenient time, to be agreed on by their chairman, meet in the conference chamber, and state to each other verbally, or in writing, as either shall choose, the reasons of their respective Houses for and against the amendment, and confer freely thereon.

The committee abovementioned further reported.

That two chaplains, of different denominations, be appointed to Congress for the present session, the Senate to appoint one, and give notice thereof to the House of Representatives, who shall, thereupon, appoint the other; which chaplains shall commence their services in the Houses that appoint them, but shall interchange weekly.

Which was also accepted.

Saturday, April 25, 1789

The Right Reverend SAMUEL PROVOST was elected Chaplain [of the Senate].

Friday, May 1, 1789

The House then proceeded by ballot to the appointment of a Chaplain to Congress on the part of this House. Upon examining the ballots, it appeared that the Rev. WILLIAM LINN was elected.

Reprinted from *The Debates and Proceedings in the Congress of the United States* (Washington, D.C.: Gales and Seaton, 1834), 1:19, 24, 242.

September 22, 1789

Chap. XVII.—*An Act for Allowing Compensation to the Members of the Senate and House of Representatives of the United States, and to the Officers of both Houses.*

SEC. 4. *And be it further enacted,* That there shall be allowed to each chaplain of Congress, at the rate of five hundred dollars per annum during the session of Congress; to the secretary of the Senate and clerk of the House of Representatives, fifteen hundred dollars per annum each, to commence from the time of their respective appointments; and also a further allowance of two dollars per day to each, during the session of that branch for which he officiates: and the said secretary and clerk shall each be allowed (when the President of the Senate or Speaker shall deem it necessary) to employ one principal clerk, who shall be paid three dollars per day, and an engrossing clerk, who shall be paid two dollars per day during the session, with the like compensation to such clerk while he shall be necessarily employed in the recess.

Reprinted from *The Public Statutes at Large of the United States of America,* ed. Richard Peters (Boston: Charles C. Little and James Brown, 1845), 1:70–71.

An Act to Provide for the Government of the Territory Northwest of the River Ohio [Northwest Ordinance] (August 7, 1789)

Whereas in order that the ordinance of the United States in Congress assembled, for the government of the territory north-west of the river Ohio may continue to have full effect, it is requisite that certain provisions should be made, so as to adapt the same to the present Constitution of the United States.*

Reprinted from *The Public Statutes at Large of the United States of America,* ed. Richard Peters (Boston: Charles C. Little and James Brown, 1845), 1:50–52.
  * See page 237 for the text relevant to this collection.—Eds.

An Act for the Punishment of Certain Crimes against the United States (April 30, 1790)

The medieval practice of "benefit of clergy" allowed clerics to be tried in ecclesiastical rather than civil courts. Ecclesiastical courts in England lost jurisdiction over all criminal matters in 1576, but the benefit of clergy evolved into a tool that allowed first-time offenders—clergy and nonclergy alike—to avoid the death penalty in some cases. America never had ecclesiastical courts that substituted for secular courts, and the legal benefit of clergy was specifically rejected by Congress in 1790. The following text is included in this collection only because it is thought by some to concern church-state relations in America.

Reprinted from *The Public Statutes at Large of the United States of America,* ed. Richard Peters (Boston: Charles C. Little and James Brown, 1845), 1:119.

SEC. 31. *And be it further enacted,* That the benefit of clergy shall not be used or allowed, upon conviction of any crime, for which, by any statute of the United States, the punishment is or shall be declared to be death.

Military Chaplains and Regulations (1791, 1806)

Following the example of the Continental and Confederation congresses, Congress provided for paid military chaplains and established regulations intended to promote religion and virtue in the armed forces.

Chap. XXVIII.—An Act for Raising and Adding Another Regiment to the Military Establishment of the United States, and for Making Farther Provision for the Protection of the Frontiers (March 3, 1791)

SEC. 5. *And be it further enacted,* That in case the President of the United States should deem the employment of a major-general, brigadier-general, a quartermaster and chaplain, or either of them, essential to the public interest, that he be, and he hereby is empowered, by and with the advice and consent of the Senate, to appoint the same accordingly. And a major-general so appointed may choose his aid-de-camp, and a brigadier-general, his brigade-major, from the captains or subalterns of the line. *Provided*

Reprinted from *The Public Statutes at Large of the United States of America,* ed. Richard Peters (Boston: Charles C. Little and James Brown, 1845), 1:222–23.

always, That the major-general and brigadier-general so to be appointed, shall respectively continue in pay during such term only, as the President of the United States in his discretion shall deem it requisite for the public service.

SEC. 6. *And be it further enacted,* That in case a major-general, brigadier-general, quartermaster, aid-de-camp, brigade-major and chaplain should be appointed, their pay and allowances shall be, respectively, as herein mentioned: The major-general shall be entitled to one hundred and twenty-five dollars, monthly pay, twenty dollars allowance for forage monthly, and for daily subsistence fifteen rations, or money in lieu thereof at the contract price. The brigadier-general shall be entitled to ninety-four dollars, monthly pay, with sixteen dollars allowance for forage monthly, and for daily subsistence twelve rations, or money in lieu thereof at the contract price. That the quartermaster shall be intitled to the same pay, rations and forage, as the lieutenant-colonel commandant of a regiment. That the aid-de-camp be entitled, including all allowances, to the same pay, rations and forage, as a major of a regiment. That the brigade-major be entitled, including all allowances, to the same pay, rations and forage, as a major of a regiment. That the chaplain be entitled to fifty dollars per month, including pay, rations and forage. . . .

Chap. XX.—An Act for Establishing Rules and Articles for the Government of the Armies of the United States (April 10, 1806)

Be it enacted by the Senate and House of Representatives of the United States of America in Congress assembled,

Reprinted from *The Public Statutes at Large of the United States of America,* ed. Richard Peters (Boston: Charles C. Little and James Brown, 1845), 2:359–60.

That from and after the passing of this act, the following shall be the rules and articles by which the armies of the United States shall be governed:

Article 1. Every officer now in the army of the United States, shall, in six months from the passing of this act, and every officer who shall hereafter be appointed, shall, before he enters on the duties of his office, subscribe these rules and regulations.

Article 2. It is earnestly recommended to all officers and soldiers, diligently to attend divine service; and all officers who shall behave indecently or irreverently at any place of divine worship, shall, if commissioned officers, be brought before a general court martial, there to be publicly and severely reprimanded by the president; if non-commissioned officers or soldiers, every person so offending shall, for his first offence, forfeit *one sixth of a dollar,* to be deducted out of his next pay; for the second offence, he shall not only forfeit a like sum, but be confined twenty-four hours; and for every like offence, shall suffer and pay in like manner; which money, so forfeited, shall be applied by the captain or senior officer of the troop or company, to the use of the sick soldiers of the company or troop to which the offender belongs.

Article 3. Any non-commissioned officer or soldier who shall use any profane oath or execration, shall incur the penalties expressed in the foregoing article; and a commissioned officer shall forfeit and pay for each and every such offence *one dollar,* to be applied as in the preceding article.

Article 4. Every chaplain, commissioned in the army or armies of the United States, who shall absent himself from the duties assigned him (excepting in cases of sickness or leave of absence) shall, on conviction thereof before a court martial, be fined not exceeding one month's pay, besides the loss of his pay during his absence; or be discharged, as the said court martial shall judge proper.

An Act Regulating the Grants of Land Appropriated for Military Services, and for the Society of the United Brethren, for Propagating the Gospel among the Heathen (June 1, 1796)

In 1788 the Confederation Congress reserved 12,000 acres of federal land for use by the "United brethren or the society of the said brethren for propagating the Gospel among the heathen." In 1796 Congress reauthorized its predecessor's act with the following legislation.

Sec. 5. *And be it further enacted,* That the said surveyor general be, and he is hereby, required to cause to be surveyed three several tracts of land, containing four thousand acres each, at Shoenbrun, Gnadenhutten, and Salem; being the tracts formerly set apart, by an ordinance of Congress of the third of September, one thousand seven hundred and eighty-eight, for the society of United Brethren for propagating the gospel among the heathen; and to issue a patent or patents for the said three tracts to the said society, in trust, for the uses and purposes in the said ordinance set forth. . . .

Treaty of Peace and Friendship between the United States of America and the Bey and Subjects of Tripoli, of Barbary (1797)

In 1796 Joel Barlow (1754–1812), an American poet, political theorist, and sometimes diplomat, negotiated a treaty intended to protect American shipping from Barbary pirates. President Adams sent the treaty to the U.S. Senate, where it was ratified unanimously with no reported discussion. There is some dispute about the content of the Arabic version of the treaty, but there is every indication that the following language was in the version of the treaty ratified by the U.S. Senate. Subsequent treaties with Tripoli and other Barbary states do not contain similar statements regarding the relationship between the United States and Christianity.

UNITED STATES, *May 26, 1797*
Gentlemen of the Senate:

I lay before you, for your consideration and advice, a treaty of perpetual peace and friendship between the United States of America and the Bey and subjects of Tripoli, of Barbary, concluded, at Tripoli, on the 4th day of November, 1796.

JOHN ADAMS

Reprinted from *The Public Statutes at Large of the United States of America,* ed. Richard Peters (Boston: Charles C. Little and James Brown, 1845), 1:49.

Reprinted from *The Debates and Proceedings in the Congress of the United States, Fifth Congress: May 15, 1797–March 3, 1799* (Washington, D.C.: Gales and Seaton, 1851), 3094, 3095–96.

ART. II. As the Government of the United States of America is not, in any sense, founded on the Christian religion; as it has in itself no character of enmity against the laws, religion, or tranquillity, of Mussulmen; and, as the said States never entered into any war, or act of hostility against any Mahometan nation, it is declared by the parties, that no pretext, arising from religious opinions, shall ever produce an interruption of the harmony existing between the two countries.

Treaty with Kaskaskia Indians (1803)

William Henry Harrison (1773–1841), future (and shortest serving) president of the United States, negotiated the following treaty with the Kaskaskia Indians in 1803. Jefferson sent the treaty to the U.S. Senate where it was ratified without recorded dissent.

Reprinted from U.S. Congress, *American State Papers: Indian Affairs* (Washington, D.C.: Gales and Seaton, 1834), 1:687.

The Kaskaskia and Other Tribes

Communicated to the Senate, October, 31, 1803
Articles of a Treaty made at Vincennes, in the Indiana territory, between William Henry Harrison, Governor of the said territory, Superintendent of Indian Affairs, and commissioner plenipotentiary of the United States for concluding any treaty or treaties which may be found necessary, with any of the Indian tribes northwest of the river Ohio, of the one part; and the head chiefs and warriors of the Kaskaskia tribe of Indians, so called, (but which tribe is the remains and rightfully represent all the tribes of the Illinois Indians, originally called the Kaskaskia, Mitchigamia, Cahokia, and Tamoria,) of the other part.

ART. 3. . . . *And whereas* the greater part of the said tribe have been baptised and received into the Catholic church, to which they are much attached, the United States will give, annually, for seven years, one hundred dollars towards the support of a priest of that religion, who will engage to perform for said tribe the duties of his office, and also to instruct as many of their children as possible, in the rudiments of literature. And the United States will further give the sum of three hundred dollars, to assist the said tribe in the erection of a church. The stipulations made in this and the preceding article, together with the sum of five hundred and eighty dollars, which is now paid, or assured to be paid, for the said tribe, for the purpose of procuring some necessary articles, and to relieve them from debts which they have heretofore contracted, is considered as a full and ample compensation for the relinquishment made to the United States, in the first article. . . .

RECOMMENDATIONS FOR FURTHER READING

Antieau, Chester James, Arthur T. Downey, and Edward C. Roberts. *Freedom from Federal Establishment: Formation and Early History of the First Amendment Religion Clauses.* Milwaukee: Bruce, 1964.

Hutson, James H. *Religion and the Founding of the American Republic.* Washington, D.C.: Library of Congress, 1998.

Lambert, Frank. *The Founding Fathers and the Place of Religion in America.* Princeton: Princeton University Press, 2003.

Novak, Michael. *On Two Wings: Humble Faith and Common Sense at the American Founding.* San Francisco: Encounter Books, 2002.

CHAPTER ELEVEN

Religion and Politics in the Election of 1800

THE PRESIDENTIAL ELECTION of 1800 was one of the most bitterly contested in American history. The campaign featured the incumbent president Federalist John Adams, who was opposed by Republican Thomas Jefferson. The election revealed a fundamental flaw in the constitutional voting process. Each member of the electoral college cast two ballots without specifying which was a vote for president and which was for vice president. The candidate receiving the most votes was to be elected president and the candidate with the second-highest tally was to become vice president. Electors intending to elect the Republican ticket, however, cast an equal number of votes for Thomas Jefferson and for his putative running mate Aaron Burr, both of whom received more votes than third-place finisher John Adams. With Jefferson and Burr tied with seventy-three electoral votes each, the election was thrown into the U.S. House of Representatives, where each state had one vote to be decided by a majority of the state delegation. The electoral crisis deepened when Burr did not disclaim presidential ambition, inclining Jefferson's opponents to shift their support to Burr. The deadlock was not broken and Jefferson elected until the thirty-sixth ballot was cast in the House. (The Twelfth Amendment, adopted in 1804, avoided this problem in future elections by requiring electors to vote separately for president and vice president.)

Religion, especially Jefferson's religion or the alleged lack thereof, emerged as a pivotal issue in the campaign. The religion controversy was encapsulated by a slogan in the Federalist *Gazette of the United States*, which declared that every American voter must ask himself one question: "Shall I continue in allegiance to GOD—AND A RELIGIOUS PRESIDENT [John Adams]; or impiously declare for JEFFERSON—AND NO GOD!!!" Jefferson was said to be an infidel. Proof of his political atheism, detractors claimed, was found in his authorship of the Virginia Statute for Establishing Religious Freedom (1786), which allegedly evidenced indifference toward organized religion's vital place in civic life; his apparently unorthodox statements in his *Notes on the State of Virginia*, which revealed skepticism about certain biblical claims and basic tenets of Christianity; and his sympathy for a revolution in France that had lately turned bloody and anti-Christian. Adams was also the target of political smears. He was accused of being an anti-republican Anglophile and an advocate for the establishment of a national church. This latter charge, especially, alarmed religious dissenters who feared persecution by a state church.

Both men were deeply wounded by the vicious attacks on their characters and their political opponents' ruinous campaign tactics. The bitterness lingered long after both had left public office, and it was many years before there was a rapprochement in their personal relationship. In private correspondence with family and other confidants, both expressed pain and disappointment from this episode.

The election of 1800 was an early test of the place of religion in national politics. What role could religion appropriately play in a constitutional system that disallowed religious tests for federal officeholders and a national ecclesiastical establishment but guaranteed free religious exercise? Although conceding that "neither the constitution, nor any law forbids his election," the Reverend William Linn warned in an 1800 pamphlet that a vote for the radical, heterodox Jefferson "must be construed into no less than rebellion against God." The promotion of an infidel to such high office "by the suffrages of a Christian nation," he continued ominously, would encourage public immorality and licentious manners and lead to the "destruction of all social order and happiness."

Jeffersonian partisans denied that their candidate was an atheist and introduced into American political discourse a separationist principle that would eventually exert much influence. "Religion and government are equally necessary," intoned Tunis Wortman in response to the Reverend Linn, "but their interests should be kept separate and distinct. No legitimate connection can ever subsist between them. Upon no plan, no system, can they become united, without endangering the purity and usefulness of both—the church will corrupt the state, and the state pollute the church."*

In this early national debate, two competing impulses emerged that continue to shape the political landscape: a desire for religion and religious values to inform politics, and a desire to separate religion from the political process.

* Timoleon [Tunis Wortman], "A Solemn Address, to Christians & Patriots, Upon the Approaching Election of a President of the United States: In Answer to a Pamphlet, Entitled, 'Serious Considerations,' &c." (New-York, 1800), in Ellis Sandoz, ed., *Political Sermons of the American Founding Era: 1730–1805* (Indianapolis: Liberty Fund, 1991), 1488.

PAMPHLETS (1800)

The election of 1800 generated scores of political pamphlets for or against the presidential candidates. One of the most provocative and widely discussed was *Serious Considerations on the Election of a President: Addressed to the Citizens of the United States,* which denounced candidate Thomas Jefferson as an infidel. *Serious Considerations* was published anonymously so that, the reader was told, its arguments would "be fairly judged by its own merits" and not by its author's identity. It was a poorly kept secret that the Reverend William Linn (1752–1808), a prominent Dutch Reformed clergyman in New York City and the first chaplain of the U.S. House of Representatives, had penned this tract. Earlier pamphleteers in the election of 1796 and succeeding years had questioned Jefferson's religious orthodoxy and fitness for high office, but *Serious Considerations* concisely and pointedly framed the debate in the 1800 campaign, and prominent pamphleteers both for and against Jefferson's candidacy responded to Linn's arguments. The New York politician DeWitt Clinton (1769–1828) ably defended Jefferson in *A Vindication of Thomas Jefferson; against the Charges Contained in a Pamphlet Entitled, "Serious Considerations," &c.,* written under the pseudonym "Grotius." Linn's and Clinton's tracts are reprinted below. (Two other influential tracts from the 1800 election season, *The Voice of Warning, to Christians, on the Ensuing Election of a President of the United States,* by John Mitchell Mason [1770–1829], and *A Solemn Address, to Christians & Patriots, Upon the Approaching Election of a President of the United States: In Answer to a Pamphlet, Entitled, "Serious Considerations," &c.,* by Tunis Wortman [d. 1822], are reprinted in Ellis Sandoz, ed., *Political Sermons of the American Founding Era: 1730–1805* [Indianapolis: Liberty Fund, 1991], 1447–1528).

Serious Considerations on the Election of a President: Addressed to the Citizens of the United States (1800)

[WILLIAM LINN]

Serious Considerations

FELLOW-CITIZENS,

THE time is drawing near, when you will be called to give your voice in the election of a President. In the exercise of this important privilege, it will be granted, that great deliberation is necessary; and that upon the choice of a suitable person depends, under Divine Providence, the prosperity of our nation. A few considerations, therefore, will be received by you with candour, and allowed all the weight to which you may think them entitled. The writer of them has neither held, nor does he expect ever to hold any office under government; he means not to be an advocate for any particular man; he is not actuated by a mere regard to the political principles of any party; but, if his heart deceive him not, by a sincere desire for the public welfare.

IT is well understood that the Honorable Thomas Jefferson is a candidate for the Chief Magistracy of the United States, and that a number of our citizens will give him all their support. I would not presume to dictate to you *who* ought to be President, but entreat you to hear with patience my reasons why *he* ought not.

TO the declarations of disinterestedness and sincerity already made, I think it proper to add, that I have no personal resentment whatever against Mr. Jefferson, and that it is with pain I oppose him; that I never was in his company, and would hardly know him; that I honor him as holding a high office in government; that I admire his talents, and feel grateful for the services which he has been instrumental in

Reprinted from [William Linn], *Serious Considerations on the Election of a President: Addressed to the Citizens of the United States* (New York: John Furman, 1800), 3–36.

SERIOUS CONSIDERATIONS

ON THE

ELECTION

OF A

PRESIDENT:

ADDRESSED TO THE

Citizens of the United States.

[By William Linn]

NEW-YORK:

Printed and sold by John Furman, at his Blank, Stamp, and Stationary Shop,
opposite the City Hall.

1800.

Audi, This is a pretty sensible, judicious & wise pamphlet on the subject discussed.

rendering to his country; and that my objection to his being promoted to the Presidency is founded singly upon his disbelief of the Holy Scriptures; or, in other words, his rejection of the Christian Religion and open profession of Deism.

NOTWITHSTANDING the general character of Mr. Jefferson, and the proofs of his Deistical principles which have been partly published, at different times, there are some who still doubt; or, if they admit the truth, are disposed to say that he is no worse than his opponents. Whether he is worse or not will be shown hereafter. When the spirit of party is so violent as we have seen it in this country, and the vilest calumnies have been propagated respecting the best characters, it is not surprising that the reports which are circulated should be received with caution, especially when there is not ready access to the highest and most infallible sources of information. I shall endeavour in this address, to present to your view the collective evidence of Mr. Jefferson's principles as to religion, and show you why such a man ought not to be honored and entrusted with the office of chief magistrate. This I hope to do principally from Mr. Jefferson's own writings, and in such a manner that neither he or any of his friends shall be able justly to charge me with the least misrepresentation.

BESIDES the publications acknowledged by a man, some dependence may be fairly placed upon his general character, and his conversation as related by men of intelligence and veracity. The world is seldom mistaken as to a man's talents and moral principles; and we safely rely upon respectable testimony. The avowal, therefore, of sentiments in conversation which shall be related, cannot be doubted, from the nature of the authority; and our belief will be strengthened when this is viewed in connection with the written evidence.

IN the work of Mr. Jefferson, entitled "*Notes on the state of Virginia,*" what he says on the subject of the deluge, is a clear proof of his disrespect for divine revelation. He opposes the opinion, that the shells found on the tops of high mountains ought to be considered as a proof of an universal deluge. He endeavours to show, that if the whole contents of the atmosphere were water, the lands could be overflowed to the height of 52½ feet only, and that in Virginia this would be a very small proportion even of the champaign country. He rejects a second opinion, that "the bed of the ocean, has, by some great convulsion of nature, been heaved to the heights at which we now find shells and other remains of marine animals." He rejects likewise a third solution suggested by Voltaire.—"There is a wonder," says Mr. Jefferson, "somewhere; is it greatest on this branch of the dilemma, on that which supposes the existence of a power, of which we have no evidence in any other case; or on the first, which requires us to believe the creation of a body of water, and its subsequent annihilation? The three hypotheses are equally unsatisfactory, and we must be contented to acknowledge, that this great phaenomenon is as yet unsolved. Ignorance is preferable to error; and he is less remote from the truth who believes nothing, than he who believes what is wrong."*

LET it be remarked here, that could Mr. Jefferson found, what he thought evidence, that the waters had ever covered the highest mountains, he would have admitted that solution as to the shells; but he attempts to show the improbability of such a quantity of water being produced, and consequently discredits the sacred history. The account given by the inspired writer, is, "All the fountains of the great deep were broken up, and the windows of heaven were opened, and the rain was upon the earth forty days and forty nights. And the waters prevailed exceedingly upon the earth; and *all the high hills that were under the whole heaven were covered.* Fifteen cubits upwards did the waters prevail; and *the mountains were covered.*"† Moses mentions two causes of the deluge; *the fountains of the great deep were broken up, and the windows*

* Page 28, to p. 31.—The edition which I use is that printed in Philadelphia, 1788. Mr. Jefferson has published, so late as the present year, an appendix to this work; but it relates wholly to the murder of Logan's family. There is not a retraction of, or even an apology for any of his sentiments, though he knows they have been repeatedly censured.

† Genesis vii. 11, 12, 19, 20.

of heaven were opened; but Mr. Jefferson does not so much as name this old philosopher, while he indirectly denies the facts, or, like other infidels, cannot still get water enough to cover the mountains. Even a miracle is not sufficient with him, or rather his faith is too weak to receive *a miracle. Requires us,* says he, *to believe the creation of a body of water and its subsequent annihilation.* He is at liberty to philosophize if he pleases, on the causes of the deluge; it is not my business at present (and I beg that it may be remembered) to refute his principles; but only to show their inconsistency with the Holy Scriptures. I am not called then to controvert his positions, that *ignorance is preferable to error,* and that *he is less remote from the truth who believes nothing, than he who believes what is wrong;* but I will be permitted to say, that it is safest for him to believe the Mosaic account of the deluge, though he should never find out a satisfactory solution; yea, though he should adopt a wrong one.

AGAIN, upon the question, Whence the first inhabitants of America originated? Mr. Jefferson is of opinion, that there are among the Indians a great variety of languages radically different, and from this circumstance, he argues the impossibility of their having emigrated from Asia. His words are, "Arranging them under the radical ones to which they may be palpably traced, and doing the same by those of the red men of Asia, there will be found probably, twenty in America, for one in Asia, of those radical languages, so called, because if they were ever the same, they have lost all resemblance to one another. A separation into dialects may be the work of a few ages only, but for two dialects to recede from one another till they have lost all vestiges of their common origin, must require an immense course of time; perhaps not less than *many people give to the age of the earth.* A greater number of those radical changes of language having taken place among the red men of America, proves them of greater antiquity than those of Asia."* I will not ask him here, what time *he* gives to the age of the earth? Whether he believes the scrip-

ture chronology? Or, whether he believes the earth to be fourteen thousand years old, judging by the lavas in the neighbourhood of Mount Etna? Whether he depends most on the authority of Moses, or of Canonico Recupero?† What I wish to be remarked is, that if the Indians did not emigrate from Asia, and are even of greater antiquity than the Asiatics, then the opinion is insinuated that they are a distinct race of men originally created and placed in America, contrary to the sacred history that all mankind have descended from a single pair. This was the opinion of Lord Kames, and is supported by the same argument of a variety of languages, in his Sketches of the history of Man.‡ This is evidently the opinion of Mr. Jefferson; an opinion repugnant to sacred history, to the express declaration of the apostle, that "God hath made of one blood all nations of men for to dwell on all the face of the earth," and striking at the root of the plan of salvation revealed in the gospel. To whom is the gospel to be preached? To the posterity of Adam only. To those of whom Adam was the natural and federal head. Salvation is purchased, and can be offered to no other race. "As in Adam all die, even so in Christ shall all be made alive. The first man Adam was made a living soul, the last Adam was made a quickening spirit."§

EVERY doubt will be removed as to the sentiment of Mr. Jefferson, when we consider what he asserts more plainly respecting the negroes. After mentioning some distinctions between them and the white people, he says, "There are other physical distinctions proving *a difference of race.*" He makes the blacks inferior to the whites in reason and imagination. He professes to take his examples not in Africa, but

---

* Page 108.

† This man has been engaged in writing the history of Mount Etna. He has discovered a lava which, he says, must have flowed from the mountain at least fourteen thousand years ago. The Bishop of the Diocese advised him to take care not to make his mountain older than Moses. I have not heard the issue.

‡ See an excellent Essay on the causes of the variety of complexion and figure in the human species. To which are added, Strictures on Lord Kames' discourse on the original diversity of mankind. By the Rev. Dr. Samuel S. Smith. This work has justly acquired reputation in America and Europe, and has been translated into several languages.

§ 1 Cor. xv. 22, 45.

among the blacks born in this country, and who have enjoyed considerable advantages. He denies "that their inferiority is the effect merely of their condition of life;" says, that they improve by mixture with the whites; compares them with the Roman slaves who excelled in arts and science, but who "were of the race of whites;" and after a long discussion of the subject, concludes in this singular manner. "I advance it therefore as a suspicion only, that the blacks, whether originally a distinct race, or made distinct by time and circumstances, are inferior to the whites in the endowments both of body and mind. It is not against experience to suppose, that different species of the same genus, or varieties of the same species, may possess different qualifications. Will not a lover of natural history then, one who views the gradations in all the races of animals with the eye of philosophy, excuse an effort to keep those in the department of man as distinct as nature has formed them?"*

Can any man now doubt of Mr. Jefferson's real opinion, and of that opinion being directly opposite to divine revelation? In his conclusion he betrays, like a true infidel, an inconsistency with himself. Having laboured to point out physical and moral distinctions between the Whites and the Blacks, he advances it at last "as a *suspicion* only," that the latter were inferior to the former; having expressly asserted, that the distinctions mentioned, "*prove a difference of race*," now he modestly conveys the doubt, "whether originally a distinct race, or made distinct by time and circumstances." Would a man who believes in a divine revelation even hint a suspicion of this kind? The last sentence, however, though curious, is clear enough as to Mr. Jefferson's real sentiment. It seems that he views his discussion as "an effort to keep those in the department of man as distinct as nature has formed them," and he prays to be *excused.* Observe that he pleads only for a *department,* a *distinct* one. Will the philosopher promise, if we indulge him, not to use his arguments hereafter in favor of the Ourang Outang? Will he engage not to trouble us, by the varieties

of colour, shape, and size, to fit up numerous other departments? The matter is too serious to jest with. Sir, we excuse you not! You have degraded the blacks from the rank which God hath given them in the scale of being! You have advanced the strongest argument for their state of slavery! You have insulted human nature! You have contemned the word of truth and the mean of salvation! And, whether you will excuse *us* or not, we exclude you, in your present belief, from any department among Christians!

Though the sentiment of Mr. Jefferson is evident enough to every attentive reader, yet it may not be amiss to know the light in which it is understood in Europe. The Monthly Reviewers in London, in reviewing his Notes, say, "It is observable, that the Virginians, soon after the assertion of Independence, appointed a committee to revise their code of laws, and though the emancipation of negroe slaves, entered into the plan of reformation, yet the idea of their being an inferior species of the human genus, governed their regulations." After quoting the whole passage respecting the Blacks, they add, "We recollect a tract relating to the sugar trade, written in the name of John Gardner Kemys, esq. a Jamaica planter, in which the same argument was extended, by an appeal to facts, to connecting the negroes with the Ourang Outang."† This latter writer endeavoured "to prove that many negroes are connected in blood with the Ourang Outang, and that the importation of them contributed to humanize the descendants of brutes."‡

Upon a plan proposed for the institution of schools in the state of Virginia, Mr. Jefferson says, "Instead of putting the Bible and Testament into the hands of children, at an age when their judgments are not sufficiently matured for religious inquiries, their memories may here be stored with the most useful facts from Grecian, Roman, European and American history. The first elements of morality too may be in-

---

* Page 147 to p. 154.

† Vol. 78, p. 379.

‡ In justice to Mr. Jefferson, it must be said that he is an advocate for the emancipation of the blacks; though unhappily, be has raised one of the greatest obstacles, by denying them to be the same species with the whites.

stilled into their minds; such as, when farther developed as their judgments advance in strength, may teach them how to work out their own greatest happiness, &c."* He mentions the Bible at last; for what purpose is easily seen. When the deluge and the origin of the blacks are under discussion, we do not hear a word about it. Moses is treated as an historian utterly unworthy of his notice.

I HAVE heard objections made to the Bible as a school-book, but never for the reason here given. A large part of the Bible consists of history, or is a relation of facts; and one would think that the minds of children are as equal to these as to any other; and that they would be more useful to them than the facts contained in profane history. The Bible is the most ancient, and the only authentic history in the world. Mr. Jefferson admits that "the first elements of morality may be instilled into the minds of children." Why not the first elements of religion, which are the foundation of all sound morality? Are the minds of children *matured* for the one, and not for the other? He has not told us when it is proper to teach them a little religion; and how we may prevent, in the mean time, irreligious principles. Indeed we hear no more about religion or the bible; nor does he think it necessary, for these elements of morality *may teach them how to work out their own greatest happiness.* If this be not a deistical education, I know not what is. Had he prized the bible, and been properly acquainted with its contents, he would have known that the facts related in that book are the most ancient, the most authentic, the most interesting, and the most useful in the world; that they are above all others level to the capacities of children, calculated to impress their tender minds, and form them to live to God, to their country, and to themselves.

AFTER what has been produced, who can refuse his belief of what I shall now relate? When the late Rev. Dr. John B. Smith resided in Virginia, the famous MAZZEI happened one night to be his guest. Dr. Smith having, as usual, assembled his family for their evening devotions, the circumstance occasioned some discourse on religion, in which the Italian made no secret of his infidel principles. In the course of conversation he remarked to Dr. Smith, "Why, your great philosopher and statesman, Mr. Jefferson, is rather farther gone in infidelity than I am;" and related, in confirmation, the following anecdote; that as he was once riding with Mr. Jefferson, he expressed his "surprise that the people of this country take no better care of their public buildings." "What buildings?" exclaimed Mr. Jefferson. "Is not that a church?" replied he, pointing to a decayed edifice. "Yes," answered Mr. Jefferson. "I am astonished," said the other, "that they permit it to be in so ruinous a condition." "*It is good enough,*" rejoined Mr. Jefferson, "*for him that was born in a manger!!*" Such a contemptuous sling at the blessed Jesus, could issue from the lips of no other than a deadly foe to his name and his cause.†

THERE is another passage in Mr. Jefferson's Notes which requires the most serious attention. In showing that civil rulers ought not to interfere with the rights of conscience, and that the legitimate powers of government extend to such acts only as are injurious to others, he says, "It does me no injury for my neighbour to say there are twenty gods, or no god. It neither picks my pocket, nor breaks my leg."‡ The whole passage is written with a great degree of spirit. It is remarkable for that conciseness, perspicuity and force which characterize the style of Mr. Jefferson. Some have ventured, from the words I have quoted, to bring even the charge of atheism against him. This is a high charge, and it becomes us carefully to examine the ground upon which it rests. Though the words themselves, their connection, and the design for which they are introduced may be insufficient to support it, yet there are concurrent circumstances to

† This story I had from Dr. Smith more than once, and he told it to, I know not how many. I applied to one gentleman, who I knew had heard it from Dr. Smith, and we agreed in the relation. There is no possibility of contradicting it, except by the improbable supposition that Mazzei told a downright falsehood. Dr. Smith was one of the most faithful, zealous, and successful ministers in all this country. His memory will long be precious to those who knew him.

* Page 157.

‡ Page 169.

be taken into consideration, and which will fix at least a suspicion. These circumstances are, the general disregard of religious things, the associates at home and correspondents abroad, and the principles maintained in conversation. With these things I am not so well acquainted as many. I shall only mention what passed in conversation between Mr. Jefferson and a gentleman of distinguished talents and services, on the necessity of religion to government. The gentleman insisted that some religious faith and institutions of worship, claiming a divine origin, were necessary to the order and peace of society. Mr. Jefferson said that he differed widely from him, and that "he wished to see a government in which no religious opinions were held, and where the security for property and social order rested entirely upon the force of the laws." Would not this be a nation of Atheists? Is it not natural, after the free declaration of such a sentiment, to suspect the man himself of Atheism? Could one who is impressed with the existence of a God, the Creator, Preserver, and Governor of all things, to whom we are under a law and accountable; and the inseparable connection of this truth with the social order and the eternal happiness of mankind, express himself in this manner?

PUTTING the most favorable construction upon the words in the Notes, they are extremely reprehensible. Does not the belief influence the practice? How then can it be a matter of indifference what a man believes? The doctrine that a man's life may be good, let his faith be what it may, is contradictory to reason and the experience of mankind. It is true that a mere opinion of my neighbour will do me no injury. Government cannot regulate or punish it. The right of private opinion is inalienable. But let my neighbour once persuade himself that there is no God, and he will soon pick my pocket, and break not only my *leg* but my *neck*. If there be no God, there is no law; no future account; government then is the ordinance of man only, and we cannot be subject for conscience sake. No colours can paint the horrid effects of such a principle, and the deluge of miseries with which it would overwhelm the human race.

HOW strongly soever Mr. Jefferson may reason against the punishment by law of erroneous opinions, even of atheism, they are not the less frightful and dangerous in their consequences. He admits the propriety of rejecting the testimony of an atheist in a court of justice, and of fixing a stigma upon him. Just such a stigma the United States ought to fix upon himself. Though neither the constitution, nor any law forbids his election, yet the public opinion ought to disqualify him. On account of his disbelief of the Holy Scriptures, and his attempts to discredit them, he ought to be rejected from the Presidency. No professed deist, be his talents and acquirements what they may, ought to be promoted to this place by the suffrages of a Christian nation. The greater his talents and the more extensive his acquirements, the greater will be his power and the more extensive his influence in poisoning mankind.

SOME of the friends of Mr. Jefferson, being ashamed that he should be reputed an infidel and wishing that he had a little religion, were it ever so little, whisper that he is a sort of a Christian. Rather than give him up, they hint that he is as good a christian as Dr. Priestley, or thereabouts. I shall not dispute a moment whether he is as good as Dr. Priestley, or Dr. Priestley as bad as him; but ask for the proofs of his professing christianity in any shape. How does he spend the Lord's day? Is he known to worship with any denomination of christians? Where? When? How often? Though going to church is no certain sign of a man not being an infidel, any more than his pretending a regard for the christian religion in his writings, yet a total or habitual neglect of public worship, must be admitted as a strong proof against him. That wretch Voltaire partook of the sacrament of the supper, while he blasphemed Christ, and endeavoured, with the malice of a devil, to extirpate his religion from the earth. Hume, Kames, Gibbons, and many infidels pretended a regard for divine revelation, while they sought indirectly and secretly to destroy its credibility. I have exhibited proofs of Mr. Jefferson's infidelity. I wait for the proofs that he is as good as even Dr. Priestley, which will be still bad

THE PROVIDENTIAL DETECTION

The Providential Detection, c. 1800. A political cartoon by an unknown Federalist artist depicting an American eagle, directed by a Divine eye, snatching from Jefferson's hand the U.S. "Constitution & Independence" before he can sacrifice it on a fiery "Altar to Gallic Despotism." Used by permission of The Library Company of Philadelphia.

enough; and I shall exceedingly rejoice if any man should be able to prove him better.

Let me ask your attention farther, while I briefly point out the effects which the election of Mr. Jefferson would produce.

1. It would give us an unfavorable character with foreign nations. We are as yet a young nation, under a government recently formed; and it is of considerable importance that we obtain respect and confidence abroad. There are now jealousies of us entertained, and reproaches cast upon us. Two nations with whom we are most connected and from whom we have the most to fear, carefully watch us, and will conduct toward us according to the opinion which they have of us. We have nothing to fear from either of them, if we show a proper spirit, deal justly with all, and reverence the commands of the Most High. I devoutly pray that we may have no connection with any nation farther than is necessary for the purpose of commerce; and that we may boast only of being Americans.

Some may suppose that by the election of Mr. Jefferson we will please the French nation. Were this true, still it would be a question, whether it is prudent to do this, without necessity, at the risk of displeasing another nation. But the truth is, in my opinion, that by his election, America would expose herself to the just derision of both. My blood mounts, when I think for a moment of either British or French giving my country a President. I despise their threats, and I suspect their caresses. Let them mind their own business. I will please myself, and take care of my own concerns. How desirable soever a reputation with them may be, unless it is founded on a regard to God and our country, it cannot be solid and lasting.

What would be the natural reflections of foreigners, were Mr. Jefferson our President? Would they not say? "Either the Americans have little impressions of religion and of its being essential to morality and good government, or they have few men versed in the science of government, or they are most dangerously torn by party spirit; otherwise they would not have exalted by a voluntary choice such a man to the seat of the first magistrate. Just returning

from the tomb of the great and good Washington, they seem to have buried all their virtue with him. They appear now to be a weak, a divided, and an irreligious people, doomed to dissentions among themselves, and to be an easy prey to their ambitious neighbours."—Yes, my fellow citizens, there was a Washington. We shall "never look on his fellow again." "Two Washingtons come not in one age." His name was, under God, our shield and defence. He honored God, reverenced his sabbaths, and attended upon the institutions of his worship. He has borne testimony in his farewel address, that, "religion and morality are indispensable supports of political prosperity;" inseparably "connected with private and public felicity." He raised his country to honor and happiness by the exertion of his talents, and still more by the magic of his virtue. Let us not insult his ashes, and debase ourselves in the sight of the world by the appointment of an improper successor.

2. Consider the effects which the election of any man avowing the principles of Mr. Jefferson would have upon our citizens. The effects would be, to destroy religion, introduce immorality, and loosen all the bonds of society. Will it be said, that he is a man of too much understanding and prudence to meddle with religion, and seek to disseminate his own principles? What assurance have we of this? We remember that Hazael, when forewarned of the crimes which he would commit, answered, "But what! is thy servant a dog that he should do this great thing?"* And yet he afterwards did it. But Mr. Jefferson tells us openly what his principles are; and we are to presume that he will act upon them. It is a light thing with him to say there is *no God*. He wishes to see a government where the people have *no religious opinions and forms of worship*. If he should endeavour to carry these principles into operation, and we should complain, he might say, "What right had you to expect otherwise? I told you before hand; and after this information you entrusted me. Had I not a better right to conclude, that you rather approved of my

* II Kings, viii. 13.

principles, than expected me to renounce them?" Mr. Jefferson indeed has shown us, that his conduct will correspond with his principles. We have not forgotten the sunday-feast of him and his friends at Fredericksburgh, in Virginia, on his return from the second seat in government.

To do Mr. Jefferson, however, more than justice, let us suppose that he will make no attempts either by word or act to unsettle the religious belief; that he will not try his favorite project of a government without religion; and that he will not think it "high time for this country to get rid of religion and the clergy;"* will not the station of President alone have a most baneful influence? Does not every person acquainted with human nature, and who is attentive to the state of manners in society, know that the principles and manners of those called the higher ranks, and especially of those in the administration of government, soon pervade all classes? Let the first magistrate be a professed infidel, and infidels will surround him. Let him spend the sabbath in feasting, in visiting or receiving visits, in riding abroad, but never in going to church; and to frequent public worship will become unfashionable. Infidelity will become the prattle from the highest to the lowest condition in life, and universal desoluteness will follow. "The wicked walk on every side, when the vilest men are exalted."†

Though there have been some infidels whose lives appeared to be outwardly regular, occasioned, it may be, by the constitution of body or peculiar restraints, yet they have been generally vicious. It is certain that infidelity leads to licentious manners; and these again to the destruction of all social order and happiness. Principles are the fountain which, if corrupted, will send forth impure streams. Epicurus, it is said, was exemplary in his life; but his doctrine that the supreme good of man consisted in pleasure, ru-

ined the morals of the people. His disciples, taking his words in a gross sense, placed all their happiness in bodily pleasures and debauchery. Hume was amiable in his manners and seems to have been carried away by the pride of philosophy; but thousands have embraced his principles as an excuse for, and an encouragement in their wickedness.‡ Surely, when we consider the principles which have been industriously circulated in this country, and the hold which they have taken upon the minds of many; the want of subordination in families; the dissipation; the mercenary disposition; the party interests, and the party rage; we have just occasion of great alarm. Instead of encouraging in the smallest degree what would promote and systematize (if the expression be proper) these evils, every virtuous man ought boldly to stem the torrent, and to warn aloud his countrymen of the impending danger. Indifference or despondency is ruin. A little longer and it will be too late. The malady will have seized the vitals. The whole mass will be corrupted and dissolution ensue. Who can tell, whether yet by the union and exertion of the portion of virtue left us, God may cause *that we perish not.*

3. Let me mention one consideration more of a very serious nature, and that is, the dishonor which would be done to God, and the fear of his displeasure, if an opposer of Christianity should be preferred. Were our government not elective, there would be an excuse for a weak or a bad man being exalted to the highest place. But when this depends upon our own choice, the blame must rest entirely upon ourselves; and the voice of the nation in calling a deist to the first office must be construed into no less than rebellion against God. What he said respecting the Israelites when they requested a king, he would say respecting us, "They have rejected me, that I should not reign over them."§ Though there is nothing in the constitution to restrict our choice, yet the open and

---

* This sentiment was expressed to one of the first characters in Philadelphia, by a pupil and admirer of Mr. Jefferson. *Sequitur passibus aequis.*—I have mentioned only in one instance the name; but all I relate depends on the best authority. I shall not relate several other things, merely because I do not sufficiently know the authority.

† Psalm xii. 8.

‡ Lord Rochester, during his last illness, often exclaimed, "Mr. Hobbes and the philosophers have been my ruin;" then putting his hand upon a large bible that lay beside him, he cried out with great rapture, "This, this is the true philosophy."

§ I Sam. viii. 7.

warm preference of a manifest enemy to the religion of Christ, in a Christian nation, would be an awful symptom of the degeneracy of that nation, and I repeat it, a rebellion against God. Whatever might be the intention, the conduct would bespeak nothing else. The want of a test or a provision that the supreme magistrate should be a professor of Christianity would show the temper of the nation the more clearly, and render their conduct the more striking. We now freely declare our own choice. Would Jews or Mahometans, consistently with their belief, elect a Christian? And shall Christians be less zealous and active than them? Shall we who profess to honor the Son of God, willingly and deliberately promote a man who dishonors him; one who, if he acts upon his belief, must oppose the propagation of what he deems an imposition upon mankind and the source of miseries. Most merciful God! forgive the thought of the heart, to take council together against thee, and against thine ANOINTED.

THE friends of Mr. Jefferson may be divided into three classes; one, who are the more intent upon his election because they believe him to be an infidel; another, who are attached to his political principles, but do not wish, on account of his infidelity, to see him President; and a third, who are in danger of being deceived and led astray by the side which they have espoused. With the first, no argument of mine can be expected to prevail. The softest name which I shall receive from them is bigot, zealot, and enthusiast. They will prefer Electors, if they can ensure them, who are infidels; and if Electors themselves, they will vote for Mr. Jefferson. To the second class nothing need be said, for they feel and will do their duty. It is with the third and last class I would reason a little, in the most solemn, affectionate, and earnest manner.

Do you believe that Mr. Jefferson is an opposer of divine revelation? Can any doubt remain in your minds after the evidence which has been produced? Or have you only a bare suspicion of him? Then you ought not to promote his election. Conscience is not safe, while there is a doubt or suspicion. Do you admit the remotest danger of the consequences which have

been pointed out? Why then would you choose him? Where is the necessity of any risk at all? Are there not other characters against whom there are not the same objections, and who are qualified to administer the government? Do not apprehend me to be an advocate for the other candidates.* At the same time I will say nothing against them. They are, I have reason to believe, irreproachable. But there are many others, and you know that there are, who would fill the office of President with reputation and usefulness. Necessity, therefore, you cannot plead; and I will venture it as my serious opinion, that rather than be instrumental in the election of Mr. Jefferson, it would be more acceptable to God and beneficial to the interests of your country, to throw away your votes.

Do you say that there has long been a complaint against the measures of government; we wish to make a change; and at any rate, there can be no harm in trying other men? Be it so. But let your change be wise and prudent. Have a regard for the honor of God, and the welfare of your country. Beware of approaching near to a surrender of judgment and conscience to any political views.

SOME time hereafter you will thank me for what I am now going to say, and pronounce it to be a salutary truth. At present you will hardly bear it. If Mr. Jefferson should be the President, and should administer the government with the highest political wisdom, your complaints will be as numerous and as grievous, in the space of a short time, as they are now. It never has been, never will be, and never can be otherwise in the present state of human affairs. Mankind are impatient under just government. The *outs* murmur against the *ins*. All the expectants of office cannot be gratified. The greater part, change ever so often, must be wofully disappointed. "Party is the madness of many for the gain of a few." "The gamester always complains that the cards are badly shuffled until he gets a good hand."

YOU may hear, as usual, many stories circulated, and much abuse. You may hear the ministers of

---

* Mr. Pinckney and Mr. Adams.

Christ assailed. You may hear the facts which I have stated denied or misrepresented. If admitted, some may offer to be sureties for Mr. Jefferson, that he will not interfere with religious concerns. I beg you not to depend upon sureties who may themselves be bankrupts in the faith. Such will seek to banter you out of your conscientious scruples, and if they cannot, will give you strong assurance. It is a case in which you cannot admit a surety. The question is not what he will *do,* but what he *is.* Is he an infidel? then you cannot elect him without betraying your Lord. No circumstance can warrant your preference of him. I beg you also to remark, that a character must be suspicious when great pains are thought necessary to clear it up. Why all these pains, and what need of sureties? There is a short and easy way to settle the whole business. Let Mr. Jefferson only set his name to the first part of the apostle's creed. "I believe in God, the Father Almighty, maker of heaven and earth. And in Jesus Christ, his only begotten Son, our Lord." Can the ministers of the gospel, who are jealous for the glory of God, and the people to whom Christ is precious, require and expect less?—You will hear it said, that whatever may be the character of Mr. Jefferson, he is not worse than many of those who censure him. Were this true, it would not excuse his election. To choose a bad man because others are bad, can never be a sufficient reason, unless all are equally bad. That we have no unexceptionable characters, I aver is not true. Besides it is not true that Mr. Jefferson is as good as his opponents, in the sense in which it ought to be taken. Though a man professing christianity may be as immoral in his conduct as a man professing infidelity, yet who of these two is the best man to put into a place of high trust and extensive influence, is totally a different question. I contend that the man professing christianity is infinitely safer; and that christians cannot consistently with the dictates of their conscience, and the obligations which they owe to their Divine Redeemer, voluntarily choose any other. The profession will have great weight with the community; it will more or less restrain the man himself, and may operate in time to the entire reformation of his

life. But on the infidel we have no hold. In what way will you bind him who has broken the bands of religion asunder and cast away its cords from him?

WILL you then, my fellow-citizens, with all this evidence, and all these consequences before you, vote for electors who you believe will vote for Mr. Jefferson; or, if you are electors will you vote for him yourselves? Can you do either of these with a clear judgment, a peaceful conscience, and an unshaken hand? If you can, do it. Let nothing warp you from that line of conduct which an enlightened conscience directs, and the great Judge of all will approve. As to myself, were Mr. Jefferson connected with me by the nearest ties of blood, and did I owe him a thousand obligations, I would not, and could not vote for him. No; sooner than stretch forth my hand to place him at the head of the nation, "Let mine arm fall from my shoulder-blade, and mine arm be broken from the bone."* I can exalt no man who reviles my Saviour. We have seen tokens of the divine displeasure for several years past; and should the Presidental chair be permitted to become "the seat of the scornful," I must consider it as an awful frown from Heaven, and the beginning of miseries. Natural pestilence is mercy compared with moral; and no nation can be more unhappy than to forsake God, and to be given up by him. If to this we are doomed, may the years be shortened! and may even you, the unwary instruments of drawing down the calamities, be sheltered, and obtain the forgiveness of God and your country!

To conclude, I have not set my name to this address; not because I am either afraid or ashamed; but because I wish it to be fairly judged by its own merits distinct from every other consideration. On this account I wish to be always concealed; at the same time, if any apparent necessity should occur, I shall immediately become known. I would feel criminal had I expressed myself with less warmth. I rather fear that I have not risen to what the cause demanded. Against Mr. Jefferson I have no personal resentment. He and I can never be competitors for any place of honor and

* Job xxxi. 22.

emolument. Separate him from his principles, and I could write his eulogium. Let me farther repeat, that no answer is intended in this address to his philosophical and religious principles; that the single thing intended, is to show that these principles are contrary to what we are taught in the holy scriptures, and that for this reason alone, he ought not to be honored and entrusted with the Presidency of the United States of America.

Postscript

BESIDES the passages which I have quoted from Mr. Jefferson's Notes, there is one of so extraordinary and dangerous a nature, that it ought not to escape animadversion. In page 100, he says, "Were it made a question whether no law, as among the savage Americans, or too much law, as among the civilized Europeans, submits man to the greatest evil, one who has seen both conditions of existence, would pronounce it to be the last: and that the sheep are happier of themselves, than under care of the wolves. It will be said, that great societies cannot exist without government, The savages therefore break them into small ones." Here is a preference plainly given of savage to civilized life. When this is taken in connection with the sentiment advanced about the belief of a God, those who have read Robison and Barruel will clearly perceive the principles of the ILLUMINATI in Europe. Their leading principles, are no religion and no government; that the institution of these has introduced misery; and that they must be banished before mankind can enjoy that happiness for which nature intended them.

WHO are we to understand by the *wolves?* Will Mr. Jefferson say, that he means despots or tyrants? This would be shifting the question; for he speaks of nations in which the *law* governs. In absolute governments, the *will* of the monarch, and not the *law* is supreme. In such governments, there is not *too much,* but *too little* law. It has ever been thought best in a free government to establish every thing by law, and to leave as little as possible to the arbitrary will

of men; and if evil arises from the multiplicity of laws, it is a less evil than to have no law. If Mr. Jefferson means that any government is a *wolf,* in this he contradicts the apostle Paul, who calls government, "The ordinance of God," and the officers, "God's ministers."* What he compares is *no law,* and *too much law.* Does he mean that the American savages have no law? In this he is mistaken. They have a government and laws which custom has established. Or, does he mean that their form of government is the best? Then he prefers monarchy or aristocracy to democracy; for their government by Sachems or chiefs partakes more of the former than of the latter. In short, I see no way to reconcile Mr. Jefferson with himself, much less with the opinions of the wisest men, and the precepts of religion. As to the savages breaking the *great societies into small ones,* I need only say that by so doing, room is made for more Sachems, but I doubt whether more freedom and happiness are introduced. Were the United States broken into several republics, more ambitious men would be gratified, but the people would be less happy.

WHAT I have principally in view, is to fix the attention upon the spirit of infidelity which the passage breathes. Some insist that before the gospel can be preached with success to the Indians, they must be civilized. If this opinion be just, then Mr. Jefferson, thinking them happier in their uncivilized state, must be opposed to preaching the gospel among them. Others assert with myself, that to preach the gospel among them is the great mean to civilize them. If this opinion be just, still Mr. Jefferson opposes the preaching of the gospel. *The sheep,* says he, *are happier of themselves,* than *under care of the wolves.* Thus, the happiest state of man is, according to the sage of Monticello, to be without law, without government, and without religion; to continue just as he was born, "a wild asses colt."

---

* Romans xiii. 2. 6.

A Vindication of Thomas Jefferson; against the Charges Contained in a Pamphlet Entitled, "Serious Considerations," &c. (1800)

GROTIUS [DEWITT CLINTON]

No. I

It is now pretty well ascertained, that a great majority of the people of the United States concur in political opinion with Mr. Jefferson, and are determined to confer upon him the highest office in the country, as a mark of their confidence and esteem, and as a reward for his tried talents and virtues, and his long and distinguished services. The party in opposition to him, seeing all their aspiring projects on the point of being blasted, and yet not daring to attack him by a fair exposition of his political opinions, have, with their usual rancour, revived an obsolete and exploded slander, originally invented by our *pilot boat ambassador*,* and with their usual industry have dissemi-

nated over the community, that Mr. Jefferson is a *deist*, if not an *atheist*.

Our honest zeal for religion is thus to be perverted into the impure channels of faction, and the name of its holy author is to be blasphemed, by being coupled with the rise and fall, the struggles, victories, and defeats of contending parties. In the hour of adversity, like most other sinners, the leaders of the aristocratic faction call upon that religion for assistance and support, which in the full tide of prosperity they either neglected or despised. The newspapers, particularly in the eastern states, have recently abounded with calumnies on this head, against Mr. Jefferson.

The *feeble Morse* and the *clumsy Dwight*† have mounted their steeds of illuminatism, and armed with ten-fold brass, have ventured again to brandish their weapons of scurrility. The disgrace was however

---

Reprinted from Grotius [DeWitt Clinton], *A Vindication of Thomas Jefferson; against the Charges Contained in a Pamphlet Entitled, "Serious Considerations," etc.* (New York: David Denniston, 1800), 3–47.

* *William Smith*, of South Carolina, ambassador at Lisbon. This man was, during the revolution, in England.—He returned with all the feelings and sympathies of a British subject, and in Congress appeared more like a British agent, than the representative of an independent people. His seat in congress was contested on the ground of his not being an American citizen, and although decided in his favor, yet the propriety of the decision is extremely questionable. When the state debts were about to be assumed, he availed himself of his public situation to amass a large fortune, by dispatching swift-sailing boats to the southern states to purchase up public securities at a low price. He was afterwards reproached with this in congress, by one of his colleagues, commodore Gillon, and was silent. Gillon, in reply to some angry observations of Smith, observed, "what makes the gentleman angry, I did not say a word about pilot-boats." Previous to the last presidential election, he published pamphlets under the signature of Phocion, abounding with the most gross flattery of Mr. Adams, and the most shameful calumnies against Mr. Jefferson. In one instance, he made use of a garbled quotation to prove the latter an atheist. This is the religious, virtuous and worthy gentleman who first raised the hue and cry about Mr. Jefferson's religion. The next act of Mr. Adams's administration, after appointing his son ambassador, was, I believe, to send this man in a diplomatic capacity to Lisbon. When our commissioners landed at Lisbon to proceed to Paris, he took an opportunity to express his dislike to the mission, by treating them cavalierly.—At a ball

to which he invited them, it is said, he was particularly polite and courteous in person, to some British officers who were there, and that he eyed the commissioners at a distance through his glass, and desired his secretary to attend to those gentlemen. This marked inattention did not escape the notice of some of the company, who knew the real situation and character of the commissioners. One of the British officers observed to an American gentleman with the commissioners, "why your ambassador don't seem to take much notice of you; but I suppose you are old acquaintance?" Smith has, I am informed, sold his lands and negroes in South Carolina, and it is easy to see where he means to transfer himself and property. The expences of foreign intercourse, since the establishment of our government, amount to nearly three millions of dollars; and this immense expenditure has in part gone to support in pomp and luxury, men who, in general, have probably acted more in subserviency to foreign views and impressions, than the real interests of their country.

† Two eastern clergymen, who have made themselves supremely ridiculous by retailing the idle dreams of the crazy professor Robison, and the jesuit Barruel, about illuminatism. Morse distinguished himself at college, by writing elegies on sick mice and dead squirrels, and has since compiled some books on geography, which have given him the reputation of considerable ability, to those who do not know him. He tried to gain an establishment in the Presbyterian church in this city; but the good sense of the people created such an opposition as induced him to withdraw his pretensions.

Dwight is now denominated the Pope of Connecticut. His most elaborate work is an epic poem, called "The Conquest of Canaan," and is one of the most successful opiates I ever tried. The British reviewers have placed it on the same shelf with the works of Sir Richard Blackmore, one of the heroes of the Dunciad. These men, *par nobile fratrum* [a noble pair of brothers], have set themselves up as a kind of politico-religious alarmists, rectifiers and new-lights. It is rumoured that Dwight, attended by his faithful squire Morse, intends shortly to explore the United States for illuminati, as Nicholai did Germany for jesuits.

reserved for this city, to give the slander the shape of system, and to veil it under the mask of piety in the abstract.

A pamphlet entitled "Serious considerations on the election of a President, &c." has recently made its appearance among us, and as it will hardly rank the author with the under-strappers of the Dunciad, I should think it unworthy of the least attention, were it not that a lie often repeated and confidently asserted, without being sometimes refuted, may gain belief—and as it professes to contain all that can be said against Mr. Jefferson's religion, I trust I shall in its refutation, afford cause of exultation to his friends, and of mortification to his enemies.

The writer says, that his objection to Mr. Jefferson's being promoted to the Presidency, is founded singly on his disbelief of the holy scriptures; or, in other words, his rejection of the christian religion, and open profession of deism. After this we would naturally expect to find evidence of Mr. Jefferson's *having avowed* himself an infidel. Not a shadow of proof, however, to this effect, has this writer produced or attempted to produce. An *open profession* means a full and unequivocal acknowledgement. Has he fixed any thing of this kind upon Mr. Jefferson? Has he shewn from conversation or writings a confession of this nature? No—this was totally out of his power. What then are we to think of a writer, who in the very threshold of his work, asserts, knowingly, a palpable falsehood, with a view to deceive? Who with christian meekness in his mouth, and hell-born malice in his heart, attempts to enlist religion on the side of faction, to blacken the reputation of a distinguished character, and to mislead his fellow-citizens on a point in which their essential political interests are deeply involved.

This writer has however attempted, by *certain inferences* from the writings and supposed conversations of Mr. Jefferson, to fix upon him the charge of deism. It shall be my business to examine, first, whether these deductions are well drawn; and secondly, I shall shew, from the writings of Mr. Jefferson, that we have the strongest reasons to believe that he is a *real christian*.

The christian world is divided into a great variety of sects, differing in their doctrines and discipline, but all agreeing in the divinity of the religion of Christ, and all admitting each other to be entitled to the denomination of christians. Some disbelieve in plenary inspiration—others in certain books, chapters, and verses of the holy scriptures; and yet I do not know that they have been charged with infidelity on that account. Calvinists, Arminians, and Universalists, Trinitarians, Arians, and Socinians, Presbyterians, Episcopalians, and Roman Catholics, are all considered constituent members of the great christian community. Any peculiar opinions which do not go directly to a disbelief of the divinity of the religion, but which are in themselves erroneous, may be named heretical, but can by no means come under the description of deistical. I may construe the scriptures differently from you without impeaching their authority. I may be in sentiment a pre-Adamite, and suppose that other races of men were created before Adam—that the red men of America and black men of Africa sprang from these sources, and yet I may believe in the holy scriptures. I make these preliminary observations, not because I consider them of essential importance to Mr. Jefferson's vindication, but merely because this writer has represented a belief in a particular creed, as essential to constitute a christian, and also with a view to shew, that if Mr. Jefferson's sentiments on these points were even as represented, yet no fair inference can be drawn of his infidelity. Deism is a disbelief of the whole scriptures; heresy of a part, or a misconception of the real meaning thereof. I trust, however, that I shall be able to shew that Mr. Jefferson's opinions do not even subject him to the latter imputation.

The first proof produced against Mr. Jefferson's religion, is his disbelief of an *universal* deluge deduced from a variety of considerations; while he admits that there have been *partial* deluges at different periods. The only controversy between him and the writer, then, is, whether the deluge, recorded by Moses, was universal or not. That it was not *universal* has been the opinion of a number of christian divines, and

A

VINDICATION

O F

THOMAS JEFFERSON;

AGAINST THE CHARGES CONTAINED IN

A *PAMPHLET* ENTITLED,

" *Serious Confiderations,*" &c.

By GROTIUS.

[DeWitt Clinton]

" OMNES ALUID AGENTES, ALIUD SIMULANTES, PERFIDI,
" IMPROBI, MALITIOSI SUNT." CICERO.

NEW-YORK,
PRINTED BY DAVID DENNISTON.

1800.

Courtesy, American Antiquarian Society.

scholars of the first celebrity for piety and learning, and whose orthodoxy has never been questioned. The intention of the deluge was to destroy all the posterity of Adam, for their sins, except the family of Noah. The Deity does nothing in vain: to deluge that part of the world which was not inhabited, might not have embraced the object of his wise dispensations. It is true Moses says, that "all the high hills that were under the whole heaven were covered." But are we always to understand the bible in a literal sense? Is not its language frequently highly figurative? St. Paul says, "I please *all men* in *all things.*" Does this mean that he pleased all men *with whom he communicated,* in all things which were *lawful?* or does it mean that he pleased the *wicked* and the *righteous,* and those whom he *did not know* as well as those with whom *he was acquainted,* in *evil* and *good* things indiscriminately. Surely no man of common sense will hesitate to embrace the first construction. The expression of Moses may in like manner be considered as a synecdoche, a figure in rhetoric, where the whole is put for a part, or a part for the whole. *All the high hills under the whole heaven* may be taken in a qualified sense, and construed only to intend all the high hills in the inhabited countries under the heavens. The deluge might therefore have been *universal* with regard to mankind, but not so with respect to the earth itself. The pious and learned Dr. Burnet was of opinion with Mr. Jefferson, that there was not water enough to cover the earth in its present shape; and in his sacred theory, he has a singular hypothesis to account for it. The celebrated Vossius says—"To effect an universal deluge, many miracles must have concurred—but God works no miracles in vain. What need was there to drown those lands where no men lived, or are yet to be found."

But when I mention the name of *Stillingfleet,* bishop of Worcester, that great champion of the christian church, on the same side of the question, surely this superficial writer must be covered with shame.

The bishop's zeal for religion was so great, that he fancied he discovered a tendency to Atheism, in Mr.

Locke's doctrine respecting innate ideas, and the most remarkable controversy on record ensued between those able writers. In speaking of the deluge, this learned divine expresses himself as follows:—"I cannot see, says he, any urgent necessity from the scripture, to assert that the flood did spread itself all over the surface of the earth. That all mankind (those in the ark excepted) were destroyed by it, is most certain according to the scriptures. When the Lord said that he would destroy man from the face of the earth, it could not be any particular deluge of so small a country as Palestine, as some have ridiculously imagined; for we find an universal corruption in the earth mentioned as the cause; an universal threatening upon all men for this cause; and afterwards, a universal destruction expressed as the effect of this flood. So then it is evident the flood was universal with respect to mankind; but from thence follows no necessity at all for asserting the universality of it, as to the globe of the earth, unless it be sufficiently proved that the whole earth was peopled before the flood, which I despair of ever seeing proved; and what reason can there be for extending the flood beyond the occasion of it, which was the destruction of mankind?

The only probability then of asserting the universality of the flood as to the globe of the earth, is from the destruction of all living creatures, together with men. Now, though men might not have spread themselves over the whole surface of the earth, which beasts and creeping things might, which were all destroyed by the flood; for it is said, "that all flesh that moved upon the earth, both of fowl and of cattle, and of every creeping thing that creepeth upon the earth, and every man."

To what end should there be not only a note of universality added, but such a particular enumeration of the several kinds of beasts, creeping things and fowls, if they were not all destroyed? To this, I answer, I grant that as far as the flood extended, all things were destroyed: But I see no reason to extend the destruction of these beyond that compass and space of the earth where men inhabited, because the punishment of the beasts was occasioned by, and could not but be concomitant with the destruction of man; but (the occasion of the deluge being the sin of man, who was punished in the beasts that were destroyed for his sake, as well as in himself) where the occasion was not, as when there were animals and no men, there seems no necessity of extending the flood thither. But to what end will it therefore be replied; did God command Noah with so much care, to take all kinds of birds, beasts and creeping things into the ark with him, if all those living creatures were not destroyed by the flood? I answer, because all those things were destroyed wherever the flood was. Suppose, then, the whole continent of Asia was peopled before the flood, (which is as much as in reason we can suppose:) I say all the living creatures in that continent were destroyed; or if we may suppose it to have extended over our whole continent of the ancient known world, what reason would there be, that in the opposite part of the globe, which we suppose to be unpeopled then, all the living creatures there should be destroyed, because men had sinned in this? And would there not have been, on this supposition, a sufficient reason to preserve creatures in the ark for future propagation?"

I think it must now obviously appear, that Mr. Jefferson's ideas, with respect to the flood, are not singular, and do not subject him even to the suspicion of infidelity—And although I am inclined to differ from him in opinion, I should be as unwilling to blame him on this account, as I should be to assert that his flimsy calumniator writes with the charity of a christian, the politeness of a gentleman, the honesty of a patriot, or the ability of a scholar.

No. II

A good cause often suffers more from the imprudence of its real, and the hypocrisy of its pretended friends, than from the opposition and violence of its open enemies. We are too apt to confound principles with men; and when we see canting hypocrisy, and a virulent spirit of persecution assume the robes of sanctity, to imbibe a disgust against the latter. Hence it is that unworthy and wicked priests, in all ages have

been more instrumental in diffusing infidelity, than the most ingenious writers who have wielded their pens in that untenable cause. Those men assume a certain set of *dogmas* as the only true and infallible faith, and denounce the least deviation as the vilest infidelity; they wickedly attempt to violate the sanctuary of private opinion, and to point the thunderbolts of almighty vengeance at the sincere followers of truth. They hunt after heresy and infidelity, with an appetite as keen as death; they scent them out in the minutest trifles, and in the gravest labors; in the sports of fancy, as well as in the researches of philosophy; and men often appear in their black list of deists, who have from their infancy followed the religion of Christ with undeviating steps, and who in all the bustle of active life, and amidst all the vanities of sublunary things, have kept their eyes steadily fixed upon the great consoling truths of religion.—The only way to disarm the fury of those unhallowed intruders into the christian church, is to approach them with adulation and with douceurs. The Ethiopean, then, changes his skin, and the leopard his spots.— the lewd man becomes chaste—the knave honest, and the infidel a christian; and moral excellencies and religious merits, are measured by extent of homage and quantity of money, not by soundness of doctrine or purity of life. The writer of "*Serious Considerations*," has strongly exemplified the force of these remarks; he can openly cultivate a professed adulterer, with all the ardor of friendship and the enthusiasm of admiration, and can see the principles of christianity flourishing in his bosom, as in their native and appropriate soil: but in Mr. Jefferson, whose life has been virtuous and exemplary, he beholds through the distorted medium of a crooked mind and a black heart—

"Perverse all monstrous, all prodigious things,
Abominable, inutterable, and worse
Than fables, yet have feign'd or fear conceiv'd
Gorgons, and Hydras, and Chimeras dire."

I have been insensibly drawn into these observations, from a contemplation of the disingenuous and unworthy arts practised by this writer, to torture some speculative notions of Mr. Jefferson on philosophy, into a disbelief of christianity. A man must read, but "with a lust to misapply," and sit down predetermined to make him a deist, who can deduce it from his observations respecting the red men of America, and Asia, and the black men of Africa. Even the unblushing Smith, this writer's predecessor in calumny, had too much prudence to resort to so sandy a foundation for his edifice of slander and falsehood.

The most authentic account of the origin and migration of nations, is to be found in the holy scriptures. The traditions and histories, of all the ancient nations of the world, corroborate in a wonderful manner the writings of Moses; to them we must look up, as a light to guide us through the darkness of antiquity; as a standard by which to regulate our opinions of the early period of the human race; and as a certain mean of solving many perplexing difficulties, which beset us in our researches into ancient history, and our views of the present appearances of men and nations. We are informed by Moses, that all men are descended from one pair, and we should be extremely puzzled to reconcile with this fact, not only the great variety, but the essential, radical and entire difference of languages prevalent in the world, did not scripture furnish us with a solution of this otherwise inexplicable aenigma.

We are told in the eleventh chapter of Genesis, that sometime after the flood, all the human race were assembled together on a plain in the land of Shinar; that the whole earth was of one language, and of one speech; that they impiously attempted to counteract the intentions of the deity, by building a city which should serve as a habitation for them all, and prevent their dispersion over the earth; that the Lord interfered in a miraculous manner, and created a diversity of languages among them, by which means their work was left unfinished, and they were scattered abroad upon the face of all the earth. This great plain was then a common centre from which mankind diverged in every direction over the earth. How many different languages were originally established, we are not informed of by the scriptures; but we have every reason to believe, that they were as various as the original families and tribes which eventually expanded into nations. A sameness of complexion and figure no doubt existed, as well as an identity of speech, and the diversities of color which now exist, must be attributed to a variety of physical and moral causes, but principally to climate and the state of society. That *white* was the original complexion of the human species, is, I believe, the opinion of the most intelligent writers on this subject. The tribes which emigrated to America, after the confusion of tongues might have settled there, long before migrations took place in the parts of Asia, now inhabited by red men, and their complexion would in course of time be changed from white to red, by the operation of natural causes. There is no difficulty with respect to the passage from Asia to America; these two continents if parted at all, are only separated by a narrow strait. We may therefore say that the red men of America are of greater antiquity than the red men of Asia, or in other words, that red men were settled in America, before they were settled in Asia, without impugning the authority of the scriptures. Every body would smile, if the writer would denominate one an infidel, for saying that the black men of Africa are of greater antiquity than the black men of Asia, and yet the cases are exactly parallel.

Mr. Jefferson infers from the greater number of radical languages among the red men of America, that they are of greater antiquity than the red men of Asia; but he expressly confines the remark to *red* men, and no where insinuates that men were originally created in America. That the population of America is very ancient, has not only been deduced from the above circumstance, but from many other considerations. The Americans had no knowledge of the people of the old continent, nor the latter any account of the migration of the former to the new world. They wanted those arts and inventions, which, when once discovered, are never forgotten; such, for example, as those of wax and oil for light, which are very ancient in Europe and Asia, and are not only highly useful, but necessary. And it is said, that the polished nations of the new world, and particularly those of Mexico, preserve in their traditions and paintings, the memory of the creation of the world, the building of the tower of Babel, the confusion of languages, and the dispersion of the people, although blended with some fables; and that they had no knowledge of the events which happened afterwards in Asia, in Africa, or in Europe; although many of them were so great and remarkable, that they could not easily have gone from their memory. The learned author of the history of Mexico, the Abbe Clavigero, a christian divine, is of opinion, that the Americans do not derive their origin from any people now existing in the ancient world; not only from the circumstance of the great diversity of languages, but from the total want of affinity between them and any of the languages of the old world. He therefore infers, that the Americans are descended from different families, dispersed after the confusion of tongues, and have since been separated from those others who peopled the countries of the old continent.

The next charge against Mr. Jefferson, is drawn from some observations on the inferiority of blacks to whites—and here again the writer has betrayed his usual want of candor, by suppressing those parts which would explain any ambiguity, and destroy any ill impression that might result from a quotation of insulated passages. If I rightly understand the writer, he means to insinuate as Mr. Jefferson's opinion, that the blacks are an order of beings inferior to the whites. In page 237, 2d American edition of the Notes on Virginia, Mr. Jefferson expressly admits that the blacks are of the human race; but in other parts of his work, he endeavors to prove what cannot be denied, that they are inferior in complexion, beauty and form, to the whites, and he also seems to adopt an opinion, which is probably erroneous, that they are inferior in the faculties of reason and imagination. He sums up his ideas on the subject with the following remarks: "To justify a general conclusion, requires many observations, even where the subject may be submitted to the anatomical knife, to optical glasses, to analysis by fire, or by solvents. How much more then, where it is a faculty, not a substance, we are examining; where it eludes the research of all the senses; where the conditions of its existence are various and variously combined; where the effects of those which are present or absent bid defiance to calculation; let me add too, as a circumstance of great tenderness, where our conclusion would degrade a whole race of men from the rank in the scale of beings, which their creator may perhaps have given them. To our reproach, it must be said; that though for a century and an half, we have had under our eyes, the races of black and of red men, they have never yet been viewed by us as subjects of natural history. I advance it, therefore, as a suspicion only, that the blacks, whether originally a distinct race, or made distinct by time and circumstances, are inferior to the whites in the endowments both of body and mind. It is not against experience to suppose, that different species of the same genus, or varieties of the same species, may possess different qualifications." Now it must require more than common acuteness, to discover any thing in the above observations, which militate against the Mosaic account of the creation. A distinct race means a distinct generation or family, and does by no means, *ex vi termini* [from the force of the term, i.e., by definition], exclude the idea of a common origin. If the blacks do not appertain to the human race, then it is no more anti-christian to say so, than it is to assert it of the Orang Outang, or the monkey. If they do belong to it, we may suppose them a distinct race, made so by time and circumstances, and inferior in the endowments both of body and mind to the whites, without impeaching the doctrine of a first pair. We must admit them "a variety of the same species," and inferior in complexion and physical conformation; but all this may have resulted from adventitious circumstances, and their original ancestors may have been white. Sir William Jones (who was a christian from conviction, and possessed of the most extensive acquirements in language, of any man living in his time) asserts, from a comparison of the Sanscrit and Arabic languages, that they "are totally distinct, and must have been invented by two *different races of men*," and that "the Tartarian language has not the least resemblance either to Arabic or Sanscrit, and must have been invented by a *race of men wholly distinct* from the Arabs or Hindoos."* And yet he concludes that these three stocks had one common root; or in other words, proceeded from one pair. In like manner, although Mr. Jefferson has asserted that the blacks are inferior to the whites in certain respects, yet as he has in unequivocal terms, admitted them to be of the human race, we have every reason to suppose that he believes that they and the whites are branches of the same stem, and children of the same common parents; especially as in a letter to Benjamin Banneker, which has been published, he declares himself convinced "that nature has given to our black brethren, talents equal to those of other colors, and the appearance of a want of them is owing merely to the degraded condition of their existence both in Africa and America."

No. III

Before the revolution, the church of England was established by law in Virginia; and although two thirds of the inhabitants were dissenters, they were obliged to contribute to the support of the ministers of that persuasion. At the revolution a partial reform only took place; the crime of heresy at common law and its punishment by burning, still remained in full force; and some of the colonial statutes which bore hard upon particular sectarians, were left unrepealed. This peculiar state of his countrymen, enjoying the benefits of civil liberty, and at the same time exposed to the evils of religious slavery, naturally attracted the attention of the enlightened author of the declaration of American independence; and his reasoning respecting it, perfectly accords with his uniform and ardent zeal in favor of the rights of human nature. "The error (says he) seems not sufficiently eradicated, that the operations of the mind, as well as the acts of the body, are subject to the coercion of the laws. But our

rulers can have authority over such natural rights only as we have submitted to them. The rights of conscience we never submitted. We could not submit. *We are answerable for them to our God.* The legitimate powers of government extend to such acts only as are injurious to others. But it does me no injury for my neighbor to say there are twenty Gods or no God. It neither picks my pocket nor breaks my leg: If it be said his testimony in a court of justice cannot be relied on, reject it then, and be the stigma on him. Constraint may make him worse by making him a hypocrite, but it will never make him a truer man. It may fix him obstinately in his errors, but will not cure them." The writer of "Serious Considerations," after agreeing with Mr. Jefferson, that "a mere opinion of my neighbor will do me no injury, government cannot regulate or punish it. The right of private opinion is inalienable," (see page 19) intimates, first, That Mr. Jefferson says, "that it is a matter of indifference what a man believes:" This insinuation is totally false. Secondly, he tries to impress it as Mr. Jefferson's opinion, "that a man's life may be good, let his faith be what it may." This idea, whether true or false, is not in the remotest degree conveyed—And thirdly, he asserts, that there is ground to fix a suspicion of atheism on Mr. Jefferson. He would, no doubt, with equal readiness and equal probity, have declared that there was *positive proof;* but this would have been too much at war with the general tenor of his publication: He had previously labored hard to prove the object of his calumny a deist—Now, if the evidence to this effect is substantiated, then the suspicion of atheism is ill-founded, because deism and atheism cannot exist in the same creed. But, if I am not egregiously mistaken, the very sentiment conveyed by Mr. Jefferson, is also more comprehensively advanced by this writer in different and less elegant language: The one says, "It does me no injury for my neighbor to say there are twenty Gods or no God."—The other declares, "A mere opinion of my neighbor will do me no injury." The only difference which can possibly be designated, is, that Mr. Jefferson's observation is confined to Polytheistical and Atheistical opinions; and the

---

* Asiatic Researches, 1st vol. p. 125–157.

writer's embraces all opinions whatsoever, good, bad and indifferent, and consequently *Atheistical,* agreeably to the maxim, *Omne majus continet in se minus;** so that, upon his own admission, we may venture to bring the charge of Atheism against him. But I am fatigued with brushing away these cobwebs. Let us attend to the spirit and legitimate meaning of Mr. Jefferson's reasoning in favor of the rights of conscience. The scope of his argument goes to prove that government has no right to punish *mere opinions,* but only the *overt acts* resulting from them, which are contrary to the peace and good order of society. To elucidate his ideas in the strongest point of view, he takes the *two extremes of error respecting religion, Polytheism and Atheism,* and declares that government has no right to punish them, because *they are opinions only, and not actions detrimental to the property or persons of individuals.* I am persuaded that every liberal, candid and intelligent friend of civil and religious liberty will sanction this sentiment; and yet would it be fair, would it not be dishonest to infer from this that he supposes them, or either of them, free from error or harmless in tendency? If we can, with propriety, fix the charge of Atheism upon Mr. Jefferson from those expressions, we have also equal reason to declare him a Polytheist, because, in his illustration of his reasoning, he puts them on the same footing with respect to freedom from persecution—Moreover, in the next preceding sentence he expressly, and, in the most pious manner, recognizes the existence and attributes of the Deity, and asserts the doctrine of human accountability, by declaring, that *"We are answerable for the rights of conscience to our God."* In truth, the only candid exposition of his meaning is, that although Atheistical and Polytheistical opinions are fundamentally wrong and have a mischievous tendency, yet, that they ought not to be the subject of legal coercion until they become injurious in action—that, in the mean time, the oath of an Atheist or Polytheist ought not to be admitted in courts of justice, because he does not believe in that God to whom an oath is

an appeal. If Atheism, or an approbation of Atheism, or a leaning towards Atheism, or a suspicion of Atheism, can be logically deduced from this, then we can have no confidence in the elements of just reasoning, or the foundations of rational belief. All the faculties of the mind must be unhinged and jumbled together in chaotic darkness. It will be seen by a marginal reference in the notes on Virginia, that Mr. Jefferson has borrowed some of his ideas on this subject from the writings of the Rev. Dr. Philip Furneaux, one of the ablest advocates of religious freedom.—The distinction between principles and their tendency on the one hand, and those overt acts which affect the public good on the other, is so ably taken and so irresistibly enforced by this excellent writer, that I should not do justice to my subject without quoting him at length; for I am confident that it will totally destroy this absurd calumny in the minds of all who read and all who understand. "But it will be said, hath the magistrate no concern with those principles which destroy the foundation of moral obligation? That is, if I understand you right, which have a tendency to introduce immorality and licentiousness. I allow he may encourage, amongst all sects, those general principles of religion and morality on which the happiness of society depends. This he may and should do as conservator of the public weal.

"But with regard to the belief or disbelief of religious principles or religious systems; if he presumes to exercise his *authority as a judge,* in such cases, with a view of restraining and punishing those who embrace and profess what he dislikes, or dislike and explode what he embraces on account of the supposed ill tendency of their principles; he goes beyond his province, which is confined to those effects of such principles, that is, to those actions which affect the peace and good order of society; and every step he takes, he is in danger of trampling on the rights of conscience, and of invading the prerogative of the only arbiter of conscience, to whom alone men are accountable for professing or not professing religious sentiments and principles. For if the magistrate be possessed of a power to restrain and punish any principles relating to religion, because of their tendency, and he be the judge of that tendency, as he must be, if he be vested with authority to punish on that account; religious liberty is entirely at an end, or which is the same thing, is under the controul, and at the mercy of the magistrate according as he shall think the tenets in question affect the foundation of moral obligation, or are favorable or unfavorable to religion and morality. But if the line be drawn between mere religious principles and the tendency of them on the one hand, and those overt acts which affect the public peace and order on the other; and if the latter alone be assigned to the jurisdiction of the magistrate, as being guardian of the peace of society in this world, and the former as interfering only with a future world, be referred to a man's own conscience, and to God the only sovereign Lord of conscience; the boundaries between civil power and liberty in religious matters are clearly marked and determined, and the latter will not be wider or narrower, or just nothing at all, according to the magistrate's opinion of the good or bad tendency of principles. If it be objected, that when the tendency of principles is unfavorable to the peace and good order of society, as it may be, it is the magistrate's duty then, and for that reason, to restrain them by penal laws: I reply that the tendency of principles, though it be *unfavorable,* is not *prejudicial* to society, till it issues in some *overt acts,* against the public peace and order; and when it does, *then* the magistrate's authority to punish commences; that is, he may punish the *overt acts* but not the *tendency,* which is not actually hurtful; and therefore his penal laws should be directed against *overt acts* only, which are detrimental to the peace and good order of society, let them spring from what principles they will, and not against *principles* or the *tendency* of principles. The distinction between the tendency of principles and the overt acts arising from them, is, and cannot but be observed in many cases, of a civil nature, in order to determine the bounds of the magistrate's power, or at least to limit the exercise of it in such cases. It would not be difficult to mention customs and manners as well as principles, which have a tendency unfavorable to so-

ciety, and which nevertheless cannot be restrained by penal laws, except with the total destruction of civil liberty: And here the magistrate must be contented with pointing his penal laws against the evil overt acts resulting from them. In the same manner he should act in regard to men's professing or rejecting religious principles or systems. Punishing a man for the *tendency* of his principles, is punishing him *before* he is guilty, for fear he *should be* guilty. Besides, if the magistrate in one country hath a right to punish those who reject the religion which is there publicly professed, the magistrates of all other countries must have the same right, and for the same reason, namely, to guard against the evil tendency of renouncing a religion, the maintenance of which they think of great importance to society. If those persons who reject christianity are to be punished in England, those who embrace it are to be punished in Turkey.—This is the necessary consequence of allowing any penal laws to be enacted and to operate in support or suppression of any religious system; for the magistrate must and will use his power according to his own religious persuasion."*

In treating of the Indians of Virginia, Mr. Jefferson describes them as never having submitted themselves to any laws, any coercive power, any shadow of government; and that notwithstanding crimes are rare among them, "Insomuch, (says he) that were it made a question, whether no law, as among the savage Americans, or too much law, as among the civilized

---

* Letters to Blackstone, page 33. In addition to this, permit me to quote a passage from Locke on Toleration, which will furnish a good lesson of charity and moderation to all persecuting bigots. "No private person (says this enlightened philosopher) has any right in any manner, to prejudice another person in his civil enjoyments because he is of another church or religion. All the rights and franchises that belong to him as a man, or as a denizen, are inviolably to be preserved to him. These are not the business of religion. No violence nor injury is to be offered him, whether he be Christian or Pagan. Nay we must not content ourselves with the narrow measures of bare justice; charity, honesty, and liberality must be added to it. This the gospel enjoins—this reason directs; and this that natural fellowship we are born into requires of us. If any man err from the right way it is his own misfortune, no injury to thee; nor therefore art thou to punish him in the things of this life, because thou supposest he will be miserable in that which is to come." Locke on tol. p. 57, Glasgow ed.

Europeans, submits man to the greatest evil; one who has seen both conditions of existence would pronounce it to be the last: and that the sheep are happier of themselves than under the care of the wolves." The writer of "Serious Considerations," has, with his usual acumen and perspicacity, discovered an enmity to all religion and government in this passage.— "Thus, says he, the happiest state of man is, according to the sage of Monticello, to be without law, without government, and without religion, to continue just as he was born, a wild ass's colt." It is evident that Mr. Jefferson is comparing two evils together, and pronouncing which, in his opinion, is the greater. By asking which of them, no law or too much law, submits man to the *greatest evil,* is clearly admitting, that the savage state without government is an evil; but he proceeds to state, that it is a less one than the condition of the civilized Europeans, where *too much law,* or, in other words, despotism prevails. "The sheep, says he, are happier of themselves than under the care of the wolves;" that is, it is better for man to be without government, than in subjection to one that devours and destroys him. Is this declaring that a state of no law is preferable to a state of neither too much nor too little law? Can an opinion that no government is better than tyranny, be construed to mean that it is also preferable to a free one? In saying that anarchy is a less evil than despotism, do I assert that it is a greater good than civil liberty? And yet all these absurdities the writer has put into the mouth of Mr. Jefferson. It is obvious that Mr. Jefferson uses *law* and *government* in this place synonimously, and that he does not refer to a multiplicity of laws, but to an oppressive government. The writer also infers from this passage, as the opinion of Mr. Jefferson, "That the Indians are happier in their uncivilized state, than if they were civilized." If I say that *a savage without law* is happier than *a civilized slave,* does this amount to a declaration that he enjoys superior felicity to a *civilized freeman,* or to man under every modification of improved society? Meanly as I think of this writer's discernment, I cannot suppose that his glaring and palpable perversion of Mr. Jefferson's remarks on this

subject arose from ignorance—No—a child could not have fallen into such a gross error: it must have been done with design; and to such as may still think the author a man of candor, honesty or truth, or may entertain a high opinion of his talents, I recommend a perusal of the whole commentary as an effectual antidote. The little ingenuity he, indeed, possesses, consists in compressing a great deal of nonsense into a small compass; and the only candor he exhibits is in spreading so diaphanous a veil over his calumnies, that they become apparent to the most obtuse vision.

It is a question which has been much discussed, and upon which the most pious christians have taken different sides, whether the bible ought to be used as a school book? It is not now necessary to go into a minute consideration of this debate, or to assign at length all the arguments which have been advanced. It is sufficient to remark, that the primary design of sending children to school, is to *learn to read and write, not to learn religion.* That to teach the latter is a more appropriate duty and concern of parents and clergymen. That if the bible ought not to be employed as a book from which to be taught spelling and reading, it does not follow that it ought not to be adopted as an infallible source of religious education and instruction; and that if it be inexpedient to resort to it in the school, it may be still obligatory to use it in the family, and to teach it from the pulpit. The reasons of Mr. Jefferson are highly honorable to religion. "Instead (says he) of putting the Bible and Testament into the hands of children at an age when their judgments are not sufficiently matured for religious enquiries," &c. *The plain inference is, that when their judgments are sufficiently matured, then the bible and testament ought to be put into their hands*—and is it not more respectful to the holy scriptures to say that they should be studied with ripe understandings and enlightened minds, than to assert that the faculties of infants are adequate to this important task.

I have now fully considered all the written proofs produced by this writer against Mr. Jefferson's religion, and I trust have shewn them to be as "baseless as the fabric of a vision." I shall in my next proceed to expose the futility of his oral and circumstantial evidences. But I cannot conclude this number without remarking that the writer has said, "*It is a light thing with Mr. Jefferson to say there is no God.*" (see p. 24.) Let me, sir, address you in the first person, and ask you if this is *not a charge of the blackest dye exhibited against one of our most respectable citizens?* Mr. Jefferson, sir, is *either a friend of atheism, or you are a base unprincipled calumniator.* There is no other alternative. Try not to evade an enquiry by saying that it is a mere slip of the pen, or that you heard it from this or that man, or inferred it from this or that expression. Your charge, sir, is direct, positive, and unqualified. Produce then your proofs, but remember that the weight of evidence must be in proportion to the magnitude of the charge. The public, sir, will not be satisfied with evasion or silence, and I call upon you by that holy religion you extol—by that sacred calling you disgrace—by that love of country you profess—and by that regard for character which even the most abandoned entertain, to come forward and support your allegation. Remember that you now stand upon your defence before the high tribunal of public opinion, and that the least faltering will blast you forever.

No. IV

Addressed to the Author of
"Serious Considerations"

A letter to an Italian of the name of Mazzei, ascribed to Mr. Jefferson, has been much employed to injure his political consequence, and to prove him an enemy of the constitution, and a calumniator of its administration.

Although it is not ascertained whether this letter be genuine or spurious, yet whenever the cause of the party is to be served or supported, it is brought forward as a sword to attack and a shield to defend. As it was fondly hoped that the name of Mazzei would have the same magical effect in religion, one of the most idle stories that was ever attempted to be palmed upon the public, has been advanced by you, with as much gravity, as if you really believed it your-

self, and with all that parade and ostentation which cunning and hypocrisy prescribe as necessary to subserve the cause of delusion. It abounds, sir, with so many absurdities, and improbabilities, and is so defective in all the properties of sound evidence, that no man of the least sagacity, unless he labours under the most violent prejudices, can be deceived by it. I will, however, bestow a few remarks upon it, as you have passed it off as a discovery of the greatest importance. The first, and most natural observation, is the circuitous route in which this story has proceeded. It does not come directly from Mr. Jefferson, but passes through three persons before it reaches the public; and I need not remark to you, sir, how liable to be perverted and to be misunderstood in every stage of its transit. Many years must have elapsed since Mazzei visited this country. It does not appear that the story was ever reduced to writing before you exhibited it to the public. The omission of a single word, or a single circumstance, may have altered its whole complexion. Memory, sir, is frail—prejudice is deceptious, and oral evidence cannot well be relied on after such an efflux of time. You heard it from Smith, who heard it from Mazzei, who heard it from Jefferson. This is, in the language of the law, a hearsay of a hearsay: and what would not be admitted as testimony in a court of justice to deprive a man of a farthing, is now gravely adduced to rob one of our most eminent and respectable fellow-citizens, of the most sacred of all property—the most invaluable of all possessions—the esteem, the love, and the respect of his country. I am well aware that in discussions of this nature, the strictness and severity of legal evidence ought not to be exacted, but certainly there should be some striking lineaments of resemblance—some leading traits of analogy required, or else the most innocent characters may be sacrificed. I have seen you, sir, charged in one of the morning papers with being a deist, upon a report said to have emanated from your family; and although I believe it to be an idle fiction, yet mark with what facility you might be ruined, if we were to mete for you with the same measure with which you have measured for Mr. Jefferson. It is more direct than your report—it proceeds from a quarter that ought to know your real sentiments, and from a source interested in guarding, instead of injuring your character. Private enmity has not mingled its gall, nor party spirit its poison in the composition; and it has been published for some time, and not contradicted by you or your friends. On the other hand, a report of an ancient date has been raked up, on the eve of the most important election in the United States, when all the passions of the human heart are in a storm of fury—when personal rivalry, ambition, avarice, and political preferences, unite to depreciate, to calumniate, and to deceive. This story too has passed through several hands, has been artfully fortified against detection and refutation, by being fastened in one instance upon a dead man, and in another upon a foreigner many thousand miles distant; and the name of the last propagator can only be acquired through the medium of conjecture. It bears with it also internal marks of imposture and fabrication. Is it probable that Mr. Jefferson would commit himself to a stranger and a foreigner, by an avowal of opinions, which being an outrage on the public sentiment, are generally concealed from the most intimate friends, and cautiously locked up in the secret depositaries of the heart. Is it probable that Mazzei, who travelled in the character of a gentleman, and a man of letters, and who it seems was hospitably received by both Mr. Jefferson and Doctor Smith, would, without any conceivable motive, betray the confidence of the former, and, in violation of all propriety and decorum, insult the feelings of the latter, by vilifying a religion to which he was ardently attached, in his own house too, and shortly after he had been performing one of its most solemn offices? Is it probable that Dr. Smith, who wisely avoided the errors of his brother, by keeping aloof from the contentions of parties, would all at once have deserted those maxims of prudence and propriety which had governed the uniform tenor of his life, and stand sponsor for a report dubious and uncertain in the highest degree, and which would infallibly expose him to ill-will, and destroy in a great degree his usefulness to his country, and to the cause

of science and religion? And here let me remark, sir, how unchristian-like in you to rake up the consecrated ashes of the venerable dead; and to descend into the dark recesses of the tomb for the unhallowed cause of faction, and the execrable purposes of calumny. If we can in any stage of the story suppose a fabrication, or a perversion of meaning through intention, misunderstanding, or defect of memory more probable, than that Mr. Jefferson should insult our holy religion, then the credit of your charge is at an end. But if Mazzei had been correct in his opinion of Mr. Jefferson's infidelity, would he not have been able to have produced some stronger proof than a mere inference from a casual and hasty conversation? Let us, however, suppose, for the sake of argument, that the story is true—Is it not susceptible of a good as well a bad meaning. In my opinion it may well admit of three constructions—either as a sarcasm upon christianity, the way in which you take it, or as a sneer of this kind at the infidelity of Mazzei. "What! you express a concern at the bad architecture of a building intended for the purposes of a religion you despise—for the worship of a Being you represent to be a mere man, born in the lowest style of poverty and obscurity!"—or it may be considered as a serious sentiment, that as "the Lord dwelleth not in temples made with hands"—as he made his appearance in the most humble state, costly and magnificent churches are as nothing in his sight, and are oftener monuments of human pride and vanity than evidences of sincere piety. I leave it to the good sense and christian charity of my readers, to say which construction ought to be adopted. It must be evident after all, that Mr. Jefferson's real meaning could only be collected from *the manner of his communication,* and of this Mazzei was a very incompetent judge. He was a stranger to Mr. Jefferson; and it requires a considerable acquaintance to infer at all times from a man's manner whether he is *serious* or in *jest.* Besides, Mazzei was a foreigner, and probably knew little of the language in which the idea was conveyed.

Your other story about Mr. Jefferson's having declared to a gentleman of distinguished talents and services, that "he wished to see a government in which no religious opinions were held, &c." is liable to many of the preceding objections. It differs however in some particulars, which redound more to its discredit. You have cautiously omitted all circumstances of time and place—You have not given us the name of your informer, nor furnished us with any clue by which to find him—You have only told us that he is distinguished for his talents and services—but you have not informed us whether he is renowned for his candor and veracity, and whether he is free from prejudice, interest, enmity, or any undue bias that may warp and discredit his testimony: and the very circumstance of your mentioning the other narrators and concealing the name of this, has a very suspicious aspect. You could bring them forward because they are either in Europe or in the grave, but this one you carefully keep out of view. A man will often whisper a calumny in a corner, who will not dare to utter it to the public. If you have been made the innocent dupe of an artful, ambitious, rancorous and unprincipled enemy of Mr. Jefferson, let us know it, and then we will transfer our censure from your heart to your head. You allow Mr. Jefferson to be a man of talents, and I believe you must also admit him to be possessed of extensive knowledge in politics, history and philosophy. How then, sir, can you ascribe to him a sentiment repugnant to all just theory and all sound experience, that a community in which no religious opinions are held would be eligible?—a sentiment more fit for the meridian of a Bedlamite, than for the mind of a statesman and philosopher. And yet you try to palm all these absurdities upon us! You measure the facility of our faith by the extravagance of your charges; and you really seem to think us ready to exclaim, *"We believe because it is impossible."*

I hope, sir, you do not seriously expect that Mr. Jefferson stands in need of vindication against a sentiment expressed by another person: namely, "that it is high time for this country to get rid of religion and the clergy." Surely one man is not blameable for the mischievous opinions or actions of another, unless he inculcated or instigated them. To render this charge

of any effect, you ought to prove that he borrowed the idea from Mr. Jefferson—This, indeed, you have insinuated by the words *pupil and admirer.* It has been a long time since Mr. Jefferson practised law, and I am yet to learn that he ever taught school. A student at law is not a polemic in divinity. Mr. Jefferson probably taught him Coke and Blackstone instead of Hobbes and Hume; and at any rate, he may possibly, after such a lapse of time, have imbibed bad notions from other quarters. But to be serious, if we are to impute to Mr. Jefferson the vices of his friends, we ought also in all justice to impute to him their good qualities. I know a warm, intimate and confidential friend of his, who has declared that the christian religion is the great prop of good government, and the only way to eternal happiness. Now, according to your mode of reasoning, I have proved Mr. Jefferson an excellent christian. Remember the maxim, that it is a bad rule that will not work both ways. But, sir, if we were to bring you to this test, bending as you are under a load of sanctity, you must suffer from the application. I have already pointed out one of your most intimate friends: were I to mention another, whom nature has endowed with shining talents, and education has polished with the most insinuating manners; but whose whole life has been a practical burlesque on religion, decency and good morals; who, to the profligacy of a Chartres, and the impiety of a Wharton, unites the impudence of a Cappadocian, and the lewdness of a Sybarite; and were I to ascribe the errors, the faults, the vices, the sins and the crimes of this man to you, would not sound discrimination recoil, and real morality frown awfully at the enormity of the injustice?

You speak, sir, of Mr. Jefferson's disregard of religious things; of his associates at home and correspondents abroad, as concurrent circumstances with a passage from his works, to fix a suspicion of Atheism on him. You profess, however, not to be so well acquainted with these things as many; you ask, "is he known to worship with any denomination of christians? Where? When? How often?" And you say, "We have not forgotten the Sunday feast of him and his friends at Fredericksburgh, in Virginia, on his return from the second seat of government." I have always understood that Mr. Jefferson belongs to the Episcopal church. How often he attends it I have not enquired, but I believe he does with as much sincerity as Mr. Adams, and full as frequently as Mr. Pinckney. That he corresponds with literary men of all sects, of all parties, and of all civilized nations, I am willing to admit. Robertson corresponded with Hume and Gibbon; and I believe Mr. Adams has been very intimate with Dr. Priestly, whom you hardly rank among christians. The truth is, the intercourse which exists in the literary world, is no proof of identity of sentiment or principle. This interchange of ideas is for the important purpose of communicating and receiving light respecting new discoveries, new inventions, and new systems in the arts and sciences, and has little or no connection with religious creeds.

That Mr. Jefferson may have dined with some of his friends on Sunday, on his return to his family, I am willing to concede, and also to allow you every advantage resulting therefrom in favor of your assertions; but as you have not informed us that it was an ostentatious parade of a festival, and a deliberate violation of the Sabbath; as you have not depicted any scenes of Bacchanalian orgies or disgraceful revelry, I must confess I do not perceive any infidelity in it.

But you seem to have attained the very acme of modesty when you say that Mr. Jefferson ought to subscribe a certain creed, and that the ministers of the gospel, &c. cannot expect less—That is, in plain language, that the clergy should propose a religious test for his subscription, and thereby violate the spirit of that constitution which he has sworn to support— Would you, sir, after the pretended proofs you have produced, believe in the sincerity of the act? Would you not exclaim that it was hypocritical, fraudulent and insincere? Has not all experience shewn, that tests and subscription articles never interpose obstacles to the wicked, and only serve as snares for the righteous? And would not his friends justly consider him "as the meanest of mankind" if he would submit to have certain declarations of faith exacted from him by an unauthorised body of men, as a necessary passport to office? Surely he may reply to you in the words of the poet—*Timeo danaos et dona ferentes.**

No. V

The writings of Mr. Jefferson abound with just and elevated ideas of the Deity and his attributes. The declaration of independence, that masterly production of his pen, appeals to the Supreme Judge of the universe, and, in a strain of exalted piety, expresses a firm reliance on the protection of divine Providence. If Mr. Jefferson had really wished that our national character should be dishonored by Atheism and irreligion, would he have inserted in *the act which called us into being as a nation,* a recognition of the creator and ruler of the world? But I am persuaded, it is not necessary to pursue this absurd calumny any further—An Atheist is a kind of *lusus naturae* [joke of nature] in the moral and intellectual world—Many intelligent persons entirely disbelieve in the existence of such a character. A man must voluntarily shut his eyes against the light which is bursting upon him in every direction, and abandon the use of his reason and his senses, if he does not perceive the finger of God in every department of nature.

The enemies of Mr. Jefferson have employed particular passages of the Notes on Virginia to prove him an infidel; and, by garbled quotations, illogical inferences, and perverted constructions, have made some impression upon the minds of many of the pious and patriotic. Their attacks would, however, have been fruitless and unavailing, if they had exposed to the public eye, those passages of his works which indicate him to be a believer in the truths of christianity. His writings, in the view of an enlightened community, will operate like the spear of Achilles, and cure the wounds they have inflicted in the assassin hands of his enemies.

* I fear Greeks, even when they bring gifts (Virgil's *Aeneid*, bk. III, l. 49).—Trans.

After expatiating upon the evils resulting to the manners, morals and industry of the people from the existence of slavery, Mr. Jefferson breaks out into the following animated strain of pious exclamation: "Can the liberties of a nation be thought secure when we have removed their only firm basis, a conviction in the minds of the people that these liberties are of *the gift of God?* That they are not to be violated but with his wrath? Indeed I tremble for my country when I reflect that *God is just;* that *his justice cannot sleep forever:* that considering numbers, nature and natural means only, a revolution of the wheel of fortune, an exchange of situation is among *possible* events: that it may become *probable* by *supernatural interference!* The Almighty has no attribute that can take side with us in such a contest."* The most remarkable trait in the above passage is, "*It may become probable by supernatural interference.*" Is not this the language of christianity? Deism disavows *particular interferences* of the Deity, and pretends that the Almighty rules entirely by general laws, and that preternatural interpositions are repugnant to his attributes, and betray imperfection in his system of government. On the other hand, christianity declares that when mankind are deeply immersed in wickedness, the Deity has sometimes produced a deviation from the general course of nature in order to *reclaim or to punish;* and that suffering virtue and uncommon goodness have been often protected or rewarded by special interpositions of his benevolence.

Again, when reasoning in favor of religious liberty, he says, "Reason and free enquiry are the only effectual agents against error. Give a loose to them they will support the *true religion,* by bringing every false one to their tribunal, to the test of their investigation—They are the natural enemies of *error,* and of error only. *Had not the Roman government permitted free enquiry, christianity could never have been introduced.*"†—The ideas conveyed in this quotation are a clear admission of the truth of christianity. The best

supports, says he, of true religion, are reason and free enquiry. Free enquiry was permitted at the introduction of christianity; it prevailed, and by the force of reason, routed the superstitions of the times, and demolished the altars and temples of Heathenism. *Give reason and free enquiry fair play, and they will establish the true religion—They had fair play and christianity predominated.* This is a faithful abridgement of his observations, and if it contain not the sentiments of a believer, then faith is a word without meaning, and like sounding brass and the tinkling cymbal. And here let us, with humble gratitude, acknowledge the gracious providence and sublime wisdom of the Deity in opening the road for christianity. One of the predisposing causes of its introduction was the toleration allowed by the Roman government. The Deity thus disposed its enemies to favor its establishment, and prepared the way for its final triumph by such a series and co-operation of secondary causes, that it has withstood the arms as well as the arts of its foes, and, fortified by the hand of truth, it still stands a monument of mercy and happiness to mankind.

I have already narrated the evils which the people of Virginia laboured under respecting religious tyranny, but I have not mentioned that Mr. Jefferson brought forward a remedy. In the year 1786, a bill for establishing religious freedom in that state was drafted by him, and laid before the legislature, who passed it into a law. The preamble states the reasons for the act, and is a master-piece of elegant and perspicuous language, and cogent and impressive reasoning. It says, "Well aware that Almighty God hath created the mind free; that all attempts to influence it by temporal punishments or burdens, or by civil incapacitations, tend only to beget habits of hypocrisy and meanness, and are a departure from the plan of the *holy author of our religion,* who being Lord both of body and mind, yet chose not to propagate it by coercions or either as was in *his Almighty power* to do; that the impious presumption of legislators and rulers, civil as well as ecclesiastical, who being themselves but fallible and uninspired men, have assumed dominion over the faith of others, hath established

---

* Jefferson's Notes on Virginia, p. 257, 2d Am. ed.
† Jefferson's Notes on Virginia, p. 232.

and maintained false religions over the greatest part of the world, and through all time," &c.* Here is an express declaration of the truth of christianity, of the reality of inspiration, and of the divinity and God-head of Christ, made by him in his public character as a legislator, and in the presence of God and man. It in fact comprehends the substance of the religious creed proposed for his subscription by the author of Serious Considerations. And here let me remark a most striking and impressive circumstance: In putting all religions upon the same footing in law, one would have thought that it would have best comported with the impartiality of the act to have done it upon the ground of natural right, moral fitness, and sound policy. If Mr. Jefferson had been a Deist, he would most certainly have proceeded in this way only, but being a christian, he reasons upon the ground of christianity; he appeals to it as the most venerable and conclusive authority, and reprobates persecution, as "*a departure from the plan of the holy author of our religion, who being Lord both of body and mind, yet chose not to propagate it by coercions on either as was in his Almighty power to do.*"

The all-seeing eye of God can alone penetrate into the secret thoughts of men. Professions may be deceitful, and actions may be hypocritical. I have vindicated Mr. Jefferson from the same sources through which he has been attacked, and I feel persuaded that he is a believer. The unaffected warmth of his expressions in favor of religion indicates sincerity, and the whole current of his life strongly corroborates the impression. Exemplary in morals, and performing all the relative and social duties with singular felicity in this licentious age, he is entitled at least to a favorable hearing. Beloved by his family and friends—esteemed by his country—exalted in the ranks of science, and peculiarly distinguished for the liberality of his mind and the benignity of his heart, I feel happy to hail him a *christian.* And let me add as a fact which cannot be controverted, that he has for a long time supported out of his own private revenues, a worthy

minister of the christian church—an instance of liberality not to be met with in any of his rancorous enemies, whose love of religion seems principally to consist in their unremitted endeavors to degrade it into a hand-maid of faction.

No. VI

Addressed to the Author of "Serious Considerations"

Omnes aliud agentes, aliud simulantes, perfidi, improbi, malitiosi sunt.   Cicero

In the course of my strictures I have been compelled to use strong language. It was impossible, sir, to view your pitiful attempt to delude the public mind under the mask of religion, without feeling the keenest emotions of contempt; and it was still more impossible to behold a minister of the Most High God descending from his exalted station, and with polluted hands, offering up sacrifices to the infernal furies of faction, without feeling that contempt ripen into indignation, and without uttering that indignation in the warmest language of the passions. I shall now, sir, enter more fully into the subject, and I entreat you to follow me with patient attention. If it cannot reform your hypocrisy, it may admonish your prudence; and if it should fail in purifying your heart, it may at least clothe you with the decent exteriors of virtue.

It requires but little acquaintance with mankind, to know that it is one of the hackneyed refinements of calumny to preface it with praise—to enumerate certain good qualities, and to regret that they should be accompanied by certain imperfections and defects. This gives an air of candor to the proceeding, and prepares the mind to receive more impressively what is to follow. In your assumed character of a religious man, it was incumbent on you to adopt this line of conduct. If you had in the first instance betrayed the gall of bitterness, the suspicions and jealousies of your readers would have been excited at the commencement of your progress, and have accompanied you in every stage of your career. This you endeavor to avoid,

---

* Appendix to Jefferson's Notes on Virginia, No. 3.

by declaring, that "it is *with pain* you oppose Mr. Jefferson—that you admire his talents, and feel grateful for the services he has been instrumental in rendering to his country—that you have no personal resentment against him, and that you honor him, as holding a high office in government."* But, alas! these vernal blossoms of candor and liberality are quickly blasted. The cloven foot soon makes its appearance. You represent him as an avowed deist; you declare that there is ground *at least* to fix a suspicion of Atheism upon him, and in the plenitude of your charity and wisdom, you denounce his exaltation to the presidency as rebellion against God, and as the harbinger of an endless train of calamities to the religion, morals, and best interests of the country. But why, sir, all this anxiety and concern? Why all these heavy charges? These terrific forebodings? Do they arise from a sincere desire to promote the cause of religion, or are they intended to answer the ends of a party?

You know, sir, that the people of the United States are divided into two great parties; that the most numerous is decidedly in favor of Mr. Jefferson for President; that the real candidate of the other is Mr. Pinckney, and the nominal one Mr. Adams; that the minority despair of carrying their point unless they create a division among the friends of Mr. Jefferson; that it is one of their first and leading wishes to secure the election of Mr. Pinckney; that no other candidate besides Mr. Jefferson can be fixed upon on the republican side with the same chance of success, and without producing a schism; and that the public opinion and public sensibility are now warmly in his favor. The tendency of your pamphlet is, by rendering him odious, to defeat his election, and this is also your avowed design. It therefore embraces a political object; takes the side of a party, and is intended to produce a great political effect. This you will say is a mere incidental circumstance; for, that you employ religious arguments only, and with the sole view of subserving the cause of christianity. If I can prove that this ground is wholly untenable; if I can clearly shew

that you have urged political considerations against his election, in open violation of your solemn declaration to the contrary,[†] then your mask will fall to the ground; your views will be exposed; all your subterfuges destroyed, and your only door of escape from the contempt, will be, in the pity of a generous community.

"Some (you say) may suppose that by the election of Mr. Jefferson we will please the French nation. Were this true, still it would be a question, whether it is prudent to do this without necessity, at the risk of displeasing another nation."[‡]

Here you insinuate strongly that Mr. Jefferson is supported by a French party, and you menace us with the displeasure of Britain, if we presume to elect him. True it is, that you afterwards assume a lofty tone, and tell us your *blood mounts* when you think a moment of either British or French giving your country a President: that you despise their *threats and suspect their caresses.* This gasconade, sir, cannot deceive us; your real meaning was previously declared, and you only introduce it to throw dust into our eyes.

Again you endeavor to represent the great political contest in the United States as a mere struggle for the loaves and fishes. You say, "the outs murmur against the ins; all the expectants of office cannot be gratified. Party is the madness of many for the gain of a few. The gamester always complains that the cards are badly shuffled until he gets a good hand."[§] This attempt, sir, to discredit patriotism, is not novel: it is the language of all tyrants and sycophants. You think if you can make the people believe that there is no essential difference in the political principles of parties, and that it is a mere struggle for power and emolument, they will become indifferent and careless, and be more apt to swallow your calumnies. But, sir, they know better; they feel the effects of the baneful poli-

---

† My objection to his (Mr. Jefferson's) being promoted to the presidency, is founded singly on his disbelief of the Holy Scriptures. Serious Considerations, p. 4.

‡ Page 22.

§ Serious Considerations, p. 31. This allusion is rather light when writing on such a subject. I dare say the parson has *played* in his time, aye, and *shuffled* too.

---

* Serious Considerations, p. 24.

tics of your party, in their consumptions and in their taxes. They see them in the misapplication and waste of the public treasures, in standing armies, navies, alien and sedition acts, and an infamously partial administration of criminal justice; and they recognize them in the unconstitutional extension of the executive powers; in the lofty star-chamber doctrines of *legislative privilege, and in the design,* no longer concealed, of destroying our free constitutions of government, and resorting to hereditary establishments. Tell us not in one breath that *you are not an advocate for Mr. Pinckney and Mr. Adams,* and in the next, that *you believe them irreproachable.** This *hocus pocus* will not answer. The bait is too apparent; the artifice too obvious; the fraud too palpable. You think, sir, even if you have failed in discrediting our politics, that you have atchieved a deed of mighty note, in creating a clashing between our political and religious attachments. You flatter yourself that it will operate like the mixture of an acid and alkali, and produce neutrality; and you most artfully tell us, forsooth, that rather than be instrumental in the election of Mr. Jefferson, it will be *more acceptable to God, and beneficial to the interests of the country, to throw away our votes.*†

This miserable attempt upon our understandings excites pity rather than indignation. If you can prevail upon us to throw away only a few votes, you think the election of Mr. Pinckney secure, and to accomplish this pious object you freely make use of the name of God. The doctrine, that all things are lawful for the saints, and the maxim of the Jesuits, that the end will justify the means, are the grounds upon which you proceed. To set yourself up as the herald of the will of the Almighty, and "to snatch from his hand the balance and the rod," will perhaps serve the cause of your party, and is therefore in your opinion, not only your apology but your incumbent duty.

Conscious that your charges against Mr. Jefferson cannot bear the light of enquiry and the test of argument, you resort to *suspicion* as your dernier strong-

hold. If evidence will not convict, let us only suspect him to be an infidel, and then we ought not to promote his election, "*conscience is not safe while there is a doubt or suspicion.*"‡ Destroyed he must be at all events, and if we cannot conquer him in fair battle, let us take him off by poison or assassination. If argument will not prevail, if evidence should fall short, why, then we must resort to the vagaries of the imagination, and conscience will decide against him, for it prefers the company of suspicion and fancy to the society of reason and evidence. I will venture, sir, to say that this high court of suspicion in which you propose to try Mr. Jefferson, is a tribunal unknown to christianity, to common sense, or common justice. Its model can only be found in the bloody tribunals of the inquisition, or in the infernal judicatory of Rhadamanthus, as described by the poet.

> *Gnossius haec Rhadamanthus habit durissima regna,*
> *Castigatque, auditque dolos, subigitque fateri.*
>
> VIRGIL§

I have now, sir, done with you, I hope for ever—Nothing could have induced me to strip the vizor from your brow, and to expose you in your naked deformity to the public, but an imperious sense of duty and a sincere attachment to my country. Let me intreat you, before we take a final adieu, to consider well the real injury you have done to religion. As poison in certain cases may have a favorable operation in medicine, so, sir, your conduct, detrimental as it is, may not be without its use—it may serve as a beacon to alarm the wavering, and a shade to heighten the lustre of the virtuous. When we turn from you and elevate our view, the barren waste becomes fertile, and the gloomy prospect brightens into sunshine. What a source of heartfelt joy does it afford to behold such characters as a Provost and a Rodgers, a Livingston and a McKnight, a Beach and a Kunzie, a Moore and a Miller, attending to the high behests of their sacred

---

* Vide page 3. Serious Considerations.

† Serious Considerations, p. 30.

‡ Page 30.

§ Rhadamanthus of Crete holds this harsh rule: He punishes, hears lies, and forces confessions. . . . (Virgil's *Aeneid,* bk. VI, ll. 566–67).—Trans.

callings with exemplary purity and fidelity; rendering unto Caesar the things which are Caesar's, and unto God the things which are God's, and maintaining the rights of private opinion, without violating the great duties which they owe to religion. They live enthroned in the affections, and they will die embalmed in the hearts of their countrymen.*—While busy factious and ambitious priests, who degrade themselves into the† Sacheverells of party, must expect and ex-

* Although I speak of these divines from a personal acquaintance, yet as I can never be known to them as the writer of Grotius, I will not be suspected of any impure motive, when I say, that they combine more genuine piety, moral worth, intellectual excellence, literary acquisition and general respectability, than the whole body of political clergymen who have enflamed instead of allaying the deadly animosities which prevail in the community: I know that some of them differ from me in opinion, but I do not respect them the less on that account—Their errors, if I may call them so, are respectable. I shall not wound their feelings by contrasting them with an eastern clergyman who has sounded the political trumpet in the pulpit, in order to excite public curiosity, and thereby reap a more extensive profit from the sale of his sermons—Nor shall I, out of pity, mention the names of some of the divines in this city, who have endeavored to pervert the religious confidence of their flocks into a political ascendancy; and whose audacious intermeddling in our political controversies betrays more of the hardened depravity of age, than of the impetuous spirit of juvenile indiscretion.

† When the tories, in the reign of Queen Ann, wished to eject the whigs from the administration, they employed an inglorious instrument of the name of Sacheverell to preach up *that the church was in danger*. He inflamed the ignorant and deluded populace to an astonishing degree, and was followed by them every where in immense crouds, crying out *High church and Sacheverell forever!* His famous sermon, for which he was impeached, is inserted in the collection of state trials, and is a real curiosity. It has served as a model for, and contains the substance of all *alarum sermons* since delivered. I have carefully compared it with the printed discourses of Dwight, Morse, and other clerical alarmists in this country, and find such a striking resemblance, that I cannot but suspect them of plagiarism. In his dedication to the Lord Mayor of London, he boldly asserts the right of the clergy to preach politics from the pulpit; he says, "We are told by these men who would fain shut both our eyes and our mouths, in order the more effectually to undermine and destroy us, that the pulpit is not a place for politics: and that 'tis the business of a clergyman to preach peace, and not sound a trumpet in Sion, so expressly contrary to the command of God to cry aloud and spare not." He took for his text, "In perils, among false brethren," and every one who did not implicitly embrace the doctrines of the high church, was, according to him, a false brother, if not an Atheist. There is a passage in this sermon so analagous to the calumnies uttered against Mr. Jefferson, upon account of some philosophical opinions, which are not more repugnant to the scriptures than the Copernican system, that I shall now quote it, to shew how the same tricks are attempted, at different times, to be played off upon the public—"Whosoever presumes to recede the least title from the express word of God, or to explain the great CREDENDA of our faith in new fangl'd terms of *modern philosophy*, must publish a new gospel, ungod his Saviour, and de-

perience the debasement of contempt—the severity of indignation—the keenest reproaches of conscience, and the bitterest pangs of remorse.

GROTIUS

The following was intended as a note to refer to the word HERESY *in the 7th page.*

I am sensible that in order to place the subject in the strongest light, I have given too great a latitude to the meaning of *heresy*. In strictness it is applicable to *fundamental* (and some think *wilful*) errors only.

The succeeding note was also designed as a comment on that part of the quotation from "the notes on Virginia" contained in the 18th page, as follows,

stroy his revelation; and, by unsettling the universal receiv'd doctrine of the church, give up christianity into scepticism and atheism, and to speak the least of his character is false both to his God and his religion," &c. The express word of God and the great credenda of our faith, were, with Sacheverell, the doctrines of the high church exclusively. It may serve as an useful lesson to his imitators, to learn that Dean Swift, who was afterwards one of the chief jugglers behind the curtain, represents him in his confidential letters in the most contemptuous point of view. His popularity was owing to the ignorance and bigotry of his hearers. It is to be hoped that his followers here will always find that they address themselves to a liberal and enlightened people; and that at all events they will act agreeably to the excellent sentiment of the Reverend Dr. Linn, who, in a preface to a sermon preached 26th November, 1795, says, "Sufficiently aware that a minister of the gospel ought not to interfere in the politics of any party, he trusts that he has advanced nothing which can be, reasonably, so construed."

The name of Dr. Linn naturally brings to mind another sermon of his entitled "The blessings of America," pronounced on the 4th of July, 1791. In it he observes; "Making due allowance for our age and numbers, we have produced as many eminent men as fall to our share." In a note he fortifies the remark by introducing the authority of Mr. Jefferson in the following manner:—"See this matter fairly and ingeniously stated by Mr. Jefferson in his notes on Virginia. It is, perhaps, not strange that foreigners should inconsiderately adopt prejudices against us; but if there be any who reside in this country, enjoy all the blessings of it, and who, notwithstanding, undervalue what gives them bread and importance, one would hardly know, whether to pity their folly, or to contemn their insolence." If Dr. Linn, eagle-eyed as he is to espy infidelity, had found any irreligious sentiments in this work, certainly he never would have referred to it with approbation nor mentioned the author with respect, particularly in a note to a sermon.

I would not wish to be understood, by any thing I have said, as denying respectable talents to Dr. Dwight—They have, however, been as much over-rated as perverted. I trust I produce a sufficient sample of his christian charity, candor and liberality, when I say that he declared some time ago in this city, that "no honest man could be opposed to the administration of the general government." Of Morse it may be truly said that he is a mere *vox et praeterea nihil* [a voice and nothing else].

viz. "Constraint may make him (i.e. the atheist or polytheist) *worse* by making him a hypocrite but it will never make him a *truer man*. It may fix him obstinately in *his errors* but will not cure them." The conclusion is irresistible, that Mr. Jefferson is of opinion that atheism &c. are not only erroneous, but positively *bad* or *wicked*. How *candid* then is the author of "Serious Considerations" to assert—"But it is a light thing with Mr. Jefferson to say there is no God!"

PRIVATE CORRESPONDENCE

In the midst of the 1800 electoral season and the days that followed, Thomas Jefferson complained bitterly to close friends and political confidants about the unrelenting, ruinous assault on his character that he believed to be directed by the Federalist New England clergy. He complained that his tormentors were unenlightened men who dangerously united the church with the engine of civil government. A September 1800 missive to Dr. Benjamin Rush (1745–1813) is Jefferson's most passionate and famous statement on the interjection of religion into politics. Similar themes were expressed in letters written to political allies shortly after the election.

Letter from Thomas Jefferson to Benjamin Rush

Monticello Sep. 23. 1800

Dear Sir

I have to acknolege the receipt of your favor of Aug. 22. and to congratulate you on the healthiness of your city. still Baltimore, Norfolk & Providence admonish us that we are not clear of our new scourge. when great evils happen, I am in the habit of looking out for what good may arise from them as consolations to us: and Providence has in fact so established the order of things as that most evils are the means of producing some good. the yellow fever will discourage the growth of great cities in our nation; & I view great cities as pestilential to the morals, the health and the liberties of man. true, they nourish some of the elegant arts; but the useful ones can thrive elsewhere, and less perfection in the others with more health virtue & freedom would be my choice.—I agree with you entirely in condemning the mania of giving names to objects of any kind after persons still living. death alone can seal the title of any man to this honour by putting it out of his power to forfeit it. there is one other mode of rewarding merit which I have often thought might be introduced so as to gratify the living by praising the dead. in giving, for instance, a commission of chief justice to Bushrod Washington it should be in consideration of his integrity and science in the laws, and of the services rendered to our country by his illustrious relation &c. a commission to a descendant of Dr Franklin, besides being in consideration of the proper qualifications of the person, should add that of the great services rendered by his illustrious ancestor B. F. by the advancement of science, & by inventions useful to man, &c. I am not sure that we ought to change all our names imposed during the regal government. sometimes indeed they were given through adulation, but often also as the reward of the merit of the times, some-

Reprinted from *The Library of Congress Quarterly Journal of Current Acquisitions* 1, no. 2 (1944): 6–8.

times for services rendered the colony. perhaps too a name when given should be deemed a sacred property.

I promised you a letter on Christianity, which I have not forgotten. on the contrary it is because I have reflected on it, that I find much more time necessary for it than I can at present dispose of. I have a view of the subject which ought to displease neither the rational Christian or Deist; & would reconcile many to a character they have too hastily rejected. I do not know however that it would reconcile the genus irritabile vatum, who are all in arms against me. their hostility is on too interesting ground to be softened. the delusions into which the XYZ plot shewed it possible to push the people, the successful experiment made under the prevalence of that delusion, on the clause of the constitution which while it secured the freedom of the press, covered also the freedom of religion, had given to the clergy a very favorite hope of obtaining an establishment of a particular form of Christianity thro' the US. and as every sect believes it's own form the true one, everyone perhaps hoped for it's own: but especially the Episcopalians & Congregationalists. the returning good sense of our country threatens abortion to their hopes, & they believe that any portion of power confided to me will be exerted in opposition to their schemes. and they believe truly. for I have sworn upon the altar of god eternal hostility against every form of tyranny over the mind of man. but this is all they have to fear from me: & enough too in their opinion; & this is the cause of their printing lying pamphlets against me, forging conversations for me with Mazzei, Bishop Madison &c which are absolute falshoods without a circumstance of truth to rest on; falshoods too of which I acquit Mazzei & Bishop Madison for they are men of truth.—but enough of this. it is more than I have before committed to paper on the subject of all the lies which have been preached or printed against me.—I have not seen the work of Sonnoni which you mention. but I have seen another work on Africa, Parke's, which I fear will throw cold water on the hopes of the friends of freedom. you will have seen an account of an attempt at insurrection in this state. I am looking with anxiety to see what will be it's effect on our state. we are truly to be pitied.—I fear we have little chance to see you at the Federal city or in Virginia, & as little at Philadelphia. it would be a great treat to receive you here. but nothing but sickness could effect that: so I do not wish it: for I wish you health & happiness, and think of you with affection. Adieu.

TH: JEFFERSON

Letter from Thomas Jefferson to Dr. Joseph Priestley

Washington, March 21, 1801

DEAR SIR,—I learned some time ago that you were in Philadelphia, but that it was only for a fortnight; and I supposed you were gone. It was not till yesterday I received information that you were still there, had been very ill, but were on the recovery. I sincerely rejoice that you are so. Yours is one of the few lives precious to mankind, and for the continuance of which every thinking man is solicitous. Bigots may be an exception. What an effort, my dear Sir, of bigotry in politics and religion have we gone through! The barbarians really flattered themselves they should be able to bring back the times of Vandalism, when ignorance put everything into the hands of power and priestcraft. All advances in science were proscribed as innovations. They pretended to praise and encourage education, but it was to be the education of our ancestors. We were to look backwards, not forwards, for improvement; the President himself declaring, in one of his answers to addresses, that we were never to expect to go beyond them in real sci-

Reprinted from *The Writings of Thomas Jefferson*, ed. Andrew A. Lipscomb and Albert Ellery Bergh, Monticello Edition (Washington, D.C.: Thomas Jefferson Memorial Association, 1904), 10:227–30.

ence. This was the real ground of all the attacks on you. Those who live by mystery and *charlatanerie*, fearing you would render them useless by simplifying the Christian philosophy,—the most sublime and benevolent, but most perverted system that ever shone on man,—endeavored to crush your well-earned and well-deserved fame. But it was the Lilliputians upon Gulliver. Our countrymen have recovered from the alarm into which art and industry had thrown them; science and honesty are replaced on their high ground; and you, my dear Sir, as their great apostle, are on its pinnacle. It is with heartfelt satisfaction that, in the first moments of my public action, I can hail you with welcome to our land, tender to you the homage of its respect and esteem, cover you under the protection of those laws which were made for the wise and good like you, and disdain the legitimacy of that libel on legislation, which, under the form of a law, was for some time placed among them.[1]

As the storm is now subsiding, and the horizon becoming serene, it is pleasant to consider the phenomenon with attention. We can no longer say there is nothing new under the sun. For this whole chapter in the history of man is new. The great extent of our republic is new. Its sparse habitation is new. The mighty wave of public opinion which has rolled over it is new. But the most pleasing novelty is, its so quietly subsiding over such an extent of surface to its true level again. The order and good sense displayed in this recovery from delusion, and in the momentous crisis which lately arose, really bespeak a strength of character in our nation which augurs well for the duration of our republic; and I am much better satisfied now of its stability than I was before it was tried. I have been, above all things, solaced by the prospect which opened on us, in the event of a non-election of a President; in which case, the federal government would have been in the situation of a clock or watch run down. There was no idea of force, nor of any occasion for it. A convention, invited by the republican members of Congress, with the virtual President and

Thomas Jefferson, by Gilbert Stuart.
© Burstein Collection/CORBIS.

Vice-President, would have been on the ground in eight weeks, would have repaired the Constitution where it was defective, and wound it up again. This peaceable and legitimate resource, to which we are in the habit of implicit obedience, superseding all appeal to force, and being always within our reach, shows a precious principle of self-preservation in our composition, till a change of circumstances shall take place, which is not within prospect at any definite period.

But I have got into a long disquisition on politics when I only meant to express my sympathy in the state of your health, and to tender you all the affections of public and private hospitality. I should be very happy indeed to see you here. I leave this about the 30th instant, to return about the 25th of April. If you do not leave Philadelphia before that, a little excursion hither would help your health. I should be much gratified with the possession of a guest I so much es-

---

1. In the margin is written by the author, "Alien law."

teem, and should claim a right to lodge you, should you make such an excursion.

Accept the homage of my high consideration and respect, and assurances of affectionate attachment.

Letter from Thomas Jefferson to Moses Robinson

WASHINGTON, March 23, 1801
Dear Sir,—I have to acknowledge the receipt of your favor of the 3d instant, and to thank you for the friendly expressions it contains. I entertain real hope that the whole body of your fellow-citizens (many of whom had been carried away by the x. y. z. business) will shortly be consolidated in the same sentiments. When they examine the real principles of both parties, I think they will find little to differ about. I know, indeed, that there are some of their leaders who have so committed themselves, that pride, if no other passion, will prevent their coalescing. We must be easy with them. The Eastern States will be the last to come over, on account of the dominion of the clergy, who had got a smell of union between Church and State, and began to indulge reveries which can never be realized in the present state of science. If, indeed, they could have prevailed on us to view all advances in science as dangerous innovations, and to look back to the opinions and practices of our forefathers, instead of looking forward, for improvement, a promising ground-work would have been laid. But I am in hopes their good sense will dictate to them, that since the mountain will not come to them, they had better go to the mountain; that they will find their interest in acquiescing in the liberty and science of their country, and that the Christian

Reprinted from *The Writings of Thomas Jefferson,* ed. Andrew A. Lipscomb and Albert Ellery Bergh, Monticello Edition (Washington, D.C.: Thomas Jefferson Memorial Association, 1904), 10:236–37.

religion, when divested of the rags in which they have enveloped it, and brought to the original purity and simplicity of its benevolent institutor, is a religion of all others most friendly to liberty, science, and the freest expansion of the human mind.

I sincerely wish with you, we could see our government so secured as to depend less on the character of the person in whose hands it is trusted. Bad men will sometimes get in, and with such an immense patronage, may make great progress in corrupting the public mind and principles. This is a subject with which wisdom and patriotism should be occupied.

I pray you to accept assurances of my high respect and esteem.

Letter from Abigail Adams to Thomas Jefferson (July 1, 1804)

In May 1804, Abigail Adams (1744–1818) wrote to President Thomas Jefferson, the man who had defeated her husband in the election of 1800, expressing condolences on the death of his daughter, Mary Jefferson Eppes (1778–1804). This initiated an exchange of correspondence in the ensuing months that soon shifted from family matters to a frank airing of grievances arising from the acrimonious presidential contest four years earlier. Mrs. Adams sharply criticized Jefferson for financially assisting and pardoning James Thomson Callender (1758–1803), a Scottish immigrant and partisan pamphleteer who had been fined and imprisoned in 1800 under the Sedition Act for his rabid attacks on President Adams and other Federalists. (Callender later turned against Jefferson, disseminating rumors that the Virginian had fathered

Reprinted from *The Adams-Jefferson Letters: The Complete Correspondence between Thomas Jefferson and Abigail and John Adams,* ed. Lester J. Cappon (Chapel Hill and London: University of North Carolina Press, 1959/ 1987), 271–74. © 1959 by the University of North Carolina Press, renewed in 1987 by Stanley B. Cappon. Used by permission of the publisher.

children with one of his slaves.) Mrs. Adams's poignant missive of July 1, 1804, revealed that wounds from the bruising campaign had not yet healed.

Quincy July 1st 1804

SIR

Your Letter of June 13th came duly to hand; if it had contained no other sentiments and opinions than those which my Letter of condolence could have excited, and which are expressed in the first page of your reply, our correspondence would have terminated here: but you have been pleased to enter upon some subjects which call for a reply: and as you observe that you have wished for an opportunity to express your sentiments, I have given to them every weight they claim.

"One act of Mr. Adams's Life, and *one* only, you repeat, ever gave me a moments personal displeasure. I did think his last appointments to office personally unkind. They were from among my most ardent political enemies."

As this act I am certain was not intended to give any personal pain or offence, I think it a duty to explain it so far as I then knew his views and designs. The constitution empowers the president to fill up offices as they become vacant. It was in the exercise of this power that appointments were made, and Characters selected whom Mr. Adams considered, as men faithfull to the constitution and where he personally knew them, such as were capable of fullfilling their duty to their country. This was done by president Washington equally, in the last days of his administration so that not an office remaind vacant for his successor to fill upon his comeing into the office. No offence was given by it, and no personal unkindness thought of. But the different political opinions which have so unhappily divided our Country, must have given rise to the Idea, that personal unkindness was intended. You will please to recollect Sir, that at the time these appointments were made, there was

not any certainty that the presidency would devolve upon you, which is an other circumstance to prove that personal unkindness was not meant. No person was ever selected by him from such a motive—and so far was Mr. Adams from indulging such a sentiment, that he had no Idea of the intollerance of party spirit at that time, and I know it was his opinion that if the presidency devolved upon you, except in the appointment of Secretaries, no material Changes would be made. I perfectly agree with you in opinion that those should be Gentlemen in whom the president can repose confidence, possessing opinions, and sentiments corresponding with his own, or if differing from him, that they ought rather to resign their office, than cabal against measures which he may think essential to the honour safety and peace of the Country. Much less should they unite, with any bold, and dareingly ambitious Character, to over rule the Cabinet, or betray the Secrets of it to Friends or foes. The two Gentlemen who held the offices of secretaries, when you became president were not of this Character. They were appointed by your predecessor nearly two years previous to his retirement. They were Gentlemen who had cordially co-opperated with him, and enjoyed the public confidence. Possessing however different political sentiments from those which you were known to have embraced, it was expected that they would, as they did, resign.

I have never felt any enmity towards you Sir for being elected president of the United States. But the instruments made use of, and the means which were practised to effect a change, have my utter abhorrence and detestation, for they were the blackest calumny, and foulest falshoods. I had witnessed enough of the anxiety, and solicitude, the envy jealousy and reproach attendant upon the office as well as the high responsibility of the Station, to be perfectly willing to see a transfer of it. And I can truly say, that at the time of Election, I considered your pretentions much superior to his [Mr. Burr's], to whom an equal vote was given. Your experience I venture to affirm has convinced you that it is not a station to be envy'd. If you feel yourself a free man, and can act in all cases, according to your own sentiments, opinions and judgment, you can do more than either of your predecessors could, and are awfully responsible to God and your Country for the measures of your Administration. I rely upon the Friendship you still profess for me, and (I am conscious I have done nothing to forfeit it), to excuse the freedom of this discussion to which you have led with an unreserve, which has taken off the Shackles I should otherways have found myself embarrassed with.—And now Sir I will freely disclose to you what has severed the bonds of former Friendship, and placed you in a light very different from what I once viewd you in.

One of the first acts of your administration was to liberate a wretch who was suffering the just punishment of the Law due to his crimes for writing and publishing the basest libel, the lowest and vilest Slander, which malice could invent, or calumny exhibit against the Character and reputation of your predecessor, of him for whom you profest the highest esteem and Friendship, and whom you certainly knew incapable of such complicated baseness. The remission of Callenders fine was a public approbation of his conduct. Is not the last restraint of vice, a sense of shame, renderd abortive, if abandoned Characters do not excite abhorrence. If the chief Majestrate of a Nation, whose elevated Station places him in a conspicuous light, and renders his every action a concern of general importance, permits his public conduct to be influenced by private resentment, and so far forgets what is due to his Character as to give countanance to a base Calumniater, is he not answerable for the influence which his example has upon the manners and morals of the community?

Untill I read Callenders seventh Letter containing your compliment to him as a writer and your reward of 50 dollars, I could not be made to believe, that such measures could have been resorted to: to stab the fair fame and upright intentions of one, who to use your own Language "was acting from an honest conviction in his own mind that he was right." This Sir I considerd as a personal injury. This was the Sword that cut assunder the Gordian knot, which could not be

untied by all the efforts of party Spirit, by rivalship by Jealousy or any other malignant fiend.

The serpent you cherished and warmed, bit the hand that nourished him, and gave you sufficient Specimens of his talents, his gratitude his justice, and his truth. When such vipers are let lose upon Society, all distinction between virtue and vice are levelled, all respect for Character is lost in the overwhelming deluge of calumny—that respect which is a necessary bond in the social union, which gives efficacy to laws, and teaches the subject to obey the Majestrate, and the child to submit to the parent.

There is one other act of your administration which I considerd as personally unkind, and which your own mind will readily suggest to you, but as it neither affected character, or reputation, I forbear to state it.

This Letter is written in confidence—no eye but my own has seen what has passed. Faithfull are the wounds of a Friend. Often have I wished to have seen a different course pursued by you. I bear no malice I cherish no enmity. I would not retaliate if I could— nay more in the true spirit of christian Charity, I would forgive, as I hope to be forgiven. And with that disposition of mind and heart, I subscribe the Name of

ABIGAIL ADAMS

Letter from John Adams to Benjamin Rush (June 12, 1812)

In a letter to Dr. Benjamin Rush (1745–1813), written long after he left public office, John Adams mused that his presidential appointment of days for "humiliation, fasting, and prayer" had been used by po-

Reprinted from *The Spur of Fame: Dialogues of John Adams and Benjamin Rush, 1805–1813,* ed. John A. Schutz and Douglass Adair (San Marino, Calif.: Huntington Library, 1966), 224, 226. © Huntington Library, 1966. Reprinted with the permission of the Henry E. Huntington Library.

litical adversaries to depict him erroneously as a proponent of the establishment of a national church. This proved to be an effective tactic in denying him the political support of Americans who feared and disapproved of religious establishments and, ultimately, he reported, cost him the election of 1800.

─────────────────

June 12, 1812

DEAR SIR,

. . . I agree with you, there is a germ of religion in human nature so strong that whenever an order of men can persuade the people by flattery or terror that they have salvation at their disposal, there can be no end to fraud, violence, or usurpation. Ecumenical councils produce ecumenical bishops, and both, subservient armies, emperors, and kings.

The national fast recommended by me turned me out of office. It was connected with the General Assembly of the Presbyterian Church which I had no concern in. That Assembly has alarmed and alienated Quakers, Anabaptists, Mennonites, Moravians, Swedenborgians, Methodists, Catholics, Protestant Episcopalians, Arians, Socinians, Arminians, &c., ... A general suspicion prevailed that the Presbyterian Church was ambitious and aimed at an establishment as a national church. I was represented as a Presbyterian and at the head of this political and ecclesiastical project. The secret whisper ran through all the sects, "Let us have Jefferson, Madison, Burr, anybody, whether they be philosophers, Deists, or even atheists, rather than a Presbyterian President." This principle is at the bottom of the unpopularity of national fasts and thanksgivings. Nothing is more dreaded than the national government meddling with religion. This wild letter, I very much fear, contains seeds of an ecclesiastical history of the U.S. for a century to come.

I recollect a little sparring between Jefferson and me on some religious subject, not ill-natured, however, but have forgotten the time and the particular subject. I wish you would give me the circumstances of the whole anecdote. . . .

I must come to an end of my letter, though I shall never find an end of my regards to Mrs. Rush or her husband notwithstanding her just admonition to the incurable, incorrigible scribbler.

John Adams

RECOMMENDATIONS FOR FURTHER READING

Lambert, Frank. "'God—and a Religious President . . . [or] Jefferson and No God': Campaigning for a Voter-Imposed Religious Test in 1800." *Journal of Church and State* 39 (1997): 769–89.

Lerche, Charles O., Jr. "Jefferson and the Election of 1800: A Case Study in the Political Smear." *William and Mary Quarterly*, 3d ser., 5 (1948): 467–91.

Luebke, Fred C. "The Origins of Thomas Jefferson's Anti-Clericalism." *Church History* 32 (1963): 344–56.

McDonald, Robert M. S. "Was There a Religious Revolution of 1800?" In *The Revolution of 1800: Democracy, Race, and the New Republic*, edited by James Horn, Jan Ellen Lewis, and Peter S. Onuf, 173–98. Charlottesville: University of Virginia Press, 2002.

O'Brien, Charles F. "The Religious Issue in the Presidential Campaign of 1800." *Essex Institute Historical Collections* 107, no. 1 (1971): 82–93.

CHAPTER TWELVE

Thomas Jefferson and the "Wall of Separation"

AMONG THE MOST influential expressions in American church-state discourse are "separation of church and state" and its attendant metaphoric formulation of a "wall of separation between church and state." Although the wall of separation metaphor has been a part of church-state discourse since at least the Protestant Reformation, it is today generally attributed to the pen of Thomas Jefferson. The First Amendment to the U.S. Constitution, Jefferson wrote in an 1802 missive to a Connecticut Baptist association, had built a "wall of separation between Church & State."

The wall of separation is accepted by many Americans as a concise description of the constitutional principles governing church-state relations. Since the mid-twentieth century, many jurists have adopted the figurative phrase as the organizing theme of church-state jurisprudence, even though it is not found in the text of the U.S. Constitution. When asked, in *Everson v. Board of Education* (1947), to interpret the First Amendment's prohibition on laws "respecting an establishment of religion," Justice Hugo L. Black, writing for the U.S. Supreme Court, opined: "In the words of Jefferson, the clause against establishment of religion by law was intended to erect 'a wall of separation between church and State.' . . . That wall must be kept high and impregnable." In *McCollum v. Board of Education* (1948), the following

judicial term, the Supreme Court revealed the extent to which it had constitutionalized the wall metaphor: "The majority in the *Everson* case, and the minority . . . , agreed that the First Amendment's language, properly interpreted, had erected a wall of separation between Church and State."

This controversial trope has been endorsed by proponents of a prudential and constitutional separation between the concerns of religion and the civil state and denounced by those who oppose the secularization of public life and believe religion must play a vital role in civic matters. Antagonists have long debated what exactly the wall separates, and whether the U.S. Constitution compels the erection of a wall of separation. Is there a constitutional wall that requires a complete separation between religion and public life, or is there a wall that merely recommends a separation between the institutions of a particular church and the civil state? Still others suggest that, as a matter of federalism, Jefferson deliberately erected his wall between the national and state governments on matters pertaining to religion (such as religious day proclamations) and not, more generally, between religion and *all* civil government.

Some advocates for a separating wall argue that it promotes private, voluntary religion and freedom of conscience in a secular polity. A wall prevents reli-

gious establishments and other forms of government assistance for religious objectives and avoids conflict among denominations competing for government favor and aid. A regime of strict separation, defenders contend, is the best, if not the only, way to promote religious liberty, especially the rights of religious minorities.

Critics counter that reliance on an extraconstitutional metaphor almost inevitably distorts constitutional principles governing church-state relationships. A complete or absolute separation is neither mandated by the Constitution nor possible to achieve. Opponents argue that a wall redefines First Amendment principles. Jefferson's trope emphasizes *separation* between church and state—unlike the First Amendment, which speaks in terms of the nonestablishment and free exercise of religion. Moreover, a wall is a bilateral barrier that inhibits the activities of both the civil government and religion—unlike the First Amendment, which imposes restrictions on civil government only. A wall of separation, critics conclude, excludes religious perspectives and citizens from public affairs and restricts religion's ability to influence public life, thus exceeding the limitations imposed by the Constitution.

The wall of separation continues to be a frequently referenced, yet controversial, figurative phrase in popular, political, and legal discourse.

ROOTS OF THE METAPHOR

Although Thomas Jefferson is widely credited with coining the wall of separation metaphor, he was not the first to use it. Examples of the metaphor's use in a church-state context can be found in Western literature as early as the Protestant Reformation. The sixteenth-century Anglican theologian Richard Hooker (1554–1600) denounced the erection of "walles of separation between . . . the *Church* and the *Commonwealth*" that prevented a Christian king from exercising leadership over both corporations. The seventeenth-century founder of Rhode Island, Roger Williams (1603?–83), supported a "hedge or wall of separation between the garden of the church and the wilderness of the world" to safeguard the religious purity of Christ's church from corrupting external influences. The eighteenth-century Scottish dissenter James Burgh (1714–75), whose writings influenced political thought in revolutionary America, proposed building "an impenetrable wall of *separation* between things *sacred* and *civil*" to avoid the ecclesiastical corruption that he thought inevitably arises from granting a church the exclusive, legal favor of the civil state.

Of the Laws of Ecclesiastical Polity (1590s)

RICHARD HOOKER (1554–1600)

Book VIII, Chapter 1, Section 2
An Admonition Concerning Men's Judgements
About the Question of Regal Power

According to the pattern of which example the like power in causes *Ecclesiastical* is by the laws of this Realm annexed unto the *Crown*. And there are which imagine, that kings being mere lay persons, do by this means exceed the lawful bounds of their calling. Which thing to the end that they may persuade, they first make a necessary separation perpetual and personal between the *Church* and *Commonwealth*. Secondly they so tie all kind of power *Ecclesiastical* unto the *Church* as if it were in every degree their only right, which are by proper spiritual function termed *Church-Governors* and might not to *Christian Princes* any wise appertain. To lurk under shifting ambiguities and equivocations of words in matters of principal weight is childish. A *Church* and a *Commonwealth* we grant are things in nature the one distinguished from the other, a *Commonwealth* is one way, and a *Church* another way defined. In their opinion the *Church* and the *Commonwealth* are corporations not distinguished only in nature and definition, but in subsistence perpetually severed, so that they that are of the one can neither appoint, nor execute in whole nor in part the duties which belong unto them, which are of the other, without open breach of the law of *God*, which hath divided them, and doth require that being so divided they should distinctly and severally work as depending both upon *God* and

Bk. VIII, chap. 1, sec. 2, reprinted from *Of the Laws of Ecclesiastical Polity*, ed. A. S. McGrade (Cambridge, U.K.: Cambridge University Press, 1989), 129–31, which was reprinted by permission of the publishers from The Folger Library Edition of *The Works of Richard Hooker*, vol. 3, *Of the Laws of Ecclesiastical Polity*, ed. P. G. Stanwood (Cambridge, Mass.: The Belknap Press of Harvard University Press, 1981). © 1981 by the President and Fellows of Harvard College.

not hanging one upon the other's approbation for that which either hath to do.

We say that the care of religion being common unto all *Societies* politic, such *Societies* as do embrace the true religion, have the name of the *Church* given unto every of them for distinction from the rest. So that every body politic hath some religion, but the *Church* that religion, which is only true. Truth of religion is that proper difference, whereby a *Church* is distinguished from other politic societies of men. We here mean true religion in gross, and not according to every particular for they which in some particular points of religion do swerve from the truth, may nevertheless most truly, if we compare them to men of an heathenish religion, be said to hold and profess that religion which is true. For which cause there being of old so many politic *Societies* established throughout the world only the *Commonwealth* of *Israel* which had the truth of religion, was in that respect the *Church* of *God.* And the *Church* of *Jesus Christ* is every such politic society of men as doth in religion hold that truth which is proper to *Christianity.* As a politic *Society* it doth maintain religion; as a *Church* that religion which *God* hath revealed by *Jesus Christ.* With us therefore the name of a *Church* importeth only a *Society* of men first united into some public form of regiment and secondly distinguished from other *Societies,* by the exercise of *Christian* religion. With them on the other side the name of the *Church* in this present question importeth not only a multitude of men, so united and so distinguished, but also further the same divided necessarily and perpetually from the body of the *Commonwealth.* So that even in such a politic *Society,* as consisteth of none but *Christians,* yet the *Church* of *Christ* and the *Commonwealth* are two corporations independently each subsisting by itself. We hold that seeing there is not any man of the *Church* of *England,* but the same man is also a member of the *Commonwealth,* nor any man a member of the *Commonwealth* which is not also of the *Church* of *England,* therefore as in a figure *triangular* the base doth differ from the sides thereof, and yet one and the selfsame line, is both a base and

also a side; a side simply, a base if it chance to be the bottom and underlie the rest: So albeit properties and actions of one kind do cause the name of a Commonwealth, qualities and functions of another sort the name of a *Church* to be given unto a multitude, yet one and the selfsame multitude may in such sort be both and is so with us, that no person appertaining to the one can be denied to be also of the other. Contrariwise (unless they against us should hold that the *Church* and the *Commonwealth* are two both distinct and separate societies, of which two the one comprehendeth always persons not belonging to the other) that which they do, they could not conclude out of the difference between the *Church* and the *Commonwealth;* namely, that *Bishops* may not meddle with the affairs of the commonwealth because they are governors of another corporation, which is the *Church,* nor *Kings,* with making laws for the *Church* because they have government not of this corporation, but of another divided from it, the *Commonwealth,* and the walls of separation between these two must forever be upheld. They hold the necessity of personal separation which clean excludeth the power of one man's dealing in both, we of natural which doth not hinder, but that one and the same person may in both bear a principal sway.

Mr. Cottons Letter Lately Printed, Examined and Answered (1644)

ROGER WILLIAMS (1603? – 1683)

The faithfull labours of many Witnesses of *Iesus Christ,* extant to the world, abundantly proving, that the Church of the Jews under the Old Testament in the type, and the *Church* of the Christians under the

Excerpt reprinted from *The Complete Writings of Roger Williams,* ed. Reuben Aldridge Guild (New York: Russell & Russell, 1963), 1:392.

New Testament in the Antitype, were both separate from the world; and that when they have opened a gap in the hedge or wall of Separation between the Garden of the Church and the Wildernes of the world, God hath ever broke down the wall it selfe, removed the Candlestick, &c. and made his Garden a Wildernesse, as at this day. And that therfore if he will ever please to restore his Garden and Paradice again, it must of necessitie be walled in peculiarly unto himselfe from the world, and that all that shall be saved out of the world are to be transplanted out of the Wildernes of world, and added unto his Church or Garden. . . .

Crito, or Essays on Various Subjects (1767)

JAMES BURGH (1714–75)

Let nobody persuade you, that *exposing* the *dissimulation* of your *clergy* (if they be found guilty of dissimulation in the matter of subscription) is wounding *religion*. That is no better than stale and baffled cant; which ought to be beneath the attention of your enlightened times. On the contrary, the detection of dissemblers, of *whatever denomination*, is taking the part of *truth* against her worst *enemies;* which is the indispensable *duty* of every wise and good man. With a very ill grace, therefore, will your trimming clergy, if any such you have among you, pretend to lament the *decay* of *virtue* and *religion* among the *people;* while they *themselves*, by their scandalous dissimulation, set so execrable an *example;* giving the laity reason to suspect, that they are ready to declare assent and consent, to whatever is, by *authority*, proposed to them, how little soever they may *believe* of it.

Do not set up a scheme for *worldly* honours and advantages, a system of posts, places, and preferments, to be given to those who make a *trade of religion*, by those who *have no religion*, and call this worldly scheme a *holy church*.

A church is nothing more than a community of persons united together in affection and esteem, by their holding the same religion, and stands wholly unconnected with *secular* concerns. The combination of a sett of idle and greedy men, who, supported by *power*, set themselves up for *lords* over the *consciences* of others, and who unite together, under the pretext of being religious *rulers*, for carrying on a sordid plan of *power* and *riches;* is an execrable *conspiracy*, which all friends of mankind ought to join together to *overturn* from the *foundation*.

No matter from what precedents I draw my conclusions; but I will fairly tell you what will be the consequences of your setting up such a mixed-mungrel-spiritual-temporal-secular-ecclesiastical establishment. You will make the dispensers of religion *despicable* and *odious* to all men of sense, and will destroy the *spirituality*, in which consists the whole *value*, of religion. If you should cloath your bishops in lawn, from head to foot, people of true piety will cry, "Shame on those men, who have perverted what was, by its heavenly Author, intended for *disengaging* mankind from riches, honours, and pleasures, to a trade in all that is sordid and luxurious! Wo be to those, who pretend to call themselves the *authorised successors* of him, who had not where to *lay his head,* and demand, as their hire for preaching, or for neglecting to preach, his pure religion, the revenues of *princes*. Ill fare those worthless worldly men, who, instead of leading the people, both by doctrine and example, to lay up for themselves treasures in heaven, and not on earth; set them the example of adding field to field, and sum to sum, while the poor are in want of bread*."

---

* It must be only *R. Catholic* bishops, the author means to reflect on. For our *English* Fathers of the church are notoriously of a contrary disposition. Accordingly two of those respectable persons, who died lately, left no more than three hundred thousand pounds to their heirs.

Reprinted from [James Burgh], *Crito, or, Essays on Various Subjects, vol. 2. and Last* (London: Dodsley et al., 1767), 115–21.

Shew yourselves superior to all these follies and knaveries. Put into the hands of the *people* the clerical emoluments; and let them give them to whom they will; *choosing* their public teachers, and maintaining them decently, but *moderately,* as becomes their *spiritual* character. We have in our times a proof, from the conduct of some among us, in respect of the appointment of their public administrators of religion, that such a scheme will answer all the necessary purposes, and prevent infinite corruption;—*ecclesiastical* corruption; the most odious of all corruption.

Build an impenetrable wall of *separation* between things *sacred* and *civil.* Do not send a *graceless* officer, reeking from the arms of his *trull,* to the performance of a *holy* rite of *religion,* as a *test* for his holding the command of a regiment. To *profane,* in such a manner, a religion, which you pretend to *reverence;* is an impiety sufficient to bring down upon your heads, the roof of the sacred building you thus defile.

If your leading men be not the great *encouragers* and *examples* of political wisdom, of sincere religion, and true virtue, but, on the contrary, the chief *tempters* of your people to debauchery and perjury; and the most notorious *despisers* and *mockers* at whatever is honourable, and whatever is sacred, I shall not think much more highly of you, than of the people of a certain distinguished age, which shall be nameless. Yet you ought to consider, that you will have a couple of centuries advantage of us, besides that of the many useful *lessons* we have set you, by our blunders, and our knaveries, the *number* of which, you must own, is not small; nor the edification you may, with a little attention, obtain from the observation of their *effects* on us, and the state, in our times, inconsiderable. I hope, therefore, you will remember, that you will have more to answer for, than we shall, and that you will behave accordingly. . . .

Your *sincere* friend,
CRITO

JEFFERSON AND THE "WALL OF SEPARATION" METAPHOR

The Danbury Baptist Association was an alliance of approximately two dozen churches located primarily in the Connecticut Valley. The Baptists perceived themselves to be a persecuted religious minority in a state that retained legal privileges for the officially established Congregational Church. In October 1801, the Danbury Baptists wrote to President Thomas Jefferson congratulating him on his recent election to the "chief Magistracy in the United States" and commending his long-standing commitment to religious liberty. They hoped President Jefferson would bring to the entire nation the same zeal for religious liberty that he had exhibited in his native Virginia. Jefferson responded with a letter written on January 1, 1802, in which he famously stated that the First Amendment had built a "wall of separation between Church & State." The following documents are the Danbury Baptist Association's letter to President Jefferson; correspondence between the president and Attorney General Levi Lincoln (1749–1820) and Postmaster General Gideon Granger (1767–1822), Jefferson's two cabinet members from New England, in which the president solicited political advice on the content of his reply to the Connecticut Baptists; and the final text of Jefferson's address to the Danbury Baptist Association.

Letter from Danbury Baptist Association to Thomas Jefferson (October 7, 1801)

The Address of the Danbury Baptist Association, in the State of Connecticut; Assembled October 7th. AD 1801.

To *Thomas Jefferson* ESQ. President of the united States of America.

Sir,

Among the many millions in America and Europe who rejoice in your Election to office; we embrace the first opportunity which we have enjoy'd in our collective capacity, since your Inauguration, to express our great satisfaction, in your appointment to the chief Magistracy in the United States: And though our mode of expression may be less courtly and pompious than what many others clothe their addresses with, we beg you, Sir to believe, that none are more sincere.

Our Sentiments are uniformly on the side of Religious Liberty—That Religion is at all times and places a Matter between God and Individuals—That no man ought to suffer in Name, person or effects on account of his religious Opinions—That the legitimate Power of civil Government extends no further than to punish the man who *works ill to his neighbour:* But Sir. our constitution of government is not specific. Our antient charter, together with the Laws made coincident therewith, were adopted as the Basis of our government, At the time of our revolution; and such had been our Laws & usages, & such still are; that Religion is consider'd as the first object of Legislation; & therefore what religious privileges we enjoy (as a minor part of the State) we enjoy as favors granted, and not as inalienable rights: and these favors we receive at the expence of such degrading acknowledgements, as are inconsistent with the rights of fre[e]men. It is not to be wondered at therefore; if

those, who seek after *power* & *gain* under the pretence *of government* & *Religion* should reproach their fellow men—should reproach their chief Magistrate, as an enemy of religion Law & good order because he will not, dares not assume the prerogative of Jehovah and make Laws to govern the Kingdom of Christ.

Sir, we are sensible that the President of the united States, is not the national Legislator, & also sensible that the national government cannot destroy the Laws of each State; but our hopes are strong that the sentiments of our beloved President, which have had such genial Effect already, like the radiant beams of the Sun, will shine & prevail through all these States and all the world till Hierarchy and tyranny be destroyed from the Earth. Sir, when we reflect on your past services, and see a glow of philanthropy and good will shining forth in a course of more than thirty years we have reason to believe that America's God has raised you up to fill the chair of State out of that good will which he bears to the Millions which you preside over. May God strengthen you for the arduous task which providence & the voice of the people have cal'd you to sustain and support you in your Administration against all the predetermin'd opposition of those who wish to rise to wealth & importance on the poverty and subjection of the people———

And may the Lord preserve you safe from every evil and bring you at last to his Heavenly Kingdom through Jesus Christ our Glorious Mediator.

Signed in behalf of the Association,
    Neh'h Dodge   )
    Ephm Robbins   )   The Committee
    Stephen S. Nelson)

Transcribed by the editors from Library of Congress originals.

Letter from Thomas Jefferson to Attorney General Levi Lincoln (January 1, 1802)

Th: J. to mr. Lincoln

Averse to receive addresses, yet unable to prevent them, I have generally endeavored to turn them to some account, by making them the occasion, by way of answer, of sowing useful truths & principles among the people, which might germinate and become rooted among their political tenets. the Baptist address now inclosed admits of a condemnation of the alliance between church and state, under the authority of the Constitution. it furnishes an occasion too, which I have long wished to find, of saying why I do not proclaim fastings & thanksgivings, as my predecessors did. the address to be sure does not point at this, and it's introduction is awkward. but I foresee no opportunity of doing it more pertinently. I know it will give great offence to the New England clergy: but the advocate for religious freedom is to expect neither peace nor forgiveness from them. will you be so good as to examine the answer and suggest any alterations which might prevent an ill effect, or promote a good one among *the people?* you understand the temper of those in the North, and can weaken it therefore to their stomachs: it is at present seasoned to the Southern taste only. I would ask the favor of you to return it with the address in the course of the day or evening. health & affection.

Jan. 1. 1802

Letter from Attorney General Levi Lincoln to Thomas Jefferson (January 1, 1802)

The President) Jany 1s. 1802—
of the U. States)

Sir I have carefully considered the subject you did me the honor of submiting to my attention. The people of the five N England Governments (unless Rhode Island is an exception) have always been in the habit of observing fasts and thanksgivings in performance of proclamations from their respective Executives. This custom is venerable being handed down from our ancestors. The Republicans of those States generally have a respect for it. They regreted very much the late conduct of the legislature of Rhode Island on this subject. I think the religious sentiment expressed in your proposed answer of importance to be communicated, but that it would be best to have it so guarded, as to be incapable of having it construed into an implied censure of the usages of any of the States. Perhaps the following alteration after the words "but subject here" would be sufficient, vis [?], only to the voluntary regulations & discipline of each respective sect, as mere religious exercises, and to the particular situations, usages & recommendations of the several States, in point of time & local circumstances. With the highest esteem & respect.

yours, Levi Lincoln

Letter from Postmaster General Gideon Granger to Thomas Jefferson (December 1801)

G. Granger presents his compliments to The Presidt. and assures him he has carefully & attentively perused the inclosed Address & Answer—The answer will undoubtedly give great Offence to the established Clergy of New England while it will delight the Dissenters as they are called. It is but a declaration of Truths which are in fact felt [held?] by a great Majority of New England, & publicly acknowledged by near half of the People of Connecticut; It may however occasion a temporary Spasm among the Established Religionists yet his mind approves of it, because it will "germinate among the People" and in time fix "their political Tenets"—He cannot therefore wish a Sentence changed, or a Sentiment expressed equivocally—A more fortunate time can never be expected.————

Transcribed by the editors from Library of Congress originals.

Letter from Thomas Jefferson to Messrs. Nehemiah Dodge, Ephraim Robbins, and Stephen S. Nelson (January 1, 1802) (final version)

To messrs. Nehemiah Dodge, Ephraim Robbins, & Stephen S. Nelson, a committee of the Danbury Baptist association in the state of Connecticut.

Gentlemen

The affectionate sentiments of esteem and approbation which you are so good as to express towards me, on behalf of the Danbury Baptist association, give me the highest satisfaction. my duties dictate a

Transcribed by the editors from Library of Congress originals.

faithful & zealous pursuit of the interests of my constituents, & in proportion as they are persuaded of my fidelity to those duties, the discharge of them becomes more and more pleasing.

Believing with you that religion is a matter which lies solely between Man & his God, that he owes account to none other for his faith or his worship, that the legitimate* powers of government reach actions only, & not opinions, I contemplate with sovereign reverence that act of the whole American people which declared that *their* legislature should "make no law respecting an establishment of religion, or prohibiting the free exercise thereof,"† thus building a wall of separation between Church & State. adhering to this expression of the supreme will of the nation in behalf of the rights of conscience, I shall see with sincere satisfaction the progress of those sentiments which tends to restore to man all his natural rights, convinced he has no natural right in opposition to his social duties.

I reciprocate your kind prayers for the protection & blessing of the common father and creator of man, and tender you for yourselves & your religious association, assurances of my high respect & esteem.

Th: Jefferson
Jan. 1. 1802

---

* Most published collections of Jefferson's writings incorrectly transcribed this word as "legislative." The mistranscription apparently originated from *The Writings of Thomas Jefferson*, ed. H. A. Washington, 9 vols. (Washington, D.C.: Taylor and Maury, 1853–54), 8:113–14.—Eds.

† U.S. Constitution, Amend. I.—Eds.

To mess^{rs.} Nehemiah Dodge, Ephraim Robbins, & Stephen S. Nelson a committee of the Danbury Baptist association in the state of Connecticut.

Gentlemen

The affectionate sentiments of esteem & approbation which you are so good as to express towards me, on behalf of the Danbury Baptist association, give me the highest satisfaction. my duties dictate a faithful & zealous pursuit of the interests of my constituents, and in proportion as they are persuaded of my fidelity to those duties, the discharge of them becomes more & more pleasing.

Believing with you that religion is a matter which lies solely between man & his god, that he owes account to none other for his faith or his worship, that the legitimate powers of government reach actions only and not opinions, I contemplate with sovereign reverence that act of the whole American people which declared that their legislature should make no law respecting an establishment of religion, or prohibiting the free exercise thereof, thus building a wall of eternal separation between church and state. Congress thus inhibited from acts respecting religion, and the Executive authorised only to execute their acts, I have refrained from prescribing even those occasional performances of devotion prescribed indeed legally where an Executive is the legal head of a national church, but subject here, as religious exercises only to the voluntary regulations and discipline of each respective sect. adhering to this expression of the supreme will of the nation in behalf of the rights of conscience, I shall see with sincere satisfaction the progress of those sentiments which tend to restore to man all his natural rights, convinced he has no natural right in opposition to his social duties.

I reciprocate your kind prayers for the protection and blessing of the common father and creator of man, and tender you for yourselves and your religious association, assurances of my high respect & esteem.

Th Jefferson
Jan. 1. 1802.

20593

(265)

UNDERSTANDING
JEFFERSON'S METAPHOR

In his letter to Attorney General Levi Lincoln (1749–1820), President Thomas Jefferson stated that his response to the Danbury Baptist Association "furnishes an occasion too, which I have long wished to find, of saying why I do not proclaim fastings & thanksgivings, as my predecessors [presidents George Washington and John Adams] did." The president was eager to address this controversial topic because in the early days of his administration political opponents had demanded religious proclamations and then denounced him as an enemy of religion when he declined to issue them. On at least two other occasions during his presidency, Jefferson addressed this same controversy: his second inaugural address in March 1805 and a letter to the Reverend Samuel Miller (1769–1850) in 1808. These two statements, which offer commentary on the subject matter of Jefferson's missive to the Danbury Baptists, indicate that, as a matter of federalism, he concluded that authority to issue religious proclamations was not delegated to the nation's chief executive but was retained by state officials and private societies.

Thomas Jefferson, Second Inaugural Address (March 4, 1805)

In matters of religion, I have considered that its free exercise is placed by the constitution independent of the powers of the general [i.e., federal] government. I have therefore undertaken, on no occasion, to prescribe the religious exercises suited to it; but have left them, as the constitution found them, under the direction and discipline of State or Church authorities acknowledged by the several religious societies. . . .

I shall now enter on the duties to which my fellow citizens have again called me, and shall proceed in the spirit of those principles which they have approved. I fear not that any motives of interest may lead me astray; I am sensible of no passion which could seduce me knowingly from the path of justice; but the weakness of human nature, and the limits of my own understanding, will produce errors of judgment sometimes injurious to your interests. I shall need, therefore, all the indulgence I have heretofore experienced—the want of it will certainly not lessen with increasing years. I shall need, too, the favor of that Being in whose hands we are, who led our forefathers, as Israel of old, from their native land, and planted them in a country flowing with all the necessaries and comforts of life; who has covered our infancy with his providence, and our riper years with his wisdom and power; and to whose goodness I ask you to join with me in supplications, that he will so enlighten the minds of your servants, guide their councils, and prosper their measures, that whatsoever they do, shall result in your good, and shall secure to you the peace, friendship, and approbation of all nations.

Excerpts reprinted from *The Writings of Thomas Jefferson*, ed. Andrew A. Lipscomb and Albert Ellery Bergh, Monticello Edition (Washington, D.C.: Thomas Jefferson Memorial Association, 1904), 3:378, 383.

Letter from Thomas Jefferson to the Reverend Samuel Miller (January 23, 1808)

Washington, January 23, 1808

Sir,—I have duly received your favor of the 18th, and am thankful to you for having written it, because it is more agreeable to prevent than to refuse what I do not think myself authorized to comply with. I consider the government of the United States as interdicted by the Constitution from intermeddling with religious institutions, their doctrines, discipline, or exercises. This results not only from the provision that no law shall be made respecting the establishment or free exercise of religion [First Amendment], but from that also which reserves to the States the powers not delegated to the United States [Tenth Amendment]. Certainly, no power to prescribe any religious exercise, or to assume authority in religious discipline, has been delegated to the General [i.e., federal] Government. It must then rest with the States, as far as it can be in any human authority. But it is only proposed that I should *recommend*, not prescribe a day of fasting and prayer. That is, that I should *indirectly* assume to the United States an authority over religious exercises, which the Constitution has directly precluded them from. It must be meant, too, that this recommendation is to carry some authority, and to be sanctioned by some penalty on those who disregard it; not indeed of fine and imprisonment, but of some degree of proscription, perhaps in public opinion. And does the change in the nature of the penalty make the recommendation less a *law* of conduct for those to whom it is directed? I do not believe it is for the interest of religion to invite the civil magistrate to direct its exercises, its discipline, or its doctrines; nor of the religious societies, that the General Government should be invested with the power of effecting any uniformity of time or matter among them. Fasting and prayer are religious exercises; the enjoining them an act of discipline. Every religious society has a right to determine for itself the times for these exercises, and the objects proper for them, according to their own particular tenets; and this right can never be safer than in their own hands, where the Constitution has deposited it.

I am aware that the practice of my predecessors may be quoted. But I have ever believed, that the example of State executives led to the assumption of that authority by the General Government, without due examination, which would have discovered that what might be a right in a State government, was a violation of that right when assumed by another. Be this as it may, every one must act according to the dictates of his own reason, and mine tells me that civil powers alone have been given to the President of the United States, and no authority to direct the religious exercises of his constituents.

I again express my satisfaction that you have been so good as to give me an opportunity of explaining myself in a private letter, in which I could give my reasons more in detail than might have been done in a public answer; and I pray you to accept the assurances of my high esteem and respect.

Reprinted from *The Writings of Thomas Jefferson*, ed. Andrew A. Lipscomb and Albert Ellery Bergh, Monticello Edition (Washington, D.C.: Thomas Jefferson Memorial Association, 1904), 11:428–30.

THE METAPHOR
AND AMERICAN LAW

The wall metaphor's influence in modern church-state discourse stems from its extensive use by the U.S. Supreme Court. The figurative phrase entered the legal lexicon in *Reynolds v. United States* (1879). The Supreme Court opined that Thomas Jefferson's letter to the Danbury Baptist Association "may be accepted almost as an authoritative declaration of the scope and effect of the [first] amendment thus secured." (The justices, however, were apparently drawn to language in the letter other than the wall metaphor.) The trope's current fame and influence in popular, political, and legal discourse date from its invocation in the landmark "establishment of religion" case, *Everson v. Board of Education* (1947). The justices referred to the metaphor more than a dozen times in *McCollum v. Board of Education* (1948), the following term, confirming the prominence of Jefferson's figurative language in church-state jurisprudence. Several justices have denounced the court's reliance on the metaphor, none more forcefully than Chief Justice William H. Rehnquist, dissenting in *Wallace v. Jaffree* (1985). The following excerpts from selected Supreme Court rulings illustrate the part played by the wall metaphor in church-state jurisprudence.

Reynolds v. United States,
98 U.S. 145, 162–64 (1879)

The word "religion" is not defined in the Constitution. We must go elsewhere, therefore, to ascertain its meaning, and nowhere more appropriately, we think, than to the history of the times in the midst of which the provision was adopted. The precise point of the inquiry is, what is the religious freedom which has been guaranteed.

Before the adoption of the Constitution, attempts were made in some of the colonies and States to legislate not only in respect to the establishment of religion, but in respect to its doctrines and precepts as well. The people were taxed, against their will, for the support of religion, and sometimes for the support of particular sects to whose tenets they could not and did not subscribe. Punishments were prescribed for a failure to attend upon public worship, and sometimes for entertaining heretical opinions. The controversy upon this general subject was animated in many of the States, but seemed at last to culminate in Virginia. In 1784, the House of Delegates of that State having under consideration "a bill establishing provision for teachers of the Christian religion," postponed it until the next session, and directed that the bill should be published and distributed, and that the people be requested "to signify their opinion respecting the adoption of such a bill at the next session of assembly."

This brought out a determined opposition. Amongst others, Mr. Madison prepared a "Memorial and Remonstrance," which was widely circulated and signed, and in which he demonstrated "that religion, or the duty we owe the Creator," was not within the cognizance of civil government. Semple's Virginia Baptists, Appendix. At the next session the proposed bill was not only defeated, but another, "for establishing religious freedom," drafted by Mr. Jefferson, was passed. 1 Jeff. Works, 45; 2 Howison, Hist. of Va. 298.

United States, Supreme Court, vol. 98, *Cases Argued and Adjudged in the Supreme Court of the United States, October Term, 1878,* reported by William Otto (Boston: Little, Brown, 1898), 162–64.

In the preamble of this act (12 Hening's Stat. 84) religious freedom is defined; and after a recital "that to suffer the civil magistrate to intrude his powers into the field of opinion, and to restrain the profession or propagation of principles on supposition of their ill tendency, is a dangerous fallacy which at once destroys all religious liberty," it is declared "that it is time enough for the rightful purposes of civil government for its officers to interfere when principles break out into overt acts against peace and good order." In these two sentences is found the true distinction between what properly belongs to the church and what to the State.

In a little more than a year after the passage of this statute the convention met which prepared the Constitution of the United States. Of this convention Mr. Jefferson was not a member, he being then absent as minister to France. As soon as he saw the draft of the Constitution proposed for adoption, he, in a letter to a friend, expressed his disappointment at the absence of an express declaration insuring the freedom of religion (2 Jeff. Works, 355), but was willing to accept it as it was, trusting that the good sense and honest intentions of the people would bring about the necessary alterations. 1 Jeff. Works, 79. Five of the States, while adopting the Constitution, proposed amendments. Three—New Hampshire, New York, and Virginia—included in one form or another a declaration of religious freedom in the changes they desired to have made, as did also North Carolina, where the convention at first declined to ratify the Constitution until the proposed amendments were acted upon. Accordingly, at the first session of the first Congress the amendment now under consideration was proposed with others by Mr. Madison. It met the views of the advocates of religious freedom, and was adopted. Mr. Jefferson afterwards, in reply to an address to him by a committee of the Danbury Baptist Association (8 id. 113), took occasion to say: "Believing with you that religion is a matter which lies solely between man and his God; that he owes account to none other for his faith or his worship; that the legislative powers of the government reach actions only, and not opinions,—I contemplate with sovereign reverence that act of the whole American people which declared that their legislature should 'make no law respecting an establishment of religion or prohibiting the free exercise thereof,' thus building a wall of separation between church and State. Adhering to this expression of the supreme will of the nation in behalf of the rights of conscience, I shall see with sincere satisfaction the progress of those sentiments which tend to restore man to all his natural rights, convinced he has no natural right in opposition to his social duties." Coming as this does from an acknowledged leader of the advocates of the measure, it may be accepted almost as an authoritative declaration of the scope and effect of the amendment thus secured. Congress was deprived of all legislative power over mere opinion, but was left free to reach actions which were in violation of social duties or subversive of good order. . . .

Everson v. Board of Education, 330 U.S. 1, 15–16, 18 (1947)

The "establishment of religion" clause of the First Amendment means at least this: Neither a state nor the Federal Government can set up a church. Neither can pass laws which aid one religion, aid all religions, or prefer one religion over another. Neither can force nor influence a person to go to or to remain away from church against his will or force him to profess a belief or disbelief in any religion. No person can be punished for entertaining or professing religious beliefs or disbeliefs, for church attendance or nonattendance. No tax in any amount, large or small, can

United States Reports, vol. 330, *Cases Adjudged in the Supreme Court at October Term, 1946*, Wayne Wyatt, reporter (Washington, D.C.: GPO, 1947), 15–16, 18.

be levied to support any religious activities or institutions, whatever they may be called, or whatever form they may adopt to teach or practice religion. Neither a state nor the Federal Government can, openly or secretly, participate in the affairs of any religious organizations or groups and *vice versa*. In the words of Jefferson, the [First Amendment] clause against establishment of religion by law was intended to erect "a wall of separation between church and State." *Reynolds v. United States,* [98 U.S. 145, 164 (1879)].

. . . That wall must be kept high and impregnable. We could not approve the slightest breach. . . .

Wallace v. Jaffree, 472 U.S. 38, 91–92, 106–7, 112–13 (1985) (Rehnquist, J., dissenting)

Thirty-eight years ago this Court, in *Everson v. Board of Education,* 330 U.S. 1, 16 (1947), summarized its exegesis of Establishment Clause doctrine thus:

> "In the words of Jefferson, the clause against establishment of religion by law was intended to erect 'a wall of separation between church and State.' *Reynolds v. United States,* [98 U.S. 145, 164 (1879)]."

This language from *Reynolds,* a case involving the Free Exercise Clause of the First Amendment rather than the Establishment Clause, quoted from Thomas Jefferson's letter to the Danbury Baptist Association the phrase "I contemplate with sovereign reverence that act of the whole American people which declared that their legislature should 'make no law respecting an establishment of religion, or prohibiting the free exercise thereof,' thus building a wall of separation

between church and State." 8 Writings of Thomas Jefferson 113 (H. Washington ed. 1861).*

It is impossible to build sound constitutional doctrine upon a mistaken understanding of constitutional history, but unfortunately the Establishment Clause has been expressly freighted with Jefferson's misleading metaphor for nearly 40 years. Thomas Jefferson was of course in France at the time the constitutional Amendments known as the Bill of Rights were passed by Congress and ratified by the States. His letter to the Danbury Baptist Association was a short note of courtesy, written 14 years after the Amendments were passed by Congress. He would seem to any detached observer as a less than ideal source of contemporary history as to the meaning of the Religion Clauses of the First Amendment. . . .

It would seem from this evidence that the Establishment Clause of the First Amendment had acquired a well-accepted meaning: it forbade establishment of a national religion, and forbade preference among religious sects or denominations. Indeed, the first American dictionary defined the word "establishment" as "the act of establishing, founding, ratifying or ordaining," such as in "[t]he episcopal form of religion, so called, in England." 1 N. Webster, American Dictionary of the English Language (1st ed. 1828). The Establishment Clause did not require government neutrality between religion and irreligion nor did it prohibit the Federal Government from providing nondiscriminatory aid to religion. There is simply no historical foundation for the proposition that the Framers intended to build the "wall of separation" that was constitutionalized in *Everson.*

Notwithstanding the absence of a historical basis for this theory of rigid separation, the wall idea might well have served as a useful albeit misguided analytical concept, had it led this Court to unified and principled results in Establishment Clause cases. The opposite, unfortunately, has been true; in the 38 years

---

United States Reports, vol. 472, *Cases Adjudged in the Supreme Court of the United States at October Term, 1984,* Henry C. Lind, reporter of decisions (Washington, D.C.: GPO, 1988), 91–92, 106–7, 112–13.

* *Reynolds* is the only authority cited as direct precedent for the "wall of separation theory." 330 U.S., at 16. *Reynolds* is truly inapt; it dealt with a Mormon's Free Exercise Clause challenge to a federal polygamy law.—Eds.

since *Everson* our Establishment Clause cases have been neither principled nor unified. Our recent opinions, many of them hopelessly divided pluralities, [footnote omitted] have with embarrassing candor conceded that the "wall of separation" is merely a "blurred, indistinct, and variable barrier," which "is not wholly accurate" and can only be "dimly perceived." *Lemon v. Kurtzman,* 403 U.S. 602, 614 (1971); *Tilton v. Richardson,* 403 U.S. 672, 677–678 (1971); *Wolman v. Walter,* 433 U.S. 229, 236 (1977); *Lynch v. Donnelly,* 465 U.S. 668, 673 (1984).

Whether due to its lack of historical support or its practical unworkability, the *Everson* "wall" has proved all but useless as a guide to sound constitutional adjudication. It illustrates only too well the wisdom of Benjamin Cardozo's observation that "[m]etaphors in law are to be narrowly watched, for starting as devices to liberate thought, they end often by enslaving it." *Berkey v. Third Avenue R. Co.,* 244 N.Y. 84, 94, 155 N.E. 58, 61 (1926).

But the greatest injury of the "wall" notion is its mischievous diversion of judges from the actual intentions of the drafters of the Bill of Rights. The "crucible of litigation," *ante,* at 52, is well adapted to adjudicating factual disputes on the basis of testimony presented in court, but no amount of repetition of historical errors in judicial opinions can make the errors true. The "wall of separation between church and State" is a metaphor based on bad history, a metaphor which has proved useless as a guide to judging. It should be frankly and explicitly abandoned. . . .

If a constitutional theory has no basis in the history of the amendment it seeks to interpret, is difficult to apply and yields unprincipled results, I see little use in it. The "crucible of litigation," *ante,* at 52, has produced only consistent unpredictability, and today's effort is just a continuation of "the sisyphean task of trying to patch together the 'blurred, indistinct and variable barrier' described in Lemon v. Kurtzman." [*Committee for Public Education & Religious Liberty v. Regan,* 444 U.S. 646, 671 (1980)] (STEVENS, J., dissenting). We have done much straining since 1947, but still we admit that we can only "dimly perceive"

the *Everson* wall. *Tilton, supra.* Our perception has been clouded not by the Constitution but by the mists of an unnecessary metaphor.

The true meaning of the Establishment Clause can only be seen in its history. See *Walz* [*v. Tax Comm'n,* 397 U.S. 664, 671–673 (1970)]; see also *Lynch, supra,* at 673–678. As drafters of our Bill of Rights, the Framers inscribed the principles that control today. Any deviation from their intentions frustrates the permanence of that Charter and will only lead to the type of unprincipled decisionmaking that has plagued our Establishment Clause cases since *Everson.*

The Framers intended the Establishment Clause to prohibit the designation of any church as a "national" one. The Clause was also designed to stop the Federal Government from asserting a preference for one religious denomination or sect over others. Given the "incorporation" of the Establishment Clause as against the States via the Fourteenth Amendment in *Everson,* States are prohibited as well from establishing a religion or discriminating between sects. As its history abundantly shows, however, nothing in the Establishment Clause requires government to be strictly neutral between religion and irreligion, nor does that Clause prohibit Congress or the States from pursuing legitimate secular ends through nondiscriminatory sectarian means.

The Court strikes down the Alabama statute because the State wished to "characterize prayer as a favored practice." *Ante,* at 60. It would come as much of a shock to those who drafted the Bill of Rights as it will to a large number of thoughtful Americans today to learn that the Constitution, as construed by the majority, prohibits the Alabama Legislature from "endorsing" prayer. George Washington himself, at the request of the very Congress which passed the Bill of Rights, proclaimed a day of "public thanksgiving and prayer, to be observed by acknowledging with grateful hearts the many and signal favors of Almighty God." History must judge whether it was the Father of his Country in 1789, or a majority of the Court today, which has strayed from the meaning of the Establishment Clause. . . .

RECOMMENDATIONS FOR FURTHER READING

Dreisbach, Daniel L. *Thomas Jefferson and the Wall of Separation Between Church and State.* New York: New York University Press, 2002.

Hamburger, Philip. *Separation of Church and State.* Cambridge: Harvard University Press, 2002.

Hutson, James H. "Thomas Jefferson's Letter to the Danbury Baptists: A Controversy Rejoined." *William and Mary Quarterly,* 3d ser., 56 (1999): 775–90.

———. "Jefferson and the Church-State Wall: A Historical Examination of the Man and the Metaphor." *Brigham Young University Law Review* 1978 (1978): 645–74.

CHAPTER THIRTEEN

Christianity, the Common Law, and the American Order

THE MOST FOUNDATIONAL question that can be asked about a legal and political order concerns the source of its rules and laws. Americans, no less than their European forebears, have pondered this question. In the Anglo-American legal tradition, the question typically presented is whether Christianity is the basis of the common law. With its profound implications for the relationship between Christianity and law, this question engaged leading intellectuals of the late eighteenth and early nineteenth centuries, including Thomas Jefferson and eminent jurists James Kent and Joseph Story. A popular, but not unchallenged, notion was that Christian precepts were incorporated into American jurisprudence by way of the common law. Insofar as the U.S. Constitution accredited the common law, the American people made Christianity part of their organic law upon ratification of the Constitution.

The English developed and exported to their American colonies the system of jurisprudence known as common law. As distinguished from statutory or civil law, common law comprises the body of laws derived from principles, customs, and prior decisions of judicial tribunals (precedents). The principal doctrine of the common law is *stare decisis,* which requires adherence to legal principles set forth in prior cases.

Whether or not Christianity is a part of the common law has been debated for centuries. In the early nineteenth century, this question once again began to agitate the public mind. Two leading figures in the discussion were Thomas Jefferson and Joseph Story, associate justice of the U.S. Supreme Court and a preeminent authority on the common law. In a posthumously published essay entitled "Whether Christianity Is Part of the Common Law?" Jefferson argued "that Christianity neither is, nor ever was, a part of the common law." In his inaugural lecture as Harvard University's Dane Professor of Law, Justice Story countered that "[t]here never has been a period in which the common law did not recognize Christianity as lying at its foundations."*

Political conservatives and religious traditionalists complained bitterly that Jefferson gave legitimacy to a discredited legal theory and, thereby, accelerated the secularization of law and policy by giving plausible grounds to eschew public prayers, fast-day proclamations, religious oaths, Sabbathday observances, and other manifestations of a

---

* Joseph Story, "The Value and Importance of Legal Studies: A Discourse Pronounced at the Inauguration of the Author as Dane Professor of Law in Harvard University, August 25, 1829," in *The Miscellaneous Writings of Joseph Story,* ed. William W. Story (Boston: Charles C. Little and James Brown, 1851), 517.

Christian nation. Jefferson's critics scrutinized constitutional, statutory, and case law, as well as learned treatises on the subject, affirming that in adopting the common law of England the American people made Christianity part of their fundamental law. They cited with approval New York judge James Kent's precedent-setting opinion in the blasphemy case of *People v. Ruggles* (1811) and the influential opinion of the Pennsylvania Supreme Court in *Updegraph v. Commonwealth* (1824). These and many other cases affirmed the proposition that general Christianity is and always has been a part of the common law. The conclusion drawn from these authorities was unmistakable. Christianity was made a part of the Constitution—the supreme law of the land—which, by explicit reference, retained and sanctioned the operation of the common law.

The founding and succeeding generations understood the paramount importance of this debate. It was germane to the enduring question whether the laws of civil society are purely positivistic or whether they are derived from transcendent sources. It also had implications for a long-standing debate between those who believed America is a Christian nation and those who contended that America is a strictly secular polity. An inquiry into whether or not Christianity is or ever was a part of the common law offers insight into the intellectual and religious foundations of the republic and the prudential and constitutional role of religion in American public life.

ESSAYS AND LETTERS

In 1764, a twenty-one-year-old Thomas Jefferson wrote a provocative essay rejecting the widely accepted proposition that Christianity was the basis of the common law. To his detractors, the essay confirmed that Jefferson was an infidel, contemptuous of established judicial, legal, and religious authorities that almost without exception affirmed the Christian basis of the common law. Jefferson's thesis, by implication, challenged the notion that America was in any legal sense a Christian nation. The essay was not published until shortly after Jefferson's death, perhaps because of its highly controversial content. This short dissertation, which was published as an appendix to a legal compilation prepared by Jefferson, was apparently the original brief expounded in several private letters on the topic Jefferson wrote late in life, including missives to John Adams in 1814, Thomas Cooper in 1814, and Major John Cartwright in 1824.

Whether Christianity Is Part of the Common Law?

THOMAS JEFFERSON (1743–1826)

[1764?]

In Quare impedit, in C. B. 34. H. 6. fo. 38, the defendant, Bishop of Lincoln, pleads that the church of the plaintiff became void by the death of the incumbent; that the plaintiff and I. S. each pretending a right, presented two several clerks; that the church being thus rendered litigious, he was not obliged, by the ecclesiastical law, to admit either until an inquisition *de jure patronatus* [concerning the right of a patron] in the ecclesiastical court; that, by the same law, this inquisition was to be at the suit of either claimant, and was not *ex officio* [by virtue of the office] to be instituted by the Bishop, and at his proper costs; that neither party had desired such an inquisition; that six months passed; whereon it belonged to him of right to present as on a lapse, which he had done. The plaintiff demurred. A question was, How far the ecclesiastical law was to be respected in this matter by the Common law court? And Prisot c. 5. in the course of his argument, uses this expression, "à tiels leis que ils de seint eglise ont en ancien scripture, covient à nous à donner credence; car ceo common ley sur quel touts manners leis sont fondés. Et auxy, Sir, nous sumus obligés de conustre lour ley de saint eglise. Et semblablement ils sont obligés de conustre nostre ley, et, Sir, si poit apperer or à nous que l'evesque ad fait come un Ordinary fera en tiel cas, adonq nous devons ceo adjuger bon, ou autermont nemy,"* etc. It does not appear what judgment was given. Y. B. ubi supra, 3. c. Fitzh. Abr., Qu. imp. 89. Bro. Abr. Qu. imp. 12. Finch mis-states this in the following manner: "to such laws of the church as have warrant in *holy scripture,* our law giveth credence;" and cites the above case, and the words of Prisot in the margin. Finch's law, b 1. c. 3. published 1613. Here we find "ancien scripture," converted into "holy scripture," whereas it can only mean the antient written laws of the church. It cannot mean the scriptures, 1st. Because the term

---

"Whether Christianity Is Part of the Common Law?" in *Reports of Cases Determined in the General Court of Virginia, from 1730 to 1740, and from 1768 to 1772* (1829). Reprinted from *The Works of Thomas Jefferson,* ed. Paul Leicester Ford, The Federal Edition (New York and London: G. P. Putnam's Sons, 1904), 1:453–64.

---

* This French passage is replicated on page 543 and, in part, on page 544. Part of the debate concerns how it should be translated. The following translation is meant to provide the overall gist, not to enter into the same debate: "To such laws as those of the holy church which are in ancient writings, it is fitting for us to give credence; as it is the common law on which all kinds of law are founded. And also, sir, we are obligated to be acquainted with their law of the holy church. And similarly they are obligated to be familiar with our law, and, Sir, if it would appear to us that the bishop had done what an ordinary person would have done in such a case, then we ought to approve it, or otherwise not."—Trans.

antient scripture must then be understood as meaning the *Old* Testament in contradistinction to the *New*, and to the exclusion of that; which would be absurd, and contrary to the wish of those who cite this passage to prove that the scriptures, or *Christianity*, is a part of the common law. 2nd. Because Prisot says, "ceo (est) Common ley sur quel touts manners leis sont fondés." Now it is true that the ecclesiastical law, so far as admitted in England, derives its authority from the common law. But it would not be true that the scriptures so derive their authority. 3rd. The whole case and arguments shew, that the question was, How far the ecclesiastical law in general should be respected in a common law court? And in Bro's Abr. of this case, Littleton says, "les juges del Common ley prendra conusans quid est lex ecclesiae vel admiralitatis et hugus modi."* 4th. Because the particular part of the ecclesiastical law then in question, viz. the right of the patron to present to his advowson, was not founded on the law of God, but subject to the modification of the law-giver; and so could not introduce any such general position as Finch pretends. Yet Wingate (in 1658) thinks proper to erect this false quotation into a maxim of the common law, expressing it in the very words of Finch, but citing Prisot, Wing. Max. 3. Next comes Sheppard (in 1675) who states in it the same words of Finch, and quotes the Y. B. Finch and Wingate. 3 Shep. Abr. tit. "Religion." In the case of the King and Taylor, Sir Matthew Hale lays it down in these words; "Christianity is parcel of the laws of England." 1 Ventr. 293. 3 Keb. 607. But he quotes no authority. It was from this part of the supposed common law that he derived his authority for burning witches. So strong was this doctrine become in 1728, by additions and repetitions from one another, that in the case of the King *v.* Woolston, the court would not suffer it to be debated, Whether to write against Christianity was punishable in the temporal courts, at common law? saying it had been so settled in Taylor's case, ante, 2 Stra. 834. Therefore

---

* The judges of the Common law consider what is the law of the church or of the admiralty and of this rule.—Trans.

Wood, in his Institute, lays it down, that all blasphemy and profaneness are offences by the common law, and cites Strange, ubi supra. Wood, 409. and Blackstone (about 1763) repeats, in the words of Sir Matthew Hale, that "Christianity is part of the laws of England," citing Ventr. and Stra. ubi supra. 4 Bl. 59. Lord Mansfield qualified it a little, by saying in the case of the Chamberlain of London *v.* Evans, 1767, that "the essential principles of revealed religion are part of the common law." But he cites no authority, and leaves us at our peril to find out what, in the opinion of the judge, and according to the measures of his foot or his faith, are those *essential* principles of revealed religion, obligatory on us as a part of the common law. Thus we find this string of authorities, when, examined to the beginning, all hanging on the same hook; a perverted expression of Prisot's; or on nothing. For they all quote Prisot, or one another, or nobody. Thus, Finch quotes Prisot; Wingate also; Sheppard quotes Prisot, Finch and Wingate; Hale cites nobody; the court, in Woolston's case, cite Hale; Wood cites Woolston's case; Blackstone that and Hale; and Lord Mansfield, like Hale, ventures it on his own authority. In the earlier ages of the law, as in the Year books for instance, we do not expect much recurrence to authorities by the judges; because, in those days, there were few or none such, made public. But in later times we take no judge's word for what the law is, further than he is warranted by the authorities he appeals to. His decision may bind the unfortunate individual who happens to be the particular subject of it; but it cannot alter the law. Although the common law be termed *Lex non scripta* [an unwritten law], yet the same Hale tells us, "when I call those parts of our laws *Leges non scriptae* [unwritten laws], I do not mean as if all those laws were only oral, or communicated from the former ages to the latter merely, by word. For all these laws have their several monuments in writing, whereby they are transferred from one age to another, and without which they would soon lose all kind of certainty. They are for the most part extant in records of pleas, proceedings and judgments, in books of reports, and judicial decisions, in tractates of learned men's arguments and opinions, preserved from antient times, and still extant in writing": Hale's Com. Law, 22. Authorities for what is common law, may, therefore, be as well cited as for any part of the *lex scripta* [written law]. And there is no better instance of the necessity of holding the judges and writers to a declaration of their authorities, than the present, where we detect them endeavoring to make law where they found none, and to submit us, at one stroke to a whole system, no particular of which, has its foundation in the common law, or has received the "*esto* [let it be so]" of the legislator. For we know that the common law is that system of law which was introduced by the Saxons, on their settlement in England, and altered, from time to time, by proper legislative authority, from that, to the date of the *Magna Charta,* which terminates the period of the common law, or *lex non scripta,* and commences that of the statute law, or *lex scripta.* This settlement took place about the middle of the fifth century; but Christianity was not introduced till the seventh century; the conversion of the first Christian King of the Heptarchy, having taken place about the year 598, and that of the last about 686. Here, then, was a space of two hundred years, during which the common law was in existence, and Christianity no part of it. If it ever, therefore, was adopted into the common law, it must have been between the introduction of Christianity and the date of the *Magna Charta.* But of the laws of this period, we have a tolerable collection, by Lambard and Wilkins; probably not perfect, but neither very defective; and if any one chooses to build a doctrine on any law of that period, supposed to have been lost, it is incumbent on him to prove it to have existed, and what were its contents. These were so far alterations of the common law, and became themselves a part of it; but none of these adopt Christianity as a part of the common law. If, therefore, from the settlement of the Saxons, to the introduction of Christianity among them, that system of religion could not be a part of the common law, because they were not yet Christians; and if, having their laws from that period to the close of the common law, we are

able to find among them no such act of adoption; we may safely affirm (though contradicted by all the judges and writers on earth) that Christianity neither is, nor ever was, a part of the common law. Another cogent proof of this truth is drawn from the silence of certain writers on the common law. Bracton gives us a very complete and scientific treatis of the whole body of the common law. He wrote this about the close of the reign of Henry III, a very few years after the date of the *Magna Charta.* We may consider this book as the more valuable, as it was written about the time which divides the common and statute law; and therefore gives us the former in its ultimate state. Bracton, too, was an ecclesiastic, and would certainly not have failed to inform us of the adoption of Christianity as a part of the common law, had any such adoption ever taken place. But no word of his, which intimates anything like it, has ever been cited. Fleta and Britton, who wrote in the succeeding reign of E. I., are equally silent. So also is Glanvil, an earlier writer than any of them, to wit, temp. H. 2.; but his subject, perhaps, might not have led him to mention it. It was reserved for Finch, five hundred years after, in the time of Charles II., by a falsification of a phrase in the Year book, to open this new doctrine, and for his successors to join full-mouth in the cry, and give to the fiction the sound of fact. Justice Fortescue Aland, who possessed more Saxon learning than all the judges and writers before mentioned put together, places this subject on more limited ground. Speaking of the laws of the Saxon Kings, he says, "the ten commandments were made part of their law, and consequently were once part of the law of England; so that to break any of the ten commandments, was then esteemed a breach of the common law of England; and why it is not so now, perhaps, it may be difficult to give a good reason." Pref. to Fortescue's Rep. xvii. The good reason is found in the denial of the fact.

Houard, in his Coutumes Anglo-Normandes, 1. 87, notices the falsification of the laws of Alfred, by prefixing to them, four chapters of the Jewish law, to wit, the 20th, 21st, 22nd and 23rd chapters of Exodus; to which he might have added the 15th of the Acts of the Apostles, v. 23 to 29, and precepts from other parts of the scripture. These he calls Hors d'oeuvre of some pious copyist. This awkward monkish fabrication, makes the preface to Alfred's genuine laws stand in the body of the work. And the very words of Alfred himself prove the fraud; for he declares in that preface, that he has collected these laws from those of Ina, of Offa, Aethelbert and his ancestors, saying nothing of any of them being taken from the scripture. It is still more certainly proved by the inconsistencies it occasions. For example, the Jewish legislator, Exodus, xxi. 12, 13, 14, (copied by the Pseudo Alfred § 13) makes murder, with the Jews, death. But Alfred himself, Ll. ccvi. punishes it by a fine only, called a weregild, proportioned to the condition of the person killed. It is remarkable that Hume (Append. I. to his history) examining this article of the laws of Alfred, without perceiving the fraud, puzzles himself with accounting for the inconsistency it had introduced. To strike a pregnant woman, so that she die, is death by Exod. xxi. 22, 23, and pseud. Alfr. § 18. But by the Ll. Alfred ix. the offender pays a weregild for both the woman and child. To smite out an eye or a tooth, Exod. xxi. 24–27. Pseud. Alfred. § 19, 20, if of a servant by his master, is freedom to the servant; in every other case, retaliation. But by Alfred Ll. xl. a fixed indemnification is paid. Theft of an ox or a sheep, by the Jewish law, xxii. Exod. 1. was repaid five fold for the ox, and four fold for the sheep; by the Pseudograph § 24, double for the ox and four fold for the sheep. But by Alfred Ll. xvi. he who stole a cow and calf, was to repay the worth of the cow, and 40s. for the calf. Goring by an ox, was the death of the ox, and the flesh not to be eaten; Exod. xxi. 28. Pseud. Alfr. § 21. By Ll. Alfr. xxiv. the wounded person had the ox. This Pseudograph makes municipal laws of the ten commandments: § 1–10, regulate concubinage; § 12, makes it death to strike, or to curse father or mother; § 14, 15, give an eye for an eye, tooth for tooth, hand for hand, foot for foot, burning for burning, wound for wound, stripe for stripe; § 19, sells the thief to repay his theft; § 24, obliges the fornicator to marry the woman he has lain with; § 29, forbids in-

terest on money; § 28, 35, make the laws of bailment, and very different from what Lord Holt delivers in Coggs v. Bernard, and what Sir William Jones tells us they were; and punishes witchcraft with death, § 30, which Sir Matthew Hale 1. P. C. ch. 33, declares was not a felony before the stat. 1. Jac. c. 12. It was under that statute, that he hung Rose Cullender, and Amy Duny, 16. Car. 2. (1662) on whose trial he declared, "that there were such creatures as witches, he made no doubt at all; for 1st. The scriptures had affirmed as much. 2nd. The wisdom of all nations had provided laws against such persons—and such hath been the judgment of this kingdom, as appears by that act of parliament which hath provided punishments proportionable to the quality of the offence." And we must certainly allow greater weight to this position "that it was no felony till James's statutes," deliberately laid down in his H. P. C., a work which he wrote to be printed and transcribed for the press in his lifetime, than to the hasty *scriptum* [writing], that "at common law, witchcraft was punished with death as heresy, by writ *de heretico comburendo* [concerning heretics who ought to be burned]," in his methodical summary of the P. c. pa. 6.; a work "not intended for the press, nor fitted for it and which he declared himself he had never read over since it was written." Preface. Unless we understand his meaning in that to be, that witchcraft could not be punished at *common law as witchcraft*, but as a *heresy*. In either sense, however, it is a denial of this pretended law of Alfred. Now all men of reading know that these pretended laws of homicide, concubinage, theft, retaliation, compulsory marriage, usury, bailment, and others which might have been cited from this Pseudograph, were never the laws of England, not even in Alfred's time; and of course, that it is a forgery. Yet, palpable as it must be to a lawyer, our judges have piously avoided lifting the veil under which it was shrouded. In truth, the alliance between church and state in England, has ever made their judges accomplices in the frauds of the clergy; and even bolder than they are; for instead of being contented with the surreptitious introduction of these four chapters of Exodus, they have taken the whole leap, and declared at once that the whole Bible and Testament, in a lump, make a part of the common law of the land; the first judicial declaration of which was by this Sir Matthew Hale. And thus they incorporate into the English code, laws made for the Jews alone, and the precepts of the gospel, intended by their benevolent author as obligatory only in *foro conscientiae* [forum (or court) of conscience]; and they arm the whole with the co-ercions of municipal law. They do this, too, in a case where the question was, not at all, whether Christianity was a part of the laws of England, but simply how far the *ecclesiastical law* was to be respected by the common law courts of England, in the special case of a right of presentment. Thus identifying Christianity with the ecclesiastical law of England.

Letter from Thomas Jefferson to Dr. Thomas Cooper

Monticello, February 10, 1814
Dear Sir,—In my letter of January 16, I promised you a sample from my common-place book, of the pious disposition of the English judges, to connive at the frauds of the clergy, a disposition which has even rendered them faithful allies in practice. When I was a student of the law, now half a century ago, after getting through Coke Littleton, whose matter cannot be abridged, I was in the habit of abridging and common-placing what I read meriting it, and of sometimes mixing my own reflections on the subject. I now enclose you the extract from these entries which I promised. They were written at a time of life when I was bold in the pursuit of knowledge, never fearing to follow truth and reason to whatever results

Reprinted from *The Writings of Thomas Jefferson*, ed. Andrew A. Lipscomb and Albert Ellery Bergh, Monticello Edition (Washington, D.C.: Thomas Jefferson Memorial Association, 1904), 14:85–97.

they led, and bearding every authority which stood in their way. This must be the apology, if you find the conclusions bolder than historical facts and principles will warrant. Accept with them the assurances of my great esteem and respect.

Common-place Book

873. In Quare imp. in C. B. 34, H. 6, fo. 38, the def. Br. of Lincoln pleads that the church of the pl. be-came void by the death of the incumbent, that the pl. and J. S. each pretending a right, presented two sev-eral clerks; that the church being thus rendered liti-gious, he was not obliged, by the *Ecclesiastical law* to admit either, until an inquisition *de jure patronatus* [concerning the right of a patron], in the ecclesiastical court: that, by the same law, this inquisition was to be at the suit of either claimant, and was not *ex-officio* [by virtue of the office] to be instituted by the bishop, and at his proper costs; that neither party had desired such an inquisition; that six months passed whereon it belonged to him of right to present as on a lapse, which he had done. The pl. demurred. A question was, How far the *Ecclesiastical law* was to be respected in this matter by the common law court? and Prisot C. 3, in the course of his argument uses this expression, "A tiels leis que ils de seint eglise ont en *ancien scripture*, covient a nous a donner credence; car ces common ley sur quel touts manners leis sont fondés: et auxy, Sir, nous sumus obligès de conustre nostre ley; et, Sir, si poit apperer or à nous que lié-vesque ad fait comme un ordinary fera en tiel cas, adong nous devons ces adjuger bon autrement nemy," etc. It does not appear that judgment was given. Y. B. *ubi supra* [where above]. S. C. Fitzh. abr. Qu. imp. 89. Bro. abr. Qu. imp. 12. Finch mistakes this in the following manner: "To such laws of the church as have warrant in *Holy Scripture*, our law giveth cre-dence," and cites the above case, and the words of Pri-sot on the margin. Finch's law, B. 1, ch. 3, published 1613. Here we find "ancien scripture" [*ancien writing*] converted into "Holy Scripture," whereas it can only mean the *ancien written* laws of the church. It cannot mean the Scriptures, 1, because the "ancien scripture"

must then be understood to mean the "Old Testament" or Bible, in opposition to the "New Testament," and to the exclusion of that, which would be absurd and contrary to the wish of those who cite this passage to prove that the Scriptures, or Christianity, is a part of the common law. 2. Because Prisot says, "Ceo [est] common ley, sur quel touts manners leis sont fondés." Now, it is true that the Ecclesiastical law, so far as admitted in England, derives its authority from the common law. But it would not be true that the Scriptures so derive their authority. 3. The whole case and arguments show that the question was how far the Ecclesiastical law in general should be respected in a common law court. And in Bro. abr. of this case, Littleton says, "Les juges del common ley prendra conusans quid est *lax ecclesiae*, vel admiralitatis, et trujus modi." 4. Because the particular part of the Ecclesiastical law then in question, to wit, the right of the patron to present to his advowson, was not founded on the law of God, but subject to the modification of the lawgiver, and so could not introduce any such general position as Finch pretends. Yet Wingate [in 1658] thinks proper to erect this false quotation into a maxim of the common law, expressing it in the very words of Finch, but citing Prisot; Wing. max. 3. Next comes Sheppard [in 1675], who states it in the same words of Finch, and quotes the Year-Book, Finch and Wingate. 3 Shepp. abr., tit. Religion. In the case of the King *v.* Taylor, Sir Matthew Hale lays it down in these words, "Christianity is parcel of the laws of England." 1 Ventr. 293, 3 Keb. 607. But he quotes no authority, resting it on his own, which was good in all cases in which his mind received no bias from his bigotry, his superstitions, his visions about sorceries, demons, etc. The power of these over him is exemplified in his hanging of the witches. So strong was this doctrine become in 1728, by additions and repetitions from one another, that in the case of the King *v.* Woolston, the court would not suffer it to be debated, whether to write against Christianity was punishable in the temporal courts at common law, saying it had been so settled in Taylor's case, *ante*, 2 Stra. 834; therefore, Wood, in his Insti-

tute, lays it down that all blasphemy and profaneness are offences by the *common law*, and cites Strange *ubi supra*. Wood 409. And Blackstone [about 1763] repeats, in the words of Sir Matthew Hale, that "Christianity is part of the laws of England," citing Ventris and Strange *ubi supra*. 4 Blackst. 59. Lord Mansfield qualifies it a little by saying that "the essential principles of revealed religion are part of the common law." In the case of the Chamberlain of London *v.* Evans, 1767. But he cites no authority, and leaves us at our peril to find out what, in the opinion of the judge, and according to the measure of his foot or his faith, are those essential principles of revealed religion obligatory on us as a part of the common law.

Thus we find this string of authorities, when examined to the beginning, all hanging on the same hook, a perverted expression of Prisot's, or on one another, or nobody. Thus Finch quotes Prisot; Wingate also; Sheppard quotes Prisot, Finch and Wingate; Hale cites nobody; the court in Woolston's case cite Hale; Wood cites Woolston's case; Blackstone that and Hale; and Lord Mansfield, like Hale, ventures it on his own authority. In the earlier ages of the law, as in the year-books, for instance, we do not expect much recurrence to authorities by the judges, because in those days there were few or none such made public. But in latter times we take no judge's word for what the law is, further than he is warranted by the authorities he appeals to. His decision may bind the unfortunate individual who happens to be the particular subject of it; but it cannot alter the law. Though the common law may be termed "Lex non Scripta [unwritten law]," yet the same Hale tells us "when I call those parts of our laws Leges non Scriptae [unwritten laws], I do not mean as if those laws were only oral, or communicated from the former ages to the latter merely by word. For all those laws have their several monuments in writing, whereby they are transferred from one age to another, and without which they would soon lose all kind of certainty. They are for the most part extant in records of pleas, proceedings, and judgments, in books of reports and judicial decisions, in tractates of learned men's arguments and opinions, preserved from ancient times and still extant in writing." Hale's H. c. d. 22. Authorities for what is common law may therefore be as well cited, as for any part of the Lex Scripta [written law], and there is no better instance of the necessity of holding the judges and writers to a declaration of their authorities than the present; where we detect them endeavoring to make law where they found none, and to submit us at one stroke to a whole system, no particle of which has its foundation in the common law. For we know that the common law is that system of law which was introduced by the Saxons on their settlement in England, and altered from time to time by proper legislative authority from that time to the date of Magna Charta, which terminates the period of the common law, or Lex non Scripta, and commences that of the statute law, or Lex Scripta. This settlement took place about the middle of the fifth century. But Christianity was not introduced till the seventh century; the conversion of the first Christian king of the Heptarchy having taken place about the year 598, and that of the last about 686. Here, then, was a space of two hundred years, during which the common law was in existence, and Christianity no part of it. If it ever was adopted, therefore, into the common law, it must have been between the introduction of Christianity and the date of the Magna Charta. But of the laws of this period we have a tolerable collection by Lambard and Wilkins, probably not perfect, but neither very defective; and if any one chooses to build a doctrine on any law of that period, supposed to have been lost, it is incumbent on him to prove it to have existed, and what were its contents. These were so far alterations of the common law, and became themselves a part of it. But none of these adopt Christianity as a part of the common law. If, therefore, from the settlement of the Saxons to the introduction of Christianity among them, that system of religion could not be a part of the common law, because they were not yet Christians, and if, having their laws from that period to the close of the common law, we are all able to find among them no such act of adoption, we may safely affirm (though

contradicted by all the judges and writers on earth) that Christianity neither is, nor ever was a part of the common law. Another cogent proof of this truth is drawn from the silence of certain writers on the common law. Bracton gives us a very complete and scientific treatise of the whole body of the common law. He wrote this about the close of the reign of Henry III., a very few years after the date of the Magna Charta. We consider this book as the more valuable, as it was written about the time which divides the common and statute law, and therefore gives us the former in its ultimate state. Bracton, too, was an ecclesiastic, and would certainly not have failed to inform us of the adoption of Christianity as a part of the common law, had any such adoption ever taken place. But no word of his, which intimates anything like it, has ever been cited. Fleta and Britton, who wrote in the succeeding reign (of Edward I.), are equally silent. So also is Glanvil, an earlier writer than any of them, (viz.: temp. H. 2,) but his subject perhaps might not have led him to mention it. Justice Fortescue Aland, who possessed more Saxon learning than all the judges and writers before mentioned put together, places this subject on more limited ground. Speaking of the laws of the Saxon kings, he says, "the ten commandments were made part of their laws, and consequently were *once* part of the law of England; so that to break any of the ten commandments was then esteemed a breach of the common law, of England; and why it is not so now, perhaps it may be difficult to give a good reason." Preface to Fortescue Aland's reports, xvii. Had he proposed to state with more minuteness how much of the Scriptures had been made a part of the common law, he might have added that in the laws of Alfred, where he found the ten commandments, two or three other chapters of Exodus are copied almost verbatim. But the adoption of a part proves rather a rejection of the rest, as municipal law. We might as well say that the Newtonian system of philosophy is a part of the common law, as that the Christian religion is. The truth is that Christianity and Newtonianism being reason and verity itself, in the opinion of all but infidels and Cartesians, they are protected under the wings of the common law from the dominion of other sects, but not erected into dominion over them. An eminent Spanish physician affirmed that the lancet had slain more men than the sword. Doctor Sangrado, on the contrary, affirmed that with plentiful bleedings, and draughts of warm water, every disease was to be cured. The common law protects both opinions, but enacts neither into law. See *post*, 879.

879. Howard, in his Contumes Anglo-Normandes, 1. 87, notices the falsification of the laws of Alfred, by prefixing to them four chapters of the Jewish law, to wit: the 20th, 21st, 22d and 23d chapters of Exodus, to which he might have added the 15th chapter of the Acts of the Apostles, v. 23, and precepts from other parts of the Scripture. These he calls a *hors d'oeuvre* of some pious copyist. This awkward monkish fabrication makes the preface to Alfred's genuine laws stand in the body of the work, and the very words of Alfred himself prove the fraud; for he declares, in that preface, that he has collected these laws from those of Ina, of Offa, Aethelbert and his ancestors, saying nothing of any of them being taken from the Scriptures. It is still more certainly proved by the inconsistencies it occasions. For example, the Jewish legislator, Exodus xxi. 12, 13, 14, (copied by the Pseudo Alfred § 13,) makes murder, with the Jews, death. But Alfred himself, Le. xxvi., punishes it by a fine only, called a Weregild, proportioned to the condition of the person killed. It is remarkable that Hume (append. 1 to his History) examining this article of the laws of Alfred, without perceiving the fraud, puzzles himself with accounting for the inconsistency it had introduced. To strike a pregnant woman so that she die, is death by Exodus xxi. 22, 23, and Pseud. Alfr. § 18; but by the laws of Alfred ix., pays a Weregild for both woman and child. To smite out an eye, or a tooth, Exod. xxi. 24–27, Pseud. Alfr. § 19, 20, if of a servant by his master, is freedom to the servant; in every other case retaliation. But by Alfr. Le. xl. a fixed indemnification is paid. Theft of an ox, or a sheep, by the Jewish law, Exod. xxii. 1, was repaid five-fold for the ox and four-fold for the sheep; by the Pseudo-

graph § 24, the ox double, the sheep four-fold; but by Alfred Le. xvi., he who stole a cow and a calf was to repay the worth of the cow and forty shillings for the calf. Goring by an ox was the death of the ox, and the flesh not to be eaten. Exod. xxi. 28, Pseud. Alfr. § 21; by Alfred Le. xxiv., the wounded person had the ox. The Pseudograph makes municipal laws of the ten commandments, § 1–10, regulates concubinage, § 12, makes it death to strike or to curse father or mother, § 14, 15, gives an eye for an eye, tooth for a tooth, hand for hand, foot for foot, burning for burning, wound for wound, strife for strife, § 19; sells the thief to repay his theft, § 24; obliges the fornicator to marry the woman he has lain with, § 29; forbids interest on money, § 35; makes the laws of bailment, § 28, very different from what Lord Holt delivers in Coggs *v.* Bernard, *ante*, 92, and what Sir William Jones tells us they were; and punishes witchcraft with death, § 30, which Sir Matthew Hale, 1 H. P. C. B. 1, ch. 33, declares was not a felony before the Stat. 1 Jac. 12. It was under that statute, and not this forgery, that he hung Rose Cullendar and Amy Duny, 16 Car. 2 (1662), on whose trial he declared "that there were such creatures as witches he made no doubt at all; for first the Scripture had affirmed so much, secondly the wisdom of all nations had provided laws against such persons, and such hath been the judgment of this kingdom, as appears by that act of Parliament which hath provided punishment proportionable to the quality of the offence." And we must certainly allow greater weight to this position that "it was no felony till James' Statute," laid down deliberately in his H. P. C., a work which he wrote to be printed, finished, and transcribed for the press in his lifetime, than to the hasty scripture that "at *common law* witchcraft was punished with death as heresy, by writ de Heretico Comburendo [concerning heretics who ought to be burned]" in his Methodical Summary of the P. C. p. 6, a work "not intended for the press, not fitted for it, and which he declared himself he had never read over since it was written;" Pref. Unless we understand his meaning in that to be that witchcraft could not be punished at common law as witchcraft, but as heresy.

In either sense, however, it is a denial of this pretended law of Alfred. Now, all men of reading know that these pretended laws of homicide, concubinage, theft, retaliation, compulsory marriage, usury, bailment, and others which might have been cited, from the Pseudograph, were never the laws of England, not even in Alfred's time; and of course that it is a forgery. Yet palpable as it must be to every lawyer, the English judges have piously avoided lifting the veil under which it was shrouded. In truth, the alliance between Church and State in England has ever made their judges accomplices in the frauds of the clergy; and even bolder than they are. For instead of being contented with these four surreptitious chapters of Exodus, they have taken the whole leap, and declared at once that the whole Bible and Testament in a lump, make a part of the common law; *ante*, 873: the first judicial declaration of which was by this same Sir Matthew Hale. And thus they incorporate into the English code, laws made for the Jews alone, and the precepts of the Gospel, intended by their benevolent Author as obligatory only in *foro conscientiae;* and they arm the whole with the coercions of municipal law. In doing this, too, they have not even used the Connecticut caution of declaring, as is done in their blue laws, that the laws of God shall be the laws of their land, except where their own contradict them; but they swallow the yea and nay together. Finally, in answer to Fortescue Aland's question why the ten commandments should not now be a part of the common law of England? we may say they are not because they never were made so by legislative authority, the document which has imposed that doubt on him being a manifest forgery.

Letter from Thomas Jefferson to Major John Cartwright

MONTICELLO, June 5, 1824
DEAR AND VENERABLE SIR,—I am much indebted for your kind letter of February the 29th, and for your valuable volume on the English Constitution. I have read this with pleasure and much approbation, and think it has deduced the Constitution of the English nation from its rightful root, the Anglo-Saxon. It is really wonderful, that so many able and learned men should have failed in their attempts to define it with correctness. No wonder then, that Paine, who thought more than he read, should have credited the great authorities who have declared, that the will of Parliament is the Constitution of England. So Marbois, before the French Revolution, observed to me that the Almanac Royal was the Constitution of France. Your derivation of it from the Anglo-Saxons, seems to be made on legitimate principles. Having driven out the former inhabitants of that part of the island called England, they became aborigines as to you, and your lineal ancestors. They doubtless had a constitution; and although they have not left it in a written formula, to the precise text of which you may always appeal, yet they have left fragments of their history and laws, from which it may be inferred with considerable certainty. Whatever their history and laws show to have been practised with approbation, we may presume was permitted by their constitution; whatever was not so practiced, was not permitted. And although this constitution was violated and set at naught by Norman force, yet force cannot change right. A perpetual claim was kept up by the nation, by their perpetual demand of a restoration of their Saxon laws; which shows they were never relinquished by the will of the nation. In the pullings and haulings for these ancient rights, between the nation, and its kings of the races of Plantagenets, Tudors and

Reprinted from *The Writings of Thomas Jefferson*, ed. Andrew A. Lipscomb and Albert Ellery Bergh, Monticello Edition (Washington, D.C.: Thomas Jefferson Memorial Association, 1904), 16:42–52.

Stuarts, there was sometimes gain, and sometimes loss, until the final reconquest of their rights from the Stuarts. The destruction and expulsion of this race broke the thread of pretended inheritance, extinguished all regal usurpations, and the nation re-entered into all its rights; and although in their bill of rights they specifically reclaimed some only, yet the omission of the others was no renunciation of the right to assume their exercise also, whenever occasion should occur. The new King received no rights or powers, but those expressly granted to him. It has ever appeared to me, that the difference between the Whig and the Tory of England is, that the Whig deduces his rights from the Anglo-Saxon source, and the Tory from the Norman. And Hume, the great apostle of Toryism, says, in so many words, note AA to chapter 42, that, in the reign of the Stuarts, "it was the people who encroached upon the sovereign, not the sovereign who attempted, as is pretended, to usurp upon the people." This supposes the Norman usurpations to be rights in his successors. And again, C, 159, "the commons established a principle, which is noble in itself, and seems specious, but is belied by all history and experience, *that the people are the origin of all just power.*" And where else will this degenerate son of science, this traitor to his fellow men, find the origin of *just* powers, if not in the majority of the society? Will it be in the minority? Or in an individual of that minority?

Our Revolution commenced on more favorable ground. It presented us an album on which we were free to write what we pleased. We had no occasion to search into musty records, to hunt up royal parchments, or to investigate the laws and institutions of a semi-barbarous ancestry. We appealed to those of nature, and found them engraved on our hearts. Yet we did not avail ourselves of all the advantages of our position. We had never been permitted to exercise self-government. When forced to assume it, we were novices in its science. Its principles and forms had entered little into our former education. We established, however, some, although not all its important principles. The constitutions of most of our States assert,

that all power is inherent in the people; that they may exercise it by themselves, in all cases to which they think themselves competent, (as in electing their functionaries executive and legislative, and deciding by a jury of themselves, in all judiciary cases in which any fact is involved,) or they may act by representatives, freely and equally chosen; that it is their right and duty to be at all times armed; that they are entitled to freedom of person, freedom of religion, freedom of property, and freedom of the press. In the structure of our legislatures, we think experience has proved the benefit of subjecting questions to two separate bodies of deliberants; but in constituting these, natural right has been mistaken, some making one of these bodies, and some both, the representatives of property instead of persons; whereas the double deliberation might be as well obtained without any violation of true principle, either by requiring a greater age in one of the bodies, or by electing a proper number of representatives of persons, dividing them by lots into two chambers, and renewing the division at frequent intervals, in order to break up all cabals. Virginia, of which I am myself a native and resident, was not only the first of the States, but, I believe I may say, the first of the nations of the earth, which assembled its wise men peaceably together to form a fundamental constitution, to commit it to writing, and place it among their archives, where every one should be free to appeal to its text. But this act was very imperfect. The other States, as they proceeded successively to the same work, made successive improvements; and several of them, still further corrected by experience, have, by conventions, still further amended their first forms. My own State has gone on so far with its *premiere ebauche* [first draft or outline]; but it is now proposing to call a convention for amendment. Among other improvements, I hope they will adopt the subdivision of our counties into wards. The former may be estimated at an average of twenty-four miles square; the latter should be about six miles square each, and would answer to the hundreds of your Saxon Alfred. In each of these might be, 1st, an elementary school; 2d, a company of militia, with its officers; 3d, a justice of the peace and constable; 4th, each ward should take care of their own poor; 5th, their own roads; 6th, their own police; 7th, elect within themselves one or more jurors to attend the courts of justice; and 8th, give in at their folk-house, their votes for all functionaries reserved to their election. Each ward would thus be a small republic within itself, and every man in the State would thus become an acting member of the common government, transacting in person a great portion of its rights and duties, subordinate indeed, yet important, and entirely within his competence. The wit of man cannot devise a more solid basis for a free, durable and well-administered republic.

With respect to our State and federal governments, I do not think their relations correctly understood by foreigners. They generally suppose the former subordinate to the latter. But this is not the case. They are co-ordinate departments of one simple and integral whole. To the State governments are reserved all legislation and administration, in affairs which concern their own citizens only, and to the federal government is given whatever concerns foreigners, or the citizens of other States; these functions alone being made federal. The one is the domestic, the other the foreign branch of the same government; neither having control over the other, but within its own department. There are one or two exceptions only to this partition of power. But, you may ask, if the two departments should claim each the same subject of power, where is the common umpire to decide ultimately between them? In cases of little importance or urgency, the prudence of both parties will keep them aloof from the questionable ground; but if it can neither be avoided nor compromised, a convention of the States must be called, to ascribe the doubtful power to that department which they may think best. You will perceive by these details, that we have not yet so far perfected our constitutions as to venture to make them unchangeable. But still, in their present state, we consider them not otherwise changeable than by the authority of the people, on a special elec-

tion of representatives for that purpose expressly: they are until then the *lex legum* [law of laws].

But can they be made unchangeable? Can one generation bind another, and all others, in succession forever? I think not. The Creator has made the earth for the living, not the dead. Rights and powers can only belong to persons, not to things, not to mere matter, unendowed with will. The dead are not even things. The particles of matter which composed their bodies, make part now of the bodies of other animals, vegetables, or minerals, of a thousand forms. To what then are attached the rights and powers they held while in the form of men? A generation may bind itself as long as its majority continues in life; when that has disappeared, another majority is in place, holds all the rights and powers their predecessors once held, and may change their laws and institutions to suit themselves. Nothing then is unchangeable but the inherent and unalienable rights of man.

I was glad to find in your book a formal contradiction, at length, of the judiciary usurpation of legislative powers; for such the judges have usurped in their repeated decisions, that Christianity is a part of the common law. The proof of the contrary, which you have adduced, is incontrovertible; to wit, that the common law existed while the Anglo-Saxons were yet pagans, at a time when they had never yet heard the name of Christ pronounced, or knew that such a character had ever existed. But it may amuse you, to show when, and by what means, they stole this law in upon us. In a case of *quare impedit* [for what purpose does he hinder] in the Year-book 34, H. 6, folio 38, (anno 1458,) a question was made, how far the ecclesiastical law was to be respected in a common law court? And Prisot, Chief Justice, gives his opinion in these words: "A tiel leis qu' ils de seint eglise ont en *ancien scripture*, covient à nous à donner credence; car ceo common ley sur quels touts manners leis sont fondés. Et auxy, Monsieur, nous sumus oblèges de conustre lour ley de saint eglise; et semblablement ils sont obligé de consustre nostre ley. Et, Monsieur, si poit apperer or à nous que l'evesque ad fait come un ordinary fera en tiel cas, adong nous devons cee adjuger bon, ou auterment nemy,"* etc. See S. C. Fitzh. Abr. Qu. imp. 89, Bro. Abr. Qu. imp. 12. Finch in his first book, c. 3, is the first afterwards who quotes this case and mistakes it thus: "To such laws of the church as have warrant in *holy scripture,* our law giveth credence." And cites Prisot; mistranslating *"ancien scripture,"* into *"holy scripture."* Whereas Prisot palpably says, "to such laws as those of holy church have in *ancient writing,* it is proper for us to give credence," to wit, to their *ancient written* laws. This was in 1613, a century and a half after the dictum of Prisot. Wingate, in 1658, erects this false translation into a maxim of the common law, copying the words of Finch, but citing Prisot, Wing. Max. 3. And Sheppard, title, "Religion," in 1675, copies the same mistranslation, quoting the Y. B. Finch and Wingate. Hale expresses it in these words: "Christianity is parcel of the laws of England." 1 Ventr. 293, 3 Keb. 607. But he quotes no authority. By these echoings and re-echoings from one to another, it had become so established in 1728, that in the case of the King *vs.* Woolston, 2 Stra. 834, the court would not suffer it to be debated, whether to write against Christianity was punishable in the temporal court at common law? Wood, therefore, 409, ventures still to vary the phrase, and say, that all blasphemy and profaneness are offences by the common law; and cites 2 Stra. Then Blackstone, in 1763, IV. 59, repeats the words of Hale, that "Christianity is part of the laws of England," citing Ventris and Strange. And finally, Lord Mansfield, with a little qualification, in Evans' case, in 1767, says that "the essential principles of revealed religion are part of the common law." Thus ingulfing Bible, Testament and all into the common law, without citing any authority. And thus we find this chain of authorities hanging link by link, one upon another, and all ultimately on one and the same hook, and that a mistranslation of the words *"ancien scripture,"* used by Prisot. Finch quotes Prisot; Wingate does the same. Sheppard quotes Prisot, Finch and Wingate. Hale cites nobody. The court in Woolston's case, cites Hale. Wood cites

Woolston's case. Blackstone quotes Woolston's case and Hale. And Lord Mansfield, like Hale, ventures it on his own authority. Here I might defy the best-read lawyer to produce another scrip of authority for this judiciary forgery; and I might go on further to show, how some of the Anglo-Saxon priests interpolated into the text of Alfred's laws, the 20th, 21st, 22d, and 23d chapters of Exodus, and the 15th of the Acts of the Apostles, from the 23d to the 29th verses. But this would lead my pen and your patience too far. What a conspiracy this, between Church and State! Sing Tantarara, rogues all, rogues all, Sing Tantarara, rogues all!

I must still add to this long and rambling letter, my acknowledgments for your good wishes to the University we are now establishing in this State. There are some novelties in it. Of that of a professorship of the principles of government, you express your approbation. They will be founded in the rights of man. That of agriculture, I am sure, you will approve; and that also of Anglo-Saxon. As the histories and laws left us in that type and dialect, must be the text-books of the reading of the learners, they will imbibe with the language their free principles of government. The volumes you have been so kind as to send, shall be placed in the library of the University. Having at this time in England a person sent for the purpose of selecting some professors, a Mr. Gilmer of my neighborhood, I cannot but recommend him to your patronage, counsel and guardianship, against imposition, misinformation, and the deceptions of partial and false recommendations, in the selection of characters. He is a gentleman of great worth and correctness, my particular friend, well educated in various branches of science, and worthy of entire confidence.

Your age of eighty-four and mine of eighty-one years, insure us a speedy meeting. We may then commune at leisure, and more fully, on the good and evil which, in the course of our long lives, we have both witnessed; and in the meantime, I pray you to accept assurances of my high veneration and esteem for your person and character.

---

* See p. 539 n.—Trans.

Christianity a Part of the Common Law (April 1833)

JOSEPH STORY (1779–1845)

The publication of Thomas Jefferson's essay "Whether Christianity Is Part of the Common Law?" and his letter to Major John Cartwright (1740–1824) drew immediate rebuttal from critics, many of whom thought these writings confirmed that Jefferson was an infidel. The most learned respondent was Joseph Story, associate justice of the United States Supreme Court and Harvard University's Dane Professor of Law. Story's refutation of Jefferson's thesis was published in the *American Jurist and Law Magazine*, the leading legal journal of the day.

MR. JEFFERSON, in a letter to Major Cartwright, recently published, insists that the maxim, that Christianity is a part of the common law, has no foundation in the cases cited to support it, they all referring to the year book 34 Henry 6, 38, 40; which he says has no such meaning.

The substance of the case in 34 Henry 6, 38, 40, is this. It was a quare impedit against the bishop and others; and the bishop pleaded that the church was in litigation between the plaintiff and his co-defendant, as to the right of patronage. The argument in one part of the case by counsel was that every advowson and right of patronage depended upon *both laws,* viz. the *law of the church* and the *common law;* for every presentment commenced at the common law and took effect by the law of the church, as to the ability or non-ability of the clerk presented or his being criminal. And it was said by *Ashton,* that if the bishop

Reprinted from [Joseph Story], "Christianity a Part of the Common Law," *American Jurist and Law Magazine* 9 (April 1833): 346–48.

should refuse the clerk on account of alleged inability, and a quare impedit was brought, and the bishop excused himself on that account, and the parties were at issue upon the fact of ability, another judge should decide that, viz. the metropolitan. But that was denied by *Danby,* who said it should be tried by the jury. *Ashton,* however, persisted in his opinion, arguing that the right of advowson must be tried by both laws, and that before judgment was given, knowledge ought to be had of the ecclesiastical law. *Prisot* then said: 'A tiels leys, que eux de sainte Esglise ont *en aucien Scripture* convenit pur nous a doner credence, quia ceo est comen ley, sur quel toutes maners leys sont fondues; et, auxi, sir, nous sumus obliges de conustre leur ley de sainte Esglise; et semble, ils sount obliges de conustre notre ley.' The literal translation is, 'As to those laws, which those of holy church have in ancient scripture, it behoves us to give them credence, for this is common law, upon which all manner of laws are founded; and thus, sir, we are obliged to take notice of their law of holy church; and it seems they are obliged to take notice of our law.'

Mr. Jefferson supposes that the words 'auncien scripture' do not refer to the Holy Scriptures or Bible, but to *ancient writings,* or the written code of the church.

But if this be so, how could *Prisot* have said that they were common law, *upon which all manner of laws are founded?* Do not these words suppose that he was speaking of some superior law, having a foundation in nature of the Divine appointment, and not merely a positive ancient code of the church?

Mr. Jefferson asserts, that in subsequent cases, which he refers to, the expression has been constantly understood as referring to the Holy Scriptures; but he thinks it a mistake of Prisot's meaning. Now it is some argument in favor of the common interpretation, that it has always been cited as clear—Mr. J.'s interpretation is novel.

This case is cited in Brook's Abridg. Title Quare Impedit [for what purpose does he hinder] pl. 12, and in Fitzherbert's Abridg. s. t. 89; but no notice is taken of Prisot's saying.

Mr. Jefferson quotes sundry cases where this saying has been relied on in proof of the maxim that Christianity is a part of the common law.

Thus in Taylor's case, 1 Vent. 293, indictment for blasphemous words, *Hale*, C. J. said, Such blasphemous words are not only an offence against God and religion, but a crime against the laws and government, and therefore punishable in this court, &c. and *Christianity is a part of the laws of England;* and therefore to reproach the Christian religion is to speak in subversion of the law. In the same case in 3 Keble, 607, Hale, C. J. is reported to have said, 'Religion is a part of the law itself, therefore injuries to God are as punishable as to the King or any common power.' The case of 34 Hen. 6, 38, 40, is not here cited by the court as a foundation of their opinion. But it proceeds upon a general principle.

So in Rex *v.* Woolston, 2 Strange R. 834, S. C. Fitzgibb. 64, the court said they could not suffer it to be debated whether to write against Christianity in general was not an offence punishable in the temporal courts, at common law, it having been settled so to be in Taylor's case, 1 Vent. 293, and Rex *v.* Hall, 1 Strange R. 416. No reference was here made to the case in 34 Hen. 6.

A reference is made by Mr. J. to Sheppard's Abridgment, title Religion; but the only position there found is, 'that to such laws as have warrant in holy Scripture our law giveth credence;' and laws made against the known law of God are void: and for these positions he cites, among others, the case of 34 Hen. 6, 40.

But independently of any weight in any of these authorities, can any man seriously doubt, that Christianity is recognised as *true*, as a revelation, by the law of England, that is, by the common law? What becomes of her whole ecclesiastical establishment and the legal rights growing out of it on any other supposition? What of her test acts, and acts perpetually referring to it, as a divine system, obligatory upon all? Is not the reviling of any establishment, created and supported by the public law, held a libel by the common law?

J. S.

See Rex *v.* Williams, Holt's Law of Libel, p. 69, note (e). Smith *v.* Sparrow, 4 Bing. R. 84, and particularly what is said by Mr. Justice Park in page 88. Omichand *v.* Barker, Willes R. 548. [—J. S.]

Is Christianity a Part of the Common-Law of England? (March 1836)

Many conservative Christians viewed Thomas Jefferson's thesis as an assault on Christianity and its privileged place in American public life. More specifically, many feared the denial of the Christian basis of the common law undermined religion and virtue as the great supports of social order and political prosperity. Accordingly, Jefferson's arguments demanded a response. "Is Christianity a Part of the Common-Law of England?" published anonymously in a leading Christian intellectual periodical, provides a vigorous rebuttal of Jefferson's thesis.

As christian spectators, we feel bound to notice the various attacks made upon religion, from whatever quarter they may come. It may not, however, be evident to every one, what connection the question at the head of this article has with religion, at least in this country. To such, it may be sufficient to say, that the *common-law of England* has been adopted in this

Reprinted from "Is Christianity a Part of the Common-Law of England?" *Quarterly Christian Spectator* 8 (March 1836): 13–22.

country, with such modifications as our situation and circumstances require; in some states, by an express provision of their constitutions, and in others, by the uniform usage of the courts, with the approbation of their different legislatures.* Now, inasmuch as the free exercise of all religions are guaranteed to the people of this country, it is claimed, (with how much truth we stop not to inquire,) by those who deny that christianity is part of, or sanctioned, by the common-law, that all legislation, having for its object the punishment of offenses against the christian religion, is unconstitutional, and all adjudications of our courts of justice on this subject, "legislative usurpation." The attempt to disprove this maxim, is an effort on the part of those who deny or reject the gospel, indirectly to undermine the principles of religion and virtue, and to break down those barriers which have been erected by the gospel against irreligion and infidelity. It is possible, indeed, that some who deny the truth of the maxim, that christianity is sanctioned by the common-law, may not desire the effects which the course pursued by their coadjutors tends directly to produce.

At the head of those who, in this country, have denied the truth of the foregoing principle, we are sorry to be obliged to place the name of a writer and statesman of celebrity, Thomas Jefferson. We are the more sorry for this, because we are aware of the extensive influence which the opinion of Mr. J. will exert upon his and our countrymen.

But we are unwilling that error should at any time go uncontroverted, and more especially when sanctioned by the authority of great names, and are fully called upon to expose every attack upon religion, though it be at the expense of those who make the charge.

We learn from Mr. Jefferson, that Major John Cartwright, an Englishman, had written a work on the British Constitution, in which he undertook to prove, "that christianity could not be part of the common-law, inasmuch as the common-law existed among the Anglo-Saxons, while they were pagans, before they had heard the name of Christ pronounced, or knew that such a character had ever existed;" and Mr. J. pronounces this proof *incontrovertible.* He then proceeds to show in what manner the law was stolen in upon us, and claims to have proved, that all the books and cases in which this principle is recognized, rest ultimately for authority on a dictum of Ch. J. Prisot, made 34 Hen. 6. Year-Book, fol. 38, (A.D. 1458,) and that the opinion of Prisot means no such thing. The mistake, or forgery, (as he terms it,) arose from a mistranslation of the words *ancien scripture,* by Finch, in his first book of the law, c. 3. 1613, who renders these words by *holy scripture,* in which he is followed by Wingate, in 1666, who sets down this mistranslation as a maxim of the law, (*Wing. Max.* 3.) and cites Finch, as Sheppard, in 1675, copies the same and cites Finch and Wingate. Ch. J. Hall, a few years after, said, Rex vs. Taylor, 1. Vent. 293. s. c. 3. Rob. 307, that *christianity is the parcel of the laws of England,* and cites nobody. In 1728, the court in the case of the King vs. Woolston, 2. Strange, 834, would not suffer it to be debated, whether it was an offense at common-law to write against christianity. Wood, 409, gives the same principle, and cites 2. Strange, and Blackstone, in 1773. Com. 459, cites Ventris and Strange, as authority for the same assertion. In 1767, Lord Mansfield decided a similar principle, and quoted nobody. Thus, says Mr. J., we find this chain of authorities hanging link by link one upon another, and all ultimately upon one and the same hook, and that a mistranslation of the words, *"ancien scripture,"* used by Prisot, and adds, "I might defy the best-read lawyer to produce another scrip of authority for this *judiciary forgery.*"[†] In a letter to the Hon. E. Everett, some time after, he holds the same language in reference to the same subject.[‡]

---

* 1. Kent's Com. Am. Law. p. 472. 1. Swift's Dig. p. 9. Knowles vs. the State. 3. Day's Rep. 103. State vs. Danforth, 3. Comes, 112. Commonwealth vs. Knowlton, 2 Mass. Rep. 530. U.S. vs. Williams, 2. Cranch. 182. Const. Mass. N.Y. N.J. and Maryland.

† Letter to Major John Cartwright. Jefferson's works, 4 vols. 8vo. vol. 4, p. 239 and on.
‡ Vol. 4, p. 408.

The biographer of Mr. J., B. L. Rayner, quotes so much of the letter as relates to this subject, and says: "The part we quote contains the detection, through a long labyrinth of legal authorities, of a fundamental heresy, which, at an early period, through a palpable mistranslation of two words, crept into the common-law, and finally, by a series of cumulative adjudications, became firmly embodied in the text."*

The only answer that, so far as we are aware, has been made to this principle, so confidently insisted upon, is a very brief one, contained in the *American Jurist*,† made by some person apparently desirous of denying the truth of Mr. J's positions, without directly contradicting him. It is treated there, however, strictly as a legal question, and therefore does not dispense with the necessity of a further examination.

The above quotations from Mr. J. contain two propositions: the first asserts, that christianity cannot be a part of the common-law, because that law existed among the Anglo-Saxons while they were pagans; and the second, that the maxim which declares it to be so, is a *"judicial usurpation,"* crept in through the mistake or chicanery of its judges.

That neither of these positions are true, we shall prove by showing,—

1. That the *common-law* has been progressive, and that the principles which compose it, have been drawn from the customs of the primitive Britons, the Saxons, Danes and Normans.

2. That the Britons were christians long before they were conquered by the Saxons, and that the Saxons became so immediately after their settlement in Britain.

3. That crimes against the christian religion were punishable at common-law before the time of Prisot.

4. That christianity was considered as part of the common-law before the time of Prisot.

5. That the authorities cited by Mr. J. do not warrant the conclusion he has drawn.

1. The common-law has been progressive.

To determine this, we must first ascertain what composes the common-law. "The common-law," says Chancellor Kent, "consists of a collection of principles, to be found in the opinions of sages, or deduced from universal and immemorial usage, and receiving progressively the sanction of the courts."‡ The definitions of Sir W. Blackstone§ and Lord Coke,¶ are to the same effect. But it is not necessary to prove, that a given custom has been in existence from time immemorial, to justify courts and juries in finding such an usage; for it has been repeatedly decided, that an usage for twenty-years, unexplained and uncontradicted, is sufficient for that purpose;‖ and if contradicted, need not date back farther than Richard I. 1189.**

The very definition of the common-law, shows, that it has been progressive, and consequently could not have existed among the Anglo-Saxons when they were pagans; but we proceed to show from history, that the customs which make up that law, have been derived from various sources.

Fortescue, who was chief justice in the reign of Edward IV., and cotemporary with Prisot, says, "the realm of England was first inhabited by the Britons, then the Romans possessed it, then the Britons again. Afterwards the Saxons, then the Danes; after, the Saxons, and then the Normans had possession of the country; and yet during all these times the country has been governed by the same customs:"†† upon which Mr. Selden observes, that the truth seems to be, that there never was any formal exchange of one system of laws for another; but that the Saxons made a mixture of their own customs with those of the Britons, the Danes those of their own with those of the Britons and Saxons, and the Normans likewise.‡‡

---

* Life of Jefferson, 8vo. N.Y. 1832. p. 31.
† Vol. 9. p. 336.

‡ Com. Am. Law, vol. i. p. 72. 2d edition.
§ Com. Eng. Law, b. i. p. 62.
¶ Coke Litt. sec. 171 and 214.
‖ Black. Com. 35. 6. East. Rep. 214.
** 2. Black. Com. 31. 1. Sanders Pl. and Ev. 399.
†† De Laudibus Legum Angliae, c. 17, p. 30. Eng. Trans. fol. Savoy, 1737.
‡‡ Selden's Notes on For. abr. sup. and 1. Black. Com. 64.

Upon every irruption and conquest by a foreign nation, new laws and customs were introduced, and incorporated with those already in force; and therefore the common-law of England, like the language of that country, has originated from a variety of sources. The histories of that period fully justify this view of the subject.

The variety of local customs prevalent in the days of Alfred, gave rise to the *dome-boc, dom-boc, liber judicialis;* but in the eleventh century, this code of Alfred had fallen so much into disuse, or been superseded by other customs, that we find no less than three systems of laws prevailing in England, called the *Mercian-lage,* partaking most of the old British customs; the *West Saxon-lage,* coming nearer to the code of Alfred; and the *Dane-lage,* partaking, as its name imports, of the customs of the *Danes.**

Upon the accession of William of Normandy, these three systems of laws were digested, and such alterations and additions made as the situation of the country required.[†] One of the changes made at this time was the establishment, if not the introduction, of the feudal system, which has exerted such an extensive influence upon the estates of Europe for centuries.[‡] All these customs, with such modifications as a progressive state of civilization, of literature, science and the arts, would work, together with such as these things have given rise to now, compose the common-law. It follows, therefore, from the foregoing facts, that the first position of Mr. J. and Major C. is entirely wrong.

We now proceed to show,—

2. That the Britons were converted to christianity before their conquest by the Saxons, and the Saxons immediately after that conquest.

As early as A.D. 180, we find Tertullian declaring, that "the extremities of Spain, and the different nations of Gaul and Britain, inaccessible to the Roman arms, had been subdued to Christ."[§]

Eusebius, about 324, says, the first preachers of christianity "passed over the ocean, to those which are called the British isles."[¶]

Gildas, himself a Briton, who wrote about 560, dates the first introduction of christianity about 61,—and in this he is supported by the ancient British documents preserved in the Welsh Triads.[‖]

Clement of Rome, about 90, says that Paul reached the *furtherest extremity* of the west, by which it seems that Britain was intended.[**]

The Romans left Britain about 410, and the Saxons were invited to England about 450. From this time war raged with varied success between the Britons and those from whom they sought protection, until about 590. As late as 527, the Britons obtained a considerable victory over the Saxons, which was followed by a peace of forty years; and in 585, they obtained another considerable victory.[††] The Saxons seem to have obtained a permanent settlement in Kent as early as 580; and in 596, St. Austin, with forty missionaries from Rome, landed in that kingdom, and in two years converted and baptized the king of Kent, with more than ten thousand of his Anglo-Saxon subjects.[‡‡]

---

* 1. Black. Com. 64, 65. Hale's Hist. Com. Law, p. 55.

† Crabb's Hist. Eng. Com. Law, c. v. p. 44. 8vo. Burlington. 1831.

‡ Spelman Orig. Feudes. Hall. H. C. and 203. Black. Com. c. iv. Crabb, H. E. C. and c. v. Coke Litt. 191. a. Butler's Additional Notes.

§ Adv. Jud. c. 7. p. 189. fol. ed. 1675.

¶ Demons. Evang. c. 3. p. 112. fol. ed. 1628.

‖ Rob. Calmet. Bib. Dic. on Christianity.

** Clem. Rom. Ep. 1. c. 5 Trans. Chevalier, p. 4. 12mo. N. Y. 1834. p. 148. Le Clerc. Apos. Pat. vol. i. fol. 1698. Plutarch Vit. Caesar. Euseb. Vit. Cons. lib. i. c. 25, 41. L. 2. c. 28. Nicephor. Hist. L. 1. c. 1. Theodoret in Ep. 2. ad Tim. iv. 7. Theod. Rel. Hist. c. 26. tom. 3. p. 881. D. Edit. Paris, 1642. Hier. in Amas. c. 5. tom. 3. p. 1412. Ed. Benedict. Catullus Carm. 29 and 11. Horace, Carm. 1. 35. Stillingfleet. Antiq. Brit. Ecc. c. 1. vol. 3. fol. 1710, in 6 vols. from which it will be evident, that by the *furthest west,* Briton was intended. See also Bede's Hist. Ecc. lib. i. c. 4 p. 44. fol. Cont. 1722. Selden's Hist. Tithes, c. 9, sec. 1. p. 1206. vol. iii. ap. fol. Lond. 1726. Ledwich's Antiq. Ireland. p. 54. 4to. Dublin. 1722. Stone's Chron. Eng. p. 36. fol. London. 1631. Mosheim by Murdock, b. 1 cent. 2. Par. 1. c. 1. note.

†† Anc. Univ. Hist. vol. xvii. pp. 124, 129.

‡‡ Bede's Ecc. Hist. lib. i. c. 27. lib. ii. c. 4. Hume's Hist. of Eng. vol. i. Gibbon's Dec. and Fall of the Rom. Emp. vol. iii. c. 45. p. 210. 4 vols. 8vo. N. Y. 1831. Turner's Hist. Anglo-Saxon, vol. i. B. 2d. 8vo. 3 vols. London. 1828. It is common for those who desire the fact to be so, to represent this as the first introduction of christianity into Britain. So Hume and

The way seems to have been prepared for the easy introduction of christianity among the Saxons, by the influence and example of the Britons, with whom the Saxons associated; and the latter appear to have borrowed their alphabet, literature, and much of their civilization, from the persons from whom they had taken their possessions.*

The christian religion was introduced into Northumbria by a resolution of the *wittem-gemote* [ruling council], as the established religion, 625. It was introduced into Mercia 655, Essex 659, by a resolution of the king and his counselors; and in less than a century from this time, it had become common for the Anglo-Saxon kings to abdicate their thrones, and give themselves up to religious pursuits.†

The piety of Alfred had led him to introduce into his laws, not only the essential principles of christianity, not before recognized by law, but also many of the enactments of the Levitical code.‡

It is not unreasonable to suppose, that a nation who had just emerged from barbarism, had acquired letters, literature, and a degree of civilization, would find

it necessary to change many of those customs, which, before that time, had had the force of law. Indeed, we find that such was the fact; for among the Saxons, before their conversion, murder, and all other high crimes and misdemeanors, were only punished by a fine, varying in amount, according to the rank of the person injured. Every man had, in fact, at that period, a legal valuation set upon him.§ But no man will pretend, that murder is not now punishable with death by the *common-law*. We might instance many other customs, prevalent among the Saxons, which the progressive state of the common-law has entirely changed; but it is unnecessary.

We shall now show,—

3. That crimes against the christian religion, were punishable at common-law, long before the time of Prisot, 1458. If we can prove this, it will not be contended, that some of the principles of christianity were not recognized by the common-law; for nothing can be more absurd, than the idea that crimes against religion are punishable at common-law, and yet that the common-law does not recognize the principles of religion, against which those crimes are committed.

Bracton, who was justice in eyre in the reign of Henry 3d, in a work entitled *De Legibus et Consuetudinibus Angliae*, written about 1266,¶ and which, it is said, "contains nothing but what had been admitted by legal authorities into our jurisprudence," expressly declares, that "apostates from the christian religion were to be burnt to death."‖ So *Britton*, about 1280, declares that sorcerers, sodomites and heretics, were burnt, by the common-law.** It is also said by *Fleta*, about 1285, that apostates, sorcerers, and the like, are to be burnt.†† To the same effect, the *Mirror*, about

---

Gibbon are entirely silent as to the conversion of the Britons before their conquest by the Saxons.

    * Wood's Rel. in Brit. p. 75. 8vo. London. 1835. Cambrian Reg. vol. iii. p. 150. Henry's Hist. Great Britain, b. ii. c. 2. sec. ii. Turner's Hist. Angl. Sax. b. iii. c. 7. vol. i. p. 358; b. iii. c. 8. p. 365; b. ix. c. 1. p. 389. Bede's Ecc. Hist. lib. iii. cc. 25 and 27; b. ii. c. 4. pp. 234–241. Camden. Brit. vol. p. 1316. fol. 2 vols. London. 1722.

    It has been said, that the almost entire absence of Celtic words in our language, is good evidence that the primitive Britons were completely eradicated by the Saxons; but to this it may be replied, that Britain was inhabited by the Britons, Angles and Jutes, before the arrival of the Saxons, and that the two latter, together with the Saxons, were coeval twigs of the same barbaric race, descended from the same Teutonic branch of the Scythian or Gothic tree, as appears from their identity of language. Turner's Hist. Angl. Sax. b. i. c. 5. Camden. Brit. c. lib. ix. Procopius De Bell. Goth. lib. iv. And further, the Cimbric, or German Celtic, the language of the Britons when conquered by the Romans, though of a Celtic character, abounds with words of a Gothic origin—*Varieties of the Human Race, by J. G. Percival, M. D.* p. 3. *in an appendix to Goldsmith's Geographical View of the World.*

    † Turner's Hist. Angl. Sax. b. iii. cc. 2, 7, 8, 22, and others. Bede's Hist. Ecc. lib. v.

    ‡ Wilkins' Leges. Ang. Sax. Leg. Alfred. fol. Lond. 1721. Turn. Hist. Angl. Sax. b. v. c. 6. vol. ii. p. 149. Mr. J. pronounces these spurious; but Mr. Turner, than whom, no man living is better able to judge, declares them genuine, and Wilkins gives them without any doubt of their authenticity. See also Holt's Law of Libel, p. 32. 8vo. N.Y. 1818.

    § Wilkins' Leg. Angl. Sax. Turn. Hist. Angl. Sax. ap. 1. b. iii. c. 4 and 5.

    ¶ Reeve's Hist. Com. Law. lib. lxxxvi. Crabb's Hist. Com. Law. pp. 164–5.

    ‖ Tract. 2. c. 9. fol. 123. Lond. 1569. Crabb, p. 164. 4 Black. Com. p. 43.

    ** Britton, 8vo. Lond. 1762. c. 9. p. 60. and c. 17. Fitzherbert's Natura Brevium. p. 601. 8vo. Dublin. 1793.

    †† Fleta seu Commentarius Juris Anglicani. lib. i. c. 37. 4to. Lond. 1685. Crabb's Hist. E. Com. Law. c. 14. Hale's Hist. Com. Law. vol. i. p. 270. Holt's Law of Libel, p. 33. 8vo. 1818.

1300, says, that heresy was to be punished by excommunication, degradation, disinheriting and burning.*

The same author defines *heresy* to be a false and evil belief, arising out of error of the christian faith. It includes witchcraft and divination.†

The order by which such persons were consigned to the flames, was entitled the writ *de haeretico comburendo* [concerning heretics who ought to be burned], and was a common-law process.‡ In the time of Prisot, the definition of heresy was still more comprehensive, and included *all disbelief of the Catholic faith, neglect to attend her worship, and disobedience of her decrees.*§

These authorities must remove all doubts concerning the question whether offenses against religion were punishable at common-law, before the time of Finch, who, Mr. J. says, mistook the meaning of Ch. J. Prisot.

4. Christianity was considered as part of the common-law, long before the time of Prisot. Horne, in the *Mirror of Justice,* A.D. 1300, says, his "predecessors had divided the law into two volumes; into the canon-law, which consists in amendment of spiritual offenses, and the written [common] law, which consists in the punishment of temporal offenses." This written law he defines to be *"the written law of the antient usages warranted by the holy scripture."*¶

This statement of the *Mirror,* one hundred and fifty years before the decision by Prisot, is sufficient evidence that such was the opinion of the ancient sages of the law; and it is supported by the history of those times. Immediately after the Romans left Britain, there were *thirty-three* independent provinces, or republics, each having a bishop, who regulated the ecclesiastical affairs, and had some power in civil mat-

ters.‖ The bishops among the Saxons had also jurisdiction of many civil cases.** The religious establishment of England and the payment of tithes, seems to have been coeval with the conversion of the Anglo-Saxons to christianity;†† and we are told by the *Mirror,* that at first, (that is, immediately after the conversion of the Saxons,) *"they made the king swear to maintain the* CHRISTIAN FAITH, *with all his power."*‡‡ The dome-book, which contained the diversity of customs prevailing in the days of Alfred, recognizes many principles of the christian religion among those customs.§§

Mr. Selden, in his notes on Fortescue, says, the common-law of England is grounded on six points; the second of which, he says, is *"the Law of God;"* and the *Mirror* declares, that whatever is contrary to holy scripture, is not law.¶¶ The same principle was decided in the court of king's bench, in 1827.‖‖ These authorities prove conclusively, that the essential principles of religion were recognized by the common-law, before the time of Prisot.

We shall now show,—

5. That the authorities cited by Mr. J. do not warrant the conclusion he has drawn.

The original of Prisot, from which Mr. J. says the principle in question was drawn, is, "A tiel leis qu'ils de seint eglise out *en ancien scripture,* covient a nous a donner credence; car ceo common ley sur quels touts manners leis fondes. Et anxy, Sir, nous sumus obliges de conustre lour ley de seint eglise, et semblablement ils sont obliges de connustre nostre ley."

A literal translation of this passage is, "as to those laws, which holy church have in *ancient scripture,* it be-

---

* Mirror des Justices, c. 4. sec. 14. p. 194. 8vo. Lond. 1768.

† C. 1. sec. 4.

‡ Hawkins' Pleas of the Crown, b. i. c. 2. Fitz. Nat. Brev. p. 601. Reeves' Hist. Com. Law. vol. iii. p. 235. 4 vols. 8vo. Lond. 1787. Co. 3. Inst. p. 44. Crabb's Hist. E. Com. Law. pp. 314, 348. 4 Black. Com. p. 42–46. Wood's Institute, Eng. Law. b. iii. c. 3. p. 422. fol. Savoy. 1775.

§ 4 Black. Com. p. 45. Lyndewoode of heretics. Stat. 2. Hen. 4. c. 15.

¶ C. 1. sec. 1.

‖ Turner's Hist. Angl. Sax. b. ii. c. 8. pp. 192, 193.

** Wilkins' Leg. Angl. Sax. LL. Edg. c. 5. LL. 6. on c. 17. Bede, lib. iii. c. 25. Crabb's Hist. E. Com. Law. pp. 20, 22.

†† Selden on Tithes, c. 10. Crabb, p. 22.

‡‡ C. 1. sec. 2.

§§ Holt's Law of Libel, pp. 31, 32. Selden, on Law and Government. 1 Black. Com. p. 64–5. Hale's Hist. Com. Law. p. 55. Mirror, c. 4. sec. 18. p. 207.

¶¶ De Laud. Leg. Ang. c. 15. p. 28. Mirror, c. 5. sec. 1. p. 224. c. 1. sec. 3. p. 6.

‖‖ Smith *vs.* Sparrow. 4. Bing. 93, 13. Com. Law. 351. See also Fennel *vs.* Ridler. 5. Bane *vs.* Cris, 406. 11. Com. Law Rep. 261.

hoves us to give credence, for this is common-law, upon which all manner of laws are founded; and thus, Sir, we are obliged to take notice of their law of holy church; and it seems they are obliged to take notice of our law."*

Finch,† says Mr. J., and after him Wingate‡ and Sheppard,§ translate *ancien scripture,* by holy scripture; Wingate quoting Finch, and Sheppard both Finch and Wingate. Finch gives the original of Prisot in the margin; and therefore both Wingate and Sheppard had it before them when they said, "That to such laws of the church as have warrant in holy scripture our law giveth credence." It will be remarked, that this passage is not a translation of Prisot, but the statement of a principle, with reference to the Year Books, as authorizing the statement.

The language of the Year Books, is marvelously like that we have already quoted from the *Mirror of Justice.* Prisot says in effect, that the common-law, upon which all other laws are founded, is the law contained in *ancien scripture;* and the *Mirror,* that the common-law consists of the ancient customs, warranted by *holy scripture.* That both refer to the same thing, seems too evident to admit of a doubt.

It is no small argument in favor of the principle laid down by Finch, that it has been copied by several authors, all having the original before them, and that its falsehood had never been detected, until pointed out by Mr. J.

But it is not Finch alone, who is chargeable with blinking the truth; for it will be recollected, that Mr. J. defies the "best-read lawyer, to produce another scrip of authority for this judiciary forgery." Now Finch not only cites the Year Books, but also Hobart, 148, and Plowd. 265, both of which are omitted by Mr. J.

In the case of Colt and Glover *vs.* the Bishop of Coventry and Litchfield, reported by Hobart, it was decided, "that the laws of the realm do admit of nothing contrary to the law of God."

The assertion of lord chief justice Hale,¶ that *christianity was part of the common-law of England,* seems to have been predicated upon the opinion of lord Coke, who had asserted the same long before that time;‖ but of the assertion of lord Coke, Mr. J. has taken no notice.

But whether the translation or assertion of Finch be true or false, the chain ends with Sheppard, lord Hale not citing it.

Again, in the case of the King *vs.* Woolston, the court would not permit it to be debated, whether to write against christianity was an offense at common-law; giving as a reason, that it had been so decided in Rex *vs.* Taylor, and Rex *vs.* Hall;** but Mr. J. has taken no notice of the case of Rex *vs.* Hall, in which the same principle was asserted, as one well known and established, without reference to authority. So too lord Mansfield, in Evans' case, took it for granted, that this principle was so well established, as to be beyond question. The inference, therefore, that lord Hale or lord Mansfield made their decisions upon the authority of the Year Books, Finch, Wingate, or Sheppard, is wholly gratuitous, and unsupported by the facts. So far then, is this whole controversy from proving "a conspiracy between church and state," as alledged by Mr. J., that it is wonderfully like a conspiracy against the former; and as such, we have felt it our duty to expose it.

P. S. Since the foregoing was prepared for the press, the writer has seen in the *American Quarterly Review,* for June, 1835, No. 34, an article on the subject of the present inquiry.

The first position of the reviewer, that christianity is not recognized in the constitution of the United States, and of the various states, is in accordance with the assumptions of the foregoing article. The other part of the argument is based on Mr. J's. letter under

---

* 34. Hen. 6. fol. 38. Trans. from Am. Jurist. vol. ix. p. 346.
† Book of the Law, c. 3.
‡ Wingate, Max. 3.
§ Tit. Religion.

¶ Rex *vs.* Taylor. 1 Vent. 293. S.C. 3 Rel. 607.
‖ 2. Inst. 220. Holt on Law of Libel, p. 32.
** 1. Vant. p. 293. 1. Strange, p. 416.

consideration, and must fall with it; and the article, therefore, requires no further answer. To this it may be added, he inadvertently omitted to state, that it has been said by the Superior Court in Pennsylvania, that christianity has been part of the common-law since the days of Bracton. 11. Serg. and Rawle, p. 400.

JUDICIAL OPINIONS

The question of whether Christianity was the basis of common law was, most importantly, debated in judicial chambers. Both federal and state judges in the early nineteenth century opined on the place of Christianity in the nation's laws. The following three influential state blasphemy cases illustrate judicial debate on this fundamental question.

People v. Ruggles,
8 Johnson 290 (N.Y. 1811)

KENT, Ch. J. delivered the opinion of the Court. The offence charged is, that the defendant below did "wickedly, maliciously, and blasphemously utter, in the presence and hearing of divers good and christian people, these false, feigned, scandalous, malicious, wicked and blasphemous words, to wit, "*Jesus Christ* was a bastard, and his mother must be a whore;*" and

Reprinted from William Johnson, *Reports of Cases Argued and Determined in the Supreme Court of Judicature; and in the Court for the Trial of Impeachments and the Correction of Errors, in the State of New York* (New-York: Printed by Isaac Riley, 1811), 8:290–98.

the single question is, whether this be a public offence by the law of the land. After conviction, we must intend that these words were uttered in a wanton manner, and, as they evidently import, with a wicked and malicious disposition, and not in a serious discussion upon any controverted point in religion. The language was blasphemous not only in a popular, but in a legal sense; for blasphemy, according to the most precise definitions, consists in maliciously reviling God, or religion, and this was reviling christianity through its author. (*Emlyn's Preface to the State Trials,* p. 8. See, also, *Whitlock's Speech, State Trials,* vol. 2. 273.) The jury have passed upon the intent or *quo animo* [in what spirit] and if those words spoken, in any case, will amount to a misdemeanor, the indictment is good.

Such words, uttered with such a disposition, were an offence at common law. In *Taylor's* case, (1 *Vent.* 293. 3 *Keb.* 607. *Tremaine's Pleas of the Crown,* 226. S.C.) the defendant was convicted upon information of speaking similar words, and the court of *K. B.* said, that christianity was parcel of the law, and to cast contumelious reproaches upon it, tended to weaken the foundation of moral obligation, and the efficacy of oaths. And in the case of *Rex* v. *Woolston,* (*Str.* 834. *Fitzg.* 64.) on a like conviction, the court said they would not suffer it to be debated whether defaming christianity in general was not an offence at common law, for that whatever strikes at the root of christianity, tends manifestly to the dissolution of civil government. But the court were careful to say, that they did not intend to include disputes between learned men upon particular controverted points. The same doctrine was laid down in the late case of *The King* v. *Williams,* for the publication of *Paine's "Age of Reason,"* which was tried before Lord *Kenyon,* in *July,* 1797. The authorities show that blasphemy against God, and contumelious reproaches and profane ridicule of Christ or the Holy Scriptures, (which are equally treated as blasphemy,) are offences punishable at common law, whether uttered by words or writings. (*Taylor's* case, 1 *Vent.* 293. 4 *Blacks. Com.* 59. 1 *Hawk.* b. 1. c. 5. 1 *East's P. C.* 3. *Tremaine's Entries,*

225. *Rex* v. *Doyley*.) The consequences may be less extensively pernicious in the one case than in the other, but in both instances, the reviling is still an offence, because it tends to corrupt the morals of the people, and to destroy good order. Such offences have always been considered independent of any religious establishment or the rights of the church. They are treated as affecting the essential interests of civil society.

And why should not the language contained in the indictment be still an offence with us? There is nothing in our manners or institutions which has prevented the application or the necessity of this part of the common law. We stand equally in need, now as formerly, of all that moral discipline, and of those principles of virtue, which help to bind society together. The people of this state, in common with the people of this country, profess the general doctrines of christianity, as the rule of their faith and practice; and to scandalize the author of these doctrines is not only, in a religious point of view, extremely impious, but, even in respect to the obligations due to society, is a gross violation of decency and good order. Nothing could be more offensive to the virtuous part of the community, or more injurious to the tender morals of the young, than to declare such profanity lawful. It would go to confound all distinction between things sacred and profane; for, to use the words of one of the greatest oracles of human wisdom, "profane scoffing doth by little and little deface the reverence for religion;" and who adds, in another place, "two principal causes have I ever known of atheism—curious controversies and profane scoffing." (Lord *Bacon's Works,* vol. 2. 291. 503.) Things which corrupt moral sentiment, as obscene actions, prints and writings, and even gross instances of seduction, have, upon the same principle, been held indictable; and shall we form an exception in these particulars to the rest of the civilized world? No government among any of the polished nations of antiquity, and none of the institutions of modern *Europe,* (a single and monitory case excepted,) ever hazarded such a bold experiment upon the solidity of the public morals, as to permit with impunity, and under the sanction of their tribunals, the general religion of the community to be openly insulted and defamed. The very idea of jurisprudence with the ancient lawgivers and philosophers, embraced the religion of the country. *Jurisprudentia est divinarum atque humanarum rerum notitia.* (*Dig.* b. 1. 10. 2. *Cic. De Legibus,* b. 2. *passim.*)

The free, equal, and undisturbed, enjoyment of religious opinion, whatever it may be, and free and decent discussions on any religious subject, is granted and secured; but to revile, with malicious and blasphemous contempt, the religion professed by almost the whole community, is an abuse of that right. Nor are we bound, by any expressions in the constitution, as some have strangely supposed, either not to punish at all, or to punish indiscriminately the like attacks upon the religion of *Mahomet* or of the grand *Lama;* and for this plain reason, that the case assumes that we are a christian people, and the morality of the country is deeply ingrafted upon christianity, and not upon the doctrines or worship of those impostors. Besides, the offence is *crimen malitiae,* and the imputation of malice could not be inferred from any invectives upon superstitions equally false and unknown. We are not to be restrained from animadversion upon offences against public decency, like those committed by Sir *Charles Sedley,* (1 *Sid.* 168,) or by one *Rollo,* (*Sayer,* 158,) merely because there may be savage tribes, and perhaps semibarbarous nations, whose sense of shame would not be affected by what we should consider the most audacious outrages upon decorum. It is sufficient that the common law checks upon words and actions, dangerous to the public welfare, apply to our case, and are suited to the condition of this and every other people whose manners are refined, and whose morals have been elevated and inspired with a more enlarged benevolence, by means of the christian religion.

Though the constitution has discarded religious establishments, it does not forbid judicial cognisance of those offences against religion and morality which have no reference to any such establishment, or to any particular form of government, but are punishable because they strike at the root of moral obligation, and weaken the security of the social ties. The object of the 38th article of the constitution, was, to "guard against spiritual oppression and intolerance," by declaring that "the free exercise and enjoyment of religious profession and worship, without discrimination or preference, should for ever thereafter be allowed within this state, to all mankind." This declaration, (noble and magnanimous as it is, when duly understood,) never meant to withdraw religion in general, and with it the best sanctions of moral and social obligation from all consideration and notice of the law. It will be fully satisfied by a free and universal toleration, without any of the tests, disabilities, or discriminations, incident to a religious establishment. To construe it as breaking down the common law barriers against licentious, wanton, and impious attacks upon christianity itself, would be an enormous perversion of its meaning. The *proviso* guards the article from such dangerous latitude of construction, when it declares, that "*the liberty of conscience hereby granted,* shall not be so construed as to excuse acts of licentiousness, or justify practices inconsistent with the peace and safety of this state." The preamble and this *proviso* are a species of commentary upon the meaning of the article, and they sufficiently show that the framers of the constitution intended only to banish test oaths, disabilities and the burdens, and sometimes the oppressions, of church establishments; and to secure to the people of this state, freedom from coercion, and an equality of right, on the subject of religion. This was no doubt the consummation of their wishes. It was all that reasonable minds could require, and it had long been a favorite object, on both sides of the *Atlantic,* with some of the most enlightened friends to the rights of mankind, whose indignation had been roused by infringements of the liberty of conscience, and whose zeal was inflamed in the pursuit of its enjoyment. That this was the meaning of the constitution is further confirmed by a paragraph in a preceding article, which specially provides that "such parts of the common law as might be construed to establish or maintain any particular denom-

ination of christians, or their ministers," were thereby abrogated.

The legislative exposition of the constitution is conformable to this view of it. Christianity, in its enlarged sense, as a religion revealed and taught in the Bible, is not unknown to our law. The *statute for preventing immorality* (*Laws,* vol. 1. 224. *R. S.* 675, s. 69, *et seq.*) consecrates the first day of the week, as holy time, and considers the violation of it as immoral. This was only the continuation, in substance, of a law of the colony which declared, that the profanation of the Lord's day was "the great scandal of the christian faith." The act *concerning oaths,* (*Laws,* vol. 1. p. 405. [2 *R. S.* 407, s. 82,]) recognises the common law mode of administering an oath, "by laying the hand on and kissing the gospels." Surely, then, we are bound to conclude, that wicked and malicious words, writings and actions which go to vilify those gospels, continue, as at common law, to be an offence against the public peace and safety. They are inconsistent with the reverence due to the administration of an oath, and among their other evil consequences, they tend to lessen, in the public mind, its religious sanction.

The court are accordingly of opinion that the judgment below must be affirmed.

Judgment affirmed.

Updegraph v. Commonwealth, 11 Sergeant & Rawle 394 (Pa. 1824)

DUNCAN, J. This was an indictment for blasphemy, founded on an act of assembly, passed in 1700, which enacts, that whosoever shall wilfully, premeditatedly and despitefully blaspheme, and speak loosely and *profanely* of Almighty God, Christ Jesus, the Holy

Reprinted from Thomas Sergeant and William Rawle, Jr., *Reports of Cases Adjudged in the Supreme Court of Pennsylvania* (Philadelphia: Printed by McCarty and Davis, 1826), 11:398–411.

Spirit, or the Scripture of Truth, and is legally convicted thereof, shall forfeit and pay the sum of *ten pounds.*

It charges the defendant with contriving and intending to scandalize and bring into disrepute, and vilify the Christian religion, and the scriptures of truth; and that he, in the presence and hearing of several persons, unlawfully, wickedly, and premeditatedly, despitefully and blasphemously, did say, among other things, in substance, as follows: "that the Holy Scriptures were a mere fable, that they were a contradiction, and that although they contained a number of good things, yet they contained a great many lies:" and the indictment concludes, to the great dishonor of Almighty God, to the great scandal of the profession of the Christian religion, to the evil example of all others in like case offending, and against the form of the act of assembly in such case made and provided.

The jury have found that the defendant did speak words of that substance, in the temper and with the intent stated. This verdict excludes everything like innocence of intention; it finds a malicious intention in the speaker to vilify the Christian religion and the scriptures, and this court cannot look beyond the record, nor take any notice of the allegation, that the words were uttered by the defendant, a member of a debating association, which convened weekly for discussion and mutual information, and that the expressions were used in the course of argument on a religious question. That there is an association in which so serious a subject is treated with so much levity, indecency and scurrility, existing in this city, I am sorry to hear, for it would prove a nursery of vice, a school of preparation to qualify young men for the gallows, and young women for the brothel, and there is not a skeptic of decent manners and good morals, who would not consider such debating clubs as a common nuisance and disgrace to the city. From the tenor of the words, it is impossible that they could be spoken seriously and conscientiously, in the discussion of a religious or theological topic; there is nothing of argument in the language; it was the out-

pouring of an invective, so vulgarly shocking and insulting, that the lowest grade of civil authority ought not to be subject to it, but when spoken in a Christian land, and to a Christian audience, the highest offence *contra bonos mores* [against good morals]; and even if Christianity was not part of the law of the land, it is the popular religion of the country, an insult on which would be indictable, as directly tending to disturb the public peace.

The bold ground is taken, though it has often been exploded, and nothing but what is trite can be said upon it—it is a barren soil, upon which no flower ever blossomed—the assertion is once more made, that Christianity never was received as part of the common law of this Christian land; and it is added, that if it was, it was virtually repealed by the constitution of the United States, and of this state, as inconsistent with the liberty of the people, the freedom of religious worship, and hostile to the genius and spirit of our government, and with it, the act against blasphemy; and if the argument be worth anything, all the laws which have Christianity for their object—all would be carried away at one fell swoop—the act against cursing and swearing, and breach of the Lord's day; the act forbidding incestuous marriages, perjury by taking a false oath upon the book, fornication and adultery, *et peccatum illud horribile non nominandum inter Christianos**—for all these are founded on Christianity—for all these are restraints upon civil liberty, according to the argument—edicts of religious and civic tyranny, "when enlightened notions of the rights of man were not so universally diffused as at the present day."

Another *exception* is taken. However technical it may be and however heinous the offence, still, if it be not charged as the law requires, the plaintiff in error is entitled to the full benefit of the exception. The objection is, that the words are not laid to have been spoken profanely.

---

* and that horrible sin which ought not to be named among Christians (perhaps an allusion to Ephesians 5:30, where "fornication should not be named among you, as is appropriate for those who are holy").—Trans.

We will first dispose of what is considered the grand objection—*the constitutionality of Christianity*—for, in effect, that is *the question.* Christianity, general Christianity, is and always has been a part of the common law of Pennsylvania; Christianity, without the spiritual artillery of European countries; for this Christianity was one of the considerations of the royal charter, and the very basis of its great founder, William Penn; not Christianity founded on any particular religious tenets; not Christianity with an established church, and tithes and spiritual courts; but Christianity with liberty of conscience to all men. William Penn and Lord Baltimore were the first legislators who passed laws in favor of liberty of conscience; for before that period, the principle of liberty of conscience appeared in the laws of no people, the axiom of no government, the institutes of no society, and scarcely in the temper of any man. Even the reformers were as furious against contumacious errors, as they were loud in asserting the liberty of conscience. And to the wilds of America, peopled by a stock cut off by persecution from a Christian society, does Christianity owe true freedom of religious opinion and religious worship. There is, in this very act of 1700, a precision of definition, and a discrimination so perfect between prosecutions for opinions seriously, temperately, and argumentatively expressed, and despiteful railings, as to command our admiration and reverence for the enlightened framers.

From the time of Bracton, Christianity has been received as part of the common law of England. I will not go back to remote periods, but state a series of prominent decisions, in which the doctrine is to be found. In The King *v.* Taylor, Vent. 93; 3 Keb. 607, the defendant was convicted on an information for saying, that Christ Jesus was a bastard, a whoremaster, and religion a cheat. Lord Chief Baron HALE, the great and the good Lord HALE (no stickler for church establishments), observed, "that such kind of wicked and blasphemous words were not only an offence against God and religion, but against the laws of the state and government, and therefore punishable; that to say, religion is a cheat, is to dissolve all those obligations by which civil societies are preserved; and that Christianity is part of the law of England, and therefore, to reproach the Christian religion is to speak in subversion of the laws."

In the case of The King *v.* Woolasten, 2 Str. 834; Fitzg. 64; Raym. 162, the defendant had been convicted of publishing five libels, ridiculing the miracles of Jesus Christ, his life and conversation; and it was moved in arrest of judgment, that this offence was not punishable in the temporal courts, but the court said, they would not suffer it to be debated, "whether to write against Christianity generally was not an offence of temporal cognisance." It was further contended, that it was merely to show that those miracles were not to be taken in a literal but allegorical sense: and therefore, the book could not be aimed at Christianity in general, but merely attacking one proof of the divine mission: but the court said, the main design of the book, though professing to establish Christianity upon a true bottom, considers the narrations of scripture as explanative and prophetical, yet that these professions could not be credited, and the rule is *allegatio contra factum non est admittendum.** In that case, the court laid great stress on the term *general,* and did not intend to include disputes between learned men on particular and controverted points, and Lord Chief Justice RAYMOND, Fitzg. 66, said "I would have it taken notice of, that we do not meddle with the difference of opinion, and that we interfere only where the root of Christianity is struck at."

The information filed against the celebrated Wilkes was for publishing an obscene and infamous libel, tending to vitiate and corrupt the minds of the subjects, and to introduce a total contempt of religion, morality and virtue, to blaspheme Almighty God, to ridicule our Saviour, and the Christian religion.

In the justly-admired speech of Lord MANSFIELD, in a case which made much noise at the time—Evans *v.* Chamberlain of London; Furneaux's Letters to Sir William Blackstone; App'x to Bl. Com,

---

* a charge against the deed is not to be heard.—Trans.

and 2 Burns' Ecc. Law, p. 95: Conscience, he observed, is not controllable by human laws, nor amenable to human tribunals; persecution, or attempts to force conscience, will never produce conviction, and were only calculated to make hypocrites or martyrs. There never was a single instance, from the Saxon times down to our own, in which a man was punished for erroneous opinions. For atheism, blasphemy, and reviling the Christian religion, there have been instances of prosecution at the common law; but bare non-conformity is no sin by the common law, and all pains and penalties for non-conformity to the established rites and modes are repealed by the acts of toleration, and dissenters exempted from ecclesiastical censures. What bloodshed and confusion have been occasioned, from the reign of Henry IV., when the first penal statutes were enacted, down to the revolution, by laws made to force conscience. There is certainly nothing more unreasonable, nor inconsistent with the rights of human nature, more contrary to the spirit and precepts of the Christian religion, more iniquitous and unjust, more impolitic, than persecution against natural religion, revealed religion, and sound policy. The great and wise and learned judge observes, "The true principles of natural religion are part of the common law; the essential principles of revealed religion are part of the common law; so that a person vilifying, subverting or ridiculing them may be prosecuted at common law; but temporal punishments ought not to be inflicted for mere opinions."

Long before this, much suffering, and a mind of a strong and liberal cast, had taught this sound doctrine and this Christian precept to William Penn. The charter of Charles II. recites, that "Whereas our trusty and beloved William Penn, out of a commendable desire to enlarge our English empire, as also to reduce the savages, by gentle and just measures, to the love of civil society, and the Christian religion, hath humbly besought our leave to translate a colony, &c. The first legislative act in the colony was the recognition of the Christian religion, and establishment of liberty of conscience. Before this, in 1646, Lord BALTIMORE passed a law in Maryland in fa-

vor of religious freedom, and it is a memorable fact, that of the first legislators, who established religious freedom, one was a Roman Catholic and the other a Friend. It is called the great law of the body of laws, in the province of Pennsylvania, passed at an assembly at Chester, the 7th of the 12th month, December. After the following preamble and declaration, viz: "Whereas ye glory of Almighty God, and ye good of mankind, is ye reason and end of government, and therefore, government in itself is a venerable ordinance of God; and forasmuch as it is principally desired and intended by ye proprietary and governor, and ye freemen of ye province of Pennsylvania, and territorys thereunto belonging, to make and establish such laws as shall best preserve true Christian and civil liberty, in opposition to all unchristian, licentious and unjust practices, whereby God may have his due, Caesar his due, and ye people their due, from tirranny and oppression on ye one side, and insolency and licentiousness on ye other, so that ye best and firmest foundation may be laid for ye present and future happiness both of ye governor and people of this province and territorys aforesaid, and their posterity: Be it therefore, enacted by William Penn, proprietary and governor, by and with ye advice and consent of ye deputys of ye freemen of this province and counties aforesaid in assembly mett, and by ye authority of ye same, that these following chapters and paragraphs shall be the laws of Pennsylvania, and the territorys thereof.

"Almighty God, being only Lord of conscience, Father of lyghts and spirits, and ye author as well as object of all divine knowledge, faith and worship, who only can enlighten ye minds, and persuade and convince ye understandings of people in due reverence to his sovereignty over the souls of mankind: It is enacted by the authority aforesaid, y^t no person, at any time hereafter living in this province, who shall confess and acknowledge one Almighty God to be ye creator, upholder and ruler of ye world, and that professeth him or herself obliged in conscience to live peaceably and justly under ye civil government, shall in any wise be molested or prejudiced for his or her conscientious persuasion or practice, nor shall he or she, at any time, be compelled to frequent or maintain any religious worship, plan or ministry whatever, contrary to his or her mind, but shall freely and fully enjoy his or her Christian liberty in y^t respect, without any interruption or reflection; and if any person shall abuse or deride any other for his or her different persuasion and practice in a matter of religion, such shall be lookt upon as a disturber of ye peace, and shall be punished accordingly." And to the end that looseness, irreligion and atheism may not creep in under the pretence of conscience, it provides for the observance of the Lord's day, punishes profane cursing and swearing, and further enacts, for the better preventing corrupt communication, "that whoever shall speak loosely and profanely of Almighty God, Christ Jesus, the Holy Spirit, or Scriptures of Truth, and is thereof legally convicted, shall forfeit and pay five pounds, and be imprisoned for five days in the house of correction."

Thus this wise legislature framed this great body of laws, for a Christian country and Christian people. Infidelity was then rare, and no infidels were among the first colonists. They fled from religious intolerance, to a country where all were allowed to worship according to their own understanding, and as was justly observed by the learned chancellor of the associated members of the bar of Philadelphia, in the city of Philadelphia, in his address to that body, 22d of June 1822, the number of Jews was too inconsiderable to excite alarm, and the believers in Mahomet were not likely to intrude. Every one had the right of adopting for himself whatever opinion appeared to be the most rational, concerning all matters of religious belief; thus securing by law this inestimable freedom of conscience, one of the highest privileges, and greatest interests of the human race. This is the Christianity of the common law, incorporated into the great law of Pennsylvania, and thus, it is irrefragably proved, that the laws and institutions of this state are built on the foundation of reverence for Christianity. Here was complete liberty of conscience, with the exception of disqualification for office of all who did not profess faith in Jesus Christ. This disqualification was not contained in the constitution of 1776; the door was open to any believer in a God, and so it continued under our present constitution, with the necessary addition of a belief in a future state of rewards and punishments. In this the constitution of the United States has made no alteration, nor in the great body of the laws which was an incorporation of the common-law doctrine of Christianity, as suited to the condition of the colony, and without which no free government can long exist.

Under the constitution, penalties against cursing and swearing have been exacted. If Christianity was abolished, all false oaths, all tests by oath, in the common form, by the book, would cease to be indictable as perjury; the indictment must state the oath to be on the holy Evangelists of Almighty God; the accused, on his trial, might argue that the book by which he was sworn, so far from being holy writ, was a pack of lies, containing as little truth as Robinson Crusoe. And is every jury in the box to decide as a fact whether the scriptures are of divine origin?

Let us now see what have been the opinions of our judges and court. The late Judge WILSON, of the Supreme Court of the United States, Professor of Law in the College in Philadelphia, was appointed in 1791, unanimously, by the House of Representatives of this state to "revise and digest the laws of this commonwealth, to ascertain and determine how far any British statutes extended to it, and to prepare bills containing such alterations and additions as the code of laws, and the principles and forms of the constitution, then lately adopted, might require." He had just risen from his seat in the convention which formed the constitution of the United States, and of this state; and it is well known, that for our present form of government we are greatly indebted to his exertions and influence. With his fresh recollections of both constitutions, in his course of Lectures (3d vol. of his Works 112), he states that profaneness and blasphemy are offences punishable by fine and imprisonment, and that Christianity is part of the common-law. It is in vain to object that the law is obsolete; this is not so; it has seldom been called into operation because this, like some other offences, has been rare. It has been retained in our collection of laws now in force, made by the direction of the legislature, and it has not been a dead letter.

In the mayor's court in the city of Philadelphia, in 1818, one Murray was convicted of a most scandalous blasphemy. He attempted, by advertisement, to call a meeting of the enemies of persecution; but this ended in mere vapor; the good sense of the people frowned upon it, and he was most justly sentenced. An account of the proceedings will be found in the Franklin Gazette of the 21st of November 1818. If the doctrine advanced in the written argument delivered to the court was just (and it is but justice to the counsel for the plaintiff in error, for the court to acknowledge the propriety of his conduct, in preferring this course to a declamation in open court), impiety and profanity must reach their acme with impunity, and every debating club might dedicate the club-room to the worship of the Goddess of Reason, and adore the deity in the person of a naked prostitute. The people would not tolerate these flagitious acts, and would themselves punish; and it is for this, among other reasons, that the law interposes to prevent the disturbance of the public peace. It is sometimes asked, with a sneer, why not leave it to Almighty God to revenge his own cause? Temporal courts do so leave it. "Bold and presumptuous would be the man who would attempt to arrest the thunder of heaven from the hand of God, and direct the bolts of vengeance where to fall." It is not on this principle courts act, but on the dangerous temporal consequences likely to proceed from the removal of religious and moral restraints; this is the ground of punishment for blasphemous and criminal publications; and without any view to spiritual correction of the offender. 4 Bl. Com. 59; Fitzg. 67; Starkie on Libel 487.

"Shall each blasphemer quite escape the rod,
And plead the insult 's not to man but God?"

It is not an *auto-da-fe*, displaying vengeance; but a law, punishing with great mildness, a gross offence against public decency and public order, tending directly to disturb the peace of the commonwealth. Chief Justice SWIFT, in his System of Laws, 2 vol. 825, has some very just reasoning on the subject. He observes, "To prohibit the open, public and explicit denial of the popular religion of a country, is a necessary measure to preserve the tranquillity of a government. Of this, no person in a Christian country can complain; for, admitting him to be an infidel, he must acknowledge that no benefit can be derived from the subversion of a religion which enforces the purest morality." In the Supreme Court of New York, it was solemnly determined, that Christianity was part of the law of the land, and that to revile the Holy Scriptures was an indictable offence. The case assumes, says Chief Justice KENT, that we are a Christian people, and the morality of the country is deeply engrafted on Christianity. Nor are we bound by any expression in the constitution, as some have strangely supposed, not to punish at all, or to punish indiscriminately the like attack upon Mahomet or the Grand Lama. The People *v.* Ruggles, 8 Johns. 290. This decision was much canvassed in the New York convention, 1821. Debates 463. An article was proposed in the new constitution, declaring that the judiciary should not declare any particular religion the law of the land. This was lost by a vote of 74 to 41.

It is a mistake, to suppose that this decision was founded on any special provision in the constitution. It has long been firmly settled, that blasphemy against the Deity generally, or an attack on the Christian religion indirectly, for the purpose of exposing its doctrines to ridicule and contempt, is indictable and punishable as a temporal offence. The principles and actual decisions are, that the publication, whether written or oral, must be malicious, and designed for that end and purpose; both the language of indictments, and the guarded expressions of judges show, that it never was a crime at the common-law, seriously and conscientiously to discuss theological and religious topics, though in the course of such discussions doubts may have been created and expressed, on doctrinal points, and the force of a particular proof of

Scripture evidence casually weakened, or the authority of particular important texts disputed; and persons of a different religion, as Jews, though they must necessarily deny the authenticity of other religions, have never been punished as blasphemers or libellers, at common law for so doing. All men of conscientious religious feeling ought to concede outward respect to every mode of religious worship.

Upon the whole, it may not be going too far, to infer, from the decisions, that no author or printer, who fairly and conscientiously promulgates the opinions with whose truths he is impressed, for the benefit of others, is answerable as a criminal; that a malicious and mischievous intention is, in such a case, the broad boundary between right and wrong, and that it is to be collected from the offensive levity, scurrilous and opprobrious language, and other circumstances, whether the act of the party was malicious; and since the law has no means of distinguishing between different degrees of evil tendency, if the matter published contains any such evil tendency, it is a public wrong. An offence against the public peace may consist either of an actual breach of the peace, or doing that which tends to provoke and excite others to do it. Within the latter description fall all acts and all attempts to produce disorder, by written, printed, or oral communications, for the purpose of generally weakening those religious and moral restraints, without the aid of which mere legislative provisions would prove ineffectual. No society can tolerate a wilful and despiteful attempt to subvert its religion, no more than it would to break down its laws—a general, malicious and deliberate intent to overthrow Christianity, general Christianity. This is the line of indication, where crime commences, and the offence becomes the subject of penal visitation.

The species of offence may be classed under the following heads—1. Denying the being and providence of God. 2. Contumelious reproaches of Jesus Christ; profane and malevolent scoffing at the scriptures, or exposing any part of them to contempt and ridicule. 3. Certain immoralities tending to subvert all religion and morality, which are the foundations of all governments. Without these restraints no free government could long exist. It is liberty run mad, to declaim against the punishment of these offences, or to assert that the punishment is hostile to the spirit and genius of our government. They are far from being true friends to liberty who support this doctrine, and the promulgation of such opinions, and general receipt of them among the people, would be the sure forerunners of anarchy, and finally, of despotism. Amidst the concurrent testimony of political and philosophical writers among the Pagans, in the most absolute state of democratic freedom, the sentiments of Plutarch, on this subject, are too remarkable to be omitted. After reciting that the first and greatest care of the legislators of Rome, Athens, Lacedaemon and Greece in general, was by instituting solemn supplications and forms of oaths, to inspire them with a sense of the favor or displeasure of Heaven, that learned historian declares, that we have met with towns unfortified, illiterate and without the conveniences of habitations; but a people wholly without religion, no traveller hath yet seen; and a city might as well be erected in the air, as a state be made to unite, where no divine worship is attended. Religion he terms the cement of civil union, and the essential support of legislation.

No free government now exists in the world, unless where Christianity is acknowledged, and is the religion of the country. So far from Christianity, as the counsel contends, being part of the machinery necessary to despotism, the reverse is the fact. Christianity is part of the common law of this state. It is not proclaimed by the commanding voice of any human superior, but expressed in the calm and mild accents of customary law. Its foundations are broad and strong, and deep; they are laid in the authority, the interest, the affections of the people. Waiving all questions of hereafter, it is the purest system of morality, the firmest auxiliary, and only stable support of all human laws. It is impossible to administer the laws, without taking the religion which the defendant in error has scoffed at, that scripture which he has reviled, as their basis; to lay aside these is, at least, to weaken the confidence in human veracity, so essential to the purposes of society, and without which no question of property could be decided, and no criminal brought to justice; an oath in the common form, on a discredited book, would be a most idle ceremony. This act, was not passed, as the counsel supposed, when religious and civil tyranny were at their height; but on the breaking forth of the sun of religious liberty, by those who had suffered much for conscience' sake, and fled from ecclesiastical oppression.

The counsel is greatly mistaken in attributing to the common law the punishment at the stake and by the faggot. No man ever suffered at common law for any heresy; the writ *de haeretico comburendo* [concerning heretics who ought to be burned], and all the sufferings which he has stated in such lively colors, and which give such a frightful, though not exaggerated picture, were the enactments of positive laws, equally barbarous and impolitic. There is no reason for the counsel's exclamation, are these things to be revived in this country, where Christianity does not form part of the law of the land!—it does form, as we have seen, a necessary part of our common law; it inflicts no punishment for a non-belief in its truths; it is a stranger to fire and to faggots, and this abused statute merely inflicts a mild sentence on him who bids defiance to all public order, disregards all decency, by contumelious reproaches, scoffing at and reviling that which is certainly the religion of the country; and when the counsel compared this act against blasphemy to the act against witchcraft, and declared this was equally absurd, I do not impute to him that which I know his heart abhors, a scoffing at religion, but to the triteness of the topics. It is but a barren field, and must contain a repetition of that which has been so often advanced and so often refuted; it is not argument. He has likewise fallen into error with respect to the report of the Judges of the Supreme Court on the British statute *de religiosis*, and of *mortmain*, parts of which are not incorporated, as being inapplicable to the state of the country; these statutes were made to resist the encroachments of religious bodies, in engrossing great landed estates, and holding them in *mortmain*, but these are adopted so far as relates to the avoidance of conveyances to the use of bodies corporate, unless sanctioned by the charter declaring void all conveyances to superstitious uses. The present statute is called *de religiosis*, from the initiatory words of the act. It clipped the wings of ecclesiastical monopoly, and voided conveyances to superstitious uses, but had no more relation to the doctrines of Christ than of Mahomet; the counsel has confounded the name *de religiosis* with the doctrines of Christianity, and drawn a false conclusion; because the statute *de religiosis* was not applicable to the country, therefore, religion itself was not, and because they incorporated only part of the statute avoiding conveyances to superstitious uses, therefore, Christianity was superstition, and is abolished. This argument is founded on misconception, and is a nullity. The plaintiff in error has totally failed to support his grand objection to this indictment, for Christianity is part of the common law; the act against blasphemy is neither obsolete nor virtually repealed; nor is Christianity inconsistent with our free governments or the genius of the people.

As I understand this writ of error was taken out with a view to decide the question, whether Christianity was part of the law of the land, and whether it was consistent with our civil institutions, I have considered it a duty to be thus explicit. No preference is given by law to any particular religious persuasion; protection is given to all by our laws; it is only the malicious reviler of Christianity who is punished. By general Christianity is not intended the doctrine of worship of any particular church or sect; the law leaves these disputes to theologians; it is not known as a standard by which to decide political dogmas. The worship of the Jews is under the protection of the law, and all persecutions against Unitarians have been discontinued in England. The statute of William III. ch. 3, with its penalties against antitrinitarians, is repealed, and it never was punishable at common law; and no partial mode of belief or unbelief was the object of coercion by the civil magistrates. Whatever doctrines were heretical, were left to the ecclesiastical judges, who had a most arbitrary latitude allowed to them. Freedom from the demon of persecution, and the scourge of established churches, was not on the European, but on our side of the Atlantic. I do not by this allude to any particular church, for the Puritans in turn became persecutors, when they got the upper hand; by an ordinance of 23d August 1645, which continued until the restoration, to preach, write, or print anything in derogation, or disapproving of the directory to the established puritanical form of worship, subjected the offender, when convicted, to a discretionary fine, not exceeding 50 pounds. Scofill 98.

While our own free constitution secures liberty of conscience and freedom of religious worship to all, it is not necessary to maintain that any man should have the right publicly to vilify the religion of his neighbors and of the country; these two privileges are directly opposed. It is open, public vilification of the religion of the country that is punished, not to force conscience by punishment, but to preserve the peace of the country by an outward respect to the religion of the country, and not as a restraint upon the liberty of conscience; but licentiousness, endangering the public peace, when tending to corrupt society, is considered as a breach of the peace, and punishable by indictment. Every immoral act is not indictable, but when it is destructive of morality generally, it is, because it weakens the bonds by which society is held together, and government is nothing more than public order. This was the opinion of the court in the case of *Commonwealth* v. *Sharpless*, 2 Serg. & Rawle, 91, 101. It is not now, for the first time, determined in this court, that Christianity is part of the common law of *Pennsylvania*. In the case of the *Guardians of the Poor* v. *Green*, 5 Binn. 55. Judge BRACKENBRIDGE observed, the church establishment of *England* has become a part of the common law, but was the common law in this particular, or any part of it, carried with us in our emigration and planting a colony in *Pennsylvania?* Not a particle of it. On the contrary, the getting quit of the ecclesiastical establishment and tyranny, was a great cause of the emigration. All things

were reduced to a primitive Christianity, and we went into a new state. And Chief Justice TILGHMAN observes, that every country has its own common law; ours is composed partly of our own usages. When our ancestors emigrated from *England,* they took with them such of the English principles as were convenient for the situation in which they were about to be placed. It required time and experience to ascertain how much of the *English* law would be suitable to this country. The minds of *William Penn* and his followers, would have revolted at the idea of an established church. Liberty to all, preference to none; equal privilege is extended to the mitred Bishop and the unadorned Friend.

This is the Christianity which is the law of our land, and I do not think it will be an invasion of any man's right of private judgment, or of the most extended privilege of propagating his sentiments with regard to religion, in the manner which he thinks most conclusive. If from a regard to decency and the good order of society, profane swearing, breach of the Sabbath, and blasphemy, are punishable by civil magistrates, these are not punished as sins or offences against God, but crimes injurious to, and having a malignant influence on society; for it is certain, that by these practices, no one pretends to prove any supposed truths, detect any supposed error, or advance any sentiment whatever.

The reasoning of the counsel of the plaintiff in error is quite conclusive on the subaltern objection to the form of the indictment. The word *profanely* used in the act, should have been inserted in the indictment. It is a description of the offence, and though the words blasphemously and despitefully, may be synonymous with profanely, and tantamount in common understanding, yet as the legislature has adopted this word as a description or definition of the crime, the omission is fatal. As for blasphemy at the common law, the indictment cannot be sustained, for the sentence is founded on the act of assembly, and distribution of the fine to the poor, is not a part of a common law punishment. The general rule is, that all indictments on statutes, must state all the circum-

stances which constitute the definition of the offence, so as to bring the defendant precisely within it; and not even the fullest description of the offence, even the terms of a legal definition, would be sufficient, without keeping to the expressions of the act. A case directly in point is the indictment for perjury, on the statute; the word wilfully must be inserted, because it is part of the description the act gives of the crime; though in indictments for some offences at common law, that precise term is not essential, but may be supplied by others conveying the same idea; and in indictments on the black act, the term wilfully is essential, as being used by the legislature, and maliciously, will not suffice. 1 *Chitty's Crim. Law*, where the various authorities are referred to. The judgment is for this reason reversed. I very much incline to think the indictment is defective on another ground. It should have stated the very words: here it is laid, that among other things, he said in substance as follows. In all indictments for words, the words themselves ought to be set out. In an accusation of this nature, particularly, the words ought to be set out, for it is from the mode and manner the words were spoken, that the malicious intention must appear. One individual attending a long sermon, with particular dogmas of his own always uppermost in his head, and with strong prejudice against the speaker and his sect, whose opinions he might hold to be heretical, and who, from that very prejudice, would put the worst construction on all he said, might conclude from an argument in which no vituperative language was used, that in substance, the speaker said the Scriptures were fabulous, and contained many lies. He might conscientiously suppose, because some favourite opinion of his own was touched, it in substance, amounted to a declaration that the Scriptures were a fable and a lie. When a man undertakes to give an account of the substance of what he has heard or read, he by no means undertakes for the accuracy of expressions; he avoids that; he only states what was his own conclusion from the whole discourse of writing; the speaker in substance intended it; it would be dangerous either to speaker or preacher, if this latitude were allowed. The thing

itself, must be stated explicitly and directly, in such an open and palpable form, that any one who heard the words, shall know the law to be infringed. A very serious, conscientious discourse, on a subject or text of Scripture, on which the different sects thought differently, might make the preacher the victim of ignorance, prejudice, fanaticism, or ill will, by taking up a sentence and disjoining it from the whole discourse and scope of reasoning of the speaker. Even in a declaration in slander in *England*, it is not sufficient to state, that the defendant among other things said in substance as follows; the words must be set out, though it would be sufficient to prove the substance. But it has been determined in this court, that in an action of slander the words may be so laid, but it never has been carried so far as to say, this would do in indictments. In an indictment for a libel, *Commonwealth* v. *Sweney*, 10 Serg. & Rawle, 173, it was decided, that this mode of laying written slander would not be sufficient.

I am not required to give an opinion on this point, and only throw out this hint to gentlemen who may have occasion to draw bills of this nature.

Judgment reversed.

———————

State v. Chandler, 2 Harrington 553 (Del. 1837)

J. M. C L A Y T O N, *Chief Justice:*—The questions arising out of these records are—First, whether the offence charged in these indictments is within the purview of the statute of this state against blasphemy, passed on the 8th Feb. 1826; and secondly, whether that statute be inconsistent with the state constitution.

Reprinted from Samuel M. Harrington, *Reports of Cases Argued and Adjudged in the Superior Court and Court of Errors and Appeals of the State of Delaware* (Dover: Printed by S. Kimmey, 1841), 2:553–79.

The act of the 8th of February, 1826, directs, that "If any person shall be guilty of the crime of blasphemy, every person so offending upon conviction thereof, shall forfeit and pay to the state a fine not exceeding fifty dollars, and shall suffer imprisonment in solitary confinement for any term not exceeding two months, and may, in the discretion of the court, be required to find sureties for good behavior for one year after discharge from prison."

This is a part of the general statute providing for the punishment of crimes and misdemeanors. It does not define the crime of blasphemy; nor does it define treason, murder, rape, perjury, sodomy and many other crimes, for the punishment of which it specially provides, as it does for that of blasphemy. We go for the legal definition of each of these crimes to the common law, and to that we must apply for the legal definition of the crime charged in each of these indictments. The legislature, using technical legal terms to describe the offences they intended to punish, had reference of course to the meaning of those terms as understood and defined in the only books which contain any legal definition of them, which we can notice; and those books are the works of the common law writers on crimes and misdemeanors. These authorities do not leave room for any doubt on the question whether the words charged in these indictments and found by the several verdicts upon them, to have been pronounced in manner and form as there alledged, do constitute the crime of blasphemy.

It appears to have been long perfectly settled by the common law, that blasphemy against the Deity in general, or a malicious and wanton attack against the christian religion individually, for the purpose of exposing its doctrines to contempt and ridicule, is indictable and punishable as a temporal offence. The cases of *The King vs. Taylor, Vent.* 293, 3 *Keble's Rep.* 607; of *Clendon & Hall,* E. T. 10 *Ann,* cited *Str.* 789, H. T. 79, *Str.* 416; *The King vs. Woolston,* in *Str.* 834, *Fitzg.* 64, 66, *Barnard.* 162; *The King vs. Williams,* before Lord Kenyon, C. J., at Guildhall, 1797, 3 B. & A. 161; *Att'y. Gen'l. vs. Pearson,* 3 *Meriv.* 352; *The King vs. Waddington,* 1 *B. & C.* 26; with the criminal infor-

mations against *Jacob Ilive, Peter Annett, John Wilkes and Daniel Isaac Eaton,* referred to in the elementary books of the common law, (See *Stark. on Slander,* 440–1, &c.; *Holt on Libel,* 66; *Russel on Crimes,* 209, 217;) fully establish this principle. And it further appears that although a written publication of blasphemous words, thereby affording them a wider circulation, would undoubtedly be considered as an aggravation of the offence, and affect the measure of punishment, yet so far as respects the definition and legal character of the offence itself, it is immaterial whether the publication of such words be oral or written. They equally constitute the crime of blasphemy in either case. *King vs. Atwood, Cro. J.* 421, *King vs. Taylor,* 3 *Keb. Rep.* 607; *Stark. on Slander,* 441. In the case of *The People vs. Ruggles,* 8 Johns. Rep. 291, Kent, C. J. delivered the opinion of the Supreme Court of the State of New York, that blasphemy against God and contumelious reproaches and profane ridicule of Christ or the Holy Scriptures, are offences punishable at common law, whether uttered by words or writing; and that wantonly, wickedly, and maliciously uttering the words "Jesus Christ was a bastard and his mother must be a whore" was a public offence, punishable by the *common law* of New York.

The Supreme Court of Pennsylvania in *Updegraph vs. The Commonwealth,* (11 *Serg. & Rawle,* 400–1,) which was the case of an indictment for blasphemy, have fully affirmed the principles of Ruggles' case, and have declared that, "from the time of Bracton, christianity was part of the common law of England." To the list of authorities already cited which sustain this opinion may be added, *Tremaine's Pleas of the Crown,* 226, *Rex vs. Doyley, Emlyn's preface to the State Trials,* 8; 2 *State Trials,* 273, *Whitlock's Speech; Raym.* 162; 4 *Blac. Com.* 59; 1 *Hawk. b.* 1 c. 5; 1 *East's P. C.* 3; 3 *Burns. Ec. Law,* 202; 1 *St. Trials,* 302. And in the case of the *Chamberlain of London vs. Allen Evans, Esq.* in 1767, upon a writ of error to the house of lords (*Blac. Com.* appendix to Bell's edition, vol. 5, p. 145,) Lord Mansfield says, "The eternal principles of natural religion are part of the common law; the essential principles of revealed religion are part of the common law; so that any person reviling, subverting, or ridiculing them, may be prosecuted at common law."

This is the true meaning of the English maxim as usually applied. It was never pretended that the common law punished the violation of every precept of christianity. No judge at common law ever decided, that he who did not to others as he would that they should do unto him, which is one of the most sublime of all the precepts of the author of that religion, or that he who did not repent and believe in christianity, was therefore liable to a penalty, or punishment at common law. Indeed, in the very speech of Lord Mansfield already referred to, which was a noble and most successful effort in behalf of the dissenters, and the great cause of religious liberty, he says "there never was a single instance, from the Saxon times down to our own, in which a man was ever punished by the common law for erroneous opinions concerning rites, or modes of worship. The common law of England, which is only common reason or usage, knows of no prosecution for mere opinions. For atheism, blasphemy and reviling the christian religion, there have been instances of persons prosecuted and punished upon the common law; but bare nonconformity to established rites and modes (of worship,) is no sin by the common law." The common law was, as Lord Coke expressed it in *Sir William Harbert's case, 3 Rep.* 42 *b.,* "the preserver of the common peace of the land;" and, therefore, we find it punished outrages on, or breaches of the peace of society, and also acts whose tendency was to disturb that peace. The union between church and state in England, by which the christian religion became connected with the government itself, induced a series of penal statutes to protect and prefer that religion as a part of the government itself. But even in England, christianity was never considered as a part of the *common law,* so far as that for a violation of its injunctions, independent of the established laws of man, and without the sanction of any positive act of parliament made to enforce those injunctions, any man could be drawn to answer in a common law court. It was a part of the common law "so far that any person reviling, subverting or rid-

iculing it might be prosecuted at common law," as lord Mansfield has declared; because, in the judgment of our English ancestors and their judicial tribunals, he who reviled, subverted or ridiculed christianity, did an act which struck at the foundation of their civil society, and tended by its necessary consequences as they believed, to disturb that common peace of the land of which (as Lord Coke had reported) the common law was *the* preserver. The common law never lighted the fires of Smithfield on the one hand, nor preferred the doctrines of infidelity, (which is proved by all history to be in character not less intolerant than fanatacism) on the other. It adapted itself to the religion of the country just so far as was necessary for the peace and safety of civil institutions; but it took cognizance of offences against God only, when by their inevitable effects, they became offences against man and his temporal security. It was never pretended by any common law court that he who did not "love his neighbor as himself;" or he who did not "visit the widow and the fatherless in their affliction, and keep himself unspotted from the world" was, therefore, indictable at common law. The same is equally true of the laws of God as revealed in the old testament. No lawyer ever framed an indictment in a common law court, charging that the defendant did not honor his father and mother, or merely coveted his neighbor's property. True, there are many instances in which the divine precepts have been enacted into statutes, and in case of a violation of these, or of any divine mandate which had been adopted into the common law, because the peace and safety of civil society could not be secured without it, the common law courts became the avengers of the public wrong. And in all cases where the tendency of any man's acts or words was, in the judgment of a common law court, to disturb the common peace of the land of which it was the preserver and protector, or to lead to a breach of it and the good order of society, considered merely as a *civil* institution, the common law avenged the wrong done to civil society alone. He, therefore, who subverted, reviled or ridiculed the religion of our English ancestors, was punished at common law, not for his offence against his God, but for his offence against man, whose peace and safety as they believed, was endangered by such conduct. Whether their belief in this respect was well or ill founded is not the question. To sustain the soundness of their opinion, their descendants point us to the tears and blood of revolutionary France during that reign of terror, when infidelity triumphed and the abrogation of the christian faith was succeeded by the worship of the goddess of reason, and they aver that without this religion no nation has ever yet continued free. They insist too, that all history demonstrates that no nation without the light of their common law, has ever been able to preserve any system of rational and well regulated liberty. But suppose all their opinions in these respects to be erroneous: still the question is not whether their law was well founded, *but what was their law?*

The defendant's counsel, in the progress of the argument on this subject, referred to a letter written by Thomas Jefferson to major Cartwright, dated June 5, 1824, and published in the fourth volume of his posthumous works. This letter we notice, because respectable counsel have cited it. It is phrased in terms more becoming the newspaper paragraphs of the day, than the opinion of a grave jurist who feels respect for the memory of the eminent lawyers of England, because he knows and can appreciate their worth. The opinion of Lord Mansfield, who was one of the brightest luminaries of the common law, palpably misunderstood by this writer, is by him denounced as a *"judicial forgery."* He considers and so states, that by this maxim mentioned by Lord Mansfield, which recognizes revealed religion as a part of the common law, his lordship had "engulphed bible, testament and all into the common law;" whereas, this mode of garbling a remark, and then replying to it, has done gross injustice to that great man whose celebrated argument for religious toleration in the English house of lords in the case of Evans does by no means justify the imputation cast upon him. So far from meaning that bible and testament were parts of the common law for other purposes than that of punishing for the

subversion, reviling or ridiculing them; so far from pretending that any man could be punished by the common law for mere infidelity, or for worshipping God as he pleases, or for any violation of any divine precept not expressly adopted by man as human law, which would make courts and juries the regulators of every man's conscience, Lord Mansfield expressly says "conscience is not controllable by human laws, nor amenable to human tribunals. Persecution, or attempts to force conscience, will never produce conviction; and are only calculated to make hypocrites or martyrs." "There is nothing," he adds, "more unreasonable, more inconsistent with the rights of human nature, more contrary to the spirit and precepts of the christian religion, more iniquitous or unjust, more impolitic, than persecution. It is against natural religion, revealed religion, and sound policy."

Mr. Jefferson endeavors to show that the maxim that christianity is a part of the common law of England is entirely derived from an opinion of Prisot in the *Year Book* 34, *H.* 6, *folio* 38, (145–8.) In a case quare impedit a question was made, how far the ecclesiastical law was to be respected in a common law court. And Prisot gives his opinion in these words: "Prisot—a tiels Leys que ils de saint Eglise ont en *auncient scripture* covient pur nous a doner credence; car ceo est common Ley sur quels touts manner Leys sont fondues," &c. (See *Fitz. abr. qu. im.* 89. *Bro. abr. qu. imp.* 12.) The whole of Mr. Jefferson's complaint is, that Finch has mistaken this passage, by translating "auncient scripture" *holy scripture.* Mr. Jefferson translates Prisot's Norman French so as to make him decide "that to such laws of holy church as have warrant in *ancient writing* it is proper for us to give credence;" while, says he, Finch interprets the passage "to such laws of the church as have warrant in *holy scripture* our law giveth credence." Now the question which the judge was considering when he delivered this opinion was, whether the sentence of the bishop or ecclesiastical court should have faith and credit at common law. He made the same decision which was afterwards made in the case reported in 11 *H.* 7, 9, and again in *Caudrey's* case, reported by Sir Edward Coke,

5 *Rep.* 1. In Caudrey's case "it was resolved by the whole court, that the sentence given by the bishop, by the consent of his colleagues, was such as the judges of the common law ought to allow to be given according to the ecclesiastical laws; for seeing their authority is to proceed and give sentence in ecclesiastical law, and they have given a sentence in a cause ecclesiastical upon their proceedings, by force of that law; *the judge of the common law ought to give faith and credit to their sentence, and to allow it to be done according to the ecclesiastical law.* For cuilibet in sua arte perito credendum est [you ought to believe one who is an expert in their art]. And this, says Lord Coke, "is the common received opinion of all our books," for which he then cites the very case, 34 H. 6, 14, where the opinion is given by Prisot. The point decided was the legal principle that the sentence of a competent court of exclusive and peculiar jurisdiction is conclusive, where that sentence comes incidentally in question in another court. The judge, therefore, concluded that "if it could appear to us (the common law judges) that the bishop has done as an ordinary may do in such a case," (that is, has not exceeded his jurisdiction,) "then we ought to adjudge these good, or otherwise." According to what Mr. Jefferson calls Finch's interpretation, the judge decided that the sentence of the ecclesiastical tribunal when warranted by the *holy scriptures,* shall be credited in a common law court as the decision of a competent tribunal, provided the ecclesiastical tribunal did not exceed its jurisdiction. According to Mr. Jefferson's version the judge decided that the same sentence, when warranted by the "ancient written laws," should be so acknowledged and credited. What these written laws were, Mr. Jefferson does not inform us; but the common law was emphatically the *lex non scripta,* or unwritten law as contra-distinguished from the statute law, and Mr. Jefferson probably knew that: he must have intended either statutes of parliament or the written laws of the church. The statutes of parliament could not have been intended, for they did not regulate the ecclesiastical jurisdiction; and the words *"car ceo est common ley sur que touts manner leys sont fon-*

dues," when applied to them would be nonsense.* For how could they be said to be the foundation of all human laws. If by written laws, Mr. Jefferson meant the written laws of the church at that day, they, at that day, credited the holy scriptures and professed to be built upon them. The ecclesiastical tribunals, as we know from Caudrey's case, assumed jurisdiction of all offences purely against God and the holy scriptures *pro salute animae* [for the salvation (or health) of the soul], without reference to the mere effect of such offences on the peace of society, which the common law never did. But the common law judges by yielding up that jurisdiction to the ecclesiastical courts, refusing to reverse or to revise their decisions when incidentally or collaterally presented in a common law court, thus simply recognizing those decisions as ecclesiastical and not as common law, did no more intend by that to acknowledge the laws of holy church as *common law,* than they intended to acknowledge admiralty law as common law when they gave faith and credit to an admiralty decision. It is not within our knowledge that any common law judge has cited this case in the Year Book, or referred to it in any manner to prove his position in deciding a case of blasphemy that the malicious reviling of christianity was punishable at common law. The labor with which Mr. Jefferson has searched the Year Book to convict Finch of a mistranslation would have been saved had he been aware that he was only proving by his own construction of the passage, that the ecclesiastical law was founded in the *written laws of the church* and not in the *scriptures* alone. As friends of religious liberty, we would prefer that the common law should have "engulphed bible and testament," rather than the laws of the church as understood at that day, which not only professed to comprise the bible and testament, but usurped an entire control over the consciences of men; and *pro salute animae* issued their writ *de heretico comburendo* [that heretics ought to be burned], or burnt the body under pretext of saving the soul.

Having thus seen Mr. Jefferson's premises, let us next consider the argument built upon them to convict Mansfield of judicial forgery. He says that Hale decided that christianity was parcel of the laws of England, but quoted no authority; that by such echoings and re-echoings from one to another, in 1728 the court (composed of Lord C. J. Raymond; and Page, Reynolds and Probyn, justices,) in the case of *The King vs. Woolston*, for blasphemy, 2 *Str.* 834, would not suffer it to be debated whether writing against christianity *in general*, was punishable in the temporal courts at common law; that justice Blackstone adopts Hale's opinion, and cites the adjudged cases; and finally, that Lord Mansfield had used the words before quoted, as delivered by him in Evans' case, "that the essential parts of revealed religion are parts of the common law:" thus, says Mr. Jefferson, engulphing bible, testament, and all into the common law, without citing any authority. "And thus far" he adds, "we find this chain of authorities hanging link by link one upon another, *and all ultimately upon one and the same book, and that a mistranslation of the words auncient scripture used by Prisot.*" He concludes that he "might defy the best read lawyer to produce another scrip of authority for this judicial forgery." This letter writer then first admits expressly that neither Hale nor Mansfield had cited any authority for their opinions, and immediately after, charges the principles for which their great names are cited, with hanging upon what he calls a mistranslation of the words used by Prisot. He thought that his erudition had enabled him to detect the very source from which their ignorance and folly, or their knavery, had sprung. Had Hale and Mansfield quoted the passage from Prisot, which Mr. Jefferson has thus plumed himself upon the translation of, as the foundation for a judicial opinion, then they would have been responsible for the translation of the passage, but neither of them quoted the Year Book; they had no occasion to quote any authority. Long before Lord Hale decided that christianity was a part of the laws of England, the Court of Kings Bench, 34 *Eliz.* in *Ratcliff*'s case, 3 *Coke Rep.* 40, b. had gone so far as to declare, that "in almost all cases, the common law was grounded on the law of God, which it was said was *causa causans*," and the court cited the 27th chapter of Numbers, to show that their judgment on a common law principle in regard to the law of inheritance, was founded on God's revelation of that law to Moses. Mr. Hargrave, in his note on *Co. Lit.* 11, b. observes, that "This inference from God's precept to Moses is unwarranted, unless it can be shown that it was promulgated as a law for mankind in general, instead of being, like many other parts of the Mosaical law, a rule for the direction of the Jewish nation only." The author of the reports and the commentary on Littleton was a professor of christianity, as is visible in all his writings. That Hale with such an authority before him should not have deemed it necessary to cite Coke, familiar as his writings were to the profession, at a time when his works were the principal text-book of every lawyer, cannot be the subject of much wonder; and we know, notwithstanding Mr. Jefferson's defiance, that even Finch himself had quoted 8 *H.* 8, "Ley de Dieu est Ley de terre," the law of God is the law of the land, *Doc. & Stud. lib.* 1, c. 6, *Plowd.* 265, to sustain his position that the holy scripture is of sovereign authority, and to show the extent and meaning of the maxim. But, independent of Lord Coke or any other judge, Sir Matthew Hale was an authority of himself, and is considered as a sufficient authority for a common law principle in every case when there is no contrary authority. What sources of legal knowledge his great erudition may have consulted on this subject, we have no means of certainly knowing, nor is it necessary to inquire.

As for the alledged translation of Finch, we have examined the whole passage, and are well satisfied that if Finch construed *"auncient scripture"* to mean *holy scripture*, such a translation of the Norman french would be the true translation. But in fact Finch has not ventured any translation of the passage whatever, notwithstanding Mr. Jefferson professes to copy the *very words* in which he has translated it. We speak with the work of Henry Finch, of Gray's Inn, Book 1st, chap. 3, published in London 1759, before us. Mr.

Jefferson has made a translation for Finch in words with inverted commas, then attempted to prove his translation false, and failed to do it. Finch evidently believed that Prisot spoke of the holy scripture, and therefore, he cited the Year Book with other authorities to sustain a general position in the text, that the scriptures were of sovereign authority; a position which, like that of every other compiler, was good to the full extent of his authorities and no further, and which is sustained by the Year Book so far as to show that the common law did recognize the decisions of ecclesiastical courts, which were founded on the scriptures, *as conclusive when brought collaterally in question in a common law court.* Lord Mansfield's alledged judicial forgery stood, as the cases we have cited prove, upon other and many other authorities than Mr. Jefferson appears to have ever read.

It is true, that the maxim of the English law, "that christianity is a part of the common law" may be liable to misconstruction, and has been misunderstood. It is a current phrase among the special pleaders, "that the almanac is a part of the law of the land." (*Chit. Pl.* 221, &c.) By this it is meant, that the courts will judicially notice the days of the week, month and other things, properly belonging to an almanac, without pleading or proving them. In the same sense it is sometimes said that the *lex parliamentaria* [parliamentary law] is a part of the law of the land. So too, we apprehend, every court in a civilized country is bound to notice in the same way, what is the prevailing religion of the people. If in Delaware the people should adopt the Jewish or Mahometan religion, as they have an unquestionable right to do if they prefer it, this court is bound to notice it as their religion, and to respect it accordingly. In England christianity, notwithstanding the dicta of Mr. Jefferson and Major Cartwright, has been the prevailing religion of its people for a time beyond that of legal memory, if the best English historians are entitled to credit. While the ecclesiastical courts were often disgraced by all that bigotry could do, the common law in giving faith and credence to their decisions, did only acknowledge them as the sentences of a *separate and independent jurisdiction,* without assuming the responsibility of their judgments. It noticed the decrees founded on the laws of revealed religion as the laws of another tribunal, whose sole province it was to punish for a violation of those laws. It did not partake of the guilt; it did not share in the degradation of those who condemned a fellow man to human punishment for an alleged violation of the laws of God; unless an offence against man's peace and safety was embraced in it. It became the preserver of the peace and good order of society throughout the land, and noticed what was the religion of the people, to the end that it might preserve that peace and good order. It sustained indictments for wantonly and maliciously blaspheming God, or the founder of the christian religion, because such blasphemy tended to subvert the peace and good order which it was bound to protect. But it sustained no indictment for a mere sin against God as a common law offence, where these objects of its care were not affected. It did not look to the condition of man in another world to punish and thus prepare him for it in this. That was the loathsome duty of some ecclesiastical commissioner; some fiery bigot, or star chamber judge. While these punished blasphemy as a spiritual offence *pro salute animae,* the common law only punished it when it tended to create a riot or break the peace in some other mode, or subvert the very foundation on which *civil* society rested. It took cognizance of, and gave faith and credit to the religion of Christ, as the religion of the common people; it acknowledged their right voluntarily to prefer that religion and to be protected in the enjoyment of it; and it carried that protection to the full length of punishing any man who outraged the feelings of the people and insulted civil society, by wantonly and maliciously reviling or ridiculing the religion which they had freely preferred, and upon which they had staked all their hopes of happiness both here and hereafter. The declarations of Lord Hale, Lord Raymond and others, who pronounced christianity to be parcel of the common law, are all to be taken in reference to the cases of blasphemy before them; and for the purpose of punishing such blasphemies as they condemned, they noticed that christianity was the religion of England, and in this sense a part of the common law of the land. The dictum of Lord Mansfield expressly confines the maxim to the object of so noticing it—the punishment of the crime of insulting or subverting that on which the affections of the people were placed; and it has been considered as a fair inference from all the principles and decisions of the common law courts in England, "that no author or preacher who fairly and conscientiously promulgates the opinions with whose truth he is impressed, for the benefit of others, is for so doing amenable as a criminal; that a malicious and mischievous intention is in such a case the broad boundary between right and wrong; and that if it can be collected from the offensive levity with which so serious a subject is treated, or from other circumstances, that the act of the party was malicious; then, since the law has no means of distinguishing between different degrees of evil tendency, if the matter published contain any such tendency, the publisher becomes amenable to justice." *Stark. on Sland.* 444, and authorities there cited.

Having thus seen that the offence charged in these indictments is within the common law definition of blasphemy, and therefore, within the purview of the statute of this state against that crime, the question whether that statute be *inconsistent with the state constitution,* now remains to be considered.

The first section of the first article of the constitution of Delaware, which has been the subject of much discussion both at home and abroad, is in these words: "Although it is the duty of all men frequently to assemble together for the public worship of the author of the universe, and piety and morality, on which the prosperity of communities depends are thereby promoted; yet no man shall or ought to be compelled to attend any religious worship, to contribute to the erection or support of any place of worship, or to the maintenance of any ministry against his own free will and consent; and no power shall or ought to be vested in or assumed by any magistrate that shall in any case interfere with, or in any manner control the rights of conscience in the free exercise of religious worship;

nor a preference given by law to any religious societies, denominations, or modes of worship."

In connection with this subject the following sections have been quoted—

"Art. 1, sec. 2. No religious test shall be required as a qualification to any office or public trust under this state."

"Art. 8, sec. 9. The rights, privileges, immunities and estates of religious societies and corporate bodies shall remain as if the constitution of this state had not been altered. No ordained clergyman, or ordained preacher of the *gospel* of any denomination, shall be capable of holding any civil office in this state, or of being a member of either branch of the legislature while he continues in the exercise of the pastoral or clerical functions."

These passages are the same in the constitution of June 12, 1792, and the revised constitution of December 2, 1831, save that in the former the word "ordained," in sec. 9, art. 8, is omitted.

It clearly appears from the works of Campanius, Proud and other writers, as well as by the ancient laws and records of the colony, and the more recent laws and records of the state, that since the settlement of Delaware by the Swedes and Fins, which was one of the earliest settlements on this continent, down to the present day, christianity has been that religion which the people as a body have constantly professed and *preferred.* The Swedes who were ever zealous christians, were succeeded by the Dutch, who equally professed and practised the same religious faith; and the English, who afterwards took possession of the province, also professed the same belief in Jesus Christ, as the savior of man. About seventy years after the landing of the Swedes, and perhaps fifty years after the settlement of this ancient town, where we still meet for the administration of justice, William Penn, the first English proprietary and governor of this territory, signed that bond with our ancestors called the "charter of privileges." This deed, which bears date 13 William III, (October 28th 1701,) 1 *Del. Laws,* app. 37, while it professed "to secure perfect liberty of conscience to every person who should confess and acknowledge one Almighty God, the creator, upholder and ruler of the world, and profess himself obliged to live quietly under the civil government" ordained, that "all persons who also professed to believe in Jesus Christ, the savior of the world, shall be capable (notwithstanding their other persuasions and practices in point of conscience and religion) *to serve this government in any capacity both legislatively and executively,* he or they solemnly promising when lawfully required, allegiance to the king as sovereign, and fidelity to the proprietary and governor, *and taking the attests as now established by the law made at New Castle in the year* 1700, entitled 'An act directing the attests of several officers and ministers as now amended and confirmed.' So that while by his charter, liberty of conscience was thus far secured to all who professed to believe in a God, none but those who professed to believe in Jesus Christ, the savior of the world, could serve the government under this charter of William Penn, in any official capacity whatever.

Seventy-five years after the date of this charter, on the 11th September, 1776, the "declaration of rights and fundamental rules of the Delaware State," (1 *Del. Laws,* app. 79,) was adopted, the second and third sections of which are in these words:

"Sec. 2. That all men have a natural and unalienable right to worship Almighty God according to the dictates of their own consciences and understandings; and that no man ought or of right can be compelled to attend any religious worship, or maintain any ministry contrary to or against his own free will and consent, and that no authority can or ought to be vested in, or assumed by any power whatever that shall in any case interfere with, or in any manner control the right of conscience in the free exercise of religious worship.

"Sec. 3. That all persons professing *the christian religion* ought forever to enjoy equal rights and privileges in this state unless, under colour of religion, any man disturb the peace, the happiness or safety of society."

Thus we see that at the breaking out of that struggle for civil and religious liberty, in which the people of this state bore a part which was not less distinguished for bravery in the field and wisdom in councils than any of her sister states, equality of religious rights and privileges was still expressly restricted to persons professing the *christian religion.*

On the 20th September, 1776, the first constitution of the Delaware State was adopted, the 22d article of which provided, that "every person who shall be chosen a member of either house, or appointed to any office or place of trust, before taking his seat or entering upon the execution of his office, shall take the following oath, or affirmation if conscientiously scrupulous of taking an oath, to wit:—'I A. B. will bear true allegiance to the Delaware State, *submit to its constitution and laws,* and do no act willingly, whereby the freedom thereof may be prejudiced:' and also make and subscribe the following declaration, to wit:—'I, A. B. *do profess faith in God the father, and in Jesus Christ his only son, and in the Holy Ghost, one God blessed for evermore; and I do acknowledge the holy scriptures of the old and new testament to be given by divine inspiration.'"*

The 25th article of this constitution provided that "*the common law of England,* as well as so much of the statute laws as have been heretofore adopted in practice in this state shall remain in force, unless they shall be altered by a future law of the legislature, such parts only excepted as are repugnant to the rights and privileges contained in the constitution *and the declaration of rights, &c., agreed to by this convention,*" 1 *Del. Laws,* app. 89.

The act of 13 *Geo.* 2, (1 *Del. L.* 174,) punished "wilful or premeditated blasphemy by setting the offender in the pillory for the space of two hours, branding in the forehead with the letter B, and public whipping on the bare back with thirty-nine lashes, well laid on." By the same act swearing, in the hearing of a justice of the peace, was punishable by a fine. By an act of the 17 *Geo.* 2, to enable religious societies of *protestants* to purchase for burying grounds, churches, houses of worship, schools, &c., the statutes of *mortmain* were partially repealed for the benefit of protestants alone. (*Digest Del. L.* 457–8.) This distinction between protestants and others made by this act, was not preserved in the subsequent act of 1787, (*Dig. D. L.* 459,) which extended the same and other benefits to, "each and every religious society or congregation of *christians* of whatever sect, order, or denomination;" provided, "that such society should consist of at least fifteen families *statedly assembling at one place of worship,* BEING SUPPORTERS OF THE GOSPEL IN SAID SOCIETY OR CONGREGATION. (*Dig. D. L.* 462.) And finally, by the act of 6th February, 1795, the performance of "any worldly employment, labour or business whatsoever upon the Lord's day, commonly called Sunday," and all Sabbath breaking, was made punishable by fine. (*Dig. Del. L.* 483.) The present statute against blasphemy was passed thirty-one years after this.

We hold these to be legal proofs of what has been and now is the religion *preferred* by the people of Delaware. And, independent of these and other evidence existing on the statute book of the state, we are bound to notice as judges acting under the authority of the people at all times, what is that religion which they have voluntarily preferred. We know, not only from the oaths that are administered by our authority to witnesses and jurors, but from that evidence to which every man may resort beyond these walls, that the religion of the people of Delaware *is christian.*

The next step which we take in discussing this subject is, that the people have secured to them by their constitution and laws the full and perfect right of conscience, the right to prefer any religion they think proper, and the corresponding and correlative right to protection in the exercise of this and all other their religious principles.

The distinction is a sound one between a religion preferred by law, and a religion preferred by the people, without the coercion of law; between a legal establishment which the present constitution expressly forbids in the 1st article already quoted, and a religious creed freely chosen by the people for themselves, and for the full and perfect enjoyment of which, without interruption or disturbance, they may claim the protection of law guarantied to them by the constitution itself.

We hold, and have already said, that the people of Delaware have a full and perfect constitutional right to change their religion as often as they see fit. They may tomorrow, if they think it right, profess Mahometanism or Judaism, or adopt any other religious creed they please; and so far from any court having power to punish them for such an exercise of right, all their judges are bound to notice their free choice and religious preference, and to protect them in the exercise of their right. Put the case, then, that they repudiate the religion of their fathers and adopt Judaism; and that their legislature in obedience to their wishes, ordains that to write or ridicule the Jewish creed shall be blasphemy, and punishable as blasphemy is now punished. On an indictment against any man for maliciously reviling Moses in public, in the language of this defendant, and publishing the Jewish religion as a villainous imposition, are we or are we not bound to sentence him according to the statute? Suppose the people then abjure Judaism, adopt the koran, and profess the religion of Mahomet. If their legislature enact that to revile or ridicule the prophet shall be blasphemy, may we or may we not against him who shall go into their public places, and with a loud voice maliciously, or with a mere intent to revile and ridicule him, publish in their presence that Mahomet was "a bastard and his mother was a whore," denounce the penalties of their statute?

On what principle would this court, acting under a constitution which prohibits any preference by law to a religious denomination, punish in either of the above stated cases? Not on the ground that the offender was a non-conformist or a dissenter; not because he did not profess the same religion with the rest of the people. The constitution proclaims in language never to be mistaken, that no man is responsible to his fellow men for a mere spiritual offence. For the sin against his God, it leaves every man to heaven, and to the thorns in his own bosom. It stamps with the highest possible sanction of authority the great truth which Lord Brougham says has now gone forth to all the ends of the earth, that man shall no more render an account to man for his belief over which he himself has no control. But in the cases supposed, does any man doubt that the offender would be guilty of an outrage on civil society, tending so directly to create a breach of the peace, that either Jews or Mahometans, especially in the absence of a law to punish him, would visit him with summary vengeance? The history of both these religions shows, that for less offences against society among either Jews or Mahometans, the cross or the bow string has often avenged the insult, and disgraced the human character, under the directions of an outraged mob.

The constitution provides that the existing laws of the land not inconsistent with it, shall remain in force until duly repealed; and it was intended by it to continue in force all the great principles of the common law, which still retains its character of "the common preserver of the peace of the land," and punishes as public offences against man, acts tending to create a breach of the public peace, and to endanger the public safety. He who disinters the dead and exposes the corpse to the public gaze; he who appears naked in the streets of a populous town, as Sir Charles Sedley did in London; every one who outrages decency so far as to incite others to a breach of the peace, is indictable at common law, although his conduct actually should inflict personal violence upon no one. On this principle, indictments for malicious mischief are constantly sustained. In the case of *The People vs. Smith*, (5 Cowen, 258,) it was held that acts injurious to private persons, which tend to excite violent resentment and thus produce a disturbance of the peace are indictable; and that on this ground an indictment lies for *maliciously, wickedly and wilfully killing a cow.* To the same effect are the cases of *The Commonwealth vs. Leach, 1 Mass. 59; Com. vs. Taylor, 5 Binney, 277;* and *Com. vs. Teischer, 1 Dall. 355,* where M'Kean, chief justice, observed that the poisoning of chickens had been indicted in Pennsylvania, on the same general rule. The principle on which a libel, or the sending a challenge to fight a duel is indictable, at common law is the same. The libel or the challenge does not break the peace: it only tends to produce that result. Can any man then, by merely making a religious theme

the butt of his raillery and the object of his outrage, claim an immunity for conduct which would otherwise be indictable? Shall the mere circumstance that he has abused religion, and thus provoked a riot, be a *shield* to protect him from the consequences which would befall him if he had but equally outraged public feeling in some other way? If the people preferred the religion of Mahomet, must we under our constitution, in despite of all legislative enactment to the contrary, suffer a man to insult civil society and provoke a mob and a riot, by gibbetting the image of the prophet in view of the public, or burning the koran by the hands of the common hangman? If the religion of the Jews be known to us to be the religion of our people, does that constitution compel us, although the legislature command the contrary, to permit any man to provoke the vengeance of that people, by burning the prophets in effigy or maliciously stamping the pentateuch under foot in the presence of the multitude.

But this is not putting the case strongly. The christian believes that his savior was conceived by the virgin Mary, and is the son of his creator. He also believes that to sin against the holy ghost is the unpardonable sin. He views the utterance of the words laid in these indictments as infinitely more horrible and blasphemously wicked than a follower of Mahomet or Moses could think them when spoken of the founder of his faith. One believes these words are spoken of his God, and the God of his fathers; the being before whom all the wisdom and virtue of his ancestors have bowed the knee in adoration for centuries which are gone; the others would believe that the same words, when spoken of the founders of their religion, were spoken of man only, though inspired. The danger to the public peace is, therefore, so much the greater in every such a case as that actually before us. If a man may blasphemously revile the founder of the religion which the people have preferred in Delaware by words, he may by acts also. Suppose then one should exhibit publicly over his own door, in view of the whole people of the city of Wilmington, the image of Him on the cross whom they believed to be their God; and, to show his contempt for their feelings and their God, should proceed to hang it and make a bonfire of it before their faces; suppose that to gratify his malice, he proceed to exhibit a naked figure which he shall call the mother of Christ, in the act of prostitution: can he shield himself by saying that he conscientiously believed Christ was a bastard and his mother was a prostitute, and that he had an honest intent to publish the fact to the world? The subject is too awful for further public discussion by this mode of illustration. But in the cases put, will any man say that the public vengeance would not probably break out in open acts of violence against the author of such insults, especially were it once understood that there exists no law to punish him? It would be in vain to expect that a populace enraged by such means could be restrained by being informed that the constitution protected him. That disgraceful law of the mob called "Lynch law" would, it is to be feared, be inflicted in despite of every effort to restrain them. The professing and devout christian would indeed look on the scene more in sorrow than anger, but his relatives and friends, who are not strictly professors of christianity or members of any church or sect, and the great mass who have been educated in the christian's belief, though not professing to act up to it, would probably do as outraged and insulted men have in all ages been accustomed to do. We do not mean that their conduct would be justifiable, but viewing men as they are and not as they should be, looking as we are bound to do, to the motives and feelings which practically regulate and control mankind, we say we cannot doubt that the public peace would be endangered. Every man can put this question home to himself for a fair solution. Let him ask himself whether, if the words contained in these indictments and found by these verdicts to have been published, were uttered by any one in *his* house, and in presence of *his* family, he would not instantly resent the outrage by an order to leave his premises, and enforce that order if necessary by the strength of his own arm? The response of a great majority of the people of Delaware, without including the actually pious and

professing christians, would solve the true question upon which this defendant's cases depend.

But it may and will be objected by some (for the question has excited deep interest among the writers of the day) that this mode of considering the subject is open to the remark, that the law may forever change with the religion and customs of the people. Thus it may be said that the christian himself may live to see the day when he shall not dare to proclaim publicly that the religion of Mahomet, or the impostures of Joe Smith, are the just topics of his ridicule and contempt. We answer that when that distant day shall arrive (if come it must) in which the people shall forsake the faith of their forefathers for such miserable delusions, no human power can restrain them from compelling every man who lives among them to respect their feelings. A new code of laws and a new constitution would at once spring into existence, if they found those under which we live did not protect them from such insults. But in that event, no man could justify himself under the *present* civil institutions of the state in endangering the public peace. He might feel himself impelled by a stern sense of religious duty, to brave public opinion and become a martyr for his zeal. All this he might do, and justify himself in his own opinion for it before God. So too that resistance to government which would be rebellion or treason in a court of law, may be patriotism and virtue *in foro conscientiae* [in the court of the conscience]. He who forcibly resists a bad religion, is thus far like him who resists a bad government; if successful in his resistance, he may become a great reformer of men or a hero; if unsuccessful, a martyr or a traitor. But a court of law is not merely the *forum conscientiae* [court of the conscience]. When human justice is rightly administered according to our common law and our constitution, it refuses all jurisdiction over crimes against God, unless they are by necessary consequence crimes against civil society, and known and defined as such by the law of man. It assumes that for sin against our Creator, vengeance is his and he will repay. It adapts itself to the condition of man as he is. In the language of Lord Coke (*Co.*

Lit. 97, *b.*) "by many successions of ages it hath been fined and refined by an infinite number of grave and learned men; and Lord Mansfield describes the common law as a pure stream, which as it runs, refines. So far from its being true that it cannot suit itself to the religion, the moral code and the ever varying condition of the people whenever they voluntarily prefer to change them, it tolerates every change in either, prohibits no reformation; and keeping constantly in view that its great object is to preserve the public peace and good order of society, without dictating what religion will best sustain it, or prohibiting any reformation in religious matters, it tolerates under all circumstances, every attempt to change, which does not by some overt act endanger the public peace and safety. It is emphatically a law for the protection of religious liberty; and no law can be truly such which does not equally protect the public peace from insults and outrages upon public opinion, when freely established and known to be so, whether that opinion be for christian or infidel, Jew or Turk. In the second volume of the *Encyclopaedia Americana,* by Leiber, p. 130, it is remarked by a writer on blasphemy, "viewing this subject in a philosophical, religious, or political view, it would be difficult to lay down any general principles applicable to different states of society; but the prevailing opinion on this subject in the United States, and that to which the laws and opinions of other countries are strongly tending, is, that any one may profess or oppose any doctrine, provided he inculcates his principles, whether orally or in writing, in such manner as not to commit a flagrant violation of decorum; *what acts or words will constitute such an outrage must evidently depend upon the state of society.*" If the violation of decorum here mentioned, be so flagrant as to endanger the peace of society, the principle of law thus limited and expressed is one, which had it been engrafted into the civil institutions of other countries, would have superseded the necessity of revolutionizing their governments with every change or reformation in religion; and rivers of blood which have been poured out in the conflicts of contending factions, might thus have been spared to mankind.

It will be seen then that in our judgment by the constitution and laws of Delaware, the christian religion is a part of those laws, so far that blasphemy against it is punishable, while the people prefer it as their religion, and no longer. The moment they change it and adopt any other, as they may do, the new religion becomes in the same sense, a part of the law, for their courts are bound to yield it faith and credit, and respect it as their religion. Thus, while we punish the offence against society alone, we leave christianity to fight her own battles, and so far we fully accord with the sentiments of a late writer, whose essay was cited at the bar, that "*christianity* requires no aid from force or persecution; she asks not to be guarded by fines and forfeitures. She stands secure in the armour of truth and reason. She seeks not to establish her principles by political aid and legal enactments. She seeks mildly and peaceably to establish them in the hearts of the people." (*Am. Quar. Review, No.* 34, *June,* 1835, p. 338.) But we would reply to all who would reason as this writer has on the main question before us, that while christianity requires no aid from force, the peace and order of civil society do require much aid from it to repel force and to prevent persecution; that while christianity asks not to be guarded by fines and forfeitures, man has been compelled to make courts and prisons to guard him both by fines and forfeitures; that while christianity stands secure in the armour of truth and reason, the public peace, which is altogether a different thing, has never stood secure in the armour of mere truth and reason, without the co-operating aid of some public punishment to assist them; that political and legal enactments are among the best means by which the peace has been preserved, in every country, and that while the law too, seeks mildly and peaceably to establish her precepts in the hearts of the people, yet if the people will the law to stand, it must be so administered as to compel obedience from such as do not yield it without force. The vice of this writer's essay is the common fault of the argument of those who have arrived at the same conclusion with him. He confounds the spiritual and temporal offence together, or rather fails to discriminate between the sin against God, which it would be presumptive arrogance and extreme folly to punish, and the offence against man alone, which in certain cases, necessarily grows out of his crime against the Deity. When the ecclesiastical court in England had jurisdiction of the former, the common law had it of the latter. But while the ecclesiastical courts punished blasphemy as an offence against God, their punishments superseded the necessity of any procedure at common law for the mere temporal offence. Blasphemy, when viewed as a *spiritual* offence, was enumerated by Coke in Caudrey's case, as an offence entirely within the jurisdiction of the ecclesiastical courts, and "not within the conisance of the common law courts." The petition of Carlisle, who was convicted of publishing Paine's "Age of Reason," was presented to parliament in 1825, by Lord Brougham, and it betrays the same mistake of the true boundaries of the respective jurisdictions of the ecclesiastical and common law courts which this writer, who quotes that petition to enforce his own argument, every where exhibits. In fact, Carlisle actually quotes Lord Coke in Caudrey's case as an authority contrary to Hale, and says he was always considered as good an authority as Sir Matthew Hale. So indeed he was. But his report of Caudrey's case no where clashes with what Hale afterwards said was the common law jurisdiction in cases of blasphemy. Lord Coke expressly says, that "in causes ecclesiastical and *spiritual* as blasphemy, heresies, &c., the conisance whereof belongeth not to the common law, the same are to be determined by the ecclesiastical judges;" and he adds, that the conisance of *such* causes (to wit, for the spiritual offence,) is not within the common law. But Lord Coke never said that blasphemy, considered as a temporal offence, was not within the conisance of the common law. After the decay of the ecclesiastical courts and the abolition of the star chamber, the common law jurisdiction was necessarily brought into active exercise. The Court of King's Bench became, as was then said, the *custos morum* [guardian of morals], and the law which had slept, but was not dead, awoke to defend the good order of the nation

with a vigor which was fully adequate to the real wants of society, and demonstrated that there was no necessity for the tyrannical powers of the ecclesiastical commissioner, or the infamous oppressions of the star chamber court.

We are aware that there is danger in the administration of any law which man ever yet laid down for the government of human action. On this subject there may be danger from both licentiousness and bigotry. We have endeavored to mark down the length, width, height and depth, of the only principle upon which, as we think, blasphemy can be punished under our state constitution. We again repeat, that the only legitimate end of the prosecution is to preserve the public peace. It is sometimes said that our courts are the conservators of morals. This is true just so far as a breach of morals may necessarily tend to a breach of the peace, and no further. We are not the *custodes morum* [guardians of morals] in any sense, except with this qualification. Yet nothing is more common, even in our American reporters, than judicial declarations that the object of certain common law punishments is to preserve good morals. *We know no other code of ethics which we can enforce than that which our laws teach us,* and we do not find, after sifting them as well as we may, that we can assume the power to punish any man for a breach of morals. Such a doctrine would lead us to usurp authority to punish for every sin against God as well as man. When the breach of morals is such an outrage on society as by fair legal intendment must lead to a breach of the peace, as in Sedley's case, (1 *Sid.* 168,) or Rolle's case, (*Sayer,* 158,) or in the case of Sharpless, (2 *Serg. & Rawle,* 101,) or in this case and others of this character, we have no right to interfere one inch further than is necessary to prevent outrage and infractions of the peace in return for it. A man may say the horrible words set forth in this indictment in private, where he thinks no ear can hear him, and yet he is no more answerable to the law of man for that, than he who strips himself in his own chamber; for the wilful publication is the essence of his offence. A man may write a libel, no matter how blasphemous or seditious in its tendency; yet if it sleep in his desk until dragged forth by the ministers of the law, it is not indictable, although it may be a great sin against God.

Franklin, though his name is cited as an unbeliever, in a letter to president Stiles in 1790, speaks of christianity as the "best system of religion and morals the world ever saw or is like to see." (*Franklin's works*, vol. 6, p. 34, 241.) He thought it the best religion for the mere purposes of civil government. Concurring with him in this as we do, were we the conservators of morals, should we not be called upon by a sense of duty to punish every sin against the religion of Him whom we believe to be the son of God and the savior of man? Yet nothing is more clear, than that our state constitution denies to us such an exercise of power as that of punishing any man for a mere difference of religion. This, indeed, is the just boast of those who made our constitution; who, as we know well, were educated in the christian faith and believed in the christian religion; that they gave religious liberty to every man who sets his foot upon the soil of Delaware; and never sought, as men of other religions have done, to make proselytes by coercion. Our ancestors had seen too much of oppression and intolerance under the penal statutes (not the common law) of England, to suffer those principles to take root among us, and their descendants have profited by their example. We say, therefore, that we cannot keep the consciences of men. And in general, we conclude, that mere impiety is never indictable unless the peace of society is endangered by it. In all cases where the tendency to excite to a breach of the peace is (as it must be in every indictment for blasphemy) the leading question; that is, a question for the jury as well as the court. Both must concur to find its tendency, for both are judges of the law.

But it has been said that it is dangerous to entrust any tribunal with power to judge of the mere tendency of acts or words, and that by this means a court and jury of fanatics and fiery bigots may finally decide, that every sin or mere impiety has a tendency to break the peace. We answer that this argument proves merely that this, like all other human power, may be abused. But to prove that power may be abused, is not to prove that power does not exist. The same kind of reasoning would break down every useful institution of man. We could no longer, according to this made of demonstration, punish any libeller; because, in any case of libel the court must necessarily judge of the tendency and effect of the libellous words.

At the same time it is due to the subject to add, that there may undoubtedly be danger in many cases of indictment for blasphemy, of mistaking the *tendency of the words* when of doubtful effect. In such cases the common law furnishes the best possible security for the accused in those great rules, that both jurors and judges are equally bound to decide the law, and that no man should be condemned if there be a rational doubt, in the minds of either judges or jurors, of his guilt. They are answerable both to God and their country for the justice of their decisions.

Let it not be supposed, that by laying down the rule that courts and juries are to judge of the tendency of words or overt acts amounting to blasphemy, we are establishing the rule, that they are to assume the power to judge the tendency of principles or systems of religion. On this subject we fully concur in the sentiments of Dr. Furneaux, in his letters to Mr. Justice Blackstone, (5 vol. *Blac. Com. app'x.* 34.) "With regard to the belief or disbelief of religious principles or religious systems, if the magistrate presumes to exercise his *authority as a judge,* in such cases, with a view of restraining and punishing those who embrace and profess what he dislikes, or dislike and explode what he embraces, on account of the supposed ill tendency of their principles, he goes beyond his province, which is confined to those effects of such principles, that is, to those actions which affect the peace and good order of society; and every step he takes, he is in danger of trampling on the rights of conscience, and of invading the prerogative of the only arbiter of conscience, to whom alone men are accountable for professing or not professing religious sentiments and principles. For, if the magistrate be possessed of a power to restrain and punish any principles relating to religion because of their tendency, and he be the judge of that tendency, as he must be, if he be vested with authority to punish on that account; religious liberty is entirely at an end; or, which is the same thing, is under the control, and at the mercy of the magistrate, according as he shall think the tenets in question affect the foundation of moral obligation, or are favorable or unfavorable to religion and morality. But if the line be drawn between mere religious principle and the tendency of it, on the one hand, and those overt acts which affect the public peace and order, on the other; and if the latter alone be assigned to the jurisdiction of the magistrate, as being guardian of the peace of society in this world, and the former as interfering only with a future world, be referred to a man's own conscience, and to God, the only sovereign Lord of conscience; the boundaries between civil power and liberty, in religious matters, are clearly marked and determined; and the latter will not be wider or narrower, or just nothing at all, according to the magistrate's opinion of the good or bad tendency of *principles*." (a)

In the cases before us, we have the verdicts of two impartial juries to sustain us in the opinion, that the offences laid in these indictments are "against the peace of the state," and punishable as blasphemy by

(a) Furneaux continues: "If it be objected, that when the tendency of principles is unfavorable to the peace and good order of society, as it may be, it is the magistrate's duty then, and for that reason, to restrain them by penal laws; I reply, that the tendency of principles, though it be *unfavorable*, is not *prejudicial* to society, till it issues in some overt acts against the public peace and order; and when it does, *then* the magistrate's authority to punish commences: that is, he may punish the *overt acts*, but not the *tendency*, which is not actually hurtful; and, therefore, his penal laws should be directed against overt acts *only*, which are detrimental to the peace and good order of society, let them spring from what principles they will; and not against *principles*, or the *tendency* of principles.

"The distinction between the tendency of principles, and the overt acts arising from them is, and cannot but be, observed in many cases of a civil nature, in order to determine the bounds of the magistrate's power, or at least to limit the exercise of it, in such cases. It would not be difficult to mention customs and manners, as well as principles, which have a tendency unfavorable to society; and which, nevertheless, cannot be restrained by penal laws, except with the total destruction of civil liberty. And here the magistrate must be contented with pointing his penal laws against the evil overt acts resulting from them. In the same manner he should act in regard to men's professing or rejecting, religious principles or systems. Punishing a man for the *tendency* of his principles, is punishing him *before* he is guilty, for fear he *should be guilty*."

our state constitution. We have also the opinion of the Supreme Court of the State of New York, in *Ruggles'* case, 8 *Johns. Rep.* 225, which was fully considered, that under their constitution, which, after a comparison of it with our own, we find was intended to be as ample a guard for liberty of speech as ours, this identical offence was indictable as blasphemy at common law, and without the aid of any statute such as ours to specify blasphemy as a punishable crime.

The principles laid down in the year 1824, by the Supreme Court of Pennsylvania also, in the case of *Updegraph vs. The Commonwealth*, which was a trial for blasphemy under their statute, clearly establish that under their state constitution, the charge in these indictments is for an offence which they would not hesitate to punish as blasphemy. Judge *Duncan*, delivering the opinion of the court in that case, said "even if christianity was no part of the law of the land, *it is the popular religion of the country*, an insult on which would be indictable, as directly tending to disturb the public peace;" and again, "it is the open, public vilification of *the religion of the country* that is punished, not to force conscience by punishment, *but to preserve the peace of the country*, by an outward respect to the religion of the country, and not as a restraint upon the liberty of conscience; but *licentiousness endangering the public peace*, when tending to corrupt society, is considered as a breach of the peace, and punishable by indictment. 11 *S. & R.* 399, 400–8.

It is no objection to the validity of these indictments that they describe the offence as done "to the dishonor of Almighty God, and in contempt of religion," though such charges indicate a spiritual offence. The intent to blaspheme God and the savior of man are laid to show the malice of the offender, and in the first case both are found by the jury. But the gist of the misdemeanor is contained in the charge, that the words were *published unlawfully and blasphemously against the peace*. This charge after verdict, does "*ex vi terminorum* [from the force of the terms]" imply that the offence was committed wantonly and maliciously; for, without the malice, there can be no unlawful blasphemy. Whether expressly laid in such an indictment as this (which counts upon a statute and may follow its words,) or not, the malice or intent of the offender is always traversable as an essential part of the unlawful blasphemy. Thus, if another man was indicted for uttering these words, and the proof should be that he only uttered them in reply to a question what this charge was, without any intent to revile, but merely to satisfy the inquiry, it could not be pretended that the proof sustained the indictment for unlawful blasphemy.

The only question remaining to be considered is, whether judgment can be rendered by the rules of the common law on the verdict which does not find "the intent to blaspheme God."

This verdict convicts the defendant on the whole indictment "except as to the intent to blaspheme God." The question which arises is, whether it is necessary to prove the offence charged in the indictment to the whole extent laid. It is fully settled, that in criminal cases it is sufficient for the prosecutor to prove so much of the charge as constitutes an offence of the same grade punishable at law. (4 *B. & C.* 330, *Rex vs. Hollingberry.*) And an unnecessary averment may be rejected altogether, unless it be *descriptive* of the *identity* of that which is legally essential to the charge in the indictment. Without going at large into this distinction, the following cases are sufficient to decide the question before us. In *Rex vs. Evans*, 3 *Stark.* 35, where the prisoner was indicted for having published a libel of, and concerning certain magistrates, with intent to defame those magistrates, and also with intent to bring the administration of justice into contempt, Bailey, judge, informed the jury, that if they were of opinion that the defendant had published the libel with either of those intentions, they ought to find the prisoner guilty. In *Rex vs. Dawson*, 3 *Stark. Rep.* 62, where the indictment charged the prisoner with having assaulted a female child, with intent to abuse and carnally to know her, and the jury found that the prisoner assaulted the child with intent to abuse her, but negatived the intention charged car-

nally to know her; Holroyd, J., held that the averment of the intention was divisible, and that the prisoner might be convicted of an assault with intent to abuse simply. And in the case of *Rex vs. Hill, Russ. & Ry.* 190, upon an indictment for obtaining money under false pretences, it was held not necessary to prove the whole of the pretence charged: proof of part of the pretence, and that the money was obtained by such part was considered sufficient. These cases with those of *Rex vs. Ellens, Russ. & Ry.* 183; *Carson's* case, *Russ. & Ry.* 303; and *Rex vs. Hunt*, 2 *Campb.* 583; *Rex vs. Williams*, 2 *Campbell*, 646, fully establish the principle that such averments as those contained in this indictment, charging the intent to blaspheme God, and the intent to revile the christian religion, are *divisible averments;* and either of these intents being found by the jury, is sufficient to sustain the indictment. The fair intendment from this verdict is, that the jury believed from the evidence, that the defendant was an infidel in creed. We cannot otherwise perceive how the rest of the indictment, which charges him with an intent to revile and blaspheme Christ and the christian religion to the dishonor of Almighty God, could have been found by the jury as it has been, without also finding the intent to blaspheme God. At the trial the defendant urged that he was of opinion that the words used by him were true. The question raised by the verdict then is, whether one of his belief can claim an exemption from the penalty of the statute, when a believer in christianity cannot. The law denies to his class as well as to every other, any right to blaspheme. If one class may thus do an act tending to a breach of the peace, all must have the same immunity from punishment, and the statute is a dead letter.

Motion in arrest of judgment refused.

The Court then proceeded to pass sentence on the defendant, to wit: in each case a fine of ten dollars, ten days' solitary confinement, and to find sureties of the peace himself in $200, and two sureties in $100 each, for one year after his discharge from imprisonment.

RECOMMENDATIONS FOR FURTHER READING

Banner, Stuart. "When Christianity Was Part of the Common Law." *Law and History Review* 16 (1998): 27–62.

Chilton, Bradley S. "Cliobernetics, Christianity, and the Common Law." *Law Library Journal* 83 (1991): 355–62.

Kenny, Courtney. "The Evolution of the Law of Blasphemy." *Cambridge Law Journal* I, no. 2 (1922): 127–42.

Stoner, James R., Jr. "Christianity, the Common Law, and the Constitution." In *Vital Remnants: America's Founding and the Western Tradition,* edited by Gary L. Gregg II, 175–209. Wilmington, Del.: ISI Books, 1999.

CHAPTER FOURTEEN

Reflections on the American Church-State Experiment

AMERICAN APPROACHES TO religious liberty and church-state relations changed significantly in the three hundred years following the Mayflower Compact. Notably, during and shortly after the War of American Independence, states either disestablished their official churches or adopted a system of multiple or plural establishments. In 1833 Massachusetts became the last state to end its formal religious establishment. As well, the First Amendment to the U.S. Constitution prohibited Congress from establishing a national church. Of course many states, and in some instances the national government, continued to promote or favor Christianity by issuing calls for prayer and fasting, hiring chaplains, providing financial support for religious organizations, and so forth. By any measure, however, Americans had rejected European models of religious establishment.

At the same time, the scope of religious liberty was broadened significantly. Not only were religious minorities increasingly tolerated, but also religious liberty came to be seen as an inviolable natural right. Virtually all Americans agreed with James Madison's conviction that civil governments should not "compel men to worship God in any manner contrary to their conscience."* To be sure, debates continued about the ex-

tent to which religious minorities should be exempted from obeying neutral, generally applicable laws, or required to support institutions or programs with which they disagreed, or exposed to government-supported religious practices or expressions. It is difficult to point to any time or place in human history prior to the 1830s where religious liberty was better protected.

Did disestablishment and the expansion of religious liberty help or hurt the cause of religion in the United States? Did Americans go too far, or not far enough, in separating church and state? What were the implications of the American approach to religious liberty and church-state relations for society and politics? By the third and fourth decades of the nineteenth century, such questions were debated by newcomers to, and veterans of, the search for the proper relationship between church and state. This chapter contains some of the most famous reflections on the successes and failures of the American experiment. The following texts illustrate important disagreements about the extent to which the national and state governments should support religion. There is remarkable agreement, however, that disestablishment and the vigilant protection of the sacred rights of conscience made religion healthier and that this outcome was beneficial for American society and politics.

* Debate over the First Amendment, page 427 above.

Detached Memoranda (c. 1817)

JAMES MADISON (1751–1836)

After retiring from the presidency, Madison recorded his thoughts on select issues he addressed in public life. Scholars estimate that he wrote the memoranda between 1817 and 1832. William Cabell Rives quoted from the memoranda in his multivolume biography of Madison (1859–68), and the section on monopolies was published by *Harper's Magazine* in 1914, but otherwise the document was not published until 1946.

James Madison, detail of an oil painting on canvas, by Asher B. Durand, 1833. Collection of The New-York Historical Society.

The danger of silent accumulations & encroachments by Ecclesiastical Bodies have not sufficiently engaged attention in the U.S. They have the noble merit of first unshackling the conscience from persecuting laws, and of establishing among religious Sects a legal equality. If some of the States have not embraced this just and this truly Xn[1] principle in its proper latitude, all of them present examples by which the most enlightened States of the old world may be instructed; and there is one State at least, Virginia, where religious liberty is placed on its true foundation and is defined in its full latitude. The general principle is contained in her declaration of rights, prefixed to her Constitution:[2] but it is unfolded and defined, in its precise extent, in the act of the Legislature, usually named the Religious Bill, which passed into a law in the year 1786.[3] Here the separa-

tion between the authority of human laws, and the natural rights of Man excepted from the grant on which all political authority is founded, is traced as distinctly as words can admit, and the limits to this authority established with as much solemnity as the forms of legislation can express. The law has the further advantage of having been the result of a formal appeal to the sense of the Community and a deliberate sanction of a vast majority, comprizing every sect of Christians in the State. This act is a true standard of Religious liberty: its principle the great barrier agst usurpations on the rights of conscience. As long as it is respected & no longer, these will be safe. Every provision for them short of this principle, will be

Excerpt reprinted from "Madison's Detached Memoranda," ed. Elizabeth Fleet, *William and Mary Quarterly,* 3rd series, vol. 3 (October 1946): 554–62. Reprinted by permission of the Omohundro Institute of Early American History and Culture.

1. Christian.

2. Madison was a member of the committee of the Convention of 1776 which framed the famous Virginia bill of rights and constitution. George Mason dominated the committee. Irving Brant, *James Madison, The Virginia Revolutionist* (New York, 1941), 234.

3. In the bill of rights originally drafted by Mason, religious tolerance

rather than freedom was provided. Madison suggested an amendment which, if accepted in full would have given the state complete religious freedom. Instead, the struggle of 1786 was necessary. Gaillard Hunt, "James Madison and Religious Liberty," *Annual Report of the American Historical Association for the Year 1901* (Washington, 1902), I, 166–167.

found to leave crevices at least thro' which bigotry may introduce persecution; a monster, that feeding & thriving on its own venom, gradually swells to a size and strength overwhelming all laws divine & human.

Ye States of America, which retain in your Constitutions or Codes, any aberration from the sacred principle of religious liberty, by giving to Caesar what belongs to God, or joining together what God has put asunder, hasten to revise & purify your systems, and make the example of your Country as pure & compleat, in what relates to the freedom of the mind and its allegiance to its maker, as in what belongs to the legitimate objects of political & civil institutions.

Strongly guarded as is the separation between Religion & Govt in the Constitution of the United States the danger of encroachment by Ecclesiastical Bodies, may be illustrated by precedents already furnished in their short history. (See the cases in which negatives were put by J. M. on two bills passd by Congs and his signature withheld from another. See also attempt in Kentucky for example, where it was proposed to exempt Houses of Worship from taxes.)[4]

The most notable attempt was that in Virga to establish a Genl assessment for the support of all Xn sects. This was proposed in the year   by P. H.[5] and supported by all his eloquence, aided by the remaining prejudices of the Sect which before the Revolution had been established by law.[6] The progress of the measure was arrested by urging that the respect due to the people required in so extraordinary a case an appeal to their deliberate will. The bill was accordingly printed & published with that view. At the instance of Col: George Nicholas, Col: George Mason & others, the memorial & remonstrance agst it was drawn up, (which see)[7] and printed Copies of it circulated thro' the State; to be signed by the people at large. It met with the approbation of the Baptists,

the Presbyterians, the Quakers, and the few Roman Catholics, universally; of the Methodists in part; and even of not a few of the Sect formerly established by law. When the Legislature assembled, the number of Copies & signatures prescribed displayed such an overwhelming opposition of the people, that the proposed plan of a genl assessmt was crushed under it: and advantage taken of the crisis to carry thro' the Legisl: the Bill above referred to, establishing religious liberty. In the course of the opposition to the bill in the House of Delegates, which was warm & strenuous from some of the minority, an experiment was made on the reverence entertained for the name & sanctity of the Saviour, by proposing to insert the words "Jesus Christ" after the words "our lord" in the preamble, the object of which, would have been, to imply a restriction of the liberty defined in the Bill, to those professing his religion only. The amendment was discussed, and rejected by a vote of   agst   (See letter of J. M. to Mr Jefferson dated   .)[8] The opponents of the amendment having turned the feeling as well as judgment of the House agst it, by successfully contending that the better proof of reverence for that holy name wd be not to profane it by making it a topic of legisl. discussion, & particularly by making his religion the means of abridging the natural and equal rights of all men, in defiance of his own declaration that his Kingdom was not of this world. This view of the subject was much enforced by the circumstance that it was espoused by some members who were particularly distinguished by their reputed piety and Christian zeal.

But besides the danger of a direct mixture of Religion & civil Government, there is an evil which ought to be guarded agst in the indefinite accumulation of property from the capacity of holding it in perpetuity by ecclesiastical corporations. The power

4. On Feb. 21, 1811, Madison vetoed a bill for incorporating the Episcopal Church in Alexandria and on Feb. 28, 1811, one reserving land in Mississippi territory for a Baptist Church. James D. Richardson, *Messages and Papers of the Presidents* (Washington, 1896–1899), I. 489–490.

5. Proposed in 1784 by Patrick Henry.

6. The Episcopal church.

7. Madison, *Letters*, I, 162–169.

8. On Jan. 9, 1785, Madison wrote Jefferson a long letter from Richmond reviewing the accomplishments of the "tedious session" of the Virginia legislature just closed. The following statement is probably that to which he refers: "In a committee of the whole it was determined, by a majority of 7 or 8, that the word 'Christian' should be exchanged for the word 'Religious.'" Madison, *Letters*, I, 131.

of all corporations, ought to be limited in this respect. The growing wealth acquired by them never fails to be a source of abuses. A warning on this subject is emphatically given in the example of the various Charitable establishments in G. B. the management of which has been lately scrutinized. The excessive wealth of ecclesiastical Corporations and the misuse of it in many Countries of Europe has long been a topic of complaint. In some of them the Church has amassed half perhaps the property of the nation. When the reformation took place, an event promoted if not caused, by that disordered state of things, how enormous were the treasures of religious societies, and how gross the corruptions engendered by them; so enormous & so gross as to produce in the Cabinets & Councils of the Protestant states a disregard, of all the pleas of the interested party drawn from the sanctions of the law, and the sacredness of property held in religious trust. The history of England during the period of the reformation offers a sufficient illustration for the present purpose.

Are the U.S. duly awake to the tendency of the precedents they are establishing, in the multiplied incorporations of Religious Congregations with the faculty of acquiring & holding property real as well as personal? Do not many of these acts give this faculty, without limit either as to time or as to amount? And must not bodies, perpetual in their existence, and which may be always gaining without ever losing, speedily gain more than is useful, and in time more than is safe? Are there not already examples in the U.S. of ecclesiastical wealth equally beyond its object and the foresight of those who laid the foundation of it? In the U.S. there is a double motive for fixing limits in this case, because wealth may increase not only from additional gifts, but from exorbitant advances in the value of the primitive one. In grants of vacant lands, and of lands in the vicinity of growing towns & Cities the increase of value is often such as if foreseen, would essentially controul the liberality confirming them. The people of the U.S. owe their Independence & their liberty, to the wisdom of descrying in the minute tax of 3 pence on tea, the

magnitude of the evil comprized in the precedent. Let them exert the same wisdom, in watching agst every evil lurking under plausible disguises, and growing up from small beginnings. Obsta principiis [oppose the beginnings].

> see the Treatise of Father Paul on beneficiary matters.[9]

Is the appointment of Chaplains to the two Houses of Congress consistent with the Constitution, and with the pure principle of religious freedom?

In strictness the answer on both points must be in the negative. The Constitution of the U.S. forbids everything like an establishment of a national religion. The law appointing Chaplains establishes a religious worship for the national representatives, to be performed by Ministers of religion, elected by a majority of them; and these are to be paid out of the national taxes. Does not this involve the principle of a national establishment, applicable to a provision for a religious worship for the Constituent as well as of the representative Body, approved by the majority, and conducted by Ministers of religion paid by the entire nation.

The establishment of the chaplainship to Congs is a palpable violation of equal rights, as well as of Constitutional principles: The tenets of the chaplains elected [by the majority] shut the door of worship agst the members whose creeds & consciences forbid a participation in that of the majority. To say nothing of other sects, this is the case with that of Roman Catholics & Quakers who have always had members in one or both of the Legislative branches. Could a Catholic clergyman ever hope to be appointed a Chaplain? To say that his religious principles are ob-

9. In the "Theological Catalogue for the Library of the University of Virginia" which Madison at Jefferson's request forwarded to him on Sept. 20, 1824 (See Madison, *Letters*, III, 450) there is listed, "Council of Trent, by F. Paul." The reference is evidently to Paolo Sarpi (1552–1623), Venetian patriot, scholar and anti-papal reformer who republished the conciliar theories of Gerson in his *History of the Council of Trent* (1619). Madison's catalogue is found in Rives, *Madison*, I, 642–644.

noxious or that his sect is small, is to lift the evil at once and exhibit in its naked deformity the doctrine that religious truth is to be tested by numbers, or that the major sects have a right to govern the minor.

If Religion consist in voluntary acts of individuals, singly, or voluntarily associated, and it be proper that public functionaries, as well as their Constituents shd discharge their religious duties, let them like their Constituents, do so at their own expence. How small a contribution from each member of Congs wd suffice for the purpose? How just wd it be in its principle? How noble in its exemplary sacrifice to the genius of the Constitution; and the divine right of conscience? Why should the expence of a religious worship be allowed for the Legislature, be paid by the public, more than that for the Ex. or Judiciary branch of the Govt?

Were the establishment to be tried by its fruits, are not the daily devotions conducted by these legal Ecclesiastics, already degenerating into a scanty attendance, and a tiresome formality?

Rather than let this step beyond the landmarks of power have the effect of a legitimate precedent, it will be better to apply to it the legal aphorism de minimis non curat lex [the law is not concerned with lesser matters]: or to class it cum "maculis quas aut incuria fudit, aut humana parum cavit natura [with faults which either carelessness has spilled or human nature is little concerned with]."

Better also to disarm in the same way, the precedent of Chaplainships for the army and navy, than erect them into a political authority in matters of religion. The object of this establishment is seducing; the motive to it is laudable. But is it not safer to adhere to a right principle, and trust to its consequences, than confide in the reasoning however specious in favor of a wrong one. Look thro' the armies & navies of the world, and say whether in the appointment of their ministers of religion, the spiritual interest of the flocks or the temporal interest of the Shepherds, be most in view: whether here, as elsewhere the political care of religion is not a nominal more than a real aid. If the spirit of armies be devout, the spirit out of the armies will never be less so; and a failure of religious instruction & exhortation from a voluntary source within or without, will rarely happen: and if such be not the spirit of armies, the official services of their Teachers are not likely to produce it. It is more likely to flow from the labours of a spontaneous zeal. The armies of the Puritans had their appointed Chaplains; but without these there would have been no lack of public devotion in that devout age.

The case of navies with insulated crews may be less within the scope of these reflections. But it is not entirely so. The chance of a devout officer, might be of as much worth to religion, as the service of an ordinary chaplain. [were it admitted that religion has a real interest in the latter.] But we are always to keep in mind that it is safer to trust the consequences of a right principle, than reasonings in support of a bad one.

Religious proclamations by the Executive recommending thanksgivings & fasts are shoots from the same root with the legislative acts reviewed.

Altho' recommendations only, they imply a religious agency, making no part of the trust delegated to political rulers.

The objections to them are 1. that Govts ought not to interpose in relation to those subject to their authority but in cases where they can do it with effect. An *advisory* Govt is a contradiction in terms. 2. The members of a Govt as such can in no sense, be regarded as possessing an advisory trust from their Constituents in their religious capacities. They cannot form an ecclesiastical Assembly, Convocation, Council, or Synod, and as such issue decrees or injunctions addressed to the faith or the Consciences of the people. In their individual capacities, as distinct from their official station, they might unite in recommendations of any sort whatever, in the same manner as any other individuals might do. But then their recommendations ought to express the true character from which they emanate. 3. They seem to imply and certainly nourish the erronious idea of a *national* religion. The idea just as it related to the Jewish nation under a theocracy, having been improperly adopted by so many nations which have embraced Xnity, is too apt to lurk in the bosoms even of Americans, who in general are aware of the distinction between religious & political societies. The idea also of a union of all to form one nation under one Govt in acts of devotion to the God of all is an imposing idea. But reason and the principles of the Xn religion require that all the individuals composing a nation even of the same precise creed & wished to unite in a universal act of religion at the same time, the union ought to be effected thro' the intervention of their religious not of their political representatives. In a nation composed of various sects, some alienated widely from others, and where no agreement could take place thro' the former, the interposition of the latter is doubly wrong: 4. The tendency of the practice, to narrow the recommendation to the standard of the predominant sect. The 1st proclamation of Genl Washington dated Jany 1. 1795 (see if this was the 1st) recommending a day of thanksgiving, embraced all who believed in a supreme ruler of the Universe.[10] That of Mr Adams called for a *Xn* worship. Many private letters reproached the Proclamations issued by J. M. for using general terms, used in that of Presidt W——n; and some of them for not inserting particulars according with the faith of certain Xn sects. The practice if not strictly guarded naturally terminates in a conformity to the creed of the majority and a single sect, if amounting to a majority. 5. The last & not the least objection is the liability of the practice to a subserviency to political views; to the scandal of religion, as well as the increase of party animosities. Candid or incautious politicians will not always disown such views. In truth it is difficult to frame such a religious Proclamation generally suggested by a political State of things, without referring to them in terms having some bearing on party questions. The Proclamation of Pres: W. which was issued just after the suppression of the Insurrection in Penna and at a time when the public mind was divided on several topics, was so construed by many. Of this the Secretary of State himself, E. Randolph seems to have had an anticipation.

The original draught of that Instrument filed in the Dept. of State (see copies of these papers on the files of J. M.) in the hand writing of Mr Hamilton the Secretary of the Treasury. It appears that several slight alterations only had been made at the suggestion of the Secretary of State; and in a marginal note in his hand, it is remarked that "In short this proclamation ought to savour as much as possible of religion, & not too much of having a political object." In a subjoined note in the hand of Mr. Hamilton, this remark is answered by the counter-remark that "A proclamation of a Government which is a national act, naturally embraces objects which are political" so *naturally*, is the idea of policy associated with religion, whatever be the mode or the occasion, when a function of the latter is assumed by those in power.[11]

During the administration of Mr Jefferson no religious proclamation was issued. It being understood that his successor was disinclined to such interpositions of the Executive and by some supposed moreover that they might originate with more propriety with the Legislative Body, a resolution was passed requesting him to issue a proclamation (see the resolution in the Journals of Congress).[12]

It was thought not proper to refuse a compliance altogether; but a form & language were employed, which were meant to deaden as much as possible any claim of political right to enjoin religious observances by resting these expressly on the voluntary compliance of individuals, and even by limiting the recommendation to such as wished simultaneous as well as voluntary performance of a religious act on the occasion. . . .

11. Issued on January 1, 1795. The original with marginal notes as quoted by Madison is now in the National Archives in Proclamations, 1791–1861.

12. The resolution is given in *Niles' Register*, July 18, 1812. Proclamations in response were issued by Madison on July 9, 1812 (Richardson, *Messages and Papers of the Presidents*, I. 513); July 23, 1813 (Ibid., I. 532–533); November 16, 1814 (Ibid., I. 558); March 4, 1815 (Ibid., I. 560–561).

10. The first was issued by Washington on October 3, 1789. "Thursday, the 26th day of November next to be devoted . . . to the services of that great and glorious Being. . . ." Richardson, *Messages and Papers of the Presidents*, I, 64.

Letter from James Madison to Robert Walsh (March 2, 1819)

Robert Walsh (1784–1859), an attorney turned journalist and publisher, wrote to former president Madison to inform him of his intention "to vindicate our Country against misrepresentations propagated abroad" and to request information on the subjects "of Negro slavery, of moral character, of religion, and of education in Virginia, as affected by the Revolution, and our public institutions." Excerpts from Madison's response concerning religion are printed below.

With respect to the moral features of Virga. it may be observed, that pictures which have been given of them are, to say the least, outrageous caricatures even when taken from the state of Society previous to the Revolution; and that so far as there was any ground or colour for them, then, the same cannot be found for them now.

Omitting more minute or less obvious causes tainting the habits and manners of the people under the Colonial Govt., the following offer themselves. . . .

3. the indolence of most & the irregular lives of many of the established Clergy, consisting, in a very large proportion, of foreigners, and these in no inconsiderable proportion, of men willing to leave their homes in the parent Country where their demerit was an obstacle to a provision for them, and whose degeneracy here was promoted by their distance from the controuling eyes of their kindred & friends, by the want of Ecclesiastical superiors in the Colony, or efficient ones in G. B. who might maintain a salutary

Reprinted from *The Writings of James Madison*, ed. Gaillard Hunt (New York and London: G. P. Putnam's Sons, 1908), 8:427–28, 430–32.

discipline among them, and finally by their independence both of their congregations and of the Civil authority for their stipends. . . .

That there has been an increase of religious instruction since the revolution can admit of no question. The English church was originally the established religion; the character of the clergy that above described. Of other sects there were but few adherents, except the Presbyterians who predominated on the W. side of the Blue Mountains. A little time previous to the Revolutionary struggle the Baptists sprang up, and made a very rapid progress. Among the early acts of the Republican Legislature, were those abolishing the Religious establishment, and putting all Sects at full liberty and on a perfect level. At present the population is divided, with small exceptions, among the Protestant Episcopalians, the Presbyterians, the Baptists & the Methodists. Of their comparative numbers I can command no sources of information. I conjecture the Presbyterians & Baptists to form each abt. a third, & the two other sects together of which the Methodists are much the smallest, to make up the remaining third. The Old churches, built under the establisht. at the public expence, have in many instances gone to ruin, or are in a very dilapidated state, owing chiefly to a transition desertion of the flocks to other worships. A few new ones have latterly been built particularly in the towns. Among the other sects, Meeting Houses, have multiplied & continue to multiply; tho' in general they are of the plainest and cheapest sort. But neither the number nor the style of the Religious edifices is a true measure of the state of religion. Religious instruction is now diffused throughout the Community by preachers of every sect with almost equal zeal, tho' with very unequal acquirements; and at private houses & open stations and occasionally in such as are appropriated to Civil use, as well as buildings appropriated to that use. The qualifications of the Preachers, too among the new sects where there was the greatest deficiency, are understood to be improving. On a general comparison of the present & former times, the balance is certainly & vastly on the side of the present, as to the number of religious teachers the zeal which actuates them, the purity of their lives, and the attendance of the people on their instructions. It was the Universal opinion of the Century preceding the last, that Civil Govt. could not stand without the prop of a Religious establishment, & that the Xn. religion itself, would perish if not supported by a legal provision for its Clergy. The experience of Virginia conspicuously corroborates the disproof of both opinions. The Civil Govt. tho' bereft of everything like an associated hierarchy possesses the requisite stability and performs its functions with complete success; Whilst the number, the industry, and the morality of the Priesthood, & the devotion of the people have been manifestly increased by the total separation of the Church from the State. . . .

Letters from James Madison and Thomas Jefferson to Jacob de la Motta (1820)

Jacob de la Motta (1789–1845), a native of Savannah, Georgia, served as a surgeon in the War of 1812 and practiced medicine in New York before returning to the city of his birth. In 1820 he delivered the consecration address for Savannah's new synagogue. He sent copies of his discourse to former presidents Madison and Jefferson, whose responses are reprinted below.

Letter from James Madison to Jacob de la Motta

Montpellier, Aug., 1820

SIR,—I have received your letter of the 7th inst. with the Discourse delivered at the Consecration of the Hebrew Synagogue at Savannah, for which you will please to accept my thanks.

The history of the Jews must forever be interesting. The modern part of it is, at the same time so little generally known, that every ray of light on the subject has its value.

Among the features peculiar to the Political system of the U. States, is the perfect equality of rights which it secures to every religious Sect. And it is particularly pleasing to observe in the good citizenship of such as have been most distrusted and oppressed elsewhere, a happy illustration of the safety & success of this experiment of a just & benignant policy. Equal laws protecting equal rights, are found as they ought to be presumed, the best guarantee of loyalty & love of country; as well as best calculated to cherish that mutual respect & good will among Citizens of every religious denomination which are necessary to social harmony and most favorable to the advancement of truth. The account you give of the Jews of your Congregation brings them fully within the scope of these observations.

I tender you, Sir, my respects & good wishes

———

Reprinted from *The Writings of James Madison,* ed. Gaillard Hunt (New York and London: G. P. Putnam's Sons, 1910), 9:29–30.

Letter from Thomas Jefferson to Jacob de la Motta, September 1, 1820

Th. Jefferson returns his thanks to Doct. de la Motta for the eloquent discourse on the Consecration of the Synagogue of Savannah which he has been so kind as to send him. it excites in him the gratifying reflection that his own country has been the first to prove to the world two truths, the most salutary to human society, that man can govern himself, and that religious freedom is the most effectual anodyne against religious dissension: the maxim of civil government being reversed in that of religion, where it's true form is 'divided we stand, united, we fall.' he is happy in the restoration, of the Jews particularly, to their social rights, & hopes they will be seen taking their seats on the benches of science as preparatory to their doing the same at the board of government. he salutes Dr. de la Motta with sentiments of great respect.

The text of the Jefferson letter is from the Thomas Jefferson Papers, Manuscript Division, Library of Congress.

Letter from James Madison to Edward Livingston (July 10, 1822)

Edward Livingston (1764–1836), son of the statesman Robert Livingston, was an attorney and politician who, as a member of the lower house of the Louisiana legislature, was entrusted with the task of revising Louisiana's criminal law. His plan for doing so was published and widely praised, although his actual revisions were not accepted by the legislature. Livingston sent Madison a copy of his plan in 1822. Excerpts from the former president's response to the plan that concern religion are reprinted below.

I observe with particular pleasure the view you have taken of the immunity of Religion from civil jurisdiction, in every case where it does not trespass on private rights or the public peace. This has always been a favorite principle with me; and it was not with my approbation, that the deviation from it took place in Congs., when they appointed Chaplains, to be paid from the Natl. Treasury. It would have been a much better proof to their Constituents of their pious feeling if the members had contributed for the purpose, a pittance from their own pockets. As the precedent is not likely to be rescinded, the best that can now be done, may be to apply to the Constn. the maxim of the law, de minimis non curat [it is not concerned with lesser matters].

There has been another deviation from the strict principle in the Executive Proclamations of fasts & festivals, so far, at least, as they have spoken the language of *injunction,* or have lost sight of the equality of *all* religious sects in the eye of the Constitution. Whilst I was honored with the Executive Trust I found it necessary on more than one occasion to follow the example of predecessors. But I was always careful to make the Proclamations absolutely indiscriminate, and merely recommendatory; or rather mere *designations* of a day, on which all who thought proper might *unite* in consecrating it to religious purposes, according to their own faith & forms. In this sense, I presume you reserve to the Govt. a right to *appoint* particular days for religious worship throughout the State, without any penal sanction *enforcing* the worship. I know not what may be the way of thinking on this subject in Louisiana. I should suppose the Catholic portion of the people, at least, as a small & even unpopular sect in the U.S., would rally, as they did in Virga. when religious liberty was a Legislative topic, to its broadest principle. Notwithstanding the general progress made within the two last centuries in favour of this branch of liberty, & the full establishment of it, in some parts of our Country,

Reprinted from *The Writings of James Madison,* ed. Gaillard Hunt (New York and London: G. P. Putnam's Sons, 1910), 9:100–103.

there remains in others a strong bias towards the old error, that without some sort of alliance or coalition between Govt. & Religion neither can be duly supported. Such indeed is the tendency to such a coalition, and such its corrupting influence on both the parties, that the danger cannot be too carefully guarded agst. And in a Govt. of opinion, like ours, the only effectual guard must be found in the soundness and stability of the general opinion on the subject. Every new & successful example therefore of a perfect separation between ecclesiastical and civil matters, is of importance. And I have no doubt that every new example, will succeed, as every past one has done, in shewing that religion & Govt. will both exist in greater purity, the less they are mixed together. It was the belief of all sects at one time that the establishment of Religion by law, was right & necessary; that the true religion ought to be established in exclusion of every other; And that the only question to be decided was which was the true religion. The example of Holland proved that a toleration of sects, dissenting from the established sect, was safe & even useful. The example of the Colonies, now States, which rejected religious establishments altogether, proved that all Sects might be safely & advantageously put on a footing of equal & entire freedom; and a continuance of their example since the declaration of Independence, has shewn that its success in Colonies was not to be ascribed to their connection with the parent Country. If a further confirmation of the truth could be wanted, it is to be found in the examples furnished by the States, which have abolished their religious establishments. I cannot speak particularly of any of the cases excepting that of Virga. where it is impossible to deny that Religion prevails with more zeal, and a more exemplary priesthood than it ever did when established and patronised by Public authority. We are teaching the world the great truth that Govts do better without Kings & Nobles than with them. The merit will be doubled by the other lesson that Religion flourishes in greater purity, without than with the aid of Govt.

My pen I perceive has rambled into reflections for which it was not taken up. I recall it to the proper object of thanking you for your very interesting pamphlet, and of tendering you my respects and good wishes.

J. M. presents his respects to Mr. [Henry B(?)]. Livingston and requests the favor of him to forward the above inclosed letter to N. Orleans or to retain it as his brother may or may not be expected at N. York.

The Relation of Christianity to Civil Government in the United States (1833)

JASPER ADAMS (1793–1841)

In 1833 Jasper Adams, scion of the famous Massachusetts family and president of the College of Charleston, preached the following sermon before the South Carolina convention of the Protestant Episcopal Church. He sent the published version of his sermon to a plethora of important Americans and received responses from, among others, Chief Justice John Marshall, Justice Joseph Story, and former president James Madison. The sermon, and these three responses, are reprinted in full below.

Be ready always to give an answer to every man that asketh you a reason of the hope that is in you, with meekness and fear.
—*I Peter* iii. 15.

Righteousness exalteth a nation, but sin is a reproach to any people. —*Proverbs* xiv. 34.

The kingdoms of this world are become the kingdoms of our Lord and of his Christ; and he shall reign for ever and ever.
—*Revelation* xi. 15.

Excerpts reprinted from *Religion and Politics in the Early Republic: Jasper Adams and the Church-State Debate*, ed. Daniel L. Dreisbach (Lexington: University Press of Kentucky, 1996), 39–58.

As Christianity was designed by its Divine Author to subsist until the end of time, it was indispensable, that it should be capable of adapting itself to all states of society, and to every condition of mankind. We have the Divine assurance that it shall eventually become universal, but without such flexibility in accommodating itself to all the situations in which men can be placed, this must have been impracticable. There is no possible form of individual or social life, which it is not fitted to meliorate and adorn. It not only extends to the more transient connexions to which the business of life gives rise, but embraces and prescribes the duties springing from the great and more permanent relations of rulers and subjects, husbands and wives, parents and children, masters and servants; and enforces the obligation of these high classes of our duties by the sanctions of a judgment to come. We find by examining its history, that, in rude ages, its influence has softened the savage and civilized the barbarian; while in polished ages and communities, it has accomplished the no less important end, of communicating and preserving the moral and religious principle, which, among a cultivated people, is in peculiar danger of being extinguished amid the refinements, the gaiety, and the frivolous amusements incident to such a state of society.

The relation which the prevailing system of religion in various countries and in successive ages, has sustained to civil government, is one of the most interesting branches of the history of mankind. According to the structure of the Hebrew Polity, the religious and political systems were most intimately, if not indissolubly combined: and in the Mosaic Law, we find religious observances, political ordinances, rules of medicine, prescriptions of agriculture, and even precepts of domestic economy, brought into the most intimate association. The Hebrew Hierarchy was a literary and political, as well as a religious order of men. In the Grecian States and in the Roman Empire, the same individual united in his own person, the emblems of priest of their divinities and the ensigns of civil and political authority. Christianity, while it was undermining, and until it had over-

thrown the ancient Polity of the Jews on the one hand; and the Polytheism of the Roman Empire on the other; was extended by the zeal and enterprize of its early preachers, sustained by the presence of its Divine Author[1] and accompanied by the evidence of the miracles which they were commissioned to perform. It is not strange, therefore, that when, under the Emperor Constantine, Christianity came into the place of the ancient superstition, it should have been taken under the protection, and made a part of the constitution of the Imperial government. It was the prediction of ancient prophecy, that, in the last days, kings should become nursing fathers and queens nursing mothers to the Church;[2]—and what was more natural than to understand this prophecy as meaning a strict and intimate union of the Church, with the civil government of the Empire. Ancient usage, with all the influence which a reverence for antiquity is accustomed to inspire, was on the side of such a union. We may well believe, then, that Christianity was first associated with civil government, without any intention on the part of civil governors to make it the odious engine of the State which it afterwards became. And if the Roman Emperors had been satisfied to receive and to continue the new religion without distinction of sects, as the broad ground of all the great institutions of the Empire, it is impossible to shew or to believe, that such a measure would not have been both wise and salutary. The misfortune was, that there soon came to be a legal preference of *one form* of Christianity over *all others*. Mankind are not easily inclined to change any institution which has taken deep root in the structure of society, and the principle of the union of *one form* of Christianity with the imperial authority under the Roman Emperors, had acquired too many titles to veneration to be relinquished, when the new kingdoms were founded which rose upon the ruins of the Roman Empire. This principle has always pervaded

---

1. Matthew xxviii. 20.

2. Isaiah xlix. 23. [Bishop of London, Robert] Lowth says of this prophecy: "It was remarkably fulfilled, when Constantine and other Christian princes and princesses, showed favour to the Church."

and still pervades the structure of European society, and the necessity of retaining it is still deeply seated in the convictions of the inhabitants of the Eastern continent.

The same principle was transferred to these shores when they were settled by European colonists. In Massachusetts and some other Northern colonies, no man could be a citizen of the Commonwealth, unless he were a member of the Church as there established by authority of law.[3] In Virginia and some of the more Southern colonies, the Church of England was established by law.[4] In this State [South Carolina], legal provision was made for the establishment of religious worship according to the Church of England, for the erecting of churches and the maintenance of clergymen; and it was declared, that "in a well grounded Commonwealth, matters concerning religion and the honour of God, ought in the first place, (i.e. in preference to all others,) to be taken into consideration."[5]

It is the testimony of history, however, that ever since the time of Constantine, *such* an union of the ecclesiastical with the civil authority, has given rise to flagrant abuses and gross corruptions. By a series of gradual, but well contrived usurpations, a Bishop of the Church claiming to be the successor of the Chief of the Apostles and the Vicar of Christ, had been seen for centuries, to rule the nations of Christendom with the sceptre of despotism. The argument against the use of an institution arising from its abuse, is not valid, unless, when, after sufficient experience, there is the best reason to conclude, that we cannot enjoy the use without the accompanying evils flowing from

Jasper Adams. Courtesy of the archives at the Warren Hunting Smith Library, Hobart and William Smith Colleges, Geneva, New York.

the abuse of it. Such perhaps is the case in regard to the union between any particular form of Christianity and civil government. It is an historical truth established by the experience of many centuries, that whenever Christianity has *in this way* been incorporated with the civil power, the lustre of her brightness has been dimmed by the alliance.

The settlers of this country were familiar with these facts, and they gradually came to a sound practical conclusion on the subject. No nation on earth, perhaps, ever had opportunities so favorable to introduce changes in their institutions as the American people; and by the time of the Revolution, a conviction of the impolicy of a further union of Church and State *according to the ancient mode,* had so far prevailed, that nearly all the States in framing their new constitutions of government, either silently or by direct enactment, discontinued the ancient connexion.

3. In 1631, the General Court of Massachusetts Bay passed an order, "that for the time to come, none should be admitted to the freedom of the body politic, but such as were Church-members."—1 *Story's Commentaries,* 39, 73.

4. 1 Tucker's Blackstone, p. 376.—Under the crowns of France and Spain, Roman Catholicism was the religion of Louisiana exclusive of all others. As late as 1797, the instructions of Governor Gayoso to the commandants for the regulation of the province, speak thus:—"Art. 8. The commandants will take particular care, that no Protestant Preacher, or one of any sect other than the Catholic, shall introduce himself into the province. The least neglect in this respect, will be a subject of great reprehension."—*Documents annexed to Judge Peck's trial,* p. 585.

5. Act of November 30, 1706.

A question of great interest here comes up for discussion. In thus discontinuing the connexion between Church and Commonwealth;—did the people of these States intend to renounce all connexion with the Christian religion? Or did they only intend to disclaim all preference of one sect of Christians over another, as far as civil government was concerned; while they still retained the Christian religion as the foundation of all their social, civil and political institutions? Did Massachusetts and Connecticut, when they declared, that the legal preference which had heretofore been given to Puritanism, should continue no longer, intend to abolish Christianity itself within their jurisdictions? Did Virginia and S. Carolina when they discontinued all legal preference of the Church of England as by law established, intend to discontinue their observance of Christianity and their regard for its Divine authority? Did the people of the United States, when in adopting the Federal Constitution they declared, that "Congress shall make no law respecting an establishment of religion or prohibiting the free exercise thereof," expect to be understood as abolishing the national religion, which had been professed, respected and cherished from the first settlement of the country, and which it was the great object of our fathers in settling this then wilderness to enjoy according to the dictates of their own consciences?

The rightful solution of these questions has become important to the religion, the morals, the peace, the intelligence, and in fact, to all the highest interests of this country. It has been asserted by men distinguished for talents, learning and station,[6] and it may well be presumed that the assertion is gradually gaining belief among us, that Christianity has no connexion with the law of the land, or with our civil and political institutions. Attempts are making, to impress this sentiment on the public mind. The sentiment is considered by me, to be in contradiction to the whole tenor of our history, to be false in fact, and in the highest degree pernicious in its tendency, to all

6. 4 Jefferson's Works, p. 397.

our most valuable institutions, whether social, legal, civil or political. It is moreover, not known to the preacher, that any serious effort has been made to investigate the relation which Christianity sustains to our institutions, or to enlighten the public understanding on the subject. Under these circumstances, I have thought it a theme suitable for discussion on an occasion, when the clergy of the diocese and some of the most influential laymen of our parishes, are assembled in convention. I may well expect to prove inadequate to the full discussion, and still more to the ultimate settlement of the principles involved in the inquiry. But I may be permitted to presume, that when it is once brought to the notice of this Convention, any deficiency of mine in treating the subject will not long remain to be satisfactorily supplied.

The relation of Christianity to the civil institutions of this country cannot be investigated with any good prospect of success, without briefly reviewing our history both before and since the Revolution, and making an examination of such authorities as are entitled to our respect and deference. It is an historical question, and to arrive at a sound conclusion, recurrence must be had to the ordinary means which are employed for the adjustment of inquiries of this kind.

I. The originators and early promoters of the discovery and settlement of this continent, had the propagation of Christianity before their eyes, as one of the principal objects of their undertaking. This is shewn by examining the charters and other similar documents of that period, in which this chief aim of their novel and perilous enterprize, is declared with a frequency and fulness which are equally satisfactory and gratifying. In the Charter of Massachusetts Bay, granted in 1644 by Charles I., the colonists are exhorted by "theire good life and orderly conversation, to winne and invite the natives of that country to the knowledge and obedience of the onely true God and Saviour of mankind and the Christian faith, which in our royall intention and the adventurers' free profession, (i.e. the unconstrained acknowledgment of the colonists,) is the principal end of this plantation."[7] In the Virginia Charter of 1606, the enterprize of planting the country is commended as "a noble work, which may, by the providence of Almighty God, hereafter tend to the glory of his Divine Majesty, in propagating of Christian religion to such people as yet live in darkness and miserable ignorance of the true knowledge and worship of God;"—and the Pennsylvania Charter of 1682, declares it to have been one object of William Penn, "to reduce the savage nations, by gentle and just manners, to the love of civil society and Christian religion."[8] In the Charter of Rhode Island, granted by Charles II. in 1682–3, it is declared to be the object of the colonists to pursue "with peace, and loyal minds, their sober, serious and religious intentions of godly edifying themselves and one another, in the holy Christian faith and worship, together with the gaining over and conversion of the poor ignorant Indian natives to the sincere profession and obedience of the same faith and worship."[9] The preceding quotations furnish a specimen of the sentiments and declarations with which the colonial Charters and other ancient documents abound.[10] I make no apology for citing the passages without abridgment. They are authentic memorials of an age long since gone by. They make known the intentions and breathe the feelings of our pious forefathers; a race of men who, in all the qualities which render men respectable and venerable, have never been surpassed; and who ought to be held by us their offspring, in grateful remembrance. We very much mistake, if we suppose ourselves so much advanced before them, that we cannot be benefited by becoming acquainted with their sentiments, their characters and their labours. The Christian religion was intended by them to be the corner stone of the social and political structures which they were found-

ing. Their aim was as pure and exalted, as their undertaking was great and noble.

II. We shall be further instructed in the religious character of our origin as a nation, if we advert for a moment to the rise and progress of our colonial growth. As the colonists desired both to enjoy the Christian religion themselves, and to make the natives acquainted with its divine blessings, they were accompanied by a learned and pious Ministry; and wherever a settlement was commenced, a Church was founded. As the settlements were extended, new Churches were established. Viewing education as indispensable to Freedom, as well as the handmaid of Religion, every neighbourhood had its school. After a brief interval, Colleges were instituted; and these institutions were originally designed for the education of Christian Ministers.[11] Six days of the week they spent in the labours of the field; but on the seventh, they rested according to the commandment, and employed the day in the duties of public worship, and in the religious instruction of their children and servants. Thus our colonization proceeded on the grand but simple plan of civil and religious freedom,

7. Almon's Collection of Charters, p. 63.

8. Almon, pp. 68, 104.

9. Idem, p. 34.

10. See Note A. [Notes indicated by capital letters refer to Adams's sermon notes, which are not reprinted here. They can be found in Daniel L. Dreisbach, ed., *Religion and Politics in the Early Republic* (Lexington: University Press of Kentucky, 1996), 59–110.—Eds.]

11. Scarcely had the Massachusetts' colonists arrived at their new scene of labour, when their thoughts were turned to the establishment of a College; and in 1636, Harvard University was founded. Dr. C. Mather says:— "The ends for which our fathers chiefly erected a College were, that so scholars might there be educated for the service of Christ and his Churches in the work of the Ministry, and that they might be seasoned in their tender years, with such principles as brought their blessed progenitors into this wilderness. There is no one thing of greater concernment to these Churches in present and after-times, than the prosperity of that society. They cannot subsist without a College."—*Magnalia, B. V.* The inscription, "Christo et Ecclesiae," on the seal of the University, is at once emphatic evidence, and a perpetual memorial of the great purpose for which it was established. In the year 1662, the Assembly of Virginia passed an Act to make permanent provision for the establishment of a College. The preamble of the Act establishing it recites, "that the want of able and faithful Ministers in this country, deprives us of those great blessings and mercies that always attend upon the service of God;"—and the Act itself declares, "that for the advancement of learning, education of youth, supply of the ministry, and promotion of piety, there be land taken up and purchased for a College and Free School; and that with all convenient speed, there be buildings erected upon it for the entertainment of students and scholars. In 1693, the College of William and Mary was founded."—*Quar. Register.* vol. iii. p. 268. Quotations of similar import might be made pertaining to Yale, Nassau Hall and in fact, to all the Colleges first established in this country.

of universal industry, and of universal literary and religious education.

The Colonies, then, from which these United States have sprung, were originally planted and nourished by our pious forefathers, in the exercise of a strong and vigorous Christian faith. They were designed to be Christian communities. Christianity was wrought into the minutest ramifications of their social, civil and political institutions. And it has before been said, that according to the views which had prevailed in Europe since the days of Constantine, *a legal preference of some one denomination over all others,* prevailed in almost all the colonies. We are, therefore, now prepared:

III. To examine with a good prospect of success, the nature and extent of the *changes* in regard to Religion, which have been introduced by the people of the United States in forming their State Constitutions, and also in the adoption of the Constitution of the United States.

In perusing the twenty-four Constitutions of the United States with this object in view, we find all of them[12] recognising Christianity as the well known and well established religion of the communities, whose legal, civil and political foundations, these Constitutions are. The terms of this recognition are more or less distinct in the Constitutions of the different States; but they exist in all of them. The reason why any degree of indistinctness exists in any of them unquestionably is, that at their formation, it never came into the minds of the framers to suppose, that the existence of Christianity as the religion of their communities, could ever admit of a question. Nearly all these Constitutions recognise the customary observance of Sunday, and a suitable observance of this day, includes a performance of all the peculiar duties of the Christian faith.[13] The Constitution of Vermont declares, that "every sect or denomination of Christians, ought to observe the Sabbath or Lord's

Day, and keep up some sort of religious worship, which to them shall seem most agreeable to the revealed will of God."[14] The Constitutions of Massachusetts and Maryland, are among those which do not prescribe the observance of Sunday: yet the former declares it to be "the right, as well as the duty of all men in society, publicly and at stated seasons, to worship the Supreme Being, the great Creator and Preserver of the Universe;["][15]—and the latter requires every person appointed to any office of profit or trust, to "subscribe a declaration of his belief in the Christian religion."[16] Two of them concur in the sentiment, that "morality and piety, rightly grounded on Evangelical principles, will be the best and greatest security to government; and that the knowledge of these is most likely to be propagated through a society, by the institution of the public worship of the Deity, and of public instruction in morality and religion."[17] Only a small part of what the Constitutions of the States contain in regard to the Christian religion, is here cited; but my limits do not permit me to cite more.[18] At the same time, they all grant the free exercise and enjoyment of religious profession and worship, with some slight discriminations, to all mankind. The principle obtained by the foregoing inductive examination of our State Constitutions, is this:—THE PEOPLE OF THE UNITED STATES HAVE RETAINED THE CHRISTIAN RELIGION AS THE FOUNDATION OF THEIR CIVIL, LEGAL AND POLITICAL INSTITUTIONS; WHILE THEY HAVE REFUSED TO CONTINUE A LEGAL PREFERENCE TO ANY ONE OF ITS FORMS OVER THE OTHER. In the same spirit of practical wisdom,

---

12. The author has not seen the *new* Constitution of Mississippi, and, therefore, this assertion may possibly not apply to that document.

13. See Note C.

14. Art. 3.

15. Part I. Art. 2.

16. Art. 55.

17. The quotation here is from the Constitution of New-Hampshire; (*Part* i. *Art.* 6.) and the concurrence is substantial, not verbal. The parallel passage in the Constitution of Massachusetts runs thus:—"The happiness of a people, and the good order and preservation of civil government, essentially depend upon piety, religion and morality, and these cannot be generally diffused through the community but by the institution of a public worship of God, and of public institutions, (instructions) in piety, religion and morality."—*Part* i. *Art.* 3.

18. See Note B.

moreover, they have consented to tolerate all other religions.

The Constitution of the United States contains a grant of specific powers, of the general nature of a trust. As might be expected from its nature, it contains but slight references of a religious kind. In one of these, the people of the United States profess themselves to be a Christian nation. In another, they express their expectation, that the President of the United States will maintain the customary observance of Sunday; and by parity of reasoning, that such observance will be respected by all who may be employed in subordinate stations in the service of the United States.[19] The first amendment declares, that "Congress shall make no law respecting an establishment of religion, or prohibiting the free exercise thereof."[20] This leaves the entire subject in the same situation in which it found it; and such was precisely the most suitable course. The people of the United States having, in this most solemn of all their enactments, professed themselves to be a Christian nation; and having expressed their confidence, that all employed in their service will practice the duties of the Christian faith;—and having, moreover, granted to all others the free exercise of their religion, have emphatically declared, that Congress shall make no change in the religion of the country. This was too delicate and too important a subject to be entrusted to their guardianship. It is the duty of Congress, then, to permit the Christian religion to remain in the same state in which it was, at the time when the Constitution was adopted. They have no commission to destroy or injure the religion of the country. Their laws ought to be consistent with its principles and usages. They may not rightfully enact any measure or sanction any practice calculated to diminish its moral influence, or to impair the respect in which it is held among the people.[21]

If a question could be raised, in regard to the soundness of the view, which has now been taken, of the relation in which our Constitutions of government stand to the Christian religion, it must be settled by referring to the practice which has existed under them from their first formation. The public authorities both in our State and National Governments, have always felt it to be required of them, to respect the peculiar institutions of Christianity, and whenever they have ventured to act otherwise, they have never failed to be reminded of their error by the displeasure and rebuke of the nation. From the first settlement of this country up to the present time, particular days have been set apart by public authority, to

19. See Note C.

20. The meaning of the term "establishment" in this amendment unquestionably is, the preference and establishment given by law to one sect of Christians over every other. This is the customary use of the term in English history and in English law, and in our colonial history and law. See 3 Story's Comm. 722–731, where the author has commented on this amendment with his usual learning and candour.

21. It has sometimes been concluded, that Christianity cannot have any direct connexion with the Constitution of the United States, on the ground, that the instrument contains no express declaration to this effect. But the error of such a conclusion becomes manifest, when we reflect, that the case is the same with regard to several other truths, which are notwithstanding, fundamental in our constitutional system. The Declaration of Independence says, that "governments are instituted among men, to secure the rights of life, liberty and the pursuit of happiness;" and that "whenever any form of government becomes destructive of these ends, it is the right of the people to alter or to abolish it, and to institute a new government." These principles lie at the foundation of the Constitution of the United States. No principles known to the Constitution are more fundamental than these. But the instrument contains no declaration to this effect; these principles are no where mentioned in it; and the references to them are equally slight and indirect with those which are made to the Christian religion. The same may be said, of the great republican truth, that political sovereignty resides in the people of the United States. If then, any one may rightfully conclude, that Christianity has no connexion with the Constitution of the United States, because this is nowhere expressly declared in the instrument; he ought, in reason, to be equally convinced, that the same Constitution is not built upon and does not recognize the sovereignty of the people, and the great republican truths above quoted from the Declaration of Independence. This argument receives additional strength, when we consider that the Constitution of the United States was formed directly for political, and not for religious objects. The truth is, they are all equally fundamental, though neither of them is expressly mentioned in the Constitution.

Besides, the Constitution of the United States contemplates, and is fitted for such a state of society as Christianity alone can form. It contemplates a state of society, in which strict integrity, simplicity and purity of manners, wide diffusion of knowledge, well disciplined passions, and wise moderation, are the general characteristics of the people. These virtues, in our nation, are the offspring of Christianity, and without the continued general belief of its doctrines, and practice of its precepts, they will gradually decline and eventually perish. See Note D.

acknowledge the favour, to implore the blessing, or to deprecate the wrath of Almighty God. In our Conventions and Legislative Assemblies, daily Christian worship has been customarily observed. All business proceedings in our Legislative halls and Courts of justice, have been suspended by universal consent on Sunday. Christian Ministers have customarily been employed to perform stated religious services in the Army and Navy of the United States. In administering oaths, the Bible, the standard of Christian truth is used, to give additional weight and solemnity to the transaction. A respectful observance of Sunday, which is peculiarly a Christian institution, is required by the laws of nearly all, perhaps of all the respective States.[22] My conclusion, then, is sustained by the documents which gave rise to our colonial settlements, by the records of our colonial history, by our Constitutions of government made during and since the Revolution, by the laws of the respective States, and finally by the uniform practice which has existed under them.[23] Manifold more authorities and illustrations might have been given, if such a course had been consistent with the limits which it was necessary to prescribe to myself on this occasion. But the subject is too important to be brought to a close without some further observations.

1st. We cannot too much admire the wisdom displayed by the American people in establishing such a relation between the Christian religion and their political institutions. To have abolished Christianity, or to have shewn indifference to its sacred nature and claims in framing their political institutions, would have been committing a great national sin. It would have been, also, to forget the Divine warning, that "except the Lord build the house, they labour in vain that build it."[24] To have given a legal preference to any one form of Christianity over another, would have

been to depart from the usage of primitive times, and to sanction abuses to which it was no longer necessary to adhere. To have refused to others the free exercise of their religion, whatever this might be, would have been illiberal and at variance with the spirit of the age.[25] They wisely chose the middle course;—the only course in fact warranted by Scripture, by experience and by primitive usage. They rightly considered their religion as the highest of all their interests,[26] and refused to render it in any way or in any degree, subject to governmental interference or regulations. Thus, while all others enjoy full protection in the profession of their opinions and practice, Christianity is the established[27] religion of the nation, its institutions

---

22. "All the States of the Union, I believe, (twenty-three of them certainly,) by explicit legislative enactments, acknowledge and declare the religious authority of Sunday."—*Speech of Mr. Frelinghuysen of New-Jersey, in the Senate of the United States, 8th May,* 1830.

23. See Note E.

24. Psalm 127. 1.

25. The Constitution of S. Carolina, contains this provision; "The free exercise and enjoyment of religious profession and worship, without discrimination or preference, shall, forever hereafter, be allowed within this State to all mankind: *Provided,* that the liberty of conscience thereby declared, shall not be so construed as to excuse acts of licentiousness, or justify practices inconsistent with the peace or safety of this State." The Constitutions of New-York, of the dates both of 1777 and 1821 contain this same provision, and as it appears to be frequently misunderstood, the author adds Ch. J. [James] Kent's exposition of it, contained in 8 Johnson, 296. He speaks of it thus:—"This declaration (noble and magnanimous as it is, when duly understood) never meant to withdraw religion in general, and with it the best sanctions of moral and social obligation, from all consideration and notice of the law. It will be fully satisfied by a free and universal toleration, without any of the tests, disabilities or discriminations, incident to a religious establishment. To construe it as breaking down the common law barriers against licentious, wanton and impious attacks upon Christianity itself, would be an enormous perversion of its meaning." The proviso, continues he, guards the article from such dangerous latitude of construction when it declares, that "*'the liberty of conscience hereby granted,* (declared) shall not be so construed as to excuse acts of licentiousness, or justify practices inconsistent with the peace or safety of this State.'" "The proviso is a species of commentary upon the meaning of the article. The framers of the Constitution intended only to banish test oaths, disabilities and the burthens and sometimes the oppressions of Church establishments; and to secure to the people of this State, freedom from coercion, and an equality of right on the subject of religion. This was no doubt the consummation of their wishes. It was all that reasonable minds could require and it had long been a favourite object, on both sides of the Atlantic, with some of the most enlightened friends to the rights of mankind, whose indignation had been roused by infringements of the liberty of conscience, and whose zeal was inflamed in the pursuit of its enjoyment."

26. The great interests of a country may be ranked thus:—1. Its religious and moral interests. 2. The peace of the country both in regard to foreign enemies and internal convulsions. 3. The intellectual interests, or the interests of education. 4. The pecuniary interests.

27. The term "established" is here used as well as at p. 11 [45], in its usual and not in its legal or technical sense, see p. 13 [46].

and usages are sustained by legal sanctions, and many of them are incorporated with the fundamental law of the country.[28]

2. The doctrine against which I am contending; to wit, that Christianity has no connexion with our civil Constitutions of government, is one of those which admit of being tested by the absurd and dangerous consequences to which they lead. It cannot be disguised, that a general belief, that Christianity is to receive no regard and no countenance from our civil institutions, must tend to degrade it and to destroy its influence among the community. It has hitherto been believed, that Christian morals, Christian sentiments, and Christian principles ought to form the basis of the education of our youth; but this belief cannot continue to prevail, if the opinion in question shall once become general. It has hitherto been supposed, that our judges, our legislators, and our statesmen ought to be influenced by the spirit, and bound by the sanctions of Christianity, both in their public and private conduct; but no censure can be rightfully attached to them for refusing to comply, if nothing of this kind is required by the commissions under which they act, and from which their authority is derived. If the community shall ever become convinced, that Christianity is not entitled to the sustaining aid of the civil Constitutions and law of the country, the outposts of the citadel will have been taken, and its adversaries may successfully proceed in their work of undermining and destroying it. In this country, where the authority of law is comparatively feeble, every enterprise must be accomplished by influencing public opinion; and the strength of public opinion is irresistible and overwhelming. In fact, under a belief, that such a conviction has been wrought in the public

mind, the adversaries of Christianity have begun to break new ground against it; and this too with renewed confidence of ultimate success. It is announced from stations usually supposed to be entitled to respect and confidence, that the Scriptures of the New Testament expressly forbid all praying in public;—that the Christian Clergy are an unnecessary and useless order of men;—and that the setting apart of Sunday, is not authorized in any part of the Christian dispensation. These are novel and sweeping assertions, and they have already been repeated so often, that they sound less harsh than they once did, in the ears of our community. Those who attempt to impose such assertions upon us, must calculate with much confidence, either on our willingness to be deceived, or on our having too little acquaintance with the subject to detect their mistakes, or on our feeling too much indifference to our religion to take an interest in refuting them. Who believes, that without an order of men to administer the sacraments, to illustrate the doctrines and enforce the duties of Christianity, without public worship, and without the general and respectful observance of Sunday, there would be the least vestige of religion among us at the end of half a century[?] As well might we expect the preservation of public order and civil obedience in the community, if our laws were permitted to remain in the statute-book, without a Judiciary to explain their import, or an Executive to enforce their observance.

3. Let us not forget what is historically true, that Christianity has been the chief instrument by which the nations of Christendom have risen superior to all other nations;—but if its influence is once destroyed or impaired, society instead of advancing, must infallibly retrograde. This superiority of the nations of Christendom is a fact, and as such can only be accounted for by assigning an adequate cause. "With whatever justice other lands and nations may be estimated," says [Arnold] Heeren,[29] "it cannot be denied that the noblest and best of every thing, which

28. "Let us not forget the religious character of our origin. Our fathers were brought hither by their high veneration for the Christian religion. They journeyed by its light and laboured in its hope. *They sought to incorporate its principles with the elements of their society, and to diffuse its influence through all their institutions, civil, political or literary.* Let us cherish these sentiments, and extend this influence still more widely; in the full conviction, that that is the happiest society, which partakes in the highest degree of the mild and peaceable spirit of Christianity."—*Webster's Discourse at Plymouth*, p. 54. See Note F.

29. Politics of Ancient Greece, translated by Mr. [George] Bancroft, p. 1.

man has produced, sprung up or at least ripened, on European soil. In the multitude, variety, and beauty of their natural productions, Asia and Africa far surpass Europe; but in every thing which is the work of man, the nations of Europe stand far above those of the other continents. It was among them," continues he, "that by making marriage the union of but two individuals, domestic society obtained that form without which so many parts of our nature could never have been ennobled;—and it was chiefly and almost exclusively among them, that such constitutions were framed, as are suited to nations who have become conscious of their rights. If Asia, during all the changes of its extensive empires, does but shew the continued reproduction of despotism, it was on European soil that the germ of political freedom unfolded itself, and under the most various forms, in so many parts of the same, bore the noblest fruits; which again were transplanted from thence to other parts of the world." These remarks, though applied by the author to Europe only, have respect equally to the descendants of Europeans on this side of the Atlantic. They are true of all Christian nations. These golden fruits are what Christianity has produced, and they have been produced by no other religion. If, then, we permit this chief cause of all our choicest blessings to be destroyed or counteracted in its effects; what can we expect from the dealings of a righteous Providence, but the destiny of a people who have rejected the counsel of God against themselves?[30] If we refuse to be instructed by the Divine assurance, we shall be made to feel by the intensity of our sufferings, "that righteousness exalteth a nation, and that sin is a reproach to any people."

4. No nation on earth, is more dependent than our own, for its welfare, on the preservation and general belief and influence of Christianity among us. Perhaps there has never been a nation composed of men whose spirit is more high, whose aspirations after distinction are more keen, and whose passions are more strong than those which reign in the breasts of the American people. These are encouraged and strengthened by our systems of education, by the unlimited field of enterprise which is open to all; and more especially by the great inheritance of civil and religious freedom, which has descended to us from our ancestors. It is too manifest, therefore, to require illustration, that in a great nation thus high spirited, enterprising and free, public order must be maintained by some principle of very peculiar energy and strength;—by some principle which will touch the springs of human sentiment and action. Now there are two ways, and two ways only by which men can be governed in society; the one by physical force; the other by religious and moral principles pervading the community, guiding the conscience, enlightening the reason, softening the prejudices, and calming the passions of the multitude. Physical force is the chief instrument by which mankind have heretofore been governed; but this always has been, and I trust will always continue to be inapplicable in our case. My trust, however, in this respect, springs entirely from a confidence, that the Christian religion will continue as heretofore to exert upon us, its tranquilizing, purifying, elevating and controlling efficacy. No power less efficacious than Christianity, can permanently maintain the public tranquillity of the country, and the authority of law.[31] We must be a Christian nation, if we wish to continue a free nation. We must make our election:—to be swayed by the gentle reign of moral and Christian principle, or ultimately, if not soon, by the iron rod of arbitrary sway.

Nor will it be sufficient for any of us to say, that we have not been active participators in undermining and destroying our religion;—we cannot escape crime, if it shall be destroyed by our neglect or indifference. The guilt of nations which have never been evangelized, for not rendering to Jehovah the glory due to his name, must be very much palliated by their ignorance; which is, in some respects, and in a considerable degree, invincible. But how can we escape, if we neglect, or abuse, or fail to improve the Chris-

---

30. Luke vii. 30.

31. See Note G.

tian inheritance which has come down to us from our fathers, and which it cost them such sacrifices to acquire. Have we forgotten the saying of our Saviour, that the damnation of Sodom, in the day of judgment, will be tolerable when compared with the sufferings which will, on that day, be inflicted upon Capernaum, which had been exalted to heaven by being made the scene of his miracles, but which still persisted in its impenitence?[32] In the Divine administration, then, the principle applies to nations, as well as to individuals, that their punishment will be severe in proportion to the advantages which they have neglected to improve, and the blessings which they have undervalued and despised. If, therefore, Christianity is permitted to decline among us, we cannot fold our arms in silence and be free from all personal responsibility. As a citizen of our community, no man can escape criminality, if he believes in the truth of Christianity, and still, without making resistance, sees its influence undermined and destroyed.

We are accustomed to rejoice in the ancestry from which we are descended, and well we may, for our ancestors were illustrious men. One of the colonial governors said in 1692, "God sifted a whole nation, that he might send choice grain over into this wilderness."[33] And the present Lord Chancellor of Great Britain has thus spoken of them:—"The first settlers of all the colonies, says he, were men of irreproachable characters. Many of them fled from persecution; others on account of an honorable poverty; and all of them with their expectations limited to the prospect of a bare subsistence in freedom and peace. All idea of wealth or pleasure was out of the question. The greater part of them viewed their emigration as a taking up of the cross, and bounded their hopes of riches to the gifts of the spirit, and their ambition to the desire of a kingdom beyond the grave. A set of men more conscientious in their doings, or simple in their manners, never founded any Commonwealth. It is, indeed, continues he, the peculiar glory of North America, that with very few exceptions, its empire was originally founded in charity and peace."[34] They were, in truth, men who feared God and knew no other fear.[35]

In no respect, therefore, were these illustrious men so peculiar, for no trait of character were they so distinguished, as for the strength of their religious principles. The perilous enterprise in which they were engaged, was chiefly a religious enterprise. To enjoy their religion according to the dictates of their own consciences, and to effect the conversion of the native Indians,[36] we have seen, were the great objects of their toils and sufferings. The principles which supplied them with the high motives from which they acted, were perseveringly taught to their children, and aided by their own bright example, became the vital sentiment of the new communities which they founded. What must have been the strength of the conviction of Christian Truth in the American mind, when the popular names of [Benjamin] Franklin[37] and of [Thomas] Jefferson among its adversaries, have not been able *much* to impair its influence. May Christianity, clear and convincing as she is in her evidences, pure in her doctrines, conservative in her moral influences, imperishable in her destiny, the last consolation of those who have outlived all earthly hopes, and the last restraint of those who are above all earthly fear, continue, with her benign reign, to bless our country, to the end of time, the crowning glory of the American name.[38]

The conspiracy formed in Europe to destroy Christianity in the last century, has been overthrown and put to shame on that continent, by the overwhelming convulsions, distress and ruin brought upon its guilty nations, through the dissemination of its destructive principles.[39] In the whirlwind and storm of this mighty moral tempest, its seeds were

32. Matthew xi. 23.
33. Am. Q. R. No. xviii. p. 128.

34. Brougham's Col. Pol. vol. i. p. 59.
35. Je crains Dieu, cher Abner, et n'ai point d'autre crainte.—*Racine.* [I fear God, dear Abner, and have no other fear.]
36. Note H.
37. Note I.
38. Note K.
39. Mr. Macaulay's Speech in House of Commons, April 17th, 1833.

wafted to our shores. They have taken root in our land, and we are threatened with their pestilential fruit in disastrous plenty. Infidelity advanced at first in this country with cautious steps, and put on the decorous garb of rational and philosophical enquiry; until at length, having examined its ground and prepared its way, it has assumed the attitude of open and uncompromising hostility to every form and every degree of the Christian faith.

Our regard for the civil inheritance bequeathed us by our fathers, leads us to guard it with the most jealous vigilance. And shall we permit our religious inheritance, which in their estimation was of still higher value and is of infinitely more enduring interest, to be taken from us without a struggle? Are we not convinced, that if our religion is once undermined, it will be succeeded by a decline of public and private morals, and by the destruction of those high and noble qualities of character, for which as a community we have been so much distinguished?[40] Christianity, in its integrity, will never perish; the gates of Hell, shall never prevail against the Church of God.[41] But it has perished and may perish again in particular districts of [the] country. Are we accustomed to reflect on the consequences of a decline of the influence of Christianity among us, and along with it, of public and private morals? And on the other hand, are we sensible of the consequences which must attend the introduction and general belief of the infidel system in our land? The Christian and infidel systems have been long known in the world, and their opposite moral effects on mankind, have been manifested by the most ample experience. A tree is not more unequivocally known by its fruit, than are these two systems by the results which they have respectively produced. What has Christianity done for the nations which have embraced it? It has done much, very much. It has diminished the horrors of war. The spirit of ancient war, was a relentless and sanguinary vengeance, which knew not how to be satisfied but by the de-

struction of its victim. This fell spirit has in a goodly measure, been softened in the conduct of modern warfare. It has meliorated the calamitous lot of captives. Anciently, death, slavery, or an enormous ransom, was their customary doom every where; and this still continues to be the case in all countries not Christian. And when Christian principles, motives and feelings shall have become universal, "glory to God in the highest, and on earth peace, good will towards men," will universally prevail.[42] In arbitrary governments, it has relaxed the stern rigour of despotic sway. It has suppressed infanticide. It has secured the life and limbs of the slave against the caprice or passion of a tyrannical master. The frequent periodical recurrence of a Day of Rest, has elevated the character and meliorated the state of the labouring classes of every Christian country. It has restored the wife from a condition of humiliation and servitude, to be the companion, the associate, the confidential adviser and friend of the husband. It has restored marriage to the standard ordained "at the beginning,"[43] the indissoluble union of two individuals, called by St. Paul a great mystery symbolical of the spiritual union between Christ and his Church; and has thus furnished the only reasonable security for domestic tranquillity, and the suitable nurture and education of children. Under its influence, the combats of gladiators, the impurities of superstitious rites, and unnatural vices, are no longer tolerated. The poor, the sick and the forsaken, are relieved by the numerous hospitals and asylums which are provided in all countries in which its authority is acknowledged. Moreover, it has been chiefly instrumental in rendering the nations of Christendom superior in virtue, intelligence and power, to all the other nations of the earth. Nor are we to estimate its principal benefits by what is visible. "The Kingdom of God cometh not with observation;" it does not consist in external splendour; its chief influence is unseen, renewing and

---

40. Note L.
41. Matthew xvi. 18.

42. Milton says;—"He shall ascend / The throne hereditary, and bound his reign / With earth's wide bounds, his glory with the heavens."
43. Matthew xix. 4–6.

sanctifying the hearts of the multitude who throng the obscure and humble walks of life. Again, what has Christianity done for our own nation? The answer is once more; much, very much. It was the moving cause which led our ancestors to transfer themselves to these shores, and to procure for us the fair inheritance which we now enjoy. It was an intimate and practical acquaintance with the doctrines, history and spirit of Christianity, which imparted to them that entire dependence on God, that unhesitating confidence in the protection of his Providence, that deep conviction of his favour, and those commanding moral virtues which shone in their lives with so resplendent a lustre. Especially it is to Christianity, that we are indebted for the steady self-control, and power of habitually subjecting our passions to the sway of reason and conscience, which have preserved us to this day, a free and a united people. May the future historian never record of us, that becoming wise above what is written, and forsaking the paths of our pious forefathers, we brought the judgments of Heaven upon our guilty land, and were made to drink to the dregs of the cup of national humiliation and shame. And what has Christianity done for us personally? The answer is not only much, very much, but every thing. In infancy it may very possibly have saved us from death by exposure; no uncommon fate wherever Christianity has not prevailed. Born, as we were by nature, children of wrath, she received us by baptism into the fold of Christ, and made us heirs of the promises, the hopes and the consolations of the Gospel. Sensibly alive to the transitory nature of all human connexions, and the instability of all earthly prospects, she provided sureties, who, in case of the demise or default of our natural guardians, might feel themselves responsible for fitting us to receive the Christian inheritance, to which we were admitted in prospect, by baptism. On arriving at years of discretion, she confirmed us in the privileges of our high estate; and as we journey onward in the thorny path of life, she feeds us with "that bread which came down from Heaven," rescues us from temptation, strengthens us amid our infirmities, and animates our weary steps by the kind voice of en-

couragement. Aided and animated by her divine guidance, when we shall come to the end of our path, we shall not be overwhelmed with fearful apprehensions. We shall contemplate the solitude of the grave without dismay. She will not leave us within its narrow and lonely precincts. She will guide and sustain us through the dark valley of the shadow of death, and will bring us to mansions of immortality and glory. And what has the infidel system to give us in exchange for the Christian promises, hopes, virtues, consolations and final inheritance which it destroys? What has it done for those who have embraced it? And in case we embrace it, what effects may it be expected to produce on our national destinies, on our domestic tranquillity, on ourselves personally, and "on all estates and orders of men?" We can have no difficulty in answering these questions;—we have the oracular voice of the experience of the last half century. These will be the burthen of its teachings, the fruit of its instructions. By excluding a Supreme Being, a superintending Providence, and a future state of rewards and punishments, as much as possible, from the minds of men, it will destroy all sense of moral responsibility; for, the lively impression of an omnipresent Ruler of the Universe and a strong sense of moral obligation, have, in the history of mankind, always accompanied each other; and whenever the former has been weakened, it has never failed to be followed by a corresponding moral declension. Now what is to preserve an habitual reverence for Almighty God in the public mind, if the institution of public worship ever comes to be disregarded, if the Christian Ministry shall be rendered odious in the eyes of the community, if the observance of Sunday shall be generally neglected, and if the Scriptures shall be brought into general discredit? Yet with just such a state of things we are threatened. Let us not refuse to look at the real nature of the case. The fact is, that a man's sense of duty, his moral sensibility, is the conservative element of his character; and no man can receive so great an injury himself, or inflict so great a calamity on another, as the impairing or the destruction of this grand principle. Of all unpromising indications in a youth, is not insensibility to moral considerations, the most decisive and unequivocal? When the sense of duty is extinguished in an individual, he becomes a burthen to himself and a nuisance to others, the sport of every wind of caprice and passion. From infecting individuals, a moral taint soon comes to infect a nation, which now becomes, in the natural order of a descending course, the theatre of every crime which can degrade individuals, disturb society and brutalize mankind. In such a community, all the virtues which procure respect and esteem, and still more, those which elevate and adorn society, must decline and perish. The security of society depends on the conviction which we habitually feel, that those among whom we dwell, are governed in their conduct by humanity, justice, moderation, kindness, integrity and good faith. When these main pillars of moral and social order are overthrown, general confidence between man and man must be exchanged for universal suspicion, every individual will be seized with apprehension and terror, the mild authority of law must cease its reign, and the dark and fearful passions of selfishness, lust and revenge break forth with unbridled violence and fury. During the last half century, where are the achievements of the infidel system to be seen, but in the ruin of hundreds of thousands of estimable families, unexampled distress of nations, general anarchy and convulsions, and in the devastation of much of the fairest portion of the earth. Encouragement of the infidel system among us, will dissolve all the moral ties which unite men in the bonds of society. Circumvention and fraud will come to be esteemed wisdom, the sacred mystery of "plighted troth" will be laughed to scorn, wise forbearance will be accounted pusillanimity, an enlightened practical benevolence will be supplanted by a supreme regard to self-gratification and an insensibility to the welfare of other men, the disregard of Almighty God will be equalled only by a corresponding contempt of mankind, personal aggrandizement will be substituted for love of country, social order and public security will be subverted by treason and violence;—

these, and all these have been, and may again be the fruits of the infidel system.[44]

Finally, let us in the strength of Almighty God, cling with fresh earnestness and new resolution to our religion, as to the last anchor of our hope and safety. "It is not a vain thing for us, it is our life." It is our only imperishable treasure. In it are comprised, at once, the great causes of peace, of virtue, of intelligence, of freedom, of good government and of human happiness.

---

44. Gouverneur Morris resided in France during the first part of the Revolution, and in a letter to President Washington, dated Paris, April 29, 1789, he thus speaks of the state of morals.

"Every one agrees that there is an utter prostration of morals; but this general position can never convey to an American mind the degree of depravity. It is not by any figure of rhetoric or force of language, that the idea can be communicated. A hundred anecdotes and a hundred thousand examples, are required to shew the extreme rottenness of every member. There are men and women who are greatly and eminently virtuous. I have the pleasure to number many in my acquaintance; but they stand forward from a back ground deeply and darkly shaded. It is, however, from such crumbling matter, that the great edifice of freedom is to be erected here. Perhaps, like the stratum of rock, which is spread under the whole surface of their country, it may harden when exposed to the air, but it seems quite as likely that it will fall and crush the builders. I own to you that I am not without such apprehensions, for there is one fatal principle which pervades all ranks. It is, perfect indifference to the violation of engagements. Inconsistency is so mingled in the blood, marrow and very essence of this people that when a man of high rank and importance laughs to-day at what he seriously asserted yesterday, it is considered as in the natural order of things. Consistency is a phenomenon."—*Life by Sparks,* vol. ii. p. 68.

Again, p. 255, under date December 21, 1792, "the morals, or rather the want of morals in this country, places every one at his ease. He may be virtuous if he pleases, but there is no necessity either to be or to appear so. The open contempt of religion, also, cannot but be offensive to all sober minded men."

For the best expositions of the character of modern infidelity, see Dr. [Timothy] Dwight's Sermons on Infidelity.—[Edmund] Burke's Reflections on the Revolution in France, works, vol. iii.—Letters on France and England, published in the American Review, 1811 and 1812.—Rev. R[obert] Hall's Sermon on Ephesians, ii. 12.

Letter from John Marshall to Jasper Adams

Richmond May 9th 1833

Reverend Sir,

I am much indebted to you for the copy of your valuable sermon on the relation of Christianity to civil government preached before the convention of the Protestant Episcopal Church in Charleston, on the 13th of Feby. last. I have read it with great attention & advantage.

The documents annexed to the sermon certainly go far in sustaining the proposition which it is your purpose to establish. One great object of the colonial charters was avowedly the propagation of the Christian faith. Means have been employed to accomplish this object, & those means have been used by government.

No person, I believe, questions the importance of religion to the happiness of man even during his existence in this world. It has at all times employed his most serious meditation, & had a decided influence on his conduct. The American population is entirely Christian, & with us, Christianity & Religion are identified. It would be strange, indeed, if with such a people, our institutions did not presuppose Christianity, & did not often refer to it, & exhibit relations with it. Legislation on the subject is admitted to require great delicacy, because fredom of conscience & respect for our religion both claim our most serious regard. You have allowed their full influence to both.

With very great respect,
I am Sir, your Obedt.,
J. Marshall

Letter from Joseph Story to Jasper Adams

Cambridge May 14th 1833

Dear Sir,

I am greatly obliged to you for the copy of your convention sermon, which you have been pleased to send me. I have read it with uncommon satisfaction, & think its tone & spirit excellent. My own private judgement has long been, (& every day's experience more & more confirms me in it,) that government can not long exist without an alliance with religion *to some extent*; & that Christianity is indispensable to the true interests & solid foundations of all free governments. I distinguish, as you do, between the establishment of a particular sect, as the Religion of the State, & the Establishment of Christianity itself, without any preference of any particular form of it. I know not, indeed, how any deep sense of moral obligation or accountableness can be expected to prevail in the community without a firm persuasion of the great Christian Truths promulgated in your South Carolina constitution of 1778. I look with no small dismay upon the rashness & indifference with which the American People seem in our day to be disposed to cut adrift from old principles, & to trust themselves to the theories of every wild projector in to [?] religion & politics.

Upon the point, how far the constitution of 1790 has, on the subject of religion, superseded that of 1778, it is somewhat difficult for me to form a decisive opinion without some additional documents, showing the authority of the convention, which framed it, & the effect given to it. If (as I suppose was the case) the object of the constitution of 1790 was, to supersede that of 1778, & to stand as a substitute, (which has been the general construction in like cases of a *general new*[?] constitution) then, it seems to me, that the constitution of 1778 is by necessary implication repealed, except so far as any of its provisions are ex-

Reprinted from *Religion and Politics in the Early Republic: Jasper Adams and the Church-State Debate*, 113.

Reprinted from *Religion and Politics in the Early Republic: Jasper Adams and the Church-State Debate*, 115–18.

pressly retained. It does not strike me that the 2d section of the 8th article of 1790 retains any thing of the religious articles of that of 1778, but only provides that the *existing rights* &c. of religious societies & corporate bodies shall remain unaffected by the change of the constitution. The rights &c., here provided for, are the more private rights of those bodies, such as the rights of property, & corporate immunities; but not any rights as Christians or as Protestants to be entitled to the superior protection of the State. The first section of the 8th article seems to me intended to abolish all distinctions & preferences, as to the state, between all religious persuasions, whether Christian or other wise. But I doubt exceedingly, if it ought to be construed so as to abolish Christianity as a part of the antecedent Law of the Land, to the extent of withdrawing from it all recognition of it as a revealed religion. The 23d section of art. 1st seems to me manifestly to point to a different conclusion.

Mr. Jefferson has, with his accustomed boldness, denied that Christianity is a part of the common Law, & Dr. [Thomas] Cooper has with even more dogmatism, maintained the same opinion. I am persuaded, that a more egregious error never was uttered by able men. And I have long desired to find leisure to write a dissertation to establish this conclusion. Both of them rely on authorities & expositions which are wholly inadmissible. And I am surprised, that no one has as yet exposed the shallowness of their enquiries. Both of them have probably been easily drawn into the maintenance of such a doctrine by their own skepticism. It is due to truth, & to the purity of the Law, to unmask their fallacies.

I am gratified by your favourable opinion of my Commentaries on the constitution. If I shall be thought to have done anything to aid in perpetuating the true exposition of its rights & powers, & duties, I shall reap all the reward I desire. The Abridgment for colleges & schools will be published next week. I hope it may be found a useful manual.

I cannot conclude this letter without thanking you again for your sermon. These are times in which the friends of Christianity are required to sound the alarm, & to inculcate sound principles. I fear that infidelity is make rapid progress under the delusive guise of the freedom of religious opinion & liberty of conscience.

> Believe me with great respect,
> Your obliged servant,
> Joseph Story

Letter from James Madison to Jasper Adams

Montpelier September 1833. *private*

Dear Sir,

I received in due time, the printed copy of your convention sermon on the relation of Christianity to civil government, with a manuscript request of my opinion on the subject.

There appears to be in the nature of man, what ensures his belief in an invisible cause of his present existence, & an anticipation of his future existence. Hence the propensities & susceptibilities, in the case of religion, which, with a few doubtful or individual exceptions, have prevailed throughout the world.

Waiving the rights of conscience, not included in the surrender implied by the social state, & more or less invaded by all Religious establishments, the simple question to be decided, is whether a support of the best & purest religion, the Christian Religion itself, ought not, so far at least as pecuniary means are involved, to be provided for by the Government, rather than be left to the voluntary provisions of those who profess it. And on this question, experience will be an admitted umpire the more adequate as the connexion between government & Religion, has existed in such various degrees & forms, & now can be com-

Reprinted from *Religion and Politics in the Early Republic: Jasper Adams and the Church-State Debate*, 120–21.

pared with examples where the connexion has been entirely dissolved.

In the papal system, Government & Religion are in a manner consolidated; & that is found to be the worst of Governments.

In most of the governments of the old world, the legal establishment of a particular religion without any, or with very little toleration of others, makes a part [pact?] of the political & civil organization; & there are few of the most enlightened judges who will maintain that the system has been favourable either to Religion or to government.

Until Holland ventured on the experiment of combining a liberal toleration, with the establishment of a particular creed, it was taken for granted that an exclusive establishment was essential, and notwithstanding the light thrown on the subject by that experiment, the prevailing opinion in Europe, England not excepted, has been, that Religion could not be preserved without the support of Government, nor Government be supported without an established Religion, that there must be at least an alliance of some sort between them.

It remained for North America to bring the great & interesting subject to a fair, & finally, to a decisive test.

In the colonial state of this country, there were five examples, Rhode Island, New Jersey, Pennsylvania & Delaware, & the greater part of New York, where there were no religious establishments, the support of Religion being left to the voluntary associations & contributions of individuals; & certainly the religious condition of those colonies, will well bear a comparison, with that where establishments existed.

As it may be suggested, that experiments made in colonies more or less under the controul of a foreign government had not the full scope necessary to display their tendency, it is fortunate that the appeal can now be made to their effects, under a compleat exemption from any such controul.

It is true that the New England States have not discontinued establishments of Religion formed under very peculiar circumstances; but they have by successive relaxations, advanced towards the prevailing example; & without any evidence of disadvantage, either to Religion or to good government.

And if we turn to the Southern States where there was previous to the Declaration of Independence, a legal provision for the support of Religion; & since that event, a surrender of it to a spontaneous support of the people, it may be said that the difference amounts nearly to a contrast, in the greater purity & industry of the pastors & in the greater devotion of their flocks, in the latter period than in the former. In Virginia, the contrast is particularly striking to those whose memories can make the comparison.

It will not be denied that causes other than the abolition of the legal establishment of Religion are to be taken into view, in accounting for the change in the religious character of the community. But the existing character, distinguished as it is by its religious features, & the lapse of time, now more than fifty years, since the legal support of Religion was withdrawn, sufficiently prove, that it does not need the support of Government. And it will scarcely be contended that government has suffered by the exemption of Religion from its cognizance, or its pecuniary aid.

The apprehension of some seems to be, that Religion left entirely to itself, may run into extravagances injurious both to Religion & social order; but besides the question whether the interference of Government *in any form,* would not be more likely to increase than controul the tendency, it is a safe calculation that in this, as in other cases of excessive excitement, reason will gradually regain its ascendency. Great excitements are less apt to be permanent than to vibrate to the opposite extreme.

Under another aspect of the subject, there may be less danger that Religion, if left to itself, will suffer from a failure of the pecuniary support applicable to it, than that an omission of the public authorities, to limit the duration of the charters to Religious corporations, & the amount of property acquirable by them, may lead to an injurious accumulation of wealth from the lavish donations & bequests prompted by a pious

zeal or by an atoning remorse. Some monitory examples have already appeared.

Whilst I thus frankly express my view of the subject presented in your sermon, I must do you the justice to observe, that you have very ably maintained yours. I must admit, moreover, that it may not be easy, in every possible case, to trace the line of separation, between the rights of Religion & the Civil authority, with such distinctness, as to avoid collisions & doubts on unessential points. The tendency to a usurpation on one side, or the other, or to a corrupting coalition or alliance between them, will be best guarded against by an entire abstinence of the Government from interference, in any way whatever, beyond the necessity of preserving public order, & protecting each sect against trespasses on its legal rights by others.

I owe you, Sir, an apology for the delay in complying with the request of my opinion on the subject discussed in your sermon, if not also for the brevity, & it may be thought, crudeness of the opinion itself. I must rest the apology on my great age now in its 83d. year, with more than the ordinary infirmities, & especially on the effect of a chronic rheumatism, combined with both, which makes my hands & fingers, as averse to the pen as they are awkward in the use of it.

Be pleased to accept, Sir, a tender of my cordial & respectful salutations.

James Madison

Democracy in America (1835)

ALEXIS DE TOCQUEVILLE (1805–59)

Tocqueville, a French aristocrat, came to America in 1831 to study the nation's penal system. Drawing from his eighteen-month journey, he wrote a classic study

Reprinted from *Democracy in America,* trans. Henry Reeve (London: Longman, Green, Longman, and Roberts, 1862), 1:359–73.

of the United States, *Democracy in America,* which was published in two volumes in 1835 and 1840. The following excerpts contain some of his analysis of religion in America in the early 1830s.

Indirect Influence of Religious Opinions upon Political Society in the United States

Christian morality common to all sects.—Influence of religion upon the manners of the Americans.—Respect for the marriage tie.—In what manner religion confines the imagination of the Americans within certain limits, and checks the passion of innovation.—Opinion of the Americans on the political utility of religion.—Their exertions to extend and secure its predominance.

I HAVE just shown what the direct influence of religion upon politics is in the United States; but its indirect influence appears to me to be still more considerable, and it never instructs the Americans more fully in the art of being free than when it says nothing of freedom.

The sects which exist in the United States are innumerable. They all differ in respect to the worship which is due from man to his Creator; but they all agree in respect to the duties which are due from man to man. Each sect adores the Deity in its own peculiar manner; but all the sects preach the same moral law in the name of God. If it be of the slightest importance to man, as an individual, that his religion should be true, the case of society is not the same. Society has no future life to hope for or to fear; and provided the citizens profess a religion, the peculiar tenets of that religion are of very little importance to its interests. Moreover, almost all the sects of the United States are comprised within the great unity of Christianity, and Christian morality is everywhere the same.

It may be believed without unfairness, that a certain number of Americans pursue a peculiar form of worship, from habit more than from conviction. In the United States the sovereign authority is religious, and consequently hypocrisy must be common; but there is no country in the whole world in which the Christian religion retains a greater influence over the souls of men than in America; and there can be no greater proof of its utility, and of its conformity to human nature, than that its influence is most powerfully felt over the most enlightened and free nation of the earth.

I have remarked that the members of the American clergy in general, without even excepting those who do not admit religious liberty, are all in favor of civil freedom; but they do not support any particular political system. They keep aloof from parties, and from public affairs. In the United States religion exercises but little influence upon the laws, and upon the details of public opinion; but it directs the manners of the community, and by regulating domestic life, it regulates the State.

I do not question that the great austerity of manners which is observable in the United States, arises, in the first instance, from religious faith. Religion is often unable to restrain man from the numberless temptations of fortune; nor can it check that passion for gain which every incident of his life contributes to arouse; but its influence over the mind of woman is supreme, and women are the protectors of morals. There is certainly no country in the world where the tie of marriage is so much respected as in America, or where conjugal happiness is more highly or worthily appreciated. In Europe almost all the disturbances of society arise from the irregularities of domestic life. To despise the natural bonds and legitimate pleasures of home, is to contract a taste for excesses, a restlessness of heart, and the evil of fluctuating desires. Agitated by the tumultuous passions which frequently disturb his dwelling, the European is galled by the obedience which the legislative powers of the State exact. But when the American retires from the turmoil of public life to the bosom of his family, he finds in it the image of order and of peace. There his pleasures are simple and natural, his joys

Alexis de Tocqueville, by Chassereau.
© Bettmann/CORBIS.

are innocent and calm; and as he finds that an orderly life is the surest path to happiness, he accustoms himself without difficulty to moderate his opinions as well as his tastes. While the European endeavors to forget his domestic troubles by agitating society, the American derives from his own home that love of order, which he afterwards carries with him into public affairs.

In the United States the influence of religion is not confined to the manners, but it extends to the intelligence of the people. Among the Anglo-Americans, there are some who profess the doctrines of Christianity from a sincere belief in them, and others who do the same because they are afraid to be suspected of unbelief. Christianity, therefore, reigns without any obstacle, by universal consent; the consequence is, as I have before observed, that every principle of the moral world is fixed and determinate, although the political world is abandoned to the debates and the experiments of men. Thus the human mind is never left to wander across a boundless field; and, whatever may be its pretensions, it is checked from time to time by barriers which it cannot surmount. Before it can perpetrate innovation, certain primal and immutable principles are laid down, and the boldest conceptions of human device are subjected to certain forms which retard and stop their completion.

The imagination of the Americans, even in its greatest flights, is circumspect and undecided; its impulses are checked, and its works unfinished. These habits of restraint recur in political society, and are singularly favorable both to the tranquility of the people and to the durability of the institutions it has established. Nature and circumstances concurred to make the inhabitants of the United States bold men, as is sufficiently attested by the enterprizing spirit with which they seek for fortune. If the minds of the Americans were free from all trammels, they would very shortly become the most daring innovators and the most implacable disputants in the world. But the revolutionists of America are obliged to profess an ostensible respect for Christian morality and equity, which does not easily permit them to violate the laws that oppose their designs; nor would they find it easy to surmount the scruples of their partisans, even if they were able to get over their own. Hitherto no one, in the United States, has dared to advance the maxim, that everything is permissible with a view to the interests of society; an impious adage, which seems to have been invented in an age of freedom, to shelter all the tyrants of future ages. Thus while the law permits the Americans to do what they please, religion prevents them from conceiving, and forbids them to commit, what is rash or unjust.

Religion in America takes no direct part in the government of society, but it must nevertheless be regarded as the foremost of the political institutions of that country; for if it does not impart a taste for freedom, it facilitates the use of free institutions. Indeed, it is in this same point of view that the inhabitants of the United States themselves look upon religious be-

lief. I do not know whether all the Americans have a sincere faith in their religion; for who can search the human heart? but I am certain that they hold it to be indispensable to the maintenance of republican institutions. This opinion is not peculiar to a class of citizens or to a party, but it belongs to the whole nation, and to every rank of society.

In the United States, if a political character attacks a sect, this may not prevent even the partisans of that very sect from supporting him; but if he attacks all the sects together, every one abandons him, and he remains alone.

While I was in America, a witness, who happened to be called at the Assizes of the county of Chester, (State of New-York,) declared that he did not believe in the existence of God or in the immortality of the soul. The judge refused to admit his evidence, on the ground that the witness had destroyed beforehand all the confidence of the Court in what he was about to say.* The newspapers related the fact without any farther comment.

The Americans combine the notions of Christianity and of liberty so intimately in their minds, that it is impossible to make them conceive the one without the other; and with them this conviction does not spring from that barren traditionary faith which seems to vegetate in the soul rather than to live.

I have known of societies formed by the Americans to send out ministers of the Gospel into the new Western States, to found schools and churches there, lest religion should be suffered to die away in those remote settlements, and the rising States be less fitted to enjoy free institutions than the people from which they emanated. I met with wealthy New Englanders who abandoned the country in which they were born, in order to lay the foundations of Christianity and of

---

* The New York Spectator of August 23, 1831, relates the fact in the following terms: "The Court of Common Pleas of Chester County, (New York,) a few days since rejected a witness who declared his disbelief in the existence of God. The presiding judge remarked, that he had not before been aware that there was a man living who did not believe in the existence of God; that this belief constituted the sanction of all testimony in a court of justice: and that he knew of no cause in a Christian country, where a witness had been permitted to testify without such belief."

freedom on the banks of the Missouri or in the prairies of Illinois. Thus religious zeal is perpetually stimulated in the United States by the duties of patriotism. These men do not act from an exclusive consideration of the promises of a future life; eternity is only one motive of their devotion to the cause; and if you converse with these missionaries of Christian civilization, you will be surprised to find how much value they set upon the goods of this world, and that you meet with a politician where you expected to find a priest. They will tell you that "all the American Republics are collectively involved with each other; if the republics of the West were to fall into anarchy, or to be mastered by a despot, the republican institutions which now flourish upon the shores of the Atlantic Ocean would be in great peril. It is therefore our interest that the new States should be religious, in order to maintain our liberties."

Such are the opinions of the Americans: and if any hold that the religious spirit which I admire is the very thing most amiss in America, and that the only element wanting to the freedom and happiness of the human race is to believe in some blind cosmogony, or to assert with Cabanis the secretion of thought by the brain, I can only reply, that those who hold this language have never been in America, and that they have never seen a religious or a free nation. When they return from their expedition, we shall hear what they have to say.

There are persons in France who look upon republican institutions as a temporary means of power, of wealth, and distinction; men who are the *condottieri* [conductors] of liberty, and who fight for their own advantage, whatever be the colors they wear: it is not to these that I address myself. But there are others who look forward to the republican form of government as a tranquil and lasting state, towards which modern society is daily impelled by the ideas and manners of the time, and who sincerely desire to prepare men to be free. When these men attack religious opinions, they obey the dictates of their passions to the prejudice of their interests. Despotism may govern without faith, but liberty cannot. Religion is much more necessary in the republic which they set forth in glowing colors, than in the monarchy which they attack; and it is more needed in democratic republics than in any others. How is it possible that society should escape destruction if the moral tie be not strengthened in proportion as the political tie is relaxed? and what can be done with a people which is its own master, if it be not submissive to the Divinity?

Principal Causes Which Render Religion Powerful in America

Care taken by the Americans to separate the Church from the State.—The laws, public opinion, and even the exertions of the clergy concur to promote this end.—Influence of religion upon the mind, in the United States, attributable to this cause.—Reason of this.—What is the natural state of men with regard to religion at the present time.—What are the peculiar and incidental causes which prevent men, in certain countries, from arriving at this state.

THE philosophers of the eighteenth century explained the gradual decay of religious faith in a very simple manner. Religious zeal, said they, must necessarily fail, the more generally liberty is established and knowledge diffused. Unfortunately, facts are by no means in accordance with their theory. There are certain populations in Europe whose unbelief is only equalled by their ignorance and their debasement, while in America one of the freest and most enlightened nations in the world fulfils all the outward duties of religion with fervor.

Upon my arrival in the United States, the religious aspect of the country was the first thing that struck my attention; and the longer I stayed there, the more did I perceive the great political consequences resulting from this state of things, to which I was unaccustomed. In France I had almost always seen the spirit of religion and the spirit of freedom pursuing courses diametrically opposed to each other; but in

America I found that they were intimately united, and that they reigned in common over the same country. My desire to discover the causes of this phenomenon increased from day to day. In order to satisfy it, I questioned the members of all the different sects; and I more especially sought the society of the clergy, who are the depositaries of the different persuasions, and who are more especially interested in their duration. As a member of the Roman Catholic Church I was more particularly brought into contact with several of its priests, with whom I became intimately acquainted. To each of these men I expressed my astonishment and I explained my doubts: I found that they differed upon matters of detail alone; and that they mainly attributed the peaceful dominion of religion in their country, to the separation of Church and State. I do not hesitate to affirm that during my stay in America, I did not meet with a single individual, of the clergy or of the laity, who was not of the same opinion upon this point.

This led me to examine more attentively than I had hitherto done, the station which the American clergy occupy in political society. I learned with surprise that they filled no public appointments;* not one of them is to be met with in the administration, and they are not even represented in the legislative assemblies. In several States† the law excludes them from political life; public opinion in all. And when I came to inquire into the prevailing spirit of the clergy, I found that most of its members seemed to retire of their own accord from the exercise of power, and that they made it the pride of their profession to abstain from politics.

---

* Unless this term be applied to the functions which many of them fill in the schools. Almost all education is entrusted to the clergy.

† See the 'Constitution of New York,' art. 7. § 4:

"And whereas the Ministers of the Gospel are, by their profession, dedicated to the service of God and the care of souls, and ought not to be diverted from the great duties of their functions: therefore no minister of the Gospel, or priest of any denomination whatsoever, shall at any time hereafter, under any pretence or description whatever, be eligible to, or capable of holding any civil or military office or place within this state."

See also the Constitutions of North Carolina, art. 31. Virginia. South Carolina, art. 1. § 23. Kentucky, art. 2. § 26. Tennessee, art. 8. § 1. Louisiana, art. 2. § 22.

I heard them inveigh against ambition and deceit, under whatever political opinions these vices might chance to lurk; but I learned from their discourses that men are not guilty in the eye of God for any opinions concerning political government, which they may profess with sincerity, any more than they are for their mistakes in building a house or in driving a furrow. I perceived that these ministers of the Gospel eschewed all parties, with the anxiety attendant upon personal interest. These facts convinced me that what I had been told was true; and it then became my object to investigate their causes, and to inquire how it happened that the real authority of religion was increased by a state of things which diminished its apparent force: these causes did not long escape my researches.

The short space of threescore years can never content the imagination of man; nor can the imperfect joys of this world satisfy his heart. Man alone, of all created beings, displays a natural contempt of existence, and yet a boundless desire to exist; he scorns life, but he dreads annihilation. These different feelings incessantly urge his soul to the contemplation of a future state, and religion directs his musings thither. Religion then, is simply another form of hope; and it is no less natural to the human heart than hope itself. Men cannot abandon their religious faith without a kind of aberration of intellect, and a sort of violent distortion of their true natures; but they are invincibly brought back to more pious sentiments; for unbelief is an accident, and faith is the only permanent state of mankind. If we only consider religious institutions in a purely human point of view, they may be said to derive an inexhaustible element of strength from man himself, since they belong to one of the constituent principles of human nature.

I am aware that at certain times religion may strengthen this influence, which originates in itself, by the artificial power of the laws, and by the support of those temporal institutions which direct society. Religions, intimately united to the governments of the earth, have been known to exercise a sovereign authority derived from the twofold source of terror and of faith; but when a religion contracts an alliance of this nature, I do not hesitate to affirm that it commits the same error, as a man who should sacrifice his future to his present welfare; and in obtaining a power to which it has no claim, it risks that authority which is rightfully its own. When a religion founds its empire upon the desire of immortality which lives in every human heart, it may aspire to universal dominion: but when it connects itself with a government, it must necessarily adopt maxims which are only applicable to certain nations. Thus, in forming an alliance with a political power, religion augments its authority over a few, and forfeits the hope of reigning over all.

As long as a religion rests upon those sentiments which are the consolation of all affliction, it may attract the affections of mankind. But if it be mixed up with the bitter passions of the world, it may be constrained to defend allies whom its interests, and not the principles of love, have given to it; or to repel as antagonists men who are still attached to its own spirit, however opposed they may be to the powers to which it is allied. The Church cannot share the temporal power of the State, without being the object of a portion of that animosity which the latter excites.

The political powers which seem to be most firmly established have frequently no better guarantee for their duration, than the opinions of a generation, the interests of the time, or the life of an individual. A law may modify the social condition which seems to be most fixed and determinate; and with the social condition every thing else must change. The powers of society are more or less fugitive, like the years which we spend upon the earth; they succeed each other with rapidity like the fleeting cares of life; and no government has ever yet been founded upon an invariable disposition of the human heart, or upon an imperishable interest.

As long as religion is sustained by those feelings, propensities and passions which are found to occur under the same forms, at all the different periods of history, it may defy the efforts of time; or at least it can only be destroyed by another religion. But when religion clings to the interests of the world, it becomes almost as fragile a thing as the powers of earth. It is the only one of them all which can hope for immortality; but if it be connected with their ephemeral authority, it shares their fortunes, and may fall with those transient passions which supported them for a day. The alliance which religion contracts with political powers must needs be onerous to itself; since it does not require their assistance to live, and by giving them its assistance it may be exposed to decay.

The danger which I have just pointed out always exists, but it is not always equally visible. In some ages governments seem to be imperishable, in others the existence of society appears to be more precarious than the life of man. Some constitutions plunge the citizens into a lethargic somnolence, and others rouse them to feverish excitement. When governments appear to be so strong, and laws so stable, men do not perceive the dangers which may accrue from a union of Church and State. When governments display so much inconstancy, the danger is self-evident, but it is no longer possible to avoid it; to be effectual, measures must be taken to discover its approach.

In proportion as a nation assumes a democratic condition of society, and as communities display democratic propensities, it becomes more and more dangerous to connect religion with political institutions; for the time is coming when authority will be bandied from hand to hand, when political theories will succeed each other, and when men, laws, and constitutions will disappear or be modified from day to day, and this not for a season only, but unceasingly. Agitation and mutability are inherent in the nature of democratic republics, just as stagnation and inertness are the law of absolute monarchies.

If the Americans, who change the head of the Government once in four years, who elect new legislators every two years, and renew the provincial officers every twelvemonth; if the Americans, who have abandoned the political world to the attempts of innovators, had not placed religion beyond their reach, where could it abide in the ebb and flow of human opinions? where would that respect which belongs to it be paid, amidst the struggles of faction? and what would become of its immortality in the midst of perpetual decay? The American clergy were the first to perceive this truth, and to act in conformity with it. They saw that they must renounce their religious influence, if they were to strive for political power; and they chose to give up the support of the State, rather than to share its vicissitudes.

In America, religion is perhaps less powerful than it has been at certain periods in the history of certain peoples; but its influence is more lasting. It restricts itself to its own resources, but of those none can deprive it: its circle is limited to certain principles, but those principles are entirely its own and under its undisputed control.

On every side in Europe we hear voices complaining of the absence of religious faith, and inquiring the means of restoring to religion some remnant of its pristine authority. It seems to me that we must first attentively consider what ought to be *the natural state* of men with regard to religion, at the present time; and when we know what we have to hope and to fear, we may discern the end to which our efforts ought to be directed.

The two great dangers which threaten the existence of religions are schism and indifference. In ages of fervent devotion, men sometimes abandon their religion, but they only shake it off in order to adopt another. Their faith changes the objects to which it is directed, but it suffers no decline. The old religion then excites enthusiastic attachment or bitter enmity in either party; some leave it with anger, others cling to it with increased devotedness, and although persuasions differ, irreligion is unknown. Such, however, is not the case when a religious belief is secretly undermined by doctrines which may be termed negative, since they deny the truth of one religion without affirming that of any other. Prodigious revolutions then take place in the human mind, without the apparent co-operation of the passions of man, and almost without his knowledge. Men lose the objects of their fondest hopes, as if through forgetfulness. They are carried away by an imperceptible current which they have not the courage to stem, but which they

follow with regret, since it bears them from a faith they love, to a scepticism that plunges them into despair.

In ages which answer to this description, men desert their religious opinions from lukewarmness rather than from dislike; they do not reject them, but the sentiments by which they were once fostered disappear. But if the unbeliever does not admit religion to be true, he still considers it useful. Regarding religious institutions in a human point of view, he acknowledges their influence upon manners and legislation. He admits that they may serve to make men live in peace with one another, and to prepare them gently for the hour of death. He regrets the faith which he has lost; and as he is deprived of a treasure which he has learned to estimate at its full value, he scruples to take it from those who still possess it.

On the other hand, those who continue to believe are not afraid openly to avow their faith. They look upon those who do not share their persuasion as more worthy of pity than of opposition; and they are aware, that to acquire the esteem of the unbelieving, they are not obliged to follow their example. They are hostile to no one in the world; and as they do not consider the society in which they live as an arena in which religion is bound to face its thousand deadly foes, they love their contemporaries, while they condemn their weaknesses, and lament their errors.

As those who do not believe conceal their incredulity; and as those who believe display their faith, public opinion pronounces itself in favor of religion: love, support, and honor are bestowed upon it, and it is only by searching the human soul, that we can detect the wounds which it has received. The mass of mankind, who are never without the feeling of religion, do not perceive anything at variance with the established faith. The instinctive desire of a future life brings the crowd about the altar, and opens the hearts of men to the precepts and consolations of religion.

But this picture is not applicable to us; for there are men among us who have ceased to believe in Christianity, without adopting any other religion; others who are in the perplexities of doubt, and who already affect not to believe; and others, again, who are afraid to avow that Christian faith which they still cherish in secret.

Amidst these lukewarm partisans and ardent antagonists, a small number of believers exists, who are ready to brave all obstacles, and to scorn all dangers, in defence of their faith. They have done violence to human weakness, in order to rise superior to public opinion. Excited by the effort they have made, they scarcely know where to stop; and as they know that the first use which the French made of independence was to attack religion, they look upon their contemporaries with dread, and they recoil in alarm from the liberty which their fellow-citizens are seeking to obtain. As unbelief appears to them to be a novelty, they comprise all that is new in one indiscriminate animosity. They are at war with their age and country, and they look upon every opinion which is put forth there as the necessary enemy of the Faith.

Such is not the natural state of men with regard to religion at the present day; and some extraordinary or incidental cause must be at work in France, to prevent the human mind from following its original propensities, and to drive it beyond the limits at which it ought naturally to stop.

I am intimately convinced that this extraordinary and incidental cause is the close connexion of politics and religion. The unbelievers of Europe attack the Christians as their political opponents, rather than as their religious adversaries; they hate the Christian religion as the opinion of a party, much more than as an error of belief; and they reject the clergy less because they are the representatives of the Divinity, than because they are the allies of authority.

In Europe, Christianity has been intimately united to the powers of the earth. Those powers are now in decay, and it is, as it were, buried under their ruins. The living body of religion has been bound down to the dead corpse of superannuated polity; cut the bonds which restrain it, and that which is alive will rise once more. I know not what could restore the Christian Church of Europe to the energy of its earlier days; that power belongs to God alone; but it may be the effect of human policy to leave the Faith in the full exercise of the strength which it still retains.

RECOMMENDATIONS FOR FURTHER READING

Dreisbach, Daniel L., ed. *Religion and Politics in the Early Republic: Jasper Adams and the Church-State Debate.* Lexington: University Press of Kentucky, 1996.

Noonan, John T., Jr. *The Lustre of Our Country: The American Experience of Religious Freedom.* Berkeley: University of California Press, 1998.

Reichley, A. James. *Religion in American Public Life.* Washington, D.C.: Brookings Institution, 1985.

Schaff, Philip. *Church and State in the United States; or, The American Idea of Religious Liberty and Its Practical Effects.* New York: G. P. Putnam's Sons; American Historical Society, 1888.

West, John G., Jr. *The Politics of Revelation and Reason: Religion and Civic Life in the New Nation.* Lawrence: University Press of Kansas, 1996.

Witte, John, Jr. *Religion and the American Constitutional Experiment: Essential Rights and Liberties,* 2d ed. Boulder, Colo.: Westview, 2005.

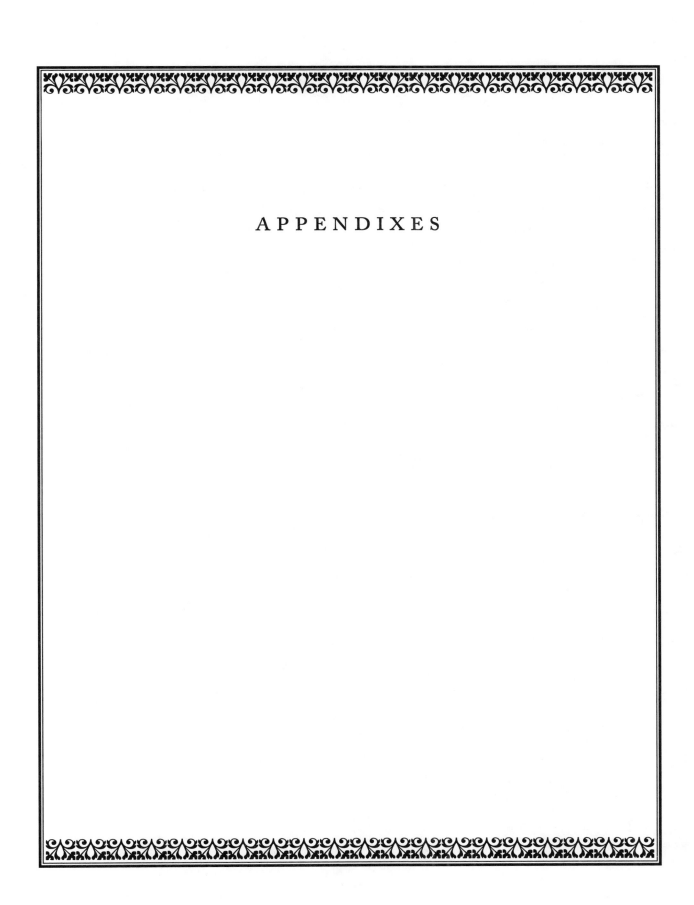

APPENDIXES

HISTORICAL CHRONOLOGY, 1607–1833

1607   The first permanent English settlement in North America established at Jamestown, Virginia.

1611   Thomas Dale, sent by the Virginia Company, arrives in Virginia and issues "Lawes Divine, Morall and Martiall" punishing, among other things, impiety, blasphemy, and neglect of religious duties.

1611   Authorized (King James) Version of the Holy Bible published in England.

1614   Dutch States-General issues an edict of toleration prepared by the jurist Hugo Grotius.

1618   Thirty Years' War begins in central Europe, involving a struggle between Protestants and Catholics for supremacy in Europe.

1619   First representative body of legislators constituted in North America convenes in Jamestown (Virginia) Church.

1620   Pilgrims arrive in North America and establish a colony at Plymouth. November 11: Male passengers aboard the *Mayflower* sign a compact establishing a "civil Body Politick."

1628   Reformed Church in America founded by Dutch settlers in New Amsterdam.

1629   Puritans, led by John Winthrop, establish the Massachusetts Bay Company following a Calvinist model for a Christian commonwealth. Settlers arrive in Massachusetts in 1630.

1632   English crown grants a charter to establish the colony of Maryland, which was intended to be a haven for Roman Catholics.

1635   Roger Williams is banished from the Massachusetts Bay colony and, the following year, founds a settlement he names Providence. Committed to a policy of toleration, the community becomes a haven for dissenters.

1636   Harvard College founded by Puritans at Cambridge, Massachusetts, the first college in British North America. The college is founded, according to an early College pamphlet, "to advance *Learning* and perpetuate it to Posterity" and so as not "to leave an illiterate Ministery to the Churches, when our present Ministers shall lie in the Dust." *New England's First Fruits* (1643).

1637   The Providence (Rhode Island) Agreement is adopted, endorsing majority rule and limiting town meeting business to "civil things."

1637   Anne Hutchinson is tried for heresy and shortly thereafter banished from the Massachusetts Bay colony.

1638–1639   First Baptist congregation in America formed in Rhode Island.

1639   Fundamental Orders of Connecticut, the first written constitution in North America, adopted.

1640   Providence (Rhode Island) Plantations Agreement provides for "liberty of Conscience."

1640   *Bay Psalm Book,* first book published in North America, printed at Cambridge, Massachusetts.

1641   Massachusetts "Body of Liberties," an early and influential colonial bill of rights, adopted.

1642   English "civil war" between parliamentary and royal forces commences.

1643   New England Confederation formed by Massachusetts Bay, Plymouth, Connecticut, and New Haven colonies for their "mutual safety and welfare."

1644   Roger Williams obtains a patent for Providence (Rhode Island) Plantations, affirming the rights of conscience.

1644   Roger Williams publishes *The Bloudy Tenent, of Persecution, for cause of Conscience,* a strong appeal for religious liberty. The Puritan clergyman John Cotton responds to Williams in *The Bloudy Tenent, Washed, and made White in the Blood of the Lambe* published in 1647. Williams returns to the debate in *The Bloody Tenet yet more Bloody* published in 1652.

1646   John Cotton publishes *The Controversie concerning liberty of conscience in matters of Religion truly stated . . . ,* an early American work dealing with liberty of conscience.

1647   Four Rhode Island colonies form a confederacy with a code of laws, concluding

with the words: "And otherwise than this, what is herein forbidden, all men may walk as their consciences persuade them, every one in the name of his God."

1647   Massachusetts adopts *The Book of the General Lawes and Libertyes.*

1647   Massachusetts Bay colony adopts first public education law in North America with an objective of promoting a knowledge of the Scriptures.

1648   A synod of the Congregational Church in Massachusetts adopts the Westminster Confession of Faith in matters of faith and sets forth their government and discipline in the Cambridge Platform.

1648   Peace of Westphalia brings end to the Thirty Years' War in Europe and advances the general presumption that each jurisdiction will maintain internal religious uniformity.

1649   January 30. Charles I is beheaded and the Puritan Commonwealth in England is created under the de facto leadership of Oliver Cromwell.

1649   April 21. An Act Concerning Religion adopted by the Maryland General Assembly. One of the most expansive seventeenth-century legislative pronouncements on religious toleration, the Toleration Act extended religious freedom to all Trinitarian Christians.

circa 1650   George Fox founds the Religious Society of Friends—also known as the Quakers. The Quakers oppose external interference with religion by the civil state and espouse religious toleration.

1651   *Leviathan* by Thomas Hobbes published.

1652   *Ill Newes from New-England Or a Narrative of New-England[']s Persecution* by John Clarke, a denunciation of persecution in Massachusetts and a defense of religious liberty, published in London.

1654   Henry Dunster, president of Harvard College, becomes a Baptist and resigns his office.

1656   Quakers arrive in Boston and are arrested, imprisoned, punished, and banished for their religious beliefs.

1656   Peter Stuyvesant, governor of New Netherland (New York), issues a proclamation forbidding religious meetings differing from the established religion set forth by the Synod of Dordt. In 1663, West India Company authorities write Stuyvesant rebuking him for the religious repression under this regime and instructing him "not [to] force people's consciences, but [to] allow every one to have his own belief, as long as he behaves quietly and legally, gives no offence to his neighbors and does not oppose the government."

1660   Mary Dyer hanged on Boston Common for defying law banning Quakers from the colony. She is only one of several Quakers executed in Massachusetts during this period.

1661   First Test Act, established under Charles II of England, makes receiving communion in the Church of England a prerequisite to holding public office.

1662   Massachusetts Congregationalists adopt the "Halfway Covenant," an arrangement permitting persons baptized in infancy to have limited membership privileges, including the ability to participate in civil affairs, without giving evidence of a spiritual conversion. This plan sacrificed spiritual purity for greater participation in civil affairs.

1663   Puritan minister and missionary to New England Indians John Eliot completes translation of the Bible into the Algonquian language.

1663   Rhode Island and Providence Plantations, established by Roger Williams in 1647 as "a Shelter for Persons Distressed for Conscience" under a Parliamentary charter secured by him three years before, obtains a royal charter through the efforts of John Clarke. Williams sought permission "to hold forth a livelie experiment . . . with a full libertie in religious concernments."

1670   William Penn writes *The Great Case of Liberty of Conscience* while incarcerated in Newgate prison.

1672   The Quaker George Fox arrives in America and promotes the spread of Quakerism throughout the colonies.

1672   Charles II of England issues a Declaration of Indulgence, granting toleration for Catholics and religious nonconformists. The following year, however, Parliament adopts the Test Act, which requires all persons filling any office, civil or military, to swear an oath of allegiance and to abjure papal supremacy and Catholic doctrine.

1677   "Laws, Concessions and Agreements" of the proprietors, freeholders, and inhabitants of West New Jersey gives full freedom of conscience in religious matters. The principle was reiterated in the law of the first assembly of West Jersey in 1681.

1681   William Penn receives a royal charter and founds the colony of Pennsylvania, which was intended to be an experiment in freedom and a haven for Quakers. Penn wanted the toleration of all Christians.

1682   William Penn sets out in *Frame of Government* his model for a Christian commonwealth.

1683   New York's first representative assembly adopts Charter of Liberties and Privileges embodying various civil liberties and religious toleration for all Christians.

1684   Massachusetts Bay Company's charter revoked by the crown, and the crown requires that liberty of conscience be extended to all persons.

1685　Edict of Nantes revoked by Louis XIV of France, depriving Protestants of rights in France and prompting many Huguenots to immigrate to America.

1687　James II of England issues a Declaration of Indulgence suspending the Test Act of 1673, suspending the execution of penal laws against nonconformists, and granting all subjects the free exercise of their religion.

1688　James II abdicates the throne of England.

1689　Parliament adopts the English Bill of Rights and Toleration Act. The Bill of Rights, which places strict limits on royal prerogatives, is passed by Parliament and assented to by King William III and Queen Mary II as the culmination of the "Glorious Revolution." The Toleration Act provides that the religious exercises of Trinitarian Protestant dissenters (Catholics and Unitarians, among others, are excluded from its protections) are to be tolerated and legal penalties for religious nonconformity are to be lifted, although subjects are required to take certain oaths of allegiance.

1689　John Locke's *Two Treatises on Government* published. The Latin text of *Epistola de tolerantia* published the following year. His second and third *Letters Concerning Toleration* appear in 1690 and 1692 respectively.

1691　In Massachusetts a new charter is granted, replacing the charter annulled in 1684, bringing an end to the Puritan commonwealth and, thereby, opening the way for the gradual development of wider toleration, as suffrage is no longer restricted to Church members. The new charter grants "liberty of Conscience in the Worshipp of God to all Christians (Except Papists)."

1692　Witch trials conducted in Salem, Massachusetts, followed by the executions of those found guilty of witchcraft.

1693　College of William and Mary in Virginia, the second college in British North America, granted a charter by King William III and Queen Mary II. The college was founded so that "the Church of Virginia may be furnished with a Seminary of Ministers of the Gospel, and that the Youth may be piously educated in good Letters and Manners, and that the Christian Faith may be propagated amongst the Western Indians, to the Glory of Almighty God."

1698　*Discourses Concerning Government,* Algernon Sidney's defense of republicanism, published posthumously.

1701　William Penn grants Delaware a charter declaring that no inhabitant "who shall confess and acknowledge One almighty God . . . shall be in any Case molested or prejudiced" on account of religious persuasion or practice.

1701　Yale College founded by Congregationalists in 1701 as Collegiate School, moved to New Haven, Connecticut, in 1716, and renamed Yale College in 1718.

1702　Maryland establishes the Church of England as the colony's official church. The Maryland assembly had made the Church of England the established church in 1692, which was confirmed by an act in 1700 and finalized in 1702.

1706　South Carolina assembly establishes the Church of England and disenfranchises nonconformists.

1706　First American presbytery organized in Philadelphia.

1707　The Philadelphia Baptist Association, the first major fellowship of Baptist churches in America, organized.

1708　Connecticut adopts the Toleration Act and the Saybrook Platform. The Saybrook Platform contains a Confession of Faith and essentially establishes the Congregational Church. The same legislative act adopting the platform provides a toleration of religious exercises of dissenting churches.

1713   Treaty of Utrecht brings an end to Queen Anne's War and permits Frenchmen in North American territory ceded to Great Britain by this treaty to "enjoy the free exercise of their religion, according to the usage of the church of Rome, as far as the laws of Great Britain do allow the same."

1727   Episcopalians in Connecticut are exempted from paying taxes to support the established Congregational Church. (Episcopalians in Massachusetts are granted a similar exemption.) By the end of the decade, Quakers and Baptists are granted similar exemptions.

circa late 1720s–mid-1730s   William Tennet, a Presbyterian minister and educator, establishes the "Log College" to prepare young Presbyterians for the ministry.

1732   George II of England grants a charter for the colony of Georgia providing that "forever hereafter, there shall be a liberty of conscience allowed in the worship of God, to all persons, . . . and that all such persons, except papists, shall have a free exercise of religion."

mid-1730s–1740s   Religious revivals, described as a "Great Awakening" and led by Jonathan Edwards, Gilbert Tennet, George Whitefield, and other preachers, transform colonial religious culture, especially in New England and the mid-Atlantic colonies.

1736   John and Charles Wesley arrive in America as Church of England missionaries to the colony of Georgia.

1738   May 24. John Wesley experiences a spiritual conversion in London that ultimately leads him to found the first Methodist society.

1738   George Whitefield, a leading evangelist of the Great Awakening, makes the first of his seven trips to America.

1741   Congregationalist minister Jonathan Edwards delivers his famous sermon, "Sinners in the Hands of an Angry God."

1742   Connecticut enacts legislation severely restricting the activities of itinerant preachers. Further restrictions on dissenters are enacted the following year.

1744   David Brainerd begins missionary work among the Indians in the middle colonies. He dies in 1747.

1746   College of New Jersey, later renamed Princeton University, founded by "New Side" Presbyterians; however, pursuant to its charter, scholars "of every Religious Denomination may have free and Equal Liberty and Advantage of Education in the Said College."

1748   *The Spirit of the Laws* by Montesquieu published.

1751   College of Philadelphia, later renamed University of Pennsylvania, founded in Philadelphia with the assistance of Benjamin Franklin.

1754   *Freedom of the Will*, a theological treatise by Jonathan Edwards, published.

1754   King's College, later renamed Columbia University, granted a charter by George II. That charter forbids the governors of the Anglican-affiliated college to make any laws "to exclude any person of any religious denomination whatever from equal liberty and advantage of education, or from any of the degrees, liberties, privileges, benefits, or immunities of the said college, on account of his particular tenets in matters of religion."

1762   *The Social Contract* by Jean-Jacques Rousseau published.

1763   *Treatise on Toleration* by Voltaire published.

1763   Treaty of Paris brings an end to the Seven Years' War (French and Indian War) and confirms Great Britain's dominance in North America.

1763   Patrick Henry argues the "Parsons' Cause" case in Virginia.

1764   College of Rhode Island, later renamed Brown University, founded by Baptists.

circa 1766   First Methodist societies in America organized in New York City and Maryland.

1766   Queens College in New Jersey, later renamed Rutgers University, chartered by George III in response to a petition from the Dutch Reformed Church.

1768   Presbyterian minister John Witherspoon arrives in America to become the president of the Presbyterian College of New Jersey (Princeton). He later emerges a patriot leader and signer of the Declaration of Independence.

1769   Franciscan missionary Father Junipero Serra establishes San Diego Mission, the first Spanish mission in present-day California.

1769   Dartmouth College founded in New Hampshire by the Reverend Eleazar Wheelock, a Congregationalist minister.

1770   *A Seasonable Plea for Liberty of Conscience* by the Reverend Isaac Backus, a New England Baptist leader, published.

1773   *An Appeal to the Public for Religious Liberty, Against the Oppressions of the Present Day* by the Reverend Isaac Backus published.

1774   June 22. Great Britain's Quebec Act gives the inhabitants of Quebec the right to "the free Exercise of the Religion of the Church of Rome."

1774   September 6. First Continental Congress, as one of its first actions, resolves to open its sessions with prayer. A clergyman opens the proceedings the following day with prayer.

1775   April 19. Shots fired at Lexington and Concord, Massachusetts, outside Boston, the first military engagements of the War for American Independence.

1775   June 7 and 12. Congress recommends the first general "day of public humiliation, fasting and prayer" to be observed on July 20. This is the first of several fast day proclamations issued by Congress.

1775   July 20. In observance of a "day of public humiliation, fasting and prayer," congressional delegates attend services at an Anglican church in the morning and a Presbyterian church in the afternoon.

1776   *Common Sense* by Thomas Paine published in Philadelphia.

1776   *The Wealth of Nations* by Adam Smith published.

1776   New Jersey adopts a constitution prohibiting the "establishment of any one religious sect" and guaranteeing "That no person shall ever . . . be deprived of the inestimable privilege of worshipping Almighty God in a manner agreeable to the dictates of his own conscience."

1776   Delaware adopts a constitution stating that "There shall be no establishment of any one religious sect in this State in preference to another" and a Declaration of Rights providing "That all Men have a natural and unalienable Right to worship Almighty God according to the Dictates of their own Consciences and Understandings" and "That all Persons professing the Christian Religion ought forever to enjoy equal Rights and Privileges in this State."

1776   Pennsylvania adopts a constitution with a Declaration of Rights recognizing "That all men have a natural and unalienable right to worship Almighty God according to the dictates of their own consciences and understanding."

1776   Maryland adopts a constitution with a Declaration of Rights stating that "all persons, professing the Christian religion, are equally entitled to protection in their religious liberty; wherefore no person ought by any law to be molested in his person or estate on account of his religious persuasion or profession, or for his religious practice; . . . yet the Legislature may, in their discretion, lay a general and equal tax, for the support of the Christian religion."

1776 North Carolina adopts a constitution declaring "That there shall be no establishment of any one religious church or denomination in this State," and a Declaration of Rights affirming "That all men have a natural and unalienable right to worship Almighty God according to the dictates of their own consciences."

1776 April 5. Congress sets a precedent for adjourning on Good Friday.

1776 June 12. The Virginia Convention adopts a Declaration of Rights, framed by George Mason, asserting in Article 16 that "all men are equally entitled to the free exercise of religion, according to the dictates of conscience."

1776 July 4. American colonies declare independence from Great Britain.

1776 July 9. The Reverend Jacob Duché appointed the first chaplain to Congress. He is succeeded by the Reverend Patrick Allison and the Reverend William White, elected chaplains to Congress later the same year (December 23). The Reverend George Duffield is appointed to replace Allison who declined the appointment (October 1, 1777).

1777 Georgia adopts a constitution providing that "All persons whatever shall have the free exercise of their religion; . . . and shall not, unless by consent, support any teacher or teachers except those of their own profession."

1777 New York adopts a constitution expressly abrogating all laws that might "be construed to establish or maintain any particular denomination of Christians or their ministers" and protecting "the free exercise

and enjoyment of religious profession and worship, without discrimination or preference."

1777 Vermont adopts a constitution with a Declaration of Rights providing "That all men have a natural and unalienable right to worship ALMIGHTY GOD, according to the dictates of their own consciences and understanding, regulated by the word of God."

1777 Articles of Confederation adopted by Congress and submitted to the states for ratification.

1777 November 1. Congress recommends setting apart December 18 as a day for "solemn thanksgiving and praise." This is the first of many thanksgiving proclamations issued by Congress.

1778 South Carolina adopts a constitution declaring "That all persons and religious societies who acknowledge that there is one God, and a future state of rewards and punishments, and that God is publicly to be worshipped, shall be freely tolerated. The Christian Protestant religion shall be deemed, and is hereby constituted and declared to be, the established religion of this State."

1779 Virginia legislature enacts a bill permanently terminating direct tax support for the formerly established church and its clergy.

1779 Thomas Jefferson's Bill for Establishing Religious Freedom introduced in Virginia legislature, but fails to gain passage.

1779 First Universalist congregation formed in Massachusetts. Universalism officially organized at a convention in 1790.

1780 Massachusetts adopts a constitution with a Declaration of Rights stating that "no subject shall be hurt, molested, or restrained, in his person, liberty, or estate, for worshipping God in the manner and season most agreeable to the dictates of his own conscience." It further states that "As the happiness of a people and the good order and preservation of civil government essentially depend upon piety, religion, and morality," civil government shall have authority "to make suitable provision" for their support.

1781 Articles of Confederation go into effect, creating "a firm league of friendship" among the states, providing for "the security of their Liberties," and promising "to assist each other" against attacks "on account of religion," and so forth.

1781 October 19. Cornwallis surrenders to George Washington at Yorktown, Virginia.

1781 October 24. Members of Congress in Philadelphia give thanks for the victory at Yorktown in a service held in the Dutch Lutheran Church.

1782 The United States and the Netherlands sign a treaty recognizing each other as sovereign nations and providing religious freedom for each other's nationals. Subsequent treaties containing similar provisions are signed with Sweden (1783) and Prussia (1785).

1782 Unitarian congregation formed in Boston.

1782 Robert Aitken of Philadelphia prints, with a congressional endorsement, the first complete English-language Bible published in North America.

1782 June 20. Great Seal of the United States adopted by Congress.

1783 June 8. George Washington writes the Circular Letter to the States resigning as commander in chief of the Continental Army and opining that Americans should demean themselves "with that Charity, humility and pacific temper of mind, which were the Characteristicks of the Divine Author of our blessed Religion, and without an humble imitation of whose example in these things, we can never hope to be a happy Nation."

1783 September 3. Treaty of Paris is signed, recognizing American independence from Great Britain. The treaty is endorsed by Congress in early 1784.

1784 New Hampshire adopts a constitution with a Bill of Rights stating that "Every individual has a natural and unalienable right to worship GOD according to the dictates of his own conscience, and reason" and authorizing civil government "to make adequate provision . . . for the support and maintenance of public protestant teachers of piety, religion and morality."

1784 Connecticut passes the Toleration Act, which exempts religious dissenters from the tax for the established Congregational Church upon certification that they are active members of another religious body.

1784 Methodist Episcopal Church in America formally organized. It flourishes as an influential denomination in America.

1785 James Madison writes his "Memorial and Remonstrance Against Religious Assessments" in opposition to a general assessment bill in the Virginia legislature for the support of "teachers of the Christian religion."

1786 January 16. Virginia Statute for Establishing Religious Freedom, authored by Thomas Jefferson, is adopted in Virginia. The Statute provides "That no man shall be compelled to frequent or support any religious worship, place, or ministry whatsoever, nor shall be enforced, restrained, molested, or burthened in his body or goods, nor shall otherwise suffer on account of his religious opinions or belief; but that all men shall be free to profess, and by argument to maintain, their opinion in matters of religion, and that the same shall in no wise diminish, enlarge, or affect their civil capacities."

1787 Northwest Ordinance adopted by Congress, stating that "Religion, morality and knowledge being necessary to good government and the happiness of mankind" and providing that "No person demeaning himself in a peaceable and orderly manner shall ever be molested on account of his mode of worship or religious sentiments."

1787   May 25. Federal convention convenes in Philadelphia for the purpose of revising the Articles of Confederation.

1787   September 17. A proposed United States Constitution, which includes the provision that "no religious Test shall ever be required as a Qualification to any Office or public Trust under the United States," signed by delegates present at the convention and, later, submitted to the states for ratification.

1788   U.S. Constitution ratified by the states.

1789   Georgia adopts a constitution stating that "All persons shall have the free exercise of religion, without being obliged to contribute to the support of any religious profession but their own."

1789   First federal Congress elects the Reverend William Linn and the Right Reverend Bishop Samuel Provoost as chaplains to the House of Representatives and Senate respectively, with an annual salary paid from the national treasury.

1789   The French Revolution begins.

1789   First federal Congress reauthorizes the Northwest Ordinance.

1789   First federal Congress drafts and adopts amendments to the U.S. Constitution (Bill of Rights), including a provision (First Amendment) prohibiting the Congress from making "law respecting an establishment of religion or prohibiting the free exercise [of religion]."

1789   The first Roman Catholic diocese established in the United States (Baltimore). Father John Carroll consecrated the first Bishop of Baltimore the following year.

1789   First Catholic college in the United States founded by Father John Carroll at Georgetown.

1789   A general convention of the Church of England in America adopts a new church constitution and formally becomes the Protestant Episcopal Church in the United States of America.

1789   April 30. George Washington inaugurated in New York City as the first president of the United States of America. The inauguration is followed by a divine service in St. Paul's Chapel attended by the new president, vice president, and members of Congress.

1789   July 14. French mob storms the Bastille.

1789   August 26. The National Constituent Assembly in France adopts the "Declaration of the Rights of Man and of Citizens," which states that "no one shall be molested on account of his opinions, even religious opinions, provided that their outward expression does not disturb the public order as established by law."

1789   November 26. First national thanksgiving designated by congressional resolution (September 25) and President George Washington's proclamation (October 3).

1790s–   The Second Great Awakening, a series of
1800s   religious revivals involving diverse denominations, sweeps various regions of the country.

1790   President George Washington writes a letter to the Newport (Rhode Island) Hebrew Congregation celebrating religious liberty.

1790   South Carolina adopts a constitution providing for "The free exercise and enjoyment of religious profession and worship, without discrimination or preference."

1791   *The Rights of Conscience inalienable, and therefore Religious Opinions not cognizable by*

Law by the Baptist minister John Leland published.

1791   December 15. Bill of Rights (first ten amendments to the U.S. Constitution), including the First Amendment, ratified by three-fourths of the states and becomes part of U.S. Constitution.

1791–1792   *The Rights of Man* by Thomas Paine published.

1792   Delaware adopts a constitution protecting "the rights of conscience, in the free exercise of religious worship" and disallowing "preference [to] be given by law to any religious societies, denominations, or modes of worship."

1794–1795   *The Age of Reason* by Thomas Paine published.

1796   September 19. In a Farewell Address published in *American Daily Advertiser,* President George Washington remarks that "Of all the dispositions and habits which lead to political prosperity, Religion and morality are indispensable supports."

1797   Treaty of Tripoli, a treaty of peace between the United States and North African Mohammedan authorities, asserts that "the government of the United States of America is not, in any sense, founded on the Christian religion." This clause is omitted when the treaty is renewed in 1805.

1798   Georgia adopts a constitution providing that "No person within this State shall, upon any pretence, be deprived of the inestimable privilege of worshipping God in a manner agreeable to his own conscience. . . . No one religious society shall ever be established in this State, in preference to another; nor shall any person be denied the enjoyment of any civil right merely on account of his religious principles."

1798   Thomas Jefferson drafts the Kentucky Resolutions and James Madison drafts the

Virginia Resolutions in opposition to the Alien and Sedition Acts (1798).

1799   December 14. George Washington dies at Mount Vernon.

1801   John Marshall appointed Chief Justice of the U.S. Supreme Court.

1801   A revival at a Presbyterian camp meeting in Cane Ridge, Kentucky, marks the expansion of a Second Great Awakening.

1802   January 1. Thomas Jefferson writes a letter to the Danbury (Connecticut) Baptist Association in which he states that the First Amendment built "a wall of separation between Church & State."

1803   U.S. Supreme Court establishes principle of judicial review in *Marbury v. Madison.*

1807   Vermont, the first state admitted to the Union after the original thirteen, makes support of religion entirely voluntary.

1808   The first Bible society in America founded in Philadelphia.

1810   Congress enacts legislation requiring post offices to be open "every day on which a mail, or bag, or other packet or parcel of letters shall arrive." This portion of the law was reenacted in 1825. Many Christian traditionalists objected to this provision, and petitioned Congress to repeal it, because they thought it failed to acknowledge the Christian Sabbath and deprived postal employees required to transport and deliver mail on Sunday the opportunity to attend public worship services.

1810   American Board of Commissioners for Foreign Missions, the first American foreign missions agency, founded in New England.

1811   Massachusetts passes the "religious freedom act," which exempted religious dissenters, upon certification of membership in a nonestablished religious society, from taxation for support of the established church and allowed such persons to direct their tax support to their own religious society.

1811 In *People v. Ruggles*, a criminal case upholding a conviction for blasphemy, Chief Justice James Kent gives the opinion of the New York Supreme Court that "Christianity, in its enlarged sense, as a religion revealed and taught in the Bible, is not unknown to our law."

1816 The American Bible Society founded in New York City.

1817 The American Sunday School Union organized in Philadelphia as the Sunday and Adult School Union. The name is changed to American Sunday School Union in 1824.

1818 Connecticut adopts a new constitution with a Declaration of Rights terminating legal preference for the Congregational Church and recognizing the free "exercise and enjoyment of religious profession and worship."

1819 New Hampshire terminates legal preference for the formerly established church and places all Christian sects on an equal footing.

1824 In the criminal blasphemy case of *Updegraph v. Commonwealth*, the Pennsylvania Supreme Court opines that "Christianity, general Christianity, is and always has been a part of the common law of Pennsylvania."

1826 After an eight-year legislative struggle, Maryland enacts the "Jew Bill," which allows Jews to hold public office.

1827 Massachusetts enacts an education law that prohibits the selection of schoolbooks "calculated to favor any particular religious sect or tenet."

1828 The Reverend Ezra Stiles Ely publishes his July 4, 1827, oration, *The Duty of Christian Freemen to Elect Christian Rulers*, in which he proposes "a Christian party in politics."

1829 Committees in both chambers of the U.S. Congress issue reports on the controversial practice of delivering mail on Sunday.

1830 *Book of Mormon* first published by Joseph Smith, Jr.

1833 The Reverend Jasper Adams, president of the College of Charleston, preaches his sermon, *The Relation of Christianity to Civil Government in the United States*, before the South Carolina Convention of the Protestant Episcopal Church.

1833 *Commentaries on the Constitution of the United States*, an influential three-volume treatise, published by Joseph Story, associate justice of the U.S. Supreme Court.

1833 In *Barron v. Baltimore*, the U.S. Supreme Court declares that the Bill of Rights protects individuals from the national government only and not the states. This principle affirms that jurisdiction in religious matters is left to the respective states and citizens cannot make claims against state governments for the violation of First Amendment guarantees.

1833 Massachusetts becomes the last state to end a formal establishment.

SUMMARY OF DELIBERATIONS IN THE FIRST FEDERAL CONGRESS ON THE FIRST AMENDMENT RELIGION PROVISIONS, 1789

I. HOUSE OF REPRESENTATIVES

A. June 8. Amendments offered by James Madison in the U.S. House of Representatives.

1. James Madison's Fourth Proposal (to be inserted in Article I, section 9, between clauses 3 and 4):

"The civil rights of none shall be abridged on account of religious belief or worship, nor shall any national religion be established, nor shall the full and equal rights of conscience be in any manner, or on any pretext, infringed."

2. James Madison's Fifth Proposal (to be inserted in Article I, section 10, between clauses 1 and 2):

"No State shall violate the equal rights of conscience, or the freedom of the press, or the trial by jury in criminal cases."

B. July 28. Amendments reported by the House Select Committee.

1. Madison's Fourth Proposal redrafted:

"No religion shall be established by law, nor shall the equal rights of conscience be infringed."

2. Madison's Fifth Proposal redrafted:

"No State shall infringe the equal rights of conscience, nor the freedom of speech, or of the press, nor of the right of trial by jury in criminal cases."

C. August 15. Full debate in the House of Representatives on Madison's Fourth Proposal. At the close of debate the House adopted Samuel Livermore's revision of the amendment.

Samuel Livermore's Proposal:

"Congress shall make no laws touching religion, or infringing the rights of conscience."

D. August 17. House of Representatives rejected Thomas Tucker's motion to strike out Madison's Fifth Proposal and agreed to Samuel Livermore's alternative version.

Samuel Livermore's Proposal:

"The equal rights of conscience, the freedom of speech or of the press, and the right of trial by jury in criminal cases, shall not be infringed by any State."

E. August 20. House of Representatives agreed to a motion by Fisher Ames to replace Livermore's version of Madison's Fourth Proposal that had been adopted at the close of debate on August 15.

Fisher Ames's Proposal:

"Congress shall make no law establishing religion, or to prevent the free exercise thereof, or to infringe the rights of conscience."

F. August 24. On or before August 21 Ames's version of Madison's Fourth Proposal, adopted on August 20, was slightly altered by the House during its consideration of the report of the Committee of the Whole. Livermore's version of Madison's Fifth Proposal, adopted on August 17, was also revised on or before August 21. On August 22 the House appointed a committee on style "to prepare and report a proper arrangement of, and introduction to the articles of amendment to the Constitution of the United States, as agreed to by the House." On August 24 the House ordered the proposed amendments to be sent to the Senate for its concurrence.

 1. "(Art. III) Congress shall make no law establishing religion, or prohibiting the free exercise thereof, nor shall the rights of conscience be infringed."

 2. "(Art. IV) The Freedom of Speech, and of the Press, and the right of the People peaceably to assemble, and consult for their common good, and to apply to the Government for a redress of grievances, shall not be infringed."

 3. "(Art. XIV) No State shall infringe the right of trial by Jury in criminal cases, nor the rights of conscience, nor the freedom of speech, or of the press."

II. SENATE

A. September 3. U.S. Senate considered several versions of Article III in quick succession.

 1. Proposed and rejected, and passed on reconsideration:

"Congress shall make no law establishing one religious sect or society in preference to others, nor shall the rights of conscience be infringed."

 2. Motion that Article III be stricken out rejected.

 3. Proposed and rejected:

"Congress shall not make any law, infringing the rights of conscience, or establishing any religious sect or society."

 4. Proposed and rejected:

"Congress shall make no law establishing any particular denomination of religion in prefer-

ence to another, or prohibiting the free exercise thereof, nor shall the rights of conscience be infringed."

 5. Proposed and rejected (Article III as it came from the House of Representatives):

"Congress shall make no law establishing religion, or prohibiting the free exercise thereof, nor shall the rights of Conscience be infringed."

 6. Proposed and passed (Article III as proposed by the House of Representatives, amended by striking out the "rights of Conscience" clause):

"Congress shall make no law establishing religion, or prohibiting the free exercise thereof."

B. September 7. Article XIV prohibiting states from infringing the "rights of conscience," derived from Madison's Fifth Proposal, rejected without recorded comment.

C. September 9. Senate approved new version of Article III and returned it to the House of Representatives. Portions of Article IV were incorporated into Article III.

"Congress shall make no law establishing articles of faith or a mode of worship, or prohibiting the free exercise of religion, or abridging the freedom of speech, or the press, or the right of the people peaceably to assemble, and petition to the Government for the redress of grievances."

III. CONFERENCE COMMITTEE

A. September 21. House of Representatives requested formation of Joint Conference Committee.

 1. Committee members:

  a. Representatives James Madison (Virginia), Roger Sherman (Connecticut), and John Vining (Delaware).

  b. Senators Oliver Ellsworth (Connecticut), Charles Carroll (Maryland), and William Paterson (New Jersey).

2. Committee version (final version): "(Art. III) Congress shall make no law respecting an establishment of religion, or prohibiting the free exercise thereof; or abridging the freedom of speech, or of the press; or the right of the people peaceably to assemble, and to petition the Government for a redress of grievances."

B. September 24. Accepted by the House of Representatives.

C. September 25. Accepted by the Senate.

IV. RATIFICATION

Ratified by the required three-fourths of the States in 1791.

SELECTED BIBLIOGRAPHY

Adams, Arlin M., and Charles J. Emmerich. *A Nation Dedicated to Religious Liberty: The Constitutional Heritage of the Religion Clauses.* Philadelphia: University of Pennsylvania Press, 1990.

————. "William Penn and the American Heritage of Religious Liberty." *Journal of Law and Religion* 8 (1990): 57–70.

Ahlstrom, Sydney E. *A Religious History of the American People.* New Haven: Yale University Press, 1972.

Albanese, Catherine L. *Sons of the Fathers: The Civil Religion of the American Revolution.* Philadelphia: Temple University Press, 1976.

Aldrich, P. Emory. "The Christian Religion and the Common Law." *American Antiquarian Society Proceedings* 6 (April 1889–April 1890): 18–37.

Alley, Robert S., ed. *James Madison on Religious Liberty.* Buffalo: Prometheus Books, 1985.

Amos, Gary T. *Defending the Declaration: How the Bible and Christianity Influenced the Writing of the Declaration of Independence.* Brentwood, Tenn.: Wolgemuth and Hyatt Publishers, 1989.

Anderson, M. B. "Relations of Christianity to the Common Law." *Albany Law Journal* 20 (4 October 1879): 265–68, (11 October 1879): 285–88.

Antieau, Chester James, Arthur T. Downey, and Edward C. Roberts. *Freedom from Federal Establishment: Formation and Early History of the First Amendment Religion Clauses.* Milwaukee: Bruce, 1964.

Bailyn, Bernard, ed. *Pamphlets of the American Revolution,* 1750–1776. Vol. 1, 1750–1765. Cambridge: The Belknap Press of Harvard University Press, 1965.

Bainton, Roland H. *The Travail of Religious Liberty.* New York: Harper and Brothers, 1951.

Baird, Robert. *Religion in America; or, An Account of the Origin, Progress, Relation to the State, and Present Condition of the Evangelical Churches in the United States. With Notices of the Unevangelical Denominations.* New York: Harper and Brothers, 1844.

Baldwin, Alice M. *The New England Clergy and the American Revolution.* Durham: Duke University Press, 1928.

Banner, Stuart. "When Christianity Was Part of the Common Law." *Law and History Review* 16 (1998): 27–62.

Banning, Lance. "James Madison, the Statute for Religious Freedom, and the Crisis of Republican Convictions." In *The Virginia Statute for Religious Freedom: Its Evolution and Consequences in American History.* Edited by Merrill D. Peterson and Robert C. Vaughan. New York: Cambridge University Press, 1988.

Barton, David. *Original Intent: The Courts, the Constitution, and Religion.* Aledo, Tex.: WallBuilder Press, 1996.

Bellah, Robert N. "Civil Religion in America." *Daedalus: Journal of the American Academy of Arts and Sciences* 96 (1967): 1–21.

Bercovitch, Sacvan. *The American Jeremiad.* Madison: University of Wisconsin Press, 1978.

Berman, Harold J. "Religion and Law: The First Amendment in Historical Perspective." *Emory Law Journal* 35 (1986): 777–93.

Beth, Loren P. *The American Theory of Church and State.* Gainesville: University of Florida Press, 1958.

Billington, Ray Allen. *The Protestant Crusade, 1800–1860: A Study of the Origins of American Nativism.* New York: Macmillan, 1938; reprinted New York: Rinehart, 1952.

Blakely, William Addison, ed. *American State Papers on Freedom in Religion.* 3d ed. Washington, D.C.: Religious Liberty Association, 1943.

Blau, Joseph L., ed. *Cornerstones of Religious Freedom in America.* Boston: Beacon Press, 1949.

Bodo, John R. *The Protestant Clergy and Public Issues, 1812–1848.* Princeton: Princeton University Press, 1954; reprinted Philadelphia: Porcupine Press, 1980.

Boles, John. *The Great Revival, 1787–1805: The Origins of the Southern Evangelical Mind.* Lexington: University Press of Kentucky, 1972.

Boller, Paul F., Jr. *George Washington and Religion.* Dallas, Tex.: Southern Methodist University Press, 1963.

———. "George Washington and Religious Liberty." *William and Mary Quarterly*, 3d ser., 17 (1960): 486–506.

Bond, Edward L. *Damned Souls in a Tobacco Colony: Religion in Seventeenth-Century Virginia.* Macon, Ga.: Mercer University Press, 2000.

———, ed. *Spreading the Gospel in Colonial Virginia: Preaching Religion and Community: With Selected Sermons and Other Primary Documents.* Lanham, Md.: Lexington Books, 2005.

Bonomi, Patricia U. *Under the Cope of Heaven: Religion, Society, and Politics in Colonial America.* New York: Oxford University Press, 1986.

Borden, Morton. *Jews, Turks, and Infidels.* Chapel Hill: University of North Carolina Press, 1984.

Botein, Stephen. "Religious Dimensions of the Early American State." In *Beyond Confederation: Origins of the Constitution and American National Identity.* Edited by Richard Beeman, Stephen Botein, and Edward C. Carter II. Chapel Hill: University of North Carolina Press, 1987.

Bradford, M. E. *Founding Fathers: Brief Lives of the Framers of the United States Constitution.* 2d ed., rev. Lawrence: University Press of Kansas, 1994.

———. "Religion and the Framers: The Biographical Evidence." *Benchmark* 4, no. 4 (1990): 349–58.

Bradley, Gerard V. *Church-State Relationships in America.* Westport, Conn.: Greenwood Press, 1987.

———. "The No Religious Test Clause and the Constitution of Religious Liberty: A Machine That Has Gone of Itself." *Case Western Reserve Law Review* 37 (1987): 674–747.

Brady, Joseph H. *Confusion Twice Confounded: The First Amendment and the Supreme Court.* South Orange: Seton Hall University Press, 1954.

Brann, Eva T. H. "Madison's 'Memorial and Remonstrance': A Model of American Eloquence." In *Rhetoric and American Statesmanship.* Edited by Glen E. Thurow and Jeffrey D. Wallin. Durham: Carolina Academic Press, 1984.

Brant, Irving. *The Bill of Rights: Its Origin and Meaning.* Indianapolis: Bobbs-Merrill, 1965.

Brauer, Jerald C., ed. *Religion and the American Revolution.* Philadelphia: Fortress Press, 1976.

Brewer, David J. *The United States a Christian Nation.* Philadelphia: John C. Winston, 1905.

Bridenbaugh, Carl. *Mitre and Sceptre: Transatlantic Faiths, Ideas, Politics, and Politics, 1689–1775.* New York: Oxford University Press, 1962.

Buckley, Thomas E. *Church and State in Revolutionary Virginia, 1776–1787.* Charlottesville: University Press of Virginia, 1977.

———. "The Political Theology of Thomas Jefferson." In *The Virginia Statute for Religious Freedom: Its Evolution and Consequences in American History.* Edited by Merrill D. Peterson and Robert C. Vaughan. New York: Cambridge University Press, 1988.

Butler, Jon. *Awash in a Sea of Faith: Christianizing the American People.* Cambridge: Harvard University Press, 1990.

Butts, R. Freeman. *The American Tradition in Religion and Education.* Boston: Beacon Press, 1950.

Calhoon, Robert M. *Evangelicals and Conservatives in the Early South, 1740–1861.* Columbia: University of South Carolina Press, 1988.

Carroll, Peter N., ed. *Religion and the Coming of the American Revolution.* Waltham, Mass.: Ginn-Blaisdell, 1970.

Carwardine, Richard J. *Evangelicals and Politics in Antebellum America.* New Haven: Yale University Press, 1993.

Cherry, Conrad, ed. *God's New Israel: Religious Interpre-*

tations of American Destiny. Englewood Cliffs: Prentice-Hall, 1971.

Clebsch, William A. *From Sacred to Profane America: The Role of Religion in American History.* New York: Harper and Row, 1968.

Cobb, Sanford. *The Rise of Religious Liberty in America: A History.* New York: Macmillan, 1902.

Cogan, Neil H., ed. *The Complete Bill of Rights: The Drafts, Debates, Sources, and Origins.* New York: Oxford University Press, 1997.

Cole, Franklin P., ed. *They Preached Liberty.* Indianapolis: Liberty Fund, 1976.

Conkin, Paul K. "The Religious Pilgrimage of Thomas Jefferson." In *Jeffersonian Legacies.* Edited by Peter S. Onuf. Charlottesville: University Press of Virginia, 1993.

Cord, Robert L. "Original Intent Jurisprudence and Madison's 'Detached Memoranda.'" *Benchmark* 3, nos. 1–2 (1987): 79–85.

———. *Separation of Church and State: Historical Fact and Current Fiction.* New York: Lambeth Press, 1982.

Cornelison, Isaac A. *The Relation of Religion to Civil Government in the United States of America: A State Without a Church, but Not Without a Religion.* New York: G. P. Putnam's Sons, 1895.

Corwin, Edward S. "The 'Higher Law' Background of American Constitutional Law." *Harvard Law Review* 42 (1928–29): 149–85, 365–409.

Costanzo, Joseph F. *This Nation under God: Church, State and Schools in America.* New York: Herder and Herder, 1964.

Cousins, Norman, ed. *"In God We Trust": The Religious Beliefs and Ideas of the American Founding Fathers.* New York: Harper and Brothers, 1958.

Curry, Thomas J. *The First Freedoms: Church and State in America to the Passage of the First Amendment.* New York: Oxford University Press, 1986.

Davis, Derek H. *Religion and the Continental Congress, 1774–1789: Contributions to Original Intent.* New York: Oxford University Press, 2000.

De Jong, Norman, with Jack Van Der Slik. *Separation of Church and State: The Myth Revisited.* Jordan Station, Ontario, Canada: Paideia Press, 1985.

Dickson, Charles Ellis. "Jeremiads in the New American Republic: The Case of National Fasts in the John Ad-ams Administration." *New England Quarterly* 60 (1987): 187–207.

Dorchester, Daniel. *Christianity in the United States: From the First Settlement Down to the Present.* New York: Hunt and Eaton, 1889.

Drakeman, Donald L. *Church-State Constitutional Issues: Making Sense of the Establishment Clause.* Westport, Conn.: Greenwood Press, 1991.

Dreisbach, Daniel L. "The Constitution's Forgotten Religion Clause: Reflections on the Article VI Religious Test Ban." *Journal of Church and State* 38 (1996): 261–95.

———. "George Mason's Pursuit of Religious Liberty in Revolutionary Virginia." *Virginia Magazine of History and Biography* 108, no. 1 (2000): 5–44.

———. "In Search of a Christian Commonwealth: An Examination of Selected Nineteenth-Century Commentaries on References to God and the Christian Religion in the United States Constitution." *Baylor Law Review* 48 (1996): 927–1000.

———. "A New Perspective on Jefferson's Views on Church-State Relations: The Virginia Statute for Establishing Religious Freedom in Its Legislative Context." *American Journal of Legal History* 35 (1991): 172–204.

———. *Real Threat and Mere Shadow: Religious Liberty and the First Amendment.* Westchester, Ill.: Crossway Books, 1987.

———. "Thomas Jefferson and Bills Number 82–86 of the Revision of the Laws of Virginia, 1776–1786: New Light on the Jeffersonian Model of Church-State Relations." *North Carolina Law Review* 69 (1990): 159–211.

———. *Thomas Jefferson and the Wall of Separation between Church and State.* New York: New York University Press, 2002.

———, ed. *Religion and Politics in the Early Republic: Jasper Adams and the Church-State Debate.* Lexington: University Press of Kentucky, 1996.

Dreisbach, Daniel L., Mark D. Hall, and Jeffry H. Morrison, eds. *The Founders on God and Government.* Lanham, Md.: Rowman and Littlefield, 2004.

Dunn, Charles W., ed. *American Political Theology: Historical Perspective and Theoretical Analysis.* New York: Praeger, 1984.

Eckenrode, Hamilton James. *Separation of Church and*

State in Virginia: A Study in the Development of the Revolution. Richmond, Va.: Davis Bottom, 1910.

Eidsmoe, John. *Christianity and the Constitution: The Faith of Our Founding Fathers*. Grand Rapids: Baker Book House, 1987.

Eisgruber, Christopher L. "Madison's Wager: Religious Liberty in the Constitutional Order." *Northwestern University Law Review* 89 (1995): 347–410.

Elazar, Daniel J. "The Political Theory of Covenant: Biblical Origins and Modern Developments." *Publius: The Journal of Federalism* 10, no. 4 (Fall 1980): 3–30.

Elliott, Emory. "The Dove and the Serpent: The Clergy in the American Revolution." *American Quarterly* 31 (1979): 187–203.

Engeman, Thomas S., and Michael P. Zuckert. *Protestantism and the American Founding*. Notre Dame: University of Notre Dame Press, 2004.

Esbeck, Carl H. "Dissent and Disestablishment: The Church-State Settlement in the Early American Republic." *Brigham Young University Law Review* 2004 (2004): 1385–592.

Estep, William R. *Revolution within the Revolution: The First Amendment in Historical Context, 1612–1789*. Grand Rapids: William B. Eerdmans, 1990.

Evans, M. Stanton. *The Theme Is Freedom: Religion, Politics, and the American Tradition*. Washington, D.C.: Regnery, 1994.

Field, Peter S. *The Crisis of the Standing Order: Clerical Intellectuals and Cultural Authority in Massachusetts, 1780–1833*. Amherst: University of Massachusetts Press, 1998.

"First Amendment Religion Clauses: Historical Metamorphosis." *Northwestern University Law Review* 61 (1966): 760–76.

Fleet, Elizabeth, ed. "Madison's 'Detached Memoranda.'" *William and Mary Quarterly*, 3d ser., 3 (1946): 534–68.

Foote, Henry Wilder. *The Religion of Thomas Jefferson*. Boston: Beacon Press, 1947.

Foster, Charles I. *An Errand of Mercy: The Evangelical United Front, 1790–1837*. Chapel Hill: University of North Carolina Press, 1960.

Frohnen, Bruce, ed. *The American Republic: Primary Sources*. Indianapolis: Liberty Fund, 2002.

Gaustad, Edwin Scott. "A Disestablished Society: Origins of the First Amendment." *Journal of Church and State* 11 (1969): 409–25.

———. *Faith of Our Fathers: Religion and the New Nation*. San Francisco: Harper and Row, 1987.

———. *Liberty of Conscience: Roger Williams in America*. Grand Rapids: William B. Eerdmans, 1991.

———. *A Religious History of America*. Rev. ed. San Francisco: Harper and Row, 1990.

———. *Sworn on the Altar of God: A Religious Biography of Thomas Jefferson*. Grand Rapids: William B. Eerdmans, 1996.

Gifford, Frank Dean. "The Influence of the Clergy on American Politics from 1763 to 1776." *Historical Magazine of the Protestant Episcopal Church* 10 (June 1941): 104–23.

Glenn, Gary D. "Forgotten Purposes of the First Amendment Religion Clauses." *Review of Politics* 49 (1987): 340–67.

Gould, William D. "The Religious Opinions of Thomas Jefferson." *Mississippi Valley Historical Review* 20 (1933): 191–208.

Greene, Evarts B. *Religion and the State: The Making and Testing of an American Tradition*. New York: New York University Press, 1941.

Greene, M. Louise. *The Development of Religious Liberty in Connecticut*. Boston: Houghton, Mifflin, 1905.

Griffin, Keith L. *Revolution and Religion: American Revolutionary War and the Reformed Clergy*. New York: Paragon House, 1994.

Hall, David W. *The Genevan Reformation and the American Founding*. Lanham, Md.: Lexington Books, 2003.

Hall, J. Lesslie. "The Religious Opinions of Thomas Jefferson." *Sewanee Review* 21 (1913): 164–76.

Hall, Mark David. "Jeffersonian Walls and Madisonian Lines: The Supreme Court's Use of History in Religion Clause Cases." *Oregon Law Review* 85 (2006): 563–614.

———. *The Political and Legal Philosophy of James Wilson*. Columbia: University of Missouri Press, 1997.

Hall, Thomas Cuming. *The Religious Background of American Culture*. Boston: Little, Brown, 1930.

Hall, Timothy L. *Separating Church and State: Roger Williams and Religious Liberty*. Urbana: University of Illinois Press, 1998.

Hamburger, Philip A. "A Constitutional Right of Religious Exemption: An Historical Perspective." *George Washington Law Review* 60 (1992): 915–48.

———. *Separation of Church and State.* Cambridge: Harvard University Press, 2002.

Hamilton, Marci A. "The Calvinist Paradox of Distrust and Hope at the Constitutional Convention." In *Christian Perspectives on Legal Thought.* Edited by Michael W. McConnell, Robert F. Cochran, Jr., and Angela C. Carmella. New Haven: Yale University Press, 2001.

———. "The Reverend John Witherspoon and the Constitutional Convention." In *Law and Religion: A Critical Anthology.* Edited by Stephen M. Feldman. New York: New York University Press, 2000.

Handy, Robert T. *A Christian America: Protestant Hopes and Historical Realities.* 2d ed. New York: Oxford University Press, 1984.

Hart, Benjamin. *Faith and Freedom: The Christian Roots of American Liberty.* Dallas, Tex.: Lewis and Stanley, 1988.

Hartnett, Robert C. "The Religion of the Founding Fathers." In *Wellsprings of the American Spirit.* Edited by F. Ernest Johnson. New York: Cooper Square, 1964.

Hatch, Nathan O. *The Sacred Cause of Liberty: Republican Thought and the Millennium in Revolutionary New England.* New Haven: Yale University Press, 1977.

Headley, J. T. *The Chaplains and Clergy of the Revolution.* New York: Charles Scribner, 1864.

Healey, Robert M. *Jefferson on Religion in Public Education.* New Haven: Yale University Press, 1962.

Heimert, Alan. *Religion and the American Mind: From the Great Awakening to the Revolution.* Cambridge: Harvard University Press, 1966.

Holmes, David L. *The Religion of the Founding Fathers.* Charlottesville, Va.: Ash Lawn–Highland; Ann Arbor, Mich.: The Clements Library, 2003.

Hood, Fred J. *Reformed America: The Middle and Southern States, 1783–1837.* University: University of Alabama Press, 1980.

———. "Revolution and Religious Liberty: The Conservation of the Theocratic Concept in Virginia." *Church History* 40 (1971): 170–81.

Horwitz, Robert H., ed. *The Moral Foundations of the American Republic.* Charlottesville: University Press of Virginia, 1977.

Hudson, Winthrop S. *Religion in America: An Historical Account of the Development of American Religious Life.* 3d ed. New York: Charles Scribner's Sons, 1981.

———, ed. *Nationalism and Religion in America: Concepts of American Identity and Mission.* New York: Harper and Row, 1970.

Humphrey, Edward Frank. *Nationalism and Religion in America, 1774–1789.* Boston: Chipman Law, 1924.

Hunt, Gaillard. "James Madison and Religious Liberty." *Annual Report of the American Historical Association for the Year 1901,* 2 vols. (Washington, D.C.: Government Printing Office, 1902), 1:163–71.

Huntley, William B. "Jefferson's Public and Private Religion." *South Atlantic Quarterly* 79 (1980): 286–301.

Hutson, James H. *Forgotten Features of the Founding: The Recovery of Religious Themes in the Early American Republic.* Lanham, Md.: Lexington Books, 2003.

———. *The Founders on Religion: A Book of Quotations.* Princeton: Princeton University Press, 2005.

———. *Religion and the Founding of the American Republic.* Washington, D.C.: Library of Congress, 1998.

———. "Thomas Jefferson's Letter to the Danbury Baptists: A Controversy Rejoined." *William and Mary Quarterly,* 3d ser., 56 (1999): 775–90.

———, ed. *Religion and the New Republic: Faith in the Founding of America.* Lanham, Md.: Rowman and Littlefield, 2000.

Hyneman, Charles S., and Donald S. Lutz, eds. *American Political Writing during the Founding Era: 1760–1805.* 2 vols. Indianapolis: Liberty Fund, 1983.

Ives, J. Moss. *The* Ark *and the* Dove: *The Beginning of Civil and Religious Liberties in America.* New York: Longmans, Green, 1936.

———. "The Catholic Contribution to Religious Liberty in Colonial America." *Catholic Historical Review* 21 (1935): 283–98.

Jacoby, Susan. *Freethinkers: A History of American Secularism.* New York: Metropolitan Books, 2004.

James, Charles F. *Documentary History of the Struggle for Religious Liberty in Virginia.* Lynchburg, Va.: J. P. Bell, 1900.

"Jefferson and the Church-State Wall: A Historical Examination of the Man and the Metaphor." *Brigham Young University Law Review* 1978 (1978): 645–74.

Jeffries, John C., Jr., and James E. Ryan. "A Political History of the Establishment Clause." *Michigan Law Review* 100 (2001): 279–370.

Jones, Archie Preston. "Christianity in the Constitution:

The Intended Meaning of the Religion Clauses of the First Amendment." Ph.D. diss., University of Dallas, 1991.

Joyce, Lester Douglas. *Church and Clergy in the American Revolution: A Study in Group Behavior.* New York: Exposition Press, 1966.

Kerr, Harry P. "The Election Sermon: Primer for Revolutionaries." *Speech Monographs* 29 (1962): 13–22.

———. "Politics and Religion in Colonial Fast and Thanksgiving Sermons, 1763–1783." *Quarterly Journal of Speech* 46 (December 1960): 372–82.

Kessler, Sanford. "Locke's Influence on Jefferson's 'Bill for Establishing Religious Freedom.'" *Journal of Church and State* 25 (1983): 231–52.

———. *Tocqueville's Civil Religion: American Christianity and the Prospects for Freedom.* Albany: State University of New York Press, 1994.

Ketcham, Ralph L. "James Madison and Religion—A New Hypothesis." *Journal of the Presbyterian Historical Society* 38 (June 1960): 65–90.

Knoles, George Harmon. "The Religious Ideas of Thomas Jefferson." *Mississippi Valley Historical Review* 30 (1943): 187–204.

Koch, G. Adolf. *Republican Religion: The American Revolution and the Cult of Reason.* Gloucester, Mass.: Peter Smith, 1964.

Kramer, Leonard J. "Muskits in the Pulpit: 1776–1783." *Journal of the Presbyterian Historical Society* 31 (December 1953): 229–44; 32 (March 1954): 37–51.

———. "Presbyterians Approach the American Revolution." *Journal of the Presbyterian Historical Society* 31 (June 1953): 71–86; (September 1953): 167–80.

Kramnick, Isaac, and R. Laurence Moore. *The Godless Constitution: The Case against Religious Correctness.* New York: W. W. Norton, 1996.

Kruse, Clifton B. "The Historical Meaning and Judicial Construction of the Establishment of Religion Clause of the First Amendment." *Washburn Law Journal* 2, no. 1 (1962): 65–141.

Kurland, Philip B. "The Origins of the Religion Clauses of the Constitution." *William and Mary Law Review* 27 (1986): 839–61.

Kurland, Philip B., and Ralph Lerner, eds. *The Founders' Constitution,* 5 vols. Chicago: University of Chicago Press, 1987.

Lambert, Frank. *The Founding Fathers and the Place of Religion in America.* Princeton: Princeton University Press, 2003.

———. "'God And a Religious President . . . Or Jefferson and No God': Campaigning for a Voter-Imposed Religious Test in 1800." *Journal of Church and State* 39 (1997): 769–89.

Laycock, Douglas. "'Noncoercive' Support for Religion: Another False Claim about the Establishment Clause." *Valparaiso University Law Review* 26 (1991): 37–69.

———. "'Nonpreferential' Aid to Religion: A False Claim about Original Intent." *William and Mary Law Review* 27 (1986): 875–923.

Lerche, Charles O., Jr. "Jefferson and the Election of 1800: A Case Study in the Political Smear." *William and Mary Quarterly,* 3d ser., 5 (1948): 467–91.

Levy, Leonard W. *The Establishment Clause: Religion and the First Amendment.* 2d ed. Chapel Hill: University of North Carolina Press, 1994.

Lindsay, Thomas. "James Madison on Religion and Politics: Rhetoric and Reality." *American Political Science Review* 85 (1991): 1321–37.

Littell, Franklin Hamlin. "The Basis of Religious Liberty in American History." *Journal of Church and State* 6 (1964): 314–32.

———. *From State Church to Pluralism: A Protestant Interpretation of Religion in American History.* Garden City, N.Y.: Doubleday, 1962.

Little, Lewis Peyton. *Imprisoned Preachers and Religious Liberty in Virginia.* Lynchburg, Va.: J. P. Bell, 1938.

Luebke, Fred C. "The Origins of Thomas Jefferson's Anti-Clericalism." *Church History* 32 (1963): 344–56.

Lutz, Donald S., ed. *Colonial Origins of the American Constitution: A Documentary History.* Indianapolis: Liberty Fund, 1998.

———. "From Covenant to Constitution in American Political Thought." *Publius: The Journal of Federalism* 10, no. 4 (Fall 1980): 101–33.

———. "The Relative Influence of European Writers on Late Eighteenth-Century American Political Thought." *American Political Science Review* 78 (1984): 189–97.

Lynch, Joseph M. "Madison's Religion Proposals Judicially Confounded: A Study in the Constitutional Law of Conscience." *Seton Hall Law Review* 20 (1990): 418–77.

Maclear, James Fulton. "'The True American Union' of Church and State: The Reconstruction of the Theocratic Tradition." *Church History* 28 (1959): 41–62.

———, ed. *Church and State in the Modern Age: A Documentary History*. New York: Oxford University Press, 1995.

Malbin, Michael J. *Religion and Politics: The Intentions of the Authors of the First Amendment*. Washington, D.C.: American Enterprise Institute, 1978.

Mapp, Alf, Jr. *The Faiths of Our Fathers: What America's Founders Really Believed*. Lanham, Md.: Rowman and Littlefield, 2003.

Marnell, William H. *The First Amendment: The History of Religious Freedom in America*. Garden City, N.Y.: Doubleday, 1964.

Marsden, George M. "America's 'Christian' Origins: Puritan New England as a Case Study." In *John Calvin: His Influence in the Western World*. Edited by W. Stanford Reid. Grand Rapids: Zondervan, 1982.

Marty, Martin E. *The Infidel: Freethought and American Religion*. Cleveland, Ohio: Meridian Books, 1961.

May, Henry F. *The Enlightenment in America*. New York: Oxford University Press, 1976.

McBrien, Richard P. *Caesar's Coin: Religion and Politics in America*. New York: Macmillan, 1987.

McClellan, James. "The Making and the Unmaking of the Establishment Clause." In *A Blueprint for Judicial Reform*. Edited by Patrick B. McGuigan and Randall R. Rader. Washington, D.C.: Free Congress Research and Education Foundation, 1981.

McConnell, Michael W. "Coercion: The Lost Element of Establishment." *William and Mary Law Review* 27 (1986): 933–41.

———. "The Origins and Historical Understanding of Free Exercise of Religion." *Harvard Law Review* 103 (1990): 1409–517.

McDonald, Robert M. S. "Was There a Religious Revolution of 1800?" In *The Revolution of 1800: Democracy, Race, and the New Republic*. Edited by James Horn, Jan Ellen Lewis, and Peter S. Onuf. Charlottesville: University of Virginia Press, 2002.

McLoughlin, William G. *New England Dissent, 1630–1833: The Baptists and the Separation of Church and State*. 2 vols. Cambridge: Harvard University Press, 1971.

———. *Revivals, Awakenings, and Reform: An Essay on Religion and Social Change in America, 1607–1977*. Chicago: University of Chicago Press, 1978.

———. "The Role of Religion in the Revolution: Liberty of Conscience and Cultural Cohesion in the New Nation." In *Essays on the American Revolution*. Edited by Stephen G. Kurtz and James H. Hutson. Chapel Hill: University of North Carolina Press, 1973.

———. *Soul Liberty: The Baptists' Struggle in New England, 1630–1833*. Hanover, N.H.: University Press of New England, 1991.

Mead, Sidney E. "American Protestantism during the Revolutionary Epoch." *Church History* 22 (1953): 279–97.

———. *The Lively Experiment: The Shaping of Christianity in America*. New York: Harper and Row, 1963.

———. *The Nation with the Soul of a Church*. New York: Harper and Row, 1975.

Meyer, Jacob C. *Church and State in Massachusetts: From 1740 to 1833*. Cleveland, Ohio: Western Reserve University Press, 1930.

Miller, Howard. "The Grammar of Liberty: Presbyterians and the First American Constitutions." *Journal of Presbyterian History* 54 (1976): 142–64.

Miller, Perry. "The Contribution of the Protestant Churches to Religious Liberty in Colonial America." *Church History* 4 (1935): 57–66.

———. *Errand into the Wilderness*. Cambridge: The Belknap Press of Harvard University Press, 1956.

———. *The Life of the Mind in America: From the Revolution to the Civil War*. New York: Harcourt, Brace and World, 1965.

Miller, William Lee. *The First Liberty: America's Foundation in Religious Freedom*. Washington, D.C.: Georgetown University Press, 2003.

Moehlman, Conrad Henry. *The Wall of Separation between Church and State: An Historical Study of Recent Criticism of the Religious Clause of the First Amendment*. Boston: Beacon Press, 1951.

Moore, Frank, ed. *The Patriot Preachers of the American Revolution, 1766–1783*. New York, 1860.

Morgan, Edmund S. *Roger Williams: The Church and the State*. New York: Harcourt, Brace and World, 1967.

Morris, B. F. *Christian Life and Character of the Civil Institutions of the United States, Developed in the Official and Historical Annals of the Republic*. Philadelphia: George W. Childs, 1864.

Morrison, Jeffry H. *John Witherspoon and the Founding of the American Republic*. Notre Dame: University of Notre Dame Press, 2005.

———. "John Witherspoon and 'The Public Interest of Religion.'" *Journal of Church and State* 41 (1999): 551–73.

Morton, R. Kemp. *God in the Constitution*. Nashville, Tenn.: Cokesbury Press, 1933.

Muñoz, Vincent Phillip. "George Washington on Religious Liberty." *The Review of Politics* 65 (Winter 2003): 11–33.

———. "James Madison's Principle of Religious Liberty." *American Political Science Review* 97 (February 2003): 17–32.

Murray, Iain H. *Revival and Revivalism: The Making and Marring of American Evangelicalism, 1750–1858*. Carlisle, Pa.: Banner of Truth Trust, 1994.

Nelson, John K. *A Blessed Company: Parishes, Parsons, and Parishioners in Anglican Virginia, 1690–1776*. Chapel Hill: University of North Carolina Press, 2001.

Nichols, James Hastings. "John Witherspoon on Church and State." *Journal of Presbyterian History* 42 (1964): 166–74.

Niebuhr, H. Richard. *The Kingdom of God in America*. New York: Harper and Brothers, 1937.

Noll, Mark A. *America's God: From Jonathan Edwards to Abraham Lincoln*. New York: Oxford University Press, 2002.

———. *Christians in the American Revolution*. Washington, D.C.: Christian University Press, 1977.

———. *A History of Christianity in the United States and Canada*. Grand Rapids: William B. Eerdmans, 1992.

———, ed. *Religion and American Politics: From the Colonial Period to the 1980s*. New York: Oxford University Press, 1990.

Noll, Mark A., Nathan O. Hatch, and George M. Marsden. *The Search for Christian America*. Westchester, Ill.: Crossway Books, 1983.

Noonan, John T., Jr. *The Believer and the Powers That Are: Cases, History, and Other Data Bearing on the Relation of Religion and Government*. New York: Macmillan, 1987.

———. *The Lustre of Our Country: The American Experience of Religious Freedom*. Berkeley: University of California Press, 1998.

Noonan, John T., Jr., and Edward McGlynn Gaffney, Jr. *Religious Freedom: History, Cases, and Other Materials on the Interaction of Religion and Government*. New York: Foundation Press, 2001.

Novak, Michael. *On Two Wings: Humble Faith and Common Sense at the American Founding*. San Francisco: Encounter Books, 2002.

O'Brien, Charles F. "The Religious Issue in the Presidential Campaign of 1800." *Essex Institute Historical Collections* 107, no. 1 (1971): 82–93.

O'Neill, James M. *Religion and Education under the Constitution*. New York: Harper and Brothers, 1949.

Parsons, Wilfrid. *The First Freedom: Considerations on Church and State in the United States*. New York: Declan X. McMullen, 1948.

Perry, William Stevens. *The Faith of the Signers of the Declaration of Independence*. Tarrytown, N.Y.: William Abbatt, 1926.

———. *The Influence of the Clergy in the War of the Revolution*. N.p., 1891.

Peterson, Merrill D., and Robert C. Vaughan, eds. *The Virginia Statute for Religious Freedom: Its Evolution and Consequences in American History*. New York: Cambridge University Press, 1988.

Pfeffer, Leo. *Church, State, and Freedom*. Boston: Beacon Press, 1953; rev. ed. 1967.

———. "Madison's 'Detached Memoranda': Then and Now." In *The Virginia Statute for Religious Freedom: Its Evolution and Consequences in American History*. Edited by Merrill D. Peterson and Robert C. Vaughan. New York: Cambridge University Press, 1988.

Plumstead, A. W., ed. *The Wall and the Garden: Selected Massachusetts Election Sermons, 1670–1775*. Minneapolis: University of Minnesota Press, 1968.

Reichley, A. James. *Religion in American Public Life*. Washington, D.C.: Brookings Institution, 1985.

"Rethinking the Incorporation of the Establishment Clause: A Federalist View." *Harvard Law Review* 105 (1992): 1700–1719.

Rice, Charles E. *The Supreme Court and Public Prayer*. New York: Fordham University Press, 1964.

Rutland, Robert Allen. *The Birth of the Bill of Rights, 1776–1791*. Chapel Hill: University of North Carolina Press, 1955.

Sandler, S. Gerald. "Lockean Ideas in Thomas Jefferson's *Bill for Establishing Religious Freedom*." *Journal of the History of Ideas* 21 (1960): 110–16.

Sandoz, Ellis. *A Government of Laws: Political Theory, Religion and the American Founding*. Baton Rouge: Louisiana State University Press, 1990.

———. "Religious Liberty and Religion in the American Founding Revisited." In *Religious Liberty in Western Thought*. Edited by Noel B. Reynolds and W. Cole Durham, Jr. Atlanta: Scholars Press, 1996.

———, ed. *Political Sermons of the American Founding Era: 1730–1805*. Indianapolis: Liberty Fund, 1991.

Sanford, Charles B. *The Religious Life of Thomas Jefferson*. Charlottesville: University Press of Virginia, 1984.

Sarna, Jonathan D., and David G. Dallin. *Religion and State in the American Jewish Experience*. Notre Dame: University of Notre Dame Press, 1997.

Schaff, Philip. *Church and State in the United States; or, The American Idea of Religious Liberty and Its Practical Effects*. New York: G. P. Putnam's Sons; American Historical Society, 1888.

Schulz, Constance B. "'Of Bigotry in Politics and Religion': Jefferson's Religion, the Federalist Press, and the Syllabus." *Virginia Magazine of History and Biography* 91 (1983): 73–91.

Shain, Barry Alan. *The Myth of American Individualism: The Protestant Origins of American Political Thought*. Princeton: Princeton University Press, 1994.

Sheldon, Garrett Ward, and Daniel L. Dreisbach, eds. *Religion and Political Culture in Jefferson's Virginia*. Lanham, Md.: Rowman and Littlefield, 2000.

Sheridan, Eugene R. "Liberty and Virtue: Religion and Republicanism in Jeffersonian Thought." In *Thomas Jefferson and the Education of a Citizen*. Edited by James Gilreath. Washington, D.C.: Library of Congress, 1999.

Singer, C. Gregg. *A Theological Interpretation of American History*. Rev. ed. Phillipsburg, N.J.: Presbyterian and Reformed, 1981.

Singleton, Marvin K. "Colonial Virginia as First Amendment Matrix: Henry, Madison, and Assessment Establishment." *Journal of Church and State* 8 (1966): 344–64.

Smith, Elwyn A. *Religious Liberty in the United States: The Development of Church-State Thought since the Revolutionary Era*. Philadelphia: Fortress Press, 1972.

———, ed. *The Religion of the Republic*. Philadelphia: Fortress Press, 1971.

Smith, Rodney K. *Public Prayer and the Constitution: A Case Study in Constitutional Interpretation*. Wilmington, Del.: Scholarly Resources, 1987.

Smith, Steven D. *Foreordained Failure: The Quest for a Constitutional Principle of Religious Freedom*. New York: Oxford University Press, 1995.

Smylie, James H. "Madison and Witherspoon: Theological Roots of American Political Thought." *Princeton University Library Journal* 22 (Spring 1961): 118–32.

———. "Protestant Clergy, the First Amendment, and Beginnings of a Constitutional Debate, 1781–1791." In *The Religion of the Republic*. Edited by Elwyn A. Smith. Philadelphia: Fortress Press, 1971.

Stokes, Anson Phelps. *Church and State in the United States*. 3 vols. New York: Harper and Brothers, 1950.

Stout, Harry S. *The New England Soul: Preaching and Religious Culture in Colonial New England*. New York: Oxford University Press, 1986.

———. "Religion, Communications, and the Ideological Origins of the American Revolution." *William and Mary Quarterly*, 3d ser., 34 (1977): 519–41.

———. "Rhetoric and Reality in the Early Republic: The Case of the Federalist Clergy." In *Religion and American Politics: From the Colonial Period to the 1980s*. Edited by Mark A. Noll. New York: Oxford University Press, 1990.

Strout, Cushing. *The New Heavens and New Earth: Political Religion in America*. New York: Harper and Row, 1974.

Sweet, Douglas H. "Church Vitality and the American Revolution: Historiographical Consensus and Thoughts towards a New Perspective." *Church History* 45 (1976): 341–57.

Sweet, William Warren. *Religion in Colonial America*. New York: Charles Scribner's Sons, 1942.

———. *Religion in the Development of American Culture, 1765–1840*. New York: Charles Scribner's Sons, 1952.

Thornton, John Wingate, ed. *The Pulpit of the American Revolution; or, The Political Sermons of the Period of 1776*. Boston: Gould and Lincoln, 1860.

Turner, James. *Without God, without Creed: The Origins of Unbelief in America*. Baltimore: Johns Hopkins University Press, 1985.

Tuveson, Ernest Lee. *Redeemer Nation: The Idea of America's Millennial Role*. Chicago: University of Chicago Press, 1968.

Van Tyne, Claude H. "Influence of the Clergy, and of Religious and Sectarian Forces, on the American Revolution." *American Historical Review* 19 (October 1913): 44–64.

Weber, Donald. *Rhetoric and History in Revolutionary New England.* New York: Oxford University Press, 1988.

Weber, Paul J. "James Madison and Religious Equality: The Perfect Separation." *Review of Politics* 44 (1982): 163–86.

West, John G., Jr. *The Politics of Revelation and Reason: Religion and Civic Life in the New Nation.* Lawrence: University Press of Kansas, 1996.

West, Thomas G. "Religious Liberty: The View from the Founding." In *On Faith and Free Government.* Edited by Daniel C. Palm. Lanham, Md.: Rowman and Littlefield, 1997.

Wilson, John F. *Public Religion in American Culture.* Philadelphia: Temple University Press, 1979.

———, ed. *Church and State in America: A Bibliographical Guide; The Colonial and Early National Periods.* Westport, Conn.: Greenwood Press, 1986.

Wilson, John F., and Donald L. Drakeman, eds. *Church and State in American History: Key Documents, Decisions, and Commentary from the Past Three Centuries.* 3d ed. Boulder, Colo.: Westview Press, 2003.

Wilson, John K. "Religion under the State Constitutions, 1776–1800." *Journal of Church and State* 32 (1990): 753–73.

Withington, Ann Fairfax. *Toward a More Perfect Union: Virtue and the Formation of American Republics.* New York: Oxford University Press, 1991.

Witte, John, Jr. "The Essential Rights and Liberties of Religion in the American Constitutional Experiment." *Notre Dame Law Review* 71 (1996): 371–445.

———. "How to Govern a City on a Hill: The Early Puritan Contribution to American Constitutionalism." *Emory Law Journal* 39 (1990): 41–64.

———. "'A Most Mild and Equitable Establishment of Religion': John Adams and the Massachusetts Experiment." In *Religion and the New Republic: Faith in the Founding of America.* Edited by James H. Hutson. Lanham, Md.: Rowman and Littlefield, 2000.

———. *Religion and the American Constitutional Experiment: Essential Rights and Liberties.* Boulder, Colo.: Westview Press, 2000.

Wood, James E., Jr., E. Bruce Thompson, and Robert T. Miller. *Church and State in Scripture, History, and Constitutional Law.* Waco, Tex.: Baylor University Press, 1958.

INDEX

The typeface used in this book is Adobe Caslon Pro, a recent interpretation by Carol Twombly of the classic face cut in the 1720s by the English typographer William Caslon (1692–1766).

This book is printed on paper that is acid-free and meets the requirements of the American National Standard for Permanence of Paper for Printed Library Materials, z39.48-1992.⊗

Book design by Erin Kirk New,
Watkinsville, Georgia

Printed and bound by Edwards Brothers, Inc.,
Ann Arbor, Michigan